THE WAR
ILLUSTRATED

Photo, Pictorial Press

CHIANG KAI-SHEK, GENERALISSIMO OF CHINA

THE WAR
Illustrated

Complete Record of the Conflict
by Land and Sea and in the Air

Edited by
SIR JOHN HAMMERTON

Volume Five

The FIFTH VOLUME OF THE WAR ILLUSTRATED
contains the issues numbered 101 to 130, which cover the period
from mid-July 1941 until early June 1942 ; in some ways the
most sensational and diversified period through which the War
has so far passed. With the treacherous entry of Japan, America's
stand for Democracy against all the forces of aggression and
oppression, and the almost unanimous adhesion of the Latin
American Republics to the cause for which the U.S.A. had determined to fight with the entire mobilization of industry, wealth,
armaments and man-power, what might aptly be described as
the World's First Total War had come into being. It is inconceivable there can be a second !

Our own pages give evidence of the difficulties of the times
through which we are passing. The paper famine, due to restricted imports of wood-pulp, has profoundly changed the com-
plexion of British publishing. We had been able to maintain
our issues weekly through the first four volumes only at the cost
of frequent and drastic cuts in circulation to keep within the permitted quota. But very soon it was necessary to limit our issues
to three each month, and finally to effect certain modifications
and publish the numbers fortnightly. All these changes are reflected in the pages of this Fifth Volume and rather increase than
detract from its appearance or its interest. And so we hope to
continue as the only current picture-record of this most thrilling
period in world history.

Published 2000
Cover Design © 2000
TRIDENT PRESS INTERNATIONAL
ISBN 1-58279-104-X Single Edition
ISBN 1-58279-021-3 Special Combined Edition*
*Contains Volume 5 & 6 Unabridged
Printed in Croatia

General Index to Volume Five

THIS Index is designed to give ready reference to the whole of the literary and pictorial contents of THE WAR ILLUSTRATED. Individual subjects and persons of importance are indexed under their own headings, while references are included to general subjects such as Libya War in; Pacific; U.S.A.; etc. Page Numbers in italics indicate illustrations.

List of Maps and Plans

Index of Special Drawings and Diagrams

Errata and Addenda

Volume 4.
Page 746. Caption under bottom photograph, 3rd line, *For* "Tribal" type *read* "W" and "V" type.

Volume 5.
Page 103. 3rd col., 4th line from end. *For* "May 28" *read* "March 28."
Page 116, col. 2, line 9 from bottom, *For* K.O.R.R. *read* K.R.R.

Page 135, last line of bottom caption. *For* "General Military Commander" *read* "German Military Commander."
Page 260, 3rd line of caption, *For* "267" *read* "247."

Page 362, 3rd and 4th line of caption, *read* "November 8" *read* "December 8."
Page 502, caption under bottom photograph, 2nd line, *For* "ahead" *read* "astern."
Page 595, last paragraph.

For "H.M.A.S. Stronghold" *read* "H.M.S. Stronghold," and *for* H.M.S. Yarra "read H.M.A.S. Yarra."
Page 690, 1st line of caption, *For* "Covenanter" *read* "Mark IV A."

Registered at the G.P.O. as a Newspaper

The War Illustrated, August 8th, 1941

Vol 5 The War Illustrated Nº 101

Edited by Sir John Hammerton

FOURPENCE

WEEKLY

ON BOARD H.M.S. NELSON, members of the South African division of the Royal Naval Volunteer Reserve with the Fleet are ammunitioning ship with 16-in. shells. South Africa has included a division of the R.N.V.R. among the defence forces of the Union for many years, and some of its officers and men served with the Grand Fleet during the 1914-18 war. In peacetime members of the S.A.R.N.V.R. serve under the orders of the Commander-in-Chief at Simonstown.

Photo, British Official: Crown Copyright.

The Way of the War

MOSCOW CALLING! MESSAGE FOR FRAU KREMER!

Russia Strikes the Human Note in Propaganda

"Moscow calling! Moscow calling! We have a message for Frau Erna Kremer of Ebenstadt. She will be terribly interested. Frau Erna Kremer! Erna Kremer . . ."

From beyond where millions grapple in the racket and rumble of war, across eleven hundred miles of Europe sunk in the night of Hitlerdom, the voice comes to the blacked-out Rhineland, to the humble home where Frau Kremer sits waiting (with an eye and an ear for the Gestapo spy prowling without). We know nothing of her save that she is a soldier's wife and the mother of a soldier's children. Perhaps she has just finished putting the children to bed; perhaps her hands are still wet from washing up. Perhaps —but the voice from Moscow persistently splits the silence.

"It is with the deepest regret we have to inform you," says the voice, "that your husband, Lance-Corporal Ludwig Kremer, of the 116th Infantry Regiment, has just died. He fell, shot through the lung, on the River Beresina. For 18 hours he was in our hospital, and he died holding photographs of you and your two children in his hands. From papers he left behind we know that your husband was a good soldier. He fought in Poland, in Bulgaria and Yugoslavia. He was decorated with the Iron Cross, first and second class. In a few days you will receive a letter from the German military authorities, notifying you that your husband died fighting for his country's honour.

"But, we ask you, Frau Kremer, why was your husband on the Beresina, and what use are the crosses to your children? Is it right to go into other people's homes, to kill their women and children? Ludwig Kremer didn't want to do that. In your last letter to him you said that you hoped he would soon be home again with you and your children, and that peace would soon come.

"You all want peace. We all want peace. But Hitler doesn't. He wants war. He knows nothing of the sufferings of a wife who has lost her husband, the sufferings of a child who has lost its father, or the sufferings of the father himself. He is wifeless and childless. Now we are giving you this sad news so that you should tell others that enough blood has been spilt. Tell all your relatives, your friends and neighbours, that you are defending a bad cause. Do all you can . . ."

This broadcast, so moving in its simplicity so direct in its appeal, struck a new note in war-time propaganda. It showed that in Moscow psychology has been married to publicity. But if Moscow can move to pity it can as easily strike the note of relentless hate. Soon the air shivered with the waves of vituperation, crackled with the atmospherics of invective, rumbled with the thunder of passion and fiery denunciation. Words that burn and flay, that sting and pierce even the thick hide of a Nazi thug, words calculated to make the medals rattle on Goering's breast and reduce Goebbels to gibbering impotence. ("If that is true," remarked Lozovsky after reading out one of

the Nazi bulletins, "then Dr. Goebbels is an Apollo.")

But the most biting phrases, the most bitter taunts, are reserved for the all-highest Fuehrer himself. "Who is Hitler?" demanded Moscow of Germany a few nights ago. "We will tell you. He is the greatest coward who ever wore an Iron Cross he never earned. He is a bloody vampire who has already cost you countless lives. Wake up! Rid yourselves of this Nazi reptile—this liar who was once a beggar and now owns millions. Destroy him before he destroys the German people!"

With calculated care the Moscow propagandists make their appeal, to this class and to that. One night they coolly borrowed the Nazi slogan, and flung it at the heads of German youth. "The Soviets are your friends," cried the announcer. "Trust the Red Army and mighty Britain. We will liberate you, but you must help. Destroy war material! Slow down the war machine! Refuse to be used as cannon fodder! *Deutschland, erwache!* " (Germany, awake!).

Russian workers are brought to the microphone to speak to their German comrades. "We know you want to help; we'll tell you what you can do. You're a transport worker? Then just slow things up a bit;

just don't put everything into it—and the war will be over more quickly. You've done it before; you can do it again. You're a woman making munitions? Just handle your machine a little more slowly—and your husband will be back sooner. Always remember: Every dud shell is a direct hit for peace."

German soldiers have received a grim warning that "you and your families are doomed to death on the land, on the sea, and in the air. It is not too late, even now, to turn your bayonets against Hitler . . ."

German peasants and farmers have heard the voice of "the free and happy German collective farmers" in the autonomous Soviet republic on the banks of the Volga. The women of Russia have been brought to the microphone to speak to the women of Germany and of the world. "Mothers, sisters, wives—Hitler has made the German woman a slave, a servant. Let us show him our worth! We call on all the women, even the women of Germany, Italy, Finland, Hungary, and Slovakia, to tell their men that Hitler is the greatest enemy of humanity. Women of the world, save your children!"

In all the broadcasts—strange when we think that Russia is a totalitarian state; strange, yet immensely encouraging in its strangeness—the personal note is struck time and again. The appeal is made to the common people, to the men and women who work and weep, to the ordinary folk who strive and suffer. The Russians realize that the soldier is not just a number in a rank; the worker is not a mere robot, a figure on a card; the housewife is something more than a unit in a statistical enquiry—that, in a word, the masses are made up of individuals.

And because they are individuals, they are not to be lumped together in one swastika-branded mass, easy to think about and as easy to condemn. Each has a body that feels the kicks, each has a soul that can answer to the call of a common humanity. Lozovsky and his men don't make the mistake so generally associated with the name of Vansittart. Just as in the Anglo-Russian Pact the enemy is "Hitlerite Germany," so in the Moscow broadcasts the "true Germans" are separated from Hitler and his gang. "German people—people of the nation of Goethe and Schiller, Wagner and Beethoven—our quarrel is not with you, but with the Nazis who enslaved you before they turned to enslave others. We and they are your brothers. Why should you want to kill your brothers? Come, let us join and kill the bloody Fascists. Then we can all live in peace together." *Royston Pike*

THE VOICE OF MOSCOW! Here is A. Lozovsky, Russia's Vice-Commissar for Foreign Affairs, who is responsible for the propaganda—so original, so dramatic, so highly effective—put out by the Soviet radio stations, and has himself given some of the most biting and pungent of the broadcasts. Born in 1878, Lozovsky was a master of the art of propaganda when Goebbels was still a schoolboy.   *Photo, Planet News*

First Soviet War Photographs from the Front

CAPTURED NAZIS, taken prisoner during the battles on the Eastern front, are being marched to the rear. This photograph was radioed from Moscow to New York and came by Clipper plane to London.

CRASHED NAZI PLANE, one of the hundreds destroyed by the Russians. The special interest of this photograph lies in the fact that it was the first ever to be transmitted direct from Moscow to New York by radio as an experimental transmission from Soviet Government sending apparatus, overcoming serious technical difficulties.

AIR RAID VICTIMS have been numerous among the civilian population of the Ukraine as a result of Nazi bombing. Here are some of three thousand casualties laid out for identification by the grief-stricken relatives.

RED ARMY TROOPS are seen above awaiting the Nazi advance. By a happy coincidence the Soviet Star contains no fewer than five V for Victory symbols. Right, Soviet A.A. guns which shot down three Nazi planes during one raid.

Photos, Keystone, Associated Press

Russia's Canals in Their Background of Strategy

As the Russian armies make their fighting retreat into the interior of the vast Soviet land, the importance of the canal system, both as a channel of communication and supply and as "interior lines" for the Red Navy must become ever more marked. In this article we give an account of the principal canal systems, to be read in close conjunction with the map opposite.

QUITE early in the Russo-German war it seemed possible, perhaps probable, that the Red Fleet would be bottled up in the Gulf of Finland, and must sooner or later become a prey to the Nazis advancing along the Baltic coast. But the gloomy prophets and the Nazi boasters forgot that, thanks to the vision of the Russian planners and the skill and energy of their engineers and workers, the Baltic is no longer a bottleneck but a highway.

Since 1933 a continuous ribbon of water has linked the Baltic to the White Sea and the Arctic beyond. This link is the Baltic-White Sea Canal, and its strategic value has already been demonstrated in this war, since along it a number of the submarines of the Soviet Baltic Fleet have been evacuated into the open waters of the north. In an attempt to prevent the evacuation, the Germans concentrated in Finland large forces of dive bombers which could ill be spared from the Central Russian front, and delivered a series of heavy day-and-night attacks on the waterway; but the submarines got through, and the damage to the Canal was made good.

Strategic reasons were mainly responsible for the construction of the **Baltic-White Sea Canal**, whose length, including the canalized portions of the Rivers Neva and Svir and the Stalin Canal, is 560 miles. The **Stalin Canal** is its most northern portion, cutting through Karelia from Lake Onega to the White Sea; 140 miles in length, it is the longest canal in the world. Built on the initiative of Stalin, it was one of the largest constructions of the first Five-Year Plan. Begun in 1930, it was completed in June 1933, and opened for navigation a year later. For its building, we are told, 21 million cubic metres of soil were excavated, and 390,000 cubic metres of concrete work were carried out in the remarkably short period of 20 months. Two and a half million cubic

metres of rock had to be blown out by dynamite, while in the construction of the spillways and dams and wooden-walled locks some 2,800,000 logs from the forests of Karelia were used. In its length there are 19 locks—each 379 ft. long, 50 ft. wide, and 15 ft. deep; 15 weirs, 12 flood-gates, 49 dams, and 33 artificial canals. The depth of water in the Canal is about 12 ft.

Since the Baltic-White Sea Canal's opening, it is no longer necessary to sail the whole length of the Baltic and round the coast of Norway, past the North Cape, to reach Archangel and Murmansk. Instead of a stormy 17-day journey, quite large ships now make the voyage from Leningrad to Murmansk—Russia's ice-free port in the north, whence ships sail all the year round to and from the Atlantic—in six days, sailing through the sombre forests and over the peaceful fenlands of Karelia.

Linking Leningrad to Rybinsk on the River Volga is the **Marinski System**. It is suitable only for barges up to 800 tons, and since there are 43 locks the transit from Rybinsk to Leningrad is slow. Plans for its modernization include increasing the depth and reducing the number of locks to six.

Moscow's Links with the Sea

The Baltic-White Sea Canal and the Marinski System are only part of a vast unified system of waterways which the Soviet rulers have planned; a system which, when completed, will link Moscow—as "inland" a capital as any in the world—with five seas, the Baltic and the White Sea in the north, the Caspian, Sea of Azov and Black Sea in the south. Throughout, the depth of the system is to be such as to allow light cruisers to be transferred from one area to another on "interior lines." The military value of the scheme is too obvious to be stressed.

Second only in importance to the Baltic-White Sea Canal is the **Moscow-Volga Canal**. This is 80 miles in length, and was completed in 1937 as part of the second Five Year Plan. It provides the Russian capital with a splendid supply of pure water—the Stalin Waterworks are the greatest in Europe; but even more important, it gives Moscow direct access by water to the great industrial centres and regions of the south. It is designed to take vessels drawing 15 to 18 feet, but at present it is not being used by vessels of this draught, owing to the incomplete state of the reconstruction of the general canal system.

Immediately below Stalingrad is the **Volga-Don Canal**, which when completed will link up the Black Sea with the main canal system. Work on the canal was commenced early in 1939, but it is not likely that it will be completed for some time. The system from the Sea of Azov via the River Don is designed for a minimum depth of 21 feet. Its completion will probably solve the problem set by the falling level of the Caspian Sea, since it will be possible to harness the waters of the Don to the Lower Volga, and so make up for the loss due to evaporation. When the Volga-Don Canal is in full working order, ships will be able to pass right across Russia from the Black Sea to the Atlantic.

Because of the Caspian's falling level and the navigational difficulties arising therefrom in the increasingly shallow waters, work on the **Manych System**, which was planned to connect the headwaters of the rivers Manych and Kuma, and so link the Black Sea with the Caspian, has now been abandoned, although considerable lengths have been completed.

Still our survey of Russia's canal system is not complete. Mention should be made of the **Tikhvinski** and **Vishnivolotski** systems, which connect the Volga with the Baltic, the **Hertzog Wurtembergski Canal**, which joins the Northern Dvina and the Volga, so linking Europe's greatest river with the White Sea, and the **Sergeitch Canal** in the Minsk region which joins the rivers Dnieper and the Western Dvina, via the Berezina; in this way the Black Sea is connected with the Baltic at Riga. Then there is the **Dnepropetrovsk Canal**, which runs past the rapids on the River Dnieper, and was constructed as part of the great Dnieproges power-station scheme. It was opened for steamer traffic in the first half of 1932.

To sum up. Already ships up to the size of large destroyers can pass between the Baltic and the White Sea. Ships up to the size of light cruisers will be able to pass between the Baltic and the White Sea when work now in hand is completed—it is believed in the near future. Ships of the same size will be able to pass between the Baltic and Black Sea when the Volga-Don Canal is completed. This is unlikely to be within the next three or four years.

THE MOSCOW-VOLGA CANAL, here seen from the top of Lock No. 7, was built during the second Five Year Plan and opened to traffic on July 15, 1937. The canal is remarkable not only from the point of view of technical achievement but also on account of its architecture. Locks, dams, landing-stages, stations and buildings on the canal are faced with marble, granite, labradorite and diorite, are decorated with statuary and fountains, and surrounded by many beautiful parks and gardens. The position of the canal is shown on the map in the opposite page. *Photo, Planet News*

Ribbons of Water that Make Moscow a Port

THE STALIN CANAL is one of the most important of Russia's new inland waterways shown on the map in this page. This canal, which was opened on August 2, 1933, is in 32 sections and is over 140 miles long. Before the canal was built, ships going from Archangel to Leningrad had to round the Scandinavian peninsula and make a journey of nearly 3,000 miles. Now the journey is reduced to about 700 miles. The five-pointed star, seen in the bottom photograph, is a memorial to the construction of the canal. It stands by the last lock at Soroka, on the edge of the White Sea. Top right, Russian freight steamers have just entered one of the locks on the Stalin Canal.

Photos, Planet News

They Keep the Heart of Britain Beating True

A convoy shepherded by destroyers and Lockheed Hudsons (not seen in the photograph) approaching a British port. Here are the ships and men that are keeping Britain alive.

Think of them always, these ships of all classes from the liner to the creaking tramp, and of their anonymous skippers, true sons of Britain, ready to die at any moment that the old country shall live.

Help them in their devoted work by economizing to the utmost limit in food, in petrol, and upon all those things which you personally need.

Circle, captains of merchant ships who will form the next convoy in conference somewhere underground in secret warrens built of steel and concrete. They are receiving instructions concerning the route to be taken and learn how the naval escort will protect them. In these subterranean labyrinths officers and men of the Royal Navy, Royal Naval Reserve and Royal Naval Volunteer Reserve work in close cooperation with the R.A.F. and the Merchant Navy. The small photograph on the left shows bluejackets in the wireless-room in these underground headquarters of the Battle of the Atlantic.

Beneath, Mr. A. V. Alexander, First Lord of the Admiralty, receives information from a convoy commodore on the latter's return to port after a voyage across the Atlantic.
Photos, British Official, Topical, and Associated Press

BATTLE OF THE ATLANTIC
Merchant Shipping Losses : Last Monthly Report

	June 1941	Jan.-June 1941	Monthly Average Jan.-June	Totals Sep. 1939-June 1941
British				
Ships	52	397		1,078
Tons	228,284	1,783,692	297,300	4,605,132
Allied				
Ships	19	162		334
Tons	82,727	710,941	118,500	1,498,047
Neutral				
Ships	8	31		326
Tons	18,285	98,161	16,400	1,014,834
TOTALS: tons gross	329,296	2,592,794	432,200	7,118,013

Note.—Total enemy tonnage, captured, sunk or scuttled, from beginning of the war was 3,391,000 tons gross. The monthly average of British, Allied and neutral losses from Sept. 1939 to June 1941 was 324,000 tons, about equal to actual losses in June 1941. The Admiralty announced that the June figures would be the last of the records of losses to be published in that form. Figures in table corrected to June, 1941.

Women Wield the Paintbrush on Board Ship

IN THE ROYAL DOCKYARDS women have taken on many jobs and enabled men to be released for more vital work. These seen here are busily engaged on their wartime task of painting ships, a job which they perform deftly and neatly. Their husbands are serving in the Forces and are doubtless proud, and rightly so, of the part which their womenfolk are playing in the national effort.   *Photo, British Official ; Crown Copyright*

Our Searchlight on the War

FANTASTIC WAR CARGOES

WAR materials have been exchanged between Britain and Russia. They were contained within the space of two aeroplanes and constituted the most precious cargo ever sent by this means. The plane bound for Russia carried diamonds to be used for industrial purposes in Soviet war factories ; the one that flew to England brought platinum for use in manufacturing British bombs and shells. All arrangements were made with the utmost secrecy and dispatch, and both aircraft reached their respective destinations at the scheduled time.

R.O.F. BADGE

BY his sanction of a new war badge (shown in the drawing on the left) to be worn by men and women engaged in the Royal Ordnance filling factories, King George acknowledges the debt owed by Britain to workers engaged in one of the most dangerous occupations of these dangerous times. The badge consists of a crossed bomb and shell in silver colour, with the letters R.O.F. and the inscription " Front Line Duty."

'LATE ARRIVALS' CLUB

IN the Western Desert there exists a highly exclusive club which has been called the " Late Arrivals." Those eligible for membership are airmen who have been shot down in action, and have, by exercising initiative and courage, succeeded in eluding the enemy and returning to their own lines. They include a D.S.O. and many D.F.C's. At least three South Africans and two Free French fliers belong to the Club. Some members are doubly eligible, as they have escaped more than once. The " Late Arrivals " are entitled to wear a special badge in blue and white enamel ; this depicts a winged flying boot, an indication that most members have come on foot from behind the enemy lines.

RUSSO-CZECH ALLIANCE

DIPLOMATIC relations between the Union of Soviet Socialist Republics and the Czechoslovak Republic were restored on July 18 by the signing of an agreement in London. By its terms the two Governments " mutually undertake to aid and support each other in every way in the present war against Hitlerite Germany," and the formation is authorized of Czechoslovak contingents on Russian territory to take part in the campaign. The Agreement is welcomed by the British Government, which has taken this occasion to announce their full recognition of President Benes' Government, hitherto regarded as only Provisional.

FACE ON THE POSTER

SERGEANT OBSERVER Ernest John Holland, whose features and urgent pointing finger have become familiar to the poster-conscious citizens of Britain, was reported missing, believed very soon after sitting for the photograph from which the poster was reproduced. The Ministry of Information, at whose Bloomsbury studios this and similar appeals were designed, asked the Air Ministry to send along three young airmen to act as models. Tests showed Sergeant Holland to be the most " photogenic," and the result was one of the best efforts in pictorial propaganda issued by this department. In civil life Sergeant Holland, who was only 22, was a stonemason in Birmingham.

HOIST WITH HIS OWN PETARD

HITLER'S policy of hounding out all Jews from Nazi territories is having a disconcerting effect on his war plans. Many of these refugees from racial persecution are brilliant scientists, and Germany is feeling the lack of their inventive knowledge, so much so that attempts have been made to get them back. Britain is making good use of her scientists to devise counter-measures against enemy attacks from air and sea, and is able, moreover, to call upon the services of many friendly aliens—doctors, technicians and the like—whose one aim is to banish from the world the deadly menace of Hitlerism.

PRESENT FROM TEXAS

ABOUT 1,340,000 barrels of oil, one day's production of all the Texas oil wells, may reach Britain as the gift of the producers if the plan first suggested by Mr. John Camp, of Dallas, Texas, is put into action. He proposed that the title to one day's output should be given to President Roosevelt, who is empowered, under the Lease and Lend Act, to send it to England. Mr. Roosevelt, replying to the offer, said : " This gift demonstrates that democracy in action is no meaningless phrase ; it symbolizes the spirit of patriotism."

SGT.-OBSERVER E. HOLLAND, of Birmingham, since reported " missing, believed killed," was the original of this striking poster.

SECRET FLAG FROM POLAND

BATTLE colours have reached the airmen of Poland who, one year after the formation of the first R.A.F. Polish squadron, now number many thousands. The flag, which was handed over to the senior squadron at a Polish bomber station by General Sikorski on July 17, has a romantic origin. At the suggestion of a young flight lieutenant who escaped to France, more than 150 women of his home town set about the clandestine task of making and embroidering this white and scarlet emblem of Poland's belief in victory. In the spring of 1940 the flag was finished and the still more dangerous task of smuggling it to Britain was undertaken by a Polish girl. After a hazardous journey across Germany she managed to enter Belgium, but was cut off by the invasion and forced to return to Poland. A second attempt was made, this time through Scandinavia, and one morning last March a code message in the B.B.C. Polish broadcast told the heroic girl and her dauntless companions that the flag had arrived.

BURGOMASTER DEFIES THE NAZIS

LIKE M. Max, his famous predecessor, the present Burgomaster of Brussels, M. van de Meulebroeck, has refused to become a tool in the hands of the enemy in occupation, and, like M. Max, is being punished for his courage and loyalty. In June the Nazis, incensed by his undaunted resolution, dismissed him, pretending that he had voluntarily retired. The Burgomaster protested against this violation of the Hague Convention in a proclamation which was posted up on the city walls. The posters were torn down by the enraged Nazis, only to be immediately and secretly replaced. Thereupon M. van de Meulebroeck was arrested, and a fine of 5,000,000 francs imposed on the population. Posters announcing this were left untouched, but beneath a number of them citizens of Brussels threw small coins as a sign of the contempt they felt for the German penalty.

CENTENARIANS V. HITLER

IN Russia neither age nor sex is a bar to waging war against Hitler. Not only is there reported to be a women's battalion, but Russian girls have been found fighting side by side with men. And even if you are a centenarian you can still, apparently, contribute to the war effort in a practical manner. Moscow radio recently broadcast the following story : The day after the announcement of the Nazi attack on the Soviet, 110-year-old Abbas and his friend Teymour, who is 100 years of age, turned up for work in the fields in Azerbaijan. They are still quite hearty and scarcely yielded to the young in the amount of work performed. Before going to work Abbas is reported to have remarked to his lifelong friend Teymour : " While the enemy lives we must not die." May their wish be granted !

A RUSSO-CZECH AGREEMENT was signed in London on July 18, 1941, restoring diplomatic relations between the Soviet Union and the Czechoslovak Republic and authorizing the formation of Czechoslovak contingents on Russian soil. Above, M. Maisky, Russian Ambassador, signs the pact, watched by M. Masaryk, Czechoslovak Foreign Minister (seated). *Photo, P.N.A*

Russia's Magnificent Stand Against the Invader

While the world's greatest battle was in progress on the Eastern Front, there was little news of the fighting beyond what was given in the (invariably contradictory) communiqués issued by one side and the other. This article gives a valuation of the position so far as it could be judged after five weeks of war.

How long can the Nazis keep it up ? This was the question on everybody's lips when, after five weeks of most furious fighting, the invaders had still inflicted no decisive defeat on the Red Army on any one of the three main battlefields ; when neither Leningrad nor Moscow, neither Kiev nor Odessa, had fallen to the German arms. How long (it was asked) can the tremendous drain on the Nazis' war material be maintained ? Are their supplies of petrol inexhaustible—and of men ? How long will the overstrung nerves of the German people at home stand the strain of the enormous losses and, with the lengthening nights, the ever-growing menace of British and Russian air raids on a colossal scale ?

Often promised, the crowning victory still escaped the Germans, though its imminence was prophesied more than once in their communiqués—and as often falsified by the event. For the Russians were fighting magnificently, and though their front was still endangered—particularly in the central sector where the main Nazi punch had been delivered with a view to smashing through to Moscow —there was little to substantiate the German claims that the Russians were disintegrating under the hammer-blows of the second big offensive, launched on July 12, and that the Germans were now engaged in mopping-up the fragments. True, the Russians had withdrawn several hundred miles. True, they had been forced to abandon to the enemy a vast

Radioed from Moscow to New York and sent by Clipper to London, this photograph shows a Moscow woman A.R.P. motor-cyclist on duty in the capital.   *Photo, Keystone*

THE ANGLO-RUSSIAN PACT being signed in the Kremlin on July 12, 1941. M. Molotov and M. Stalin are standing behind Sir Stafford Cripps as he signs.

territory. But that territory was now nothing more than a scorched waste. The Germans claimed an enormous bag of prisoners and a huge booty, but there was little to justify their claims. Indeed, there was reason to believe that their own losses were as great. Thus the Russians picked up on the battlefield a copy of an order issued by Major General Naehring, Commander of the 18th German Tank Division, which stated that "losses in equipment, arms and machines are unusually heavy, and considerably exceed the material captured. This situation cannot be tolerated, otherwise we will go on scoring victories until we ourselves perish."

After the first rush, when (it seemed clear) the Russians were taken by surprise, the German advance slowed down almost from day to day. The Nazis had plenty of excuses. German military spokesmen in Berlin emphasized the "superhuman difficulties" of the terrain ; the battle areas, they pointed out, were worse than in any previous European campaign. There were huge tracks of swamps, traversed by a close network of rivers and

streams and surrounded by vast, almost impenetrable forests. Everywhere lurked Russian guerillas in readiness for nocturnal sallies, so that the Nazi supply lines were constantly menaced. Moreover, it was pointed out, the great Russian rivers formed natural defence lines, most difficult to overcome.

Then stress was laid upon the "unexpected savagery" and the "fatalistic resistance" of the Red soldiers. "Russian troops," said a spokesmen of the Nazi High Command in a broadcast on July 23, "although at times completely surrounded, defend themselves desperately, and time and again attempt to break out in every direction. They fight to the death and do much more than their duty. While the battlefields are covered with dead, we hardly take any prisoners these days. The Russian Command continuously push forward their troops into fresh counter-attacks." Very different was this battle from what the Nazis experienced on the Western Front where, to quote the spokesman again, " enemy resistance broke down because the officers gave in, or because the individual soldier realized the futility of further resistance." Altogether, the present phase of the German campaign in the East presented a strange picture. "'If such a state of affairs as has developed in Russia had been suggested as a plan for peacetime manoeuvres in Germany, every military expert would have turned it down as utterly impossible. Forms of strategy have developed that have hitherto been completely unknown"

To add to the invaders' difficulties, the weather showed signs of breaking. In places there were heavy rains, so that now the complaint was not of blinding dust storms but of morasses of mud in which the German tanks and lorries were heavily bogged.

The Nazis still advanced, more particularly in the Smolensk area. They drew a little nearer to Leningrad, and at the opposite end of the immensely long front Bessarabia had now been completely overrun. But every day that passed was an immense gain to the Russians. Hundreds of thousands of reserves were pouring into the depôts ; new armies were springing out of the earth far behind the fighting front. All Russia nerved itself as never before at the call and under the leadership of Stalin, who

EASTERN FRONT after one month of war. The black arrows show how the main Nazi thrusts developed, and the white arrows the Russian counter-attacks. The neighbourhood of Smolensk was the most easterly point reached by the Nazis after the first month's fighting.
Photo, British Official ; Map, G.P.U.

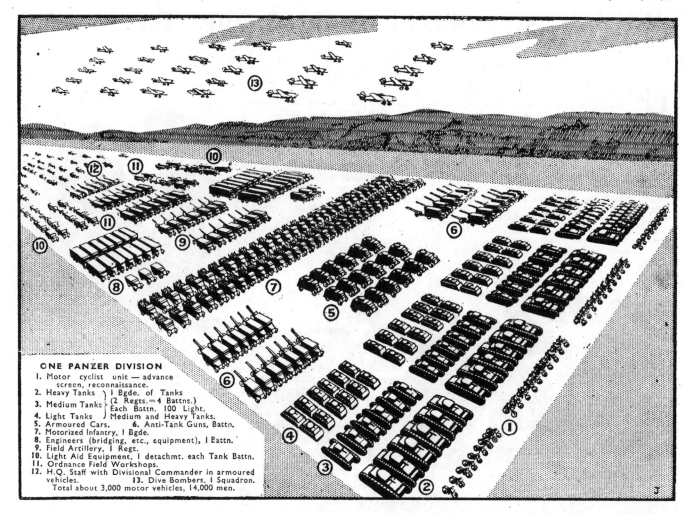

ONE PANZER DIVISION

1. Motor cyclist unit — advance screen, reconnaissance.
2. Heavy Tanks ⎫ 1 Bgde. of Tanks
3. Medium Tanks ⎬ (2 Regts.= 4 Battns.) Each Battn. 100 Light,
4. Light Tanks ⎭ Medium and Heavy Tanks.
5. Armoured Cars.   6. Anti-Tank Guns, Battn.
7. Motorized Infantry, 1 Bgde.
8. Engineers (bridging, etc., equipment), 1 Battn.
9. Field Artillery, 1 Regt.
10. Light Aid Equipment, 1 detachmt. each Tank Battn.
11. Ordnance Field Workshops.
12. H.Q. Staff with Divisional Commander in armoured vehicles.   13. Dive Bombers, 1 Squadron.
    Total about 3,000 motor vehicles, 14,000 men.

Speed! Speed! Speed!
How the Whirlwind Advances of the Panzer Divisions Are Made

1. The advance is prepared and assisted by artillery and dive bombing attacks on anti-tank gun positions and traps; close co-operation between bombers and tanks and headquarters staff is maintained by radio.

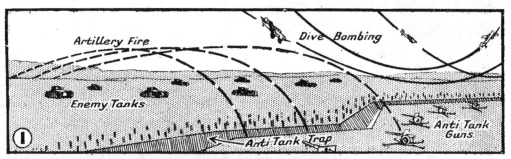

THE keynote of Hitler's European successes was the breathtaking speed of advance of his mechanized forces, crushing armoured strength being used regardless of cost in life and pressed forward relentlessly. Centres of resistance unsubdued have been by-passed to be dealt with later. In the wide spaces of Russia panzer units, having penetrated deep defence zones, have often pressed on 100 miles or more without widening the gaps.

2. Having created a gap in the defences, tanks, brought by radio orders, advance and, by sheer weight of numbers, break through and widen the gap by spreading out and attacking each flank.

3. Some tanks are sacrificed in forcing a minefield, and the tanks following up avail themselves of gaps made clear.

Specially drawn for THE WAR ILLUSTRATED *by War Artists Ltd.*

Have the Germans Found Their Match at Last?

SMOLENSK, with its old fortifications in the foreground. The Germans reported its capture on July 16, but Marshal Timoshenko counter-attacked and dislodged General Kleist's panzer units from the outskirts of the town on July 19. On the right, Nazi troops are seen threading their way along a road towards a village that has just been fired by Russian soldiers. *Photo, E.N.A.*

by a decree of the Presidium of the Supreme Soviet issued on July 20 was appointed People's Commissar for Defence—in effect, supreme commander of the Russian forces—with Marshal Timoshenko as Assistant Commissar.

Another decree of the Presidium on July 17 reintroduced the office of Military Commissar in the Red Army. Specially selected and trained men, it was stated, would be assigned to all military units, and their tasks would be those which had been carried out with such conspicuous success by their predecessors during the Civil War of twenty years ago when, to quote "Pravda," "Military Commissars and Political Instructors inspired the Red Army with their personal examples of unselfishness and courage. They encouraged those who were exhausted. They strengthened and restored the fighting spirit of those whose strength flagged. They urged forward men who subsequently became heroes."

What, then, was the position after five weeks of war? On the northern front the Finnish thrust had reached Petrozavodsk on the north-west shore of Lake Onega, and was aiming to join up with Nazi divisions advancing from Latvia and Estonia to the encirclement of Leningrad. A Finnish division under General Siilasvuo was threatening the Leningrad-Murmansk railway and the Stalin Canal, but a strong Soviet counter-attack was being mounted. On the central front the Germans had driven in two deep salients near Smolensk and Kiev, and were striving desperately to drive south and north so as to enclose the Russian forces still fighting desperately and successfully along the Dnieper line. In the Ukraine the German High Command claimed that "German, Rumanian, Hungarian, and Slovak troops were pressing forward in relentless pursuit." Then Moscow was bombed for the first time on July 21, and again on successive nights. The Germans claim that the raids were highly successful : the Kremlin had been hit several times and the city was a sea of flame. But these claims were scouted by the Russians, in common with most of the claims which the Nazis made in that hour of supreme testing.

SOVIET SOLDIERS crossing a river by pontoon bridge on their way to attack the Nazis. On the right are motorized German troops passing through a blazing Russian town, while the oval photograph shows Russian mechanics loading a bomb into the bay of a plane in readiness for an aerial attack on the enemy columns. Up to the end of July none of the great objectives on the Russian front had been captured by Hitler. Leningrad, Moscow and Kiev still remained in Soviet hands, and the German blitzkrieg in the east may be said to have failed. *Photos, British Official*

Hedge-hopping Over Holland, Britain's Air

How low our pilots flew when they made their daylight attack on the Rotterdam docks on July 16 may be judged by these remarkable photographs. Above and below right, Blenheims are seen on the outskirts of the city where farmers can be seen at work in the fields. Right, our aircraft, flying less than 200 feet above the Rotterdam streets, are watched with interest by the inhabitants. One woman (black arrow) has stopped on the edge of the kerb and gazes upwards. No one runs for cover, for the Dutch know the R.A.F. bombs its target. Only the ducks on the lake (white arrow) are disturbed by the roar of the aircraft.

n Write 'V' for Victory in the Dutch Sky

AT ROTTERDAM, on July 16, Blenheim aircraft of Bomber Command made a daring low-level daylight attack on enemy shipping in the docks. On the left, British bombs are seen bursting in the target area alongside the river. Seventeen ships, totalling some 100,000 tons, were put out of action in this raid, while two warehouses and a factory were left in flames.

Photos, British Official : Crown Copyright

With the Royal Navy in the Syrian Campaign

Fresh from their laborious and dangerous exertions off Crete, light units of our Mediterranean Fleet played a considerable part in the campaign in Syria. It may be added that at the same time the Navy was responsible for supplying the forces in Tobruk, our submarines were ranging the Mediterranean, searching out enemy tankers and supply ships, while Admiral Cunningham's main fleet had to be ready in case the Italians put to sea to create a diversion.

BESIDES having to carry out almost daily bombardments of Vichy positions out of reach of our own field guns ashore, our naval forces engaged in the Syrian warzone had had to guard the coast so that Vichy destroyers could not bombard our troops. On one or two occasions Vichy destroyers did manage to slip out of Beirut and engaged our land forces from very close range—so close, in fact, that the soldiers ashore could see the officers on the bridge observing through their glasses. The guns ashore replied to the Vichy fire from the sea and claimed a hit, but before any damage had been done British cruisers and destroyers

spotted by the reconnaissance planes of the Fleet Air Arm. Immediately a torpedo attack was launched, and one torpedo was seen to hit the destroyer fair and square. Daylight reconnaissance showed oil and wreckage, and finally Vichy announced that they had lost a destroyer.

One night—a beautiful moonlight night with very good visibility—there was a short brisk action with the Vichy destroyers, seen by our forces against the distant lights of Beirut. There was a quiet order of "Alarm port," and simultaneously our ships opened fire. Our shells were seen falling all round

SYRIA, off whose coast naval units of the British Mediterranean Fleet collaborated with the Allied land forces during the successful Syrian campaign.

BRITISH WARSHIPS of the Mediterranean Fleet are here seen in action against strongly fortified Vichy positions along the Syrian coastal road. This naval cooperation was of immense help to the Imperial troops during their advance towards Beirut.   *Photo, British Official*

arrived on the scene and the Vichy naval force retired behind a smoke screen.

Cooperation between the Navy, the Army, and the Air Force was once again the feature of this short campaign: and the Australian and British forces on the coastal road have said how comforting it was to look out to sea day after day and find there five or six—sometimes more—ships of the Royal Navy steaming a few miles offshore. The Australians always cheered whenever our destroyers turned up off the coast, and after one of these bombardments when our destroyers knocked out a battery of twelve French 75s harassing our columns, the Brigadier commanding the coastal columns sent to the squadron this signal: "Thank you very much. Navy saved our bacon today!"

There were times when our destroyers came very close in, and then could thoroughly enjoy themselves. Once a destroyer was watching one part of this coastal road and within a few minutes it engaged and destroyed the following targets: a saloon car, two armoured fighting vehicles and three supply lorries. Someone who was there at the time described it as being rather like a shooting gallery at moving targets. Tanks and armoured cars were picked off as if it were a rifle range. If no moving targets presented themselves, then our ships searched out and destroyed bridges and artillery positions behind the Vichy lines.

During these operations our ships were subject to air attack, and they had always to be ready night or day for sudden sorties by the Vichy destroyers from Beirut. One Vichy destroyer which was on her way to reinforce the small squadron in Beirut was

the enemy, sending up great white waterspouts, and several times, although the enemy were firing, there was the unmistakable flash—different from a gun flash—which showed that our shells were going home. But as our ships raced up at thirty knots to complete their destruction, the enemy destroyers turned and got safely back to Beirut.

As our troops grimly fought their way up the coastal road towards Beirut one Vichy centre of resistance after another fell, and at last the French withdrew from Sidon, which had just undergone a twenty-four hour bombardment from a British naval force of nine units. From Sidon the advance continued, and finally we came up against the extremely strong position at Damour. Then

our destroyers closed in to hammer the position, and methodically steamed up and down the coast, backwards and forwards, so close in that they could hear their own shell bursts echoing around the ravines. This bombardment helped our troops to cross the River Damour and to force a position which the enemy thought was impregnable. From then on our troops advanced closer and closer upon Beirut; and with them, supporting them from the sea, were our naval forces.

By now the citizens of Beirut had become extremely apprehensive. They had no wish for naval 6-in. and 4·7-in. shells to be flying around their city, and they made urgent demands that it should be declared an open town and the French withdraw beyond it. The threat of air and naval bombardment certainly helped to persuade the Vichy authorities to ask for an armistice.

GUEPARD, one of three Vichy destroyers—Valmy and Vauquelin being the other two—which escaped from Syria to Toulon before the Convention, by which all French ships in the vicinity of Syria were to be turned over to Britain, came into force.   *Photo, Planet News*

Theirs Was a Fine Contribution to the Victory

Gun flashes from a British warship seen at water level, a photograph taken during a night encounter between our naval units and Vichy vessels. On the left, British destroyers approaching the coast of Syria in the dawn to cooperate with our land forces are attacking strongly fortified positions.

OFF SYRIA, British destroyers in formation returning to harbour after being in action against the Vichy forces. Certain ships of the Royal Australian Navy took part in those actions intended to help the advance of our army along the coast road to Beirut. On one occasion the Vichy ships took refuge in Beirut harbour, and subsequent aerial reconnaissance established the fact that a Vichy destroyer was lying there badly damaged, probably as a result of our bombing or gunfire.

Photos, British and Australian Official : Crown Copyright

Our Diary of the War

SUNDAY, JULY 20, 1941   687th day

Sea.—Admiralty announced that H. M. drifters Devon County and Lord St. Vincent had been sunk.

Air.—Offensive cross-Channel sweeps resumed. Enemy tanker set on fire.

Sustained night attack on Cologne. Other targets in Rhineland and docks at Rotterdam were also bombed. Fighter Command attacked enemy aerodromes in France.

Russian Front.—Fierce fighting in areas of German thrusts towards Leningrad, Moscow, and Kiev. Germans claimed successes on Finnish and Bessarabian fronts.

Africa.—During night of 19-20 British and Indian patrols at Tobruk carried out series of successful raids on enemy positions.

R.A.F. made heavy night attacks on Benghazi and Tripoli.

Mediterranean.—Heavy bombers raided Naples on night of 20-21, damaging harbour and railway sidings.

General.—Mr. Brendan Bracken appointed Minister of Information in place of Mr. Duff Cooper, proceeding on mission to Far East.

German Minister to Bolivia expelled by Government following discovery of subversive activities centralized in German Legation.

MONDAY, JULY 21   688th day

Air.—R.A.F. made daylight attack on Lille and on enemy shipping off French coast. Eight enemy fighters down for loss of three.

Night raids on industrial targets and railways at Frankfurt and Mannheim. Docks at Cherbourg and Ostend and aerodromes in northern France were also attacked.

Russian Front.—Stubborn fighting round Smolensk and in sectors north and south of German wedge. In south Russians completed strategic retreat from Bessarabia to lines behind the river Dniester.

German High Command claimed that in southern sector enemy was being pursued.

During night of 21-22 German aircraft raided Moscow for first time, but caused comparatively little damage. Attempts to raid Leningrad were intercepted by Russian aircraft, and 19 enemy planes were shot down.

Home.—Few enemy aircraft crossed coast during night. Bombs fell at points in East Anglia. Enemy bomber collided with R.A.F. machine over Home Counties ; both destroyed and crews killed.

General.—German Government protested against expulsion of German Minister from La Paz, and ordered Bolivian Chargé d'Affaires in Berlin to leave.

TUESDAY, JULY 22   689th day

Sea.—Enemy convoy off island of Pantellaria, Mediterranean, attacked by R.A.F. and Fleet Air Arm ; three ships sunk and destroyer damaged.

Air.—R.A.F. attacked shipbuilding yards at Le Trait, west of Rouen. Extensive sweeps over northern France. Four enemy fighters destroyed for loss of three.

Night raids on Rhineland industries, main targets being Frankfurt and Mannheim. Docks at Dunkirk, Ostend and Rotterdam also bombed.

Russian Front.—Moscow reported heavy fighting in four principal sectors of front. Germans claimed that Soviet defence line had been broken up into isolated groups which were being annihilated.

Another night raid on Moscow Russians stated they destroyed 15 enemy bombers.

Africa.—Patrols at Tobruk made another sortie on night of 21-22. Heavy bombers attacked Benghazi on night of 22-23.

WEDNESDAY, JULY 23   690th day

Air.—R.A.F. made daylight attacks on enemy shipping off France and Low Countries. One vessel sunk, another damaged. Inland targets near St. Omer bombed. Eleven fighters destroyed. We lost 10 fighters and 5 bombers.

Reconnaissance machines discovered that battleship Scharnhorst had been moved from Brest to La Pallice, 240 miles south. There she was attacked with heavy armour-piercing bombs. During night further attacks made on Scharnhorst and on Gneisenau at Brest.

Night offensive against Frankfurt and Mannheim. Port of Cherbourg was also bombed, and docks at Le Havre and Ostend.

Russian Front.—Smolensk stated still in Russian hands despite German claim of capture on July 16. Fighting continued in Petrozavodsk sector, north-east of Lake Ladoga. Enemy renewed attacks in Porkhov sector, south-east of Leningrad.

Germans claimed to be pursuing " beaten enemy " in Ukraine. Battle in progress round Zhitomir.

Another mass night attack on Moscow attempted ; most raiders intercepted before reaching city.

Africa.—Further offensive patrols from Tobruk. R.A.F. made night attack on Benghazi.

Mediterranean.—R.A.F. fighters destroyed an E-boat and two Junkers.

R.A.F. bombed shipping at Trapani, Sicily, and aerodromes at Trapani and Marsala.

Home.—One day and two night bombers shot down during widespread but small-scale raids on Britain. Bombs also fell in Northern Ireland and Eire.

General.—Vichy announced that Japan had been granted temporary bases in French Indo-China.

THURSDAY, JULY 24   691st day

Air.—Coastal Command bombed railway yards at Hazebrouck. Twelve enemy fighters destroyed for loss of six.

Daylight attacks on Scharnhorst and Gneisenau. In the two days' operations R.A.F. destroyed 33 enemy fighters. We lost 15 bombers and 7 fighters.

Heavy night raids on Kiel and Emden. Lesser ones on Wilhelmshaven and docks at Rotterdam. Fighter Command attacked airfields in France.

Russian Front.—Moscow reported furious fighting in regions of Porkhov, Polotsk-Nevel, Smolensk and Zhitomir. German report made no new claims and referred to strong Russian resistance.

Home.—Enemy bomber shot down off east coast of Scotland.

FRIDAY, JULY 25   692nd day

Sea.—Admiralty announced that during naval operations connected with passage of British convoy through Mediterranean our forces suffered series of heavy dive-bombing and E-boat attacks. H.M. destroyer Fearless sunk.

Air.—R.A.F. night offensive centred on Hanover and Hamburg. Berlin also raided. Fighter Command attacked aerodromes in northern France.

Russian Front.—Russians launched counter-attack in Battle of Smolensk and claimed to have destroyed 5th German infantry division.

General.—Great Britain and U.S.A. froze Japanese assets.

OUTSIDE ST. PAUL'S, on a beautifully warm and sunny July day, the band of the Royal Marines is playing to an appreciative audience. This was one of a series of lunchtime and evening band concerts arranged for Londoners during the summer. Thanks to the R.A.F., for which the Luftwaffe now has a wholesome respect, no apprehensive glances at the sky distract from their enjoyment. *Photo. Associated Press*

AIR VIEWS OF HAMBURG: WHAT DO THEY SHOW?

A Critical Commentary by the Editor

Although written before Mr. Brendan Bracken's appointment this is by way of an open letter to the new Minister of Information, in whose energy and youthful daring I have great confidence. British propaganda has been—and is—adversely criticized. It is up to him to effect the much-needed change. M. Maisky might be worth consulting, as the Soviet officials have quickly shown that their closer relations with Goebbels since September 1939 have taught them much.

HAS the M.O.I. done a wise thing in issuing these two air photos of a scene in Hamburg before and after camouflage ? I don't think so. They horrify me. I am haunted by the fear that we are not " giving it " to Hamburg as generously as we have been led to believe. Look at the photos ; examine them with care ; you will agree that the Hamburg Hun did a good job in making the Binnen Alster, the lesser of the two lakes in the centre of his city, look like a " built-up area." But to what purpose our thousands of heavy explosives and incendiaries in our 80 raids on the city ? Not a sign of destruction can I make out. The main building blocks look the same before and after camouflage ; indeed, they are more sharply defined in the later photograph ; nowhere do I detect acres of ruin, no thoroughfares show any breakages, all streets, broad and narrow, follow their old straight lines or curves, even the railway station appears to be undamaged. A refugee from the city has reported that while there was a near-miss at the station it had not actually been hit when he left the place.

Like millions of my fellow-citizens I have listened almost every day for months to the reports of our bombers over Hamburg and the vast fires they could see when they were forty miles away on their return journey, and I believe them implicitly. Not the least little indication of the devastation in which I have so fondly believed jumps to the eye that critically examines these amusing but otherwise disappointing " releases " from our Ministry of Information. Nothing is here to comfort the inhabitants of the East End of London, the business men of the City, the bombed-out tenants of the Temple, our homeless friends in Coventry, Bristol, Plymouth, and many another of our bombed and fire-wrecked cities—nothing at all to make us realize that Hamburg has been made to suffer. Only that they have got some ingenious experts in the art of camou-

flage there. How bewilderingly ineffective our propaganda people do seem to be ! Why cannot they obtain the release of at least a few photographs that would give us the long-denied satisfaction of clear evidence of damage ?

There is a possible (but highly unlikely) explanation of these absolutely futile photos. They may have been taken twelve months ago and are now thought fit for release. Not too great a lapse of time in the languorous judgement of the M.O.I. Meanwhile the central station, the real Lombards-Bruecke, as well as the dummy one shown in the " after camouflage " photo, and all the closely-built areas included in the amusing snapshots may have been reduced to shapeless rubble, *as they ought to have been*, if the oft-repeated tales of our heavy attacks on Hamburg have been worth the listening. If so, would it not have been far more worth while to let us have some photographic records of the consequent chaos ? Surely that is not only a sensible question but also an urgent one. If our aerial cameras can

record so clearly the effects of camouflaging, so that its purpose is nullified, could they not equally record the effects of our " beautiful bombs " and incendiaries ?

Unhappily all my inquiries and perquisitions lead me to think that these photographs were actually taken quite recently, and most people can only conclude that the inhabitants of this part of central Hamburg have enjoyed an immunity from British bombs that is totally at variance with the experience of those of us in central London, whose fate it is to endure the attentions of the Nazi bombers. The great dock area, which we are told has been enormously damaged, is only three-quarters of a mile from the outer edge of the district covered by these air views. Photographs of that damaged area would be very acceptable.

I suggest in all seriousness that the effect of these two official photos—completely useless as propaganda—will be most disturbing to anyone who brings to their study even a moderate capacity for investigation. But they are quite in line with the childishness that has informed so many of the futilities for which we taxpayers are providing an unstated number of millions sterling.

Goebbels will not be up to his accustomed form if he doesn't re-issue them to his Nazi pictorial press as a present from his opposite number in London showing how well Hamburg has stood up to the R.A.F. bombing and how neatly his colleagues of the camouflage have done their job ; there can be no reason else for his concealing them. Let the pundits of Senate House, Bloomsbury, try again with something more instructive and a little more consolatory. But in the meantime they might, in fairness to the efforts of our brave lads of the Bomber Command, " condescend upon a date " by letting the public know how long it is since the centre of Hamburg was looking as spick and span as it does in the second of these two photographs.

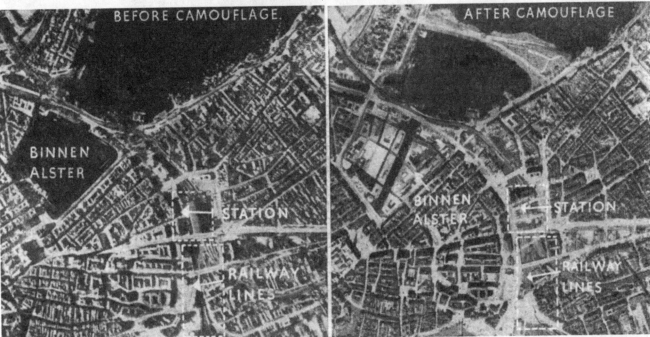

BEFORE CAMOUFLAGE.   AFTER CAMOUFLAGE

BINNEN ALSTER   STATION   RAILWAY LINES

Photos, British Official ; Crown Copyright

Glimpses of Life in Once-Great France

FRENCH WAR PRISONERS, a few of whom have recently been released in keeping with an accord reached between Vichy and the Nazis, are on their way home. Each prisoner has had a white line placed on his back by the Nazis.

DEMOLISHED BRIDGES, remnants of the bitter struggle of 1940, are now being repaired in France. These steel reinforcement rods droop sadly from the wreckage of a concrete railway bridge.

MARSHAL PÉTAIN (carrying cane) listens to explanations by Gen. Jean Bergeret, Minister of Aviation in the Vichy Government, as he examines bombs at the French air base at Aulnat. Against whom are they destined to be used ?

The notice in this window of a baker's shop in Vichy France reads : " Our products are made with flour sent by the United States of America. Our thanks to the Americans." Behind is a bag of flour labelled " Gift of the people of U.S.A. to the people of France, through the intermediary of the American Red Cross. 98 lb. flour."

GERMAN SOLDIERS and the Luftwaffe's maintenance men are busy levelling the ground of an airfield in Occupied France after the R.A.F. have passed over on an " offensive sweep."

Photos, Wide World, Associated Press, Keystone

Only a 'V'—But It Spells Hitler's Doom!

THE most effective propaganda so far devised against the Nazi tyranny is the V campaign invented by M. Victor de Laveleye, head of the Belgian station at the B.B.C. It has brought hope to the occupied territories. The letter V which appears mysteriously anywhere and everywhere means victory for the Allies. The Nazis are so perturbed by this symbol that they have tried to steal it, but the German people must know that *Viktoria* is not the right German word for victory. In Hun language it is *Sieg*. There is a significant V in German, and it is *Vernichtung* meaning destruction, and this is coming to the Nazis.

A Pétain poster in Marseilles, Unoccupied France, has been marked with two significant "Vs," meaning British victory, in answer to the pusillanimous policy of collaboration with Germany on the part of the Vichy Government.

The "V" in Morse code and as a letter chalked up on a London wall. On the right a "V" wreath placed on the Foch statue in London. *Photos, Associated Press and "Daily Mail"; cartoon by Wyndham Robinson from the "Star"*

Where the 'Bombed Out' Are Sure of a Welcome

COLOUR, cheerfulness, and "none of that Nosy Parker business"—these are among the chief impressions I brought away from a tour of several of the Rest Centres run by the Social Welfare Department of the London County Council. They must mean a lot to the unfortunate folk for whom these Centres have been established—people who, emerging from their Andersons or public shelters in the early morning light, find that their homes and all their worldly goods have been blown to pieces or buried beneath debris, or at least covered with a thick layer of dirt and dust. They themselves are likely to be a bit dirty, too, particularly if bombs have been stirring up the elements round about them. Some of them, as they step along the white line which guides them through the children's playground to the school where the Centre is established, are dressed in their night-clothes only, or maybe they have next to nothing on save a blanket.

No sooner are they inside the Centre, however, than they find a deck-chair awaiting them, a cup of tea and a cheery smile. Then there is hot water for a wash, heaps of shoes and piles of clothes from which any deficiency in dress may be speedily repaired. There are no questions asked; no payment is demanded, nor is it taken if it is offered, though some of the inmates—we had better call them guests, as that is the official term—may stay as long as a week, until their homes have been made fit for them to go back to, or a neighbour has offered the use of his spare room, or they can be evacuated into the country.

SCATTERED about London are numbers of these Rest Centres, and, of course, in other great cities, too. The first-line Centres are L.C.C. schools, where accommodation is available since so many children have been evacuated. These have been carefully adapted for their new use; floors have been strengthened, windows blocked up, and gas-proof rooms provided. The second line consists of church and public halls, which are used as over-flows. Then there is a third line brought into use only during the very bad "blitzes," consisting of chapels, mission premises, Quaker meeting-houses, and the like. A considerable proportion of the staff is drawn from the ranks of the teachers, but many have been specially recruited, and the whole are under the direction of the permanent staff of the L.C.C.'s Social Welfare Department.

The Centres of the first line are reminiscent of the hostels which have become so popular amongst holiday-makers of recent years. In each there is a

Bombed out of their home, this little family, after rescuing what they can in the way of personal belongings, make their way to an Emergency Rest Centre.

reception-room, a large communal dining-room, a recreation-room for games, and a children's nursery; the latter in particular is an altogether charming place, with its chintz curtains, its jolly pictures and its wealth of toys—mostly second-hand but none the less desirable for that. There are rocking-horses, building bricks, dolls' houses big enough to get into, shops and garages, and chairs just big enough for the comfort of juvenile posteriors.

Then upstairs there is a rest-room—and what a collection of armchairs, settees, sofas, and other relics of bygone days have been rescued from bombed homes! Now they are enjoying a further lease of usefulness in surroundings altogether un-dreamed of by the mid-Victorian newly-weds who first gave them a place in their homes. Every-where there are bright colours. The rooms are known as the green room, the yellow room; the deck-chairs are painted vivid reds and blues, and even the bins in the kitchen are distinctively coloured: "That one with the rice in, is black because niggers eat it." Then there are the bedrooms with piles of mattresses ready to be laid on the bunks; on the door of the women's room is the notice, "Gentlemen withdraw when the first lady retires."

Down below, well beneath street level, is the Control Room where, when the Alert is sounded and the bombs are dropping—and heaven knows, every street in this thickly-populated area of North-East London has its wounds—the officer-in-charge directs his little army of workers. Sometimes he is hard put to it to find room for all his guests, but as many as 1,800 have sought admission in a single night. Sought admission, and found it—and a welcome, too.

E. R. P.

They reach the Rest Centre, which is housed in a school building, and the first thing they do is to have a good meal, right, before making plans for the future.

Circle, an experienced lady interviewer has a chat with them about their future plans, gives some useful advice, and offers any further assistance they may need. *Photos, Keystone*

I Was There! ....Eye Witness Stories of the War

We Went in a Motor-Boat from Crete to Africa

One party of soldiers and airmen who escaped from Crete crossed the Mediterranean to North Africa in a boat designed for calm coastal waters. Their story is told here by an Australian sergeant air-gunner.

MY aircraft had to make a forced landing on the beaches of Crete. The other three members of the crew and I all got clear of the machine, and not far away we found some Army and Royal Air Force personnel awaiting evacuation. We stayed the night and following day with them, and next evening another British aircraft made a forced landing within 500 yards of our own machine. We were joined by its crew, and at about the same time a Hurricane pilot arrived.

Next morning the Germans began bombing a near-by village, so we moved. It was good to see them bombing two wrecked aircraft on the beach. The German pilots must have made fantastic claims of successes, because the wrecks were set on fire several times.

During the night we sent out patrols to forage and they brought back onions, lettuces, beans and green mulberries. I was scrounging in a fowlhouse when a German plane dropped bombs close by. The fowlhouse was demolished and fell on top of me.

Eventually we met some more British and Australian troops and decided to try to launch a flat-bottomed landing craft which had been washed up and abandoned on the beach. Men of various regiments were detailed to find fuel and rations. The Australians were to try to launch the craft, while the Air Force was made responsible for its navigation. Launching seemed an impossible task, but we were hastened by the Germans firing tommy-guns. A patrol in a rowing boat was fired on and one officer was wounded. Other members of the crew jumped over the side and towed the boat out of range before climbing back and returning to us.

That evening we got our craft away and set course for North Africa. There were about 77 of us. The sea, which had been beautifully calm for two days, became rough, and we found that the compass from my aircraft was useless. Our boat, 50 feet long with a 10-foot beam, had a flat bottom and little freeboard, so we had to bale out all the way over. Most of us were horribly seasick. We navigated with a small pocket compass in daytime and in darkness by the stars.

Early next morning we sighted a submarine. Somebody on board the submarine said something in English which cheered us up no end. We soon found it was not one of ours, for it opened fire across our bows and stopped us. Our senior officer was ordered to leave, and he swam across to the submarine which afterwards came alongside and took off all the officers except the wounded Australian. The submarine commander then told us that we were free, but that we must return to Crete.

Instead, we reset our course for North Africa. Only one of the engines was working and we had to check our course continually. Our supply of water was very foul, and for food we had one quarter of a tin of bully beef per man twice daily. There were also a few onions.

Early during the afternoon of the third day we had our first sight of land and thought at first we had fallen into the hands of the Germans, because we saw a tank which did not look like one of ours. Two of us swam ashore to investigate and discovered we were within four miles of the point we had aimed at. We all swam ashore, to be warmly welcomed by South African troops.

How I Plodded 200 Miles Across Libyan Sands

" Moore's March " was one of the epics of the Libyan campaigns. The remarkable story of how four wounded British soldiers, with practically no food or water, set out to walk over 200 miles through the desert is told here by Trooper Ronald Moore himself.

WE were on patrol when the " Eyeties " spotted us at Hadje Bishara, some miles south of Koufra. There were several trucks in one patrol, under Major Clayton, and we returned their fire with our machine-guns as our drivers bumped, all out, over the sand.

Very soon my truck got cut off from the others, and it wasn't long after that that she caught fire, and we thought it was all up. I yelled to the others, " Shall we go or surrender ? " and somebody yelled back, " Beat it." We piled out—four of us and an Italian prisoner we had with us—and made for some rocks a short way ahead.

There was Guardsman John Easton, of Edinburgh, who was wounded in the throat; Pte. Alfred Tighe, of Manchester, Guardsman Alexander Winchester, of Glasgow, and myself (a New Zealander), but Major Clayton and two others, who were wounded, remained behind and were captured.

We hid among the rocks until nightfall, not daring to move, as enemy planes were circling overhead. But after dark we got together, and as we had neither food nor water with us, debated whether we should give ourselves up or set out across the desert in the hopes that another of our patrols would pick us up. We decided to make a bid for it, and set out at dawn, taking our prisoner along with us. We headed south, where we thought it most likely we would run across another British, or perhaps a French, patrol.

I had had a piece of shrapnel in my foot some days previously, and John Easton's wound was hurting him, but we managed to cover forty miles that first day. We had no food or water, and I remember my tongue sticking to the roof of my mouth, so that I couldn't speak. Then, late in the afternoon, we saw a car, and our hopes rose.

We walked towards it—about two miles—when we saw without doubt it was Italian. We sat in the sand then, out of sight, behind a dune, and again debated whether we should surrender. We were nearly mad with thirst, and decided to give ourselves up. The " Eyetie " led the way in front, and we followed in line up a wadi with our hands up. But we got closer and closer with nothing happening and, when finally we reached the car, we found it had been abandoned—shot to pieces, evidently by one of our own patrols.

The first thing we did was to search for food and water, but the water tanks had also been riddled by bullets, and every drop had leaked out. There was no food either, and all we could find were some empty condensed milk cans that had been thrown away, and the dried-up leaves that someone had emptied from a teapot.

We scraped the remains of the milk with our finger-nails from the insides of the cans, but it was hard and full of sand. We tried to chew the dried tea-leaves, but with no saliva in our mouths we couldn't swallow, and we were about to give up when I found a water tank among the debris of the car that had about a gallon and a half of water in it.

We took a condensed milk can, and in it we boiled up some of the dried tea-leaves. It looked awful, and tasted worse, but, oh boy ! that was the finest cup of tea I've ever had.

We left the " Eyetic " there—he had a

THIS AUSTRALIAN signaller, alone in an open boat, escaped from Crete and made his way across the Mediterranean to the N. African coast between Sidi Barrani and Mersa Matruh. His only compass was a penknife stuck into the deck, he was fired at by the Germans as he left the Cretan coast, and then was machine-gunned by an enemy plane. When ten miles off the African coast his boat fell to pieces and he finished the journey floating on this two-gallon water tin. *Photo, British Official*

The thrilling story of "Moore's March" is related in this page. Above, after they had been picked up, are Trooper Ronald Moore (left) and Pte. Alfred Tighe.
Photo, "Life" Magazine

chance of being picked up. Then the four of us set out again across the sand.

It was bitterly cold that night. None of us had more than just our shirts and shorts—so we dug a hole in the sand and lay, with our arms round each other, trying to keep warm. We had found a field dressing that morning, so had been able to dress Easton's wound and bandage my foot. I don't think I could ever have gone on without that dressing.

Our water we rationed out among the four of us, drinking only a mouthful or so, night and morning—but we had no food. I remembered where, a few days ago, we had camped in the sand. Cookie had given us lentils for supper. None of us liked lentils, and we all had thrown them away—we had cursed poor Cookie, too.

That was at Sarra—125 miles from where we took to the sand. I kept thinking of those lentils, and, as it was on our way south, we made for our old camp, and we got there in four days. We found the lentils, but they had been dried out by the sun, and were so salty we couldn't eat them. Again we scraped out the milk cans that had been thrown away.

We were all very weak by now, and as Alfred Tighe was in a pretty bad shape, he decided to remain at Sarra, thinking there would be more chance of being picked up there than there would be farther south.

There was not much water left by now, but we divided what little there was, putting Tighe's share in an empty lentil bottle we found at the camp, and the three of us went on alone. Later, when I saw Tighe again, I learned the bottle we had put his water in had so much salt in it from the lentils that the water was like brine and he couldn't drink it.

I lost all count of time after that. We just walked on, heading south and stopping every hour for a few minutes' rest. Each night I thought I would never live to see

another day—the cold was so intense, and it was always some time before I could get my legs to work when we set out again at dawn.

Then, one morning, I think it must have been the second after leaving Tighe, John Easton could not get up. Winchester and I rubbed his legs to start the circulation, and, finally, got him to his feet, but he could not stand for long—just stumbled a few paces and dropped in the sand.

He did this several times, trying all he could to keep going, but I knew, somehow, by the staring look in his eyes that he was done. He asked for water, and I gave him half of what was left, but it was no good, and in a few moments he died.

We just buried him where he was, in the sand, and Winchester and I went on alone. We divided the few mouthfuls of water we had left, equally, and set out south again. We could not walk far at a time, so stopped for frequent rests. We had lost our shoes somewhere, and were walking in our bare feet. It is easier, I think, in the soft sand.

I don't remember very clearly what happened after that, except plodding hour after hour through the hot sand. I didn't dare drink the last few drops of water I had, so just swilled my mouth out with it and spat it back into the bottle to use again.

And then, one day, Winchester conked

out. He could go no farther. I just scraped a hollow in the sand for him to lie in. I left him there and went on.

By this time I could only go a mile or so without resting, but I went as far as I could each time before sitting down in the sand. And I saw two lorries away off on the horizon, and I waved at them, but they didn't see me, and soon disappeared among the dunes.

It was the next day that I got picked up—on the Jef Jef, 225 miles south of where we started—and I found, later, I had taken ten days to get there—ten days without food and only three pints of water.

When I first saw the lorry approaching, I couldn't believe my eyes. I thought it must be a mirage or something, and just kept on stumbling along. I remembered I was thinking about the bones at the time that lay along the route every few hundred yards, bleached white. They were only camels' bones, but I thought, if even the camels died, what chance had I?

From the drivers of the truck I learned that both Tighe and Winchester had been picked up. Tighe first, the day before, but, being unable to speak French, he had not been able to make them understand that they would find us also, somewhere south.

It was not until the next day, after they found someone who spoke English, that they set out in search of us.—*Time and Life, Ltd.*

What a Pity the 'Enemy Ships' Were Dummies!

The Royal Navy are the world's foremost exponents of torpedo-bombing, and this picture of the Fleet Air Arm at practice shows how the pilots develop their skill in this difficult technique.

Pilots, observers, air-gunners—and myself—were called at 3.30 a.m., and, after a sandwich and a cup of tea in the air station wardroom, put on fur-lined jackets, Mae Wests, (an elaborate form of water-wings), parachute harness and helmets. Then we listened to the squadron leader outlining the plan of attack.

Under a dark and angry sky, with a 40-m.p.h. wind, we climbed into our planes, and my earphones were connected up so that I was in touch with the pilot. The rear-gunner satisfied himself all was ready for the pilot to fire his guns if enemy planes were encountered, then sat on a tiny collapsible stool behind the one on which I was perched, the engine's throb rose to a roar—and we were off.

Almost at once thick swirling mist and

cloud engulfed us. Despite this the planes leapt into the air smartly, one after another, and quickly assumed formation. Damp fields slid away to be replaced by leaden sea.

For an hour we sped on, our wing-tips nearly touching. "Don't worry," came my pilot's voice down the tube. "We often fly closer than this." Frequently clouds blotted out the sea, leaving us in a grey world empty save for the planes of our flight alongside us. Most of the time the rest of the squadron were hidden.

Through a gap I suddenly spotted two black dots moving on the slate-coloured sea, with thin grey streaks trailing out behind them. They looked like tiny kites with tails, floating in a storm-laden sky. These were the "enemy battleships"; smaller dots around them were "escorting destroyers."

FAIREY ALBACORES are the latest torpedo-spotter-reconnaissance biplanes of the Fleet Air Arm. How their pilots practise is described above. This aircraft has folding wings to save stowage space on aircraft-carriers and succeeds the Fairey Swordfish.   *Photo, Central Press*

IIIIIIIIIIIIIIIIIIIIIIIIIIIIIIIII I WAS THERE! IIIIIIIIIIIIIIIIIIIIIIIIIIIIIIIII

Our leader shot ahead and the planes on either side broke away. Rapidly we manœuvred for the best striking position. Then, from clouds now dawn-tinged with pink, we swept down, one after another.

Had they been real enemy ships they would hardly have had time to train their guns on us before we swooped, launched our torpedoes (special practice ones) and were back again behind the clouds. As we dived the water appeared to rush up to meet the plane. One half of me was sure we should hit it. The other remembered the pilot had done this many times before, and knew all would be well.

When nearly on the water, the plane dropped its load, banked sharply, sickeningly, and as I clung grimly to my "handle-bar," it seemed the wings must catch in the water. We flattened out, waltzed drunkenly to avoid imaginary shells hurtling at us from hundreds of barrels on the "battleships," now twisting to avoid the torpedoes and leaving pale green wakes like wriggling snakes.

Now the sea was dropping away as we climbed steeply back into the clouds. Behind us other planes were diving and hurtling away to regain station. Soon we were wheeling in readiness for another attack, and down we plunged again . . .

Two hours later I was breakfasting with a number of young pilots who had still further increased their skill with a weapon that must be the terror of Axis warships.—*Reuter*.

My First Flights Over the Enemy's Country

Pilot Officer Dan McIntosh, a young Canadian from Saskatchewan, who is serving in a heavy bomber squadron of the R.A.F., told of his experiences over Germany and Italy in a broadcast. His vivid first-hand story is printed below.

I DON'T suppose any member of a bomber crew—whether he's a pilot, air gunner, wireless operator or navigator—will ever forget his first operational flight. I made mine on November 5 last year, Guy Fawkes' Day, a very appropriate day as it turned out. I was flying as second pilot then to get experience. My captain was a young Flying Officer who has since been awarded the D.F.C. He was not long down from Oxford and just the coolest customer you ever saw.

On this particular night we were going to Hamburg. I got my baptism of fire all right then, because it turned out to be a really hot spot; in fact, I've never seen anything quite so hot since. I remember saying to the captain when I saw all the anti-aircraft fire coming up and the searchlights all over the plane, " Do you have to go through that stuff ? " It looked to me as if there wasn't a square inch where you could get through safely. He said, " Oh, yes, we'll fix that all right." And then he just sailed in, jinking—or, in other words, dodging about to put the ground defences off. He got on to the target, levelled out, bombed, and came out again, as coolly as you please. When we'd got clear I said, " It doesn't seem so bad as it looks," and then I remember saying, " But it *is* pretty, isn't it ? " He laughed his head off at that. On the way back we ran through some more searchlights and he handed the controls over to me so that he could show me how to dodge them. I had one more trip with another pilot, this time to the Krupps works at Essen, before I started with my own crew who had come with me from the Operational Training Unit. First we were sent to bomb the German submarine base at Lorient, then we had raids on Cologne, Bremen—I've been three times to Bremen—Mannheim and Ludwigshaven, Gelsenkirchen, Düsseldorf, Wilhelmshaven, Hamburg and a good many other less well-known places. We also had a go at some of the invasion ports on the Channel coast, and then we had the Italian trip.

This was to bomb the Royal Arsenal at Turin, and it meant a flight of about thirteen hundred miles and, of course, we had to cross the Alps twice. It was a perfect moonlight night—one of the best nights I've ever been out on—and as it turned out it was a more or less straightforward trip both going and coming back. The Alps were the grandest sight I've ever seen, with a bright moon shining on the snow. Some of the other people from the squadron went through a mountain pass, flying below the level of the peaks on either side of them, but I decided to go right over the top and we made the crossing at about 16,500 feet.

When we got to the other side of the Alps there was Turin right in front of us. As I came down over the foothills I could see the Italian guns loosing off at somebody who was just coming out of the pass, and while I was bombing there was another chap over the target at the same time. We saw his bombs just before our own went off. Then when we'd made our attack, we had to climb again to cross the Alps a second time. It seemed a very long way back and nothing much happened except that the guns at one German aerodrome in Occupied France opened fire.

The pilot officer who relates his experiences in this page has been three times to Bremen. This is the kind of thing his captain alluded to when he said, " It is pretty, isn't it ? "—tracer bullets, bursting shells and searchlights seen from a Bremen rooftop. *Photo, Keystone*

We landed again after about nine hours flying. If you can imagine driving for nine solid hours in the black-out you'll get some slight idea of what a flight like that means.

ABBREVIATIONS USED BY THE FOUR SERVICES
The Royal Air Force

A.A.F. Auxiliary Air Force.
A.A.F.G.L. Auxiliary Air Force General List.
A.A.F.R.O. Auxiliary Air Force Reserve of Officers.
A.ᶠCmdre. Air Commodore.
AC Aircraftman (followed by 1 or 2 to denote class).
A.C.A.S. Assistant Chief of Air Staff.
ACH Aircrafthand.
A.C.M. Air Chief Marshal.
A.Ct. Air Commandant (W.A.A.F.).
A.M. Air Marshal.
A.M.P. Air Member for Personnel.
A.M.S.O. Air Member for Supply and Organization.
A.M.T. Air Member for Training.
A.O.C. Air Officer Commanding.
A.O.C.-in-C. Air Officer Commanding-in-Chief.
A.P.O. Acting Pilot Officer.
A.S.I. Air Speed Indicator.
A.S.O. Assistant Section Officer (with A.A.F.).
A.T. Anti-tank.
A.V.M. Air Vice Marshal.

(B.) Balloon Branch Officer.
B.P.S.O. Base Personnel Staff Officer.

C.A.S. Chief of Air Staff.
Ch. Chaplain.
Cpl. Corporal.
C.T.T.B. Central Trade Test Board.

(D.) Dental Branch Officer.
D. A.F.L. Director of Allied Air Cooperation and Foreign Liaison.
D.B. Ops. Director of Bomber Operations.
D.C.A.S. Deputy Chief of Air Staff.
D.F. Ops. Director of Fighter Operations.
D.F.T. Director of Flying Training.
D.G.C.A. Director-General of Civil Aviation.
D.G.D. Director of Ground Defence.
D.G.E. Director-General of Equipment.
D.G.M.S. Director-General Medical Service, R.A.F.
D.G.O. Director-General of Organization.
D.G.W. Director-General of Works.

D.M.C. Director of Military Co-operation.
D.M.O. Director Meteorological Office.
D.M.S. Director of R.A.F. Medical Service.
D. of I. Director of Intelligence.
D. of M. Director of Manning.
D. of P. Director of Postings.
D. of Plans. Director of Plans.
D. of S. Director of Signals.
D.O.N.C. Director of Operations (Naval Co-operation).
D.O.O. Director of Operations (Overseas).
D.O.T. Director of Operational Training.
D.P.R. Director of Public Relations.
D.P.S. Director of Personal Services.
D.R.S. Director of Repair and Service.
D.T.T. Director of Technical Training.
D.W.A.A.F. Director of the Women's Auxiliary Service.

(E.) Equipment Branch Officer.
E.F.T.S. Elementary Flying Training School.
E.O. Education Officer.

F.A. Financial Adviser.
F/Lt. Flight Lieutenant.
Fl.O. Flight Officer (W.A.A.F.).
F/O. Flying Officer.
F/Sgt. Flight Sergeant.

(G.) Air Gunner-Officer.
G.C. Group Captain.
G.O.C. (-in-C.) General Officer Commanding (-in-Chief).

(I.) Intelligence Officer.
(I.A.F.) Indian Air Force Officer.
I. of R. Inspector of Recruiting.
I.T.W. Initial Training Wing.

J.A.G. Judge Advocate-General of the Forces.

(L.) Legal Branch Officer.
LAC Leading Aircraftman.
L. of C. Line of Communication.
L./T. Line Telegraphy.

(M.) Medical Branch Officer.
(Mc.) Marine Craft Officer.
M.D.S. Main Dressing Station.
(Met.) Meteorological.
M.L.O. Military Landing Officer.
M.R.A.F. Marshal of the Royal Air Force.

(N.) Navigation Instructor Officer.
N.T.O. Naval Transport Officer.

(O.) Observer Officer.
O.T.U. Operational Training Unit.

P. Det. Port Detachment.
(Ph.) Photographic Officer.
(P.M.) Provost Marshal Duties Officer.
P.M.N.S. Princess Mary's R.A.F. Nursing Service.
P/O. Pilot Officer.
(P.T.). Physical Training Officer.
P. U.S. Permanent Under-Secretary of State.

Q.F. Quick Firing.
Q.M.G. Quartermaster-General.
Qr.M. Quartermaster.

R.A.A.F. Royal Australian Air Force.
R.A.F.O. Reserve of Air Force Officers.
R.A.F.V.R. Royal Air Force Volunteer Reserve.
R.C.A.F. Royal Canadian Air Force.
R.N.Z.A.F. Royal New Zealand Air Force.

S.A.S.O. Senior Air Staff Officer.
Sgt. Sergeant.
S.F.T.S. Service Flying Training Squadron.
S.I.O. Senior Intelligence Officer.
S/Ldr. Squadron Leader.
S.O. Section Officer (W.A.A.F.).
S. of S. Secretary of State.
Sq.O. Squadron Officer (W.A.A.F.).
S.P. Service Police.
(Sp.) Special Duties.

(T) (a) Armament Officer.
(T) (e) Engineer Officer.
(T) (s) Signals Officer.

V.C.A.S. Vice Chief of Air Staff.

W.A.A.F. Women's Auxiliary Air Force.
W.A.A.F. (Fl.O.). Women's Auxiliary Air Force, Flight Officer.
Wg. Cr. Wing Commander.
Wg. O. Wing Officer (W.A.A.F.).
W.O. Warrant Officer.
W.O.2. Warrant Officer Class 2.

The Editor's Postscript

IN offering the first number of our Fifth Volume I do not propose further to enlarge upon the difficulties we have had to overcome to arrive thus far in our progress. All too soon, mayhap, events may shape our ends differently from our own designing. In these days, indeed, "master of the event" is an outmoded concept. But we enter upon the second century of our issues with determination to keep our flag flying, and if another hundred and yet another hundred numbers of THE WAR ILLUSTRATED should be called for I hope that the immense public whom we serve will never be able to say we failed them. "Circumstances beyond our control," must, of course, be allowed for.

WHEN we set out on our adventurous journey in September 1939 there were many who doubted if we would get the necessary pictorial and literary material to carry on our current chronicle of the War. The War went slowly in those days. But I never imagined that we should fail for any lack of picture or story. Equally I did not at the outset envisage a time when the material wherewith to print and multiply our issues would so lessen that we should, week by week with diminished space, be overwhelmed with ever more embarrassment of matter worthy of presenting to our readers. I assure you that were paper available we should have no difficulty in publishing three numbers every week instead of looking apprehensively to a day when we might have to limit our issues to no more than that per month !

BUT I am convinced that my readers, whose goodwill has so manifested itself in all the mutations of the last few trying months, will continue to support us with their loyalty and tolerance in whatever the misfortunes of war may bring upon us, assured as they are that we of THE WAR ILLUSTRATED regard our job of maintaining this pictorial record of civilization's gravest hour as a work of national importance.

NOR do I think it may be wishful thinking on my part when I reaffirm my belief that we shall "win through" with our chronicle as the nations that are fighting for freedom win through against the powers of evil that have assailed them. I believe that Mr. Churchill was in no degree exaggerating the trials that await us when mass air attacks are resumed. Such precautions as are humanly possible have been taken by our publishers to enable us to carry on should we, by ill luck, have the present not-too-even tenor of our way made still more uneven.

COMING up to Town today by my customary route I was struck by the absolutely prodigious display of roses : England's queen of flowers. Everywhere at cottage doors and in the gardens of the more pretentious houses the roses were smothering their bushes with prodigal blossom. But what most impressed me was that in the southward suburbs, which had suffered most during the raids on outer London, here and there one saw a villa that had lost its roof and windows (not to say its unfortunate tenants) yet clambering over the porch and spilling down from the shattered trellis were gorgeous masses of roses, pink and white. Lots of " Dark Red Roses," too, which reminded me of Stacy Aumonier and the lovely film made out of his famous short story so named. Adapting a line from a once popular sentimental song, " These roses round the door made me hate Hitler more ! "

MANY years ago—in the days of the Irish " difficulties "—Mr. Churchill, with his characteristic gift of using the right yet unfamiliar word to express his thought, said in the House of Commons, " We must now put these grave matters to

THE RT. HON. BRENDAN BRACKEN, appointed Minister of Information in succession to Mr. Duff Cooper. Mr. Bracken is M.P. for North Paddington, and was formerly the Prime Minister's Private Parliamentary Secretary.

the test." I remember being mildly amused to watch in the journalism of the period how writers forthwith proceeded to make use of " grave " in their phrases on all appropriate and inappropriate occasions : the grave this and the grave that were dragged in until even a dispute about some small financial scandal in a Football Club was described as " a matter of grave dishonesty." In the intervening quarter-century the use of " grave " has rather gone out, its more literal implication as a substantive having become much too common.

THE pet word of our day is " pattern." Not a bad word either, but now somewhat overdone. There is a pattern of life, of thought, of poetry, of prose, of philosophy ; but I enter a mild protest against " The Pattern of Victory," which is the heading of a letter (I have not read it) in " The Times " today. There is no more possibility of a pattern of victory than of a pattern of defeat. I should not be surprised if somebody talks about the pattern of chaos one of these days. One of the evening papers a day or two ago headed its leader " The Eagle has Wings." Could anything be sillier ? Imagine the eagle without wings ! It was merely a thoughtless adaptation of " The Lion has Wings." One is almost ashamed to explain the latter as cleverly indicating that the British Lion had been transformed into a symbolic creature of the upper air, but it is an insult to one's intelligence to suggest that the American Eagle has ever been wingless.

IN these latter days the qualities of success are certainly poorer and less picturesque than in the days of my youth. I cannot help marvelling at the reasons for the popularity of certain individuals whose abilities strike me as extraordinarily ordinary. The film and the radio are largely to blame. Fame is frightfully cheap today. What more stupid than a process of things whereby a daring young man who has the luck to make a successful flight across the Atlantic achieves a world-wide popularity which induces him to pose as an authority on the high politics of Europe and America ? The proper way to treat Lindbergh and his obstructive attitude to the Democracy under which he flourishes is to remember that nothing in his life justifies the least consideration for anything he has got to say other than how to oil up an aero engine and manipulate the controls.

THERE begins and ends the achievement of this man whose opinion on world affairs is engaging serious attention on both sides of the Atlantic. But you see the mob know his name, and that means 99 per cent of his right to talk. Another instance of this—but on a minuscule scale —amused me some years back. A gentleman who, so far as I am aware, has achieved nothing much nearer to greatness than a certain popularity arising from his putting gramophone records on a machine and making some remarks about them while he is in the act of touching the switch, was chosen by a national daily as one of six eminent personages to write an article on " The Lord's Prayer." Straining to the utmost such powers of thinking as I possess, I failed to discover any link between gramophone records and the Lord's Prayer.

MY congratulations to Mr. George C. Curnock, a colleague of old years, on his very admirable piece of work just issued by George Allen & Unwin, Ltd., " Hospitals Under Fire." It was a fine idea to make a complete survey of the inhuman destruction wreaked upon London's hospitals during the heaviest of the air raids. More damning testimony to the deliberate savagery of the Germans in attacking women and children could not have been marshalled and all who are interested in hospital work would do well to acquaint themselves with Mr. Curnock's remarkable compilation.

JOHN CARPENTER HOUSE
WHITEFRIARS, LONDON. E.C.4.

Registered at the G.P.O. as a Newspaper

The War Illustrated, August 15th, 1941

Vol 5 The War Illustrated Nº 102

Edited by Sir John Hammerton

FOURPENCE

WEEKLY

WOMEN OF RUSSIA are working, even fighting, beside their menfolk in defending the Soviet state and civilization from the hordes of Nazi barbarism. While the fighting services are bearing the brunt of the attack, women, old men, boys and girls have organized themselves in regiments of factory or agricultural workers. In this photograph as far as eye can see are many hundreds of peasants—women for the most part—digging trenches calculated to put a sudden and disastrous stop to the onslaught of Hitler's Panzer units. *British Paramount News*

The Way of the War

JAPAN STILL TREADS THE AGGRESSOR'S PATH
Is There No Alternative to 'Expand or Explode'?

Through the streets of Hsinking came a host of Japanese flags ; then, led by an officer, some 50 or 60 Japanese soldiers, each carrying before him a square wooden box covered with a white cloth supported by another cloth round the neck. Behind the soldiers walked a number of women and civilians. Each of the boxes contained the ashes of a Japanese trooper, killed up in the stern northern hills, now being borne back to the land of his fathers f r honourable burial.

That is what Hessell Tiltman saw in the capital of Japanese-controlled Manchukuo. The procession was a reminder of the price of empire-building in Asia—or anywhere else. The Chinese roads are filled with those grim caravans ; and to Japan, across the China Sea, ships make regular journeys with cargoes of those little urns. Already in what the Japanese still call the " Chinese incident " a million Japanese soldiers have been converted into handfuls of burnt dust ; a million women in " Cherry-blossom Land " have wept beneath the wistaria and iris, and wiped away their tears on the sleeves of their bright-hued kimonos. The price of empire ; and the price is not paid yet.

Not just frantic greed and sheer aggressiveness have launched Japan along that road which leads through lakes of blood and seas of fire. Japan is one of the most densely populated countries in the world, and large tracts are mountainous and barren. Every inch of the land is cultivated, and the terraced hillsides and irrigated fields are a monument to the patient toil of the Japanese peasant, one that puts to shame our England where even in wartime so much is left to go waste and sour. The peasants are poor, terribly poor ; although, it is doubtful whether any Oriental peasant is better off. In 1935, the last year before Japan's armies began to flounder in China, the excess of births over deaths in Japan was over a million, and even of late years, when so many of the fathers-that-might-be are at the front, the figure is not far short of 700,000. Japan has, in fact, an Oriental birth-rate combined with an Occidental death-rate.

What then should be done? Birth control? But the Japanese population is already over a hundred millions, and although the practice of contraception is spreading it can hardly make much immediate difference to the problem. Besides, one factor making for large families is the absolute necessity, in Japanese eyes, of having sons, or at least a son, to hand on the family name and traditions. Emigration ? Japan's capital has flowed freely into Manchukuo, but few Japanese have

followed, since they take not at all kindly to the land's fog, rain and cold. The U.S.A. and the British Commonwealth ban Japanese emigrants. Brazil, which has received 180,000 Japanese since 1908, has now imposed a quota. To the islands of the South Seas there is a steady flow of Japanese ; and the desire to secure Indo-China—and perhaps the Dutch East Indies, Malaya and the Philippines—has a population incentive just as it has a commercial. If in the past Japan has been able to find food for her hungry millions, it has been due to the ingenuity and enterprise of her industrialists and the ill-paid toil of her industrial population, who between them have made the words " Made in Japan" known throughout the world. But here again difficulties are encountered, for in Japan as in Britain machines are supplanting human labour ; and by tariffs, quotas, and other restrictions on the free flow of commerce, foreign countries are doing their utmost to stem the flood of Japanese goods.

Then in the matter of the distribution of territory and raw materials, Japan feels that she has had a raw deal. Other empires have vast territories which they may exploit, huge areas which they can convert into closed markets for their goods. It is only natural that Britain should see to it that the Malayans are clad, if clad at all, in cotton garments made in Lancashire ; but the Japanese think it is just as natural that they should be permitted to trade their cotton lengths, made in

Osaka, for the Malayan tin and rubber of which they are so desperately in need. Manchukuo is providing Japan with coal, iron ore, timber, wheat, and soya bean. From China they hope to get rice. But it is the tropical products which they need most, and these products—oil, rubber and tin in particular—are certainly not to be had for the asking. Indo-China, with its far-spreading rice fields, its plantations of tea and maize, its forests of hardwood and bamboo, may fall an easy prey. But for the riches of Malaya and the Indies Japan will have to fight—and fight with the dice loaded heavily against her.

Other factors making for an imperialistic policy are the exceptionally strong and privileged position of the fighting services in Japan as compared with the civil service. Army and Navy officers hold all the key positions in the State ; and they do so, it would seem, with the almost complete approval of the Japanese people. Indeed, it is not too much to say that in Japan the Army *is* the people, and its soldiers living on two-pence a day and its caste of officers condemned by the salary scale to the most frugal existence compare most favourably with the bureaucrats and big industrialists who get rich on the profits of war contracts. The militarists are apt to discount economic considerations, and when the economists urge that Japan is being beggared in the process of empire-building, they reply that without that empire Japan must sink into a position of penury and hopeless subordination to the countries of the West.

This brings us to the nationalistic urge, which finds its centre and its inspiration in the person of the Emperor. The Japanese, it has been well said, live in two worlds, the modern and the feudal. To take an example, the business man who works in an office equipped with every modern appliance, who dictates in English to his stylishly-attired and coiffured stenographer, removes his shoes as soon as he crosses the threshold of his house, changes his suit, and takes his meal of rice and fish in traditional fashion, seated on a cushion on the floor. The Japanese have no difficulty in reconciling their belief in the divinity—yes, the divinity—of the Emperor with all the adjuncts of western life.

Finally, there is the almost mystic conception of Japan's Pan-Asiatic mission. Asia for the Asiatics is her war-cry—with the Japanese as the privileged overlords.

These are some of the reasons which have persuaded Japan to take the aggressor's road. There is another : the impossibility of turning back. Ahead lies disaster—perhaps ; but at least, too, the possibility of tremendous triumph. But to retreat spells disaster and death.   E. Royston Pike

SOLDIER OF THE MIKADO. Some may find in this Japanese soldier all the sinister craftiness popularly associated with the Oriental. In others, however, the suspicion will be diluted by pity for the humble pawn, destined to suffer and perhaps to die, as a million of his fellows have suffered and died, in the windswept wastes of Manchukuo and the treacherous yellow mud of the Chinese valleys.   *Photo, Natori, Tokyo*

American 'Liberators' Fly in Freedom's Cause

WITH the coming autumn and winter the British public will strengthen their air-raid discipline. Make no mistake, the Hun will come again. But we are now in 1941, and if London and provincial towns could "take it" when we had little defence and means of retaliating, the position is now mightily changed for the better.

Lord Halifax, on a tour of the Consolidated Aircraft Factory at San Diego, California, made this significant remark:

"As the nights get longer the 'Liberator' bombers you send us will be sent over Berlin, and we hope to be able to alter the outward appearance of that city and make some parts of it look like London looks now."

In this page are some photographs of the famous four-engined "Liberators." They and other American aircraft are being turned out in thousands, and likewise thousands of British pilots are being trained to fly them. As Hitler squanders his machines and petrol on the east front Britain is piling up her resources on what is, in effect, her far west front in the United States and Canada. There indeed is our greatest reservoir of mechanical strength.

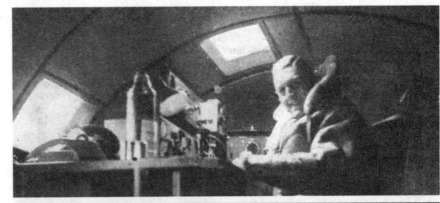

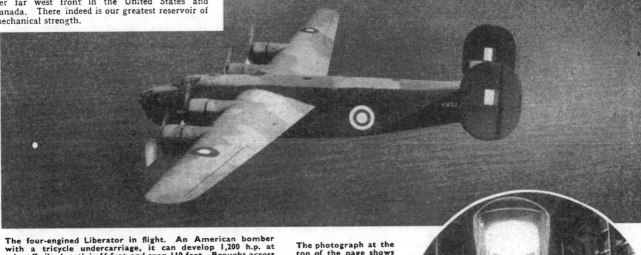

The four-engined Liberator in flight. An American bomber with a tricycle undercarriage, it can develop 1,200 h.p. at take-off. Its length is 66 feet and span 110 feet. Brought across the Atlantic by an Anglo-American crew, landfall was made in 8 hours.

The photograph at the top of the page shows the wireless operator aboard a Liberator. "There are a hundred more like this on the way to help you finish the job," Lord Halifax wrote to Mr. Churchill on the tail of a machine before it took off.

An American from Cuba, who has joined the Air Transport Auxiliary, in the tail of a Liberator. Many American pilots and mechanics are helping, like their compatriots, in the factories in the great cause against the Nazi tyrants.

BENEATH THE WINGS of a Liberator. Setting off from the Atlantic coast, this machine arrives in England in less time than it takes for a train to reach Scotland from London.

Photos, British Official :• Crown Copyright

IN his broadcast from London on July 28 Mr. Harry Hopkins, Mr. Roosevelt's special envoy to Britain, promised us more and more planes. Saying that he did not come from America alone, but with twenty other bombers made in America, he gave us heartening news of the tremendous work that is being done in the United States to assist the Allied cause. "The President is one with your Prime Minister in his determination to break the ruthless power of that sinful psychopathic of Berlin." Mr. Hopkins continued, "I have learned that most of the war material America has shipped to this island has arrived here, although some of the precious cargoes have gone to the bottom of the sea."

This welcome American, who is controller of the Lease and Lend programme, made it clear that the verbal messages of sympathy and good cheer have now been reinforced with the practical help of the whole of the United States industry.

Giving a brief summary of what is really being done, Mr. Hopkins remarked that "during the past several months aeroplanes numbering thousands made in American factories have been flown or shipped across the Atlantic. These range from the largest bombers to the fastest fighters. They are in combat now. I have seen in the past week the great Boeing four-engine bombers return from Germany. A vast programme for building thousands of these giants of the air is far advanced."

IF Hitler imagines that he can win this war before the industrial might of America can take effect, Mr. Hopkins reassured us with these words. "The Nazis will never be able to move their war factories far enough away to keep them from the eyes of the combined air strength of our countries. The enormous amount of war material which is en route now will reach here safely. President Roosevelt promised that he would take steps to ensure the delivery of the goods consigned to Britain. Our President does not give his word lightly."

What Is Your Picture of an 'Offensive Sweep?'

When in a B.B.C. news bulletin it is announced that our bombers and fighters have carried out yet another offensive sweep over Northern France, what sort of picture does it conjure up in our minds? That was the question asked by a spokesman of the Air Ministry who came to the microphone after the 9 o'clock news on July 22; and here is the answer he gave.

IF you could hear the cheers that go up daily from the towns, villages and the fields of Kent, from the hearts of those who go down to the sea in ships; if you could see our bombers escorted by squadron upon squadron, wing upon wing, of our fighters, pass overhead, you would know these daily offensive operations are not mere "tip and run" raids. I'm told the sight of them in a summer sky over Kent is one never to be forgotten, as fair a sight as can be seen in war. A majestic, awe-inspiring sight, one that makes you catch your breath as each squadron wheels into its allotted fighting position. Surely as moving a sight to "Men of Kent" and "Kentish men" as, long ago, the sight of Drake's ships shaking the wind into their sails and setting their course across the sea, to seek out and destroy the enemy, must have seemed to that little knot of people on Plymouth Hoe.

Unfortunately, it is given to but few to see this sight. I wish it were otherwise; I wish it were possible for all of you who are listening to me now, particularly those of you who have helped to build those aeroplanes, to see it just once. There'd be so great a surge of pride and gladness in your hearts as would, I'm sure, make the daily task of each one of you take on a new meaning. But as we can't all see it, if you'll bear with me for a few moments I'll try to tell you some of the history behind these "sweeps," as they're so often called—what we're doing, what they mean.

You know, we're a curious race, we British—we're always ready to belittle and decry our own efforts and abilities, yet ever ready to laud up to the skies the efforts of other nations, and *their* ability to wage war. For instance, we always think of the German as a past-master of organizing ability. We credit him with remarkable foresight and ability to plan and to arrange each action and battle right down to the minutest detail, to a precise timetable, and with a thoroughness that inspires success. Well, believe it or not, that virtue is not the sole prerogative of the Hun. If deep thought, careful planning, thoroughness—inspire success, then these fighter-bomber operations of ours, far into France, in broad daylight, also deserve the success they are achieving.

The talk of those who prepare the plans for these operations is, at times, an exacting business. Racing against the clock—targets to be chosen—what's the weather?—cloud and wind conditions over France—position of the sun? Hundreds of pilots to be "briefed"—speeds to be calculated—timetables worked out to a split minute—every squadron, every wing assigned to its task: where it will fight, how, its height, its route, its role, its time of arrival over the target, or to the area allotted to it either as support or to cover the withdrawal of the main force. Every squadron must also know, not only what it has got to do, but where every other squadron, every other wing, is going to be, and what they are going to do at the same time.

And then, when zero hour arrives, in an Operations Room far below the ground, as if by magic we see our cavalcade set out, not as you who live in south-east England see it, in all its brave splendour and array, but as coloured counters on a table map. Far beyond the range of human eye *we* see them go—wing converging upon wing at the appointed place as the impending battle unfolds before our eyes.

Now the boot is on the other foot, and it's the Hun who stands on the defensive in

WING COMMANDER EDWARDS, who won the D.F.C. for his part in an attack upon an enemy convoy off the Dutch coast in June 1941 has now had conferred upon him the Victoria Cross.

Hugh Idwal Edwards joined the Royal Australian Air Force in 1935, and in 1936 became a pilot officer in the R.A.F. Later given command of No. 105 squadron, in May 1941 he was promoted Acting Wing Commander.

His V.C. was awarded for skill and bravery shown in planning and leading a daylight attack upon Bremen on July 4. Despite heavy anti-aircraft defences of the town he brought his formation 50 miles overland to the target, which was attacked at a height of little more than 50 feet.

Photo, British Official: Crown Copyright

Northern France, as once we stood last year in Southern England.

Last year our lads were fighting over London; now it's Lille. What the Hun found unprofitable last year over here in England we are now doing daily, sometimes twice and three times a day—escorting our heaviest bombers in broad daylight to targets farther into Occupied France than London stands within our shores. We get the fighting now all right—they can't ignore our "heavies." Why, in the 31 days from June 14 to July 14 our fighter pilots in these offensive sweeps have destroyed 311 German aircraft for certain, and probably destroyed or damaged many others, for a loss of 99 of our pilots.

I wish you could see the Hun now as I see him upon his Western Front; once so sure of himself and so arrogant—he's apprehensive now—all of a "jump" and on his toes—never knowing when and where the next attack is coming. Already he is showing a marked disinclination to fight. This relentless "coming for him" over his own aerodromes is having its effect. The man-for-man ascendancy our pilots won last year is being added to daily, and the effect of all this on his

morale, barely noticeable as yet, will, of course, pave the way to his ultimate defeat—for when morale is broken, victory is swift.

And of our Fighter Pilots, what am I to say? I know what *they* would say if you asked them: "It's just a piece of cake." But, believe me, it's not. They're having to fight as hard as they fought last year and a great deal farther from home. It's just their way of saying their tails are up, there's nothing wrong with their morale. Many of them are the same youngsters who fought all through the Battle of Britain—only they aren't youngsters any more, but veterans of experience, leading now their flights and squadrons—some their wings. Throughout Fighter Command they are known personally not by their surnames, but by their Christian names—"Victor," "Douglas," "Harry," "Adolf," or "the Admiral."

As you hear each day in the future as a matter of course the brief announcement in the "News," perhaps those words will now paint a warmer picture in your mind—a picture of great beauty as our vast formations set out beneath a summer sky, a picture such as our fighter pilots see when each hour is fully charged with excitement, deadly earnestness, breathless hope that turns to exhilaration as in the heat of battle Messerschmitts go tumbling down, and in other fleeting moments charged with fear of a crippled aircraft in a sky that seems full of Huns.

And if you're very quiet you'll hear the cheers in Kent that speed our boys upon their way; and fainter still, perhaps, the ones that welcome their arrival over France—the silent cheers that live in all true Frenchmen's hearts, who understand the purpose of our coming.

How high must run their hopes as they look up and see this great spearhead of our air offensive speed across their skies! As the shadow of our "V" formations dance across their café tables, in your imagination you will see the many broken matches Frenchmen leave behind them there and in the street—to taunt the Hun; broken matches, paper strips, shaped to the letter "V"—for Victory.

OUR AIR WAR ON ENEMY SHIPPING
Over 73 Vessels (200,000 tons) Sunk or Hit in Three Weeks

Date	Targets	Time	Aircraft	Results
July 1-5	3 S.S.	Day	Bl, Be,	1 5-6,000 tons S.S. torpedoed
	1 Convoy		Hu, B, F	1 4,000 ton, 1 6,000 ton in convoy hit
	Barges			1 3,000 ton S.S. sunk, 1 barge destroyed
6-10	Patrol Ships	Day	B, Bl,	1 Liner at Brest hit
	Docks	and	C.C.	5 patrol ships sunk, 3 damaged
	2 Convoys	Night		7 S.S. in convoy hit
	S.S.			6 S.S. 20,000 tons, total loss, 2 hit
11-15	Minesweeper	Day	Hu, Bl,	1 Minesweeper on fire
	Patrol Vessels		Be	2 6,000 ton mcht. ships hit in dock
	Mcht. Ships			1 6,000 ton, 1 3,000 ton in convoy hit
	1 Convoy			1 1,500 ton escort hit
16-20	2 S.S.	Day	Bl, Be,	2 S.S., 3,500 and 6,000 tons, hit
	2 Convoys	and	Hu, B, F,	7 convoy ships, 38,000 tons, hit and fired
	3 Tankers	Night	C.C.	1 tanker, 6,000 ton, torpedoed; 2 10,000 and 7,000 tons on fire
	Shpg. at Rotterdam			17 at Rotterdam hit, 90-100,000 tons out of action
	Shpg. (at sea)			5 at Rotterdam hit, 40-45,000 tons, severe damage
	Motor Ship			4 at sea, 11,000 tons total, hit
21-28	S.S.,	Day &	Bl, Be	1 tanker, 1,500 tons fired
	Patrol	Night		2 S.S. sunk

S.S.=Supply Ships; Bl=Blenheim Bomber; Be=Beaufort (Coastal); Hu=Hudson (Coastal); B=Bomber; F=Fighter; C.C.=Coastal Command.

Note. In the first 3 weeks covered by the table, 30 attacks were made, resulting in destruction or severe damage of 73 or more vessels with a tonnage (supply, convoy, ships and tankers alone) of over 200,000 tons (other tonnage figures not available). This exceeds British merchant shipping losses for the whole month of June.

R.A.F. attacks on shipping in the Middle East, July 1-28: 21 ships, over 75,000 tons hit, mostly destroyed.

From the Stratosphere Our Boeings Bombed Brest

A FLYING FORTRESS (or Fortress I aircraft, to use the official R.A.F. title of the Boeing B.17) is here seen about to land after the daylight attack on the Gneisenau at Brest.

Off to Brest to attack the Gneisenau on July 23, the crew of a Flying Fortress enter their aircraft. Manned by picked crews and flying at a tremendous height, these powerful four-engined bombers formed the spearhead of the attack.

At such a height did the Boeings fly that Brest, in the words of a pilot, "seemed no bigger than my thumb." Oxygen masks and electrically heated clothing were worn by the crew because of the rarified air and bitter cold.

Left, a Boeing crew enjoy a cup of hot tea before taking off. Above, the harbour at Brest, with two French cruisers, the Duguay-Trouin and Dupleix, at anchor. The map shows the route taken by the Scharnhorst after she left Brest on July 22. She was spotted by reconnaissance planes and on July 23 and 24 was heavily bombed at La Pallice.

Photos, British Official : Crown Copyright. Map by courtesy of the " Daily Mail "

Attack by Blenheims

A Close-up of the Great Bristol Master-piece of Engineering at the Moment of Striking the Enemy

Specially drawn by Haworth for
THE WAR ILLUSTRATED

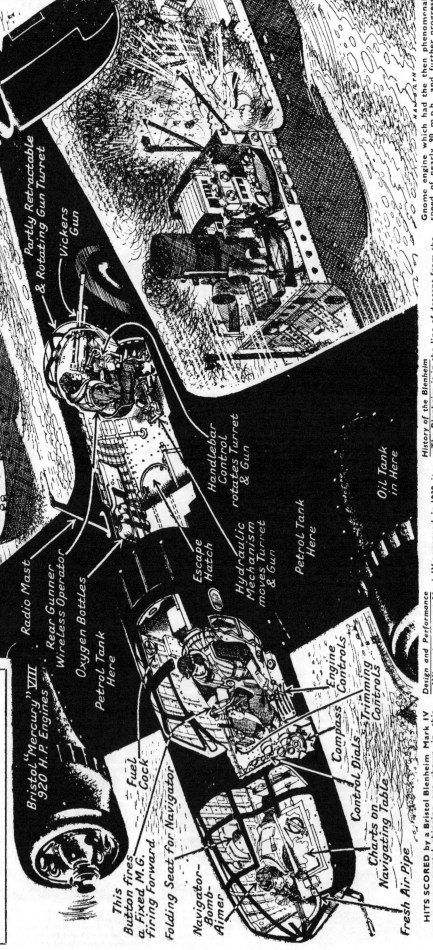

Bristol "Mercury" VIII
920 H.P. Engines

Radio Mast

Rear Gunner
Wireless Operator

Oxygen Bottles

Petrol Tank
Here

This
Button fires
a Fixed M.G.
firing Forward

Folding Seat For Navigator

Navigator-
Bomb-
Aimer

Fresh Air Pipe

Fuel
Cock

Charts on
Navigating Table

Control Dials

Compass

Trimming
Controls

Engine
Controls

Oil Tank
in Here

Petrol Tank
Here

Hydraulic
Mechanism
moves Turret
& Gun

Escape
Hatch

Handlebar
Control
rotates Turret
& Gun

Vickers
Gun

Partly Retractable
& Rotating Gun Turret

HITS SCORED by a Bristol Blenheim Mark IV on enemy coastal shipping are shown in this diagram. This incident will have been repeated many times during the recent heavy attacks by Blenheims of Coastal and Bomber Commands on the enemy seaborne traffic (see table in page 28).

The Bristol Blenheims, which have taken part in a great many raids, including the first raid of the war made on Wilhelmshaven, can claim a large share in the R.A.F.'s bid for air superiority. Since 1936, when the first Blenheim appeared, as the result of modifications to a fast transport monoplane called the Bristol 142, these aircraft have been in use by the R.A.F.

Design and Performance

When the present Mark IV appeared, in 1938, it was christened the "long-nose" Blenheim—previous models had a very stubby front. The new design improved the speed and manoeuvrability, and made room for the navigator's table, plus better space for the bomb-aiming arrangements. Speed, range and bomb-carrying capacity were also increased. The last will now have new type of bombs, which have greater destructive power for a given weight. The speed of the Blenheim is about 295 m.p.h. at 15,000 ft.; range is 1,900 miles (at about 200 m.p.h.), and service ceiling is 27,280 ft.

History of the Blenheim

The Blenheim is in the line of descent from the old Bristol Fighter (nicknamed the Brisfit) of the last war. Its evolution is part of the romance of Sir George White's mobile-minded genius, for it was this enterprising merchant-venturer who registered the British and Colonial Aeroplane Company, Ltd., in the infancy of flying. Sir George liked things that moved quickly. He bought up the old horse-drawn tramways and electrified them. He gave Bristol the most efficient bus and taxi service in England.

In 1913 Frank Barnwell, the Scottish engineer, produced a small biplane with a 50 h.p. rotary Gnome engine which had the then phenomenal speed of nearly 90 m.p.h., and further progress may be traced in many successful experiments and revisions of types. We had the Bristol Bullet, Fighter and Bulldog, all of which made aeroplane history.

It was in 1935 that Lord Rothermere, looking ahead with patriotic vision and warning Britain of her peril, presented the latest Bristol to the R.A.F. Upon this machine the famous Blenheim is founded. At this supreme moment of Britain's danger and heroism let us think gratefully of the pioneers who by their skill and industry also helped to put the R.A.F. " on top."

The Convoy Got Through—But Not the Italians

Towards the end of July there were two memorable achievements by our forces in the Mediterranean. One was the successful passage of an important convoy through the Sicilian Channel in the face of intense enemy attacks ; the other was the complete repulse of a sea attack upon the harbour of Valetta.   Both are described in what follows.

"THE convoy must go through." This order to the Western Mediterranean Fleet was given by Vice-Admiral Sir James Somerville just before an important British convoy, which for three days and nights was subjected to incessant enemy attacks by sea and air in the Sicilian Channel, set out from its assembly point. How important this convoy was may be judged from the broadcast message of thanks from the First Lord of the Admiralty, given in the panel on this page ; how well the units of the Mediterranean Fleet played their part is shown by the fact that the convoy arrived safely at its destination.

The convoy was spotted on July 22, its second day out, and that night an attack was made by an enemy U-boat. This was unsuccessful and it is thought that the U-boat was destroyed by prompt counter-action.

The next morning the first of a series of air attacks developed, an eye-witness account of which is given in page 45. These attacks were made by torpedo-carrying aircraft and high-level bombers. Of six torpedo-carrying aircraft which got within range, three were shot down by A.A. fire. In this action one British destroyer, H.M.S. Fearless, was hit by a torpedo and had subsequently to be sunk by our forces.

The high-level bombing attack was unsuccessful ; two of the bombers were shot down by naval aircraft, and two others were thought to be destroyed. During the afternoon of July 23 there were further attacks, but these, too, were abortive, two S.79s being shot down by British fighters. Another attack that evening, when the convoy was very close to enemy bases, was rendered fruitless by the superb handling of our ships. Enemy aircraft were seen to be searching unsuccessfully for the convoy and around midnight the sea was lit up by flares.

Early on the morning of July 24 six E-boats made an attack which lasted about an hour, and it was during this attack that the only ship of the convoy to receive any damage was hit. Nevertheless, she was able to continue and was subsequently twice unsuccessfully attacked. One E-boat was sunk and another probably damaged.

There followed three more air attacks. In none of these were any of our ships hit. One German dive-bomber was shot down by A.A. fire, and our fighters accounted for two Cants and two S.79s, while another S.79 was damaged. Altogether, in this long series of heavy air attacks at least 12 enemy aircraft are known to have been destroyed and several others were badly damaged. Apart from the loss of the Fearless, the only damage inflicted upon the units of the fleet was upon one cruiser and this resulted in a small number of casualties. Although the route of the convoy compelled it from time to time to pass close to enemy bases all the dangers of sea and air attack were successfully defied and the ships were brought safely to port.

Shortly after this significant naval event, another, no less significant, took place at Malta. Just before 5 a.m. on Saturday, July 26, a naval attack was made upon the harbour of Valetta. Italian E-boats were seen off the

ITALIAN E-BOAT of the type classed as Motoscafi Anti-Sommergibili or Anti-Submarine Motor-boats. These craft have a range of some 250 miles, are manned by a crew of about 12 and carry an armament of shell-firing automatic guns, as well as two side-firing torpedo tubes. Their speed is about 45 knots.   *Photo, "Jane's Fighting Ships"*

harbour entrance and the defences at once engaged the enemy. So accurate was the fire that one of the E-boats blew up on being hit and four others were destroyed. It was then discovered that the E-boats were acting as a covering screen for small torpedo-carrying craft which tried to penetrate the harbour defences. Not one succeeded in the task, and eight of them were either blown up or sunk by gunfire from the shore defences.

Seeing that the attempt was doomed to failure, the remaining E-boats withdrew but were pursued by R.A.F. fighters which sunk four more of them and damaged others. Then the R.A.F. encountered enemy aircraft which were trying to give support to the retreating naval units. Three of these were shot down into the sea for the loss of one British fighter, the pilot of which was saved.

It would seem, from the reports, that the assault on the harbour was made by eight small torpedo-carrying craft, not one of which survived the attempt. Judging from accounts published in Italian newspapers, the "secret" torpedo-carrying craft used in this ill-fated attempt were of the type used when on October 30, 1940, an abortive attempt was made to sink ships in the harbour of Gibraltar. According to the Rome press, the crews, wearing bathing suits, cork belts and crash helmets, man the torpedoes, which are fitted with a device for climbing over boom defences, and afterwards detach themselves, returning in a tiny boat fitted with an outboard motor which is attached to the torpedo on the outward trip. Not without reason the men are called "suicide sailors," but in this case their suicide seems to have been to little purpose. The "Times of Malta," describing the attack, said : "The enemy has now been made aware that Malta's coastal defences are not less powerful than the air barrage. . . . To Malta goes the honour of having repelled the first sea attack on British territory." The Maltese themselves, says Reuter, are proud of the part they played in this engagement. They had been waiting a long time to have a chance of using their guns and they made the most of it alongside the British garrison.

There was only one man among them who was disappointed—a Maltese gunner with 34 years' service with the Malta Artillery who had taken a day's leave inland. Cursing his luck in two languages and a few odd dialects, he swore he would not take another day's leave until he, too, had "had a go" at the E-boats. Such is the spirit of the Maltese, but it is doubtful whether this man will have another chance, for it is believed in authoritative quarters that the Italians will be in no hurry to repeat an attack from the sea.

H.M.S. FEARLESS, lost while escorting a convoy through the Sicilian Channel on July 23, 1941, was a destroyer of 1,375 tons, launched and completed in 1934. She normally carried a complement of 145, and the Admiralty communiqué stated that the number of casualties was not large. She was one of eight destroyers of the class to which she gave her name.   *Photo, Wright & Logan*

Our Searchlight on the War

AMERICAN TRIBUTE TO THE R.A.F.

THE "War Birds of the Royal Air Force" is the name of an American organization composed of 150 business and professional men who served as pilots and observers in the R.A.F. during the Great War. They have their headquarters at Detroit, Michigan, and many are again actively engaged either with the R.A.F. or the U.S. Air Corps. There arrived recently at the Air Ministry a large envelope containing a parchment scroll bearing the winged emblem and seal of the "War Birds" and a resolution passed at their last annual reunion, in which they salute the R.A.F. and pledge themselves to uphold the "ideals of American democracy for which our common forbears died that we might live as free men." Accompanying the scroll was a letter which read : "We daily view with intense admiration the reports of the magnificent exploits of present members of the R.A.F. in their struggle with the enemies of free peoples, and have complete confidence that their herculean efforts will be rewarded with ultimate victory."

HELP FOR THE BOMBED-OUT

FIRST the mobile canteen sped to heavily raided areas, carrying its welcome freight of food and drink. Now comes the office on wheels, set up by the Assistance Board. The first of a fleet of twelve of these units was recently on view in Hyde Park, London. It is staffed by fourteen civil servants, and speeds to the aid of blitz victims with money and coupons to tide them

A MOBILE OFFICE of the Assistance Board, the first of its kind, will tour heavily raided areas to bring relief in money and coupons to blitzed towns. The crew comprises fourteen Civil Servants who between them speak many languages.
Photo, Planet News

over the first days of homelessness and desolation. Members of these crews are carefully chosen, and between them they speak many languages, so that claims may be settled immediately and relief given on the spot.

POLICE—BUT NO CONQUEST!

GERMANY, it would seem, has long had in mind the conquest of the Ukraine. For some time a police college has been in existence at Przemysl, where Ukrainian candidates are trained to act as quisling police. Two days after the outbreak of the German-Soviet war, the Nazis, feeling that the moment was propitious, published in "Krakauer Zeitung" an illustrated article on the college and its courses of instruction. Pending the occupation of the Ukraine, some of these trained police have already been sent to serve in parts of German-occupied Poland.

NAZI PERSONA NON GRATA

BOLIVIA'S German Minister, Ernst Wendler, was given 24 hours to leave the country on July 20, when a state of siege was proclaimed following the discovery of pro-Axis intrigues centralized in the German Legation at La Paz. Colonel Murillo, Bolivian Minister of the Interior,

responsible for this prompt action, declared that the Government has documentary proof of political intervention by a foreign nation to undermine public order. Several propagandist newspapers, including the Socialist "La Calle," were suppressed, and the editors arrested. Two days later Germany issued an indignant protest, asserting that the charges were unfounded. At the same time the Bolivian Chargé d'Affaires in Berlin was given his congé.

FIRST M.C. ON BRITISH SOIL

THE first Military Cross to be won in this country, in this war, has been awarded to Second-Lieut. J. D. K. Hague, of the Scots Guards. The exploit that earned him the honour occurred during the Battle of Britain. One day last August dive-bombers swooped down over the airfield where he was in charge of a detachment, and wrecked his headquarters. Oblivious of a badly injured shoulder, Mr. Hague extricated himself, collected his men and shepherded them to shelter 100 yards away. More bombs fell within a few yards of the party, and they were subjected to machine-gun attacks from enemy 'planes. Two N.C.O.s received the Military Medal for their share in this disciplined withdrawal.

DRAMATIC R.A.F. RESCUE

UNDETERRED by rifle fire from a large and hostile crowd of Arabs, a Coastal Command Swordfish recently landed in French Morocco to pick up the crew of a wrecked Blenheim. Aircraft

had been sent to look for the Blenheim, which was overdue at her base, and the burnt-out shell of the bomber was first sighted by a Sunderland flying-boat, which also spotted the crew of three apparently uninjured. The Swordfish, which was assisting in the search, was summoned, and made a neat landing near the stranded airmen. The three scrambled aboard and, despite the load of five men in place of the normal two, the Swordfish took off without mishap and made a safe return. No one was injured, and only two bullet holes in the fuselage bore witness to the volley of fire under which the rescue was effected.

'D. K. S.'

IN Denmark a little badge has made its unobtrusive appearance. It consists of three letters, and in these days of initial short-cuts, might pass unnoticed, were it not worn in nearly everybody's buttonhole. It consists of the letters "D. K. S.," standing for "Den kolde Skulder" (the cold shoulder), and its wearers are pledged to this method of frigid passive resistance against the Germans in occupation. They have many ways of presenting the cold shoulder. German military bands play to empty seats ; restaurants frequented by the Nazis are avoided by the Danes ; German soldiers find that shopkeepers have mysteriously run out of commodities for which they ask, although Danes manage to get what they want. Of all the occupied countries Denmark is the best treated, suffers the fewest restrictions, has the most food. Nevertheless, the Danes persist in turning the cold shoulder.

RUSSIA'S DEFENCE CHIEFS

WHEN, by a decree of the Presidium of the Supreme Soviet issued on July 20, Stalin was nominated People's Commissar for Defence, he thus took over in name the supreme command of the Russian forces which he had in fact possessed since the beginning of the war with Germany. At the same time Marshal Timoshenko was made Assistant Commissar for Defence, with five vice-commissars : Army Commander Shadenko, Lt.-Gen. Fedorenko, in charge of tanks, Lt.-Gen. Zhigareff, in charge of the Air Force, Lt.-Gen. Khruleff, in charge of supplies,

FIRE BROOMS, made of twigs, like those above, have been placed up and down the countryside for use should crops be fired by incendiary bombs.
Photo, "Daily Mirror"

and Mr. Peresipkin. Stalin's genius for organizing supplies and administration brought him into prominence during the Revolution, and in recent years he has overhauled all Russia's military reserves and communications.

FLIGHT OF THE SCHARNHORST

DURING the night of July 22-23 the Scharnhorst was moved from Brest to La Pallice, near La Rochelle, 240 miles south. The Germans attempted to conceal the fact that she was gone by retaining the camouflage netting over her old berth and simulating her familiar outline by mooring beneath it a 530-foot oil tanker, with small ships at bow and stern to give the required length, all fitted with devices to resemble the battle cruiser's superstructure. But the R.A.F. were not taken in by this decoy. Patrols systematically searched every yard of the Breton coast, contemptuously ignoring further attempts at deception in the shape of smoke screens, tracks of oil and the like. Almost simultaneously several aircraft signalled that they had discovered the Scharnhorst inside the pierhead of the outer jetty at La Pallice, and that day and night she was again attacked with heavy armour-piercing bombs. Later she was reported to be again at Brest.

KING GEORGE OF THE HELLENES (left) is here seen with Major-General FREYBERG, V.C., after inspection and bestowal of decorations upon the N.Z. bodyguard which attended him in Crete and during the evacuation.
Photo, British Official: Crown Copyright

Britain's Guns Fire Across the Channel

THE SUPER-HOWITZER is seen below in action. It is skilfully concealed from enemy observation by camouflage netting, and the barrel is only visible at the moment of firing. The shells for this monster are kept in a well-protected and well-hidden ammunition store. The fire of these giant guns is directed from control posts situated in the rear. Recently Mr. Churchill, visiting the coastal batteries, fired a shell from one of these guns by pressing a button.

Photos, British Official: Crown Copyright

About to reply to the German guns on the other side of the Dover Straits, this British gun awaits a shell from the hoist. This gun (and there are others still larger) is manned by gunners of the Royal Marines. It has been named "Winnie," presumably as a compliment to the Prime Minister.

Some idea of the calibre of our cross-Channel guns may be gained from this photograph of a gunner walking along the top of the barrel, the rifling of which can be clearly seen.

'The Worst War Germany Has Had to Fight'

After five weeks the second wave of the German offensive against Russia had spent itself, and a third, so it was reported, was about to be launched. But the Russian armies were still intact, and behind the German lines their guerilla detachments were very much in action. The stories of guerilla fighting given below are taken from the "Soviet War News"—that remarkable piece of wartime propaganda issued by the Soviet Embassy in London. It is said it has a staff of four—which compares not unfavourably with the 1,801 at our Ministry of Information.

"ONE huge horror." This expressive phrase occurs in a letter written by a German soldier, and quoted in a Swiss newspaper. It sums up his experiences of the Russian war in which he is playing the part of a humble pawn. "This is the worst war which Germany has had to fight," he says. "It is a war to win or perish against soldiers who fight with desperate obstinacy, even in hopeless situations."

Another German—Lieut. Soldan, war correspondent of the Berlin newspaper "Voelkischer Beobachter"—complains that the German blitzkrieg against Russia has degenerated into a "confused jumble of friend and foe," and goes on to describe how the huge battle is apparently dissolving into individual conflicts. "Nobody has any time; everything is rushing backwards or forwards. The front is everywhere. To the half-right, behind me, 100 miles away, infantry are fighting against the encircled enemy front. German detachments are also fighting farther forward. But there still remain enemy forces between them." He admits that German divisions continually thrust forward, "knowing that the gap behind them instantly closes, cutting them off from communications and supplies."

Another German war correspondent, this time of the "Stuttgarter Kurier," puts the blame on the bad roads for the slowness of the German advance. "One mile advance in the war in the east is comparable to roughly 100 miles in the Western war." The German troops, he says, are now forced to construct and repair roads day and night, and an enormous amount of time and material are needed to make it possible for them to advance in the muddy country.

Then General Liebmann, writing in the Berlin "Boersen Zeitung," makes the significant admission that the Russian resistance is such that "it is necessary to throw into the battle the entire German Army, the majority of which consists of unmotorized infantry and horse-drawn wagons and batteries."

'Quite a Different Kind of War'

Finally we may quote from a review of the first five weeks' fighting in the "Frankfurter Zeitung." "The war in the East has developed into quite a different kind of war from that in the West. It has become the most adventurous war in history. Our tank units are often separated from the infantry, fighting in the confidence that the Luftwaffe and motorized units will come in answer to their desperate need. Although our tank troops realize that, after breaking through the oncoming wave of enemy troops, it will ever and again close behind them, they do not retreat. Everything depends on whether reinforcements arrive in time. Lately the Russian troops have developed the same tactic of deeply penetrating our lines. Therefore it is difficult today to give our exact positions. Actually our front is split into many confused fighting centres." Whereas, he concludes, the French General Staff completely neglected every military idea of offensive warfare, so inducing a sense of moral inferiority among their troops, the Soviet General Staff is determined to oppose the German attack not merely with defensive measures but with its own offensive.

In the fifth week of the campaign in Russia one of the most outstanding features

MARSHAL TIMOSHENKO, commanding the Soviet troops in the central sector of the Russian front, is here seen in a trench with one of his men who is scanning the enemy position.

was the guerilla warfare proceeding along the whole front. Everywhere guerilla detachments were operating in the rear of the Nazis, in some places 100 or even 200 miles behind the "front." It is a mistake to think of these guerilla detachments as being undisciplined mobs of half-armed *franc tireurs*. True, many of them are composed of armed workers and peasants, who perform isolated deeds of heroic resistance and, in particular, "scorch the earth" against the coming of the invader. But more are regular

EASTERN FRONT, showing the main German thrusts and the Soviet counter-attacks at the end of July 1941, by which time the German blitz appeared to have been held.
Map by courtesy of "The Times"

units formed out of highly-trained and well-armed Soviet troops specially picked and detailed for this work. Some are "battalions of destruction" who, using flame throwers, dynamite and special equipment—such as the machine which rips up railway lines and sleepers and tears open the surface of the track—blow up bridges, destroy public buildings, block roads and railways, and set fire to the forests. Others are squads charged with particular small-scale tasks. Yet others are in fact small armies whose job it is to harass, to delay, and to destroy before being themselves destroyed.

Many are the stories which are told of the guerillas. One detachment, composed of a number of collective farmers, discovered 20 large German tanks halted in a hollow owing to a shortage of fuel. The guerillas felled trees across the road, and intercepted two German fuel tanks which ere long made their appearance. Both lorries were blown up, and next morning Soviet dive-bombers smashed the stranded tanks.

Near a small town a guerilla party attacked an enemy tank group, moving along a forest lane during the night. The leading tank fell into a well-camouflaged trap. The second crashed against the first. Those that followed turned off the road, but they too fell into deep traps. In this way, within a few minutes five tanks were captured by the guerillas. Then another five were attacked with hand grenades and destroyed.

Ambushes in the Forest

In a forest a guerilla detachment discovered the strongly-guarded headquarters of a German formation. Reinforced by a military unit, the irregulars attacked and destroyed the headquarters. Many soldiers and officers were killed, including a general. The headquarters documents and a group of officers were taken and delivered by the irregulars to the Soviet command.

Here is a report from Major Meltzer, commander of a German tank column, which was captured in a Nazi whippet tank heading for the headquarters of the German 18th Tank Division. "I have to inform you," Major Meltzer writes, "that many soldiers in private conversation express dissatisfaction at the shortage of food. It is impossible to carry out your instructions regarding the necessity of getting food on the spot. Counter to all our expectations, the Russian peasants have proved so fanatical that they leave together with the Red Army, and destroy their whole property.

"Within the last six days I have lost a number of picked men who were sent on trucks to surrounding villages to get food. Only three soldiers returned out of 23, and even they brought nothing. The rest were apparently killed or taken prisoner by guerillas, who harass us day and night. I insistently request the urgent dispatch of food. It is desirable that the transport be strongly escorted, otherwise it will inevitably fall into guerilla hands."

Such incidents as these could be multiplied indefinitely. Every day hundreds of new guerilla detachments are formed, and thousands of attacks are launched by the irregulars, on bridges, communications, transport and warehouses. Peasants who are not actually members of the guerilla detachments help in every possible way as scouts and guides to where the enemy is lying. The fear of the irregulars, it is reported, is making the soldiers nervous. The orderly movement of the columns is upset, and an attack causes panic amongst the Nazi soldiery.

How the Nazis Hate and Fear the Red Guerillas!

RUSSIAN ARMED BANDS, some of whom are seen above after they had been rounded up, have caused great havoc behind the German lines. Wherever the Nazis broke through, the Russians before withdrawing their main bodies left strong guerilla bands to harass enemy communications, commit acts of sabotage, and carry out an offensive-defensive in depth.

Above, an instructor of the Red Army is giving instruction in the use of hand grenades to guerillas who will work behind the enemy lines. Right, mounted guerillas riding out of a wood in which they have been concealed to take part in the war of nerves which they are inflicting upon the hard - pressed Nazi divisions.

Photos, Associated Press

Where the War Is Carnage in Endless Space: Fr

RED ARMY TANKS camouflaged with leaves moving along a forest road on the eastern front. In the circular photograph on the right, a Russian doctor is attending the leg wound of a Finnish prisoner of war. Beneath, a Nazi soldier stealthily advances in spite of the fact that the cornfield and farm buildings have been fired by the retreating Russians. Fanatical courage, tanks, planes and "scorched earth" in one great combination have made a myth of Nazi invincibility.

line Glimpses of the Struggle of Slav and Teuton

A RUSSIAN NURSE giving water to captured Nazi soldiers. In the circular photograph at the top, General Tyulenev (centre figure), Commander of the Moscow Military Area, is discussing plans with some of his staff. Top right, Red Army amphibian tanks crossing a river on the eastern front. Thanks to fine organization, intelligent application of the lessons of the French collapse, and two years in which to consolidate its defences, the Red Army has completely broken the blitz-krieg tradition. *Photos, P.N.A., British Official, Associated Press, Planet News, Keystone*

Russia's 'R.A.F.' Is Very Much Alive!

In the first exuberance of their offensive the Nazis claimed that the Russian R.A.F. had been
destroyed in the first few days' fighting. Thousands of planes had been shot down, they said,
and thousands more destroyed on the ground. But six weeks later the Red Air Force was giving
the Luftwaffe as good as it got. Here we tell something of its composition and strength.

FOUR weeks after the Red Air Force had been wiped out (according to the Nazis) a German war reporter, one Joachim Richter, made this front-line record for broadcasting to the German people at home ; it was tapped by the "Daily Express" radio. "We are attacked almost continuously by Russian Rata (fighter) planes. They sweep over us all of a sudden and don't give us a chance to get our A.A. guns into action. Here is one coming now," he yelled excitedly, "and she is machine-gunning us. She's over us ! *Take cover !* Hell—we can't reply with our guns . . . These Russian planes attack us everywhere, coming out of the blue. Now here is another one ! *Achtung !* Again she is over us, and off she goes after a burst from her guns."

Then Richter had a conversation with the commander of a German battery whose gun had just been put out of action. "These Russian planes simply won't be driven off," shouted the artillery officer. "Such ceaseless raids we've never experienced b e f o r e. The devil knows where they all come from. They must have been transferred from other sectors of the front. I can't explain these masses of Soviet planes

otherwise." Then he, too, began to yell. "Here is one of them over us again—and another one—and another . . ."

Up to quite recently the Red Air Force was as big a mystery as the Red Army. We know today that it is a match for the Luftwaffe and that it may be compared not unfavourably with our own R.A.F., but we are still in the dark as to its real strength, its full potentiality. As long ago as 1937 the German air expert, Colonel von Bülow, reckoned that

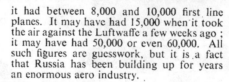

it had between 8,000 and 10,000 first line planes. It may have had 15,000 when it took the air against the Luftwaffe a few weeks ago ; it may have had 50,000 or even 60,000. All such figures are guesswork, but it is a fact that Russia has been building up for years an enormous aero industry.

Between 1919 and 1933 there was considerable cooperation between Russia and Germany in aeroplane manufacture, and factories were built at Leningrad, Moscow, Kazan, and Saratoff, where German aeronautical experts built aeroplanes of German design ; it has been alleged that the planes which Germany managed to secure during those years when she was supposed to be disarmed were built in Russian aeroplane factories. In 1936 it was stated that between 4,000 and 5,000 planes were produced in five Russian factories, and there has been an enormous increase in productive capacity since then. It is stated that there are now 350 aeroplane factories in Russia, most of them situated in the centre of the country, far away from the frontier, and that they employ nearly 250,000 workers. The principal plant is at Fili, near Moscow, where 40,000 workers are employed in eight-hour shifts throughout the 24 hours, and are said to be

capable of producing over 300 twin-engined bombers per annum. At Gorki Plant No. 21 is said to be turning out five single-seater fighters a day. It is not unreasonable to suppose, then, that the Russian factories are capable of turning out 20,000 machines a year.

Of the types little is known, although quite a number have been mentioned. In the early days of the Five Year Plans American aero-engines and aircraft companies, e.g. Douglas, Glen Martin, Curtiss Wright and Consolidated, built aero-engines and aeroplanes under licence in Russian factories and also supplied a number of complete aircraft from their works in America. But of recent years attention has been concentrated on the production of Russian types. Of single-seater fighters we know of the Chato, the Rata, and the I 17, whose maximum speeds are respectively 236, 285 and 304 miles per hour. Then there are the J 15 and J 16 machines, whose speed is given as 260 m.p.h. Just before the war the ZKB 19 was produced, with a speed of about 300 m.p.h. During the last few weeks we have been told of the I 18, designed by Nikolai Polikarpov, which may be regarded as the Russian equivalent of our Spitfire and Hurricane. It is a single-seater all-metal monoplane, and an improvement on the I 17, which had a top speed of 310 m.p.h., an armament of one 20 mm. forward-firing cannon and four machine-guns in the wings, and a Hispano-Suiza engine.

About half the Red Air Force strength consists of bombers. Some are medium, like the SB 2, with a top speed of 264 m.p.h. and a maximum bomb load of 1,760 lb. and range of 1,428 miles. Heavy bombers include the TB 3, whose bomb load is stated to be 4,400 lb. and its range 2,000 miles. The engines include Gnôme Rhône, Wright Cyclone, Hispano-Suiza, and the Soviet AM 34.

Pilots of the Red Air Force are handpicked from the enormous supplies available of Russian youth. As in Britain, men called up for service may volunteer for the R.A.F. Physical standards are higher than for the Red Army, and the men sign on for three years instead of two. Quite a number of women are employed on the ground staff, and some also fly.

The Red Air Force, although separated from the Red Army, is trained to work in the closest cooperation with it. Stationed in each military district is an air force group, and there is also an independent bombing force which is entrusted with such strategical bombing as has of late weeks been visited upon Ploesti and Constanza.

According to a communiqué issued from Hitler's headquarters on July 5 Russia had increased since 1939 the number of her airfields along the German frontier from 90 to 814. But only a day or two before Goebbels had stated that "the reason why we were able to destroy more than 4,000 planes in the first week of war was that Russia has only a limited number of airfields along the border. As many as 250 planes were often ranged on one airfield. German dive-bombers, therefore, had an easy task in destroying masses of Soviet planes." But when Goebbels wrote that, he had not realized that the crafty enemy had constructed a very large number of faked aerodromes, complete with hundreds of dummy aeroplanes made of plywood and cardboard. That, we may presume, is one reason why the Red Air Force, though it has been destroyed time and again on paper, is still very much alive.

THIS RED PILOT has shot down the Nazi bomber seen in the larger photograph: hence his victory smile. It is believed that the Germans have lost at least 3,000 aeroplanes on the east front.   *Photo, British Official*

The Red Air Force Springs a Surprise

What Marshal Voroshilov termed, in 1939, a " good Soviet strait-jacket for aggressors," the Soviet Air Force has proved its mettle in combat with the Luftwaffe.   Above, a flight of Russian planes in formation.   Top left, Capt. A. Vyaznikov, one of the Soviet's ace pilots.

This new and secret Soviet fighter monoplane is possibly a new version of the ZKB 19, which was reputed to have a speed of over 300 m.p.h.   It is comparable in several points with our own Spitfire and with the Curtiss Tomahawk and Vultee Vanguard.   In 1937 the Soviet Government acquired constructional rights for several American aircraft designs, including Vultee.

Left, bombs dropping from a Soviet bomber during an attack on enemy mechanized units. Above, a photograph radioed from Russia via New York showing a Soviet bomber, concealed by camouflage netting, being loaded with bombs behind the line.   *Photos, Wide World, British Paramount News, Planet News*

Our Diary of the War

SATURDAY, JULY 26, 1941   *693rd day*

Air.—Flying Fortress bombed Emden. Offensive patrols carried out over French coast.

Russian Front.—Moscow reported fierce battles in areas of Porkhov, Nevel, Smolensk and Zhitomir, but no important change. It was claimed that 104 enemy planes were destroyed.

German communiqué reported vague advances.

Africa.—During night of 25–26 Indian patrol from Tobruk attacked four enemy strong points and bayoneted the garrisons. British and Australian patrols also operated deep into enemy positions. Enemy retaliatory raid on 26–27 driven off by rifle fire.

Night raid by heavy bombers on Benghazi.

Mediterranean.—Attack on Valletta harbour, Malta, by E-boats and torpedo-carrying craft successfully repelled by fixed defences and R.A.F. fighters. Reports indicated that none of assaulting forces survived.

SUNDAY, JULY 27   *694th day*

Air.—Night raids on Dunkirk docks and aerodromes in Northern France. Mines extensively laid in enemy waters.

Russian Front.—Moscow reported strenuous battles in progress near Smolensk and Zhitomir, and claimed that two German infantry divisions had been crushed.

Berlin announced fall of Leningrad, but there was no confirmation.

Africa.—Heavy night attack on Benghazi.

Home.—Night air activity over S.E. England. London had first raid for seven weeks, but not on heavy scale. Four enemy bombers destroyed.

MONDAY, JULY 28   *695th day*

Russian Front.—Moscow announced continued fighting near Nevel, Smolensk and Zhitomir. Soviet aircraft bombed oil depots at Constanza, Rumanian Black Sea port. Ten German machines shot down during attempted mass raid on Moscow during night.

Africa.—Strong fighting patrol from Tobruk routed large party of Italians occupying post two miles from our lines.

Benghazi again raided by heavy bombers on night of 28–29.

Mediterranean.—R.A.F. made onslaught on four aerodromes in Sicily; 34 aircraft destroyed and many others damaged without British loss.

Home.—Bombs fell during night at three points in East Anglia.

TUESDAY, JULY 29   *696th day*

Sea.—Berlin claimed that 19 ships, totalling 116,500 tons, were sunk by U-boats in attacks on British convoy in Atlantic lasting over some days.

Russian Front.—Moscow reported continued fighting in direction of Nevel, Smolensk and Zhitomir. U-boat sunk by Soviet bomber.

Berlin claimed that Rumanian troops in Bessarabia had reached mouth of R. Dniester, and that Akkerman had been occupied.

Africa.—Four enemy bombers and two fighters, attacking British shipping off Libya, shot down by R.A.F.

Home.—Bombs fell at a few points near East Coast.

WEDNESDAY, JULY 30   *697th day*

Air.—R.A.F. bombed enemy convoy in Heligoland Bight; four ships hit, two sunk.

Naval aircraft attacked German shipping in harbour of Kirkenes and Petsamo, N. Finland. Warship Bremse twice hit; at least four supply ships damaged.

Night attacks on Aachen and Cologne.

Russian Front.—Stubborn fighting continued in Nevel, Smolensk and Zhitomir sectors. Germans claimed to have repulsed powerful Russian counter-attacks near Smolensk.

Mediterranean.—R.A.F. attacked aerodrome and seaplane base at Elmas, Sardinia, causing great destruction to aircraft.

General.—Russian-Polish Agreement signed in London by which Soviet-German Treaty of 1939 is declared no longer valid. Both sides agreed to combine against Hitlerite Germany.

THURSDAY, JULY 31   *698th day*

Air.—Several offensive operations over Channel and French coast.

Russian Front.—No change in area of fighting. Russians claimed to have driven enemy back at Smolensk.

Heavy night raid on Moscow attempted, but few bombs were dropped.

Africa.—Patrols from Tobruk made deep penetration into enemy lines during night of 30–31.

R.A.F. heavy bombers attacked Benghazi on nights of 30–31 and 31–1 August. Gazala and Bardia also raided. In Tripolitania, one aircraft destroyed and others damaged on airfield at Zuara.

Mediterranean.—Fleet Air Arm made night attack on convoy in Central Mediterranean. Hit obtained on one vessel.

Shipping in Messina Harbour bombed by R.A.F. during day.

General.—President Roosevelt set up U.S. Economic Defence Board.

FRIDAY, AUGUST 1   *699th day*

Air.—Convoy attacked off Belgian coast by Blenheim bombers; one 2,000-ton ship left sinking.

Russian Front.—German advance slowed down at all points. Fierce but undecisive fighting continuing around Smolensk.

Moscow stated that Russian aircraft had sunk enemy destroyer in Baltic and severely damaged two others.

Berlin claimed that Russian counter-attacks in Smolensk area were broken, with heavy loss to attackers.

Africa.—R.A.F. heavy bombers attacked motor transport concentrations near Sidi Omar.

Mediterranean.—Day attack on shipping at Lampedusa Island, two ships being wrecked. Aerodrome at Borizzo, Sicily, was also bombed.

R.A.F. made heavy night raid on enemy aerodromes in Crete, including Candia and Maleme.

Home.—Few night raiders dropped bombs at points in S.W. England and in Scotland, but there were no casualties or damage.

General.—Officially announced that diplomatic relations with Britain and Finland had been severed.

State of emergency declared throughout Norway.

Announced that Third Canadian Division, a fully trained force, had arrived safely in Britain.

Gen. Sir H. MAITLAND WILSON signing the Convention which brought hostilities in Syria to a close on July 14, after thirty-five days of fighting. General Catroux, who led the Free French delegates, is seen second from the left. The ceremony took place in the military schoolroom of the Sidney Smith Barracks, Acre, in Palestine, and the terms of the Convention placed Syria under Allied protection for the duration of the war. The end of the Nazi-Vichy conspiracy in Syria consolidated the British position in the Eastern Mediterranean and restored our prestige among the peoples of that area.

Photo, British Official : Crown Copyright

Preparing for the Century's Greatest Harvest

FELTWELL FEN, right, a 6,000 acre tract that was recently nothing, but peat and bog, is being made fit for cultivation under a Ministry of Agriculture scheme. A tractor is at work clearing the land of weeds and bushes. Below, a part of the fen already reclaimed and, producing beet. On the left of this photograph and also in the circle is the "Bread and Butter Express," which runs over a 20-mile stretch of railway specially laid down to serve the needs of the farmers. In the circle Mr. R. S. Hudson is seen driving the "express" at the inaugural ceremony.

Photos, Fox and "News Chronicle"

Below, a field of oats being cut on a farm in Herts—opening yield of 1941's bumper harvest. "It's a grand crop," was the farmer's comment.

"ASSUMING reasonable weather between now and the middle of September," said Mr. R. S. Hudson, Minister of Agriculture, speaking in the House of Commons on July 24, "I think we can rely on the farmers producing a greater weight and output of food than in any previous year this century."

Then he gave an estimate of the amount of food he considered would be available in the third year of the war, despite an inevitable reduction owing to shipping losses in the quantity to be imported. His words agreeably surprised his auditors, for he said :

"Despite that reduction—and it is a very substantial reduction—it should be possible, owing largely to the increased produce grown at home, to assure the people of this country that in the third year of war the quantity of food, in terms of food values, will be not only greater than it was in the second year of the war, but at least as great as it was in peacetime ; and quite possibly it may be greater."

Indo-China Is Now 'Protected' by Japan

Not content with the occupation of Manchukuo and the "Chinese Incident," Japan took another step along the aggressor's path when she demanded—and received—from Vichy France the right to establish bases in the great French colony of Indo-China. The move and its immediate repercussions in Japan and the democratic camp are outlined below.

"JAPAN," said an official spokesman in Vichy on July 23, "has demanded bases in French Indo-China as a temporary military measure to defend Indo-China against the de Gaullists, Chinese, and British. There are," he went on, "Chinese troop concentrations in Yunnan, and British troops and aircraft in Burma and Malaya, leading Japan and France to fear an Anglo-Chinese attempt to occupy · Indo-China. France cannot defend Indo-China alone. We had proof of that in Syria. Japan's intervention comes within the 1940 agreement (the Tripartite Pact) which recognized Japan's predominant position in the. Far East and her responsibility in maintaining peace in Asia."

and Thailand. "I welcome this opportunity, therefore, to state that the alleged designs of Great Britain in both these countries are entirely non-existent."

If any aggression were contemplated it was on Japan's part. As the "Daily Telegraph" pointed out, by the occupation of Camranh, Indo-China's magnificent harbour, the Japanese naval and air forces would establish themselves less than 800 miles from the United States naval base in the Philippines. At Saigon, farther south, their forces would be within 600 miles of Singapore, and about the same from the Dutch East Indies. The possession of airfields in Indo-China would enable Japan to deliver heavier attacks on

Reactions to Japan's new move were swift in their coming. In Washington Mr. Sumner Welles, Under-Secretary of State, issued a formal denunciation of Japan's attitude. The course taken by the Japanese Government was "a clear indication that it is determined to pursue an objective of expansion by force or the threat of force." There was not the slightest ground, he went on, for the belief that the Governments of the United States, Britain or the Netherlands had any territorial ambitions in Indo-China, or had been planning any moves which could have been regarded as threats to Japan. The American Government could, therefore, only conclude that Japan's action had been undertaken because of the estimated value of her bases in Indo-China, primarily for purposes of further and more obvious movements of conquest in the adjacent areas. Japan had never been denied the right to purchase tin, rubber, oil, or other raw materials in the Pacific area on equal terms with other nations, but the step she had just taken tended to jeopardize the procurement by the U.S.A. of essential materials, such as tin and rubber, necessary for America's normal economy and for the consummation of her defence programme. "The step which the Japanese Government has taken," he concluded, "also endangers the safety of other areas in the Pacific, including the Philippines. The Government and.people of this country fully realize that such developments bear directly upon the vital problem of our national security."

From July 26 Great Britain and the Dominions imposed a ban on dealings in Japanese balances, gold and securities, thus "freezing" the bulk of Japan's cash resources throughout the Empire. Sir Robert Craigie, the British Ambassador in Tokyo, informed Admiral Toyoda, who on July 18 succeeded Mr. Matsuoka as Japanese Foreign Minister, that the Empire's commercial treaties with Japan had been denounced.

America took similar action. President Roosevelt announced that all Japanese assets in the United States were to be "frozen" as from the opening of business on July 26. Although China is regarded as a friend of the United States, Chinese assets were included in the order "at the specific request of the Generalissimo, Chiang Kai-Shek, and for the purpose of helping the Chinese Government," since otherwise the Japanese might be able to evade the order by operating their commerce with America through the ports they have occupied in China. Then President Roosevelt also ordered the incorporation of the Philippine Army of some 150,000 men, and appointed Lt.-Gen. Douglas MacArthur to the command of the United States Armed Forces in the Far East. Then at the same time the Netherlands East Indies' extended the licensing system to all exports from the Dutch colonies in Asia to Japan.

To these moves—which might well spell disaster, since Japan relies for 90 per cent of her war needs on overseas sources—Japan retaliated with orders "freezing" American and British assets in Japan.

So Japan struck another blow at the balance of power in the Pacific. That she contemplated other blows none could doubt. Would the next fall in the south or in the north against Russia's maritime provinces and Vladivostok ? Such a move would, no doubt, please Hitler, and perhaps he had asked for it ; but as yet (it seemed) Japan felt it advisable to make the easy conquests, and to wait to see how the battle of the Stalin Line was going before she "took on" Soviet Russia.

JAPANESE TROOPS are here seen on the march during the campaign in China. Service in the Japanese army (or navy) is compulsory. All persons physically capable of bearing arms are divided into two classes, the "fit" and the "very fit," the latter category forming the first line army.
Photo, Natori, Tokyo

In conclusion, the Vichy spokesman insisted that the Japanese occupation would not be permanent ; and he denied, too, the allegation that pressure had been brought to bear on France by Germany to satisfy Japan's demands. Negotiations had been conducted at Hanoi between Vice-Admiral Jean Decoux, Governor-General of Indo-China, and Major-General Sumita, head of the Japanese Military Mission, and had been brought to conclusion at 8 o'clock that evening.

The suggestion that Britain had had any designs on the integrity of Indo-China was indignantly scouted by Mr. Eden in the House of Commons on July 23. In a written reply to a question he declared that the Government were aware of persistent reports that the Japanese Government intended to take action to obtain naval and air bases in southern Indo-China. The reports were the more significant since they coincided with a Japanese press campaign of innuendo against Great Britain in respect of both Indo-China

the Burma Road, by which American and British trade with China is maintained. If Japan's drive to the south were continued, then it might disturb the security of Australia and India, besides interrupting the essential supplies of tin and rubber which America draws from Malaya, of the tungsten which she imports from China, and of the mica which she receives from India.

Japanese troops to the number of 40,000 began disembarking in Camranh Bay on July 28, and in anticipation of their arrival French and Japanese planes roared over Saigon, Indo-China's capital. It was announced that the invaders were about to occupy eight airfields, viz: Saigon ; Nahtrang, 40 miles to the north ; Siemreap, on the border of Thailand ; Tourane, in the middle of the Annam coastline, north of Camranh ; Bienhoa, near Saigon ; Soctrang, at the mouth of the Mekong River ; Kompongitom, near the great lake of Cambodia ; and Pnompenh, the capital of Cambodia.

War Clouds Blow Up On the Eastern Horizon

Air Chief Marshal Sir H. R. M. BROOKE-POPHAM (left), Commander-in-Chief of British Forces in the Far East. Right, Admiral JEAN DECOUX, who succeeded Gen. Catroux, when the latter joined General De Gaulle, as Governor-General of French Indo-China.

SAIGON, the harbour of which is seen above, is the capital of Cochin-China and the main French military and naval base in the Far East. It has a population of over 110,000, of whom about 10,000 are Europeans.

JAPANESE WARSHIPS, steaming in line ahead, seen from the battleship Nagato, a ship of 32,720 tons armed with eight 16-in. guns. Japan has a large fleet, so far untried in action.

Below, one of the great guns which defend the approaches to Singapore; above, it is seen while a gun crew are pulling a swab through the barrel after firing. The gun is well camouflaged against its tropical surroundings.

FRENCH INDO-CHINA, where the Vichy Government has surrendered strategic bases to Japan following an ultimatum, is seen on this map in relation to the Dutch East Indies, long coveted by the Japanese, the British strategic base of Singapore, and the U.S. outpost in the Philippine Islands.

Photos, Wide World, Associated Press, Topical, Dorien Leigh; Map, " News Chronicle "

Sweeping the Swastika from the Atlantic

A BRITISH CORVETTE destroys a German submarine, which is seen sinking on the left. Having come up for the last time as a result of depth charges, the U-boat was attacked by gunfire and is now taking the final plunge. Small boats stand-to to pick up survivors. Beneath, a Focke-Wolf Kurier shot down by a Lockheed-Hudson.

A FEW weeks ago the Battle of the Atlantic had reached a critical stage. There was no question of Hitler's finally winning this far-flung conflict, but the position was a matter of grave concern.

Since then the situation has improved somewhat. Quoting from Mr. Churchill's speech of July 29, " the Battle of the Atlantic, although far from being won, has, partly through American intervention, moved impressively in our favour."

When Hitler announced that he intended to wipe us off the sea in this area of the war, and ordered swarms of U-boats and flocks of planes to do his bidding, Britain had some cause for anxiety though none for fear. Let us be thankful for American aid. It is vital to us and to our friends across the Atlantic, but let us never forget the indomitable host of British seamen of all kinds and classes who are bearing and have borne the brunt of this grim strife.

GERMAN U-BOAT MEN lined up at a quayside after being landed at a British port as prisoners. Above, on the right, more German sailors, taken prisoner when their ship was sunk, being led ashore blindfolded lest they should notice features of the naval base through which they are going en route for the internment camp, and in the event of subsequent escape pass the information on to the enemy.

Photos, British Official : Crown Copyright; Associated Press and Central News

I Was There! .... Eye Witness Stories of the War

I Saw Beirut's Welcome to Our Victorious Troops

The welcome which the Imperial troops entering Beirut received from the inhabitants—French as well as Arab—in their relief at the ending of hostilities is described in this dispatch from Reuter's special correspondent at the front in Syria.

THE streets of Beirut were thronged with people cheering and clapping as a long convoy of advance Imperial troops entered the suburbs of the city before the formal entry on July 16.

From a point just past the radio station some eight miles outside the capital, which shows the grim marks of British artillery fire, Arabs and Syrians were gathered in little knots on the roadside and on the tops of houses, waving and calling out greetings in English. Girls on bicycles hung on to the backs of lorries, talking to the Australians and giving them sweets. The rooftops and balconies of the Arab houses were crammed to breaking point.

There was evidence, however, that the Vichy forces had been determined to defend the Lebanese capital to the last possible moment. I saw sand dunes south of the city laced with barbed wire. Ammunition dumps were spread out among the trees on the roadside. Expressions of relief were seen on the faces of the civilian population, but some of the Vichy soldiers looked dejected and depressed. I called at the barracks in the centre of the town and found some black Spahi soldiers rolling up the French tricolour and preparing to evacuate. They sprang smartly to attention upon our arrival and were very friendly.

At the chief military hospital I found about forty British wounded prisoners of war. They told us that the French had treated them magnificently and could not have been kinder. "The French nurses have been kindness itself," said a wounded Australian. "They give us anything we want, but we are longing for a cup of tea. We can't get one here." His face lit up when I told him that the Australians were already in the town, and that soon he would get as much tea as he wanted.

The town itself was pleasantly peaceful. Many Free French flags fluttered from the rooftops. I learned that only a few of the inhabitants had been evacuated. All were sure that the British would not attack the capital itself. Many houses were flying the Union Jack, and opposite the hotel there is a bar named "The Australian Bar," whose name remained unaltered even during the hostilities.

Despite the stream of Imperial forces, tanks, armoured vehicles, and lorries arriving from every direction, there was an air of gaiety about the capital which seemed to show the relief felt by Syrians and French alike at the final ending of Nazi intrigue and influence in the country.

The Navy's 'Most Brilliant Convoy Action'

This eye-witness account of "the most brilliant convoy action of the war" (see also page 31) was written by Norman Smart of the "Daily Express," who witnessed the assaults of bombers and E-boats from the bridge of one of our cruisers.

MY ears still ring with the noise of the most brilliant convoy action fought by the Navy in this war.

For 27 hours on end we were subjected to continuous attacks from bombers—high-level, dive, and torpedo—and E-boats as we, with another cruiser and destroyers, convoyed merchantmen through the Mediter- ranean. All the merchantmen got through, obeying Admiral Somerville's signal : "Convoy must go through." Ark Royal fighters who were with us from the first day, on July 23, with the Renown, took off to engage Italian aircraft soon after breakfast.

"Tally-ho!" We hear their battle-cry over the radio as they engage the enemy

ENTERING BEIRUT, Australian troops were welcomed, as Reuter's Correspondent tells above, by acclamations from the crowds who thronged the streets. Another correspondent, with the A.I.F. relates how the Australians marched into the town behind an Australian band playing the "Anzac March." The crowd, made up of French, Syrian, and Lebanese onlookers, numbered well over 20,000 The band then stood in front of the Cenotaph playing many rousing airs, including, of course, "Waltzing Matilda," while the infantry marched past. *Photo, British Official*

46   *The War Illustrated*   *August 15th,* 1941

|||||||||||||||||||||||||||||||||||||||||||||||||||||||||||||||||||||||||||||||| **I WAS THERE!** ||||||||||||||||||||||||||||||||||||||||||||||||||||||||||||||||||||||||||||||||

on the skyline. Terrific battles are being fought over there as the machines swoop and soar with the rattle of machine-guns. Twenty minutes later we hear the boom of destroyers' guns as they open fire against the enemy formations ahead.

Here they come. I can see them clearly with the naked eye coming slap down the middle of the convoy. The sky is filled with the puffs of bursting shells as the first bombs plop into the sea 100 yards starboard, spouting water 50 feet high. Some open fire with deafening cracks of main armaments, mingling with the staccato thunder of pom-poms, sounding like a man beating a big kettle-drum. A column of black smoke from the Fearless as she is hit, and at the same moment the look-out shouts : "Italian plane hit."

see the plane swoop down to the water, and two Italians clamber into a rubber boat. Another has its wings plucked off like a butterfly, and falls like a stone into the sea.

There is a brief pause in this fantastic din. The commander at the microphone coolly announces : "Two planes shot down, and one destroyer hit," so that the crew below decks may know what is going on.

The second wave of Italians cannot face the terrific barrage and drop a hail of bombs harmlessly into the water a few miles away and flee, pursued by the Ark Royal's fighters.

Far astern the Fearless, now almost enveloped in smoke, blows up as she is torpedoed by another destroyer, after the survivors have been rescued. We cannot stop to assist her because "the convoy must go through." More of the Ark Royal

green train in the blue water. The look-outs shout in chorus, and the captain skilfully swings the ship. The torpedo slides past 15 yards to the starboard.

At 7.45 p.m. another big formation attack, and more bombs fall, erecting soundless columns of spray around us. The Italians flee before the withering barrage which shatters the tea cups on the bridge, and spills the tea on the navigating officer's chart. Two Italians are shot down. Empty shell cases fill the washhouses and overflow into the crew's recreation space.

There is a lull until 3 a.m. next day, when Italian E-boats attack. In the inky blackness the cruisers open fire at dim targets, pom-poms spouting across the sea like fireworks. There is terrific excitement now as the look-outs, with eyes glued to glasses, scan the sea.

Suddenly there is a flood of light ahead as a cruiser boldly switches her searchlight on for half a minute, and I see an E-boat, like a black beetle, scudding through the water to escape the shells. The E-boat twists and turns to escape the showers of metal hurled from the

guns, but the flying woodwork seen by the look-out means a direct hit.

Ten minutes, and there is a big explosion astern as a merchantman is torpedoed, but she carries on and we and a destroyer are detached to assist her.

Seven-twenty a.m. and eight Junkers 87 dive-bombers come screaming to the attack. We watch them fascinated. They deliver two attacks, and wheel into position in the sky, slowly, oh so slowly.

Look out, here come the bombs ; one hitting the sea 40 yards from us, and raising a waterspout 60 feet high. The merchantman is gallantly plodding along near us, with a heavy list, and swings away just in time as a bomb drops almost beside her.

Our guns are still firing, and the air is filled with the stench of cordite, as black puffs skyward like baby clouds, near the Germans, show our gunners are well on the target. One is down. And, yes, there's a second hitting the sea now.

Altogether we were at action stations 60 hours, sleepless, red-eyed and unshaven.

The Russians Shot All Our Tanks to Pieces

The narrow escape of the German General Rudolf Schmidt from a Russian tank-trap was described in a broadcast interview between a Nazi war correspondent and men of the general's unit.

GENERAL SCHMIDT was leading a tank detachment which was to clear an important road and protect an infantry division moving a short distance behind. One of the tank crew survivors said :

We had just turned a bend in the road when a hail of hand grenades and continuous bursts from machine-guns greeted us. At first the fire came only from the left of the road, but we had hardly realized what was happening when hell broke loose from the right as well, and finally from our rear.

Our general had to halt the tanks, but before he could deploy them for defence against the "invisible enemy" the Russians' fire became so intense that we had to run for our lives. We jumped out of our tanks and threw ourselves flat into a ditch. We could see we had run into a tight pincer. Before we had regained our breath every one of our tanks had been shot to pieces.

Then the Russians fired into the ditch where we were lying, causing a good few more casualties. It was impossible for us to stay. We had to crawl away on our stomachs, and our general wriggled back just as we did. He threw away his mackintosh so as to be able to wriggle more quickly.

After a few hundred yards of this we got up just in time to see the Russians leaving their hiding-place and charging towards us. Fortunately we had a good start, and, running as fast as we could, we and the general just managed to jump into a lorry which took us back to our base.—*Daily Express.*

fighters take off in the smoke of battle as enemy formations are reported.

The bridge where I am is a kind of orderly madhouse of signals, shouts and orders. The commander, pausing a moment between 10 other jobs, orders water for the men in the stuffy gun turrets. Says he : "They'll need it by the end of the day."

We ate a supper of soup and sandwiches at action stations.

At 7 p.m. torpedo bombers attack from starboard. Through glasses I see them skimming the water towards us like birds, shells bursting around them, and pompoms shooting a hail of fire into their snouts. I see the torpedoes plop on the water, as they swing away after the attack, one appearing to be hit.

"I wish I had a death ray," grins the gunnery officer, sweating in the burning sun.

From the bridge I can see one torpedo coming straight for us, leaving a pretty pale

FLEET AIR ARM planes, operating from the famous aircraft-carrier Ark Royal (seen above, viewed from a patrolling Swordfish), did magnificent work during the enemy attack on an important convoy in the Mediterranean described above and in page 31. Top, one of the Fairey Fulmars, two-seat Fleet Fighter monoplanes, from H.M.S. Ark Royal in flight, *Photos, British Official*

IIIIIIIIIIIIIIIIIIIIIIIIIIIIIIIIIIIIIIIIIIIIIIIIIIIIIIIIIIIIIIIIIIIIII **I WAS THERE!** IIIIIIIIIIIIIIIIIIIIIIIIIIIIIIIIIIIIIIIIIIIIIIIIIIIIIIIIIIIIIIIIIIIIII

How We of the Red Army Smashed the Nazi Tanks

This dramatic story telling how a Soviet unit destroyed 39 out of 70 German tanks in a fourteen-hour battle was sent direct from the front by M. Simonov, military correspondent of " Izvestia."

DURING the night scouts reported to our H.Q. that German tanks were concentrated in a forest at two points previously under Soviet fire, ready to attack. At 3.30 seventy German tanks were seen emerging from the forest ; they opened a hurricane of fire with artillery and machine-guns.

Soviet anti-tank guns held their fire without disclosing their position. Supporting artillery, however, immediately opened up. After losing several tanks the Germans were compelled to launch the attack before they had adequately prepared it with artillery. They deployed and began firing indiscriminately as they advanced. In their path was an anti-tank ditch. A group of tanks skirted this, but in doing so came on a minefield. Seven tanks were blown up

stationed near the highway then opened up with head-on fire. Three tanks were destroyed and the caterpillar wheels of a heavy tank were damaged. This tank halted, but continued firing. Sergeant Tarasevich crept up to it and hurled a bottle of benzine at the red-hot exhaust pipe. The tank burst into flames and the crew jumped out. Tarasevich shot one with his revolver and destroyed the rest with a hand grenade. Seeing the blazing tanks, the German infantry who were preparing to move into action from the forest, flung themselves down.

During this time the Nazi tanks in the centre had rounded the anti-tank ditches and the minefield and had arrived within about four hundred yards of our infantry. The tanks were followed by trailers in the form of armoured platforms bearing infantry.

A tank commander of the Red Army, one of the men who are doing so much to stem and hamper the German advance in Russia.
Photo, Planet News

Some of the infantry crouched on the rear of the tanks themselves under cover of their armour. Our anti-tank guns then opened fire, putting ten tanks out of action, but being themselves partly put out of action. The German infantry now leapt from the armoured platforms and tanks, hurling hand grenades into the Soviet trenches. Captain Gavrushin opened fire with anti-tank guns and machine-guns from the depth of the defence zone. Then the German infantry fled through a field of tall rye, throwing away their arms and tearing off rank marks from their uniform. At the outskirts of the forest they were met by the fire of our howitzers.

The battle had lasted fourteen hours. Afterwards I saw dead German soldiers lying in groups in the rye field. Thirty-nine enemy tanks, two motor lorries and a staff car were destroyed, about two companies of infantry wiped out. We had captured a considerable quantity of motor-cycles, bicycles, rifles, machine-guns and ammunition. —*Soviet War News.*

GERMAN TROOPS IN RUSSIA are everywhere encountering strong resistance, as the military correspondent of "*Izvestia*" points out in this page. These Nazis are entering a Russian village which, in accordance with Stalin's policy, has been set alight. Profiting by past experience at the hands of snipers, they hold hand grenades " at the ready."
Photo, Associated Press

in a few seconds. From our trenches the Nazi tank men could be seen jumping out through the hatches and being mown down by machine-gun fire. The remaining tanks skirted the ditch on two sides and appeared before the beginning of the defence zone.

At this point a German staff car and several lorries laden with soldiers emerged from the forest on to the road—apparently imagining that victory was already assured. A minute and a half later the entire area surrounding the forest was covered with dead German soldiers. The occupants of the staff car were killed on the spot. A similar fate was met by two companies of German infantry which emerged from the forest in close order. Their intention was apparently to launch a " psychological " attack.

Meanwhile the tanks continued to advance, several of them coming on to the main road. Lieutenant Khoroshev gave sappers the order to explode a mined bridge on the road. After allowing the first tank to pass, the sappers blew up the bridge under the noses of the remaining tanks. Soviet batteries

Siftings From the News

The King contributed twelve bottles of 1815 Waterloo brandy to Red Cross wine sale.

Women Post Office workers may discard stockings, but must wear skirts, not trousers, if serving at counters.

New type of British tank has been named " Crusader " in view of work it accomplished in Middle East.

Nazis are endeavouring to acquire rail trucks from Spain, as these fit wide gauge in Russia.

Dr. Colijn, former Netherlands Prime Minister, has been sent to a German concentration camp.

Five hundred Cretan women were deported to Germany for taking part in defence of their island.

Special spectacles for use with Service gas mask are to be provided for Home Guards who need them.

New secret anti-Hitler broadcasting station, calling itself " Christian Radio," sends out messages in five languages.

Germans have taken a census of poultry in Belgium. Only one chicken per inhabitant is to be allowed.

Two-thirds of British Columbia's total 1941 production of tinned salmon is to be shipped to Britain.

Shops of asbestos sheets on timber frame, built in a day, are now open in Coventry.

Prospective mothers are to be given 50 coupons to provide baby clothes.

Meat, bacon and eggs are now practically unobtainable in Norway.

Curfew at 8 p.m. was imposed on citizens of Liége as punishment for acts of sabotage.

Postage stamps are now lighter in shade, in order to save valuable dyes.

Over 650,000 airgraph letters have been received from British Forces in Middle East.

Aeroplanes, not films, are now the chief product of Los Angeles.

Russian broadcaster stated casualties in five weeks of Soviet-German war reached 3,000,000.

A mule which saw active service in the last war is now working on a farm in Gloucestershire.

Long-distance transmitting radio was found in diplomatic baggage of German Embassy official in Buenos Aires.

Shell splinters from Hampstead raids, auctioned in U.S.A., raised enough to provide a Y.M.C.A. tea car for Enfield.

Flags at half-mast at Constance, Baden, led to reports that Russians had annihilated entire Constance regiment.

The Editor's Postscript

HERE is an idea of which Mr. Brendan Bracken might think well. Have already expressed it in a letter published in the "Daily Telegraph," but owing to the promise of success in the V campaign believe it worth repeating. Our fighters in their flights over Occupied France, Belgium and Holland might blaze their sky trails by writing occasional Vs in the same way that commercial planes used to advertise various articles. In November last, when discussing in my Jottings in No. 65 of THE WAR ILLUSTRATED the vaporous vision revealed, alas, only to two or three local village women, in the sky over Firle Beacon of the Saviour on the Cross supported by "six angels on each side," I mentioned my own experience in the same vicinity a week or two later "a vast V-shaped blaze in the sunset sky." The left limb of the [mile-or-more-high letter thinned away at the top into white vapour, but the letter as a whole stood solid and vividly aflame, retaining its volume and density for nearly 20 minutes of my journey. I offered the explanation that "a bright young Hurricane pilot had shot down the three-engined enemy bomber I also saw that afternoon, and in his ecstasy of victory traced this gigantic V by making a dive of a mile or so and zooming up to the same height again at the appropriate angle."

HEARD Miss Dorothy Thompson's broadcast tonight while staying at a country hotel. Felt that here is a Voice of incalculable value to the Anglo-American cause : the charming accents of the feminine expressing a masculinity of thought. This was the first time one had the pleasure of listening to her without the distortion which always accompanies a relay or recording of a talk from U.S.A., as she was speaking in person from an unidentified studio of the B.B.C. At the moment I find it difficult to write even this brief impression, as my writing table is within earshot of an American bar (why are these so called : is it the noise ?) where a number of modern young ladies are screeching with laughter in the company of their military menfolk (wonder what can be so funny for all that !) ; but, there, just heard them setting off in their cars (whence the petrol ?) and all is delightfully quiet once more.

Noise is certainly a common American characteristic ; but could anything be more remote from the noisy than the low dulcet tones of Miss Thompson's cultured voice which carry her admirable phrasing and fine, confident, thoughtful observations so clearly across the ether ? When the time comes to assess the individual contributions to the winning of the War and the downing of Hitlerism, Dorothy Thompson, by virtue of both pen and personality, is assured of a high place. More power to her.

I READ with some interest today that Sir Nicholas Gratton-Doyle, who has just died, was " one of the few M.P.s who still kept to the top hat, a black hat in the winter

and grey in summer." It is interesting to know that any Member of Parliament still lagged so far behind the changing fashions of our times, and I look back a little incredulously upon my own days when I arrived in town each morning with a silk hat and frock coat to carry on my editorial work, which was so much better discharged in an old jacket and a loose collar, as soon as I discarded the conventional garb of respectability and sat down at my desk. Sir Oswald Mosley's grandfather was distinguished for little else than having worn to the end of his days an old-fashioned silk hat of the shape that Tony Weller wore when seated on the dickey of his stage coach —that and being the founder of the standard bread movement in 1911.

Another Splendid Volume for Your Bookshelf

The War Illustrated—Volume 4

To make THE WAR ILLUSTRATED of real permanent value you should have the weekly numbers bound as each volume is completed. Number 100 completed the Fourth Volume. The publishers have produced specially attractive binding cases. They are made of stout boards covered with durable Dark Red Cloth with side and spine bearing appropriate designs in two inks and blind blocking. You can obtain these cases, together with title page, index, frontispiece, etc., through your newsagent or bookstall for 2/6 each or direct from THE

WAR ILLUSTRATED (Binding Dept.), Bear Alley, Farringdon Street, London, E.C.4, when 7d. extra for postage must be enclosed for each case ordered.

Subscribers who would prefer an extra special binding for this work can secure our DE LUXE CASE, which is made of dark blue half leather with blue cloth sides, also blue leather corners, and spine blocked in gilt and blind. It can be obtained through your newsagents, price 6/6. (Postage 7d. extra if ordered direct from the Publishers.)

See Announcement in Number 91 for

PUBLISHERS' SPECIAL BINDING OFFER

The publishers will undertake to bind the weekly numbers of THE WAR ILLUSTRATED into volumes at a special inclusive charge of 6/- per volume for the Standard Binding or for the De Luxe Binding 10/6 per volume. These charges include cost of binding case, packing and return carriage. It is important that the details given in the announcement on the back cover of Number 91 of THE WAR ILLUSTRATED be complied with.

THE clinging to fashions that have become entirely obsolete is, in my thinking, an indication of a certain personal vanity, just as the wearing of anything so stupid as a silk hat forty years ago was the opposite—for it was conforming to the general. But to break away from a foolish, long-established custom by introducing something more practical need carry no suspicion of vanity about it. The late Kennedy Jones, who was Lord Northcliffe's very competent associate in the founding of the "Daily Mail" was one of the first, if not the very first, to get rid of the silk hat and frock coat habit by appearing in Fleet Street with a "boater" and lounge suit. And now the boater is almost as obsolete as the "tile," having succumbed to the Trilby. I hope that our new and unexpected collaboration with Soviet Russia may not presage a vogue for the cloth cap of the coalminer, the cowherd, and the golfer ! But fashion's freaks are beyond controlling, and one never knows.

I still have two or three top hats stowed away somewhere ; the most up to date has, like Dick Phenyl's dress trousers, " been going to funerals for years," also to weddings, and not infrequently to dinner parties until Hitler put the lid on that side of our social enjoyment.

A LETTER from one of my correspondents in Canada states that the writer has been a reader of THE WAR ILLUSTRATED from the first issue and only lately, owing to the severe restrictions imposed upon our paper supplies to meet the perplexities of an unprecedented situation, has he experienced occasional difficulty in getting his weekly copy. His last letter begins : " Since the start of this present European unpleasantness I have been receiving (with occasional jerks) your wonderful magazine . . ." I believe that his circumlocution for the Second World War is one that is still used in Ireland in the past tense, where the Rebellion of 1916 is known as the " late unpleasantness." " The present emergency " as an official description of a state of war is most time-honoured of all those evasions, and I think I have already mentioned in my jottings that I found it used several times over by Plutarch in his " Lives " in connexion with the civil wars of Rome and even the classical campaigns of Alexander and his generals !

THE verb " to rubber " used to be very popular in U.S.A. Perhaps it is no longer in vogue —knowing Americans. But rubbering implied curiosity, and, in my opinion, that is one of the divinest qualities in man : to be interested in the manifestations of life, active and " still," which surrounds each of us from the cradle to the coffin. I've done a lot of rubbering in my time, but never merely from idle curiosity. I've rubber-necked (again Americanese) my way through many countries and hundreds of foreign and far cities ; so that I have some sympathy with those who crowd to London's ruins " to see for themselves."

BUT certainly I have no sympathy with those who impede the A.R.P. men in their urgent tasks. A friend of mine, who hasn't been in London since the first bomb fell and had to go through it yesterday on her way north, declined a suggestion I made to guide her through the Temple, the City, round about West End clubland, and other historic areas of the London which she has loved for so many years, on the plea that she wants to remember these only as she knew them. Personally, I think it is a duty to acquaint oneself with the effects of London's ordeal. " See all, nor be afraid." Else is illusion.

REVERTING to rubbering. A good story worth recalling. A passenger in a New York tram was tempted to look occasionally at an appallingly ugly infant which a woman opposite him was nursing. The mother, annoyed at his furtive glances, after a while exclaimed in a loud voice—you need a loud voice in New York trams—" Rubber ! " that being the noun in use then for the over-inquisitive. " Thank God," he retorted, " I was afraid it was real ! "

JOHN CARPENTER HOUSE.
WHITEFRIARS, LONDON, E.C.4.

Printed in England and published every Friday by the Proprietors, The Amalgamated Press, Ltd., The Fleetway House, Farringdon Street, London, E.C.4. Sole Agents for Australia and New Zealand : Messrs Gordon & Gotch, Ltd. ; and for South Africa : Central News Agency, Ltd.   August 15th, 1941.   - S.S.

Registered at the G.P.O. as a Newspaper

The War Illustrated, August 22nd, 1941

Vol 5 *The War Illustrated* Nº 103

Edited by Sir John Hammerton

FOURPENCE

WEEKLY

H.M.S. NELSON, 34,000-ton battleship operating with the Western Mediterranean Fleet, was one of the naval units protecting the very important convoy which successfully defied the dangers of the Sicilian Channel towards the end of July, 1941. The story of the desperate enemy attacks made upon this convoy and an eye-witness account of the successful naval defence are given in pages 31 and 45 of this volume. Above is an actual photograph of H.M.S. Nelson taken during the three-day period of incessant attacks.   *Photo, British Paramount News*

The Way of the War

THE TRAGIC IRONY OF INDIA AT WAR
Four Hundred Millions in Search of —— What?

Even in this country, where not one in a thousand has read anything about India save Macaulay's glowing accounts of those imperial swashbucklers, Clive and Warren Hastings, and the even more colourful pages of Katharine Mayo, who investigated—and smelt—the Indian scene with truly American intelligence and zest, there are many who are surprised, even a little perturbed, when they are told that in India the prisons are full of men whom, if they were anything but Indians, we should be proud to acknowledge as friends.

Men who hate Nazism even more than they hate British imperialism, who denounced appeasement of the aggressors when it was the policy of his Majesty's Government, who are (by all accounts) better democrats and more liberal-minded than the leaders of the Labour Party—by the hundred and thousand they are being gaoled ; former prime ministers, hundreds of Indian M.P.s, Trade Union officials, leaders of cultural organizations and of the women's movement, Moslems and Hindus and Christians, men of high caste and of none . . . And while these are going to prison we are still on excellent terms with the Indian princes, petty despots some of them and autocrats nearly all . . .

The situation in India today is, indeed, filled with a tragic irony. The Indian democrats are in prison or concentration camps because they are Nationalists. They want to see achieved in India what Britain and her Allies are fighting for in the world at large.

India is in the war. The great mass of Indians, whatever their caste and class, their race and religion, want Britain to win, for they see clearly enough what would be India's fate in a world dominated by the spirit of totalitarianism, whether that be expressed in the Japanese or in Hitler's swaggering bullies, made drunk on the heady rubbish of racialism. But when war was declared in 1939, though Britain asked Canada to stand by her, asked Australia, asked New Zealand and South Africa, she did not ask India. India, whose 400 millions outnumber all the peoples of Britain and the Dominions, was not consulted. Instead, the Viceroy made a simple declaration that India was at war.

"The declaration by the British Government of India as a belligerent country, without any reference to the people of India, and the exploitation of India's resources in this war, is an affront which no self-respecting and freedom-loving people can accept or tolerate." So the All-India Congress has declared—Congress, the largest Indian political party, representative of the great mass of the Hindus, and to a considerable extent of the Moslems, too. Since 1939 Congress has declared time and again that, though it is still as strongly opposed as ever to Nazism, it cannot and will not cooperate with Britain in the war until Britain gives India her freedom. Similar declarations have been made by the Moslem League, chief rival of Congress, and the Indian Liberals.

What do they mean by freedom? Before the war Britain promised India dominion status, and that promise still holds good, although its fulfilment has been deferred until after the war. Many Indians believe that a renewal of that promise would go far to close the breach between Britain and India, since it might well secure the support of the more moderate elements in the Nationalist camp. But Congress is committed to complete independence ; it demands that Britain shall make a formal acknowledgement of India's independent status, and as an immediate step should set up at Delhi a truly national government.

Then there is Mr. Jinnah, leader of the Moslem League : he, too, wants independence, but he also wants to be assured that under no circumstances will India's 90 million Moslems be placed under the rule of the Hindus, from whom they are separated by a vast gulf of religion and ways of life. Mr. Jinnah is committed to the "Pakistan Movement," which advocates the creation of a Moslem-controlled state in the Punjab and the surrounding provinces. The Hindus protest most strongly against this "vivisection of India," while the Sikhs declare that the Punjab, should it pass out of British hands, must revert to them.

Nor shall we receive much enlightenment if we inquire of the two Indians whose names are known even in England . . . Mr. Nehru declares that "We want to be completely free, with no reservations or exceptions except such as we ourselves approve in common with others, in order to join a federation of nations or a new world order." He thinks that India should be closely associated in a federation with China, Burma, Ceylon, Afghanistan and Persia. "We are prepared to take risks and face dangers. We do not want the so-called protection of the British Army or Navy. We shall shift for ourselves . . ."

Then Mahatma Gandhi, he wants *Purna swaraj*, which may be translated as self-government. He dreams of an India in which Hindu-Moslem rivalry will be at an end and "untouchability" no more, when village industries will have been established, when the peasant will be educated not only in letters but hygiene and husbandry, when there will be a common language (at present there are some 220) and a general economic equality.

There Mr. Gandhi shows his realism. He knows how foolish are the claims made by some Indian writers that only with the British did there enter into India misery and wrong. Was there no caste before Clive ? Were there no untouchables, no widows who died on their husbands' pyres, no little children sold into unnatural marriage ? Were there no horrible worships, no sly and hypocritical priests, no throngs of temple prostitutes, male and female servants of the gods—and those gods foul, obscene, bloodstained, altogether horrible ? Was Benares in those days a model city, or did the Ganges run then, as now, a filth-filled stream, washing with its fetid tide banks of sewage ? India's burden is made up of Nature's pestilences, famines and floods, of Man's inhumanity to man. So great a burden that only the cooperation of India and Britain can ease it, and then perhaps only a little . . .

E. Royston Pike

GANDHI and NEHRU, most prominent spokesmen of Indian nationalism, are here seen together at Allahabad in 1939. Mahatma (Great Soul) Mohamdas Karamchand Gandhi was born in 1869, and for many years has been the leader of the non-violent civil disobedience movement in India. Pandit (Great Scholar) Jawaharlal Nehru is 20 years younger, and in spite of his Harrow and Trinity College, Cambridge, education, is even more left wing and anti-British in his views.   *Photo, Planet News*

'Beautiful Bombs' Ready for the Boche

British spokesmen have promised that the Nazi air blitzes on the cities of Britain will be repaid with interest. Some of the British bombs which will be unloaded on vital military objectives in the Reich are seen in this page. Top, along a miniature railway passes a load of destruction from an underground ammunition dump. Above, Canadian crew of a Wellington bomber examine their cargo with satisfaction. Left, stacking bombs in an underground dump: the first stage on their journey to Germany.

Photos, British Official ; Fox

America's New Army in the Making

Until little more than a year ago the American Army was a small-scale professional organization
since it was not contemplated that it would ever again have to go overseas as it did in 1917-18.
But following the increasing appreciation of the Nazi menace to the security of the Western
Hemisphere, the U.S.A. has now embarked upon a huge policy of Army expansion.

LITTLE more than a year ago the Regular Army of the U.S.A. numbered 265,000, or, with the addition of the National Guard (243,000), about half a million. Last March it passed the million mark for the first time since the World War. The latest available detailed figures are those for April 12 last, when it comprised 487,000 Regulars, 286,000 National Guard, 38,000 reserve officers recalled to duty with the colours, and 374,000 selective service trainees—a total of 1,185,000. Its present strength is said to be in the neighbourhood of 1,500,000.

The U.S. Regular Army consists of volunteers. In the first instance men enlist for one or three years, but all re-enlistments are for three-year periods. A newly enlisted private receives 21 dollars per month—say 3s. 6d. per day; after four months' service his pay is raised to 30 dollars per month. The highest non-commissioned rank is that of Master Sergeant, who receives 126 dollars per month, though what with free quarters and service, ration allowance, uniform, underwear, medical care, and so forth, his total emoluments are well in excess of 200 dollars a month—say £50 at the present rate of exchange. In addition, soldiers receive an increase of 10 per cent of their basic pay for each four years of army service, up to a total increase of 25 per cent. Then there is also additional pay for specialists, up to a maximum of 30 dollars per month.

The National Guard is a kind of militia, and dates in its present form from 1933, though the name goes back to 1824. In peacetime it is a State, not a Federal establishment. The men are required to do 48 drill periods yearly, each of not less than one and a half hours' duration, and also to put in 15 days' training in camp or on manoeuvres, during which time they receive pay, subsistence and travel allowances at the same rate as the regulars. For each of the 48 drill periods a man is entitled to receive a day's pay. The National Guard may be called out by the President with the concur-

GEN. G. C. MARSHALL, Chief of Staff of the U.S.A. Army. He saw service in the Philippines and in France during the Great War. Under the American constitution the President is C.-in-C. of the Army. *Photo, Keystone*

rence of Congress, and this was done on September 2, 1940, when the President called out 60,000 National Guardsmen for 12 months' active duty as from September 16, so that they might be trained in modern warfare and also later aid the existing army personnel in training conscripts.

The Officers Reserve Corps consists of officers of all grades, and has a strength of some 125,000; the higher ranks in particular are composed very largely of officers who served during the Great War. Officers may be called up for training not exceeding 15 days each year, and be ordered to go on active service at any time and for any period, although if a state of national emergency has not been declared this must be with their own consent. There is also a Reserve Officers Training Corps, consisting in the main of students at universities and secondary schools who must complete four years' military training before being transferred to the O.R.C. Its strength in 1940 was 170,000. Finally there is the enlisted Reserve Corps, consisting of men whose qualifications are such as to make them eligible for enlistment in the Regular Army; a year ago it numbered 28,000.

Millions of Trainees

So much for the volunteer forces. These are, it will be realized, though small, highly trained and keenly efficient. They are the basis on which is being formed the vast American army of tomorrow, an army recruited by conscription. In the U.S.A. this dates from last year. The Selective Training Bill, as it was called, was introduced into the Senate by Senator Burke and into the House of Representatives by Mr. Wadsworth on June 20, 1940; it proposed the registration of all men from 18 to 65, numbering 40 million, of whom those between the ages of 21 and 45 would be eligible for eight months' compulsory military training, the men chosen being selected by lot. The Bill was hotly debated since the opposition to conscription —in peacetime, too—was as great in the States as in Britain. General Marshall, U.S. Chief of Staff, told the Senate Military Affairs Committee that the War Department

favoured compulsory military training as the only possible way of immediately bringing the Army up to its full strength; what the U.S.A. needed, he said, was a completely trained and equipped army of at least two million men if it was to defend the Western Hemisphere. Discussion on the Bill dragged on for many weeks until early in August President Roosevelt forthrightly declared that conscription was the most fair and effective means of obtaining man-power for the Army, and said that while it was true that during the last war the United States had been able to build up an army of four million men after war was declared, she would never be so fortunate again; it had been, he said, just sheer luck. But still the debate dragged on, and the President was not able to sign the Bill until September 13. In its final form it applied to all men between 21 and 35 years of age inclusive—about 16,500,000 in all—and it was also enacted that conscripts should not be required to serve outside the Western Hemisphere and American possessions, including the Philippines, and that the number of conscripts under training at any one time should not exceed 900,000. It was laid down that the conscripts should be paid at the rate of 21 dollars a month, rising to 30 dollars after the first four months of training, i.e. the same as the regulars. The period of service of the trainees was originally fixed at a year, but a Bill is now before Congress making the service period thirty months.

All male United States citizens between the ages specified, and all aliens who have declared their intention of becoming United States citizens, without any discrimination on grounds of race or colour, were required to register on October 16. Registration took place at 125,000 local registration offices throughout the country, and the total number who registered was 17,000,000. On October 29 the drawing which determined the order in which the first 800,000 men should be called up for training took place at Washington; and Mr. Stimson, Secretary for War, announced that by June 15, 1941, the full 800,000 would have been called up for training.

The Army of Tomorrow

In 1939 the Regular Army of the U.S.A. was based on three divisions, and even those three were little more than cadres. By the end of May 1940 there were five well-equipped infantry divisions, and within a few months this number had been increased to nine infantry divisions, one cavalry division, and two armoured divisions. As at present visualized, the new American Army will consist of nine army corps, each composed of one regular " triangular " division (i.e. one with three infantry regiments, 14,000 men in all) and two National Guard " square " divisions (i.e. one with four infantry regiments, each division being composed of 18,300 men), plus Corps, Army and G.H.Q. units. There will also be four mechanized divisions and two horsed cavalry divisions. The total strength will be 850,000, but in addition some hundreds of thousands of men are required for the overseas garrisons, the Army Air corps, and coastal and anti-aircraft defences. General Marshall has stated that the eventual goal is 45 infantry divisions completely equipped and 10 armoured divisions, which means upwards of 2,000,000 men.

That, however, is a matter for the future. At present America's problem—and that a very great and pressing one—is that of equipping the enormous man-power available.

'TIN HATS' in the American Army are of two patterns. In this photograph the sergeant on the left is equipped with the new type, while his comrade wears the old helmet. *Photo. Wide World*

Uncle Sam Goes In for Mechanization

HEAVY ARTILLERY of the U.S. Army includes 155 mm. guns of the type seen above. Tractor-drawn and mounted on huge balloon tires for mobility, this gun can throw 95-lb. shells a distance of 14-15 miles. Top left, a demonstration of the U.S. Army's new flame-thrower.

U.S. SECOND ARMOURED DIVISION reviewed at Fort Benning, Georgia. Some 2,000 motor vehicles were on parade, including midget cars, scout cars, motor-cycles and six-wheeled trucks. Here three army planes are roaring over the parade ground. In the circle a soldier is seen in one of the U.S. Army's new camouflage suits. These suits, which are cut both as raincoats and as uniforms, effectively blend snipers into a background of trees and bushes.

Photos, Keystone, Wide World, Planet News

In Syria the R.A.F. Were On the Job

A Bristol Blenheim releasing a stick of bombs over a target in Syria. The top photograph shows two Blenheims following the Syrian coastline on their way to attack enemy positions. A winding river with its interesting delta formation is seen as in a relief map.

Vichy's collusion with her Nazi masters is clearly proved by this photograph of a ruined French aeroplane. A thin coat of paint bearing the Vichy markings only partly obscures Hitler's swastika beneath.

HURRICANE PILOTS who played a victorious part in the Syrian campaign. Right photograph, Vichy France Air Force General Jenneken (left), a member of the French Armistice Convention, chatting with Air Commodore Brown, Chief of the R.A.F. in Palestine, after the close of Syrian hostilities.

Photos, British Official : Crown Copyright

Roar of Battle 'mid Palmyra's Time-scarred Ruin

BRITISH BREN GUN CARRIERS, rumbling through the arches of Palmyra after it had been occupied by the Allies on July 3, strike an incongruous note as they pass beneath an archway forming part of the splendid ruins which testify to the city's former greatness, when, under the Roman Empire, it was a great commercial centre. The capture of Palmyra, said an official Vichy statement, followed a " powerful attack by a British armoured force." Another photograph of Palmyra and an account of the British advance in that sector are given in page 686, Vol. 4.

Photo, British Official : Crown Copyright

Our Searchlight on the War

DUKE OF KENT IN CANADA

FIRST member of the Royal Family to fly the Atlantic, the Duke of Kent arrived in Montreal from England on July 29. His purpose is to inspect R.A.F. training centres under the Commonwealth Air Training Plan, and his tour of every province to see the operations of the Air Force, together with visits to factories and

DUKE OF KENT (bareheaded) talking to his equerry, Sir Louis Greig, before taking off on his flight to Canada to inspect Empire Air Training Schools.

Photo, British Official : Crown Copyright

shipyards, and a schedule of other engagements, presents an arduous programme which will engage him for about six weeks. His Royal Highness will visit President Roosevelt towards the end of August, and will also inspect the naval facilities at Norfolk, Virginia, and the Martin Aviation factories at Baltimore. The Duke, who holds a pilot's certificate, made the crossing in a Liberator, an 18-ton American four-engined bomber, one of the ferry service planes in which pilots flying bombers to this country make the return trip. He was accompanied by Group Captain Sir Louis Greig and Flight-Lieut. P. J. Ferguson. The flight took about nine hours and the Duke described it as " reasonably comfortable but very tiring."

GIANT R.A.F. BOMBER

MR. CHURCHILL recently visited a Bomber Command aerodrome and inspected the famous Short Stirling. This enormous aircraft has a wing span of 99 feet, a length of 87 feet 3 inches, and a height of 22 feet 9 inches. There are four 14-cylinder engines generating 1,400 h.p., which enable the Stirling, which itself weighs 35 tons, to carry more than four tons of bombs at a rate of over 350 miles per hour. " In bombers of British production alone," said the Prime Minister in the House of Commons on July 29, " we have doubled our powers of bomb discharge on Germany at 1,500 miles range." Berlin is one of the cities which has recently been punished by this terrible avenging machine.

GERMAN TRICK EXPOSED

BEIRUT suffered a good deal of bombing before hostilities in Syria came to an end, and the inhabitants were deeply resentful because residential areas had apparently been attacked in preference to military objectives. When the British entered the city they found craters and destruction in the most unexpected places, tending to show that British airmen had either disobeyed orders or been singularly unskilful in marksmanship. So an inquiry was undertaken. This

revealed several curious facts.' First, a 2,000 lb. German land mine had been dropped (this was examined by experts) ; second, two German three-engined bombers were found to have been shot down during raids ; third, the city had been attacked on nights when it was known that British machines were not over the town. The only damage that could be definitely attributed to British bombs was that done to the docks and harbour works.

BRITISH SYMPATHY WITH RUSSIA

CAMBRIDGE University recently sent a cable to the Academy of Sciences of the U.S.S.R., signed by the Vice-Chancellor and seventeen professors and other eminent members of staff. It read : " Warmest greetings and support for your country's heroic fight against the common foe." In his reply the Vice-President of the Academy of Sciences said : " Soviet scientists are convinced that in joining their forces and uniting the peoples of the Soviet Union and Great Britain, they will triumph in the historic struggle for culture and liberty against Fascist tyranny." Other messages of sympathy have been exchanged by the artists of the Soviet Theatre and the British Actors' Equity Association. The Durham Miners' Association, a body both generous and practical, have informed their miner comrades at Donbass, in the Don Valley, that they are giving a donation from their political fund to purchase six ambulances —one for each of their county wards—for the Anglo-Russian Ambulance Corps. These would act as a symbol of fellowship between the workers of Britain and Russia.

TOUGH LITTLE ISLAND

WHEN Malta was attacked on July 26 by E-boats the Royal Malta Artillery put up a tremendous defence and not one of the raiding boats survived (see p. 31.) The colours of this gallant regiment bear only one battle honour, namely Egypt, 1882, but the Maltese have always been ready to take up arms against any invasion of their island. In 1565, with the Knights of St. John, they fought against the Turks ; at the end of the 18th century, side by side with the English, they gave battle to the army left there by Napoleon. Today the splendid harbour batteries bear the brunt of attack by enemy sea-borne forces, while

GEN. DAUFRESNE DE LA CHEVALERIE, commander of a Belgian Army division, who escaped from internment in Holland and has now reached England via the U.S.A.

Photo, Planet News

air raiders are discomfited by the accurate marksmanship of the Maltese A.A. gunners.

PRESS-BUTTON S O S

ONE of the latest life-saving devices now carried in most ships is a radio transmitter powerful enough to be heard 200 miles away, and yet so compact that it is built into a suitcase which is water-tight and buoyant. The set is used if the crew have to take to the boats, and an unskilled person can send out the signal by merely pressing a button. Its value was recently proved in a practical way, for 17 men in a lifeboat were saved within seven hours, because the S O S they sent out was picked up 90 miles away.

NAZI INTRIGUES IN ARGENTINA

GREAT anger and discomfiture have been aroused among German circles in Argentina by the detention of three diplomatic bags by a Parliamentary Committee set up to investigate totalitarian activities in that country. The bags, refused entry into Peru, had been returned by the German Legation in Lima to the Embassy in Buenos Aires, and were removed from the aeroplane at Cordoba by order of the Committee and taken under guard to the Chamber of Deputies. It was later stated that they contained amongst other things a powerful short-wave transmitting and receiving set ready for use, several copies of the book " America Must Be Saved," by Theodore Dreiser, propagandist photographs and lists of German propagandist films. Tucked inside the wireless set was a code message ordering all Nazi agents in Peru and Bolivia to follow instructions issued by the four Nazi envoys in South America at their meeting in Santiago, Chile, last March. The discovery of this message proves that Argentina is the centre of Nazi organizations to promote war, revolutions and internal strife in South America

THE SHORT STIRLING heavy bomber, seen above in flight, is Britain's latest bomber. The upper photograph shows Mr. Churchill inspecting one of these giant machines during a visit to a Bomber Command aerodrome. The Stirling, which is driven by either Bristol Hercules or Wright Cyclone engines developing 1,400 h.p., has a very heavy defensive armament. The wing span of the air-craft is 99 ft. and its length 87 ft. 3 in. Undercarriage and tail wheels are retractable.

Photos, British Official : Crown Copyright

Poles and Russians Are Friends Again

Since September 1939, when, following the crushing of Polish armies by the Nazis, the Russians invaded and occupied most of Eastern Poland—territory which for the most part was included in the Tsar's dominions before 1917—Poland and Russia have been at war. On July 30, 1941, however, representatives of the two countries signed in London an agreement which, though it left many points still to be settled, united Poland and Soviet Russia in the struggle against their common foe, Hitlerite Germany.

IT was in Mr. Eden's room at the Foreign Office in London that the Russian-Polish Agreement was signed on the afternoon of July 30. Mr. Churchill was in the chair and seated at the table with him were Mr. Eden; M. Maisky, the Soviet Ambassador, and Mr. Novikov, representing the Soviet Government; and General Sikorski, the Polish Prime Minister.

There was little ceremony. First the documents (a translation of the main clauses of the Agreement is given on the right, prepared in Russian and Polish, were signed by M. Maisky and General Sikorski. Then Mr. Eden handed General Sikorski a Note, stating that " in conformity with the Agreement of Mutual Assistance between the United Kingdom and Poland of August 25, 1939, His Majesty's Government of the United Kingdom have entered into no undertaking towards the U.S.S.R. which affects the relations between that country and Poland," and giving an assurance that they " did not recognize any territorial changes which have been effected in Poland since August 1939 "; to which the General handed a reply expressing the Polish Govern-

RUSSIAN-POLISH AGREEMENT

1. The Government of the Union of Soviet Socialist Republics recognizes the Soviet-German Treaties of 1939 regarding territorial changes in Poland as having lost their validity. The Government of the Republic of Poland declares that the Republic of Poland is not bound by any agreement with any third Power which is directed against the U.S.S.R.

2. Diplomatic relations will be restored between the two Governments upon the signing of this Agreement and an immediate exchange of Ambassadors will be effected.

3. The two Governments mutually undertake to render each other assistance and support of all kinds in the present war against Hitlerite Germany.

4. The Government of the Union of Soviet Socialist Republics consents to the formation on the territory of the Union of Soviet Socialist Republics of a Polish army under a command appointed by the Government of the Republic of Poland in agreement with the Soviet Government. The Polish army on the territory of the Union of Soviet Socialist Republics will be subordinated, in regard to all operations, to the Supreme Military Command of the Union of Soviet Socialist Republics, which will include a representative of the Polish army. All details as to organization, command and employment of this force will be settled in a subsequent agreement.

Protocol—As from the resumption of diplomatic relations, the Government of the Union of Soviet Socialist Republics grants an amnesty to all Polish citizens now detained on the territory of the Union of Soviet Socialist Republics either as prisoners of war or on other sufficient grounds.   *London, July 30, 1941*

The meeting was brought to an end by a few words from Mr. Churchill. " Here, as the result of the labours of the last few days," he said, " is a pact of friendship, signed between the Russians and the Poles, whose long history has been chequered and darkened by their quarrels, whose future can be lightened by their comradeship. It is a sign and proof of the fact that hundreds of millions of men all over the world are coming together on the march against the filthy gangster Power which must be effectively and finally destroyed."

Announcing the news of the new pact to the House of Commons that afternoon, Mr. Eden declared that the signature constituted a historic event, one on which both parties were to be warmly congratulated. The House cheered the announcement, and the news of the Agreement was generally welcomed, although Mr. Zaleski, Poland's Foreign Minister in London, resigned.

Broadcasting to Poland and Poles throughout the world on July 31, General Sikorski defended the Agreement as one which was both honourable and dignified—one which could not but result in a considerable

SIGNING THE RUSSIAN-POLISH AGREEMENT at the Foreign Office on July 30, whereby 200,000 Poles detained in the U.S.S.R. were freed, and an agreement was entered into on the formation of a Polish army to fight with the Russians against the Nazis. The Russo-German Treaties of 1939 dividing up Poland are now null and void. In this historic photograph those seated from left to right are Gen. Sikorski, Polish Prime Minister, Mr. Eden, Mr. Winston Churchill, and M. Maisky, Soviet Ambassador.   *Photo, British Official; Crown Copyright*

ment's sincere satisfaction with the British Government's Note.

Following the signature of the Agreement, Mr. Eden expressed the belief that it was fair and advantageous to both sides. It would lay a firm foundation for fruitful collaboration between the two countries in the war against the common enemy, and was therefore a valuable contribution to the Allied cause and would be warmly welcomed in all friendly countries, and not least by public opinion in the United Kingdom. General Sikorski declared that this was a turning-point in history. Not every question between Russia and Poland had been settled in the Agreement, but a basis was provided for useful collaboration. The future would depend on the goodwill of both sides, and they possessed

that goodwill. He, too, stressed the fact that the solidarity of all freedom-loving peoples against Hitlerite Germany would provide the basis for the common victory, and in conclusion he thanked the British Government, and especially Mr. Eden, for their share in the great work. Then M. Maisky, in his turn, expressed his country's gratitude to the British Government and to Mr. Eden. The peoples of the Soviet Union, he went on, had very friendly feelings towards the people of Poland. They had a common enemy in Hitlerite Germany, against whom they would fight side by side.

This would pave the way to form a solid friendship between the two peoples in the future, when the time came to build up a new Europe, after the war had been won on the principle of self-determination of nations.

strengthening of Poland's alliance with Britain, and a tightening of her bonds of friendship with the U.S.A.

And here, to conclude, is a pregnant passage taken from a leader in London's German newspaper *Die Zeitung*. " The Russian-Polish alliance, concluded through British mediation, ends a national enmity of a century-and-a-half, and at the same time, through brotherhood-in-arms against the common deadly foe, lays the foundation for a future genuine friendship between the two great Slav peoples. It loses nothing of its value from the fact that it leaves open the question of frontier-drawing. In the economically and militarily united Europe of the future frontiers will have lost much of their old significance."

Now Was Launched the Third German Offensive

When the campaign in Russia had entered its seventh week the Germans launched their third
great offensive, one which they hoped (so it was believed) would carry them to Kiev and beyond.
The position of the opposing armies at this critical moment in the campaign is given below so far
as it might be ascertained.

HITLER's armoured train, with the Fuehrer inside it, was reported to have arrived on August 6 in the southern sector of the vast Russian front. Germany's supreme war lord inspected his Rumanian allies and decorated General Antonescu with the Knight's Cross of the Iron Cross for his "liberation of Bessarabia." But the Fuehrer had more important business than this on hand. He had come to discuss with the puppet general and his own military chiefs what were described as the final plans for the capture of Kiev and the rest of the Ukraine. Those plans were even now in operation. For the third time in seven weeks the German armies were thrusting themselves forward in a huge offensive ; and although fierce fighting continued along the whole front, particularly at Smolensk and near Kexholm on the Finnish front, it was in the Kiev sector that the Germans hoped this time to make a really effective break-through.

The switching of the German drive to the Ukraine front was indicated by the Soviet communiqué issued in the early hours of August 4, when it reported fighting in two new regions to the north and south of Zhitomir : round the railway junction of Korosten, 100 miles north-west of Kiev, and Byelaya Tserkov, 45 miles south-west of the Ukrainian capital. It seemed that General Schmidt's Panzer division had succeeded in pushing through the Russian armies in a new pincers drive, while the main body of German infantry was still held up 80 miles to the west of Kiev, in the neighbourhood of Zhitomir. The situation did not look too good for the Russians, but Marshal Budenny's armies were reported to be fighting tenaciously.

As yet only a small portion of the Ukraine had been occupied by the Germans, and that portion was still a battlefield. Early in August Marshal Budenny issued an appeal to the population in the Nazi-occupied zone, urging those who were able to handle arms to "join guerilla detachments, create new lines, annihilate the hateful German troops, exterminate Fascists like mad dogs. Derail their trains, interrupt communications, blow up dumps, see that not a single ounce of grain is left to the enemy. Gather as much as you need for the near future, and destroy the rest. Destroy plantations of industrial crops — beetroot and flax. The hour of our victory is at hand. Make every effort to fight the enemy and exterminate him." Such was the Marshal's proclamation, and it was obeyed with an eager efficiency.

But great as was the destructive work of the guerilla bands, greater still was that done by organized units of the Red Army which were still in being in the back areas. There was one Russian unit caught in Poland by the German advance, Colonel Novikov's division. In 32 days, so the Russian newspaper, "Red Star," revealed, days of raiding and fighting, they killed at least 3,000 Germans, destroyed one motorized division, captured over 300 trucks loaded with munitions, food and clothing, as well as hundreds of motor bicycles, bicycles and armoured cars. Eventually, by a combination of fighting and stratagem for 500 miles through forests and swamps, the division succeeded in crashing through the German lines and joined Marshal Timoshenko's main army.

On August 6 the Nazi High Command deemed it time to issue another special announcement concerning the course of the war. It was dated from the Fuehrer's headquarters and read out over the German wireless. As usual, the most sweeping successes were claimed. The total of Russian prisoners, it was declared, now amounted to 895,000, while there had been destroyed or captured 13,145 armoured cars, 10,388 guns, and 9,082 aircraft. " The bloody losses of the enemy, fighting with extreme tenacity and stubbornness, far exceeded the number of prisoners taken." Yet " the German forces have achieved almost superhuman feats of bravery and endurance in these battles with the bitterest enemy we have met so far." Reviews were given of the fighting on the various fronts.

In the north, Field-Marshal Ritter von Leeb's army had been allotted the task of breaking through the Stalin Line along the Latvian-Soviet border. In a daring assault the army commanded by Col.-Gen. Busch, and the Panzer group under Col-Gen. Hoeppner, broke through south of Lake Peipsi and captured Ostrov, Porkhov and Pskov. In spite of bad roads, embittered enemy resistance, and the enormous strain on the Nazi soldiers, the German left wing had been able to advance up to Narva. In Estonia, Col-Gen. von Kuechler's army had taken Dorpat.

Red scout on horseback reporting to his commanders : an incident in the conflict in eastern Europe. Scouting in this war of "no fronts" must be a more than usually perilous part of military duty.

Photo, Planet News

In the southern sector, an army group under Field-Marshal von Rundstedt had had to overcome particularly difficult terrain, unfavourable weather, and the resistance of a numerically superior enemy. The armies of General Stuelpnagel and Field-Marshal von Riechenau, supported by General Kleist's tank force, had to fight their way forward beyond Zhitomir as far as the gates of Kiev, thus enabling the German forces to sweep southward on a broad front between the Dniester and the Dnieper so as to cut off the enemy's retreat and start the "great battle of encirclement which is still in progress." At the same time German and Rumanian detachments under General Antonescu had forced their way across the Pruth and driven the Russians out of Bessarabia. Since then the army commanded by General Ritter von Schobert had advanced to the north-east across the Dniester.

Finally, in the central sector the army group of Field-Marshal von Bock had " gloriously concluded " the great battle of Smolensk. In almost four weeks of fighting the armies of Field-Marshal von Kluge, Col-Gen. Strauss and Colonel von Weicks, together with the tank formations under General Guderian and General Hoth, had inflicted enormous casualties on the enemy. The Air Force units under Field-Marshal Kesselring had also decisively contributed to their victory.

But, interesting as was this catalogue of Nazi war chiefs, the Fuehrer was still unable to claim any decisive advantages, nor did he say what the German losses had been, although in Berlin it was admitted that they were terrific. Early in August Mr. Lozovsky, the Soviet propaganda chief, stated that on the Eastern Front the Germans had lost already more than 1,500,000 men, and he went on to claim that the process of the disintegration of the German Army had begun. Its morale was broken, a sure sign of its nearing ruin and rout. " The Germans now explain," he said, " that the Russians are fighting fanaticallly and fatalistically owing to their poverty and the misery which makes life not worth living. By that token the Italians and Rumanians should be the world's best soldiers and the English the worst."

GERMAN THRUSTS into Russia are here marked with black arrows. The map shows the position at August 7.
Courtesy of the "Daily Mail"

With the Red Army on the Ukraine Front

The peculiar photograph above shows one Russian method of dealing with hostile river transport. Obstacles, placed in the River Bug, are covered by the rising tide, making navigation extremely hazardous. Right, Marshal Budenny (left), commanding the Red Army in the Ukraine sector, seen with some of his officers in the field.

Left, a 'brigade commander of a Red Army tank unit examines with his men a relief model of the surrounding countryside before going into action.

This Soviet soldier is carrying one of Russia's secret weapons, a new type of automatic rifle. With a flash eliminator on the muzzle, it bears some resemblance to the Bren gun.

German motorized troops passing an abandoned Russian tank somewhere in the Ukraine sector.

Photos, Keystone, Planet News and Sport & General

Behold the Beaufighter, Britain's Formidable Ne

THE existence of the Bristol Beaufighter was first revealed to the British public some months ago when Beaufighter pilots were credited with the destruction of a considerable number of German night bombers. Now a few official details concerning Britain's "Night fighter No. 1" have been released for publication. Though best known, so far, as a night fighter, the Beaufighter is essentially a long-range fighter aircraft and will probably be increasingly employed as an escort to day bombers. Incidentally, the aircraft which made the highly successful attacks on Sicilian air fields on July 28, when between thirty and forty enemy planes were destroyed on the ground, were Beaufighters.

An all-metal mid-wing monoplane, the Beaufighter is fitted with two Bristol Hercules engines developing 1,400 h.p. each. The wing-span is 57 ft. 10 in., the length is 41 ft. and the all-up weight is in the neighbourhood of 21,000 lb. The Beaufighter's top speed is over 300 m.p.h. and it has a range of 1,500 miles.

Its armament is exceptionally heavy for a fighter plane. It consists of four 20 mm. Hispano-Suiza cannon guns and six Browning machine-guns ; the cannon are mounted in the fuselage and the machine-guns in the wings. Thus its fire-power is terrific, and often a German plane has been literally blown to pieces after an en-

BRISTOL BEAUFIGHTERS, seen flying in formation, top left, and in close up (oval), are among the "latest summer aircraft fashions" to which Mr. Churchill referred in the House recently. They are being built in ever-increasing numbers, and, above, a partly completed Beaufighter is being removed by workmen from the assembly jig. Soon it will shoot more German planes from the skies.   *Photos, British Official: Crown Copyright*

Warplane Which Can Fight All Round the Clock

unter with a patrolling Beaufighter. Many a
aufighter is said to have landed after a night
gagement with the enemy, its wings and
selage covered with wreckage from a dis-
egrated Nazi bomber.

EVERAL novel features are incorporated in
the Beaufighter's general design, including
new type of cabin heating system and an
ergency signalling system between pilot and
server so that both can be ready, in case of
ergency, to leave the machine at the same
e. Other equipment includes a cine-camera
it, a de-icing system for the air-screws and a
vice for jettisoning fuel in case of emergency.
o special hatches give entrance to the pilot's
d observer's seats, and these can also be used
emergency exits if the crew has to bale out.
ditional emergency exits are provided in the
m of a knock-out panel on the starboard side
the pilot, a hinged window above the pilot's
ad, and a hinged hood above the observer.

factories all over Britain the new "ten-gun
Beau" is being turned out by men and
men workers in ever-increasing numbers, and
this page two stages in the production of
istol Beaufighters are depicted : one is a heavy
, for which the men are better adapted—the
er is particularly suited to the nimble fingers
the women workers. To prevent production
ng held up by air attacks, Beaufighter parts are
ade in several factories and assembled in others.

NIGHT FIGHTER No. 1, as the Beaufighter has come to be called, is also designed and fitted for day operations.
Top right, a Beaufighter in flight is seen from directly underneath. It has all that a fighter pilot could desire :
speed, manoeuvrability, and, above all, fire-power. Women, as well as men, are helping to build this scourge of
the enemy, and girls are here assembling controls and instruments. *Photos, Sport & General and Central Press*

R.A.S.C.—The Army's 'Maid-of-All Work'

In pages 594-595 of Vol. 4 we gave an account of the Royal Army Ordnance Corps.
Now we tell something of the Royal Army Service Corps, on which the troops rely
for their food, supplies and transport.

WITH the departure of the G.S. wagon into the limbo of past wars, the derisive epithet of "Ally Sloper's Cavalry" can no longer be hurled at the R.A.S.C. Not that it was ever really deserved, for the Army Service Corps (it did not become " Royal " until 1918) did fine work throughout the last war. Along with the old G.S. wagon the Divisional Train is now a thing of the past—and the R.A.S.C. has been completely reorganized.

The duties of the R.A.S.C. fall under three headings : Supply, Transport, and Barrack Services ; and the Corps has been described by Major Gordon Dickson as " a very efficient combination of Mr. Sainsbury, the L.P.T.B., Carter Paterson, and Shell Mex. "

Today, just as in Napoleon's time, an army marches on its stomach, and the gigantic task of feeding millions of men is one special province of the Supply branch. A division is estimated to eat 17 tons of food a day, and though this may be comparatively easy to deliver to troops stationed at home, the task of getting rations to an army constantly on the move, as in the Western Desert or Italian East Africa, is almost superhuman.

Problems of Desert Supply

In the years of stationary warfare from 1915 to 1918 it was a relatively easy task to supply the front line, but today, when mechanized forces advance rapidly, it is no easy matter to work out how the necessary supplies, both of rations and ammunition, can be got to a given place by a given time. And in the case of desert warfare the " water men " must move up thousands of gallons of water a day, chlorinate it and distribute it to men parched with the heat of battle. Ambulance men and medical supplies have to keep pace with the advance, and the signal companies, often strung over hundreds of miles of territory, must be kept going. The term " supplies " means more than food alone. It includes mails, ammunition, hospital stores and any material an army may want brought from its bases.

An instance of the difficulties which can face the R.A.S.C. in wartime is the evacuation of the B.E.F. from Dunkirk, when small boats laden with provisions and water stored in petrol cans braved undreamt-of dangers to feed the men who still waited on the beaches. And when these men were safely evacuated, the famished army which arrived back in " Blighty " had to be fed under abnormal conditions. How the R.A.S.C. rose to the occasion has been thus described by a correspondent of " The Times " :

For 12 almost sleepless days and nights men from every cookhouse, workshop, and station company in the area fought the physical problems of food at the centres established at Headcorn, Faversham, and Paddock Wood. An average of 100 trains a day passed through. They halted for about eight minutes, and in that time every man—there were sometimes as many as 800— was roused from exhausted slumber and fed through the windows of the compartments.

At three hours' notice the depot baked 60,000 lb. of bread a day in their Aldershot ovens at Shorncliffe in place of the normal 20,000 lb. ; another 50,000 lb. was provided by private contractors. Meat was cooked over trench fires on long spits hurriedly improvised for the purpose by the workshops ; there were mountains of bread and butter on the platforms ; men made tea and cut sandwiches for 24 hours a day ; and, in the words of one of their officers, they knew what it was to see 5,000 eggs at a time and cook them.

As part of the Divisional organization the R.A.S.C. is divided into three companies : the Supply Column, the Ammunition Company, and the Petrol Company. The Supply Column is subdivided into two echelons, and while one of these is bringing up rations the other is busy at Railhead collecting supplies for the next day's delivery. The general principle underlying the supply system is to have two days' rations on wheels ahead of Railhead.

Since it is impossible to calculate closely the expenditure of ammunition and petrol, a different system of supply has to be adopted. The underlying principle is that front line reserves are replaced by those in the rear. For instance, as a soldier uses up his ammunition it is replaced by the Company reserve of small-arm ammunition, which draws on the Battalion reserve. This is kept replenished by the Divisional Ammunition Company, which in turn is fed from the Divisional Ammunition sub-park of the Corps Ammunition Park, lying near Railhead. The supply of petrol is dealt with in much the same way to ensure that every vehicle has a full tank before any move. The vehicles of each unit fill up from the unit reserve, and these reserves draw their supplies from a Petrol Point established by the Petrol Company lying near Railhead.

But important as these three companies of the R.A.S.C. are, with their three great systems of supply stretching out in an endless chain from bases and railheads to the forward formations, they represent but part of the vital work carried out by the Corps. There are, in addition, the mechanical transport companies, responsible for the troop-carrying vehicles of the army, the field bakeries and butcheries, the technical transport which carries the heavy bridging material of the R.E.s, and the Motor Ambulance Companies and Convoys.

Loaves by the Million

Here is what a correspondent of " The Times " saw when he visited a Divisional Supply Company where recruits were being trained under field conditions :

At the Command bakery 35,000 2-lb. loaves a day are being turned out in the great range of ovens, and the master baker, an " artist by inclination " who has practised his art in many climes during long years of service, spoke with pride of the quality of Army bread, which he said has improved since the war began. He put the number of complaints made at one in 5,000,000 lb. of bread. Over the way was the master butcher, responsible for storing and issuing 80,000 lb. of meat a day. The cutting of the Army ration from 10 oz. to 8 oz. a day saved 11,000 lb. a day in this depot alone.

The period of training has been condensed to a minimum, yet the driving battalion I saw, receiving 120 raw recruits each week, is turning them out as qualified drivers of lorries and staff cars in nine weeks, and their first month is wholly occupied with the military training.

Some of the drill squads I watched might almost have been members of the Guards, and this excellent standard was nowhere more marked than in a detachment from the boys' battalion being drilled by a youthful little sergeant, who outbawled the sergeant-major.

This mention of the boys' battalion opens up yet another aspect of the R.A.S.C. These boys are recruited between the ages of 15 and 18. They enlist for three years, and are given ordinary schooling as well as military and technical training. The boys are trained as fitters, turners, electricians, carpenters, etc., and by the time they have finished their training have a useful trade at their finger-tips.

R.A.S.C. Drivers at one of the Training Centres in the Northern Command out on the road for driving practice in convoy. Other aspects of the Corps' work may be seen in Vol. I, page 607 and Vol. 2, pages 85, 326 and 475.   *Photo, Keystone*

'Sainsburys' and 'Carter Patersons' All in One

The sewing machine has no mysteries for the soldier trained in the art of making army necessities in fabric or canvas. Here is an R.A.S.C. " trimmer" dealing deftly with a problem of stitches and canvas.

WITH THE R.A.S.C., this lance-corporal is working on a turret lathe in the maintenance workshops at the depot. Keeping machines "fit" in modern war is no less important than keeping physically fit.

In the photograph to the right, R.A.S.C. men are guiding a pack-horse down a steep incline. Horses are kept in reserve, and frequently come in useful, for a horse can go sometimes where a machine is hindered or breaks down. Already on the Eastern Front horses have been used for transport purposes.

Beneath, spraying a car with the regulation army paint, two R.A.S.C. men are keeping the vehicle spick and span. They, incidentally, have to wear nose-protectors against fumes.

The Sergeant-Major explains what you have to do when you come to a road junction. He has all the answers and the road signs in the R.A.S.C. School of Motoring. And they don't allow L drivers to waste time, since they are expected to be efficient at the wheel after five weeks' intensive training.

Photos, Topical, Fox, Associated Press

Our Diary of the War

SATURDAY, AUG. 2, 1941   *700th day*

Air.—Docks at Kiel and targets on Dutch coast bombed by day. Fighters made offensive patrols over northern France.

Very heavy night raid on Berlin. Intense attacks also on ports of Hamburg and Kiel. Dock area of Cherbourg bombed.

Russian Front.—Moscow reported fighting in sectors of Novorzhev, Nevel, Smolensk and Zhitomir. German 137th Division said to have been routed near Smolensk. Two raiders down during another night attack on Moscow. German High Command claimed success in Ukraine.

Mediterranean.—Enemy aircraft attacked H.M. ships off N. African coast; four bombers and one fighter destroyed by our fighters.

SUNDAY, AUG. 3   *701st day*

Sea.—Admiralty announced that British submarine had torpedoed and probably sunk Italian cruiser of Garibaldi class in Mediterranean.

Our submarines also sank two supply ships and torpedoed a floating dock near Italy.

Air.—Night attacks on industries and communications at Hanover and Frankfurt-am-Main. Calais docks also bombed.

Russian Front.—Moscow reported fighting in two new areas in Kiev sector, Germans apparently attempting pincer movement from north-west and south-west. Fighting also reported from Estonia and Smolensk.

Africa.—Squadrons of S.A.A.F. heavily attacked enemy gun positions in Tobruk area.

R.A.F. bombed shipping at Tripoli. Night attacks on Benghazi and on Berka aerodrome. Fleet Air Arm bombed aerodrome at Gambut.

Mediterranean. — Successful attack by R.A.F. on Italian fighters on ground at Reggio, Italy.

Home.—Heavy bombs dropped during day raid on south-east coast town. Enemy bomber shot down in Channel. At night a few bombs fell in east and south England.

MONDAY, AUG. 4   *702nd day*

Sea.—Admiralty announced that H.M. minesweeper Snaefell had been sunk.

H.M. trawler Norland shot down German bomber.

Russian Front.—Battle for Smolensk still

regarded as crucial. On Finnish front enemy has made no advance, and there were reports that Russians were attacking. Battle in progress for possession of Sortavala, north of Lake Ladoga.

Africa.—R.A.F. bombers made night raids on Derna, Gazala and Martuba, and on enemy shipping off coast near Apollonia.

Mediterranean.—Night raid on Suez Canal area, causing damage and casualties.

TUESDAY, AUG. 5   *703rd day*

Sea.—Admiralty announced naval raid on Porto Conte, Sardinia, on August 1; seaplane bases and harbour defences shelled. Aerodrome at Alghero bombarded and later bombed by naval aircraft.

Air.—Large force of bombers attacked Mannheim, Frankfurt, and Karlsruhe. Other targets were Aachen and Ostend. Hits observed on large supply ship at Nantes.

Russian Front.—Russian communiqué reported fighting in Kholm, new point in attack against Leningrad. No change on other fronts.

Germans claimed to be widening a breach 60 miles south-east of Smolensk.

Africa.—During nights of 4-5 and 5-6 R.A.F. and S.A.A.F. made series of attacks on Benghazi, Gazala, Tmimi and Derna. Schooner sunk off Misurata.

WEDNESDAY, AUG. 6   *704th day*

Air.—R.A.F. attacked small convoy off Dutch coast; one ship left sinking.

Night attacks on Frankfurt, Mannheim and Karlsruhe. Aerodromes in Northern France and one in Norway raided. Enemy ship off Norway torpedoed by Beaufort aircraft.

Russian Front.—Third German offensive in progress, directed mainly against Kholm region in north and against Ukraine. Germans claimed capture of Kholm.

Nine German planes shot down during night raid over Moscow.

Russian submarine sank enemy troops and munition transport in Baltic.

Africa.—Third consecutive day of heavy bombing attack on Gondar, Abyssinia.

Mediterranean.—During night of 5-6 Fleet Air Arm bombed submarine base at Augusta.

Fleet Air Arm attacked convoy of six merchant ships escorted by destroyers off

Lampedusa. Two freighters sunk, one probably sunk and one badly damaged.

Home.—Night raiders dropped bombs at few points in east and south-east England. Two destroyed.

THURSDAY, AUG. 7   *705th day*

Air.—Main night attack on Essen. Dortmund and Hamm were also heavily raided. Other forces bombed docks at Boulogne, aerodromes in Northern France, aerodromes and other targets in Denmark, and shipping off Dutch coast.

Russian Front.—Fighting intensified in the Ukraine. German attack towards Leningrad making little headway.

First night raid on Berlin by Russian bombers.

Africa.—R.A.F. attacked Benghazi, Tripoli, and other ports and targets in Libya.

FRIDAY, AUG. 8   *706th day*

Sea.—Netherlands Admiralty announced that Dutch submarine sank enemy supply ship in Mediterranean convoy.

Air.—Heavy night raids on naval base at Kiel and targets at Hamburg and elsewhere in N.W. Germany.

Enemy supply ships in fjord north of Bergen were bombed.

Russian Front.—Moscow reported fierce fighting at Kexholm, on Lake Ladoga, at Smolensk and in the Ukraine. Russian night bombers again reached outskirts of Berlin.

Mediterranean.—R.A.F. bombed harbour at Catania, Sicily.

SATURDAY, AUG. 9   *707th day*

Sea.—Heinkel shot down at night by minesweepers' A.A. gunfire.

Air.—Eighteen enemy fighters destroyed over France during offensive sweeps. Ten British fighters missing.

Russian Front.—Germans announced capture of Korosten, 100 miles N.W. of Kiev. Russians reported no change in areas of fighting.

German bombers made night raid on Moscow; eight shot down.

Africa.—Night raids on Libyan ports, including Tripoli, Bardia, Benghazi and Derna.

A VALENTINE TANK, the 16-ton infantry tank formerly known as the "Mark III" type, led the procession which, starting from the Mansion House, London, inaugurated the Tank Tour of the country which began on August 1. The ceremony was performed by the Lord Mayor of London, Sir George Wilkinson. Similar tours, intended to show what are being manufactured and what are wanted, started from Edinburgh, Macclesfield and Cambridge. Facing the camera, in the tank, is Captain Barker, who was in charge of the British tanks in Libya. *Topical Press*

They Have Won Honours in Freedom's Cause

Insp. Michael McHugh, P.L.A. Police, **G.M.,** for removing naval ammunition to a place of safety during a raid on docks.

P.C. Douglas Barr, P.L.A., **G.M.,** for assisting in the removal of the ammunition to safety during the same raid.

P.C. J. E. Fletcher, P.L.A., also received the **G.M.** for heroic work in connexion with this Dockland incident.

War Res. P.L.A. Constable H. P. Odell, G.M., for taking part in the removal by truck of the ammunition.

Constable William Turner, the fifth recipient of the **G.M.,** for removing the ammunition under incendiary and H.E.

P.C. Edward G. Walker, G.M., for conspicuous courage and devotion to duty during several heavy raids.

Captain John Epps, Dockmaster at Millwall, **G.M.,** for courage in organizing fire-parties.

Lieut. R. E. Moore, G.C., for conspicuous courage and skill in the execution of his duties.

Gunner J. H. Clinton, of the Merchant Navy, **B.E.M.,** for skill, resource and courage.

Able Seaman S. J. Tuckwell, G.C., for great gallantry and undaunted devotion to duty.

Temp. Lieut. H. R. Newgass, R.N.V.R., **G.C.,** for setting a fine example of courage on all occasions.

Chief Officer H. Post, M.B.E., for skill, courage and seamanship in a lifeboat.

Commander L. Newman, R.N.V.R., **O.B.E.,** for exceptional bravery on convoy duties.

Captain V. Power, Merchant Navy, **O.B.E.,** for outstanding bravery and skill.

Lt.-Commander Bramwell, Fleet Air Arm, **D.S.O.,** for conspicuous gallantry.

Commander E. F. Anderton, O.B.E., for outstanding courage in connexion with his duties.

Vice-Admiral W. Whitworth, awarded the **K.C.B.** He was recently made Second Sea Lord.

Vice-Admiral H. D. Cunningham, awarded the **K.C.B.** in recognition of distinguished services.

Major H. Barefoot, R.E., **G.C.,** for carrying out hazardous work in a brave manner.

Lt.-Col. William G. Harriott, M.C., R.A., **O.B.E.,** Military Division, for distinguished services.

Col. C. M. Barber, Queen's Own Cameronians, **D.S.O.,** for meritorious service.

Corpl. J. P. Scully, G.C., for great courage and strength in saving two people trapped in debris.

Major-Gen. A. E. Percival, D.S.O., O.B.E., M.C., the **C.B.** He is the new G.O.C. Malaya.

Lieut. J. A. Langley, M.C., Coldstream Guards, **M.B.E.,** in recognition of his distinguished services.

Mrs. M. E. Bolton, Matron of Sir R. Jeffrey's Home, Eltham, **G.M.,** for rescuing two old ladies from a burning building.

Miss C. M. Heard, Liverpool A.R.P., **B.E.M.,** for helping to free a man trapped by debris, though bombs were falling.

Miss E. M. Smyth, Organizing Secretary of Women's Land Army, **M.B.E.,** for devotion to duty and great ability.

Miss W. P. Hollyer, Croydon A.R.P., **G.M.,** for remaining at her post in telephone-room though severely wounded.

Mrs. Hayes, Lady County Superintendent of Hampshire, **M.B.E.,** for distinguished services in connexion with the war.

Miss A. Eke, Women's Land Army, **Sustained Courage Badge,** for devotion to duty under bombs.

Mr. C. A. Baines, P.L.A. Docks Superintendent, **M.B.E.,** for gallant work in putting out incendiary bombs.

Mr. S. C. Farmer, Food Executive Officer, Southampton, **G.M.,** for bravery in fighting fire during a heavy blitz.

District Warden S. Woolfson, Stepney, **G.M.,** for brave rescue work when a Stepney building was hit by H.E.s

Mr. W. H. Willson, G.M., for rescue work at Bromley when a German bomber crashed on two houses.

Mr. F. E. Marvell, of Stoke Newington, **G.M.,** for courage, initiative, and endurance when bombs were dropped.

Mr. C. D. Lindsey, electrical foreman, P.L.A., **G.M.,** for cutting off electric current under heavy bomb attack.

Are All Our Aerodromes 'Invasion-proof'?

Attacking troops in position during manoeuvres near London designed to test the defences of a fighter-station. This trial of our preparedness against invasion was inspected by Captain Margesson, Secretary of State for War, in company with the Army commanders and other senior officers.

In the photograph beneath is a camouflaged machine-gunner making use of natural cover in defence of an aerodrome. The exercise was carried out with great thoroughness, and included air-borne troop landings. G.H.Q. Liaison kept contact throughout with all "enemy" landings and movements. The successful defence of aerodromes is the essential preliminary in modern war.

HOME-DEFENCE PATROL taking cover by a bracken-lined path. On the right, members of the R.A.F. undergoing bayonet practice in a smoke-screen. They are part of a Balloon Command Personnel stationed on the South Coast, and their duties include infantry training should they be called upon to repel invader troops who might be landed in or near airfields and stations. In the last resort such attacks must be accounted for by hand-to-hand fighting.

Photos. British Official: Crown Copyright; Fox

In America They're Training for the R.A.F.

R.A.F. CADETS who recently arrived for flight training at Riddle Aerodrome, Arcadia, Florida, found other mounts besides training planes awaiting them, for Arcadia cowboys were there to greet them with their cow ponies.

Group Captain Carnegie congratulates a young Flight Leader upon being the first British cadet to take off from Carlstrom Field, Arcadia. The instructor looks on.

A STEARMAN TRAINER, one of the aircraft on which British cadets in the U.S.A. will learn to fly, passing over Carlstrom Field. The Stearman Aircraft Division is now an integral part of the Boeing Airplane Co., which makes "Flying Fortresses."

Several hundred R.A.F. Cadets were recently sent to the United States for a 30 weeks' course of flight training at American training centres. One of them is seen above being greeted by his American instructor at Maxwell Field, Alabama.

Right, some of the British cadets who are doing their training in America are seeing their new quarters for the first time after their arrival in Florida.

Photos, British Official: Crown Copyright; Keystone

Should It Have Happened on Bank Holiday?

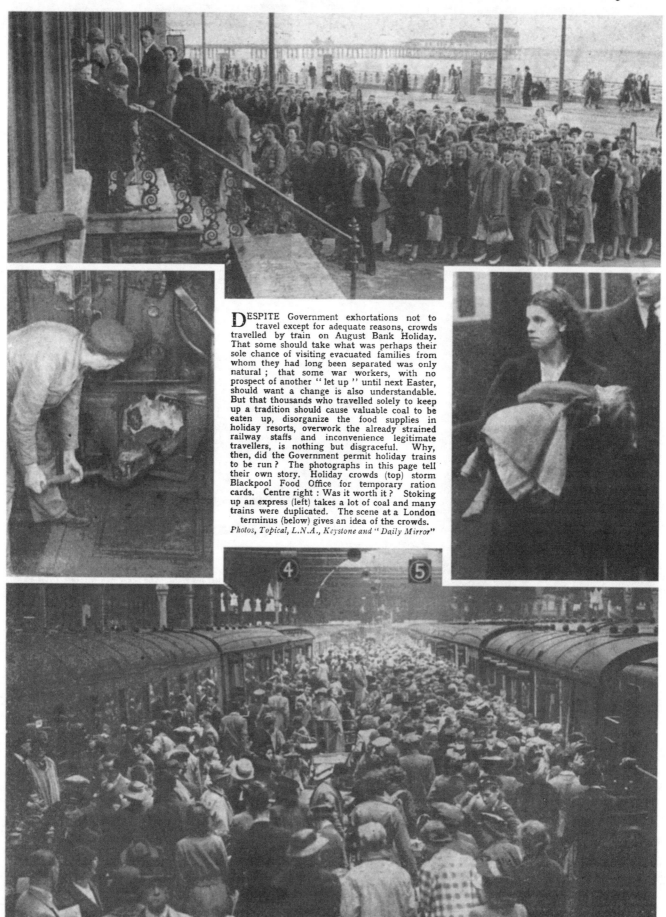

DESPITE Government exhortations not to travel except for adequate reasons, crowds travelled by train on August Bank Holiday. That some should take what was perhaps their sole chance of visiting evacuated families from whom they had long been separated was only natural ; that some war workers, with no prospect of another " let up " until next Easter, should want a change is also understandable. But that thousands who travelled solely to keep up a tradition should cause valuable coal to be eaten up, disorganize the food supplies in holiday resorts, overwork the already strained railway staffs and inconvenience legitimate travellers, is nothing but disgraceful. Why, then, did the Government permit holiday trains to be run ? The photographs in this page tell their own story. Holiday crowds (top) storm Blackpool Food Office for temporary ration cards. Centre right : Was it worth it ? Stoking up an express (left) takes a lot of coal and many trains were duplicated. The scene at a London terminus (below) gives an idea of the crowds.

Photos, Topical, L.N.A., Keystone and " Daily Mirror"

I Was There! .... Eye Witness Stories of the War

I Saw How Moscow Took Her First Air Raid

In the fifth week of their war with Russia, the Germans began to bomb Moscow by night, having been unable to do so by day. Here the "Daily Telegraph" correspondent, A. T. Cholerton, describes the failure of the first raid on July 21.

FROM dusk to dawn last night (July 21) the Moscow region was stubbornly attacked in raids lasting five and a half hours, but although the Luftwaffe launched more than 200 planes against the Russian capital, only isolated machines actually got over the city. Casualties were slight, and although several dwelling-houses were set on fire, no military objectives or national monuments were hit.

For the most part the raiders concentrated on the use of incendiary bombs. Hundreds of them must have been dropped, and during the night I saw a number of ugly-looking fires, but they were all well under control by dawn.

My respect for Moscow's professional fire brigade was immensely increased by the night's events, and from what I saw of the amateur fire-fighting the boys made a grand job of it.

One boy on the roof opposite my house dived at an incendiary as if he had been doing it all his life, fielded it with fire-proof gloves and threw it down into the courtyard before it blazed up—a particularly risky proceeding. I saw three other incendiaries got off this roof with the same speed, and I saw two boys go at a blazing incendiary in our garden like terriers, splashing sand at it and then scooping up soil on it with their hands.

This rather aimless raid must have been made from a distance of 400 miles at least, and the bombers attacking the capital in the last hour of the raid had to fly home over the Russian lines in broad daylight.

Therefore I believe the Russian claim to have brought down 22 of the raiders. Such a raid was not worth the loss of so many bombers ; it merely tickled up the Muscovites without hurting them much.

The best compliment I can pay to the people of Moscow is to say that they behaved like Londoners. It was their first raid, mind you. Those who were not fire-fighting remained perfectly calm and quiet. The fire-fighters, too, were pretty quiet, except for their rallying cry of " Tovaritschi "— " Comrades."

It was a moonless night, with an overcast sky. The German planes seemed to be flying low over the city. The first raiders dropped a large number of flares. Meanwhile the city's A.A. defences put up a spectacular display with flaming onions, tracer bullets and searchlights. The noise of gunfire was heavy and practically continuous.

When the Alert sounded the streets were immediately cleared, the police escorting people to the shelters. There was no rushing, no panic. Everybody was obliged to stay in their homes or in shelters with the exception of the fire-watchers on the roofs and the police, wardens and nurses, who remained in the streets.

Down in one Tube station there were about 2,000 men and women and a few children. Some were talking of the raid, others were already fast asleep beneath their blankets. There was complete calm and no grumbling.

Touring the city immediately after the All Clear I saw the crowds emerge from their shelters. None showed any signs of panic. Within a matter of hours workmen had cleared away practically all traces of bomb damage. Public utility services ran as usual.

Youthful firemen of Moscow, members of the Young Pioneers, who have gallantly stood the test of Nazi air raids and rendered useful help to the professional fire brigades.   *Photo, Planet News*

We Flew From Belgium in an Ancient Plane

Two Belgian Air Force officers who made their escape to England in a ramshackle aeroplane navigated by home-made instruments told the following story of their adventures.

THE two officers were captured by the Germans during the invasion of Belgium, but were afterwards released. Back in Antwerp they made up their minds to get to England. One of them told the following story :

We remembered there was an old training airplane belonging to the Belgian Army in a stable.

We went to make sure it was still there. German sentries were posted close, and we had to be careful not to attract their attention. By using a pocket torch battery we were able to peep through the keyhole of the stable door, and see that the old machine was still there.

Our next step was to make false keys to open the door. Once inside we found that all the instruments had been taken out of the airplane. For months we worked at night preparing the machine, with German sentries less than 400 yards away. We procured a compass and an altimeter, and by using an ordinary clock spring we were able to make an air-speed indicator. A cheap clock served as a chronometer.

Our next task was to obtain petrol. This was easy. The Germans wanted money, and so we were able to get petrol. They had no suspicion of the use to which we intended to put the petrol. As it was not aviation spirit we had to distil it ourselves.

During our many night visits to the stable, we could often hear the R.A.F. 'planes on their way to bomb the Ruhr, while we were working on our old bus.

On the first occasion when we took it out of the stable, the carburetter would not work. Next night at about 2.30 a.m. we were able to start up the engine. Because the German sentries were so close, we dared not wait to allow the engine to warm up. Fortunately, the airplane got off the ground immediately.

We had to take off from a very small field, and we nearly crashed into the trees bordering the meadow. Over the Channel the engine began to misfire, and we came down very low over the sea. But the engine picked up again and we were just able to reach the English coast and make a forced landing in a field.—*Evening Standard.*

MOSCOW RAID DAMAGE is shown in this photograph radioed to New York and flown to London. It shows how the blast from a German bomb stripped the rear wall from an apartment house, exposing all the rooms. An eye-witness account of Moscow's first air raid, in which 22 enemy raiders were brought down, is given above.   *Photo, Associated Press*

70   *The War Illustrated*   *August 22nd,* 1941

IIIIIIIIIIIIIIIIIIIIIIIIIIIIIIIIIIIIIIIIIIIIIIIIIIIIIIIIIIIIIIIIIIIIIIIIIIIIIIIIIIII **I WAS THERE!** IIIIIIIIIIIIIIIIIIIIIIIIIIIIIIIIIIIIIIIIIIIIIIIIIIIIIIIIIIIIIIIIIIIIIIIIIIIIIIIIIIIIIIIIII

The Dutch Waved to Us Over Rotterdam

The " bad spirit " which the Germans have admitted still prevails among the people of the Netherlands is typified in the following stories of the reception given to the R.A.F. when they bomb the port of Rotterdam.

A TWENTY-ONE-YEAR-OLD Air Gunner who took part in a big raid on Rotterdam shipping said :

The first I saw of Rotterdam was a sky-line of high cranes over the docks ; fat columns of black smoke were already climbing as high as the cranes themselves from the shipping that had been successfully bombed by the first formation of Blenheims.

I was in the second formation and watched the leading squadron cross the Dutch coast in V formation, only a few feet above the sandy beaches, and people waved us on. I had expected the countryside to be flat and it was, astonishingly so, but what did surprise me was that the country Dutchmen really do wear baggy trousers and vivid blue shirts.

Nearly everyone we saw gave us some kind of cheery gesture, though one man was evidently frightened, because he crouched against a telegraph pole, and cows galloped nervously over the fields. We were so low that some of my friends brought back evidence of it ; one pilot, for instance, not only cut straight through a crane cable but got a dent in the belly of his aircraft, and some red dust from the Dutch chimney-pots was stuck to the fuselage. The same pilot had evidently been corn-cutting in between the hedges, because he came home with a small sheaf of it in a niche in the leading edge of his wing.

We bombed Rotterdam at 4.55 in the afternoon. As we flashed across the docks the observer saw our ship—a bulky black hull with one funnel, I should say about 4,000 tons. We nipped across the last building, let our load drop from mast height, and we were away over towards the town.

In ship-bombing of this kind you often

can't see your results, but I had a very clear view of ours this time. There was a terrific explosion and smoke and flames leapt up instantaneously. I have seen lots of these explosions by now, but this one was by far the biggest. Over to the left we saw a good many enemy supply vessels burning from the attack by our first wave, though burning warehouses obstructed our view to a certain extent. However, on our way out of the town, with white tracer whipping under us, we got a good view and could see great pillars of smoke springing up from all the other ships we had bombed.

A Dutch girl who succeeded in reaching Lisbon told of the heavy damage in Rotterdam and of the spirit of the Dutch people. She said :

The Germans admit the suspicion that British bombers have been guided to their objectives by Dutch patriots using secret radio sets.

R.A.F. planes have often been seen over Rotterdam on their way to Germany. People stand in the streets or lean out of their windows and wave to them. Hundreds of people stroll backwards and forwards over the Maas and Wilhelmina bridges solely to get a glimpse of the damage in the forbidden zone.

On nights when the sky is red from oil tank fires and the air heavy with smoke, people call to each other from their houses : " Come and look at this beautiful English sunset." —" *The Listener* " *and Daily Express.*

R.A.F. BOMBS EXPLODING during a daylight raid on Waalhaven, Rotterdam, when our Blenheims came down very low to attack a concentration of German shipping in Rotterdam docks. Estimated tonnage destroyed on this occasion was 100,000, and two warehouses and a factory were left in flames. The Blenheims arrived in V formation, and this victory symbol heartened the Dutch people who waved the R.A.F. on. Other photographs of R.A.F. attacks on Rotterdam will be found in pages 12-13 of this volume.

Photo, British Official: Crown Copyright

ıllı||||||||||||||||||||||||||||||||||||||||||||||||||||||||||| **I WAS THERE!** ıllı||||||||||||||||||||||||||||||||||||||||||||||||||||

We Were 8½ Days in Our Rubber Dinghy

At 2.30 in the morning of July 1 an aircraft of the Bomber Command came down in the sea; at 12.30 p.m. on July 9 the crew—all sergeants— were picked up by a rescue launch. The story of how they survived their 8½ days' ordeal is told here by the pilot.

ENGINE trouble caused the bomber to turn back from a raid on Germany. The pilot hoped to reach the English coast, but was forced to come down in the sea. He said:

When the bomber hit the water the dinghy was automatically released and the crew got out on to the wing and clambered into it. The bomber sank. We thought that we were only about 12 or 20 miles out from the English coast. Actually, we were much farther out, and in a minefield! If we had known that, I don't think we should have been quite as happy as we were. We arranged ourselves in the dinghy as comfortably as possible and just sat there waiting for something to turn up. The wireless operator had sent out an S O S, but it was not received.

All we had in the way of signalling equipment were two distress flares. We had no compass. We had a few boiled sweets, a tin of food tablets, a few ounces of concentrated chocolate, about a pint of water and a small bottle of rum. We thought it would be only a few hours before we were picked up.

About half an hour later a bomber passed overhead on its way back to England. We tried to attract attention, but the distress flare failed to work. Occasionally, too far away or too high to be seen from the dinghy, other aircraft could be heard returning. Daybreak came, but the day passed without any sign of rescue. We dried our clothes and stripped our parachute harnesses of all metal to make them lighter. At night we lay packed uncomfortably in the bottom of the dinghy. We had ripped up the wireless operator's Sidcott suit and spread it over ourselves. We all had bad cramp and no one got any real sleep.

The next day was cloudy and there was a fairly heavy sea. The waves were washing over the side of the dinghy and we had to bale out all the time with a small canvas bag in which our chocolates and tablets had been kept. When night came again we kept two-hourly watches, two men at a time.

So the days and nights went on. We rationed our food and water. The sweets and the tablets lasted about four days. After the second day we didn't feel hungry. What we wanted was water. We began by allowing ourselves a tablespoonful each twice a day and we measured it out in the lids of the tins. I was the official measurer. After three days we cut the water down to a tablespoonful a day and on the seventh day our ration only just wet the bottom of the lid.

We still thought we were not far off the English coast. We saw house-flies and a lot of green flies, and at times we could see white specks in the distance which looked like cliffs. Sometimes we could hear the sound of motor-boat engines, and once we heard a noise under the water, which we took to be the engines of a submarine. Soon afterwards there were three violent explosions which seemed to be under the water. On the fourth day we saw three British aircraft coming straight towards us. They were low down over the water and they passed us about 200 yards away. We stood up and waved scarves and handkerchiefs and flashed two mirrors that we had. We thought at first that they must have seen us and were going on to finish a job before they came back to us. But they didn't come back and we knew that they hadn't seen us.

We were all growing beards and had a daily inspection. We made a fishing line about forty feet long, by unravelling a piece of cord from the dinghy and tying the pieces together. Then we made a spinner from a piece of tin. We could see plenty of fish, but none of them would bite. Each day we played about sluicing our heads in the sea and pouring water over each other's neck to cool ourselves off.

One day, when we were trying to see who could hold his head under the water longest, the navigator lifted his head out of the water with a terrific shout. "There's a damn great mine down here," he said. We all had a look, and there it was, covered with barnacles, one of those great big circular affairs with knobs on. We began to realize then why we hadn't seen any ships. Just after we had spotted the mine we saw three motor torpedo-boats coming straight at us, but when they were about two miles off they turned at right angles.

Seven R.A.F. men keeping themselves afloat in a rubber dinghy. These rescue craft are fitted with a pump, repair-outfit, distress signals, anchor, hand-paddles (being used by two of the crew) and rations. A rubber dinghy adventure is told in this page. *Photo, Associated Press*

SGT. JAMES ALLEN WARD, the 22-year-old New Zealander who won the 7th V.C. awarded to the R.A.F. in this war. He received the award for putting out a fire aboard an aeroplane returning from a raid over Munster. When crossing the Zuyder Zee his aircraft was attacked by a Messerschmitt 110, and fire broke out near the starboard engine. Sgt. Ward climbed through the narrow astro-hatch, and, breaking the fabric to make hand- and foot-holds where necessary, he descended three feet to the wing and proceeded to a position behind the engine. In great danger of being blown off the aircraft Sgt. Ward smothered the flames in the wing and endeavoured to push an engine-cover which had been used as a cushion through a hole in the wing on to a leaking pipe where the fire originated. The peril was averted, the flight home was made possible by his great courage, and the damaged plane was landed.

Photo, British Official

We made up our minds we'd try to paddle towards where we thought the coast was. We started at 11 o'clock one morning, and kept it up till eight that night, working two at a time in half-hour shifts. The next day we had a go at it from eight in the morning till eight in the evening, but we had to keep on taking rests. The day after we tried to keep it up through the night as well, but our strength was going and we couldn't. I found then that I couldn't even stand up in the dinghy. We had to keep pumping the dinghy up with the hand pump, and we were so weak that we couldn't do more than a dozen strokes at a time. When we saw aircraft passing without seeing us, we kept on saying, "Our luck's bound to change," and each day we expected to find a ship or see the coast at dawn. Each night we could hear our bombers crossing over, and sometimes we saw them returning in the half light before dawn.

On the eighth evening a Hampden escorted by two Hurricanes appeared from the west at 2,000 feet and then turned north almost above us. We all waved, but they did not see us. By now we were out of drinking water and our tongues were beginning to swell and crack. We rinsed out our mouths with sea water but we didn't drink any. I think another two days would have been as much as we could have managed.

At 8.20 in the morning of the ninth day a Hampden came out of the sun at about 2,000 feet and passed us a quarter of a mile away. We waved and flashed our mirrors at it. The Hampden did a half-turn, banked, put its nose down, and then we realized that we had been seen. We all joined hands and sang "Auld Lang Syne." The Hampden signalled by Aldis lamp, "Help coming." Then it dropped its own dinghy on the water about 30 yards away from us. We paddled over, got the water bottle from the dinghy and shared out the water. Then we hitched the two dinghies together and sat waiting. The Hampden had wirelessed, and it circled round keeping us in sight for four hours. Then two Blenheims came on the scene, followed by two fighters. Soon afterwards we saw a terrific spurt of foam which quickly got nearer and nearer, and then we saw a launch. When we got on board we couldn't walk without help. The boat's crew gave us something to eat and drink, and somebody gave me a cigarette, but I couldn't smoke it.

The skipper of the launch said that when he saw the dinghy the sergeants were waving their hands and shouting. When they got on board they each drank about a quart of water. I took them downstairs and suggested they should lie down on the bunks, but they said it wasn't necessary. They stayed in the wardroom for about half an hour and then came on deck and took an interest in what was happening. They all wanted tea.

The Editor's Postscript

WHERE I am writing far away from home, rarely by day, and only in slightly less degree by night, does so long a spell as ten minutes pass without the burbling of bombers in our local sky. Several aerodromes not very far away. Not one of them damaged so far; little unoffending villages here and there have had to take the Nazi bombs intended for the nesting grounds of our bombers that have produced many a headache in Germany. Over their home terrain these bombers fly so low that one is able to distinguish them with the aid of the little silhouettes which I give in the "A B C of the R.A.F."; but I'm surprised how quickly the young boys here can tell you the exact category of any machine.

IN the earlier days of motoring the youngsters of the last generation made a hobby of spotting the different makes of cars, and their successors of today have developed equal dexterity in the more exciting game of aeroplane spotting. Mention of the "A B C of the R.A.F." reminds me that this little manual very quickly became a best seller. Some two hundred thousand copies have already been bought, and there are bound to be various new and improved editions to follow. Appropriately the motto of the publishers is "The sky's our limit." But there is unfortunately another limitation—paper supply. The brilliant success of the little book, however, and its great usefulness may induce the paper controller to provide the necessary paper to enable the Amalgamated Press to meet the persistent demand of the bookselling Oliver Twists.

AWAY from London when the raids are being resumed, I'm wondering how I shall take to the wailing of the sirens on my return. My firm conviction is that we must accustom ourselves to a state of war for some years to come and carry on our lives as best we may, cherishing no vain illusions about Germany blowing up from the inside in another month or two, or that the beastly people, reinforced by the fouler elements of Vichy, Italy, Japan, Rumania, Bulgaria, Hungary and Spain (to say nothing of unhappy Finland) will not be able to stand another winter of war. An R.A.F. padre in the train in which I travelled the other day talked a lot of nonsense about an early end to the War which made me write him down as the most unreliable of sky pilots. That is the most foolish sort of optimism. Let us realize we are in for a long War, and let our every action be conditioned accordingly. That way lies Victory . . . that way only.

So when I return to the London front in another week or so, it will be with the well-grounded anticipation of many another night of blitz to be faced with fortitude . . . not with joy or even equanimity, but with trepidation and resolution. I do not admire the bravery of the thoughtless. To know where danger threatens and

avoid it as far as humanly possible is the proper attitude of mind that enables us to "take it"—a lesson I learned long ago in Chile's earthquake zone. Only the "gringos" (like myself) were at first indifferent when "temblores" occurred: the natives who had been accustomed to them and to "terremotos" all their lives were the first to run for safety. Those of us who have been caught in any of the London blitzes will be last to be found out of doors sky watching. Myself, I have faithfully practised the carrying of my gas mask, and I think I am going to find it useful one of these days.

A NEW and cheap edition of that classic of the Napoleonic wars, "Memoirs of Sergeant Bourgogne," which I read in the original long years ago, has just been published, and I am promising myself an early

MR. HARRY HOPKINS, intimate friend of President Roosevelt and supervisor of the U.S. Lease and Lend programme, left Moscow for England on August 3, after a flying visit during which he conferred with M. Stalin and members of the Russian Government and staff.
Photo, Topical

re-reading of it, for its graphic descriptions of the occupation of Moscow and the great retreat through the country which is again "in the news" with the clash of modern Hun and a new and unbelievable Muscovite will take on an enthralling new interest when re-read with Smolensk and the Beresina figuring every few hours in the wireless bulletins. Especially do I recall at this moment Kipling's "A St. Helena Lullaby." Perhaps you remember the lines:

"How far is St. Helena from the Beresina ice?"
A longish way—a longish way—with ten year more to run.
It's south across the water underneath a falling star.
(*What you cannot finish you must leave undone!*)

How apt is this, save that the carpet-biting paranoiac will know no St. Helena other than a cup of poison as the easy way out for the beast that he is!

IN these days when so much of our news bulletin is unintelligible unless checked up on the largest scale maps to which we have access, it is worth reminding readers that where the maps are based on Mercator's projection we can go greatly wrong in our notion of territories the nearer we follow the news toward the poles. Mercator's method of representing the globe on a flat and square area can be compared to cutting the skin of an orange into segments, after splitting it down one side and leaving it unbroken along the middle (or equatorial latitude). When this is done the North and South poles, each of which may be regarded as mere spots affording footage for just one person, become co-terminous with the equator! Thus Greenland, Arctic America and Russia as shown on a Mercator map must be grossly distorted and look many times vaster than they are in reality.

THIS convention of cartography should be borne in mind when map-reading, and the perpendicular lines of longitude that intersect the horizontal lines of latitude are to be thought of as all curving towards the poles where they would eventually unite. There are various other projections in use, but one only, the Equal Area projection, which is usually drawn in the form of two wide ovals like two halves of an orange skin flattened out without splitting them into segments, shows the areas of the world's geographical divisions in approximation to their actual dimensions. The Dominion of Canada on an Equal Area map and on a Mercator are two very different things. It would take all my space to make this quite clear to the uninitiated, and as I'm writing where I have no choice of maps at hand I am attempting only to touch upon the misleading nature of the old Mercator projection, which I have seen much in use lately, with the northward movement of the War.

QUITTING London and the South for a much needed respite in another part of England where unusual heat has given way for the greater part of two days to rain, I have had another reminder of the protean attainments of the English climate. Not in years have I witnessed such needless wealth of water. "And the Rains Came!" After a few days of excessive heat we have had a genuinely tropic display which has been maintained for nearly two whole days at the intensity of rain artificially produced for film scenes— you know what I have in mind. How seriously such sudden changes would have thrown a tank division out of its stride I cannot guess, but I feel sure that a few days of unremitting downpour such as we have had here would make a mighty difference to the mobility of these mechanical monsters and might easily bring disaster where a day or two earlier all had looked set for success.

JOHN CARPENTER HOUSE.
WHITEFRIARS, LONDON E.C.4

Printed in England and published every Friday by the Proprietors, The Amalgamated Press, Ltd., The Fleetway House, Farringdon Street, London, E.C.4. Sole Agents for Australia and New Zealand: Messrs. Gordon & Gotch, Ltd.; and for South Africa: Central News Agency, Ltd. August 22nd, 1941.   S.S.

Registered at the G.P.O. as a Newspaper

The War Illustrated, August 29th. 1941

The War Illustrated

Vol 5   N°104

Edited by Sir John Hammerton

FOURPENCE   WEEKLY

THE NAVY TO THE RESCUE. Not long since a merchant ship was attacked in the Atlantic by a German U-boat. When the torpedo struck, an S O S was picked up by one of our destroyers, which raced to the scene. Abandoning their doomed ship (seen in the background), the merchant sailors on a raft, and in two lifeboats, are nearing safety. Saved from death, they ask only to serve again.

Photo, "Daily Mirror," Exclusive to THE WAR ILLUSTRATED

The Way of the War

AFTER TWO YEARS: A WORD TO THE WISHFUL

BY THE EDITOR

As the second anniversary of the outbreak of the War will have passed before our next number appears, the occasion suggests some reflections prompted mainly by a recent sojourn at a certain English Spa where I had the refreshment of meeting a number of my compatriots whose opinions on the War startled me in their complete detachment from what I regard as reality.

What shall I say of an R.A.F. officer who wore the rings of a Wing Commander but only in a nominal way, as he has never flown a plane and joined the service at the age of fifty in a strictly technical capacity ? A most valuable man, mind you. He looked to an early end of the War —possibly this year, certainly next. Of a retired colonel with distinguished service and " Poona " experience, who expected the whole business to be over by next Christmas ? A sturdy optimist from Glasgow, who has done worthy work in the real spirit of national service, open to wager a large sum that 1942 would see the collapse of Nazism. What of him ? And of several dear old ladies who were " figuring " (as the Americans say) on returning to their evacuated homes at Eastbourne, Folkestone and St. Margaret's Bay " in the Spring " ?

Well, I fear they all wrote me down a dismal pessimist, little knowing that I am one of the real optimists : those, who, having faced the stark, staring, staggering facts, decide to march on, chin up. In this I take my cue from no less a person than our heaven-sent Prime Minister, without whose splendid energy and gift of expression I hate to think where we should find ourselves.

No man alive could have guessed beforehand what was going to happen in these two years. As the scroll of the War unrolls it is easier to hazard a guess at the succeeding chapters of its history, though the ultimate and most crucial not even its most prescient student can forecast. But we have seen enough in the past six months to prepare us for events of early happening such as we only vaguely dreamed of when our imagination was running riot fifteen months ago.

Japan (still licking her greedy chops after the jackal meal of Indo-China) might be in the War up to the neck before these words can get into type ; Vichy France will be an active and shameful partner of the Hun possibly as soon or sooner ; certainly ere long Spain will be ripe—if not already rotten—as an adjunct of Nazi Europe ; Portugal might be overrun by Hunnish hordes and have to move her loyal government to the Azores ; eventually the U.S. must fight, and fight even more thoroughly than they have forged

" the tools " for us ; South America will have to do far more than suppress Nazi agents in her ten republics : Thailand, Turkey, Egypt, Iraq, Arabia may all have to take up arms somehow—and soon. Even that valiant race of neutrals inhabiting the adjacent land of Eire may not for ever elude the maelstrom ! Do I exaggerate ? Make a careful study of the Nazi conquests before answering.

What has Germany done ? In two years she has subjugated Poland, Denmark, Norway, Sweden (don't tell me that tricky country is else than Nazi-dominated), and all the Baltic lands (excepting only Russia), Holland, Belgium, France (and much of the French Empire by implication), Bulgaria, Hungary, Rumania, Yugoslavia, Greece . . . are there any others ? Yes, Italy, and her comic-opera " kingdoms " on the Adriatic, while Spain (with Portugal to follow) is already in Hitler's pocket.

Just think of that, ye wishful thinkers. And do please forget about next Christmas, or the one after, as a time for " the best wishes of the season " and goodbye to the Nazis for ever ! Go on believing, if you like—and I would not dissuade you except as to your dating of the event—in the collapse of Germany from within. Until that takes place there can be no end to the War, but it can take place only when every German, with the exception of the small liberal and communistic elements that are already anti-Hitler, has been convinced that the War is not going to be a paying business. The millions of Germans who will eventually

welcome the Allied armies when they march into Berlin and occupy all the great cities of Hunland, are hoping for Britain's collapse before American aid and Russian resistance can prove effective. The very Jews of Germany would as readily bow the knee to a victorious Hitler today and take a chance under Nazidom as wait to welcome—and they assuredly will—the triumph of the Allies.

Now, none of this, I insist, is pessimism. It is an unperturbed facing of discernible facts. Don't tell me this vast conquest of Europe, achieved in so large a measure by the connivance of the defeatist French, can be brought to naught in a few months, or a year or so. It cannot ; despite our own rapidly growing strength and the solid achievements with which we have off-set our earlier losses. All the theorizing one reads about Germany's hunger for oil and metals and grain notwithstanding. I assert, at the end of two years of war, that we are in for a Long War to which these two years are but the opening chapters. And before it ends the profoundest changes will take place in the economic and social life of Britain and every country fighting alongside Britain for the freedom of mankind.

So thinking, I would urge upon every reader the need to orient his life in accordance with the new conditions in which he will have to live it. To cease chattering about an early end to it all. To contemplate in all seriousness the possibilities of having to live for years to come, if not in conditions of actual, active hostilities, at least in a state of war, the end of which few of the older generation will survive to see, and which will potently affect the lives of the younger generation to their last days.

Above all, my reading of the situation demands an unceasing sacrifice from each one of us to help the Allied war effort, so that, although " we are still very far from winning the War," as Mr. Duff Cooper frankly announced on his arrival in America the other day, the cause of freedom—the right to determine the conditions of our own lives apart from State compulsion, concentration camps and subservience to a breed of official bullies—will prevail, and the War and the Peace shall eventually be won.

But certainly that won't be by next Christmas, nor next Spring ; possibly next Autumn, or perhaps the following Christmas ; but more probably the succeeding winter will at least see the beginning of the end. All which implies for us a tightening of the belt, a gritting of the teeth, and a deep resolve to " finish the job." And as I am no pessimist, but a firm believer in our eventual victory, my slogan is " once more unto the breach, dear friends ! "

J. A. HAMMERTON

VIGIL IN ENGLAND. Whatever the course of the great battle that is raging on the Russian plains, Britain remains as the chief and ultimate objective of Hitler's hatred. As Mr. Churchill warned us on July 29, " The invasion season is at hand. . . . We have to reckon on a gambler's desperation . . . If we fall all fall together." *Photo, British Official : Crown Copyright*

Soviet Women Have Their Place in the Vanguard

Every individual of both sexes and all ages in Russia are standing up to the Nazis. Of this group of guerilla fighters, captured by the Germans, three are women.

Wives of the commanders of a Soviet air unit refilling machine-gun belts. Housewives everywhere have left their kitchens and gone into the war factories.

Comrades-in-arms, this Russian soldier and his girl fought side by side until taken prisoner by the Germans. Like the Amazons of old, many Russian women are taking a militant part in the war.

D URING the years of the Russian Civil War Soviet women worked in first-aid detachments, guarded factories, fought in the firing line, joined guerilla detachments, and derailed enemy trains. Today they are again in the vanguard as active helpers of their husbands, sons and brothers in the war for the defence of the fatherland.

Housewives are entering war factories to take the place of their menfolk, and are showing a high standard of skill and production. Women are daily achieving new records in many trades. More than a hundred women, formerly housewives, are now working in coal mines. Women are also giving an excellent account of themselves in metallurgical work. At the Lenin Metallurgical Plant women are doing the work of assistant blacksmiths very efficiently.

I N the Moscow region alone the Trade Unions have organized during the last few days 177 groups of Red Cross nurses and 250 groups of volunteer Red Cross detachments, in which approximately 20,000 women, drawn from 350 enterprises, are studying in their spare time. The wives of Soviet scientists, artists, teachers, and all sections of the intelligentsia are training to be nurses. Many women have volunteered for blood transfusion. Others are organizing the dispatch of comforts for the troops both at the front and in the hospitals. The women members of the A.R.P. services have already displayed exceptional courage during enemy air raids, both in fire-fighting squads and night patrols.

Klavdia Nikolayeva, leading Russian woman Trade Unionist and Secretary of the Soviet Central Council of the Trade Unions in Moscow.

A lathe-operative can be as useful as a tank-driver in the mechanized war, and many thousands of Russian women, employed as typists and clerks, have turned to making munitions and other specialized work in the war factories. Here is one who was lately a warehouse keeper applying her hand and brain in the great cause of humanity against Hitlerism.

A group of Russian nurses, having just arrived at a forward position on the east front, are receiving final instructions. Note how their keenness is reflected on their faces.

Photos, Associated Press, British Official, Keystone

To Have or to Hold These, Millions Fight

ODESSA, Russian Black Sea port, is a prime objective of the Nazi drive in the Ukraine. On August 14 it was stated that Marshal Budenny had left behind him a force of 100,000 men to hold the fortress and naval base of Odessa, and thereby block the German rush towards the Crimea. This photo shows the City Hall.

Russian coalminers (above) of the Donetz basin, another of Hitler's elusive prizes, descending a pit. In the lower part of the Donetz river, a tributary of the Don, there are extensive coal beds which have helped greatly in the industrialization of the Soviets.

Beneath : tractor parts being placed on a conveyor at the Ordzhonikidze works in the Caucasus. The fine quality and immense number of Russian tanks are inherent in the mass-production of tractors turned out specially to deal with vast areas of agricultural land.

Photos, Planet News, and E.N.A.

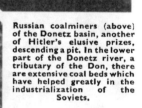

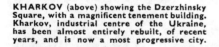

KHARKOV (above) showing the Dzerzhinsky Square, with a magnificent tenement building. Kharkov, industrial centre of the Ukraine, has been almost entirely rebuilt, of recent years, and is now a most progressive city.

KIEV (below) capital of the Ukraine. On the right bank of the Dnieper, 280 miles above Odessa, it is an important rail centre and air station, and the Nazis have been making desperate efforts to capture it.

This Is the Ukraine That Hitler Wants

In the Ukraine, Russia's south-western republic, a tremendous battle is raging as Marshal von Rundstedt strives to defeat—still more important, to annihilate—the opposing armies of Marshal Budenny. Below we give some facts concerning the appearance of this vast country, its agriculture and industries, and of the people who now at Stalin's call are converting the fair and fruitful countryside into a scorched desert.

ONLY Hitler knows why he ordered the attack on Russia. One of the reasons, however, was almost certainly that he wished to secure for the German Reich the riches of the Ukraine.

Hitler's greed is understandable enough. The Ukraine is a country worth many a sacrifice to win. With its 170,000 square miles it is considerably larger than Italy, about the same size as Sweden, and not much smaller than the Germany in which Hitler rose to supreme power. For the most part it is one great plain—just made for tanks, as the German generals must oftentimes have remarked. "It is so flat," Mr. I. Macdonald, Diplomatic Correspondent of "The Times," has written in that journal, "that the ripening cornfields seem merely like the gilt frame to a picture that is all blue sky and pearly cloud. Most of the hills, where there are hills, rise and fall hardly more than Piccadilly and the Haymarket. . . . The Ukraine has its larches, willows and birches, signs to the traveller that he is coming to a village. But mainly there is only the great plain, fenceless, hard under foot, with the wind shaking the barley, and the cattle—Friesians by the look of them—standing knee-deep and glum in a millennial feast of sweet pasture."

For centuries the Ukrainian steppes have been the happy hunting ground of the Cossack horsemen ; for centuries, too, the land has been amongst Europe's most productive farmlands. Some 40 million of its acres lie in the Black Earth region, that is, they are covered by a thick layer, 18 inches to four and a half feet in depth, of black humus or leaf-mould, which is infinitely fertile. Here are grown immense crops of rye and barley and oats, sugar beet, potatoes, sunflowers, flax, maize, even tobacco and cotton. Before 1918 over half the land—and that the best—was in the hands of the large landowners, monasteries and *Kulaks*, but these were swept away long ago. The old-fashioned strip system of cultivation has been abandoned and practically all the farming is now done collectively. Mr. Macdonald has told how great has been the change brought about by the years of collectivization. The picture he draws is one of an up-to-date agricultural economy. He describes how each peasant family in their log cabin have hens and rabbits and their own cabbage patch, from which they sell the produce in Kiev market. "The men were healthy and the women happy, asking about the latest fashions in London and slimming exercises. Of an evening we sat in the orchard where the crab apples were dropping like bright red beads through the sunlight . . ."

Times without number the Ukraine has been called the granary of Russia. It is still *a* granary, although it is no longer *the* granary that it once was, since of recent years other regions of the U.S.S.R. have forged ahead in agricultural development. But, even so, the Ukraine produces about a quarter of Russia's total grain production.

To be really up to date we should describe the Ukraine as Russia's South Wales. In the Donetz Basin, the "Donbass," it possesses one of the largest coalfields in Europe, with resources, so it is estimated, of 55,000,000,000 tons, and an annual production of 67,000,000 tons. Large deposits of iron ore are being worked near Krivoi Rog, and the Dnieper has been harnessed to produce electrical power; the power-station at Dnieproges is one of the largest in the world. Manganese deposits are worked at Nikopol.

Kramatorsk has great machine-building plants. Kharkov produces machine-tools and tractors by the tens of thousands. Voroshilovgrad is famed for locomotives. Kiev is earning new renown today as an industrial centre. At Zaporozhie special steels are made. Today the Ukraine produces about 80 per cent of the coal mined in the Soviet Union, 70 per cent of its pig-iron, 50 per cent of its steel, more than 60 per cent of its iron ores, 70 per cent of its agricultural machinery, 72 per cent of its aluminium, and 35 per cent of its manganese.

And the people ? They number just over 30 millions, of whom the great majority are described as Ukrainians ; the minorities are Jews, Germans, Greeks, Armenians, Poles, White Russians, and many others. They are all citizens of the Ukrainian Socialist Soviet Republic, which is one of the eleven republics constituting the U.S.S.R.

The Ukraine, towards which the new German offensive is aimed, is shown shaded on this map of S.E. Europe. By mid-August the Russians were on the line of the Dnieper.

UKRAINE'S HARVEST, threatened by the German invasion, is now, thanks to the stubborn resistance of the Red Army, being safely garnered. Above, reaping machines on a collective farm. Left, a Ukrainian "partisan" ready to defend his wheatlands.   *Photos, Associated Press and E.N.A.*

Thailand May Soon Become a Battlefield

For generations, Thailand—or Siam, as it was called until 1939—has been in a backwater, remote from the full stream of world politics. Now, however, following Japan's virtual occupation of the neighbouring French colony of Indo-China, it is on the verge of the war zone, and may itself soon become a victim of Japan's aggression. An account of its recent "war" with Indo-China has been given in page 354 of Volume 4 of "The War Illustrated."

VERY surprised were most people at the vehement tone of a broadcast made from Bangkok on August 10. The Thailanders (or Siamese) have been generally regarded, and with reason, as an essentially gentle folk, light-hearted and easy-going, the very personification of kindliness. But one would not think so from this radio declaration. Here is what the announcer said :

" The Thai forces will not yield an inch of territory. They will use every possible means of annihilating the enemy. They will fight to the last drop of blood, and will adopt even the scorched earth policy and, if need be, gas. The Thai will die to the last man rather than surrender their freedom. If we have to retreat, we must burn our houses and destroy everything—food and communications, even the crops in the fields, leaving nothing to the enemy. Any invader who succeeds in over-running Thailand will find only the vast cemetery of the Thai nation.''

Thai means " the free people,'' and the Thailanders call their country *Muang Thai*, the land of the free. They pride themselves on their independence ; indeed, they are amongst the very few peoples of Asia who has succeeded in retaining their sovereign status. Up to a few years ago, Europeans enjoyed " extra-territorial '' privileges in the kingdom of Siam as they once did in China, but these have now been given up, and by a series of treaties negotiated with Britain, America, France, Japan, Germany, and the rest, Thailand has regained her full autonomy. About the same time Siam's absolute mon-archy was abolished, and under the constitution granted by King Prajadhipok in 1932 supreme power belongs to the nation, while the legislative power is exercised by the King, with the advice and consent of the Assembly of the

A boat in Thailand laden with rice sheaves taking the crop to a central threshing ground. On the bank are women peasant harvesters waiting to be ferried across the river. *Photo Black Star*

Council of Regency has the conduct of affairs. The Prime Minister—he is also Minister of Defence, Foreign Affairs, and the Interior—is Luang Bipul Song-gram.

Thailand has an area of over 200,000 square miles, and is thus almost as big as France and a little bigger than Spain. In the north it is mountainous, and the precipitous thickly-forested slopes should present almost insuperable difficulties to an invader coming, as the Japanese might be expected to come, from Indo-China. The only lines of advance would be along the deep river gorges. In the east is an extensive low-lying plain, sandy and almost barren, subject to floods in the rainy season and to drought in the dry. The heart of the kingdom is the great alluvial plain which slopes down to the Gulf of Siam. Then finally there is a narrow strip of territory in the Malay Peninsula, separating Burma from the Malay States. At its narrowest point, the Kra Isthmus, the Japanese (so it has been reported at intervals for years past) have had in mind the construction of a canal which, when completed, would largely deprive Singapore of its present commercial and strategical importance.

In this country of mountain jungle and fertile plain some 15 million people have their homes. Most of them are Siamese and Laos, but there are about half a million Chinese—in their hands much of the country's trade is concentrated—and numbers of Malays, Cambodians, Burmese Indians, Annamites, and so on. The great majority are peasants, living in the most primitive circumstances. Their needs are few, and those few are easily satisfied. The staple food is rice, which is grown easily enough on the great mud expanses. It is supple-mented by fish and sometimes by meat.

The houses are huts, made of poles and brushwood generally built on the edge of

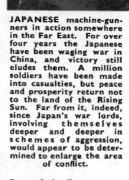

JAPANESE machine-gun-ners in action somewhere in the Far East. For over four years the Japanese have been waging war in China, and victory still eludes them. A million soldiers have been made into casualties, but peace and prosperity return not to the land of the Rising Sun. Far from it, indeed, since Japan's war lords, involving themselves deeper and deeper in schemes of aggression, would appear to be deter-mined to enlarge the area of conflict.

People's Representa-tives, half of whose members are nominated by the King and the other half elected by the votes of all men and women over 20 years of age. The actual gov-ernment of the state is exercised by the State Council of 14 to 24 members—the majority of whom are chosen by the King from the Assembly. The present King is Ananda Mahi-dol, a boy of 16, who succeeded to the throne on the abdication of his uncle, Prajadhipok ; during his minority a

IN BANGKOK, Thailand, a young Thai passes by the monument to the Constitution commemorating the overthrow of the absolute monarchy on June 24, 1932. Formerly Siam, the country has revived the original nomenclature, Muang Thai, the land of the free. "Thai-landers will die rather than surrender to any invader," said their premier on August 10. *Photos, Black Star & Natori, Tokyo*

Japan's Militarists Still Greedy for Conquest

THE FAR EASTERN ARENA of war and possible war can be studied in this comprehensive map showing in solid black Japan and her island of Formosa and Japanese territory on the mainland—Manchukuo and Korea. Japan also occupies the tract of China indicated in dark shading now being administered by the puppet government at Nanking. To the south, French Indo-China has recently come under Japanese control, and Thailand is threatened. At a glance we see how far Japan's dream of Asia for the Asiatics has progressed since she became empire-conscious. Her latest moves are a threat to British and American interests in Malaya, the Philippines, and other Pacific positions.

By Courtesy of " The Sphere "

a stream, into which the refuse is most conveniently dropped through a hole in the floor. The principal garment of the Thailanders, both male and female, is the one-piece *panoong*, which is passed round the body. But in the towns men may be found wearing coats of European cut and soft felt hats, and the ladies of the upper class—there are not many of them—go in for blouses, silk stockings and high-heeled shoes, sometimes even skirts in place of the *panoong*. Polygamy is permitted, but few men can afford more than one wife. Slavery has not been completely abolished, but there is no system of rigid caste as in India, so that low birth is no bar to advancement. Nor are there any hereditary titles.

In the nineties of last century it seemed likely that Siam would be incorporated by the French in their colonial empire in the Orient, but in 1896 Siamese independence was guaranteed by both France and Britain. Now her independence is threatened afresh, but this time it is Japan who is the menace—Japan, who having established bases and secured aerodromes in Indo-China, is believed to be striving to obtain similar facilities in Thailand, with a view to hostile action against the British in Burma and Malaya, and against Chiang Kai-shek's China to the north.

On August 6 Mr. Eden stated that any Japanese move against Thailand must inevitably give rise to a most serious situation,

while Mr. Cordell Hull declared that it would be a step menacing American security. On which Thailand remarked through Bangkok radio that both Britain and Japan had pledged their word to respect Thailand's integrity, and that Thailand trusted both. It added " Thailand is quite strong enough to protect herself, and has no need for any other nation to come to protect her."

But how far Thailand's brave words could be maintained in deed is open to conjecture. Her army consists, so it is reported, of some 50,000 men ; she has a tiny air force ; and a navy chiefly composed of small craft, several of which were sunk or damaged by the French in the brief hostilities of January.

Our Searchlight on the War

INDIAN HEROES of the Merchant Navy. Mr. Toraboola (right) and Mr. Abdul Lotiff, leaving Buckingham Palace after having received the Medal of the British Empire.
Photo, Planet News

RAIDERS OVER BERLIN AND MOSCOW

DURING the night of August 7 the Russian Air Force bombed Berlin—or at least its outskirts--for the first time. This achievement was said to have been one of the greatest operational feats of the present war, for the raid was undertaken from bases and in conditions which made the flight even more difficult than it is for the R.A.F. Moscow was reticent about the damage done ; in fact, the first news that the raid had taken place came from Berlin itself. Germany's night attacks on Moscow have failed in their aim to reduce the Russian capital to a second Warsaw, for very few of the enemy planes have been able to evade the city's interception system. Moscow is equipped with the newest detector device, an American invention based on the use of high-frequency wireless waves, which makes it possible for enemy aircraft to be located with exactness, despite darkness and fog, at a distance of 50-60 miles. This early warning of their approach allows time for fighters to intercept the raiders. Any that

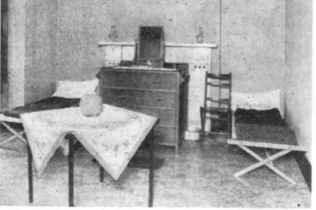

NEW HOMES for the bombed out are now being supplied by the Ministry of Health. Here is a typical bedroom-suite, neat and serviceable, consisting of two camp-beds, chest of drawers, table, etc. The full equipment numbers 43 articles.
Photo, L.N.A.

get through have to meet A.A. gunfire made devastatingly accurate by the technical perfection of the detector.

FRANCE GOES FASCIST

IN a broadcast on August 12 Marshal Pétain announced twelve new measures which impose on France what is virtually a Fascist constitution. By these all political activities are forbidden, the powers of the police are doubled and those of the regional prefects strengthened, all secret societies are to be destroyed, sanctions will be taken against Freemasons holding Government or public positions, and a Council of Political Justice is created to speed up the trial of men said to be responsible for the national disaster. The announcement of this programme followed the appointment of Admiral Darlan, already Vice-Premier and Foreign Minister, as head of the new Ministry of National and· Empire Defence. He is now in 'supreme control of all naval, air and land forces.

SOCIETY HOSTESS'S WAR MEDAL

MARSHAL PETAIN has awarded the Croix de Guerre to Mrs. James Corrigan, widow of the American steel magnate, who, in pre-war years, entertained in London and Paris on a princely scale. When war broke out she was in Paris, and at once threw herself into work for the troops. She became the "marraine" of the 110th Regiment, and herself supplied and packed most of the comforts for the men, as well as for those of the 27th Tank Regiment, of which she was appointed Honorary Corporal. When France collapsed she went to Vichy, and from here provided and personally delivered comforts of all kinds to soldiers in neighbouring camps. When the dollar was blocked she set about selling her jewelry and other valuables, in order to be able to stay and continue her efforts on behalf of the soldiers and their stricken families.

BRITISH STILL FIGHTING IN GREECE

FROM the mountain caves in which they live side by side with bands of unsubdued Cretans, about a thousand British soldiers and Marines are waging guerilla warfare against the

Germans in occupation of the island. They were cut off from escape at the time of the evacuation ; their present chance of rescue or escape is small, but, rather than surrender, they snipe and ambush the Germans by day, raid their food supplies and stocks of ammunition by night, and in the caves, which are their home, lead the hardy but romantic existence of outlaws. Many Cretan families fled from the towns into the mountains to escape the German bombers, and amongst these some of the British have found brides, to whom they have been married by a priest in a cave now consecrated to worship. So apprehensive are the youthful Nazi garrison of these tough, desperate men that no attempt has been made to round them up in their mountain fastnesses.

G.H.Q. LIAISON REGIMENT

STARTING life as a very small unit in Belgium —where it began with the colonel who still commands it, one clerk and a motor-car—this new specialized force of the British Army forms a direct link between field formations and the Commander-in-Chief. In Flanders, where normal communications were being constantly wrecked by swift enemy assaults, it was found that the only way of sending news of a battle to French or British H.Q. was by means of a small motorized detachment. Even under less chaotic conditions this new direct delivery of dispatches saves an enormous amount of delay, and proved invaluable in Greece. As the essential qualities demanded are speed, both of mind and of action, all members of this unit are picked men, and include many expert rough-riders in motor-cycle trials. In addition, the regiment has a fleet of fast little cars equipped with wireless, and even small aircraft which are piloted by the men themselves. All members are trained in map-reading and in military observation. It is not surprising that the exciting, adventurous life attracts speed-lovers from nearly every regiment in the Army.

BRAVE INDIAN SEAMEN

AT a recent investiture at Buckingham Palace, King George presented British Empire Medals (Civil Division) to two out of four Indian seamen who were awarded them for displaying great gallantry when their respective ships were sunk by enemy action. Abdul Lotiff, 1st deck Tindal, employed by the Ellerman City Line, was serving in a ship which was torpedoed in April 1941. "With entire disregard for his own safety he remained with the Chief Officer assisting, until all passengers and crew were clear of the vessel and he was told to leave." Toraboola, an engine-room Serang, had served with the Ellerman Line for 25 years, and during the last war was torpedoed while in s.s. Katlamba. When again torpedoed in April 1941 he showed great devotion to duty, searched the bunkers for possibly disabled men, rescued an engine-room hand who was badly injured, and afterwards stayed at the emergency lighting plant until ordered to leave ship.

A YEAR'S SAVINGS IN A WEEK

A NEW form of War Weapons Week, devised by the Leatherhead and District War Savings Committee and since adapted for national use, has had striking results. Here each Savings Group in road, society, school or business firm runs its own War Weapons Week, aiming at saving enough to buy a particular weapon, such as a rifle (£7) or Bren gun (£50), which it has on show during the Week. In a 12 weeks' drive 144 Savings Groups in this district—which includes Ashtead, Bookham, Fetcham and Leatherhead—saved enough to equip a battalion. Their ordinary savings in one week would have amounted to only £770. They increased this to over £42,000, or over 54 times their normal—equal to more than a year's savings in a week.

BREN AND ANTI-TANK GUN demonstration in a timber yard at Great Bookham, Surrey, to members of the War Savings Group in the yard. It was hoped to provide £95 to purchase these two weapons, but so splendid was the response that this small Group raised £1,443 during its War Weapons Week—enough to buy 15 Brens and 15 anti-tank rifles.
Photo, Keystone

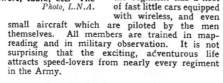

New 'Tubes' Will Keep the Londoners Safe

Photo, Planet News

DEEP UNDERGROUND SHELTERS are being tunnelled near London's Underground Railway stations, and this is one of many which are being made. The shelters will be divided into two storeys and bunks will be provided in each section. Each shelter, when finished, will accommodate some thousands of people, and admission will be by ticket, a large proportion of the accommodation being reserved for urgent cases, such as families bombed out of their homes. The shelter seen above will be finished and ready for use by November

'Arabian Tales': Russia Ridicules the Nazi Claims

In a recent article (see page 58) we summarized the review of six weeks' war that emanated from the Fuehrer's headquarters on the Russian front on August 6. Four days later the Russians issued their reply, in which, as will be seen from the extracts quoted below, the German claims were exposed as absurd falsifications. All the same, by mid-August the Nazis had not been checked in their advance, and particularly in the Ukraine their thrust had assumed dangerous proportions.

Is there a Stalin Line? The Germans would seem to have no doubt of its existence. They have breached it time and again, in this place and in that. But the Russians—and they ought to know—maintain that no special Stalin Line exists, or ever has existed.

"German propaganda," said the Soviet Information Bureau in an announcement issued on August 18 under the heading, "Arabian Tales of the German High Command, or the First Six Weeks of the War," "while concealing from the German people the real losses of the German Army in the war against the U.S.S.R., feeds them on absurd lies. In its endeavour to explain the heavy losses suffered by the Germans, and the reason for their protracted marking time, German propaganda attempts to create a legend about the existence of a ' powerful, fortified Stalin Line.' It is to be noted that the Stalin Line appears wherever German troops encounter the stubborn resistance of the Red Army and suffer particularly heavy losses."

Of course, went on the announcement, the Soviet Government have created fortified points wherever they were deemed to be necessary, but these did not and do not constitute anything which may be described as a line. The enormous German losses are attributable not to the existence of a Stalin Line but to the fact that "The Red Army and the Soviet people are defending their native country with the greatest bravery and gallantry, and are transforming every inch of their native land into a fortified zone."

No less absurd, continued the statement, are the Nazi "estimates" of the number of prisoners taken and the amount of booty captured by the German Army on the eastern front. The German High Command has claimed that the Soviet losses during the first six weeks of the war were 895,000 prisoners, 13,145 armoured fighting vehicles, 10,388 guns, and 9,082 aeroplanes. "Here, Nazi propaganda has surpassed itself. The technique of these mendacious 'estimates' is as follows: after occupying a Soviet area, the Nazis immediately proceed to forcibly mobilize for all kinds of hard labour the entire population of peasants, Soviet workers, and women, or they drive them to the rear, declaring that they are prisoners of war. Certainly in this way one might count not only 895,000 prisoners of war, but very many more. . . ."

The same clumsy trick is resorted to by the German propaganda department when it publishes data about the number of war trophies captured —Soviet guns, tanks and aircraft. In concocting this data the Nazis apparently take first of all their own losses, add to this the Soviet losses, and then add to these extravagant figures any other number they care to think of.

Since Hitler's G.H.Q. has shirked giving the truth about these losses, the Soviet Information Bureau in Moscow is ready to

MARSHAL VON RUNDSTEDT, in charge of four Nazi armies operating in the Ukraine, commanded an army group in the Polish campaign and was responsible for breaking the Ardennes and Meuse lines in France.
Photo, Planet News

fill the gap. "During six weeks of war, Fascist Germany has lost over a million and a half soldiers killed, wounded, and taken prisoners. These enormous losses account for the fact that the Germans are more and more often throwing into the battle soldiers of over 45 and youngsters of 17."

The Russian losses in killed, wounded and prisoners (the Russian statement goes on) amount to about 600,000 men. The Red Army has seized or destroyed over 6,000 German tanks ; its own losses are about 5,000 tanks. The Red Army has captured or destroyed over 8,000 German guns as against a loss of about 7,000. The losses of the Germans in aircraft amount to over 6,000 ; the Red Air Force has lost about 4,000 aircraft.

So much for the Russian statement. But mendacious as their claims undoubtedly are, the Germans have made great progress in their invasion of Russia. The third offensive which was launched at the end of July carried the German armies well into the Ukraine. The Russian "front" at Belaya Tserkov, to the south-west of Kiev, was penetrated, and Marshal von Runstedt's troops swept down the corridor between the rivers Dnieper and Bug, so that the Russians on the southern sector of the Ukraine front were in imminent danger of being cut off. But Marshal Budenny is a masterly strategist, and he succeeded in extricating most of his divisions from the German trap, while leaving a considerable force to hold Odessa. The Germans claimed to have isolated Odessa and they succeeded in taking Nikolaev, but they did not succeed in their main object—the annihilation of the Russian armies in the Ukraine. Fighting tenaciously, Budenny withdrew his troops to take up fresh positions on the Dnieper ; much valuable territory had to be abandoned in particular the great iron-producing region about Krivoi Rog. But still great Russian armies barred the way to Kharkov and the Donetz basin, vital centre of Russia's war production, and the as vital oil-producing region of the Caucasus. Elsewhere on the 1,500-mile front, the Germans were still pressing hard, but their progress was not so marked.

THE EASTERN FRONT after seven weeks of war. Though considerable, the German advances fell far short of what the Nazis had anticipated, and no break-through had been made.

Miles
0 50 100   200
U.S.S.R. Frontier since 22 Sept. 1939.

APPROXIMATE EXTENT OF GERMAN ADVANCE for week ending
28 June 5 July 12 July
19 July 26 July 2 Aug.
9 Aug.

Here and There on the War's Eastern Front

KING CAROL BRIDGE across the Danube near Cernavoda is reported to have been destroyed by Soviet aircraft on August 11. About 60 planes under Comrade Kulikov took part in the attack and direct hits were scored, one huge span disappearing into the river. The entire railway communications with the Rumanian coastal areas were paralysed as a result, and a pipe-line which ran along the bridge was also broken.

In the German photograph below, two Russian soldiers are seen inspecting a giant statue of Lenin torn from its pedestal by Nazis.

This photograph, radioed direct from Moscow to London, shows a Red Army soldier lying in ambush with " Molotov cocktails "—bottles full of benzine —waiting to hurl them at an approaching Nazi tank.

RUSSIAN ARMOURED TRAIN moving up to the front. A soldier scans the sky, ready to turn his multiple machine-guns against hostile aircraft.

The end of a German raider, brought down by Soviet air defences. Russian soldiers and collective farmers stand by as the plane burns itself out.

Photos, E.N.A., Associated Press.
Planet News.

It Was 'Blenheims, Blenheims All the Way' When

Here are some of the men who bombed the power stations at Quadrath and Knapsack on August 12. The pilot on the extreme right of the photograph above went over the target at a height of only 30 feet. In the oval is the crew of one of the Blenheims. The pilot (left) is a 19-year-old Canadian. *Photos, " News Chronicle," Exclusive to* The War Illustrated

It Was 'Blenheims, Blenheims All the Way' When

R.A.F. Bombed Germany's Biggest Power Stations

THE great daylight raid of August 12 on the power stations of Quadrath and Knapsack, near Cologne, was one of the best organized raids in the history of the R.A.F.

Scores of Blenheim bombers, roaring low over fields and villages, often flying within fifty feet of the ground, dropped their bombs with precision right in the middle of the targets, leaving them, to quote the words of one pilot, "looking pretty sick."

The Blenheims flew in at a very low level to surprise the Germans and their tactics proved highly successful. A Canadian who took part in the raid summed up his impressions in this way : "The first lot went in very low and every one of their bombs was smack on the target. Others followed at about 800 feet to get out of the way of the bomb bursts. The defenders were so surprised that at first there was no flak at all."

Though swarms of German fighters awaited the Blenheims on their return from these successful operations they were held off by Spitfires which came inland to escort the bombers back.

Photos, British Official : Crown Copyright

Blenheims in formation, as seen top right, bombed the great power station at Knapsack heavily and effectively. On the left is a general view of the attack taken just after the aircraft seen in the foreground had dropped its bombs, while above, more bombs are seen falling upon the target, the great power station, from a low level. The bombs have just been dropped from a 'plane travelling in the direction of the foot of the page.

'Wherever I Go, Bright Eyes and Smiling Faces'

THEIR MAJESTIES IN BERMONDSEY, during a tour of East End air-raid shelters on August 1. Wherever the foul horrors of war have afflicted their, people, they have, by their sympathy and by their own devotion to duty, cemented the bond between Crown and commoner.

WE, like yourselves, love peace, and have not devoted the years behind us to the planning of death and destruction . . . It is only now that we are beginning to marshal around us in their full strength the devotion and resources of our great British family of nations, which will in the end, please God, assuredly prevail.

Through these waiting months a heavy burden is being borne by our people. As I go among them I marvel at their unshakable constancy . . . Yet hardship has only steeled our hearts and strengthened our resolution. Wherever I go I see bright eyes and smiling faces, for though our road is stony and hard it is straight, and we know that we fight in a great cause.

It gives us strength to know that you have not been content to pass us by on the other side ; to us, in this time of our tribulation you have surely shown that compassion which has been for 2,000 years the mark of the good neighbour . . . To you tyranny is as hateful as it is to us ; to you the things for which we will fight to the death are no less sacred. To my mind, at any rate, your generosity is born of your conviction that we fight to save a cause which is yours no less than ours ; of your high resolve that, however great the cost and however long the struggle, justice and freedom, human dignity and kindness, shall not perish from the earth.—*From H.M. the Queen's broadcast to the Women of the United States, August* 10, 1941

H.M. THE QUEEN, accompanied by the two Princesses, presenting a miniature sword to the most efficient cadet (A. H. Taylor), after the "Passing Out" parade of a company of Sandhurst Cadets at Sandhurst College.

Accompanied by King George, the Queen passes through some of the worst of Hull's bombed areas. She has seen at first-hand what, in her broadcast, she termed " the bitter but also proud sorrow of war."

Photos, British Official : Crown Copyright ; "Daily Mirror"

See the Americans Made Welcome in Iceland

UNITED STATES MARINES in Iceland make friends with British soldiers amid the congenial surroundings of the ubiquitous Y.M.C.A. Right, American naval men chat with a member of the R.A.F. beneath the monument to Jon Sigurdsson, Iceland's national hero, in Reykjavik.

AT REYKJAVIK, capital of Iceland, some of the first Americans to land come ashore. The secret of the landing was well kept and was first publicly announced by President Roosevelt in a special message to Congress on July 7, 1941. In his message the President declared that the United States could not permit "the occupation by Germany of strategic outposts in the Atlantic to be used as air or naval bases for an eventual attack against the Western Hemisphere." The action was arranged in the most friendly way with the Icelandic Government.

Photos, Associated Press, L.N.A., Sport & General

Our Diary of the War

SUNDAY, AUG. 10, 1941 *708th day*

Sea.—Admiralty announced that H.M. destroyer Defender had been sunk.

Air.—Day attacks on enemy shipping.

Russian Front.—Germans advanced nearer Kiev and threatened to turn the line of the Dniester. In north, Kexholm still in Russian hands and Karelian defences unbroken.

Soviet aircraft bombed Berlin by night. Moscow raided by German planes, five of which were destroyed.

Africa.—Post on outer perimeter of Tobruk routed Italian troops attacking by night.

On night of 9-10 R.A.F. attacked Bardia and Gazala.

Home.—During night bombs fell at a point in Scotland.

General.—The Queen broadcast to the women of America.

MONDAY, AUG. 11 *709th day*

Air.—R.A.F. made night raids on Ruhr towns of Krefeld, Rheydt and Munchen-Gladbach. Rotterdam docks also attacked.

Russian Front.—Moscow reports referred to fighting in Uman area, in Southern Ukraine. Germans claimed to have advanced to within 40 miles of Black Sea port of Nikolaiev.

German thrusts east of Lake Ladoga and in Estonia were halted.

Red Air Force destroyed important bridge over Danube, cutting communication between Bucharest and Black Sea ports. Night raid on Berlin.

Africa.—R.A.F. made very heavy attack on Benghazi during night of 10-11. Fleet Air Arm attacked Bardia and Tripoli.

Mediterranean.—R.A.F. bombed chemical works at Cotrone, S. Italy, and military buildings at Cariati. Enemy collier sunk off Lampedusa.

Fleet Air Arm sank ship in Syracuse harbour and bombed Gerbini aerodrome.

TUESDAY, AUG. 12 *710th day*

Air.—Heaviest day raid of war made by Blenheim and Fortress aircraft on Cologne power stations and other targets in N.W. Germany. Other forces attacked railways near St. Omer and power station at Gosnay. Fortress aircraft bombed aerodrome at De Kooy and port of Emden. We lost 12 bombers and 8 fighters.

Widespread night raids over Germany, main targets being objectives in Berlin, industries in Magdeburg and Hanover districts and Krupps works at Essen. Aerodromes in Holland and Le Havre also attacked.

Russian Front.—Main German effort concentrated in Ukraine in attempt to capture Donetz industrial area. Russians reported that fighting continued in Uman area. Lull on Finnish front.

Africa.—During night of 11-12 R.A.F. bombed Gazala, Bardia and Derna. Sustained raid on Tripoli harbour.

Home.—Few bombs fell in scattered night raids over Midlands and east of England.

France.—Admiral Darlan appointed head of new Ministry of National and Empire Defence.

WEDNESDAY, AUG. 13 *711th day*

Russian Front.—Soviet High Command reported no important change on any front. German claim to have reached Black Sea and encircled Odessa not confirmed. Russians admitted that evacuation of Smolensk had taken place.

Africa.—During night of 12-13 R.A.F. bombed Bardia and Tripoli.

Mediterranean.—Fleet Air Arm bombed aerodromes at Catania and Gerbini.

Home.—Few bombs fell on N.E. coast.

THURSDAY, AUG. 14 *712th day*

Air.—R.A.F. made day attack on docks at Boulogne. Fourteen enemy fighters destroyed for five British.

Large forces of night bombers attacked Hanover, Brunswick and Magdeburg. Smaller raids on docks at Rotterdam and Boulogne. Supply ship off Frisian Islands left sinking.

Russian Front.—Moscow officially denied German claim to have encircled Odessa, and stated that there had been no important operations on any front.

Africa.—Heavy bombers attacked Tripoli. Tobruk patrol wiped out enemy strong point.

Mediterranean.—During night of 13-14 R.A.F. heavily bombed Corinth Canal. Heraklion aerodrome attacked.

Fleet Air Arm attacked submarine base at Augusta (Sicily) and barracks at Syracuse.

Home.—Night raiders dropped few bombs in north-east, east and Midlands.

General.—Announced that Mr. Churchill and Mr. Roosevelt had had a 3-day conference at sea, at which a joint declaration of peace aims was drawn up.

FRIDAY, AUG. 15 *713th day*

Russian Front.—Moscow reported stubborn fighting in four main regions of Kexholm, Staraya Russa, Smolensk and Odessa.

German High Command repeated that Odessa was encircled and iron ore centre of Krivoi Rog captured.

Africa.—Aerodromes of Berka and Benina and ports of Bardia and Benghazi bombed on night of 15-16.

Mediterranean.—R.A.F. attacked two tankers and two schooners, hitting all and probably sinking tankers.

Fleet Air Arm made night attack on convoy; two merchant vessels and one destroyer sunk, and another vessel damaged.

During nights of 14-15 and 15-16 R.A.F. heavily raided Catania, Sicily. Augusta harbour and aerodromes of Gerbini and Trapani also bombed.

SATURDAY, AUG. 16 *714th day*

Sea.—One German bomber destroyed and two damaged when they unsuccessfully attacked a British convoy.

Air.—During two daylight offensives R.A.F. bombed railways and aerodromes near St. Omer. Nineteen enemy fighters destroyed for four British. Fortress aircraft bombed Brest docks.

Main targets of night raids were Cologne, Düsseldorf and Duisburg. Docks at Rotterdam and Ostend also bombed.

Russian Front.—Soviet communiqué reported continued fighting all along front. Russians withdrawing east of R. Dnieper. Germans admitted large pockets of Russian resistance in southern Ukraine.

Finns claimed capture of Sortavala.

Mediterranean.—Night raids on Catania and Syracuse.

Home.—Night raiders dropped bombs in eastern and south-eastern areas. Enemy bomber shot down off S.W. coast.

General.—Stalin accepted proposal of Mr. Roosevelt and Mr. Churchill to hold 3-Power conference at Moscow.

British and Soviet Governments signed trade agreement.

MOBILE POST OFFICES are among the new experiments now being tried out in order to overcome some of the difficulties resulting from heavy air raids. The object of the scheme is to provide postal facilities in any part of London where the local post office has been put out of commission through enemy action. Each of these post offices on wheels will have a staff of counter clerks, and messenger boys will be in attendance to take telegrams to the nearest telegraph office. The first, seen above, was opened experimentally in the City on August 6, 1941. *Photo, Topical*

They're Ready for War in Tropical Malaya

For Malaya's defence the anti-aircraft batteries of the peninsula, manned by British and Indian troops, have been constantly strengthened. Here are men of the Hong Kong-Singapore Royal Artillery.

Aid from the U.S.A. has been sent direct to Singapore under the Lease and Lend Bill. An American ship, which has just discharged war material, is seen with the Stars and Stripes on its hull.

JUNGLE WARFARE has been closely studied in the Malay Peninsula, and the fieldcraft is now of a high order. The R.A.S.C. in Malaya recruits almost entirely Asiatic drivers, Malays and Indians, for transport, and Asiatic dispatch riders are here seen making their way over the densely wooded country of the peninsula. In the circle is Lieut.-General A. E. Percival, British G.O.C. Malaya. He knows the country well, as he was G.S.O., First Grade, Malaya from 1936 to 1938. Gen. Percival was on the General Staff of the 1st Corps. B.E.F.. from 1939 to 1940.   *Photos British Official*

The Marines Fought Magnificently in Crete

Apart from their work on H.M. ships, Royal Marines are playing a great part on land in this war. Iceland and the Faroes were first occupied by Royal Marines ; members of the Corps were in action in Norway ; and at the Hook of Holland, Boulogne and Calais they covered the withdrawal of troops and demolition parties. Then they were in Crete, where of 2,000 nearly 1,100 failed to return. Here is the story of their gallant rearguard action. See also page 93.

THE Royal Marine Forces in Crete consisted of heavy and light anti-aircraft batteries, a searchlight battery and coast defence batteries for the defence of the naval base at Suda Bay and the aerodromes at Maleme and Heraklion. A signal company 200 strong also landed. Although specialist units, each man had his rifle, since it is customary in the Corps that the basic training should be that of infantry, and this includes, of course, training in the use of the rifle and bayonet. They were not, however, in the first instance organized infantry battalions.

After the main attack broke on May 20 the searchlight battery in the Suda Bay area was organized as an infantry battalion and put into the line south of Canea. The areas in which these troops were holding positions were in olive groves with small fields of fire, and the shortage of wire and digging tools had not enabled proper positions to be prepared. It is difficult to portray the situation at this period, when there was a complete absence of our own air support and formations of German bombers and fighters kept up a continuous " blitz " of the front and back areas, flying very low.

Worsting the Parachutists

By day, no movement of any sort was possible. Motor transport and dispatch riders were immediately shot up, and any area which showed any activity was " strafed." Communications were difficult to maintain, and all supplies had to be delivered to units by night. Two platoons of Royal Marines improvised from signallers and searchlight crews, gallantly led by Captain A. L. Laxton, distinguished themselves on this day by driving a large force of parachute troops out of a 3·7-in. gun position south of Canea which had been captured by the enemy.

Some of these small local actions required great courage and leadership, as in all cases the Germans were armed with Tommy guns, hand grenades and mortars, and when once they had taken up a defensive position were very difficult to dislodge, especially by troops armed only with a rifle.

The A.A. batteries, like those of the Army, were heavily strafed by low-flying aircraft during the whole attack and suffered corresponding casualties. The guns were in action in improvised sites up to the moment of withdrawal. At Maleme, where air-borne troops landed close to the A.A. batteries and drove the gun's crews from the guns, these crews remained to fight as infantry soldiers for the rest of the day and until they retired, when the position was evacuated. At Heraklion, where there were some light and heavy A.A. batteries, these guns had great success in the preliminary stages in shooting down German fighters and troop carriers. Later, when parachutists in large numbers were dropped near and in the gun positions, the detachments had to man their rifles, and succeeded in killing large numbers whilst still in the air. One Royal Marine manning a Lewis gun himself brought down two aircraft and killed many parachutists even before they reached the ground. The closeness of the fighting can be judged by the fact that the Royal Marine officer commanding this battery shot two Germans with his revolver.

In this area it is estimated that at least 2,000 parachute troops were definitely killed on the first day of the attack. In the later stages German reinforcements were dropped outside the main defences, and in one case surrounded an Australian patrol, who never-

theless fought their way back with the bayonet and brought in a large number of prisoners.

All these A.A. positions at Heraklion were successfully held until May 28, when all the troops, totalling 4,000, were evacuated by sea. During this period the enemy repeatedly attacked our positions both by air and from the ground, and on several occasions the Royal Marine A.A. guns were used in a direct fire role against ground troops. When the line broke in the Canea sector on May 26, the Royal Marine searchlight battalion near Mournies was the last battalion to remain in the line and marched out in good order. Thereafter the credit for the rearguard action belongs to the New Zealand and Australian units, who fought magnificently throughout.

'JOLLIES' from a British cruiser, typical of those who fought so magnificently in Crete, are here seen boarding a picket boat for a brief spell ashore.   *Photo, Fox*

The outstanding incident in the Suda area at this time was a counter-attack at 11.30 hours on May 27, ending in a bayonet charge by Australian and Maori battalions which drove the Germans back a thousand yards and enabled other troops of the rearguard to disengage. It was not until Thursday, May 29, that reinforcements were required for the rearguard, and a Royal Marine battalion was organized from the remaining units and brought in the line. The enemy made a determined attack on the rearguard south of Imvros on May 30. Their advanced parties were brought under fire from several forward positions well in advance of the main rearguard position, and this still further delayed the enemy.

A company of Royal Marines under Lt. T. W. Retter was detached from the main rearguard to prevent the Germans working round the right flank of the main position. The quick deployment of this company frustrated the threat from this flank and

caused many casualties. Contact with the main rearguard position was again made by the enemy later in the day, when a further attack was not pressed. From then onwards the Royal Marine battalion were in contact with the enemy and, with the Australian Infantry battalion, who had been in action throughout the rearguard operations, were the last to retire from the hills overlooking the beaches.

When the final order to withdraw to the beaches was given, the Royal Marine battalion was still under heavy machine-gun fire. Only twenty minutes' notice was given to withdraw. In order to distract the enemy's attention, so as to enable the main party to disengage from the action, a diversion was created by throwing grenades down a ravine in which it was known a force of the enemy had infiltrated. These grenades were set so that the full length of the fuse was used, and the grenades exploded amongst the enemy force down in the ravine. Long-range fire was also used to keep the enemy at a distance. This enabled the whole of the battalion to withdraw according to plan.

The terrain over which this rearguard fought was alpine in the extreme, and ill-suited for evacuation. There was only one road, which dropped from the top of the mountains about 2,000 feet high to a narrow plain below in a series of acute hairpins, the lower half of the road being unfinished and covered with loose road metal, coming to an abrupt end on the hillside about 500 feet above sea level. The plain below was of the roughest scrub and limestone, crossed only by a few ill-defined tracks. The supply of rations and water to the rearguard was of the utmost difficulty, and during the last two and a half days the force was on reduced rations.

It was unfortunate that the Royal Marines and Australians who held the rearguard positions to the end were unable to be re-embarked on the final night of the evacuation, but by their actions they enabled large numbers of British and Imperial troops to be successfully evacuated. This composite Royal Marine battalion, under the command of Major R. Garrett, consisted of the A.A. searchlight battery, parts of a heavy and light A.A. battery, two coast batteries and a number of signalmen. All these men had been trained in the use of a rifle and light machine-gun and gave a good account of themselves as an improvised infantry battalion. A senior officer present remarked that " they were a tribute to the versatility of the Corps." Thus ended the rearguard action in Crete—although in August there came stories that some of the men left behind were engaging in guerilla war against the Nazis. (See p. 80).

Great Traditions Maintained

The splendid achievements of the Royal Marines in Crete were recognized by Mr. Alexander, First Lord of the Admiralty, in a speech on June 27. " I shall not readily forget," he said, " the thrill which I felt when the signal came from Crete, and I knew that the Royal Marines had again been chosen for a part of great danger. Once again they had maintained the great traditions of the Corps. They displayed remarkable courage, which enabled us to evacuate from Crete more troops than otherwise could have been done." Then General Wavell in a message to General Weston on May 31 said, " General Freyberg has told me how magnificently your Marines fought, and of your own grand work." (See page 671, vol. 4.)

Waiting for the Next Round in Libya

INDIAN REGIMENTS are still playing a splendid part in the forays of the Western Desert. Here Indian troops are seen on parade at an Indian reinforcement camp. Their drill is impeccable.

Desert post office where mail for the troops is being unloaded. The O.C. Army Postal Service has charge of 200 sub-post offices in the Western Desert.

A.R.P. IN THE DESERT. This notice is erected on the outskirts of Tobruk, where air raids are incessant. The red flag is hoisted because transport drivers and dispatch riders cannot always hear the noise of aircraft above the noise of their own engines.

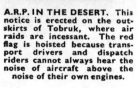

Circle, Gen. Ettore Bastico, Italy's new C.-in-C. in N. Africa and Governor of Libya in succession to Graziani. He commanded the Italian Volunteer Force in Spain in the Civil War.

"Tin Can Alley," right, leads to a small desert camp; without the lines of empty cans which mark the roadway, even the most experienced driver could easily get lost in an attempt to locate the site of the camp.

Photos, British Official: Crown Copyright; Sport & General

Bombs on Egypt : Alexandria's Worst Raid

ALEXANDRIA was heavily raided by Axis bombers on the night of June 7, 1941, the second severe raid on the city in four nights. Hundreds of civilians were killed or injured and considerable damage, some of which is seen above, was done in European and Arab residential quarters.   Below, an Italian bomber, brought down by ground defences at Alexandria, is shown to the Egyptians.   *Photos, Associated Press, Fox*

I Was There! .... Eye Witness Stories of the War

The Norwegians Gave Us the 'V' Signal

A sergeant-pilot from a Beaufort torpedo-bomber squadron of the R.A.F. Coastal Command broadcast the following account of a successful patrol off the Norwegian coast in August

I KNEW I was going to have a good trip that morning. The Beaufort torpedo-bomber which I was piloting is called the Wreck . . . W-R-E-C-K. It is the aircraft which torpedoed a German pocket battleship a few weeks ago. Its own crew were on leave and I was told to take their Beaufort on Norwegian patrol.

It was still fairly dark when I climbed on board, and the flight across the North Sea was monotonous; we didn't see a thing until we made landfall at the extreme southern tip of Norway. It was daylight by then, and I turned and followed the coast for a minute or two. I could see for miles.

Then I spotted a ship in the distance, just off the Norwegian coast. I put the nose of the aircraft down, and as we dived on the ship I saw it was heavily loaded. There were crates stacked all over the deck and it looked a pretty good target. From mast height I laid a stick of bombs across the ship. I didn't see the bombs drop, but Mac, the rear-gunner, yelled over the inter-comm in a broad Scots accent—"There's one on the deck."

I banked and turned and saw the ship's crew climbing into their lifeboats. They couldn't get away fast enough. They just rowed like mad in the direction the boat's nose happened to be pointing. I let them get away. Then we shot up the vessel from stem to stern. Every gun on the plane let rip. After that we decided it was time to get on with our patrol. As we left the ship I saw it drifting on to the rocks, while its seamen were still rowing away like a boatrace crew. Then we flew farther along the coast.

Everything looked very quiet and peaceful in the early morning light. Suddenly I was deafened by a short yell from the rear turret.—"Messerschmitts"! Hard on the warning came the rattle of the rear-gunner's guns. There was one long burst of fire—then another excited yell from the turret—"I've got him! I've got him!" There was a short silence. Then came the news: "He's in the drink!" I heard the navigator ask where the other fighter was. "I don't know," Mac shouted back. "I can't see a damn thing. I think he's gone home!"

The whole incident was over in a few seconds. When I got the rear-gunner's warning I turned to port to make the Beaufort a more difficult target for Jerry. At that moment I saw a few tracer bullets whizz past over the wing, but that was all I saw of the scrap. The fighter had dived down on us from astern. The rear-gunner held fire until the German filled his wing sight—then he pressed the trigger. The Messerschmitt never pulled out of that dive. It plunged straight into the sea.

We weren't the only ones to have a good bag that morning. One of my companion Beauforts got a 1,500-ton oil tanker just off the north of us. This happened only minutes after Mac had shot down the Messerschmitt. The pilot dropped one of his bombs slap on the tanker and smoke and flames shot up. When the Beaufort flew away the crew was trying to beach the blazing ship. It won't carry any more oil for Hitler.

I must tell you of another interesting event which happened the same morning. During our patrol we flew over some Norwegian fishing smacks. My navigator picked up his signalling lamp and flashed the letter "V" in Morse. Down below I saw lamps winking back the answer—three dots and a dash. It was repeated several times—V for Victory.

Our 10-day Voyage from Crete to Sidi Barrani

Here, as a postscript to the story of the Royal Marines in Crete (see page 90), is the account of the hazardous escape to North Africa of 139 Marines and other units, told by Major R. Garrett.

THE Royal Marines in Crete fought until dusk on May 31, when, under cover of darkness, they were able to get to the beach of Sphakia Bay, on the south side of the island.

There they found men from many different units, as well as a boat which had two petrol engines and twin screws, but was like a flat-bottomed lighter built up with screens fore and aft.

Into this piled 139 men, Marines, Australians, New Zealanders, Maoris, Palestinians, Maltese, Military Police, and other Army details and Naval ratings.

Early on June 1 [said Major Garrett] I got away on one engine, the port screw being jammed by wire. We stopped at the little island of Podvopula, 20 miles south of Crete, where I had every conceivable container filled with water. For food we had bully beef and biscuits, but, not knowing how long we were going to be at sea, I restricted the rations to inch-and-a-half cubes of bully beef and half a biscuit twice a day.

With every drop of water we could load we only felt safe in issuing one-third of half a pint per man each 24 hours. It was enough to rinse the mouth every four hours.

Having cleared the port screw at Podvopula, we tried to put as much distance between ourselves and the enemy by using both engines. We had covered about 80 miles by June 2 when the petrol was exhausted from the port motor. Efforts to get it to fire while it was still hot on a fuel called Zieselite were ineffective. Then the starboard clutch began to slip so badly that recourse was had to sail—improvised from blankets sewn together with spun yarn.

At this time we had a fair wind and we made about a knot, but later the vessel, flat-bottomed as she was and with this built-up stern, was the game of every puff.

Once she got off her course, neither rudders nor improvised oars would pull her back. So we had to send men over the side, and as they swam their combined efforts were able to push her stern round until we were on our course again.

Meantime, inside the boat exhausted men were labouring at the engines—because we had discovered that tins which were thought to contain water proved to contain eight gallons of petrol. We did not know whether we were glad or sorry, for our water position was then desperate.

Still, by bullying the mechanics, I fear, I managed to get the gearbox of the port engine put in place of the starboard unit, whose clutch was slipping. By the morning of June 5 we were completely out of petrol.

That day and the next we turned to make an improvised craft which would proceed

OFF NORWAY an R.A.F. bomber has just secured a direct hit on a 2,500-ton motor vessel. The plane came down to within 50 feet of the ship, and in the photo is seen rising to the left of the smoke. This photograph might well be of the incident described in this page.
Photo, British Official : Crown Copyright

more swiftly than our miserable 20 miles a day. First we tried a raft made of oil tins, but it was too buoyant, and threw the men off. Next day we rigged up a canvas canoe, but it would only hold one man—and all of us were too weak to risk being the one to be sent ahead in the canoe for aid.

Finally, on the 7th, we concentrated on making more sail with blankets, and rigging up some sort of jib. This left us bitterly cold at night. On the 8th two men died.

By this time we would all have died had we not rigged up apparatus for distilling sea water. This consisted of two petrol tins joined together with piping. We boiled sea water in one, using the hitherto despised Zieselite as fuel, and condensed the steam by wrapping wet towels round the pipe, so that it dripped pure water into the second tin.

Finally, we sighted land 12 miles off, and at 1.30 a.m. on the morning of June 10 landed west of Sidi Barrani.

Within a quarter of an hour two Maoris, by what they called "Maori instinct," discovered a well of fresh water. This enabled the crew to sustain a march of five miles. Then we were picked up by a unit of the Western Desert Army, and given a hot meal of bully beef and potatoes, which tasted wonderful. The disappointments of the

ROYAL MARINES undergoing their arduous training with bayonet and gas-mask on the summit of obstacles.
Photo, Topical

journey included two occasions when they thought they were sighted by British aeroplanes.—"*Daily Mail.*"

It Seemed as if Our Whole Hospital Was Lifted Up

Badly wounded and shocked by a bomb explosion at the Royal Chest Hospital, City Road, London, the staff remained on duty until all the patients had been removed to safety. Their story is told by Miss Catherine McGovern, Assistant Matron, who, with Dr. Bathfield and Staff Sister Marmion, was awarded the George Medal.

It was between three and four in the morning. I was sitting in front of the fire with two Sisters in the board-room of the hospital on the ground floor. Dr. Bathfield [see page 160, Vol. 4] was standing talking to us. It was no night for bed ; the Alarm had gone, we had heard bombs exploding, and were ready to receive casualties.

It came all of a sudden—it seemed as if the whole hospital was lifted up and would fall down on top of us. The blast threw us all in a heap. Electric cables, gas and water pipes were broken. Everything went black ; the air was full of choking dust. The ceiling had come down ; the walls and windows had come out. We were hit by everything that could move—the glass from the windows, the frames of the windows, the plaster from the walls, furniture and medicine bottles. There wasn't one of us who was not cut, mostly in the head, arms, or legs, and eye injuries, and afterwards everyone wondered how we managed to get out of the heap of stuff that poured on to us.

At first we didn't know what had happened. It was quite plain that the face of the hospital was blown out. I thought as I got to my feet, "What has happened upstairs ? " There were also the maids to think of. They were sleeping on mattresses in the basement, and what a miraculous

ROYAL CHEST HOSPITAL, City Road, London, after a raid in September 1940. Many of the staff and patients were wounded. The story of the bombing is told in this page by Miss McGovern, G.M., Assistant Matron, and is reproduced by permission from " Hospitals Under Fire," edited by G. C. Curnock (Allen & Unwin). (See also illus. page 325, Vol. 3.)
Photo, Planet News

escape they had ! That big bomb went straight down just in front of and under the main steps and exploded on its way. Those maids were brave ; they came up the broken stairs bringing stretchers and the porters with them.

Dr. Bathfield was bleeding all the time from wounds in his face, but he thought only about the patients and how they could be taken out of their beds. Staff Sister Marmion [see page 620, Vol. 4], in charge of the men's ward, had a terrible time. Wounded as she was by glass, she first of all had to deal with a poor fellow who had lost his whole family two nights before. He went crazy when the bomb struck us, and, calling out, " It's finished—this isn't going to happen to me again ! " he was making his way to throw himself from the great hole in the wall where the window had been, when Sister Marmion caught him. She thinks it was the sight of the blood streaming down her face that brought him back to his senses. He said to her, " Let me be. You look after the others," and then made his own way downstairs.

She then went to a man who was pinned down by a heavy window-frame. His legs had already been broken in another raid. She got him to put his arms around her neck, and so lifted him on to her back and

August 29th, 1941　　　　　　　　　　*The War Illustrated*　　　　　　　　　　95

IIIIIIIIIIIIIIIIIIIIIIIIIIIIIIIIIIIIIIIIIIIIIIIIIIIIIIIIIIIIIIIIIIIIIIIIIIIIIIIIII **I WAS THERE!** IIIIIIIIIIIIIIIIIIIIIIIIIIIIIIIIIIIIIIIIIIIIIIIIIIIIIIIIIIIIIIIIIIIIIIIIIIIIIIIIIIIIIIIIIIIIIIIIIIII

carried him downstairs into the basement. As soon as they saw what had happened, the police and wardens came in to help us. Fortunately the building did not catch alight, but the business of getting the patients out of the beds and into the ambulances through all the darkness was not easy. No one knew what they might be stepping into or what might fall on them.

I felt I could not leave. The Matron was away, and I was in charge. The others felt the same. The police urged us to go with the patients for treatment. I suppose we were not a very pretty sight. I had seven wounds and was bleeding badly. While I was standing there, watching the last of the patients being carried out, the " All Clear " went. It seemed to me that that old devil of a Hitler was saying, " We've done our damnedest, you can go ! "—*From " Hospitals Under Fire," edited by G. C. Curnock, published by George Allen & Unwin, Ltd.*

We Put the Bombs Right on the Dot in Mannheim

Those readers who have seen the R.A.F. film " Target for Tonight " will remember the crew of the Wellington bomber " F for Freddie." Some of them took part in the big attack on Mannheim on July 5, and they tell their stories below.

THREE of the film crew—the first pilot, the Scots navigator, and the sergeant gunner with a shock of black hair— were together in one aircraft over Mannheim. Here is the story of the navigator :

We saw the coast and got a pin-point there. There was some anti-aircraft fire as we crossed the coast, but we soon left it behind. After that we flew through cloud. Then we came into perfectly clear weather, and from that point I just map-read the way to the target. It was so light that I didn't even need a light to read the print on the map. I could pick out the different colours of the fields below. We picked up the Rhine, but we didn't fly down the river because it was lined with searchlights.

When we started the run-up I could see the target all right, but when we had got half-way drifting cloud hid it. When we came out of cloud again I heard my pilot say, " there it is down below as clear as day." But by that time we had got past it, and over open field, so we did another circuit. This time we ran up into the moon, and you could see things on the ground more clearly. There were three cones of searchlights, each of about 30 lights. When I first saw them there was a bomber caught in each of the cones and the guns were filling the cones with flak, flying up into the apex. We ourselves got a clear run in and weren't attacked. I put the bombs right on the dot.

Then the searchlights caught us. The guns opened up and we started dodging and diving to avoid them. We came down to try to get away. There was a banging and rattling all round the aircraft. Shrapnel was hitting against the fuselage and in the rear of the Wellington there was a smell of cordite from exploding shells. We were held in the searchlights for four minutes ; then, when we got clear, the wireless operator shook everybody by calling up and saying, " Hello, captain, do you know the port engine's on fire ? " Apparently one of the pipes had been split

This " still " from the R.A.F. film " Target for Tonight " shows, smoking his pipe, the first pilot of the Wellington bomber, " F for Freddie," which is featured in the film. He took part in the big attack on Mannheim on July 5, and his story is told in this page.

and there was a sheet of flame a foot high which kept flickering out of the top of the cowling. It was rather like a big gas jet. The pilot just carried on, nursing the engine and not forcing it. After a time one forgot all about it. We ate our rations and made

up our minds that if anything worse was going to happen it would have happened already. The flames were still coming out of the cowling when we landed, and they only went out when the engine was cut off. We counted 37 shrapnel holes in the aircraft afterwards.

The pilot of the new " F for Freddie " which has now replaced the one in the film was also over Mannheim. He said :

Over Germany the moon was so bright that you could see for 30 miles all round. I've never had a trip like it before. You could see the hedges and the roads, even the smallest streams and railway lines as well. We had been to Mannheim before. It was easy. We picked up the Rhine and then turned on to the target. There was an awful lot of light flak and a good deal of heavy. As we were bombing, my rear gunner told me there was a Hampden on our tail, keeping almost to the same course. At one time we counted at least twelve flares in the air and you could see that other bombers were at work farther away.

We laid our bombs across the docks. Then, coming home, we gave the two gunners a night out. First we had a go at the railway station in a fair-sized town just west of Mannheim. We went down to 500 feet to wake the stationmaster up, and to give the gunners some exercise. There were three rows of trucks on the sidings and some warehouses beside them. We raked them with fire from both turrets. The station had a glass roof and we made a mess of it ; you could see the bullets smashing the glass. As soon as we began to fire the Germans started on us with pom-poms, so we thought we'd get along to the next place. We found some goods yards and warehouses in another town and machine-gunned them from 300 feet. There was no opposition at all there. All the time we were in Germany the gunners kept calling me up whenever they saw a town. " There's a likely-looking place, sir," they said, " there must be a railway station there." But we had to save some ammunition in case we met fighters, so after the second town we came quietly home.

The pilot of another bomber which attacked a large chemical factory at Ludwigshaven on the same night said :

We saw a great explosion, and enormous orange-red flames leaped up hundreds of feet into the air. My rear gunner said he could see the glow in the sky when we were a hundred miles away, and we only lost sight of it because we ran into cloud."

The Editor's Postscript

WE are now into our **V** Volume ! And if all goes well it should be the best of the series. I have had a "dummy" bound up and am satisfied that one volume can comfortably contain thirty-six parts, so that our subscribers who are binding the loose numbers will have only one volume to bind at the end of twelve months—an economy which I hope they will appreciate. The current issue went to press before we could adequately deal with that truly dynamic episode of this year—the Anglo-American meeting off the coast of Britain's oldest colony : Newfoundland. In our next number a fine selection of the official photographs recording this never-to-be-forgotten event will form its main pictorial feature.

"THE Eight Points" will resound in history to better purpose than Wilson's "Fourteen," yet I have never been excessively anxious about "War aims." If a thug is trying to bash my features while I defend myself at my own door, behind which there is something he desires for himself, I don't begin to ask myself what are the ideals for which I am defending my abode, or nicely to distinguish between Christian, Moslem, or Pagan ideals before I start bashing back, lest I might have to admit with one of W. W. Jacobs's old salts : "There you are now, my fatal beauty spoiled at last !" We can do with less talk about our war aims so as not to divert our attention from the winning of the War. It is enough to know that we are fighting to prevent ourselves from being downed.

BUT I will admit that there will be lots of ideals to strive for after we've settled with the thugs. Social honesty, for one. Nineteen hundred years of Christian teaching has done astonishingly little to eliminate dishonesty in social relationships. Already I have given some striking examples of this. Here is another. A Glasgow friend has just told me that in a certain "service club" in that "no mean city," where social workers have been labouring devotedly to help the members of the services that are to stand between us and annihilation, it was arranged to supply good hot baths and the use of soap and towels to the men at the nominal cost of twopence. Result : an average of two dozen towels and cakes of soap borrowed (I had nearly written "stolen") every week. Scottish caution has been equal to the occasion, however, by making each man pay eighteenpence on receiving his towel and soap and refunding fifteenpence to him when these are returned. The borrowing habit has been cured and one penny per head added to the amount received for the excellent service provided.

WITH Cardinal Newman, "I do not ask to see the distant scene," and the winning of the War will be "one step enough for me" . . . and for all of us. That a new order of social life will have to be fashioned, nobody outside of our enlarging mental homes will deny, but all those who are urging the definition of the new order while we are in the thick of our fight against another new order, which

has been only too clearly defined by its originators, are not helping us to attain even so much as that one step that is essential : those who are two-stepping it to Bertie Bonehead and His Boys are quite as serviceable at the moment. They are at least keeping a light heart, without which there will be no standing up to the renewed assaults upon our morale with the lengthening nights that are coming all too soon.

AND this reminds me that, travelling in the Hull train a few days ago, I was regaled with the most hair-raising account of the last blitz on that city by one of its citizens. I shall not repeat the figures of the killed (which were up to the highest I have heard of Glasgow, Plymouth, Bristol or Coventry), but I am not surprised to read in a local daily paper that "a scheme to stop gossip

---

IMPORTANT ANNOUNCEMENT

CONTINUED pressure of War conditions involves a change in our publishing dates as the only alternative to further curtailment of circulation. To comply with the latest restrictions of the Paper Control and continue weekly publication, it would [be necessary either to reduce still further the contents of THE WAR ILLUSTRATED or to disappoint many thousands of readers by limiting the number issued.

The Editor and his publishers are of opinion that in its present form THE WAR ILLUSTRATED represents the minimum of contents necessary for a well-balanced picture-record of the War and as such it should be maintained. Of its original very large circle of readers there must be upwards of 100,000 who, to the great regret of the publishers, have been unable to get it on account of the reduced quantities printed in accordance with the paper quota officially permitted from time to time.

The only way to retain its present very important circulation and so to avoid further disappointment for would-be readers, is to modify the number of issues each month. Beginning with No. 105, which will be published on Wednesday, September 10, THE WAR ILLUSTRATED will thereafter appear on the 10th, 20th and 30th of each month. These dates have been fixed as easiest to remember, involving a minimum of confusion to distributors and readers alike. When the 10th falls upon a Sunday our periodical will be on sale everywhere on the preceding Saturday, and in certain districts, where transport facilities permit, it will usually be obtainable on the day preceding the date which the issue bears.

The Editor will be glad, therefore, if his readers will make a note of this new arrangement, and he hopes they will appreciate that it has been decided upon with a view to disappointing none of the present subscribers or involving regular readers in the loss or occasional breaking of the continuity of interest so essential to the intelligent unfolding of the story of the War.

It is assumed, of course, that every reader has already given a firm order to his newsagent to deliver or reserve each successive number of THE WAR ILLUSTRATED for him, but please make a note that on the 10th, 20th and 30th of each month (naturally excepting February, when it will appear on the 28th) our publication should either be delivered by your newsagent or reserved for you.

No. 105 will be published Wednesday, Sept. 10th

---

by the prompt publication of air-raid casualty figures in Hull is to be prepared by the town clerk and medical officer of health." The Lord Mayor of the town stated that "the death-roll is nothing like the figure quoted by the rumour-mongers, who do great disservice to the community." But who's to blame ? Those in high places who have decided to withhold details from the press and lump the casualties for the month. My view is that the cold, stark facts are never so terrifying as the rumour-swollen figures suggest. If we cannot stand up to the truth we are far less likely to stand up to rumour. Every reporter knows that the commonest accident assumes the most formidable proportions until he has investigated it. What a man on the perimeter of a crowd will tell you has no relationship whatever to what a man at the centre of the crowd can see.

A BOOK society to which I subscribe sent me a "choice" volume just as I went off on my brief holiday. It is by an author of repute none of whose limited writings I had read : Richard Hughes. It is entitled "In Hazard," a phrase that means no more to me now that I have read the book than it did before. I thought I had struck something new, moving, great, after I had read a few pages and regretted that I had not read the author's earlier work, "A High Wind in Jamaica." I have never been so caught by the description of a modern steamship : the soul of the ship analysed and laid bare, as it were, vivid, instinct with the actuality of truth, so I read on and on as the description of a terrific hurricane was developed . . . until I got seasick of ship and hurricane and didn't care a bean what happened to either.

BUT why do authors who don't know the Scots language attempt to write it ? There are passages in "In Hazard" that are laughably grotesque ; as grotesque as if I had attempted to write a line or two of colloquial German, knowing mighty little of the mother tongue. I ask my Scottish readers to listen to this :

"Weel, noo. Are ₁we to tak' it that a human Chreestian is compoondit o' three pairts : his body, his min', an' his speerit ?" . . . "The body dees, the speerit leeves ?" . . .

"Than whit o' the mín' ? That's nayther speerit nor body. Yet it's vera boont up wi' the body. A disease o' the body can disease the min'. A blow on the body can blot oot the min'. The min', like the body, graws auld an' decays. The daith o' the body, than, is that the daith o' the min' tae ?"

"Allooin' it be," said MacDonald.

"Than the future life canna be of a vera pairsonal nature, A'm thinkin' ; it is a saft, imbecile sort o' thing ma speerit would be wi'oot ma min'."

NEVER have I heard a Scot speak like that. Nor can I approve Mr. Hughes when he makes MacDonald say of the Chinese, "They dinna min' daith, whit way a whit' mon min's it." Although every Englishman may think so, no Scot ever, ever said "mon" for "man" ("mun" would be an approximation) nor "whit way" (which implies a question) when he would surely have said "th' wey," and when I read "In the Next Worrld Man (not Mon this time) casts Reason, Mr. Soutar, as I tau'd ye," I can neither accept the needless capitals nor "tau'd" for told ; tell'd or telt would have passed. The whole phrase is absurd to any Scotsman. I'm sure that all the interesting and fascinating things Mr. Hughes tells me about a ship in a hurricane are truer to life than his "Scotch" is to the Scots with which I am familiar. Apropos of this, I had to point out many years ago to my old friend F. Frankfort Moore when he attempted some Scottish dialogue (which ought to have come easy to an Ulster man) in one of his many popular novels, that "Laird" is not the Scots equivalent of "Lord." He had written "By the Laird I hae ye the noo." Which being English would read "By the Squire I have you now."

JOHN CARPENTER HOUSE.
WHITEFRIARS. LONDON. E.C.4.

Vol 5 — No 105

The War Illustrated

Edited by Sir John Hammerton

FOURPENCE

SEPT. 10TH. 1941

MR. CHURCHILL RESPONDS to the cheers from the crew of H.M.S. *Prince of Wales* on disembarking at a British port after his return from the Atlantic conference with President Roosevelt. The battleship was escorted by destroyers and a patrol of Catalina flying boats. Other photographs and a description of the historic meeting with President Roosevelt appear in pages 107 to 110, and page 117.

Photo, British Official : Crown Copyright

THOSE TWO YEARS: THINGS TO REMEMBER

Two years have passed since that Sunday morning when, standing round our wireless sets, we heard that we were at war again.

Two years—and what years! In those swiftly pursuing hours, those heavy drops of time, we have known terrible experiences and fearful joys; we have felt the exultant thrill of victory and the cold stab of defeat; we have been lifted up on the wings of boundless hope only, ere long, to be plunged into the deeps where reigns a grim and comfortless gloom.

From its very beginning this war has been vastly different from the last. We entered it in a mood of sober realism; not for us in 1939 the trumpetings and flag-waving, the glamour and glee with which we and our fathers went to war in 1914, when war was still a great adventure, supremely glorious, noble, uplifting, inspiring. We know better today. Only Sir Arthur Keith strangely insists that war is a beneficent pruning-hook. We have no Bottomley bellowing his " patriotic " bilge. We still have our stay-at-home patriots, our armchair warriors; but those of us who remember the vulgar, senseless clamour of a generation ago cannot but be impressed by the present absence of foolish depreciation of our enemy. We know today that though the Germans are dirty fighters they are also brave, bold, and resolute. Then in this war we have had no white-feather girls who (poor things!) tried to show their patriotism by pinning the emblem of cowardice on the lapels of young men they met in the street. Our girls have found something better to do, whether it be punching tickets or making shells, driving a tractor or an ambulance through the blitz.

For us in these days war is no distant adventure, so interesting to read about and to see pictured when it is being fought many miles away by bands of mercenaries. We have heard the swish of falling bombs, the crash of gunfire, the noise of buildings collapsing like a castle of cards caught in the draught of an opening door. War has come very near to us, into our own land, our own city or village, our own street, even our own home. We now know war for what it really is: as the most dirty, disgusting, degrading, and desperately dull activity to which human beings can descend. War has been debunked. But we know, too, that though it is all these things it is something which we have got to get on with and finish as soon and as thoroughly as we possibly can.

Looking back along the road which we have travelled in these two years, what are the features that catch the eye? First, those months when Gort's men stood side by side with Gamelin's and *watched* Todt's engineers toiling on the other side of the Rhine . . . Then we spy little groups of khaki soldiery straggling and struggling in the mountain passes of Norway. The scene shifts to the Low Countries, deluged by the flaming horror of modern war. The whole of the Western Front leaps into a roaring activity. We see the survivors of the once great— nay, still great—British Expeditionary Force burrowing in the sands of Dunkirk, waiting with a stoical patience for the little ships which by a miracle of deliverance took most of them across the Channel to safety.

Since Dunkirk we have had other evacuations. After the first triumphant rush to Benghazi our sorely denuded forces in the Western Desert were driven back into Egypt. We went to Greece, and after a tremendous rearguard action we were again forced to take to our ships and sail away. Crete was the same story. Each one of these was a masterly evacuation, but wars, as Mr. Churchill found it necessary to remind us, are not won by evacuations. Others have reminded us, too, that wars are not won by speeches, however fine . . .

Though we have known disappointments, we have had our moments of compensation. Perhaps the first was in the war's early days when the Royal Navy showed that Hitler's minelayers, U-boats, and surface raiders were not going to rule the waves. Even greater was the Battle of Britain of a year ago, when Goering's Luftwaffe strove desperately to drive the R.A.F. from the skies. High above us was waged the tremendous duel. We watched the smoke trails painted on the azure sky. We saw " Slap-happy Hermann's " young men dive to the ground in smoke and flames. An American journalist said that Hitler had taken London but didn't know it; on which we may comment that the Londoners didn't know it, either . . . Our gaze shifts to the ever-rolling ocean, and we watch the *Graf Spee* shot off the Atlantic, and the *Bismarck* shelled and bombed into an unmanageable hulk. Then in the far distance we glimpse the peaks of Abyssinia, and try to form a picture of that amazing war in which a little army of British and Indians, South Africans and Africans from the West and East, sent the flimsy fabric of Mussolini's Ethiopian Empire crashing into the dust.

In these two years we have known the joys of comradeship, but we have known, too, the pangs of severed friendship. We have seen our allies torn from our side, and bludgeoned into submission. Never since the crisis of the Napoleonic wars or the struggle with new-born America was Britain so lonely as in the months following the collapse of France. We realized our loneliness, and, in the Biblical phrase, we girded up our loins as never before—must we add, as never since ? But the darkness of that dread time began to lift as from across the Atlantic the great American republic roused herself to assist Britain in the fight which is America's too.

As the years have passed, the character of the war has changed. I do not refer entirely to matters of strategy and tactics, though tanks and dive-bombers, parachutists, Fifth Columnists, defence in depth, and scorched earth have made all the military text books just museum lumber. What I have in mind is the change that has been worked in the war's objectives. When it began two years ago we realized that we were fighting for our self-preservation, for our homeland and the Commonwealth, for the maintenance of our liberties, our traditions, our culture, our own ways of life. But by degrees we are coming to stand for something greater even than self-preservation. Our war aims have now a positive ring. Only the other day they were put down on paper when Mr. Roosevelt and Mr. Churchill met somewhere in the broad Atlantic.

The years since the last war have been filled with disillusion and disappointment. We had such high hopes of the world to which we were returning from the trenches and the high seas. We thought the politicians meant it when they orated about " homes for heroes " and " an England fit for heroes to live in." We thought that " No more war " was not just a pious aspiration. We thought that the League of Nations was something more than an imposing palace on Lake Geneva . . . We were deceived, and great was the reaction to our disillusionment.

Now, however, there is a new spirit abroad in the world. Once again we dare to hope. Once again we talk of a new world, and think that it may be worth while to turn our attention to planning it, since we may have an opportunity of building it. Under the stress and strain of totalitarian aggression a new " freedom front " is painfully being brought to birth, and in its construction, in the re-orientation of our wartime purpose, the yeoman's part has been played by Franklin Roosevelt. If the world is ever to live at peace, he has told us, then we must have freedom of speech and expression, freedom to worship God in our own way, and freedom from fear, but we must also have—and here he strikes the note which Mill omitted in his classic exposition—freedom from want. In the light of that hope surely even those of us who have no more illusions left to lose, can find inspiration and encouragement when we go out to meet all that the third year of war may bring.

DO YOU REMEMBER THIS? Hardly had Mr. Chamberlain told us that we were at war with "the evil things" when the policemen rode through the streets warning us to take cover. Only two years ago! *Photo, Topical Press*

E. Royston Pike

Few German Raiders Get Through to Moscow

NAZI PLANE brought down near Moscow being inspected by foreign journalists. More than a hundred others have met a similar fate near the Soviet capital.

A.A. GUN in action during a German raid on the Russian city, where defences against the night-flying Hun are remarkably effective, in guns, fighters and all departments of A.R.P. Highly trained and brave men and women are reducing the danger of night-bombing to a minimum.

Salvaging pieces of a Heinkel 111 which hit a barrage balloon cable and crashed into the Moskva River (left). The Germans are finding it very difficult to get through Moscow's A.A. fire. On one occasion they announced that 500 raiders had attacked Moscow, but, in fact, not one was able to get over the city.

In the photograph beneath, a member of the Moscow A.R.P. stands silhouetted against the beam of a searchlight.

A MOSCOW SCHOOL after it had received a direct hit in the course of a German air raid. On the right of the photograph may be seen members of the city's A.R.P. searching the debris.

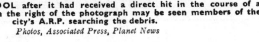

Photos, Associated Press, Planet News

Western Russia: Europe's Eastern War Zone

Specially drawn for THE WAR ILLUSTRATED by D. Dalton

After Two Months: The Russians at Bay

*" The first two months of the war," claimed Moscow on August 22, " prove that the Red Army
is not only not destroyed but its powers of resistance are increasing with each day of the war."
But, nevertheless, the weeks of terrible strain and loss had left their mark, and (as we show here)
the situation of the armies of our gallant ally gave occasion for considerable anxiety.*

"NINE weeks ago today," said Mr.
Churchill in his broadcast on
Sunday, August 24, " Hitler hurled
millions of soldiers upon the neighbour he had
called his friend. ' Let Russia be blotted out !
Let Russia be destroyed ! Order the armies
to advance ! '—such were his decrees.
Accordingly, from the Arctic Ocean to the
Black Sea six or seven millions of soldiers
are locked in mortal struggle."

" Ah, but this time it was not so easy,"
went on the Premier. " This time it was not
all one way. The Russian armies and all the
peoples of the Russian Republic have rallied
to the defence of their hearths and homes.
For the first time Nazi blood has flowed in
a fearful flood. Certainly a million and a
half, perhaps two millions, of Nazi cannon-
fodder have bitten the dust of the endless
plains of Russia. The tremendous battle
rages along nearly 2,000 miles of front. The
Russians fight with magnificent devotion.
The aggressor is surprised, startled, staggered;
for the first time in his experience mass
murder has become unprofitable."

Then Mr. Churchill went on to say that
our generals who had visited the Russian
front line had expressed their admiration of
the efficiency of the Russian military organization and the excellence of their equipment.
The next day there was published a statement made by one of the generals in question,
Lt.-Gen. F. N. Mason Macfarlane, of the
British Military Mission sent to Moscow.
He told a press conference that he had just
seen a counter-attack by a Soviet division
in the Smolensk region. " The division I
saw in action," he said, " was obviously
well trained, full of fight, and was fighting
well. The men looked very good, hardened
and well-fed. I was impressed by the most
efficient cooperation of all arms—infantry,

artillery, tanks, field-guns and air force, and
also by the smooth organization of supply."

For two months Hitler's gigantic armies
had been battering at the Russian front.
That front still stood unbroken in spite of
all the Nazi claims. Leningrad, Moscow, and
Kiev were still intact. But, all the same, the
Germans had scored indisputable successes.
They had overrun all the recently-acquired
provinces of Russia, and had even made
considerable inroads into the main body of
the Soviet Union. On each of the three great
fronts the situation seemed full of menace
for the defenders.

In the north the Germans and their Finnish
allies were drawing closer to Leningrad.
Narva and Kingisep had fallen, and on
August 25 the Russians admitted the evacuation of Novgorod ; the next day the Russians
announced that the enemy were at the city's
approaches. But in front of the advancing
Germans lay a solid fortified region 50 miles
deep, constituting one of the strongest fortresses in the world and defended by a well-
trained and splendidly-equipped army of at
least a million men. Dr. Goebbels's propaganda machine threatened that Leningrad
would be " ground to rubble " by the
Luftwaffe, and bade the Russians remember
the fate of Warsaw. But in the city there was
never a suggestion of surrender. Most of the
noncombatants had been evacuated months
before, and those who remained toiled in
improving the city's defences and men and
women alike shouldered rifles and took their
places in the line beside the garrison. They
were nerved to do and die by a stirring
proclamation from Marshal Voroshilov
issued on August 20.

" The enemy is attempting to penetrate into
Leningrad," he said. " But this will not be.
Leningrad has never been and never will be in
the hands of the enemy. He will never set foot
in our beautiful city . . . Women, inspire your
husbands, your sons and brothers. Young men,
join the detachments for defence. Workers and
engineers, work for the defence of the country,
the defence of your own city. Increase the production of munitions and arms. Let us all rise
up in the defence of our city, our children,
freedom and honour." In answer to the Marshal's
appeal, a wave of revolutionary fervour spread
through the city which was the birthplace of the
Soviets, and " Leningrad can take it " became
the slogan of the indomitable multitude.

In the central sector there was little change
to report. The German drive beyond
Smolensk had slackened, and there were
reports that the Nazis were digging in. This
did not suit the Russian book, however, and
Marshal Timoshenko launched a series of
vigorous counter-attacks which not only
disturbed the German plans but succeeded
in wresting from them a number of villages.
One of these counter-attacks was directed
by General Koniev, whose troops routed a
German infantry division, killing at least
3,000 officers and men and destroying 130
tanks and a large number of guns, lorries
and ammunition. This gallant action was
recognized in a special Order of the Day by
Marshal Timoshenko, in which the units
concerned were congratulated on having
" inflicted a major defeat on the enemy."

Timoshenko's counter-attacks were dictated at least in part by the desire to relieve
the pressure on Budenny's armies to the
south, and also to do something to retrieve
the situation arising from Von Bock's break
through at Gomel, east of the Pripet Marshes.
Von Bock's aim obviously was to separate
Timoshenko from Budenny, and if he did
not succeed in this, at least the way lay open

The Eastern front from Kexholm in the north
to Nikolayev, Nikopol and Dniepropetrovsk in
the Ukraine, showing the progress of German
drives up to August 23. Note the all-import-
ant bridges across the Lower Dnieper.

for a march south along the right bank of
the river in the direction of Kiev. Much
more dangerous was the situation to the south
of Kiev, where Von Rundstedt was making
very rapid progress. Maybe Budenny was
out-generalled, but at least his retreat was
generally considered to have been masterly
in the circumstances. Odessa was left behind
as a strongly-defended fortress, and the
Germans soon claimed that it was surrounded
and that their troops had occupied the Black
Sea ports of Nikolayev and Kherson lying
beyond it. There was talk of a stand on the
River Bug, but the Germans still advanced ;
very soon they had penetrated into and overrun the highly-industrialized region of Krivoi
Rog in the bend of the Dnieper. Budenny,
still retreating, managed to get a very large
proportion of his troops across the Dnieper,
here a wide-flowing river with but four bridges
beyond the two at Kiev : at Cherkassy,
Kremenchug, Dniepropetrovsk, and Zapor-
ozhye. The Germans strove their utmost to
hamper his retreat, and claimed to have
successfully dive-bombed the vital bridges,
and to have taken Dniepropetrovsk. From
various sources came the news that the
Russians had destroyed the famous
Dnieper dam near Zaporozhe and blown
up the power-station, and this was confirmed
from Moscow on August 28th.

SOVIET GUERILLAS, secretly known as L. and
Senior Lieut. T., in command of Unit X. These
men, typical of thousands, have done valiant
work in wrecking railways, enemy tanks and
transport. Note the sub-machine-gun in
Lieut. T.'s hand.　　　　*Photo Planet News*

War's Tide Reaches Russia's Monster Dam

A general view of the town of Zaporozhe (above), where the workers at Dnieproges, the great hydro-electric station, live. Fine tenements and scientific town-planning are the pride of modern Russia, as also are such engineering works as the Dnieper Dam (top photograph), which provides the power for one of the greatest hydro-electric plants in the world. Spanning the river for half a mile, the dam provides a generating capacity of 900,000 h.p., and most of the industries in the Dnieper valley are dependent upon it.

A soldier-compositor setting type for one of the Soviet Army's news-sheets which are circulated regularly among the troops. On the right, a Nazi officer's car trying to pass through a Russian town where heavy rains have turned the road into a quagmire. The violent struggle for the industrial Ukraine is taxing the Nazi armies to their utmost. In a desperate effort to control the Dnieper bridgeheads the Germans claimed to have captured Dniepropetrovsk, the great steel city north of the dam. on August 25.   *Photos, Planet News and Keystone*

How Yugoslavia Upset Hitler's Time-Table

Yugoslavia's resistance against the Nazis was crushed in a campaign of 12 days, and the country was overrun by Hitler's hordes. Yet her stand was not in vain, as is made clear in this article, which takes its inspiration from a broadcast by General Simovitch, the Yugoslav Prime Minister, now in England, to his people on June 27, 1941.

WHEN last spring dawned the Balkans must have made a very satisfactory picture in Hitler's eyes. Rumania was in the occupation of German troops, and General Antonescu, the head of the Rumanian Government, was nothing more than the Fuehrer's puppet. Yugoslavia was on very friendly terms with the Reich, as was seen on March 25 when Premier Tsvetkovitch signed the Vienna Pact which bound his country to the Axis. Bulgaria was already a member of the Axis family, and, like Rumania, was filled with German troops ; it was destined, indeed, by Hitler to be the jumping-off ground for his next act of aggression in Europe.

The German Army in the Balkans was under the command of Field-Marshal List. The plan of campaign was as brilliantly conceived as it was carefully prepared for. Its general shape has now been revealed by General Simovitch, former Chief of the Yugoslav Air Force, who on March 28 captained the coup d'état which resulted in the overthrow of Tsvetkovitch and his pro-Nazi friends and the establishment in his place of a pro-Ally Government under General Simovitch himself (see pages 362 and 386, Volume 4).

" There is some evidence based on the disposition of troops," said General Simovitch in his broadcast to the Yugoslav people, " that Germany intended to conquer Turkey in April, and to create there a base for a further attack first in a southern direction against Suez, and later to the north against Russia in the direction of the Caucasus, coordinating this latter move with a frontal attack from Rumania and Poland against the Ukraine and Central Russia."

The ground had been well prepared. Turkey, so the Germans considered, would not fight if she were attacked. Russia was still Germany's friend, and the time had not yet come to disillusion her. Syria was in the hands of Vichy France, and day by day was receiving more Axis agents who were preparing the ground for a large-scale invasion by Nazi air-borne troops. Then in Iraq pro-Nazi Raschid Ali had organized a rebellion timed for April 3, which, we may now presume, was the date when the Germans intended to be on the march through Turkey. This march was to start from Bulgaria, where List had his main army close to the Turkish frontier, opposite Adrianople.

Another German force was in the southwest of Bulgaria, well placed for an advance against Salonika to the south.

This, then, was in Hitler's mind. Already he must have seen in imagination his armies sweeping southwards into Greece (thus by-passing the great fortress of Adrianople), through European Turkey to the Straits, and then across them along the Anatolian coast or across the Black Sea in Rumanian and Bulgarian ships to the Caucasus. Information in the possession of General Simovitch leads us to suppose that the campaign was to be launched between March 15 and April 1, and was to be completed in from six weeks to two months.

But a hitch developed, and a very serious one. On the night of March 27-28 General Simovitch seized power in Belgrade, and List was quick to realize that now he had on his right flank not a friendly power but a definitely hostile one. Wasting no time, he switched his main army across Bulgaria and on April 6 invaded Yugoslavia and struck south against Salonika. The Yugoslavs, fighting with their traditional bravery but hopelessly outnumbered, were speedily compelled to capitulate, since they were invaded at one and the same time by Italians from the west, Hungarians and Germans from the

north, and Germans and Bulgarians from the east. After 12 days organized resistance was at an end. But fighting went on in Greece until June 1, when the last of the British troops were withdrawn from Crete.

The ground might now seem to have been cleared for the prosecution of Hitler's plan, but much valuable time had been lost. The Iraq rising had been crushed, and on June 8 Syria was invaded by Wilson's army. The situation, in a word, had been transformed.

Another fortnight, and Hitler launched his attack on Russia. His new plan was but a ghost of the old. Originally (so General Simovitch surmises, seemingly with good reason) Hitler had planned that the advance through the Ukraine should be timed to coincide with the one through Turkey in the direction of the Caucasus. At the same time another German army was to be sent across Turkey into Iran to invade Russia by way of the east side of the Caspian Sea. If this pincer movement had been carried out, then Russian resistance might well have been hamstrung. Nor was this all. These strokes were to be accompanied by an advance of General Rommel's army in Libya through Egypt to the Suez Canal, there to join up with another German army, which should march southward from Turkey, through Syria, Iraq and Palestine.

Such was the plan, but, as we have seen, there was a hitch. General Simovitch's action in overturning the pro-Nazi government in Yugoslavia upset Hitler's time-table. Several precious weeks had to be spent in crushing the resistance of the Yugoslavs and the Greeks, supported by our own Forces of the Empire. Yugoslavia, by her dramatic reversal of policy on May 28, saved her soul. She also did much to save the situation for the Allies in the Near East. That must not be forgotten.

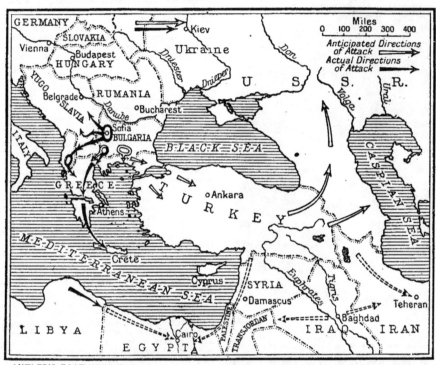

HITLER'S EASTWARD PLAN, the time-table for which was upset by Yugoslavia's unexpected resistance, is illustrated in this map. According to Gen. Simovitch, Hitler had planned a double pincer movement: the northern arm was to advance through Turkey and the Ukraine, while the southern arm of the pincer was to take the form of an advance from Libya.   *Courtesy of " The Times"*

M. Ninchitch, left, Foreign Minister of the Yugoslav Government now in Britain, and Gen. Simovitch, the Prime Minister and C.-in-C. of the Yugoslav army.   *Photo, Associated Press*

Our Searchlight on the War

A NEW LEG BY PARACHUTE

WING CMDR. D. R. BADER, D.S.O., one of the most indomitable airmen in the R.A.F., was reported on August 14 to have baled out of his burning plane and to be now a prisoner of war. This famous pilot, who had lost both his legs in 1933 at an air pageant rehearsal, badgered the authorities, when war broke out, into giving him a flying test, and passed it brilliantly. He led the Canadian Squadron of Fighter Command in the Battle of Britain, and shot down at least 15 German machines. More recently he had played a prominent part in the daylight sweeps over Northern France. It was

SOUND LOCATOR, for finding people trapped under debris, is the invention of a Brighton man, Mr. R. Moore. The locator enables the trapped to hear the voices of the rescue squad, and they in turn can hear sounds of the victims below them. The horn is of special composition ; rescuers speak through a microphone and listen through earphones.
Photo, Hamlin, Brighton

stated that one of Bader's metal legs was damaged when he baled out, so on August 19 one of the "spares" he kept at his air station was dropped from a plane of an R.A.F. squadron flying over enemy territory to bomb a distant target.

DE GAULLE'S AERIAL FLAGSHIP

PILOTED by Mr. J. H. Mollison to Brazzaville, French Equatorial Africa, the "Flying Wing" has arrived safely after a journey of 6,500 miles over sea and jungle, much of which was flown at night in order to avoid Vichy and

Axis aircraft. This is an experimental aeroplane of unusual design, destined to transport Free French officers and military mail to distant parts of the great wilderness extending from the Congo watershed to the edge of the Libyan desert. Col. Pierre Carettier, commander of the Free French Air Force in Africa, and his staff made a test flight in this remarkable plane, in which passengers and freight are accommodated not in the fuselage but in the wings.

PROTECTION FOR TANKER CREWS

AFTER consultation with the representatives of tanker companies, the Ministry of War Transport has adopted a plan whereby the crews of British tankers proceeding within danger areas are to be supplied with a special garment designed to protect them against burning oil. This one-piece garment is made of light, flame-proof fabric, and consists of a cape, gauntlets and a hood with eye-piece of mica ; it is intended for the protection of face and hands while boats are being launched. The hull of each lifeboat, the mast, oars, canvas hood and sail cover, are to be fireproofed, and the boats are to be equipped with a manual bilge pump adapted for spraying water.

DOUBLE AIR TRAGEDY

ON August 10 a transoceanic aircraft flew into a hillside shortly after taking off from a British airport, and all the passengers and crew, totalling 22, were killed. They included several pilots and radio operators engaged in ferrying American aircraft across the Atlantic for the R.A.F., and there were nine Americans among them. All were buried with naval honours on August 15, the mourners being fortunately unaware that an almost identical disaster had taken place the night before. Again a transatlantic aircraft crashed within a minute of taking off for a flight to Canada, and, as before, the 22 passengers and crew lost their lives. Among them was Mr. Arthur Purvis, chairman of the British Supply Council in North America and well known as head of the British Purchasing Commission. This distinguished Canadian had been responsible for the supply of well over £500,000,000 worth of aircraft, arms and supplies.

'VOLUNTEERS' AGAINST RUSSIA

BELGIUM has been recently combed for recruits " to fight Communism," but despite all their propagandist efforts the Germans were only able to muster about 1,000 Flemish nationals and 900 French-speaking Fascists (Rexists) willing to take up arms for Hitler. Leon Degrelle, leader of the Rexist party, presented the volunteers with the flag of the old Dukes of Burgundy—which suggests that some Flemish extremists look to the creation of a State which would comprise Holland, Belgium, Alsace and adjacent parts of Switzerland.

ANGLO-SOVIET PLEDGE TO TURKEY

DECLARATIONS were presented at the Turkish Foreign Office in Ankara by the British and Soviet Ambassadors on August 10. They were to the effect that both Governments had no claims whatever with regard to the Dardanelles, that they were " prepared scrupulously to observe the territorial integrity of the Turkish Republic," and, while fully appreciating the desire of the Turkish Government not to be involved in the war, they " would nevertheless be prepared to render Turkey every help and assistance in the event of her being

NORWEGIANS ESCAPE to England very frequently through the offices of a vast underground Escape Club which helps those desiring to do so to reach this country. This is called " taking the Shetland bus." Among those who have taken the risk are Nelley, a 26-year-old nurse, and Nils, junior house physician in a hospital on the Norwegian coast. They are now engaged, and work in a Norwegian hospital in London. *Photo, Keystone*

attacked by a European Power." The Declarations were warmly received and should do much to reassure Turkey as to her neutrality and her independence, while also making more remote the possibility of her country becoming a battle-ground in the present struggle.

WE LAND GOODS AT TANGIER

NO British freighter had unloaded at Tangier from the moment of the collapse of France until August 13, when a merchant ship arrived with a cargo of green tea, soap and other supplies. The Italian colony demanded to know how the ship had been able to slip through the Axis blockade. Irritated German residents watched in silence the goods being discharged on to the quays. But the Moorish and Spanish population welcomed the supplies with pleasure and with outspoken disbelief in the Axis propaganda which still tries to spread the legend of starvation in England.

AFTER-THE-RAID PLANS

THE Minister of Health, Mr. Ernest Brown, has been making a special drive to bring all target areas up to a higher standard of preparedness against air attack. In June there were about 10,000 Rest Centres in England and Wales, with accommodation for well over a million people, who will find there food, a place to sleep, help and advice ; but this provision should be doubled, and local authorities are setting about the task of acquiring or erecting suitable buildings which the Ministry of Health will then equip with furniture, crockery, etc. In addition to this, Mr. Brown is anxious that individual families should make a " mutual-aid pact " with friends or relatives living in another part of the town, if possible not nearer than half a mile. If one family is bombed out, members can go straight to the other house.

THE FLYING WING, piloted to Brazzaville by J. H. Mollison, is an aircraft of revolutionary design, passengers and freight being carried in the centre section of the wing. The aircraft is powered by two 870 h.p. Bristol Perseus engines. *Photo, British Official: Crown Copyright*

Wren's Masterpiece Revealed by War's Havoc

ST. PAUL'S CATHEDRAL, now that the raid-damaged buildings in the vicinity have been cleared away, is more visible from the southern side than ever before in its history.   Originally Sir Christopher Wren had planned a colonnade to enclose a large piazza forming a clear space around the church, but the value of City sites militated against this proposal.   When London is rebuilt, will Wren's original idea be reconsidered, so that the City's proud cathedral can at last be given a proper setting ?

Photo, Keystone

Britain and Russia Take Action Against Iran

Just as in April British troops were landed in Iraq to destroy the nest of Nazi intriguers, and in June invaded Syria to counter the menace deriving from the presence of Axis agents, so in August Britain—but this time acting in close conjunction with Soviet Russia—sent an army into Iran. For once Hitler was forestalled.

THE first news of the invasion of Iran was given by Moscow radio at 1 a.m. on August 26 : " Soviet troops crossed the Iranian frontier early yesterday morning and are moving in the direction of Ardebel and Tabriz. They have covered twenty-eight miles and the advance continues."

The trouble which thus came to a head had long been simmering. For many months past Nazi influence in Iran had been all too obviously on the increase. Large numbers of German " tourists " were reported to be arriving in the country, and many of those Axis agents who, when Britain took action in Iraq, found it advisable to flee the country, made for Teheran—prominent among them being Herr Grobba, former German minister in Baghdad. Then there were also numbers of German technicians who had succeeded in occupying most of the key-positions in the Iranian railways, air-routes, and such important industries as spinning and sugar-production. The numbers of these German immigrants were estimated at from 500 to 5,000. Then the Iranian intelligentsia were reputed to be of Nazi sympathies since many of them had received their technical education in Germany, and had brought back with them German wives.

The presence of so many Germans in Iran was seen to constitute a direct menace not only to the British oil interests in the country —the interests on which the financial stability of Iran depends, indeed its continued existence as a modern state—but also to India and to the Russian oil fields in the Caucasus. This last menace became particularly marked following Hitler's onslaught on the Soviets.

So it was that representations were made to the Shah, Riza Khan Pahlevi, that extraordinary figure who has endeavoured to repeat in Persia the achievements of Mustapha Kemal in Turkey. He was asked to send the German " tourists " and technicians home, but the representations and the warnings which accompanied them went unheeded. A few Germans were indeed sent out of the country, but only a mere handful. At last the situation had grown so acute that it could be tolerated no longer, and at 4 a.m. on August 25, Sir Reader Bullard, the British minister in Teheran, and his Soviet colleague, Mr. Smirnoff, called on the Iranian Prime Minister, Ali Mansur, and presented what the last-named described as " threatening memoranda," notifying him that the British and Soviet forces were already crossing the frontier.

Iran. At the same time they stressed that they had no intentions whatever against Iranian territorial integrity or national independence. The military measures taken were against the danger created by the activities of Germans in Iran, and as soon as this danger

RIZA KHAN PAHLEVI rose from a private soldier of the Persian Cossack Brigade to be dictator and Shah of Iran in 1925.

IRAN, formerly Persia, which was entered by the British and Soviet troops on August 25, thereby forestalling a Nazi coup d'état to take control of the country. The Russians marched through the Caucasus, the British advancing from the south. On the right, an oil field at Baku, chief centre of the Russian oil industry.   *Photos, Planet News: Map by courtesy of " News Chronicle"*

GEN. SIR A. WAVELL (right), Commander-in-Chief of the British Forces in India, some of whom are operating in Iran. He is chatting with Sir Hugh Dow, Governor of Sind. *Assoc. Press*

Within a few hours the text of the Russian note was broadcast from Moscow, and it was found to contain the most circumstantial details of the German penetration of Iran. A number of Germans were mentioned by name, and they were accused of having organized " tourist " groups in Baku, and to be preparing a military coup d'état in Iran itself. The German Legation in Teheran was stated to have organized armed bands in certain frontier districts in Iran, sending them to Baku and to other particularly important Soviet centres with the object of sabotage on Soviet territory. German agents, the note went on, had munition dumps at their disposal at different places in Iran, particularly in the north ; and under cover of hunting parties they had created near Teheran a military training course for their accomplices. " In their criminal activities these Germans grossly disregarded the elementary demand for respect of the territorial sovereignty of Iran by transforming Iranian territory into an arena for preparation for military invasion of the Soviet Union."

So the Soviet Union and Britain had found it necessary to take military action against

was averted the troops would be withdrawn.

The British troops invading Iran were part of General Wavell's command in India. The first communiqué describing their progress was issued from Simla on August 26.

It stated : " British and Indian troops entered Iran at three points early on Monday morning (August 25). Naval and air cooperation enabled the landing of a force at Abadan and a small detachment of Indian troops also secured Bandar Shapur (Persian Gulf), where there were two damaged German ships and three Italian ships only slightly damaged. Two further German ships which had been beached were captured with their crews. Steps were taken by air-borne troops to give protection to British families in the employ of the Anglo-Iranian Oil Company. British and Indian troops, including infantry and armoured units, advanced simultaneously into Iran from Khanaqin (Iraq). The oil installation at Naft-i-Shah and the small town of Qasr-i-Shirin were occupied without serious opposition. Leaflets were dropped by R.A.F. bombers on Teheran and other towns explaining the reasons for the operations and stressing that we have no quarrel with the Iranian people and no designs on their independence or territory."

Then on August 29th came the news that Teheran had asked for an armistice.

HIGH DRAMA on the HIGH SEAS

A Pictured Record of the Churchill-Roosevelt Meeting

ON August 14 the world learned from Mr. Attlee's broadcast that the two great leaders of Democracy had met and drawn up an 8-point Anglo-American Declaration.

Amplifying the facts of this historic meeting, Mr. Churchill stated in his broadcast on August 24 "There are two distinct and marked differences in this joint declaration from the attitude adopted by the Allies during the latter part of the last war, and no one should overlook them. The United States and Great Britain do not now assume that there will never be any more war again. . . . We intend to take ample precautions to prevent its renewal in any period we can foresee by effectively disarming the guilty nations while remaining suitably protected ourselves.

"The second difference is this : That instead of trying to ruin German trade by all kinds of additional trade barriers and hindrances, as was the mood in 1917, we have definitely adopted the view that it is not in the interests of the world and of our two countries that any large nation should be unprosperous or shut out from the means of making a decent living for itself and its people by its industry and enterprise."

H.M.S. PRINCE OF WALES, Britain's new 35,000-ton battleship, aboard which Mr. Winston Churchill and President Roosevelt had one of their historic meetings. On the left, Admiral Sir Dudley Pound, General Sir John Dill, the Premier, and Air Chief Marshal Sir Wilfrid Freeman confer in the admiral's quarters on the Prince of Wales.

In the photograph beneath, President Roosevelt is seen arriving aboard the Prince of Wales with his son, Captain Elliott Roosevelt. He is shaking hands with the Commander of the ship, Captain J. C. Leach, M.V.O., R.N. The Prime Minister is standing between the two British naval officers on the left. Coming along the gangway is Mr. Sumner Welles, U.S. Under-Secretary of State.

Photos, British Official: Crown Copyright

Beneath, President Roosevelt engages Mr. Churchill in earnest conv
On the right, Divine Service aboard H.M.S. Prince of Wales ; Mr.
and the President are seated in front.   Behind them, numbered l
Captain Elliott Roosevelt, Ensign Franklin Roosevelt, Gen. Arnol
Mr. Sumner Welles, Mr. Harry Hopkins, Lord Cherwell (Prof. Lin
Mr. Averill Harriman, Major Gen. E. M. Watson (U.S.),
Air Chief Marshal Sir W. Freeman, Adm. King(U.S.), Gen.
G. Marshall (U.S.), Gen. Sir John Dill, Adm. Stark (U.S.).

MR. CHURCHILL GREETS
MR. ROOSEVELT (top left)
as, on the arm of his son
Captain Elliott Roosevelt, he
comes aboard the Prince of
Wales. On the left, the
Prime Minister visits the
President on the American
cruiser Augusta and hands
him a personal letter from
King George. The meeting,
which took place somewhere
in the Atlantic, symbolized
the increasing strength of
the Democracies. It sealed
the entente between the
Anglo-Saxon peoples.

BRITISH AND U.S. CHIEFS on board H.M.S. Prince of Wales.   Left to right, Air Chief Marshal Sir W. Freeman, Gen. Arnold (Chief of
Air Staff, U.S.), Adm. Stark (U.S. Naval Operations Chief), Adm. Sir Dudley Pound, Adm. King (Commander of U.S. Atlantic Fleet),
Gen. G. Marshall (U.S. Army Chief of Staff), Gen. Sir John Dill, Adm. Turner (Dep. Chief of U.S. Naval Staff).   On the right, U.S.
seaplanes flying over the ship during Divine Service.

Photos, British Official : Crown Copyright

Mr. Churchill, at the rail of H.M.S. Prince of Wales, watches the departure of the U.S. destroyer McDougal with President Roosevelt aboard. Below right, the Prime Minister, with Mrs. Churchill, on his arrival back in London on August 19.

Photos, British Official and L.N.A.

THE 'ATLANTIC CHARTER'
The Anglo-American Declaration of August 1941

The President of the United States and the Prime Minister, Mr. Churchill, representing his Majesty's Government in the United Kingdom, being met together, deem it right to make known certain common principles in the national policies of their respective countries on which they base their hopes for a better future for the world.

First, their countries seek no aggrandizement, territorial or other.

Second, they desire to see no territorial changes that do not accord with the freely expressed wishes of the peoples concerned.

Third, they respect the right of all peoples to choose the form of government under which they will live ; and they wish to see sovereign rights and self-government restored to those who have been forcibly deprived of them.

Fourth, they will endeavour, with due respect for their existing obligations, to further the enjoyment by all States, great or small, victor or vanquished, of access, on equal terms, to the trade and to the raw materials of the world which are needed for their economic prosperity.

Fifth, they desire to bring about the fullest collaboration between all nations in the economic field, with the object of securing for all improved labour standards, economic advancement and social security.

Sixth, after the final destruction of Nazi tyranny, they hope to see established a peace which will afford to all nations the means of dwelling in safety within their own boundaries, and which will afford assurance that all the men in all the lands may live out their lives in freedom from fear and want.

Seventh, such a peace should enable all men to traverse the high seas and oceans without hindrance.

Eighth, they believe all the nations of the world, for realistic as well as spiritual reasons, must come to the abandonment of the use of force. Since no future peace can be maintained if land, sea or air armaments continue to be employed by nations which threaten, or may threaten aggression outside of their frontiers, they believe, pending the establishment of a wider and permanent system of social security, that the disarmament of such nations is essential. They will likewise aid and encourage all other practicable measures which will lighten for peace-loving peoples the crushing burden of armaments.

Announced by Mr. Attlee, as Deputy Prime Minister, over the wireless on August 14, 1941

New Bombers for Britain's New Squadrons

Off to attack enemy shipping in the Channel, one of the latest type Blenheims is seen (circle) just after taking off, with the under-carriage being retracted. Above, a Leading Aircraftman examines the 500-lb. bombs in the racks of a Blenheim.   *Photos, Associated Press and Sport & General*

EVERY day more and more new bombers are coming off the assembly lines as British industry gathers still greater momentum. As they leave the factories they are sent to a maintenance pool where they are fitted with their armament and bomb racks. They are then allocated to a particular bomber group, and eventually reach the squadrons who are to fly them. Though spick and span when it reaches the squadron, the new bomber soon loses its shining brightness under a coat of dull paint. Then on the nose is painted the crew's own badge, the choice of which is left to the captain of the aircraft, and on the fuselage is painted the squadron and flight number. It receives no further decoration until it has made its first attack—then a little yellow bomb is painted on the fuselage. As the new bombers arrive the old ones are handed over to a new crew, which has not yet done any operational-flying, and the experienced crews take over the new machines. But they don't, as a rule, look forward to this ; they have become attached to their old familiar bomber.

Laden with miscellaneous equipment, including "Mae West" and parachute, this R.A.F. sergeant hurries from the briefing room to jump into his plane for another Channel sweep.

Right, one of the new Stirling bombers encounters enemy "flak" as it draws near to the French coast. The Short Stirling is a giant bomber with four 14-cylinder engines. It weighs 35 tons and can carry more than four tons of bombs.

Our Diary of the War

SUNDAY, AUG. 17, 1941   715th day

Air.—Main night objectives were port of Bremen and industrial districts at Duisburg.

Russian Front.—Germans claimed capture of Black Sea port of Nikolaiev and town of Nikopol. Russians reported fighting all along front and much air activity.

Africa.—Considerable enemy bombing at Tobruk. British patrols continued offensive.

Mediterranean.—During night of Aug. 16-17 Fleet Air Arm successfuly attacked harbour at Syracuse and barracks at Cape Passero.

Home.—Single enemy aircraft dropped bombs at point near S.E. coast of Scotland. Night raid on Hull. One enemy bomber destroyed.

MONDAY, AUG. 18   716th day

Sea.—Admiralty announced that H.M. minesweeper No. 39 had been sunk.

Air.—Day attack on Lille. Three enemy patrol vessels sunk off Dutch coast.

Night attacks on Cologne and Duisburg. Other forces bombed Dunkirk docks and enemy airfields.

Russian Front.—Russian forces in Western Ukraine continued to retreat in good order across R. Dnieper. Germans believed to have renewed offensive against Leningrad.

Africa.—Benghazi and Tripoli heavily raided on night of 17-18.

In Wolchefit, Debarech and Gondar areas of Abyssinia aircraft of R.A.F. and S.A.A.F. continuously attacked enemy positions.

Mediterranean.—Attempt by large force of German fighters to attack shipping off Egyptian coast beaten off by R.A.F.

During night of 17-18 Fleet Air Arm attacked enemy convoy; one vessel sunk, tanker fired, second freighter hit and later set on fire.

Home.—Small-scale night raids on east coast of England and Scotland.

TUESDAY, AUG. 19   717th day

Sea.—Admiralty announced that H.M. submarine Cachalot must be considered lost.

Air.—Day attacks on shipping in Ostend harbour, railway yards at Hazebrouck, and shipping off Dutch coast. Night raids on Kiel and occupied aerodromes.

Russian Front.—Moscow reported stubborn fighting along whole front, including Novgorod area. Kingisepp (Yamburg), 70 miles south-west of Leningrad, evacuated. Successful counter-attacks near Smolensk.

Germans claimed to have occupied all country west of R. Dnieper except Odessa and some bridgeheads.

Africa.—Tripoli harbour heavily bombed during night of 18-19.

Home.—Few bombs fell at night near east and south-east coasts. One raider destroyed.

WEDNESDAY, AUG. 20   718th day

Air.—Day raid on Dutch aerodrome.

Russian Front.—German three-pronged offensive continued. Leningrad now seriously threatened. In centre Russians reported fierce fighting near Gomel. Germans claimed success in attacks on Dnieper bridgeheads.

Africa.—Night attack on Benghazi.

Mediterranean.—R.A.F. attacked Syracuse harbour; three balloons shot down in flames and a number of seaplanes damaged.

General.—Mr. Mackenzie King, Canadian Premier, arrived in England for discussions. On Aug. 19 and 20 10,000 Jews were arrested in Paris.

THURSDAY, AUG. 21   719th day

Air.—Three day attacks; one on iron and steel works at Ymuiden, Holland, two on industrial targets and railways in St. Omer and Bethune areas. E-boats in Channel bombed.

Russian Front.—Germans claimed to have captured Novgorod, Kingisepp and Narva, south of Leningrad, and Kherson, at mouth of Dnieper. Russians evacuated Gomel.

Africa.—Day attacks on enemy landing-grounds at Gambut and Menastir.

Home.—Few night raiders dropped bombs near east coast. One destroyed.

FRIDAY, AUG. 22   720th day

Air.—Two enemy fighters destroyed during R.A.F. patrols over Channel and French coast. Heinkel shot down off east coast.

Night attacks on Mannheim, harbour at Le Havre, docks at Ostend and Dunkirk, and many aerodromes.

Russian Front.—Moscow reported strong resistance to German offensive in Leningrad sector. Stated that Russian bombers had attacked German transports in Black Sea; two sunk, third set on fire, others damaged.

Africa.—During night of 21-22 R.A.F. dropped 25 tons of bombs on Tripoli.

SATURDAY, AUG. 23   721st day

Russian Front.—Soviet communiqué reported continuous fighting along entire front, and in south claimed to have wiped out Rumanian 15th Division.

Unofficial German reports, later confirmed, stated that Nazi troops were 60 miles east of Gomel and that Cherkasy, on Dnieper south-east of Kiev, had been captured.

Africa.—During night R.A.F. dropped 20 tons of bombs on Tripoli and also attacked encampments at Sollum, Bardia and Gambut.

General.—Owing to activities of revolting Serbs, Italy placed entire Croatian coast under military occupation.

SUNDAY, AUG. 24   722nd day

Sea.—Announced that H.M. trawler Brabant had shot down a Dornier.

H.M. submarine Union overdue and considered lost.

Air.—Daylight offensive patrols over Northern France. Sharp night attack on Düsseldorf.

Russian Front.—Moscow reported fierce battles near Odessa, where 3rd Rumanian Division was annihilated. Russian counter-attacks in region of Gomel. Four German transports sunk in Baltic.

Germans claimed to have forced Russians back in Lake Ilmen area, south of Leningrad, capturing 10,000 prisoners. Great tank battle in progress. Helsinki claimed that Finnish troops had surrounded Viipuri.

Berlin admitted that Russian bombers had destroyed power station at Zaporoje, on R. Dnieper.

Africa.—Heavy night attack on Tripoli.

MONDAY, AUG. 25   723rd day

Sea.—Announced that 14 merchant ships out of British convoy of 21 attacked for four days by U-boats and aircraft had arrived in the Tagus.

Air.—R.A.F. made heavy night raids on Mannheim and Karlsruhe.

Russian Front.—In south Russians continued fighting retreat to Dnieper. Fierce battle near Dniepropetrovsk. Enemy operations against Leningrad-Moscow railway held in check, but Germans claimed that Leningrad was now under artillery fire.

Iran.—British and Russian forces crossed frontier. Imperial troops occupied Abadan and Bandar Shapur on Persian Gulf. At latter, seven Axis ships were captured. Other forces advanced from Khanikin and occupied Qasr-i-Shirin and Naft-i-Shah. Russians advanced towards Tabriz and Ardebil.

TUESDAY, AUG. 26   724th day

Sea.—Admiralty announced loss of H.M. corvette Picotee.

Announced that ex-American destroyer Bath, manned by Norwegian Navy, had been sunk.

Air.—Two convoys attacked off German and Dutch coasts. Two ships sunk; others hit. Large-scale night raid on Cologne. Docks at Le Harve and Boulogne, and enemy aerodromes, also bombed.

Russian Front.—Germans claimed capture of Dniepropetrovsk, west of R. Dnieper. They also claimed to have taken Luga, 90 miles south of Leningrad.

Iran.—British and Russian troops continued to advance, meeting so far only slight resistance. Russians occupied Tabriz, Ardebil, Dilman and Lissar.

Mediterranean.—Announced that naval aircraft had bombed military targets north and south of Tempio, Sardinia. Junkers shot down and Cant floatplane heavily damaged.

Home.—Few bombs fell at night at widely separated places, including Scilly Isles.

General.—War Office announced creation of new East African Command, to be held by Lt.-Gen. Sir William Platt.

CUTTING THE CORN: Land Girls reaping a 400-acre field in Sussex. Said to be the largest wheat plot in England, the field has been brought back to cultivation by the East Sussex County War Agricultural Committee after lying fallow for twenty years.
Photo, Topical Press

They Have Won Honours in Freedom's Cause

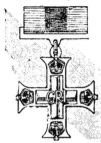

THE MILITARY CROSS

Mrs. Ida Hacker, Rest Centre Service organizer, **B.E.M.,** for gallantry when the Rest Centre was damaged in a raid.

Miss " Biddy " Harris, A.F.S., **B.E.M.,** for aid in rescuing trapped people. She worked for 12 hours in a heavy raid.

Mrs. Mary Fitzgerald, G.M., for carrying on under heavy bombardment after her ambulance had been wrecked.

Miss Joan Hobson, London A.F.S., **B.E.M.,** for improvising a fire pump and playing a hose on a blazing building.

THE MILITARY MEDAL

Pilot Officer K. W. Mackenzie, " Ulster's air ace," **D.F.C.,** for ramming a Messerschmitt and sending it crashing into the sea.

Flt.-Lt. R. E. Hunter, No. 240 Squadron, **D.F.C.,** for bravery on important duties, often involving long flights in adverse weather conditions.

Air Vice-Marshal F. H. M. Maynard, A.F.C., **C.B.,** in recognition of his services as Air Officer commanding R.A.F., Mediterranean.

Flt.-Lt. J. E. H. Marshall, D.F.C., for gallant services in the Middle East. Before the war he was a member of the Stoke-on-Trent Police Force.

Rev. S. W. Harrison, R.A.F. chaplain, **G.M.,** for rescuing members of the crew of a blazing aircraft in circumstances of great danger.

Flt.-Sergeant G. P. Jones, No. 77 Squadron, **D.F.M.,** for devotion to duty in the execution of air operations. He is a wireless operator air gunner.

Flt.-Lt. P. H. M. Richey, No. 609 Squadron, **D.F.C.,** for skill and coolness on operational missions. He has destroyed at least 9 enemy aircraft.

Ldg. Aircraftman C. L. Wheatley, G.M., for climbing under the fuselage of a bomber which caught fire and subduing the flames.

Flying Officer A. Watson, No. 203 Squadron, **D.F.C.,** for rescuing a fellow pilot and his observer during operations in Iraq.

A Wing Commander P. F. Webster, D.F.C. and bar, No. 21 Squadron, **D.S.O.,** for leadership during an attack on Rotterdam docks.

Sergeant Bowen, R.A.F., **D.F.M.,** for bravery on operational missions with a bomber squadron in Syria. He shot down 7 enemy aircraft.

A C I K. E. W. Clifton, D.F.M., for taking over controls of an aircraft over Ramadi when the pilot was shot and bringing the plane safely back.

Harold Dingle, Rescue Party, **G.M.,** for helping to rescue a family trapped in a basement where water was rising.

James Ward, Rescue Party, Stoke Newington, **G.M.,** for the part he played in the same gallant rescue.

Oliver Clarke, Rescue Party, Stoke Newington, **B.E.M.,** for the part he played in this dangerous rescue work.

E. V. Hignett, employee of the Gas Light and Coke Co., **B.E.M.,** for heroism in preventing fires from spreading during a raid.

S. J. Ffitch, employee of the Gas, Light and Coke Co., **B.E.M.,** for tackling and subduing fires during an air raid.

Stanley Pembertny, Plymouth labourer, **G.M.,** for removing a large quantity of cordite from a blazing building.

Edward Hacker, Supervising Officer, L.C.C. Rest Centre, **B.E.M.,** for bravery shown when the Rest Centre was bombed.

Brian Vaughan, 15-year-old Southampton A.R.P. messenger, **B.E.M.,** for rescuing a mother and baby from a ruined house.

Major A. W. Richards, Home Guard, Barking, **O.B.E.,** for gallantry displayed during two heavy air raids.

F. H. Brooks, employee of the Gas, Light and Coke Co., **B.E.M.,** for gallantry in preventing fires from spreading during a raid.

A. H. Lambert, Lambeth Warden, **O.B.E.,** for his heroic rescue work during enemy air raids on his district.

E. W. Clark, G.M., for diving into water under a building to make sure no one was left, after rescuing a woman.

Col. Hedley White, awarded the **D.S.O.,** for meritorious service.

Capt. E. A. W. Williams, who has been awarded the **M.C.**

Capt. F. H. Lawder, Argyll and Sutherland Highlanders, **M.C.**

Lieut. Hugh Campbell, Argyll and Sutherland Highlanders, **M.B.E.**

Major Lorne Campbell, Argyll and Sutherland Highlanders, **D.S.O.**

Sergt. L. E. Waters, R.A., who won the **M.M.** for gallantry in Belgium.

The Why and the How of the Syrian Campaign

In earlier pages we have given a week-to-week account of the war in Syria. Now we are able
to print what may be described as the official story. For the first time the campaign is reviewed
as a whole and—still more interesting—the units engaged in the fighting are named and their
individual contributions to the victory acknowledged.

WE went into Syria on June 8 because the Germans had gone there first. During the troubles in Iraq German aircraft used the Syrian aerodromes as bases for action against our troops on the Euphrates, and German ground staffs, experts, agents and agitators arrived steadily by air. There was a very real possibility that they would be followed by troops in large numbers, and in this case our ally, Turkey, would have been isolated, and our own position in the Middle East jeopardized.

That threat was forestalled by our invasion of Syria. As soon as the Allied troops crossed the frontier there was a hasty exit of Axis personnel. Most of the German air staffs and officials were flown back to the Dodecanese, while others were evacuated by train through Turkey. Vichy France's protest that we had no excuse for our invasion since there were no Germans or Italians in Syria was distinctly naïve. They had been there; they might come back, and others with them; so the invasion proceeded, to make sure that they had gone for good.

The Vichy French had long recognized the probability of our advancing into Syria, and General Dentz had made his arrangements accordingly. He had under his command about 35,000 troops, comprising 20 battalions of Colonial and Foreign Legion infantry and 11 battalions of locally recruited *troupes speciales*, Syrians, Circassians and White Russians. He had also a considerable force of artillery (upwards of 80 guns), 90 tanks, and a small air force, which during the operations was largely reinforced from North Africa. About 2,000 fresh troops also arrived by air during the campaign. The General retained detachments in the north, but his main defences had been organized on the line Kiswe (south of Damascus) -Rasheiya-Al Wadi-Jezzin-Sidon. On the coast he had a second line on the river Damour.

General Wilson's army went into battle on June 8 in three columns. The first, or eastern, operating in the open country east of Mt. Hermon, with Damascus as its objective, was formed of the 5th Indian Brigade with one Field Regiment of the R.A., a squadron of the Royals, and elements of the Transjordan Frontier Force. On their right were the Free French under General Catroux, and beyond them again Colonel Collet's cavalry. The Indian Brigade with the Royals captured Dera, Sheik Meskin and Ezra on June 9; the Free French passed through them at Sheik Meskin and pushed on towards Kiswe, where they were held; Colonel Collet's force reached Kiswe on June 11, but the position was too strong for frontal attack.

In the central sector the second column, made up of the 25th Australian Brigade and the Royal Fusiliers, moved up the valley between Mt. Hermon and the Lebanon range in the direction of Kayot. The Fusiliers captured Quneitra on June 9, and the Australians, starting from the Metulla salient, took Merj Ayun on June 11 after heavy fighting on the frontier, and then advanced north to Nabatiyeh.

The third column moved along the coast, making for Beirut. It was composed of the 21st Australian Brigade with the

Cheshire Yeomanry (horsed) on their right flank. The Yeomanry brushed aside Vichy opposition at Ras Naqura (the frontier), and with part of the Australian brigade pushed inland through the hills towards the upper valley of the Litani, occupying Mazra'st ech Chouf and Mrousti, north of Jezzin. The rest of the 21st Brigade, although

AUSTRALIANS advancing into Syria. The 25th Australian Brigade moved up the valley between Mt. Hermon and the Lebanon range.
Photo, British Official: Crown Copyright

delayed by demolitions at Iskanderoun, captured Tyre on June 8 and advanced to the Litani river at Kimiye. Here the bridge had been blown up and stubborn resistance was offered by the enemy.

On the night of June 8-9 the Royal Navy landed a sea-borne detachment north of the Litani, in the face of heavy and well organized opposition, and on June 10 the Australians crossed the river and advanced five miles up the coast beyond its mouth.

Up to June 13, therefore, progress on all points was fairly good. Then Vichy resistance stiffened. They had used our attempts at parleys to withdraw their forward troops to the main lines of defence: they were probably encouraged by our failure to secure an immediate success at Damascus, where Kiswe was proving a formidable obstacle and a flanking movement by tanks had forced the Free French to withdraw; and they were certainly embittered by having the Free French in the field against them.

On June 15-16 they counter-attacked. On the east, taking advantage of their superiority in armoured fighting vehicles, they drove two mechanized squadrons of the Transjordan Frontier Force out of Ezra and recaptured the village. Quneitra was heavily attacked by their A.F.V.s and infantry, and the garrison of the Royal Fusiliers was compelled to surrender after exhausting its ammunition. In the centre, Merj Ayun was heavily bombarded, and on June 15 Vichy

SYRIA, showing the places involved along the coast and in the interior during the victorious campaign waged by British and Free French against the forces in the Levant of Vichy France. General Maitland Wilson's army went into battle on June 8, and hostilities were closed by the signing of the Armistice Convention on July 14.

Here General Wilson's Men Thrust to Victory

During the advance of the Allied forces in Syria British Bren carriers pass a destroyed Vichy armoured car on the outskirts of a town. Right, a British machine-gunner on the hills overlooking the Damascus-Beirut road.

RIVER LITANI, which runs into the Mediterranean north of Tyre, was reached by Imperial troops on June 9, when the bridge across it was found to he blown up. Sappers are seen above making a temporary one.

Photos, British Official: Crown Copyright

Five Weeks' War Described From Day to Day

Armoured forces played a great part in the Syrian campaign, and this photograph, taken during the occupation after the signing of the Convention, shows men of British armoured vehicles having a friendly chat with Turkish soldiers patrolling the Turkish-Syrian frontier.
Photo, British Official

troops gained a foothold in the town, which was hotly disputed by the Scots Greys. On the coast, by clever use of mortars and tanks, they held up our advance south of Sidon. But the set-back was only temporary, for by June 17 Quneitra had been retaken by the Australians and the Queen's R.W.S., and Ezra by a mixed force of the Free French and Transjordan Frontier Force. An attack on Merj Ayun on June 17 was only partially successful, but farther north, in the Jezzin area, we inflicted severe casualties on the Vichy forces and captured several armoured cars.

Jezzin itself had been captured by the Australians and the Border Regiment on June 15, though it was not held for long. On the same day the Kiswe position was evacuated by the Vichy troops, and Sidon fell to combined action by the Australians of the 21st Brigade and the Royal Navy. On June 18 the 1st Australian Corps H.Q. took over command of the Syrian operations.

On our extreme right the desertion of considerable numbers of Druse cavalry weakened the Vichy position, but the citadel of Suweida held out till the " cease fire." Meanwhile, however, the attack on Damascus made progress. The 5th Indian Brigade, with the Royals, advancing along the foothills west of Kiswe, took Mezze, after heavy fighting, while the Free French, after an unsuccessful attempt on Jebel Kelb, advanced towards the town by way of Al Qadem and threatened to outflank the Vichy forces. On June 21 they entered Damascus.

In the central sector, where the Staffordshire Yeomanry and the Scots Greys were with the 21st Australian Brigade, a " platoon commanders' battle " continued round Merj Ayun. Here our troops were north and west of the town, while the Vichy forces were dug in the town itself and held the hills to the east and along the Hasbaya road. On the coastal sector we had advanced to positions just south of Damour, the Australians holding the general line Jezzin-Ras Nebi Yunus with Yeomanry patrol on the flank.

But in the meantime from Iraq a column consisting of Household Cavalry, the Wilts Yeomanry, the Warwickshire Yeomanry, the Essex Regiment, a Field Regiment of the

R.A., and part of the Arab Legion, with R.A.F. armoured cars, was advancing across the desert. On June 22 it reached Palmyra, a strong position defended with numerous concrete pill-boxes and resolutely held by a small but stubborn garrison consisting of a company of the Foreign Legion (half Germans and half Russians) and a Desert Company.

Part of our force gradually encircled Palmyra, while patrols by-passed it and at Qariatein linked up with the Free French who had pushed up from Damascus. A second column from Iraq, the 10th Indian Division, advanced on July 1 from Abu Kemal towards Deir Ez Zor, and its patrols made contact with those of the Palmyra column at Sukne, where the Arab Legion under Glubb Pasha on July 1 accounted for 17 Vichy A.F.V.s from Deir Ez Zor. On June 26 the Free French captured Nebk, and four days later repulsed a Vichy counter-attack and knocked out four tanks. The Leicesters and the Queens (who had captured Qatana on June 23) and the K.O.R.R. had moved westwards into the hills to cut the Damascus-Beirut road, and were now holding the southern slopes of Jebel Mazar, which overlooks the road and railway. In the central sector the Australians reoccupied Merj Ayun on June 24, and our Yeomanry patrols maintained contact with the French cavalry on the eastern flank.

On the desert side, therefore, the position at the beginning of July was that a small Vichy force was hemmed in by the Druses at Suweida and another by the Iraqi column at Palmyra, but otherwise the eastern desert was clear of enemy forces. Vichy still held the Damascus-Beirut road north of Jebel Mazar and the whole of the Beka'a down to Hasbaya and the Lebanon through Hasrout south of Beit ed din to the coast just south of Damour.

Here the 7th Australian Division controlled operations between the sea and the Merj Ayun area. On June 29 it had been reinforced by the 23rd Infantry Brigade, which included the Border Regiment and the D.L.I. who were engaged in the inland sector, while the 7th Australian Division itself was on the coast. In the north, part of the 10th Indian Division cleared up the " duck's bill " salient between Turkey and Iraq, capturing Tel Kotchek, Kamchliq Masseche and Nusaybin, and compelling the Vichy forces in the Jezirch area to fall back westwards, whilst the main force took Deir Ez Zor on July 3 and Raqqa on July 5, to advance thence to Meskine and threaten Aleppo.

Farther south, Palmyra surrendered on July 3, and the British and Arab troops pushed west, occupied Furqlus on July 8, and on July 10 had cut the Homs-Baalbek railway south of Homs. In the Damascus sector the 6th Division captured Jebel Mazar on July 10. In the Merj Ayun sector there was little change, but in the hills to the west the Cheshire Yeomanry, advancing through rough country, overcame enemy resistance at Mrousti, while the 2/33 Australian Infantry Battalion recaptured Jezzin. On the same day, July 9, the Australian troops in the coastal area, supported by a naval bombardment, outflanked and captured the whole of the Vichy line of defence on the Damour and advanced to Khalde, about five miles south of Beirut.

On July 10 General Dentz requested armistice terms, and at midnight July 11-12 the " cease fire " was sounded in Syria.

IN ALEPPO, the British armoured vehicles which entered the city during the occupation of the country by Allied forces became a centre of attraction for the inhabitants, some of whom, no doubt, had witnessed a previous occupation by British forces on October 26, 1918.
Photo, British Official: Crown Copyright

I Was There! .... Eye Witness Stories of the War

We Met Mr. Churchill in the Atlantic

On board one of the destroyers which formed the escort of the Prince of Wales, homeward bound with Mr. Churchill following his Atlantic conference with the American President, was Reuter's Special Correspondent with the Royal Navy. Here is his account of his experiences on this never-to-be-forgotten occasion.

IT was a glorious afternoon as we sailed out of the naval base to keep our rendezvous with the Prince of Wales, somewhere in the North Atlantic, and at that time no one except the captain of the ship knew the importance of the task which lay ahead of us.

Early one morning, some days after leaving the naval base, we sighted a smudge on the horizon, and as we approached we could see through our glasses the immense

was paying them this novel visit. We saw men running to hoist the " V " signals in flags, while others stood on deck cheering and waving.

Prince of Wales was a proud sight. She had cocked up all her great 14-inch guns to their highest levels, and, if Mr. Churchill was thrilled, it was nothing to the excitement that it caused amongst the vessels of the convoy.

We steamed on to perhaps two miles

time to hoist flags and the crews lined the rails, waving hats and shouting.

We wished them God-speed and then resumed our original course, which was to bring us to Iceland. Here we made the day's stay and in the evening sailed again for England.

Earlier in the day on which we met the convoy Prince of Wales carried out a practice shoot with her anti-aircraft guns, watched by the Prime Minister and his party. She first fired a smoke shell, which exploded into a compact ball of smoke high up in the sky. Using this as a target, she let loose with her A.A. guns, plastering the area round the ball of smoke with exploding shells. This was followed up by an exhibition of barrage fire, using every anti-aircraft gun on board. The battleship's sides seemed to be constantly flaming, so great was the rate of fire, while the air all round her was black with exploding projectiles. It seemed unbelievable that one ship could put up so devastating a barrage.

FROM H.M.S. PRINCE OF WALES, on which ship this photograph was taken, Mr. Churchill, returning from his meeting with President Roosevelt, saw, as here related, a great convoy pass—over eight miles of ships, all bound for Britain. Men aboard the merchant ships ran to hoist the " V " signals in flags, while others stood on deck cheering and waving. To enable Mr. Churchill to inspect the vessels closely, the Prince of Wales steamed right through the convoy, then turned about and passed again through the line of ships.
Photo, British Official : Crown Copyright

outline of the giant battleship, flanked on both sides by Canadian destroyers. The great ship was truly a noble sight, plunging through the Atlantic swell and throwing up great clouds of white spray as she dipped her bows into the waves.

We approached from head on, and as we swooped in to take our positions there was a sudden flurry of destroyers all around the battleship. In a very few minutes, however, we had turned round and with a slight increase of speed we had taken our positions and were zigzagging with the other warships.

During the afternoon Catalina flying-boats patrolled the air over us, and one of them reported that there was a large convoy some 50 or 60 miles ahead bound for Britain. The Prime Minister had never seen a large convoy at sea, so, with a slight alteration of course, we made towards them.

After two or three hours we could see the convoy on the horizon. It was an incredible sight. As far as the eye could see there were ships—tankers, freighters, supply ships, big ships, little ships, ships of every conceivable size and sort, all loaded down to the water-line. They were ranged in lines—in all over 8 miles of ships. Around them scurried their escort of corvettes and former American destroyers, keeping stragglers in line and always ready for the possible approach of danger.

We steamed straight towards them and then passed right through the middle of the convoy. Each of Prince of Wales' escorts chose its opening amongst the ships, and as we dashed through the lines of the merchantmen we could see that they realized who it

ahead of the convoy, and then Prince of Wales and her escort turned round, and once more we all went through the lines of wallowing ships. If there had been enthusiasm before it was nothing to what greeted us the second time. Every merchantman had had

The journey from Iceland to Britain was quite uneventful. With her escorts screening her, Prince of Wales, plunging ahead at speed, reached home safely after what must surely come to be regarded as the most remarkable transatlantic voyage of the war.

My Submarine Sank 17 Nazi and Italian Ships

One of our newest submarines operating in the Mediterranean accounted, according to the official statement, for seventeen enemy vessels in the course of two patrols in July. The following account of these exploits was given by the submarine commander.

PROUDLY pointing to a large " Jolly Roger," which is presented to each submarine entering Mediterranean service, and on which is stitched a white symbol denoting the type of vessel sunk after each patrol, the commander of the submarine said :

We were patrolling the Aegean in the early morning when we sighted two troopships escorted by an Italian destroyer and a single aircraft. Owing to the calm sea I was not able to approach too closely, but fired torpedoes at long range at each ship and then dived quickly. The ships were heading westward, and the larger troopship which we thought to be the City of Tripoli was hit and, I believe, definitely sunk.

We were then attacked with depth charges for about one hour, but nothing fell near us, though the distance is difficult to judge. The noise of depth charging carries under water for more than 100 miles, near explosions causing an unpleasant sound like broken glass raining down the sides of the submarine.

Two days later we sighted a solitary caique which we sank by gunfire on coming to the surface. On the same afternoon a schooner laden with troops, apparently carrying reinforcements to the Greek islands, was also sunk. We fired about twenty rounds, perforating the sides of these ships, whereupon the Germans jumped into the sea, or crowded into small boats which they carried. The next day we dispatched a further caique in like manner.

Our next encounter was during a moonlight night, when we came to the surface to charge our batteries, and sighted a convoy composed of a schooner and three caiques on their way to Crete. One caique returned our fire with high anti-aircraft fire, but this was soon silenced as the caique burst into flames. We had to deal with each ship in turn and one caique managed to escape.

The schooner blazed for hours, and the flames from the burning ships, which were carrying petrol and ammunition in addition to a number of troops, presently attracted

118   *The War Illustrated*   *September 10th, 1941*

||||||||||||||||||||||||||||||||||||||||||||||||||||||||||||||||||||||||| **I WAS THERE!** |||||||||||||||||||||||||||||||||||||||||||||||||||||||||||||||||||||||||||||

the attention of some passing enemy aircraft. Although these aircraft made our continued presence difficult we went alongside one caique and were met by cries of " The captain is Greek ! '' shouted in English. But when my sub-lieutenant replied in German, they all broke in in German, apparently thinking that we were a German submarine. They were then ordered to abandon ship, and pile into their small boat, which they unwillingly did after we had taken their swastika flag. We then destroyed the caique with an explosive charge and carried on with our patrol.

Our final success came the following morning, when the Italian tanker Strombo, which had undergone temporary repairs at Istanbul, was intercepted on her way to Italy. This completed our patrol and we then made for our base.—*Reuter.*

The exploits of one of our latest submarines are told in this and the preceding pages. Here a Petty Officer on a submarine is explaining the working of a torpedo. *Photo, L.N.A.*

romancing when he gets home. A small boy who presented me with a sweet was in charge of his mother and baby sister, for his father is at the front. Armed with two flasks of iced water almost as big as himself, he conducted the family underground and found them places to sleep. Then, after making a general inspection, he curled up and did not wake until the all-clear.

Red Cross girls, who parade the tunnel all night, wear rubber shoes so as not to disturb the sleepers. So do the white-robed women who come round with hot rolls and sweets which they sell for a few coppers.

Sanitation is good, the air sweet and constantly changing, and there is an adequate supply of drinking water.

The shelterers are much quieter than their opposite numbers in London, and, though they are ready enough to joke about most things, they do not joke about bombing. It makes them very angry.—" *Daily Express.* ''

I Spent a Raid Night in the Moscow Tube

Moscow's famous tube railway is used, like those of London, as an air-raid shelter. An English newspaper correspondent sent this descriptive dispatch after a night among the Russian shelterers.

D URING one of Moscow's longest raids —it lasted 5½ hours, and the Germans, risking the semi-daylight journey both ways, lost nine planes—I went underground to compare Moscow's Metro shelters with London's Tube.

Though the station I chose was hardly deeper than, say, Lancaster-gate, it was sound-proof, and it is obvious that whoever designed and built the Metro—credit is given in every station to Kaganovitch—did not forget that one day the tunnels might be needed as air-raid shelters. They are lined with what appears to be a considerable thickness of concrete.

I found conditions much better than they were in London in the early days, but not as good as they are in London now. There are no bunks, and, as one is not allowed to remain in the station itself, but is forced on to the lines and far up the tunnels, it is difficult to see how bunks can be introduced.

The current is switched off, at each end of the platform a ramp is thrown over the lines, and the shelterers march down this in an orderly, quiet way. Bedding is then spread between the rails and walls. Discipline is first-class, and

there is really no need for so many policemen to be on duty.

All, without respect for rank, dignity or what not, are compelled to use the shelters. Near me last night a senior general slept beside an ancient peasant who must have come from some remote Tartar region— where, perhaps, air raids will always be unknown and where they will think he is

MOSCOW'S METRO, with its beautiful stations richly decorated with marble columns, is being used, like the London Underground, to provide shelter against air raids for the city's vast population. An account of a night spent among the shelterers is given above. Aspects of German raids on Moscow are shown in p. 99. *Photo, Planet News*

I Flew Between the Chimneys at Knapsack

On August 12, 1941, Blenheims of the Bomber Command, in greater numbers
than had ever visited Germany by daylight, bombed the Knapsack and
Quadrath power-stations near Cologne. Some of the airmen who took
part here tell the story in their own words.

"IT was one wild, mad dash over, in and
out and back." This was how one
pilot summed up the R.A.F.'s daylight
swoop over Cologne. He went on :

We just skimmed the North Sea. We
could see people waving to us all the way
across Holland. They were thrusting their
thumbs into the air. They were making the
V sign with their fingers. They were jumping
up and down with their hands above their
heads in the form of a V. We saw them
cheering—we thought we could even hear it
above the roar of the engines.

But when we got over Germany it was a
different story. We knew we were across the
frontier at once. No cheers. People simply
ran like mad, and some
fell on their faces in the
ditches.

The moment we got
into Germany some of the
lads began blowing off
everything they had. One
of us set a cornfield ablaze.
We machine-gunned a
mansion. We fired at
everything moving we saw.

Another pilot took up
the tale :

When we reached the
target we were supposed
to go up to 800, but I
went up to 1,000 to avoid
the slips caused by the
machines ahead of me.
Everywhere I looked there
were Blenheims — right,
left and ahead of me, and,
my air gunner says,
behind.

The air gunner re-
marked :

I got a bit of flak on my
tin hat that dented it, but I
didn't seem to notice it somehow. All I heard
was a crump. I ducked and I straightened up.

A Canadian pilot took up the story,
saying :

My air gunner wanted me to get into closer
formation—it's "curtains" if you straggle
when the Me.s are up. He said, "Close up,
close up for God's sake." I told him that if
he wanted the crate to go any faster, he could
get out and push. We were doing over 300.

The pilot who was captain of the last
flight to bomb the Knapsack power-station
had a very good view of all the destruction
that had already been done. He said :

Over Germany we flew below the level of
the trees. My observer called me up when
we were seven minutes from the target, and
at that moment another squadron of Blenheims crossed our paths. They were on their
way to the other power-station. The air
seemed alive with British bombers. We were
nearly there when my rear gunner cried,
"Tailyho, fighter to port." I felt the aircraft jar twice and saw cannon shells hitting
the port wing. I told my flight to take
evasive action. Then the flak became
intense. I could see it bursting among
bombers in front of me and I looked on the
ground to see where it came from. I saw
flashes from a gun emplacement and went
straight for it. We passed about three feet
over the gun and I saw soldiers in a trench
hit by a stream of bullets. The gun ceased fire.

You couldn't miss the target. There were
the twelve chimneys—a row of four and a

parallel row of eight—standing dark against
the sky. The sun was to our port bow.
There were smoke and flames coming from
the plant, so we climbed to attack. The
flames were 50 feet high and the smoke too
thick to let us bomb accurately from any
lower. Inside the buildings we could see the
sudden red glow of explosions under the
smoke. I flew straight between the chimneys.
I was watching my observer's elbow as he
pulled back the release lever, and then I
heard him call "bombs gone."

I did a steep turn over a belt of trees down
into a sandstone quarry to get away from
the flak. I should think we went about
thirty feet below the level of the ground. As

The bombing of Knapsack power-station on August 12 (see pp. 84-85) is
described in this page by airmen who took part in it. On the same day
another force bombed the Fortuna power station at Quadrath, when
the upper photograph, showing bombs bursting on the target, was
taken. Right, men who bombed the power-stations and returned
home in time for lunch.
Photos, British Official and "News Chronicle"

we came up there was a great deal of crackling
in the earphones and I couldn't quite catch
something my rear gunner said. But then I
heard him repeat it. It was "fighter again,"
and at the same moment a piece of my port
wing fell away. I heard no more from my
rear gunner, and it must have been then that
he was wounded. I tried more evasive action.

A bullet came in behind my head and
another smacked the armour plating at my
back. My observer said that he could see a
stream of bullets coming between his legs. I
turned to the right to give
the fighter a more difficult
angle of fire and this seemed
to work. He sprayed the
air above us. While we
twisted about I hit the top
of a telegraph post and
chipped one air screw. I
could see that the yellow
tips were uneven as they
turned and the note of the
air-screws' roar was a little
different. But this didn't
seem to affect our flying.
There was a film of oil over
my perspex. I didn't see a
church spire and my
observer told me of it just
in time to let me miss it. I
banked sharply and caught
the tip of my wing in a tree.
Once more we were lucky
and we managed to catch
up with the others.

The worst of the attack was over then, but
I have never known anything so welcome as
the squadrons of British fighters which came
out to meet us. They staved off the attacks
of more Messerschmitts and then I had time
to think of my rear gunner. I tried to call
him up and then he passed me a note he had
written on his knee-pad. "Please get here
quickly. Bleeding badly," it said. I gave
the observer a bandage and he crept through
to the gunner. I made straight for base ; our
undercarriage had been damaged and would
not go down. The observer had to hold the
rear gunner while we made a belly landing.

The breezy talk of pilots, observers and air
gunners made light of this magnificent
bombing flight, but a Wing Commander said :

When I first heard that the raid was
projected, there was a hell of an argument.
We all thought they had gone mad ; it
seemed impossible to penetrate into Germany
150 miles in daylight. The operation, however, was brilliantly organized. It was a bit
tricky, but I've never seen anything handled
so well. It was really A 1. "*News Chronicle*"
and *Air Ministry News Service.*

The Editor's Postscript

Here is the first of our ten days' issues. I am no believer in the latest theory that Time is the Fourth Dimension. That time doesn't " pass "; that we do the passing through the " dimension." All I know is that today isn't yesterday and last year isn't this or the next. And that ten days are more than seven. Nothing but the exigencies of the paper situation could have induced us to alter the incidence of our issues. A week is an easier period of time (whatever Time may be) to think of than ten days, and we should all have liked to carry on from week to week. But ten days is like " Paddy —the next best thing." It has the value of the decimal (what's happened to our once numerous advocates of " decimal coinage " by the way ?—all dead I imagine) and it is easy to remember : ten, twenty, thirty —not to continue, as in the old song, " forty, fifty years ago." You can't forget these numerals. I shall not recapitulate the reasons for the change which I fully explained in our last number ; but I will add that I should not be surprised if *before* the War comes to an end (note that) we may be able to resume our weekly issue. It would take too much space to explain why I think this ; but at some later day I may have the opportunity.

" What a beastly boy ! " I remember exclaiming these very words as I lay abed one night in Neuilly, reading Bertrand Russell's masterly treatise on " Power " . . . The name of the beastly boy was given as Bruno Mussolini, and I have just read with sincere joy that this spawn of Italy's evil genius has been killed in an air accident. What prompted my exclamation that night three years ago were some expressions attributed to Bruno in describing his achievements in the Abyssinian campaign when the Italian aerial assassins had it all to themselves, bombing and gunning a totally unprotected and inoffensive people. " We had set fire to the wooded hills, to the fields and little villages . . . It was all most diverting . . . The bombs hardly touched the earth before they burst out into white smoke and an enormous flame and the dry grass began to burn . . . I thought of the animals. God, how they ran . . . After the bomb racks were emptied I began throwing bombs by hand . . . It was most amusing : a big zariba surrounded by tall trees was not easy to hit. I had to aim carefully at the straw roof and only succeeded at the third shot. The wretches who were inside, seeing their roof burning, jumped out and ran like mad. Surrounded by a circle of fire about five thousand Abyssinians came to a sticky end. It was like hell."

Well, that was little Bruno's way, as I put it when I quoted these passages later in print. The bestial young man (he was twenty-four when he came to *his* sticky end) may know more about hell now. But just as I am going to press with these notes I am told that Russell was wrong in crediting the expressions to Bruno ; Vittorio, that other spawn of Benito's, was the guilty one— and his sticky end is still to come ! We may

be sure, however, that in this matter their two black hearts beat as one. For let us remember that the vile spirit of these vermin is the spirit of all Fascist airmen : they are a race of absolute assassins. Indeed, it is a truism that the Italian as a fighter is formidable only when the circumstances make assassination easy. That a creature such as Bruno could have been given a state funeral and the certainty that Vittorio will be similarly honoured when his turn comes, provide an index of the moral condition to which Italy has sunk under Fascism.

I assert that no living Englishman could have written of sadistic joys such as these horrid Mussolini offspring shared and

MICHAIL I. KALININ, who has been President of the Presidium of the Supreme Council of the U.S.S.R.—in other words, President of the Soviet Union—since 1938. He is 66, and in his early days was a metal worker. At 20, he joined the " Union for Struggle for the Freedom of the Working Class."   *Photo, Planet News*

have retained a shred of respect from any of his compatriots. There are relatively few Germans for whom I can think that a decent Englishman should have any respect, but many Italians whom we would all be glad to call our friends : none of these, however, have been inoculated with the Fascist virus, and all of them I am sure will be rejoicing in the extinction of this true specimen of the vulture's brood. A day will come when *they* will be our friends again, but will such day ever dawn in Germany ? I'm whole-heartedly with Lord Vansittart in a comprehensive loathing of Germans ; quite otherwise as regards the Italians, in which I am sure that brilliant diplomatist would agree.

For the first time I have listened tonight to our incomparable Prime Minister with a tinge of disappointment—not as to the manner of his superbly phrased speech, but the matter. He has seldom spoken more eloquently, more inspiringly. Yet when he had finished did you know more than the

newspapers had told you a week before in pictures and paragraphs ? I didn't. I was left with the impression that, while one of the greatest events in history must have taken place " somewhere in the North Atlantic," at a spot which in all likelihood Hitler could mark with a pin prick on his map of the North Atlantic, we were left speculating on the inner significance of the meeting.

Those " Eight Points " might have been agreed upon by long-distance telephone without the movement of great battleships and protective flotillas of destroyers. From which we must conclude that they do not represent the total outcome of the magnificently-staged "High Drama on the High Seas," as I have headed it in our pictorial record of the event—not by a long chalk. Mr. Churchill's speech, masterly and moving as it was, must be regarded as one of those that are no less eloquent in what they leave unsaid than in what they reveal. In one respect, however, I should not complain, for, in common with Mr. Herbert Morrison's on the preceding day (not to mention " Woe, Woe," Ansaldo's), it warns us to expect a long war, and I have already done my little bit in that way.

The common mind in wartime seems to go questing back for memories of happier days if one may judge from the flood of theatrical revivals and the vogue of old musical favourites on the radio. Among the former I note a production by the Mercury players of " L'Enfant Prodigue," that delightful musical play without words. I saw the original company with Mlle. Jane May at the old Royalty in Glasgow fifty years ago—a thrilling experience which I have never forgotten. The incident of hunting an imaginary bluebottle, whose buzzing was most realistically imitated by the bassoon, was a little gem of mimetic comedy which stays in the mind. The play was revived for a brief season some five or six years ago, and my friend of later years, and long my next-door neighbour in John Carpenter Street when he was Principal of the Guildhall School of Music, Sir Landon Ronald, who had so brilliantly played the continuous piano accompaniment to the actions of the mimes in the original production, resumed his place at the piano !

Sir Landon told me one day how nervously he was looking forward to the performance and how he was having his fingers massaged with ointment to restore to them some of the suppleness they possessed when he was only nineteen, his age when I saw him in Glasgow. I foolishly missed the opportunity of witnessing the revival, regretting this more for the sake of seeing Landon at the piano again after so many years than for the play itself. Indeed, I'm not sure that I want to see it again ; that might rub off some of the ethereal bloom which " fond memory " still leaves upon the original. When one recalls the furore it created and the fact that no other wordless plays have ever caught on with the British public, one can only suppose that the art of miming on so artistic a plane has no strong appeal to playgoers who enjoy good singing, and the spoken word, or eye-engaging ballet, which is to say the generality of British playgoers.

JOHN CARPENTER HOUSE,
WHITEFRIARS, LONDON, E.C.4.

Printed in England and published on the 10th, 20th and 30th of each month by the Proprietors, The Amalgamated Press, Ltd., The Fleetway House, Farringdon Street, London, E.C.4. Registered for transmission by Canadian Magazine Post. Sole Agents for Australia and New Zealand : Messrs. Gordon & Gotch, Ltd. : and for South Africa : Central News Agency, Ltd. September 10th, 1941.   S.S.

Vol 5 # The War Illustrated № 106.

Edited by Sir John Hammerton

FOURPENCE

SEPT. 20TH. 1941

A SOVIET GRANARY destroyed by the retreating Russian soldiers. Searching the still smouldering ruins are a few Soviet peasants, gleaning what the fire has not reduced to ashes, lest even a handful should be left for the oncoming Nazi invaders. The destruction of all things—grain, houses, machinery—likely to assist Hitler, is one of the greatest patriotic gestures in history. Russia is willing to sacrifice her material progress to preserve ultimately her freedom.

Photo. Associated Press

NO. 107 WILL BE PUBLISHED TUESDAY, SEPT. 30

The Way of the War

FROM 14 TO 8: OUR WAR AIMS TAKE SHAPE

"Fourteen Commandments? Why, *le bon Dieu* himself had only ten !" This was "Tiger" Clemenceau's comment on the peace proposals put forward by President Wilson in January 1918. The cynical old freethinker might have been less contemptuous of the "Atlantic Charter": Mr. Churchill and President Roosevelt between them have produced only eight points...

Wilson formulated his "Points" in an address to Congress. Of the fourteen, the first five were of general application. Open covenants of peace—open diplomacy, in other words: freedom of the seas ; removal of economic barriers; reduction of armaments; and an adjustment of colonial claims based upon the principle that the interests of the populations must have equal weight with the claims of the governments concerned. Then followed eight concerned with rectifications of the political map of Europe. Finally, the Fourteenth Point ran : "A general association of nations must be formed under specific covenants for the purpose of affording mutual guarantees of political independence and territorial integrity to great and small States alike."

That was in 1918. Now in 1941 we have the "Atlantic Charter" (see page 110). None of its Eight Points is concerned with frontier revision, whether because the two statesmen who framed them think it is too early to make detailed proposals, or because it is assumed that we shall bear in mind Mr. Churchill's frequent declarations that all the territorial wrongs worked by Hitler of recent years shall be made good. In 1941 the draftsmen are concerned with broad principles. Britain and America seek no aggrandizement, desire no territorial changes that do not accord with the freely expressed wishes of the peoples concerned, respect the right of all peoples to choose their own form of government and wish to see the restoration of sovereign rights and self-government to those who have been forcibly deprived of them.

Following these expressions of political resolve and intention are two "Points" in the economic sphere. The one declares that Britain and America will endeavour, "with due respect for their existing obligations"—some have hastened to point out that if this reservation means anything it may well mean danger to our hopes and plans for a permanent improvement in international relations—to see that "all States, great or small, victor or vanquished," shall have equal access to the trade and raw materials of the world needed for their economic prosperity. The other, by way of corollary, expresses the desire that there should be the fullest collaboration between all nations in the economic field, with the object of "securing for all improved labour standards, economic advancement, and social security."

The next Point expresses the hope that after the destruction of Nazi tyranny there will be established a peace which will afford to all nations the means of dwelling in safety within their own boundaries, which will afford assurance that all men—the emphasis is on the *all*, as Mr. Attlee was at pains

to show when he read out the declaration over the wireless—in *all* lands may live out their lives in freedom from fear and want. Here surely we have an echo of Roosevelt's "Four Freedoms" speech of a few months ago.

That the peace shall permit all men to traverse the high seas and oceans without hindrance is hardly an improvement on Wilson, since he demanded "freedom of the seas" alike in times of war and times of peace. Then the eighth and last Point declares that all the nations of the world must come to the abandonment of the use of force. Yet since peace cannot be maintained if armaments continue to be employed by the aggressor nations, these nations must be disarmed until a wider and permanent system of general security is established. Wilson could hope and work for a world in which there would be no more war. A quarter of a century later all we may expect is that "all practical measures" will be taken to "lighten for peace-loving peoples the crushing burden of armaments."

Here is the first of the two distinct and marked differences which Mr. Churchill has pointed out between the Atlantic Charter and the attitude adopted by the Allies during the latter part of the last war. The possibility of future war cannot be ruled out ; hence, while disarming the nations guilty of having broken the peace, we must remain "suitably protected" ourselves. And the second difference is that whereas after the last war we tried to ruin German trade, now "we have definitely adopted the view that it is not in the interests of the world and of our two countries that any large nation should be unprosperous or shut out from the means of making a decent living for itself and its people by its industry and enterprise."

In my opinion it is unlikely that the Atlantic Charter will find a place of high honour among the great declarations of the world, among the charters of emancipation of the human race. It has not the ring of immortality. Where in this document is there such a line as Paine's, "These are the times that try men's souls," or Jefferson's, "We hold these truths to be self-evident"? Of a surety there is here never a suggestion of the gorgeous tapestry of Burke, the grand simplicity of Lincoln or Bright, the classic power of Asquith or the joyous lilt of Lloyd George. It is a draft rather than a finished document, a bald statement of working principles rather than a clarion-call to the human spirit.

Nevertheless, the declaration has been warmly and widely welcomed, and by none more enthusiastically than by Mr. H. G. Wells, who is himself a pastmaster in the outlining of "things to come". Mr. Wells has called it "the great declaration," and says that we have only to compare its Eight Points with "the petty Fourteen Points of President Wilson to realize the profundity and vastness of the change" which has come over the human situation since the end of the last war. We may not agree with Mr. Wells's devaluation of Wilson's efforts, but his tribute is all the more remarkable since he himself has been largely responsible for a "Declaration of Rights" which may well have been in the mind of Mr. Churchill—or if not, ought to have been. I have no space here to give it in detail, but it may be read in full in a sixpenny "Penguin"—Mr. Wells's "The Commonsense of War and Peace." Suffice it to say that it consists of eleven main provisions : the right to live, the protection of minors, the duty of every man to give his quota of service to the community, the right to knowledge, the right of freedom of thought and worship, the right to work, the right to enjoy personal property, freedom of movement, personal liberty, freedom from violence, and the right to have a part in the making of the laws. In some directions Mr. Wells goes farther than either Wilson or Roosevelt-Churchill. He realizes the vast revolutionary changes which have come over the world during the last few generations, the last few decades. He knows that we live in a world of potential plenty ; he realizes the "out-of-dateness" of national boundaries, that "sovereignty" is so old-fashioned as to be positively dangerous. But such vision and understanding are only to be expected in one who is not a statesman but a seer.

Some there are who scoff at this "Utopia-building." Why waste time discussing what we shall do with our victory when we are as yet so far from having won it ? But such critics have no conception of the might of words, of the power of ideas to send men's feet clattering adown strange, untrodden and (as often as not) better and brighter paths. So may it be that the "Points," whatever their number, whoever their author, may help us to glimpse the light at the end of our present long and gloomy tunnel.

E. Royston Pike

PRESIDENT ROOSEVELT acknowledging the cheers of the crowd at Rockland, Maine, on his return from the historic meeting with Mr. Churchill.   *Photo, Associated Press*

Stronger Grows Our Life-Line to the West

The Battle of the Atlantic continues, but the total tonnage of British and Allied merchant shipping sunk in July, 1941, was the lowest since April 1940, when it was 135,372 tons. Right, women and children gather on a headland to cheer the safe arrival of a convoy bringing food.

The R.A.F. sends crews out with convoys to gain first-hand experience. Below, a Pilot Officer sits on the bridge of a destroyer with the commander. The net is to prevent them being blown overboard.

ENEMY SHIPPING LOSSES

Tonnage Captured, Sunk or Scuttled since Sept. 3, 1939

	Sep. 3, '39–Sep. 2, '40	Sep. 9–Oct. 31	Jan. 7–May 10, '41	May 11–June 10, '41	June 11–July 9	July 10–August 16	Whole War Period
German —	923,000	209,639	623,361	132,000		433,000	2,321,000
Italian —	273,000	92,661	724,339	149,000		294,000	1,533,000
					180,000 (Not analysed)	34,000 (Finnish)	34,000 (Finnish) 180,000
Under Enemy Control	32,000	12,190	21,810	18,000		35,000	119,000
Total Tons	1,228,000	314,490	1,369,510	299,000	180,000	796,000	4,187,000

Note : In 5-week period July 10 to August 16, Russians claim to have sunk about 200,000 tons (51 ships) in the Baltic and Black Seas. Of the remainder in Col. 6, a substantial part was due to the R.A.F. and a certain proportion to British submarines. (See *also* Table of R.A.F. sinkings in page 28.)

	Pre-War Strength	Loss
German :	4,492,708	51%
Italian :	3,448,453	44%

For twenty hours these men have been continuously on duty as their ship watches over a convoy. Even now they can only take a cat nap.

U-BOAT SURVIVORS clambering to safety up the netting of the British destroyer which they tried to sink. In this case it was the destroyer which did the sinking.

Photos, "Daily Mirror"

How the Nazi Snake Was Scotched in Iran

In page 106 the circumstances leading up to the Anglo-Soviet intervention in Iran were described.
Here is an account of the military operations which led to the surrender of the Iranian forces.

IT was on the morning of August 25 that British and Indian troops of General Wavell's command, under Lt.-Gen. E. P. Quinan, launched a three-point attack in Western and South-western Iran, while Soviet forces marched into the country from the north.

Starting from Basra in the early hours of that Monday morning, Lt.-Gen. Harvey of the Indian Army, in charge of the forces attacking from the south-west, pushed in three lines of attack. One made a surprise landing at Abadan, where the Anglo-Iranian Oil Co. has large refineries, machine shops, storage tanks, and shipping facilities for dealing with its oil ; the second force made an all-night march across sandy desert and captured Khorramshah from the north ; the third headed towards Ahwaz, an important town on the pipe-line. The landing at Abadan was made with the help of naval and air cooperation. After sailing down the Tigris, tugs and sloops landed Indian troops direct at the Abadan waterfront. Considerable opposition was encountered here, but after seven hours of hand to hand fighting the town was captured and the Iranian forces retired northwards.

While this was going on, naval units put out of action two Iranian gunboats which opened fire, set on fire the Iranian escort vessel Babr, and captured several Axis ships found lying in the harbour at Bandar Shapur, in the Persian Gulf, which was occupied by another detachment of Indian troops.

During the first hours of the attack Admiral Beyendor, head of the Iranian navy, met his death while organizing resistance near Khorramshah.

Spearhead of the Attack

Meanwhile, another force, operating from Khanikin, crossed the western frontier of Iran, passed through Qasr-i-Shirin, and advanced along the road to Kermanshah. A British Hussar regiment, belonging to an Indian armoured brigade, formed the spearhead of the attack. Crossing the frontier a few miles north of Chosroes the Hussars circled round Qasr-i-Shirin, cutting the town's communications with west and north and then getting astride the main road between Qasr-i-Shirin and Kermanshah. Here they met a detachment of Ghurkas and led them towards the Paitak Pass. Another column crossed the frontier at Chosroes and headed south-east towards Gilan with the object of trying to get in the rear of any Iranian force which might attempt to hold the strong defensive position of the Paitak Pass, where the road crosses the Zagros range.

Gilan was occupied after very slight resistance and British troops entered Shahabad within 48 hours of leaving Iraq. The measures taken to counter resistance in the Paitak Pass proved highly successful. Patrols sent out to reconnoitre the approaches to the pass encountered, not Iranian, but Indian army troops approaching them from the opposite direction. To avoid encirclement the Iranian troops had retired. As the British forces continued their advance it became

evident that the Iranians were putting up no more than a token resistance, and on Wednesday, August 27, a new Iranian government was set up. The premier of the new government, Ali Furanghi, told the Iranian parliament of his government's decision to cease fighting, and as this was unanimously approved orders were at once given to the Iranian troops to cease fire.

East of Shahabad there was some fighting when the Warwickshire Yeomanry were sent out to take up a position on the Zibiri ridge, about seven miles east of Shahabad. The Warwickshires were caught in an ambush and one truckload was captured, though eventually all but one escaped. Artillery then came to their support and the Warwickshires held the ridge for the night, being relieved the next day by Wiltshires. The Wiltshires came in for a certain amount of shelling, but just as the British troops were assembling upon the heights preparatory to making a swift dash across the plain, Major Abdullah Massoud of the Iranian cavalry arrived at British Headquarters to ask for a cessation

of hostilities. The British divisional general named his terms for a cessation of hostilities and thereupon the British attack was suspended for two hours to enable the Iranians to consider their reply. An acceptance was given to General Quinan and the British and Indian troops marched peacefully across the plain of Krukur to Kermanshah, which under the agreement was to be evacuated within two days. Into that town they entered on Saturday morning, the actual campaign having lasted only three and a half days. As a special concession the Indian Army Command allowed a token force of Iranians to remain in the barracks and fly the Iranian flag.

In the south-west the situation remained calm. The people showed themselves friendly and were agreeably impressed by the British action of importing at once into the areas they had occupied 650 tons of wheat from Iraq, for there was much destitution in the country. Tempted by favourable credit terms offered by the Germans, the Iranian government had sold for export almost all the year's grain harvest, as well as stocks of tea and sugar, with a total disregard for the welfare of their own people.

In the southern sector the Indian detachments had reached a point only eight miles from Ahwaz when Iranian resistance ceased and the Iranian General Mohamed Shahbakhti surrendered. Shortly afterwards the Indians entered the town.

British Air-Borne Troops

During the campaign British airborne troops were landed in the largest-scale operation of its kind so far attempted by the R.A.F. Several battalions are stated to have been carried from their base in Iraq by plane.

While these operations were progressing, the Russians, on their side, were making equally rapid progress. In addition to the forces moving into Iran from the Trans-Caucasus, Soviet troops made landings from the Caspian sea.

On the first day of their advance the Soviet forces penetrating into Iran from Trans-Caucasia progressed to a depth of 25 miles in the directions of Tabriz and Ardebil, and these towns, together with Dilman and Lissar were occupied by the Red Army on August 26.

On Sunday, August 31, less than a week after the opening of the campaign, British and Russian forces met at Kazvin, 95 miles north-west of Teheran, and Indian forces advancing along the Baghdad-Teheran road met Soviet troops at Sehneh. As soon as the Iranian forces gave up the fight British and Indian mobile columns moved swiftly over the country taking over strategic points pending the signature of armistice terms. By September 2 it was announced that an agreement had been reached upon the broad principles which would govern the Anglo-Russian-Iranian armistice terms, although some difficulty arose over the insistence of the Allies that all legations under German control should be closed and Nazis sheltering in the compound of their legation handed over.

IRAN, where armed intervention by Britain and Russia removed the dangers of Nazi control. The arrows show the points from which the British and Soviet attacks were launched.
By courtesy of "The Times"

The Gate to India is Now Barred to the Nazis

NEAR TABRIZ, on the road to Marand, Iran. Tabriz, sixty miles from the Caucasian border, is an Iranian keypoint linking the country by rail with Russian Tiflis on the Batum-Baku line and the Turkish city of Erzerum. The Soviet forces entered Iran on August 26.

A bridge on the Trans-Iranian railway, which was completed in 1938, the system comprising nearly a thousand miles of line.

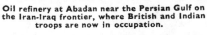

Oil refinery at Abadan near the Persian Gulf on the Iran-Iraq frontier, where British and Indian troops are now in occupation.

THIS GATEWAY, Teheran, one of the twelve covered with glazed brick, was erected in the 19th century. It is in picturesque contrast to the modern industrial buildings in the Iran capital. On the left, the new high road called the Great Western, linking Teheran to Bagdad in the south-west and to Tabriz in the north-west.

Photos, "Daily Mirror," Black Star, Lubinsk

Soviet Striking Power

Powerful Modern Weapons of the Red Army and Air Force Shown in Panorama Form

Specially drawn by Haworth for THE WAR ILLUSTRATED

RUSSIAN MECHANIZATION. This panoramic drawing, showing a number of Russian fighting vehicles making their way along narrow, winding terraces through low hills, gives some idea of the varied and highly mechanized character of the Red Army.

Tanks: Five Varieties. The tanks shown are: (1) Fast cruiser tanks of 16 tons with 2-inch quick-firing cannon. Bundles of stout branches called fascines are slung on the rear of these tanks and are used to assist the tank over deep ditches or traps. (2) 30-ton tanks whose main armament is a 3-inch gun. Small

two-wheeled trailers are pulled behind, carrying drums of oil for replenishing the fuel tanks. (3) Small 8½-ton tank, equipped with 45 mm. cannon, being carried slung on its own trailer. This saves the tracks and suspension mechanism from needless strain. The trailer can also be used for taking the tank back to the repair depot if it is damaged. (4) Flame-throwing tanks, similar to those used by the Russians in Spain. (5) An amphibious tank, which can cross fords and small streams without having to wait for a bridge.

Mechanized Artillery. Russia has many of these heavy guns (6), which can be manoeuvred over difficult

country by means of their caterpillar carriage. (7) Small mobile anti-tank guns. (8) Anti-Aircraft guns. (9) Fast armoured cars for reconnaissance. (10) Quadruple machine-guns mounted on lorries to protect troops against low-flying planes. (11) Light field gun and carriage.

Fighter Planes. In the lower left corner fighter planes of the Red Air Force are being serviced and re-fuelled whilst hidden among bushes and trees surrounding the airfield. The planes shown are: (12) The I-15 B Chato single-seat fighter, which is armed with 4 machine-guns and has a speed of 240 m.p.h. (13) The I-16 B Rata—speed 290 m.p.h., armed with 2 cannon

and 2 machine-guns. (14) One of Russia's latest fighters, heavily armed with cannon and machine-guns, which is reported to have a speed of 350 m.p.h. and to reach 15,000 ft. in four minutes.

The planes seen in the sky are SB-1 medium bombers, which closely resemble the American 'Martin.' Their top speed is 250 m.p.h. and bomb load 1,100 lb. They are powered with Wright Cyclone engines. A later development, the SB-2, has a greater speed and longer range. Most of Russia's aircraft bear signs of American inspiration but the armament of later models has been suggested by British experience.

The Red Army Holds On and Hits Back

After two months of fighting on a scale never before known in history, with losses in men amounting to millions, and in machines to many thousands, the mighty conflict between German and Russian continues unabated. Hitler has been unable to force a decision, his armies are being wasted in the Russian inferno, the rains and snow will increase his difficulties, and as each day passes the German people, promised victorious peace for so long, must resign themselves to another grim and fearful winter of war.

ON August 26 Berlin authorities, obviously perturbed that they could not implement their promises of rapid victory over the Russians, let it be known that there must be a breathing space. There were difficulties, communications were long, the Soviet armies from one end of the front to the other had remarkable powers of co-ordination.

To put it simply, the Germans had failed to blitzkrieg Russia into a quick knock-out. They had hoped, by driving great wedges into the three main Russian armies under Marshals Voroshilov, Timoshenko and Budenny, to roll them up in irresistible outflanking movements.

Critical as was the position of Budenny's forces in the Ukraine he had saved the greater part of them in his retreat across the Dnieper, and had left large bodies of Russian troops behind to harass the advancing Nazis. Significant was the fact that Odessa continued to remain in Soviet hands, a kind of Russian Tobruk standing like a great rock in the surging sea of Nazi invaders, aided by units of the Russian Black Sea Fleet.

The increasing pressure on the southern sector could only be relieved by a strong counter-attack in the centre, and this had been proceeding for many days. On August 28 the news that General Koniev was near Gomel, accepted at first with reserve, indicated the terrific power of a Russian offensive against General von Bock, a manoeuvre which frustrated the Nazis' plan to smash between the Red armies operating in the centre and south and turn Budenny's retreat into a rout. As Koniev's attack developed it was seen to be one of the most important in the Russo-German conflict so far, and likely to have a far-reaching effect on the whole campaign along the Eastern front. The fury of the thrusts between Gomel and Smolensk was such as to embarrass von Bock, who was apparently unprepared for it, and compelled to withdraw from his advanced positions. It also gave Budenny the opportunity to counter-attack from his positions beyond the Dnieper.

The Great Dnieper Dam Destroyed

The destruction of the Dnieper dam was confirmed on August 28. Having made use of the fine road along the dam at Zaporozhe, Budenny gave instructions for this great work to be blown up. Hundreds of millions of gallons, in a mighty wall of water, leapt forth, causing immense devastation on both banks of the river.

While Koniev and Budenny in the centre and Ukraine respectively were hitting back, a third counter-offensive was developing between Kholm and Toropets in the north in an effort to break through between Pskov and Ostrov, and so threaten the rear of General von Leeb's army advancing on Leningrad.

On August 29 the Germans claimed the capture of Tallinn, the Estonian capital. It fell after many weeks of fighting, the Nazis losing at least 30,000 in this area. The last scenes in the burning city were among the most horrible and violent since the war against Hitler began. Continuous Nazi bombardment was punctuated with louder explosions as the retreating Russians blew up the port's quays and warehouses. Soviet planes and Stukas met in sky duels over the flaming town while Russian warships and transports, with 50,000 men aboard, fought their way out to sea. Though Soviet casualties were heavy, the Russian Baltic fleet was

reported to be intact as a fighting unit, and was acting as an important auxilliary in the defence of Leningrad by shelling the Germans advancing along both sides of the Gulf of Finland.

A diversion in the campaign on the East front began to manifest itself at the end of August in rumours of peace between Finland and the Kremlin with American and British mediation. It was also announced that Voroshilov had withdrawn from Karelia. Popular opinion in Finland was said to demand peace as soon as the Finns drew near

This is not Mr. Wells's "invisible man," but an example of Russian ingenuity which caused the Nazis to waste quite a lot of ammunition.
Photo, Associated Press

to their 1939 Soviet frontier. The Russian move was thought, at first, to be a political one, but it is far more likely to have been a purely military measure to concentrate the strongest possible force in defence of Leningrad. The Nazis had been gradually drawing nearer to the second city of the Soviets, and claimed on September 2 to have begun to storm the outer defences, but official Russian sources expressed the greatest confidence that Leningrad would not be taken. As a proof of the city's powerful defences in fighter squadrons and A.A. guns 500 Nazi planes had been destroyed round about Leningrad during the fortnight ending September 2, Voroshilov's armies were fighting against von Leeb's storm divisions with indefatigable heroism, and six dictators, including the Marshal himself, had been appointed to defend Leningrad to the last.

While the situation on the East front is still obscure, and decisive battles have yet to be fought, one thing at least is clear. The Russians have thwarted and are still thwarting the enemy in his main objectives. His territorial gains are large, but the destruction of material and the deliberate ruin of vast industrial works as a result of the "scorched earth" policy have left the Germans in possession of a no-man's-land which may well become more of a liability than an asset.

Germany has, in fact, little to compensate herself for the losses she has incurred. That these are colossal may be gathered from the fact that she has had to draw on her western reserves. Prisoners captured by the Russians say that they had been transferred suddenly from garrisons in France, Belgium and Holland.

On September 2 Moscow announced that in two months fighting 170 German divisions had been wiped out, the enemy's casualties in the series of battles amounting to 2,500,000 killed and wounded. In the first three weeks of August the Nazis lost 12 armoured divisions, 37 infantry divisions, 8 motorized divisions, 17 infantry regiments and several storm troop divisions. The losses in machines—tanks, aeroplanes and guns—have caused an appeal in Germany for more and better weapons, an admission that Hitler's military might has been seriously damaged by the Red armies.

Approximate German Front, Aug. 12 ......●●●●●●●
        "   "   "   Sep. 1 .....————

The Eastern front, showing the approximate position of the front line on Sept. 1. The dotted line shows the approximate German front on August 12.
By courtesy of "The Times"

Our Searchlight on the War

HEROIC NURSE IN CRETE

MISS JOAN STAVRIDI, daughter of a London banker, was visiting her sister in Athens when Greece was invaded. She at once volunteered as a nurse and, at the fall of Greece, was evacuated to Crete. Here she became Chief Superintendent of " Hospital 7," situated in no-man's-land between two strategical points. Three times during the campaign the hospital changed hands. All the regular doctors were killed by German machine-guns while out swimming. They were replaced, but Miss Stavridi, at that time the only nurse in Western Crete, remained unrelieved. On one occasion, although clearly marked, the hospital was bombarded for two and a half hours, and at last she ordered the evacuation of patients to the only available place, caves on the Aegean shore. The injured included German paratroops with broken thighs, and by that time only one vial of morphine remained for hundreds of acutely suffering cases. Food and water were also running very short. Miss Stavridi spread sheets on

FIRE GUARD armlet, 1,800,000 of which have been ordered as well as a million " patches " for sewing on Street Fire Party armlets.   *Photo, British Official*

a slab of rock outside the cave mouth and stood by while operations were performed. She sewed enormous red crosses on to other sheets in an attempt to stop bombardment of the caves. But the shells continued to come over. When after 10 days' heavy fire she was discovered by German staff officers, they insisted on putting her on a plane taking wounded to Athens—where she is still nursing

FAREWELL TO 300,000 LISTENERS

EARLY in August the inhabitants of towns and villages along the north, west and south coasts of Norway were compelled to hand over their wireless sets to the Nazi authorities. Mr. Olaf Rytter, Director of the Norwegian State Broadcasting Corporation in London, gave a farewell address over the wireless to 300,000 listeners who are thus cut off from truthful news. " From all Norwegians," said he, " working on Allied soil and sailing on all the oceans, we send greetings, the last until we can once more meet in some way or other, saying that the bond which, during this

FREDDIE HARRISON, six-year-old London air raid hero, who rescued his little sister from the bomb-wrecked bedroom of his house and then went back to rescue his other sister. He received a cheque for his bravery from an American, and letters and presents from all parts of the world, including this huge engine. With him are his father and one of the sisters he rescued,   *Photo, G.P.U.*

year of struggle and suffering, has been strengthened between the home front and the front abroad, can never be broken. The enemy are now trying to break the tie between the two fronts. That is why they have confiscated the wireless receivers. . . . The whole decree is a defeat, morally, for the enemy. It is an admission that the truth is a danger to their cause, and at the same time an admission that their own propaganda machine has proved a failure."

THE VOICE

ON August 21 a new irritation was inflicted upon the Berlin wireless authorities, already harassed by R.A.F. interference and illicit listening-in to foreign broadcasts. That evening musical programmes on the long-wave station Deutschlandsender were interrupted by a harsh Voice that denounced Hitler, the war and the sufferings of the German troops in the Ukraine, many of whom were mentioned by name. Sometimes the music drowned the Voice, but in the softer parts it was clearly audible. The next night officials at the station were prepared, and the moment the Voice was heard jamming started. They also tried to squeeze out the interrupter by non-stop transmission, one item following immediately on another and the announcer starting to read the news while the last bars were being played. But despite these and other elaborate efforts the Voice has continued its loud inexorable utterance of home truths, rising above the orchestra, interpolating mocking comments in the announcer's shouted speeches. So successful was the interrupter that on August 29 the Deutschlandsender closed down, and listeners were asked to tune in to Breslau for the news. It is assumed that the pirate is installed at a Soviet station, for on September 3 he read a message signed by a number of German officers and airmen taken prisoner in Russia, imploring the Germans to stop fighting.

HOLIDAY CAMP AT GIBRALTAR

GIBRALTAR garrison has been provided with a novel rest camp to which a hundred men at a time may repair for three days of respite from work and the monotony of life in the fortress. Originally designed for prisoners of war, this barbed-wire enclosure contains comfortable huts for sleeping (with the proviso that the men may get up when they like), for meals, indoor games, reading and writing, an outdoor cinema, a garden laid out with rock plants, and access to two perfect bathing beaches. The food provided is claimed to be the best in Gibraltar, and includes such items as mixed grill, meat pie, melon and lemonade. Band concerts or talkies are given nightly. The sole rule is that men must be back in camp by 11 p.m. It is hoped that every soldier in the garrison will in time have a spell at this holiday camp. Visitors are invited to make suggestions, and the one most often proposed is that those using the camp should be allowed to stay longer than three days.

A.B.C.A.

"THEIRS not to reason why, theirs but to do and die," is an attitude of mind regarding the private soldier which is now, fortunately, nearly dead. The last nail is knocked in its coffin by the creation of a new branch of the Army the Army Bureau of Current Affairs, known as A.B.C.A. for short. Cromwell's famous definition of the citizen-soldier was one who " must know what he fights for, and love what he knows." This thought is the motive behind the new scheme, which aims at keeping the soldier abreast of current affairs. This training of men in Current Affairs will be conducted by Regimental Officers in training time, will be under the general direction of the Director-General of Army Welfare and Education, and will be run by a body of specialists. Officers will be supplied with weekly bulletins on the basis of which they can inform and instruct their men

about current affairs and the progress of the war. There will also be discussion circles, travelling exhibitions, panels of special speakers, etc. The Director of A.B.C.A. is Mr. W. E. Williams, who for many years has directed the British Institute of Adult Education.

ATTEMPT TO KILL LAVAL

UNREST in France, steadily growing from day to day, reached a climax on August 27, when Pierre Laval, former Prime Minister and supporter of collaboration with Germany, was shot and seriously wounded by Paul Colette, a 20-year-old native of Mondeville in the Calvados. The shooting took place at the Borgnis des Bordes barracks at Versailles, during an enrolment ceremony of French volunteers to fight against Russia. Two other men were wounded, but less seriously, by Colette's five shots Marcel Déat, editor of the Paris newspaper " L'Œuvre " and president of the French pro-Nazi party, and Major Durvy, a member of the French Fascist party. The attempt on Laval's life has caused the French authorities to take further drastic measures against Communists.

MID-OCEAN REVIEW

WHEN Mr. Churchill was returning in the Prince of Wales from the historic meeting with President Roosevelt, the giant battleship diverged from her course to overhaul a large convoy bound for Britain. It was composed of ships of all sizes, ranged in lines and stretching over 8 miles, shepherded by an escort of corvettes and ex-American destroyers. There followed an unpremeditated and amazing review of British and Allied shipping, as the Prince of Wales' escort destroyers threaded the lines of the merchantmen and the great battleship herself passed up the convoy, running up a show of signal flags : " Churchill wishes you a pleasant voyage." The convoy's flagship responded by proudly raising

CHURCHILL signal flying at the upper yard of H.M.S. Prince of Wales and made to the convoy which the battleship met in mid-ocean.
Photo, British Official

the " V " signal in flags. Immediately the cue was taken up by warships and merchantmen alike, and brilliant rows of red, white and blue flags began to flutter in the sunshine from every bridge. Having passed through the convoy and about two miles ahead, the Prince of Wales, with her escort vessels, wheeled round and again went through the lines of gaily dressed ships, with their wildly cheering crews and passengers, before resuming her original course towards Iceland.

ARK ROYAL ONCE MORE

SEEKING in vain to engage the elusive Italian fleet, our still unsunk warship Ark Royal cruised for an hour off Valencia, while her aircraft gave the astonished Spaniards a free show. Fifteen fighters roared over the town, their formation making an enormous " V." Then a formation of 18 bombers took off and, flying with their escort of fighters just outside the three-mile limit, again impressed the Victory sign on the populace. Just previous to this light-hearted air display, planes from the Ark Royal had attacked and set blazing about 16 miles of an important cork forest in Sardinia. Several hundred 25-pound explosive fire bombs were dropped, and a cork factory near Tempio was also set on fire. Flames were visible 75 miles away. The Italians were evidently not expecting a raid in this area, for only one A.A. gun went into action, and no fighters appeared. In a message of congratulation the Admiral signalled : " Estimate enough burnt cork to give every Nazi a Hitler moustache."

Where Nazi Gains Are Bought at Fearful Cost

Two Nazis hammering their way into other people's property, an incident on the East front that perfectly expresses the eternal Hunnish spirit.

When the Russians cannot stop the Nazi tanks with shells they just ram them with their own tanks. Here is a German machine (left), one of three crushed by Captain Kukushkin's tank.

Nazi motorized units impeded in the waters released by the Soviet's destruction of a dam higher up the river. On the right, a Russian soldier escorting prisoners of the 94th German infantry regiment to headquarters.

HITLER and Field-Marshal von Rundstedt after a conference somewhere on the southern sector of the Nazi front against Russia. Hitler's headquarters are now a fleet of lorries in which he and his staff camp, generally near a wood. On the right, Soviet submarines which were under construction in the naval yards at Nikolaiev, near Odessa. They were destroyed prior to General Budenny's retreat across the Dnieper.

Photos, British Official; Crown Copyright; Associated Press, Sport & General, Keystone

There's Another Russia Beyond the Urals

Even if Hitler succeeds in taking the Ukraine and the Caucasus, Soviet Russia will not necessarily
be knocked out. Far to the east beyond Moscow, in the Urals and the vast plain that stretches
across Asia to the Pacific, a great new Russia has come into existence of recent years—one which
is largely independent and capable of the most prolonged and determined resistance.

Not so many years ago Asiatic Russia—
that vast mass of territory extending
from the Urals on the eastern edge
of Europe to the Pacific facing Japan, from
the icebound waters of the Arctic to the
torrid mountains of the " roof of the world "
close to India—was lumped together as
" Siberia." The very word was a symbol
of barbaric backwardness. One had visions—
there was plenty of substance for them in
actual fact—of a barren expanse across which
staggered the chain gangs made up of the
Tsar's political prisoners, men and women
sent to labour in the forests and mines
because they had dared to suggest reforms,
even to work and agitate for them. Very
different is the Siberia of today. It is Siberia
no more, not even in name ; instead, it is a
second Canada in the making, a land where
cities have sprung up almost overnight,

local raw materials in local factories, driven by
local power plants, and spreading culture and
newness of life to local inhabitants. Robbery and
exploitation of Russian colonies ceased."

The most important of these new centres
of economic life is in the Ural Mountains,
which lie where Europe and Asia meet.
Here there are being worked vast deposits of
iron ore, and already the Urals are the most
important centre of Russian iron ore production, yielding 60 per cent of the total
Soviet output. Sverdlovsk (pop. 426,000)
and Chelyabinsk (pop. 273,000) are two of its
most important centres ; a third is Magnitogorsk, which is surely one of the most romantic
creations of recent years. As recently as
1929 its site was occupied by the obscure
village of Magnitnaya (Magnet Mountain),
inhabited by Cossack peasants, and herds
of cattle browsed on the slope of the Atach

of Kuznetsk on the banks of the Yenisei, and
even at Pechori in the frozen Arctic. In
addition to pig iron, steel and coal the Ural-
Kuznetsk Combine also produces non-ferrous
metals and manufactures machinery of every
kind. The entire region has been electrified.

From one end of the Urals to the other
stretches a chain of oil wells, sited on an
extension of the oil-bearing strata running
north from Baku in the Caucasus. Derricks
tower above the ice at Pechori, and they break
the skyline at Cherdyn and Perm, line the
banks of the Kama and the Emba, are prominent at Sterlitamak, south of Ufa, and Makat,
at the head of the Caspian Sea. Altogether
this district bids fair to become what it is
sometimes called, a " second Baku," since
already it is producing 2,500,000 tons of oil a
year—about half the production of the
Rumanian oilfields before the war.

South of the Ural-Kuznetsk region lies
Kazakhstan, a huge, dry, woodless plain,
with an area five times that of France. Only
a decade or two ago the Kazakhs were nomads
living in felt tents. Now they work in collective
farms, in the coal mines of Karaganda, and
at the oil wells on the river Emba, in copper
smelting works and railway yards. Alma-
Ata, Kazakhstan's capital, is a garden city,
linked by railway with Kuznetsk and Tashkent.

From Squalor to Modern Industry

Tashkent is another city which of late
years has been transformed out of all recognition. It is the capital of the Uzbek
Socialist Soviet Republic, in what used to be
called Russian Turkistan. This is the land
of Bokhara and Samarkand, famed in history
and romance. Until after the Great War
they were ruled over by emir and khan ; the
women went veiled, polygamy was the
custom, ignorance was universal, poverty
supreme. Behind the façade of oriental
glamour was a life of stinking squalor. How
different is the picture today ! In 1928 the
first of the cotton mills were erected in
Uzbekistan, and Tashkent and Fergana are
now busy centres of industrial life. Nitrogen
is extracted from the air to fertilize the
fields, since the development of agriculture
has kept pace with that of industry. Uzbekistan is now Russia's chief cotton producing
area. But perhaps its most remarkable
development is the complete emancipation of
the Uzbek women ; the veils with which they
used to cover their faces have been discarded,
and women and girls go to school and work
side by side with the men.

Still farther to the east has spread the wave
of progress. Where in Tsarist days lived
tribes of miserable natives, amongst whom
were dumped from time to time batches of
political prisoners—there industry expands,
minerals are worked, towns are born and
grow to vigorous life. Yakutsk, only a short
time ago a wretched village, is now a city
of 25,000 souls. The same story of rapid
development can be told of the Far East.
The Russian colonies on the Pacific coast
have been revolutionized. Immense lumber
combines have been set up ; the fishermen
go to sea in motor-boats, and fish-canning
factories are dotted along the coast. New
collieries have been started, together with
engineering and shipbuilding industries.
Sakhalin has a flourishing oil industry. Here
too there are cities whose names are becoming
increasingly famous : Khabarovsk, for instance, and Komsomolsk on the edge of the
forest near the mouth of the Amur. And
everyone has heard of Vladivostok, Russia's
principal gateway on to the Pacific.

**MAGNITOGORSK, in the Urals, north-east of the Caspian Sea. A decade ago it was little more
than the village of Magnitnaya (Magnet Mountain). Today, as can be seen from this photograph,
it is an industrial town of power plants, coke-ovens and blast-furnaces, with a population of over
150,000 living under the best modern conditions.**
                                                                                              Photo, E.N.A.

where large-scale industry flourishes and
agriculture is making the desert blossom,
where people whose fathers were unlettered
nomads go to up-to-date schools and have
a literature, even a drama, of their own.

Since the Soviet Union, under Stalin's
guidance, became the subject of the Five
Year Plans, there has been a marked tendency
for industry to shift eastwards to the Urals
and beyond. The regions about Leningrad
and Moscow, the Ukraine, and the Caucasus
are still the prime centres of Russian industrial
and mineral production, but they are too
near the western frontier to be really safe
and comfortable—too near, that is, to
Hitler's bombers and tanks. So new industrial centres have been deliberately constructed hundreds of miles, even thousands
of miles, to the east. Not only the question
of safety has dictated this decentralization.

" The Soviet Union," writes Hewlett Johnson
in " The Socialist Sixth of the World," " aimed
at immediate and radical distribution of industry. Railways and roads thrust out north,
south, east and west to the districts where raw
material was found. Agriculture penetrated into
lands hitherto neglected. Marshes were drained,
deserts irrigated, forests removed, controlled or
replanted, and soil enriched. New industrial
centres sprang into being overnight, operating

mountain, which has been described as one
vast lump of iron ore. Today a great city
of 150,000 people stands there, with huge
power plants, batteries of coke-ovens, and
tremendous blast-furnaces. Great ledges have
been cut in the mountain, and the ore has
been extracted—the raw material of tractors,
as of tanks. Where so recently there was a
squalid village, there are now, we are told,
17 great blocks of workers' flats, each with
its own department store, school, restaurant,
and crèches, while each apartment has running
water, electric light, gas, and central heating.

Although there is coal in the Urals, there
is not sufficient, or rather, it is not of the right
coking quality for the iron works and their
chemical subsidiaries. Hence now Kuznetsk
(Kuzbas) at the foot of the Altai Mountains
on the borders of Mongolia comes into the
picture. It is 1,400 miles from the Urals,
but it has excellent coking coal. So the
Ural-Kuznetsk Combine has been formed ;
while coal from Kuznetsk is carried by rail to
Magnitogorsk, ore from Magnitogorsk is
taken to Kuznetsk, and at either end are
a number of metallurgical undertakings.
Another source of coal is Karaganda, on the
steppes of Kazakhstan, some 700 miles from
the Urals ; still other coalfields lie to the north

In Asia the Soviet Builds a Second Canada

MONGOLIAN CAVALRY, part of the army of Outer Mongolia, where, after the death of the last theocratic ruler in 1924, was set up the Mongolian People's Revolutionary Government run on Soviet lines. The photograph at the top is of the Soviet Siberian port of Vladivostok, through which United States' supplies for Russia are passing in spite of Japanese protests. Beneath, on the left, Kazakhs of the Soviet Republic of Kazakhstan are curious about a railway switch on the Turkistan-Siberian line. Circle: Russian guard on the Soviet-Manchukuo frontier.   *Photos, Planet News*

The Colossus of European and Asiatic Russia

THE SOVIET UNION stretches from the Baltic in the west to the Pacific in the east, from the Arctic in the north to India in the south. Its total area is square miles, and the population revealed by the census of 1939 is over 170 millions. Far to the east of Moscow a great new Russia has come into existence where many cities have sprung up and industry and agriculture are making the most of the enormous resources of the Russian soil. Should Moscow fall—Ukraine be lost—Russia beyond the Urals could still put up a prolonged resistance. Russia in Europe is seen in greater detail in p. 100.

Heavy industry (cars, farm machinery, munition, tool, transport and general machinery)
Oil fields   Oil refineries   Oil pipe lines   Coal   Shipbuilding
Aluminium   Copper   Iron   Water power   Railways

arly One-Sixth of the World's Land Surface

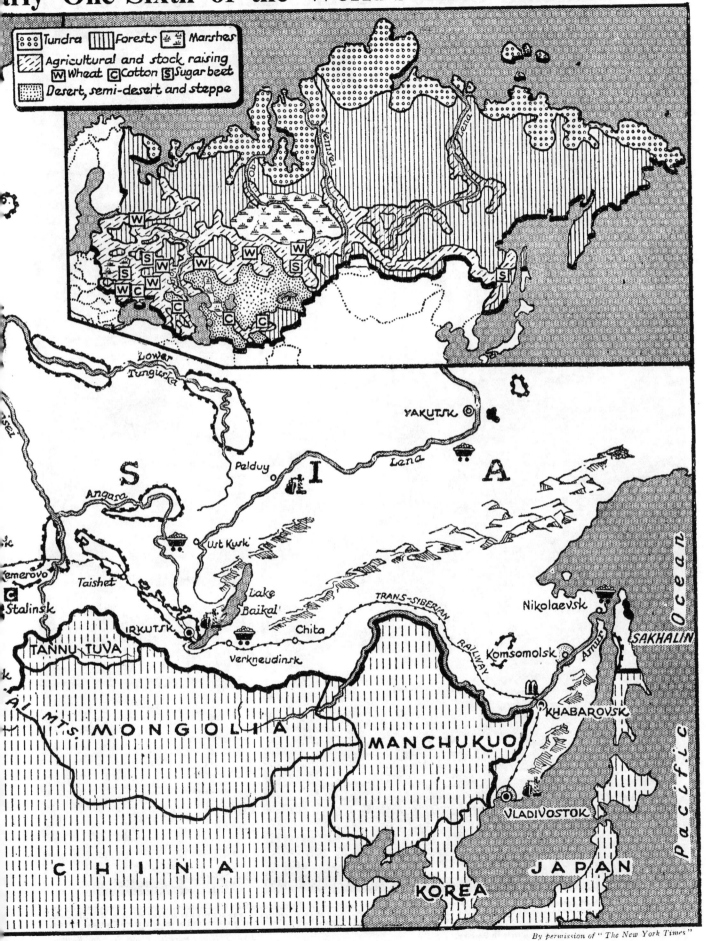

Tundra   Forests   Marshes
Agricultural and stock raising
W Wheat   C Cotton   S Sugar beet
Desert, semi-desert and steppe

Lower
Tunguska

YAKUTSK

S

I

A

Angara

Pelduy

Lena

Kemerovo

Ust Kursk'

Taishet

Stalinsk

Lake
Baikal

TRANS-SIBERIAN

Nikolaevsk

Ocean

SAKHALIN

IRKUTSK

Chita

RAILWAY

Komsomolsk

Amur

TANNU-TUVA

Verkneudinsk

KHABAROVSK

AI MTS. MONGOLIA

MANCHUKUO

Pacific

VLADIVOSTOK

CHINA

JAPAN

KOREA

The 'Churchill Convoy' Comes Safe Home to Port

FOOD FROM CANADA arrives safely in Britain. In page 117 is a striking photograph of the convoy which Mr. Churchill inspected at sea passing the Prince of Wales, and also an eye-witness account of the episode. Since then every ship of that eight-mile-long convoy has arrived safely in British ports, and above are scenes at the unloading. Left, bags of Canadian wheat being loaded into a barge. Top right, a crane-load of cheeses from Canada. Circle, girls examine a consignment of orange juice, while bottom right, another girl gazes gleefully at stacks of chopped ham. The Battle of the Atlantic still goes on, but it is being won by the British Empire.

Photos, "News Chronicle," Planet News and Keystone

In France Today: Patriots Defy the Quislings

IN France the spirit of resistance grows ever stronger, and ever larger grows the body of Frenchmen who repudiate the "collaboration" policy of Vichy and the quislings there assembled. The photograph on the left is one of a series smuggled out of France by an escaped Belgian prisoner of war. It shows a manifestation at Marseilles in front of the monument to the memory of King Alexander of Yugoslavia and M. Louis Barthou, who were assassinated in that city in 1934 by terrorists instigated by Ante Pavelitch, now the Croatian quisling. This manifestation took place on March 28, 1941, when it was learned that King Peter, the murdered Alexander's son, had decided to resist German aggression

Despite the orders of the Germans, who, when they learned of an intended manifestation, closed all the florists' shops, scores of wreaths were placed at the foot of this monument in Marseilles (see panel, right).　*Courtesy of "France."*

The Nazis having confiscated France's stocks of petrol, Paris takes to electric cars, of the kind seen above.

The parvis of Notre Dame, Paris (right centre), once crowded with sightseers from all over the world, is today deserted save for a few Nazi soldiers. Above right, two of the first French sailors, prisoners of war, to be repatriated. Above left, M. Laval, who was seriously wounded by a young Frenchman on August 27 while attending a parade of the Anti-Bolshevik Legion at Versailles, is seen at an exhibition seated with (right to left) Consul-General Quiring, M. de Brinon, and Gen. von Stuelpnagel, General Military Commander of Paris.

Photos, Keystone, Wide World and Associated Press

Our Diary of the War

WEDNESDAY, AUG. 27, 1941 *725th day*

Air.—Ten enemy fighters destroyed during large-scale sweeps over northern France. Eight British fighters missing.

Heavy night attack on Mannheim. Smaller raids on other targets in Germany and on docks at Boulogne, Ostend and Dunkirk.

Russian Front.—Stated that Germans have not crossed Dnieper below Gomel. They claimed capture of Velikiye Lugi, between Smolensk and Lake Ilmen.

Russians repulsed Finnish attacks by land and sea on Hango. Enemy conducting determined offensive against Tallinn. Fierce struggle for Viipuri.

Iran.—Abadan area cleared of Iranian troops. In Persian Gulf British naval forces have sunk two Iranian sloops and captured eight Axis merchantmen.

Africa.—Benghazi heavily raided on nights of 26-27 and 27-28.

Mediterranean.—Night attack by Fleet Air Arm on escorted convoy of four merchant ships. One hit.

General.—Attempt to assassinate Laval.

THURSDAY, AUG. 28 *726th day*

Air.—Offensive patrols over northern France. Shipping in Rotterdam docks attacked and much damage done.

Heavy night raid on Duisburg. Many other targets bombed, including Ostend.

Russian Front.—Main weight of German attack transferred to north, but enemy still held 50 miles from Leningrad.

Moscow announced that Russians have destroyed great dam over Dnieper and that troops have withdrawn from Dnepropetrovsk.

Iran.—British having penetrated 100 miles from west, and Russians 120 miles from north, Iran ordered "Cease Fire."

Africa.—S.A.A.F. heavily attacked enemy dump near Bardia.

Mediterranean.—Two enemy vessels attacked and hit by R.A.F. Powerful night raid on aerodromes in Greece and Crete, over 30 tons of bombs being dropped.

Home.—Few bombs from night raiders at points in eastern England.

General.—Mr. Menzies resigned Australian premiership. Mr. A. W. Fadden succeeded.

FRIDAY, AUG. 29 *727th day*

Air.—Ten enemy aircraft destroyed during offensive operations over northern France and off coasts of Low Countries. Ten British fighters missing.

Russian Front.—Germans claimed capture of Tallinn and port of Baltiski. Russians counter-attacked between Kholm and Toropets.

Widespread floods reported in Ukraine following destruction of Dnieper dam.

Africa.—Heavy night raid on Tripoli; five ships set blazing and harbour damaged. Benghazi and Bardia also bombed.

Mediterranean.—Fleet Air Arm bombed Gerbini aerodrome, Sicily.

General.—Announced that Hitler and Mussolini had had 5-day meeting.

SATURDAY, AUG. 30 *728th day*

Air.—R.A.F. shot up two "flak" ships off French coast. Enemy shipping off Norway attacked. Night attack on Cherbourg docks and ground defences near Dutch coast.

Russian Front.—Stubborn fighting along entire front, but few indications of definite trend of battle. Odessa still holding out.

Finns claimed capture of Viipuri. Berlin claimed that 57 Russian ships trying to escape from Tallinn had been sunk.

Africa.—Another heavy night raid on Tripoli, causing fires among shipping. Fleet Air Arm bombed dumps at Bardia.

Mediterranean.—R.A.F. bombed munition factories at Licata, Sicily. Night raids on aerodromes at Maritza and Calato, Rhodes. Fleet Air Arm torpedoed merchant vessel near Lampedusa Island.

SUNDAY, AUG. 31 *729th day*

Sea.—Admiralty announced further successes of submarines in Mediterranean Fleet, which included sinking of two enemy schooners and two supply vessels.

H.M. trawler Thorbryn reported sunk.

Air.—Day targets included railway communications and aerodromes. Night raids on objectives in Ruhr and Rhineland, particularly Essen and Cologne. Docks at Boulogne also bombed.

Russian Front.—Fierce fighting continued along entire front. Finns claimed advance beyond Viipuri. Germany admitted Russian counter-attacks north and south of Kiev.

Home.—Sharp night raid on Hull. Slight damage elsewhere. One raider destroyed.

MONDAY, SEPT. 1 *730th day*

Air.—Night raid on Cologne.

Russian Front.—Armies interlocked in almost stationary struggle. German salient at Gomel threatened by Russian forces on flank. Stubborn defence of Leningrad continued despite ceaseless enemy dive-bombing.

Iran.—Armistice terms reported signed. British and Russian troops met at Sehneh and Kazvin before separating.

Africa.—About 100 enemy aircraft made dive-bombing attacks on Tobruk, but damage and casualties were negligible. Tripoli and Bardia heavily raided on night of 31-1. Considerable enemy shelling in frontier area.

Mediterranean.—R.A.F. attacked Pozzallo, Sicily, and Cotrone, S. Italy. Fleet Air Arm bombed aerodromes at Gerbini and Comiso, Sicily, on night of 31-1.

Home.—Night bombers attacked north-east coast towns, causing damage and casualties. Two raiders destroyed.

TUESDAY, SEPT. 2 *731st day*

Air.—Daylight raid on Bremen. Low-level attack on heavily guarded supply ship off Dunkirk; two hits made.

Heavy night raids on Frankfurt and Berlin. Lesser attacks on Mannheim and other towns in Germany and on Ostend and Dunkirk.

Russian Front.—Fierce battle raging near Leningrad. Reported that during past three days Russians had bombed enemy Black Sea ports, troop concentrations and supplies.

Reported that Finns were negotiating for separate peace with Russia based on restoration of 1939 frontiers.

Africa.—Heavy raids on Tripoli and Benghazi during night of 1-2. S.A.A.F. bombed landing-ground at Gazala.

Mediterranean.—Fleet Air Arm bombed Sicilian aerodromes of Gerbini and Comiso.

WEDNESDAY, SEPT. 3 *732nd day*

Sea.—Admiralty announced that British submarine attacked Axis convoy near Libyan coast, sinking two schooners.

Air.—Night raid on Brest docks.

Russian Front.—Marshal Voroshilov now in charge of operations round Leningrad and directing counter-attacks.

Africa.—R.A.F. attacked Derna, Gazala and Bardia during night of 2-3. S.A.A.F. shot down five enemy fighters near frontier.

Mediterranean.—Fleet Air Arm attacked escorted convoy of five merchant vessels east of Sardinia during night of 2-3. One large ship blown up, another hit, and two smaller ones damaged.

THURSDAY, SEPT. 4 *733rd day*

Sea.—Admiralty announced that H.M. cruiser Hermione had rammed and cut an Italian submarine in half.

Air.—Fortress aircraft bombed Rotterdam. Eleven enemy fighters shot down during day.

Russian Front.—Voroshilov launched counter-attack at centre of German advance on Leningrad. Finns claimed to have reached old frontiers at all points except near Murmansk.

Mediterranean.—Nine enemy aircraft shot down over Malta; many others damaged.

Fleet Air Arm sank enemy destroyer outside Tripoli harbour and hit large merchant ship during night of 3-4.

R.A.F. attacked shipping at Cotrone, S. Italy. Night attacks on aerodromes at Gerbini and Catania.

FRIDAY, SEPT. 5 *734th day*

Sea.—Admiralty announced that our submarines in Mediterranean had damaged 10,000-ton cruiser near Messina, torpedoed large liner and sunk tanker and supply ship.

Russian Front.—Germans still 50 miles from Leningrad. Russian counter-attacks continued here and in Ukraine.

Africa.—During night of 4-5 bombing raids were made on Tripoli, Barce and objectives at other points.

General.—Announced that U.S. destroyer Greer had been attacked by submarine while carrying mails to Iceland.

ITALIAN PRISONERS, now being employed on agricultural work in England, unloading stores from a lorry. Many hundreds of Mussolini's "invincible" army are doing really useful work in draining, ditching and general farm labour, thus helping to solve Britain's food problems.   *Photo, Planet News*

The Flight of Bombs from Plane to Target

A DAYLIGHT ATTACK provides opportunity for explaining a confusing matter. In page 85 bombs dropped on Knapsack seem to be going nose upwards. Here, in a series taken during a raid by Short Stirlings on the Potez aircraft factory at Méaulte, near Albert on the Ancre, the sequence is clearly shown. Top, bombs have just left the plane. Centre, the bombs are half-way down and the target appears on the right. Bottom, the target is hit : (1) machine-gun shops: (2) shops and main assembly hangars; (3) assembly shops.

Photos, British Official

This is What Tobruk is Like Today

Since the middle of April Tobruk has been besieged, though it is in no sense cut off from the world as the approach to it by sea is still open. Recently it was visited by a number of War Correspondents, and here we have an account, largely based on Richard Capell's dispatches to the " Daily Telegraph," of what they saw.

L ucknow, Mafeking, Ladysmith—these are three of the beleaguered places in our Imperial story where " ever upon the topmost roof our banner of England blew." Now to the heroic company is to be added the name of Tobruk.

Judging from the descriptions of the people who have been there, it is not exactly a pleasure resort. Even in peacetime, when it was just one of a chain of Italian towns scattered at intervals along the Libyan shore, it had few attractions, and now it has all the drawbacks of a place in the war's front lines. It is usually approached by sea, since on the landward sides, on the east and south and west, the ring of Italian and German troops is drawn tight. " Tobruk, as seen from the sea at night," Richard Capell reports, " rather suggests the Ypres salient in the old days, with an elaborate display of rockets, Very lights, gun flashes and bursting ack-ack shells." Daylight reveals the spacious harbour as a graveyard of ships ; the wrecks number the best part of a hundred, including the old Italian cruiser " San Giorgio." Tobruk town itself is in process of being demolished by daily bombing, not to speak of occasional shelling ; and the white city, with its hospital, school, wine shops and shady arcades, now lies battered and wrecked. For the rest, the 100 square miles—about the size of the Isle of Wight—contained within the

perimeter presents hardly a landmark. From the harbour one ascends to the first plateau, where thousands of motor vehicles left by the Italians last winter lie stranded. In the sheltered valleys near the sea occur a few palms, fig trees and prickly pears, but on the windy plateaux, scorched by driving sand, only camel thorn struggles for life.

In this unprepossessing place a little garrison has stood at bay since last April, and still stands, and is determined to stand until the wave of British victory for the second time washes its walls. " Although Australia is the predominant partner in the defence " (to quote Mr. Capell again), " many British counties are represented too, and the coming years will hear yarns of tawny Cyrenaica, its tyrannical sun, its withering sandstorms, its flies and fleas and its invariably ultramarine sea, told in the village inns of the North Country, the Midlands and East Anglia."

" Tobruk," he goes on, " is an epic of intercontinental comradeship. Australian infantrymen call the British gunners incomparable, and while our men equally admire the grit and daring of the Australians who sortie into the unknown, these men in their turn think that the Indians, rich in North-West Frontier experiences, are the supreme masters of patrolling."

So there the little army live, with their backs to the sea and their faces to the illimitable desert where the enemy lies in wait. Some of the defenders have their quarters in the ruined houses of the little port, while others live in caves in the hillside or in trenches cut in the rock, in the open desert or in the beds of dried-up streams. Yet others are stationed in the outer perimeter, in the line of Italian-constructed fortifications which makes an arc 30 miles long in the desert at an average distance of eleven miles from the port. Air raids are a daily, almost hourly, occurrence, and the A.A. guns are almost constantly in action. The log-book of one battery records some 1,200 incursions and alerts. Between April 9 and July 31 there were 437 bombing raids—277 in daylight, including 48 carried out by dive-bombers, and the remaining 160 at night. It was estimated that during this period the raiders dropped some 350 tons of bombs. Yet the casualties have been remarkably light, thanks in large measure to the caves with which the district is liberally supplied.

There is No Beer in Tobruk

Save for the raiding, life in Tobruk is uneventful enough, but it is far from easy. There are none of the amenities of garrison life. There is sufficient food, but the mainstay is bully—bully—bully. Fresh vegetables and fruit are hard to come by, and tinned herrings are not particularly appetizing in that torrid climate. There are no girls, no cinemas, no canteens. The water is brackish, coming from wells or from the distilling plant which the Italians left behind them ; it is apt to spoil the whisky—when whisky is to be had. And as for beer—well, there is no beer. That, perhaps, is the garrison's chief grievance. Sweltering in the blazing sun they think longingly of the bars they used to know. One of them, an Australian lieutenant, has been moved to write an ode which runs as follows :

Oh, sleek brown shape, thou prize of my desiring,
Mine inner man cries out for thee ;
Mine eager lips, my thirsty throat aspiring
To taste thee, brew sublime and free.
In dreams I see thee held aloft and shining ;
Thy sparkling fluid trembleth near ;
Ah ! bliss divine, what need now my repining ?

A British naval rating on duty at Admiralty House, Tobruk. This Libyan harbour is a veritable graveyard of ships, some of which can be seen in this photograph.

Soon, soon I'll taste thee, precious beer.
Thus dream I soon that it will be my lot
Beneath thy lips to hold mine eager pot.

Books and papers are sadly lacking, though the men print and publish several news-sheets. One is " The Tobruk Truth Dinkum Oil " (Australian slang for " the real truth "), whose motto is " always appears." Another is a very lively production known as " Mud and Blood."

After ten days in the line the men are given two days off. Occasionally the more fortunate may spend a few days in Cairo ; but for the most part the leisure hours are passed in Tobruk or lazing on the beach.

Since Tobruk is one of the dustiest places on earth, sea-bathing is very popular. Sometimes it has its excitements. " One moment," writes Richard Capell, " the whole land steamed in a deep hypnotism under the Libyan sun. The next it was spitting fire like an irritated dragon. We bathers wriggled as best we could into the sand, meanwhile gazing fascinated at the swooping aircraft, the tracer bullets and ack-ack shell bursts, a spectacle stranger than all those ancient lands' mythology could afford."

Then the men have their competitions, e.g. a flea-catching contest, on which it may be commented that it was not confined to fleas but comprised all kinds of vermin. " Mud and Blood " printed a table of comparative values : 1 bug equals 3 fleas ; 1 rat, 10 fleas ; 1 gazelle, 300 fleas ; 1 Italian prisoner, 200 fleas—plus all fleas found on him. William Forrest, Special Correspondent of the "News Chronicle," tells of a cartoon in " Mud and Blood " depicting an Italian surrendering to an Aussie. " Don't kill me ! " cries the Italian. " Kill you, be —— ! " replies the Aussie. " You mean about 700 fleas to me !" This is a sample of the more mild instances of humour that is rife in Tobruk. But " Mud and Blood " is not a family newspaper, and as an excuse for not publishing some more vigorous specimens, William Forrest reminds us that there are no ladies in Tobruk !

The " latest " from the " Tobruk Truth," a news sheet which contrives to appear daily. The editor moves his office whenever enemy action interferes with the editorial scheme of things. *Photos, British Official : Crown Copyright*

Their Backs to the Sea, Their Faces to the Desert

The Italian cruiser, San Giorgio, lies battered in Tobruk harbour. She was damaged and beached during a bombing attack by the Fleet Air Arm at Tobruk, June 11, 1940.

" Cave-men " who have put a spoke in the Axis wheel in North Africa, these Australian soldiers round about Tobruk live and work thus protected from Nazi bombs.

Australian reinforcements making their way towards the outer defences of beleaguered Tobruk. The area still in British hands is about 100 square miles.

A FULL HOUSE for amateur theatricals at Tobruk where men of the R.A.F. and A.I.F. are entertaining comrades. On the wall is a piece of Italian rant about Fascism.

Photos, British Official

Home Guards Show a Really Offensive Spirit

A realistic attack by "German" paratroops operating from behind a smoke screen against a railhead. Porters, goods-checkers and signalmen of the Home Guard rush into action and score a local victory over the "enemy." On the left, an "invader" is captured by a Home Guard and threatened with his own revolver. Tanks were used by the defenders in driving off the parachute troops.

SHORT SHRIFT FOR LOOTERS in a Home Guard exercise at Birkenhead. An incident in the "battle" between Home Guards and Dutch Army troops who played the part of the "invaders." Though the Home Guards accounted for 50 per cent of the attackers, and stubbornly resisted them everywhere, the "enemy" captured the town. In the circle above, a Home Guard crew with their Northover Projector in an ambush post during similar manoeuvres on Epsom Downs. The Northover Projector is used for throwing Molotov cocktails at advancing tanks and enemy blockhouses.

Photos, "News Chronicle," Sport & General, Keystone and Associated Press

I Was There! .... Eye Witness Stories of the War

How We German Parachutists Captured Maleme

Here is a German eye-witness story, issued by the German propaganda, of the capture of Maleme aerodrome in Crete. Told by Lieut. Ernst Kleinlein of the First Division of Parachute Troops, it is published here by arrangement with "Life."

Lieutenant Kleinlein's story begins when he is flying out from Greece in a Junkers transport plane. He says :

The hand on my small silver watch stands close to 4 a.m. We still have 15 minutes more flying. I look out of the plane window. The other planes in the squadron have closed up. Behind us flies the second company, behind it the third. I count to see whether a plane has been left behind—12, 15, 23, 30, 52—as I come to 60 I give it up. From the cobalt-blue vapour between sky and water the planes rise behind us like an army of scaled dragons. The lance-sergeant taps my shoulder. He points through the opposite window. There it is : the small narrow beach, the first ridges in the foreground and behind the second terrace the white rocky peaks of the mountains of Crete.

The lance-sergeant again taps my shoulder. "*Herr Oberleutnant.*" Yes, I know. Again there is that pressing feeling in my stomach which comes to me when the plane descends.

"Door open." The sergeant stands at the door. He gives the signal to leap with a rap of his left hand on the back of every man who quickly appears in front of the plane door. Schroeder, Grammelsberg, Hansen, Berg, Wenstaedt, now the lance-sergeant, now me.

I have four-and-a-half seconds from the time the parachute opens until landing. The wind carries us directly to the hill. Our bombers hurtle against the airport batteries from above like catapulted knives. Now I notice the whining whistle of the plane swooshing down only 50 metres from us—there is a dry rattle of its cannons. There comes the next one. In the distance hollow bomb detonations thud. Over there, our first machine-gun begins. Lieutenant W. is attacking already. Then I myself am down.

Will the English Fighters Come ?

The lance-sergeant stands in the bomb crater next to the machine-gun ; next to him, Schroeder ; next, the sergeant. The bombers have withdrawn and circle about like swallows in the air. Will the English fighters come ?

None come. From our hill we can look down on the field (Maleme aerodrome). To the right, the hangar, made of old clay, wooden pillars and planks. Now and again a small gun crackles from the shadowy depth. Four khaki figures advance and fall together. From here they look like freed marionettes. We did not see the gunfire.

I nod to the lance-sergeant. He goes with three men toward the clay building from the rear. It is 4.25 a.m. We have been on the ground for ten minutes. The bombers are no longer to be seen. In their place new transport planes soar in the sky. They are to land at 4.30 a.m. The sergeant has taken up the machine-gun of the lance-sergeant. A flare goes up from the other side of the field. It is 4.26 a.m. and the edge of the field is filled with a flock of men. The British khaki is intermingled with the grey cloth of our men. A British tank clatters over the airport. It is only of medium size. We must hurry.

Now everything goes according to manoeuvres. "Fire." The sergeant shoots as if prompted by a stop-watch. The western edge of the field lights up. Hand grenades tear out the side of the clay hangar. It is 4.30 a.m. We have it. Eighty prisoners, one gun, some munitions.

Junkers transports sink low and descend with their load. There are still two Bedford trucks with broken axles lying on the runway. We should have removed them, but now there is no time. They explode into the air from our hand grenades. Immediately the first Junkers rolls into the midst of the splintered ruins. Now everything comes : radio apparatus, munitions, one sack of Wittler bread from Berlin, packages of bandages, trench mortars, lemons, our new rapid-firing cannon of manganese alloy, the folding gun carriage. The propellers of the Junkers do not stop. It blows as if God and the general wanted to give us special ventilation for the hot battle. The Junkers climbs. The next comes down. The bicycle detachment steps out: The third, the fourth. Down, up, down, up.

"Lance-Sergeant, what has become of that British tank ? " He doesn't know. We find that a bomber took care of it for us. Since Greece our bombers have received small but effective cannon and are as useful to us as though we had the anti-tank guns.

Land, take off, land, take off, land, and take off again and again. The sun already is high and hot. My ears have become deaf from the roar of motors. After 60 transports have landed and taken off again, the advance to the sea begins. But we are to remain at the field. Toward noon we are supposed to be picked up and then go on again—to Heraklion. But I don't tell my men.

We look around the vicinity. Burned-out Mausers, tent sections which were drenched with lime and now break like paper, rifles, munition cases. In the disintegrated shed the lance-sergeant has discovered a supply of corned beef. " May we breakfast ? " he asks. " Permitted," I say. They make themselves a stove from a petrol tank which withstood the blowing up of the truck barricades, and start a fire. The sergeant is wounded. Lieutenant W. has lost two men.

Meanwhile I look over the prisoners. They are almost all New Zealanders. " We had no idea of this kind of war," says one fellow, tall as a tree. We captured the majority in shirts and shorts. They were more surprised than outfought—the affair went that fast. " We expected you ever since Saturday," the tall one says. " So we were on guard for three nights and got no sleep. Today you surprised us."

" Impolite of us," I say, and the entire group laughs.

I permit my men to gather up and fold the parachutes and then order quiet. At 10 o'clock the prisoners are transported away in empty Junkers. At 11 a.m. the last Junkers brings new sealed orders.

I stroll about the country a bit. Spread-out detachments have pushed up to the tank nest. The air battle apparently has moved out to sea and to the west. The sun burns on bare stones. A large lizard in strange colours shoots along between the cliffs. Now we lie here between Europe and Africa and wait . . .

NAZI PARATROOPS, three of whom are seen in the foreground, with others coming down, on the island of Crete. A detailed description of the German air-borne invasion of Crete appears in this page from the pen of a Nazi lieutenant of the First Division of Parachute Troops taking part in the capture of Maleme aerodrome.

Photo, Planet News

The German Officer Shot Me in Cold Blood

In a special hospital in Moscow for men severely wounded in the head
and face lay V. Dolgin, a 26-year-old Ukrainian, who was maltreated
and left for dead by the Germans on the Smolensk front. Here is his
story, as reported in " Soviet War News."

IT was on July 16, and we had received
orders to occupy the village of Demidovo,
near Smolensk, and to advance to the
highway. When we had gone a little way
the Germans opened fire on us, but we
answered them. It was in this battle that I
was wounded in the arm and leg. The
commander urged me to go back, but I was
a machine-gunner and wanted to turn my
ammunition over to the other gunners. As
I was trying to reach them, something
crashed on my head and I was knocked
unconscious.

I lay where I was for about four hours
and regained consciousness only when I
felt someone kicking me. I opened my eyes
and saw a German officer and two soldiers
standing over me. The officer ordered me to
stand up, but I could not stand. The two
soldiers pulled me to my feet, but when the
officer hit me in the face with his fist I fell
down again. Then the officer demanded
that I tell him the whereabouts of the Soviet
troops and how many tanks we had. I
refused, and he became angry and hit me
again. I still remained silent ; and then he
took a gun from one of the soldiers and shot
me twice. The second bullet tore through my
tongue and knocked out several teeth.
Thinking I was dead, they left me. I was
very weak, for I was bleeding badly. I
wanted to dress my wounds, but I was
afraid that, if they saw the white bandage,
they would know I was alive and come back
again. Finally, I decided to remain as I was
until the night and then try to reach the
village. The whole day I lay on the ground
in a semi-conscious state. I had illusions
that I saw my comrades, and I wondered
why they did not come to my rescue. I
tried to call to them, but I could not speak,
and I could not stand up.

Finally, it grew dark and I began to crawl
to the village. I was terribly thirsty ; and
I think it was the thirst that saved my life,
for every time I fell down the thirst drove me
on again. At last I reached the village and
found water, and then I felt better. I met
two old peasants and asked them to direct
me to the Soviet troops. My tongue was
so swollen from the wound that I could only

mutter and they could not understand me.
They thought I was a German soldier.
Reluctantly, they said I might sleep on the
hay near their house, and I stayed there until
the morning. When the morning came I
heard firing, but I did not know whether it

was our troops or the Germans. I crept out
of the hay, and after I had gone a little
way I ran into a Red Army man from the
signal corps. He took me to the hospital,
where my wounds were dressed, and then I
was sent to Moscow. That is all.

Nobody, if they have never experienced
the torture that I did, can imagine that
men can be so cruel and do the terrible things
that the Germans did to me. It is horrible
to recall it now, and every time I think of it
I feel as if I am beginning a second life.

I Posed as a Traitor to Get Out of France

A young French infantry officer, who volunteered for service in Syria in
order to have a chance of getting out of France, here gives a revealing
account of the attitude of the people in the Occupied zone towards cooperation with the Germans.

IN June I was garrisoned with an infantry
regiment near the border of Occupied
France. Like many comrades who left
the military school at the same time as
myself, I entertained the secret hope of
joining the Free French. A heaven-sent
opportunity arose when a secret circular
arrived, asking for reinforcements in officers
and N.C.O.s for the Levant. I signed on
immediately, and towards the middle of
June we left, 700 of us, by special train.

Every time our train stopped in Occupied
France people, often in the presence of
German officers, did not hide their contempt
for the " volunteers ," brandishing a threatening fist at us, calling us " traitors " and
shouting all sorts of insulting epithets.

At Mulhouse groups of people, notably
women, gathered in front of the train windows
shouting " Shame ! Shame ! " and pelted
us with stones. Many windows were broken.
The police had great difficulty in moving
hostile groups from the platform. An aged
peasant shouted in front of my carriage
window : " You are all traitors. I hope
you will be killed by the Free French or
drowned in the sea." Many of us tried to
buy cigarettes and refreshments at the
station buffet, but no one would serve us.

All the places through which we passed
bore signs of the real feeling of the population, like the immense " Darlan has sold
himself " chalked up on the wall of a factory
beside the railway line.

We were particularly disgusted when we
arrived at the German frontier. Then it
became clear whom we were about to fight
for. The Nazis, officers and men, were most
polite, almost obsequious. The clanking of
boots and spurs, the shaking of hands, the
robot-like salutes, the refreshments specially
prepared for us, the toasts to German
victory and the new order in Europe—if
some credulous or misled people were taken
in by them, most of us felt more like crying.
The same ceremony was repeated during the
crossing of Germany and the occupied
Balkans.

We left the train to be taken by air to
Aleppo. The plane which took me and
several other officers to Athens must have
been sabotaged in some way or other, for we
had scarcely got in the air when we lost one
propeller. Then three engines out of four
refused to work properly. The pilot managed

This Free French soldier fought alongside the
British in Syria. After the Allied victory
many of the Vichy troops came over to the
cause of Free France.   *Photo, P.N.A.*

to land safely in a field near the aerodrome
where we had started.

We arrived in Syria a few days before the
armistice was signed. As soon as we arrived,
a great many of us made arrangements to
join the Free French Forces. One day I
hailed an Australian motor-lorry on the
Tripoli road, and two hours later I was at
the Free French headquarters.—*Free French
Newsletter.*

My First Six Months as a Land Girl

By the summer of 1941 it was hoped to raise the total of recruits fo the
Women's Land Army over the last war figure of 16,000. Here E. M.
Barraud, who was one of the first thousand, tells the story of her first six
months on the land.

ONE September morning my employer
led me, with what I now know to be
mutual doubts, out to his orchards
to start picking plums ; and there he left
me, with a completely uncontrollable ladder,
two picking baskets and a pile of empty half-
sieves. I had no idea of the lay-out of the
farm, and when he disappeared into the blue,
I felt more alone, lost, desolate and incompetent than ever in my life before.
Apart from anything else, I have a horror

of heights, and ladder-heights in particular !

I can laugh at that day now, but at the time
it was almost unmitigated horror. I nearly
killed myself lugging that ladder about. I
could never find the right place or angle in
which to set it, and when I *had* managed to
coax it into position, as soon as I set foot on
it, it lurched ominously, with creaking and
cracking of branches. I had no idea how
many baskets of the wretched plums I was
expected to fill, or by what time. But the

**V. DOLGIN, young Russian machine-gunner,
who describes above how he was shot by the
Nazis although wounded.** *Photo, British Official*

Astride her horse, this land girl is homeward bound with a load of hay. In this page a land girl describes her experiences.

real sore spot is that, in my ignorance, and working alone, I did not know for a week that it was the local custom to take half an hour for lunch at ten o'clock—and when it came to Friday night, and I found out, I hadn't the nerve to charge my employer for those five half-hours !

It all seems a very long way off now, now that I am a hardened farm hand. In the second week a new terror lay in wait for me —my first handling of a farm horse. A man fell out of the harvest field, and I was put on to lead loaded carts back to the rickyard and empty ones out to the field. Then I was roped in to pitch sheaves down in the field. Then to help with the stacking.

Those were the days when every fresh job meant a fresh set of unused muscles to ache, till I began to think I would never come to the end of the pain, and be able to say, " Now there isn't another inch of me to discover." Because no sooner were my arm muscles fairly tough than they gave me the job of horse-raking through the stubble, and I got it in my legs, so that when at last I dared to climb down from the seat I found I could not stand. (It was that day when I first had to

stable my horse, and ended up, after a hectic twenty minutes, with his collar round my neck and the harness a glorious tangle at my feet.)

Summing up those first two or three weeks, I can only say that had anyone realized how utterly ignorant and inept I was, I might never have survived. As it was, it was taken for granted I could do this and that—and, to save my face, somehow I managed to do it ! I hasten to say, however, that there was no lack of friendly help and advice when I did ask for it. I have the deepest gratitude for all the patience everyone has shown me as I have been learning. But I have always preferred to learn by " watching points " rather than by asking questions, and in the rush of those harvest days I was allowed to give full rein to my preference.

My farm is one of some 200 acres, mainly arable—wheat, barley, oats, beans, potatoes —with just enough cows to supply the house and one or two cottagers with milk, and some couple of dozen calves running on, upwards of fifty pigs, about seventy head of poultry and some thirty rabbits. At first I had nothing to do with stock : a young German refugee trainee attended to these, with occasional assistance. Early in November, when the

Martha Ferris, once a shop assistant, now has a very different job. Her new customers include these three-month-old calves.

harvest work proper was really at an end, and I began to wonder how soon I, in common with the other already dwindling team of harvest workers, should be " stood off," and what would happen then, the German boy found he was not suited for farm work, and left.

I shall not forget that bitter November morning, when I was half-way up my legs in water, wrestling with a hedge and ditch which had not been touched for three years, and my employer came down to tell me the boy had left, and ask me if I would take on the milking. It meant I had my chance to go " on the staff." I started milking that afternoon. Within a week I had charge of the feeding of the calves, poultry and rabbits, and the shadow of being " stood off " on wet days was lifting rapidly. My proving handy with a saw and hammer banished it for good. I did not have one day at home all through the winter.

London friends wrote to me, " I suppose there is not much doing on the farm this weather." Not much doing ? Hedging and ditching (one of my favourite jobs), muck-carting, all the concentrated high-speed work of threshing and chaff-cutting, artificial manure distributing, fence repairs, barbed wire work, dressing wheat, barley, oats, thatching, and all the other endlessly different tasks that crop up in the farming year.

And in October my employer wondered, Could I manage the tractor ? He worked with me for an hour—then strode away and left me to go on ploughing a ten-acre stubble. Since then I have done my share of ploughing and drilling and harrowing and rolling, too.

I am afraid I laughed a little bitterly when I heard a broadcast about the training of Land Girls—how they were given I don't know how many hours' technical instruction, etc. I laughed still more bitterly—though there was some triumph in it, too—when I heard a Dorset farmer enumerate some of the jobs you couldn't ask a woman to do. I had done them all ! And the triumph was definitely on top next morning, when my employer commented on the broadcast, and our foreman added, " Ah well, master, we've got one in a hundred ! "

Well, there it is, the record of my first six months. I still say to myself, " Gosh, you're being *paid* to do this ! " Because, having beaten my typewriter into a ploughshare, I know I shall never now be able to bear going back.—" *The Land Girl* "

Siftings from the News

Empress of Abyssinia has flown home to Addis Ababa.

New Liberator bomber crossed from Newfoundland to Ireland in 7½ hours.

Bags of tea, sent from Dutch East Indies, were dropped by R.A.F. over Holland.

Wing Cmdr. J. W. Gillan, who in 1938 flew at speed of 408·75 m.p.h., was reported missing.

Hitler has presented Mussolini with a great astronomical observatory to be built near Rome.

Germany has appealed to Rumania for loan to help " the Reich to carry on the Holy Crusade of liberation."

In Plymouth 52,000 bombed dwellings have been repaired, some of them two, three or even more times.

One hundred and eighteen air officers and airmen from New Zealand have already won awards.

Hard-rock miners of Royal Canadian Engineers reported rapid progress on engineering project deep in Rock of Gibraltar.

Estimated that during first eight weeks of egg control scheme 170,000,000 out of 305,000,000 delivered were bad.

Rioters at Goering Steel Works, Linz, Austria, being refused rise in wages, blew up two main blast furnaces.

A New Zealand torpedo-bomber squadron is to be formed in Britain.

Three citizens of Liége sentenced to death for concealing shot-down British airman.

Canadian Air Force has lost a total of 557 reported killed and missing since war began.

Quisling, sufferer from insomnia, has been gravely ill after overdose of sleeping tablets.

Nazi leader at Sandefjord, Norway, was thrown into the harbour by crowd singing Norwegian National Anthem.

" Berlin slaughters the Red Army with an adding machine," commented New York evening paper P.M.

Dutch Boy Scouts defied Nazi ban on their camp at Putten and police had to use arms, wounding one.

Five members of Yugoslav Cabinet will set up H.Q. in Montreal, cooperating with rest of Government in London.

During first week of outward Airgraph service 170,000 letters were photographed and dispatched to Middle East.

Nearly one in ten of population of Australia —600,000 men—will soon be in fighting services, and another 150,000 in munitions.

Argentine Committee investigating Axis activities discovered Gestapo index of 3,000 prominent anti-Nazi Argentines.

Paddy Coleman has exchanged typewriter for tractor and now works on a farm not fifteen miles from Piccadilly Circus.　　*Photos, Topical*

Editor's Postscript

SURELY not even the deepest attachment to the democratic right of free speech can justify any government in time of war allowing a self-advertising citizen to broadcast notorious untruths about a friendly state. Isn't this hot-airman Lindbergh just getting too much rope ? . . . Happily, we know what he may do with that later on . . . His latest reported distortion of truth—truth which no future historian will ever dare to question—is that Britain " turned against France " and " turned against Finland," so that Americans have no guarantee she may not yet " turn against " the U.S.A. !

SUCH mischievous vapourings leave one gasping : leave one, indeed, with the feeling that Lindy's little admirer Goebbels would gladly have supplied the script of some of these speeches for him to broadcast. Goebbels certainly has invented nothing more foully false : not even his big Athenia lie, doubtless accepted by America's anti-British propagandist as a statement of fact. Has the man forgotten that Norway and Sweden barred, by the laws of a strict but futile neutrality, all plans and proposals for effective help to Finland when the Allies could have given that help and might have remained Allies thereby ? Does he know that Finland " turned against " Britain when she joined with the Nazis in attacking the Soviets, for whom the strangely changed conditions of the War demanded Britain's utmost measure of help ? Has he forgotten Churchill's passionate appeal to a corrupt and confused government of France to stand in with Britain on a basis of equal citizenship—perhaps the most daring gesture ever made by one valiant and undefeated ally to another, stunned, stupefied, vacillating, disintegrating ? A self-sacrificing offer whose rejection should gladden all Britons today, for it fell on ears unworthy and hearts untuned to its greatness. *We* turned against them ! What are the rulers of America going to do about this dangerous fictionist ; this lucky airman whom the Nazis have flattered into posing as a violent leader of America's minority of Anti-British factions ?

" **O**PHELIA of the Ages, deckt in woeful weed and daisy "—thus Meredith of his Victorian age, and so many another poet from Juvenal to Joyce, in varying words, but to the same purpose, of his own age. To the moralist his own particular age is always deckt in woeful weed and daisy, merging into madness. I was tempted so to ruminate last night at the Player's Theatre, where I was the appreciative guest of Mr. Leonard Sachs with his delightful presentation of " Ridgway's Late Joys," which originated, if I'm not mistaken, in Covent Garden some time before the War. The entertainment was exclusively pastiche—but, as such, entirely charming. Yet it left me sad, for I saw in it —just like listening to the Wireless in these days—the end of an era. I'm an old playgoer, who has seen the early days, the heyday and death of the Music Hall, that peculiarly British institution which went out—nor will

it ever come back—with the rise of the so-called " revue," which has never, save under the aegis of C. B. Cochran, approximated to the French original, and then only when it was associated with that other dramatic form known as " spectacle."

HAVING seen Lottie Collins do " Ta-ra-ra-boom-de-ay " with an abandon and a vivacity that the very title of the song can still bring to life in memory's movies, there was a tear in my applause for the young lady who faintly revived for me at the Joys last night that picture of a distant past. " The days of the Kerry dancers " did not come back to

GEN. KONIEV, whose troops made a highly successful counter-attack on the central sector of the German armies in Russia, routing a Nazi infantry division and retaking many villages.
Photo, Planet News

me, but to the younger generation, gathered under the chairman's hammer of Mr. Sachs, I could perceive that all was well—they were seeing as a new thing an old thing renewed. But all the spirit of it gone with the winds of fifty years ! " Playmates," " Josh-u-a," " Clementine," and other early joys of my youth were all reproduced—with a new archness and *finesse* of satire, let it be said— but sheer nostalgia was their effect on me.

NOW I do not wish to be " nothing if not critical," where I saw so much talent, but all this harking back by the young generation to the days of old—of which they know little more than they do of the Greek theatre —seems to me foreboding. What I missed and what I long for is " the rapture of the forward view " (another Meredithism by the way)—and that's what I miss in all those Broadcasts that are built upon " old favourites." Old favourites be hanged ! It's a sterile world we are living in if we can't get even a rationed supply of new favourites. All the listeners to the Wireless are not so old

as I am, and I can attribute only to sheer decadence this continual insistence on the old. I'm all for the new. That is the good way of life : the " forward view."

I HAVE seen all the old favourites : Jenny Hill, Dan Leno, Arthur Roberts, T. E. Dunville, Vesta Victoria, Marie Lloyd, Bessie Bellwood, James Fawn, Chirgwin, John Jolly Nash, George Formby (senr.), Harry Randall, Harry Weldon, aye, and a hundred more, some of whom are still surviving and " in wery good 'ealth," notably Harry Lauder, George Robey, Charles Coborn, Vesta Tilley ; but it is sad to see so much genuine talent in the younger generation being spilled even on good reproductions instead of exploiting new ideas, new personality, new interpretations of this new and totally different age. An age in which the art forms are all looking back for inspiration means that we have come to an end instead of an advance. In the thing that is new there is always a verve, an enthusiasm, that no subsequent reproduction can recapture. Look forward, Mr. Leonard Sachs (who might be a *revenant* Lewis Waller), not back ! But thanks no less for a bitter-sweet evening.

I AM told by the Binding Department of THE WAR ILLUSTRATED that, despite their stipulation that only loose numbers untorn, and not disfigured by writing or otherwise, can be accepted for binding, some subscribers ignore this condition. This is especially the case since I have re-modelled the publication in order that the whole of each number can be bound up. It is obvious, since the paper restrictions have forced us to abandon the original wrapper pages, that those who intend to bind should take extra care in the handling of the loose numbers, and ought not to make marginal notes on any of them. Fortunately, when we consider the large number of volumes that are being bound, these instances are extremely few, but as it is not always possible to ensure that each set when bound goes back to the original sender (which explains why " only loose numbers in good condition can be accepted for binding "), I do hope that binding subscribers will take greater care than was previously necessary to preserve their loose numbers.

A PROPOS of this, I have this very day received a letter from a Scottish subscriber who tells me that he keeps the cardboard box in which the bound volume is posted to him by our Binding Department and places his current numbers, after he reads them, into the box to preserve them for eventual binding. What an ingenious idea ! Nothing could be simpler or more practical. So I pass on the idea without delay to all subscribers who look to binding their loose numbers in volume form. When the total for making up a volume has been collected in the cardboard box, all that need be done is to send it and its contents with the necessary postal order and instructions as to style of binding, name and address of sender, the whole securely tied up and directed to our Binding Department, and in due course back comes your lovely and valuable volume !

JOHN CARPENTER HOUSE.
WHITEFRIARS LONDON. E.C.4.

Printed in England and published on the 10th, 20th and 30th of each month by the Proprietors, The Amalgamated Press, Ltd., The Fleetway House, Farringdon Street, London, E.C.4. Registered for transmission by Canadian Magazine Post. Sole Agents for Australia and New Zealand : Messrs. Gordon & Gotch, Ltd. ; and for South 1941

Vol 5 # The War Illustrated Nº107

Edited by Sir John Hammerton

FOURPENCE

SEPT. 30TH, 1941

IN THE MEDITERRANEAN on a dark night : roar and flash, and the anti-aircraft guns, port and starboard, beat off an attack by enemy planes. The silence is torn to shreds, and sea and sky are illuminated with brilliant hostile flashes, momentarily revealing the superstructure of the ship, and making it possible to take this night action photograph, the first obtained under real war conditions.
Exclusive to THE WAR ILLUSTRATED

NO. 108 WILL BE PUBLISHED FRIDAY, OCT. 10

BUT EVEN NOW AMERICA IS NOT AT WAR

AMERICA took another big step towards war with the Axis Powers when President Roosevelt, in his broadcast on September 11, uttered the warning that though " we have sought no shooting war with Hitler and do not seek it now," yet neither " do we want peace so much that we are willing to pay for it by permitting him to attack our naval and merchant ships while they are on legitimate business." Nazi submarines and raiders, those " rattlesnakes of the Atlantic," were declared to constitute a menace, a challenge to American sovereignty. " From now on, if German or Italian vessels of war enter the waters the protection of which is necessary for American defence, they do so at their own peril. The orders which I have given as Commander-in-Chief to the United States Army and Navy are to carry out that policy—at once." What those orders were was not made public, but commentators supposed to be " in the know " said that they meant " shoot at sight."

STILL, however, though it may be true to say that America is *in* the war, she is not yet *at* war, and there are still many signs of a reluctance to take the final, irrevocable step. These signs have multiplied since the German attack on Soviet Russia.

Nor need we be surprised that this should be so. After all, we ourselves watched the conversion of Manchuria into Manchukuo and the Japanese invasion of China with equanimity, if not worse. We watched, even aided, the suppression of Czechoslovak democracy, the extinction of the state of Masaryk and Benes. The Far East seems a long way from our English fields, and even Czechoslovakia is out of earshot. But neither one nor the other could have seemed more distant to us than the war zones of Europe must appear to the men and women of Montana, whom Senator Wheeler represents, or to those who read the paper which Senator Vandenberg edits in a small town in Michigan.

WHEN the war began two years ago the American masses had the excited feeling that they were watching from comfortable seats in the grandstand a really thrilling baseball display. Many, perhaps most, of them still have that feeling, and this although nearly all the responsible leaders of American opinion, from the President downwards, have striven their hardest to remove the blinkers from their eyes. In 1939 the American farmers and artisans, the American housewives and business executives, thought that the war was not their war : they are still not altogether convinced to the contrary. Too many of them still feel that, whatever the President may say, American security is not *really* threatened, the happiness of their lives is not *really* menaced by anything that Hitler may say or can do.

Not only distance contributes to this state of mind. There is that distrust of Europe so deeply engrained in the children of those who left Europe generations ago because of religious persecution and political oppression—a distrust which was fostered by the disappointing results of the Great War, when President Wilson's plans for a new order of society were frustrated (so the Americans are told) by the cynical cunning of the Old World politicians. Then we must allow for that lack of knowledge and understanding of England and the English which can be matched only by our ignorance and mis-understanding of the Americans. Even quite well-educated Americans profess to believe that Britain is not democratic. They talk of the " Cliveden set." They point to our titled aristocracy. They have a vision of a countryside still ruled by rector and squire. Not even the actual presence of King George VI has been able to wipe out the memories of George III, that honest old pighead who lives in history because he lost an empire.

Then we must not forget that the American newspaper-reading public are probably the best informed in the world ; and just as they knew about King Edward and Mrs. Simpson months before a Yorkshire bishop gave us the first inkling of the approaching abdication crisis, so they long anticipated our condemnation of the Chamberlain regime, and knew quite a lot about the real Daladier and Gamelin when we were still being led to suppose that these were men of the calibre of Foch and Clemenceau.

ABOUT a year ago the American attitude towards the war became much more intimate. When Hitler threw off the mask and wantonly attacked Norway and Denmark, Holland and Belgium, neutrality was seen to be an exceedingly poor raincoat for use in a time of political storm. Then the substitution of Mr. Churchill for Mr. Chamberlain was universally welcomed ; and even those who had no concern with or knowledge of English literature were moved by his phrase about blood and tears, toil and sweat, and were stirred by his declaration that the British would fight on the beaches, on the hills and fields and in the streets. Their admiration went up and up when the news came through of Dunkirk, of the Battle of Britain, and the grit and grim humour of the populace under pitiless bombardment from the skies.

THROUGHOUT the length and breadth of the great republic " Aid For Britain " became the popular slogan, and the Isolationists seemed to be fighting a losing battle. There was a great swing of public opinion towards sympathy with Britain and all that Britain stood for, and in this swing every section of the people was represented. Whereas in 1917 the German-Americans constituted a most dangerous pro-German element, in 1940 the great mass of the German population of the States were most decidedly anti-Nazi. Mayor La Guardia of New York, the most conspicuous American of Italian blood, spoke for practically the whole of the Italian section in denouncing Hitler and all his works. The Scandinavians, too, who a generation ago were pronouncedly Isolationists, were now, Lindbergh notwithstanding, vociferous in their demand for full aid to Britain.

During the last war President Wilson was hampered and finally overthrown by his political opponents of the Republican party ; but in this war the Republican leader, Mr. Wendell Wilkie, rivals Mr. Roosevelt, the Democrat chief, in his advocacy of aid for the Allies. Even the Irish, who for so many generations have poisoned Anglo-American relations, have showed a tendency to leave to the history-books the England of red coats, of absentee landlords and an alien clergy, and to see instead an England which is a break-water, protecting Eire from the storms that have ravaged the continent.

This was the state of mind that generally prevailed in America up to a few short months ago. That the Isolationists have been able to secure a better hearing of late weeks must be attributed to the confusion arising out of Russia's entry into the war. There is no country more anti-Communist than America, and the Americans are finding it just a little difficult to adjust their ideas so as to receive Joe Stalin and the Reds as their allies in a war for civilization and human freedom. They were ready to go all out for Britain ; they are not so ready (so it would seem) to go all out in a war which, in their view, may well be won by Russia.

IF that is, indeed, the opinion in the States today, it is unlikely that it will prevail very long. The President has no ideological affinities with Moscow, yet he is as convinced as ever that American aid is absolutely necessary if the Allies are to win the war. Before long we may expect that America will view the conflict with just that urgency and sympathy which were so marked until quite recently. This is the spirit displayed by one gigantic sergeant of police in Boston—an Irishman, of course—who, when he had told James Bone of the " Manchester Guardian " where he could get a drop of another kind of spirit, exclaimed : " And ye're from London ! We niver thought you had it in ye. Ye're putting up a grand fight—that you are. We'll be over, yes, we'll be over. Good luck to ye ! "

E. ROYSTON PIKE

FRIEND OF BRITAIN. Here is William Allen White, 73-year-old editor of the "Emporia Gazette," way down in Kansas, who, as founder of the "Committee to Defend America by Aiding the Allies," has made the U.S.A. aid-for-Britain-conscious.

In Capturing a U-Boat the Hudson Made History

EARLY one morning a Hudson of the R.A.F. Coastal Command took off and headed out over the Atlantic. Visibility was poor, frequent rainstorms swept across the sea. The water below was angry and rough, covered with white caps. The plane was "toddling along with George (the automatic pilot) doing most of the work," when suddenly there was a shout from the navigator's cabin in the nose of the aircraft. "There's one just in front of you !" shouted the navigator. The pilot gazed out and there, about 1,200 yards away on the port bow, was a U-boat. The pilot thrust the plane's nose down, and dived.

The navigator stood with his face pressed to the cockpit window, keeping the submarine in sight. "Let me know when it's time to drop, Jack," called the pilot quickly. The navigator nodded, and a few seconds later yelled "Now !" The rear-gunner, who had been winding in the aerial, popped his head into the astrodome in time to see a column of water shooting high into the air.

Then the pilot turned the Hudson steeply, and climbed. And as he watched the U-boat came surging up through a mass of foaming water. The navigator reached for his camera, and called to the rest of the crew : "Machine-gun them, let's machine-gun them !" The wireless operator dropped to the floor, and rapidly wound down the belly-gun. Then the aircraft dived across the U-boat, all guns blazing.

WHEN the Hudson dived the U-boat' conning-tower hatch opened, and about a dozen of the crew tumbled out and dropped on to the deck. The Hudson crew thought they were manning the guns, and so they kept their own guns firing hard. The red streaks of the tracers were peppering into the conning-tower, and kicking up little spurts of water all round the U-boat. This was too much-for the Germans. Those who were already on the deck turned and ran back into the conning-tower, those who were coming up from below still tried to push outwards. For a few moments there was "an awful shambles" in the conning-tower. All the figures seemed to be capless, and were distinctly visible from above, in their bright yellow life-saving jackets.

Four times the Hudson roared over the U-boat, guns streaming, banking steeply, while the rear-guns and the belly-gun kept up the fire. All the pilot remembers hearing was the navigator muttering, "I've lived all my life to see those baskets scrambling out of a conning-tower."

As the Hudson was coming round for the fifth attack the U-boat surrendered. One of its crew held a white shirt up from the conning-tower. The airmen ceased fire, but continued to circle with guns trained, watching suspiciously. The Germans followed them anxiously round with the shirt, and then held up some sort of white board. "They've shoved a white flag up," called the wireless operator triumphantly. By then the entire U-boat crew had crowded into the conning-tower, some thirty to forty of them. "And a very glum lot they looked," the pilot said afterwards.

The U-boat now lay stopped in the water, slightly down by the bows, with the waves breaking over her decks, and sometimes right over the conning-tower, drenching the crew. Her crew had surrendered, but—how were they to be taken into custody ? Swiftly the navigator prepared a message for base, and the wireless operator's

hand rattled up and down on the key. Meanwhile, the pilot was circling the U-boat, keeping his eyes glued to it. He did that for three and a half hours. All this while, too, as the navigator and wireless operator were working away at their signals, the rear-gunner kept his guns trained ceaselessly on the U-boat crew. The message reached base, and it was determined to bring that U-boat to shore. Never before had an under-water

craft surrendered to a land aircraft. A Catalina was at once sent off to relieve the Hudson, and arrived in the early afternoon. When the Hudson crew saw the Catalina approaching they were afraid it might bomb and sink the U-boat. So they signalled anxiously to it : "Look after our, repeat OUR, submarine which has shown the white flag !"

"O.K.," signalled back the Catalina. Then the Hudson crew, satisfied, dived twice more over "their" U-boat to have a last look at it. One or two of the Germans waved mournfully to them. The pilot waved cheerfully back, and set course for home. Many hours later the U-boat was "run in" by British warships.

A Carley float from a British warship is seen approaching the U-boat to receive the surrender of the enemy submarine after it had been attacked and held captive by a Hudson aircraft as described in this page. Below, the U-boat photographed from one of the Catalina flying-boats which were sent to relieve the Hudson.   *Photos, British Official*

CREW OF THE HUDSON which captured the U-boat. 1, the Captain, 32-year-old Squadron-Leader J. Thompson, from Hull. 2, Flying Officer W. J. O. Coleman, navigator, 28, hails from Berkhampstead. 3, Sergeant rear-gunner, aged 20, an agricultural student from Oxford. 4, Sergeant wireless-operator, 21, comes from Wimbledon.

Even London Can Learn From Moscow's A.R.P.

Soviet A.R.P. volunteers soon learned the trick of dealing with fire-bombs, and here are four in the attic of a Moscow apartment house extinguishing an incendiary. Beneath, in the circle, a member of the staff of Moscow University and leader of a first-aid squad. The organization to deal with the effects of aerial bombardment is remarkably thorough. The Government has enlisted every office, every factory and every household in A.R.P. work.

Beneath, on the left, a fire-fighting squad on duty at a convenient well, buckets of water, sandbags and shovels in readiness; while in the photograph on the right pupils of School No. 613 in Moscow take part in anti-gas drill. The Soviet capital has no delusions as to the ruthlessness of Hitler's intentions. A recent order commanded every individual house to be put in a state of " winter defence."

Photos, " Soviet War News "

This is how Russia Deals with German Bombs

Profiting largely by the experience of other countries, Russia has set up an elaborate A.R.P.
system which includes many highly efficient methods. When British experts visited the
Soviet capital recently they learned almost as much as they were able to teach, and London will
doubtless adopt some of Moscow's technique.

MODERN Russia is not a country which leaves things to chance, optimistically hoping to "muddle through." Long ago she foresaw the dangers which threatened her, and silently made her plans. When the first German planes raided Moscow the city was ready to cope with the danger.

On July 7, 1941, the Commander of the Garrison of Moscow ordered compulsory enlistment of all persons of both sexes between the ages of 16 and 55 for house fire parties. Moreover, any fire-watcher absent from his post during an air-raid alarm is treated as a deserter. Disobedience to orders may entail a fine of 1,000 roubles or six months' imprisonment. But the Russians do not grumble; they know that the only way to meet "total war" is by "total war," and since property is vested in the community they realize that it is up to the community as a whole to protect it.

Colonel Guy Symonds, Fire Adviser to the Home Office, who recently spent seven weeks in Moscow as one of a British mission sent there to study and advise on fire defence and A.R.P. services in general, has had many interesting comments to make on the Russian A.R.P. system. Moscow's A.R.P. organization, he tells us, is based on the "house-manager" who is the janitor or concierge in charge of each block of flats. He is held responsible for the efficiency of the A.R.P. service in his particular block of flats, and the inhabitants take their orders from him. He it is who appoints the A.R.P. squads and superintends their training.

Although this compulsory fire-fighting service was not introduced until war had broken out, many fire-fighting teams were in existence long before the war, each with a house committee, women and boys playing their part with as much enthusiasm as the men. Civil Defence in Russia is under the direction of Osoaviakhim, the Society for Defence against Chemical and Aerial Warfare, a voluntary organization open to civilian men and women of all ages. Each block of flats has an A.R.P. committee and wardens all working under Osoaviakhim. In this organization training and equipment are standardized so that should a member move to another district he can at once take his place in the local branch, and these branches may be found even in the remotest villages.

Every factory in the big cities has its own self-contained fire-fighting service in addition to the city's regular fire-brigades, and equipment everywhere is up to date. Colonel Symonds, who watched nineteen raids on Moscow, paid tribute to the Moscow Fire Brigade, which, he said, was very strong in personnel and training, uncommonly quick, and with some very interesting appliances.

Colonel Symonds found, too, that Moscow's civilian fire-watchers dealt swiftly and effectively with incendiary bombs. They endeavour, he said, "to handle it while it is still a bomb, before it becomes a mass of molten metal, lifting it with tongs or a gloved hand and plunging it into a cask of water."

Sand is found on every landing, on every staircase and even on window-sills.

Against the menace of high explosives good shelters have been constructed in the basements and cellars of tenements by shoring them up stoutly with pit-props and wooden ceilings, a job at which the Russian peasant is past-master. There are also vast numbers of trenches, revetted with wooden stays, and, of course, Moscow's "Metro," the deep middle sections of which provide complete protection. (A photograph of one of Moscow's underground stations and a description of a night spent amid shelterers in the Moscow tube appear in page 118, while in page 69 Mr. A. T. Cholerton gives a vivid account of Moscow's first air raid.)

One of the most remarkable features of the Russian campaign has been the success of the anti-aircraft defences in the night raids

on Moscow. Very few of the large numbers of Nazi bombers sent to raid the capital have managed to penetrate the defences, and the losses suffered by the Luftwaffe were very heavy. The Russian Observation Corps is a very efficient body, and it is impossible for enemy planes to approach within twenty-five minutes' flight of Moscow without their presence being known in the capital. Equally efficient are the Soviet A.A. gunners. Moscow is said to be equipped with new American-invented detectors based on the use of high-frequency wireless waves which permit the aiming of guns directly at an unseen plane. These detectors also make it possible for the numbers of enemy aircraft to be located with precision, even in darkness or fog, at a distance of 50 to 60 miles, thus allowing time for the raiders to be intercepted by fighters and for the A.A. defences to get fully ready.

Russian A.R.P. poster indicating how to dispose of an incendiary which has fallen into the roof. "Take up the fire bombs boldly and throw them on to the pavement," says the notice. On the right another poster shows how to safeguard the home by means of fire alertness. There are fire-watchers in the attic, the bath on the top floor is filled with water, sand and buckets stand outside; each flat door and an A.R.P. liaison officer at the entrance to the building.

Photos, British Official

Caucasus: Land of the Oil that Hitler Must Have

We may be sure that one of Hitler's prime objectives in invading Russia was to secure the Caucasus, the richest oil-producing region in the Old World. But although his armies have made great progress they have still some hundreds of miles to go before they glimpse the snow-capped peaks of the mountains that tower above the derricks of Baku.

RUSSIAN oil production is the second largest in the world—it ranks next to that of the U.S.A., though a long way after—and 90 per cent of Russia's oil comes from the Caucasus, using the word in a broad sense to include the whole of that extreme corner of south-eastern Europe which lies between the Black Sea and the Caspian. Modern war cannot be waged without oil—millions of tons of it; and it is not "wishful thinking" to believe that Hitler is getting anxious about his oil supplies. Small wonder, then, that he has sent his armies clattering in the direction of the Caucasus.

But the Caucasus has more than oil to tempt the greedy Fuehrer. It is a land of immense natural riches above ground as well as below. Its mountains (several of whose summits are higher than the highest Alps, and which present as a whole a variety of the most beautiful and romantic scenery) contain in their bowels manganese and iron, coal and nickel, copper, lead, zinc and asbestos.

Vast deposits of these and other minerals have already been discovered and are being worked, while others are being constantly sought for by the Soviet geologists. The mountain heights are covered with thick forests, the basis of a great and ever-growing timber industry. The soil in the lowlands is exceedingly fertile, and the climate is all that can be wished: the Black Sea coast well deserves the title of the Soviet California. In this sub-tropical region, indeed, three or four harvests a year are not unusual. Here are grown peaches, pears, oranges and lemons; here there are tobacco plantations and tea gardens, and valleys filled with roses which are picked in January and from whose petals is distilled the most fragrant attar.

The silk industry of the Caucasus is already one of the largest in the world, though only yesterday it was in the handicraft stage. The wool of the Caucasus sheep is famous. There is even a natural rubber plant; and large areas are given up to cotton and to rice, the seed for which is dropped from aeroplanes.

IN TIFLIS, capital of the Georgian and Transcaucasian republics, these Soviet peasants are about to buy a drink at a soda fountain.
Photo, Paul Popper

But oil constitutes the region's chief wealth. Some 75 per cent of the total Russian annual output of 30,000,000 tons of oil is obtained from the wells at Baku on the Caspian, and another 15 per cent comes from the oilfields at Grozny and Maikop on the northern side of the Caucasus mountains.

With a population exceeding 800,000, Baku ranks fifth among the cities of the Soviet

THE CAUCASUS area of the U.S.S.R., between the Black and Caspian Seas, and bordering on Turkey and Iran. It is now a vital strategic link between Britain and Russia.

Union; part of it is old with traces of Arab and Persian occupation, but for the most part it is a new creation, an industrial metropolis with numerous factories and, of course, huge petroleum refineries. It is the capital of the Azerbaijan Socialist Soviet Republic, one of the chief constituents of the Soviet Union.

From Baku the oil pipe-line runs across the Caucasus to Batum—or, rather, two pipe-lines, one for crude petroleum and the other for petrol. Batum, too, is an ancient city, with a cathedral, churches and mosques set in a frame of pleasant parks and gardens, bright with flowers and shady with palms. But oil is its very life blood; indeed, the city smells of oil. It was the oil traffic that called it into being, and it is the oil traffic that maintains and increases its prosperity. Not so long ago it was just an old-fashioned little harbour; now it is a model city and one of the most important of the Black Sea ports. It is the capital of the Adzhar autonomous S.S.R., which forms part of the Georgian S.S.R. The capital of Georgia is Tiflis (pop. 520,000), which is also the capital of the whole region of Transcaucasia. With its more than a hundred factories and large works, Tiflis is a highly important industrial centre, but it is also a spa, thanks to its warm sulphur springs; while its universities, polytechnics, teachers' institutes and other educational establishments constitute it a cultural centre. Not far away is the little village of Gora where Stalin was born in 1879.

In the Soviet Riviera

North of the Caucasus mountains lie a little group of autonomous republics, all included in the R.S.F.S.R., or Russia proper. Through them runs another rich belt of oil-bearing strata, and there is an oil pipe-line from Makhach Kala, on the Caspian, through Grozny and Ardavir, to Tuapse on the Black Sea. A branch line links Ardavir with Rostov on the Don, whence the oil is distributed to Western Russia.

Like Batum, Tuapse has many large oil refineries. To the south is Sochi, one of the most favoured spots on the Soviet Riviera, with many sanatoriums and rest homes for the Russian workers; the whole coast, indeed, is dotted with health resorts.

Very interesting is the picture of the Caucasus given in a recent article in the "New Statesman." We are shown a land

in which vast new areas for cultivation have been created by irrigation. "From the air, when flying from Erivan to Tiflis," says the writer, "I could see the effects of irrigation very clearly. On the dry, yellow-brown earth below were many patches and lines of green, interlaced with channels of water, where crops were growing, and these were spreading rapidly, year by year, like a green rash."

Around Batum, dangerous swamps have been drained and are now covered with groves of citrus fruits, while along the hillsides one may drive for miles through endless tea plantations where a few years before had been only a tangle of sub-tropical forest.

Fostering Local Culture

Whereas in Tsarist days it seemed to be Moscow's aim to keep the 45 different nationalities of the Caucasus fighting each other for their existence, today they cooperate for the common good. Each of the nationalities has autonomy, and even the smaller divisions have a very large measure of self-government. Collectivization has been introduced slowly and carefully; example rather than compulsion has been the rule among the strongly individualistic people. Education has been fostered. Every village has its own school. There is no attempt at Russification; on the contrary, the native languages and centres are fostered, and Armenians, for instance, learn Russian as their first foreign language. The "New Statesman" correspondent drove over the Georgian Military Highway, which runs from the North Caucasus to Tiflis across the mountains. Within living memory caravans and travellers were constantly beset with robbers and bandits drawn from the neighbouring villages. Today travellers pass over it in perfect safety.

If report speaks true, Hitler is expecting to find amongst the peoples of the Caucasus a considerable element of Fifth Columnists, and until recently German agents in Iran were doing their best to enlist the support of Caucasian refugees. But, to quote again: "Hitler stands about as much chance of creating revolt in the Caucasus as the old White Russians of Paris do in Moscow itself." Why, he was told, even the Jews are happy in the Caucasus.

In the Wonderland 'twixt Black Sea and Caspian

BATUM, the waterfront of which is seen above, stands on the S.E. coast of the Black Sea and is linked with Baku, 600 miles east, by the Trans-Caucasian railway. As the palms suggest, its climate is sub-tropical.

THE DARIEL PASS, five miles long, is in the Terek valley, midway between the Black Sea and the Caspian. It is the chief pass through the mighty Caucasus range and carries the far-famed Georgian Military Highway across the mountains. This great road runs from Tiflis to Ordjonikidze, seen below with its old church in the Byzantine style.

ROSTOV on the Don, capital of the N. Caucasian area, is an important railway junction. This photograph shows peasants from the surrounding districts selling their produce in the local market.　　　　*Photos, J. Allan Cash and Paul Popper*

Our Searchlight on the War

FOOD LAUNDRY

BRITAIN'S first " food laundry " has been established in Hornsey. It is a building for the decontamination of food affected by war gases, and was organized by local food traders. At a demonstration given to Sir Ernest Gowers, London Regional Commissioner, a number of foodstuffs, including meat, sugar, rice, potatoes, haricot beans, split peas, and a variety of tinned

NEW CIVIL DEFENCE uniform for a District Warden. Stripes are worn on the shoulder, and the letters C D under a crown with the name of the district concerned replace the original A R P. *Photo, British Official : Crown Copyright*

when they were sighted and picked up by a British destroyer. Now safe with their comrades, they are ready to take an active part in the liberation of their country from Nazi slavery.

GERMANS SENT TO SIBERIA

TO circumvent possible fifth-column activities, Stalin has ordered the transfer to Siberia of the entire German population of the Volga area.

A decree, of the Supreme Soviet of the U.S.S.R., states : " There are thousands and tens of thousands of diversionists and spies among the German population in the Volga region who are prepared to cause explosions in these regions at a signal from Germany . . . In order to forestall serious bloodshed it has been found necessary to resettle the entire German population of the Volga region in other regions on condition that those resettled in this way are allotted land and given State aid to establish themselves in the new regions. The resettled Germans will be given land in the Novosibirsk and Omsk districts, the Altai region, and the Kazakhstan Republic, and neighbouring localities where the land is rich and fertile."

A population of 600,000 is affected by the order. Two-thirds of them are of German stock, their ancestors having emigrated at the request of Catherine the Great in the 18th century. The Volga German region is on the borders of European Russia, about 470 miles south-east of Moscow, and is one of the autonomous Socialist Soviet Republics contained in the R.S.F.S.R.

U.S. AIR CHIEF IN CAIRO

MAJOR-GENERAL BRETT, Chief of the U.S.A. Army Air Corps and a member of the U.S.A. War Supply Mission to Moscow, recently visited Cairo, having flown to Egypt in a Liberator bomber. His primary task, he stated, was to look into the maintenance and supply of air equipment and all problems connected with keeping planes in active service once they had been delivered. His schedule will be one of considerable magnitude, since the Middle East is a vital supply area for the tremendous fighting front which stretches from Spitzbergen to Tobruk.

NEW CIVIL DEFENCE BADGES

LOCAL A.R.P. services will in future be known as Civil Defence services. A device consisting of the letters " C.D." under a crown, in

gold, with the name of the town or county underneath if desired by local authorities, will replace the present letters A R P on new uniforms. The new badge will not, however, be worn on greatcoats. There will also be a shoulder title for each service—" Warden," " Ambulance," etc.— and a system of rank badges will be introduced for junior supervisory officers and also for certain senior officers. The badges of rank will be in the form of thick and thin bars, 2½ ins. long, for senior officers, and chevrons will be worn by junior officers. No special uniform has been authorized for senior officers, but they will be allowed to wear the neck of the uniform open, provided they wear a light blue or grey shirt and collar and a plain dark blue tie. This ruling applies to both sexes, but shirts are not part of the uniform.

FRENCHMEN SWIM TO JOIN DE GAULLE

THE 11,996-ton Vichy liner Providence was one of three ships sent to Beirut to repatriate Vichy troops from Syria. A 19-year-old Parisian youth, who wanted to join the Free French, signed on before the liner left Toulon. When the liner dropped anchor off Beirut he wriggled through a porthole and swam ashore. On reaching dry land his surprise was great to find that over a hundred other members of the crew had done the same. Next day Senegalese Vichy troops were posted on the liner to prevent further escapes. The entire crew of the Providence had been picked from a special camp of Vichy sailors near Toulon, but it turned out that not one of the 120 men who joined forces with De Gaulle was really a sailor. In consequence the Vichy government has issued a decree providing for 20 years' imprisonment for non-seamen posing as sailors.

INDIA'S EFFORT

INDIA'S factories are producing an evergrowing stream of war material. Since the war the country has exported more than 150,000,000 rounds of S.A. ammunition and 600,000 rounds for guns, besides meeting its own needs. Yearly production of guns is five times greater than pre-war output, and of completed shells, 24 times. India is turning out rifles, machine-guns, ammunition, artillery and shells, tractors, bodies and plating for armoured vehicles, web equipment, boots, blankets and uniforms. India's fighting forces have expanded to 500,000 men, excluding those sent overseas.

A CAMOUFLAGE NET, many of which are being made by twenty-five women volunteers in South London. Such nets are used to camouflage working parties, and their making demands great concentration and physical effort. The volunteers comprise a charwoman, secretaries, housewives and shop-assistants. *Photo, Planet News*

and bottled goods, which were assumed to have been salvaged from stores affected by mustard gas, were " decontaminated." It was, however, pointed out that sealed tins and drums and glass bottles with well-fitting stoppers give complete protection from gas, and even waxed cartons and cellulose wrappings afford a certain measure of protection. In the case of non-persistent gases, airing goods of this kind for about 48 hours is often enough to make them perfectly safe for human consumption.

IRAN ACCEPTS ALLIED TERMS

ON September 9 Sir Reader Bullard, British Minister in Teheran, was informed that the Iranian government accepted the terms put forward by the British and Soviet governments. These terms include the closing of the German, Italian, Hungarian and Rumanian Legations and the handing over to the British and Russians of German subjects. They also provide for the withdrawal of Iranian troops to the south of a line running from a point south of Lake Urmia through Kazvin, Semnan, east of Teheran, and Shahi. Iranian troops are also to be withdrawn east and north of a line running from Khanikin, Kermanshah, Khorrambad, Dizful, Masid-i-Sulaiman and Haft Khel to Bandar Dilam on the Persian Gulf. On Sept. 16 the Shah abdicated, and on the next day British and Russian troops reached Teheran.

TO FREEDOM IN A CANOE

TWO young Dutch Army officers recently escaped from Holland and crossed the North Sea in a canoe. They set out from the mainland with an outboard motor, but when about a mile from shore the engine failed. Unable to put it quickly to rights, and aware of the danger of delay, they jettisoned it and hoisted sail. For four days they struggled along in their frail craft, and were within twenty miles of the English coast

BY PADDLE AND SAIL across the stormy North Sea came these two Dutch army officers determined to escape to Britain and fight for Holland. Their motor failed, but eventually (as told in this page) they were picked up by a British destroyer. *Photo, Keystone*

Cyprus Is Resolved Not to Be Another Crete

A Bren-gun carrier in its garage on the island of Cyprus. Top right, men of the Royal Artillery reading the Cyprus Post. In the circle, a gun-crew busy cleaning one of the large guns. It was announced from Cairo on September 5 that Gen. Sir Claude Auchinleck, C.-in-C. Middle East, had just made a comprehensive inspection in Palestine, Syria and Cyprus. Since the evacuation of Crete the Cyprus defences have been heavily reinforced. Many new aerodromes have been built.

Beneath, on the left, men of a light infantry regiment boarding Bren-gun carriers in the course of a training exercise. On the right, light infantry on the march in the warm Mediterranean sunshine. Cyprus is now a kind of Gibraltar at the other end of the Mediterranean. The lesson and example of Crete have been learned, and Cyprus, which is only 55 miles from the Turkish coast and 127 from Beirut, in Syria, is an essential bulwark to our Middle East position.

Photos, British Official : Crown Copyright

From Leningrad to Odessa the Battle Raged

On July 13 the German News Agency proclaimed that Leningrad was immediately threatened,
that Kiev was about to be occupied, and that the road to Moscow lay open to the German armies.
Two months later neither Leningrad nor Kiev had fallen, still less Moscow ; but, all the same,
the Nazis had bitten deeply into the Russian defences, and the Soviet situation was critical.

As the September days passed, Marshal Ritter von Leeb's troops drew ever nearer to Leningrad, second city of the Soviet Union. In German circles it was suggested that the city was about to be stormed, but Von Leeb knew better. Not only had the Luftwaffe not won command of the air, but he realized full well the immense strength of the city's defences and the fanatical spirit of its well-armed and numerous defenders. Moreover, Leningrad was reported to contain vast stocks of food and war material, which would be of immense value to the conquerors if they could be secured intact, while for the same reason it was desirable that the city's many factories and armament works should be preserved from destruction.

Leningrad was indeed a hard nut for the Nazi war machine to crack. Before the war it was claimed that the city, with its great chain of surrounding fortresses and its garrison of 800,000 men, was the strongest point in the Russian front. Now its garrison was immensely strengthened, and strong forces of tanks and the most modern planes had been accumulated to help in its defence.

The sea approaches were guarded by the great naval fortress of Kronstadt, on an island in Leningrad Bay, and by thickly-sown minefields and powerful anti-aircraft and heavy gun batteries mounted on the shore. Even if the Russians were driven from their outer defences, they swore that they would defend the city street by street, block by block. Leningrad has more canals than Venice ; across its centre runs the Neva, over half a mile wide and spanned by a mere handful of bridges, all of which could be easily blown up by the retreating Russians.

In a special communiqué issued by their High Command on September 8, the Germans claimed that their mobile divisions had reached the river Neva, east of Leningrad, on a broad front. " German troops have also stormed the town of Schluesselburg, on Lake Ladoga. The German and Finnish ring round Leningrad has thus been closed, and Leningrad is cut off from all communications by land." But this claim was premature. It was true that the Nazis had cut the main railway line to Moscow, but a secondary line through Vologda remained open, and reinforcements and supplies were poured into the city.

All the same, the German pressure on Leningrad was tremendous and sustained. Given terrific support from dive-bombers, artillery barrages and flame-throwers, the Nazi infantry were flung against the Russian guns without any regard for casualties. Special " storm blasters " with demolition charges tackled the Russian casemates and machine-gun posts. The forests and marshes around Leningrad were covered with Nazi dead, and everywhere were shattered fuselages of swastika-marked planes.

Russian Victory at Yelnya

To relieve the pressure on Marshal Voroshilov's army in Leningrad, Marshal Timoshenko delivered a formidable counter-attack in the Yelnya (Velyna) sector. The push was made by his right-wing forces under the command of Major-General Rakovski. Yelnya lies some 45 miles southeast of Smolensk, and the town represented the limit of the Nazi push after taking the ancient cathedral city. That was in July, and since then they had not advanced a step.

On August 12 the Russians struck back, and the fighting developed into what " Pravda's " correspondent called " a mincing-machine for the German regiments." After 26 days of fierce struggle, reported Moscow on September 9, " the fighting for Yelnya ended in the routing of an enemy S.S. division, the 15th Infantry Division, the 17th Motorized Division, the 10th Tank Division, the 137th Austrian Division, and the 178th, 292nd, and 268th Infantry Divisions. The remnants of the enemy's divisions are hastily retreating in a westerly direction. Our troops occupied Yelnya."

Within a few days Rakovski had retaken 50 villages, and his advance units were reported to be within 14 miles of Smolensk. At the same time Timoshenko's left wing, under General Koniev, which halted Von Bock's thrust north of Kiev three weeks before, delivered another successful counter-attack in the direction of Gomel, to the north-east of Kiev.

But now Von Bock again assumed the offensive, striking with his right wing south-east from Gomel, thus threatening to take Kiev in the rear and to outflank Marshal Budenny's hastily prepared defences on the

NAZI PRISONERS, some of the thousands captured by the Russians, enjoying a smoke after their arrival at a Red Army base.
Photo, British Official : Crown Copyright

right bank of the Dnieper. The gravity of the situation was revealed in a communiqué from Moscow on September 12, which stated that after stubborn fighting the Russian troops had been obliged to evacuate the town of Chernigov, on the Desna, some 85 miles north-east of Kiev. Then two days later came the further news of the Soviet forces' withdrawal from Kremenchug, on the east bank of the Dnieper, south-east of Kiev. Thus the German thrust was developing on both sides of the Ukrainian capital. Kremenchug is one of the few bridgeheads on the Dnieper, and with its fall Budenny's position on the farther bank was made much more difficult, even dangerous, as the river formed the last great natural barrier between the Nazis and the vitally important industrial area of the Donetz basin.

Meanwhile, Odessa, far to the south, blazed defiance. " During the last ten days," reported the Russian High Command on September 9, " the Rumanian troops on the approaches to Odessa have lost 20,000 officers and men. The battlefield is strewn with the corpses of Rumanian soldiers. A Rumanian Guard division, and the 11th, 21st, and 1st Frontier Guard divisions of the Rumanian Army have suffered exceedingly heavy losses."

Odessa Roars Defiance

" For a whole month this heroic city has been beating off the savage Fascist attack," broadcast Kolybanov, secretary of the Odessa Communist Party, on September 8, " but the enemy will never take our city. Our motto is not one backward step. Blood for blood, death for death ; victory will be ours." From Kiev, too, came the defiant cry, " Our city was and will remain the Russian capital of the province of the Ukraine, despite all the enemy's efforts to storm it." And, to complete the trio, Leningrad radio answered Von Leeb's dramatic Order of the Day to his armies battering in the rain across a shell-torn countryside : " Leningrad must be captured at any cost within the next few days," with Voroshilov's exhortation to the Leningrad garrison and people : " Fight like lions ! Death for death ! Blood for blood ! "

THE EAST FRONT, showing the situation up to September 11, with the names of opposing German and Soviet generals.
Courtesy of the " Daily Mail "

Victory Turns to Ashes in the Nazis' Path

CROSSING THE STYR in inflated rubber boats, a party of Nazis are silhouetted against the light of a burning wooden bridge set alight by the Soviet troops to hinder the German advance. Along this river battles between the Russians and Austro-Germans were fought in 1915-16.

NAZIS IN A HOLE, the blitzkrieg having failed. Faced with solid resistance, the Nazi infantry have been forced to adopt old-time tactics and creep from hole to hole in the "scorched earth." Left, Marshal Timoshenko, commanding the Red Armies in the central sector, visits a strong point. On his right is his Chief of Staff, Gen. Zhukov

Photos, "News Chronicle," Pictorial Press, Associated Press

'Now, City of Peter, Stand Thou Fast, Fourso

Above left, the Narvski district of Leningrad seen from the air. (1) the Narva triumphal arch; (2) the Narvski House of Culture ; (3) the district Kitchen-Factory. Circle, St. Isaac's Cathedral.

ENVIRONS OF LENINGRAD, formerly Petrograd and earl Prospekt, the most celebrated thoroughfare in the city, where Russian flats on the north bank of the Neva.

Like Russia': Leningrad Echoes Pushkin's Call

A general view of Leningrad. Foreground, the Admiralty building facing the Garden of the Toilers, with the Winter Palace to the right and the river Neva flowing in the background.

TAIPALE KONEVITSA SORTAVALA SCHLÜSSELBURG

L. LADOGA

R. NEVA

ENINGRAD

KOLPINO

PULKOVO

DETSKOYE SELO

urg. Left, the Prospekt of October 25, the old-time Nevski 's most important buildings stand. Right, a typical block of

hotos, Planet News, E.N.A., Paul Popper; Map, " News Chronicle "

War in the Arctic: The Spitzbergen Raid

Far to the north of Norway, on the very edge of Europe's frozen north, lies the archipelago of Spitzbergen. But distant as it is from the main stream of human life, it is not too far removed to escape the flood of war. Below we tell the story of the raid, news of which was given to the world on September 9, 1941.

SPITZBERGEN, or Svalbard as the Norwegians call it, is an archipelago lying within 500 miles of the North Pole, some 360 miles north of Norway, and 1,300 miles from Britain. It is one of the world's most inhospitable lands. For four months of the year it sees perpetual daylight; for eight months it is plunged in perpetual darkness. Not a tree grows there, hardly a bush. For the most part its soil is icebound, its coasts are swept by gales and dangerous seas.

Yet even in winter, when Spitzbergen is covered with a thick mantle of snow, the white tracks crossing the wilderness are sooty with coal dust, since here are some of the richest coal deposits in the world. The development of the island's coal resources dates from 1905, when an American, whose name is perpetuated in Longyear City, began to exploit them. Twenty years later the archipelago was officially annexed by Norway. Until recently there were six mining settlements inhabited all the year round by Norwegians and Russians, the former being in the neighbourhood of Longyear City, while the Russians were at Barentsberg, 25 miles away. Last winter between 700 and 800 Norwegians, miners and their families, were living in the Longyear settlement, while the Russian mines employed about 2,300. In 1938 the export of coal was 606,000 tons.

Until Russia entered the war, life in Spitzbergen went on much as usual, in spite of the occupation of Norway by the Nazis. A small German military delegation, consisting of three officers or mining experts, paid it a visit, but after an inspection of the mines they soon departed. Possibly the existence of the Russian mining concession contributed to the German hesitation about occupying the place. In due course reports arrived in this country from Germany to the effect that the Germans in the course of

was made without any interference, probably because the Nazis were unable to spare the necessary naval force to oppose it.

The Canadians, supported by a formidable flotilla of Royal Navy warships, Fleet Air Arm planes and detachments of British and Norwegian troops, were the first to land. Speedily they manned the guns and con-

CANADIAN commander of a signals detachment and two N.C.O.s take over a radio station after the occupation of Spitzbergen. The raid was carried out by Canadian, British and Norwegian troops, the whole force being under the command of a Canadian officer.
Photo, British Official: Crown Copyright

structed defence positions on the island; but there was not a single air raid, nor indeed any indication that the Germans were aware of the invasion. After more unopposed landings at various parts of the coast, the Canadians lived with the Norwegians and Russians in the settlements, receiving everywhere the most hospitable treatment.

"I left an English camp with the troops recently," said a Canadian correspondent, the only newspaper man with the Canadian forces, on his return to Britain, "being told that we were going on Army exercises somewhere in Britain. Only a few senior officers knew that it was anything more than this. First we went to a special coastal training area, where the units were instructed in invasion tactics and beach assaults as a prelude to the expedition. Then this special operational force was chosen, but still we did not know where we were heading or what the assignment was. The flotilla sailed and wild rumours and speculations floated around the ship. Guesses about our destination ranged from the coast of Norway to Biscay, but nobody picked Spitzbergen.

"Warships shielded the troopships and the seagoing arsenal of anti-aircraft guns was manned by Canadians every hour of the voyage. The round-the-clock daylight in the Arctic increased the need for keen naval vigilance. One day out from Spitzbergen the commander gave his officers their operational orders.

"It was not known whether there were Germans on the island, so plans were prepared for opposed and unopposed landings. Warm clothing was

issued all round—leather jerkins, sheep-skin coats, woollen underwear, gloves, and socks. The men looked like Arctic explorers as they stood their watches by their guns.

"The flotilla reached Spitzbergen about 6 a.m., after a destroyer and aircraft of the Fleet Air Arm had reconnoitred ahead to determine that there were no Germans there and that the Allied landing would probably be unopposed. At sea a lieutenant and some signalmen had transferred to a destroyer, and they made the first landing to take over a wireless station which communicated with the Germans in Norway.

"Loaded into small boats, with Bren guns in the bows, the Canadians were ready for a fight, but Norwegians rushed out of their shacks to greet them warmly and helped them to occupy the wireless station. The next party ashore took over another wireless station.

"After these initial sorties the commander and interpreters went ashore for an official landing at a Russian town. The commander was first ashore, climbing to the dock aided by Russian miners. Officials of the town met him there. There was no sign of animosity. As the troops climbed up the stairs to the centre of the community miners touched their hats and grinned.

"In the communal centre the Russian Commissar ceremoniously greeted every Canadian, and a British officer passed around long Russian cigarettes. Negotiations were rapidly carried out."

By this time 200 men had been put ashore and were drawn up in the town square. Despite language difficulties, the Russians and Canadians were soon fraternizing, and the miners loaded the troops with Russian cigarettes, candy, and souvenirs of one kind or another. While destroyers, trawlers, Russian lighters and motor boats brought the Canadians, ammunition, explosives and supplies ashore, another destroyer hustled the Norwegian detachment and a Canadian landing party to the Norwegian settlement of Svalbard, down the fjord. Here a Norwegian major, representing King Haakon's Government in London, landed with his troops, marched down the main street, and after a parley with the civilian Governor, read a proclamation informing the people of what was being done. The Canadians got on well with the Norwegians, as with the Russians, and officers and men were billeted in private houses as well as in community buildings. Then in view of the approach of the Norwegian winter, it was decided to evacuate the island, but not before the coal, so vital to the German war machine in Norway, had been destroyed.

The young folk, at least, among the Norwegians seemed glad to leave Spitzbergen. They held farewell parties, and on the eve of their departure there was a last-night dance, when Norwegian girls danced with Canadian, Norwegian, and British soldiers to the music of Norway's folk songs and tunes. Then in the morning the evacuees, loaded with their personal belongings, went to the ships. At midnight the flotilla set sail for Britain and, after an uneventful journey, safely arrived. The Russians were similarly evacuated.

SPITZBERGEN, the Norwegian archipelago in the Arctic Ocean, where the Allied soldiers landed as described in this article. The total area of the Spitzbergen islands is 24,294 square miles, and they are rich in coal deposits.
Courtesy of "News Chronicle"

preparing their campaign against the Soviet Union were laying their hands on the coal which was being sent from Spitzbergen, as well as on the coal stocks in Norway itself. The fuel was needed for the Nazi transports operating along the Norwegian coast. In the light of this information, the Allies decided to send an expedition to Spitzbergen, with a view to destroying its usefulness to the enemy. This expedition was made up of Canadian, British, and Norwegian troops under Canadian command, and the landing

Britain Checkmates the Nazi in the Far North

CANADIAN TROOPS about to leave a Norwegian settlement on Spitzbergen to make another landing farther down the fjord. A British warship awaits them at the jetty.

At Barentsberg, on one of the islands, a power house is burnt out. An exciting incident was when engineers fired a large dump of coal.

SAFELY ARRIVED in the transport after their 1,500-mile expedition, a landing force of Canadian troops disembarking for the shore unopposed.

SPITZBERGEN NORWEGIANS, with their baggage, waiting to board ship for Britain. The islanders welcomed the Allied troops with patriotic enthusiasm, and were reconciled to leaving their homes. Many expert miners, with other Norwegian men and women, will now be able to play their part in the liberation of Norway from Nazi tyranny. In the circle a Norwegian mother expresses her delight at being safe in England.

Photos, British Official: Crown Copyright ; Wide World

Our Diary of the War

SATURDAY, SEPT. 6, 1941   735th day

Sea.—Admiralty announced that submarines in Mediterranean had sunk strongly escorted 11,000-ton Italian liner Esperia and 4,000-ton ship of Ramb class.

Air.—Fortress aircraft attacked shipping at Oslo. Night raid on rubber factory at Huls, Rhineland. Coastal Command attacked harbour at Bergso Island, Norway.

Russian Front.—Struggle for Leningrad continued. Farther south fierce fighting along line of R. Lovat, north of Kholm, and on southern flank of Smolensk salient.

All attacks on Odessa being repulsed.

Africa.—On night of 5-6 R.A.F. sank merchantman at Tripoli, and bombed Derna, Martuba, Bardia and aerodrome at El Adem.

Mediterranean.—Germans made night raid on Suez Canal area.

SUNDAY, SEPT. 7   736th day

Air.—Day attack on shipping off Dutch coast; supply ship set on fire, escort vessel blown up.

Very heavy night raid on Berlin. Shipyards at Kiel and docks at Boulogne bombed.

Russian Front.—Continuous fighting along whole front. Successful Russian counter-attacks in Kexholm and Gomel areas.

Finns having resumed offensive, forces driving southward from N.E. of Lake Ladoga arrived at R. Svir.

Africa.—Night bombing raids on Benghazi, Barce, Berka and landing-grounds in Libya.

Mediterranean.—On night of 6-7 Fleet Air Arm attacked convoy, hitting two ships out of three. Three Sicilian aerodromes raided.

MONDAY, SEPT. 8   737th day

Sea.—Announced that U-boat, having surrendered to Hudson aircraft in Atlantic, was later boarded by naval party and towed in.

Announced that forces of British, Canadian and Norwegian troops had recently landed on Spitzbergen and taken measures to deprive enemy of use of coalmines.

Enemy convoy of two supply ships attacked at night by naval patrols in Channel. Both ships torpedoed, accompanying E-boat probably sunk, and armed trawler set on fire.

Air.—Flak ship destroyed off Ostend by Spitfire. Night raid on Kassel. Objectives at Munster and elsewhere in Germany, and docks at Cherbourg, also attacked.

Russian Front.—Battle for Leningrad continued with violence. Germans announced that mobile units had reached R. Neva and captured Schlüsselburg, 25 miles east of city.

U.S.A.—Announced that U.S. steamer Steel Seafarer had been bombed and sunk in Red Sea on Sept. 5.

Home.—One night raider destroyed.

TUESDAY, SEPT. 9   738th day

Sea.—Admiralty announced that light naval forces have been operating against German convoys supplying troops on Murmansk front. Enemy destroyer, armed trawler and another vessel sunk.

Light cruiser Bremse, damaged on July 30 off Kirkenes, now reported sunk.

Announced that large Italian schooner had been sunk by British submarine in central Mediterranean.

Russian Front.—Leningrad bombed day and night. Soviet forces in central zone have recaptured Elnya and advanced beyond it. Fifty villages said to have been retaken.

Africa.—R.A.F. raided landing-grounds at Tmimi, Martuba, Derna and Gazala.

R.A.F. heavily bombed Corinth Canal on night of 8-9, making many direct hits. Heraklion aerodrome, Crete, also attacked.

Other forces bombed Palermo harbour and aerodromes at Catania and Gerbini.

Iran.—Announced that Iranian Govt. had accepted British and Soviet terms.

U.S.A. — Washington announced that Panamanian ship Sessa, operated by New York firm, was torpedoed without warning and sunk by U-boat off Iceland on Aug. 17.

WEDNESDAY, SEPT. 10   739th day

Sea.—Announced that Italian tanker Maya had been sunk by British submarine in Aegean Sea.

Russian Front.—Enemy still held outside Leningrad. Russians maintaining heavy pressure at several points in German centre.

Africa.—Fleet Air Arm bombed aerodromes at Gambut and Menastir on night of 9-10.

Mediterranean.—Heavy R.A.F. bombers made night raid on Turin. On night of 9-10 aerodrome at Castelvetrano was bombed and Messina heavily raided.

THURSDAY, SEPT. 11   740th day

Sea.—Admiralty announced loss of H.M. auxiliary Tonbridge.

Enemy bombers made night attack on convoy in North Sea. One shot down. One small freighter damaged but safe.

Air.—Fighter Command made offensive sweeps over Northern France and Low Countries. Night attacks on Kiel and Rostock. Docks at Le Havre and Boulogne also bombed. Coastal Command bombed docks at Haugesund, aerodrome near Stavanger, and enemy shipping.

Russian Front.—In Karelian sector Russian forces reported to have recaptured important strategic positions. Renewed fighting near Murmansk. In central sector Russian counter-offensives continued.

Africa.—During night of 10-11 R.A.F. raided Benghazi, Martuba, Gambut and Derna. Benghazi heavily bombed on 11-12.

Mediterranean.—R.A.F. sank one of two escorted merchantmen in Ionian Sea.

U.S.A.—President Roosevelt broadcast warning to Axis ships against entering American waters.

U.S. cargo steamer Montana torpedoed and sunk in Icelandic waters.

FRIDAY, SEPT. 12   741st day

Air.—Enemy convoy attacked off Dutch coast; one ship set on fire. Naval aircraft attacked shipping in Bodo area of Norwegian coast and military targets in vicinity. One supply ship sunk, others damaged.

Night attacks on Frankfurt and elsewhere in Rhineland, Cherbourg and St. Nazaire.

Russian Front. — Continued Russian counter-attacks outside Leningrad, in central sector and on Lower Dnieper. First snow fell in Leningrad area.

Africa.—S.A.A.F. bombed landing-grounds at Gambut and Gazala. At night Fleet Air Arm raided Bardia and Gambut.

Mediterranean.—Fleet Air Arm and R.A.F. made night and day attacks on convoy bound for Tripoli. Every ship hit.

On 11-12 R.A.F. attacked ships and dry dock at Palermo; Fleet Air Arm bombed factory at Licata and railway at Ragusa.

Home.—Two night raiders destroyed.

SATURDAY, SEPT. 13   742nd day

Air.—R.A.F. set on fire German supply ship off Borkum. Heavy night raid on docks at Brest. Other aircraft bombed Le Havre.

Russian Front.—Kiev threatened by encirclement as result of fall of Chernigov, 80 miles to N.E. Soviet communiqué recorded continuance of stubborn fighting along whole front. Great air battles in Leningrad area.

Mediterranean.—R.A.F. bombed Cretan aerodromes during night of 12-13, and Fleet Air Arm those at Gerbini and Catania, Sicily.

SUNDAY, SEPT. 14   743rd day

Russian Front.—Germans claimed to have pierced outer fortifications of Leningrad. Russians attacking in Schlüsselburg area.

Germans reported to have gained strong bridgehead at Kremenchug, east of Dnieper.

Africa.—Cairo announced deep penetration from Tobruk into enemy's lines, and successful raids by patrols.

R.A.F. fighters attacked large concentration of aircraft at Gambut; eight left in flames and others damaged.

During night of 13-14 heavy bombers raided Tripoli, Benghazi and Barce.

MONDAY, SEPT. 15   744th day

Air.—R.A.F. sank enemy ship in convoy off Friesian Islands, attacked shipping at Haugesund, and shot down Junkers off Norfolk coast.

Heavy night raid on Hamburg. Other targets were Bremen, Cuxhaven, Wilhelmshaven and Le Havre.

Russian Front.—Germans claimed to have reached suburbs of Leningrad. Moscow announced that four enemy transports and a destroyer were sunk on Sept. 13 when Germans attempted to land on Oesel Is.

Two-day attack on Odessa repulsed.

ON BOARD H.M.S. ILLUSTRIOUS as Lord Louis Mountbatten, the great aircraft carrier's new commander, takes over. Her late commander, Capt. Denis Boyd, was recently promoted Rear-Admiral.   *Photo, Keystone*

When the R.A.F. Bombed Nazi Ships in Holland

On the left, Blenheim bomber making an attack from mast-high on a cargo-liner of the Noordam type in Rotterdam docks on August 28, 1941. Two bombs have fallen astern, but a direct hit has been scored with the third, proved by the photographic record above, showing the liner lying on her side. Beneath, an enemy vessel which had her stern blown off when Blenheims swept the Dutch coast on Aug. 18. *Photos, British Official.*

OUR AIR WAR ON ENEMY SHIPPING

(Continued from page 28, Vol. 5.)

Date	Targets	Time	Aircraft	Results
July 30-Aug. 3	2 Convoys 1 Tanker at Ostend E-boats Patrol Ships	Day	Bl, Be, F	5 in convoy hit (47,000 tons). 1 sunk 1,200 tons, 1 1,500 tons and 1 2,000 seen sinking. 1 Tanker torpedoed, 1 Patrol fired
Aug. 4-8	2 Convoys Patrol ships 2 Tankers 5 S.S. (1 large at Nantes)	Day and Night	Be, F, C.C., B	3 Patrol ships hit 2 in convoy hit—1 2,000 tons 1 Tanker fired 4 S.S. hit, 1 torpedoed
9-13	S.S. and harbours A.A. Ships	Day and Night	Bl, F	1 S.S. hit and fired 2 A.A. ships hit Norwegian harbours attacked
14-18	1 S.S. 4 Patrol Ships 1 Tanker	Day	Bl, Be	4 S.S. sunk 1 Patrol fired 1 Tanker torpedoed
19-21	Shipping off coast 1 S.S. (Ostend harbour) Patrol ships E-boats in Channel	Day and Night	Bl, C.C., F	Many hits, 1 sunk 1 S.S. hit 2 E-boats hit

S.S. = Supply Ships ; Bl = Blenheim Bomber ; Be = Beaufort (Coastal) ; B = Bomber ; F = Fighter ; C.C. = Coastal Command.

Note.—In the period covered by the table (July 29-Aug. 21) the 28 attacks made, mainly on coastal shipping, achieved the destruction or severe damage of **more than 35 vessels**—tonnage not stated, but unlikely to be less than **100,000 tons** destroyed. Attacks off coasts of Belgium, France, Holland, Norway, and Germany. R.A.F. and F.A.A. attacks on shipping in **Mediterranean**, July 28-Aug. 18 : **26 ships**. over **70,000 tons** hit, mostly destroyed. 2 Destroyers hit, 1 presumed sunk.

After Four Years of War China is Undaunted

IN CHUNGKING, the most bombed city in the world, a Chinese anti-aircraft battery goes into action as a squadron of Japanese bombers is sighted.

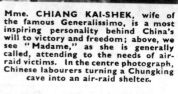

Mme. CHIANG KAI-SHEK, wife of the famous Generalissimo, is a most inspiring personality behind China's will to victory and freedom; above, we see "Madame," as she is generally called, attending to the needs of air-raid victims. In the centre photograph, Chinese labourers turning a Chungking cave into an air-raid shelter.

HWEI SEN BRIDGE, in the prosperous business section of Chungking, China's wartime capital; the photograph was taken before it was bombed. Centre right, Hwei Sen Bridge as it appeared after one of the heaviest air bombardments. Right, another part of the same thoroughfare.

Still a Buttress for the Freedom Front in Asia

CHINESE MACHINE-GUNS, home-manufactured stocks, being checked by arsenal technicians (left). China can now supply from her own factories a high percentage of her needs in rifles, machine-guns and light artillery.

Below, a Chinese squadron-leader gives final instructions to his men before they set off on an operational flight. The Chinese air force, which at the beginning of the war with Japan in 1937 was almost nil, is now expanding rapidly with outside help.

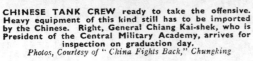

CHINESE TANK CREW ready to take the offensive. Heavy equipment of this kind still has to be imported by the Chinese. Right, General Chiang Kai-shek, who is President of the Central Military Academy, arrives for inspection on graduation day.
Photos, Courtesy of "China Fights Back," Chungking

Fighters With a Sting

Two American-built Fighter Planes Now Coming off the Assembly Lines for Delivery to the Royal Air Force

Specially drawn by Haworth for THE WAR ILLUSTRATED

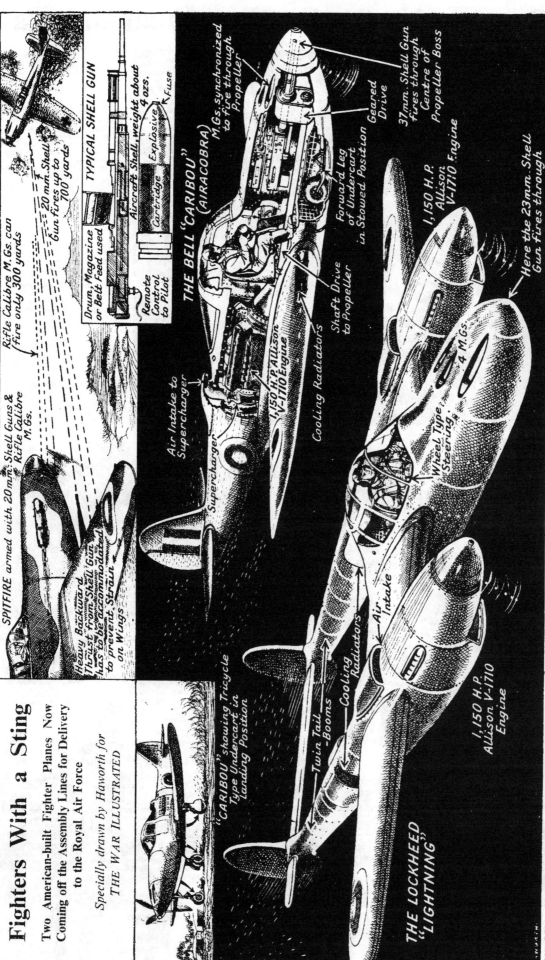

SPITFIRE armed with 20 mm. Shell Guns & Rifle Calibre M.Gs.

Rifle Calibre M.Gs. can fire only 300 yards

20 mm. Shell Gun fires up to 700 yards

TYPICAL SHELL GUN

Aircraft Shell weight about 4 ozs.

Fuse

Explosive

Cartridge

Drum, Magazine or Belt Feed used

Remote Control to Pilot

Heavy Backward Thrust from Shell Gun has to be centrally mounted to prevent Strain on Wings

THE BELL "CARIBOU" (AIRACOBRA)

M.Gs. synchronized to fire through Propeller

37 mm. Shell Gun fires through Centre of Propeller Boss

Geared Drive

Forward Leg of Undercart in Stowed Position

Shaft Drive to Propeller

1,150 H.P. Allison V-1710 Engine

Cooling Radiators

1,150 H.P. Allison V-1710 Engine

Here the 23 mm. Shell Gun fires through

Air Intake to Supercharger

Supercharger

"CARIBOU" showing Tricycle Type Undercart in Landing Position

Twin Tail Booms

Cooling Radiators

Air Intake

Wheel Type Steering

4 M.Gs.

THE LOCKHEED "LIGHTNING"

1,150 H.P. Allison V-1710 Engine

THE BELL "CARIBOU," known in the U.S.A. as the Bell P-39 Airacobra, is one of the latest types of single-seat fighter. A low-wing all-metal monoplane, it has a length of 29 ft. 9 ins. and a span of 34 ft. It has a gross weight of 6,662 lb., carries 140 gallons of fuel, has a maximum speed of 400 m.p.h. at 15,000 ft., and a range of nearly a thousand miles at a cruising speed of 335 m.p.h. An unusual feature of the design is that behind the pilot's cockpit is mounted amidships the Allison V-1710 engine. This engine is electrically-operated airscrew by way of an eight-foot shaft. This gives the pilot a very clear forward outlook. American workmen who are turning

out this aircraft in ever-increasing numbers have nicknamed it the "tank buster."

THE LOCKHEED "LIGHTNING," another American single-seat fighter monoplane, is also of unusual design in that it has twin fuse-lages, each housing a 12-cylinder Allison V-1710 engine. The central streamlined nacelle accom-modates the pilot's cockpit and mounts the arma-ment in the nose. The length of this aircraft is 37 ft. 10 ins., and the span 52 ft. Top speed is given as 400 m.p.h. at 16,000 feet, and the maximum cruis-ing range, with an overload of fuel, is over 1,000 miles at a cruising speed of 350 m.p.h. It is believed,

however, that the latest Allison engines develop sufficient horse-power to give it a maximum speed of about 450 m.p.h. The Allison aero-engine with which both these aircraft are fitted is the only liquid-cooled high-powered engine from America at present in service with the R.A.F. It is used in the Curtiss Tomahawk (see Vol. 4, pp. 448, 487). The Lightning takes off very quickly and can climb at a rate of 2,860 feet a minute.

BOTH the Caribou and Lightning are well armed, being equipped with a shell-firing cannon and machine-guns of .30 and .50 calibre. The Caribou is stated to carry a greater amount

of ammunition than any other single-engined fighter now in service. Its gun, which fires through the hub of the airscrew, can fire 120 shells a minute, explosive, armour-piercing or tracer. It has .50 calibre heavy machine-guns housed in the nose, with a rate of fire of 850 per minute, and in the wings .30 cal. machine-guns firing at 1,200 per minute. Each type has an undercarriage of the retractable tricycle pattern. These are considered to give maximum security on landing. The Allison V-1710, used in both aircraft, is said to be America's finest liquid-cooled aero-engine. Cool-ing is carried out with ethylene glycol by a pump driven off the back of the crankshaft.

I Was There! .... Eye Witness Stories of the War

My Visit to One of Moscow's A.A. Batteries

English A.R.P. experts on their return from Moscow paid high tribute to the efficiency of the Russian A.A. barrage, and here A. T. Cholerton, "Daily Telegraph" correspondent, tells of a visit to a typical battery in Moscow's outer line of defences.

Moscow's A.A. barrage proved the worth of patient planning and training over a number of years in the first raid on the capital, and went on improving during succeeding Alerts.

One day I was taken on a visit to a typical A.A. battery in the city's outer line of defence. I would like to have been there on the night when, firing 198 shells, they played their part in stopping what appeared to be a serious raid developing against the capital itself.

But it is true that one cannot really see much at an A.A. battery by night—one can only glimpse highly trained, eager men quietly handling their guns, detectors and predictors.

I visited this battery at high noon under the pure late summer sunlight. It is situated in the midst of a field of oats on a collective farm—one of those vast, flat Russian fields which make one know instinctively that Russia is a very big place indeed, going on for thousands of miles. Moscow's daylight fighter patrols droned in high key overhead, but the larks still sang joyously.

In that wide Russian field this cunningly concealed battery of guns of the latest type was as invisible from the air as the larks' nests.

Nor could it be seen from the ground until, when I had approached to within 50 yards, the gunners, by order of Lt. Boyarinoff commanding, poked out their noses from their lairs like so many young Russian bears ending their hibernation, and swiftly worked their guns.

The camouflage of this battery, their sound detecting and predictor instruments, their shell dumps, their underground rest posts, their dormitory and dining-rooms a little farther back and also underground, impressed me chiefly by their admirable simplicity. I cannot imagine a job more effectively or cheaply done.

Those guns and the equipment stirring them into precise, deadly fire spelt the costly output of the most modern technique. All the rest spelt the old frugal peasant wisdom.

The discipline and training of the men—many of them had served in 60 deg. of frost on the Finnish frontier or in the blinding sand of Outer Mongolia—appeared admirable.

We hear so much nowadays about the guerillas that we may sometimes forget this fact about the regular Russian Army in being. Lt. Boyarinoff's battery is so highly trained that its gunners do their job like one person. The men are justly proud because they have got four bombers already.

I saw good, clean bedding and plentiful tasty food in the well-built dug-outs. The men's dinner consisted of Ukrainian bortsch soup with meat in it, followed by pork chops and potatoes, washed down with *kvass*—a near beer made from black bread.

How We Sweep the Channel for Our Convoys

Shelled from the French coast, bombed and machine-gunned from the air, threatened by E-boats, the minesweeping trawlers daily clear the Channel for our convoys. Here is the story of a typical day's sweep.

The long-range guns mounted on the French coast are shelling the harbour as our four minesweeping trawlers cast off and get under way for the day's sweep.

As we put to sea the shelling, directed by a German spotter plane overhead, follows us. Some of the shells are very wide; some are uncomfortably near. But the Channel must be swept clear of the mines for our convoys on the trade routes.

If we sweep successfully no praises will be sung; none are expected. If we are mined there will be a curt notice in the Press a few days later: "The Admiralty regrets to announce the loss of H.M. Minesweeping Trawler . . ."

The clear blue sky is combed with swirls of white exhaust in fantastic designs as our fighter aircraft dive in and out of the German formations. Twenty thousand feet up the Battle of Britain is being waged. At that great height it all seems infinitely slow; it is hard to realize that these microscopic dots are planes, twisting and turning in deadly combat at more than 300 miles an hour.

Now we have reached our allotted station, the trawlers have altered course, sweeps have been veered, and the day's work begins. In a short while the look-out man sights an aircraft shadowing us; we must expect trouble. Guns are manned and all eyes are turned skywards.

Soon the drone of engines is heard. The sky sounds to be full of planes, but our attention is held by a minute speck busy drawing a wide vapour circle directly above us. We know from experience that this means trouble. The bombers will fly over the circle and release their load in the centre.

The first formation rapidly approaches the circle. We are in an unenviable position; having sweeps out, we are unable to take violent evasive action. There is a shrieking roar as the first stick of bombs crashes into the sea a few cables astern, and this is followed by a veritable shower of bombs. We escape them all.

But the Germans are determined to stop our sweeping. The aero engines develop a venomous, whining howl as the second formation swings and dives to the attack. It is as if a swarm of locusts were descending on us as the sun glints on their dark green cowlings. The guns' crews hold their fire for what seems an eternity until the planes are within range; then the ship reels as the guns bark their defiance. Clouds of smoke and ladders of tracer bullets appear between ourselves and the planes, which swerve, bank steeply and climb away with machine-guns and cannon blazing. Our opposition has proved too much for them.

Towards midday the visibility worsens and a heat mist shrouds everything except the trawler immediately astern.

A signal is received from the last ship of the line that E-boats are in the vicinity.

This Russian multiple machine-gun is in operation by the side of a road, protecting advancing columns of troops from low-level attacks by enemy aircraft. Enemy dive-bombers have not had matters all their own way in Russia as they did during the 1940 campaign in the West.

Photo, British Official : Crown Copyright

While "surface action stations" is still sounding three sleek, grey, ghost-like shapes are discerned travelling very fast across our course. Almost instantly they are swallowed up in the mist ; had they seen us they would most certainly have attacked, as this is ideal weather for E-boats—when they can make a quick assault and disappear before the guns can be brought to bear.

For a while we are left in peace, but just when we are contemplating hauling in the sweep at the end of a good day's work, a grey seaplane of German type, marked with a Red Cross, alights a couple of cables ahead of us. Since Jerry has been found using such planes for reconnaissance and mine-laying, we have recently received orders to fire on them on sight, but as the guns are being trained suddenly, with engines shut off, two Messerschmitt 110s dive on us from opposite directions with cannon and machine-guns firing, raking our ship.

For what seems ages, though in reality only seconds, bullets fly in all directions ; the ship's guns let go with everything they have got, but the raiders have come and gone before accurate aim can be taken. Bridge, wheelhouse, decks, life-saving floats, life-boats, funnel and ventilators are left a mass of twisted iron and smouldering timber with the stench of gunfire. It seems impossible that anyone could have survived, but, apart

from an officer slightly wounded, there are no casualties.

It is a battered sweeper that returns, but with a satisfied crew aboard who have defied bombs, machine-gun and cannon fire, E-boats and mines, and have cleared the Channel for convoys.—"Daily Telegraph."

We Slipped Over to Have a Look at Calais

While the R.A.F. sweep the skies over Northern France, the Navy are sweeping the Channel right up to the German-occupied coast. Here is an account of a trip in one of the fast rescue-boats which come to the aid of airmen in distress.

DURING an air attack by the Fighter Command I was out in the Straits of Dover in one of the fast rescue boats which were on patrol, and I can testify that the narrow strip of water between ourselves and the Germans can still be truly described as the English Channel.

The two young sub-lieutenants in command of the fast motor-boats treated the adventure of crossing to the enemy-occupied coast as lightly as holiday-makers enjoying an afternoon outing in a pleasure boat.

"We'll just slip over and have a look at Calais," they said, when we were out in the Channel. Without another word they headed straight for the French coast at a rate of knots equal to 40 miles an hour.

These boats have a crew of only eight, including a radio operator, and a gunner who sits on a swivelling turret with a double-barrelled pom-pom for use against hostile aircraft. They are built for speed, and are no bigger than a fair-sized motor launch, but they raced towards the German-occupied coastline with all the assurance of battleships armed with 15-in. guns.

Over the water we roared and bounced with our tiny white ensigns at the mast-heads, and a long trail of white foam in our wake, until the cliffs of England faded in the distance and the coast of France began to take shape.

Friendly British fighters passed overhead. The two sub-lieutenants exchanged messages with their flashing signalling lamps.

Nearer and nearer we came to the enemy coastline without a sign of activity on his part until we could see clearly the roofs of Calais, the chimneys of factories, and the cranes in the dock.

Yeoman of the signals, aboard a minesweeper, flashing instructions to other minesweepers. Top, a minesweeper steaming back to port.
Photos, Criterion Press and Lubinski

We swept along the coast within three or four miles of the German batteries. One of the crew stood perched on the tiny deck with his hands on his hips and a look expressive of complete boredom. "It gets ruddy monotonous," he complained. "Always the same ; nothing ever happens."

Four Messerschmitts came out to have a look at us as we were on our way back. Two took up a position from which they could dive at us out of the sun, while the two others made wide circles round us and seemed to be on the point of making an attack.

Suddenly they disappeared, and a few moments later the sky was filled with British fighters returning from a sweep.

We rescued one pilot shot down in that sweep. A protective screen of Spitfires came back with him as he glided towards the English coast, but he was losing height too rapidly to reach the coast. We saw him turn his Spitfire on its back and float down with his parachute into the sea.

As we raced towards him with the powerful engines of our speed boats going all out, one Spitfire circled over the spot where the pilot had come down. Within a few moments we had reached him squatting in his rubber dinghy. He was dazed but uninjured. By the time we had returned to our base, an ambulance was waiting and he was whisked off to hospital.—"Evening Standard."

Saved from the sea, this sergeant-pilot of a Spitfire Squadron is being helped aboard the naval rescue launch after his machine had crashed in the Channel. A similar incident is described in this page.
Photo, Topical

‖‖‖‖‖‖‖‖‖‖‖‖‖‖‖‖‖‖‖‖‖‖‖‖‖‖‖‖‖‖‖‖‖‖ **I WAS THERE!** ‖‖‖‖‖‖‖‖‖‖‖‖‖‖‖‖‖‖‖‖‖‖‖‖‖‖‖‖‖‖‖‖‖‖‖‖‖‖

We Sank a German Ship on Hitler's Doorstep

*The Free French submarine Le Jour de Gloire, after sinking a German
ship almost on Germany's doorstep, was crippled by depth-charges and
had to spend three days on the surface in enemy waters. The story of this
exploit is told here by the submarine's commander.*

Free French sailors of the submarine Le Jour
de Gloire arriving back in Britain after the
adventure related in this page.
Photo, " Daily Mail "

WHEN the crew of *Le Jour de Gloire*
returned safely to their Scottish base,
their British comrades were full of
praise for their skill and bravery. In the
words of a British officer, there has rarely
been such a successful combination of
" damned cheek and wonderful pluck and
endurance."

Here is the Free French submarine commander's own story :

We were very deep into the Hun's own
territory when we sighted a convoy. We
picked the biggest ship, of about 4,000 tons,
and let fly.

Eh bien! We hit her. She started sinking
almost at once. But a sweeter sight to us was
the panic and confusion among our enemy.
There was a great scuttling to and fro. His
ships dashed here and there.

Soon the escort vessels began to make
things uncomfortable for us with their depth-
charges. They shook our ship. We submerged, but could see the fun through our
periscope. They hunted us for several hours,
and we had to remain submerged for
a considerable time before the coast
was properly clear.

At one time an armed trawler passed
quite close to us, but her captain,
whom we could see plainly on the
bridge, was so intent on peering ahead
that he did not notice us on his port
side, and we had a good laugh about
that.

When they had given up the chase
we surfaced. It was then quite dark.
We did not realize we had been
crippled until we tried to submerge
again and found we could not. It was
an uncomfortable discovery because
we were so far into enemy waters.

Our batteries had been damaged, and
when we surfaced quarters below deck

had been filled with poison gas. We started
to move off, but only very slowly and we had
to repair the damage.

This was a tricky business because of the
poison gases, but every member of the crew,
wearing masks, took five-minute spells below.
It was exhausting work. They had to be kept
going by doses of aspirin, but they were
always cheerful. We kept this up for two
days and two nights until we were sighted
on the third day by a British ship.

All the time we expected attack from the
sea or the air, for throughout those two days
we were in enemy waters. I do not know
how we were not sighted and sunk. It
would have been such an easy job for any
ship or plane to make an end of us. We
were indeed lucky.

Even during those two days men who were
not working below sunbathed on the deck.
Fortunately the weather held good and we
were thankful when the British ship came along
to escort us throughout our third day's
surface ride.—"*News Chronicle.*"

TWO YEARS OF AXIS AND BRITISH AIRCRAFT LOSSES						
September 1939—September 1941						
	AXIS			**R.A.F.**		
	1939	1940	1941	1939	1940	1941
Over Gt. Britain and shores	23	3,038	568	—	847	37
At Sea	6	27	5	—	—	—
Western Front	14	943	—	5	374	—
Scandinavian Campaign	—	56	—	—	55	—
Germany and Occupied Territory	20	45	625	26	349	959
Middle East	—	421	1,666	—	78	305
Royal Navy	3	241	319	—	—	—
Totals	—	66	4,771	3,183	31	1,703	1,301
Grand Totals		8,020			3,035	

*Note.—German aircraft losses on the Russian front, in addition to
those above, have been variously estimated at from 4,000 to 7,200, the
latter figure being given by the Soviet Army organ " Red Star." Losses
in the Middle East include many Italian planes. Net German losses
may be estimated at not less than 11,000 and not more than 14,000.*

The first two boats got away in five
minutes, the third in eight or maybe
nine. There were slight injuries in
getting into the boats, but none were
serious. The Captain, myself, and
one sailor, Robert Cartwright, stayed
aboard until the decks were awash.
The Seafarer went down in twenty
minutes.

After twelve hours' rowing in a
choppy sea we reached land at 11
o'clock next morning.

When we landed on the island the
Egyptians were most helpful. They
enabled us to send a signal giving our
position and requesting another vessel
to search for our missing boat.

The crew of a Royal Naval craft
eventually picked us up. They gave us
everything we wanted. The only thing
I am sore about is that I had carried my
money and my watch in my belt until the
day of the attack, when I locked them up
in a drawer, and have lost everything.

James Abernethy, the radio operator, who
was one of the last to leave the ship, said :

The aerial crashed down and the emergency
transmitter was put out of action. It was a
miracle that no one was seriously hurt,
although our quarters were a shambles, with
chairs, radio sets, and dishes smashed by the
force of the explosion.—*Reuter.*

I Was on the Bombed Steel Seafarer

*Although she was not blacked out, and her markings must have been clearly visible
in the moonlight, the American vessel Steel Seafarer was dive-bombed and sunk
in the Red Sea on September 5, as described here by members of her crew.*

WHEN 24 members of the crew of the
Steel Seafarer arrived at an
Egyptian port on board a vessel
of the Royal Navy, the Seafarer's first
officer, Mr. Ralph S. Pratt, gave a first-hand
account of the sinking of his ship. He said :

The plane came over
at 11.30 on Friday night
Sept. 5. It dived down
with its engines shut off,
and opened the throttle
with a roar when the
bomb dropped. There
were two explosions, in
No. 5 oil tank and amid-
ships. At the time we
were steaming northwards
and were not in convoy.
The plane swooped over
just between our masts.
The bomb—or it may
have been an aerial tor-
pedo—seemed to hit and
explode just under the
water.

I was asleep at the
time. The washstand fell
down, and all the lights
went off. Sliding into my
slippers, I reached the

bridge in thirty seconds. The plane had
flown off. The ship was sinking rapidly
with a list to starboard.

The Captain said : " We are hit aft." We
got two of the port boats out and one starboard, which were sufficient for the crew.

STEEL SEAFARER, a U.S. merchantman, was sunk by a Nazi plane on Sept. 5 in the Red Sea. Some of the crew, after
landing on an island, were picked up by a Royal Naval craft. The story is given in this page, and above is a photograph of Steel Scientist, sister ship to Steel Seafarer.
Photo by courtesy of Frank Bowen

Editor's Postscript

DURING my weekly toil in London I pass by a certain bomb crater at least four times a day. It is a legacy of a blitz in April, and I have already written about it, as the explosion produced not a ha'p'orth of damage to any of the buildings that stand no more than twenty feet from the centre of the hole ! A month or two after the event the drains, gas-pipes, telephone wires and water-pipes had been repaired with what commercial people used to call " expedition and dispatch." But now for more than five months the street has been cluttered up while innumerable wagonloads of old rubble have been dug out and carted away and as many wagonloads of new material brought back (I can't guess why) to fill in the hole, which by digging (for Victory ?) down and along gradually extended lengthwise to about twenty times its original dimensions, electric drills doing their soul-shattering share in the agonizing process for many weeks.

BUT more usually, as I have passed by any time in the last four months, ten or a dozen men armed with pick and shovel have been engaged upon the titanic task of filling up this originally modest and unassuming crater. I wish to put it on record that not once in all that time have I seen these " workers of the world unite " in digging or shovelling ; on every occasion the majority of them have been leaning languorously on their pick or shovel, lighting cigarettes, or blandly discussing matters of power politics— or beer. I have even seen some of the younger men taking their ease stretched out on a plank down in the ever-yawning hole . . . and not at dinner-time, either ! I fancy that this happy little band of brothers (one of whom in the early days of their joyous occupation used to entertain his fellow-toilers by imitating with noteworthy skill the noise of a whistling bomb) may here have found that " better 'ole " of Old Bill's derision and are loath to leave it. But the net result is the traffic of a once busy street is slowed down for months (it will take another fortnight from now to put on the finishing touches) which with ordinary energy and organization might have been its old self again by the end of June. If the repairing of ruined London were to proceed at this snail's speed—even should not another bomb drop on it—those in their twenties now will be well into the sixties when the job is done.

MY first introduction to Yoga dates back half a century, on a day when my friend Acton Bond and I cycled from Birmingham to Stratford-on-Avon to see a performance in the old Memorial Theatre. Acton Bond has spent most of his long life in the service of Shakespearian drama, and not much of it, I suspect, in perfecting himself as a Yogi. Strange that the other afternoon, when we chanced to meet at Victoria, among the books I was taking home for my week-end study was " The Hidden Teaching Beyond Yoga," by Dr. Paul Brunton ! So little time had I given to the study of Yoga, in all these years (though I have talked to an English Yogi about his philosophy), that I am still somewhat distant from its " hidden teaching," and I doubt if the enthusiast of fifty years ago has made any closer approach, as I cannot recall in any of our hundreds of subsequent meetings ever seriously discussing this system of Hindu philosophy with him.

As it is, I fear I shall now go down to the tomb or the crematorium without its innermost secrets being revealed to me, for my week-end has been clouded by wading through Dr. Brunton's massive tome of 150,000 words on the vainest of quests. Such prolixity, such loquacity, I have seldom

VOROSHILOV, C.-in-C. of the Russian Northern Army, whose heroic defence of Leningrad is one of the greatest episodes of the war. " Take up your arms and defend the city at all costs," he told the people.
Photo, Planet News

encountered in any book. I am told with a great fluency of phrase a multitude of things familiar to all students of science and philosophy, things that I know as well as Dr. Brunton, and nearly all which I have already been responsible for publishing in works I have edited (e.g. " The Encyclopedia of Modern Knowledge "), but devil a trace can I find of that hidden teaching, and when, arriving near the end of the wordy work, I read : " Hence if we must close this study with the questions, ' What is thought ?' and ' What is mind ?' regretfully left unanswered, that is because those answers belong to the further and final stage of our journey, which not merely the necessities of space and the compulsions of time bid us reserve for a later volume, but other reasons which are more important still," I can only say in the immortal words of Sam Goldwyn that in any further stage of that journey Dr. Brunton can " include me out."

As a contrast I have just read " The Myth of the Mind," by Frank Kenyon, which in some 20,000 words presents a crystal-clear treatise on the thesis that the mind is essentially a function of the brain and not an abstract something that exists apart from it and persists somewhere in space after death. Not that I subscribe to all Mr. Kenyon's opinions, but his little book is a model of clean-cut expression and clear thinking, free from all the pretentious jargon and mushy phrasing in which so many of our writers on philosophic subjects love to splurge. I suggest the hidden teaching of Yoga might be summed up into half a dozen words : " Mind is all, the body nothing." For myself a good enough ideal is supplied by one's earliest Latin tag : " mens sana in corpore sano."

THUS a confident but not-too-well-informed critic of mine who writes purely for my private instruction, bless him, not for publication :
" Regarding your reference to Scottish language in a current issue, may I state that Gaelic is *the only* Scottish language. What you quote is merely a Lowland Scottish dialect of English."
He may not state anything of the kind ; but there are thousands of Englishmen who, never having bothered to inform themselves, would imagine him to be right. The subject is too large to discuss here, but I may tell him that the Scots language (of which a monumental dictionary has been in preparation for some years now) has closer affinities with Early English than Modern English. If the smart Alec who puts me on the mat would condescend to spend half an hour with my " Universal Encyclopedia" he would learn a good deal about Gaelic and the Scots language, of which he stands in need, and another half-hour with Jamieson's massive " Etymological Dictionary of the Scottish Language " would be instructive, if he could get a look at it in his local library.

As I have just been dealing with one critic, I may as well mention another, a youthful reader who takes me to task for attempting to mitigate our paper shortage by utilizing the outer pages of THE WAR ILLUSTRATED for pictures and reading matter, and then "disfiguring" one page with (as I think) a very unobtrusive announcement which will " spoil his book." He doesn't think my own notes worth keeping —an opinion I should not attempt to dispute —but by the same post I received a letter from a young New Zealander enclosing a Postal Order for half-a-crown (!) with the request to send him the *wrapper pages only* of an early number, as he binds these for the sake of my " Jottings " ! The wrapper of this particular number had been spoilt, but the inner pages were intact. Well, " it takes all sorts "—as we all know.

IS this the very latest addition to the comic lore of the evacuee ? Two East End mothers discussing probable duration of War : " Well, I seen it said that it may go on for thirty years." " 'Eavens above ! Why, our little Albert would be forty-two when he came 'ome from Wales ! "
JOHN CARPENTER HOUSE,
WHITEFRIARS, LONDON, E.C.4.

Printed in England and published on the 10th, 20th and 30th of each month by the Proprietors, The Amalgamated Press, Ltd., The Fleetway House, Farringdon Street, London, E.C.4. Registered for transmission by Canadian Magazine Post. Sole Agents for Australia and New Zealand ; Messrs. Gordon & Gotch, Ltd. : and for South Africa : Central News Agency, Ltd. September 30, 1941.
S.S.

Vol 5 The War Illustrated *N°108*

Edited by Sir John Hammerton

FOURPENCE

OCT. 10TH. 1941

IN ACTION IN RUSSIA, these Nazi machine-gunners are operating in a town fired by the retreating Soviet troops in accordance with the policy of leaving nothing of use to the enemy. A few snipers, however, remain to harass and delay the Nazi advance. A remarkable action photograph this—one in which the tense attitudes of the man firing the gun and the one feeding it are vividly expressed. *Photo, Keystone*

DO WE REALLY NEED AN ARMY OF MILLIONS?

NEVER in the long history of Britain have we made so great a military effort as today. Our Navy is the largest and most powerful in the world. Our Air Force cannot have far to go before it surpasses the Luftwaffe in numbers, as it surpasses it already in spirit. Our soldiers, here at home and on many a distant field, are to be counted in millions. We are trying to do what no other Great Power is attempting : we are trying to be supreme in three elements at once. And not content with this, we have embarked upon a colossal industrial effort, designed to supply not only our own needs but those of our allies.

About the necessity for a great navy and an air force as great in its own field, all men are agreed. But there is not the same unanimity about the necessity for a great army. Outside Downing Street and Whitehall there are few who know the actual strength of our present-day land forces, but Mr. Churchill told us nearly a year ago that it numbered two and a half millions (or four millions including the Home Guard), and there can be no doubt that today it is far larger.

EVERY male British subject in these islands between the ages of 18 and 41 is now liable for military service, and time and again the Schedule of Reserved Occupations has been revised so as to enable more and more men to join the colours. So extensive are the powers granted to the military authorities, and so drastically have they been exercised, that there is hardly a department of our national life which has not been adversely affected in consequence. We are likely to shiver in our homes this winter—and, much more important, our public utilities and communications are likely to be most seriously hampered—because thousands of coal-miners have been drafted into the Army. In vain it has been urged that some considerable percentage of them should be returned to the mines. The War Office is adamant : once a soldier, always a soldier, is its argument. Industry, however, is not in a position to make so firm a stand, so men who left the mines years ago because there was no work for them and secured jobs elsewhere are now being compelled to return to the mines at a lower wage.

AGAIN, tens of thousands of agricultural workers have joined the Army and must remain there, even though the harvest rots in the fields because of the lack of workers, even though good ships and gallant seamen are lost bringing food to Britain which ought to have been, and could have been, produced within our own shores. The building trade is crying out for craftsmen, and the construction of aerodromes, aircraft factories, armament works, soldiers' camps and homes for munition workers is held up because the carpenters and joiners, the plasterers and painters are forming threes on the parade ground. Our A.R.P. services are being combed week by week since the powers-that-be have decided that the defenders of our lives and property against air bombardment can be better employed in khaki. Worse still, never a day goes by but one reads of complaints that highly skilled engineers, who ought to be making aeroplanes and tanks,

shells and bombs, are pushing pens in battalion orderly rooms, washing up crockery or cleaning the barrack windows.

THERE would be fewer complaints about this misdirection of the nation's man-power if the necessity for the huge army was more clearly apparent. But there is a widespread belief that our military mandarins have been so bitten by the bug of their own importance that they consider that the Army's needs are the only needs worth consideration.

But surely it is reasonable to ask, if we have this great army, why don't we use it ? "Oh," reply the mandarins, " but we *are* using it. We have to maintain an enormous force in these islands, ready to repel the Nazi invaders. We have an army in the Western Desert and the Middle East, another in India. We have to maintain garrisons in Singapore and Gibraltar, Iceland and Abyssinia. . . Besides, the time will come when we shall be able to take the offensive in real earnest, and *then* we shall need all the men we can get."

To which the ordinary man responds with a shrug of the shoulders. To put it plainly, there is a widespread scepticism concerning the ability, and the intention, of Hitler to launch a large-scale attack on these islands at an early date. Even the Prime Minister's eloquence, even his warning that the defence services should be ready to meet an invasion by the beginning of September, have been unable to convince the sceptics. Of late weeks, since the invasion of Russia, criticism of our military policy (or lack of policy) has become ever more loud, ever more widespread. Why don't we do something to help Russia ? is the question asked in the railway carriage and the saloon bar, in the club lounge and the suburban parlour. Why don't we raid the 1,500 miles of coastline which lie so

invitingly in front of us ? Why don't we make a dash on Bergen one day and on Boulogne the next, then ring the changes on Ostend and Oslo ? Why waste any more bombs on the Gneisenau and the Scharnhorst ? Why not go into Brest and fetch them out ? Why shouldn't we recapture the dash and daring, the vigour and valour, of the last war, and repeat Sir Roger Keyes' Zeebrugge exploit of 1918 ? Some go further and urge that now or never is the time to invade the Continent—now, when Hitler, with what would seem to be a contemptuous disregard of our striking power, has denuded Western Europe of all his best troops.

Altogether unconvincing appear the replies to those questions. We are told that we cannot raid the Continent, still less invade it, because the danger of a Nazi invasion of Britain is still imminent ; because we are not even yet strong enough to invade the Continent in force ; because—this is the latest excuse—we cannot spare the ships to take our men across the Channel and the North Sea.

BUT if we are not going to invade or even raid until we have an army big enough to take on the Germans single-handed, then we shall never be in a position to do so. One does not have to be much of a mathematician to realize that a nation of 45 millions can never compete in numbers with the 120 million Germans and Italians. Thus it is not surprising that some shrewd observers argue that the *real* reason why we have not invaded the Continent is not because we fear for our security, not because we are expecting to wake up one fine morning to see the Nazi armada throbbing its way across the narrow seas, but because our Army is not yet sufficiently equipped. In other words, we are told the Germans are about to invade us because we are not yet able to invade Germany.

If it is asked why we are not even yet in a position to take the offensive, then the answer must be sought in our production policy. We have not the men, we are told ; it would be more to the point to say that we have not the tanks, the guns, the ships, the planes, the shells, the bombs. . .

MEANWHILE, we are letting slip an extraordinary opportunity—one which we had no right to expect ; one which, once it is lost, can never return. For three months our Russian ally has been standing up to the full brunt of the world's greatest military machine. At the present moment the Russians are staggering in the scorched wheat fields of the Ukraine, in the bloody quagmires before Leningrad. They may keep upright. On the other hand, they may succumb ; and then what use will our Army be, however numerous, however well-equipped ? When the Red millions have been defeated, are our comparatively tiny armies likely to fare any better ?

Surely *now* is the time of imperative need to fling into the balance all the weight which we can muster. For if Russia falls, at best the war must continue for years and years ; hardly better, the war must end in a draw ; at the worst, we, too, shall be thrust into the pit of Nazidom.

BRITAIN'S ARMY has at long last a considerable mechanized element. Above we see a division of the Royal Armoured Corps parading before the King somewhere in the Eastern Command on Sept. 12. *Photo, Keystone*

E. Royston Pike

Armoured Trains Help to Defend Leningrad

Soviet armoured train, typical of many that are being used to smash the Nazi divisions trying to capture Leningrad. Beneath, in the circle, the commander of an armoured train examining Nazi uniforms and colours draped beside the railway line. They were found in a German armoured car which had been abandoned by the crew.

On look-out for Stukas, the commander of a Soviet armoured train scans the horizon on his way up to the battle-front on the outskirts of Leningrad. On the right, a Nazi soldier beside a Soviet armoured train captured from the Russians. A bomb placed in the tender had made it unusable.

The defence of Leningrad, one of the greatest military feats in history, is the result of a combination of mechanical power and the fanatical courage of the Soviet troops and citizens resolved to die rather than surrender. How many Nazis have been killed in this inferno will never be known, but whatever happens to Leningrad now, her splendid fighting defiance will have materially helped to destroy the power of Hitlerism.

Photos, British Official: Crown Copyright; Planet News, Wide World

Black Sea Ports Menaced by the Fires of War

SEBASTOPOL, the Soviet port not far from Balaclava, Crimea, on the Black Sea. It is one of the Russian state dockyards, and has a population of about 80,000.

ZONGULDAK, a Turkish port, about 150 miles east of Istanbul. It is the chief town of a vilayet in which lies the biggest coalfield not only in Turkey but in the Balkans and the Near East.

TRABZON (Trebizond), a Turkish town not far from the Transcaucasian frontier. One of the oldest settlements on the Black Sea, it is still enclosed within Byzantine walls. Its population at the last census was 29,682.

VARNA, a Bulgarian port which is likely to play a big part in the war if the Nazis force Bulgaria to fight against Russia. This photograph shows the up-to-date bathing establishments. Population in 1934, 70,000.

YALTA, on the Crimean coast, has long been famed as a Russian health resort. Called "The Swallow's Nest," this view gives a good idea of its natural beauty. On the right, a glimpse of industrial ODESSA, which, though surrounded by the Nazis, is still holding out.

Photos, Topical Press, E.N.A. and Paul Popper

Maybe There Will Be Battles in the Black Sea

When the Germans invested Odessa, cut off the Crimea, and reached the Sea of Azov, the Black Sea was brought into the zone of active military operations. Naval operations, too, may be expected, since the sea route is the most direct from Hitler's Europe to Batum and the oil region lying in the Caucasus beyond.

ON the map the Black Sea does not look very large, but in fact it is as big as the Baltic. From Constantza on its western shore to Batum on its eastern is a matter of some 700 miles, so that Hitler's convoys—if they should actually set sail—will be five or six days making the passage.

Geographers are not too sure about the origin of the Black Sea's name. Its waters are not particularly black, but the gloomy nature of its climate may well be responsible for the adjective. In the summer months navigation is easy and safe, and the climate in some favoured regions—the Crimean coasts and the Caucasus in particular—is delightful. It is this aspect which is responsible for the Sea's ancient name, Euxine, from the Greek for hospitable. But in winter the Sea, completely enclosed as it is on every side, is swept by fierce storms, which make it well-nigh impassable for shipping. In January and February its north coasts are icebound ; though Odessa is never completely frozen up, the entrance to its harbour is made dangerous by floating ice.

Tideless, immensely deep, the Black Sea drains nearly a quarter of Europe and much of Asia Minor ; it receives many great rivers—Danube, Dniester, Bug, Dnieper, Don and Kuban in Europe, and a number of lesser streams from the mountains of Anatolia. For the most part its coasts are high—the chief exceptions are at the Danube mouth and in the Crimea ; and it is ringed with fine harbours. At its extreme south-western corner, where through the Bosporus its waters have an outlet to the Mediterranean, lies Istanbul. Proceeding northwards we come to Burgas and Varna, in Bulgaria. Then in Rumania are Constantza, and Sulina in the Danube' delta. Next we have the Russian ports : Odessa, Nikolayev and Kherson ; Sebastopol in the Crimea ; Novorossiisk beyond the Straits of Kerch, Tuapse (where the oil pipe-line from Grozny ends), and Sukhum, Poti, and Batum, terminus of the twin pipe-lines from Baku. Then along its southern shore are the Turkish harbours of Hopa, Trabzon, Samsun and Sinop.

Often the Black Sea is called a Russian lake, partly because so much of its shores are Russian, but still more because within it the Soviet Navy is predominant.

Mystery Fortress of Sebastopol

Sebastopol in the Crimea is one of the Soviet Union's principal naval bases and dockyards. It lies four miles up an estuary, one of the best roadsteads of Europe, large and deep enough to accommodate all the fleets of the continent. The chalk cliffs lining the estuary are strongly fortified ; for most of the way the width is three-quarters of a mile, but at the entrance it narrows to 930 yards. In English history Sebastopol has its place because of the great siege of 1854-5 by the English, French and Turks. After its evacuation by the Russians the Allies blew up its fortifications, and by the Treaty of Paris of the following year the Russians were bound not to re-fortify it. But in 1870 this restriction was repudiated and Sebastopol once again became a naval arsenal. It is not a commercial harbour, and no ships other than those on Government business have ever been allowed to enter it. It is indeed one of Europe's mystery fortresses ; just how strong it is, only time, and Hitler, may prove.

Second to Sebastopol as a naval base ranks Novorossisk. Nikolayev has a naval dock-

yard, and a number of warships were building there when it was captured by the Germans on August 17. The Russians claimed, however, that they would take a long time to complete. It is said that even if Sebastopol were captured or rendered untenable, the Soviet Navy could be adequately based on Novorossiisk, while the smaller ships could operate from Batum.

Strength of the Soviet Navy

The present strength of the Soviet Navy in the Black Sea is a matter of conjecture, since Russian Navy secrets are as well kept as those of Japan. The old battleship *Pariskaya-Kommuna*—formerly the *Sebastopol*, built in 1911 and reported to be decrepit—went to the Black Sea in 1930 for a refit, and is probably still there. One or two other battleships of the same class may also be there, but their fighting value is distinctly problematical. Then there may be the aircraft carrier *Stalin*, and several cruisers—*Krasni Kavkaz*, *Profintern*, and *Chervonaya Ukraina*. *Profintern* was laid down with *C. Ukraina* in 1915, but not completed until 1925 ; she was refitted in 1937 and is reported to have been renamed *Krasni Krim*. Then there are two new cruisers, *Kubyshev* and *Orjonikidze*, which were due to be completed in the summer of 1940 ; *Kubyshev*, at least, may be actually in service. But the main strength of the Soviet fleet in the Black Sea lies in its small craft. There is a destroyer flotilla numbering about 20, while there may be 30 submarines—perhaps more.

Against this force, weak as it may seem, the Germans in the Black Sea are able to oppose only one very much weaker. The German fleet can consist only of any U-boats and E-boats which they have brought down the Danube, but to these must be added the Rumanian and Bulgarian fleets. Rumania's Black Sea Division before the war consisted of four destroyers (*Regele Ferdinand*, *Regina*

Maria, *Marasti*, and *Marasesti*), three torpedo-boats, a minelayer, four gunboats, and a submarine. The Danube Division was composed of eight monitors and a patrol vessel. As for Bulgaria, she was compelled at the end of the last war to surrender all warships and submarines, but she was permitted to maintain on the Danube and along the Black Sea coast four torpedo-boats and six motor-boats.

Altogether, the Germans, Rumanians and Bulgarians cannot have more than 10 destroyers and torpedo-boats between them, to which must be added some U-boats and E-boats. Against these the Russians can oppose, as we have seen, perhaps 20 destroyers and 30 submarines. The disparity is great, but it would be much more than compensated for if the Germans could manage to introduce into the Black Sea even a small portion of the Italian Navy.

Italian Warships for Bulgaria ?

Of late weeks it has been reported that Turkey would be required to permit the passage through the Dardanelles of Italian warships " sold " to Bulgaria. Bulgaria, so the Germans have been arguing, is a neutral in the Russo-German war, and hence Turkey should allow her ships to pass through the Dardanelles, since the Montreux Convention states that in wartime, Turkey being neutral, warships of belligerents only are banned from the Straits. But it should be difficult to convince the Turks that Bulgaria is not a belligerent, more particularly since the Russian Note of September 11 which accused the Bulgarian Government of permitting their country to be used as a base for warlike operations against the Soviet Union. These warlike operations, there can be little doubt, consisted of the use of the Bulgarian ports as " invasion ports." Significant, too, is the presence in Bulgaria of Admiral Raeder, Hitler's Navy chief.

THE BLACK SEA, which may become the scene of violent battles as a result of the recent Nazi successes in the Ukraine. Odessa, the Crimea and Batum are German objectives. The Black Sea, which is seven hundred miles wide from Constantza in the west to Batum in the east, is swept by fierce storms in winter, and for some months its north coasts are icebound.

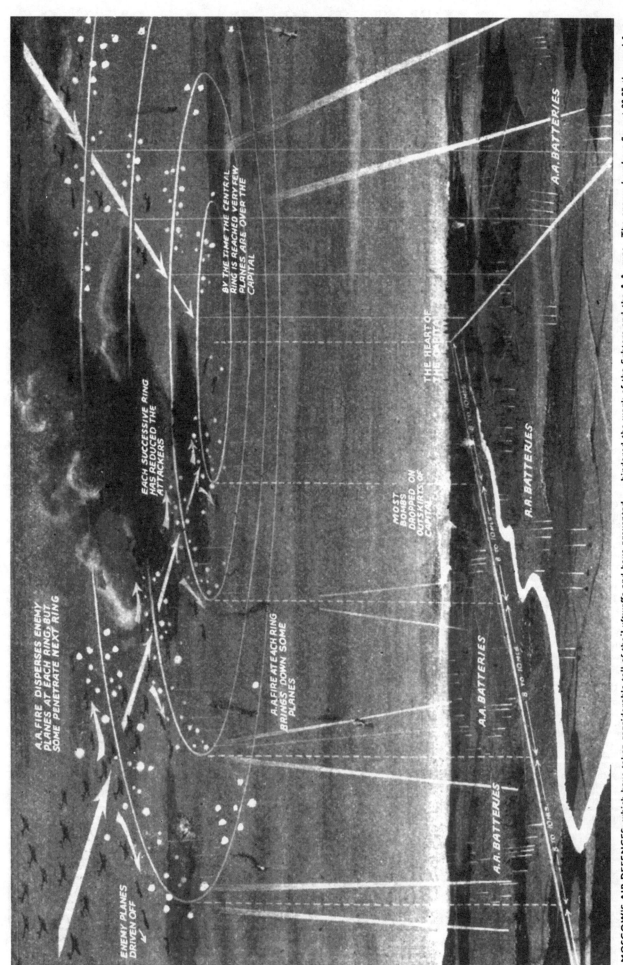

ENEMY PLANES DRIVEN OFF

A.A. FIRE DISPERSES ENEMY PLANES AT EACH RING, BUT SOME PENETRATE NEXT RING

A.A. FIRE AT EACH RING BRINGS DOWN SOME PLANES

EACH SUCCESSIVE RING HAS REDUCED THE ATTACKERS

BY THE TIME THE CENTRAL RING IS REACHED VERY FEW PLANES ARE OVER THE CAPITAL

MOST BOMBS DROPPED ON OUTSKIRTS OF CAPITAL

THE HEART OF THE CAPITAL

A.A. BATTERIES

A.A. BATTERIES

A.A. BATTERIES

R.R. BATTERIES

A.A. BATTERIES

MOSCOW'S AIR DEFENCES, which have taken considerable toll of the Luftwaffe and have prevented the German invaders from reaching the centre of the city in any great numbers, are represented above in diagram form. Major-General Gromadin, Commander of the Moscow Air Defence Zone, has described how, although the Nazi Air Command sent its best fliers over Moscow on the first raids against the Russian capital, their formations were quickly dispersed by night-fighters and coordinated gunfire. "The Moscow air defence system," he says, "works smoothly in all weathers. At times thick cloud hindered the work of the fighters and the A.A. guns. The enemy bombers flew at 20-25 thousand feet. The reply to this was a massed barrage of shell fire in the enemy's path, which caused the bombers hastily to turn back and attempt another route of approach. They tried coming in from the south, the east—and everywhere they found the same intensive barrage. The scouting planes, which generally approached Moscow in the daytime, consistently avoided battle and dodged in and out of cloud, swooping away as quickly as they could."

Drawing by E. G. Lambert, by courtesy of "The Sphere"

We Showed the Russians Our Air Defences

RUSSIAN OFFICERS of the Soviet Military Mission have been shown some of the secrets of Britain's air defences. One of them is seen above testing the weight of an A.A. shell. Top, watching a gun team at work. Right, a Russian officer who is a test pilot at the controls of a Stirling, which he flew as second pilot.
Photos, British Official; Topical and Central Press

Our Searchlight on the War

HOSPITAL IN 'THE ROCK'

DEEP down inside the great rock of Gibraltar British and Canadian tunnellers are preparing the way for the world's most remarkable hospital. This hospital, named after Lord Gort, Gibraltar's Governor and Commander-in-Chief, will accommodate 800 beds in the heart of the rock, safe from bombs, shells and gas, and will have its own operating theatre. The fortress already possesses some completed underground hospitals, fully equipped for any emergency, and a convalescent home is being built in a huge cave high up on the giant face of the rock. A large brick building, it is so placed that it would be practically immune from any attack.

COXSWAIN BLOGG, of Cromer, who has been awarded the gold medal of the Royal National Lifeboat Institution for the third time. He has also received the silver medal three times and the British Empire medal.
Photo, Associated Press

GALLANT COXSWAIN

FOR the third time Coxswain Henry Blogg, of Cromer, has been awarded the gold medal of the Royal National Lifeboat Institution—the lifeboatman's V.C. Coxswain Blogg was largely instrumental in saving 119 lives when six ships were stranded on the Haisborough Sands during a gale. Seven medals, 18 vellums, and £117 were awarded to the coxswains and crews of five lifeboats which took part in the rescue.

AN ORANGE S O S

A NEW type of distress signal for the use of shipwrecked seamen is now being put into operation, and will be fitted on every ocean-

A WEEK END WITH THE R.A.F.
Attacks of Sept. 20 and 21

Sat. Sept. 20—Biggest Daylight Offensive of the War
Bombers—Norway—fish oil factory. Germany—Emden. France—Hazebrouck, Abbeville, Rouen shipyards, Cherbourg docks. Holland—Convoy (6 ships hit).
Fighters—Escort and continuous sweep, Cherbourg and high up Dutch coast.

Sun. Sept. 21—Non-stop Daylight Raids
Bombers—France—Gosnay power station, Lille railway.
Fighters—Escort and continuous sweep over Occupied France.

Sat.-Sun. Sept. 20-21—Night Bombing
Targets—Frankfort, Berlin, N.W. Germany, Ostend Docks.

		LOSSES		
	Sept. 20	Sept. 20-21	Sept. 21	Totals
Enemy	16 MEs	—	24 MEs	40
R.A.F.	7 Fighters	—	13 Fighters	20
	3 Blenheims	4 Bombers	—	7

going British merchant ship. It is a smoke float resembling a box about two feet square. Upon a button being pressed a bright red-orange cloud of smoke rises, which hovers in the air for a considerable time and is visible in good weather from nearly forty miles distance. The boxes float, and if water reaches the chemicals inside them this merely serves to thicken the already dense cloud of smoke.

TWO NIGHTS IN A CANOE

ON September 18 five French boys landed at Eastbourne after spending two nights and a day crossing the Channel in two canoes. Their ages range from 17 to 19½. On the night of September 16 they set out from a French town and paddled down river to the sea. During the day they could not use their sails owing to the presence of German aircraft, but they eventually arrived safely in this country, though one of the canoes struck a rock and sank just off shore, and the occupants were obliged to swim to land. The young men were received by Mr. and Mrs. Churchill at Downing Street on September 22, and are now going to the Free French Cadet School.

NEW TYPE OF CARGO SHIP

CARGO ships of revolutionary design, known as Sea Otters, are now undergoing final tests in the U.S.A. This new type of vessel, which may prove of great value in combating submarines, has a six-foot propeller amidships instead of at the stern, and is driven by stock motor-car engines obtainable from any of the big car manufactures. Sixteen of them will be used in each Sea Otter. The vessels are 270 feet long, and with a displacement of 1,900 tons are comparatively light. They can carry a cargo load of 1,500 tons. Sea Otters can be built in two months by mass production methods, and can be constructed at inland yards and transported to the sea by river or canal.

CHELSEA PENSIONERS, who have already served their country faithfully and well, were among those who registered for fire-watching under the recent Order. These bemedalled old soldiers are once again answering their country's call.
Photo, Fox

MORE BALLOONS FOR W.A.A.F.

THE experiment of replacing men operators by W.A.A.F. at a number of balloon sites has proved so successful that it has now been decided to transfer to them as many sites as possible. This will free a large number of airmen for duties which cannot be performed by women. The women so far engaged on this work rapidly mastered the technique of balloon handling, and various improvements which have been made in the construction of the balloons themselves as well as in the methods of handling and bedding down have rendered this work less exacting than it was, though physical strength and endurance are still necessary qualifications. More operators are now wanted to "man" the additional sites and recruits are taken between the ages of 17 and 43. They must, however, be of first-class physique and prepared to work out of doors in all weathers, and at all hours of the day and night.

POSTWOMEN mail van drivers are to have a new hat. The old type, seen right, tended to get knocked off by the overhanging roof of the van. The new type is of felt, with a peak, and looks very smart. *Photo, Keystone*

DE GAULLE'S ARMY GROWS

M. CHARLES BARON, former Governor of French possessions in India and now leader of the Free French movement in the Far East, stated in an interview on his return from a tour in the East : "Free French forces are represented by 55,000 men at present in the fighting lines on different fronts, by thirty warships actually in service, by a third of France's merchant marine, and 1,000 airmen. These figures represent our numbers six months ago, and they have most certainly been increased since then. We know that at the present moment an army of 100,000 fighting men is being formed at Brazzaville, French Equatorial Africa."

GOERING PILLS

GERMAN airmen are drugged before action to increase their physical resistance and will power. The drug is taken in the form of tablets known as "Goering Pills." These tablets, says the Rome journal "Aquilone," contain a substance which affects the sympathetic system. They were found effective during the Norwegian campaign as a preventive of air sickness, and are also used in the German Navy to combat sea sickness. "Aquilone" goes on to say that the Italians have an even more effective drug, called Simpamina. This new drug was, it is claimed, tried out by the Italian Medical Research Institute before the German product was brought into use.

SYRIA NOW INDEPENDENT

THE independence of Syria and the termination of the French Mandate were proclaimed by the Free French authorities on Sept. 16. Sheik Tajeddine Hassani has been appointed President of the Republic. In a letter to the new President, General Catroux said : "Free France, acting in cooperation with her ally, Great Britain, has spontaneously undertaken to terminate the mandate and grant Syria the status of an independent sovereign state and to guarantee this new status by Treaty." The formal ceremony took place on Sept. 26 in Damascus amid scenes of enthusiasm. Bands played and cheering crowds paraded the streets, whilst a salute of twenty-two guns ushered in the new order. A guard of honour of Syrian militia and mounted Republican guards saluted Gen. Catroux as he rode away.

Triumph Is the Word for These Sea Stories

Men of the Soviet Baltic Fleet defending the Leningrad approaches from the sea, in action against the German dive bombers. The Russian navy has done excellent work in the Gulf of Finland, fighting off many Nazi attacks by sea and air.

Intercepted by the British in the Caribbean Sea, the crew of the German ship Hannover (above) set her on fire. The resulting list jammed a sack of grain in a hole through which the water was entering. The fire was subdued and the prize taken to Kingston, Jamaica.

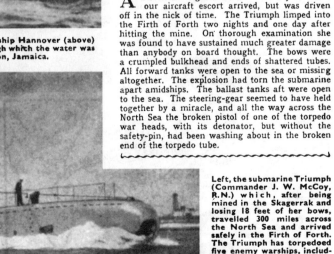

IT happened on the night of December 26, 1939. It was very dark, and the place was the Skagerrak on the German side of the North Sea minefields right inside enemy waters and 300 miles from home. The submarine H.M.S. Triumph was going slow ahead when, lifting over a wave, she came right down on a large mine. There was a shattering explosion. The whole extent of the damage could not be ascertained, but it was certain that the rear ends of the torpedo tubes had all been forced back about six inches, the foremost bulkhead was split right across and had been forced back into the tubes. Eighteen feet of the ship was missing. The Triumph had no bows and she could, not dive. She was making water fast and a rating endeavoured to plug the leaks with wooden plugs and felt.

In this crippled state she started for home at about 5 knots. The weather getting worse, speed had to be reduced to 2½ knots for a whole day— a desperately anxious day with German reconnaissance aircraft about. When the weather improved the Triumph made 10 knots.

A DORNIER sighted the submarine just before our aircraft escort arrived, but was driven off in the nick of time. The Triumph limped into the Firth of Forth two nights and one day after hitting the mine. On thorough examination she was found to have sustained much greater damage than anybody on board thought. The bows were a crumpled bulkhead and ends of shattered tubes. All forward tanks were open to the sea or missing altogether. The explosion had torn the submarine apart amidships. The ballast tanks aft were open to the sea. The steering-gear seemed to have held together by a miracle, and all the way across the North Sea the broken pistol of one of the torpedo war heads, with its detonator, but without the safety-pin, had been washing about in the broken end of the torpedo tube.

Left, the submarine Triumph (Commander J. W. McCoy, R.N.) which, after being mined in the Skagerrak and losing 18 feet of her bows, travelled 300 miles across the North Sea and arrived safely in the Firth of Forth. The Triumph has torpedoed five enemy warships, including a U-Boat, and five enemy supply ships.
Photos, British Official; Associated Press, and Wright & Logan

Kiev Falls: The Nazi Drive in the Ukraine

With the fall of Kiev and the consequent rapid penetration of the Ukraine in the direction of Kharkov, thus engulfing a still larger part of one of Russia's most vital industrial regions, the situation on the Eastern Front appeared uglier and more dangerous for our hard-pressed allies than ever before. But still the Russians maintained an unbroken front.

"THE Reich flag has been flying from the Citadel of Kiev since this morning." This was the report that came from the Fuehrer's Headquarters on September 19. " In the course of encircling operations announced today the attack against the capital of the Ukraine was begun. After a bold penetration through the strong fortifications on the west bank of the Dnieper our troops have penetrated into the town."

What the Germans described as a tremendous battle of encirclement followed the junction on September 13, 125 miles east of Kiev, of Von Runstedt's and Von Bock's armies. Employing masses of men, aided by a host of tanks and armoured cars and hordes of General Lœhr's and Field-Marshal Kesselring's dive-bombers, the Germans surrounded Kiev with a ring of fire and iron. The grand offensive against the city, which had temporarily halted while the German marshals were joining hands, was resumed on September 17. German divisions moving up the east bank of the Dnieper attacked from the north, while others advanced up the western bank from the south. On the night of September 18 German infantry, naked but for their steel helmets and carrying their arms and ammunition, swam across a little river to the south of Kiev and stormed the concrete casemates defending the inner city. For days continuous fighting had raged in the northern suburbs and the southern approaches ; piles of German dead and scores of smashed-up tanks and armoured cars (reported the correspondent of " Red Star," the Red Army newspaper) were scattered among the woods, along the roads into the southern suburbs and in the gardens of the cottages. At length a strong ring of fortifications on the west bank of the Dnieper was broken through and (so the German High Command reported on September 20) " after the higher leadership of the Soviet troops had fled, the garrison threw down their arms and ceased further resistance."

When the German troops entered Kiev they found " indescribable devastation,"

announced Berlin. " All vital supplies had been removed or blown up, the water and electricity works put out of action. The place is strewn with the wreckage of railways and bridges that have been blown up. The population had not the bare necessities of life." For a week, indeed, the city had been without water, and for three days its people had gone hungry. Its buildings were packed with wounded. Yet resistance was of the most bitter description, and the Ogpu divisions left behind by Budenny fought with desperate bravery to the last.

Great Battle of Encirclement

Following Kiev's fall, the Germans concentrated upon the destruction of Marshal Budenny's divisions, which (so the Germans claimed) were encircled to the east of the city. " The armies of General Field-Marshal von Reichenau and the panzer armies of Colonels-General von Kleist and Guderian," stated the German High Command on September 21, " have annihilated large sections of the encircled enemy, and have already taken over 150,000 prisoners and captured 151 tanks, 602 guns, and vast quantities of other war material." In the course of the next few days the German claims mounted apace, until the number of prisoners taken had risen to some 665,000, with 885 tanks and 3,718 guns captured or destroyed. But in spite of these claims Budenny's armies seemed to have plenty of

Wing-Commander H. N. G. Ramsbottom - Isherwood, from New Zealand, in command of the R.A.F. wing on the Russian front. One squadron accounted for three M.E. 109s in its first encounter, and later destroyed another four, with the loss of one British fighter and its pilot.
Photo, Vandyk

EAST FRONT (left), indicating the conflicting thrusts between Smolensk and the Black Sea up to September 24.
By courtesy of the " News Chronicle"

fighting spirit left. Nearly a week later, on September 24, a German spokesman in Berlin, after announcing that the Battle of Kiev was almost finished, that around Kiev there was chaos and some of the Russian corps were in a state of disintegration, went on to state that there was no general disintegration of the Russian forces east of Kiev. " How far they will be able to resist only time will show. Difficulties of supplies for the German forces have considerably increased. Lines of communication have been lengthened by a further 75 miles because of our advance. The Russians have blown up all the bridges and the roads—and these were bad enough before. The farther we advance east, the more difficult it will be for us to get supplies to our armies."

While this battle of encirclement was proceeding, other German forces continued to make progress through the Ukraine in the direction of Kharkov and the Donetz basin. On the same day that they announced the fall of Kiev, the Germans reported with a fanfare of trumpets that they had taken Poltava, about 85 miles south-west of Kharkov. But a week later their armoured units were still no nearer than 33 miles to the great industrial city, so hampered had they been by the forests, swamps, and rough country, and by the determined resistance put up by the Russian regulars and guerillas. To the south the line of the Dnieper between Kremenchug and Zaporozhe seemed to be still held by Budenny's troops, but between Nikopol and Kherson the river line was breached. Kherson was outflanked and the Germans, after investing Perekop on the isthmus connecting the Crimea with the mainland, swept on to the shore of the Sea of Azov.

Timoshenko's Counter-attacks

Meanwhile, in the other sectors of the front the battle raged with undiminished fury. In the centre Marshal Timoshenko continued to make progress in the neighbourhood of Smolensk ; for the first time in the present war the Germans were compelled to withdraw from territory—in some places as much as 10 or 15 miles—which they had conquered. Even Berlin admitted that Timoshenko's attacks were " very heavy."

At Leningrad the Germans continued to batter the city's steel-bound defences. Their losses were terrific, but territorially, at least, they had little to show for their immense sacrifices. Hardly anywhere were the Germans within 20 miles of the Nevski Prospekt, but on September 19 a German war correspondent in the front line with the shock troops reported that with field-glasses the men in the most advanced positions could sometimes catch the flash of Leningrad's windows in the sunlight, while factory chimneys, still blithely smoking, despite German bombing and shelling, were visible here and there. Watchers in Finland, looking across Kronstadt Bay, saw the night sky over Leningrad lit up with towering flames, saw the flash of bursting bombs and shells, and the scintillating network of searchlights and " flak " fire.

Then in the far north, in the most northern sector of the 1,500-mile front, the Germans and Austrians were still struggling vainly to capture Murmansk, and so deprive Russia of her sole ice-free port and close one of the very few channels whereby British and American support might reach the Soviet. It was on this front that the R.A.F. wing sent to Russia was reported from Stockholm to be in action.

German Guns Captured by Timoshenko's Men

NAZI ARTILLERY, comprising howitzers, light field guns and anti-tank guns, captured by Soviet troops at village "N," being examined by engineers and technical experts of the Red Army. German losses in men and material during the fighting on the Eastern front, which has been on an unprecedented scale, have been enormous. But Hitler is making use of the resources of a conquered Europe, and only unremitting toil in our own factories will enable us to gain the ascendancy in material needed for our ultimate victory.   *Photo, British Official: Crown Copyright*

With Gun and Tank, Bayonet and Bomb, Hitler

1. Russian anti-aircraft guns being used in the defence of Odessa, the seaport on the Black Sea besieged by Rumanian and German troops. 2. Col.-General Busch, chief of a Nazi army group, inspecting an A.A. position. 3. German photograph purporting to show Nazi machine-gunners attacking Russian troops. The geese seem strangely unperturbed. 4. Finnish troops, assisting the Nazis in the Karelian Isthmus, taking cover during an advance.

des Grapple with the Hosts of a Russia at Bay

5. Nazis urging on the frightened horses of a supply column through a blazing Russian town.   6. Nazi infantry and tanks advancing through the vast wheatfields of the Ukraine.   7. Radio photograph from Moscow showing an actual bayonet charge by Soviet infantry during the fight for the village of " N."   One result of this engagement is shown in page 179.

Photos, Planet News, Associated Press and Keystone

After Three Months: The Battle Line in Russia

LENINGRAD, defended by the armies of Voroshilov. The Kirov House of Culture.

SMOLENSK, taken by the Nazis in August. German motor vehicles in the main street.

KIEV, the loss of which was admitted by Moscow on Sept. 21. A residential quarter.

ODESSA, Black Sea port besieged but unconquered. Steps linking city to seafront.

TERRITORY overrun by the Nazis in twelve weeks' fighting on the Eastern Front. Although, as can be seen, the territorial gains of the German armies are very considerable, the Soviet Red Army still preserves an unbroken line from Finland to the Black Sea, and is still fighting with undiminished ardour. The Nazi gains have been bought at an enormous cost to themselves in both men and material. M. Maisky, Soviet Ambassador to Great Britain, speaking on September 23, said that the Germans had lost, "at a moderate estimate," 3,000,000 men in killed, wounded and missing, as well as something like 8,500 planes.

As September drew to a close, Leningrad still held out stubbornly in the face of Von Leeb's powerful attacks; Smolensk had been captured by the Nazis early in August, but now they were losing ground east of the city owing to Timoshenko's counter-attacks. The loss of Kiev was a severe blow to the Soviet, but Budenny's forces were still fighting hard, and Odessa, the Russian Tobruk, was proving a graveyard to thousands of Antonescu's Rumanians.

Map by courtesy of "The Manchester Guardian." Photos, Soviet War News, Associated Press, Topical Press, E.N.A.

Exit Riza Shah: A New Chapter in Persia

Vital to the defence of India and Egypt, vital to the Russian defenders of the Caucasus, Iran (or Persia, as Mr. Churchill prefers to call it) has now, following the abdication of the old Shah, been brought under the control of the Russian and British Allies.

SHAH RIZA KHAN PAHLEVI abdicated on September 16 in favour of his eldest son, the Crown Prince Shah Mohammed Riza, a young man of 22. Failing health was given as the reason, but in fact the old Shah had become altogether *non persona grata* to the Russians and British who had invaded his country on August 25, and who since then had been waiting in vain for the Nazi

NEW SHAH OF IRAN, Mohammed Riza Pahlevi, who acceded to the throne when his father abdicated on September 16, 1941.
Photo, Associated Press

intriguers to be handed over or expelled. It was only too obvious that the Nazis were being sheltered and shielded by the Court. Every difficulty was put in the way of their extradition, and some of the most "wanted" were allowed to escape over the frontier into Turkey. Nor were the Axis legations in Teheran liquidated; rather they were permitted to continue in their hostile activities. So at length, and not too soon, the Allies' patience was exhausted. From Moscow there came complaints of "insincerity" and "unforgivable slowness" in fulfilling the terms of the armistice concluded on September 9, and in effect the Shah was told that his unfriendly and unreasonable attitude could be no longer tolerated. He made his choice, and stepped down from the throne.

So fell one of the world's most picturesque rulers and, let it be admitted, one of the most capable in the whole of Asia. It is now the fashion to decry Riza Shah's achievements, but history will record that in his earlier years at least he worked wonders in a country which for centuries has been a political and social quagmire.

Born about 67 years ago, Pahlevi was the son of humble parents, and after the briefest schooling and a spell as a shepherd boy he enlisted in the Cossack division of the Persian Army. For 20 years he was a trooper before he rose to become an officer. In 1920 his abilities were recognized by two British officers, Colonel Smythe and General Sir Edmund (now Lord) Ironside, and he was appointed to the command of the Cossack division which was then operating in conjunction with British forces against the Bolsheviks. That was his first step on the

road to fame and supreme power. In 1921 he executed a *coup d'état* and seized Teheran. Two years later he was Prime Minister, and in 1925 he supplanted the old Shah, Sultan Ahmed, who preferred to spend most of his time at Deauville and Biarritz, dallying with his dancing girls. In 1926 the one-time trooper was crowned Shah.

For years he ruled as an enlightened despot. He built roads and bridges, constructed irrigation works, encouraged agriculture, established schools, some of them on co-educational lines. He introduced new legal codes, thus striking at the power of the religious courts conducted by the mullahs, did much to emancipate women. Unlike his Turkish exemplar, he did not feel strong enough to prohibit the veil, but he did everything in his power to discourage its use.

He set up factories in which he was the principal shareholder; he did much to encourage the tourist trade, and the hotels which he built on the Caspian shore were his own property. In Teheran he constructed a magnificent railway station which cost, so it is said, £30,000,000; at first there were no trains and not even rails. "Teheran," reported John Gunther, "became a mixture of primitiveness and sophistication. Splendid boulevards and dial telephones—but no sewage system. Between street and pavement are ditches filled with dogs, cats and drinking water." The construction of a splendid bourse was begun, although the building was never finished. A magnificent opera house was completed, but Iran still has no opera, just as it has no stockbrokers.

But it must be admitted that the Shah could have done few or none of these things but for the royalties paid him by the Anglo-Iranian Oil Company, of which the largest shareholder is the British Government. These made him independent of the Iranian *Majlis* or National Assembly, enabled him

to defy the Moslem mullahs and the feudal chieftains. Still more, they provided him with the funds with which he paid his troops and officials. Out of a rabble he produced a conscript army of respectable appearance and conduct, with which he was able to put down brigandage and overawe recalcitrant tribesmen. The oil royalties represent more than half the country's national income,

ALLIES IN IRAN: a representative of the Soviet forces in Iran chatting with British officers. This photograph was wired direct from Moscow to London.
Photo, British Official: Crown Copyright

but the balance had to be wrung from a people living in the most squalid poverty. His great public works were only carried out by forced labour at very low wages, and parts of the country were depopulated as the peasants fled to avoid his press gangs. Then many of the necessities of life—sugar, tea and salt, as well as foreign trade, transport, petroleum and tourism—were made state monopolies, sold to the highest bidder.

A great man in his heyday was Riza Shah Pahlevi; so great indeed that on one occasion, in 1932, he challenged the great oil company and its British Government backers. Not only did he reduce the area of its concession by half, but he demanded that instead of receiving as heretofore a share of the net profits he should be paid a specific rate per ton of oil, with the proviso that the sum paid should never fall below £750,000 per annum. After six months of haggling and angry protests his demands were conceded; in 1937 and again in 1938 the Anglo-Iranian Oil Company paid the Persian Government over £3,000,000.

But as Pahlevi grew old he revealed ever more plainly the well-known vices of the solitary autocrat. He was a one-man tyrant, intolerant of opposition, determined to have his own way in everything. Moreover, his avarice became insatiable. In particular he indulged in a passion for land-grabbing— a passion which may be traced back, perhaps, to his peasant ancestry.

Now, however, all that is gone. Most of his wealth has been restored to the Persian State, and he himself is an exile.

IN TEHERAN the British Legation is housed in this charming building. It contains a well with the only good drinking water in Teheran, which the whole town is said to use.
Photo, "Daily Mirror"

Our Diary of the War

TUESDAY, SEPT. 16, 1941   *745th day*

Air.—Seven enemy fighters destroyed during R.A.F. sweeps over northern France. Two British fighters missing. Night attack on Karlsruhe and objectives in W. Germany as well as on the docks at Le Havre.

Russian Front.—Russians reported gains in local actions near Leningrad. Germans claimed defeat of large Russian forces south of Lake Ilmen. Von Rundstedt launched powerful new offensive in Ukraine.

Africa.—39 killed and 93 injured in enemy air raid on Cairo area. Harbours and shipping at Tripoli and Benghazi attacked during night. Stores at Bardia bombed.

Iran.—The Shah abdicated, being succeeded by his son, Mohammed Riza Pahlevi.

Home.—Few bombs from night raiders at points in eastern England. One enemy bomber destroyed.

WEDNESDAY, SEPT. 17   *746th day*

Sea.—Admiralty announced loss of H.M. Submarine P.32.

Air.—Strong R.A.F. forces attacked power plant at Mazingarbe, near Bethune. 12 enemy fighters destroyed in offensive sweeps. For the second night in succession Karlsruhe raided. Night attack on St. Nazaire.

Russian Front.—Germans renewed assault on Leningrad with waves of dive bombers. Marshal Timoshenko still counter-attacking north-east of Smolensk.

Africa.—In Abyssinia, R.A.F. bombers attacked enemy positions north-east of Azozo.

Mediterranean.—Munition factories at Licata, Sicily, raided in daylight by bombers of the R.A.F.

Home.—Bombs on south-east coast towns caused a few casualties.

General.—Three Swedish destroyers were blown up near the island of Naersgarn.

THURSDAY, SEPT. 18   *747th day*

Sea.—Submarines of Mediterranean Fleet attacked an Italian convoy, destroying two liners of over 20,000 tons each and probably damaging a third.

Air.—Enemy supply ship damaged and two A.A. ships sunk off Belgian coast. Power station near Rouen bombed. In an offensive sweep over northern France, 17 enemy aircraft were destroyed. British losses, two bombers and nine fighters. At night the docks of Le Havre were attacked.

Russian Front.—Pressure on Leningrad relieved by counter-attacks. Crimea reported cut off from the mainland.

Iran.—Russian troops entered Teheran. British troops encamped on the outskirts.

U.S.A.—President Roosevelt asked Congress for an additional £1,500,000,000 for Lease and Lend supplies.

Home.—The King and Queen inspected the Third Canadian Division. Night raiders dropped bombs at a few points in South Wales and East Anglia.

General.—New Japanese offensive in Hunan.

FRIDAY, SEPT. 19   *748th day*

Sea.—Netherlands Admiralty announced that a Dutch submarine had sunk two Italian supply ships in the Mediterranean.

Air.—Night attacks included a heavy raid on the Baltic port of Stettin and objectives near Nantes, in France.

Russian Front.—Germans claimed the capture of Kiev and announced that the armies of Rundstedt and Bock had joined forces beyond that city. Germans claimed to have reached Poltava, 85 miles from Kharkov.

Iran.—A British column occupied the inner suburbs of Teheran. Other British troops occupied the Skoda machine-gun factory east of the city.

Home.—Bombs dropped in the Thames Estuary area during a daylight raid.

SATURDAY, SEPT. 20   *749th day*

Sea.—At night unsuccessful attacks on North Sea convoys were made by enemy E-boats, two of which were severely damaged.

Air.—R.A.F. attacked enemy convoys off the Dutch coast setting several ships on fire. Air attacks were also made on objectives in Norway, N.-W. Germany and occupied France. The railway junction at Hazebrouck, shipyards near Rouen, the docks at Cherbourg and the railway centre at Abbeville were bombed. Objectives at Emden and a fish-oil factory at Floro, in Norway, were also attacked. 16 enemy fighters were shot down. British losses, seven fighters and three bombers. Night attacks on Frankfurt, Berlin and N.-W. Germany as well as the docks at Ostend.

Russian Front.—Fighting continued along the whole front and was especially fierce around Kiev. Germans claimed the capture of islands of Vorms and Moon in the Baltic.

Africa.—Merchant ship bombed and sunk by R.A.F. off Kerkenah, and enemy destroyer successfully attacked off Tripoli. Benghazi raided on night of Sept. 20-21.

Home.—700 interned Fascists rioted at Peel, Isle of Man, internment camp. A few bombs were dropped by night raiders at points in south and eastern England. One enemy aircraft destroyed.

SUNDAY, SEPT. 21   *750th day*

Air.—24 enemy fighters shot down in two big sweeps by R.A.F. over northern France. Blenheims attacked power station at Gosnay, near Bethune, and Hampdens railway objectives at Lille. British losses, 13 fighters.

Russian Front.—Russians admitted evacuation of Kiev. Germans claim capture of Baltic island of Oesel. Moscow claimed an advance by Marshal Timoshenko's armies of 13 miles in the Smolensk area. Germans claimed also to have reached Sea of Azov.

Home.—South-east coast town bombed.

MONDAY, SEPT. 22   *751st day*

Air.—5,000-ton German supply ship hit by a Beaufort aircraft off Norway. Night attack on the docks at Boulogne.

Russian Front.—Soviet forces encircled east of Kiev still put up vigorous resistance. Timoshenko's armies continued their advance in the Smolensk area. Pressure on Leningrad relieved by Russian counter-attacks from the Valdai Hills. Moscow announced arrival of British and American missions.

Africa.—Harbour at Benghazi and objectives at Tripoli bombed on night of Sept. 22-23.

Home.—King George of Greece arrived in London. "Tanks for Russia" week began.

General.—Lord Linlithgow's term of office as Viceroy of India extended to April 1943.

TUESDAY, SEPT. 23   *752nd day*

Russian Front.—Nazis pushed back seven miles by Soviet counter-attacks in the Leningrad sector. German 3rd Mountain Infantry Division routed near Murmansk.

Middle East.—Announced from Cairo that Gen. Wavell had returned to India after a conference with Gen. Auchinleck somewhere in the Middle East.

Iran.—The Iranian government decided to recall its diplomatic representatives in Germany, Italy and Rumania.

Africa.—In Abyssinia enemy positions near Gondar bombed by R.A.F.

Home.—Night raiders dropped a few bombs in South Wales and south-west England. Mr. Churchill appointed Lord Warden of the Cinque Ports in succession to the late Marquess of Willingdon. Gen. de Gaulle announced Free French National Committtee.

WEDNESDAY, SEPT. 24   *753rd day*

Sea.—Admiralty announced torpedoing of an Italian minelayer, a transport and two supply ships in the Mediterranean.

Russian Front.—Germans claimed capture of Peterhov, 18 miles west of Leningrad. Budenny counter-attacked at Kherson, on the Dnieper. Officially announced that one R.A.F. squadron in Russia had shot down 7 Nazi planes for the loss of one fighter.

Mediterranean.—Announcement of successful attacks on merchant shipping by Fleet Air Arm and bombers of R.A.F.

Home.—Day raider bombed Scottish east coast village. Few night bombs on south-east coast. Allied Council, at St. James's Palace, endorsed the Atlantic Charter.

THURSDAY, SEPT. 25   *754th day*

Russian Front.—Leningrad attacked by waves of Stukas and heavy bombers. Rundstedt's southern forces began new advance from Genichesk along the coast of the Sea of Azov.

Home.—Few night bombs on east coast.

General.—Berlin admits seriousness of big guerilla risings in Serbia.

M. MAISKY, Soviet Ambassador in London, addresses workers after taking delivery of the first tank made in the Tanks for Russia Week which started on Sept. 22 and resulted in 20 per cent increase over the previous "best."
Photo, G.P.U.

New Halifaxes and Hurricanes Take the Air

HALIFAX, the formidable new Handley Page bomber in use with the R.A.F. It has a span of 99 ft., a length of 70 ft., and is 22 ft. high. Fitted with four Rolls-Royce Merlin engines, it is a midwing monoplane with twin fins and rudders, the tail gun-turret projecting well beyond the tail assembly.

Members of the ground staff at an R.A.F. station loading up the ammunition container of one of the new Spitfire cannon-guns.

AERIAL supremacy over the Nazis, numerical and technical—such is the order of the day and night. In technique, Britain has always led the way, and recent developments are very gratifying.

The Halifax, one of the largest and most formidable new machines under Bomber Command, is doing splendid service. It is an all-metal midwing monoplane with four Rolls-Royce Merlin 12-cylinder liquid-cooled engines. The fuselage is rectangular, and the bomb-aimer's position is placed under the forward turret. It carries four machine-guns in the rear turret and two in the front turret.

The Hurricane II introduces many new features to the earlier model. Fitted with a new Rolls Merlin engine, with two-speed supercharger, it extends the fighting ability in three directions, performances at height, fire-power and effective range. The machine has a better rate of climb at altitude and a greater top speed. Some Hurricane IIs carry 12 machine-guns, others four 20-mm. cannon.

HURRICANE IIs in formation. These machines are carrying four 20-mm. cannon. On the left a Hurricane II, showing the port-holes for its 12 machine-guns.
Photos, British Official: Crown Copyright; and Associated Press

Norway's Great Stand Against the Oppressor

Eighteen months have passed since the Nazis invaded Norway, and each successive month has increased their unpopularity, until today they are hated with an intensity such as only the most bitter tyranny could have aroused in an essentially tolerant and kindly people. Below we review the chief events which have marked the German occupation of Norway to date.

WHEN the Nazis invaded Norway on April 9, 1940, one of their first acts was to set up a puppet government under Major Vidkun Quisling, leader of the small Norwegian Fascist Party, the *Nasjonal Samling*. Six days later, however, Quisling was replaced by an Administrative Council headed by Herr Christensen, Chairman of Oslo Municipal Council. Then on April 27 Hitler issued a decree appointing Herr Terboven, Gauleiter of Essen, as Reich Commissioner of the German-occupied territories in Norway.

Following the occupation of the whole of Norway by the Nazi invaders, there were further changes. In September a new Administrative Council was formed by Christensen to act as a link between the Norwegian authorities and the occupying power, and on September 25 Terboven set up a *Statsrad* (State Council), nearly all of whose members were drawn from Quisling's party. A few hours before its establishment all the Norwegian political parties, save the Nasjonal Samling, were closed down, and in a few weeks the same fate had befallen most Norwegian organizations, even Masonic Lodges and Rotary Clubs. The Norwegian Trade Union Council anticipated compulsory dissolution by closing down all its organs and destroying its membership lists and documents. Then on September 28 Terboven in another pronouncement proclaimed the abolition of the Norwegian *Storting* (parliament) and monarchy, the deposition of King Haakon, and the nomination of Quisling as sole political leader in Norway. It was decreed that all portraits of King Haakon and members of the Royal Family should be burnt, and that the word "royal" should be deleted from street names and so on. On October 4 there came yet another proclamation decreeing that parliament would be replaced by a *Ringsting*, whose members would be appointed on the corporative principle.

These measures induced grave unrest throughout the country—so grave that at the beginning of November 1940 "Extraordinary People's Tribunals" were set up to enforce them and to punish loyalty to the Norwegian king and constitution. But the discontent throve on suppression. Everywhere loyalists flaunted badges bearing the portrait of King Haakon. There were frequent clashes in the streets between loyalists and Quisling's brownshirts or *Hirdmen*. Sabotage was widespread. Newspapers were so outspoken in their criticism of the regime that numbers of journalists were arrested, many papers were suppressed and others suspended for publishing disrespectful remarks of Quisling and his gang. Even in the schools anti-Quisling demonstrations were the order of the day, so that the Government threatened to close the high schools and severely punish the teachers who failed to keep their classes in order. Children who refused to give the Nazi salute or to attend the Hitler Youth Exhibition in Oslo were beaten up by Hirdmen in the streets. Undaunted, a crowd of Norwegian youths and girls paraded in front of the Royal Palace and sang the Norwegian National Anthem, while others shouted "Long live King

MAJOR VIDKUN QUISLING, leader of the Norwegian Nazi Party, was born in 1887. He was for twelve years an officer of the Norwegian General Staff, and from 1931 to 1933 was Minister of Defence.   *Photo, Keystone*

Haakon! Down with Quisling!" before the latter's headquarters.

Meanwhile the economic condition of the country was growing steadily worse as the Nazis laid their hands on all the foodstuffs that happened to be immediately surplus. Huge quantities of fish, eggs, pork and potatoes were appropriated and dispatched to the Reich, with the result that food rationing of the civilian population became ever more drastic. German soldiers of the army of occupation were reported to be going on leave with their rucksacks filled with the good things which the people at home had gone without for so long.

Things had reached such a state that last spring Himmler himself arrived in Norway, and after a tour of the country helped in the establishment of a secret police on the lines of the Gestapo. But still the agitation went on. There was another wave of arrests, and the gaols, supplemented by concentration camps, were filled to overflowing.

Then the Church entered the struggle. On February 9 the Norwegian bishops issued a pastoral letter denouncing the Quisling government's interference with church matters and severely criticizing the violent activities of

the Hirdmen. In particular, they protested against an order of December 13, which gave the police the right to require a priest to break his oath of secrecy in matters of the confessional, or run the risk of imprisonment if he refused. When the pastoral letter was read from a number of pulpits and widely distributed, Quisling ordered the police and Hirdmen to attend Divine Worship and report any priests and pastors who read the letter, or offered prayers for the Norwegian Royal Family. Already the Quisling government had attacked the Norwegian judiciary, with the result that in December all the justices of the Supreme Court resigned and were replaced by quislings.

On August 2 Terboven proclaimed a state of civil emergency throughout Norway, and followed this up with more measures of repression, including in particular the confiscation of all wireless receiving sets along the west and south coasts ; the Norwegians were showing too keen an interest in broadcasts from London. In Oslo the wireless sets were due to be given up on September 8 ; that same afternoon the R.A.F. heavily bombed shipping in Oslo Fjord, and the appearance of the British planes above the city acted as a signal for a patriotic demonstration of the most openly enthusiastic description. The same day work was stopped in the big factories, ostensibly because heavy workers did not get their milk ration ; it was true enough that the milk rations were short, since 10,000 gallons of Norwegian milk are being sent daily to Finland alone for the German troops, while further large quantities are being condensed for the use of the German forces elsewhere. Soon in the engineering industry the strike was general, 54 works being brought to a standstill.

Quisling informed the German authorities that these demonstrations were the prelude to a general strike. This was not the case, as the Germans well knew, but they seized upon an opportunity for crushing the workers' organizations, just as a year before they had suppressed the political parties. On September 9 Terboven imposed martial law on Oslo and its industrial suburbs. The Gestapo promptly occupied the offices of the Trade Union Federation, and all members of the executive as well as many local officials were arrested. A few hours later shots rang out ; Viggo Hansteen, president of the Trades Union Federation, and Rolf Wickstrom had to pay with their lives for having refused to yield to Terboven and the Gestapo. Many other Trade Unionists, engineering shop stewards and dockers were sentenced to hard labour for ten and fifteen years, and in some cases for life.

But even these atrocities have proved insufficient to crush the spirit of the Norwegian workers and of the Norwegian people as a whole. Never were King Haakon and Crown Prince Olaf more popular than now, when they are exiles in London. The British planes—"angels" as they are called—as they fly over Norway's towns and coasts are greeted with friendly waves and cheers. While, as for Quisling, he is reported to be tormented by insomnia, and an overdose of his sleeping draught has brought him to the brink of the grave.

NORWEGIAN SYMPATHIZERS at the funeral of a British airman on a small island named Austevoll, near Bergen. This lonely island was chosen for the funeral by the Nazis to avoid demonstrations of pro-British feeling, but over a thousand Norwegian fishermen and peasants journeyed from even quite distant villages to be present.   *Photo, Associated Press*

Who *Wouldn't* Hurt a Fly in North Africa ?

AN ANTI-FLY SQUAD leaving its headquarters with traps. These are baited with fresh meat, left for four days, and then collected for the catch to be destroyed.

SETTING THE TRAPS in which over a million flies have been caught in six weeks. The Anti-Fly Squad is an essential part of Western Desert Hygiene Section.

BURNING TROUGHS full of flies (right). When the traps are full the flies are sprayed with chemicals and then cremated. Above, a member of the Anti-Fly Squad emptying the traps into a trough.

The insect plague is not the least of the dangers and nuisances to which our men in North Africa are exposed. Thanks, however, to skilful organization, the breeding circles are broken up. An important order is that all refuse must be burnt in the camps and not buried, as research has proved that a fly can work its way through 8 ft. of sand.

Photos, British Official: Crown Copyright

They Have Won Honours in Freedom's Cause

The White Cross of St. Giles

Mr. A. M. Nabarro, Portsmouth A.F.S., **G.M.,** for rescuing two persons trapped in blazing wreckage, and controlling fires.

Mr. L. Stephens, Plymouth A.F.S. messenger, **B.E.M.,** for carrying on with his duty although injured by bomb-blast.

Stn. Offr. R. A. Pullinger, G.M., for helping to save patients from a hospital which was set on fire by a bomb.

Stn. Offr. G. E. Switzer, Silver Medal of National Horse Asscn. for bravery in saving 39 horses during a London raid.

National Horse Association of Great Britain

Miss M. F. Weston, White Cross of St. Giles, for saving over 500 animals from buildings destroyed by bombs.

Miss M. I. Stepnall, Matron, Royal Eye Hospital, London, **M.B.E.,** for rescuing patients and fighting fires.

Warden Janet Evans, of Plymouth, **B.E.M.,** for courage and devotion to duty during several raids.

Mrs. H. Broadberry, of Winkbourn, **B.E.M.,** for helping to rescue three Polish airmen from a crashed and burning plane.

Miss E. Kitson, M.B.E., for her work at the British Embassy in Norway during Nazi invasion.

Miss M. Monk, Rotherhithe Girl Guides, the **Bronze Cross,** for rescuing children from blazing shelter.

Stn. Insp. Ronald Noble, G.M., for rescuing a woman from a bomb-wrecked block of flats.

Sergt. G. Deacon, G.M., for gallant and devoted work in tending a man trapped in wreckage.

P.C. Eakers, of Plymouth, **B.E.M.,** for rescuing six persons from demolished property.

Det. Con. F. S. Stanley, of Plymouth, **O.B.E.,** for rescuing several persons and tending the injured.

P.C. T. A. O'Connor, B.E.M., for heroism in helping to release people trapped in debris.

Insp. John Lindsey, B.E.M., for rescue operations when Plymouth City Hospital was hit.

Telegraphist J. Stephenson, formerly A.R.P. Warden, Holborn, **G.M.,** for rescuing casualties from bombed building.

Sea Cadet H. Thomson, St. Clement Dane's Unit, **Navy League Cross,** for bravery in preventing fires.

Cdr. H. W. Biggs, R.N., **Bar to D.S.O.,** for distinguished services in the withdrawal of our troops from Greece.

Lieut. J. R. Phillimore, D.S.C., for courage and skill in the course of operations off the Libyan coast.

Chief Offr. H. Thompson, M.B.E., for bravery and navigational resource after his ship had been torpedoed.

Lieut.-Cdr. G. A. Thring, D.S.O., for bravery and skill in bringing a convoy through two U-boat attacks and a storm.

Mr. G. Davis, G.M., for turning off gas from flaming main near an unexploded bomb, during a London raid.

Mr. N. Potts, of the Gas Light & Coke Co., also awarded the **G.M.,** for bravery in the same incident.

Mr. J. F. Knape, O.B.E., for gallant work in the Plymouth A.R.P. Control Room, set on fire by bombs.

Mr. J. W. Coulthard, Liverpool A.R.P. messenger, **G.M.,** for great bravery in a bomb-wrecked blazing building.

Mr. L. J. Bell, of the Gas Light & Coke Co., **G.M.,** for controlling gas amid falling high explosives and incendiaries.

Mr. E. F. Bradley, who was also awarded the **G.M.,** for splendid resource in the same courageous exploit.

Wing-Cdr. G. T. Jarman, D.F.C., awarded the **D.S.O.,** for attacks on Gneisenau, Scharnhorst and Prinz Eugen.

Sgt. Air-Gunner Billington, D.F.M., for putting out fire in his plane by using his parachute regardless of his own life.

Squad.-Ldr D. R. Bader, D.S.O., D.F.C., the famous **legless** pilot, now a prisoner of war, awarded **Bar to D.F.C.**

Flt.-Lieut. H. P. Blatchford, D.F.C., for helping to destroy eight and damage five Nazi planes in one day.

Flying-Offr. D. V. Cotes-Preedy, G.M., for saving lives of his air-gunner and observer from crashed plane.

Wing-Cdr. J. W. Gillan, D.F.C., A.F.C., **Bar to D.F.C.,** for showing inspiring leadership and determination.

I Was There! ....Eye Witness Stories of the War

What Caught My Eye in Besieged Odessa

Since the beginning of August, Odessa, the great Russian port on the Black Sea, has been fiercely attacked by the Rumanians and their German masters. This account of life in the beleaguered city is from the pen of E. Vilenski, a Russian war correspondent.

ODESSA is encircled from the land side. The roads leading from the city are cut short at the front line which surrounds the approaches to the town. Odessa can only be reached by sea, and although the vessels may be hindered they cannot be stopped.

Odessa was the city of gaiety, the beautiful seaside town inhabited by happy, sunny southerners, where people from all parts of the country came to rest, where the parks were masses of flowers and where music could be heard everywhere.

The first sound I heard on approaching the town was the boom of guns. These belonged to a warship guarding the sea approaches, and they fired to the right at regular intervals. Our boat slid into port to the same accompaniment of artillery.

Odessa has become a different town. It is a besieged city, fighting for its liberty and its very life. And it stands with clenched fists, grim and determined. You see pass by groups of working men and women—especially women. Most of them have remained in their native city, while most of the men have gone into the firing line. Old people and children have been evacuated, despite the enemy's attempts to prevent their evacuation.

It is early, and I can see the people out on the streets carrying spades, picks, sandbags. The streets are narrow, for cobble stones and pavement stones have been torn up to build barricades, and only a narrow strip is left for motor traffic.

There is one man in Odessa whom everyone knows : Arkady Khrenov, one of the Soviet Union's best military engineers and one of those responsible for the destruction of the Mannerheim Line during the Finnish campaign. He is in charge of Odessa's fortifications. Under his direction

the inhabitants have surrounded their city with several belts of fortifications, anti-tank obstacles and trenches.

You should see them work ; old men and women, youngsters, women of every kind, carrying stones to the barricades. Their unremitting efforts have converted Odessa into an immensely strong fortress. Everything has been done to lessen the danger to the defenders. Gun turrets are cunningly concealed and the men's firing positions covered against shrapnel.

Fighting side by side with the Red Army are Odessa's People's Volunteers and the Red Navy. These Red Navy men are the object of Odessa's particular affection. You can see them in the firing line in their navy blue, with heavy cartridge belts across their chests and with a big supply of grenades.

Everyone in the city is taking part in its defence. The factories are producing all that is required at the front, and the collective farms bring in a constant supply of vegetables, fruits and other produce.

The people of Odessa never had the occasion to build tanks, but now its engineers are producing a number of armoured vehicles, which, while not conforming to standard designs, have nevertheless caused

great damage to the Rumanians attacking the city. Hundreds of thousands of mines have been made in the town's workshops ; some of them unconventionally encased in wooden boxes, large tins and even film containers.

Enemy tanks and armoured cars are encountering diverse and cleverly contrived obstacles—there are at least a million of them in the approaches of the city. Never had the Odessaites contemplated doing so much intensive digging and shovelling. Spades and picks were produced in a few days at fabulous speed. The city has organized its defence in such a way as to rely as little as possible on other towns. Odessa scientists are producing high explosives, and Odessa technicians are designing new types of arms.

The city and the front have merged into one—there is no dividing line. Workers' detachments are training in the streets. They learn to handle arms, dig trenches and camouflage. Their womenfolk see them off to the outskirts of the town where the gunfire is clearly heard. They bring their men bundles of food and then return to the city to resume work.

Odessa engineers are also repairing the tanks brought in from the front, and every factory has a group of tanks attached to it for repairs. Brigades of workers have their own tanks to look after. The electric power supply, the shops, and the telegraph and telephone services work without interruption. It is true that in the telegraph office I saw a notice : " Prompt delivery is not guaranteed," but still telegrams are being accepted. As a journalist I was particularly pleased to see that three daily papers still appear in Odessa, and the Moscow papers arrive with only two days' delay.—*Soviet War News.*

We Did a Tour of Europe as Vichy Prisoners

A British officer who spent two months as a prisoner of war, and during that time travelled through nine different countries, broadcast the following remarkable story of the bravery and spirit of people condemned to live in German-occupied countries.

DURING the fighting in Syria a few of my regiment ran out of ammunition and we were taken prisoner by the Vichy French, who sent us in batches by air to Greece. In Salonika, where we had to live like animals, we met Vichy reinforcements on their way to Syria, and these

soldiers greeted us with great friendliness, one of them saying : " We're still friends ; it's the Boche who is our enemy."

Then, after we had heard the good news of the end of hostilities in Syria, we were taken overland to France. We travelled by train, the twelve most senior officers in a second-class carriage, and were reasonably comfortable ; but the remainder of the British and Indian officers and the N.C.O.s had third-class accommodation, which was far from good, especially over so long a journey. All the time our hopes and fears were struggling with each other, and many were the theories advanced in favour of one or the other. Sometimes we wondered whether we would ever be released ; sometimes we were afraid the French might hand us over to the Hun ; the most optimistic hoped that we should be sent straight back to England.

We travelled north through Yugoslavia, passing through Bulgaria and Hungary, and then south-westward through Austria and Germany into France. On the third day of our journey, while we were still in Yugoslavia, we saw some British prisoners-of-war. We had previously heard that they had been put to work on a new *autobahn* being constructed from Austria into Yugoslavia. At first we were only able to wave to them, and sometimes throw them cigarettes if they were close enough ; but in the evening the train, for no apparent reason, stopped very near to a large party of them. They were very pleased to see us and to hear that the Allies had taken Syria, and showed splendid spirit despite all their troubles, and it was grand to hear them shouting : " Well done, the British ! " and " There'll always be an England." Although we saw lots more, we

ODESSA, beautiful seaside town as well as great port, was once a city of gaiety. Today, besieged by the Germans and Rumanians, it shows a different face, and its streets are lined with great stone barricades and strong points. How every citizen of this great Russian port is contributing to its defence is told above.   *Photo, British Official ; Crown Copyright*

190   *The War Illustrated*   October 10th, 1941

IIIIIIIIIIIIIIIIIIIIIIIIIIIIIIIIIIIIIIIIIIIIIIIIIIIIIIIIIIIIIIIIIIIIIIIIIIIIIIIII **I WAS THERE!** IIIIIIIIIIIIIIIIIIIIIIIIIIIIIIIIIIIIIIIIIIIIIIIIIIIIIIIIIIIIIIIIIIIIIIIIIIIIIIIII

After the landing of the Allied forces on Spitzbergen a Norwegian major, representing the Norwegian Government in London, informed the people that they were to be evacuated. Above, inhabitants, aided by Canadian soldiers, are gathering their belongings on the jetty preparatory to embarking.   *Photo, British Official: Crown Copyright*

never had a similar opportunity to talk to them again ; however, we threw them as many cigarettes as we could gather together, and they seemed very glad to get them.

I think it was on the evening of the fifth day that we passed Berchtesgaden ; the scenery was certainly magnificent, but one felt amused that the Fuehrer needed to have his house built in a place where one would normally only expect to find birds of prey picking the bones of what they had devoured.

Later in our journey we passed through the Black Forest, but we were disappointed not to see Goering's hunting lodge ; but we heard instead that he was languishing in gaol.

Nothing much else occurred until we reached Dijon, in German-occupied France. Here our train halted in the station for some time, and we were able to talk to quite a lot of French people. One train that was passing through for Paris welcomed us with every sign of friendship, in spite of the fact that there were lots of German sentries on

the platform ; all the windows were jammed with people waving to us and making signs that they were depending on us, and there was much blowing of kisses. In the carriage directly opposite me was a most warm-hearted and good-looking girl-guide who bore the bravest smile I have ever seen ; and we were extremely sorry when their train steamed out. As it left the station the girl waved her handkerchief, and in one corner was a miniature Union Jack.

Soon afterwards another train came in alongside us full of released French prisoners-of-war ; they were very friendly and glad to see us, and we got into conversation all along the line, and left them very much more cheerful than we had found them.

It was here that we had confirmed for us the story [see page 142] that the trains bearing French reinforcements to Syria were stoned by their own countrymen, and many shouted to them : " May you rot with good British bayonets in your bellies." Poor devils ! What a send-off to fight a war.

We then travelled down to Toulon, stopping a night at Lyons as guests of the Red Cross, who were very good to us on our journey, even in Germany, where they gave us bread and coffee. At Marseilles we stayed for four hours ; here we met only with friendliness, especially from the porters, on the platform.

In Marseilles our most confirmed bachelor was very embarrassed by the pathetic gratitude of the young girl to whom he gave a piece of soap—there's not much of that in France nowadays.

Then we went on to Toulon, and all along the line we were cheered by friendly crowds at the stations, including soldiers on leave, who we had always heard were not so inclined to like us. In Toulon we were shut up in a Napoleonic fortress, and were able to examine at leisure the signatures of past prisoners-of-war inscribed on the walls, many over a century old ; also to try-out the disadvantages of a rather inadequate vegetarian diet.

From Toulon in a ship back to Beirut, where a huge breakfast made us completely forget that we had ever been hungry. And then we finally arrived safely in Cairo.

How We Spent The Last Days on Spitzbergen

Among the Norwegians who came to England from Spitzbergen was Mrs. Mary Olsen, with her husband, Andor, and their 13-year-old daughter. Mrs. Olsen gave the following account of their last days in their Arctic home to a " Daily Mail " reporter. See pages 158-159.

WARM sunshine bathed the little Arctic town where we lived. I was at work in my timber-built cottage, my daughter Marie was playing outside with our pet " husky " dog Kiki.

Suddenly a neighbour cried out, " There are warships in the bay ! "

I took Marie by the hand and we ran to the sea, Kiki galloping at our heels. The lifting mist revealed a great fleet of ships at the entrance to the fiord.

Ship's boats packed with soldiers were coming towards the quay. As the first boat scraped alongside an officer in uniform sprang ashore.

" Good-morning," he called in Norwegian. No one in the little knot of people, mostly women and children, who had gathered to watch, answered him. We did not know who they were. We were suspicious.

Soldiers in khaki climbed out of the boat—smiling soldiers who stood smartly to attention and winked at the children clinging to our hands.

Then someone noticed the flag of Norway on the officer's shoulder. There was an audible sigh of relief. It was all right. These were British soldiers—not Germans.

Spitzbergen was being occupied. I listened uncomprehendingly to my English-speaking countrymen who were now chatting with the newcomers. I watched, wondering, until Marie suddenly said that she was hungry. We went back home. Then an excited friend told me " The Canadians have come to take us away. They are going to free our beloved Norway."

The news was a shock. I love my home. Andor, my husband, is a foreman in the mines. All our life was here. This was a big decision. Sad thoughts ran through my mind.

The story of a Norwegian family's last days on Spitzbergen before the evacuation is told in this page. Here are mothers and children from Spitzbergen on arrival in Britain, still wearing their picturesque ski costumes. Nearly 1,000 of the evacuated Norwegians are now happily settled in temporary quarters in Scotland.   *Photo, " Daily Mirror "*

" This is my dear Spitzbergen. This is our home. Andor and I have a beautiful home and a beautiful child. Oh, God, why should there be Nazis . . .''

I went on with my household work. Late in the afternoon Andor came in from the mines. We had tea.

The Canadians were busy. Everything was to go on normally ; there would be more news tomorrow.

I took out the last letter I had received from my mother months ago. There was very little in it. Away in Roros, near Trondheim, the Nazis were in possession. All the letter contained were little family details. But it did let us know that food was scarce, queues long.

Spitzbergen was beyond the war. We listened to the radio, some to Oslo, but most of us to the Norwegian news from London. We did not always believe the news from London. But we never believed the news from Oslo. That was Hitler talking. So we were often puzzled.

Days passed. The Canadians went about their own affairs and we carried on as usual— went shopping, even had one or two little house parties.

Then came the day we were told we were to sail for Britain. We could each bring 50 kilos of luggage. Fifty kilos ! What could I do with all our treasures, the home we had built, and our lovely furniture ?

I was so sad, but my Marie was in great excitement . . . '' Going to England ! What fun ! ''

Andor and I talked it over. There was nothing else to talk about. '' It is for freedom and right,'' he would reassure me. He said it over and over again.

Then the last day. There were more explosions as the Canadians went about destroying mines and machinery around Longyear.

One big explosion I welcomed. It drowned the crack of a gunshot. That was the end of poor Kiki. He had to be destroyed. One of Andor's friends did it for us. Poor Marie wept as Kiki was led away.

Mid-afternoon, Andor placed our luggage outside the door. I had one last look round. All the things I left. Little treasures I had carried from Norway. Andor locked the door and took the key. I never looked back. Now I am glad to be here. What we did was right. We know it.

This Soviet bomber crew has a fine record. Its members have taken part in twenty air combats and have bombed Constantza, Sulina and Tulcia. *Photo, British Official : Crown Copyright*

We Came from East and West to Bomb Berlin

During July and August 1941 Berlin was under fire from two sides, for the Red Air Force alternated with the R.A.F. in raiding the city. Here spokesmen of the two air forces describe their experiences.

LIEUTENANT MALININ, of the Red Air Force, described a Russian raid on Berlin in the following words :

When we started for our raid on Berlin we knew that it would not be easy. By following strictly our mapped course we had to cover several thousand kilometres under difficult weather conditions. Soon after we took off we were flying in clouds. Conditions were very unfavourable, as a large zone of cloud stretched all along the route to Berlin. Over 70 per cent of our flying time was spent flying blind about the clouds. Temperature dropped to 40 degrees below zero. On board it was completely dark except for the dim light shed by the instrument panels. When I looked down at the bank of dense black cloud I could not help wondering whether we would be able to locate our target.

We forged on through cloud and rain. According to our calculations we were already over Germany, but we could see nothing but clouds. When our time reckoning indicated that we had reached our goal we were still not quite sure of our bearings. However, there was no time to waste. With muffled engines I made for the target. Through the last layer of ragged clouds we saw the ground. Below lay Berlin. I looked at the time—exactly 1.47. Everything in order and according to our calculations.

Suddenly we saw flickering lights flashing in front of us—enemy fighters. Our navigator, Tkachenko, spotted two of them, and our wireless operator, Martyanov, saw three more. The Nazis had not seen us. What were we to do ? Hide in the clouds ? But this would mean missing our objectives. We decided to go right down below the clouds— down to 2,700 feet. From that height we could see the city quite clearly. Through a misty haze it looked like a huge field crisscrossed by ditch-like streets and squares.

So far everything was quiet—no searchlights or A.A. guns. Our plane was the first to reach the target. The enemy had either failed to notice us or was biding his time to deceive us. At 2,700 feet I manoeuvred in accordance with Tkachenko's instructions to find our strategic objectives. Time was passing—1.55 . . . 2.0. Finally, Tkachenko found what he was looking for.

Our machine shuddered as a heavy bomb was released. Below, a dazzling explosion flared up. We were dropping very heavy bombs, and from the air we could clearly see how each bomb threw up a pillar of fire. When our load had gone we flew back into the clouds. Looking back, I could see more flashes through the darkness. Our comrades were already hard at work.

Our return journey was uneventful. We climbed high and under cover of cloud made for home. At our base we were met by several comrades. '' Well, what's the news ? '' '' Everything in order,'' we reported ; and I could not help adding, '' I don't suppose Berlin will sleep very well tonight.''

MUCH more favourable weather conditions were enjoyed by the R.A.F. during the heaviest raid they had made on Berlin. A Squadron Leader of a heavy bomber squadron said :

We could see the western defences of Berlin —the flak and the searchlights—in action when we were still 40 miles away. They seemed very busy, and we knew then that the earlier aircraft were already doing their stuff. Just south of Berlin we saw one of our bombers very low down and caught in a cone of searchlights. Then an enemy fighter attacked him. I was busy keeping an eye on the flak and searchlights, but my crew said they saw tracer shooting between the two aircraft, and the next thing they reported was that the fighter had gone down in flames.

There were five big fires already going when we got to Berlin : big orange and red-coloured fires with masses of smoke and flames, two of them nearly in the centre of the city. We could see buildings ablaze and flames coming out of the windows.

Conditions were absolutely ideal for bombing. The moon was so bright that if we had been flying at the same height in daylight we could hardly have seen more. Streets and buildings and railway lines— everything stood out absolutely clearly ; I even picked out the Brandenburger Tor. There was not even a bit of haze to cover the city. We had our set target, which was one of the big railway stations, but we could have bombed from just anywhere we liked ; we had the city at our mercy, as it were.

We got to Berlin about a quarter of an hour after midnight and we left at about a quarter to one. During that time we saw a number of other people bombing, and then we dropped our bombs. We were carrying one of the new bombs. When it went off there was an explosion which lit up the sky.

We had a grand journey back—almost flak- and searchlight-free—but as we were nearing home the port engine failed. We threw out a bit of stuff to lighten the aircraft, and came along very nicely on one engine. When we got over the aerodrome that engine packed up too. I managed to land in a field, after encountering difficulties with a haystack and some telegraph wires. No sooner had we landed than up came three Home Guards with rifles at the ready, but when they saw it was a Wellington everything was all right. When we got back to the aerodrome and talked things over with the others who had been out, we agreed that this raid on Berlin was one of the most successful we had ever been on anywhere.—*Soviet War News and Air Ministry News Service.*

AFTER RAIDING GERMANY this bomber pilot (seated in cockpit) landed his plane safely in a thickly wooded plantation when his petrol supply ran out. *Photo, British Official*

Editor's Postscript

'COUNTRY life is not all it's cracked up to be,'' someone said to me the other day. And as an inveterate townsman upon whom, at a late day, the rural way of life has come less from choice than circumstance, I was inclined to agree. Harvest bugs, for example. I've made my first acquaintance with them in these autumnal days. I thought at first I had contracted some sort of blood disorder . . . itching here, itching there, and a baker's dozen of focal points of discomfort arising as I scratched from ankle upleg ! With relief I found that many others in my neighbourhood were suffering similarly. Strange how one's discomfort lessens with the knowledge that others are in like state.

I HAD suffered from the ''bicho colorado '' (*lit.* red insect) in South America, and mosquitos have at times robbed the most enchanting sub-tropical scenes of all their charm for me, but these minute harvest bugs whose acquaintance I have made so recently—'' eh, it's been a rare year fur tham dratted 'arvest mites,'' said a shepherd of the Downs to me yesterday, giving them their proper name—are as effective itch producers as any South American '' bicho.'' Nor is it any consolation to know that this absurdly tiny red devil belongs to the family of *Trombidiidae* and, as a relative of the '' bicho colorado,'' has quite a surprising life-story.

HIS abundance this year is due to the long lush grass which the August rains have engendered. Fortunately ammonia quickly reduces the irritation his activities create. But bad as the plague of insect life may be—insects preceded Man by millions of years and will probably survive him by millions more—it is nothing to what might have been, as I read in J. B. S. Haldane's '' Fact and Faith '' that if all the existing varieties of only one species of fly, *Drosophila Melanogaster*, could be suitably crossed there isn't enough matter in all the known heavenly bodies, and probably not in the universe, to make *one* fly of each of the possible kinds simultaneously ! How's that for being fruitful and occupying the Earth ? According to Maeterlinck it was really a case of touch-and-go for mastery of the Earth between the Termite (the so-called White Ant) and Man. Nature, in her infinite variety, becomes somewhat alarming to contemplate close up. The epidemics that will inevitably follow the gigantic destruction of human beings now proceeding along the Western Front of Russia will involve some epic battles between the minutest forms of insect life and the latest ingenuities of Science.

IN passing through the ruins of the Temple to-day—or rather trying to pass through, for ruin is now at its zenith there, as the housebreakers pull down the gaunt skeletons of the antique memory-haunted courts and halls—I went to see how Crown Office Row was faring. A few days more and its last brick will have been dislodged. A bit of the south wall

at hallowed No. 2, where Charles Lamb was born, still stood but was about to come down. All my life in London that quite featureless brick building has fascinated me, and I have rarely in the thousand times I have passed it failed to think back to those distant days when, having just discovered Charles Lamb, and so let a new and lovely light stream into my young mind, I read and re-read him in cheap pocket editions (Cassell's Library) under the birch trees of a little wood in the Isle of Bute. Well, like his roses that perished, his birthplace has perished too, and on another distant day when some new building will occupy its site we shall have to be content with one of those blue enamelled

MR. AVERELL HARRIMAN, President Roosevelt's Lease and Lend envoy, who heads the American Mission to Moscow for the three-power supply talks. *Photo, G.P.U.*

plaques which the L.C.C. put up at historic places reading (perhaps) '' In a house that stood on this site, destroyed by Enemy Action, in 1941, Charles Lamb (' Elia '), English Essayist, was born February 10, 1775.''

EMERGING from the bright interior of a theatre yesterday a little after eight o'clock into the dark of a moonless evening, I was suddenly conscious that the nights of gloom had actually returned. The haunting horrors of last winter, which our relatively happy months of double summertime had helped us to forget, came back in chilling memories. The empty, ghostly squares and side streets through which we passed, which were so recently traffic-thronged in ten p.m. daylight, and where last winter and spring the bombs had fallen every night or two : they all seemed scraps of a bad dream that was being dreamt again. But in the dazzling cheerfulness of the hotel lounge this mood of

brooding memory quickly vanished, and doubtless after a few more nights of outward gloom one will recover something of that stoic poise which carried us all through the worst days and nights of the Battle of Britain, apprehensive, afraid, but still undaunted. Myself, although I happened to be in many of the heavy raids during my London nights, I had the luck to escape two or three of the worst. Perhaps my luck will hold again during the coming terror we are promised ; at least I hope so, for even a limited experience of London's night raids counts for quite a lot in a lifetime.

'' SWANK'' is a quality I detest, although one may still like a friend who is '' a bit of a swanker ''—I have more than one —for the sake of his other qualities. So far as one can examine objectively one's own actions and reactions, I have always tried to do so, and have seldom felt more indignant than when an old friend wrote to me, some weeks back, breaking a long silence, and mentioned that his '' young people '' thought it was swank to mention '' my village '' in my jottings. The young sillies ! What about '' my country,'' '' my hometown,'' '' my doctor,'' '' my tailor,'' '' my tobacconist '' (who swears he hasn't '' my '' cigarettes this week) ? My friend tells me that he explained to his critical offspring that '' my village '' did not indicate any actual proprietary claims but was just '' a journalistic way '' of alluding to the place.

HIS young people must be abnormally d e n s e, or little used to our common idiom to need such enlightenment at their age, and the fun of the thing is that, although I own a good percentage of the houses in '' my village '' (more swank), I could never for a moment think of it as '' mine.'' Occasionally I derive some quiet amusement from hearing some of my colleagues refer to those immediately under their direction as '' my people.'' Not once do I recollect ever having lumped the lot as '' my people,'' and I have been directing editorial staffs for well over forty years.

THIS matter of swank was really not suggested by that letter from my friend of old years, whom I haven't met since the last war, and who wrote to me '' out of the blue '' (he might have been buried for all I knew), but by noticing today on a Sussex highway two 10 h.p. cars proudly displaying the '' G.B.'' plaques which are supplied for temporary use only when travelling abroad. I could fish out several of these from my garage dump, for I have never, on returning from any of my foreign tours, failed to remove the G.B. mark, which is totally meaningless *in* Great Britain. To wander about British roads flaunting this advertisement of your having been abroad (at least once) has always seemed to me the very apex of motoring swank. You will notice the G.B. more often on an 8 or 10 than on a 27 or 30 h.p. But to display it any time since August 1939 is sheer senseless swagger. Possibly the two instances I observed today may have originated in secondhand purchases and the buyers' ignorance of the significance of the initials. You never know. But let's be charitable.

Printed in England and published on the 10th, 20th and 30th of each month by the Proprietors, The Amalgamated Press, Ltd., The Fleetway House, Farringdon Street, London, E.C.4. Registered for transmission by Canadian Magazine Post. Sole Agents for Australia and New Zealand : Messrs. Gordon & Gotch, Ltd. ; and for South Africa : Central News Agency, Ltd. October 10th, 1941.   S.S.   *Editorial Address :* JOHN CARPENTER HOUSE WHITEFRIARS LONDON, E.C.4.

Vol 5 *The War Illustrated* N° 109

Edited by Sir John Hammerton

FOURPENCE

OCT. 20TH, 1941

NAZI PRISONERS, captured by Soviet forces, on their way to a field prison camp under an escort of Red soldiers. Since the war began last June, the German losses on the Russian Front (said Mr. Alexander Shcherbakov, Director of the Soviet Foreign Bureau in Moscow, on October 5) exceed 3,000,000 killed, wounded, missing, and taken prisoner. The Russian losses are given as 1,128,000.
Photo, British Official: Crown Copyright

NO. 110 WILL BE PUBLISHED THURSDAY, OCT. 30

NEED THE NAZIS WORRY ABOUT OIL?

WHAT a fine thing it would be if Hitler's war machine should be slowed up, perhaps brought to a full stop, not by hard and bloody fighting but because it was running short of oil ! From time to time this delightful suggestion is trotted out and paraded before our wishful eyes, and unless we are very careful we shall find ourselves once again treating as a fact what is at best but an interesting speculation.

A few weeks after the invasion of Russia was begun a group of Oxford statisticians estimated that Germany, assuming that she was employing on the Russian front 180 divisions, had an oil consumption of at least a million and a half tons a month, which meant that she must be drawing on her reserve stocks to the tune of a million tons a month. Her reserves were placed at between six and seven million tons, but it was unlikely that she would hazard more than four million tons on her Eastern offensive. Thus, it was argued, she might maintain her large-scale attack for about four months.

By the end of October, then, we ought to be seeing a diminution in the tempo of the Russian battle, not because of General Winter's arrival to aid the Russians, but because Admiral Oil has failed the Nazis . . .

Shortly after this distinctly hopeful estimate was published, there came from the Petroleum Press Service an authoritative analysis which gave a far different picture of the oil situation.

It was assumed that Germany was employing against Russia some 15 armoured divisions, 20 motorized infantry divisions, and 150 ordinary infantry divisions. The number of tanks included in this force was estimated at 6,300, and in addition there would be 72,500 motor vehicles of various kinds, and 3,750 motor-cycle combinations. The fuel consumed by these vehicles was estimated at 1,020,000 gallons per day, equivalent to 104,000 tons a month. In addition it was estimated that 72,500 lorries might be used on the lines of communication, representing an oil consumption of some 74,000 tons a month.

Then as regards the Luftwaffe, it was assumed that Germany might have in the air on the average for three hours a day 1,000 bombers and 1,000 fighters ; their total fuel consumption would be 2,000 tons daily, or 60,000 tons a month —70,000 tons when allowance is made for ground staff and supply service requirements. Another 12,500 tons a month was included in respect of lubricants, making a total of over 260,000 tons.

Still this is not all, since there must be added the consumption of the German naval forces in the Baltic and the Black Sea, and that of the Finnish, Hungarian and Rumanian armies. Altogether, it was estimated, Germany's oil expenditure in the Russian campaign might average well over 300,000 tons a month—an approximation which, it was pointed out, seemed likely to err on the low side. The discrepancy between this estimate and that first quoted is obvious.

Now, when the war on the Eastern Front is over three months old, the Petroleum Press Service has prepared another analysis of the oil situation. "It is popularly believed," writes its editor, Dr. Oscar Tokayer, "that the Nazis are hard pressed to find the liquid fuel and lubricants required for a prolonged struggle, and the only question is how long it will be before their war machine rolls to a standstill for lack of oil. Unfortunately, however, the hope of an early collapse due to this cause, though widely cherished, has little foundation in fact. From the dreadful happenings of the past three months one fact stands out clearly : despite fearful loss of men and material, the German drive has so far lost little momentum."

Suppose we attempt to draw up a sort of balance-sheet of Hitler's oil position. First we must include a figure for Germany's own coal-oil production. This was planned before the war to have an output of 3,500,000 tons by 1941, and by now this goal may not only have been reached but considerably exceeded. Certainly it seems safe to assume that the Germans are now producing from coal and lignite well over 3,000,000 tons of oil a year—sufficient perhaps to maintain the Luftwaffe in the air. At the same time, the production of crude petroleum, in Germany, Austria, Western Poland, Slovakia, and Alsace, may now approach 1,250,000 tons a year, while another half a million tons at least may be contributed by Hungary and Albania. Then the Rumanian oilfields may be expected to be now producing at the rate of 5,500,000 tons per annum, and this notwithstanding the Soviet raids on Ploesti—raids which have not been long sustained, although quantities of oil, no doubt, have been destroyed by the Russian bombers at Constantza and on the tanker routes.

While their production has been stimulated to the utmost, the Germans have made every effort to cut down oil consumption. Traffic has been diverted from the roads to the railways and waterways ; alternative motor fuels, such as liquefied gases, town gas, wood and charcoal, are being largely utilized ; while civilian consumption has been reduced to the barest minimum. Before the war German Europe was consuming over 21,000,000 tons of oil a year, but it is believed that in most European countries the actual consumption is now no more than 25 to 30 per cent of its peacetime level : hence Europe's civilian consumption of petroleum products may be now little more than 6,000,000 tons.

On the basis of these figures, it may be calculated that the total quantity of petroleum products at the Germans' disposal, for civilian and military use, exclusive of stocks, can hardly be less than 12,000,000 tons annually. This, then, represents the total on the credit side of the balance sheet. Against it we must set the debits, of which the chief are the German oil consumption on the Eastern Front estimated (as we have seen) at 300,000 tons a month or between 3,500,000 and 4,000,000 tons a year, and the civilian consumption of 6,000,000 tons, making 10 million tons in all. This leaves an annual balance of 2,000,000 tons, which is all that is available to cover all the other military needs in German Europe, e.g. the oil consumed by the armies of Italy, Rumania, Hungary, Finland, and Bulgaria, as well as to cover the losses due to aerial attack on the Rumanian oil wells and Germany's oil-production plants, not to mention destroyed tankers. This figure, concludes the Petroleum Press Service analysis, may seem so low that certain withdrawals from stocks can hardly be avoided ; but in view of the magnitude of these stocks, their depletion is unlikely to assume dangerous proportions. Moreover, with the approach of winter, military operations on the Eastern Front will probably be held up in any case, and the supply position of Germany may well show an improvement as production is whipped up and substitute fuels are employed to an ever larger extent.

"There seems, therefore, to be nothing to support the popular misconception that an oil problem is of itself likely to lead to an early collapse of the Third Reich. If oil is to become Germany's Achilles' Heel, there must be methodical, persistent and overwhelming air attack from the West and the East, resulting in the large-scale destruction of enemy-controlled refineries, coal-oil plants, storage installations, and distributing centres, wherever these may be found."

All of which gives point to Lt.-Commander Fletcher's advice concerning what people should do this winter. "If anyone says Germany is short of oil," Mr. A. V. Alexander's Parliamentary Private Secretary said the other day, "the appropriate reply is 'Oh yeah !' "

E. ROYSTON PIKE

OIL FOR HITLER. Constantza, seaport of Rumania on the Black Sea, is the main outlet for the petroleum of the Rumanian oilfields, and here oil tankers are seen being filled from the pipes which run alongside the wharves. It has been bombed by the Soviet Air Force.

From Berlin to Baku: Hitler's Thrust for Oil

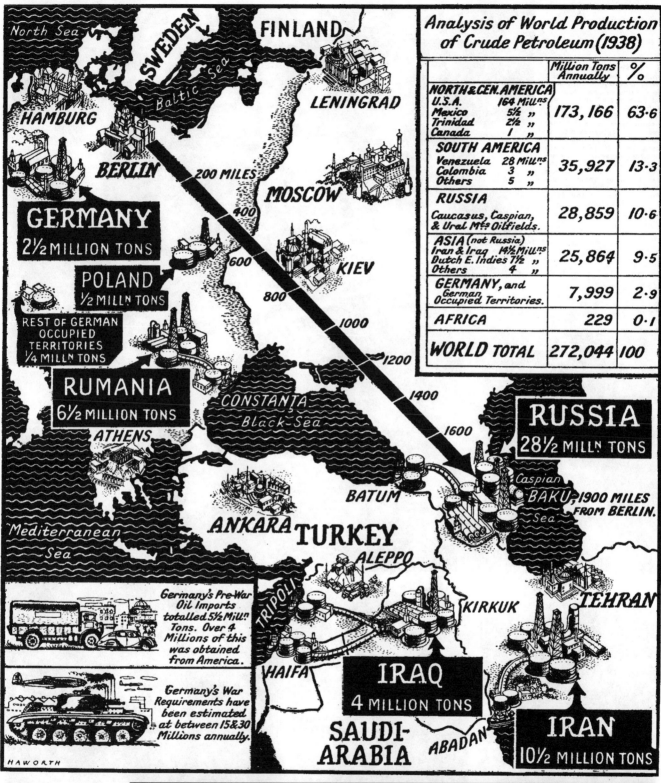

GERMANY
2½ MILLION TONS

POLAND
½ MILLⁿ TONS

REST OF GERMAN
OCCUPIED
TERRITORIES
¼ MILLⁿ TONS

RUMANIA
6½ MILLION TONS

RUSSIA
28½ MILLⁿ TONS

BAKU, 1900 MILES
FROM BERLIN.

IRAQ
4 MILLION TONS

IRAN
10½ MILLION TONS

Germany's Pre-War
Oil Imports
totalled 5½ Millⁿ
Tons. Over 4
Millions of this
was obtained
from America.

Germany's War
Requirements have
been estimated
at between 15 & 30
Millions annually.

HAWORTH

Analysis of World Production of Crude Petroleum (1938)

		Million Tons Annually	%
NORTH & CEN. AMERICA		173,166	63·6
U.S.A.	164 Millⁿˢ		
Mexico	5½ ,,		
Trinidad	2½ ,,		
Canada	1 ,,		
SOUTH AMERICA		35,927	13·3
Venezuela	28 Millⁿˢ		
Colombia	3 ,,		
Others	5 ,,		
RUSSIA		28,859	10·6
Caucasus, Caspian, & Ural Mᵗˢ Oilfields.			
ASIA (not Russia)		25,864	9·5
Iran & Iraq	14½ Millⁿˢ		
Dutch E. Indies	7½ ,,		
Others	4 ,,		
GERMANY, and German Occupied Territories.		7,999	2·9
AFRICA		229	0·1
WORLD TOTAL		272,044	100

Germany's oil situation is a matter of perpetual controversy, but here in this picture diagram we have illustrated some at least of the most important facts. Right, oil derricks at Baku, chief centre of the oilfields in the Caucasus whence Russia derives 90 per cent of her oil supplies.

Diagram specially drawn for The War Illustrated *by Haworth; Photo, Planet News*

There's No 'Weaker Sex' When Russia Calls!

In their hundreds of thousands the women of the Soviet Union have rallied to the defence of their country and have set a fine example to the women of every land. On the right a group of Russian women in a Soviet munitions factory are being shown how to fill machine-gun belts. In factories, in hospitals, on ships, and even on the field of battle, the women of the Soviet Union are throwing their whole weight into their country's effort to destroy the Nazi invaders.

The grim, determined faces of the women collective farmers who have joined the guerillas (left) bodes no good to any Nazi bands which may come their way. Below, girl students of the Leningrad Textile Institute volunteering for service in hospitals.

A SOVIET WOMAN (left) soldier in gloomy mood after being captured by the Nazis. Many of these Soviet women are fighting side by side with their male comrades. Right, a Soviet girl working as a "seaman" aboard a motor ship on the White Sea.

Photos, British Official; Crown Copyright; Associated Press, and "Soviet War News"

Soviet War Posters Show the Will to Win

"THE brightest feature of the streets of Moscow," said Mr. Vernon Bartlett recently in a broadcast from that city, "is the display of war posters. The pictorial method of bringing the issues of the war home to the people is probably the most effective and certainly the most attractive . . . There are pictorial reminders of the way in which the men at the front depend upon the men and women in the factories. There is plenty of advice about the treatment of incendiary bombs (see page 149), and many of the posters deal with the defence of the Soviet Union."

Three of the Soviet War posters are reproduced in this page. The one on the right is being sent to British factories with the admonitory caption in English: "But Russia needs the tools NOW!" Below is an exhortation to Russian guerillas, which reads: 1, Stir up guerilla warfare in the Fascists' rear. Destroy (2) communications, (3) bridges, roads, (4) combustibles, warehouses, (5) enemy bands.

Below right, a British and Russian pilot lean out of their machines to shake hands over Berlin, on which they drop a salvo of bombs. It is headed "Meeting Over Berlin" and the text beneath reads: "Over an enemy town Comrades had an appointment. This handshake bodes no good for Germany."

Filling the Gaps in Britain's Labour Front

How to make the best use of the man and woman power of the country? That is not the least of the many pressing problems that confront the Government at the moment, and it has been made all the more urgent by Hitler's conquest of so many of the centres of Russian war production. If we are to give effective aid to Russia we must mobilize our own labour power to the utmost.

ALTHOUGH there is no question of increasing the numbers of the Army, said Mr. Churchill in his review of the war in the House of Commons on September 30, it is indispensable that the normal wastage—considerable even when troops are not in contact with the enemy—should be made good and that the ranks should be kept filled; moreover, since our Army must be highly mechanized and armoured, a steady flow of skilled tradesmen and technicians will be required in order to use the weapons which the factories are now producing in rapidly increasing numbers. How and where are these men to be obtained?

In large measure the strength of the Army will be maintained through the normal influx of young men reaching military age; many more recruits will be released following the constant combing of the reserved occupations. There are still many thousands of young men in civilian industry who have not been called up. Some in the earlier age groups have expressed a preference for service in one of the specialized corps or the Navy, which at the moment have as many men as they require. Others have been exempted on grounds of hardship, domestic or business; and yet others are key-men in the employ of firms engaged on Government work. Then there are many older men who are in reserved occupations, but their number is steadily lessening as the reservation age is raised and there are changes in the Schedule.

So far as the skilled men are concerned, it is obvious that they must be secured from industry. The Beveridge Committee, set up by the Ministry of Labour and National Service under the chairmanship of Sir William Beveridge to conduct a continuous man-power survey, has reported that, in the interests of the efficiency of the armed forces, there must be a further substantial calling-up of skilled men from the engineering and allied trades; otherwise, " the machines on which the lives of fighting men and the safety of the country depend, may have to be entrusted to hands insufficiently skilled, under inadequate supervision."

Arising out of this proposal, a somewhat heated controversy developed between Mr. Bevin, Minister of Labour, and Sir Walter Citrine, General Secretary of the Trades Union Congress, and, as such, spokesman of skilled labour. Sir Walter Citrine is of the opinion that war industry cannot afford a further loss of man-power, since our Army and Air Force are not yet properly equipped, and we have also to plan and work for the re-equipment of Russia. To which Mr. Bevin made reply, in his usual downright fashion. Asking if he was entitled to send a man up in a bomber without providing a journeyman to test the bomber and see if it was safe, he went on: " No, Citrine, nobody can tell me that I shall not call on

skilled men. I mean to have sufficient of them for all the Services. "It shall not be on my conscience that I risked a single airman's life." This outburst was met by Sir Walter Citrine with the comment that " all were suffering from some degree of war strain . . ."

As these skilled men are withdrawn from the munitions works, those skilled men who are left must be spread thinner, labour must be diluted by the addition of unskilled and only partially-trained recruits, and women

MAN AND MACHINE in the drive for victory, as a heavy mechanical drill is guided through the thick armour-plating to be used in refitting a battleship, at a Royal Naval dockyard.
Photo, Keystone

must be employed to an ever-increasing extent.

In an oft-quoted line, Charles Kingsley once wrote that " Men must work and women must weep." He would not have written that today. Women nowadays have no time for weeping; they too are working, not only in shops and offices and light industry, but at the engineer's bench and in the heavy trades—not to mention the hundreds of thousands who have joined the Services, releasing men for the fighting line. There is no question of their eagerness to learn, of their suitability and capacity; nor of their bravery. The women of today have shown that what the men can stand, outside the heaviest manual labour, they can stand too.

This being so, it is all the more surprising to learn that in some districts the number of women employed is still only a small

percentage of the whole. Thus in Lancashire, where women in industry are no new thing, one engineering firm employs only five women in over a thousand employees; another, also employing over a thousand hands, has only eight per cent of women; and though some firms employ up to 30 per cent of women, the average in this type of engineering industry is only up to 10 per cent. In the new light engineering factories, on the other hand, the percentage of women employed is up to 80 per cent. These figures were given by Mr. H. N. Grundy, North-West Regional Controller of the Ministry of Labour, on September 23.

Another interesting, but far from satisfactory, fact revealed by Mr. Grundy was that the Government training centres are getting far fewer women recruits than they can take. In his region from 400 to 500 women a week are wanted to fill the vacancies, not to mention a large number of women required for training as light lorry drivers and motor mechanics. Yet of the between 8,000 and 9,000 places available in the training centres, only 20 per cent are taken by women, when the percentage aimed at is 65 per cent.

So many are the openings for female labour that last April women of 20 and 21 were required to register for industrial service. Other age groups have since been included up to 27, and all women, married and single, are required to register. On Oct. 2 Mr. Bevin disclosed that 1,823,176 women had registered, and approximately 520,000 had been interviewed up to Sept. 20.

In September it was announced that Mr. Bevin had decided to withdraw from retail trades other than food all female shop assistants between the ages of 20 and 25 inclusive. Another field of female labour which is being combed for recruits is that of domestic servants, the onus of proving the indispensability of a maid, etc., being placed on the employer.

But while these efforts are being made to obtain further recruits for industry, there are constant complaints that the man and woman power at present engaged is not employed to the best advantage. A report issued by the Select Committee on National Expenditure makes it clear that the M.P.s who investigated the question of labour-power in our munition factories discovered that there was a considerable amount of idle labour, whether because of the slow delivery of materials, breakdowns in plant, or changes over in production types. Such temporary dislocations are largely inevitable; but there can be no doubt, too, that much labour is being wasted or misapplied because of managerial muddle. There are still few firms in the country which have been geared up to their maximum capacity; yet there are few factories, too, which do not complain of a labour shortage.

Women's Work from Bench to Battery

The great part women are playing in the production of armaments to win the war is exemplified in this photograph taken at a Government Ordnance Factory. Here women from all walks of life are turning breech components for two-pounder guns.

Top right, Evelyn Duncan, who recently set up a world's record by turning out 6,130 A.A. shell components in six days, busy at her capstan lathe. Right, a British barrage in the making : thousands upon thousands of 3·7-in. anti-aircraft shell cartridges stacked in a British munitions factory.

Photos, British Official : G.P.U.

Girls from British munitions factories were invited to Salisbury Plain to see some of the shells they make fired on the ranges. Above, one of them sights a gun. Right, Mrs. Wainwright pops one in the breech.   *Photos, L.N.A. and Fox*

Our Searchlight on the War

ALEXANDRIA'S MINE SPOTTERS

CIVILIAN volunteers, cooperating with the Navy, patrol Alexandria's large harbour watching for the dropping of mines by the enemy. Every night at sunset a flotilla of strange craft—sponge-fishing caiques, Egyptian feluccas and privately owned yachts—sail for a thirteen-hour vigil at their appointed stations. The volunteers are made up of British, Americans, Swiss, Greeks and other nationalities, of all walks of life, and the secretary of this "spotting" patrol is Mrs. Valerie Goodchild, who is secretary of the British Boat Club. The spotters' duties are to take a bearing and mark with sinkers any mine seen to fall in their area. These mines are usually released from Nazi planes by means of green silk parachutes, 20 feet in diameter. All reports are submitted in writing and the Navy then proceeds to destroy the located mines.

R.A.F. IN RUSSIA

WHEN the C.O. of a North of England station received a message a few weeks ago stating that a new wing was to be formed there to proceed overseas at short notice, it marked the birth of a wing which has gone to Russia and has already shot down many Nazi planes. The first of the new wing to arrive was a squadron-leader, an original member of the City of Glasgow auxiliary squadron. There came a string of others —some from famous squadrons, some from operational training units or depots. None knew where they were going. One August morning Wing-Commander H. N. G. Ramsbottom-Isherwood (see p. 178), 36-year-old leader of the wing, gave orders to entrain and the journey to Russia began, though none of the rank and file and few of the officers knew their final destination. Besides the leader from New Zealand there are English, Scottish, Irish, Canadian and Australian pilots in the wing. The entire personnel arrived safely in Russia.

KING GEORGE OF GREECE HONOURED

THE Greek Government, meeting at their hotel in Mayfair, have recently decided to confer upon King George of the Hellenes the Greek Military Cross. This medal is the equivalent of the British V.C. and is awarded only in wartime for conspicuous bravery in the field. It is to be given to King George for his part in the Greek campaign and particularly the operations in Crete.

SCIENCE AND THE NEW WORLD

WORLD scientists met at the Royal Institution, London, on September 26, to discuss plans for using scientific knowledge in the best manner, not only in the winning of the war, but in the construction of a new framework of civilization. The conference lasted for three days, and the President of the British Association for the Advancement of Science, Sir Richard Gregory, read a Charter of Scientific Principles, in which it was declared that any policy or power which deprived men or nations of their free practice convicted itself as an agent of an iniquity against the human race. Among the speakers was Mr. H. G. Wells, who gave a warning that man might become extinct unless he adapted himself to changing circumstances.

MEDICAL SUPPLIES FOR RUSSIA

THE British Red Cross are sending to Russia at once huge quantities of medical supplies, including thirty blood transfusion sets, 53 emergency operating outfits, a ton of cotton wool, 60 miles of gauze, a thousand pneumonia jackets, 50,000 assorted bandages, 100 cases of surgical dressings, a million tablets of the " M. & B. 693 " drug, two tons each of chloroform and ether, and diphtheria and tetanus anti-toxins. Comforts such as pyjamas, scarves, balaclava helmets, blankets and sheets are also being sent. Part of the first consignment of 150 tons was inspected by Mr. Maisky, the Soviet Ambassador, on October 2. The British Red Cross and St. John War Organization has allocated £250,000 for medical supplies to be sent to Russia.

L.C.C. FARMS

THE London County Council is running Britain's largest municipal farming enterprise. Since September 1939 its acreage of cultivated land has been greatly increased, and recent additions bring the total to about 4,800 acres, while further expansion is anticipated. L.C.C. farms supply 98 hospitals and institutions with dairy produce and fresh vegetables ; on the farms 1,500 cattle are maintained, including several notable herds of the Ayrshire breed, and 3,000 pigs are kept. At the Coulsdon area farm, hospital patients are helping to preserve grass as silage, of which nearly 1,200 tons will be made by the Council this year. Royal gardens and parklands are also to grow more food next year.

LONDON STONE from bombed buildings of historic interest is being made into domestic articles, like the book-end above, and exported to America. Each piece bears this medallion.

DOLLARS FROM RUINS

ARTICLES such as table-lamps, book-ends, bird baths, ashtrays, etc., are being made from the blasted stonework of important London buildings and exported to America. Every article has been originally designed by fellows and members of the Royal Society of British Sculptors, and the sculpture is done by stonemasons at the works of London Stonecraft. Stone from historical buildings destroyed by German bombs forms the

MR. CHURCHILL is here photographed for the first time in the uniform of an Air Commodore. This was during a visit to No. 615 Fighter Squadron, of which he has been Honorary Air Commodore since 1939. With him is the Squadron C.O.   *Photo, British Official : Crown Copyright*

PREMIER VISITS No. 615 SQUADRON

MR. WINSTON CHURCHILL in his capacity of Honorary Air Commodore of No. 615 (County of Surrey) Squadron, recently paid a visit to his station, when the photograph in this page was taken. The Prime Minister and Mrs. Churchill took tea in the officers' mess. The Squadron was formed in June 1937 at Kenley, as an Army Cooperation Squadron, and converted into a Fighter Squadron in 1938. Early in 1939 Mr. Churchill was made honorary Air Commodore of the Squadron, which served in France and Belgium. Later it played a great part in the Battle of Britain, and its personnel have gained many awards.

PALACE RAILINGS FOR WEAPONS

THE King has approved the removal from Buckingham Palace of certain sections of railings and gates. These will be converted into scrap for the manufacture of war weapons. About 20 tons of metal was removed on October 3, derived from sections of the inner railings behind the main railings fronting the roadway in Buckingham Palace Road. It is estimated that the Ministry of Works will get some 500,000 tons of scrap iron from the collection of unnecessary iron gates and railings listed by local authorities throughout the country.

base or characteristic feature of each " London Fragment," and each piece is personally scrutinized by the artist responsible for the original design before it is passed for sale. Part of the profits from these goods, which are being sold in the American market to help the dollar exchange, will go to the Royal Air Force Benevolent Fund. With each article a presentation volume is given containing pictures of London life during the air raids.

CANADA'S AIR CADETS

CANADIAN boys are rolling up in their thousands to join the Air Cadet League, which was organized during the summer on a Dominion-wide basis. Boys between the ages of 15 and 18 are admitted to the League for preliminary training in aviation, which includes aero-engines, aircraft recognition, airframes, airmanship, armament, map-reading, mathematics, signals and the theory of flight. In every province, from British Columbia to Quebec, air cadet units have rapidly been formed and the boys show a keenness which rivals that of the Air Training Corps in this country. The League has its own magazine, " Canadian Air Cadet," the editor of which is Bruce Keith, formerly of the " Toronto Star." R.C.A.F. officers have been lent to the League.

KING GEORGE OF GREECE, who arrived in London on Sept. 22, inspecting a guard of honour of Grenadier Guards. With him is our King George.   *Photo, Fox*

Above the Desert Fly the Navy's Fighters

GRUMMAN MARTLETS, belonging to a Royal Naval Fighter Squadron operating in the Western Desert, are seen taking off from a desert aerodrome. This squadron works in close cooperation with the R.A.F. The Grumman Martlet, known in the U.S.A. as the Grumman G-36, is an American-built single-seat fighter now in use with the Fleet Air Arm. A mid-wing cantilever monoplane, of all-metal structure, it has a length of 28 feet 10 ins. and a span of 38 feet. It has a speed of about 330 m.p.h. at 19,500 feet, a service ceiling of 28,000 feet, and a range of 1,150 miles.

Photo, British Official: Crown Copyright

The Moscow Conference: Full Aid for Russia

While the greatest battle in history was being fought along the whole front from Leningrad to the Black Sea, the Three-Power Conference was in session in Moscow. Something of what was said and done is described below, together with some account of the channels through which British and American aid may be conveyed to Russia.

"TIME is precious," said Mr. Molotov, in his opening speech as Chairman of the Three-Power Conference that began its sessions in Moscow on Monday, September 29; "let us get to work." On which Lord Beaverbrook, head of the British Mission, commented: "Mr. Molotov is right. We will give a lesson to those who make war. We will do everything we can to bring the conqueror low"; while Mr. Averell Harriman, leader of the American delegation, after pointing out that President Roosevelt's dispatch of the American Mission was an historic departure since the United States was still a non-belligerent, added, "But we come with your ally, Britain, with the same object—to give you every assistance against the violent, uncalled-for attack upon you by Hitler and his cohorts. Your success means everything to the people of America. I am instructed to pledge you the very fullest possible support."

It was following the Roosevelt-Churchill meeting in the Atlantic that the announcement was made that Britain and America had suggested to Stalin that a Three-Power Conference on the vital question of arms supply to Russia should be held in Moscow. That was on August 15; the next day Stalin gratefully accepted the offer.

Before the Conference Began

A month elapsed before the composition of the American and British Missions was announced. Then on September 15—the day on which Mr. Averell Harriman, Mr. Roosevelt's Lease-and-Lend expert, arrived in London by air—the names were released, Mr. Harriman being leader of the American delegation, and Lord Beaverbrook of the British. Three days later Moscow announced that the Russian delegation would be headed by Mr. Molotov, Foreign Commissar, and would include Marshal Voroshilov and Admiral Kuznetzov, Commander-in-Chief of the Soviet Navy. There were many criticisms of the delay in the dispatch of the missions, but the interval had been well spent.

"The British and United States missions are now in conference with the chiefs of the Soviet at Moscow," Mr. Churchill told the House of Commons on September 30. "The interval which has passed since President Roosevelt and I sent our message from the Atlantic to Premier Stalin has been used in ceaseless activity on both sides of the ocean. The whole ground has been surveyed in the light of new events, and many important supplies have already been dispatched. Our representatives and their American colleagues have gone to Moscow with a clear and full knowledge of what we are able to give Russia month by month from now onwards."

DISTANCES TO MOSCOW	
Statute Miles Approx.	
From London	
via Murmansk or Archangel — —	3,500
via Persian Gulf (Cape route) —	15,100
From New York	
via Murmansk or Archangel — —	5,800
via Persian Gulf (Cape route) —	15,300
via Vladivostok (Panama route)—	16,400
From San Francisco	
via Vladivostok — — — — —	12,200
via Persian Gulf — — — — —	16,200

After the formal opening on September 29 the Conference at once appointed six committees—army, navy, air, transport, raw material, and medical supplies—and instructed them to work day and night so as to have a full report on Russia's war needs ready by the following Friday. Though their task was huge and difficult, they worked with such zest and urgency that their reports were ready well before time.

It was on Wednesday night, October 1, that the reports were presented to the Conference. In an accompanying statement Lord Beaverbrook and Mr. Harriman announced that an agreement had been reached to place at Russia's disposal virtually every requirement for which the Soviet military and civil authorities had asked. Russia in turn had agreed to supply to Britain and the United States large quantities of urgently required raw materials. Transport facilities had also been fully examined, and plans made to increase the volume of traffic in all directions. "In concluding this session the Conference adheres to the resolution of the three Governments, that after a final annihilation of Nazi tyranny, peace will be established which will enable the world to live in the security of its own territory, in conditions free from fear or need." Stalin

had expressed his thanks to Britain and America for "the bountiful supplies of raw materials, machine tools, and munitions" which had been promised and which would enable the Soviet forces forthwith "to strengthen their relentless defence and develop vigorous attacks."

What had been promised Stalin, said Mr. Churchill in his speech of September 30, represented sacrifices of the most serious kind; and the most extreme efforts would have to be made by the British people, and enormous new installations or conversions of their existing plants would have to be set up in the United States, with all the labour, expense and disturbance of normal life which these entailed.

Not only tanks, "the tanks for which we have waited so long," were being sent, but precious aircraft and aluminium, rubber, copper, oil, and many other materials vital to modern war. It was not only the making and giving of these commodities, but their transport and reception which had to be organized. "It may be that transportation rather than our willingness or ability to give will prove in the end the limiting factor."

Main Routes into Russia

There are three main routes from the Allies into Russia, namely, through Vladivostok, the Persian Gulf, and Archangel; until recently there was a fourth, that through Murmansk, but although Murmansk is still holding out, the railway between it and Leningrad has apparently been severed by the Finns. The use of Vladivostok depends on Japan's keeping out of the war; it is kept open by ice-breakers, but is nearly 6,000 miles by rail from Moscow. At Archangel, the main factor is the degree to which ice may interfere with the traffic; some reports indicate that the port can be kept open all the year round, but it is generally icebound from mid-November until the middle of May. The Persian Gulf route is the most favourable since the Allied occupation of Iran, and cargoes are now being landed there at Bandar Shapur and carried by rail or road to Baku on the Caspian for transfer to the Soviet authorities at convenient centres. It involves three trans-shipments, however, and Bandar Shapur is 2,460 miles from Moscow.

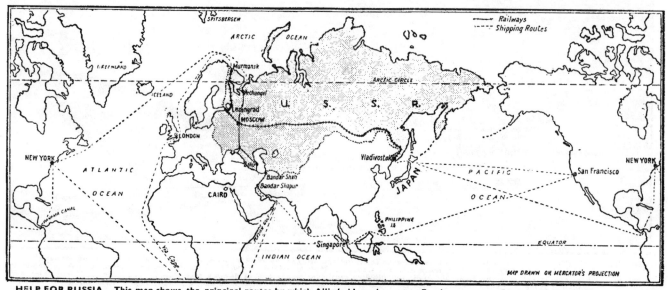

HELP FOR RUSSIA. This map shows the principal routes by which Allied aid can be sent to Russia. *Courtesy of "The Manchester Guardian."*

In the Battle Zone of the Eastern Front

When both troops and tanks were needed at a vital point on the Russian front the Soviet commander did not wait for lorries. He sent his troops up to the line mounted on the tanks, as seen above. Great initiative has been shown by Soviet officers in the field.

Left, a view in Poltava, the town whose loss was admitted by the Russians on September 30, and around which fierce fighting went on for some days. Above, a grenade section of the Red Army advancing under scanty cover towards a German position.

NAZIS TAKE COVER behind a tank on a railway siding before attempting to approach the burning ruins of a Russian station. Right, men and women of Leningrad building anti-tank defences on the outskirts of the city. Despite Nazi boasts that Leningrad would fall within a few days of the launching of Von Leeb's assault, the army of Voroshilov stood firm, inflicting bloody losses on the attackers and making many successful counter-attacks.

Photos, British Official ; E.N.A., Sport & General, and Planet News

Not Only the Red Army But the Russian Navy

The Soviet battleship Marat (above) has, together with the October Revolution, been beached near Avtovo, south of Leningrad where both vessels are used as fortresses in defence of the city. Oval, twin-engine flying boat of the Red Navy taking off for an operational flight.

Loading one of the guns on the October Revolution. The sailor on the left, judging from his cap band, formerly belonged to another ship, possibly the Krasnoye Znamya.

Photos. British Official ; Planet News and "Soviet War News"

RUSSIAN MOTOR TORPEDO BOATS have recently scored many successes against Nazi transports and supply ships in the Baltic. These swift-moving craft carry out nightly sweeps in the Gulf of Finland and Riga Bay, attacking German naval formations and convoys, sinking transports full of troops and ammunition.

How many of these motor torpedo boats the Soviet Navy possesses is not known, but in 1940 Russia had at least 130 of them and many more were building. They are of various sizes and designs, the majority, according to "Jane's Fighting Ships," being of the Italian M.A.S. type (Motoscafi Anti-Sommergibili), one of which is show photogragh in page 31 of this volume.

M.T.B. Flotilla

THE small drawing shows part of a flotilla o motor torpedo boats creeping upon an convoy under cover of morning mist, the a engines only being in use in order to approa enemy as silently as possible. When the boa approached to within effective range, they swing in a tight circle, training their twin 21-inch t tubes on the target. The main engines are then up and the torpedoes discharged.

Proved Its Mettle in Many a Hard-fought Fight

Radioed direct from Moscow to London, this photograph shows Russian sailors of the Baltic Fleet landing on an enemy-occupied island in the Baltic.

A Red Navy sailor keeping a watch along the coast. The Soviet Navy plays an exceedingly important part in the defence of Leningrad and of Odessa.

Diagram specially drawn for THE WAR ILLUSTRATED *by Haworth*

ion Stations

main picture-diagram shows the crew of a motor rpedo boat at action stations at the moment of Standing on the bridge is the captain (A), as just given his instructions to the torpedo s (B), who are seen in the act of firing one of the oes.

e small streamlined superstructure can be seen lmsman (C), the wireless operator (D), and or (E), who has left his charts to see the results attack. The whole of the streamlined forepart vessel is taken up by the high-powered aero-type s (F) which, together with the auxiliary engines

situated farther forward, are operated and controlled by the engineer (G) and his staff.

Sizes and Speeds

THE displacement of this kind of craft varies, according to design, from 6 to 35 tons. The type seer above displaces about 20 tons and is about 70 feet ir length. Those built at the Marti Yard, in Leningrad, ir 1937, were of 11 tons displacement and had a speed o 42 knots. Others have been completed more recently in Black Sea yards and are said to have speeds of from 45 to 55 knots. Judicious use of the auxiliary engines, which enable the boat to cruise at low speeds, conserves the fuel and greatly increases the range of operations.

Strange, the Czechs Don't Like Nazi 'Protection'!

Most successful of the small states that came into being at the end of the last war, Czecho-slovakia, was free and independent until 1938, when its dismemberment was ordered by the "Men of Munich." Six months later the whole country was seized by the Germans, and from then until this very hour its people have been subjected to a process of brutal Nazification.

PRAGUE and the Czechs have a new master. "Higher Group Leader Heydrich," it was announced by the German authorities in Prague on September 28, "has assumed his duties in Prague Castle as Deputy Protector of Bohemia and Moravia." Right-hand man of Himmler, and one of Europe's most unsavoury scoundrels, Heydrich took the place of Baron von Neurath, who asked to be relieved of his office as Reich Protector until his health should be restored. On the same day a state of emergency was proclaimed in Prague and five other districts of the Protectorate of Bohemia and Moravia.

Heydrich's first act was to visit the puppet President, Dr. Hacha, to inform him of his appointment and require his continued loyalty to the Nazis. He also told him that on his orders the Prime Minister of the Protectorate Government, General Elias, had been arrested on a charge of plotting high treason.

Then a veritable reign of terror developed with the shooting, after the travesty of a trial before the German People's Courts, of six men who were arrested on September 29 : they included two retired generals, J. Bily and H. Vojta, who were charged with " treason," a term which may include any-thing which the Germans regard as inimical to their rule ; two were accused of wrecking, and the other two of possessing arms. They were but the first of many victims. About 100 Czech patriots faced the firing squads on

GEN. ALOIS ELIAS, Premier of the puppet government of the Protectorate of Bohemia and Moravia, sentenced to death on a charge of plotting against German rule.
Photo, Planet News

September 30 and the following day or two, while many hundreds were arrested and thrown into prison and concentration camp. To save further slaughter, President Benes broadcast from London on Oct. 1 a warning to the Czechs that "the time for revolt will come, but it is not yet ripe."

So opened a new and more terrible phase in the Nazification of the Czech country and people. Even before this last outburst it was difficult to discern any of the features which once made Czechoslovakia the continent's model democratic commonwealth. True, there is still a President, but he is a "yes-man" of the Fuehrer ; there is still a Cabinet,

but there is no parliament, no free assembly, no free press, no freedom of speech. The Czech universities have been suppressed ; numbers of Czech schools have been closed on flimsy pretexts, while German schools have been multiplied out of all proportion to the German-speaking population. All the most important posts in the central and local governments are held by Germans, and Czech industry has been brought under German control. The great munitions works at Skoda and elsewhere are making tanks for

GESTAPO CHIEFS meet at their Berlin Headquarters. Heydrich, second from right, Himmler's right-hand man, was on Sept. 28, 1941, appointed Deputy Protector of Bohemia and Moravia in succession to Baron Von Neurath. He immediately instituted a reign of terror and hundreds of Czechs were arrested, many of them being shot by execution squads. Others in the photograph are, left to right, Nebe, Hueber, Himmler and, extreme right, Mueller.   *Photo, Central News*

Hitler's armies, guns to batter the Russians, bombs to be dropped on Britain. Czech electricity stations are producing power for the Reich. Tens of thousands of Czechs have been sent into Germany to labour there as Hitler's serfs ; some 20,000 Czech families have been ejected from their homes to make room for Germans brought back by Hitler from the Baltic states.

Town and country alike have been plundered by the Germans. Germany has first claim to all the food resources of the Protectorate. The country has become one vast refugee settlement for German industry and individual Germans. Following the R.A.F. raids on the Rhineland and the Ruhr, many key factories and armament works were transferred to the safer, because more distant, soil of Czechoslovakia. To the same haven of refuge have fled tens of thous-ands of Germans, not only from the Ruhr and the Rhineland, but from the heavily-bombed ports of the north-west.

So useful, so indispensable, indeed, has the Protectorate become to Germany at war that the Germans have seen the advantage of securing the goodwill of the population. They have striven to convince the Czechs that their country has no future outside the German orbit, and that therefore they should cooperate to the utmost in the establishment of Hitler's New Order. A flood of pro-paganda has been unloosed, designed to convince the Czechs that in the Middle Ages Czech and German culture was the same, that Prague is one of the ancient cities of the German race. Since the Czechs have proved obdurate in their ignorance of these in-teresting facts, last year there was established a " Society for Cooperation with the Ger-mans," which established a network of

semi-official offices throughout the country " to give an ideological re-education to the Czechs." This society organized com-pulsory German classes and cultural enter-tainments, intended to dissuade the Czechs from " cherishing vain hopes during the long winter evenings."

But the Czechs have resisted German blandishments, just as they have refused to be cowed by German bludgeons. Of necessity their resistance has had to be mainly passive,

since not only is the country flooded by the German police, but there is an army of occupation of at least 150,000 men. The young German soldiers, even the nicest-looking, have been cold-shouldered by the Czech girls ; the streets are emptied as the German bands begin to play ; German-controlled newspapers have been boycotted for weeks, and the people have read in train and tram nothing but the Czech classics.

Sabotage as an Art

But passive resistance has taken most dangerous forms. Sabotage is an art which has been perfected by the Czechs, who for so many generations were accustomed to under-ground agitation. Not a day goes by but the Nazis have to deal with some fresh activity of the saboteurs. Railway lines have been damaged, points put out of action, signal lights changed, loaded goods trucks left " forgotten " in the marshalling yards for weeks. Many serious train crashes have been reported, involving the deaths of German soldiers and technicians. For days at a time traffic on important railway lines has had to be suspended. In the armament factories, too, there is a similar tale to be told. Vital machines have mysteriously broken down ; the electricity has unaccountably failed ; more than one power station has been damaged by bombs placed in the machinery.

The directing brains of the saboteurs are to be found in London. Five times a day " Volá Londyn ! "—London Calling—is heard over the air as the Czech radio announcer at the B.B.C. calls to the Czechs. His message is eagerly listened to throughout the Protec-torate. Even in the heart of Prague, under the very noses of the Gestapo, the word is passed round that Jan Masaryk is to be on the air and may be heard at so-and-so's café or house.

Phases in the Far-flung Battle of the Seas

A BLENHEIM making a mast-high attack on a German tanker. Losses of Axis ships during the three months ending September 30 were about one and a half times what they were in the previous three months.

An urgent cot case, otherwise a patient needing an operation, is transferred from a destroyer, where there is little hospital space, to a British cruiser. So as not to waste valuable patrol time the trans-shipment is made under way.

A mighty column of smoke marks the end of an Italian destroyer after coming into conflict with British warships in the Mediterranean.

THE war of attrition by sea, which had reached so critical a point a few months ago, is now definitely moving in Britain's favour. Our incomparable Navy carries out its multifarious duties with heroic efficiency. Behind its shield Britain has survived and will survive, and Germany will again learn that without sea-power there can be no world-power. The aeroplane and the submarine upon which she counted so much are not enough, and, in any case, two can play that game.

The monotonous story of British sea losses in the Battle of the Atlantic is now relieved by a steep fall in such casualties, and a great rise in the tonnage of Axis ships destroyed by us. The facts as given by Mr. Churchill in his war review on September 30 are, to say the least, reassuring. He told us that "Losses by enemy action of British, Allied and neutral ships during the quarter July, August, September, have been only one-third of those losses during the quarter April, May and June. During the same period our slaughter of enemy ships, German and Italian, has been increasing by leaps and bounds. In fact, it is about one and a half times what it was in the previous three months."

H.M.S. LIVERPOOL, the 9,400-ton British cruiser which was damaged in a bombing attack off the island of Crete, undergoing repairs at the United States navy yard at Mare Island, California.

Photos, British Official ; Associated Press, Keystone

Our Diary of the War

FRIDAY, SEPT. 26, 1941   *755th day*

Air.—Minesweepers and A.A. ships attacked off Dunkirk by Fighter Command. Enemy patrol ship sunk off Cherbourg. Cologne and W. Germany, as well as docks at Calais and Dunkirk, bombed by night.

Russian Front.—Soviet troops recaptured four fortified villages. German parachute troops landed in Crimea.

Mediterranean.—Palermo harbour and railway and warehouses at Agrigento, Sicily, bombed on night of Sept. 26-27.

Iraq.—General Wavell and General Auchinleck met in Bagdad for two-day conference.

Syria.—Formal proclamation of Syrian independence at Damascus.

SATURDAY, SEPT. 27   *756th day*

Air.—Twenty-one German planes destroyed in R.A.F. sweep over Northern France. Railway at Amiens and La Bassée bombed.

Russian Front.—Bitter fighting in Crimea. New German offensive against Leningrad repulsed with heavy losses.

Africa.—Bardia and neighbourhood bombed by R.A.F. Motor transport bombed near Mersa Lukk.

Mediterranean.—R.A.F. attacks on enemy aircraft and aerodromes at Elmas, Sardinia, and at Marsala and Borizzo in Sicily. Electrical plant bombed at Porto Empedocle, Sicily. Important British convoy attacked by Italian torpedo bombers. H.M.S. Nelson hit by torpedo, but not badly damaged. Convoy went through safely with the loss of only one merchantman.

SUNDAY, SEPT. 28   *757th day*

Air.—R.A.F. sweep over Occupied France. Supply train and petrol wagons set on fire. Night attack on objectives at Genoa, Turin, Milan, and elsewhere in N. Italy. Frankfurt and St. Nazaire docks also bombed.

Russian Front.—Russian local successes in central sector. Lord Beaverbrook and Mr. Harriman arrived in Moscow and were received by M. Stalin.

Africa.—G.H.Q. East Africa announced surrender of Italian garrison of Wolchefit, Abyssinia.

Mediterranean.—British light forces shelled Italian E-boat nest on the island of Pantellaria.

Home.—A few single enemy aircraft dropped bombs at scattered points.

General.—Baron Von Neurath resigned office as Protector of Bohemia and Moravia and was at once succeeded by Heydrich, Himmler's deputy.

MONDAY, SEPT. 29   *758th day*

Air.—R.A.F. fighters attacked enemy patrol boats off Belgian coast and convoys of lorries in N. France. Night attacks on Stettin, Hamburg, and the docks at Cherbourg and Le Havre.

Russian Front.—No change in the general situation. Russians claimed to have destroyed 263 German aircraft in the two days Sept. 26-27.

Africa.—Tripoli heavily raided on night of Sept. 29-30.

Mediterranean.—Night raids on Gerbini and Comiso, in Sicily.

Home.—Slight enemy activity by night over east and south coasts. Bombs dropped on a town in N.E. Scotland.

General.—Thousands of arrests by Heydrich in Czechoslavakia. Many shot by execution squads. An Official Conference was held at Singapore.

TUESDAY, SEPT. 30   *759th day*

Air.—Offensive operation by R.A.F. over N. France. Coastal Command attacked German convoy off Norway. Armed enemy merchant vessels bombed off Cherbourg.

Night attacks on Stettin, Hamburg and Cherbourg.

Russian Front.—Russians claimed 15 villages recaptured in one day in sorties from Odessa. German drive against Kharkov developed. Russians admitted loss of Poltava.

Home.—Fairly sharp night attack on North-East coastal district. One enemy aircraft destroyed. Air Ministry announced 600 enemy planes destroyed by A.A. fire over Gt. Britain since war began.

General.—256 Czechs arrested in the Heydrich terror. 844 people arrested in Bulgarian port of Varna.

WEDNESDAY, OCT. 1   *760th day*

Air.—New type Hurricanes attacked eight E-boats off French coast. Night attacks on targets in South-West Germany.

Russian Front.—Leningrad army reported to have made successful counter-attack towards Tosno, south-east of the city. Three-Power Conference at Moscow ended.

Africa.—Naval aircraft made night attack on Bardia.

Home.—A few night raiders over S.E., East coast and Midlands.

General.—Jean Oderkerke, secretary of Belgian Rexist organization, killed by bomb explosion.

THURSDAY, OCT. 2   *761st day*

Air.—Offensive sweep over N. France. 7 enemy fighters destroyed. Night attack on the docks at Brest and docks and shipping at St. Nazaire.

Russian Front.—Russian successes claimed in the Leningrad area. Violent fighting around Poltava. Crimea drive held.

Africa.—Creation of an Eastern and Western Army in the Middle East announced from Cairo. Night bombing raid on Bardia.

Home.—Night raids over various parts of England and Scotland. Three enemy aircraft destroyed.

General.—120 Czechs reported executed in four days by Heydrich. Michele Pascolata appointed Food and Supply Dictator in Italy.

FRIDAY, OCT. 3   *762nd day*

Air.—Escorted enemy supply ship set on fire off Gravelines. One flak ship sunk and three others damaged. Blenheims attacked

Ostend docks. At night Coastal Command attacked docks at Aalborg, Denmark. Night attacks also on docks at Dunkirk, Rotterdam, Antwerp and Brest.

Russian Front.—Soviet claimed new successes in Leningrad sector. Successful counter-attacks by Voroshilov around Lake Ilmen.

Africa.—Several important raids made from Tobruk. Enemy forced to evacuate strong points. Night air attack on Bardia harbour.

Mediterranean.—Daylight raid on power station and munition factory at Marina di Catanzaro, S. Italy.

Home.—Night raid on an East Anglian coast town. One enemy aircraft destroyed.

General.—Australian premier, Mr. A. W. Fadden, resigned. Hitler, speaking in Berlin, announced a " gigantic operation " on the Russian front.

SATURDAY, OCT. 4   *763rd day*

Sea.—Admiralty announced that a German supply ship had been sunk in the Atlantic by one of H.M. ships.

Africa.—Heavy night attack by R.A.F. bombers on the harbour at Benghazi.

Russian Front.—Strong Russian counter-attack north of Sea of Azov. German attack over River Litsa, west of Murmansk, driven back with heavy losses.

General.—Dr. Otakar Klapka, former Mayor of Prague, executed by the Germans together with six other Czechs.

SUNDAY, OCT. 5   *764th day*

Russian Front.—Soviet claimed 20-mile advance in Ukraine and 30 villages recaptured in three days.

Africa.—Heavy bombers of R.A.F. made night attack on Tripoli Harbour. Benghazi also heavily bombed.

Mediterranean.—Three enemy air raids on Malta. R.A.F. raided Catania, Sicily. Aircraft of Fleet Air Arm attacked escorted enemy convoy coming from Ionian Sea. Two large merchant ships were left sinking and another was damaged.

General.—A large convoy with reinforcements reached Singapore from Australia. Conference began between British and U.S.A. commanders-in-chief in the Far East at Manila, Philippines.

BRITISH AND U.S. DELEGATES to the Three-Power talks in Moscow arriving in Russia. Left to right: A. Y. Vyshinsky, Deputy People's Commissar for Foreign Affairs; Admiral Kuznetsov, Chief of U.S.S.R. Navy; Sir Stafford Cripps; Lord Beaverbrook; Mr. Steinhardt, U.S. Ambassador; Mr. Averell Harriman; F. Molochkov, Soviet Chief of the Protocol, and K. A. Umansky, Soviet Ambassador to the U.S.A.   *Photo, Planet News*

British Tanks for the Battle of Russia

The photographs on the right of this page were taken in the Ministry of Supply tank factories while British workers responded to the appeal for a massive output of tanks for Russia. Production reached a record high level, and evidence of the British workers determination to do everything possible to help our Russian allies is seen in this line of completed tanks already on the railway.   *Photos, Fox*

SEPTEMBER 22, 1941, saw the beginning of "Tanks for Russia" week, during which all tanks made in Britain were earmarked for Russia, delivery of the first being taken by M. Maisky, the Soviet Ambassador (see page 184). The urgent need of help for Russia was stressed by many speakers during the week, for, as Mr. Chuter Ede, Parliamentary Secretary to the Board of Education, said : "Stalin will value one tank far higher than he will a theatre full of cheers." The Prime Minister, too, made an allusion to our help for Russia in his speech in the Commons on September 30. "In order to enable Russia to remain indefinitely in the field as a first-class war-making Power," he said, "sacrifices of the most serious kind and the most extreme efforts will have to be made by the British people . . . We have just had a symbolic Tank Week for Russia, and it has, I feel—I know—given an added sense of the immediate importance of their work to the toiling masses of men and women in our factories. But the output of Tank Week is only a very small part of the supplies which Britain and the United States must send to Russia and must send month after month upon a growing scale and for an indefinite period. The veriest simpleton can see how great is our interest, to put it no higher than interest, in sustaining Russia by every possible means."

What the Soldier Eats and How He Gets It

In earlier articles (see Vol. 4, p. 594 ; Vol. 5, p. 62) something has been said of the work of the Royal Army Ordnance Corps and of the Royal Army Service Corps. Here, S. G. Blaxland Stubbs presents some little known details of that part of the Quartermaster-General's huge organization which plans, gathers, cooks and serves the soldier's food to him wherever he may be and on whatever service he may be acting.

THE Quartermaster - General's Department of the British War Office is, despite the achievements of big businesses and combines in Europe and America, probably the largest and most highly organized business the world has seen. Based upon the dual principles of de-centralization and self-sufficiency to the smallest units, it has nothing of the cold detachment of big business, but welds the whole Army into a happy, if very well disciplined family. Under the Quartermaster-General is the Director of Supplies and Transport, and working for the latter are the heads of his six chief Departments, which are :

S.T.1. Water Transport (W.D. Fleet) for coastwise sea traffic and harbour work. Their vessels also tow the practice targets for our coast defences.

S.T.2. The provision and distribution of the Army's needs in petrol, lubricating oil and all other petroleum products.

S.T.3. The provision of all R.A.S.C. transport, its organization, operation and maintenance. From the railway docks or depots they carry to the whole Army everything it needs, and their ambulances return the sick and wounded.

S.T.4. The Army's catering experts. They arrange the training of messing officers and of cooks on a scale never before attempted in this country.

S.T.5. The employment of all civilian staff for R.A.S.C. services.

S.T.6. The branch that feeds the Army in every quarter of the globe, and provides, as well, its forage, its coal and electricity. They decide "how much is enough" and from what source it shall be provided. It is the one branch in the War Office which must never fail or even be too late. Not to be 12 months ahead of current events may well be too late when the planting of crops (to put into cans) has to be linked with where the Army will be and what it will be doing in a year's time.

From them comes everything that the Army consumes—except the ammunition, accoutrements and weapons it fights with—and, except for sea and rail transport, they also provide all the means of carrying everything, including ammunition and other stores, to the fighting troops.

Hunger Defeats Armies

Here, however, we will leave on one side the details of these six meticulously planned branches of the Quartermaster-General's work and responsibilities. One example, however, may be quoted. There are few people, for instance, who know that the War Department possesses a fleet of its own. Some of these W.D. vessels distinguished themselves at Dunkirk and suffered losses. Let us rather consider the work which is of direct importance to men and women in civil life as well as to serving soldiers.

Without carefully planned and distributed food supplies soldier and civilian alike must fail. Hunger will destroy the morale of them both : it defeats armies, it breaks down

the Home Front. It is a common mistake to imagine that the Army picks the best food and leaves the civil population to manage on the rest. Nothing is farther from the truth, in this war at least. Knowledge of the methods of the modern Army in the present war shows that the Q.M.G. and the Ministry of Food work in the closest and most amiable of relations. There is at the War Office a section of the Q.M.G. Department (S.T.6) which is run by officers of high rank and immense experience. There the results of many years of serious scientific research, combined with even longer experience in the field and in the barrack, are applied to the question of what the soldier shall eat wherever he be.

The broad policy of Army catering is governed by four main considerations— and the order of them is to be noted—what the soldier likes, what the Army can afford,

Soldiers on the Tobruk front filling water-bottles and petrol-tins from a captured Italian water-carrier. It is amusing to see with what professional touch somebody in our R.A.S.C. has painted in the word Wop under the Italian Acqua Potabile, which means drinking water.
Photo, International Graphic News

what the shipping policy is at the time, and what the Ministry of Food officials agree must be set aside for civilian rations.

The soldier's ration is not a fixed fact, something that is put on a plate in front of him which he has to eat, day after day, and inevitably waste. In the last great war the monotony of stew (bully beef and mutton) killed many an appetite and filled many a swill-tub. Now the rations are worked out as a result of elaborate dietetic consultations, and they are designed to meet many different needs. In 1941 there are no fewer than 89 different rationing scales, varying from those for the troops in Iceland and Libya, to men on Home Service, and to the extraordinary variety of races serving in the Armed Forces of the Crown. Even vegetarians and men of special faiths are catered for, and for those with special jobs there are special rations. Parachutists and invasion troops are obvious examples : they have two days' complete supplies in mess tins, including biscuits of delectable quality and even a packet of cigarettes.

The food experts include doctors, distinguished scientists of the Department of Medical Research, and always representatives of the Ministry of Food, who have their

say in every form of food that goes into the Army diet sheets. The diet is, in fact, varied from week to week to help the civilian situation in regard to the question of supplies of any particular form of food or shortages of special classes of food. While it is clearly recognized that the Army needs butter (actually margarine) as well as guns, it is also ensured that the civilian's interests are fully taken into account.

Scientific Communal Feeding

Much is heard from time to time of the so-called scandal of Army waste, and those who remember only too well how, in the last war, the dirtiest and most inefficient soldier was sent forward as company cook, may wrongly assume that similar conditions apply now. In fact, the catering side of the modern British Army is so organized that, with the exception of a few cases where the human factor of inefficiency spoils the organization, it can be said that the soldier's food is properly planned, properly cooked and well served. It is a form of scientific communal feeding, and it takes advantage of the many forms of modern progress. Canning has made it possible for the Army not only to have big reserves of food but many more varieties.

The catering advisers are a body of men chosen solely for their experience in management, and every Command has well-known hotel managers on its advisory staff. They are always thinking ahead and thinking in quantities, which was their specialized job in civil life. It is a very common fallacy that because women are good cooks they should therefore be called in to run the Army cooking. The average woman, of course, is a cook on a very small scale. Her "unit" is her family. The Army, on the other hand, needs mass production of well served meals, in some units of 2,000 or 3,000 meals a day. Hence the disappearance from civil life of many famous hoteliers who understand the niceties of this difficult form of mass production. In this part of his work the Q.M.G. is responsible for over 100 Army cookery training schools, and since the beginning of the war some 45,000 cooks have been trained and passed out. Even battalion commanders now have to go on a two-day catering course.

Recently the establishment of the Army Catering Corps was announced, but this is nothing new : it represents the organization built up in many years of peace, but which only now has achieved its own official title and its badge.

And lest any should think that with all this care the soldier is spoiled or likely to get less hardy, let it be pointed out that not only does he endure greater strain than we knew in 1914-1918, but that more is demanded of him both in training and in the field ; and let us remember that he is worthy of all he gets and eats. His gross pay is but 2s. 6d. per day ; in fact the greater part of his emoluments are in kind, and even these have of necessity been cut severely since the war began.

They're Real Chefs in the Army of Today

Hand and nail inspection is preliminary to cooking efforts. Trainees of the R.A.F. School of Cookery are taught all about diet, and how to use the most modern apparatus. Six civilian chefs from leading hotels in the West End of London are on the staff to give the best advice.

ARMY FOOD is no longer the crude bill of fare of Kipling's day. Cooks have to go through a complicated training, and here are some pupils at a military cookery school with their field kitchens.

A square meal and a tasty one, judging by the contented expressions of those "dining out." On the left an ex-hotel chef is giving instructions to some of the members of an Army School of Cookery.

Photos, Fox, L.N.A., "News Chronicle"

Mascot Pets Relieve the Monotony of War

Wilfred, the duck, about to try another method of flight, as he is handed into a plane en route for new quarters. In the centre, above, is Aircraftswoman Judy "jumping to it," to help to haul in a barrage balloon rope. Judy strayed into the camp and was adopted, or, as she would prefer to say, "joined up" like any good A.C.W. Right, top, Percy, the tortoise, is not as fast as a Spitfire, but he is "sporting" his wings, since he became a member of a Middle East R.A.F. Maintenance Unit. "Any Nazis about?" asks Venus (circle), the pet of a captain on a British destroyer.

Photos, British Official; Wide World

Along the bottom row, from left to right, we have Charles James (Fox, of course). He is not going to earth in these days; his life is on the ocean waves—with the minelayers, whose mascot he is. Mrs. Hedgehog and her young family are proud to display their graces to some of the South African soldiers in the Western Desert. Here is a jolly photograph of an interlude in the dreary round of desert duty. Finally, Private Whisky, pet spider monkey of a South African Medical Corps, is not averse to a "splash." He and his keeper are about to take a dip in the Mediterranean.

Photos, British Official; Fox

I Was There! .... Eye Witness Stories of the War

What We Saw on the Smolensk Battlefield

Among the correspondents—Russian and foreign—visiting the Smolensk sector after Marshal Timoshenko's successful counter-attacks was the famous Russian novelist, Mikhail Sholokhov, whose vivid description of the scene is printed below from the "Soviet War News."

ARMED with pencils, notebooks and light machine-guns, we go by car to the front, speeding past innumerable lorries carrying Red Army men, ammunition, provisions to the front-line positions. All the cars are cleverly camouflaged with branches of birch and fir ; looking down on the road from a hill one gets the impression of forests moving in a weird procession from east to west.

The booming of artillery guns from the west grows steadily louder. We are warned to expect an air attack at any moment, and take turns standing on the running-board watching the sky, but no German planes appear.

The landscape in the Smolensk region is strange to me, a native of the almost woodless Don steppes. Pine forests rise in green walls on either side of the road, giving out a cool, pungent, tarry scent. In the forest thickets there is a semi-darkness even by day, and to me there is something ominous and sinister about the gloomy silence. Now and again a bush of berries makes a splash of scarlet on the sunlit meadow of young birch trees, and then once more the forest closes in on both sides. Presently there is a sudden vision of undulating fields of rye or oats trampled by troops, and somewhere on the slope of a hill there are the black patches of villages razed by the Germans.

We switch off into a country lane. Germans were here only a few days back. Now they have been driven out, but traces of recent furious fighting are left all round : in mutilated, yawning caverns left by shells, mines and bombs. We come across the bodies of men and horses more frequently. Not far from the road lies the swollen body of a bay mare, and beside the mother a tiny colt lies dead, lifeless bushy tail outspread—so tragically unnecessary, this little dead colt on the big battlefield.

German trenches on a hill slope are ploughed up by our shells. Around the parapets of splintered roofs lie empty cartridges, empty tin cans, helmets, shapeless shreds of grey-green German uniforms, fragments of smashed weapons and torn telephone wires twisted into fantastic shapes. A direct hit from a shell destroyed the machine-gun, together with its crew. Through the doorway of a shed a mutilated anti-tank gun is visible.

A village for which furious battles were fought for several days stands on the other side of the hill. Before withdrawing the Germans razed it to the ground. Down below Red Army sappers are building a bridge over a small stream. Their sunburned backs, moist with sweat, gleam in the sunshine as do the fresh boards of the bridge covering. We drive slowly over a row of logs on to the unfinished bridge. The mud on the roadside is churned up by tank and tractor treads.

We drive into what recently was the village. There I see charred remains of houses on either side of the road. Smoke-blackened stovepipes alone remain, jutting out of the debris ; heaps of bricks where once were dwellings, fragments of broken dishes, a child's bed with the spring mattress warped by flames. Against a grim background of desolation stands a single sunflower. Its petals are slightly singed by flames, its stalk powdered with brickdust—but it is alive ! It lives on stubbornly amid a scene of death and devastation ; and it seems as if this sunflower, swaying gently in the breeze, is the only living thing in this graveyard.

But it is not so. Leaving the car we walk silently through the streets, and suddenly we see a yellow cat sitting on a black, smoke-begrimed wall. She is busy washing herself. She behaves as if she had never witnessed the horrors that deprived her of home and human friends. Observing us, she stops dead for a second and then vanishes in a flash among the ruins.

Two hens would not let us approach within forty yards of them. They were tranquilly hunting for food, pecking at a trampled vegetable patch, but the moment they saw men dressed in khaki they scuttled off without a sound. " They must have mistaken our uniforms for German," remarked one of my companions who had fought in recent battles here. " Well, we can't blame those hens for being careful," he added. " They've certainly been under fire."

It is touching to see how animals and birds grow attached to homes. In the same village I saw a flock of doves fluttering sadly over the ruins of a church demolished by German shells. They had evidently lived in the belfry and, although their home had gone, they could not fly away from the place where they had once lived in peace and comfort. In a lane a small dog crawled up to meet us, wagging his tail apologetically. He might not have possessed what is called " canine dignity," but he had the courage required to return alone through the forest to the ruins of his home. In much the same way

NEAR YELNYA, around which the armies of Marshal Timoshenko have been counter-attacking with such success, lies the village of Klimyatino, or rather what is left of it, for it is now no more than a heap of stones bearing mute witness to the thoroughness of the Soviet "scorched earth" policy. But Soviet peasants have a strong attachment for their native villages, and to this one, as to many others in the region, they have already returned. Here a peasant woman is seen cooking a frugal meal for her family on the site where her home once stood.

Photo, Planet News

women collective - farmers have a strong attachment for their own village. The men had gone to the front. The women and children took shelter in neighbouring villages when the Germans came. Now they have returned to the razed village and wander forlornly amid the ruins, rummaging in brick piles in search of some memento from their former homes. At night they take to the forests, where Red Army reserve units feed them from field kitchens. But in the daytime they go back to their villages like birds fluttering round their devastated nests.

I asked one woman where she intended living now. "Drive those accursed Germans farther away from here," she replied, "and don't bother about us. We'll manage somehow. The village Soviet will help us. We'll get along all right." The haggard faces grey with soot and ashes, the inflamed eyes of children and women, remained imprinted on my memory for a long time.

We drove on past fields with unharvested grain, a plot of faded flax with little blue flowers still growing, a Red Army sentry standing by the roadside, and a warning

notice on a pole sticking up out of the flax field : " Mined field." The retreating Germans had mined roads and ditches and had abandoned their cars, their own trenches and the corpses of their soldiers. Our sappers were busy de-mining territory ; we saw their bent, searching figures everywhere.

The cacophony of artillery firing rises to crescendo, and now we can distinguish the thunder of the Soviet heavy batteries—music to our ears. Before long we arrive at the positions of one of our reserve units. These men, almost fresh from the firing lines, now listen to an accordion playing *sotto voce* beside a dug-out. Some 20 Red Army men are standing in a circle, laughing gaily at a young, stocky fellow in the centre. Lazily he dances, patches of salt-dried sweat gleaming on the back of his green shirt. Slapping his kneeboots with huge palms, he challenges a comrade, a tall, gawky fellow : " Come on, now, shake a leg, don't be bashful ! You're from Ryazan and I'm from Orlov. Come on, let's see who can hoof it better ! "

Soon the brief twilight darkens the forest and silence descends on the camp.

even stand in comfort, owing to over-crowding, and we used to take it in turn to lie down for an hour at a time on a thwart cleared for the purpose. After about ten days the hardship and privation began to tell and each day three or four persons died.

We had no charts and our only aid to navigation was a compass, but we usually steered by sun or stars. At noon each day the three officers who had a knowledge of navigation conferred and estimated our latitude and longitude, and also average speed and distance run. Our navigation was not a great deal out, for we sighted land when we expected to and were only two degrees of latitude and three of longitude out after travelling 1,535 miles in 23 days.

Our first intimation that we were near land was the " earthy " land smell which came with the slight breeze at dawn on the Tuesday three weeks after the sinking, and when it got light enough, we were able to see that the sea was a shore green instead of deep sea blue. We were very excited, especially when we saw pieces of driftwood, which made us think we were off the mouth of a large river. At eleven-forty we sighted long, low sandhills, and by three o'clock were close to a flat beach, but as there was such a heavy surf a landing was out of the question, for the waters were shark-infested, we were very weak, and the boat would never have got through.

We saw a lighthouse and kept this in sight all night, but at daylight next morning there was no sight of land, so we altered course to S.S.W. and eventually sighted land again at noon, and by four o'clock we were close in to the shore in a small bay. We grounded in about two feet of water some 250 yards out, and I gave the order for everyone to get ashore as best he could.

With the help of another officer I threw overboard everything from the lifeboat that would float and which might be useful for building a camp, and then, carrying the ship's bag containing the papers and valuables of the men who had died, the two revolvers, the last of the first-aid gear, the few remaining matches, the ship's lamp, a can of oil, and the only remaining baling tin, we set off ourselves to wade ashore. It took a very long time, for we could only shuffle along a few yards at a time and then stop to rest. The other men got ashore in small groups, some helping each other by holding hands or arms round waists and others crawling on their hands and knees.

There Were 82 of Us in an Open Boat—44 Died

A 23-day voyage of 1,500 miles in an open boat, which is probably without precedent in naval history, was described in the following broadcast by an officer of the R.N.V.R., one of the survivors of the Anchor liner Britannia, sunk by an enemy raider in the tropics.

I WAS travelling as a passenger on a British liner when she was attacked by an enemy armed cruiser one morning about eight o'clock. She was shelled for a little over one hour and received several direct hits and near misses. We were ordered to take to the boats at nine-twenty. My own lifeboat was successfully lowered and got away before the raider sank the ship ; and after picking up persons from several rafts, there were sixty-four Indians and eighteen Europeans, a total of eighty-two persons, in a lifeboat designed to hold fifty-eight. A considerable amount of water was leaking into the boat and we had to bale frantically throughout the first day and night.

Next morning we discussed our position. We decided to try to make for the African coast and hoisted the mainsail, but found it quite impossible to go in an easterly direction as the boat would not sail into the wind, so we had no alternative but to try for the coast of Brazil, which we estimated to be 1,200 miles away. We then found that much of the water was coming in through holes made by shell splinters. We managed to plug these with bits of blanket and to nail pieces of tin over them. This made a great difference, and although we had to bale throughout the voyage, it was not such hard and continuous work as before.

We found that we had about sixteen gallons of water, forty-eight tins of con-densed milk, and two tins of biscuits. As we estimated it would take twenty-four days to reach Brazil we worked out that we could only have a third of a dipper of water each per day (that is, a little less than an eggcupful), two tins of milk divided and one biscuit each. One tin of milk was used at sunrise by dipping a spoon made from boxwood into the milk and then cleaning it on the palm of each man in turn.

The biscuit was issued at sundown followed by the water ration. After about ten days we had several storms and were able to catch some rainwater, which permitted an increase in the water ration to about a full eggcupful, and later still it was possible to double the water ration as more water was caught and the number in the boat decreased. After the second day most of us found we were unable to swallow our daily biscuit and had only

milk and water, until later in the voyage we soaked biscuits in rainwater which was too brackish to drink and so made them moist. The heat during the day was terrible, and we suffered greatly from thirst. Some of the men sucked buttons which made them feel less thirsty. It is strange that we at no time felt really hungry. Quite a number of the Indians drank salt water during the first few days, and, despite my warnings, con-tinued to do so, but it was not until after about ten days that it affected them and they eventually died.

During the first week we saw four ships and made frantic efforts to attract their attention by burning flares, but with no success. During our twenty-three days afloat we saw altogether seven ships.

We were soon all covered with salt water sores and boils and later many abscesses, and those were greatly aggravated by the crowded conditions and the constant rolling of the boat, which threw us against each other. It was also impossible to sit, lie, or

BRITANNIA SURVIVORS photographed after landing at São Luiz, Brazil. The story of their adventures and their sufferings after their ship, the Anchor liner Britannia, had been sunk by an enemy armed cruiser, is related in this page by one of the survivors; 44 men died from exposure and wounds during 23 days in an open boat.
Photo, Associated Press

It was nearly dusk when we all got ashore, and we walked up to the scrub-covered sandhills and built a fire and boiled some water from a pool for drinking and then scooped holes in the sand and lay down. Early the next morning we met some fishermen who fed us with native farinha—a meal made from mandioca roots and boiled fish. Never has food tasted so good. Later in the morning a horseman passed and we gave him a written message addressed to "anyone speaking English." This eventually reached the police and British vice-consul in São Luiz de Maranhão, a very old city in North Brazil, and they sent assistance. We eventually reached São Luiz at six-thirty a.m. on April 19 and went to hospital. Of the eighty-two persons who were originally in the lifeboat, thirteen Europeans and twenty-five natives survived.—"The Listener"

En Route to Turin We Nearly Hit the Alps

The R.A.F. made a heavy raid on North Italy on the night of September 10. Stirlings and Halifaxes led the attack, while (as told below) a squadron of Wellingtons bombed the Royal Arsenal at Turin.

WE set off at dusk. We were flying over cloud for about 400 miles. The first thing we saw was Lake Geneva, well away to one side. We were then over French territory. The rising moon was shining on the lake and you could see it for miles. We'd come down through France with very little trouble, though we had the usual flak and searchlights crossing the French coast. It was a glorious night up above the clouds, and ideal for long-distance astro-navigation. We were using the star Vega chiefly; for longitude and for latitude we used the Pole star. By these means we were fixing our position about every 30 minutes.

There'd been a following wind all the way down, which meant that we arrived at the foot of the Alps a bit earlier than we had expected, with the result that we didn't start climbing to get over them as soon as we should have done, and there we were at the foothills at only 9,000 feet. I must say it shook me a bit, because we'd intended crossing the Alps at about 13,000. We didn't want to waste time and petrol by circling and climbing, so we flew up the valleys between the peaks, slowly gaining height as we went. Way down in the valleys we could see lakes and villages, and the peaks were towering each side of us.

Nobody said anything at the time, but I think we were all wondering whether we'd get over, and what I was thinking all the time was, "Is that peak higher than we are or am I just imagining it?" The rear gunner, I remember, called up on the intercom., and said, "I hope you chaps see the next one before I do." The peaks seemed so close on either side and it seemed to take so long to get past them—all the same, one couldn't help appreciating what a mag-

nificent sight it was with the moon shining on the snow-capped peaks. But I must say I was pretty glad to stick the nose down when we got on the other side of the Alps in order to come down to bomb.

The other bombers had obviously got there before us, for as we nipped over the foothills, we could see the glow of the fires that were already burning. There were fires everywhere, some small and some large. After we'd dropped down to 2,000 feet we saw two very long factory sheds ablaze, and while we were there we saw one shed completely burnt out. The smoke from the fires was billowing up higher than our aircraft.

Our objective was the Royal Arsenal, and after we had gone round the town about ten times, we got a lovely pin point, and, using this as a datum point, we went in and bombed. We certainly knew our bombs had gone off because we felt the blast, and there was a most satisfying crump underneath the aircraft.

After that we climbed round Turin a bit to get some more height to face the Alps again. That took another quarter of an hour, so that, having arrived on the target at 20 minutes past eleven, we didn't really get away from Turin till 12.45 a.m. After our rather hair-raising experience of the outward crossing of the Alps, we made the return one a bit higher, but some of the peaks on the port side still seemed to be slightly higher than we were. Eventually, after a nine and a half hours' flight, we returned safely to base.

STIRLING four-engined bomber, type of aircraft which attacked Turin in September. The top photograph shows the bomb-aimer in the nose of a Stirling machine.
Photo, British Official: Crown Copyright

How We Escaped from Internment at Dakar

After being interned at Dakar for fourteen months, a handful of Allied merchant marine officers outwitted the Vichy authorities and sailed out in a new steamer, as told here by the captain.

TELLING his story on arriving at Cape Town, the captain said:
The ship had made only two voyages when she was trapped at Dakar at the time of the French collapse.

The crew escaped by rowing a hundred miles to a British colony in the ship's lifeboats at night. My officers were equally anxious to escape, but were determined to take the ship with them.

The French naval authorities had taken away the high-pressure lines from the engine, but for eight long months the engineer in secret modelled dummy pipes with the few tools available.

When they were ready we told the French we must have our pressure lines back in order to turn the engines, which would otherwise have been permanently wrecked.

The French agreed, but sent guards to watch us. We tested the engines, then invited the guards to have drinks and dinner on board. It did not take very long to substitute the dummy pipes for the real thing, and the French took the dummy pipes ashore without discovering the trick.

I conspired with the masters of four other ships to form a makeshift crew together with the ship's engineer, officers and two stewards.

The French had put a net across the entrance to the harbour. We planned to escape on a Saturday night, when the crews of the harbour defence usually relaxed. When the time came I retained just enough ballast to keep the ship on an even keel.

We were looking for a buoy marking a gap in the net when we saw the net almost dead ahead. It was too late to alter course. We steered straight for the net, shut off the engines, and the ship just scraped over the net without fouling the propellers.

The French naturally expected us to make for Bathurst, Gambia, so we went in another direction.

Early on Sunday we sighted a French patrol ship astern. It opened fire on us with five shells which crashed around the stern. Our speed was reduced, but we put on all the power we had got until the ship vibrated so much that we could not stand upright. Gradually we dropped the French ship behind and next morning we met a British destroyer.—*British United Press*

TURIN, showing the Mole Antonelliana, the River Po and the Lombardy Alps in the background. An airman's account of an attack on Turin is described in this page.
Photo, E.N.A.

Editor's Postscript

ONE of the pleasures of reading a good book is telling others about it. And one of the drawbacks of my editorial job is the need to examine any book about the War that bears promise of instructing me in the dominant interest of my life today ; too often do I meet with disappointment. What a reviewer describes as my " searching mind " too frequently returns empty-handed from its quest. For I read widely with no view to writing about what I have read, but for my own information or entertainment, and such books as I occasionally mention here are those odd ones that have either stirred my admiration or raised my ire.

AMONG my most recent reading I place foremost in the former category " War in the Air " by David Garnett. In 1920 I edited a hefty pictorial tome so entitled, which could it be reprinted today would " sell like hot cakes "—though I wonder if hot cakes really do sell—as it contains an unrivalled collection of expert writing and photographic documents which the Air War today has suddenly made more excitingly interesting than at the time of its publication. I mention it because I think Mr. Garnett's little masterpiece—it is nothing short of that—would be much better titled " The War in the Air," as it deals specifically in the most competent and brilliant manner with every aspect of the aerial war, from the attack on Poland to Wavell's victories in Libya and Abyssinia, not with war in the air generally. Nor will anyone ever write a better account of one of the most historic periods of British achievement in aerial combat, no matter how much greater detail may some day be available. Although many of the facts were fully known to me I have found their restatement and amplifying by a writer of genius as fascinating as a new romance. Indeed, it is a lesson in literary artistry to observe the skill with which the whole confused and inchoate data of the Air bulletins and official reports are here shaped in a clear, swift-moving story that instructs while it fascinates.

UNFORTUNATELY, I have little space here to deal adequately with Mr. Garnett's masterly account, but I hope it may yet be possible to devote space to a further and better ordered review of " War in the Air " and to draw attention to some of the more remarkable and less-known facts to which the author has had access, the opportunity of verifying, and, from his own practical experience as a flying man, correctly to assess. For the present I can note only one or two expressions of his personal opinion, and a point or two away from the main theme of his book. Referring to the " phoney " period of the War he tells us that captured German pilots revealed they had strict orders to avoid any damage to the Forth Bridge ! They came mighty near to damaging it when they tried to bomb the H.M.S. Edinburgh on October 16, 1939, as my readers will remember from the German aerial

photos which I published and commented upon at the time. But, is it possible that Hitler at that early date had his invasion plans ready and wished to preserve the Forth Bridge for the southward movement of his mechanized forces from a point somewhere to the north ? Not unthinkable !

BOTH Belgium and France at a later date helped him to their speedy conquest by obligingly leaving vital bridges undestroyed. And I agree with Mr. Garnett in thinking that if the civil population of France had been taught to destroy everything likely to be of use to the advancing Germans, France might never have been conquered. To which the only answer is that both the French army and the population behind it

MARSHAL S. M. BUDENNY, commanding the Red Armies in the Ukraine. One of the three most famous Russian leaders in the present war, he was a private during 1914-18, and rose with the Revolution. *Photo, Planet News*

(*not* the Belgian army or people, mark you) had no higher impulse at that critical moment than *sauve qui peut*. They emulated the despised Italians of Caporetto—and there were many in high places in France at the time of Caporetto who had no better spirit than our Italian allies then, seeing nothing but immediate surrender. The British had to stiffen both French and Italians at that critical hour. It has been left to the Russians to show the world what ruthless self-sacrifice can do to impede a ruthless enemy. Many may agree with Mr. Garnett in saying that when the Germans paused after their " tremendous victory " over France instead of instantly proceeding with the invasion of Britain : " I believe that this delay in the invasion of Britain will be found to have cost Germany the War. Had the Germans flung every available soldier by every available means into Britain in June, they would

perhaps have won." Well I think they didn't, just because they couldn't. *They* can seldom be accused of " letting ' I dare not ' wait upon ' I would.' "

FOR the moment, with the return of bomber's moons it is comforting to recall that " on the night of May 10, 1941, that of full moon, all records were broken and thirty-two bombers were shot down by our night Fighters during a heavy raid on London." I'm writing this in London on just such a night at the hour of 3 a.m., and have no fear that my sleep, when I do turn in, will be disturbed by bombing ; for the Hun now knows that our night Fighters, thanks to radiolocation and other devices that may not yet be mentioned, have got the measure of the bombers ; and though we may have to endure some more of the Nazi efforts at our destruction, the night is not far distant when our Fighters will have as thoroughly achieved ascendancy as they did on September 15, 1940, when Goering's bombers made their greatest daylight attack, losing 185 aircraft for the British loss of twenty-five Fighters, from which fourteen of our pilots were saved. Mr. Garnett's figures and the official ones which I give do not quite tally ; various heavy attacks followed, admittedly in *diminuendo*, before the daylight bombers had vanished from our skies save only as " single spies."

HERE is the heading to an article I have just noticed in " The New York Times Magazine ": " If we had joined the League—there might not have been a Hitler." I have not read the article, but the headline speaks volumes, and I for one think it speaks truth. Perhaps some day, twenty years from now, " Pravda " of Moscow may print an article " Did the Stalin-Hitler Pact Bring on the Second World War ? " The tendency of the moment is wilfully to forget things that happened in the recent past. Confronted as we are with many new and unforeseen relationships there is no other course if we wish, as we certainly must, to take a realistic view of the present state of international relations ; but the historian of a future day will find it difficult to ignore these two " ifs."

DEAR MR. NEWSAGENT,— Does this apply to you ? I have today seen about fifty numbers of THE WAR ILLUSTRATED in which you have written, not only in pencil but in *ink*, the address of the subscriber, thus permanently disfiguring the number for the purposes of binding. Will you please stop this ? Remember that your customer may wish to bind his numbers into volume form, and as the outer leaves are now paginated consecutively with the inner, being specially designed for binding, any disfigurement of these spoils the volume. Further, if you bind your customer's volumes locally you must warn your binders that since No. 91 the four outer pages of each issue are to be included in the volume. A subscriber has just reported to me that the local agent has delivered his volume with these pages omitted—and this despite my oft-repeated instructions to the contrary !

JOHN CARPENTER HOUSE.
WHITEFRIARS. LONDON. E.C.4.

Printed in England and published on the 10th, 20th and 30th of each month by the Proprietors, The Amalgamated Press, Ltd., The Fleetway House, Farringdon Street, London, E.C.4. Registered for transmission by Canadian Magazine Post. Sole Agents for Australia and New Zealand : Messrs. Gordon & Gotch, Ltd. ; and for South Africa : Central News Agency, Ltd. October 20th, 1941.
S.S.

Vol 5 # The War Illustrated Nº 110

FOURPENCE

Edited by Sir John Hammerton

OCT. 30TH, 1941

A STIRLING BOMBER being loaded up for an attack on industrial Germany. The four-engined Short Stirling carries a heavy bomb freight equal to that of three Wellingtons or nine medium Blenheims. It has proved a splendid machine, very light on the controls and easily manoeuvrable, while its defensive armament is formidable indeed. The Stirling has a four-gun turret in the tail, a twin-gun turret in the nose, and another turret amidships. A close-up view of its bomb racks is given over-leaf.

Photo, Keystone

NO. 111 WILL BE PUBLISHED MONDAY, NOV. 10

DEATH-WATCH BEETLES IN HITLER'S EUROPE

THERE is a war on *inside* Europe. It is a war fought by men without uniform save the dungarees of a workman, with no weapons but a screwdriver and crowbar, an oily rag and a can of petrol, perhaps a package of blasting powder. The battlefield lies in the factories and workshops where men and women toil day and night to make tanks and guns and planes for Hitler; it runs through dark byways and along woodland paths and railway embankments. No communiqués are published giving news of its progress. Its heroes are awarded no medals to wear on their breasts; instead, they go unhonoured and unsung, and often their only reward is death. The day comes when a spy speaks. There is a hurried trial —what a mockery!—a muffled figure before a firing squad, and a felon's burial.

In every corner of Hitler's Europe the saboteurs are busy, since the New Order he boasts about is old tyranny writ large. But he has the power: the truncheons and the bayonets, the police and the Gestapo, the torturers in the concentration camps. So they work against him underground, under cover of night.

"IT is a moving and terrible spectacle—a darkened Europe through which the tramp of the Nazi guards re-echoes and their voices ring into the night, challenging every sound and movement; and behind this façade of vigilance, a host of nameless men, working in silence with pliers and saws and acetylene flares, pulling at the proud structure, dislocating here a line, there a dynamo, there a storage plant, like death-watch beetles in the floor of Europe." This powerful passage from a recent article in the "Economist" well suggests the wave of sabotage which is spreading over Europe, and is not to be overborne by the counter-wave of ruthless repression and ferocious reprisal.

From Bergen to Crete, from Brest to Kiev, the war of the plain man against Hitler goes on. Never in the whole of history has one man aroused so many enemies, such bitter animosities, such undying hate. In the field his armies are faced by millions of open foes; behind their lines in the countries they have subjugated, in the very Fatherland where are their own homes, the death-watch beetles are busy in their burrows.

FROM here and there trickle tidings of the saboteurs. Trains are derailed, machines wrecked, crops are destroyed, buildings fired, power stations put out of action, workers practise ca' canny. ("How can we do a full day's work," they ask, "when you refuse us a man's rations?") In Prague the other day the Nazis offered a reward of 30,000 crowns for information leading to the arrest of those who had cut their telephone wires. It's a year's wage of a Czech workman, but so far no Judas has appeared to pick up *those* pieces of silver. In France the police have offered a million francs for information leading to the conviction of saboteurs on the railways; the million francs still goes unclaimed. In Belgium the telephone and telegraph lines of the German

Army have been cut time and again, and a few weeks ago the Nazis executed 20 hostages; but the next dark night more wires will be cut, more military vehicles damaged, more buildings in German occupation set on fire. In Holland, where German soldiers no longer walk alone along the canal banks at night, Hilversum Radio reports that: "We Dutch have all become children again. We are members of secret societies. We raise the first and second fingers of the right hand in the air, forming the letter V, to indicate the English word, Victory. We write on walls and cut telephone wires . . ."

FROM Greece there come tales of guerillas wrecking Italian troop trains, burning store dumps, setting fire to the transports in Salonika harbour. From Bulgaria the story is much the same. In the mountain fastnesses of Montenegro and Serbia bands of *Chetnics* harass and hamper the enemy columns and make their lives a misery. From Rumania comes the news that railwaymen, guilty of the "slightest attempt at sabotage," are to be shot out of hand; "the same punishment will apply to managers of industrial establishments. They are responsible for the smooth running of the machinery in their charge."

In Norway, Quisling and his Nazi friends have found it necessary to decree that: "Whoever by lockout, damage of industrial plant or equipment, by defeatist influencing of others, by deliberate slow work, or by other means, upsets the industrial processes, will be punished with penal servitude and, in serious cases, with death." Two of the Norwegian Trade Union leaders have been

shot; but when a short time ago the R.A.F. flew low over Oslo to bomb the harbour the people of Norway's capital rushed into the streets to greet them, and the hospital to which two of the wounded British flyers were taken was swamped with flowers.

It is only to be expected that Poland should be a country of saboteurs. But what of Italy, whence come stories of strikes and sabotage in factories controlled by Nazi taskmasters? And little Luxemburg? Surely there are no saboteurs there? Perhaps not; but it is a fact that the men of Luxemburg prefer to break stones on the German roads rather than work in their own country as collaborators with the Nazis. No people are more peaceloving than the Danes; what, then, are we to read into the stories of acts of sabotage against German ships in Esbjerg and other Danish ports? Was it only an accident when a large fire broke out the other day in that factory near Copenhagen which was producing tinned food for the Germans?

NOT even the thunder of the guns can drown the ominous ticking of the death-watch beetles, gnawing and nibbling through the foundations of Hitler's empire. May we assume, then, that it is tottering to destruction? May we cheer ourselves with the belief that the vast edifice, so imposing, so splendid-seeming, has feet of clay which are even now showing signs of crumbling?

Before we answer, let us remember that so far we have seen but part of the picture. We have glimpsed the saboteur at his dangerous and deadly work; we have seen in our mind's eye the flames of arson reflected in the sky; we have heard in our imagination the screams of the Nazi soldiers sent hurtling to destruction. as their train pitched over the embankment; we can understand the look on the workpeople's faces as there is a rending and crashing, and the machinery in the giant factory suddenly stops. Sabotage is grit in the machinery, admitted; but a million machines continue to grind for Hitler. The saboteur refuses to be a slave; but for every saboteur there are hundreds of thousands who toil for Hitler because they must, for bread. Three millions of foreigners are employed in Germany today, the "Frankfurter Zeitung" tells us: Poles and Czechs; French and Belgians, Dutch and Slavs. Largely discontented, often actively hostile, yet this vast army of serfs contributes enormously to the success of Hitler's schemings.

COMPARED with these, the saboteurs are few indeed. Sabotage can make Hitler pause and stumble, but it cannot make him stop. That will happen only when German production is outstripped by ours and America's. The path to victory lies through the factories. "The saboteur," concludes the "Economist," "is the far-flung advance guard of the Allied attack. Unsupported, his little effort will cost the Germans a bullet and him his life. Sabotage is a call to action, not to relaxation. The forgotten men of Europe are taking up the cry of Britain last year, 'Give us the tools. Together we can finish the job.'"   E. ROYSTON PIKE

BOMBS FOR BERLIN! Sabotage (as described in this article) can do much to disrupt Hitler's war industries, but British bombs can do more. Here we see a Stirling's bomb racks being loaded; a side view is given in the photo of a Stirling in the preceding page.

Photo, Keystone

Tobruk Holds Fast • Odessa Falls At Last

ODESSA, great Russian port on the Black Sea which had been besieged by the Rumanians and Nazis since the middle of August, was claimed by the enemy on October 17. Right, residents greeting Red Army soldiers as they made their way to the defence lines. B e l o w, bombs bursting on the quays during a Nazi dive-bombing attack.

TOBRUK, claims the "Sydney Sun," "has taken its place among the great sieges of modern military history." Centre, Bren gunners in Tobruk, hidden from the air in a ruined house, are ready for attacking Stukas. Right, an Australian O.P. outside the town; from his look-out post the observer watches the enemy's movements and obtains information which will be of great value to our patrols. Above, bombs bursting during a raid on Tobruk by enemy planes.   *Photos, British Official and Associated Press*

RECENTLY the commander of the garrison of Odessa received this telegram from the Commander of the Tobruk Garrison: " We in besieged Tobruk salute the resolution and fighting spirit which we have learned to associate with your country and with which you and your gallant garrison are facing great tasks. From our African stronghold we are following your fortunes with admiration and wish you good luck and the continuation of your successes. May the enemy soon be overthrown."

To which the commander of the Odessa Defence district replied : " We read your greetings with great satisfaction. The Soviet people will resolutely and firmly smash the Fascist bandits until these barbarians are completely annihilated . . . We send you, the valiant defenders of Tobruk, our fervent greetings. Be firm in the struggle, victory will be ours ! "

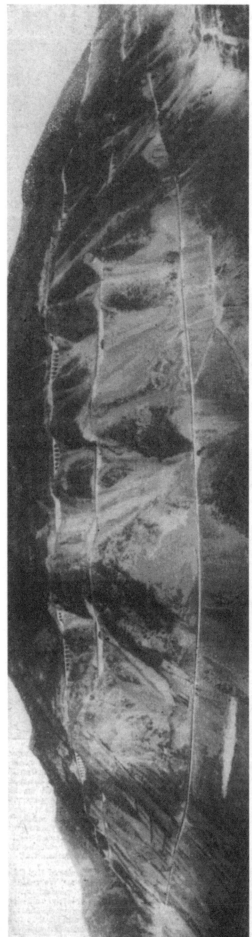

THE TRANS-IRANIAN RAILWAY, important supply route between the Persian Gulf and the Caspian Sea, was completed and inaugurated in August, 1938. Its length is 960 miles, with an additional 200 miles of branch lines. One of the greatest difficulties encountered in the construction of this railway was the crossing of the Elburz Mountains, between Teheran and the Caspian, and the top photograph shows how the line winds from the Abbas valley to within a few hundred feet of a mountain top. Left, part of the northern section of the railway, showing Mt. Demavend, 18,464 feet, in the background. Right, another link of communications, the highway between Teheran and Tabriz.

Photos, "The Times" and "Black Star"

Persia is Our Gateway into Russia

Of the routes by which Allied aid can be given to Russia, one of the most important is through
Iran (or Persia, to give it its old name). Below we describe the railway and road systems of the
country—systems which are now being modernized and extended under the urgent impetus of war.

TRANSPORT is the problem of problems
in Iran today. Everywhere the most
desperate efforts are being made to
improve and extend the road system, to
multiply the fleets of lorries, and to increase
the carrying capacity of the railways. Nor is
it forgotten that, in this wild country of
climatic extremes, four-footed transport—
horses, donkeys, mules and camels—still has
its place.

Allied aid to Russia through Iran may be
brought from the Persian Gulf, from Iraq,
and from British India via Baluchistan. Of
these, the most important is the Persian Gulf.
There is a motor road starting at Bushire,
which runs through Shiraz to Teheran and

SHIRAZ, an important
Persian town now on the
line of communications
between Russia and the
Persian Gulf. Its popu-
lation is given as 119,000.
Photo, E.N.A.

on to the Caspian ports.
This road is linked with a
second which, beginning
at Mohammerah, runs
north through Ahwaz to
Hamadan and Kasvin,
whence one road runs
north-west to Tabriz and
thence to the Caucasus,
while another drives north
across the Elburz Moun-
tains to Resht on the
Caspian. Kasvin has also
railway communication
with Teheran, and work
is in progress between
Kasvin and Tabriz.

Most important of the
routes from the Persian

IRAN has now assumed
vital importance as one
of the few countries
through which Allied aid
may be brought to
Russia. The map on the
right shows roads and
railways available.
*Courtesy of the "Manchester
Guardian"*

Gulf is the railway which runs from Bandar
Shahpur (Harbour of the King's Son) to
Bandar Shah (King's Harbour) on the
Caspian. Twelve years in the making, the
line was opened in 1938. It is 960 miles long
and is reported to have cost £30 millions,
exclusive of the cost of the two terminal
towns, which had to be specially built; in its
making, American, German, British, French,
and Danish engineers had a hand, but the
hardest sector of the track, the climb to the
great plateau, was entrusted to a British firm.
It is of the standard gauge of 4 ft. 8½ ins.

From Gulf to Sea by Rail

From Bandar Shahpur the railway has an
easy run over fairly level country to Ahwaz,
where the river Karun (navigable up to this
point) is crossed. Then it begins a long climb
up to the Bakhtiari Mountains, to cross which
involves 18 miles of tunnelling. After crossing
the great desert plateau, 3,000 feet above sea
level, there is next a run down to Teheran;
and then another formidable climb over the
Elburz Mountains (often snowbound from
November), through 25 miles of tunnels, until
the line emerges above the low-lying coastal
plain beside the Caspian. Its terminus at
Bandar Shah has a road link with Resht and
Enzeli (Pahlevi). From the latter to Baku
is about 200 miles across the water, and about
the same distance separates Bandar Shah
from Krasnovodsk, whence there is railway
communication with Russian Central Asia
and the Trans-Siberian railway, which joins
Moscow with Vladivostok.

When the Iranian Railway was first mooted
the British urged the Shah to build it east
to west, so as to link Baghdad with the
borders of India, while the Russians, for their

part, although they favoured a line joining
the Caspian with the Persian Gulf, would
have liked the northern terminus much
nearer their frontier on the west shore of the
Caspian. But since Shah Pahlevi was
suspicious of the intentions of both British
and Russians, he planned his line most carefully so that, while it suited Persia's interests,
it would give the least possible aid to British
and Russian pretentions. Hence Bandar
Shah is placed about as far as it could be
from the Caucasus boundary, while Bandar
Shahpur is inconveniently remote from Basra.

So much for the Persian Gulf. From the
west two routes enter Iran from Iraq: the
first consists of the railway from Baghdad
to Kuretu, on the frontier, whence a good
motor road, constructed by British troops
during the last war, crosses the Paitak Pass
to Hamadan, Kasvin, and Teheran. Then
more to the north a road leads from Mosul
in the oilfields through Ruwandiz to Tabriz,
whence there is a railway connexion with the
Russian railway system in the Caucasus.

Finally, there is a line of the Indian north-
western railway system which, crossing the
frontier from Baluchistan into Iran at
Mirjawa, proceeds to Duzdab; this line is
now being extended.

Many miles of new road and railways (e.g.
from Samnan to Meshed) are under construction. Progress is hampered, however,
by a shortage of motor tires and lubricating
oil, and the number of lorries available falls
far short of what is needed. Recently the
United Kingdom Commercial Corporation
has imported 2,000 lorries into the country,
while big quantities of rolling stock are
being sent for the railways from Australia.

Yugoslavia on the Conqueror's Rack

Some of history's blackest and most shameful pages tell of the partition of Poland in the eighteenth century. Today we are witnessing another partition, just as brutal and equally shameful—that of Yugoslavia, the Balkan state which in the spring of 1941 had the temerity to stand up to Hitler.

FOR a few days in April 1941 Yugoslavia waged war against the Nazis and their companion jackals—Hungarians, Italians and Bulgarians. Then her armies were compelled to capitulate, and the country which had been in existence for a brief 22 years was split into fragments at the conqueror's behest.

Italy received the lion's share of the spoil, since she was not only permitted to annex Slovenia and the Dalmatian coast, but Montenegro and Croatia were placed under her suzerainty. Montenegro was at first under the rule of an Italian High Commissioner, but on July 11 Count Mazzolini was petitioned by the "National Assembly" to re-establish the independence of Montenegro within the framework of the Italian Empire, and to appoint a regent pending the selection of a monarch. Montenegro, it may be recalled, was an independent kingdom prior to 1918, its last sovereign being King Nicholas, father of Queen Elena of Italy. On old Nicholas's death on the French Riviera in 1921, his rights passed to his grandson, Prince Michael, and it was now suggested that this young man, the Italian Queen's

nephew, should be restored to the throne of his ancestors. It was later reported, however, from Switzerland that he had refused the proffered crown.

Croatia, Italy's other puppet state, had for its first Prime Minister a notorious terrorist and gangster of the worst Balkan type—Anton Pavelitch, who was implicated in the murder of King Alexander of Yugoslavia at Marseilles in 1934, sentenced to death in his absence by a French court, and since then has lived in Italy under Mussolini's protection. Now he was elevated to the position of "leader of the Croats," while his "party," the pro-German *Ustacha*, was declared the only legal political organization in what was to be henceforth a totalitarian state. A month later Pavelitch went to Rome at the head of a Croatian delegation, and formally offered the crown of Croatia to the House of Savoy. His Imperial Majesty Victor Emmanuel, "King of Italy, Emperor of Ethiopia, King of Sardinia, King of Cyprus, Jerusalem and Armenia, Duke of Savoy," etc., etc., declined another crown, but was graciously pleased to nominate his second cousin, Prince Aimone, Duke of Spoleto,

brother of the Duke of Aosta, as sovereign of the new state, and in due course the Duke was proclaimed King Tomislav II. But he showed no great eagerness to experience his new subjects' welcome, and the real power remained in the hands of Pavelitch and his Ustachis, with strong Italian support, who engaged in the highly congenial occupation of wiping out their old enemies, the Serbs.

In the north, the Banat of Temesvar—the triangular piece of country between the Rivers Drava and Tisza which had been Hungarian up to the Great War—was restored to Hungary. The Bulgarians, for their part, occupied a considerable portion of Macedonia, in the south of Yugoslavia ; but here they came in conflict with the Italians, who had been indulging a hope of a Greater Albania, extending so as to include Salonika. Another plan revolved about the creation of an independent Macedonia—a project which has the support of the I.M.R.O. (Internal Macedonian Revolutionary Organization), whose chief, Mihailoff, is described by some as a patriot and by others as a brigand.

In the Yugoslavia carve-up the Germans appropriated for themselves a small strip of Slovenia in the far north round the town of Maribor (Marburg). At once they began a campaign of murder and expropriation, described by Dr. Miha Krek, deputy Prime Minister of the Yugoslav Government now in London, as a deliberate attempt to murder a highly-civilized European nation.

In what is left of Yugoslavia the Germans have succeeded in setting up a quisling government under General M. Neditch, who was War Minister in the Tsvetkovitch cabinet. But only where the German and Italian troops are present in force does his government function ; elsewhere the country is in the hands of patriotic bands.

In September it was said that four wars were being waged in Yugoslavia. One was being carried on by the Communists, who were working with good effect as saboteurs, their special forte consisting of derailing trains by loosening rails. The second was that of the Ustachi terrorists versus the patriots in Croatia—a matter of street clashes between gangs of partisans. Much more important was the third, which was being carried on by units of the Yugoslav regular army against the troops of the occupying powers.

Perhaps as important was the fourth war, which was, and is, being carried on by the guerilla bands (*komitadji*) of *Chetnics* (patriots). These *komitadji* are well equipped and extremely mobile, operating in groups of 15 to 50 ; they carry their own munitions and provisions, and hide, or are hidden, in villages and woods. One of their chief activities is the hampering of the Nazi engineers who are trying to rebuild the destroyed railway between Belgrade and Salonika ; what is built during the day is destroyed at night by the Chetnics.

In vain the Nazis and Italians have taken the most savage steps to counteract these hostile activities. Executions are an everyday occurrence ; hostages are seized and mercilessly shot ; heavy fines are imposed on villages alleged to have given succour to the Chetnics ; a strict curfew has been imposed. Yet the wars go on. Sabotage is perpetual, assassinations are almost as frequent as bomb outrages, savagery evokes savagery in return. And in spite of everything the Yugoslavs still believe that the day of resurrection will dawn for their martyred country.

YUGOSLAVIA today, showing how the kingdom is now being carved up and partitioned amongst Italy, Hungary and Bulgaria. But though Yugoslavia is theoretically a conquered country, strong guerilla bands throughout the land are waging war against the "conquerors."
By courtesy of "The Sphere"

Hurricanes Have Been in Action in Russia

Already the R.A.F. in Russia has given a good account of itself, and from the very first cordial relations were established with the Soviet airmen. In the circle, Wing-Cmdr. H. N. G. Ramsbottom-Isherwood, commanding the R.A.F. wing in Russia, is seen studying a chart with Soviet Flying officers preparatory to a joint sortie by the two forces. Above, a Hurricane stands under trees on the edge of a Soviet flying field. The Soviet airmen had nothing but praise for the Hurricanes with which the R.A.F. wing is equipped, and were unanimous in their opinion that this fighter plane fully justifies its name.

Photos, British Official: Crown Copyright

Our Searchlight on the War

BOMBER HERALDRY

BRITAIN'S bombers go into action with emblems and mottoes painted on their sides—some gay, some grim, but all imbued with the spirit of individuality. It is the captain's privilege to choose an emblem for his aircraft, but he does it in consultation with his crew. Then he commissions a member of the ground staff, usually a man who has been an artist or designer in civilian life, to paint the emblem upon the aircraft. These emblems take various forms. A Canadian bomber squadron boasts among its emblems a fine drawing of a Red Indian's head with the inscription " Chief Thundercloud." The captain of another aircraft, which has carried out many operational flights over Cologne, Dortmund, Essen and Hamm, has adopted as its emblem a drawing of a witch riding a bomb instead of a broomstick, with the motto, " Terror of the Ruhr." Bombers are known by their letters—like " F for Freddie," in the film " Target for Tonight." The captain of a certain " D for Donald " has, of course, a Donald Duck on the aircraft he takes over Germany, while a bomber marked " P " bears the well-known figure of Pop-eye the Sailorman. The commonest form of bomber decoration is a fresco of bombs or swastikas, each one of which denotes an operational flight. When the twenty-first attack is reached a key, symbolizing a coming-of-age, is incorporated.

' THE DUKE ' is, appropriately enough, the emblem borne by one Wellington bomber which flies over Germany. This emblem was drawn by Zec, the " Daily Mirror " cartoonist.
Issued by the Air Ministry

C.-IN-C. TALKS AT MANILA

AIR Chief Marshal Sir Robert Brooke-Popham, Commander-in-Chief Far East, recently held a three-day conference at Manila with General Douglas McArthur, Commander-in-Chief of the American Forces in the Philippines. Although denying the existence of any formal Anglo-American agreement for mutual military

NEW " TIN HAT " for British soldiers is seen above. The helmet is said to afford better protection than the type previously used.
Photo, Keystone

action in the Far East, observers believed that Sir Robert was informed of the help he might expect in the event of an Axis attack on Singapore. Others reported to have taken part in the Conference were Brig.-Gen. John Magruder, leader of President Roosevelt's military mission to Gen. Chiang Kai-Shek, Sir Earle Page, President Quezon of the Philippines, Major Grunert and Brig.-Gen. Clagett, commanding respectively the U.S. Army and Air Forces in the Philippines, Admiral Hart, commanding the U.S. Asiatic Fleet, Sir Otto Niemeyer, Gen. Ho Ying-Ching, and the Prime Minister of Burma, U Saw.

JAPAN'S DEFEAT IN CHINA

ON October 1 Japan suffered a severe defeat at the hands of General Hsueh-Yueh. Two great Japanese enveloping movements launched from Hankow and Canton to annihilate the Chinese armies in Hunan, to seize the vital Hankow-Canton railway and gain possession of

Changsha, were smashed after violent fighting. General Hsueh-Yueh, the " little tiger," commanding the Chinese forces defending Changsha, concentrated on dealing with the most dangerous Japanese thrust—the one from Hankow in the north. As the Japanese moved southwards he offered only slight resistance with his advance units, which were then withdrawn to the Japanese flanks. The enemy was allowed to get within eight miles of Changsha when, by a piece of perfect timing, the main Chinese force came into action while the advanced forces, now on the Japanese flanks, made a simultaneous attack. The fierce battle which ensued lasted for forty-eight hours, after which the Japanese, heavily defeated, retreated towards Hankow, leaving behind them 40,000 dead and wounded. With the defeat of this army the Japanese southern drive from Canton faded out and that army, harried by the Chinese, retreated towards its base.

' SWOPPING ' TOOLS

SOME eighty firms of war manufacturers in South-West England were represented recently at one of the most remarkable auctions ever held in Bristol. The object of this auction, which was really more of an exchange than an auction in the strict sense of the term, was to eliminate bottle-necks in production. Tools used in the production of planes, tanks, guns, shells and ships were bought, lent or exchanged between firms, and representatives of the firms attended with lists of tools they required to complete urgent orders. A number of machine tools were " swopped " between various firms from different parts of the country, and within the first hour over forty firms were brought into contact and more than a hundred bottle-necks eliminated. Similar auctions are to be held throughout the country.

COLDS HELP HITLER

THE Ministry of Health is launching a big campaign against the common cold and influenza, ailments which cause great loss to industry through sickness absence. Sir William Jameson, Chief Medical Officer of the Ministry of Health, has said that if one reckoned that 10,000,000 workers in this country were engaged on war production, and each of them lost no more than two days' work each year through sickness, production would be held up to the extent of 3,500 tanks, 1,000 bombers, and 1,000,000 rifles. It must be remembered, too, that sick absentees were not only absent from work during these two days, but would have been sick before they left and below par for some time afterwards. Slogans, posters, drawings, films and model lessons in school will form part of the anti-infection campaign, and two of the photographs are reproduced below.

FLT.-LT. BRENDAN FINUCANE, twenty-one-year-old Spitfire " ace " of No. 452 Squadron R.A.A.F., brought down his twenty-first enemy plane early in October. Born in Dublin in 1920 he was commissioned in August 1939. He was awarded the D.F.C. when a Flying Officer with No. 65 Squadron R.A.F. in May 1941. Since then he has won it twice more. and was recently awarded the D.S.O. " His ability and courage," says the official account, " have been reflected in the high standard of morale and fighting spirit of his unit." *Photo, L.N.A.*

AUSTRALIA'S NEW CABINET

FOLLOWING the resignation of Mr. A. W. Fadden on Oct. 2, a new Labour Cabinet was announced from Canberra on Oct. 6, with Mr. J. Curtin as Prime Minister and Minister of Defence Coordination. Mr. Curtin has been Leader of the Opposition in the Commonwealth Parliament since 1935. Editor of the " Westralian Worker," Perth, from 1917 to 1928, in the latter year he was elected a Member of the House of Representatives. He was Australian delegate to the International Labour Conference in 1924. One of the most important posts in the new Cabinet is that of Mr. J. J. Dedman, who has been given an entirely new Ministry, that of War Organization of Industry. Mr. Dedman, who is only 44, was born at Newton Stewart, Scotland. The new Army Minister is Mr. F. F. Forde, Deputy-Leader of the Labour Party. Senator J. S. Collings, who takes the Interior, is Leader of the Labour Party in the Senate, and External Affairs are in the hands of Mr. Herbert Evatt, a former judge of the Supreme Court of New South Wales. The Australian War Cabinet comprises Mr. Curtin, Mr. Forde, Mr. Chifley, Australian Treasurer, Mr. Evatt, Mr. Beasley, Minister of Supply and Development, Mr. Dedman, and Mr. Makin, Minister for Navy and Munitions. The members of the Advisory War Council have not yet been chosen.

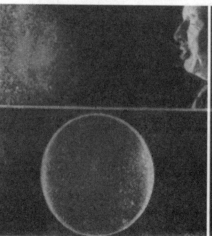
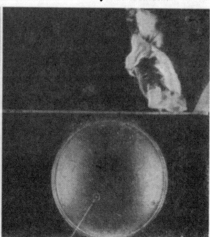

SNEEZE CAREFULLY ! Left, a careless sneezer broadcasting thousands of germ-laden droplets into the air. One of these droplets was caught in a Petri dish held three feet away and in it there grew 19,000 colonies of living germs (bottom left). Right, as the result of a careful sneezer using a handkerchief to trap the germs, a droplet caught at the same distance showed under the microscope only one colony of germs. (See paragraph above.) *Issued by the Ministry of Health*

Machines and Men in the Battle of Giants

STORMOVIK dive bombers about to take off from a Soviet airfield. Lord Beaverbrook has referred to this new type of heavily armoured plane as having proved very successful in breaking up Nazi troop concentrations advancing on Moscow.

RUSSIAN SAILORS wheeling up heavy shells for the big guns defending Leningrad. Right, an immense mobile field weapon on caterpillar wheels coming into position.

GERMAN PRISONERS captured by the Red Army in recent fighting. On the right, a Soviet soldier engaged in the perilous duty of cutting barbed wire entanglements in a wooded sector of the battlefront.
Photos, British Official ; Crown Copyright

Soviet Bombers in Action

With Devastating Effect Russia's Air Force Strikes at the German Lines of Communication

Specially drawn by Haworth for THE WAR ILLUSTRATED

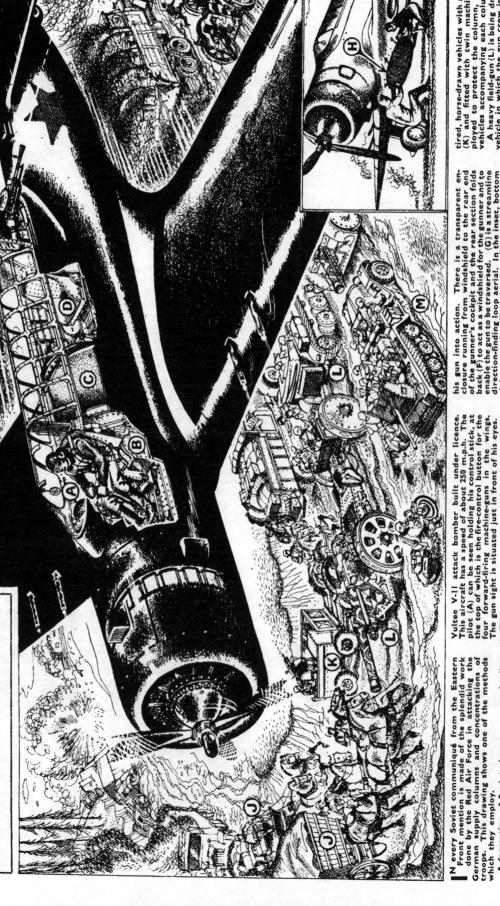

IN every Soviet communiqué from the Eastern Front mention is made of the splendid work done by the Red Air Force in attacking the German supply columns and concentrations of troops. This drawing shows one of the methods which they employ.

A formation of Soviet airmen are seen hurling their bombs at a German supply column. The aircraft depicted are the strongly built short-range R.10 attack bombers, specially designed for direct support work. This is in reality the American

Vultee V-11 attack bomber built under licence. This aircraft has a speed of about 250 m.p.h. The pilot (A) can be seen holding his control stick, at the top of which is the fire-control button for the four forward-firing machine-guns in the wings. The gun sight is situated just in front of his eyes.

The engine controls are shown on his left (B), the main petrol tank is just behind him (C), and behind that again is the observer's seat (D). The observer (E), who also combines the functions of wireless operator and rear-gunner, is seen bringing

his gun into action. There is a transparent enclosure running from windshield to the rear end of the gunner's cockpit and the rear section folds back (F) to act as a windshield for the gunner and to enable the gun to be traversed. (G) is a streamline direction-finding loop aerial. In the inset, bottom right, ground staff are loading a 500-lb. bomb to the external rack (H) of an R.10. There is also internal bomb stowage for small bombs.

Two- and four-horsed wagons (J) are a feature of the German supply organization. Small rubber-

tired, horse-drawn vehicles with armoured bodies (K) and fitted with twin machine-guns are employed to protect the column, several of these vehicles accompanying each column.

A heavy field-gun (L) is being drawn by a tracked vehicle in which the gun crew is accommodated.

An anti-tank gun (M) is mounted on a tracked vehicle of a lighter type. These guns are very mobile, and are used in great numbers to afford protection against the Soviet tank attacks. There is also a horse-drawn light field-gun (N).

Soviet Russia's Supreme Hour of Crisis

September 1940 was Britain's supreme hour of crisis. A year later it was Russia's, when Hitler flung the greatest and most powerful army ever assembled on earth against the Russian lines. Below we tell of the opening phases of this, the fourth of the great German offensives launched in the war against the Soviet.

OUTSIDE the Sportspalast in Berlin on Oct. 3 Nazi soldiers and storm troopers were rattling the collection boxes, while within the great hall the Fuehrer opened the Winter Help Campaign. But Hitler had little to say of the *Winterhilfe*; rather he had come to announce the launching of what he hoped would be the final blow against the Soviet power.

"In this very hour," he said dramatically, "a new, gigantic event is in progress on the Eastern Front. In the last 48 hours operations have been started which will assist me to smash our enemy in the east . . ." A few hours before, in his Order of the Day to the German soldiers, he had spoken in similar vein.

Opening on October 2, the "gigantic event" to which Hitler referred revealed itself as a pincers movement against Moscow delivered by the armies of Field Marshal Von Bock. The northern arm of the pincers operated from the area to the south of the Valdai Hills, 210 miles north-west of Moscow; while the southern arm came into operation from Roslavl, 75 miles south-east of Smolensk. At its outset the operation involved a front of about 160 miles, but this was ere long extended until for some 700 miles there was a fluid zone of furious war.

Onslaught Against Moscow

But in the main the offensive was directed against Moscow. Von Bock was reported to have under his command over 100 divisions, more than a million men. Many of them were fresh to the struggle; all were well equipped and organized. In the north General Hoth's panzers stormed ahead from Veliki Luki; and south of the Moscow highway General Guderian's tanks pushed rapidly ahead from Roslavl against Bryansk. Supporting them were the vast motorized infantry divisions of Field Marshal Von Kluge and General Von Strauss, while Kesselring's dive-bombers blasted a way before them. Opposed to them were Marshal Timoshenko's armies, inferior in numbers and perhaps in equipment, and tired by their counter-attacks at Yelnia.

For days the communiqués from either side were tantalizingly uninformative, although from unofficial reports issued in Moscow it was made plain that the German onslaught was the greatest, the fiercest in intensity, that had been experienced. Correspondents pictured wave on wave of dive-bombers, tremendous barrages by artillery of all calibres, hundreds of tanks locked in a deadly struggle, the plain swept by machine-gun fire, burnt by flame-throwers and loaded with wounded and dead. But Timoshenko's men were reported to be facing this inferno with their traditional bravery and without dismay; while the Red Air Force put up a performance which for brilliant audacity rivalled that of our own R.A.F. at Dunkirk.

The first concrete news of the fighting was given in a report from the Russian High Command on October 7, which said that particularly fierce fighting was taking place in the direction of Vyazma, Bryansk and Melitopol (near the Sea of Azov). Then came the significant admission that after fierce battles the Russian troops had evacuated Orel, an important railway-junction 75 miles south-east of Bryansk. The German communiqué of the same day opened by a reference to the panzer army which had advanced to the Sea of Azov and defeated the 9th Soviet Army near Melitopol; S.S. regiments had followed up the Russians to Mariupol, it

BRYANSK, about 200 miles south-west of Moscow, was evacuated by the Russians when part of Gen. Yeremenko's army had been encircled. Above are blocks of workers' flats in the town.

MURMANSK TO ROSTOV, showing the approximate battle positions in mid-October.
Photo, Planet News; Map, "Daily Telegraph"

was claimed. Then in the vital Moscow zone, "The break-through, which began in the central sector on October 2, has led to a new series of tremendous battles of destruction; in the Vyazma area alone several armies are encircled, and are proceeding irrevocably towards their destruction."

From these statements it was clear that the Russian situation was grave indeed. Both Vyazma and Bryansk lie some 60 miles to the east of the positions occupied by the Russians at the beginning of October; while as for Orel, it is separated by some 140 miles from the starting point of the vast offensive. Thus in a week the Germans had pushed Timoshenko far beyond Smolensk, and this following more than three months of almost incessant fighting and persistent attack. Timoshenko's gains in the Yelnia sector had been wiped out; and at Vyazma and Bryansk many thousands of Russian troops had been cut off. So terrific had been the punch, so swift the onset, that it says much for the Russian Marshal's generalship that he was able to withdraw most of his threatened divisions, and still maintain a fighting front before Moscow.

"Attacked by strong tank forces in the rear," announced Hitler from his headquarters on October 9, "three enemy armies are faced with annihilation in the Bryansk area. Together with troops already encircled at Vyazma, Marshal Timoshenko has sacrificed the last army capable of giving battle on the whole Soviet front." These vainglorious boastings were received with scoffing in Moscow. "Hitler's plan to encircle Timoshenko's forces has been thwarted," declared "Red Star," the Soviet Army newspaper on October 10, and the paper's correspondent described the reinforcements which were streaming to the front in endless columns.

"Fascist planes are trying to halt them, but are dealt with by our fighters," he wrote. "Column after column of lorries carrying troops and war material are passing the cross-roads I have chosen as my observation point. Infantrymen are sitting in the lorries with calm faces, gripping their tommy-guns, automatic rifles and machine-guns of all calibres . . . All the soldiers have new winter caps and warm winter greatcoats. Their underwear is warm and their boots are strong. Everything they have is new. Cavalry and artillery are following the infantry in unending columns. They are all fresh reserves. Colossal war machines are rolling along the edge of the road. They are the tanks the Germans are so afraid of."

Fall of Bryansk and Vyazma

But if Timoshenko's armies were not trapped, they were increasingly hard pressed as the German hordes drew ever nearer to Moscow. The northern arm of the pincers was encountering fierce resistance at Kalinin, south of the Valdai Hills; but the Germans at Vyazma were only 100 miles from Moscow, while their fellows in the Bryansk region to the south were now moving swiftly northwards, threatening to take Timoshenko's main forces in the rear. And all the time, while this great struggle was going on in the central sector the Germans maintained their pressure on Leningrad, and in the Sea of Azov region were claiming a fresh series of annihilating victories.

On October 12 Soviet headquarters announced the evacuation of Bryansk, and a day later that of Vyazma; both, the Germans claimed, had been left far behind by the battle. Then for a day or two there was a comparative lull. But on October 15 the drive was again in full strength, and Moscow heard at last the thunder of the enemy's guns.

At the End of the Road Piled High with Ger

Among the sights of Moscow the mausoleum (top) in which the body of Lenin lies in state ranks high in the affection of the loyal subjects of the Soviet Union. It stands in the Red Square by the walls of the Kremlin. Above is the House of the People's Commissars in Moscow.

Photos, Paul Popper, E.N.A. & Pictorial Press

ead: Moscow, Capital City of All the Russias

Sverdlov Square in the heart of Moscow, a scene of constant activity all day long. In this square stands the Grand (Bolshoi) Theatre, meeting-place of the All-Union Congress, pending the completion of the Palace of Soviets on the site of the Cathedral of the Redeemer, now pulled down.

N OF MOSCOW, capital of the U.S.S.R. The numbered sites on the (left) of the heart of the city are: 1, the Great Palace; 2, Headquarters he Central Executive Committee; 3, Cathedral of St. Basil; 4, Lenin's b; 5, Historical Museum; 6, Sverdlov Square; 7, Mostorg (Central rtment store); 8, Grand (Bolshoi) Theatre; 9, New Government se; 10, State Bank; 11, Moscow Art Theatre; 12, Moscow Soviet Hall); 13, Central Telegraph and Post Office; 14, U.S. Embassy; Moscow University (First); 16, Office of Pres. Kalinin; 17, Kremlin pital; 18, Central Market; 19, Lenin Library; 20, Palace of Soviets er construction); 21, Kammenyi Bridge; 22, Tretiakov State Art Gallery; 23, Moskva Bridge; 24, Main power station.

Left, the All-Union Lenin Library, formerly the Rumiantsev Library, one of the largest libraries in the world. Above, the offices of the Moscow Transport Board, on Krasnovorotskaia Square, seen from the entrance to the Red Gate Underground station.

Plan by courtesy of "The New York Journal-American"

The Germans are Bridging the Sahara by Rail

North African natives breaking stones to form a foundation for a great new railway across the Sahara. Right, the three-metre-high trackway.

NORTH-WEST AFRICA, showing the routes of the Trans-Saharan railway now under construction by German engineers with the support of Vichy. At Segou it will connect with the present light railway from Dakar.

THE TRANS-SAHARAN RAILWAY has made considerable progress near Colomb-Bechar. Left, natives laying the metals ; above, the foundation for the line across the desert. These photographs from a French source are proof that Nazi-controlled France is not only planning the New Order in North-West Africa, but is looking towards America ; Dakar is 1,900 miles—only eight hours' flying time—from Brazil. Thus this vast engineering project has a strategic significance.

Photos, E.N.A. and Keystone

In the Market of Athens Dejection Reigns

FROM OCCUPIED GREECE has been smuggled this remarkable photograph of the fishmarket in Athens. The empty stalls and dejected stallholders are an apt commentary on Hitler's New Order, one of whose inevitable results is the starvation of all the unhappy folk who come under his sway. The food markets of Europe have been looted to feed the Nazis. Such is the logical conclusion of " guns before butter," and the criminal ideal of a Herrenvolk. The Nazis believe themselves born to rule the world. Others may die to serve their monstrous vanity.   *Photo, Associated Press*

Our Diary of the War

MONDAY, OCT. 6, 1941   765th day
Air.—Enemy shipping attacked off Ostend.
Russian Front.—New German offensive developed into two pincer thrusts towards Moscow.
Africa.—Shipping in Tripoli harbour attacked by R.A.F. bombers on night of Oct. 5-6. Benghazi also attacked. Workshops at Bardia bombed.
Mediterranean.—Naval aircraft attacked aerodromes and seaplane bases at Marsala, Catania and Gherbini.
Home.—Few enemy planes over coastal districts by night.
General.—Five more Czechs executed and all synagogues in Czechoslovakia closed by German decree. New Australian Cabinet formed.

TUESDAY, OCT. 7   766th day
Russian Front.—Terrific German onslaught along 350 miles of the central front from Valdai Hills to Bryansk.
Mediterranean.—Admiralty announced eleven more Axis ships sunk or seriously damaged by torpedoes. Piraeus, port of Athens, attacked by bombers of R.A.F. on night of Oct. 6-7. Tripoli harbour also attacked.
Home.—Greatest Army manoeuvres ever held in Britain ended. Enemy night raiders over S. Wales and coasts of S. and W. England.
General.—Arrangements for repatriation of British and German sick and wounded prisoners of war finally cancelled.

WEDNESDAY, OCT. 8   767th day
Air.—Naval aircraft attacked enemy shipping and communications in the Vest Fjord area of Norway. Supply ships hit off Bodo on Salton Fiord.
Russian Front.—Germans claimed to have reached Vyazma. Moscow admitted evacuation of Orel. Germans claimed successes towards Melitopol, near Sea of Azov.
Africa.—Tripoli harbour and landing grounds at Gazala attacked during night of Oct. 7-8. Day attack on motor transport between Misurata and Sirte.

THURSDAY, OCT. 9   768th day
Air.—Enemy shipping attacked off Ostend and Cherbourg. Hurricanes raided Ostend and offensive sweeps were carried out over enemy occupied territory. Night attack on Aalesund, Norway.
Russian Front.—Fierce fighting in the neighbourhood of Vyazma, Bryansk and Melitopol.
Mediterranean.—Comiso aerodrome and enemy shipping in Mediterranean attacked on night of Oct. 8-9.
Home.—A few bombs on S.W. coast at night.

FRIDAY, OCT. 10   769th day
Air.—Shipping attacked off Dutch coast. Night attack over Calais area, as well as on Cologne, the Ruhr, and the docks at Rotterdam, Ostend, Dunkirk and Boulogne.
Russian Front.—Fierce fighting around Briansk. Moscow denied German claim to have encircled Timoshenko's main forces.
Africa.—Benghazi raided on night of Oct. 9-10. Aerodromes at Berka and Benina attacked.
Home.—Single enemy plane dropped bombs in open ground near E. Coast at night.

SATURDAY, OCT. 11   770th day
Air.—Offensive sweeps over Occupied France. Night attack by Coastal Command against shipping and land targets on Norwegian coast.
Russian Front.—Fierce battles still raged in the Vyazma and Orel sectors.
Africa.—R.A.F. attacked enemy shipping in Gulf of Sirte.

Home.—Bombs dropped at two points in E. England after dark. One enemy aircraft destroyed.

SUNDAY, OCT. 12   771st day
Air.—Heavy night raids on Nuremberg, Bremen and a score of objectives in North and West Germany.
Russian Front.—Russians announced loss of Briansk.
Africa.—Harbours at Benghazi and Tripoli heavily raided on night of Oct. 11-12.
Mediterranean.—Italian convoy attacked during night of Oct. 11-12. Several ships hit by torpedoes and bombs.
Home.—Enemy night activity fairly widespread. Two German aircraft destroyed.

MONDAY, OCT. 13   772nd day
Air.—20 enemy aircraft destroyed during offensive sweep over N. France when chemical works and power station were bombed near Mazingarbe, near Béthune. British losses 12 fighters and 1 bomber. Night attacks on Western Germany and on Channel ports and objectives in N. France.
Russian Front.—Enemy drive for Moscow continued, but German progress slower. Russians announced evacuation of Vyazma.
Home.—A few bombs dropped by night over E. England and Home Counties.

TUESDAY, OCT. 14   773rd day
Air.—Beauforts attacked enemy shipping off Norway. Spitfires attacked military targets in the Cherbourg peninsula. Bomber Command attacked targets in S. Germany by night.
Russian Front.—New threat to Moscow developed from the north-west. Fierce fighting around Kalinin.
Africa.—British patrol captured enemy post near Tobruk.
Home.—Few night raiders over E. Coast.
General.—77th French victim of German "reprisals" executed in Paris.

WEDNESDAY, OCT. 15   774th day
Air.—Enemy shipping attacked off Dutch coast and in the docks at Le Havre. Night attack on French coast from Dunkirk to Calais, and targets in W. Germany.
Russian Front.—Fierce fighting around Kalinin, Briansk and Vyazma. Germans claimed capture of Borodino.

General.—Air Chief Marshal Sir R. Brooke-Popham arrived at Melbourne for discussions with Australian Air Staff.

THURSDAY, OCT. 16   775th day
Air.—Offensive sweep over Holland and N. France. Heavy raid on Le Havre. Night attack on targets in Western Germany. Docks at Dunkirk, Ostend and Calais also attacked.
Russian Front.—Rumanians claimed to have marched into Odessa. A Rumanian army under Gen. Jacobici entered the town from which the Red Army defenders had been successfully evacuated by units of the Soviet fleet. Odessa's war industries were completely destroyed by its defenders before they left. Soviet Government reported to have left Moscow.
Africa.—Heavy bombers of R.A.F. raided Benghazi on night of Oct. 15-16.
Home.—A few enemy planes over E. Coast. One enemy bomber destroyed.
General.—Japanese cabinet resigned.

FRIDAY, OCT. 17   776th day
Air.—Coastal Command attacked enemy shipping off Norwegian coast. Night attack on coasts of N. France and Belgium by cannon-firing Hurricanes. Two armed trawlers set on fire.
Russian Front.—Moscow announced a successful counter-attack at Kalinin and a slackening of German pressure north of Orel. British military and diplomatic missions left Moscow at request of Soviet authorities. Guerillas in the Kalinin district killed over 1,000 German soldiers, set fire to over 200 ammunition lorries and blew up scores of bridges and pontoons.
Africa.—Bombing and machine-gun raids by R.A.F. on motor transports in Tripolitania. Aerodrome at Ez Zauia attacked.
Mediterranean.—Heavy bombers of R.A.F. raided Naples on night of October 16-17. Many factories hit. Daylight raid on seaplane base at Syracuse.
General.—General Hideki Tojo entrusted with formation of new Japanese cabinet. U.S. destroyer Kearny torpedoed in Atlantic. American House of Representatives approved arming of U.S. merchantmen.

MERCY SHIPS, the Dinard and St. Julien, floodlit at Newhaven. At the beginning of October plans were far advanced for the exchange of a number of severely wounded German prisoners for a number of British soldiers in Nazi hands. But the scheme fell through. The German were re-embarked, and the lights were extinguished in the early hours of Oct. 7.   *Photo, Fox*

Who Will Join the Women in Blue and Khaki?

WRENS have now taken over duties with the Fleet Air Arm as well as serving with the Navy. Two of them are here shown being instructed in the intricacies of packing parachutes, a job which calls for skilful fingers.

W.A.A.F. code and cipher officers have lately taken up duties with the R.A.F. Middle East Command. Above, Wing Officer F. M. Hayes discusses the business of the day with Flight Officer M. M. Bevan.

A.T.S. poster, issued in connexion with a big recruiting drive in September 1941; it was painted by Cpl. Games, R.E., War Office artist.

A.T.S. TRANSPORT SECTION at a West Country Depot taking a course of motorcycle riding are negotiating a ford under the watchful eyes of their instructors. Left, Private Mary Churchill, youngest daughter of the Prime Minister, who has just joined the A.T.S.   *Photos, British Official: Crown Copyright; Fox, Keystone, "Daily Mirror"*

Gas May Yet Be Used in This War

Nearly two years have passed since we published (Vol. I., p. 534) an article in which it was stated that expert opinion was then almost unanimous in believing that it was very unlikely that gas would be used in this war. That view has not yet been falsified by experience ; but, in view of the many warnings issued by Government spokesmen, it is obvious that the possibility—some would say, the probability—still exists.

I N the last Great War gas was used within nine months of the opening of hostilities, but it has not yet been employed in this. It was used by the Italians in Abyssinia with the most horrible results, and from time to time there have been reports of its use in China : only the other day it was said that the Japanese were using it on the Ichang front. If it *is* used against us, then it will be probably as an accompaniment to an invasion attempt, since of all the weapons in the modern armoury gas may be credited with the most panic-raising effects.

Such panic, however, would be almost certainly the result of ignorance and unpreparedness, rather than of its lethal qualities. We know something of the effects of high explosive and incendiary bombs, but as yet gas has all the terror of the unknown. Yet, judging from past experience, gas is a far less deadly weapon than the H.E. bomb.

" Mustard gas is the most humane weapon ever invented," Mr. J. B. S. Haldane has written in one of his essays. " Of the casualties from mustard gas during the late war there were 170,000 in the British Army alone. Three per cent or less died, and less than one per cent were permanently incapacitated—a very low proportion compared with the casualties from other weapons."

This view is supported by Mr. C. W. Glover in his book, " Civil Defence." In the Great War, he tells us, while gas caused 5·7 per cent of all non-fatal battle injuries, it was responsible for only 1·32 per cent of all battle deaths. Only one casualty resulted from each 230 lb. of lung gas used ; it took 60 lb. of blister gas to cause a casualty, and 650 lb. of eye, nose and chest irritant gas ; 6,000 tons of tear gas caused not a single casualty. On an average, there was only one casualty for each 192 lb. of gas. Another

point to be remembered is that in hospital gas cases recovered in about half the time that was required for other wounded.

" The judgement of future generations on the use of gas," General Hartley has written, " may well be influenced by the pathetic appeal of Sargent's picture of the first ' Mustard Gas ' casualties at Ypres, but it must not be forgotten in looking at that picture that 75 per cent of the blinded men he drew were fit for duty within three months, and that, had their limbs and nerves been shattered by the effects of high explosive, their fate would have been infinitely worse."

If There Is a Gas Attack

In the event of a gas attack against this country, poisonous gases of either non-persistent or persistent type might be discharged from aircraft, either in the form of bombs or (in the case of the latter) in the shape of liquid spray. It is possible that clouds of gas might be released from ships approaching the shore at some distance. The most dangerous and most effective attack might be by gas bombs on large cities, where the buildings are closely packed, and there is little opportunity for the gas cloud to be dissipated by cross currents of air. The attack might be made at night, when aircraft can operate most securely ; but, on the other hand, an attack in daylight might be expected to catch thousands of people in the open streets. In any case, gas bombs would probably be accompanied by high explosive, which would blast windows and walls and would destroy, or at least seriously hamper, anti-gas precautions.

When a bomb bursts in a street a poison cloud is formed which may rise rapidly to roof level and move along the street, according to the direction and velocity of the wind.

A nurse working a baby's respirator during a mock gas-attack at Esher. Mothers with infants should make a point of regular practice with baby's respirator. *Photo, Topical*

Two danger zones may be distinguished : (a) one in which concentration is so high as to be fatal to unprotected persons, and (b) one in which, though the concentration is so high that the risk of becoming a casualty is great, yet there will be plenty of time for the donning of respirators. On the fringe of this zone the gas will still be sufficiently strong to cause watering of the eyes and severe coughing. In a long street of terraced houses, with few or no side turnings, the length of the first zone may be as much as 1,200 yards ; in streets with semi-detached houses and cross-roads it may be as short as 300 yards. When there is no wind a gas cloud may take about 14 minutes to disappear in summer, and 20 minutes in winter ; though the time is affected, of course, by the closeness or otherwise of the buildings and the condition of the atmosphere. In a dense fog, or a completely enclosed courtyard, the cloud might take as long as an hour to disperse.

Against clouds of phosgene, the non-persistent gas most likely to be used as being one of the most deadly, the respirator is claimed to be a complete protection. Against mustard gas vapour and spray, the respirator protects the face, eyes, and lungs, but the outer clothing is likely to become contaminated. Moreover, while phosgene is quickly dissipated in a light wind, mustard gas is persistent, and an area splashed may remain dangerous for hours, perhaps days

Carry Your Gas Masks !

Since before the war members of the Civil Defence services have been trained in anti-gas protection, and their knowledge has been refreshed and kept up to date by frequent practice. So far as the general public is concerned they are required to do little more than to carry their gas masks. But, needless to say, they should also know how to put them on and " make it snappy." Gas, it should be stressed time and again, is preeminently a panic weapon ; against a people properly protected and possessed of a proper knowledge of what gas can and cannot do, it is likely to prove a very blunt weapon indeed.

R.A.M.C. men, wearing their anti-gas apparel, carrying a casualty out of a smoke-screen. Note how the gloves are worn over the sleeves, and the ankles are strapped to prevent gas from reaching the skin. Properly adjusted this uniform is a complete protection.

Photo, Daily Mirror

They 'Tried Out' an Invasion of Britain

SOVIET EYE-WITNESSES hear Brigadier Firebrace explaining operations during the recent large-scale manoeuvres which extended over half of England.

By night as well as by day British armoured units played a great part in these Army exercises in which hundreds of thousands of men were engaged.

Taking no chances against possible fifth-columnists, the defenders closely inspected civilians' credentials. Left, gunner of a Westland Lysander with an Army Cooperation Squadron. Right, Gen. Sir Alan Brooke, C.-in-C. Home Forces, watching the battle from an air liner.

LANDING FROM BARGES on the shores of a remote Scottish loch, British shock troops of the Combined Training Command recently showed the King the technique of modern raiding warfare. Together with a group of high naval and military officers, His Majesty watched the men practising beach landings, raids and assaults. Once the barges had grounded the steel platforms crashed down and the troops leapt ashore and at once charged towards their objectives.

Photos, British Official: Crown Copyright; Associated Press. Fox. Barratt's, Planet News, Sport & General

H.M.S. Malaya Rides the Storm of Bombs

BOMBS BURSTING close to H.M.S. Malaya. Mountainous columns of black and white smoke and spray are rising all round the battleship. At the top of the page the Malaya passing safely through the inferno. In the centre, a clear view of this 31,100-ton battleship, originally a gift to Britain from the Federated Malay States. She underwent a £1,000,000 refit a few years ago. The ship's motto is "In the care of God," and her badge is shown in the inset, top left.

Photos, Associated Press; Badge, Copyright of Controller of H.M. Stationery Office

Cheers for the Lady Shirley and Seawolf

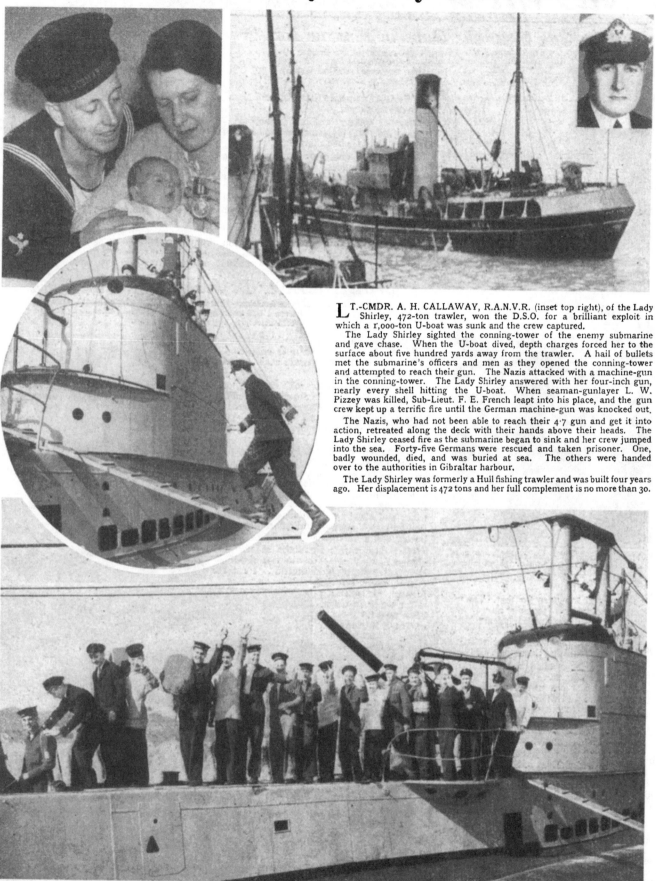

LT.-CMDR. A. H. CALLAWAY, R.A.N.V.R. (inset top right), of the Lady Shirley, 472-ton trawler, won the D.S.O. for a brilliant exploit in which a 1,000-ton U-boat was sunk and the crew captured.

The Lady Shirley sighted the conning-tower of the enemy submarine and gave chase. When the U-boat dived, depth charges forced her to the surface about five hundred yards away from the trawler. A hail of bullets met the submarine's officers and men as they opened the conning-tower and attempted to reach their gun. The Nazis attacked with a machine-gun in the conning-tower. The Lady Shirley answered with her four-inch gun, nearly every shell hitting the U-boat. When seaman-gunlayer L. W. Pizzey was killed, Sub-Lieut. F. E. French leapt into his place, and the gun crew kept up a terrific fire until the German machine-gun was knocked out.

The Nazis, who had not been able to reach their 4·7 gun and get it into action, retreated along the deck with their hands above their heads. The Lady Shirley ceased fire as the submarine began to sink and her crew jumped into the sea. Forty-five Germans were rescued and taken prisoner. One, badly wounded, died, and was buried at sea. The others were handed over to the authorities in Gibraltar harbour.

The Lady Shirley was formerly a Hull fishing trawler and was built four years ago. Her displacement is 472 tons and her full complement is no more than 30.

THE SEAWOLF off to sea again after a refit, her crew indicating their indomitable spirit with hand-waves and victory signs. Circle, the Submarine's captain strides up the gangway with confident and jaunty step. Top left, Leading Stoker Owen Wood, with his wife, baby, and the D.S.M. which he won for gallant work in that branch of H.M. Forces which Mr. Churchill, on Sept. 9, referred to as " the most dangerous of all the Services," and praised " for their skill and devotion which have proved of inestimable value to the life of our country."

Photos, " Daily Mirror," Central Press, and Press Portrait Bureau

I Was There! .... Eye Witness Stories of the War

'We Can Hear the Guns in Moscow Now'

The spirit which pervaded Moscow under the shadow of the German on-slaught was vividly depicted in the following dispatch which the Russian journalist, Ilya Ehrenburg, sent from the threatened city on Sunday, October 12, when the Germans were some 70 miles away.

W E can hear the grumbling of distant guns in Moscow now. They are the guns near Vyazma, where our brothers are fighting. Hearing them, women stop for a moment in the street, and think of what is happening out there—and then hurry on faster to their munition factories.

They pass long columns of fresh troops going out to battle. They see tanks lumbering along, and munition convoys speeding westward. At the railway stations they see many trainloads of reinforcements departing to plunge into the desperate struggle.

There is not much cheering. Everybody is

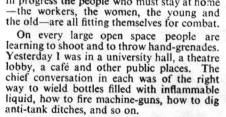

Mitya Afonin, a Russian schoolboy who put out eight incendiaries which fell on a school roof in Moscow. He is erecting a fire-extinguisher.
Photo, British Official

too busy and too stern for that. The whole vast movement is forging ahead like a machine expertly controlled. And while it is in progress the people who must stay at home —the workers, the women, the young and the old—are all fitting themselves for combat.

On every large open space people are learning to shoot and to throw hand-grenades. Yesterday I was in a university hall, a theatre lobby, a café and other public places. The chief conversation in each was of the right way to wield bottles filled with inflammable liquid, how to fire machine-guns, how to dig anti-tank ditches, and so on.

In fact, this old city has become a gigantic fortress with a garrison of millions.

I was at a big war factory the other day. I saw faces grey with tiredness. Many of the women had been there three days, refusing to leave for rest. They were helping their husbands at the front.

They worked on even when enemy bombers were directly overhead, when the noise of anti-aircraft fire was drowning the hum of their industry. They worked on even when they heard that whistling noise you in the towns of Britain know so well.

I asked one of them how many hours of sleep she was getting. She said, almost fiercely, " It is a sin to sleep now. I shall not sleep while they are dying out there." It

is difficult to persuade them that a little rest means more output.

Only for military training is work interrupted. And that is the case with all kinds of activities. Here is one example :

Classes were going on as usual at the Institute of Ceramics. Girls were painting flowers on porcelain. Suddenly one stood up and said, " We must learn to throw bottle-grenades ! We're wasting time here." All the girls supported her suggestion. They marched out to the training field.

I saw the " proposer of the resolution " later—a pleasant, snub-nosed little person called Galya. She said, " Each one of us has resolved to kill at least one Nazi—whatever

happens to us. We want to go out there now, and start." She pointed in the direction of the west.

Later, I met the actors at the Kamerny Theatre. They had been studying machine-gun parts for two hours before they put on their grease-paint. With me was a young student of literature, a disciple of Shelley. He had been digging anti-tank ditches all day.

We Russians have always imagined our capital as a woman. We see her now as our wife or mother in danger.

In churches this morning prayers went up for our defenders. Old women queued up to give their wedding rings and crucifixes to the Defence Fund. Young people practised Civil Defence.

It was all quiet and grim. And yet the German wireless announces that there is confusion here !

Our own radio answers the lie. On all the front lines, from Murmansk to the Crimea, the calm voice of Moscow is heard expressing undying resistance. The voice of the broadcaster is the voice of all the millions in this city today.—" *Daily Herald.*"

'Shall We Ever Be Picked Up?' We Asked

Three survivors of the American-owned ship Sessa, sunk by a U-boat, were landed in Iceland from a U.S. destroyer early in September, after being (as told below) 19 days adrift on a raft.

H ENRIK BJERREGAARD, Danish first officer of the Sessa, was still crippled by frostbite and exposure when he told the following story.

We left New York with a cargo of supplies for the American forces in Iceland. After some time at sea we were torpedoed at midnight, and then shelled by the U-boat as the ship sank. She went down in two minutes.

I had no lifebelt, but I grabbed a pole as I was thrown into the water. A seaman joined me, and we hung on for two hours. Then we floated to a lifeboat which was upside down, and found four more of the crew sitting astride the keel. We joined them, and stayed on the lifeboat all night. Besides myself there were three Portuguese, a Swede, and a Canadian.

Next day a raft from the ship drifted alongside, and as we could not right the boat we all jumped on the raft. I cut the canvas cover off the lifeboat, s w i m m i n g under water to do it. Then we put the cover on the raft to make a roof. After seeing we had a drum of water and tin of biscuits, I cut a sliver off the raft and started a log.

Every day at sunrise I made a notch to mark another day. After the tenth day on

SESSA, a former Danish ship which was flying the Panamanian flag when sunk in Arctic waters. Top, Henrik Bjerregaard, first officer ; centre, the log which he kept on a piece of wood until he and two companions on a raft were rescued. His story is printed in this page.
Photos, Bippa and Wide World

the raft one man died, and on the thirteenth two more died. One of the men was the Canadian, and another a Portuguese. To mark their deaths I cut a little cross into my wooden log above the day of the month.

We had a sip of water each day and hard biscuits. When the water ran out we caught rainwater. On the seventeenth day all our water went, and our throats were so parched that we could not eat anything.

The sea was moderate most of the time, but it was impossible to go right off to sleep. We should have been washed off. When I got to Reykjavik I had my first night's sleep for three weeks.

Every sunrise as I notched my log my two remaining companions, the Swede and the Portuguese, asked : " Shall we ever be picked up ? '' Every day I said " Yes. We are drifting towards Iceland. A fishing-boat will see us.''

I was quite confident that I should live through it. On the eighteenth day we saw smoke on the horizon, but to our intense disappointment it faded away.

Then on the 19th day, as I lay utterly exhausted, I heard to my joy a ship's siren and raised myself weakly to see the Stars and Stripes of an American destroyer.

There were 27 men in the Sessa, and all the others must be lost. Our ship was flying the Panama flag. We were a Danish ship taken over by the American Government.—"*Daily Express* ''

After an R.A.F. raid on Bremen more than a year ago ; today the results are much worse. A Czech writes in this page about what the R.A.F. has done in Germany.　*Photo, Keystone*

Our Life as Czech Labourers in Germany

The unhappy fate of the Czechs in their homeland is described in page 206. Here is an account of the harsh experience of Czech workers transported to Germany for forced labour, given by one of them to H. O. Brandon.

BEFORE I was sent to Germany I was helping to build a villa for a Czech mayor in my home town. Suddenly all construction work in the district was stopped by the German authorities. Only work on important factories in the neighbourhood was to be completed.

When my colleagues and I had to register as unemployed at the Labour Exchange, a German officer was present. Two days later I received a printed letter telling me to be at the railway station at a certain time to go to my next job—unspecified. Out of work and hungry I decided to go and see. My colleagues were also at the station, and only when we approached the German frontier did we know our fate.

There are now about 100,000 Czech building workers forced to labour in Germany. Members of our trade form the largest contingent ; there are about 20,000 Czech metal workers besides. Our group of Czech workers in Bremen numbered about 3,000.

Our pay, actually the only sign that we were not prisoners, was about 35 per cent less than that of Germans. Expenses for our communal kitchen were deducted beforehand, and every month we had to give different " voluntary '' donations to institutions such as the German Red Cross, " Winterhilfe,'' and so on. Our food was officially of the same standard as for prisoners of war. We had some kind of soup daily ; its ingredients could not be specified. Three of us shared one unbreakable tin plate. We slept in some kind of barracks and were watched day and night by S.S. men. We were not allowed to buy clothing, and when relatives at home were asked to send us clothes they never reached us. We were supplied with a kind of sackcloth uniform.

The Gestapo and S.S. not only watch foreigners on forced labour—they watch the German workers, too. In their own factories, indeed, the Germans are under observation like convicts. If a German worker does not perform a certain minimum of work, or if he offends against discipline, he is thrown into the factory concentration camp. I am not speaking of sabotage, for which the punishment is death, but of minor offences. It is an offence, for instance, if a word is heard that sounds like grumbling. In the concentration camp the offending worker remains a prisoner until the supervisor thinks he has been cured by the camp's disciplinary methods.

These methods vary, but prisoners will be set to work on tasks of no practical use to break their spirit. They will be set to carry steel bars from one end of the camp to the other and back again. The monotony and stupidity and strain and fatigue soon show their effects.

This is the situation of a " free German worker,'' which cannot, of course, be compared with ours ; we are foreigners, belonging to a lower race. We have no right to holidays or to visit our family ; many of the foreign labourers have not seen their relatives for 18 months. Money for their support is being deducted from wages, but no one knows whether it reaches them.

The Nazis compel foreign workers to take up work in Germany not only because their scheme is devised as one of the means by which whole nations can be annihilated. For months and years these men are being kept away from their homeland, their families, their cultural life ; they cannot read in their own language and have little opportunity to speak it.

Families are deliberately scattered all over Greater Germany, for it is a rule that a son is never sent to the same place as his father, and brother never allowed to work with brother. The young generation are thus losing contact with their own soil and with their own fellows. There is no chance for them to find a wife of their own nationality, and, of course, they are not allowed to marry a German girl. The whole scheme is designed to sap the existence of a nation.

I was shifted about a lot during my involuntary stay in Germany, being sent to Berlin, Stettin, Hamburg and Bremen. Bremen was the worst ; we had bombs everywhere, and when we arrived some days after a raid the ruins of the wrecked buildings were still smoking. We were mostly employed in clearing destroyed buildings, never the docks ; but we knew from others that there were whole districts wiped out and that traffic was stopped for days after each raid.

Although we were not allowed to go to shelters, during sudden panics I sometimes entered a public one and listened to the " Voice of the People.'' You would not believe what the Germans dare to say in public about their " beloved '' Fuehrer and his gang—things we should never dare to say in Prague. But nearly all that I heard finished up like this : " Even though we don't like our leaders, and even though we detest the war, we must fight on to the bitter end. We have gone too far. The existence of the German people is at stake. We cannot retreat now.'' The most discussed question was whether the United States would enter the war, and all who experienced the last war openly say that that will be the crucial point.—"*Daily Telegraph* ''

Siftings From the News

Turkeys have been changing hands at £3 each.

There are now about 18,000 members of the Woman's Land Army.

West Ham has been presented with a Travelling Dispensary by Philadelphia, U.S.A.

New York's Mayor La Guardia has urged the purchase of 50,000,000 gas masks.

A portrait of Paderewski by the late Princess Louise, painted in the 'nineties, has been presented to the Polish Ambassador.

The cost of repairing Croydon's bomb-damaged property up to May 31 last was £282,248.

4,500,000,000 bricks are needed for the new war factories, hostels for war-workers and first-aid repairs.

The Cyprus garrison is now the strongest in the history of the island.

Radiolocation was used in Russia in 1937 to guide fog-bound ships.

The Dutch royal family's property in Holland has been stolen by the Nazis.

People of Mufulira, N. Rhodesia, have contributed £2,500 for British war charities.

An army of 100,000 Free French fighting men is being formed at Brazzaville, French Equatorial Africa.

At 83, Mr. Cottrill of Birmingham is making essential parts for aircraft.

Coxswain Blogg, of Cromer, has been awarded the Gold Medal of the Royal National Lifeboat Institution for the third time.

Miss E. Duncan holds the world record for making 6,130 A.A. shell components in a six-day week.

Convicts in Britain's penal establishments have produced £500,000 worth of war material in one year.

Ancient Egyptian tombs, their mummies removed, are providing air-raid shelters for Siwa oasis people, in the Western Desert.

The Falls of Glomach, Ross-shire, are now part of the National Trust for Scotland.

Roast cygnet may be a wartime dish if the Ministry of Food give permission to kill cygnets for food purposes.

A.F.S. men are using Dr. Johnson's house, Gough Square, as a rest centre.

A South Norwood boy of ten is raising money for a Spitfire fund by lending books to playmates at 1d. a week.

Editor's Postscript

JOURNEYING to my country home this smiling afternoon of early autumn the thought that came uppermost in my mind was the futility of air war against a land where any good defence could be put up. Here we were in an electric express, seated in a comfortable Pullman, rushing through scenes of pastoral beauty and considerable industrial activity over which thousands of aeroplanes in numberless combats had been engaged and many thousands of tons of bombs had been dropped during two years of war, yet once beyond the suburbs not a sign of any kind to suggest there was a war on, or any war had ever been ! I would even venture to prophesy that in two years from now that same countryside will look exactly as it did this afternoon, when it looked much as I have known it over forty years and as I have passed through it several times a week for sixteen years. All over the British Isles this afternoon trains were streaming along gleaming railway lines where the heated imagination of Hitler had foreseen nothing but devastation wrought by his " finest air force in the world " which he had commanded Goering to provide for him. Rather wonderful, don't you think ? And the moral is that air power alone will conquer no country. Poland and Holland succumbed not merely to aerial attack, but to the coordination of that with mechanized land attack.

ENORMOUS ruin has been wrought in many of our great cities and coastal towns, and but for the silver streak that so fortunately separates our homeland from Hunland Hitler might not have needed to explain to his fellow-Huns why his long-threatened invasion of England had been postponed. But no silver streak, and the whole course of European history would have been changed long before Hitler ever mixed a pail of paste. Not that I have ceased to believe in the possibility of an attempt at invasion, but the improbability of its success has increased every month that has passed since Dunkirk. On the other hand, when I hear complaints about our not invading the Continent, where millions are awaiting deliverance at our hands, I realize that many a day may have to pass before we are in any position to carry the War into Germany other than by air, and though our beautiful bombs on Berlin will greatly help they cannot force a decision.

SO long as the present astrology craze amuses people and they don't take it seriously, perhaps no great harm results. There is certainly " entertainment value '.' in it. But when one reads the announcement at the annual convention of the American Federation of Scientific (*sic*) Astrologers that " Hitler's star is setting ; he is on the downgrade ; his move on Russia was a great mistake ; and although *we cannot predict the date* of his defeat, it is certain that *if* the U.S. enters the War before next spring he is doomed," one is moved less by amusement than derision and contempt. No stars are needed to tell us these things, and the

words I have italicized indicate the quackery of the business in its higher reaches.

HERE is a paragraph by an English exponent of the so-called science : " There can be no doubt of the tension which I predicted would be upon us this week-end. If you feel anxious, please remember that the tide of battle now turning cannot but make for nervousness. The main thing is that the tide goes now in *our* direction." The stars told him that . . . the stars my foot ! And also " terrific news is on the way from France." The real sources of his knowledge are many millions of miles nearer than the nearest star : what the wireless calls " agency messages."

OCCASIONALLY in an idle moment, to test these scanners of the firmament I have looked at the daily horoscope of my birthday, and while admiring the adroitness with which the words are framed to suit almost any human creature born anywhere on earth on any of the 365 days which go to make a year, I have never struck one that I could identify with my own particular case. This today is an example : " Memorable week-end. New opportunities for contact with interesting people. Welcome news arrives by post, but watch £ s. d." Wrong on every point, so far as I am concerned. But little these bright lads reck : they eat their own words as easily, and with as great a relish, as their eggs and bacon (I put egg in the plural as they can doubtless see more than I can).

NOT one " astrologer " on this planet—not one, I repeat—foresaw the date of the War : without exception they divined the message of the stars as making for Peace !

I defy the whole brood of them to predict its end ! Science, indeed ! Modern astrology has the same relationship to science as the spotting of winners for the 3.30. That, and no more. But in ancient times, before it was discovered that the earth was not the fixed centre of the universe with the sun and moon and multitudinous stars circling about it, the element of primitive science was not absent, and out of it the true science of astronomy was eventually born. The abracadabra in which its exponents deal today dates back to the dark ages before astronomy, to times when even the finest intellects in Ancient Rome believed in signs and portents, and looked for revelations in the reeking entrails of sacrificial animals.

WHY do people shout on the telephone and bellow on the microphone ? I ask this, remembering that I once had to part company with an assistant editor because he disturbed the whole staff by screaming at the pitch of his voice when using the phone and just couldn't get out of the habit. And tonight I have been listening to Lord Beaverbrook broadcasting his vivid, informative and business like talk on his most business-like mission to Moscow in accents that were better suited to a Hyde Park orator on a soap-box trying with his naked voice to gather an audience than to a broadcaster in a sound-proof room speaking in front of a world-resounding microphone.

THERE is, I think, something to do with nerves in this quite foolish habit of shouting into an instrument which can enormously magnify one's voice so that a mere whisper will go round the globe in a flash that makes Ariel's promise to girdle it in forty minutes sound extraordinarily out of date. Merchant mariner Laskier, whose very dramatic broadcast from a Liverpool café a week or so back brought him a spot of fame overnight, spoke in a tone that seldom rose above the voice of a speaker who had lost his vocal cords, yet I'm sure it was as clear and audible to the millions of listeners as Lord Beaverbrook's loudest passages, which lost from over-emphasis. There is no more surprising thing than to hear your own voice recorded for the first time. They told me at Elstree when I was recording the commentary to " Forgotten Men " years ago that a famous American stage actress got so great a fright on hearing her voice for the first time as it issued from the sound track that she fled the studio and had to be sought at her hotel in London, where she was contemplating throwing up her contract !

HAVE just had a mystery explained to me : the recurring lack of shillings in shopkeepers' tills. I had to take eight sixpences the other day in place of four shillings. At other times the familiar bob seems to be in ample supply. Explanation : gas and electric meters. When housewives are using their shilling meters a lot they save up shillings so that they may not have to go short of light or heat at a critical moment, then with the periodical clearances of the meters the accumulated shillings go back into circulation just to become scarce once more before another clearing time comes round.

MARSHAL TIMOSHENKO, 47-year-old commander of the Red armies in the central sector, is a native of Bessarabia. Conscripted into the Tsar's army in 1914, he became a Marshal of the Soviet Union in 1940. *From the portrait by V. Yakalev*

Printed in England and published on the 10th, 20th and 30th of each month by the Proprietors, The Amalgamated Press, Ltd., The Fleetway House, Farringdon Street, London, E.C.4. Registered for transmission by Canadian Magazine Post. Sole Agents for Australia and New Zealand : Messrs. Gordon & Gotch, Ltd. ; and for South Africa : Central News Agency, Ltd. October 30th, 1941.   S.S.   *Editorial Address :* JOHN CARPENTER HOUSE, WHITEFRIARS, LONDON, E.C.4.

Vol 5 # The War Illustrated Nº 111

Edited by Sir Jonn Hammerton

FOURPENCE

NOV. 10TH, 1941

WAR FLAMES IN KIEV. Soon after they entered Kiev on September 19 the Germans claimed that the capital of the Ukraine was less damaged than other towns they had occupied, although the Russians before withdrawing had destroyed the power-stations, waterworks and various war industries. But a week or so later thousands of time-bombs and radio-controlled mines began to go off, and the centre of the city was laid in ruins. Prominent in this German photograph is a Russian traffic-control signal. *Photo, Associated Press*

WHAT ARE WE TO MAKE OF GORT'S DISPATCHES?

Dated April 25 and July 25, 1940, Lord Gort's eagerly-awaited Dispatches, covering the history of the British Expeditionary Force from its landing at Cherbourg in September 1939 to its re-embarkation from Dunkirk at the end of May 1940, have just been published.* No reasons are given for the delay in publication, nor is it clear why the present moment has been chosen—unless it be, as some have suggested, that the contents of the Dispatches are calculated to answer those critics of our military effort who have been urging that a second front should be opened in the west so as to relieve the pressure on our Russian allies in the east. Certainly, in his Dispatches the B.E.F.'s Commander-in-Chief has expressed himself with a candour that is as remarkable as it is refreshing.

From the first Dispatch we learn that the existing war establishment of an infantry battalion was not designed for continental warfare, and had called for modification. The criticisms are much more detailed and comprehensive in the second Dispatch. In the opening paragraphs there is a reference to serious deficiencies in stocks which could not be made good since it had been decided that the programme of shipments to France had to be severely curtailed in February and March. On the next page Lord Gort tells us of the situation as regards equipment.

"I had on several occasions called the attention of the War Office to the shortage of almost every nature of ammunition of which the stocks in France were not nearly large enough to permit of the rates of expenditure laid down for sustained operations before the War. There was a shortage of guns in some of the anti-tank regiments of the Royal Artillery, while armour-piercing shells for field guns had not by May 10 been provided. There were also deficiencies in technical apparatus for light anti-aircraft requirements, such as Kerrison predictors, signal lights, technical and specialized vehicles of many types, and a number of smaller items . . ."

From later pages we learn that work on the lines of communication was hampered by the shortage of labour. As the battle developed there was a terrible deficiency of fighter aircraft. On May 23 the B.E.F. was placed on half rations, and the ammunition immediately available was only about 300 rounds per gun, the prospect of receiving any further supply being remote, since communications with the coast had been cut.

Another grave deficiency—perhaps the gravest of all—was that while the Germans were employing at least five armoured divisions against the British, our armoured forces in the theatre of war amounted to only " seven divisional cavalry regiments equipped with light tanks, one regiment of armoured cars of an obsolete pattern, and two battalions of infantry tanks, the latter, except for 23 Mark II tanks, being armed each with one machine-gun only." We had, it is true, an armoured division, but unfortunately it was not sent to France in time to come under Gort's command.

Against this background of shocking unpreparedness is set a story of brave and dogged achievement which

* Supplement to the London Gazette, October 17, 1941 : H.M. Stationery Office, 1s.

will be read with avid interest by all who went through Dunkirk and lived to tell the tale. Some incidents stand out from the terse, matter-of-fact narrative. We can share Gort's surprise when General Ironside, then Chief of the Imperial General Staff, descended on him at G.H.Q. in the middle of the battle, with instructions from the Cabinet that the B.E.F. was to move southwards upon Amiens, attacking all enemy forces encountered : fortunately, Ironside was swift to appreciate that the battle as seen from Wahagnies looked very different from what it did when glimpsed from Whitehall. We can ride beside the C.-in-C. in his car as it threads its slow and painful way through the crowds of refugees who blocked every road and path (" Scenes of misery were everywhere, and the distress of women, children and aged people was pitiable"). We see him opening his copy of Mr. Churchill's telegram to M. Reynaud, the French Prime Minister, demanding that " French Commanders in north and south, and Belgian G.Q.G. be given most stringent orders " to carry out the Weygand plan and "turn defeat into victory "; and a day later receiving the surprising intelligence that the French had recaptured Péronne, Albert and Amiens . . .

We can share his feelings when, following the collapse of the Belgian Army on his left, he was suddenly faced with an open gap of 20 miles between Ypres and the sea, through which enemy armoured forces might rush to reach the beaches from which the British Army was being evacuated ; and we can hear him urging General Blanchard that for the sake of France, the French Army and the Allied cause, General Prioux should be ordered back from Lille. " Surely, I said, his troops were not all so tired as to be in-

capable of moving . . ." Blanchard was obdurate, but their parting, we are told, was not unfriendly ; nor, let it be noted, is there the slightest indication in the Dispatches of any recrimination against King Leopold. The evacuation from Dunkirk was in progress before the Belgium capitulation.

Then there is the last scene when " Major-General Alexander, with the Senior Naval Officer (Captain W. G. Tennant, R.N.), made a tour of the beaches and harbour in a motor-boat, and on being satisfied that no British troops were left on shore, they themselves left for England." That was at midnight on June 2 ; in the past five days a fleet of ships, great and small, had successfully taken back across the Channel 211,532 fit men and 13,053 casualties of the B.E.F., in addition to 112,546 Allied troops.

So the B.E.F. got back to England. For eight months they had toiled like navvies in the mud, holding a tiny front beyond Lille. Then at 1 p.m. on May 10 had begun the rush into Belgium. The next day they marched into Louvain. They exchanged a few shots with the enemy, but since the German breakthrough at Sedan had left their flank in the air, they marched back again. After but 22 days of actual fighting the campaign was at an end.

Once again the Germans had proved their superiority. Lord Gort speaks admiringly of their willingness to accept risks, their exploitation of every success to the uttermost ; he emphasizes " the advantage which accrues to the commander who knows how best to use time to make time his servant and not his master." From out of hard and bitter experiences he deduces the moral that an expeditionary force, if it is to be used in a first-class war, must be equipped on a scale commensurate with the task it is to be called upon to fulfil. Strange, surely, that so obvious a lesson should have to be learnt from letters writ in blood.

The gloomy oppressiveness of the story is lightened time and again by an instance of British pluck and tenacity. Well may Lord Gort say in one of his final paragraphs that the campaign " proved beyond doubt that the British Soldier has once again deserved well of his country. The troops under my command, whatever their category, displayed those virtues of steadiness, patience, courage and endurance for which their corps and regiments have long been famous."

There is an old saying that the British are the least military of peoples but the most warlike ; that may well be true when, after our armies have been driven out of Norway, France and Belgium, Libya, Greece and Crete, they still stand proudly to arms ready and eager for battle. There is another old saying that Britain loses every battle save the last. Often History has proved this true ; we hope and expect that it will be proved true again. But, all the same, wouldn't it be a pleasant change if we were so well prepared, equipped, led and inspired that we were able to win not only the last battle but the battle before the last ?

E. Royston Pike

GEN. LORD GORT, V.C., G.C.B., with his immediate superior during the campaign in Flanders, the French General Georges ; the photograph was taken at Arras on the occasion of Lord Gort's investiture with the Grande Croix of the Legion of Honour.
Photo, British Official : Crown Copyright

These Men Brought the B.E.F. Out of the Inferno

Maj.-Gen. V. M. FORTUNE, who was in command of the 51st Division when they withdrew from the Saar to the Somme. He was taken prisoner of war with the remnant of his division at St. Valery.

Maj.-Gen. (now Lt.-Gen.) Hon. H. R. L. G. ALEXANDER (centre). When Lord Gort received instructions to embark for England from Dunkirk he selected Major-Gen. Alexander to remain in France in command of the 1st Corps and assist the French in the defence of the port. He was the last soldier to leave Dunkirk.

Maj.-Gen. H. E. FRANKLYN, who commanded the 5th Division, which joined the 50th in the Vimy area and was later known as the Frankforce. He was ordered to occupy bridgeheads on the Scarpe.

Maj.-Gen. R. L. PETRE, who commanded the 12th Division, and later a force known as Petreforce, including the 23rd Division, 36th Infantry Brigade, and the garrison of Arras.

Maj.-Gen. H. O. CURTIS commanded the 46th Division, defending the canals between Aire and Carvin. Gen. Curtis' force was known as Polforce, intended to hold St. Pol, Frevent, and Division.

Maj.-Gen. F. N. M. MacFARLANE (Director of Military Intelligence). He commanded a force which was called MacForce, formed on May 17, which went into the line from Raches to St. Amand.

Lt.-Gen. M. G. H. BARKER, who took over command of the 1st Corps from Gen. Sir John Dill, when the latter became C.I.G.S. Lt.-General Barker's force defended the Dyle position in front of Louvain.

Maj.-Gen. A. F. A. N. THORNE, commanding the 48th Division. He held the area Gravelines–St. Omer in the retreat to Dunkirk.

Lt.-Gen. Sir R. F. ADAM, who commanded the 3rd Corps, and subsequently organized the final Allied defence of the perimeter and the bridgehead at Dunkirk.

For 69 Days Odessa Stood at Bay

When the Rumanians and Nazis marched into Odessa on Oct. 16, the great Black Sea port had been already evacuated by its heroic garrison. Below we tell the story of the ten-weeks' siege ; much of the information has been gathered from articles contributed by Major-General Petrov to the Red Army newspaper " Red Star," and republished in the " Soviet War News."

I T was in the first week of August that General Antonescu's Rumanians, with a stiffening of Nazis, invested Odessa and set about its capture. Eighteen divisions under General Ciuperdea were flung against the city—almost half the entire Rumanian Army.

At first the enemy made considerable progress, but as they approached the outer defences of the city they were bloodily repulsed. Soviet troops left behind by Marshal Budenny employed every moment when they were not actually manning the guns in improving and extending the city's defences, and in this work they were eagerly supported by the entire population, which worked tirelessly day and night.

By September 1 hostilities were general along the whole perimeter. The hilly steppes, intercepted here and there by wooded groves and crossed by many a road, were a battlefield on which men fought furiously with rifle and bayonet. Villages in the outer zone were taken, lost and retaken. In the first 15 days of fighting some of the attacking divisions lost three-quarters of their effectives and half their equipment ; between September 1 and 15 the Russians estimated that the enemy troops lost over 50,000 killed, wounded and prisoners. Having received very substantial reinforcements of German artillery, bombing planes and mine-throwers, the Rumanians delivered a fresh onslaught on September 17 on a narrow sector of the front. Six infantry regiments were opposed by three Soviet infantry battalions ; over 15,000 mines and shells were fired against the Red troops. But the defenders stood fast, and the enemy waves were utterly broken. The story was repeated day after day as the Rumanians were driven afresh to the slaughter. The defenders were undaunted, and such was their spirit that many of the wounded refused to be evacuated to hospital, but after being bandaged insisted on returning immediately to the front line.

In the meantime, in Odessa itself there was never a suggestion of despondency. A Russian newspaper correspondent drew a vivid picture of the city swinging into lively activity at daybreak. " The early morning finds the streets crowded with people," he wrote. " Men and women hastening to the factories. A group of volunteer Red Cross nurses hurriedly make their way to take up duty at the hospital. Women and youngsters, armed with buckets and spades, move up the street in the direction of an almost completed barricade. Almost every street has a barricade, made of heaps of cobbles, torn from the pavements. Endless columns of lorries, skilfully camouflaged with greenery, roll along the open roads, carrying munitions to the front. Red Army units and detachments of armed workers who have exchanged their tools for rifles are also constantly moving up. Odessa's undertakings, factories and offices have sent to the front line tens of thousands of patriots who display prodigies of valour." The factories,

" manned " chiefly by women, were working at full blast, many of them far exceeding their normal output quotas. In the suburbs the collective farms finished their harvesting, and all able-bodied folk helped to gather the vegetable crop. Even the entertainments were maintained.

Supporting the Red Army were a large number of sailors from the Black Sea Fleet, and on one occasion a number of these Red Navy men were dropped by parachute behind the Rumanian lines, where they played havoc with their automatics, hand grenades and bayonets before fighting their way back to their comrades. Collective farmers from the surrounding districts and Cossacks from the steppes joined, too, in the city's defence.

Evacuation in Progress

When Odessa had stood out for nearly two months the Red Army High Command decided on evacuation since its defenders could be better used elsewhere. The date first chosen was October 6, but since industrial equipment, war materials, and the civilian population had to be got away, the operation was postponed until October 15.

For eight days, troops, tanks, guns and other

RUSSIAN SCIENTISTS assembled in the Hall of Columns, Moscow House of Trade Unions, to listen to addresses by the leading scientists of the U.S.S.R. At this meeting an appeal was broadcast to the scientists of the world " to unite their forces against Hitlerism, the greatest enemy of culture and science." Under the Nazi tyranny, all independent thought and search for truth is abolished. Many famous German scientists are either in concentration camps or exiled abroad. The Nazis in Paris recently arrested a number of eminent French scientists.
Photo, British Official : Crown Copyright

vital war materials were quietly withdrawn to the rear—to the harbour where a great fleet of transports, strongly guarded by Russian Air Force fighters, transported them across the Black Sea to Sebastopol. During those eight days the city's outer defence line was held by a mere handful of troops, but the Rumanians, who (so the Russians estimated) had by now lost 250,000 men killed, wounded and taken prisoner, were in no mood for fresh slaughter.

Embarkation of the guns, tanks, lorries, and military stores was completed by 7 p.m. on October 15, then most of the soldiers

followed. At 4 a.m. the next day the rearguard were taken on board. Then after Capt. Makarenko, Commander of the port, had assured himself that none were left behind, the last ships sailed. Even several thousand German and Rumanian prisoners were taken away. Only the noise of explosions in the city, only the sight of huge fires burning in the heart of the city—fires which, it was first put out, were caused by the German-Rumanian air arm—at length led the attackers to realize what was afoot. Then, gingerly enough, their patrols again approached the outer defences, and found the defenders flown. General Ciuperdea was promptly sacked by Antonescu for letting the enemy slip, and it was under General Jacobici that the Rumanians entered the burning and evacuated city.

" Troops of our 4th Army marched into Odessa this afternoon," triumphantly announced the Rumanians on October 16. " The last nests of resistance are being cleared up in street fighting. The population received the German-Rumanian forces with enthusiasm." The Nazis claimed that in the waters around Odessa the Luftwaffe had successfully attacked troop ships carrying the enemy " fleeing from the town."

For 69 days Odessa had bid defiance to the Nazi-Rumanian hosts. She might have maintained her stand almost indefinitely had not the Soviet Supreme High Command decided otherwise for strategic reasons. And as it was, when the German-Rumanians marched into Odessa they discovered that all the war installations had been destroyed, and that many parts of the city were nothing more than a shell. As for the garrison which had for so long defended the city, they were now strengthening the defences of the Crimea.

In Kazakhstan, One of Russia's 'Hidden' Bases

In Western Kazakhstan lies a rich oil-bearing region ; Emba Neft, top left, is the best-known centre. Kazakhstan is also rich in mineral ores, which are extracted by giant excavators (above).

KAZAKH S.S.R., shown unshaded, is 1,047,797 sq. miles in area, with a population of 7 millions.

STILL in many geography books Kazakhstan —the Kazakh Soviet Socialist Republic—is described as a dismal tract of steppeland, sterile, stony and streamless, inhabited only by nomad tribes of Kirghiz. Since the Russian Revolution, however, this region, in common with so many other regions of Soviet Asia, has been transformed. As a glance at the map above will show, it contains oilfields, coalmines, and mineral workings ; there are also extensive cotton fields and huge tracts devoted to the production of grain. Linking this once remote and still largely unknown province of the Soviet with Moscow is a railway through Kuibyshev, the second seat of government of the U.S.S.R., while the Turk-Sib Railway crosses its eastern region.

Threshing grain at a collective farm in Kazakhstan (above). Circle, the great wooden pipeline down which are borne the melted snow and rain from the Ural Mountains to the hydro-electric plant at Ulba ; right, this alert Soviet soldier symbolizes the large, fully-trained army which garrisons Kazakhstan.

Photos, British Official ; Crown Copyright ; G.P.U.

Malta—Grit in the Hub of the Axis

'IRON GREETINGS FOR MALTA,' is the inscription on a reserve of German bombs in Italy. Right, an R.A.F. pilot-defender of Malta. The Anglo-Maltese League recently entertained the R.A.F. and Fleet Air Arm and expressed Malta's gratitude.

HURRICANES ready to take off from a Maltese aerodrome. The battle of Malta goes on continuously. Mussolini imagined that the great British Mediterranean fortress would soon fall, but, though the Axis has attacked it many hundreds of times, Malta remains impregnable, and our A.A. guns and aircraft have taken a heavy toll of enemy machines. The Maltese themselves have excellent shelters cut in the limestone rock.

Photos, British Official: Crown Copyright; Associated Press

Unorthodox but Formidable : the Bell Airacobra

AIRACOBRAS IN LINE, with one machine flying over the squadron. The Airacobra, for a time christened the Caribou in this country, is a most unorthodox single-seat fighter with an Allison 1,150-h.p. engine mounted in the fuselage behind the pilot. Inset, the nose of the Airacobra showing the cannon protruding through the airscrew hub. This gun can fire at the rate of 120 shells a minute. A detailed diagram of the Airacobra is given in page 164.

Photos, British Official: Crown Copyright

Our Searchlight on the War

BRITAIN'S CATAPULT PLANES

NEW methods of protection for shipping have been put into operation in order to deal with the enemy long-range aircraft which attack ships and report the movements of shipping to U-boats. Certain ships have been fitted with catapults and provided with fighter aircraft which can be catapulted into the air to deal with enemy aircraft shadowing or attempting to attack. After shooting down or driving off enemy aircraft the fighter lands at a shore base if there is one within range. If not, the pilot has to "land" in the sea or as close to the ship as possible in order to be picked up. The fighters are piloted in some cases by pilots of the Fleet Air Arm, and in others by pilots of the Fighter Command of the Royal Air Force who have volunteered for this special duty. This new method of trade defence has already proved successful, both in averting attacks and in destroying German long-range aircraft. Lieut. Everett, who has been awarded the D.S.O. "for bravery, skill and tenacity in many hazardous operational flights in the protection of shipping," is one of the Fleet Air Arm pilots who are being

SEED ONIONS being planted in a special plot in Alexandra Gardens, Melbourne. The seed will eventually be sent to Britain to increase our onion crop.   *Photo, Associated Press*

catapulted in fighter aircraft from ships at sea. Recently he was catapulted in his fighter aircraft to deal with a Focke-Wulf Kondor which was approaching a convoy. He crashed the enemy bomber into the sea, but by the time the fight was over he was 45 miles away from his ship. He tried unsuccessfully to bale out and eventually "landed" in the sea. In a few seconds his fighter sank beneath him, but he was picked up safely. In peacetime he often rode in the Grand National, but he now realizes that as a water-jump Becher's Brook is not to be compared with the Atlantic.

CIVILIAN TECHNICAL CORPS

MEN of the new Civilian Technical Corps, many of whom come from the United States, are now settling down to work with the R.A.F. in England. This is a corps of specialists, every man of which is highly skilled in his particular trade. All members of the corps are recruited abroad, and they have come forward voluntarily to lend their technical knowledge to Britain. The status of the corps is purely civilian and its members are not required to undertake

combatant duties. They receive civilian rates of pay, and agree to serve for three years or for the duration of the war, whichever is the less. On arrival in Britain the men who have joined the corps are given a blue-grey serge uniform of R.A.F. pattern, steel helmets and anti-gas equipment. They will wear on their arms the C.T.C. title-badge, and will have flat-topped field-service caps with C.T.C. in a metal wreath on the front.

WELFARE OF THE NAVY

THERE is at the Admiralty a department whose whole and fulltime business is to look after the welfare and recreation of the men. At each naval base in home waters is stationed an experienced man with the title of Amenities Officer. His job is to see that all the recreational facilities of his port are used to the utmost. This officer keeps in direct touch with the Admiralty. Under his charge come not only R.N. and Reserve men, but Allied seamen, and, by no means least, the Wrens. Most of the Navy men's time is spent actually at sea, and that is the time when they most appreciate such gifts as woollies, cigarettes and pipe tobacco, packs of cards, books and magazines both new and old which are sent to them by the people ashore. The distribution of these gifts is arranged by an Admiralty Committee, and the Amenities Officers arrange for them to reach the ships—everything from battleships with a crew larger than the population of a small village, down to drifters manned by half a dozen or even less. Two funds at the Admiralty administer the donations —the R.N. Amenities Fund and the Minesweepers and Coastal Craft Fund. Last year they spent between them £50,000 ; it went on wireless sets, footballs and goal-posts, canteens, hostels, concert halls and sports fields. The result is that this winter, at nearly all bases round our coasts, there is a comfortable canteen where men ashore can have a good meal in pleasant surroundings. There are rooms for reading and writing letters, billiard tables, table tennis, and the inevitable dartboard. Two of the largest bases have theatres with lighting and equipment up to West End standard. Others have cinemas, concert halls for ENSA and other entertainments, and football fields. Country man-

N.A.A.F.I. to R.A.F. ; this present of the Spitfire "Counter-Attack" was bought with a subscription from the N.A.A.F.I. canteen workers.   *Photo, British Official : Crown Copyright*

sions and large town houses have been taken over and turned into really comfortable Naval Hostels. Behind all this are many voluntary organizations, and there is not an officer, rating or boy in the Navy who is not truly grateful.

LEGLESS PILOT'S LAST FIGHT

IT was originally believed that Wing-Cmdr. Douglas Bader, famous legless pilot of the R.A.F., with 22½ German planes to his credit (the half being shared with another pilot), had been shot down in the combat over France on August 9, from which he did not return. In a letter to his wife, however, Bader now reveals that he fell into the enemy's hands after colliding with an Me.109F. Giving his last order, "Come on, boys, there are plenty for all ; pick one each," Bader led his formation in a 5,000-feet dive on some Me.s, and was last seen by his squadron pursuing an Me.109F. His letter tells how he sent the Me.109F down in flames and how, in pulling up from his dive attack, he collided with another Me.109F. The enemy machine crashed, and Bader baled out from his crippled fighter.

FRENCH SAVANTS ARRESTED

ON Oct. 19 the Vichy government confirmed the arrest in Paris by the German authorities of six members of the Académie des Sciences : MM. Borel, Langevin, Lapique, Mauguin, Villey, and Cotton. M. Borel is a mathematician of world repute and a former Minister of Marine. M. Langevin, a noted physicist, was, until relieved of his post by the Vichy government, Director of the Ecole de Physique et de Chimie and professor of Physics at the Collège de France. M. Lapique, physiologist, has done a considerable amount of anthropological research and latterly devoted himself to the study of the physiology of the nervous system. M. Mauguin was professor of mineralogy at the Sorbonne. M. Villey was a noted mathematician, professor at the Faculty of Sciences at Paris University. M. Cotton is a world-famous physicist, President of the Académie des Sciences and of the Fédération des Sociétés de Physique.

HOME-GROWN SUGAR

THE main reason which lay behind Lord Woolton's recent decision to increase Britain's sugar ration was that home-grown sugar-beet now provides the whole of the domestic sugar ration, thanks to the strides which have been made in recent years in developing the sugar-beet industry in this country. During the last war Britain was almost entirely dependent on imported sugar. At one time in 1917 stocks dwindled to about sufficient for four days' consumption, and the price rose to 1/2 a lb. But today, in spite of two years of war, sugar is still cheap. The Ministry of Agriculture has announced that the acreage of sugar-beet under cultivation, now standing at about 350,000 acres, will next year be increased to some 405,000 acres. The beet pulp, incidentally, has proved of great value as foodstuff for cattle. Photographs of reclaimed fenland now producing sugarbeet are reproduced in page 41.

AMERICAN C.T.C.s—members of the Civilian Technical Corps, specialists who have volunteered for the United Kingdom to do repair and maintenance work on aircraft with the R.A.F.   *Photo, Central Press*

Round Jibuti the K.A.R.s Have Drawn a Cordon

A total land, sea and air blockade of Jibuti, the seaport of French Somaliland, is now in operation. The King's African Rifles are on a twenty-four hours' watch along certain sectors of the land frontier. Left, the C.O. of the K.A.R. is interrogating a native blockade runner, with a laden camel, detained near Warre Kafule. Right, a K.A.R. observation post at Warre Kafule.

OFF ON PATROL, a truck-load of members of the King's African Rifles taking part in the blockade of Jibuti, which lies opposite Aden. It is the capital of French Somaliland and the terminus of the railway to Addis Ababa. In the centre photograph, Free French Senegalese soldiers, on the frontier, facing the French post at Loyada, are waving greetings and invitations to troops under Vichy control to desert.

Photos, British Official: Crown Copyright

Fateful Moves on the Russian Chessboard

The lull that followed the fall of Bryansk and Vyazma (see page 227) was short-lived. By Oct. 15 a great new offensive had been launched, one that was intended not only to smash Timoshenko's armies but to capture the Russian capital. Nor was this all. In the south, too, the Nazis pushed ever farther ahead.

FROM three sides, from north and west and south, the Nazi hordes thrust fiercely at Moscow. So gigantic was the operation, so many the directions in which von Bock's armies were heavily engaged, that it was no mere "pincers movement," but rather, as Mr. Garvin described it in the "Observer," an octopus movement, meaning the fastening round the whole body of its intended victim with one tentacle after another.

News of the fresh offensive was contained in a communiqué issued by Soviet G.H.Q. at midnight on October 15. During the preceding night, it was stated, the position in the central sector of the front had deteriorated. "The German Fascist armies hurled a large quantity of tanks and motorized infantry against our units, and in one sector broke through our defences." The Russian forces opposed to the enemy were stated to be resisting heroically and inflicting heavy losses on the foe, but they had been compelled to give ground. A few hours later Moscow broadcast the grave statement that the enemy was increasing his pressure and "is now nearing the approaches to Moscow."

At first it was not clear where the breakthrough had occurred, but ere long it was revealed that it was at Mojaisk, about halfway from Vyazma to Moscow on the great highway which leads from Smolensk, and about 60 miles from the Russian capital. Evidently the Germans had discovered a weak spot; they hastened to intensify their punch, packing it with all the weight that tanks, bombing planes and heavy artillery could give. But, as the metaphor of the octopus implies, Moscow was threatened not from one direction only but from many. In particular there might be distinguished thrusts from the direction of Kalinin, an important railway junction 100 miles to the north-west; from Bryansk, 200 miles to the south-west; and from Orel, 200 miles to the south. At the end of that same October 16 Moscow reported that the battle was growing fiercer and fiercer; the enemy still held the initiative, and operations in the Moscow

sector were on a gigantic scale, not only because of the enormous quantity of men and machines taking part, but also on account of the depth of the operations. Anything in the nature of a "front" had dissolved in the fluidity of the battle; the Nazi panzers operated like knights on a chessboard, while the pawns of infantry toiled and fought the Russian pieces far behind.

As early as October 15 the Germans claimed that their troops had occupied Kalinin; General Hoth's panzers had crashed through Borodino and were battling in the district of Mojaisk, while Guderian's tanks had carried Misensk and were approaching Tula, 110 miles south of Moscow. Some of these claims, at least, were premature; two days later the Germans claimed afresh to have occupied Kalinin, and it is certain that fighting was going on in this vital sector a week later. But there was no denying the desperate gravity of the Russian situation. By October 19 Hitler's High Command felt it safe to claim that von Bock's field army, in cooperation with Kesselring's air fleet, had "annihilated the Soviet Army Group of Marshal Timoshenko, numbering eight armies, with 67 protecting divisions, six cavalry divisions, seven tank divisions, and six tank brigades."

'Annihilated' But Still Fighting

That was on October 19. Yet day after day Moscow continued to report fierce fighting at Mojaisk and Malo Yaroslavets, while guerilla detachments were waging continuous war in the Kalinin region. At Orel and Bryansk the Russians claimed—and claimed with truth—that they were counter-attacking fiercely and not without success. To account for this surprising conduct on the part of the "annihilated" enemy, officials in Berlin dilated on the extraordinary difficulties of the campaign. In particular the German soldiers were tired after so many forced marches, while as for the weather, what with sleet and snow, rain and mist, treacherous ice and seas of mud, it was foul beyond belief.

All the same, the Germans continued to make progress, and on October 23 Hitler's chiefs claimed that their troops had broken through the outer defences of Moscow, and that the spearhead was only 38 miles from the Russian capital.

In Moscow there was no attempt at hiding from the people the gravity of the situation. The Muscovites realized, as their comrades at Leningrad had realized weeks before, that soon they might have to fight for their native town and defend it, arms in hand, street by street, house by house. On October 19 Stalin issued a decree, proclaiming a state of siege in Moscow and the surrounding districts as from the following day. Although some of the Government departments, together with the foreign diplomats, military missions, and war correspondents, were evacuated to Kuibyshev (Samara), 540 miles to the south-east on the banks of the Volga, Moscow itself was placed in a state of defence. Everyone capable of handling a rifle was enlisted in workers' battalions, and thousands of people were engaged in digging trenches and raising ramparts.

While the tremendous battle for Moscow was raging, von Rundstedt resumed his offensive in the south. On October 20 a great host of German, Italian, Hungarian and Rumanian troops went into action in

EASTERN FRONT: the main military developments in the Russian campaign as October—the war's fourth month—drew to a close. *Courtesy of the "News Chronicle"*

the Donetz basin, and within 24 hours they had fought their way into Taganrog, while Stalino, too, was taken by Alpine troops. The Russians fought desperately, demanding a great price for every yard of ground; but though they counter-attacked time and again, they were still forced to abandon further huge areas of the vital Donbass industrial region. By October 25 the Germans claimed to be fighting in the approaches of Rostov; and on the same day they claimed to have occupied Kharkov. Meanwhile, in the Crimea they had driven a deep wedge into the defences across the Perekop Isthmus, only to be flung out by Russian counter-attacks.

This, then, was the position as the fourth month of the Russian campaign drew to a close. On October 9 Dr. Dietrich, head of the German official News Agency in Berlin, had declared that Russia was virtually finished as a fighting power. It must have been, then, with a shadow of apprehension that the German people heard on October 23 that the Russian Command had been reorganized; henceforth, Zhukov was commander in the north and Timoshenko in the south, while—ominous news!—Voroshiloff and Budenny had been withdrawn to take command of great new armies which Stalin was calling into being, far behind the fighting zone.

KUIBYSHEV, on the Volga, 540 miles east of Moscow, to which part of the Central Administration of the Soviet Union has been withdrawn from the capital. Other branches may go to Kazan and Sverdlovsk. *Photo, Planet News*

Action! At Close Quarters in Russia

A well-aimed Russian shell has scored a direct hit on a span of a large bridge over a wide river, thereby delaying the German advance.

Nazi infantrymen advance with caution into the streets of a town lately evacuated by Russian troops. There may be many snipers among the ruins.

Crawling forward under heavy fire, Soviet troops advance under cover of a camouflaged machine-gun post (left). Centre, Soviet tank drivers, concealed in a wheatfield, check up on the topography of their sector. Right, Soviet infantry pursuing German troops during a counter-attack through a wooded stretch of country. The soldier on the left is hurling a hand grenade while the others charge with fixed bayonets.　　*Photos, British Official, Keystone*

Russia Under Arms: Some of the Photograp

RED ARMY orderly, Zalman Grinker, carrying a wounded Soviet soldier from the battlefield on his back. Orderly Grinker saved seventy-two wounded in the course of a few days.

AFTER THE MOSCOW CONFERENCE Mr. Stalin presented to Lord Beaverbrook a number of photographs illustrative of the courage, the dogged determination and the great resources of our Russian Ally, a selection from which is given above. Left, a supply train carrying big guns and

lin Presented to Lord Beaverbrook in Moscow

ARMOURED CARS, in vast array, on parade before moving to the front. The Red Army has been the first to confront the German Army with panzer divisions on a scale approaching its own, and Lord Beaverbrook has disclosed how every available British and American tank is to be sent to make good Russian losses.

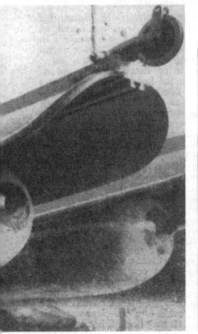

nation

tractors up towards the front. Oval, Nurse E. Vershova, one of Russia's thousands of brave nurses, who combined valuable scouting activities with first-aid work. Below, centre, torpedo gunners of the Red Navy in action. Right, a trainload of tanks on its way towards the scene of battle.

What Sort of Men Are the Japanese Militarists?

Japan has a new Cabinet, comprised largely of Generals and Admirals and pledged to maintain the policy of " Japan over Asia " which has been for so long an unsettling factor in Far Eastern politics. More than ever before the militarists are at the helm.

WHEN General Tojo became Prime Minister of Japan on October 18, he proceeded, in accordance with immemorial custom, to the Grand Shrine of Ise, to notify the Sun Goddess of his appointment. Shortly before he had offered prayers at the shrines of the Emperor Meiji (the Emperor who was " restored " in 1868, so opening the modern age in Japanese history) and of Admiral Togo (Commander-in-Chief of the Japanese Navy which annihilated the Russian fleet at Tsushima in 1905), and at the Yasukuni Shrine—the shrine in Tokyo where the Japanese war dead are deified and worshipped as the nation's patron saints, or rather gods. (Between October 16 and 21 a further 15,000 soldiers and sailors, for the most part dead in the " Chinese incident," were solemnly deified, bringing the total so commemorated to nearly 225,000).

Not only every Japanese minister and high official has to report his appointment to the Sun Goddess, but the Emperor himself visits her shrine on great occasions—to keep her informed, as it were. Thus the present Emperor, Hirohito, visited the shrine after his father's death in 1926, before and after his trip to Europe, and after his marriage to pretty little Princess Nagako ; he will go again if (as seems not unlikely) Japan should declare war. The Emperor—he is never called the Mikado by the Japanese : to them he is *Tenno* (Son of Heaven)—is, according to Japanese belief, physically descended from the Sun Goddess ; the first Emperor was Jimmu, whose date in the Japanese history books is equivalent to 660 B.C. For more than 2,600 years, then, the same dynasty has ruled in Japan.

To the western world much of this is pure mythology, but it is very real to the Japanese. To them, however educated and modern in their outlook they may be, the Emperor is divine in some mystic fashion ; by the vast majority he is regarded as not only divine, but as being a visible embodiment or incarnation of Godhead and at the same time of the Japanese race. Thus he is not merely

EMPEROR HIROHITO of Japan. Born in 1901, he succeeded his father as Tenno in 1926. Above we see him at a parade of the graduates of the Japanese Military Academy.

Photo, Wide World

head of the state as is our King ; he *is* the state. So venerated is he that very few Japanese have ever seen him ; when he approaches every eye is cast down, and when he goes in procession his loyal subjects dare not gaze at the " Son of Heaven " for fear of being stricken with blindness. No human being is permitted to look down upon him ; hence no building round his castle in Tokyo is so high as to permit a view of the castle grounds, and when he passes through the streets all blinds in upper storeys must be drawn. When passing the gates of his palace every Japanese bows deferentially, even when seated in a tramcar.

Radicals in Uniform

There are many other features of the modern Japanese state which are utterly opposed to western ideas. A monarch who rules by divine right, or rather because he is divine, is supported by a military caste which occupies a position of peculiar influence in the Japanese political system. " To die for the sake of the Emperor is to live for ever " is a statement made in a pamphlet issued a few years ago by the Japanese Army. Yet, strangely enough, the Army is intensely democratic in that there is no officer class in Japan ; the humblest recruit may rise to the highest rank. Only about one in ten of the Japanese officers are of noble or *samurai* origin ; some are specially educated from the age of 14 in the military academies, but conscript privates may enter the officer training corps up to the age of 22. Before any officer is commissioned he has to spend eight months in the ranks. As a class, Japanese officers are exceedingly abstemious and modest in their ways of life ; they have to be, since a full general receives little more than £350 per annum, and few there are who have private means.

Because the Japanese Army is drawn in the main from the peasantry and small-town folk—every year 150,000 young men of 20 are chosen by lot from those who pass the doctors as being absolutely fit—it is extremely radical in its ideas. Reading some

of the pamphlets which have been issued by the press department of the Imperial War Ministry, one discovers a medley of ideas, some Socialist, some Fascist, most of them decidedly anti-Capitalist. Capitalism in Japan is a recent growth, and not by any means a popular one. There is no great middle class as in Britain or the U.S.A. ; rather, industry is in the hands of great monopolistic families, of which the " big five " are the houses of Mitsubishi, Mitsui, Sumitomo, Yasuda, and Okura. For generations the first two have largely controlled Japanese politics through their respective parties, Minseito and Seiyukai ; now, however, political parties have been abolished and Japan is a totalitarian state.

Will the People Crack ?

Not that that is anything new. For thirty centuries Japan has been governed in accordance with the principles of totalitarianism ; even the revolution of 1868 was called a restoration. Conformity is ingrained in the Japanese temperament ; loyalty to the Emperor is paramount. The Japanese display little or no critical spirit ; they are not inclined to mistrust authority as are we English ; autocratic forms of government are quite congenial to their spirit. There are amongst them men who may be called Liberals, Socialists, even Communists (though Communism is a crime in Japan), but these are a tiny and almost uninfluential minority. Parliamentary government, liberty of the press, free speech—these things count for little with the Japanese ; seemingly they do not resent the many restrictions which have been imposed upon them, even before the Chinese war—the rationing of foodstuffs, spying, censorship, and police regulation of the details of everyday life. In the Japanese mentality, as in Japanese history, there is little to encourage those who would like to believe that under the strain of war Japan may collapse. As long as the people are fed —and, heaven knows, they need little more than a handful of rice per day per head— they may be expected to continue to fight, since it is the Emperor's will.

It is difficult to estimate the present-day worth of the Japanese Army or, indeed, of the Japanese armed forces as a whole. In the Russo-Japanese war of 1904-5 Japan won a crushing victory over Russia, but it was the Russia of Tsar Nicholas, not of Stalin. Within the last two or three years the Japanese armies have twice suffered severe reverses at the hands of the Russians, although the world's press has passed these by with little comment and smaller understanding ; one was at Changkufeng, south-east of Vladivostok, in August 1938, and the other in the summer of 1939 at Nomonhan, in the east of Outer Mongolia. At Nomonhan, indeed, there was a series of battles in which whole army corps were engaged on each side ; the Japanese admitted 18,000 soldiers killed, and there was no hiding the fact that in a struggle for a few square miles of desert their troops had been defeated. Then in China the cream of the Japanese armies have been engaged for four years in an attempt to crush the forces of Chiang Kai-shek ; so far, however, they have completely failed, although they have the enormous preponderance in military equipment and a practical monopoly of bombing planes. What would happen in the event of a first-class war it is difficult to say. It may be said, however, that the soldiers of Nippon would fight with fanatical courage just as they did at Mukden and Port Arthur 35 years ago.

GEN. HIDEKI TOJO, who on October 18 succeeded Prince Konoye as Prime Minister of Japan. Nicknamed *Lamisori*, i.e. the razor, he is a keen, sharp-witted militarist.

Photo, Wide World

Whither Japan in this Grim Hour of Destiny?

WAR AND PEACE are strangely symbolized in this photograph of a carrier-pigeon, belonging to the Japanese Carrier Pigeon Corps, perched on the soldier's rifle. Right, Japanese troops, clad in their winter uniforms, on parade at a Siberian frontier outpost; turning towards Tokyo, they are presenting arms in salute to the Emperor. Beneath, a grim irony is expressed once again in this mass of Oriental robots doing homage at the Yasukuni Shrine in honour of comrades who have been slaughtered in the interests of Japanese imperialism. Here they are dedicating themselves to any new adventure of the militarists.

Photos, Wide World, Associated Press

Our Diary of the War

SATURDAY, OCT. 18, 1941   777th day

Russian Front. — Fierce battles around Kalinin and Mojaisk. Russian Fleet reported to have sunk German cruiser and two destroyers. A second cruiser badly damaged.

Mediterranean.—Enemy convoy attacked by R.A.F. Night raid on Naples.

Home.—Lord Croft announced British Army casualties to date as 100,000, including prisoners of war. Australian, 13,000; New Zealand, 6,000

SUNDAY, OCT. 19   778th day

Air.—Offensive sweeps by R.A.F. over Cherbourg peninsula.

Russian Front.—Germans claimed capture of Taganrog. Fierce fighting around Majaisk and Malo Yaroslavets.

Africa.—Heavy night raid on Tripoli. Enemy landing-grounds in Libya bombed.

Home.—Night raiders over E. Coast. One enemy aircraft destroyed.

General.—Afghanistan announced expulsion of Axis nationals.

MONDAY, OCT. 20   779th day

Air.—R.A.F. sweep over N. France. Ammunition train blown up, and transport column near Dieppe attacked. Coastal Command bombed objectives in N. Denmark. Night raids on Bremen, Wilhelmshaven and Emden.

Russian Front.—State of siege declared in Moscow. Certain government departments moved to Kuibyshev.

Africa.—Enemy positions near Azozo, Abyssinia, bombed.

Home.—Night raiders over N.W. England and N. Wales.

General.—Lt.-Col. Holtz, commander of Nantes Military Region, shot by French patriots.

TUESDAY, OCT. 21   780th day

Air.—Offensive sweep over N. France. 13 enemy aircraft destroyed. Night raids on Bremen and N.W. Germany. Aarhus, Brest and Lorient bombed.

Russian Front.—Position stationary on Moscow front while Germans prepare new offensive. German advance in Donetz Basin area.

RUSSIA'S WAY WITH 'STICK-IN-THE-MUDS'

DURING these days of hard fighting in the distant approaches to Moscow, people are being tested and tried in the heat of battle. Lieut.-Colonel Dorontsov, for example, took nearly 24 hours to make a journey of 18 miles. Finally his car got stuck a few miles from its destination. Instead of getting out and walking, he sat in the car for seven hours and reported to his chief that he had got stuck in the mud.

Actually, he was stuck in the mud in more ways than one. He was up to his neck in the muck of his own inactivity and complacency. Such types have nothing in common with true Soviet patriots.

" Pravda," October 24.

Mediterranean.—Heavy night raid on Naples.

Africa.—Midnight bombardment of enemy gun positions near Tobruk by British warships. Benghazi raided on night of Oct. 20-21, and in daylight on Oct. 21. Enemy positions near Azozo again bombed.

General.—50 hostages shot by Germans at Nantes as reprisal for the shooting of Col. Holtz.

WEDNESDAY, OCT. 22   781st day

Air.—Night attack on French coast from Dunkirk to Boulogne also on Mannheim and the Ruhr. Docks at Le Havre and Brest attacked.

Russian Front.—Russians admitted grave situation in Donetz Basin area. Fresh German attack on Crimea held.

Mediterranean.—Night raid on Naples. Admiralty announced submarine successes against enemy convoy. Two supply ships torpedoed.

Africa.—Night raid on docks and shipping at Benghazi. Landing ground at Gasr el Aryid bombed. Enemy positions in Gondar region bombed.

Home.—Enemy night raiders over N. Wales and Merseyside. Three enemy bombers destroyed.

THURSDAY, OCT. 23   782nd day

Air.—Enemy aerodromes attacked at Calais and Lannion. Night raids on N.W. Germany. Docks at Cherbourg, Brest and Le Havre attacked.

Russian Front.—Reorganisation of Red Army Command announced. Gen. Zhukov given command of the central sector of the front. Slight German advance in Crimea. German attacks repulsed at Mojaisk and Malo Yaroslavets.

Mediterranean. — Chemical works at Cotrone, S. Italy, bombed.

Africa.—Derna aerodrome bombed.

General.—A further 50 hostages reported executed by Nazis at Bordeaux following the shooting of another German officer.

FRIDAY, OCT. 24   783rd day

Air.—Offensive sweep over N. France. 7 German fighters destroyed. Night raids on W. Germany.

Russian Front.—Germans claimed to be 20 miles from Rostov. No essential changes elsewhere.

Mediterranean.—Admiralty announced torpedoing of an Italian armed merchant cruiser. Night attack on Naples by R.A.F. bombers. Ragusa and Licata, in Sicily, also bombed.

Home.—Enemy night raiders over Merseyside.

SATURDAY, OCT. 25   784th day

Air.—Offensive sweeps over N. France and Dutch coast.

Russian Front.—Moscow denied German claim to have captured Kharkov. Heavy fighting at Kalinin and in the Crimea.

Africa.—Enemy transport at Zuara, Tripolitania, attacked by R.A.F. bombers.

Home.—Night raiders over N.W. England.

SUNDAY, OCT. 26   785th day

Air.—Enemy shipping bombed off Dutch coast. Offensive sweeps over Holland and N. France.

Russian Front.—Germans reported 10 miles from Rostov. Bitter street fighting in Kharkov. Russians admitted evacuation of Stalino, 100 miles N.W. of Rostov. Marshal Timoshenko arrived on southern front.

Home.—Night raiders over S. Wales and S.W. England.

HOLBORN VIADUCT, one of London's most famous thoroughfares, is now to be seen very much as it was when it was built between 1867 and 1869, since the demolitions and clearances made necessary by the German bombing of last spring have revealed the great arches on which it rests. Prominent in the photograph is the gutted City Temple, the " Cathedral of Nonconformity " as it has been called; next it is the shell of St. Andrew's, Holborn ; while in the foreground is the debris of the buildings on the north side of the Viaduct, east of Hatton Garden.

Photo, Topical Press

They Have Won Honours in Freedom's Cause

Lloyd's War Medal

Acting Lt.-Col. G. C. T. Keyes, M.C., for gallantry in Syria. He is a son of Admiral Sir Roger Keyes.

Sgt. J. Horsman, M.M. He escaped from a German prison camp, was caught, and escaped again.

Sergt. H. G. Preece, D.C.M., for bravery and devotion to duty in the Norway operations.

Sepoy N. Singh, Indian D.S.M., for successful reconnaissance work in the region of Keren.

Albert Medal

Cadet D. Hay, Lloyd's War Medal, for rescuing a radio officer from shark-infested sea.

Lieut. G. D. Davies, D.S.C., for devoted work in guiding convoys through the Straits.

Third Officer S. Ross, M.B.E., for keeping small boat with 10 men afloat for 16 days.

Lieut. J. Miller, G.C., for devoted work in dealing with magnetic and acoustic mines.

Lieut. Nelson B. Smith, R.N., G.M., for courage and attention to duty on all occasions.

Able Seaman Miles, Albert Medal, for helping to save a shipmate caught in hawser.

Miss Helen Mason, G.M., for bravery and devotion to duty in Hammersmith blitz.

Actg. Sectn. Officer J. Woods, of Mowlsford, **M.B.E.,** for bravery and devotion to duty.

Mrs. Armitage, London Ambulance Service, **B.E.M.,** for great resource and courage.

Miss Betty Leverton, London Ambulance Service, also awarded the **B.E.M.,** for bravery.

Acting Flight Officer H. Murdock-Grant, M.B.E., for distinction in Signals and Code work.

Wren P. G. McGeorge, B.E.M., for getting dispatches through under a heavy blitz.

Firemaster A. S. Pratten, G.M., for great skill and gallantry during an air raid on Greenock.

Patrol Officer J. Vale, B.E.M., for outstanding courage in a heavy Plymouth blitz.

Sub-Officer W. Neill, G.M., of Greenock, for exceptional courage in fighting a fire.

Dep. Chief Officer R. J. Smith, Plymouth Fire Brigade, **M.B.E.,** for devotion to duty.

Fireman J. C. Cunningham, G.M., for rescuing a man who was trapped in burning building.

Mr. H. W. Mould, A.F.S., **G.M.,** for assisting Fireman Cunningham in the same brave deed.

Acting Sqdn.-Ldr. R. W. Bungey, D.F.C., for continuous gallant and efficient leadership.

Flying Officer E. A. Morrison, U.S. citizen, **D.F.C.,** for bombing the Gneisenau.

Acting Sqdn.-Ldr. J. Harrison-Broadley, D.F.C., for attack on an enemy convoy.

Pilot Officer D. U. Barnwell, D.F.C., for shooting down four Italian planes over Malta.

Flight Lieut. L. W. Coleman, D.F.C., for bombing Munich on night of Bier-Keller speech.

Pilot Officer A. C. Lewis, D.F.C., for destroying six Nazi planes on one day, and five on another.

Mr. V. H. Sellwood, Portsmouth A.F.S. Messenger, **B.E.M.,** for splendid work in a heavy raid.

Warden M. C. Starr, G.M., for climbing a wrecked building and rescuing three persons.

Mr. E. L. Playford, G.M., for rescuing a Post Warden from a bombed Bermondsey building.

Mr. John Bradley, G.M., for assisting Mr. Playford in this conspicuously gallant action.

Mr. A. A. Webster, G.M., for rescuing two children from demolished Manchester house.

Mr. H. Broadberry, B.E.M., for saving Polish airmen from crashed and burning plane.

They Direct the Fortunes of Free France

André DIETHELM, National Commissioner for Interior, Labour and Information. At one time principal secretary to M. Mandel.

Maurice DEJEAN, National Commissioner for Foreign Affairs, is a distinguished diplomat.

René PLEVIN, Nat. Commissioner for Economy, Finance, and Colonies, hitherto Director of External Relations of Free French movement.

Post Capt. Georges THIERRY D'ARGENLIEU, Nat. Comm. without portfolio, served for 10 years in the French Navy.

GENERAL DE GAULLE, Leader of the Free French and President of the Free French National Committee.

Air Cdr. VALIN, Nat. Comm. for Air, in 1939 commanded a French Air Intelligence unit. He is a specialist in night flying.

ON September 23, 1941, General de Gaulle announced the formation of a Free French National Committee, to act with him in the direction of the policy and administration of Free France. Another body set up at the same time was a National Advisory Council, drawn from French organizations all over the world, such as the Français de Grande Bretagne in this country.

Gen. LEGENTILHOMME, Nat. Commissioner for War, was former C.-in-C. of the French Forces in Somaliland.

Prof. René CASSIN, Nat. Commissioner for Justice and Education, was formerly Professor of Law at the University of Paris.

Vice-Admiral MUSELIER, Nat. Comm. for Navy and Mercantile Marine, took several French warships to Gibraltar on June 28, 1940.

Photos by courtesy of Free French Cinematograph Service, P.N.A., Universal, and Planet News

Pitiable Is the Plight of Pétain's Subjects

MARSHAL PÉTAIN (above) delivering to M. Féricard, Vice-President of the French Legion of Veterans from two World Wars, the flag of the Organization, on the first anniversary of its foundation. Circle, the unhappy Marshal holding a food conference with French butchers in the hope of finding some way of alleviating distress during the coming winter.

GEN. HUNTZIGER, Vichy War Minister (top photo, light uniform, in centre), addressing French prisoners of war on their arrival at Sathonay Station, near Lyons, after having been released by the Germans.

Photos, Associated Press

UNOCCUPIED FRANCE is being Nazified under cover of collaboration with the Germans. These "new order" uniforms now worn by the Vichy State police (above) are obviously inspired from Berlin. Left, the inevitable food queue, this time at Grenoble, where people wait their turn for meagre rations under a Vichy scheme for national aid. Thus France, once so rich in food and wine, has been reduced to semi-starvation and beggary by Hitler's insatiable greed.

Photos, Fox and Wide World

This is My Life as an Aircraftman

Much have we read and listened to concerning the splendid achievements of the flying crews of the R.A.F. Here for a change is an article describing the life of one of the ground staff. It is written by a Volunteer Reserve Aircraftman, and his experiences may be taken as typical of thousands of those men on whom the efficiency of the R.A.F. so largely depends.

IT was in November 1939 that I joined the R.A.F. In civil life I'd been a journalist, and, having a hankering after a little excitement and variety, I volunteered at my local recruiting depot as a pilot. But they didn't want pilots just then—they were swamped out with applications and they'd a six months' waiting list. So I volunteered and was accepted as wireless operator, aircrew. But it didn't materialize, for at the last minute the recruiting people persuaded me to enlist as a teleprinter operator.

After that I signed one or two official documents, passed my medical exam. quite satisfactorily, and a few days later I was off to one of the big R.A.F. receiving depots where recruits are clothed and kitted and sorted out generally. A week later, inoculated,

my life; and after those early rigorous days I was beginning to appreciate small comforts that hitherto I had never even noticed. It was exactly like going to school all over again. Between classes held in centrally-heated wooden huts we marched in groups from one hut to another to the accompaniment of military marches relayed through loudspeakers. We lived first in huts and later in stone barrack blocks. The huts were remarkably snug, with a coal stove at each end of the room; but personally I preferred the old stone barrack blocks, which held as many as 60 men in each and which were centrally heated. By this time I had learnt how to utilize my five blankets and two sheets to the best advantage, and I became so used to sleeping on one of those

which is called for by a continuous stream of vital communications which must be passed from centre to centre accurately and rapidly.

The average layman can have no idea of the innumerable varied trades that constitute the extensive R.A.F. ground organization. Just as Britain is often referred to as a nation of shopkeepers, so the R.A.F. might well be described as a service of tradesmen. Every non-flying airman adopts a particular trade on enlistment and he receives, as I did, a full training in his special branch at one of the instructional centres. He becomes, therefore, a specialist, and he is graded and paid according to his trade classification. Among the best-paid trades in the R.A.F., for which the highest quality of workmanship is demanded, are those of instrument maker and wireless operator mechanic. Particularly skilled fitters are also highly-paid tradesmen, as are metal workers and riggers. An aircraftman second class (Group I) is paid 3s. 9d. a day, an aircraftman first class 4s. 6d., a leading aircraftman 5s. 6d. a day, a corporal 7s. 6d. a day, and so on. In addition, of course, every serviceman now gets an allowance of 6d. a day for cigarettes.

Another special group comprises such assorted trades as cook and butcher, coppersmith and motor-boat crew, and another group includes clerks, for a variety of duties, and equipment assistants. Yet another category consists of no fewer than nineteen different trades ranging from acetylene welder to photographer. A trade in this group which undoubtedly has an important place in bomber squadrons is that of armourer; armourers fit the bombs to our heavy aircraft. Wireless operators, who also come under this group, are the only air crew who are graded as tradesmen. There are, of course, many ground operators as well. In the same class as motor transport drivers, which covers both car and motor-cycle dispatch riders, are aircrafthands, who are engaged on a variety of general duties which range from ground defence to telephone operating. A separate category includes the various specialist assistants engaged in medical duties.

At the End of a Day's Work

With almost every trade represented in its ranks, not only is the whole of the R.A.F. practically self-supporting, but at the same time it keeps its personnel au fait with what are chiefly civil life occupations.

Naturally, camp life is on the whole a plain kind of existence, but there's more life and variety under the surface than might be imagined. Most of us sleep in stone barracks specially constructed as living quarters. Each room is fitted with a wireless, so that in the evenings, when our day's work is over, groups of airmen are always to be found taking their ease, listening to the wireless, reading, writing, playing cards, or just talking in what are both their living and sleeping quarters. Then there is always the N.A.A.F.I. restaurant, where there are special reading and writing rooms, in addition to the for ever busy canteen, where hot meals are in demand in the evening.

But although it can be very pleasant to spend one's evenings leisurely in camp, we all look forward to, and appreciate, a few precious hours away from the scene of our daily labours. It is refreshing indeed to renew contact with civil life—to see a film, visit a theatre, forgather at the local Toc H, or merely to stroll anywhere, drinking in the sight of civil life still in full swing.

Among the many varied trades that constitute the R.A.F. ground organization, that of armourer, as the author of the article in this page says, has a most important place. Aircraftmen are here seen armouring up a Bell Airacobra, details of which are shown in pages 164 and 267 of this volume. The guns in the wings and airscrew hub are clearly seen in this photograph. *Photo, G.P.U.*

completely uniformed, and plus a hefty kitbag containing an amazing assortment of "necessary items," I found myself, with hundreds of others, at a recruits training depot. Here we went through an intensive course of foot and rifle drill which straightened our backs and taught us something of the discipline demanded in the services.

New Year saw me at my trade training centre, a vast encampment miles from anywhere, which, with 12,000 airmen to cater for, is absolutely self-contained. There's an excellent camp cinema, two or three very lively N.A.A.F.I. canteens, and extensive playing fields. We worked hard and played hard; and by now, hardened to the vigorous R.A.F. life, I really began to feel the benefit of that intensive preliminary training. Quite honestly, I don't think I'd ever felt fitter in

iron bedsteads which we call "McDonalds" that I found an ordinary bed difficult to sleep on when I went home on leave.

Having completed our course satisfactorily, we were posted to stations in all parts of the country, and I was marked down for the headquarters of one of the Bomber Command groups. Here the whole concern is a hive of activity, and the signals section, of which teleprinting is an important part, works at high pressure 24 hours a day. The signals section of the R.A.F. is undoubtedly one of the most interesting—not to say one of the most important—in the service. Messages arrive from and are dispatched to the most remote parts of the country by wireless, telephone, and teleprinter. The teleprinter system, which is maintained by the G.P.O., affords the R.A.F. that essential secrecy

Below Ground in the H.Q. of Bomber Command

In the Operations Room of the station (above) the operation ordered by Bomber Command Headquarters is worked out in detail. What is the best route to the target? How can it be identified? What of the weather? On the right, a corner of the Intelligence Room where reports, constantly arriving from Group Headquarters and stations, are pieced together.

The entrance to Bomber Command Headquarters is a single door only, and this and the stairway are guarded by sentries. Headquarters are protected by layers of concrete, and are illuminated by a soft artificial light from half-concealed reflectors. In the Operations Room the Air Officer Commanding-in-Chief, with his staff plans the night operations, and here all data referring to the air war are minutely studied and carefully kept up to date.

Right, one of the three large pivotal tables which stand near the desk of the Commander-in-Chief, Sir Richard Peirso (seen right) in the Operations Room. The first is covered with maps, graphs and photographic records which offer a bird's-eye view of the whole field of battle. On the second there is a large map of Europe showing routes to the various objectives and other information. The third table displays facts about targets, the number of times they have been bombed, and a map of Berlin.

Photos, British Official: Crown Copyright

I Was There! .... Eye Witness Stories of the War

I Stood Beside the Sentinels in the Khyber Pass

In a recent visit to the N.W. Frontier of India, Reuter's special correspondent, as he tells below, saw something of the modern defences of the Khyber Pass, which, following the formation of a front in the Middle East, is now more than ever important.

PASSING Jamrud Fort, standing like a sentinel at the base of the Khyber Pass, as it debouches into the rich fertile plains of the frontier province and the Punjab, I drove through a narrow defile between grim, barren cliffs which for centuries past have been the silent witnesses of savage fighting, noting the squat menacing pillboxes at the top of almost every hill commanding the valley beneath.

At the Indo-Afghan border I halted, and from there slowly retraced my steps, while the enormous obstacles that face any would-be imitator of Alexander were pointed out to me. Apart from the physical advantages which would enable a defender with only a small force to hold up an enemy many times his number in the narrow portion of the Pass, I was shown ingenious defences based on the most modern methods which now stretch the whole length of the Khyber. While nothing can be revealed regarding their exact nature, it can certainly be said that they are of the most formidable character. So skilfully are they planned and camouflaged that any attempt to invade India by this historic route would be a most hazardous undertaking.

By a narrow road coiling like a snake round the sides of stark hills, with hair-raising drops of thousands of feet stretching beneath me, I reached a typical infantry post at the top of a commanding hill.

Here, in bleak, barren surroundings, India's soldiers keep watch day and night. Curving away in the distance are miles of carefully planned firing and communication trenches hewn out of the rocky hillsides, and designed for utmost mobility to meet attacks from every direction.

Since they first entered the Pass just over 100 years ago, the British have blasted a superb motor road out of the mountain side, enabling the passage of motor transport between Afghanistan and India. Moreover, a broad-gauge railway, which is a monument of engineering skill, runs as far as Landi Kotal.

Despite these developments, the great Pass is now a far tougher nut to crack than when Alexander sent a division through over 2,000 years ago during his invasion of India. And the Indian and British forces stationed there—still constantly improving

The compass, wristlet watch, alarm clock, torch and Bible which helped the five French boys in their canoe escape from France. Their adventure is told in this page.
Copyright, Free French Forces

the fortifications—are quietly confident of holding against all-comers this historic gateway to India's fertile plains and the vital industries which are now playing so large a part in the Empire war effort.

We Paddled Our Canoes Across the Channel

After thirty hours in the Channel in two canoes, five French boys between the ages of 16 and 19 reached the English coast on September 17. The boys' own story of their plucky venture is here told exclusively to "The War Illustrated."

CANOEING has always been my favourite hobby (said nineteen-year-old Pierre, who led the party), but I have always found time to have pets, too. Dogs, rabbits and cats are my favourites, and I hate to think of the pets that have had to be eaten in France because of the shortage of food.

My younger brother Jean is an ardent canoeist, too, having started to paddle his own canoe when only six years old. Renaud is a schoolfriend of ours who also owned a canoe, which got damaged, and it was while we were all three repairing it that we started to talk about the possibilities of escape from France. I asked two other fellow students to join us; they are Christian and his brother Guy.

For weeks we talked about the project,

leaving nothing to chance. We planned what stores to take—bread, army biscuits and water. We knew that bread tickets would have to be stolen, so Jean hung about a bakery, and dived under the counter and stole some when the assistant was busy. Our navigational instruments were of the simplest: a compass in each canoe; an alarm clock—this was Jean's idea—a large Bible, a gun and some rounds of ammunition.

We set off on a suitably dark night after leaving notes for our parents and dodging the German guards. For a few kilometres we were certain that we could not get away undetected because, although the night was dark, the sea was so phosphorescent that shafts of light came from our paddles each time we lifted them out of the water. We

THE KHYBER PASS, North-West Frontier "gateway" to India, may yet become a storm centre, should Hitler, like Alexander, sigh for new worlds to conquer. But the mechanized Nazi savages will find this portal to the riches of Ind heavily barred and locked with every defensive device against their lust for loot. This striking photograph shows the stern topographical realities of the frontier. These, as the writer in this page tells us, are bristling with the most modern methods for repelling an invader.
Photo, Fox

paddled most of the night ; when the wind was favourable we hoisted sail ; as the sea got choppy we shipped a lot of water and had to bale constantly. Of course, it was not long before we were all soaking wet. Because we were afraid of becoming separated I went from my own canoe into Renaud's. He had been all alone and was very tired ; soon after that I tied the two canoes together.

When dawn broke we found we had come a fair way, but were still within sight of the French coast. I became very sick and had to lie down. All day long we battled with the wind, waves, tides and currents and we were all tired, cold, wet, hungry and apprehensive when night again began to fall. But we never swerved from our determination to get to England. Shortly after dawn, about thirty hours after we had left our own coast, we were off Dungeness. I knew then that a difficult part of our trip would be the landing. Heavy breakers were rolling up the beach and, worse still, rocks were visible, even in the poor light, but what I wanted to know more than anything else was whether the shore was mined or not.

Renaud and I were lucky. We brought the two canoes safely in. We were so stiff from having been cramped up for so many hours that we all fell as we got out ; our legs just wouldn't hold us up.

Everyone was very kind to us, and it was grand to be given a hot bath, fresh clothes and a meal. We were all most surprised to get a whole cake of soap each ! We couldn't get over the quality of the woollen clothing we were given, and none of us had seen real leather-soled shoes for months—let alone had any to wear.

We enjoyed being in London for a few

days, and we saw Mr. and Mrs. Churchill and General de Gaulle. It was exciting going to No. 10 Downing Street and being received in the Cabinet room. I was not nervous with Mr. Churchill, but I must confess that I was a little frightened at the thought of meeting the General.

As soon as we have had a good rest in the country I am starting my army training. The others are too young, and must continue their studies for a time. They are going to the college at Malvern, where there are about fifty other French boys completing their studies before joining the Free French Forces.

Mr. and Mrs. Churchill entertaining in the garden of 10 Downing Street the French boys who escaped from France in a canoe. The toast is to Free France. Photo, Associated Press

fire on us. They also shelled us from the armoured cars. One of my men was wounded and died later. The back of my car was also damaged, but it was still workable. The firing of the Nazis was notably inaccurate, but we got on the move.

After covering seven miles to the east we suddenly came across two German tanks which were cutting us off. One made off as we fired at it, but the other stuck with damaged treads. We shot it full of holes ; then with tommy guns we chased the crew of five until they called " Kamerad." They all appeared to be under 20. They were not at all truculent, and were very glad to be captured without being ill-treated.

Another Nazi tank appeared while we were bundling the prisoners into our vehicles and we fired, definitely hitting it. Quite a number of the enemy were to the south and east of us, so we bustled off with our captives. Next day we returned and salvaged the damaged German tank.—*Reuter.*

Outnumbered, We Captured a Nazi Tank

Typical of small-scale encounters between British and German troops in Libya was the following incident, in which a captain and 44 men of a famous rifle regiment were engaged.

TELLING of his successful running fight with German armoured vehicles, Captain J. A Hunter said :

My platoon with two anti-tank guns was in a listening post on the centre of a track running southward from Fort Capuzzo, west of the escarpment, on the night of September 13. We heard some enemy transport on the move so I sent out a patrol who reported heavy movements. But it was not until dawn that we actually saw it was Nazi tanks to the right and rear of us, rumbling along, making a tremendous racket. Following them were Nazis in lorries.

We fired on them, causing them to halt, but as they greatly outnumbered us, we withdrew and lay in wait for them in a position five miles back.

When they approached again we fired at a thousand yards range, taking them by surprise and setting several of their vehicles on fire. They lost no time in unloading small field guns from the trucks and opening

GERMAN TANK, captured in the Western Desert, being dismantled by British engineers at a mobile workshop near the front. Encounters between British and Nazi troops are continually taking place in the areas of Tobruk and Sollum, and in this page is a description of an engagement in which a German tank and its crew fell into the "bag."

Photo, International Graphic Press

Editor's Postscript

ONE of the chief mentors of my youth was Principal Dyer, who so long ago as 1873 founded the Imperial College of Engineering at Tokyo and thus helped distantly to bring about that westernizing of the Japanese which, after the expansion of Teutonic barbarism, has done so much to land the world in its present mess. Dyer was one of Glasgow's great men, and it was fortunate for me that in my teens, when he had returned to his native city after ten years of intensive work for the emerging aggressors of the Far East, he could spare so many teatime hours in his study at Dowanhill to engage an ignorant but inquiring youngster in profitable talk. How it all began I cannot remember, but fifty years later it makes me happy to recall those sittings at his feet and a touch of pride that so fine a man could have thought so young and raw a journalist worthy of his friendship.

WHAT has sent my mind coursing back across these years today? An odd thing enough. For weeks past I have been striving to bring order to the chaos which had come upon my library consequent upon an unwished-for change of home dictated by, perhaps, a too-ready assent to an official hint to withdraw somewhat from a front-line position in the Battle of Britain. Trammelled with thousands of books for which new accommodation had somehow to be found, I have had at least the comfort in the dread process of rearranging them to discover forgotten souvenirs of a past that sometimes looks as remote as the fall of Rome, and anon as recent as yesterday.

I DID not know until today that among my many forgotten books there was " Japan in World Politics," written by Dyer in 1909, and in turning over Dyer's unremembered pages the job of arranging my bookshelves at once gave place to checking the changes of thirty years with his somewhat austere presentation of a subject on which no man at that time had a better right to be heard. I find him stating in this book of his such incontestable truths as " the ultimate solution of international politics will be reached only when an adequate idea has been formed of the meaning and object of life, both personal and national," and " no one can undertake a more important work than that of doing something, however little, to promote the fraternity of nations and the abolition or diminution of standing armies by the education of public opinion in the direction of peace." Good. But we in Britain, under the lead of such statesmen as Sir Austen Chamberlain, Viscount Cecil, Ramsay MacDonald, Earl Baldwin, Neville Chamberlain and many others, did more than a little in that direction, while an unregenerate Germany, a misled Italy, and an aggressive Japan were devoting every thought and action in the opposite direction. And in 1939 we suffered for having done that little. Give a boy a drum and tell him not to make a noise with it ! All unconsciously the idealist in Dyer was cancelled out by his making these rather

horrid Japanese machine-minded. Note here the irony of the events : years before Dyer wrote his book the late Kaiser had a cartoon drawn and widely circulated to warn us of the Yellow Peril—China's millions egged on by Japan's westernized Samurai on the way to world domination—while this Yellow Peril, so far as its Japanese component is concerned, has hitched its *panzerkraftwagen* to Hitler's star ! Yes, and China's millions have become one of the hopes of Western Democracy ! A comic world, forsooth !

DYER in 1909 was quite rightly concerned about Germany's " aggressive commercialism " as a menace to world peace, nor was he blind to Britain's rival commercialism. Then speaks the idealist : " A new way of life both individual and national," and " a combination of the ideals of the East and the West, by which the means of life and all that concerns them are subordinated to the ends of life "—that comprised his only solution. How ardently every sane man would like to think that possible ! But we all know in our hearts that ideals are unattainable—yet not the less to be pursued. Worth recording here that Dyer told me the policy of the Japs in his day was to employ the best European minds to teach them the tenets of Western civilization and immediately they had got all they could out of their preceptors to send them packing with good pensions and let little nippy Nipponese carry on in their places. Clever little rascals these Japs !

Writing so soon after the conclusion of the Russo-Japanese War, which revealed the inherent rottenness of Tsarism, just as June 1940 disclosed the inherent, deep-seated

putrescence of France's Third Republic, my mentor of these old years foresaw a Russian war of revenge . . . He did not guess that the Russia of the Tsars was already finished as a great power, and that a totally inconceivable new Russia of the Soviets would thirty years later have to face the unimagined Germany of the Nazis and the Yellow Peril of Japan in a day of war which would have been no more than a madman's dream to Dyer, but is now a living reality of horror, largely through the triumphs of engineering—to which he had devoted his life !

THE newest volume in my reassembled library is William L. Shirer's " Berlin Diary," which has been the smash hit (Hollywoodese) in America, and over here ought to number its readers by the hundred thousand. No foreign correspondent ever had a more engrossing story to tell, none has ever told his story better. It begins back in 1934 when he and his wife said good-bye to the little Spanish village where they had spent a " sabbatical-year," much needed after the preceding six of journalistic adventure far from his American homeland.

ONE can well imagine his feelings on that night of December 13, 1940, when he sailed away from Lisbon. " A full moon was out over the Tagus, and all the million lights of Lisbon . . . sparkled brightly as the ship slid down to sea. For how long ? Beyond Lisbon over almost all of Europe the lights were out. This little fringe on the south-west corner of the Continent kept them burning. Civilization, such as it was, had not yet been stamped out here by a Nazi boot. But next week ? Next month ? The month after ? Would not Hitler's hordes take this too and extinguish the last lights ?" To read Shirer's description of many Belgian and French towns, and especially of Paris, all with live personal memories for me, as seen by him when no British eye could observe them, is profoundly moving.

One passage of Mr. Shirer's book, where every page can yield several worthy of remembrance, I must give on account of its timeliness. It was written in Berlin ten months back. " Hitler's Germany can never dominate the Continent of Europe as long as Britain holds out, neither can it master the world as long as the United States stands unafraid in its path. It is a long-term fundamental conflict of dynamic forces. The clash is as inevitable as that of two planets hurtling inexorably through the heavens towards each other. As a matter of fact, it may come sooner than almost all Americans at home imagine. An officer of the High Command somewhat shocked me the other day while we were discussing the matter. He-said : ' You think Roosevelt can pick the moment most advantageous to America and Britain for coming into the War. Did you ever stop to think that Hitler, a master of timing, may choose the moment for war with America—a moment which he thinks will give him the advantage ?' I must admit I never did." Yet on October 27th, 1941, we find the U.S.A. Secretary of State saying: " The probability is that we shall not be at war until Hitler decrees that we shall." " So what ?" as they say over there.

LORD LOUIS MOUNTBATTEN who so brilliantly carries on his family's service to the British Navy has been promoted from command of the " Illustrious " to a new command of major importance which carries the rank of Commodore 1st Class.
Photo, Cannons

Printed in England and published on the 10th, 20th and 30th of each month by the Proprietors, The Amalgamated Press, Ltd., The Fleetway House, Farringdon Street, London, E.C.4. Registered for transmission by Canadian Magazine Post. Sole Agents for Australia and New Zealand : Messrs. Gordon & Gotch, Ltd., and for South Africa : Central News Agency, Ltd. November 10th, 1941. S.S. *Editorial Address :* JOHN CARPENTER HOUSE, WHITEFRIARS, LONDON, E.C.4.

Vol 5 _The War Illustrated_ Nº 112

Edited by Sir John Hammerton

FOURPENCE

NOV. 20TH. 1941

QUEEN ELIZABETH, mammoth Cunard White Star liner, is here seen entering the dock at Singapore for repairs and overhaul. Since the news was published of her arrival in New York on March 7, 1940, after her secret maiden voyage from Clydebank, little has been heard of this great vessel, which has since been used as a transport, possibly conveying some of the many thousands of reinforcements sent to Malaya. Her great length of over 1,000 feet is difficult to visualize owing to foreshortening. *Photo, Planet News*

NO. 113 WILL BE PUBLISHED SATURDAY, NOV. 29

BUT FOR BRITAIN!... THE TWO AMERICAS?

BY THE EDITOR

Not enough attention is being drawn to the role which the Latin republics may yet have to play in Hitler's War. But for Britain the grip of the Nazi would even now have been tightening upon their throat —unless the Northern continent had been plunged into chaos by the arrival of clouds of bombers over its sky-scrapers and populous cities ! We know that a single imaginative broadcast by Orson Welles, most brilliant of America's radio, stage and film personalities, created a panic throughout the States in the autumn of 1938, a few weeks after Munich. A panic of hysteria far greater than anything seen here when the air blitz was actually at its height over Britain !

But for Britain having the courage and resource to stand up to Germany on the sea and in the air with nothing more substantial than American promises of help, which even now are far from having been fulfilled, the Hun would have had his chance to panic the U.S.A. into a state of mind very different from that which now obtains throughout all America, despite the Lindberghites and Isolationists. '' But for Britain '' I have said, and let the historian of a future day underline and emphasize that phrase.

This War is as much a war for the true democracies of North and South America as for the survival of the British peoples. And the United States should have been in it long ere this—would have been were not President Roosevelt compelled to move with caution while shepherding his vast and heterogeneous mass of free citizens to that point of realism at which Hitler has now helped them to arrive.

The eternal shame of France will be that for eighteen of the most critical months in world history she has watched the Britain she deserted, and against whom her soldiers have actually fought, suffer and struggle alone to save those ideals of liberty, equality and fraternity which were so long her own guiding stars, and the very names of which the infamous Vichy government has obliterated, just as the German overlords have done, from the public buildings in France.

But for Britain there would be no more France. In that happy, but maybe far-off day, when General de Gaulle and those brave, determined French who have followed him, either in person or in spirit, stand erect in a France redeemed, somehow the name of this island fortress of their freedom should be honoured for ever, boldly linked with that of the land which British heroism will surely save from the fate the Hun has in mind for it : '' moitié potager, moitié bordel.''

Reverting to the opening sentence of this article, however, I wish to glance briefly at that once far, but now, thanks to aerial progress, easily accessible continent where in happier times I travelled and sojourned in most of its ten republics from Panama to Argentina. For in the grandiose Nazi plans for world domination the South American continent has naturally a large place.

The conquest of South America is no new ambition of Nazi Germany : it constantly preoccupied the minds of the German expansionists in the days of Kaiser William II, and the numerous Fifth Columns existing there today had for the most part been founded in his time. Brazil on the east and Chile on the west were the main centres of German penetration. The Chilean army was trained by German officers, accoutred like the Hun from pickelhaube to boot and spur. Early in the century flourishing German

communities in the two republics named looked not to the national governments under which they lived and thrived but to Berlin. Brazil in its southern regions had such towns as Porto Alegre, capital city of the State of Rio Grande do Sul, and the important seaport bearing the same name as the State, largely, almost exclusively, controlled by German colonists, and throughout the whole republic the Hun was busy digging himself in.

Chile was in similar case. Valdivia, in the south, with a population of some 20,000 in those days, had a town council so German in its membership that its Alcalde, or Mayor, had the brazen nerve publicly to cable the Kaiser on his fiftieth birthday (1909) that he had a colony of '' loyal Germans '' amounting to so many thousands in that part of the world ! Valdivia was indeed a German city not only in its population but in its material appearance, as most of its houses and business premises had been constructed sectionally in Germany and shipped out to be re-assembled (as they do with their U-boats) on Chilean soil. And very charming they looked : no South American town of its size was more attractive. Talcahuano, Concepción (near where our disastrous Battle of Coronel, Nov. 1, 1914, was fought), and dozens of other coastwise towns of Chile swarmed with Germans, many of whom did great service as spies on the British naval movements in 1914-18.

Germans in the Argentine, though numerous and powerful in the commercial and political world, did not overwhelm the other non-Latin races, though they had important daily newspapers and magazines — "Caras y Caretas," most popular of all Buenos Aires weeklies, was the product of expert German technicians—and their fingers were in every pie and plot. The same obtained in varying degree throughout all the ten republics, large and small : Paraguay had even a German president. And that was

DR. GETULIO VARGAS, President of Brazil, who, after paying tribute to the rising star of Fascism in June 1940, now utters stern warnings against " aggression, from whatever source." *Photo, Associated Press*

thirty years ago. Had the Huns of 1914 won their war all these South American '' cells '' would have speedily become focal points of revolution if the German Fleet had been able to command South American waters instead of scuttling itself at Scapa.

Under the direction of the more ambitious and infinitely abler Hitler, the Kaiser's groundwork must have been vastly extended in recent years. The prolific Teuton has multiplied his kind and Nazi teaching and intrigue have influenced great numbers of the Latin Americans, so that in the large cities, such as Buenos Aires, Rosario, Santiago, Valparaiso, the native population has been split into factions that could seriously impede the full national expression of resistance to a Nazi attack : Nazi-inspired riots have been reported in recent months in a number of important centres of the southern republics— the late president of Panama had to quit because of his avowed Fascist principles. There have been riots even in Havana engineered by the locally active Hitlerites.

All this despite the adherence of the governments of both South and Central America— Mexico here proving the most encouraging example of anti-Nazi feeling—to the declaration against foreign aggression at the Pan-American Conference at Havana, at the end of July 1940, and their determination to cooperate with the United States and Canada in resisting any and every form of European interference with the independence of the existing republican states.

There are two important declarations on which the international policy of '' The Two Americas '' is based: the Monroe doctrine and the Drago doctrine. The former is the better known: formulated in 1823 by U.S. President Monroe, it may be stated briefly as affirming that any attempt by any power outside the American continents to colonize any part of Central and South America would be regarded as a menace to the peace of North America. The Drago doctrine is in a sense a pendant to the Monroe. Its author was a famous Argentine statesman and jurist (with whom the writer had an interview in Buenos Aires a few years before his death in 1921). Drago in 1902 had persuaded the Argentine government to secure general agreement to the declaration that the independence of the Spanish-American nationalities must be recognized and that no power should be allowed to impose itself by force of arms upon any of them. In other words, what goes for European powers in the Monroe doctrine goes for the United States and Canada also. The South American republics had scant regard for " Yanquis " in those days and did not accept America's Monroe doctrine without certain reservations : hence the Drago declaration.

Such, then, is a very fragmentary sketch of the situation in Latin America, but it indicates what an enticing field of Nazi activities exists in that vast continent of 7,000,000 square miles, with its enormous natural resources and a population of some hundred million. What a continent to dive-bomb into submission to the Nazi yoke ! In the fevered dreams of Hitler that might not appear too much to attempt. But for Britain, Russia and America barring the way the attempt would assuredly be made. Meanwhile, the Nazis of South America are likely to prove more a nuisance value for Hitler than potential key pieces in the assembling of his jig-saw puzzle of the new World Order !

J. A. Hammerton

The Swastika Makes Trouble South of Panama

BRAZIL, revising its opinions, is now coming down heavily upon Nazi activities in the country. Police officers are seen removing evidence of anti-democratic activities from a Nazi headquarters.

CHILEAN NAZIS meet in Santiago. There is a Chilean flag in the foreground and a Chilean officer well in the rear ; otherwise the meeting might have been staged anywhere in Germany.

IN ARGENTINA, at Apostoles, these rifles were discovered buried in the garden of a German resident. Nazi banners were also found in the house. Evidence of Nazi intrigues have been revealed throughout Argentina.

MONTEVIDEO firemen are retrieving some of the hundred grenades thrown into the Las Brujas River by Nazi agents after their secret organization had been discovered by the authorities.

Street-fighting in Buenos Aires between students of pro- and anti- Nazi sympathies shows how the Argentine is split by faction hatreds. A policeman is arresting a student (left) who has thrown a smoke bomb.

Photos, Keystone, "New York Times Magazine," Associated Press, Wide World, Fox

Captains of Germany's Mighty War Machine

Field-Marshal VON BOCK, in command of the German armies on the Russian central front, led a German army in the Battle of France.

Field-Marshal VON RUNDSTEDT, extreme right, is seen introducing young staff officers to Hitler. Von Rundstedt, like Von Leeb, came back from retirement at the beginning of the war and now leads the German armies in the Ukraine.

Field-Marshal VON KLUGE, who commanded an army in Flanders in 1940, is now leading an army in the central sector of the Russian front.

Field-Marshal RITTER VON LEEB, whose armies are attempting the capture of Leningrad, was a major on the German Staff in 1918.

General STRAUSS, another of the successful tank generals working on the Eastern Front. He is seen in conference at his headquarters discussing his plan of operations to encircle the opposing Russian forces

Field-Marshal Wilhelm LIST, Germany's blitzkrieg expert, commands an army group in the Balkans which faces Turkey in ominous fashion.

General HOTH, Guderian's right-hand man, is an ex-infantry general who has had great success with the German panzer divisions.

General Heinz GUDERIAN, Polish-born Inspector of the Nazi tank divisions, based most of his strategy on the theories of General de Gaulle.

LUFTWAFFE LEADERS are Field-Marshal Karl KESSELRING (left), commanding a German air fleet in Russia, and (above) Field-Marshal Otto SPERRLE, commanding the German air force in Western Europe.

Photos, E.N.A., Planet News, Wide World, Associated Press, International Graphic Press, Keystone

Maybe We Can Learn From Hitler's Army

In this article our Contributing Editor, E. Royston Pike, writes of the German Army as it has
been described by two American correspondents until recently in Berlin—William L. Shirer of
Columbia Broadcasting System and Joseph C. Harsch of the " Christian Science Monitor."

Brutes and scoundrels as many of the
Nazi soldiers are, they are, it must be
admitted—well, soldiers, and first-
rate soldiers at that.   Never since Napoleon's
day has there been such a succession of victories.   In little more than two years a score
of armies has been destroyed by Hitler's war
machine ; great states have been smashed
into ruin, whole peoples enslaved, by the men
whom we used to laugh at in days gone by
because of their strutting goose-step.   The
German war machine has rolled on inexorably
—relentlessly. It has not been stopped. Not yet.

The Kaiser's army was renowned in its
day ; it used to be said that the army which
swept across France to the Marne
in the brilliant autumn sunshine of
1914 was the finest that had ever
taken the field.   But Hitler's (so it
would seem) is better than the
Kaiser's.   " A well-oiled machine
of destruction," the American
journalist, William L. Shirer,
describes it in his " Berlin Diary,"*
a book from which I am about to
quote extensively.   " A magnificent machine," he calls it on
another page ;   " a gigantic, im-
personal war machine, run as
coolly and efficiently as our auto-
mobile industry in Detroit."   So
efficient that you have to see it in
action to believe it.

Shirer asserts that, compared with
the German command of the air,
" the Allies have no eyes."   He
describes the Germans bringing up
men, guns and supplies, unhindered,
on a vast scale.   In France motor
transport was used exclusively.
Stretching across the plain, driving
along at 40 or 50 miles an hour, sped
unending mechanized columns.
" You wonder how they are kept
fed with petrol and oil, but they are.
Petrol supplies come forward with
everything else. Every driver knows
where he can tank up when he
runs short."   Absolutely no excitement, no tension.   An officer
directing artillery stopped for half
an hour to explain what he was up
to, while General von Reichenau
halted for an hour to explain to the
visiting journalists his particular job.   " A few
miles down the road two million men are trying
to slaughter one another.   He bosses almost a
million of them.   The General smiles and
jauntily says good-bye."   This is the Reichenau
who led the German van into Poland.   He
was the first to cross the Vistula River.
He swam it, says Shirer.   Now he is in Russia
driving through the Ukraine and the Donbass.

Generals in the Van

From Shirer's description of last year's
campaign in France one gets an impression
of speed—almost effortless, mechanical in its
perfection, compared with which the French
effort was almost pitifully ineffective.   Particularly striking was the comparison between
the opposing generals.   The French generals
were " civilized, intellectual, frail, ailing old
men, who stopped thinking new thoughts 20
years ago, and have taken no physical exercise for the last 10 years."   The German
generals, on the other hand, were all young ;
one of them was not yet 40, most of them
were in the forties, and only a few at the very
top were in their fifties.   And they had all

* " Berlin Diary : The Journal of a Foreign Correspondent, 1934-1941."   Hamish Hamilton, 12s. 6d.

the characteristics of youth—dash and daring,
imagination, initiative, and physical prowess.
They actually led their troops in the front
line ;   all the big German tank attacks were
led in person by the commanding generals.
" They did not sit in the safety of a dug-out,
10 miles behind the lines, directing by radio.
They sat in their tanks, in the thick of the
fray, and directed by radio and signalling
from where they could see how the battle was
going."

Quite as important as the quality of the
Nazi generals is the " fantastically good
morale " of the German Army as a whole.
Here Shirer's evidence is supported by the

VON REICHENAU, one of Hitler's General-Field-Marshals, is here
seen studying the map on the Eastern front.   Habitually monocled,
he has the reputation of being a good Nazi party man as well as a
brilliant general.
Photo, Keystone

testimony of another American correspondent in Berlin, Joseph C. Harsch, who in his
recent work " Pattern of Conquest " has much
to say of the German Army.   He tells us that
there is " a new vitality and ingenuity in
leadership, from the High Command down
to the lowest non-commissioned leader of a
platoon, which has never been approached in
modern times."   There is only one criterion
for promotion and command in Hitler's army,
and that is not birth, not personal relationships,
not even standing in the Nazi party, but—
ability.   During constant exercise and large-
scale manoeuvres the Germans in peacetime
sought ability and rejected incompetence. Men
were swiftly promoted to officer's rank, and
officers who failed in the field were as swiftly
demoted ; the same principle is employed today
under conditions of actual war.

In another passage Harsch remarks on
the freedom of the German officer from administrative work ;   unlike his British opposite
number, he spends little time in the orderly
room, but is almost constantly with his men.
His primary task is to be familiar with them,
to win their respect and loyalty, and to
practise with them the art of war.

In the Kaiser's army lieutenants and captains used to deal with their men through the
sergeants.   In Hitler's army the lower officers
know everything of a personal nature about
their men.   They have received instructions
that they must be their men's confidants
and friends.   There is a new *esprit de corps*,
based on an honest camaraderie between
officers and men.   " The old Prussian goose-
step, heel clicking, the *Jawohl* of the private
when answering an officer, are still there (to
quote Shirer again), but the great gulf between
officers and men has gone in this war.   They
feel like the members of one great family.
Even the salute has a new meaning.   German
privates salute each other, thus making the
gesture more of a comradely greeting than a mere recognition of
superior rank.   In cafés, restaurants,
dining-cars, officers and men off
duty sit at the same table and
converse as man to man."   In the
field, officers and men usually eat
from the same soup kitchen, and
in Paris " I recall a colonel who
was treating a dozen privates to
an excellent lunch in a little
Basque restaurant off the Avenue
de l'Opéra.   When lunch was over
he drew, with all the care of a
loving father, a plan for them to
visit the sights of Paris.   The
respect of these ordinary soldiers
for their colonel would be hard to
exaggerate.   Yet it was not for his
rank, but for the man."

For the Soldier the Best

One reason for the excellent
morale of the German troops is
their realization that they are receiving the very best treatment that the
nation can offer ;   their food and
clothing are far better than those of
the civilians.   Their barracks are
heated, when the people at home
often go cold.   The Nazi soldiers
may have oranges and coffee and
fresh vegetables—things unobtainable on the home front.   At Christmas the food parcels are sent home
from the front and not the other
way round.   Hitler, Shirer reminds
us, once said that as a private of
the last war he would see that the
men of his new army benefited by
the lessons he had learned.   That is almost
the only promise he has ever kept.

Knowing these things, it is perhaps a little
easier for us to understand the extraordinary
triumphs won by the German arms of recent
months.   Perhaps from the German experiences we may ourselves learn some lessons
not without value in the winning of ultimate
victory.   For no army is invincible ; and one
day, so we confidently believe and prepare for,
Hitler's army will have its " black day," just
as did Hindenburg-Ludendorff's in 1918.
" It will be beaten," says Mr. Harsch, " not
by masses of infantry bogged down in
trenches, but by relatively few men operating
large numbers of tanks and airplanes, produced by some industrial organism larger,
more productive and more sheltered than
Germany's.   And the force which defeats it
must also possess another essential of the
German military machine.   It must be
backed, as is Germany's, by a government
which can exact sacrifices from the civilian
mass behind the army beyond anything
America has ever faced."   And not only
America.   We in Britain, too, may find in
that paragraph the way to win.

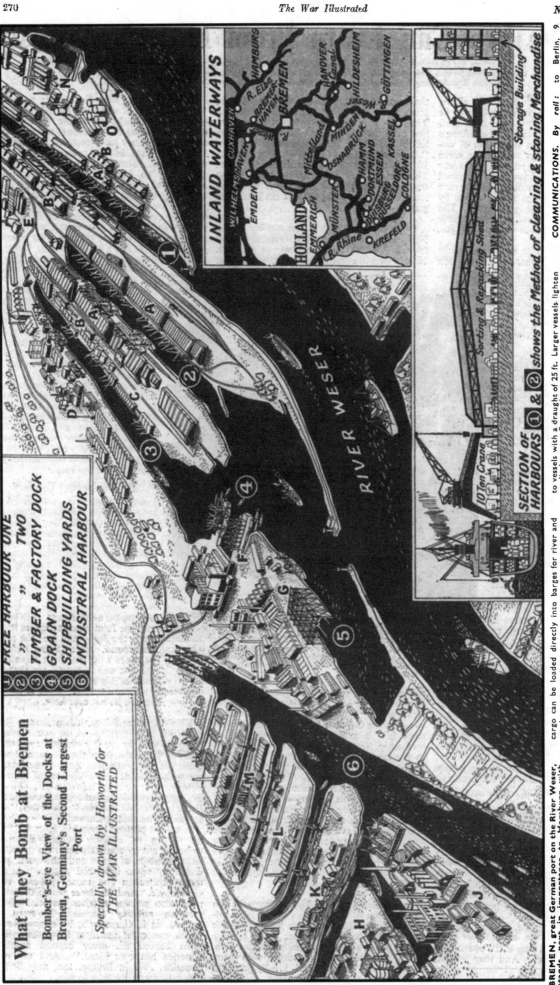

What They Bomb at Bremen

Bomber's-eye View of the Docks at Bremen, Germany's Second Largest Port

Specially drawn by Haworth for THE WAR ILLUSTRATED

1 FREE HARBOUR ONE
2 　" 　　" 　　TWO
3 TIMBER & FACTORY DOCK
4 GRAIN DOCK
5 SHIPBUILDING YARDS
6 INDUSTRIAL HARBOUR

INLAND WATERWAYS

Storage Building

Sorting & Repacking Shed

10 Ton Crane

RIVER WESER

SECTION OF HARBOURS 1 & 2 shows the Method of clearing & storing Merchandise

---

BREMEN, great German port on the River Weser, stands next in importance to Hamburg with regard to the amount of shipping it handles. The port is well equipped and laid out, and this bird's-eye view of the docks shows some of the reasons why Bremen is a frequent and important target of R.A.F. bombers.

The Basins of Free Harbours One and Two are provided with four sets of railway lines and a vast number of cranes lifting between five and ten tons, behind which are the huge sorting and repacking sheds (A). From these sheds goods are either moved by rail or road or stored in warehouses (B). Alternatively

cargo can be loaded directly into barges for river and canal transportation.

The Timber and Factory Dock is the main centre of import and storage of Baltic timber (C). Here also are oil factories (D) and jute mills (E).

In the Grain Dock the plant, the largest of its kind in Europe, has a capacity of 75,000 tons. At the two piers (F) the cargoes of four large ships can be dealt with simultaneously by automatic elevators with a capacity of 600 tons per hour.

The Shipbuilding Yards lie farther down the river (G), Bremen, although 46 miles from the sea, is accessible

to vessels with a draught of 25 ft. Larger vessels lighten or discharge at Bremerhaven.

The Industrial Harbour is closed by a lock 564 ft. long and 82 ft. wide, with a maximum depth of 28 ft. Here is situated one of Germany's largest oil refineries (H), which deals with crude petroleum from the oil-fields in the neighbourhood of Bremen and around the River Aller. Here, too, are situated blast furnaces (J) ; coal transhipment plant (K), by which 16 wagons an hour can be lifted and discharged into ships ; potash plant (L); and timber storage (M). At (N) is the Atlas Werke A.G. (shipbuilding auxiliary industry), and (O) is a mineral oil refinery.

COMMUNICATIONS. By rail : to Berlin, 9 hours. To Hamm, important junction for the industrial Ruhr, 6 hours.

By autobahnen (motor highway) : to Central and Southern Germany.

By waterways : The small map shows the network of canals and rivers connecting Bremen with most parts of Germany, including the Ruhr, and, via the Mittelland Kanal, Berlin and the Baltic port of Stettin. Along these lanes fleets of barges move cargoes vital for Germany's war effort. Any dislocation at Bremen may have important repercussions elsewhere.

Just What Damage Have We Done to Germany?

To those who are hoping that widespread and sustained bombing will bring Germany to her knees, a recently-issued report by the Air Ministry and the Ministry of Economic Warfare will prove disappointing reading. Damage is being done ; but the evidence provided by this report, at least, falls far short of what might have been anticipated from a number of ministerial pronouncements made earlier in the year.

BOMBS on Germany ! " Our raids (upon German harbours and cities) have already exceeded in severity anything which any single town has in a single night experienced over here." That is a passage taken from a speech by Mr. Churchill on April 10. Three months later, on July 15, the Prime Minister declared that " in the last few weeks alone we have thrown upon Germany about half the tonnage of bombs thrown by the Germans upon our cities during the whole course of the war." A few days before, Colonel Moore-Brabazon, Minister of Aircraft Production, had assured the House of Commons that it would not be many months before the recent enemy raids on London would be " mere child's play " compared with the raids we should be making on Berlin. Then on September 3, Sir Archibald Sinclair, Secretary of State for Air,

Loading-up a Handley Page Halifax heavy bomber. With its four Rolls-Royce Merlin engines and strong armament the Halifax is one of the most formidable types of heavy bomber in existence.

expressed the view that many Germans must be wondering how many other towns like Munster would by the Germans themselves be called unhappy, or be devastated like Aachen.

With these words in mind, let us study the statement concerning the progress of Bomber Command's intensified air offensive against Berlin and other German cities, issued by the Air Ministry and the Ministry of Economic Warfare on October 22.

Berlin is the first town mentioned. Recent attacks, the heaviest being that of September 7-8, have not been comparable in weight with the Luftwaffe's persistent raids on the London area in the autumn and winter of 1940, so it is not possible to compare the damage done. Berlin, it is declared, plays a greater part in the German industrial war effort than does London in Britain's—a statement which is the exact opposite of one which was frequently made when the public and press together were demanding " Bombs on Berlin ! " One of the engineering works hit in the past month was the Knorrbremse A.G. plant, which produces almost all the brakes used on German and European railways ; considerable destruction was caused in railway repair shops at the Schlesischer

station, and railway installations at and near Potsdamer and Anhalter stations (not unlike King's Cross and St. Pancras) were damaged. The tunnel between the two stations was hit, causing many casualties, and a number of houses in the area were also damaged. Many postal vehicles near Potsdamer Station were destroyed ; tracks serving the central meat market were hit, and the Eden and Adlon luxury hotels were hit on the same night.

Next on the list is **Bremen**. Already severe damage had been inflicted on the port and various aircraft plants ; now a number of aircraft under construction were hit, and heavy casualties caused among the factory personnel ; the completion of submarines was retarded, and launchings at the Deutsche Werfte yard were behind schedule. At **Kassel** good results were achieved on the

night of September 8-9, since the main station was hit, and the roof of the main booking hall collapsed. But the most extensive piece of destruction was the burning down of the famous Palais—home of the old Electors—and of the Friedrichs Museum.

Next we come to **Cologne**—a city, we are told, that can take a lot of punishment. But under persistent attacks, and with the use of increasing numbers of the heaviest bombs, the city centre is beginning to present an appearance comparable with that of some of the heavily raided English towns. A steadily growing strip on the left bank of the Rhine has suffered most heavily ; so has the shopping district around the Hohestrasse. A number of hits were obtained on important factories, and a large department store employing 400 hands was completely destroyed.

In **Mannheim** bombs put one of the railway lines out of action for some days in the first week of August ; sidings and warehouses were destroyed, and a gas container exploded. Considerable losses were inflicted on rolling stock. Finally, at **Karlsruhe** main and goods stations were damaged ; electric power supplies were interrupted, and amongst the buildings hit were the Schloss Hotel, the largest brewery, and the military barracks. Heavy casualties were caused when air-raid shelters received direct hits.

From this report, and from accounts which have been received from Lisbon and other neutral sources, it is obvious that our bombs have done considerable damage to Germany. But it can hardly be claimed that it is such as might be expected from the pronouncements quoted above. It is an insult to our own people, to the sorely tried citizens of London and Coventry, Bristol and Plymouth, Birmingham and Liverpool, even to suggest that their ordeal has been paralleled, let alone surpassed, by that of the people of German cities of comparable size and importance. Germany's turn is yet to come.

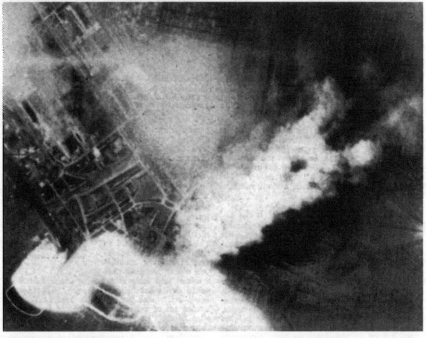

BOMBS ON EMDEN, the Prussian seaport and town at the mouth of the Ems. An important industrial centre, it has been visited frequently by the R.A.F. This photograph, taken at night, shows the effect of some of Britain's high-powered bombs on military objectives.

Photos, British Official: Crown Copyright; G.P.U.

Our Searchlight on the War

MASSACRED IN FRANCE

FOLLOWING the shooting of Lt.-Col. Holtz, German field commander of the Nantes area, at Nantes on October 20, fifty hostages were shot there and a further fifty threatened with death if the culprits were not handed over. On the following day another German officer was killed at Bordeaux ; this was followed by the execution of another fifty hostages with fifty more to follow if the assailants had not been arrested. These brutal reprisals called forth condemnation from all over the world. President Roosevelt described this deed of savagery as " revolting a world already inured to suffering and brutality." Mr. Churchill, too, issued a statement which said that his Majesty's Government associate themselves fully with the sentiments of horror and condemnation expressed by the President, and declared that " retribution for these crimes must henceforward take its place among the major purposes of the war." The Pope and the Chilean Government were among those who interceded with Berlin on behalf of the 100 hostages awaiting execution. Then Hitler himself ordered a suspension of the executions—not out of mercy, but because he had been advised that the French workers, so sorely needed to make tanks and planes for Germany, were being roused to stubborn defiance.

DOVER'S FRONT-LINE SCHOOLS

ONE thousand four hundred children of Dover, who have to sleep in cave shelters because they live within range of the Nazi cross-Channel guns, now have to go to school again, and the Dover authorities have expressed themselves as " desperately concerned " at a Board of Education ruling which has compelled the re-opening of schools closed since June 1940. The schools—six

DOVER CHILDREN, who have just returned to school after 16 months' absence, entering their cliff dug-out as part of their daily A.R.P. practice. Dover authorities think that they should be compulsorily evacuated owing to the danger from shelling.   *Photo, G.P.U.*

in all—are now open every day for part-time education. The Dover Education Committee is of the opinion that the Government should apply a compulsory evacuation order for the children still remaining in that bombarded town. " The children must be educated," they agree, " but that education should not be in a town which is regularly shelled."

DUTCH 'PIMPERNELS' AID R.A.F.

THE Free Dutch newspaper "Vrij Nederland" tells how crews of R.A.F. bombers shot down over Holland are being hidden by the population, who help them to escape to Britain. Dispatches brought from the Netherlands by a Dutch engineer who escaped state : " One of the greatest difficulties in giving these Britons refuge is the problem of feeding. Supplies are short, but our visitors get food. Everybody plays his part— for every ten who are arrested or taken as hostages, twenty new recruits fill the gap." These dispatches relate, also, how a secret wireless transmitting station, known to the Dutch as the "Germicide Sprayer," has not been discovered despite unremitting efforts by the Gestapo. Another interesting point is that after an order had been

issued that the Dutch were to surrender to the German authorities all domestic metal, mass " funerals " took place in back gardens as tons of metal were buried. More than 60,000 roof-top aerials in Amsterdam have been removed, ostensibly because they were unsightly. But the real reason was the anxiety of the Nazi authorities in Holland on account of the mass listening by the Dutch to the B.B.C. broadcasts.

RADIO IN JUNGLE RHYTHM

IN the Belgian Congo natives, educated into military radio operators, use a jungle rhythm, says the " Chicago Daily News " representative, which is a more effective method of secrecy than any secret code. This was ascertained by Belgian colonial officers talking to captured Italian officers. " At times we have had as many as eight cipher officers listening to your radio field orders," the Italians said, " but your operators' sending is so peculiarly uneven and irregular that we cannot even understand the letters they transmit, to say nothing of putting them together." The rhythm these Congo natives use is so eccentric that it is difficult for the Belgian officers themselves to decipher. But the native operators not only receive each other faultlessly, but are experts on messages sent by Italy's all-white operators. The Belgians are now using a corps of negro operators who have very quickly become proficient in their duties.

NAZI ANTI-CHRIST PLAN

A DOCUMENT outlining a Nazi plan to abolish Christianity entirely in Germany (and, naturally, in all German-dominated countries) is in the possession of the United States State Department, declared Mr. Adolf A. Berle, Assistant Secretary of State, in a speech at Columbus, Ohio.

The programme, said to have been drawn up by some of the most influential members of the German government, aims at reorganizing religion in Germany by setting up a national church, confiscating all church property, eliminating the Christian faith and substituting " Mein Kampf " for the Bible. This was probably the document to which Pres. Roosevelt referred in his Navy Day (Oct. 27) speech, commenting: " the God of Blood and Iron will take the place of the God of Love and Mercy."

SABOTAGE!

AN amusing incident which occurred while Midland troops were on manoeuvres recently is reported by the " News Chronicle." The troops were told to engage in acts of sabotage, " however small." One officer, noticing that a soldier was busy rummaging inside a Staff car, asked him what he was doing. " Sabotage, sir, small act," was the private's reply. This particular act of sabotage consisted in blunting the edge of the " enemy " general's razor. In the course of the operations the officer was " captured," and while incarcerated at enemy Staff H.Q. was able to watch the general trying to shave with the blunted razor. " It was a good piece of sabotage," was the officer's comment.

KEARNY, U.S. destroyer of the Benson Class, completed in 1940, was torpedoed 350 miles south of Iceland on Oct. 17. She is seen being assisted into port by a sister ship. The arrow points to the gash made in the Kearny's side. " Hitler's torpedo," said Mr. Roosevelt, " was directed against every American."   *Photo, Associated Press*

" Besides hacking his face, the general was so furious that he could scarcely have thought clearly for the rest of the day."

WARSHIP WEEKS BEGIN

STARTING off with a bang on October 18, the latest Campaign of the National Savings Movement, which is to last until March 1942, caught the popular imagination in so clear a manner as to ensure success. The scheme is to hold Warship Weeks all over the country in which a city or town aims at raising enough in War Savings to pay for a warship. If successful, the town then " adopts " a named warship of the class it has aimed at. In the first Warship Week the cities of Birmingham and Glasgow each aimed at raising £10,000,000 for a battleship. H.M.S. George V and H.M.S. Duke of York respectively, while

LEATHERHEAD PARADE in aid of the town's Warship Week to raise £65,000 for a minesweeper. After the costume procession, part of which is seen above, a play, " Nelson at Leatherhead," was performed.   *Photo, Fox*

Sheffield's £2,000,000 was to go for a cruiser of the Sheffield type. Natural rivalry between Birmingham and Glasgow gave the latter £13,510,509 against Birmingham's £10,088,199. A number of other places in the country also held Weeks. One town, Leatherhead, took advantage of the fact that Trafalgar Day fell in the week to revive historical associations with Nelson in procession and play ; aiming at £65,000 for a minesweeper it raised £222,510.

Dropping to Earth at Split-Second Intervals

PARACHUTE TROOPS descending in the course of manoeuvres somewhere in Britain. They use a fool-proof parachute which opens automatically, leaving the plane at the rate of ten in six to seven seconds. Circle, a parachutist ready with his sub-machine-gun. Parachute soldiers are volunteers, and are selected for special qualities of courage, initiative and determination from almost every branch of the Army. They are trained in conjunction with the R.A.F. (See pages 536-7, Vol. 4).

Photos, Central Press and G.P.U.

Now the Crimea Is Caught in the Nazi Net

As autumn gave place to winter the German armies were flung into the Crimea, and after furious
fighting overran the peninsula to the approaches of Sebastopol. At the same time the Nazi
pressure was maintained on the other fronts.

THE first German offensive against the
Crimea began on September 24.
In its opening it was successful,
since the Nazi tanks and infantry drove a
strong wedge into the Russian defences
across the Perekop Isthmus. But the Soviet
troops rallied and threw out the Germans
with heavy loss. Picked S.S. formations were
then flung into the breach, but they too were
defeated in a violent battle. Yet another
offensive was launched on October 1, and
it again was repulsed. About a fortnight
later the attack was renewed by General
von Manstein's divisions, with Lieut.-
General Pflugbeil's Air Corps, and the
Russians admitted that furious fighting was
in progress and that the danger was great.
Then on October 30 there came the claim
from Hitler's headquarters that the entrance
to the Crimea had been forced. " In breaking through the strongly-fortified defence
lines of the enemy between October 18 and
October 28 " (it continued) " 15,700
prisoners were taken and 13 tanks, 109 guns
and much other war material were either
captured or destroyed. The beaten enemy
is being pursued."

For some days subsequent to this announcement the situation in the Crimea was

Simferopol, the Crimean capital, was claimed
by the Germans on November 3, and on the
next day they claimed that their troops had
occupied Theodosia.

The weight of the Nazi offensive was
terrific. Through the torrential rain they
were hurling in wave after wave of men,
tanks and artillery, with utter disregard of
casualties. At the same time the Luftwaffe
bombarded the Russian troops in Sebastopol
and the other harbours of that shore which
in peacetime was famed for its pleasant
climate and holiday resorts, where tired
Soviet workers recuperated in the sun, but
which now was engulfed in the inferno of war.

While this dangerous situation was developing in the Crimea, the battle for Moscow
was continuing, now rising to a fresh pitch
of intensity, now subsiding into a comparative lull. Both sides brought up masses of
reinforcements, and while the Germans
employed an apparently inexhaustible
number of tanks, the Red Army revealed a
preponderance of artillery. At the price of
tremendous slaughter the Germans progressed, but their gains, territorially considered, were hardly significant. " Not a
step back " was the order issued to the
Russian troops on the Moscow front; and
it was obeyed with the
courageous stubborn-
ness for which the
Russians have long
been famed. At
Mojaisk in the centre
of the sector, at
Kalinin to the north-
west, and between
Orel and Tula to the
south, fierce fighting
was reported to be
raging day after day,
in heavy snow and in
icy winds, and at a
temperature 50 de-
grees below freezing.
An official spokesman
in Berlin expressed the
view that " the
Weather God now
seems to be either a
Russian or a Jew, be-
cause he is giving us
plenty of trouble."

Particularly bitter
was the struggle in the
Orel sector, where the
Germans were making desperate efforts to
break through and cut Russian communications to the east of Moscow. After fighting
of the fiercest description, Moscow radio admitted that General Guderian's tanks had
made some progress. At the same time a
fierce struggle was still continuing for the
possession of Kalinin, representing the tip of
the northern claw of the pincers of which the
offensive against Tula formed the southern.

Tula was mentioned for the first time in a
Russian communiqué on October 30, when
it was stated that all attacks by the German
and Fascist forces—a reference presumably
to the Finnish and Spanish volunteer divisions
trained in Germany, which had now arrived
on the Eastern Front—in the direction of
Volokolamsk, Mojaisk, Malo Yaroslavets,
and Tula—were repulsed with great losses to
the enemy. At the approaches to Tula the
Russian soldiers under General Yermakov
were fighting shoulder to shoulder with
workers of the town. Once again the Germans
put out the claim that the enemy had been
annihilated, when General Zhukov's forces
were more than holding their own. " All the

MOSCOW'S ENVIRONS, showing how the
German threat to the Russian capital had
developed by the end of October 1941.

same, the situation in the Tula area has become menacing," announced Moscow on
October 30. The highway to Tula was
reported to be littered with wrecked machines,
aircraft, burned-out tanks, and uncounted
thousands of German bodies.

Nazi Progress in the South

Meanwhile the Germans were developing
their drive in the south. The evacuation by
the Soviet troops of the great industrial city
of Kharkov in the Donetz basin was admitted in the Russian communiqué issued
at midnight on October 29. Fighting had
been continuing in the streets in the suburbs
for many days, and now the city was evacuated for strategic reasons, and not before the
Nazis had lost 120,000 killed and wounded,
450 tanks, 3,000 lorries, and 200 guns.

After abandoning Kharkov Timoshenko's
divisions continued their slow, stubborn retreat eastwards, fighting every inch of the
way against an enemy almost as exhausted
as themselves, and in weather conditions
reported to be even worse than those prevailing at Moscow. Here as elsewhere the
German casualties were exceedingly heavy,
and there was significance in the report that
a new expeditionary force had been sent by
Hungary to the Ukraine and had already
proved itself in action.

Between Kharkov and the Crimea Von
Rundstedt pushed rapidly ahead against the
Donetz basin. By early in November the
Germans were reported to be within 10 or
15 miles of Rostov at the mouth of the
Don. Here, for the time being at least, they
were halted, so fierce was the Russian resistance. To reinforce the Red Army the
miners of the Donetz basin formed themselves into regiments and, fighting side by
side with the regulars, proved themselves
most redoubtable warriors.

From other sectors of the vast front there
was little to report. Leningrad was still
holding out, its garrison counter-attacking
whenever opportunity offered; while at
Murmansk in the far north the Germans
were said to be digging-in—for warmth.

UKRAINE FRONT, showing the German advance in the Donetz basin
area and the threat to the Crimea. At the beginning of November
fierce fighting raged between Taganrog and Rostov and the Germans
were making headway in the Crimea.

obscure, but there seemed to be little doubt
that the Germans had broken through the
Perekop defences, and were now debouching
on the far-spreading plain, averaging some
100 feet above sea level, which occupies the
centre of the Crimea, gradually sloping up
into the hill country in the south. So flat is
this expanse, so devoid of natural obstacles,
that it is small wonder that the Germans,
once they had achieved a penetration,
pushed rapidly ahead, more particularly
when it is learnt that they had concentrated
five divisions, 200 aircraft, and a host of tanks
and guns on the narrow isthmus.

The defending Russians resisted fiercely;
the Germans themselves described the battle
as one of the toughest in the war. But the
Nazi war machine drove on steadily across
the rolling steppes. Soon they had reached
the foothills of the Yaila Mountains, and it
seemed that the Russian forces had been
split into two. One body was slowly retiring
along the railway from Simferopol through
Bakhchiserai towards the great fortress of
Sebastopol, while the other was moving eastwards in the direction of the Kerch Isthmus.

Millions Have Died But Millions Fight On

NAZI SOLDIERS' GRAVES near the village of Malaya Nezhoda, recently recaptured by Soviet troops.　　*Photo, British Official*

ROSTOV-ON-DON : tractor workshops in the big industrial city, key-centre of south-eastern Russia, which the Germans are making terrific efforts to capture.　*Photo, E.N.A.*

HURRICANES of the R.A.F. Fighter Command wing, now operating with the Russian army, preparing to go into action.
Photo, British Official

RUSSIAN SUBMARINE in the port of Sebastopol, the Soviet naval dockyard, which is being heavily attacked by Gen. Pflugbeil's air corps.　　*Photo, Keystone*

Will They Be in Time? Maybe These T

TANKS FOR RUSSIA being embarked at a British port. They are infantry tanks of the type popularly known as "Waltzing Matildas." At the Three-Power Conference in Moscow, Stalin said that the war was essentially a tank war, but would eventually be decided by tanks and aeroplanes in coordination. Hence, the first need of our Russian allies is an emergency supply of British and American machines made imperative by the Soviet's loss of certain highly-developed industrial regions. It is an interesting fact that help for Russia has been rendered ever since Hitler's invasion, but

f Ours Will Help Turn the Tide in Russia

during the past weeks it has risen to a commendable crescendo. The Anglo-American Mission, on the occasion of their meeting with Stalin at the Kremlin, assured the Soviet leader that all he asked for would be forthcoming, even if Britain had to forgo her share of American production. The surest way of stopping Hitler at present is to help the Russians with every machine we can spare. The second front, for the opening of which there has been so clamant a demand by press and public, is for the time being at least, in the workshops of Britain and the United States.

Convoy Raiding Is Now a 'Desperate Assault'

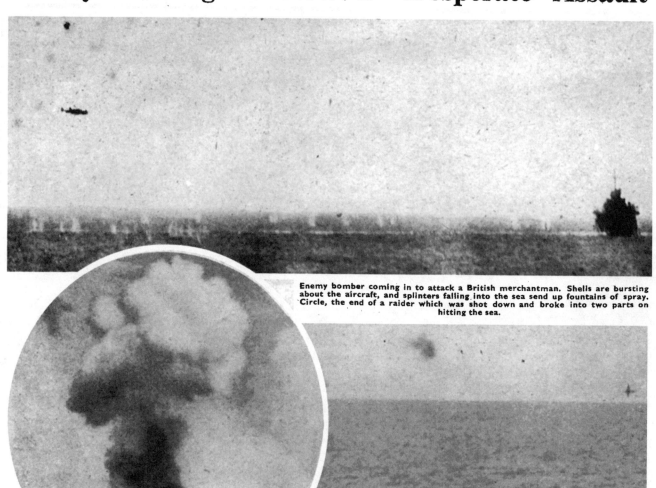

Enemy bomber coming in to attack a British merchantman. Shells are bursting about the aircraft, and splinters falling into the sea send up fountains of spray. Circle, the end of a raider which was shot down and broke into two parts on hitting the sea.

" TODAY an attack on a convoy can be compared with nothing less than a desperate assault on a mighty line of fortifications. British convoys are now always powerfully escorted by large numbers of fast and heavily armed warships ; all these encircle the convoy, keeping vigilant and sharp watch. Moreover, all the merchantmen themselves are armed with A.A. guns or machine-guns. Added to this are the cruisers with their heavy-calibre guns . . . barrage balloons with their malicious steel cables. As soon as our bombers approach a most murderous fire is opened, and they have no easy task to penetrate this hail of shrapnel, steel and iron. For them to get at the ships is to go down into the shadowland of death."   *Berlin Radio, Oct. 26*

The Italian torpedo bomber on the horizon has been attacking a British convoy ; in the foreground a gun crew is busy with the A.A. gun. Left, working the 0·5 A.A. weapon aboard a corvette, the plucky little craft which has done such admirable work in protecting convoys.

Photos, Central Press, Fox

Adrift in Mid-Ocean : Seen from a U-Boat

Taken by a German sailor aboard a U-boat, these photographs add yet another grim page to the Nazi black record of infamy and crime.

An Allied merchantman has been torpedoed, and those of her crew who survive are now afloat on the deep. What was their fate we are not permitted to know. Perhaps they were taken on board the U-boat; perhaps they were left to drift.

The photographs, from left to right down the page, are of merchant sailors in a rubber dinghy; a U-boat gunner firing at the sinking ship which has just been torpedoed; two negroes and two white sailors on a rubber dinghy, and a lone seaman standing on a frail raft.

Photos, Exclusive to The War Illustrated

Our Diary of the War

MONDAY, OCT. 27, 1941   786th day

Air.—Seaplane base at Ostend raided. Offensive sweep over N. France. Six enemy fighters destroyed.

Russian Front.—Russian troops made a successful counter-attack across the river Nara. Germans made further progress in the Donetz basin.

Mediterranean.—Goods train blown up by R.A.F. near Cotrone, S. Italy.

Africa.—Benghazi harbour raided by heavy bombers on night of Oct. 26-27. Again attacked in daylight on Oct. 27 by S.A.A.F. Store dumps near Gambut raided by medium bombers. Trenches at Deva, near Gondar, bombed by R.A.F.

General.—President Roosevelt, in a broadcast, declared that America was at her battle stations. Venezuelan Government ordered withdrawal of all consuls from Germany and German-occupied territories.

TUESDAY, OCT. 28   787th day

Air.—Offensive sweep over N. France. Hudson aircraft bombed enemy convoy off Terschelling. Night raid on objectives in S. and S.W. Germany and docks at Cherbourg.

Russian Front.—Heavy fighting continued along R. Nara. Germans claimed capture of Kramatorsk in Donetz basin. Fierce fighting in suburbs of Kharkov.

Africa.—Benghazi harbour raided by heavy bombers on night of Oct. 27-28. Daylight raid on military camp at Buerat El Hsun.

Home.—Slight enemy activity by night over West Country. One enemy bomber destroyed.

WEDNESDAY, OCT. 29   788th day

Air.—R.A.F. sweeps over enemy occupied territory. Aerodromes, trains and ships attacked. Soviet Air Force raided Berlin at night.

Russian Front. — Russians announced evacuation of Kharkov after inflicting 120,000 casualties on the enemy in that sector. Germans claimed important break-through into Crimea through Perekop Isthmus.

Mediterranean.—Comiso, Sicily, raided by naval aircraft on night of Oct. 28-29. R.A.F. bombers attacked Siderna, Soverato, Locri and Catanzaro Marino, South Italy.

Africa.—Tripoli heavily raided by R.A.F. on night of Oct. 28-29. Enemy positions south of Ambazzo, Abyssinia, effectively bombed.

General.—Vichy Government banned listening to British broadcasts. U.S. naval tanker Salinas sunk S.W. of Iceland by torpedo.

THURSDAY, OCT. 30   789th day

Air.—Coastal Command carried out devastating raid on harbour and anchorages at Aalesund, Norway, on night of Oct. 29-30.

Seven supply ships left sunk or sinking. Offensive sweep over N. France.

Russian Front.—Fierce fighting around Tula. Rundstedt's armies claimed to have reached upper reaches of the Donetz on a broad front. Battle for Rostov increased in intensity.

Mediterranean.—Heraklion and Suda Bay, Crete, raided by R.A.F. on night of Oct. 29-30.

Africa.—Tripoli, Benghazi, Tmimi and Bardia bombed on night of Oct. 29-30.

General.—U.S. destroyer Reuben James sunk by torpedo while on convoy duty.

FRIDAY, OCT. 31   790th day

Air.—Offensive sweep by R.A.F. over N. France. Night raid on shipping off Norwegian coast and Frisian Islands. Eleven ships sunk. Night attacks on Bremen, Hamburg and N.W. Germany as well as docks at Dunkirk and Boulogne.

Russian Front.—Russians held further fierce drive for Moscow. Germans made further progress on the Ukraine front and in the Crimea.

Mediterranean.—Night attack on Naples and on Licata and Palermo in Sicily.

Home.—A few bombs fell in E. Anglia by night. 2 enemy bombers destroyed.

SATURDAY, NOV. 1   791st day

Air.—R.A.F. sweep over N. France.

Russian Front.—Intense fighting in streets of Kalinin. Germans claimed to have crossed the upper Donetz. Crimea gap widened.

Home.—Raiders over N.W. England at night. 6 enemy bombers destroyed. First occasion on which A.T.S. girls directed A.A. fire against enemy planes.

SUNDAY, NOV. 2   792nd day

Air.—R.A.F. sweep over N. France. Night attack by Coastal Command Hudsons on shipping off Dutch and Norwegian coasts.

Russian Front.—Simferopol, capital of Crimea, captured by German and Rumanian troops.

Africa.—Enemy aircraft dropped bombs on Cairo area. R.A.F. bombers carried out four-hour attack on enemy aerodrome at Castel Benito, south of Tripoli.

Home.—A few bombs fell at night in E. Anglia and E. Coast of Scotland. One enemy raider destroyed.

General.—Gen. Sir Archibald Wavell arrived in Singapore.

MONDAY, NOV. 3   793rd day

Sea.—Coastal forces in Channel intercepted a strongly escorted enemy supply ship, which was hit by two torpedoes. Enemy escort heavily engaged with successful results.

Air.—Enemy positions in N. France and

2nd Lt. CHARLES UPHAM, of the New Zealand Force, who has won the V.C. for gallantry during the German invasion of Crete. He performed a series of remarkable exploits, showing outstanding leadership and tactical skill. He commanded a forward platoon in the attack on Maleme on May 22, 1941, and fought his way forward for over 3,000 yards, unsupported by any other arms, against a defence strongly organized in depth.

enemy shipping attacked off French and Belgian coasts by Spitfires of Fighter Command. Soviet aircraft made night attack on Danzig, Koenigsberg and Riga. The German battleship Tirpitz was heavily bombed at Danzig.

Russian Front.—German drive towards Crimean ports of Sebastopol and Kerch continued. In the Moscow sector Russian forces made several strong counter-attacks. Russians regained part of Kalinin.

General.—Washington announced that U.S. had warned Finland to cease military operations against Russia.

TUESDAY, NOV. 4   794th day

Sea.—Admiralty announced that five ships of a Vichy convoy carrying contraband goods were captured off S. African coast. Attempts to scuttle the ships were foiled.

Air.—Night attack on industrial districts in Ruhr and Rhineland. Ostend and Dunkirk docks bombed. Supply ship sunk off Terschelling.

Russian Front.—Another great attack launched against Moscow. In the Crimea German troops advanced towards the outer defences of Sebastopol.

Africa.—Night attacks by R.A.F. on petrol dumps at Benghazi, Berka and Benina. Motor transport at Bardia bombed.

WEDNESDAY, NOV. 5   795th day

Air.—R.A.F. sweep over N. France. Goods trains and ammunition dumps attacked.

Russian Front.—Moscow armies held new Nazi onslaught on capital. Heavy fighting in Crimea. German advance in Ukraine slowed down. Russian Black Sea Fleet reported to have left Sebastopol.

Africa.—Shipping in Gulf of Sirte, Libya, attacked by R.A.F. bombers.

General.—Turkish M.T.B. Kenah Dere torpedoed and sunk in Bosporus by an unknown submarine.

Sergt. ALFRED HULME, of the New Zealand Force, also awarded the V.C. for heroic conduct during the operations in Crete. The official citation states that he exhibited most outstanding and inspiring qualities of leadership, initiative, skill, endurance and devotion to duty from the commencement of the action on May 20, 1941, until he was wounded in the field eight days later.

Photos, British Official: Crown Copyright

Off for a 'Cruise' in Tobruk's Perimeter

DESERT PATROL in the Tobruk area is carried out by cruiser tanks such as that seen above, among others. Most of the officers and men who form the crews of these tanks have taken part in the war in Libya since it began. " Our patrols were active in the Tobruk area " is an official formula which conveys little to the man in the street, but those few words may cover many a story of strange adventure in the desert sands where British tanks are a tempting but elusive target for Axis artillery and dive-bombers.

Photo, British Official : Crown Copyright

Behind the Front: Battle of Supplies in Russia

About the actual fighting in Russia we are told all too little ; about the conditions behind the lines, the preparations for the battle, we are told even less. Here, then, is an article giving at least some idea of the enormous difficulties which have to be overcome on the one side and the other.

MILLIONS of men to be transported, fed, clothed, and armed ; many hundreds of thousands of mechanical vehicles to be kept oiled and supplied with petrol, tens of thousands of planes to be fuelled ... We have but to think of these things to realize the immensity of the supply problems which confront the German commissariat and the Russian.

Both have to contend with vast distances ; both have to make provision for enormous numbers, to supply by road and rail colossal quantities of every kind of war material. But beyond this there is little similarity. Germany's supply lines stretch for 1,000 miles beyond Berlin, across a hostile Poland and vast tracts of conquered territory which the retreating Russians have converted into a burnt desert. The roads still exist ; but the railways in many places have been destroyed, and in any case the Russian gauge is 5 ft. while the German is the same as ours— 4 ft. 8½ ins. As the Germans advance they have to reconstruct what has been destroyed, and their activities in this direction are constantly hampered by bands of Russian guerillas, or "partisans," and by innumerable acts of sabotage.

The Russians, for their part, are operating a transport system which has been vastly improved of recent years, and does not seem to have been affected to any considerable extent by German bombing. Their base towns, too, even those quite close to the front, are still intact ; while on the German side of the line most of the captured towns and villages are mere shells, having been destroyed by the Russians after all their war plant had been removed or put out of action. Thus the Germans have complained that the Zaporozhe aluminium factory on the Dnieper was empty when they reached it, that Kiev had been cleared before it was burned. It is more than likely that they found Kharkov an empty gain, since all the arms factories had been removed before the city's fall, together with the skilled workers and, indeed, most of the population.

In these circumstances all the more credit is due to those responsible for the maintenance of German supplies. There can be no gainsaying the extraordinary efficiency of the German equivalents of our Ordnance and Service Corps, but it would seem that the palm should go to the vast organization built up by Dr. Todt which, after constructing the great motor roads in Germany and the Westwall or Siegfried Line along the Rhine, is now engaged on the supply lines between Germany and the Eastern Front. At the time of the invasion of Russia its strength was reported to be about 300,000 men, and since then it has been increased considerably ; some 50,000 Jews are stated to be included in its ranks, some drawn from the Rhineland and some from German-occupied

Poland. Not a single able-bodied Jew remained under his charge, boasted Gauleiter Greiser ; all had been dispatched to work on roads behind the front in Russia.

Road construction and maintenance is the Todt Organization's chief job, but its labourers have also been employed for building fortifications, repairing damaged water and electric mains in the captured cities, repairing railway embankments and bridges. In his speech on October 3 Hitler stated that 25,000 kilometres of Russian railways had been reconstructed and put into service, while 15,000 kilometres had been switched over to the German gauge. The actual conversion seems to have been done in the main by the Army Railway Corps.

Another of the Todt Organization's activities is the construction of vast numbers of wooden barracks in which it is hoped the Nazi troops will spend the coming winter in conditions of reasonable comfort. The other day it was reported from Berlin that 1,000 portable blockhouses had been brought to

within 25 miles of the front, 50 blockhouses comprising a "village." Each blockhouse is equipped with electric or petroleum heating, each "village" has a mobile power station. The same correspondent stated that German factories are pouring out tinned goods, vitamin tablets and anti-frost preparations ; and from other sources we learn that vast quantities of special woollen underclothing, gloves and ear-warmers, bedding and comforts, are being prepared and dispatched to the German armies in Russia. Among the comforts are mentioned the finest French brandies, Dutch cigars, and Bulgarian cigarettes—all things which are quite unobtainable by the German civilian, but which Hitler, in his wisdom, deems not too good for the German warrior.

While the directing staffs in the Todt Organization are German, great numbers of the labourers are drawn from the occupied countries. In these countries, indeed, the blockhouses just referred to, as well as numbers of wooden huts, have been constructed by the forced labour of prisoners. Vast

numbers of Russian prisoners-of-war are being employed, and the Nazis are making tempting offers to those of the Russians who are still living in the occupied territory. Recently a German broadcast from Kiev appealed to Russian engineers, technicians, tradesmen, chauffeurs, locksmiths and carpenters to enlist in the Todt Organization. But it is exceedingly unlikely that the Russians will "fall for" any appeals of this description ; besides, the keyworkers have mostly been evacuated.

In some respects the Russians' supply position compares favourably with that of the Germans, but as a whole it is increasingly serious. Before the war the most vital industrial centres in European Russia were the regions about Leningrad and Moscow, the Ukraine and the Donetz Basin. All these have now been lost to Russia—if not entirely, at least in very large measure. More and more the Soviet Union is becoming dependent on outside supplies obtained through Archangel and Iran, and by way of the tremendous haul across Siberia, from Vladivostok. Her Birminghams and Sheffields have had to be abandoned one by one, their plant evacuated or destroyed ; hundreds of thousands of her most skilled workers have been taken prisoners, wounded or killed.

Not even General Winter is so good a friend to Russia as he was in Napoleon's time, since motor vehicles can make quite good progress across hard snow. But at least there is some comfort in the thought that the Red soldiers and workers are inured to the Russian winter ; while the Nazis, and still more their allies from the warmer south—the Italians in particular—are likely to find that a wooden blockhouse, heated by an oil stove, is not exactly a home from home.

SOVIET SUPPLY LINES within the Union are illustrated in this map, which shows the main rivers and railway lines as well as the position of the oil-fields and pipe-lines.
Map, Courtesy of the " Manchester Guardian "

Mud and Man Combine to Thwart the Nazis

ON THE EASTERN FRONT obstacles to progress, man-made and natural, are now being everywhere encountered by the German forces. An instance of how Nature is taking a hand in the game and impeding the German advance is given in the top photograph, which shows how bad weather conditions, combined with an abnormal amount of traffic, are wrecking Russian roads and making them almost impassable. Two more photographs from German sources show (oval) a bridge destroyed by the Russians near Repols ; and above, a diverted watercourse, which, however, is not sufficiently deep to hinder the advance of this German supply column.

Photos, Associated Press and Sport & General

After the Battle the Heavy Hours of Captivity

QUEEN VICTORIA'S RIFLES : Officers taken prisoner after the defence of Cálais, at the German camp, Oflag VII C., Laufen. The two on the left and the one on the right are unidentified ; the others, left to right, are Lieut. Courtenay, Capt. J. A. Brown, Lt.-Col. J. A. M. Ellison-Macartney, Capt. P. J. E. Monico, Capt. A. N. L. Munby, and Lieut. S. J. Saunders.

STALAG VII A. is a prisoner-of-war camp for " other ranks " at Moosburg, a small town about 40 miles north-east of Munich. Here in the castle (entrance shown above) many British soldiers are interned.

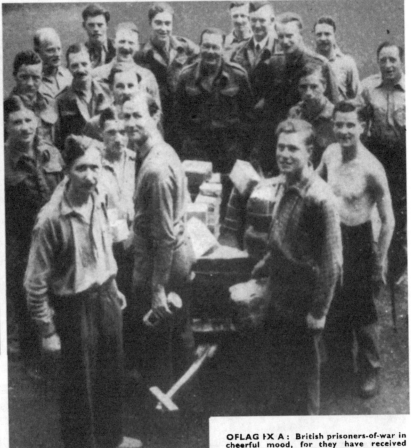

OFLAG IX A : British prisoners-of-war in cheerful mood, for they have received eagerly awaited parcels from home.

OFLAG VI B., Warburg, to which British officer prisoners recently held at Oflag VII C and Oflag VII D., have been transferred. Warburg is on the border of Westphalia and Hesse. Right, British prisoners at Stalag XX A, shown on the map in page 101, Vol. 4 to be at Thorn, in Poland. Among these soldiers are C. W. Davis (front centre), K. J. Brydson, A. Cross, H. K. Wright, M. Fox, N. C. Baker, A. Johnstone, A. H. Berrisford, F. Nurse, A. L. Gosling.

Photos, Daily Telegraph ; E.N.A. ; Keystone : Associated Press

'Commando' Men Have 'Guts' and 'Gumption'

Woodcraft is an essential part of the training of a commando. The men must be able to light a fire with as little smoke as possible so as not to give away their position. They must also be able to live on the country and they learn to kill and dress their own food (below).

BRITAIN'S COMMANDO TROOPS are encouraged to develop initiative in every possible way and must be able to adapt themselves to all sorts of circumstances. Men of a Commando unit are here seen trying some experiments with their equipment.

Severe training is undergone by men of the commando units. Physical strength and power of resistance are of prime importance to these shock troops. Commando men are trained to the utmost limit of physical endurance and think nothing of climbing a steep hillside carrying full equipment. "Tough" is a commando's second name.

"COMMANDO" first came into our language during the South African War of 40 years ago, but the word is now sometimes seen on the shoulders of soldiers in battledress.

These men are shock troops, drawn from nearly every regiment in the Army. They are trained not only to operate independently on land for long periods without the assistance of the supply and maintenance organizations which normally minister to the needs of the fighting soldier, but also in amphibious warfare, training for which is carried out in cooperation with the Royal Navy. Both officers and men are familiarized with the life of ocean-going ships and are trained in the use of small craft, including practice in rapid embarkation and disembarkation by day and night in all sorts of weather. Most of this latter training is carried out with assault landing craft and motor landing craft, flat-bottomed motor-boats with bullet-proof protection —the former type capable of landing an infantry platoon, and the latter motor vehicles or a company of infantry, direct on shore. As may be expected, great attention is paid to instruction in swimming. Everyone with "Commando" on his shoulder is able to swim short distances in full equipment with his rifle kept high above the water.

ON land the soldiers are trained to march long distances over the most difficult country, existing on the scanty rations they can carry with them. As they may have to act as guerillas, all ranks have to master map-reading, the use of the compass and the tricks of field-craft. They are also trained in the elements of ju-jitsu.

Finally, they must all be extremely skilled in the use of their own weapons, and also must have a working know-ledge of weapons which they may capture from the enemy. As shock troops they are taught how explosives can best be carried and used to the best effect. A final subject in their curriculum is the hunting of the tank.

Photos, British Official: Crown Copyright

I Was There! .... Eye Witness Stories of the War

We Sang as the Germans Shelled Us at Calais

Of the heroic garrison of 4,000 under Brigadier Nicholson which defended Calais in May 1940 (see page 627, Vol. II) only 47 escaped. Here are the first-hand stories of some of these officers and men.

I LANDED in Calais on Thursday, May 23 (said Rifleman David Hosington, D.C.M., a 35-year-old Cardiff reservist of the King's Royal Rifles). We were told that the Germans were only seven miles away, but we did not believe it, and took it as a joke. We soon found it was true. I was with a half company of 60 other ranks and two officers who were holding a canal.

I saw my first German at about four o'clock on the Friday morning. He was a member of a small reconnaissance party which loomed in the darkness on a road a few hundred yards away. I waited breathlessly, holding my fire while they loitered for five or ten minutes. Then, when they turned to retreat, I let them have it with a Bren gun. They all fell flat, but one was wounded and three others were brought in later as prisoners.

On Friday evening we were told to retire, and we occupied a large hotel adjoining the post office, from which we could command three streets. There was a great deal of sniping going on, chiefly by Fifth Columnists, most of whom seemed to be wearing blue coats and flannel trousers.

Towards lunch-time on Saturday there was a lull in the German shelling and dive-bombing, which had been almost uninterrupted, and I saw a German officer, accompanied by a French officer as guide, going to the headquarters of Brigadier Nicholson, who commanded the Calais force, with a white flag. He had come to ask us to surrender, but he got the right answer.

We expected then to be blown to bits by the German artillery, having no artillery of our own, and the only thing we hoped for was that "Jerry" might run out of ammunition. So we left one or two sentries at the top windows of the hotel and retired to a cellar. Then, when the bombardment began, we got some beer and a piano and had a sing-song. We sang "Roll out the barrel" and many other songs—there was nothing else to do.

Then the Germans began to send light tanks down the road between the blazing houses. We fired at them with anti-tank rifles with good effect. Next morning I was sniping from an upper window and I saw the Germans only 200 yards away. It was a good shoot.

At this time a duel developed between a British destroyer in the harbour and the German artillery. It was good to think they were getting something back.

More German dive-bombing started, and they must have been bombing their own troops, for the town was full of them. Later in the day we abandoned the hotel, and there was a general retirement towards the docks. It was carried out in perfect order, the men helping one another. We had hardly five rounds of ammunition apiece, but we had a few bombs, and occasionally went off to bomb out some of the Fifth Columnists who still pestered us with their sniping.

We blew up everything we could. Then we could retire no farther—the Germans were in front of us and behind us. We were out of ammunition. It was all over.

MAJOR D. TALBOT, Royal West Kent Regiment, who was brigade major to Brigadier Nicholson, described the last moments in the citadel, where the garrison consisted of some French, a party of marines sent out specially from England, and some units of searchlight men, A.A. gunners, and others who had mustered in Calais. He said:

Headquarters were in a bastion under one of the sandy 20-ft. walls of the citadel. Few of the defenders had had much sleep for six days and they had had scratch meals of biscuits and bully beef. There was little water. Then our radio and telephone communications were hit. We got no news from Dunkirk—but kept in touch by radio with England.

Dive-bombing had been going on all day without intermission. We knew little of what was happening outside. Then at four o'clock on Sunday afternoon an officer rushed in to say that the Germans were in the citadel. I do not know exactly what had happened. We ran out to find that the Germans were on top of the walls with grenades in their hands. It was the end of resistance.

A YOUNG lance-corporal in the Rifle Brigade described how the wounded were picked up by the Navy while the Germans were shelling Calais harbour. He said:

We were lying in the dressing-station, feeling there was no chance of a ship getting through to us, when, travelling at top speed, two naval speed-boats appeared. They completed a circle of the harbour before coming alongside the quay. Two naval ratings climbed out of the launches and, throwing away their cigarettes, said calmly: "Who wants a lift? Our minesweeper is waiting outside, gentlemen."

During the next half-hour British and French soldiers who could still walk loaded the more seriously wounded into the launches. Firing from near-by cranes and warehouses, hidden German snipers waited until we appeared on the wharf with a stretcher. Then they let loose, and it is a wonder any of us escaped. When the launches were loaded until they were dangerously low in the water we set out to sea, through the barrage of German shell fire. In the end we were picked up by the minesweeper. Even then we were still in danger. Four dive-bombers tried to sink us, and the last dropped a bomb ten feet from the bows, which stopped the engine and split a plate on the starboard side. However, the engineers got the engines going again and we all crowded to the port side to keep the vessel on an even keel.—"*Daily Telegraph*" *and "Evening News"*

I Shall Never Forget that First 'Blitz' Night

Hundreds of volunteer ambulance drivers stand ready to turn out by day or night to take air-raid wounded to hospital. One of them—a woman who has given her whole time to this work in London for over three years —here tells of some of her experiences.

TWELVE months before the war I joined up as a driver with the London Auxiliary Ambulance. We were given training in night-driving without lights and in gas-masks; we took courses in first-aid and direction-finding. With the outbreak of war came a flood of new recruits, but not until another twelve months had passed did the first "blitz" raid on London come.

I shall never forget that night. We heard the bombs falling, and sat tight until a call came from a street not far from the station.

HEROES OF CALAIS are seen above. They are, from left to right, Major Williams, 60th Rifles; Major Dennis Talbot, Royal West Kents; Rifleman David Hosington, D.C.M., King's Royal Rifles; and Lce.-Cpl. Richard Illingworth, Queen Victoria's Rifles. Rifleman Hosington and Major Talbot tell in this page their own stories of the epic defence of Calais in May 1940, when a small force under Brigadier Nicholson was given the task of holding the town at all costs as a check to the German advance upon Dunkirk. They held out for four days against vastly superior forces, thus helping in no small measure to save a great part of the B.E.F.

Photos, Associated Press

November 20th, 1941　　　　　　　　　*The War Illustrated*　　　　　　　　　287

|||||||||||||||||||||||||||||||||||||||||||||||||||||||||||||||||||||||||||||||||||| I WAS THERE! ||||||||||||||||||||||||||||||||||||||||||||||||||||||||||||||||||||||||||||||||||||||||||||

L.C.C. ambulance waits while rescue parties search for survivors from a bombed tenement house. Some experiences of an ambulance driver are related in this page.
Photo, Sport & General

It was my turn for duty, so I went out at once with the Station Officer. The start wasn't easy. It was getting on for midnight and every light had gone out just as we got the call. We groped our way to the garage in the darkness, started up our ambulance and were soon away. A "sitting car" followed us, to pick up walking wounded.

I can't say that I was altogether happy at the idea of going out on such a dark night with bombs and shrapnel falling. Once out on the street we didn't worry a bit about that. We have often thought since, when we've been looking over our ambulance the morning after a raid, how little we can remember, though we can see then how many pieces of shell must have struck us.

We found our street and a stretcher party waiting for us. The two of us got out at once and began, with the help of the stretcher-bearers, to take our four stretchers out of the ambulance. One was out, both of us helping at the foot-end as usual, when one of the stretcher party yelled " Get down ! "

Hearing his yell and the whiz of the bomb, we all fell flat on our faces. That one exploded in a near-by street. A second fell as we were getting the rest of the stretchers out—and down we went again . . .

We reckon our worst night was that on which a shelter was struck and many poor people badly injured. Three calls came, and one lasted three hours. Here we watched the rescue party risking everything to find someone thought or known to be under the ruins. We were back again next day to see a poor old man brought out more dead than alive, but it is amazing how many people came out alive and cheerful after a night under the rubble.

During the earlier weeks of the blitz we learned to be very grateful for our first-aid

training. We are not called on so often now to help in that way. There are more first-aid workers, and in any case the most important thing is to get the victim quickly to a hospital. We cover our people up, see that they are comfortably fixed in the ambulance, and take the smoothest road to the nearest hospital. That takes some finding on a black night, with the way possibly blocked by a fallen house or a new-made crater.

Our personal good luck has been very great. We have driven for miles over broken glass, and I cannot remember a single tire-burst. We have walked in the dark over glass, stones, bricks, and the timbers of fallen buildings, and, thanks to our rubber knee-boots, which are very wonderful, and our

" tin-hats," we have had neither cuts nor bruises to show.

Our station has had a bad time. Nine bombs have fallen in or around it. One crashed into the garage and we lost several ambulances and a perfectly good Rolls-Royce. In spite of this our personal casualties total only one. We have two day shifts of eight hours each, followed by two night shifts of sixteen hours each, and two clear days off. In addition we can take one day a month as a holiday, or as many as twelve consecutive days in one year. There are still four of us at the station who joined up in 1938, and we all hope to carry on until peace comes.—*From " Hospitals Under Fire," edited by G. C. Curnock, published by George Allen & Unwin, Ltd.*

They Showed Me a Moscow Collective Farm

While so much of Russia is being ravaged by war and turned into scorched earth, even close to the fighting zone the land is being made to bear as never before. Here is an account by Alexander Werth, Reuter's Special Correspondent in Moscow, of a visit to a market-garden in the vicinity of the city.

PRODUCTION " no matter what weather " has long been the slogan on the Soviet food front. Highly scientific and elaborate methods are employed. I have just returned from a visit to one of the market-gardening " kolkhozes " (collective farms) in the Moscow region.

There are acres and acres of tomato plants, with thick clusters of incredibly large fruit, and yet more acres of similarly prolific cabbages, cauliflowers and cucumbers. Until 1931 rye was grown on this site. The village was small and poor. Now the Kolkhoz is shown to visitors with justifiable pride.

Beyond the hundreds of acres set aside for vegetables are pastures with cows munch-ing contentedly and huge pedigree pigs. A river meanders through these pastures. From its banks children bathe in the sun. There are 400 homesteads on the Kolkhoz now, and some 400 active " Kolkhozniks." The rest are children, old people, and youthful students.

I walked over the grounds with the Kolkhoz chairman, Comrade Rusin, the moving spirit of the whole place. Later he took me to his cottage for " tea "—in reality, a gargantuan rustic meal at which everything excepting the tea itself and vodka and salt herring was produce of the Kolkhoz.

Before that we had talked to some women attending to the cows. Their husbands were all at the front. They mentioned this in a matter-of-fact, almost deliberately casual way, but there was anxiety in their eyes.

Among the people at the tea-table was an impressive and handsome twenty-nine-year-old native of the village, to which he had returned on a visit. He wore a high Soviet decoration, which, I learned, he had received for his deeds in munition making.

As the meal progressed he grew more talkative. Pointing from the veranda to the chairman's pretty garden, with beds of phlox and the acres of vegetables beyond, he said : " Look at the prosperity of this place. Without this war we would be living in a world of plenty and prosperity for all."

He talked about the numerous men who had left the Kolkhoz for the army and about the German advance. " You had a rough time in London, hadn't you ? " he said. " But now the whole weight of the Hun machine is turned against us. It won't be easy. But," he added angrily, " we shan't give up even if we have to retreat to the Urals. But, no—we shan't need to do that."

Later I was taken to the Kolkhoz office, with its elaborate charts of working hours and output, and Stakhanovite honour tables, to the school library and infirmary, and shown the enormous pedigree prize bull that is the pride of the Kolkhoz.

The air was filled with the smell of hay. A crowd of happy children were returning from a bathe, waving their coloured towels. It was hard to imagine that not so many miles away other prosperous farms were being shelled and bombed by the Germans.

Siftings From the News

A huge magnetic mine, believed to be German, has been found in the Caribbean Sea.

More women are being taken on the staff of Scotland Yard, which already employs 200.

Britain's average daily expenditure reached £17,456,490 during the week ended November 1, 1941.

New Army Tank plant costing £6,445,000 has been installed at Flint, Michigan.

Nazis are trying to stamp out freemasonry in Holland by closing lodges and confiscating funds and regalia.

Lifeboats saved 136 lives during October from ships and planes in distress.

No more eggs are being exported from Egypt.

Civil Defence uniforms in Essex will cost £100,000.

Historic and artistic railings in Hampstead have been listed with a view to " reprieve,"

A Cheshunt A.R.P. Warden has collected £70 in pennies on Sundays.

Chicago business girls have taken to wearing bright red on Mondays, in order to dispel that Monday feeling of depression.

Owing to a serious shortage of motor tires in Hungary many bus-lines have stopped.

The Nazis are taking up copper street-crossing studs in Brussels for scrap.

The average income of an American family, according to the National Resources Planning Board of Washington, is £405.

Old-age pensioners have voluntarily given up their pensions to the amount of £2,000 to help war effort.

Since 1936 the cost of living in Shanghai has increased by 600 per cent.

A British air line between Cairo and Teheran, capital of Iran, has been opened.

The pastor of the Christian Temple at Toledo, Ohio, has burned a copy of " Mein Kampf " on the altar.

Heydrich, Nazi butcher No. 1, has had 807 people put to death since he took charge of Bohemia and Moravia.

Loneliest and strangest job of the R.A.F. is the Ice-Pack patrol over the Arctic.

Kent aims to raise £10,000,000 during Warship Weeks.

The Duke of Gloucester's Red Cross and St. John Fund now amounts to £7,328,861.

The Dutch Maritime Court in London is now being held at Middlesex Guildhall.

Fifty Streatham women have formed an auxiliary to the Streatham Home Guard.

Over 20,000 names are already recorded on the Civilians' Roll of Honour.

Editor's Postscript

I SOMETIMES speculate on what might have happened had the promoters of the Channel Tunnel scheme succeeded between 1918 and 1939 in realizing their aims. It was intended to unite France and England—a France that forty-five years ago might have used it to our hurt, or sabotaged it, a France that twenty years later would have co-operated with Britain in its use against the Hun, and a Britain that in June 1940 would have had to destroy it as a protection against the effete and traitor-led French ! So good-bye to all Channel Tunnel schemes "for a thousand years," as Hitler is so fond of saying. When we remember that Japan for her own ends was our ally in the Great War, that Italy did us great service by double-crossing the Triple Alliance but as a fighting partner played her part ingloriously, that Rumania stood in with the Allies and suffered for their cause, we can appraise alliances between diverse nations at their true value. The Anglo-American alliance may, by the time this note is printed, have become a binding reality and not an indeterminate understanding, thanks to the sinking of the U.S. destroyer Reuben James, to news of which I've just been listening. The fighting alliance of the two great English-speaking powers is the one hope for today and to-morrow.

WITHIN that alliance alone do the root principles of freedom and democratic government prevail. Not that we should belittle in any sense the democratic ideals and attainments of our Scandinavian friends, the Dutch, the Belgians, the Greeks glorious even in defeat, the Yugoslavs, nor the possibilities of a renascent France or a Turkey armed ; but Britain and America are the natural partners in the defence of a democracy that is inherent in their national institutions, and in defence of which they must be the real burden-bearers. The French people we must always dissociate from their corrupt and traitorous leaders. There are millions of Frenchmen in France as loyal to the democratic way of life as any in Britain or America, and De Gaulle will surely find the means of effecting cooperation with them and the doubly valorous Frenchmen whom he leads ; but the old France we knew and loved we cannot hope to see again in all the strength and glory of the past. The chastened France that will emerge from these catastrophic times will be strangely different. If the traitors of Vichy eventually sink to "full collaboration" with their Nazi conquerors and the British Navy is forced to fight another Trafalgar (no vain idea this), then indeed will the War's end see a France that none of us three years ago had ever dimly visioned.

THE horrors of the War must not be allowed to blind us to the beauty that is everywhere around us. Perhaps the ever-present background of the Evil Things that are both consciously and sub-consciously in our minds makes the inde-structible beauty of Nature more keenly felt.

That is my own experience and I am sure it is a common one. In these autumn days of white morning sun and vast gold-fringed evening clouds my riverside London becomes the world's finest picture gallery. Never have I seen grander pictures from Nature's portfolio : the lightly veiled masses of the Parliament buildings, the Abbey, the County Hall, the picturesque muddle of commercial warehouses on the Surrey side (less pleasing in the clear light of moon) and the bridges, especially the tracery of the temporary structure amidst which the new Waterloo is evolving, the intense green of the Embankment gardens, even the ruins of the Temple,

MR. WINSTON CHURCHILL at the time of his marriage, Sept. 1908, when he was President of the Board of Trade. An interesting and little known portrait-sketch of our Prime Minister. (See below.)

From the drawing by Noel Dorville

all exhaling under the kindly draping of these early mists a sense of beauty that thrills me and suffers eclipse only when I sit down before stacks of photos from the War fronts and the latest reports of how these beastly battles are going.

FOR I must confess that to me all war has now become beastly with nothing but the hope and heroism to inspire those who are endur-ing it for freedom's sake to relieve it from the primal slime. I remember a one-time colleague of mine in the early years of this century writing a sensational novel, "The Final War." In those days the German menace of a great war was in all our minds, but had still that far-offness which made it a subject of drama and romance, no horror of reality. "The Final War ! " Can this be it ? It may be ; but happily there is no end to beauty so long as man has the senses to respond to it. And now to the sunset glories of the Embankment, which no raid, light or heavy, can take away !

THAT " well of English undefiled " (which was Dan Chaucer) is being mightily muddied in these late days with America's contribution to the mother tongue. Language is a living thing and must grow from day to day by borrowings from everywhere : must reflect every new facet of thought and fact the world over. But the well of English has suffered horrid pollution since Hollywood imposed its Americanisms on the so-called English-speaking world—one of the largest of the many undesirable contributions of the Film to our modern life and speech. It is not a matter of " borrowing " but of imposition. Myself I have always loathed " Okay," and yet I find myself by the sheer pressure of its popular usage " falling for it," like scores of other Americanisms to which I have more readily taken ; never in speaking, only as a quickly pencilled symbol O.K. on a proof slip or the like. Spoken, it is no shorter than " All right " and twice the length of " Right."

AN amusing instance of okay-ing was provided by Lord Beaverbrook in his broadcast account of his Soviet mission. To the admirably concise statement of the points on which agreement was reached between the representatives of the three signatory powers America's representative said " Agreed," and Britain's (according to Lord Beaverbrook) said " Okay." We must remember that Lord Beaverbrook is a Canadian and is perhaps less concerned about the English language than about the material survival and pro-gress of the British Common-wealth. Even so, he will surely admit on reflection that the comic element was not absent from the contrast in these two responses. I thank Mr. Harri-man for that "Agreed." One could wish that our American cousins were as successful in smothering us with the tools for fighting Hitler as with Americanisms that threaten to clog the English tongue. Here is an appropriate quotation from our little remembered sixteenth-century poet, Samuel Daniel :

And who, in time, knows whither we may vent
The treasure of our tongue, to what strange shores
This gain of our best glory shall be sent,
T' enrich unknowing nations with our stores ?
What worlds in th' yet unformed Occident
May come refin'd with th' accents that are ours ?

Who knows, indeed ! If old Samuel Daniel could awake from his three centuries of sleep to sit through a full-blooded Hollywood film he would feel that waking had been pain and take the nearest way back to his graveyard.

IN this page I am printing a very charming portrait-sketch of our Prime Minister which appeared in a London daily on Sep-tember 14, 1908, accompanying a lively account of Mr. Churchill's wedding on the preceding 12th. The leaf on which it was printed I found today in an old file of clippings where I had placed it thirty-three years ago, and thought my readers might like to see it. M. Noel Dorville was a well-known French artist who visited England early that year to make a series of drawings for an Entente Cordiale Album which had been issued a month or two before the Churchill-Hozier " event of the social season."

Printed in England and published on the 10th, 20th and 30th of each month by the Proprietors, The Amalgamated Press, Ltd., The Fleetway House, Farringdon Street, London, E.C.4. Registered for transmission by Canadian Magazine Post. Sole Agents for Australia and New Zealand : Messrs. Gordon & Gotch, Ltd. ; and for South Africa : Central News Agency, Ltd. November 20th, 1941.   S.S.   *Editorial Address :* JOHN CARPENTER HOUSE. WHITEFRIARS. LONDON. E.C.4.

Vol 5 # The War Illustrated *Nº 113*

Edited by Sir John Hammerton

FOURPENCE

NOV. 29TH, 1941

DOWN IN RUSSIA! Just one of the many thousands of Nazi planes destroyed on the East Front. Germany's European successes have been founded upon numerical air superiority. In the Battle of Britain, when fewer but better machines and men broke the Nazi legend of aerial invincibility, Germany's decline began. Since then the Russians have taken a huge toll of Nazi aircraft, and (so Mr. Churchill assured us in his Mansion House speech on November 10) Britain has now reached parity with the enemy.

Photo, British Official: Crown Copyright

NO. 114 WILL BE PUBLISHED WEDNESDAY. DEC. 10

STALIN SPEAKS, 'THAT GREAT WARRIOR STALIN'

HITLER—so the report runs—announced some time ago that he would parade his troops in Moscow's Red Square on November 7, the 24th anniversary of the Soviet Revolution of 1917. There *was* a parade in the Red Square at Moscow on November 7, but it was not the German legions who goose-stepped past Lenin's tomb; they were still floundering in the muddy morasses, the snow-filled forests, fifty or sixty miles to the east. It was the Red Army that marched past; and it was Stalin that took the salute; not Hitler.

It was bitterly cold, with an icy wind, in the Red Square that November morning. But the sky was clear, and every now and again the waiting multitudes looked up at the waves of fighter planes which kept guard above the Russian capital. Thousands of people lined the square facing the massive walls of the Kremlin, now camouflaged in red, yellow, and grey, and the squat austerity of Lenin's tomb. Their faces were set, their mood serious, even stern. It was no joyous holiday this year, but rather a re-dedication to the service of the nation. The enemy, everyone realized, was at the gate.

WHEN Stalin emerged from the Kremlin door and climbed the steps of the review-stand placed beside Lenin's mausoleum, there was a great burst of cheering. Close behind came Molotov, Commissar for Foreign Affairs, Kaganovitch, and many other of the Soviet leaders. As they took their places on the stand Marshal Budenny inspected the guard of honour composed of units of the Moscow military district. Then he too mounted the tribune and greeted Stalin and the rest. Then a deep hush fell over the Square as Stalin came to the microphone and began to speak. His voice was calm, steady, reassuring. Not for him the frenetic splutterings, the half-insane ravings of the Fuehrer.

" Soldiers, workers, collective farmers," he began, " brothers and sisters in our enemy's rear who have fallen temporarily under the yoke of the German brigands, our glorious guerillas . . . on behalf of the Soviet Government and our Bolshevik party I greet and congratulate you on this day of anniversary. We celebrate it under difficult conditions. The treacherous attack of the German brigands and the war they have forced upon us have created a threat to our country. We have temporarily lost a number of regions and the enemy has appeared before the gates of Leningrad and Moscow."

NOT the slightest attempt to conceal the seriousness of the situation, it will be noted; the losses were admitted, and the danger. But at the same time there was never a suggestion of defeatism. Stalin knows that his people can bear to hear the truth and may thus be twice armed. The country was in danger, admitted. But there was a time when it was in a still more difficult position. " Do you remember 1918," he asked, "when we celebrated the first anniversary of the Revolution? At that time three-quarters of our country were in the hands of foreign interventionists. We had temporarily lost the Ukraine, the Caucasus, Central Asia, the Urals, Siberia, and the Far East. We had no allies. We had no Red Army—we had only just begun to create it— we were short of bread, short of arms, short of clothes. At that time fourteen states were ranged against us. But we were not despondent. We did not become disheartened. Amidst the conflagration of war we organized the Red Army and converted our country into a military camp. Great Lenin's spirit inspired us . . ."

AND what happened? The interventionists were defeated. All the lost territories were restored. Victory was won. Now, a generation later, Russia is in a far better position. She is many times richer in industry, food, and raw materials. She has allies who form a united front against the German invader. She enjoys the sympathy and support of the peoples of Europe who have fallen under the yoke of the Fascist tyranny. She has no serious shortage of food, arms, or clothing; she has a splendid Army and a splendid Navy, while her resources of man-power are inexhaustible.

Russia, Stalin made it plain, can face the future with confidence. But Germany— hunger and impoverishment are reigning there. In four months of war the Reich has lost 4,500,000 soldiers. She is bleeding to death, he declared in a pregnant passage. Her resources are giving out; the spirit of revolution is spreading throughout Europe, even amongst the German people themselves who see no end to the war. " Another few months," declared the Red Leader, " another half-year, one year, maybe—and Hitlerite Germany must burst under the weight of her own crime." So he came to his conclusion. " Under the banner of Lenin, onward to victory! "

When Stalin had finished speaking, he stood at the salute beside the tomb of his master, while the stream of armed men and formidable war machines swept past. As they went by loudspeakers announced the details of each unit's achievement, giving the names of the commanders and the men who had distinguished themselves in action. Then, as is the custom at this yearly celebration, the soldiers were followed in the march-past by columns of factory workers, men and women representing every organization and aspect of the capital's life. But hundreds of thousands of the Muscovites were making the national holiday a day of voluntary labour. They were toiling in the bitter cold digging anti-tank trenches, erecting barbed wire entanglements, strengthening the already immensely strong defence ring round about Moscow.

THE day before, Stalin had delivered an anniversary speech to the Moscow Soviet. It was expressed with realism, filled with information, charged with encouragement. He pointed out how gravely the Germans had miscalculated the unity of the Soviet Union and the strength of the Red Army. The lightning war in the east had failed. All the same, the Red Army had suffered severe set-backs. But these were understandable enough when it was realized that Russia was carrying on the war of liberation alone against the concentrated power not only of the Germans but of the Finns, Rumanians, Italians, and Hungarians. Undoubtedly, said Stalin, the absence of a second front in Europe has eased considerably the position of the German Army; but he spoke in confident anticipation of the creation of such a front in the near future.

The secret (he went on) of the success of the German Army—the temporary success—was that their tanks, though not superior in quality to the Russian, were far more numerous. Had it not been for this fact, had it not been for the Nazi command not only of their own tank industry but of those of Czechoslovakia, Belgium, Holland, and France, the Red Army would long ago have smashed the German Army. " The war is a war of motors and will be won by those who possess a superiority in motor production. The U.S.S.R., Britain and the U.S.A., who are now united in a single camp, have a superiority in this respect over Germany of three to one. This is just one reason why Hitler's robber imperialism is doomed."

SO Stalin spoke. Then he went back to his room in the Kremlin. There he sits at the long baize-covered table, smoking cigarette after cigarette, studying the pile of papers lying neatly stacked before him, " doodling " occasionally as the mood takes him.

" That great warrior, Stalin," Mr. Churchill called him the other day; and Lord Beaverbrook, fresh from his visit to Moscow, has expressed himself in similar vein. " He is a great man, Stalin," he said; " the Russians are well led. If I am any judge of mankind, if I have had any experience worth while in my long life, I put my faith in that man's leadership, and I believe in the Russian resistance."

RUSSIA'S PREMIER is in cheerful mood as he talks with a young "pioneer" from Uzbekistan and a Tajik delegate at a Collective Farm conference in Moscow. Not long ago a figure of hate, Stalin now ranks with Churchill and Roosevelt in the anti-Hitler front.
Courtesy of "Soviet Russia Today"

E. ROYSTON PIKE

America's a Friend in Need to British Warships

To make good the losses sustained in the Battle of the Atlantic and to strengthen further the power of the Royal Navy, British shipyards are working to their utmost capacity. In order that these shipyards may concentrate exclusively upon this vital task of shipbuilding, America is now rendering us great assistance by repairing an increasing number of British ships in her own yards.

On the British side the work is supervized by a technical mission in Washington under Adml. Sir Wilfred French, who has stated : "The work that has been done by the U.S. naval and private yards in refitting our ships has been wonderful."

H.M.S. *Malaya*, British battleship of the Queen Elizabeth class, is seen above leaving New York harbour after refitting. Right, the aircraft carrier *Formidable*, sister ship to the *Illustrious*, in the Navy Yard at Portsmouth, Virginia, where she has been undergoing repairs. Some of her crew are standing by one of the many 4·5-in. dual purpose guns with which the aircraft carrier is equipped.

Photos, British Official : Crown Copyright; Associated Press

Burma's Coming to the Front of the Picture

Constituting a land link between India and China, French (or, should we now say, Japanese ?)
Indo-China, Thailand or Siam, and the Malay States, Burma occupies a place of great and
growing strategical importance.   Some account of the country and its people, its Government and
its communications, is given below.

Burma's Prime Minister, the Hon. U Saw, arrived in this country in October with the triple purpose of conveying to Britain and the British Government a message of goodwill from his own Government and people, of seeing for himself how we are standing up to the ordeal of war, and of obtaining a definite promise from the British Government that Burma will be granted Dominion Home Rule at an early date. After a three weeks' stay Mr. U Saw set out on his return journey at the beginning of November. " I return home disappointed and dissatisfied," he said. " Mr. Churchill was very blunt. I was blunt also.

" I have not been able to get an assurance to take back to Burma," he complained, " that she will be placed on the same level as other members of the Empire. There are no immediate prospects of that coming about. Each of the 17 million people of Burma is expected to participate in the war, yet we are not taken into the confidence of the War Cabinet like the Prime Ministers of the Dominions. In the Atlantic Charter the British Government gives as a war aim the liberation and freedom of small nations. My only request to the British Government and people is that, before they free the countries under Hitler, let them free the countries which are in the British Empire." With that aim a large body of public opinion in England will be in agreement, and it is at least satisfactory to know that U Saw has left our shores with no bitterness.

Probably the chief reason why Burma has not been granted Dominion status, or even a promise of it at a definite date, is that to do so would cause dangerous repercussions in India. But the Burmans fail to find this a good reason. They point out that the new constitution which came into force in 1937 has worked most satisfactorily. There has been no breakdown as in India. The ministry has remained in office, and the Burmese Parliament, consisting of the Senate and the House of Representatives, is function-ing well. Considerable powers are reserved to the Governor (now Sir R. H. Dorman Smith, formerly Minister of Agriculture at Westminster), the principal being currency, defence, foreign relations and ecclesiastical matters ; but for the rest the Burmans have shown themselves well capable of managing their own affairs.

Nothing irritates a good Burman more than to have his country compared with India. Burma, he points out, is not like India in the least. For one thing, it was annexed only so recently as 1886. Then there are vast differ-ences in social life and structure. The Burmans have no caste system and never have had. They have no fierce religious rivalries, nor have they a professional priest-hood. The great majority of them—843 out of every 1,000—are Buddhists, and Buddhism is practically the only religion in the world which has never attempted to make converts by force. Burmese women do much more than their fair share of the work, but they have none of the sex disabilities which so often make the lives of the Indian women a misery. On the whole, the Burmans are a most attractive people, courteous and kindly, cheerful in disposition, tolerant in all things.

Rather more than 260,000 square miles in area, Burma is about the same size as Japan, or twice the size of Italy. Of its people the majority are Burmans by race, but there are also many Shans, Karens and Kachins. The capital is Rangoon (pop. 400,000), but Rangoon is a cosmopolis rather than a Burman city. Next to it rank Mandalay (pop. 150,000) and Moulmein (pop. 65,000).

For the most part the Burmese people are cultivators of the soil ; not for nothing has Burma been called the world's rice granary. But many thousands are engaged in the oil-fields in the basin of the Irrawaddy, between Rangoon and Mandalay. Burma, indeed, has the Empire's richest oil-fields, producing more than a million tons of crude petroleum per annum. Many more are engaged in mining tungsten, copper, and lead. Then

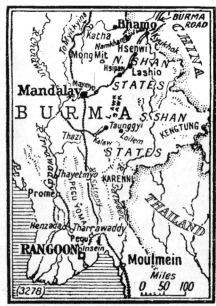

BURMA, showing the two main routes to China from Rangoon : the road and rail route via Mandalay and Lashio to the frontier at Kyukhok, and up the Irrawaddy River to Bhamo.
Courtesy of "The Times"

there are also numerous plantations of rubber and other tropical produce. The people live in little villages of wooden huts with roofs thatched with palm leaves or grass (though nowadays corrugated iron is becoming all too common). Then every village has its bazaar, where the countryfolk meet to ex-change their goods and gossip, and its pagoda, containing relics of the Buddha perhaps, attracting pilgrims from far and near.

Very largely covered with mountains as it is, Burma's communications are few and difficult. The main channel of commerce is the Irrawaddy, which is navigable up to Bhamo on the Chinese frontier, 900 miles from the sea. From Bhamo there is a road to Kyukhok on the frontier, where it joins the Burma Road from Lashio to Kunming, chief town of the Chinese province of Yunnan, and so on to Chungking, capital of Chiang Kai-Shek's Free China. This is one of the two main routes from Rangoon into China. The other and more important is the railway from Rangoon to Lashio, where the Burma Road begins (see Vol. 3, page 454).

More than half a century ago plans were prepared for the connexion of the Burman and the Chinese railway systems, but it is only now that the line is being extended from Lashio to the Chinese border at Kunlong, whence it will be continued by a Chinese line to Kunming and ultimately to Chungking. Already Lashio and Bhamo are in effect the chief supply bases of Chiang Kai-Shek's armies, but this will be even more true when the new railway is open—in perhaps two years' time—for then it will be far cheaper to transport the goods from the outside world across Burma into China. But the capacity of the Burma Road is limited, and it costs over £100 to send a ton of goods from Rangoon to Chungking. Nevertheless, 15,000 tons of goods entered China by way of the Burma Road last August ; and in spite of the monsoons and the Japanese air raids 4,000 lorries, mostly American, rolled steadily along the tortuous track. The Burma Road is in very truth Free China's life-line.

HON. U SAW, Prime Minister of Burma, a photograph taken on the occasion of his recent visit to the area of the South-Eastern Command known as Britain's front line. Whether his country will be involved in the war depends on Japanese policy.   *Photo, British Official: Crown Copyright*

Echoes of War on the Road to Mandalay

WAR in the Pacific, if precipitated by Japan, may involve Burma, whose frontier is threatened since Indo-China came under Japanese control. Hence the rearmament of Burma has been proceeding in anticipation of Japanese aggression.

A chain of air bases hacked out of the Burmese jungle has been constructed during the past few months, and should the Japanese advance either across Thailand or the north-west frontier of Indo-China they will meet with powerful opposition from squadrons of R.A.F. bombers and the new American-built Brewster Buffalo multi-gun fighters. These aerodromes, with all-weather runways, are the formidable answer to the new bases which have been built by the Japanese in Indo-China.

The Burma Defence Force comprises the Army in Burma and the Burma Frontier Force. The latter force came into being in April, 1937.

An Indian Mountain Battery, in defence of Burma, transporting its guns on Texas mules. The mountainous country often makes mechanized movement impossible.

A company of Burma Rifles marching out of the gateway of the old fort of Mandalay to keep watch on the frontier with French Indo-China.

AT RANGOON, Bren-gun carriers are being swung on to the dockside. Left, Indian mountain gunners examining the latest weapon from the West, a Tommy-gun. Since the Japanese menace became acute Burma has consolidated her defensive armaments.

Photos, British Official: Crown Copyright

If They Want War, Then Australia Is Ready

AT MELBOURNE, the first Bristol Beaufort assembled in Australia makes its maiden flight.   Right: Australia's Party Leaders at a War Advisory Council meeting at Victoria Barracks. Left to right: Messrs. Curtin (Prime Minister), Fadden and Menzies.

Close-up of a Sydney air-raid siren. Australia, like Britain, has to counter the mine menace, and, right, is a trawler in the Bass Straits engaged in sweeping operations.

AUSTRALIAN A.A. GUNNERS practising on the sea-coast at movable R.A.A.F. targets. In the last war Australia, territorially, was beyond the line of fire. This time the possibility of Japanese aggression makes a powerful home defence force essential.
Photos, Wide World, Sport & General, Keystone

SHOULD war begin in the Pacific, Australia will have her own front. She has been preparing for this eventuality, and Sir Earle Page, Australian special representative in this country, has stated that " Australia's preparedness is very much greater than they realize in Germany."

The Dominion has 450,000 men, or 25 per cent of the male population between 18 and 40, in her armed forces. Production of munitions is 20 times greater than at the outbreak of war. More than 1,000 planes have been built, and new types are in schedule. Land forces comprise 170,000 troops in the A.I.F., 200,000 in the militia and garrison battalions, and a Home Guard of 50,000. The Australian R.A.F. has expanded to over 60,000.

" To counter a blockade," Sir Earle continued, " we have laid in food stocks at city, provincial and country centres throughout Australia. Hence land transport could be used almost completely for military purposes should sea communications be seriously interfered with."

Flying the Atlantic Is Ferry Command's Job

LOCKHEED HUDSONS getting ready to take off on their transatlantic hop from a Newfoundland airfield.

Above, the control desk in the control tower of a Newfoundland airport. The O.C. control tower watches an incoming aircraft through his glasses.

CROSSING the Atlantic in an aeroplane, which, only a few years ago, was such a hazardous feat, is now a routine job. Indeed, some R.A.F. pilots look upon Atlantic ferrying as a rest from operational flying. A pilot officer, in a recent broadcast, gave two main reasons why flying the Atlantic is now such a comparatively simple job. "First," he said, "because America is building and supplying us with fine aircraft. Secondly, because each flight is planned to the last detail."

The A.O.C.-in-C., R.A.F. Ferry Command, Canada, takes delivery of American-built aircraft from the Flight Ferry Command of the U.S. Army Air Corps and is responsible to the Air Council for their delivery in Great Britain.

From the factories in Canada or America the planes to be delivered to Britain are taken to Newfoundland, where the real business of ferrying starts. Pilot and navigator are informed by the meteorological experts of weather conditions right across the Atlantic. The captain of the aircraft then decides whether and when he will take off. Next, the aircraft, which is under an armed guard, is examined in every detail, the petrol tanks are filled, and after a final conference with the weather experts the crew is ready to take off.

The coast of Newfoundland is left behind and the aircraft climbs rapidly through the clouds to a great height where there is no moisture in the air to ice up the wings and airscrews. As soon as it is dark the navigator checks his position by the stars, the automatic pilot is plugged in, and the crew settles down for the night. The navigator is the only one with much to do. The remainder read or talk and there is plenty of food and drink to sustain them on the trip.

The average duration of the trip is about ten hours. Eventually the aircraft makes its appointed landing on the other side of the ocean. As the pilot officer remarked : "It's satisfying to descend through a hole in the cloud and find yourself in exactly the right spot at the right time. It's a grand feeling."

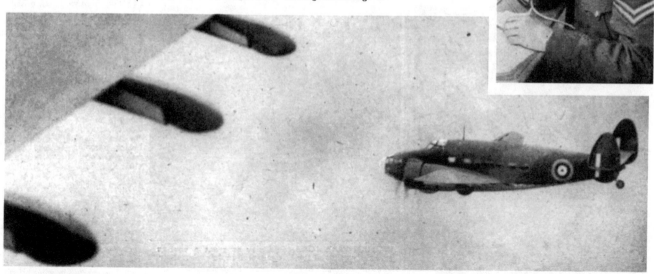

FERRY COMMAND is responsible for the organization of the service which flies aircraft built in N. America across the Atlantic to Britain. Above, a Lockheed Hudson winging its way across the vast expanse of the ocean. Above, right, an R.A.F. corporal maintaining communication between the home airport and a home-bound machine.

Photos. British Official : Crown Copyright

Our Searchlight on the War

IF WE LOSE THE WAR '— Goebbels

Recently Dr. Goebbels, Hitler's Propaganda Minister, wrote an article for " Das Reich " which created a great sensation because of its unwontedly serious note. It was called "Wann oder Wie ? " (When or How ?), the point of the heading being in the statement that the question of *how* the war is going to end is more important than the *when.*

IF Germany wins the war, writes Dr. Joseph, everything will be gained—raw materials, plenty of foodstuffs, living-space, the basis for a new social order for Germany and the other members of the Axis family. But if Germany loses the war, she will not only lose all these things but everything she has at present. " The fate of the German people is hard and bitter," he admits, but the war would have had to come even if Poland had agreed to Hitler's demands in 1939, or even if England and France had accepted the Fuehrer's peace offer after the conclusion of the Polish campaign. " We can and will win," he goes on, " but this needs a mighty national effort by the whole nation." Then the article takes a grimly sardonic turn. " When people at home complain, they should ask themselves : ' Are not the sacrifices of the conquered peoples much greater than our own ? ' " Without waiting to reply, Goebbels proceeds : " We still enjoy the highest living standard of all European nations. Every German must now give his all, and if he complains of hardships he will always be able to find another German who is suffering still more." So there's comfort for you, Grumbling Gretchen and Fretful Fritz!

ONE SAD SATURDAY

Thirty-seven of our bombers are missing from these operations over Germany and Occupied France last night. At least half of that number were forced down by bad weather.—*R.A.F. broadcast* 1 *p.m., Nov. 8th.* Fifteen of our fighters are missing from these operations today.—*R.A.F. broadcast 9 p.m., Nov. 8th.*

THIS was indeed bad hearing. In material terms it represents a loss of some £2,000,000 of aircraft within the space of one day. Think what £2,000,000 could have done for social service in peacetime ! But more serious is the loss of pilots, gunners, observers, wireless men. A total of about 200. Fortunately the death roll may have been only a fraction of that : even so, those saved are lost for the term of the War. Two questions arise : (1) Why not better knowledge of the weather ? (2) Why push on to their remoter targets in conditions of such imminent danger ? The answer to the first is that the most expert meteorologists are at . times no more able to ensure weather conditions at a distance than the trickiest astrologer his foretellings—there is always the imponderable. And here it was. " Haig's weather " it might be called, for that commander rarely planned an advance that wasn't soon held up by adverse weather. But in the end his armies beat the Boche ; and so it will be again. The answer to the second : that the motto of the service is to " get your target at all costs." This time the cost was high : a new cruiser (that might have been sunk by one lucky torpedo shot) could

have been built for the money spent on these aircraft and equipment. But the lost bombers had got their targets, and doubtless if the results of their bombs could be assessed it would be found that they had more than squared accounts with the enemy in whose behalf the weather had changed so unexpectedly.

TOTAL WAR NEEDS TOTAL EFFORT

The Russian S K F ball-bearing factory was evacuated from Moscow and set up again in its new home, hundreds of miles to the east, in an incredibly short space of time.—*" Evening Standard " Correspondent at Kuibishev*

BUT the men did not sit and wait for builders to arrive. The district was scoured for tools ; sand, bricks and cement were found. Then turners and grinders, book-keepers and office-girls set to work to rebuild their factory. On October 2 production was resumed and during the ensuing month the output of the plant was larger than during any month in Moscow ! On the day this story was published the " Daily Telegraph " announced that the Ministry of Labour was to make an immediate investigation into the recent departure of many young women of call-up age for the Isle of Man. People in that island are, thanks to the local law, not required to register under the Registration for Employment Order. The spineless have apparently gone to join the tail-less.

BUT IS IT A MAJOR MISTAKE ?

The R.A.F.'s work over the British Isles has saved England from defeat. But its work elsewhere has added up to a major British mistake of the war. I believe the mistake lies in the fact that it is an independent unit.—*Rear Adm. Harry Yarney, U.S. Navy. (retd.), in " Collier's Magazine "*

THESE criticisms and those of Major Fielding Eliot, on very similar lines, echo a campaign now being waged in the U.S.A. against the proposed separation of the air arms from the American army and navy and their union as a separate force. They recall the long-sustained controversy that raged in Britain and ended only in 1937 by the incorporation of a limited portion of the Royal Air Force into the Navy as the Fleet Air Arm. But the Admiralty still depends upon the co-operation of the Coastal and Bomber Commands of the R.A.F. for sea work which, in Germany, is under a central military control. Similar and even stronger criticisms have been directed against the Army's lack of control of the air in land operations. The German Wehrmacht obtains its air striking power by coordination and control, the British by cooperation and agreement, excellent in peacetime, but too slow in decision and action for total war. One high ranking officer in Greece is reported to have declared, says Major Eliot, that he would never accept another command in which he did not have full and undivided control of his supporting air force. Looking back over the record of this war and allowing for all the unforgettable triumphs of the R.A.F., who shall say that he is without justification ?

WASTE is folly in peacetime : in wartime it is criminal. This bread was found among refuse collected from just a few houses in an English town. Yet men risk their lives daily to bring wheat to Britain.   *Photo, " Daily Mirror "*

SHOOT STRAIGHT : DAMN DRILL !

Drill teaches movement of walking pace or quick step. In modern war men crawl or run, or lie down. . . . Drill teaches movements in unison, with men shoulder-close beside each other. In war men are in loneliness, yards apart. . . . Drill teaches straight lines. In war all straight lines are suicidal. . . .—*Tom Wintringham in " New Ways of War "*

THERE is a case for ceremonial drill, but it does not cut much ice when speedy training is of vital urgency. For guerilla warfare it is completely inessential. Therefore, ladies of the Slough Women's Guerilla (see photograph below), and all other women who wish to emulate the example of the women of Soviet Russia, don't spend a lot of time on the correct etiquette for greeting " Grand Rounds," but concentrate all your efforts on good grouping at the local rifle range. A Royal Marine, captured at Calais, said in a recent broadcast describing what he saw as he was marched under guard through France and Belgium : " We very seldom saw the Germans drilling, but you would always see targets up and men firing . . . We soon saw how quick and straight they can shoot. They were shooting all the time for sport, and to show off, at anything that happened to be about : cats and dogs, hens, men and women — anything' that came handy. And they were hitting them right in the head every time ! "

' FIRST HUNDRED THOUSAND ' ?

The Germans have now 100,000 or more guns. There has never been known such an immense assembly of guns in the world. These are all pointed in the end at Britain.—*Lord Beaverbrook*

WHY should we be surprised at this ? In addition to her own vast pre-war preparations of heavy artillery, Germany, by her long succession of quick-fire victories, came into possession of all the ordnance of Czechoslovakia, Poland, Belgium, Holland, and France —to say nothing (which is quite enough) of the British armaments abandoned in the flight from Belgium. Moreover, and even more important, the Nazis became the masters of the great Czech and French munitions factories which for nearly eighteen months have been turning out new and improved heavy artillery wherewith to hedge their immense coastline from Narvik to Biarritz. Most of these 100,000 guns may yet be needed to defend these far-stretching shores. Another winder, this, for the blithe spirits that would gaily throw British expeditionary forces against that coast in the sure and certain knowledge that destruction on a gigantic scale would await all, or most of the B.E.F.s that tried large - scale frontal attacks on beaches bristling with these endless batteries. There is a way round, even if it involves a detour of some thousand miles.

WOMEN WARRIORS could play as great a part as have the women of the Soviet Union in defending their lives and homes. But time spent in peacetime ceremonial drill (left) is time that could be better spent in practising marksmanship, as the Cambridge Women's Home Defence Corps (above) know.
Photos, Associated Press and Eastern Press Agency

Bitter and Hard Is the Fight for the Crimea

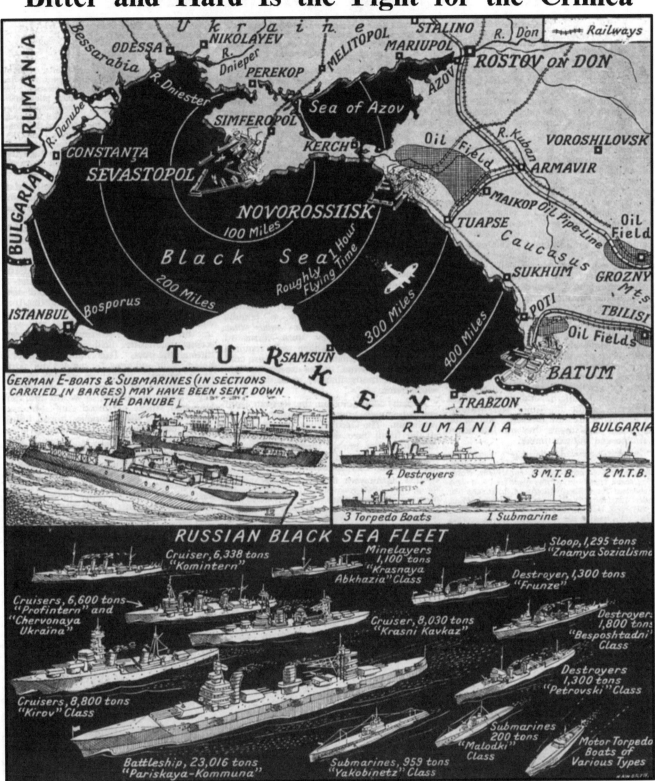

WAR IN THE BLACK SEA AREA is increasing in fury; Sebastopol, chief naval base of the Russian Black Sea Fleet, is now under German fire. On November 16, Berlin claimed that German infantry had fought their way into the streets of Kerch at the eastern extremity of the Crimea; but Gen. von Manstein's 14 infantry divisions were having to fight through heavy snowstorms and 30 degrees F. of frost. Should the Nazis occupy the whole of the Crimea they would base bombers there to attack oil-producing centres and ports in the Caucasus and the Russian Fleet. No doubt Germany has sent E-boats and submarines down the Danube to supplement the weak Rumanian and Bulgarian units under her control. They could be transported overland in sections and assembled in Balkan ports.

The Russian Fleet in the Black Sea is said to consist of one battleship with twelve 12-in. and sixteen 4·7-in. guns, four modern cruisers, two armed with 7·1-in. and 4-in. guns and two with 5·1-in. guns, one older type cruiser, about twenty modern destroyers and several older ones, roughly fifty submarines, and fifty or more motor torpedo-boats.

If Sebastopol falls, Novorossiisk—an important commercial oil port possessing good harbourage—may become the Russian Black Sea base. The photograph on the right is of the Novorossiisk cement factory. The town is an important centre for the export of cereals and cement. Batum, the only other important Black Sea port left to the Russians, has harbour facilities, but is unsuitable as a base during winter storms.

Photo, E.N.A.

Diagram specially drawn by Haworth for THE WAR ILLUSTRATED

Will Winter's Coming Halt the Russian War?

Although fierce fighting continued near Moscow and in the Crimea, as November wore on there
were signs that the fury of the German offensive had passed its peak. From various quarters
there came suggestions that the approach of winter was severely taxing the strength and the
resources of the invader.

"AT the present moment," said Mr.
Churchill in his Mansion House
speech on November 10, "the
German invading armies, after all their
losses, lie on the barren steppes exposed to
the approaching severities of the Russian
winter."

Winter in Russia ! It begins in November,
and from then until April the whole country
is frozen. Bitter winds, born in the icy
steppes of Central Asia, cut like a knife, or
rather, like a saw. The average temperature
falls below 20 degrees Fahrenheit. Even
on the Crimean Riviera the winter months
are as cold as they are in the north of Scotland. Elsewhere the rivers are solid ice ;
even the ports are ice-bound. The roads are
frozen hard, but every night their course is
almost blotted out by enormous piles of snow-
drifts. To these bitter conditions is added
an element of gloom, since daylight hours are
short and the country seems sunk in almost
perpetual night.

The Germans, it seems reasonable to
suppose, did not expect that they would have
to face a winter in Russia—at least, in the
open. They probably thought that even if
the campaign had not been brought to a
close, yet their armies would spend the winter
months snugly enough in their quarters in
Moscow and Leningrad and in the villages
and towns behind the front. But Moscow
and Leningrad are still untaken ; and as for
the villages and towns, they are just heaps
of rubble and burned timber.

"'Forward, forward,' the officers urged their
men," reported the other day a Nazi war reporter,
speaking from a radio van on the Moscow front,
"' we must reach our winter quarters.' At last
we reached the village which was to become our
winter quarters. Well, there had been a village
at this spot, but all that was left was a heap of
ruins. We had to dig deep holes in the ground
to snatch a few hours' sleep. Six to eight men
are crammed into these holes and then tanks
are moved into position over them so as to
protect them against the night attacks of the
Red Air Force."

Now, however, the Nazis have recognized
the inevitable. The spokesmen in Berlin
are trying to "put across" the story that
the Russian winter has been steadily getting
better of recent years, and that it is not to be
compared with that which brought ruin to
Napoleon's armies. Winter in the Moscow
region, they declare, is no worse than it is

near Berlin. But, all the same, extraordinary
precautions are being taken just in case
"General Winter" should prove difficult.
Huge orders for wooden huts, fur-lined
overcoats, skis, and snow-shoes have been
given out. Skis, sweaters and ski clothing,
even blankets, have been confiscated wholesale in Norway and the Baltic States. The
Finnish aircraft factory at Tampere has
been ordered to supply quantities of special
skis for the German aeroplanes. Large
numbers of prisoners-of-war have been
drafted to the clothing factories, and orders
have been issued to the German troops in
Russia to confiscate the winter clothing of the
civilian population.

'Spiritual Nourishment' for Nazis!

Then, on November 8, half a million Nazis
and their assistants spent the Saturday in a
house-to-house visitation throughout Germany, collecting bottles. These, it was
explained, would be filled with "spiritual
nourishment" in the shape of brandy,
schnapps, rum, Norwegian *Aqua vitae*,
champagne, and barley spirit—forms of
concentrated alcohol which were required
to guard the German soldiers against cold
and fatigue. Wines, it was expected, would
not be sent in any quantity, since the lighter
wines freeze.

Already conditions on the Russian front
are bad enough, and the real winter has not
yet begun. The German war correspondents
at the front have described the appalling
conditions that prevail there. Here is one
typical report quoted in "The Times" from
its Stockholm correspondent.

"The infantrymen halted. No one moved,
for movement was very difficult. Their feet were
deep in the sucking mud, stuck to their legs like
iron clamps. Shots rang out. The experienced
soldiers knew that 30 or 40 yelling men were
attacking our transport detachments behind.
Still our mud-coated men remained motionless,
their faces grey with tension. 'Forward,'
shouted the lieutenant, and the men panted on.

"The ammunition was heavy, the muddied
knapsacks heavier, but the machine-guns were
heaviest—heavier than sacks of coal. The men
cursed and groaned, and in spite of the cold
wind sweat ran down their faces in a stream.
'If only it were as hot as this at night, d——n it,'
one soldier exclaimed, and he spoke for all.

"Dusk descended as we reached the village.
The men spoke little. After marching east for
1,200 miles, after four months of constant

fighting, the men do not waste words. Our old
sergeant, the best in the whole army, also does
not talk. The night is cold, icy, hostile. Feet
are numb, like ice. The wet shirts stick to the
body like cold bandages. Three hours' sleep,
and then it is too cold. You can feel it through
your greatcoat. The mud is stiff, and it is snowing slightly. Warm coffee comes, the devil
knows where from or how. The men laugh—no,
they do not laugh, they merely draw back their
bearded lips a little, with a slight suggestion
of a smile . . ."

Compared with the Germans, the Russians
are in a much better position. For one thing,
they are hardened to the climate ; they know
what to expect and are prepared for it.
Every Russian has his sheepskin coat and his
felt boots. He thinks little of 50 degrees of
frost, and can remain in the open day and
night, when the Germans would freeze. All
the Russian clothing factories are working
non-stop, turning out huge quantities of
warm uniforms. Herds of cattle and sheep
have been driven up to just behind the front,
so as to be within easy reach of the Russian
commissariat ; they have walked, as it were,
to the stew-pots. Correspondents report
seeing numerous field-kitchens steaming
through the trees. Tremendous quantities of
bread, soup and stew are handed out as the
day's rations. So far as possible the Red
Army private has at least two solid meals a
day ; while the officers, so we are told, have
abundant stocks of tinned stuff—preserved
meat, caviare, fish, sausages, bread, butter,
cheese, beer, wine, vodka and brandy.

Then the Russians are much better off in
the matter of quarters. The towns behind
their front are not destroyed. "Woods are
interspersed with little sod mounds," the
correspondent of the "New York Times"
has written, "which prove to be roofs of
three-men dug-outs, where soldiers sleep in
trios on dirt shelves covered with straw.
This may sound neither warm nor comfortable, but if you have come in out of a
hail storm and visit one, you will realize it is."
Many headquarters along the front, he goes
on, are now provided with underground
dug-outs, some of which have sleeping
quarters, club rooms, with the wireless laid
on, a gramophone or piano, and all are warm.
The front line first-aid stations are being
transferred from tents to dug-outs, and
stores of medical supplies, including tinned
blood for quick transfusions and medicine
for frost-bite, are being distributed.

'GENERAL WINTER' is at last taking a hand in slowing down the German offensive on the Eastern Front and thereby giving the hard-pressed Red
Armies a valuable breathing-space. Snow is falling everywhere, and German broadcasts refer to appalling weather conditions. For once the
German radio speaks truth, as may be gathered from these photographs showing (left) German troops moving up along a sodden road and (right) the
mud-clogged tracks of German tanks after travelling over the waterlogged countryside.   *Photos. Keystone, Sport & General*

But As Yet the Nazi War Machine Drives On

RUSSIAN FRONT in mid-November, showing the centres of fierce fighting in the Moscow, Rostov and Crimea areas.

Motor-cycle detachment, part of reinforcements for the badly-mauled Rumanian army, crossing a pontoon bridge over the Dnieper.

Snowshoes such as are now being turned out for Russia in British factories. Below, girls stringing the shoes, which are made largely of ash.

GERMAN PANZER units (left) on the move to the Eastern Front. The dense smoke in the background probably indicates Russian application of "scorched earth" policy. Circle, a German heavy gun manned by a crew in camouflage uniforms.

Photos, Sport & General, Keystone, Associated Press. Map by courtesy of the " Daily Telegraph"

A Year Later: In Liverpool and Manch

A panoramic view taken from a building in Sout
Memorial and Lord Street. The town was heav
has been in progress for some mon

The last corner of the Victoria Buildings site, Ma
Right, the Market Place in " Cottonopolis," whi
arise on the ruins of the old.

War's Wreckage Is Being Cleared Away

...erpool show ng the neighbourhood of the Victoria ... the winter raids of 1940, but now clearance work ... open space for eventual reconstruction.

...as destroyed in raids at the end of 1940 (left photo). ...heavily. After the war a new and fairer city must

Photos, Topical Press and " Manchester Guardian "

'This Most Important and Timely Action'

H.M.S. AURORA is a cruiser of 5,270 tons displacement, completed in November 1937. Her main armament consists of six 6-in. guns.

Lt.-Commander W. F. HUSSEY, commanding H.M.S. *Lively*, one of the destroyers which took part in the action here described.

ON November 9, two days before the anniversary of the Battle of Taranto, a patrolling force of British naval units annihilated two convoys of enemy supply ships. The first enemy convoy, consisting of eight ships escorted by destroyers, was sighted south of Taranto on the afternoon of November 8 by an R.A.F. Maryland on reconnaissance. A patrolling force, consisting of the cruisers H.M.S. *Aurora* and H.M.S. *Penelope* and the destroyers H.M.S. *Lance* and H.M.S. *Lively*, were directed to intercept. They made contact with the enemy at about 1 a.m. on November 9, when it was found that the convoy had been joined by another of two supply ships escorted by two destroyers. The operation was being covered by two powerful 10,000-ton 8-inch-gun cruisers of the Trento class.

Despite the disparity of force, Captain Agnew of the *Aurora* immediately engaged. Nine of the ten enemy supply ships were set on fire and sunk, one being an ammunition ship, which blew up. The tenth, a tanker, was left blazing furiously. Of the Italian warships, it was reported that two escorting destroyers were sunk and one damaged. No casualties or damage were sustained by the British ships. Later the remnant of Italian naval escort was intercepted and attacked by a British submarine. Two enemy destroyers were hit by torpedoes and one was seen to sink. In a message of congratulation to the Admiralty, Mr. Churchill described this engagement as "this most important and timely action." The two Italian cruisers beat a speedy retreat when attacked. Mr. Alexander later disclosed that four Italian destroyers were known to have been sunk in this engagement.

Capt. W. G. AGNEW, commanding H.M.S. *Aurora*, though only 42, has been in the Navy for 30 years. He was awarded the C.B. for the brilliant Mediterranean engagement of Nov. 9.

Area south of Taranto, in the Central Mediterranean, where British naval forces annihilated two escorted convoys, sank two enemy destroyers and damaged one, which ultimately sank, without loss or casualties.

H.M.S. PENELOPE, sister ship to the *Aurora*, was completed in November 1936. Both ships are of the improved *Arethusa* class. In the Mediterranean action described above *Penelope* was commanded by Capt. A. D. Nicholl, R.N.

Photos, Wright & Logan, "Daily Mirror," Topical Press. Map by courtesy of "News Chronicle"

What Is it Like in a U-Boat in Winter?

Although the Battle of the Atlantic is not yet won, it seems to be going not too badly for us, and we are certainly much better prepared for the fray than we were a year ago. But Mr. Churchill revealed in the House of Commons on Nov. 12 that there were never so many U-boats at work as now, and they may be expected to put up a stern fight.

NEVER pleasant at the best of times, life in a U-boat in an Atlantic swept by winter gales must be a nightmare of anxiety and dangerous labour. Speaking from Zeesen the other night, a German " front reporter " told his listeners that " the last weeks have been more difficult, as you all know. They were especially taxing for the nerves of our crews. Yet our brave U-boat men fought splendidly."

U-boats are small craft, smaller as a rule than those which were employed in the war of a quarter of a century ago. The largest, the ocean-going type, has a surface displacement of about 750 tons and a length of 275 feet. The sea-going and coastal types have surface displacements of 500 and 250 tons respectively, and a length of 200 feet and 140 feet. Some of the bigger ships of von Tirpitz's U-boat fleet had a surface displacement in excess of 2,000 tons.

Even in calm weather, in a smooth sea, submarines pitch and toss considerably, and in stormy weather some of the boats are very heavy rollers. It is not at all unusual for the entire complement of a submarine to be violently seasick ; and there is always the risk of accidents, when men are flung against the sides of the little vessel or come into contact with moving machinery. When submerged the boats are often bitterly cold, since the commander may decide that he cannot spare any of his precious " juice " for the electric stoves ; when on the surface the boats are warmed by steam heaters run by the Diesel oil engines, which are the main propellants above water. In cold weather the decks may be covered with ice and snow ; the hatchways may be frozen hard, and the periscopes jammed by the ice and their glass frosted over. There can hardly be any more unpleasant job than chipping off the ice formed on a submarine's deck, when a heavy sea is rolling and the temperature is somewhere below freezing.

Firing the Torpedoes

Submariners have expressed a preference for choppy weather over the smooth seas of summer, since in the latter the periscope moving through the water leaves a feather-like trail, all too easily spotted from the air ; in a rolling sea, on the other hand, the tell-tale feather is not to be distinguished in a moving waste of " white horses." But there is a difference between a choppy sea and those seas produced by winter gales in the Atlantic. Then it is usually impossible to see any distance ahead, and a target may appear and disappear in the most tantalizing fashion. A commander usually strives to arrange matters so that he fires his torpedoes at an approaching ship from an angle of 45 degrees. In bad weather, however, it often proves impossible to take a good aim ; he must just take his chance, hoping for a lucky hit. Moreover, the torpedo is likely to be deflected from its course by the mountainous waves.

Then when the chaser becomes chased, when the U-boat's presence has been detected and the destroyers are prowling around dropping their depth charges as they go— then the U-boat's life is full of menace. To surface may be next to suicide ; but a U-boat cannot remain below water indefinitely. After about 48 hours it must be surfaced in order that it may recharge its batteries and replenish its supplies of fresh air. At full speed it cannot remain below water for more than an hour or two.

When a U-boat is cornered in deep water, it is usually sent to the bottom with the loss of all its crew ; in shallow water, however, there is a reasonable possibility of some, at least, of the men managing to escape and be picked up. Recently it was announced by the Admiralty that a total of 1,276 officers and men have been rescued from sunken enemy U-boats and are held as prisoners-of-war ; of these, 467 are stated to be Italians. For obvious reasons the Admiralty has not revealed from how many U-boats the prisoners were taken, but on the experience of the last war it has been suggested that some 190 U-boats have been sent to the bottom. It is very difficult to estimate the figure, however, since numbers of U-boats must have been sunk in deep water without leaving any trace—*spurlos versenkt*, as the Germans phrased it in the last war. But certain it is that Hitler has lost some thousands of U-boat men—men of a service in which years are required to attain proficiency.

Certain it is, too (since Admiral Raeder, Commander-in-Chief of the German Navy, has published their obituary notices), that three of Germany's U-boat aces have lost their lives : Cmdr. Prien, who sank the *Royal Oak* in October 1939, and the *Arandora Star* in July 1940, is stated to have perished on March 7 ; ten days later Lt.-Cmdr. Schepke was lost, and on May 9, Lt.-Cmdr. Lemp.

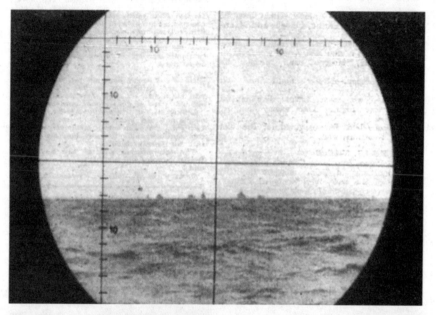

U-BOAT VIEW of a British convoy. Above, the German submarine commander scans the surface of the ocean through his periscope and is rewarded by the sight of a British convoy upon the horizon (top). The graduated black lines across the field of vision enable him to judge the size and distance of the vessels. Yet such is the efficiency of British listening devices, aerial reconnaissance and other counter-submarine measures, that few U-boats get within effective striking distance of their target.

Photos. Associated Press

Our Diary of the War

THURSDAY, NOV. 6, 1941   *796th day*
Air.—Night attacks on Wilhelmshaven, Hamburg and N.W. Germany as well as extensive mine-laying operations in enemy waters.

Russian Front.—Little change in the general situation. Germans claimed Sebastopol under fire. Stalin spoke on the occasion of the 24th anniversary of the Russian Revolution. He estimated Nazi losses in Russia at 4,500,000.

Mediterranean.—Augusta and Licata, Sicily, raided on night of Nov. 5-6. Naples raided on night of Nov. 6-7.

Africa.—Aerodrome at Castel Benito raided during night of Nov. 5-6. Benghazi also attacked.

Home.—Ban on coast visits between the Wash and the Thames and from Littlehampton to Hastings suspended until Feb. 15. A few bombs were dropped by night in E. Anglia and S.E. England.

FRIDAY, NOV. 7   *797th day*
Air.—Bomb-carrying Hurricanes took part in a sweep over N. France. Great force of bombers attacked Berlin, Cologne and Mannheim at night.

Russian Front.—Little territorial change. Great Parade of the Red Army was held in Red Square, Moscow, and another at Kuibishev.

Mediterranean.—Heavy night raid on Brindisi.

Home.—Two coast towns dive-bombed during the night. One enemy bomber destroyed.

General.—U.S. Senate voted for Revision of the Neutrality Act.

SATURDAY, NOV. 8   *798th day*
Air.—Dawn attack on German administrative buildings in Oslo. Biggest daylight sweep of the war over Occupied France. Factories at St. Pol and Lens bombed. Night attack on Essen, Dusseldorf and W. Germany, also docks at Ostend and Dunkirk.

Russian Front.—Little change in the general situation. Soviet counter-attacks on N.E. sector of Leningrad front announced by Moscow.

Mediterranean. — Successful attack by R.A.F. on enemy convoy in Central Mediterranean.

SUNDAY, NOV. 9   *799th day*
Air.—Night attack on targets in N.W. Germany.

Russian Front.—Yalta, in Crimea, occupied by Nazis. Thrust at Murmansk supply line held. Fierce fighting around Kalinin and Volokolamsk.

Mediterranean.—Two Axis convoys annihilated south of Taranto. Three escorting destroyers sunk. Another destroyer later sunk by British submarine. Naples and Brindisi raided at night by R.A.F.

Home.—Attack on S.E. coast town at night. One enemy bomber destroyed.

General.—Col. Knox announced establishment of a complete U.S. operational base at Iceland.

MONDAY, NOV. 10   *800th day*
Sea.—Admiralty announced loss of H.M.S. *Cossack*.

Air.—Mr. Churchill announced that British Air Force was now at least equal in size and numbers to the Luftwaffe.

Russian Front.—New Nazi drive to isolate Leningrad. Germans claimed capture of Tikhvin, 110 miles S.E. of Leningrad. Soviet cavalry in action on Moscow front.

Mediterranean.—Naples raided by R.A.F.

Africa.—Night raid on Benghazi.

Home.—Slight activity over E. and N.E. coasts. Two Nazi planes destroyed.

TUESDAY, NOV. 11   *801st day*
Russian Front.—Big battle around Serpukhov for the crossings of River Oka. Bitter fighting at Tula, south of Moscow. Russians announced evacuation of Bakchisarai, 24

miles N. of Sebastopol. Germans claimed Mariental, 20 miles from Kerch.

Mediterranean. — Admiralty announced sinking of six enemy supply ships and the crippling of four more by British submarines. Naples raided by R.A.F. bombers. Seaplane

MOSCOW'S TRIBUTE TO BRITAIN

AT present there is a lull on the Western Front, but this does not mean that the British people are not preparing for the fight. They are assembling all their forces and are strengthening their defences.

The British people fight bravely and stubbornly and succeed in getting out of the toughest situations with honour. After Dunkirk Hitler shouted victory, thinking that this evacuation meant the end of British resistance. This was a mistake. The British people withstood the mass German air raids on London, Coventry, Birmingham, Liverpool and other towns. They never thought of capitulating because, like the Soviet people, they do not want to live under Hitler's yoke. They are determined to fight till Hitler's final collapse.

The mighty British Navy has grown in numbers and in strength. It crushed German naval power, inflicting many cruel defeats, especially on those German ships which tried to interfere with the communications between the British Isles and the British Dominions overseas and America. The powerful fleet of our ally guards the seas and watches over the convoys with military cargoes which are constantly arriving in British and now also in Soviet ports.

THE Soviet people stand on the advanced lines of the battle-front in this great hour of trial, but the day will come when the British people will also stand on the forward positions.

Difficult days of trial are in store for us, for the people of Great Britain and for the whole anti-Nazi front, but their heroic endurance will prove that spiritually and materially they are stronger than the German bandits.

The indomitable will of the Soviet and British peoples will see this war to a victorious end.

Broadcast by M. Viktorov, November 5, 1941.

base and railway station at Syracuse attacked.

WEDNESDAY, NOV. 12   *802nd day*
Russian Front.—Nazi divisions repulsed near Tula. In Leningrad sector Russians claimed to be still holding Tikhvin. Soviet aircraft made night attack on Koenigsberg and Riga.

Mediterranean.—Naples attacked at night by R.A.F. Gela, Sicily, attacked by Hurricane bombers.

Africa.—Officially announced that Italian positions at Gondar, Abyssinia had been encircled by Allied troops, after capture of Gianda. Fayum area, S.W. of Cairo, raided by enemy aircraft.

Home.—New session of Parliament opened by King.

General.—Gen. Huntziger, Vichy war minister, killed in air crash. Finland rejected U.S. suggestion that she should cease hostilities.

THURSDAY, NOV. 13   *803rd day*
Russian Front.—Germans claimed to have broken through the defences across the Kerch Isthmus in the Crimea.

Home.—A few enemy raiders dropped bombs at night in S.W. England.

General.—Bill to Amend U.S. Neutrality Act passed House of Representatives. Japan closed Canton River, west of Hong-Kong.

FRIDAY, NOV. 14   *804th day*
Sea.—Admiralty announced loss of the aircraft carrier *Ark Royal*, torpedoed by a U-boat. Moscow announced sinking of five German transports—two in the Barents Sea and three in the Baltic.

Russian Front.—Heavy fighting in front of Sebastopol and Kerch. After a fortnight's battle Russians dislodged Nazis from heights near Naro Fominsk, by the River Nara, with the loss of 29,000 killed and wounded.

Mediterranean.—Night attack by R.A.F. on Brindisi as well as Catania, in Sicily.

Africa.—Night attacks by R.A.F. on objectives at Benghazi, Berka, Bardia and Derna. Aerodromes at Barce and Murtuba also attacked by S.A.A.F.

SATURDAY, NOV. 15   *805th day*
Air.—Offensive sweep over Occupied France by Hurricane bombers and Spitfires. Night raids on Emden and N.W. Germany.

Russian Front.—Crimea still the scene of bitter fighting. Moscow announced failure of a German landing attempt on Murmansk coast. 20 boats sunk by Russian fire and two companies of Nazi troops destroyed.

Home.—Two enemy bombers shot down off E. Coast. N.E. Coast town raided during day. Slight enemy activity at night.

THE AVRO MANCHESTER, new type of twin-engined aircraft now in service with Bomber Command, in flight (top). Beneath, the wireless operator and one of the crew inside the machine. *Photos, British Official : Crown Copyright*

Have You Ever Been Inside a Submarine ?

TORPEDO ROOM of a British submarine at a base port, showing a torpedo being loaded into the firing tube.   A reservoir of compressed air at a pressure of 2,000 lb. per sq. in. is stored in tanks to fire the torpedoes, and the actual firing is done by a compressed air cylinder, at 500 lb. pressure, which forces the torpedo out of the tube.   Since the discharge would upset the balance of the boat unless immediately compensated, torpedo-trimming tanks are placed near the torpedo tubes.   Early submarines carried only two torpedo tubes, but later models, like the Triton class, may have as many as ten.
Photo, Planet News

This 'Fertile Island' is Now a Food Factory

"Every endeavour must be made to produce the greatest volume of food of which this fertile island is capable," said the Prime Minister on November 5, 1940. A year later he was able to congratulate all who have to do with the land, farmer and farm-worker alike, on the very great expansion that they have made in our home food production.

BEFORE the war more than half our food was imported. In 1939, indeed, the farming industry was in a much less favourable position than in 1917 to cope with the great task of feeding Britain's millions.

For one thing, the land devoted to food production was 2½ million acres less—an area nearly equal to the counties of Lancashire, Cheshire and Durham. Much had been

of a million fewer than in the last war. On the other hand, whereas towards the end of the last war there were probably fewer than 5,000 tractors in use on our farms, today there are over 100,000.

Immediately the war broke out the Government launched a great "Grow More Food" campaign. The first target was an additional two million acres of grassland to be ploughed up; this was attained, even slightly exceeded,

enough barley to provide the whole of our requirements in beer. If it be asked why we are ploughing up grassland that feeds the beasts that give us meat and milk, here is one answer: ten acres of meat-producing pasture feed one person, and of milk-producing pasture, four persons; while ten acres of wheat feed 21 persons, and of potatoes, 42. Since there is less grassland for cattle and sheep, and since far less food is being imported for them, some reduction of our livestock population has been inevitable. But that reduction has been kept to the minimum since farmers are now growing more oats and beans, kale and mangolds and swedes, and turning more of their grass and other crops into silage for winter food.

But the farmers are doing much more than this; they are also using more fertilizer to get "an extra sack to the acre" of wheat or potatoes, to get extra grass and hay and root crops for their stocks. They are draining their fields, cleaning out their ditches and water courses, dealing with overgrown hedges, and tackling energetically such pests as rats and rabbits that do great damage to the crops. Rats, it is estimated, do £25 million worth of damage annually. *Every rat costs a farmer £1 a year to keep.* In Lancashire the War Agriculture Committee has offered to pay 1d. into the Red Cross Agricultural Fund for every rat's tail collected through the branches of the National Farmers' Union. Thus it is that while every live rat helps Hitler, every dead one helps the Red Cross.

More Labour for the Land!

Farm workers of every kind are not sparing themselves in the fight for food production. They are working long hours in the fields with their horses, tractors, and implements. Their numbers are being supplemented in various ways. The Women's Land Army, now numbering some 18,000, are doing grand work. Units of the Auxiliary Military Pioneer Corps have been lent as drainage gangs. Over 3,000 conscientious objectors are employed in agriculture and forestry. Schoolboys and students have spent their holidays on the land with excellent results.

The campaign is being directed by the Ministry of Agriculture through its War Agricultural Executive Committee. In each county there are an Executive Officer and a committee of practical farmers with full knowledge of local conditions. There are 7,500 of these committeemen, all voluntary workers who are doing a great job of work. The County Committees have wide powers and duties. They give directions as to the grassland to be ploughed up on each farm, and they are always ready to give the farmer advice on all his many problems—cropping, cultivation, fertilizers, foodstuffs, labour, machinery and credit. They hire out tractors and other farm implements provided by the Ministry. They can also take over, with the Ministry's consent, derelict or badly farmed land, and arrange for it to be cultivated properly. Some thousands of acres have been taken over in this way.

Finally, we must mention the "Dig For Victory" campaign—the effort of the small man, particularly the townsman, to increase home food production. Well over half a million new allotments have been taken up in England and Wales since the war began, and the total now exceeds 1½ million, not including the thousands of private and railway allotments and countless private gardens which have been turned over to vegetables.

THE PLOUGHMAN'S CRAFT is well exemplified in this scene on a West Lothian farm near Queensferry, with its straight furrows stretching to the Firth of Forth in the distance. After a recommendation by the Central Agricultural Wages Board of a national minimum wage of 56s. per week for farm workers, most of the county Wages Committees moved for a minimum wage of £3. Surely the man who draws these furrows is worth it! *Photo, Fox*

taken for aerodromes and factories, even more for garden cities and ribbon development; while thousands of acres had reverted to the waste lands of scrubland, bracken and grazing. Then the area under the plough had fallen by 4½ million acres. Yet the population to be fed had risen by 6¾ millions, from 41 millions in 1917 to 47¾ millions today. For every thousand acres cultivated in the last war there were about 1,200 people, whereas in 1940 there were over 1,500 people for every thousand acres. In 1939, too, the cattle population was a record; over 6 million tons of foodstuffs had to be imported for our farm livestock.

There were more men and more beasts to be fed from less land. There were also fewer people to do the job—about a quarter

in spite of the worst ploughing season in living memory. For 1940–41 the target was a further 1¾ million acres, making a total of 3½ million acres ploughed up since war broke out. All over the country land is now under cultivation which has never been cultivated in living memory, if, indeed, at all. Downland in the south of England, fenland in Norfolk and Cambridge, horrible stiff clayland in Huntingdon, undeveloped building land in the Home Counties, commons throughout the country, hilltops in Wales, even golf courses—have been requisitioned and are now bearing bumper crops.

To an ever greater extent our farms are growing the essential food we need: more wheat for our daily bread, enough sugar beet to supply our household sugar ration,

Thanks to Them Our Larder Is Well-Stocked

VICTOR STROBRIDGE, blown up seven times and sunk five times in this war while helping to bring supplies to Britain.

FOOD DEPOT, where thousands of 2-cwt. bags of flour are stored. The flour seen here was imported from Canada, thanks to the men of the Merchant Navy.

SAIDI ALI spent several hours in the water after his ship was sunk. "It was veddy cold," was his comment.

FOOD FOR BRITAIN arrives in increasing quantities, thanks to the protection of the Royal Navy and the devotion to duty of the men of the Merchant Service. In addition to meeting our current needs, a vast national larder has been stocked ready for any emergency and ten thousand storehouses are scattered over the country with a variety of foodstuffs apportioned between them. At every mealtime think of the man in the circle above—the only survivor of a torpedoed ship's crew—who drifted for eleven days on a raft in mid-Atlantic, with the dead bodies of two of his officers beside him. If it weren't for men like this the country might now be starving.

Photos, Ministry of Information, Keystone, Central Press

Should Animals Be Used in Modern War?

SOMEWHERE in the London area is the Army School of Dog Training, where some 60 dogs are trained to work with reconnaissance patrols, in listening posts, and in liaison duties between the front line and Company H.Q. For the most part they are Alsatians ; but included in their number are Border collies, sheep-dogs, Labradors, and even cross-breeds. All have their points, but the individual is more important than the breed.

A " recruit "—all the dogs are lent by their owners for the duration of the war—is on probation for a month or six weeks. Then, if suitable —about 30 per cent fail in their " final "—he (or she) " graduates " in two to three months as a messenger dog, and in four months for patrol duties. Scent power and silence are the qualities most prized. The dogs must never bark ; they warn by " pointing " their tails and muzzles. Gun dogs are generally unsuitable because of their scent for game. Most of the training is done in the dark, and includes subjection to sudden noises, explosions and smoke (see photo below). Already quite a number of the dogs are on active service.

Horses killed in the fighting on the East Front, where they are still used as an auxiliary to mechanical transport. So our " dumb friends " are involved in " Man's inhumanity!"

Circle, an Alsatian, one of many dogs being used for various purposes in this war, is trained to face a smoke-screen. Beneath, this photograph from an Italian source shows bombs bursting amid rebel Arabs and their camels somewhere in the Libyan Desert—a terrifying experience for the tribesmen, but surely worse far for the unhappy beasts.

A carrier pigeon just released from an aeroplane operating from a coastal aerodrome at the Cape of Good Hope. Pigeons are used to carry important messages when contact by wireless is impossible or liable to interception.

Photos, Keystone, South African Official, E.N.A.

All Together Against the Peril by Night

A.T.S. girls on duty at a predictor. They are doing valuable work in countering enemy air attacks, and some of them went into action for the first time on November 1.

THE numbers of Britain's military and civilian defence against the enemy air raider have developed since the war began into a vast and complex organization. A.T.S. girls, A.A. gunners, wardens, police, fire-fighters, are all linked together in a spirit of proud camaraderie. Profiting by our grim experiences, by new methods and rigorous training, the nation stands foursquare against any attack or possible attack that the Nazis may launch. Lull or no lull, the order of the night is "Be ready!"

In regard to civilian defence, the organization will be reinforced by the call-up of girls and youths for part-time duty, and it is proposed to bring in men in their 40s for whole-time duty.

The beam of a searchlight probes the sky for enemy raiders. In the circle, a spotter, protected by a ring of sandbags, in a chair specially adapted for its purpose, keeps vigil with powerful glasses. He is linked by telephone to the searchlight site. Left, fire-watchers report All Clear to the Wardens' Post, a scene typical of the nocturnal civilian defence of Britain.   *Photos, G.P.U., Topical*

I Was There! .... Eye Witness Stories of the War

My Life as a Boy in Much-Bombed Malta

Recently the editor received from John Mizzi, a 16-year-old reader of
"The War Illustrated" in Malta, a letter describing his experiences
during the many air raids to which that historic island has been subjected.
So vividly written is it, so interesting, that we reprint the greater part of it here.

TOURISTS used to call Malta "The Island of Sunshine and Beauty." It's now "The Island of Air-raids and Ruins." Up to the time of writing the island has had over 820 Alerts and more than 300 bombing raids.

I would be lying if I told you we were happy when Italy declared war. Far from it! When we heard the news we looked rather glum. But we were ready! Malta would remain British! We Maltese treasure freedom. We fought for it many times in past days, and we will fight for it now, if need be, again. Let them come!

They came! At 6 a.m. on the morning of June 11 Malta heard the siren for the first time. I did not, for I was sound asleep; but I soon woke up. Many who were asleep like me thought it was A.A. practice. So I thought at first, but when I went on the roof I knew it wasn't. I saw bombs bursting about two miles from where I was. Our ack-ack was merrily blazing away at the enemy planes. After half an hour came the Raiders Passed signal. But the siren wailed again. Its wailing gives you a sickening feeling. They came over eight times that day! The last raid at sunset was the worst raid I ever experienced. It was a very fierce raid. There's no harm now in telling you (as she is sunk) that H.M.S. *Terror* was their principal objective. The ship put up a magnificent fight. The ship's personnel had been drying the clothes on deck and I can still picture the crew running about among the clothes, all eager to arrive first on the guns and have a crack at the "wop." They succeeded in hitting one plane. The crew baled out, but to bale out amidst all that flying shrapnel was sheer madness. They all floated down, dead.

This first experience of air-warfare will never fade from my brain. Nor will the horrors some of the bombed-out victims related. On the morrow Malta woke up, bathed in hate for a nation so cruel, a nation who had overnight forgotten God. They would not leave us. They came again and again. But the more one tries to conquer the Maltese spirit the more we resist. Hatred gave us courage!

The Germans first came over Malta during the night. They made their first daylight appearance in the Mediterranean on January 12, when they attacked a British convoy. They sank the *Southampton*, but the *Gallant*, though broken in half, was brought safely to port; and so was the *Illustrious*. It had a gaping hole in the bows and was down at an alarming angle. A Red Cross plane in the morning flew over on reconnaissance and saw the ship. On the afternoon of January, at about 2 o'clock, the German Air Force darkened the Malta sky. They were met by the fiercest barrage ever. Their planes were either shot out of the sky, or else went to Sicily, leaving behind them a trail of smoke. They came on the following Saturday and Sunday and we shot down 39 planes in all. They only hit the *Illustrious* once, and they kept away after that. When their wounds were healed they came again. It was the aerodrome's turn now. But they found daylight bombing too costly, for we shot down a large number of their planes, and the damage done was out of proportion to the number of bombs dropped, so they took to night bombing. Their targets then were the military hospital and civilian houses. Then, on the last day of April, they came over during the night and dropped heavy bombs on Valetta and brought down half the principal shopping centre. They came on the following night and brought down almost all the other buildings in Kingsway which had escaped.

Funny Liars, the Italians!

But when Hitler invaded Russia he needed all available aircraft to hurl against the heroic Russian Air Force, so the Luftwaffe left us. The Italians started coming over again then. They used to send a reconnaissance aircraft over, escorted by as many as thirty fighters. Our fighters always shot down the reconnaissance plane. So, as a last resort, the Italians last month sent over two reconnaissance aircraft. *One* must return home, they thought. But our fighters shot both down, and three fighters for company, one of the pilots being the Italian Commander of their Air Force in the Mediterranean, General Federigi.

They changed their tactics again now. They come over during the night and drop a rain of incendiaries. As soon as they fall the incendiaries make a fine display, and the island seems to be floodlit, but they soon fizzle out. The night bombers are not having it their own way, for when more than one plane comes over, our searchlights always pick them out, and our fighters shoot many down in flames. When we shoot any down, we have at least two raidless nights. The Italians haven't got any planes to spare now. As a postscript to a raid, we switch on the Italian radio at 5 p.m. and have a hearty laugh. The Italians are funny liars!

When the Italians are overhead our bombers take off and fly over enemy territory. Even during the day our Blenheims, Marylands and "Beaus" take off and drop their bombs on enemy shipping. Even our Hurricanes now are showing an offensive spirit, and they carry out frequent sweeps over Sicily. They rarely meet any Italian fighters, but woe betide the unfortunate fellow who is occasionally seen. He is shot down. The Air Minister has congratulated the Malta Command on its offensive spirit.

When a Convoy Enters Harbour

The Navy, too, is helping us to carry on. They bring the convoys safely in, though attacked by numerous waves of bombers. You in England don't hear much about this —it's secret—but we here appreciate it immensely. When a convoy enters harbour we cheer the ships in, and later we give dances, the crews and captains of the ships in the harbour being the guests of honour.

The Royal Malta Artillery was in the news lately. Italian torpedo-boats tried to torpedo the ships of a convoy in harbour. We had had a night raid before and I was still on the roof, when suddenly the searchlights were switched on and began sweeping the sea. Then the coastal batteries opened fire. Not one of the torpedo-boats returned back to Italy. All seventeen were either sunk or captured. Some of the crews were taken prisoner. The soldiers who had manned the guns during the attack were given a fortnight's leave. It was a glorious victory for us, and another fiasco for the Italian Navy. We have had attacks from the sea and air. We are only waiting for the Italians to try to land . . .

MALTA'S DEFENCES include, naturally enough, the ubiquitous Hurricanes, some of which are here seen taking off from a Maltese airfield to intercept Italian raiders. But Malta is now passing from the defensive to the offensive and, as the Maltese boy says in the article in this page, " even during the day our Blenheims, Marylands, and ' Beaus ' take off and drop their bombs on enemy shipping." Sicily, too, is the objective of ever-increasing raids by the R.A.F., many of them being made by the new type of Hurricane bomber.

Photo, British Official : Crown Copyright

|||||||||||||||||||||||||||||||||||||||||||||||||||||||||||||||||||||||||||||| **I WAS THERE!** ||||||||||||||||||||||||||||||||||||||||||||||||||||||||||||||||||||||||

I Am Captain of a Band of Russian Guerillas

*Recently, War Correspondent Khamadan with the Red Army at the front
contacted in the heart of the forest a guerilla detachment. On parting,
the guerilla commander, Vassili G., gave Khamadan a battered note-book
from which the following extracts were taken.*

SEPTEMBER 3 : I have been appointed commander of the guerilla detachment. I took the guerillas' oath not to spare my life in the merciless struggle against the Nazi bandits.

9. Germans got on our track as soon as we left M. They surrounded the village, noticed our departure and cut us off—trying to push us on to the road. They numbered a whole company, with machine-guns and automatic rifles. We just managed to beat them off. I got my ear shot through. Comrade V. was wounded in the hand, but is not complaining. The Germans lost six dead and an undetermined number of wounded.

13. Mined the road between K. and C. Hid in the bushes alongside the road. The first to appear were four motor-cyclists with machine-guns. Then three motor lorries carrying ammunition. The first lorry blew up and the second smashed into it and caught fire. Eight soldiers were killed. Third lorry exploded. No losses on our side.

15. An old collective-farmer arrived from the village of Beliaevka. He wept as he told us about the atrocities there. The Germans threw 14 wounded Red Army men and commanders and two collective-farmers into a house, splashed the walls with kerosene and then set fire to it. Girls were violated and kept in a separate house. For three days one could hear their cries and the sound of shots. A company of Germans is in the village, one platoon keeping guard.

We promised to come to Beliaevka on September 17. We arrived during the night. First we killed the guards. The rest of the Germans were all drunk. We killed more than 50 of them with grenades. The remainder fled. We freed the girls—all of them with their hands tied, all naked, and beaten black and blue. Among them were girls of 12 to 15 years.

20. Disabled our first tank today. Serozha did it with a grenade. Well done ! It was well smashed.

23. At last we found a Nazi aerodrome with 30 planes—17 bombers and the rest fighters. A large guard, more than two companies. Serozha found the aerodrome.

24. Hard work. Only five of us in action. We crept to the aerodrome with hand-grenades. Nearing the planes, we stood up and walked the rest of the way. It was pitch dark. Some of the planes were evidently getting ready to start. Their engines were working. We threw 23 grenades. Indescribable panic. Sixteen planes were burned down. We escaped into the woods—all safe except Comrade A. who must have been killed. All glory and honour to you, our brave comrade ; you perished like a hero.

25. We spent all day sleeping in the woods —feeling a little tired. At night we went with some men to a neighbouring window. We quietly approached the former collective-farm club. Through the open windows we saw German officers. Some of them were typing in one room ; in another they were examining large maps on the walls. We threw two grenades through each window.

26. Today was a real holiday. Comrade A. returned safe and sound. He had run from the aerodrome in another direction and had got lost in the woods. He was hungry, ragged, but sound and gay.

October 1. Nazis trying hard to get at us. Their punitive detachment surrounded the whole forest. For four days we played hide-and-seek. In a skirmish our brave Comrade Gregory perished. Seven Nazis killed. Only today we got out of the encirclement—thanks to Serozha, who knows the district like the palm of his hand. I got wounded in the leg, but I can walk. The bone is sound. A scout came from a Red Army unit with an order to mine road on which Nazis are moving men and munitions.

SOVIET 'PARTISANS' listening to the instructions of the leader of the band as he outlines his plans for a coming foray. Some extracts from the notebook of a guerilla commander are given in this page.   *Photo, British Official*

3. Mined 400 yards of the road. At the same time wound up 3½ miles of telephone wire connecting German headquarters— good thick wire with rubber insulation.

6. Attacked German motorized kitchen. Burned it down. We had hardly got into the woods when a large Nazi motorized infantry column appeared. Halted by the smouldering kitchen, and then opened machine-gun fire on the woods.

8. We approached the region M. and fell on a punitive detachment. After a skirmish we retreated to the swamps. Serozha brought a Nazi leaflet from the village— written in bad Russian, about me.

We read the leaflet aloud and laughed. I

am not a Jew, but there are three Jews in our company—good warriors. We'll get this hangman, Spann.

9. Collective-farmers say Spann is scouring the woods. All his men have automatic rifles.

11. Spann hunting us, and we are hunting Spann. They don't go into the woods and swamps—afraid. We came to T. and found devastation there. This Nazi bandit Spann paid a visit there. Undressed old women, put them on the snow and whipped them. Said they had helped the partisans. Took two girls and carried them off in car.

14. Spann no longer exists. It happened this way. An old woman came this morning and told us that Spann had arrived drunk, with 18 soldiers, also drunk. No guard was posted. The Nazis were chasing the women in the village. We entered the village at both ends. Spann and two soldiers taken alive. Others fought frantically. Our losses : Partisan Moisei killed, two others wounded. We put Spann on trial. This Nazi officer fell on his knees and begged for mercy. Sentence passed and executed.—'' *Soviet War News* ''

Editor's Postscript

ONE hears, these days, much about "inflation" without quite knowing how it works or what it really means. We saw something of its effect in Germany and Russia soon after the last War, when the mark was so debased that thousands instead of twenty went to the pound, and the rouble was in much the same case. I remember gutter vendors in the Strand selling both marks and roubles at thousands for a penny! Well, early in the thirteenth century Ogadai, son and successor to Genghis-Khan, the bow-legged barbarian who had come as near to world-domination as any conqueror since the Caesars, said to his Chinese adviser, "I am told that in Cathay they stamped money out of a worthless stuff, paper. Why cannot we print money in this fashion?" "True, it was done once," was the answer, "and they called the minister who did it Lord Scrap-paper. After a while, with this same precious paper, it took ten thousand *taels* to buy one cake." Whatever the *tael* was worth in 1229, it was the equivalent of the U.S. dollar a few years ago. So inflation is no new thing, however it be brought about.

I CAME across that anecdote in a newly published book—one of the most fascinating of the many I have read this year —"The March of the Barbarians" by Harold Lamb. It's my first acquaintance with this author, who has almost a dozen books to his credit, dealing mostly with kindred subjects: the history of the Mongols. His new work discloses a vast and intimate knowledge of the rise and decline of the Mongol tribes, and contains a short, colourful portrayal of Genghis-Khan, of whom he published a full biographical narrative thirteen years ago. "The March of the Barbarians" is worth many best-selling novels so far as enthralling narrative is concerned, and is written in a peculiarly vivid style which changes its movement in accord with the shifting scenes and tempo of the times depicted. Genghis, *mutatis mutandis*, was the Hitler of his day, or the other way round. Certainly one of the most amazing characters in the world's history, and nowhere portrayed more vividly or with greater erudition than in Mr. Lamb's pages. The Germans are the Barbarians of this later age. Get the book from your library (it is published by Robert Hale Ltd. at 15s.) and see how little the veneer of modern culture has changed the Teutonic tribes who had long settled in cities while the Mongols remained nomadic.

ANOTHER parallel of the present age of barbarism with the days of Genghis-Khan and his Mongol hordes. Among the more frightening of the arrows with which these amazing horsemen of the Steppes struck terror and death into the civilized warriors of the west, Russia, Hungary, Bohemia, Austria, was one that whistled! Imagine scores of thousands of wild horsemen thundering down on the ranks of well ordered and finely caparisoned, but relatively tame cavalry, and crossbowmen discharging as they came clouds of steel-tipped arrows that whistled like a gale in the rigging! And there you have an ancient anticipation of the whistling bomb.

IN the last war the fountains in Trafalgar Square and in most of the parks were stopped and the water in their large ornamental basins drained off. This was done to prevent reflections from the water during moonlight or under the play of searchlights, which would have helped the Zepps to identify their targets—if they ever had targets more specialized than the whole of Central London. But water is now the urgent need of the fire fighters and many great ponds have now come into existence by the simple but laborious process of using the deep basements of bombed buildings, whose overground remains have been cleared away, and filling them with water to serve as priceless reservoirs when, for any reason, the regular sources that feed the hosepipes fail. A bright idea, this. Some of these ponds look quite picturesque and will possibly outlast the War for a year or two. I hear this plan is being carried out all over the country.

EARLY in the War I expressed my relief that mechanization, which had brought so many new horrors to the conflict, had got rid of at least one—the martyrdom of the horse. Horses had, of course, been destroyed in thousands when Poland was overrun owing to the foolish faith in cavalry which the Poles retained. But I was altogether too hopeful, as the horse, mule and donkey are all being used in large numbers in the worst of the battle zones. In Greece the nature of the country brought them into use in conditions of appalling misery among the snow-covered mountains of her Albanian frontier, Germans are making great use of them in supply columns, the Russians employ them by the thousand for Cossack cavalry, and they are at work in surprising numbers in North Africa and the Near East as well as in the China-Japan battle areas. The poor, dumb, suffering creatures whose complete innocence of all offence and hatreds makes their martyrdom so pathetic.

WILLIAM L. SHIRER in his "Berlin Diary" has many references to the dead horses he saw along the routes of the invaders in Belgium and France. The other day I had before me a photograph of an entire train load of Russian horses sacrificed to prevent their falling into Nazi hands. Cut off from escape, the Russians, faithful to the scorched-earth policy, ran the train conveying the horses over a cliff into the sea, where on the rocky shore their bodies were piled high amid the tangled wreckage of the train. The mind recoils from contemplating the monstrous horror of their death agonies, and yet the hard facts of war justify the Russians (who are real lovers of horses) in such an action. Their resolute destruction of the beautiful modern cities they have built up in the last ten years is the best proof of their determination to do nothing to help the enemy. It may be sheer sentimentalism, but I can't get that mountain of horses out of mind.

AN exceptional number of letters from boys and girls, so far apart as Malta, Cape Town, Wellington N.Z., Toronto, Rhyl, and Carrickfergus, coming to my desk within the last few days, has made me aware that a new impulse is urging our young people to study current affairs and attempt to express themselves. The ages of these young folk range from 13 to 17. Already I have given quotations from a very lively account of her life in Malta by Miss Cissie Vella (16), and it is again from Malta that I have received a long letter, so animated in its style and so interesting in its contents that I am giving it considerable space in our pages. Its writer, a boy this time, is also a sixteen-year-old. Not many adults could write so engagingly, even with the start of having so good a story to tell. Two such letters from Malta (where I'm told "everybody" reads THE WAR ILLUSTRATED!) suggest an unusual literary precocity in its juvenile population, the total number of inhabitants being only about 240,000.

SEVERAL of my young correspondents, like the youngest of all, Anthony Martin of Rhyl, who is just thirteen, are already hoping to become journalists some day. But what impresses me about them all is the keenness with which they are following the tremendous events of the historic times in which their youth has been cast. It promises well, I think, for the mental preoccupations of the rising generation, and one can safely prophesy that in the post-war years we shall see a vastly increased reading public interested in the more serious things of life and literature.

GENERAL ANDERS, Commander-in-Chief of the Polish Army being raised on Soviet territory, three divisions of which had been staffed and organized at the beginning of October.
Photo, Polish Ministry of Information

Printed in England and published on the 10th, 20th and 30th of each month by the Proprietors, The Amalgamated Press, Ltd., The Fleetway House, Farringdon Street, London, E.C.4. Registered for transmission by Canadian Magazine Post. Sole Agents for Australia and New Zealand : Messrs. Gordon & Gotch, Ltd. ; and for South Africa : Central News Agency, Ltd. November 29th, 1941.   S.S.   *Editorial Address*: JOHN CARPENTER HOUSE WHITEFRIARS, LONDON E.C.4.

Vol 5 # The War Illustrated № 114

Edited by Sir John Hammerton

FOURPENCE

DEC. 10TH, 1941

'GENERAL WINTER' is now perhaps only a Colonel, as Mr. Maisky has put it, but at least the mud and snow have not improved matters for the German offensive. The Nazi soldiery, grim-faced and gloomy, plod wearily through sleet and rain, and at night bivouac in the desolate countryside with a temperature below freezing-point. German soldiers in Norway and Rumania are now being asked to give up a blanket each to send to their comrades on the Eastern Front.

Photo, Associated Press

NO. 115 WILL BE PUBLISHED SATURDAY, DEC. 20

YOU WANT A MILLION WOMEN, MR. BEVIN?

So there is going to be an end of "this silly sex nonsense" in the matter of women's recruiting. "To me," Mr. Bevin stated the other day, "men and women are producing units for the war effort, and I approach the problem on terms of equality of men and women alike. I don't want these sloppy gossip column announcements about women. Women are intelligent beings, and should be treated as such." (*Chorus of women*: Thank you kindly, sir, she said.)

Certainly it is about time. Some of the appeals made of late to women to take their places in the ranks of the A.T.S. have been —well, sloppy. There have been appeals to the shy girl, the home girl, and the really intelligent girl. Columns have appeared describing the wonderful sort of work they will be asked to do, their hotel-like existence, the social advantages, the "good times" that are to be had by all. "What sort of job would you like to do?" asks the recruiting officer. "We will do our best to oblige." The uniform is being made smarter yet.

Now Mr. Bevin has frowned on this sort of thing. Posters will still have to be used to publicize the women's services—just as they were used in the early days of the last war to get recruits for Kitchener's Army— since the Minister of Labour has no power to compel anyone to become a woman in uniform. But so far as the munition factories are concerned, Mr. Bevin *has* that power, and he has declared his resolve to use it. And about time, too, many women will say. They are sick of being appealed to, cajoled, coaxed, wooed and wheedled, entreated and persuaded. They are just as indifferent to threats. If Mr. Bevin wants us, they ask, why doesn't he come and fetch us and tell us exactly what we have to do?

Since war began many hundreds of thousands of women and girls have joined the A.T.S., the W.R.N.S., and the W.A.A.F., and have taken their places in the factories and other centres of the nation's war effort. But very many more are required, if more and more men are to be released for the fighting line. Some months ago it was stated that 100,000 women were wanted for the A.T.S. alone before Christmas, and in various places recruiting campaigns have been organized, with loudspeakers, military bands and a kind of mobile Brains Trust to answer any and every question. But still not enough women have joined up. Some are held back by the desire to remain in their own localities— a matter which surely could be easily arranged; others want to be at home when their husbands come on leave; others complain of too much drill, suspect "influence" in the matter of promotion, and object to being regarded as mere substitutes for men. Then we have to remember that many women have to depend on their own resources and are obliged to think of "after the war" just as much as their brothers.

Then there is the munitions front. If the productive capacity of the country is to be utilized to the full a great army of women must be enlisted. "I have asked the younger women to leave home and go where their services are needed," said Mr. Bevin, at Middlesbrough, on November 16. "I want to get at least a million married women, either full or part-time—that is, half a day—in many of our munition works. If not in munition work, I want the married women to help in the distributive trades, in offices, and in commercial undertakings, and I want employers to utilize them for part-time, if not for full-time, work to release the younger mobile women to fill shells and make munitions. I must get these thousands of women into this terrific job."

No one will quarrel with Mr. Bevin's aim, but it is, to say the least, a little surprising to find these appeals coupled with the continued existence of considerable numbers of what have been called white-feather girls— girls, i.e. who, belonging for the most part to the more prosperous classes, are making no contribution to the war effort beyond, perhaps, an occasional attendance at the local hospital. Numbers of pin-money girls, it is said, have dodged the call-up by persuading Daddy or Uncle or a friend of Daddy's to find them comfortable and not badly-paid jobs. And this at a time when soldiers' wives are being urged to take up work in the factories. Day nurseries are to be provided for their children, true; but how much simpler it would be to pay the mother sufficient to enable her to remain at home and look after her own children? Surely *that* is a job which ought to be regarded as a reserved occupation.

To repeat, a million women are wanted urgently, at once. Mr. Bevin declares that he must have them. Why have they not come forward? One reason has been given above: that in all fairness many women feel that if the country wants them, then it should fetch them. But there are many other reasons. Here are four given by Mrs. Mavis Tate, M.P. for Frome. Uncertainty as to earnings is the first. Many women working in factories, says Mrs. Tate, are never sure what they are going to earn from one week to the next, while so low are the wages paid in many instances that a woman could not exist if it were not for the allowance she receives in respect of her soldier-husband. In other words, the State is subsidizing the private employer. A second reason is the lack of shopping facilities. Women who go out to work still have shopping to do, and when are they to do it? On leaving the factory or office after a hard day's work, they find that all the shops are shut; and if they wait until Saturday afternoons, though they may receive their rationed goods, all the un-rationed supplies have been bought up long before. Shortage of nursery schools and centres is another reason militating against the employment of married women; women with young children must have somewhere to leave them, and not everybody has a granny or an aunt conveniently available. Finally, Mrs. Tate mentions inadequate transport facilities to and from work.

Yet other reasons were advanced by Lord Samuel in the debate in the House of Lords on Nov. 25. He criticized the system of interviewing and the medical examinations, declared canteens were inadequate and crèches insufficient, while trained women were put on unskilled jobs and had to work harmfully long hours. If the Ministry of Labour paid more attention to these things, it might find its appeals more fruitful, possibly very largely unnecessary.

But even if compulsion were applied to all Britain's womanhood, it might well be found that the number of women available is nothing like so large as it is often supposed to be. Comparisons with the last war are apt to mislead, since the conditions prevailing today, when women have invaded practically every field of employment, are very different from those of 1914. When the last war began only quite a small percentage of women and girls "went out to work." Most women were employed in the home. There were thousands of girls behind shop counters, but perhaps as many men. Even the typewriter was not an exclusively feminine possession, and few but the big banks and insurance companies employed a large female staff. The North had its thousands of mill girls, but for the rest, women were domestic servants, governesses, nursery maids. Oh, yes, and barmaids.

All the more credit, then, to those gallant pioneers of 25 years ago who, casting aside the trammels of Victorian propriety, took their places at the work bench or on the land. They said goodbye to hobble skirts and tight lacing, received or took "the key of the door," stayed out late, met a lot of strange "boys," learnt the joys of a comradeship between the classes such as they had never dreamed of. They were a grand set of women and they did a grand job. But in forcing wide open the door to women's employment they made any repetition of their achievement impossible. No more than its manhood is Britain's supply of woman-power inexhaustible.

'MUNITIONETTES' OF 1917, though differing vastly in appearance from their daughters who are now carrying on the task, showed the same spirit of service and eagerness to help their menfolk at the Front.
Photo, Topical Press

E. ROYSTON PIKE

They've Answered the Call!

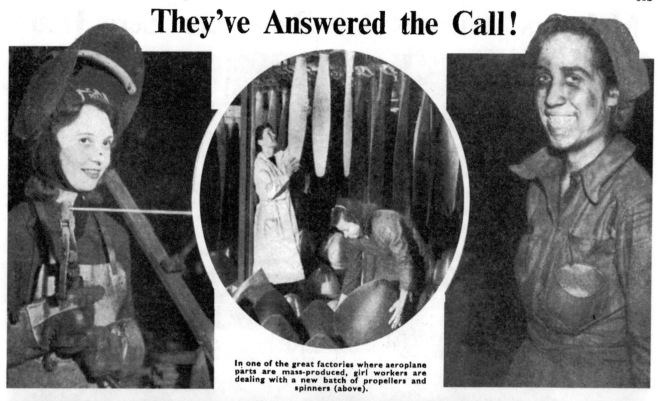

In one of the great factories where aeroplane parts are mass-produced, girl workers are dealing with a new batch of propellers and spinners (above).

IN A LONDON GASWORKS women take their turn at night-shift work in the retort house, "going to it" even during the height of air raids. Top left, a girl electric-welder employed on making goods wagons by the Southern Railway; she has thrown back the shield that protects her face. Top right, sixteen-year-old "trough" girl is happy in the laborious if somewhat dirty work of making iron gas and water pipes. By taking on such occupations women and girls are releasing men for the fighting services.

Photos, Topical, Keystone, Fox

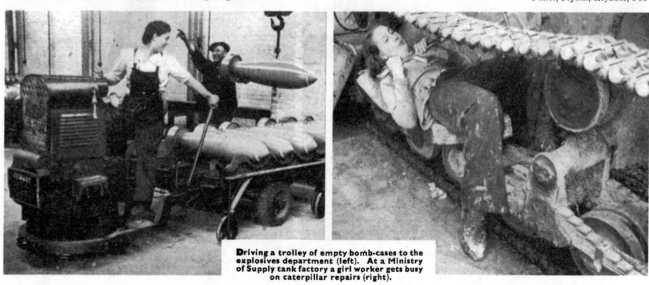

Driving a trolley of empty bomb-cases to the explosives department (left). At a Ministry of Supply tank factory a girl worker gets busy on caterpillar repairs (right).

Malaya's Defences Are Ready for Zero Hour

Air Chief Marshal Sir Robert BROOKE-POPHAM, C.-in-C., Far East, is here seen at Singapore naval base H.Q. in conference with his staff. Left, men of the A.I.F. in training advancing through pandanus palm jungle in Malaya.

A flight of Blenheim bombers about to take off from an airfield at Singapore to reinforce British defence positions in the northern part of Malaya. Considerable numbers of American aircraft have also been shipped to that country.

AT SINGAPORE the floating boom protecting the vital harbour is being overhauled by Malayan sailors (left). The floats and the cables connecting them are covered with sharp steel spikes. Right, one of the big coastal guns, with which the shore of Singapore Island is ringed, elevated for firing. The coastal artillery of Singapore has long been famous, and it has recently been powerfully reinforced.

Photos, British Official: Crown Copyright; Associated Press

What Is Behind the Strikes in America ?

In Britain, the Trade Union movement is solidly behind the national war effort. In the U.S.A.,
however, the trade unions are divided into two rival camps, and numerous strikes are hampering
the defence programme.

WHEN on Nov. 13 the House of Representatives in Washington came to vote on the Bill providing for the revision of the Neutrality Act, the Bill was carried by a majority of only 18—by 212 votes to 194. In the minority were found many generally firm supporters of President Roosevelt ; in particular, some Democrats —the President's own party—from the Southern states voted against him. But they made it clear that they would not have done so if there was any possibility of the Bill being defeated. They had not the slightest objection to American ships being permitted to carry arms to Britain ; indeed, they were strongly in favour of the proposal. But they were angered by the wave of strikes—especially the strike of 53,000 miners in the pits of the steel companies—and disgusted with the activities of certain Labour leaders. They thought that Mr. Roosevelt was not taking a sufficiently strong line on this issue, and so they voted against the Neutrality Bill by way of protest. Theirs were negative votes, as it were. They hoped that the President would realize their disgruntlement and see that the strike issue was firmly handled.

To understand the labour situation in America, one must realize that there are, in fact, two " T.U.Cs "—the American Federation of Labor and the Congress of Industrial Organizations. The A.F.L. was founded in 1881 by Samuel Gompers, who remained its president until his death in 1924, when he was succeeded by William Green. It is an organization of craft unions of skilled workers, both American and Canadian ; and, unlike the British trade unions, is non-socialist, even non-political. A year ago its membership was stated to be 4,247,000.

Mr. Lewis of the C.I.O.

The C.I.O. dates only from 1935, when eight large unions broke away from the A.F.L. under the leadership of John L. Lewis, president of the United Mine Workers Union, and established what was at first called the Committee for Industrial Organization. The C.I.O. set out to win the support of the unorganized, in large measure unskilled, workers, and its unions were based on industries instead of on crafts. From the beginning there was bitter rivalry between the A.F.L. and the C.I.O., but the C.I.O. unions went ahead rapidly, and a year ago it claimed that its membership was 3,559,000. When Mr. Roosevelt started his New Deal the C.I.O. gave it its support, both political and (so it was hinted) financial. But the relations between the Roosevelt Administration and the C.I.O. gradually cooled, particularly when many of the C.I.O. unions began to show traces of Communist influence. As Mr. Roosevelt leaned more and more towards the Allies, Mr. Lewis and the extremists in the C.I.O. became ever more hostile : in those days, it will be remembered, the Soviet was the ally of Germany. Mr. Lewis, indeed, became a leader of the Isolationists (though the C.I.O. is firmly anti-Hitler), and ere long developed into a most bitter opponent of the President, so that he was suspected of hating Roosevelt more than Hitler. Thus it was that when Mr. Roosevelt stood for a third term in the autumn of 1940, Mr. Lewis gave the C.I.O.'s backing to Mr. Wendell Willkie. Lewis, indeed, was so pronounced in his opposition that he swore that if the President were elected for a third term, he himself would resign the presidency of the C.I.O.'s Mr. Roosevelt was elected, and Mr. Lewis did

resign. But, though he made way for Philip Murray, he is still the president of the United Mine Workers, and a real power in C.I.O. politics.

Strongly opposed as they are, the A.F.L. and the C.I.O. are united on at least two issues : the closed-shop and the check-off. By the first is meant the demand that when a union has organized a substantial proportion of the workers in a particular plant or business, then the employer shall make membership of that trade union a conditional service. This was the issue that led to the coal strike of Nov. 16 ; the Lewis union had 95 per cent of the workers in the " captive " (i.e. " company ") mines of the steel companies, and called the strike to compel the remainder to join it. The check-off is sometimes insisted upon in addition ; it means that the employer is required by the trade union not only to see that all his workpeople are members of the union, but to deduct their

U.S. soldiers on guard with their machine-
guns when the army took over the N.
American Aviation Co.'s plant in Inglewood,
California, during a recent strike.
Photos, Wide World and Planet News

dues from their wage-packets and to hand them over to the union officials. Another feature of the trade union movement in the States is racketeering. British trade unions are registered under the Friendly Societies Acts, and must conduct themselves and their finances in accordance with rules laid down by the State. But in America there is no legal obligation on trade unions to publish their annual accounts, or even to hold annual conferences, so that in effect there is little or no check by the rank-and-file on the way things are run. This leads directly to racketeering, i.e. the complete subordination of every other interest to that of the inner circle of union members. Often there is an unholy combination of trade union and management executives to fleece the public more effectively.

Bearing these facts in mind, it is easier to understand the hostility against trade unions, which exists in the U.S.A. where there is no Labour Party as in England. Most

Americans cling, at least in theory, to a rugged individualism, and the " log cabin to White House " is still a living tradition with them ; perhaps it is true to say that in industrial legislation America is about fifty years behind Britain, and in business circles there are widespread criticism and opposition to Roosevelt's New Deal policies. This antagonism has been intensified by the wave of strikes which has swept over the country during the last year or two. Between August 1940 and August 1941 nearly 19 million man-days were lost through strikes.

All the same, numerous and costly though these strikes have been and are, the time lost through them represents only a very small proportion of the total man-days worked. Only about a quarter of the strikes have been due to demands for better working conditions, wages and hours, while considerably more than half are connected with the question of collective bargaining.

JOHN L. LEWIS, President of the United
Mine Workers of America, reading his letter
to President Roosevelt in which he rejected
the latter's request to order the miners back
to work. But on November 24 he called off the
strike and agreed to arbitration.

Sure, We're the Men for the Two-Ocean Navy!

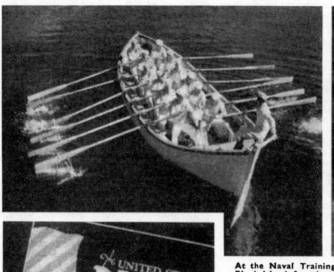

At the Naval Training Station, Newport, Rhode Island, American sailors are practising their rowing in a whale-boat race (left). Right, a group of trainees lined up for gun-duty ; all equipment is carefully studied on land before the men are posted to a ship.

WHETHER the Japanese are bluffing or not, the United States Navy is resolutely preparing for battle. Since the war began America has had her eyes looking east and west. She has had to watch Japan in the Pacific, and get ready for any eventuality in the Atlantic. Behind British sea-power the U.S. has been carrying out a two-ocean navy policy, and it is hoped to complete it by 1944.

Although the United States Navy at present is far less powerful than the combined fleets of the Axis, America is determined to overhaul this disparity. The threat of Japanese aggression has done more than Hitlerism to awaken the United States to her peril, and her concentration on sea-power is of supreme importance to Allied strategy. New ships must mean a great addition to personnel, and a popular naval enlistment campaign has been proceeding for some months in the United States. In this page we see some of the new recruits to the call of the freedom of the seas in the course of training.

U.S. SAILORS studying a model in the rigging loft of the American Naval Training Station, Newport, to accustom themselves to the lay-out of a battleship. Centre, left, a recruiting poster which is helping to draw 11,000 men a month into naval service. Centre, right, recruits learning to march and turn correctly with the aid of footprints on the training ground.

Photos, Planet News, Exclusive to THE WAR ILLUSTRATED

America Speaks! Let Aggressors Beware!

U.S.S. NORTH CAROLINA, mighty American battleship, firing a salvo from the triple 16-inch guns of her forward turret. First to be completed of six battleships of the Washington class, the North Carolina has a standard displacement of 35,000 tons and carries a main armament of nine 16-inch guns. Another photograph of this powerful unit of the U.S. Fleet appeared in Vol. 4, p. 545. Although some of the ships of this class were not originally scheduled for completion before 1943, it is probable that, in view of Japan's aggressive policy in the Pacific, they will take their fleet stations much sooner than was at first contemplated. The Washington was commissioned on May 15, 1941, and the Indiana was launched on Nov. 21.   *Photo, Sport & General*

Our Searchlight on the War

HOUR OF DESTINY

AS we go to press it is much too soon to make either pronouncement or prognosis on the new battle of Libya. But these things are clear : it began well for Britain, it came as a surprise to the Nazis. The Italians we need not consider as supplying more than animal and mineral material for desert-strewn junk that will have to be mopped up when the British Empire forces in the Western Desert have done their main job : the destruction of the two Panzer divisions, which the infamous traitors of Vichy secretly permitted the Huns to transport through French territorial waters to North Africa after the astounding British sweep of last winter, to the undoing of the improvised, and too swiftly successful advance of our Army of the Nile on Benghazi. The destruction of the Italian mechanized division will make slight demands on our forces while they are about the more serious task of destroying the Huns.

It is further clear that for the first time Britain is meeting Germany on equal terms of preparedness. Here is no Norway scramble, no hasty rush to Greece (at the cost of our Libyan defences) ; above all, no meeting of German might alongside a bemused ally dreaming of Maginot magic. But a Britain armed against a Germany no better armed, and the issue to all who believe in Britain should not long remain in doubt. It is another of the great moments of the War, and if it happens that at this stage the French traitors determine to place their sea power under German control when its collaboration with Britain would have assured an earlier end of the War and the salvaging of the French Empire, that will imply a long lengthening of the struggle and an eventual shrinkage of an Empire which those unworthy Frenchmen are willing to lose if they can but keep their jobs as helots of Hitler. The moment at which we write, with the Germans at Rostov, Japan threatening, America resolute in the Pacific, Turkey watching the Caucasian approach of the Nazis, and Britain moving against a Hitlerized North Africa, is indeed freighted with the destiny and doom of nations.   J. A. H.

GENERALS AT GENERAL POST

On December 25, 1941, General Sir John Dill, K.C.B., C.M.G., D.S.O., A.D.C., will relinquish the appointment of Chief of the Imperial General Staff, on attaining the age of 60.—"*London Gazette*," *November 18, 1941*

HERE was a paragraph that caused both surprise and puzzlement. No wonder. For many months General Dill had been one of the great figures of the war. On his shoulders had fallen the frightening burden of reorganizing the Army after Dunkirk, and of directing it through the grim and crucial days of the Battle of Britain.

Now he was to take up the post of Governor of Bombay, and in his place would reign General Sir Alan Brooke. " I have always been anxious that the young men in the Army should get on," he himself said. " That can only happen if the older men give way to them. You all know General Brooke and his fine record : I hand over the duty of Chief of Imperial General Staff to him with the greatest confidence."

What is the real reason for Dill's going ? asks the man-in-the-street. Is it just that generals are too old at 60 (and fit only to become Field-Marshals), or is it that in the more offensive phase of the war now opening we need generals of a different type ? To such questions satisfactory replies are not very obvious. But from the new men—from General Brooke, Lt.-Gen. Paget, who succeeds him as C.-in-C., Home Forces ; Lt.-Gen. Sir H. R. Pownall, who has been selected for a special appointment ; Maj.-Gen. A. E. Nye, the 45-year-old ex-ranker, who is to succeed General Pownall as Vice-Chief of the Imperial General Staff ; and Lt.-Gen. B. L. Montgomery, who takes over the South-Eastern Command in succession to Lt.-Gen. Paget—from these new men who are going to build on the foundations Field-Marshal Dill has laid the country expects much.

HE 'SANK' THE ARK ROYAL

For nearly 24 hours the German authorities hesitated to claim the sinking of the Ark Royal on November 14. Why ? Because they had already claimed to have sunk her in a dive-bombing attack in the North Sea more than two years ago, in September, 1939.

POOR Oberleutnant Franck ! He was the Luftwaffe pilot who " sank " the Ark Royal in the first month of the war. In fact, Franck never claimed to have sunk the great ship. In his original report he simply stated that he had spotted an aircraft-carrier in the North Sea and had dive-bombed it. Visibility was poor, but he believed that a 1,000-lb. bomb secured a direct hit.

That report was never released ; instead, Dr. Goebbels' Ministry of Popular Enlightenment and Propaganda got busy and sank the Ark Royal Pictures depicting every phase of the sinking appeared in the German illustrated magazines. Franck's accounts got longer and more detailed, more dramatic. But Franck never wrote them, so we are told by an American journalist, William Bayles, who met him in Berlin. The climax came when Goering sent Franck a telegram of congratulation and conferred on him the Iron Cross, First Class. Franck was photographed hundreds of times wearing his Iron Cross, and became Public Hero No. 1. When it became known that the Ark Royal had *not* been sunk, Goebbels still continued to brag about the sinking ; his ministry even prepared an illustrated children's booklet called " How I sank the Ark Royal," and put Franck's name to it. Meanwhile, Franck's position in the Luftwaffe had become quite intolerable. He became the butt of jokes, and one of the secret broadcasting stations referred to him as Baron Franckhausen. Last spring things had come to such a pass that Franck was talking of suicide ; if he could only get up into a plane again, he said, he would dive it into the first ship he could find. So far as is known he is still alive ; but his should become a classic case among those who " have greatness thrust upon 'em."

Adm. SIR ROGER KEYES, who from July 17, 1940, until Oct. 19, 1941, was responsible for the organization of the Commandos.
Photo; Press Portrait Bureau

COMMANDOS LOSE KEYES—WHY?

Since July 1940, Admiral of the Fleet Sir Roger Keyes had held an appointment for special duties—those duties being the organization and training of the special service troops known as Commandos. On November 16 it was revealed that Sir Roger's appointment had terminated on October 19.

FAMED as the commander of the glorious Zeebrugge raid on St. George's Day, 1918, Sir Roger Keyes came into prominence again in the spring of last year when in a debate in the House of Commons he made it known that he had offered to lead a naval raid on the Germans in Trondheim. His intervention in the debate was largely responsible for the fall of the Chamberlain administration. Shortly afterwards he was made British liaison officer with King Leopold, and it is largely through his advocacy that the King of the Belgians has been in some measure rehabilitated in popular esteem. Few people were aware of the fact that for the last 15 months in connexion with the Commandos (see page 285), and only recently, indeed, was the existence of these made known.

Sir Roger has been generally regarded as one of our " real live gingers " ; all the greater, then, was the surprise when it became known that he had been " sacked." The matter was raised in the House of Commons on November 25, when the Admiral complained that he had been frustrated " in every worthwhile offensive action I have tried to undertake as Director of Combined Operations " and of the " cumbrous machine " in Whitehall " by which all offensive amphibious projects are strangled at their birth, or mangled after endless discussions in the many committees."

SIR JOHN DILL, who relinquishes the post of C.I.G.S. on Dec. 25, has been appointed Field-Marshal and will succeed Sir Roger Lumley as Governor of Bombay.

Gen. SIR ALAN BROOKE, who will succeed Sir John Dill as C.I.G.S., has been C.-in-C. Home Forces since July 1940. He led the 2nd Corps in Flanders.

Lt.-Gen. SIR HENRY POWNALL, Vice-C.I.G.S. since May 1941, who, it was announced, on Nov. 18, has been selected for a special appointment.

Maj.-Gen. A. E. NYE, who will succeed Sir Henry Pownall as Vice-C.I.G.S., has risen from the ranks. During the last war he served firstly as a private.

Lt.-Gen. B. C. T. PAGET, to succeed Sir Alan Brooke as C.-in-C. Home Forces, was responsible for the evacuation of our troops from Andalsnes, without loss.

Lt.-Gen. B. L. MONTGOMERY, G.O.C.-in-C. South - Eastern Command in succession to Lt.-Gen. Paget, commanded a division in the Battle of France.

Photos, British Official: Crown Copyright; Hay Wrightson, Sport & General, Planet News, Fox, Lafayette

Bitter War in Russia's Blasted Countryside

AT KHARKOV, whose evacuation was announced by the Russians on Oct. 29, German troops cross a damaged bridge.

Circle, top right, the Hurricane presented to the Maj.-Gen. Commanding the Northern Red Fleet Air Arm by the R.A.F. The general is seen on the far side of the machine supervising adjustments. Circle, left, men of the Russian Fleet Air Arm.

ROSTOV ON DON, the remarkable New Theatre of which is seen above, was the scene of bitter street fighting when on Nov. 23 the German tanks were reported to have forced their way into the city. The Russians are leaving nothing of military value to the invading armies, and the photograph centre right shows how railway lines have been left completely destroyed as the Soviet troops fell back.

Photos, British Official: Crown Copyright ; Associated Press and Planet News

If We Have to Fight in the Caucasus

With the German tanks battling in the streets of Rostov, the threat to the Allies' position in the Caucasus became much more pronounced. At last Hitler was nearing striking distance of the oilfields which were a primary objective in the invasion of Russia. This article describes the Caucasus from a military point of view ; a more general description is given in page 150.

THE Caucasus, with Persia, Iraq, and Syria, may well prove to be the great battlefield of 1942, General Sir Archibald Wavell, C.-in-C. in India, told a special correspondent of the "Daily Telegraph" at New Delhi, on November 20. "It is difficult to predict whether any particular phase of the war will be decisive, but obviously, when and if the Germans strike out for the oil in the Caucasus and the oil in Iran, and seek to attack our mid-eastern positions, this region will become a main theatre of war. This is a possibility which we have clearly foreseen and are preparing against. In this region we should be fighting in the closest cooperation with the Russians. The main task now," the C.-in-C. went on, " is the organization of supply lines through Iraq and Iran (Persia). This is obviously work of the greatest importance and urgency, and it is now going on at full speed."

But it is these supply lines which are now being threatened by the German advance. On November 22 the Nazis claimed to have captured Rostov, the important city at the mouth of the Don through which runs the oil pipe-line from Baku and Grozny—the only pipe-line to Central Russia from the Caucasus oilfields. At the same time the Nazis had overrun the Crimean Peninsula, with the exception of Sebastopol, and were massing on the western shore of the Kerch Straits— only half a mile wide in places. From the north, then, by way of Rostov, and from the west from Kerch, the Caucasus (so generally considered to be the main economic and strategic objective of Hitler's eastern campaign) was now definitely threatened with invasion. If the Nazis could conquer the Caucasus, then not only would they be free of oil worries for years to come, not only would they secure supplies of other valuable raw materials, manganese in particular, but, just as important, they would cut the land bridge between Europe and Asia, across which Britain and America are sending aid to hard-pressed Russia.

Valuable as would be the Caucasus to Hitler, its possession is vital to the Allies in the Middle East. Indeed, it is not too much to say that the Caucasus must be successfully defended " if Russia is to continue to hold out "—to quote from an article by Heinrich Frey in " Die Zeitung," the German newspaper published in London—" not as a vast region of warring guerillas (so to speak, a Serbia multiplied a hundredfold), but as a first-class, organized military power—until the moment when the Anglo-Saxon war potential reaches its full effect."

But though the Germans are at the gates of the Caucasus, they have a hard struggle before them. Not for nothing has the region been described as one of the world's natural fortresses. The Caucasus Mountains, stretching from the Black Sea to the Caspian, are nowhere less than 250 miles in depth, and, with many peaks surpassing the height of Mont Blanc, stand like a huge wall barring the Axis from the oil-bearing region between Batum and Baku.

Across the mountains there are only two roads worthy of the name. One is Ossetian Highway, which links Batum via Kutais with the Grozny oilfields. More important is the Georgian Military Road—one of Europe's most famous highways—which connects Tiflis, the Georgian capital, with Ordzhonikidze. For 133 miles the road runs along the edge of precipices, crossing narrow ravines and deep defiles. It is one series of hairpin bends, and though its surface is good and fit for motor traffic, the road could easily

be blocked by blowing up bridges and viaducts, and so should be impracticable for mechanized warfare. There is no railway through the High Caucasus, as it is called, but the main mountain mass is enclosed within a parallelogram of railways, which are linked with the main Russian system through Rostov, and through Tiflis with the systems of Iran and Turkey.

If the Germans do decide to attack the Caucasus, then it may be presumed they would endeavour to advance along the narrow coastal strips. But on the Black Sea side the mountains fall steeply to the sea from Novorossiisk to Sukhum, and it should be an easy matter to defend the long and narrow strip of shore, even against greatly superior numbers. On the Caspian coast, too, the mountains come down close to the sea. On paper it looks possible to land troops at Batum or Poti, but an attempt is hardly likely to be made so long as the Russian Black Sea Fleet is in existence.

But it might be that the Germans would content themselves with an attack on the northern half of the Caucasus Isthmus. The oilfields at Grozny and Maikop are not so important as those at Baku, but they would. be a godsend to Hitler's panzers. Moreover, the occupation of this region would block the supply channel from Iran into Russia, which is, undoubtedly, as we have seen, now one of the German's principal objectives. We may envisage, then, Hitler's mechanized hordes fighting their way from the Don across the Kalmuck steppes in an effort to reach Astrakhan on the Caspian. Arrived there, they might then seriously interfere with the passage of the tankers from Baku—the only means left open to Russia to receive oil from the Caucasus if, as we have supposed, the isthmus was cut. But the position of the German armies would not be too favourable, since to the north there would be the constant threat of the Russian armies and, in particular, of the new armies now being raised by Marshal Timoshenko ; while to the south, holding the line of the High Caucasus, would be the Allied army of British and Russians.

For months past General Wavell has had a kind of advanced H.Q. at Tiflis, and not far away in Iraq and Persia is a formidable Empire force, already numbering, so it is said, some 60,000 men. Some of the British troops may even be in position in the Caucasus. Before long we may be reading communiqués from G.H.Q., Tiflis—communiqués which may have to announce the most important news of the war.

EASTERN FRONT'S VAST EXTENT is emphasized by this map upon which a same-scale silhouette of Great Britain is three times superimposed on the Russian front line. The dotted line shows the approximate battle line at the middle of November.
Map by courtesy of the " Daily Sketch "

Here the War's Decisive Battle May Be Fought

THE CAUCASUS REGION of Russia between the Black and the Caspian Seas and bordering upon Turkey and Iran. The Georgian Military Road is clearly marked, and the oil centres which are a principal objective of the Nazi invaders.

BATUM, a view in the Park of Culture and Rest (circle). The classic columns and entablature make a fine decorative effect against the background of the Caucasus mountains. In contrast, the top photograph shows the wild natural scenery at Kazbek not far from Ordzhonikidze.

ACROSS THE CAUCASUS between Ordzhonikidze and Tiflis, runs the Georgian Military Road, a typical stretch of which is seen right. For centuries this highway has been a caravan route between Persia and Europe. Hitler's onslaught on Kerch and Rostov is preparatory to a drive into the Caucasus. The Nazis, however, are meeting with stubborn counter-attacks in the Kerch Straits aided by heavy Soviet coastal guns, bomber and fighter aeroplanes and motor torpedo-boats.

Photos, J. Allan Cash

'The Desert Army May Add a Page to History

GENERAL ERICH ROMMEL (back to camera), in command of the German Afrika Corps in Libya, inspecting the defences of Fort Capuzzo. Right, the commander of a British supply ship, carrying munitions to Tobruk, on the look-out.

IN THE WESTERN DESER
by systematic bombing of
take their place in the batt

Will Rank With Blenheim and With Waterloo'

Photos, British Official: Crown Copyright; Sport & General

NEAR TOBRUK a Bren-gunner and his comrade attached to a British patrol are out on a coastal sortie. Our troops, operating from this long-beleaguered garrison on the Libyan coast, have played an important part in the great battle, helping powerfully to close the ring round Sidi Rezegh and so frustrate the German general's plans.

Wellington bomber are donning warmer clothing as the sun and temperature go down (left). The R.A.F. did magnificent work preparatory to the British attack ...tions, transport, aerodromes and grounded planes. Below, British crews drawn from a famous Irish regiment running to their 11-ton M3 American tanks to ...hurchill has suggested, may come to rank in history with Blenheim and Waterloo.

Photos, British Official: Crown Copyright; Sport & General

THE MEDITERRANEAN has been well described as the strategic backbone of the British Empire. Among its many islands are Cyprus (left) and Pantelleria (right), belonging respectively to Britain and Italy. After the invasion of Crete both the garrison and the defences of Cyprus were greatly strengthened. In addition to British troops a Cyprus Volunteer Force recruited from amongst the Cypriots contributes to the defence of the island. Pantelleria, 60 miles S.W. of Sicily, is only 32 sq. miles in area, but is heavily fortified and, lying between Sicily and Tunis, was considered by the Italians a second Heligoland; but despite its commanding position it has not prevented the British Navy from obtaining mastery of the Mediterranean and was heavily bombarded by British naval units on September 28. Positions of both islands and the Libyan coastline are shown in the relief map of the Mediterranean (top).

Photos, British Official: Crown Copyright; E.N.A.

The Battle of Libya : The First Phase

What was described as the greatest desert battle in history, the greatest tank battle ever fought between Britons and Germans, perhaps the greatest battle ever fought on African soil, opened on November 18, when General Auchinleck's Eighth Army advanced against the Axis forces in the Western Desert. Below we give an account of the first phase in the campaign.

"GENTLEMEN, I am taking you into my confidence," General Sir Alan Cunningham, Commander of Britain's Eighth Army, told a group of war correspondents assembled at his desert headquarters on Sunday, November 16. "At dawn on Tuesday we will advance in Libya at selected places, from the sea down to the oasis of Jarabub." Naval cooperation? Swift came the reply: "Perfect. I spoke to my brother about it."

Thirty-six hours later the offensive was launched. "Imperial Forces under the command of Lieutenant-General Sir Alan Cunningham, supported by formations of the R.A.F. under Vice-Marshal Coningham," announced Cairo on the night of November 19, "began at first light on November 18 an advance into Libya from the coast east of Sollum as far south as Jarabub. While pressure was rapidly exerted on the Axis forces holding defensive positions from Halfaya to Sidi Omar, British armoured formations, supported by New Zealand, South African, and Indian troops, crossed the frontier south of Sidi Omar. So skilfully had our fighting troops been insinuated into their concentration areas, so good were the arrangements for deception, camouflage, and dispersal, coupled with the support of our air forces, that enemy observation and interference from the air prior to and during the advance yesterday were negligible. By yesterday evening, in heavy rain, our forces had penetrated over 50 miles into enemy territory. Up to that time little or no enemy opposition had been encountered."

When the battle began, General Rommel's forces comprised two German armoured divisions, one Italian armoured division, and several divisions of Italian infantry. These were, for the most part, concentrated in the area between Tobruk and Sollum; report had it that Rommel was himself on the eve of launching an offensive. The British made no secret of the fact that their principal aim in the campaign was not the winning of territory—that could come later; the first and most important objective was the annihilation of the German panzer divisions. Cunningham's strategy was planned accordingly.

On the first day, as we have seen, the British armoured columns plunged through the wire on a 130-mile front, and swept west and north. By dark they were ranged along the escarpment from Sidi Omar to Bir el Gobi. On the next day they drove northwards, some making for Sidi Rezegh and Tobruk, while others raced past Sidi Omar in the direction of Bardia. There was a sharp brush at Gobi, where the Italian tanks were severely handled. Rezegh, 10 miles south-east of Tobruk's perimeter, was captured, although for some days yet it was to be the scene of fierce fighting. Meanwhile, the Bardia column

had had a clash with a strong German tank force, in which the American light tanks, little 11-tonners, were in action for the first time; they were successful in tackling and driving off big German Mark 3 and Mark 4 tanks of 17 and 22 tons, with much heavier armament.

On the next day (November 20) Rommel threw into the fight the main German tank force which had been held back in reserve. There was a fierce struggle in the vicinity of Sidi Rezegh, and the Germans were reported to have lost 70 tanks and 33 armoured cars before they withdrew. At dawn on November 21 a column of British tanks sallied forth from Tobruk to join up with their comrades at Rezegh; but although they made considerable progress, the gap was not completely closed. In fact, the British at Rezegh were heavily engaged in an attempt to cut off the retreat of the main German tank force, estimated at about 180 tanks, which was endeavouring to cut its way out past El Adem. With tank columns closing

in on them from three sides, and attacked at the same time from the air, the German column was soon in difficulties and was compelled to retreat towards the coast.

A vivid account of the fighting on that Friday morning came from a R.A.F. fighter pilot, who flew at 4,000 feet above the battle. "Guns were blazing on all sides as these land cruisers made for each other," he said. "It was impossible to pick out from our position which was which. Most of them were on the move, but there were several stationary and no longer firing. Several hundreds of them appeared engaged in a grim show-down. It must have been a concentrated hell of shell against shell and steel against steel. It was like looking down on some huge prehistoric area with fire-breathing, scaly-hided monsters pitted against each other in a terrific struggle, lumbering slowly forward, swinging this way and that, each intent upon the destruction of the other."

By now much of the ground in the neighbourhood of Sidi Omar had been cleared of the enemy tanks, and so it was possible to develop a thrust towards the coast at Bardia. New Zealand forces, in the face of exceptional climatic difficulties — it had been raining hard for some days so that the desert sands were churned into a sticky morass — stormed Fort Capuzzo and Sidi Aziz, and occupied Bardia, which was reported clear of the enemy. At the same time Indian troops made some progress between Halfaya Pass and Sidi Omar.

But the main battle was still in the vicinity of Sidi Rezegh, where the British and German tanks were battling furiously. Wrote Guy Harriott, of the "Daily Telegraph," who was there:

"The enemy tanks were firing with everything they had, storming forward at full speed with shells from their artillery bursting in front of them. Our gunners, firing at point-blank range as fast as they could load, smashed their shells into tank after tank, blowing off their tracks and ripping their sides. No armour in the world could withstand gunfire at that range.

"Some of the tanks crashed to a halt in ruins almost on the muzzles of our guns. Others, hard hit, tried to limp away. The charge wavered and broke. Grey-brown-clad figures leapt from the turrets of their shattered tanks and ran aimlessly across the littered desert."

At this stage of the fighting commentators in Cairo and London expressed the opinion that the first phase of the battle was over. Cunningham had succeeded in his first objective: he had, that is, split the enemy forces into fragments, since one group was centred about Sollum, another near Gambut (which was captured by the New Zealanders on November 24), a third was south of Tobruk, while a fourth was near El Gobi. The second phase was about to begin. Annihilation was the watchword.

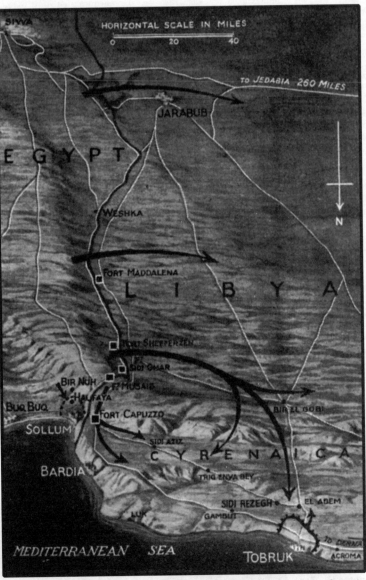

LIBYA BATTLEGROUND, showing the main lines of advance by General Cunningham's forces after the launching of the British offensive on Nov. 18. Contact was made with the Tobruk garrison on the morning of Nov. 27, and so Rommel's main road of retreat to the west was cut.

Relief map specially drawn for THE WAR ILLUSTRATED *by Félix Gardon*

Our Diary of the War

SUNDAY, NOV. 16, 1941   806*th day*

Russian Front.—German attacks renewed at Kalinin. Bitter fighting around Sevastopol and Kerch. Germans claimed to have cut railway to Vologda, near Tikhvin, in the Leningrad sector.

Africa.—Official announcement from Cairo of formation of British Eighth Army in the Western Desert.

Home Front.—Two German bombers shot down off E. Coast in daylight.

General.—Large Canadian force landed at Hong Kong.

MONDAY, NOV. 17   807*th day*

Air.—Targets in N. France attacked by Fighter Command.

Russian Front.—Particularly fierce fighting around Kalinin. German attack at Volokalamsk smashed by Gen. Rokossovski.

Mediterranean.—Night attack on Naples by R.A.F.

Home.—Bombs fell at night in E. Anglia and in S.W. England.

General. — Alfred Rosenberg appointed Reich Minister for the occupied Eastern territory. President Roosevelt signed bill to revise Neutrality Act.

TUESDAY, NOV. 18   808*th day*

Air.—R.A.F. offensive sweep over N. France.

Russian Front.—German push towards Voronej, 290 miles S.E. of Moscow held by Gen. Gordnianski's forces.

Mediterranean.—Night attack on Naples by R.A.F.

Africa.—British 8th Army, under the command of Lt.-Gen. Sir Alan Cunningham, began big drive into Libya at dawn from the coast east of Sollum as far south as Jarabub.

Home.—Important changes in the High Command of the British Army announced. E. Coast town bombed at night by two enemy raiders.

General.—Japanese envoys had three-hour talk with Mr. Cordell Hull in Washington.

WEDNESDAY, NOV. 19   809*th day*

Sea.—One E-Boat sunk, two probably sunk and others damaged during night engagement off E. Coast.

Russian Front.—Particularly fierce fighting in the Rostov, Kalinin and Volokolamsk sectors.

Mediterranean.—Naples and Brindisi raided by R.A.F.

Africa.—British forces penetrated to a depth of 50 miles on a front of 130 miles.

General. — Vichy government dismissed Gen. Weygand from his post as Delegate-General in N. Africa and C.-in-C. of French forces in Algeria. General Juin appointed C.-in-C. of French forces in N. Africa.

THURSDAY, NOV. 20   810*th day*

Sea.—Admiralty announced sinking of U-Boat presumed to have sunk the Ark Royal by the corvette Marigold. 34 of the crew captured.

Air.—Spitfires attacked E-Boats off Dutch coast.

Russian Front.—Germans launched new offensive on Moscow front. Russians announced evacuation of Kerch. Three enemy transports and a tanker were sunk in the Barents Sea.

Mediterranean.—Enemy tanker and supply ship torpedoed.

Africa.—Capture of Sidi Rezegh by British announced.

FRIDAY, NOV. 21   811*th day*

Russian Front. — Moscow reported a " serious situation " at Tula, south of the capital, where the Germans launched a very heavy new offensive.

Mediterranean. — Naples, Brindisi and Messina raided by R.A.F.

Africa.—Rapid British thrust towards Tobruk split up German armoured forces. Large force trapped in coastal area between Gambut and Capuzzo. Germans lost 130 tanks. British troops from Tobruk made a sortie supported by tanks. In Abyssinia strong enemy positions at Kulkaber and Ferroaber, east of Lake Tana, heavily attacked. The Italian garrisons surrendered. Prisoners numbered 1,800. Italian garrison at Cirda encircled.

SATURDAY, NOV. 22   812*th day*

Air.—R.A.F. offensive sweep over N. France. 6 enemy planes destroyed.

Russian Front.—Germans claimed capture of Rostov, but Russians stated that street fighting was still in progress there. Moscow attack widened. Successful Russian counter-attack near Novgorod, in the Leningrad sector.

Africa.—New Zealand forces recaptured Fort Capuzzo. Great tank battle raged in the triangle Capuzzo, Gabraleh, Sidi Rezegh.

SUNDAY, NOV. 23   813*th day*

Sea.—Admiralty announced torpedoing in the Mediterranean of an enemy cruiser and a destroyer by submarine and the torpedoing of another cruiser by a naval plane.

Air.—Offensive sweep over N. France. Night attack on docks at Lorient, Brest and Dunkirk.

Russian Front.—Russians reported to have evacuated main forces from Rostov after inflicting heavy casualties on the enemy. Fierce fighting at Kalinin and Volokolamsk.

Africa.—Gen. Rommel's forces split into four main groups. Bardia entered by New Zealanders. Another N.Z. force captured Sidi Aziz. Indian troops captured Sidi Omar Nuovo. 15,000 prisoners captured since battle began.

Home.—Two enemy raiders destroyed at night.

General.—Gen. Odic, Chief of Staff of French Air Force after the armistice and later Commander of French Air Force in N. Africa, rallied to Gen. de Gaulle. Small British raiding party landed at night on coast of Normandy. All returned.

MONDAY, NOV. 24   814*th day*

Air. — Stirlings of Bomber Command made a successful attack on enemy shipping off Dutch coast.

Russian Front.—Germans drove deep wedge into Russian lines near Klin, north-west of Moscow. Battles raged around Volokolamsk, Mojaisk, Narafominsk and Tula. Russian counter-attacks successful in Leningrad area and in Donetz sector. Germans claimed capture of Solnechaya Gora, 30 miles N.W. of Moscow.

Africa.—New Zealand units captured Gambut. Italian garrison at Gialo Oasis 150 miles south of Benghazi, overpowered by British motorised column. From Abyssinia it was reported that an Italian sortie from Gondar was defeated.

Home.—One enemy raider destroyed in slight night raid over Britain.

General.—Pres. Roosevelt authorized Lease-Lend aid to Gen. de Gaulle's forces. U.S. troops sent to Dutch Guiana to protect the bauxite mines.

TUESDAY, NOV. 25   815*th day*

Sea.—Admiralty communiqué that surface patrols in the Mediterranean sank an enemy convoy of two supply ships on Monday.

Russian Front.—Situation very serious in the Klin and Tula sectors of the Moscow front. Russia also reported hard fighting in the direction of Volokolamsk, Stalinogorsk and Rostov. Mr. Molotov sent a note to all non-Axis powers protesting against Germany's barbaric treatment of Russian prisoners.

Africa.—Cairo communiqué announced the entry of Indian troops into Augila, 100 miles S.E. of Jedabya. German attempt to smash a way out westward between the Imperial Army and the Tobruk garrison was checked by South African forces. Harbour at Benghazi bombed by R.A.F. during night of Nov. 24-25. Raids also made on aerodromes at Benina and Berka. Nairobi communiqué stated that British columns had captured Tadda Ridge, seven miles from Gondar.

Home.—Widespread but small scale activity over West of England at night. One enemy bomber was destroyed.

General.—Mr. William C. Bullitt, former U.S. Ambassador to France, given post as President Roosevelt's personal envoy in the Near East. U.S. troops arrived in Dutch Guiana. President Pedro Cerda of Chile died. Representatives of Axis countries and of puppet governments under their control went to Berlin to sign a protocol to the Anti-Communist pact.

SIGNING THE AMENDMENT of the United States Neutrality Act on November 13. The representatives standing behind the Speaker, Mr. Sam Rayburn, are, left to right, Messrs. F. T. Boland, J. W. McCormack, and Howard W. Smith.   *Photo, Associated Press*

They Have Won Honours in Freedom's Cause

D.S.O.

Lt.-Comdr. Hodgekinson, D.S.O., for conspicuous courage and skill in the course of his naval duties.

P/O O. Yeats, D.S.M., for conspicuous courage. He served on the submarine Thunderbolt, formerly the Thetis.

Ord. Seaman A. Howarth, Albert Medal, for supporting a shipmate in a raging sea, though severely wounded himself.

Capt. W. S. Coughlan, Merchant Navy, **O.B.E.,** for bringing safely to port four lifeboats of survivors from sunk ship.

FOR DISTINGUISHED CONDUCT IN THE FIELD

D.C.M.

Lieut. T. Archer, Bomb Disposal Squad, **G.C.,** for great courage in carrying out his hazardous duties.

Capt. Thomas Sharman, G.M., also for brave work in connexion with the disposal of bombs.

Sergt. Glen Moody, B.E.M., for gallant rescue work during a heavy bombing raid on Clydeside.

L.-Cpl. R. W. Etchells, M.M., for sticking to his A.A. gun, and bringing down three enemy planes.

Mr. W. A. Pullar, Edward Medal, for attempting to avert an explosion in a factory.

Sgt. Ronald Kells, D.C.M., for gallantry in the fighting around Tobruk.

F/O L. J. T. West, A.F.C., for devotion to duty. He has been in the R.A.F. for eighteen years and flying for half that time.

Sgt. Robbins, D.F.M., for carrying out a raid on military objectives in France with great skill and courage.

Flt.-Sgt. Loveitt, of Coventry, **D.F.M.,** for attacking the pocket battleship, Scharnhorst with an aerial torpedo.

Sgt.-Pilot J. Flint, D.F.M. and G.M., for flying home damaged plane and rescuing his navigator from the sea.

Flt.-Sgt. D. Kingaby, Second Bar to his D.F.M., for skill and courage; first pilot to be so honoured.

Flt.-Lieut. R. D. Max, D.F.C., for conspicuous bravery in raiding German warships at Brest and La Pallice.

P.-C. E. G. Pope, G.M., for great skill and courage in rescuing several persons during a heavy raid.

P.-C. W. Taylor, G.M., for bravery and presence of mind in rescue work during a heavy blitz.

Fireman E. Morgan, B.E.M., now receives the **G.M.,** for saving women trapped in the debris.

Fireman J. Coletta, G.M., for preventing a fire from spreading to the Wilberforce Museum, Hull.

Stn.-Offr. A. C. A. French, G.M., for saving an important London railway station and bridge.

Fireman L. Barclay Young, G.M., for rescuing two men and a girl from a bomb-crater.

Warden Alcock, of Coventry, **Bar to his B.E.M.,** for saving a man trapped in a wrecked house after a heavy raid.

Rev. A. Wellesley-Orr, Kingston-on-Thames Vicar, **M.B.E.,** for saving many lives during raids on the Kingston area.

Mr. H. F. Finch, of Finsbury, posthumously awarded the **G.M.,** for helping to rescue persons from a flooded basement.

Mr. T. J. Goodfellow, B.E.M., for being instrumental in saving several lives in the city.

Cpl. D. C. E. Wood, G.M., for walking into a minefield and helping to rescue a wounded comrade.

Mr. F. E. Mockford, G.M., for taking charge of all major incidents in the much blitzed Deptford area.

Miss B. M. Rendell, B.E.M., for brave conduct as watchroom A.F.S. attendant during the raids on Plymouth

Nurse M. Brown, of Coventry, **G.M.,** for bravery and devotion to duty in various raids on the city.

Matron A. Dolan, R.R.C., First Class, for great skill and courage during the Manchester blitzes.

Miss D. Jerome, B.E.M., for gallant work in evacuating patients from the London Chest Hospital during a raid.

Miss B. Phillips, A.R.P. Mobile Nursing Unit, **B.E.M.,** for exceptional bravery and devotion to duty.

Mrs. W. A. Tribe, B.E.M., for continuous duty with a mobile canteen under the most dangerous conditions.

Catapult Plane v. Kurier

How Britain's Fighter Aircraft Are Dealing with Hitler's Long-range Convoy Raiders

Specially drawn for
THE WAR ILLUSTRATED
by Haworth

AS great a menace to our merchantmen on the Atlantic as the submarine is the huge four-engined Focke-Wulf Kurier (see Vol. 4, p. 392), a strengthened military version of the Focke-Wulf Kondor air liner and troop carrier. These long-range bombers, operating mainly from Merignac aerodrome, near Bordeaux, can carry a bomb load of 6,000 lb., have a maximum speed of 280 m.p.h. at 18,000 ft., and have a range of about 2,300 miles. They carry a crew of five or six and are provided with a formidable armament.

To deal with attacks by these commerce raiders of the air, new methods of protection for shipping have been put into operation, and this drawing shows how certain merchantmen have been fitted with catapults from which fighter planes can be launched.

Drawing 1. A Kurier has appeared from the clouds and wheels to attack. The British fighter plane is ready on the catapult cradle, the engine is started, and the pilot, who may be a member of the Fleet Air Arm or the Fighter Command of the R.A.F., climbs into the cockpit. The crew stand by to operate the firing

mechanism of the catapult, which is power-operated. The catapult consists of a girder framework and a trolley, connected by wire ropes and pulleys to the ram of a cylinder. The cylinder is connected by a pipe to the chamber in which the charge is exploded, causing the ram to push the aircraft forward with sufficient velocity to make it air-borne at the end of its run.

Drawing 2. With a roar the fighter is air-borne and ready to intercept the raider.

Drawing 3. The Kurier has been shot down into the sea and its crew are taking to their rubber boat.

Meanwhile, the fighter plane wheels away and heads for the nearest shore base. Many of these pilots have succeeded in navigating their aircraft back to shore after a combat under the most difficult conditions. If the fighter pilot knows that he is out of reach of land, his only alternative is to land in the sea as close to the ship as possible in order to be picked up.

This method of trade defence has proved very successful, and the Commander-in-Chief, Western Approaches, has congratulated the pilots engaged in this hazardous work on the skill they have displayed.

Ships and Men in the Battle of the Seas

Survivors from a bombed ship, crowded in a whale-boat, are nearing the rescuing destroyer. Right, a convoy of merchantmen, moored temporarily at Aden, ready at any moment for the perilous voyage.

H.M.S. VICTORIOUS and H.M.S. KING GEORGE V. The 23,000-ton aircraft carrier is 753 feet long and is armed with sixteen 4·5-in. dual-purpose guns. Both ships took part in hunting down the Bismarck.

Friend or foe ? A British minesweeper in the Mediterranean takes a critical look at a passing craft. Right, a British destroyer engaged in the Atlantic battle ships a green sea.

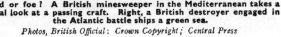

Photos, British Official : Crown Copyright ; Central Press

How They Made Ready for the Offensive

In another page (see page 327) we tell of the opening of the great offensive by Britain's Eighth Army in the Western Desert. Here in this chapter we are concerned with what went before— with the Battle of Supplies in which the opposing forces contested not only with each other but with an environment grim and difficult in the extreme.

"THIS offensive has been long and elaborately prepared," said Mr. Churchill, in the House of Commons, "and we have waited for nearly five months in order that our army shall be well equipped with all those weapons that have made their mark in this new war." Five months— that takes us back to June, when the British attack on the German-Italian positions at Sollum was thwarted. The lessons of that unsuccessful fray were carefully noted, digested, taken to heart. Some of them, indeed, were pointed out by Sir Claude Auchinleck, C.-in-C. in the Middle East, himself, when in "Parade," a weekly illustrated magazine produced by a branch of G.H.Q. in Cairo, he commented on a number of extracts from a German officer's diary. Here are some of the extracts, with the General's comments thereon italicized.

The last golden glow of the setting sun fades. I have just finished my round of the advanced posts. Everything is in order. Although they have had to sacrifice all comforts and pleasures, the lads are in good spirits. They are the German outposts in Africa ; they know it and are proud of it.

These fellows are good soldiers. They know their job and mean to do it.

At last the oppressive heat abates. We now get some respite from the flies, which nearly eat us alive here. It is hopeless arguing with these unwelcome guests. We sent about 100 into the hereafter in our tent alone —and then we gave up.

We are not the only ones to suffer discomfort. The Huns are probably worse off in this respect than we, as we know more about looking after ourselves. All the same, we must keep up to the mark in all those things which affect our health and comfort, so that we are fighting fit when the time comes.

June 16. No sleep all night. Fiendish heat. The Tommies seem to have encircled our position. Our supply column has not arrived today, or have the British nabbed it ? It is just as well we have enough " squibs " to keep us going for a long time.

When we are feeling thirsty, hungry, and tired, in fact " all in," we should remember " the other fellow " is just as bad, if not worse. The one who sticks it longest wins.

Gen. SIR CLAUDE AUCHINLECK, C.-inC. Middle East, who commands the two Armies of the Nile, one of which, the 8th Army, formerly known as the Western Desert Army, drove into Libya on Nov. 18.
Photo, British Official

A wireless message from corps, " Hold on." We promise old Rommel we will do that all right. We would have held on, even without the message, to the last man. Even if the British took the position (but it is not theirs yet) they would not take a single German soldier alive.

As I said before, these chaps have got guts and know their jobs. We have guns, too, and must know our job even better than they. As to the last sentence but one, we do get the German soldier now and again, and want a lot more of them. I hope you will get them for us.

Eating and sleeping had become things of the past. We were choking with thirst, but we finally forgot about drinking, too. No one talked. Silently and deliberately we did what had to be done.

They are tough and worth beating, these Germans.

Since the letters I wrote last week are still in my pocket I open them again and add a few words : " Everything fine. I am fit and well, and I am glad I was there when the British were given the thrashing they deserve at Sollum."

I hope we have him under the sand or in the bag before long.

Following the June fighting, the position in the Western Desert was almost stabilized. In Tobruk a considerable British force was isolated though not besieged, since the approach by sea was kept open , throughout, Tobruk was a hot spot, being bombed and shelled almost continuously, but the British Navy saw to it that it was well victualled. From time to time there was patrol activity on both sides, and the air forces were busy on reconnaissances.

As the months drew on, it became more and more clear that the enemy was becoming apprehensive. It was noticed that he was blasting rock and digging extra gun emplacements and trenches round Sollum and Tobruk and constructing a chain of observation towers reaching far out into the desert. Probably he suspected—what was, indeed, the fact—that the British forces in Egypt

and Tobruk were being largely reinforced. So improved was the British position that on November 16 it was announced in Cairo that the forces in the Western Desert had been constituted as the Eighth Army, and it was revealed that the flow of supplies—of tanks, guns, aircraft and transport—to General Auchinleck's Imperial Army from Great Britain and America was working in most satisfactory fashion.

" I was there when the first American tanks were unloaded," said Mr. Averell Harriman, Mr. Roosevelt's personal representative in this country, in his B.B.C. Postscript on November 23. " Early one morning I went with General Auchinleck to inspect them. A sergeant of our army, one of a group of American soldiers who had come out to instruct your troops in the use of the tanks, proudly explained to Gen. Auchinleck the mechanism of the tank. Then he drove him in the tank to the neighbouring desert to show how it performed. I awaited their return with some concern. Our tanks are different from your tanks. Perhaps he would find ours wanting in some essential. The tank returned. General Auchinleck pulled his large frame out of the small opening in the turret, and with typical British brevity he turned to me and said ' She'll do. It's a fine weapon, manoeuvrable and sturdy. How many can you send ? ' This same tank and and many more that have arrived in the months since have been carrying your soldiers in the battle raging on the Libyan Desert."

On the other hand, it was thought that Gen. Rommel had not been reinforced, at least to any considerable extent, since not only had his lines of communication been subjected to severe bombing, but his sea communications were now distinctly hazardous. Scores of Axis ships were torpedoed or seriously damaged, and this slaughter culminated in the annihilation of the two enemy convoys during the week-end of November 9 (see page 302), following which came reports that the bodies of 7,000 Italians had been washed ashore in Tunisia. While this submarine blitz was being maintained in the sea passage, the R.A.F. in the Middle East were subjecting the enemy to an air blitz.

All this pointed to a vast reinforcement of the R.A.F. in the Middle East ; indeed, it was reported that Air Vice-Marshal Coningham had squadrons where his predecessor in the offensive a year ago had planes.

Adm. SIR ANDREW CUNNINGHAM, C.-in-C. Mediterranean Fleet, is a brother of Gen. Cunningham who commands the 8th Army operating in Libya. *Photo, British Official*

Air Vice-Marshal ARTHUR CONINGHAM, A.O.C. Western Desert, is a 46-year-old New Zealander. He served in the Near East during the last war.   *Photo, Wide World*

America Has a Part in the Libyan Campaign

Tins of fruit and vegetables for troops engaged in the Libya offensive at a Detail Issue Depot in the advanced area ; the rations are collected and distributed by lorries, some fitted with refrigerators for fresh meat.

" Our supplies in the last few months have reached your forces in the Middle East," said Mr. Averell Harriman, the American Lease-Lend Administrator, on Nov. 23 ; " we hope and pray that our tanks and our planes are serving them well." Top right, American M 3 light tanks for General Cunningham are being landed in North Africa, while below is a huge shipload of stores which are about to be taken from the quayside to the advanced depots in the desert.

Photos, British Official: Crown Copyright ; Sport & General

I Was There! ....Eye Witness Stories of the War

One Night We Made a Bolt from Benghazi

Three British soldiers—Leading Bombardier A. H. Hasler, Gunner J. J. Cocker (both Rhodesians), and Trooper A. R. Oldham (from Surrey)—broke out of a German prison camp at Benghazi and marched across the Libyan desert for seven days before contacting a British patrol. Bombardier Hasler's story follows.

As soon as we were captured, five months ago, we made up our minds we would try to escape. We knew we would have to make our plans well—we had a long way to go to the '' wire '' (the Frontier fence erected by the Italians). First, we needed an opportunity, then we required food and water. These last two provided our major problem, because we had, so we thought, about 400 miles to go before reaching safety.

There were 300 prisoners in our camp—200 of them Australians. Once a week we organized our own concerts, and at the end we sang '' God Save the King '' as loud as we could.

The Germans fed us badly—a roll of Italian bread and some weak coffee for breakfast at 5 a.m., while at midday we had macaroni soup and, on rare occasions, meat. They worked us 14 hours a day, but later got this down to 12 hours.

Every day we stored any tinned rations—sardines and Italian bully. Just as we were set to go, I fell ill with yellow jaundice. This put us back for a bit, but I soon got better. We could only escape by night, and we had to reckon on not being missed long enough to get a good start.

On the appointed night we slipped out and took cover in the grounds of the camp. We lay quiet for a moment, and then bolted.

From our first stop it was pretty easy going. We had enough rations for a 21-day journey—enough to keep us alive anyway. We had four water bottles apiece. Our map was torn from a German illustrated newspaper, and we had a poor compass—one of those things in the top of a fountain pen. Later we lost it; but its loss was not felt because we found the sun a better guide.

The first day we made 25 miles. At night we tried our best to sleep, but at half-past three in the morning it was too cold, and we resumed our march at that time. When the sun became unbearable later in the day we rested until it became cooler in the afternoon.

So on we went for seven days. We managed to strike a water point en route, and replenished our supplies. Day after day we kept going, spurred on, when we grew tired, by the thought that every step was one nearer our own army.

Finally one night we slept in a disused building and with the morning light were surprised to see the captain of a British patrol standing near us with a tommy gun. We told him who we were and from where we had escaped. He wasn't the least taken aback, but simply said, '' would you like a lift back ? ''—*Reuter.*

HITLER OVER BERLIN ! On this bomber of a Polish squadron which took part in a recent raid on Berlin is a caricature of Der Fuehrer himself.   *Photo, L.N.A.*

Berlin's Burning—and We Poles Have Done It!

Here we reprint from '' Wings,'' the fortnightly journal of the Polish Air Force, an account of a raid by Polish airmen on Berlin—told by a Polish officer to Jerzy Głebocki.

The greatest thrill I ever had was over Berlin, because Berlin is something very special—the heart of Germany, and we Poles are over this city. The sirens wail for them as they did for us in September 1939, and their hearts are full of fear. Children cry as ours did then. Houses are thrown high, high into the air and vanish in the dust as we let the bombs fly. Then a red glare is pulling you back to drop more bombs, of which you have none left. And we, the Poles, have done it !

Berlin is my best flight—a lot of flak, so we climb fairly high. I want to drop my

POLAND'S AIR FORCE IN ACTION				
From time of arrival in Great Britain to November 11, 1941				
Fighter Squadrons				
Enemy aircraft destroyed	..	..	..	410
Probably destroyed	..	..	..	108
Damaged	..	..	..	52
Total	..	..	..	About 570
Bomber Squadrons				
Number of Bombing Raids	..	..	..	265
Number of aircraft engaged in operations	..	1,304		

bomb-load well inside the target area, so I again check our course for the pilot. As we are approaching our objective I can see clearly the A.A. barrage in front of me. It is apparent that somebody is in, as the salvos are frequent and searchlights wander widely over the sky. The heavy A.A. barrage forms an outer circle, inside of which light A.A. guns and tracer bullets give a strange, but menacing picture.

We slowly lose height over our target. I check the safety catches of the bomb hatches. Now the A.A. fire is aiming at us as well as the searchlights being after us. Suddenly one gets a direct bearing on our plane. At once several others also cross their beams on us ; the A.A. fire becomes definitely concentrated and very accurate. I lie stretched flat in the bomb aimer's turret, waiting to get a bearing with the bomb sight on to the target. I give the pilot an abrupt warning to keep on his course as we are going in !

Suddenly I feel a sharp pain in my right leg. I become overwhelmed by a rush of heat stiffness. I report that I have been wounded. The second pilot crawls into my turret in order to help me. I pull myself together after a short while in order to keep the plane on the course. We were right over the target. In front of my eyes I see green and red patches ; I am feeling giddy, but I can still see the target, and now I can see it through the bomb sight, the string well in the middle of it ; now . . . I press the button to free the bombs. In a tenth of a second I can see the parting load, then they

ESCAPED FROM BENGHAZI, these three British soldiers—from left to right, Trooper Oldham, Ldg. Bombardier Hasler, and Gunner Cocker—marched across the Libyan desert for seven days before encountering a British patrol. Their story is told above by Bombardier Hasler.
Photo. British Official ; Crown Copyright

Our 'Lady Shirley' Sent a U-boat to its Doom

After a spirited action the crew of H.M. Trawler Lady Shirley sank a
U-boat and captured the crew. This remarkable achievement is described
below by the Lady Shirley's captain, Lieut.-Commander A. H. Callaway,
who was awarded the D.S.O.

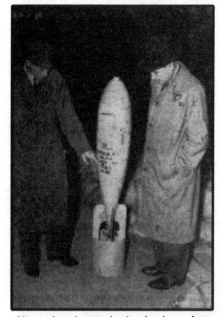

Many American-made bombs have been
dropped on Germany during raids such as that
described below. An American journalist is
shown one at an R.A.F. station. *Photo, L.N.A.*

vanish and I hear distant explosions . . . one,
two, three—all of them have detonated.

But now comes the real hell. We are
caught in innumerable searchlight beams, the
fire of hundreds of guns is concentrated on us.
The glare of the bursting shells is so strong
that I am able to see the second hand of my
watch moving forward. The noise of the
explosions is so deafening that it makes me
think that it actually burst inside the cabin.
You feel you smell the burning wood and
fumes. The second pilot helps me to get
into the navigating cabin and to fasten the
parachute. The whole craft is being thrown
about. I can hear the crackling of fragments
against the wings. It seems that in a short
while we shall fall to bits. Under us lies a
sea of light· and fire. We fly over it for
twelve minutes.

After we have come out of the barrage I
take the bearing for the shortest course home-
wards. The air gunners report much damage
and we can't rely too much on the engines.
I feel the pulse inside my head. The blood
trickles from my leg—my right boot is filled
with it. As though for spite, the bomb doors
are trapped, diminishing the speed. I finish
my calculations and give the pilot a homeward course. The rest of the crew slide a
parachute under my feet, making some sort
of bandage over it. All is in blood—a fragment penetrated my right thigh above the
knee. A shortage of oxygen is threatening
us and the base is far away.

We leave Bremen aside and avoid the
fierce A.A. barrage, climbing high. Through
the damaged parts of the craft a cold wind is
blowing ; my leg is nearly frozen. The boot,
wet from blood, has shrunk and can't be put
on. My comrades are rubbing my thumbs.
It is already dawning.

We approach our aerodrome, but the
hydraulic undercarriage is jammed. The
automatic device letting it down does not
work. We pump on the emergency pump in
order to increase the pressure. After 45
minutes the undercarriage is let down. We
ask for permission to land, and to down.
Now, after climbing out of our plane, we can
observe the result. The right tire is shot
through, and there are about 50 holes in the
wings and cowling. Even the pulley system
of the starboard wing is cut. How we have
managed to reach home I don't know.

WE were steaming in daylight when we
sighted the conning-tower of a U-boat
on the surface. We were several
miles away. We steamed at full speed
towards the submarine and saw it dive.

Immediately we reached the spot we
dropped depth charges. A bare two or
three minutes afterwards we saw the periscope
and knew the U-boat was surfacing. She
was 500 yards away. We turned to port
ready to attack with gun-fire or ram her.
We learned from the crew afterwards that
she had been badly damaged and was
leaking, with her machinery out of action.

As soon as the conning-tower opened
we swept it with machine-gun fire. We
could see the officers and men falling before
the hail of bullets. We saw a number of
men rushing to man the gun on the deck
of the submarine, but they never reached it.

Just as we opened fire with our four-inch
gun a machine-gun began to fire from the
conning-tower of the submarine. Our
first two rounds missed, but after that
practically every shell hit the submarine,
one bursting on the conning-tower and
another penetrating the well and exploding
inside.

After our first three rounds our seaman
gunlayer, L. W. Pizzey, was killed by
machine-gun bullets. Immediately Sub-Lieut.
French, in charge of the gun, leapt into his
place and with the gun crew working heroically in spite of a hail of machine-gun bullets
sweeping the entire length of the ship, we
kept up such a hot fire that the enemy
machine-gun was silenced and none of the
Germans could bring their 4·7 gun into
action against us.

They ran away from the gun. We could
see them running along the deck of the
submarine holding their hands above their
heads in token of surrender and shouting.
We ceased fire, but kept our gun trained
on her. She was badly down by the stern,

and her crew, wearing lifebelts, began to jump
overboard.

When she plunged down stern first we
cheered and then set about the business of
picking up the survivors. There were 45 of
them, 15 more than the total complement of
the Lady Shirley. A rating whose legs had
been blown off died soon after we got him
on board. I asked one of the two German
officer survivors, who spoke English, if he
would like to conduct the burial service, but
as he was wounded he asked me to do so.

~~~~~~

ANOTHER TRAWLER EPIC

THERE'S a Naval trawler on escort duty off the East
Coast ; three swastikas decorate her funnel, showing
that she has shot down three German aircraft . . . A
group of aircraft was seen coming from the English coast,
at first thought to be British. The Captain sounded the
alarm to give his crew some practice. Then the aircraft
were recognized as German. The trawler was ready and
shot down two of them. **In this little ship, with less
than thirty men, three have won decorations, five
have been mentioned in despatches, and five more
recommended for bravery in rescuing survivors
from another ship.**—*Rt. Hon. A. V. Alexander, broadcasting on Trafalgar Day, 1941.*

~~~~~~

I said I had no German flag with which
to cover the body, and I presumed they
would not wish him to be buried under
the Union Jack. Politely they agreed, and
with our ship's company and the two German
officers and five ratings standing together on
the deck I conducted the service, the body
going over the side not covered with a flag.
The Germans were obviously very touched,
and thanked me for the way in which the
service was carried out.

We rendered first-aid to eight wounded
Germans. On leaving the ship the Germans
showed no signs of Nazi arrogance. They
thanked us all for what we had done for
them. They were absolutely astonished
that such a small ship as ours could sink a
powerful submarine. Our fire, they said, was
so rapid and accurate that they could not
man their own gun.—*Reuter.*

THE LADY SHIRLEY'S crew listening as the captain, Lt.-Cmdr. A. H. Callaway, R.A.N.V.R., reads
congratulations from the Prime Minister. How this 470-ton trawler sank a U-boat and captured
the crew is told above, and a photograph of the ship is in page 237. Her captain received the D.S.O.,
Lt. Boucaut and Sub-Lt. French the D.S.C., and Seaman S. Halcrow the C.G.M. *Photo, British Official*

Editor's Postscript

FOUND a colleague yesterday busy calculating how to salvage enough old books and magazines to keep the paper mills of Britain at full strength with only a few thousand tons of sea-borne pulp—the little leaven that leaveneth the whole lump. Some optimist, this ! Yet it sounds dead easy. Population of U.K. and N. Ireland (Eire doesn't count—some of it can't even read) is approximately 46,000,000. Take an average of five persons to each household : say nine million homes. Deduct at least one million as bookless and paperless, then get the remaining eight million households to contribute one book per week (any old book) to the paper salvage scheme, and behold eight million books a week, or a good 400,000,000 a year. Assuming that so many exist (which one may doubt) the annual tonnage of salvage would make repulping one of our great national industries. To which the American " Aw, nuts ! " might not be inapposite.

WHEN I thought of the many homes I have seen where the only books have been the local telephone and residential directories, with some old school prizes, a dictionary, and (perhaps) an un-thumbed Bible somewhere in the background, I was unable to go any distance with the optimist along this new road of hope which he was eager to explore. Moreover, in this dire " scorched earth " policy which he would apply to Bookland he would have to get rid of the organization that is working night and day to collect old books not for pulping but for distributing to H.M. Forces as reading matter " to educate, to elevate, to entertain." It indicates, however, the desperate measures that one whose perplexing task is to hunt for plain paper for printing purposes, is ready to consider. For, indeed, the situation is desperate and gets desperater and desperater every day, as Alice might put it in an actual Blunderland more fantastic than her Wonderland.

IT is certainly no laughing matter, and I'm almost ashamed to have reacted so lightheartedly to that flight of fancy, for every publisher of books, newspapers, or periodicals is now engaged in a deadly struggle to keep going, even in a restricted and fractional way, for lack of paper. And it is surprising how greatly the reading public could help those who cater for them by combing their houses, especially their lumber rooms, and collecting all old, outworn, forgotten books, and stray back numbers of magazines—being careful not to overdo the combing process by parting with items whose loss might be soon regretted —all sorts of old paper documents (expired insurance policies exist in scores of thousands and are valueless for any purpose other than repulping), old greeting cards, out-of-date directories and annuals, and tradesmen's catalogues and, of course, newspapers old and new . . . in short all forms of " junk " made from paper. The machinery exists for receiving and disposing of this salvage, for which appreciable payment is obtainable

where the quantities are considerable, and I hope that none of my readers in a position to respond to this urgent Salvage Drive are holding back. Let me add, also, that it is not merely, or even primarily, to help the publishing trade that I appeal to my readers, but for our munitions factories where vast quantities of coarse paper are required for making cartridge cases, wrapping and packing bombs, grenades, and many other sorts of "tools" (*vide* Mr. Churchill) so urgently needed to " finish the job."

IT's pleasant to hear of instances where profiteering is disdained by those who might have been excused had they dabbled

LT.-GEN. SIR ALAN CUNNINGHAM, who conducted the East African campaign in such brilliant fashion, commands the Eighth Army in the Western Desert which launched an offensive into Libya on November 18.   *Photo, British Official : Crown Copyright*

in it just a little. No one needs to be told that country cottages are fetching fancy rents these days where they are free from the Rent Restriction Acts, or that tenants who enjoy the very one-sided provisions of those acts sub-let rooms at rents which enable them to reap a profit and sit rent free. Well, I heard from a friend yesterday about an actor who for some years has had a tiny country hide-out at a weekly rent of 3s. 10d. Times, have been pretty bad with him, and instead of using the cottage for week-ends only he and his wife have been constrained for economy's sake to stay most of their time in this very bijou abode. They have often wondered that the landlord has shown no sign of putting up their rent. The other week, however, a letter came from that traditional ogre, and the actor, nervously opening it, said to his wife : "Here it is at last : the fatal missive. I hope old So-and-so is not sticking us for too much." He was quite prepared in the changed

conditions to be charged anything over half-a-guinea, as the humble cot would let today for double that, being in a relatively safe area. " I am sorry," he read out to his wife in lugubrious tones, " that owing to increased costs it will be necessary to ask you for a larger rent, and I suggest that in future you pay me 4s. 2d. instead of the exisiting arrangement of 3s. 10d. I shall be glad to know if this meets with your approval." Joyous collapse of actor. So even in the landlord class simple souls may still be found.

THIS morning while I had my frugal breakfast in my bedroom, read the papers, bathed, shaved and dressed—a total process occupying very nearly one hour—a tractor with a harrow attached stood upon the village green, its engine all the while sending up a cloud of exhaust vapour to pollute the sharp morning air, for its chug, chug never ceased ! Its driver had met a pal with a tradesman's motor van and together they gossiped all that time. I am told that the tractor would be consuming paraffin, petrol being needed only to start its engine, and it might have been that its driver was afraid to stop it because of difficulty in restarting. Still, paraffin ranks next to petrol as liquid fuel and calls for strict economy in its use. Perhaps I'm fussy, but I can think of no plausible excuse for this sort of waste.

LUNCHED today with my old friend, M. Henry D. Davray, who, unique among the French journalists of our time, has given the best of his years to promoting by pen and speech the mutual understanding of the French and British peoples. And although he has been at it for more than forty years, he still found something to do in that way last week, when, at a Press conference, he drew Mr. Brendan Bracken's attention to a typical instance of misunderstanding. A photograph of General Weygand on a platform in an Algiers street " taking the salute " was widely circulated recently in the British press, most of the inscriptions asking the reader to note that Weygand, the legionaries, and the public were all giving " a modified form of the Nazi salute." This, Davray assured me, was nonsense : what they were doing was signifying their submission to the new Vichy constitution in the manner observed in France for generations before his foulness the Fuehrer (an unfriendly critic complimented me on that phrase the other day) or the Nazi party came into being. Which shows how easily a gesture can be misunderstood, especially in a photo. The orthodox Nazi salute has its counterpart in England, as every boy or girl at school is well aware.

"BE like Dad, keep Mum," the silliest of all the stupid posters issued by the M.O.I. has for some time, I was glad to think, ceased to disfigure our streets and stations. But I have not been able to escape the banality ; it pursues me on matchboxes! So that for fifty times per box it stares at me in block letters—and my dad and mum have long been one with Julius Caesar, and Napoleon! In many instances the class of reader for whom the words were originally phrased would have been served just as well as if it had read : "Be like Mum, keep Dad."

Printed in England and published on the 10th, 20th, and 30th of each month by the Proprietors, The Amalgamated Press, Ltd., The Fleetway House, Farringdon Street, London, E.C.4. Registered for transmission by Canadian Magazine Post. Sole Agents for Australia and New Zealand : Messrs. Gordon & Gotch, Ltd. ; and for South Africa : Central News Agency, Ltd. December 10th, 1941.   S.S.   *Editorial Address :* JOHN CARPENTER HOUSE WHITEFRIARS. LONDON. E.C.4.

Vol 5 | The War Illustrated | Nº 115

Edited by Sir John Hammerton

FOURPENCE | DEC. 20TH, 1941

ABANDON SHIP, the last scene in the glorious career of H.M.S. Ark Royal, when it was found impossible to save her. A destroyer packed with survivors is just leaving the doomed aircraft carrier, and some of the crew have already been taken off by small boats. Here and there a rubber dinghy floating on the waves is emergency succour for any that may have to go into the "drink." There is no panic, no fear—only regret that a fine and valiant ship has, by the fortune of war, fallen a victim to the enemy.

Photo, the "Daily Mirror," Exclusive to THE WAR ILLUSTRATED

NO. 116 WILL BE PUBLISHED TUESDAY, DEC. 30

TO WIN WE MUST HAVE 30,000 TANKS—AND MORE

THE war is being decided by tanks, Stalin told Lord Beaverbrook at the Moscow Conference. It is a tank war. " 'Is it not an aeroplane war, too?' I asked, but Stalin replied that it was essentially a tank war."

Certainly tanks have played and are playing a predominant part. On the War's very first day German tanks crashed across the frontier into Poland and carved a blood-stained path through the serried masses of horsemen, brave but so horribly doomed from the start, that the Poles flung against them. Tanks rolled along the roads and across the dykes of the Low Countries. Tanks rumbled over the bridges over the Albert Canal and the Meuse—bridges which the defenders ought to have blown up beforehand. Tanks followed the woodland paths through the Ardennes, pushed through the fatal gap at Sedan, even overran in places the Maginot Line itself.

TANKS careered across the desert in Wavell's triumphant vanguard. Tanks were the spearhead of Rommel's counter-thrust, which in a few days left only Tobruk as a reminder of Wavell's victory. It is hardly an exaggeration to say that tanks have been mentioned in every communiqué from the Russian front, whether Nazi or Soviet. We have heard and read until we were tired of Hitler's panzers, of Guderian's tanks and of von Kleist's. They battered their way through Minsk and rumbled along the road to Moscow, they crawled over the shattered houses of Kiev and Kharkov, they swept across the vast wheatfields of the Ukraine; but they are not making such good progress now when the ground is deep in snow. They clattered over the Crimea and made their way into the station yard at Rostov. (And there, at Rostov, for the first time, they were forced to reverse their tracks).

Now again, in Libya, tanks are opposed to tanks in a battle as strange as it is fateful. Every correspondent dilates upon the clash of these " fire-breathing, scaly-hided monsters," as one has called them, monsters recalling the prehistoric reptiles which " tare each other in their slime " in the ages when the earth was still clothed with tropic swamps.

Tanks dominate the vast battlefield in the desert. They rage and roar across the waste of sand and scrub seeking the enemy tanks that they may devour. They are the battleships of land warfare, and are even more defiant of the bombers of the air. In this mighty struggle there is no retreat. Theirs but to charge and charge again with the furious mêlée; to knock out before being knocked out and left a tangled, blackened and twisted wreck.

"How will the war be won?" asked General de Gaulle, leader of the Free French, when he visited recently a great munitions factory in the Midlands. " We are living in the machine age. The battles of our time are and will be won by machines of war—which means, first of all, by tanks. *When will the war be won?* The Germans conquered Poland because they had 5,000 tanks against 1,000. They conquered France because they had 10,000 tanks against 3,000. They are advancing in Russia because they have 25,000 tanks against 15,000. They will be beaten when the war machines of the defenders of liberty have gained superiority over theirs, in numbers and quality. Napoleon once said, ' Victory is won by the big battalions.' Today he would say victory is won by the big battalions of tanks."

Later in his speech General de Gaulle—who had urged upon the French General Staff the establishment of a great tank force years before the war—went on to quote Mr. Churchill, who in 1918 said that the battle of 1919 would be won by 10,000 tanks, large and small. " That," commented General de Gaulle, " was the number that M. Reynaud demanded for the French Army in 1935." When, in March 1940, Reynaud became Prime Minister, he fixed this figure as the goal to be reached by the French armament industries; but it was too late. " It is exactly the same number of tanks as the Germans sent into action in May and June, 1940, on the soil of France, Belgium and the Netherlands. They are bringing twice this number to bear today from the White Sea to the Black Sea."

WELL might Lord Beaverbrook tell the engineering shop stewards on Clydeside a few days ago that the tank has proved the most formidable weapon of the war to date. It destroyed France and would have destroyed Britain had it not been for the Channel tank trap. Furthermore, " It is the British tank in Libya which has brought the invincible army of Germany to defeat for the first time," and British tanks are in action outside Moscow. Then the Minister of Supply read a telegram received a few hours before from Stalin.

" Beaverbrook," it read, " Let me express my gratitude for the sending of aeroplanes and tanks. Some of these British-made aeroplanes and tanks are already in action in the front line. The reports of our commanders on the British-made tanks are favourable. The Hurricanes are greatly appreciated. We would like as many Hurricanes and tanks as you can send, and could you limit the number of types sent to us? It would make everything much easier."

" That is straight from the battle front," Lord Beaverbrook said, and added that when he became Minister of Supply he sent out a message to all the firms engaged on tank production, informing them that tanks would henceforth be 1A priority. But in each of the messages was the injunction, " On no account shall you put the tank ahead of the aeroplane." That rule had been observed ever since. " Aircraft," said Lord Beaverbrook, " cannot win the battle alone. The tank might. Certainly aircraft cannot. The tank and aircraft together is the form in which we want to fight this battle front."

TANKS, more tanks, and yet more tanks is, then, the slogan for today. " We want," said Lord Beaverbrook at this same meeting, " from all sources from July of next year until July 1943, in twelve months, 30,900 tanks. That will include the quota we get from America, what we can produce in Canada, and a wide plan of production which we must lay down here."

30,000 tanks! A tremendous figure, indeed. But General de Gaulle—and who should know better?—thinks even more will be required. " It is perhaps the action of 100,000 tanks, combined with that of 100,000 planes, and provided with supplies by 50,000,000 tons of shipping, which will win once and for all the victory of liberty."

To return to Lord Beaverbrook. " Stalin told me in the Kremlin that the Germans had 30,000 tanks," he said. " The Germans are producing, too, and adding to that number. So it is again the race of the tortoise and the hare. We have to get there fast to catch up on the production of German tanks."

TREMENDOUS as the figures are, they are not beyond the capacity of the combined plants of Britain and the Dominions, the United States and Russia. But we are a long way yet from full production. His audience of Clydesiders bombarded Lord Beaverbrook with questions inspired by intense criticism of the way things are done. Some Clyde employers, he was told, have the point of view of 40 years ago; and there was a frequent complaint that there is bad management, not in one factory but in all. " Bring about cooperation between management and men," declared Mr. Kirkwood in forthright tones. " The Clyde will then give you records that will make other records look like standing still."

REALLY we have no choice. We must extend our output of tanks to a degree hitherto undreamed of, we must make tank production a supreme objective of the national effort. By tanks far more than by masses of infantry, however fanatically brave and excellently equipped, far more even than by armadas of aircraft, Hitler has scored his resounding triumphs. And by tanks he will be beaten and driven along the road of defeat.

E. ROYSTON PIKE

OVER THE LIBYAN DESERT races a British tank one of the hundreds which for weeks battled furiously with the tanks, as numerous perhaps and in many cases more powerfully built, armoured, and armed, that constituted the main strength of Rommel's Afrika Korps.
Photo, British Official: Crown Copyright

American Tanks in the Desert Battle

A corporal on one of the new American tanks, specially designed for desert warfare, about to descend into the body of the machine for a test run.

A tank driver, having been instructed in the mechanism at a tactical training school, starting up somewhere behind the lines. Circle, crew of a tank jumping into their machine.

IN THE WESTERN DESERT, an American light tank goes at full speed. Right, units of the Royal Tank Corps studying one of the new American machines. In the background is a British "Matilda" tank. These American M.3 tanks have done good work in the battle for Libya. At least 150 are believed to have participated in Lt.-Gen. Sir Alan Cunningham's preliminary offensive, and since then many others are on the way.

Photos, British Official: Crown Copyright

Retreat from Rostov: Hitler's First Defeat

What was described as the first major defeat inflicted on Hitler's armies was the smashing counter-attack by Timoshenko's Russians, which in a few days expelled von Kleist's shock troops from Rostov. Here we tell of the battle and of the Nazi retreat which soon became a rout.

GREAT was the jubilation in Hitler's camp when it was announced on November 22 that General von Kleist's shock troops had, after violent fighting, captured Rostov-on-Don. The city, it was pointed out, was one of great commercial and strategical importance, one which would be of exceptional value in the contemplated invasion of the Caucasus.

It was noticeable that the Russians declined to confirm the news of the city's fall, although they admitted that the Germans had penetrated the defences of Rostov and that fighting was going on in the streets. German tanks had reached the railway station, where there was fighting of the most violent description. Stubbornly though the Russians resisted, they were borne back. Every yard of advance cost the enemy dear, however; in two days' fighting the Germans lost (so the Russians claimed) 55 tanks, many lorries, much ammunition, and thousands of men killed and wounded.

Considering the city as good as won, von Rundstedt laid his plans for a further big offensive which would carry his armies across the Don. He was forestalled, however. In the last week of November Marshal Timoshenko, who for weeks past had been quietly organizing great new armies behind the southern sector of the front, struck a surprise blow. It came with all the force of a complete surprise, and in a few hours von Kleist's picked infantry and vaunted panzers were sent reeling back.

Battle was joined when units of General Remizov's 56th Army slipped across the Don after nightfall on November 27, and at dawn the next day launched an assault against the hastily-prepared German defences in the southern suburbs of Rostov. Savage street fighting began, in which a valiant part was played by the Russian guerillas, who sniped the Nazis from the rear. During the night of November 28 Soviet troops belonging to General Kharitonov's 9th Army were ferried over the Don, up river from Rostov, between Nakhichevan and Novocherkassk, and stormed the German lines in the north-east of Rostov. At the same time Red Army shock troops under Commander Goncharov broke through a German flank.

Thus attacked from both sides, von Kleist's army group, consisting of the 14th and 16th Tank Divisions, the 60th Motorized Division, and the SS. (Nazi Black Guard) Viking Division, were trapped. Only with extreme difficulty and after suffering heavy losses did remnants of his force burst their way through the narrowing gap still left open through the

The arrow shows the direction of retreat of Gen. von Kleist's army following the successful Russian counter-attack launched at the end of November. *Courtesy of " News Chronicle "*

north-west suburbs. They retreated in disorder along the coast-road towards Taganrog, closely pursued by the triumphant Russians. No opportunity was given to the enemy for making a stand. The whole line of the Red Army's advance was littered with heaps of Nazi dead, while everywhere were abandoned tanks, tractors, lorries, guns, and dumps of ammunition. Swarms of Stormovik dive-bombers turned the retreat into a rout.

"Our booty is so tremendous," said Kharitonov in a victory speech, "that we have not yet had time to count it. Of course, the Germans may try, with the help of new reinforcements, to stop the Red Army offensive, but I am ready for such an eventuality. I possess the necessary forces to prevent any enemy counter-offensive from stopping us. My soldiers are now pursuing a beaten enemy. They will continue to do so until he is finally smashed."

Stalin was swift to send a message of congratulation to Marshal Timoshenko and to Colonel-General Cherevichenko, Soviet Commander on the southern front. "I congratulate you on the victory over the enemy," he said, "and the liberation of Rostov from the German Fascist invaders. I send greetings to the gallant troops of the 9th and 56th Armies under the command of Generals Kharitonov and Remizov, who raised our glorious Soviet banner over Rostov."

Before leaving the town the Germans indulged in an orgy of murder. Hundreds of women, children, and male civilians in the city were slaughtered, declared Moscow. German forces looted the place and set fire to the houses. In one school, it was stated, the Russians found the bodies of 20 women, together with the bullet-riddled corpses of 70 children. Piles of dead Russian civilians were found in the streets. "We shall exact a terrible punishment for this bestiality from the German people who have produced this band of inhuman gangsters," vowed Moscow.

The Germans were not without their excuses for their defeat. Rostov, they explained, had been evacuated by the German troops in accordance with orders, "so that the necessary measures of reprisal may be taken against the population who have illegally taken part in the battle in the rear of the German Army." (This confession reads strangely in the light of the previous statement made by the German propagandists that the Soviet population meets the German troops as liberators from Stalin's tyrannical yoke.) No doubt, Berlin opined, the Reds would claim the recapture of Rostov, but really there was no question of this: the German High Command had merely taken systematic methods to enforce international law. Then the officials in Berlin declared that the Germans were going to take reprisals which would turn Rostov into "a smoking pile of debris, covering tens of thousands of Russians." The destruction would be worse than that of Warsaw, Rotterdam, or Coventry.

A few days later this excuse, as ridiculous as it was infamous, was discarded. Now it was admitted that the Germans had been forced to withdraw in face of heavy enemy superiority. The Russians, it was explained, had brought up fresh reserves from Siberia and Persia and, moreover, the Soviet partisans in the city had been active. So the Nazis had decided to retire to better positions in order to avoid unnecessary loss and the better to withstand the desperate Russian counter-attacks.

There was no disguising, indeed, the fact that the Germans had been defeated—and defeated, moreover, by an army which had been "annihilated" some time earlier, if the German account had been believed. "This is not the first, and certainly not the last, decided blow dealt to the German Army," said M. Lozovsky. "The rout of Kleist's army at Rostov puts an end to the stories of the invincibility of the German Army, and bars the way to a further advance by the invaders." For the time being, at least, the threat to the Caucasus was averted.

ROSTOV-ON-DON, Russian port and industrial town, from which the Germans were driven by Soviet forces on November 29, after they had held the city for barely a week. Marshal Timoshenko's successful counter-stroke at the German right flank has checked, if it has not smashed, Hitler's plan to invade the North Caucasus. By December 4 the Russians were back in Taganrog, 50 miles west of Rostov, while the remnants of von Kleist's shattered divisions were in retreat towards Mariupol.
Photo, G.P.U.

Here and There on the Vast Eastern Front

This ingenious anti-aircraft observation post has been improvised by Soviet soldiers; here, connected by telephone with their battery, they watch for Nazi planes.

FINNISH TROOPS attacking the railway station of Jaakkima on Lake Ladoga, after the capture of the town from the Russians in advanced lines defending Leningrad.

NAZI TANK in action on the East Front. Right, exhausted German soldiers sleeping in an open trench during a lull in the fighting for Leningrad. Circle, a German soldier engaged in the dangerous task of rendering mines harmless. Like little portable wireless sets in shape these weapons are sown in vast numbers all about the Russian front, in open spaces and in towns, and have inflicted immense casualties on the Nazi machines and men.

Photo, Planet News and Sport & General

One Last Glimpse of the Ever-glorious Ark Royal

So often "sunk" by German propaganda, H.M.S. Ark Royal was torpedoed on November 13 and sank the next day. The fatal list to starboard is clearly noticeable in this photograph taken from the deck of the destroyer which rescued her crew. In the upper photograph the stricken ship is seen from another angle with some of her complement crowding over the side to be taken aboard the destroyer which, thanks to calm weather, was able to come up alongside. The Ark Royal, completed in Nov. 1938, had a displacement of 27,000 tons full load, and was armed with sixteen 4·5-in. guns.

Upper photo, British Official : Crown Copyright ; lower photo, the " Daily Mirror," Exclusive to THE WAR ILLUSTRATED.

All But One Were Saved from the 'Ark'

ARK ROYAL SURVIVORS, all smiles and congratulating themselves on their good fortune, arrive at Portsmouth. The Ark Royal was torpedoed in the Mediterranean by a U-boat on November 13. Though "officially sunk" by Goebbels on September 26, 1939, the Ark Royal continued a glorious career, taking part in the hunt for the Graf Spee and the Norwegian campaign. In the Mediterranean last November one of her aircraft torpedoed an Italian battleship. She was at the bombardment of Genoa, and in the chase of the Bismarck. *Photo, Associated Press, badge by permission of H.M.S.O.*

Our Searchlight on the War

OUR TOO HUSH-HUSH PROPAGANDA

Recently the Press was invited to a showing of Army Training film, under the auspices of the Directorate of Army Kinematography.

CONVINCED of the great power of the modern sound film, the War Office decided in August 1940—yes, as early as that—to make the fullest use of this up-to-date, successful method of instruction. A special section of the War Office was created to study and develop the use of films, a section which has now been expanded into the Directorate of Army Kinematography (note the K : long years ago the cinema used to be the kinema). Over 100 films have been put into production, and 45 of them have been completed. Three of these were shown the other day. All were quite good specimens of the cinematographer's art, but it was difficult to discover any reason why they should be described as secret.

The first—a very useful one this, particularly to A.R.P. wardens—illustrated the various types of H.E. bombs. It was humorous, yet practical ; but surely the Germans know what sort of bombs they've dropped on us ! The second film was a highly instructive, and not too easy to follow, account of the mechanism of a 25-pounder gun ; quite a number of these are now in German possession. But the real gem was the third, a Universal film designed to create "booby-trap mentality." The men who made it must have enjoyed themselves immensely, particularly those who played the enemy parts. One scene in particular sticks in the mind : two German officers come into a drawing-room, presumably French, which has been carefully "doctored" by the British before their withdrawal a few days before. They call for a drink and toast a German victory, grin and wink at the contemptuous French girl—presumably she is French—who brings it, and look long and longingly at her retreating legs as only Nazi officers can. But would *you* loll back in your chair and try to straighten a picture on the wall with your riding crop ? *Exeunt omnes :* picture, piano, room and officers " in one red burial blent " !

READY FOR THE RAIDERS ?

" Keep your knowledge of air-raid precautions continually up to date," counsels Mr. Herbert Morrison, Minister of Home Security, in his foreword to the 3d. pamphlet, " Air Raids : What You Must Know ; What You Must Do " (H.M. Stationery Office).

THE little book should be a best-seller, for it contains a mass of information of what may well prove to be of life-saving value. It gives a full description of incendiary bombs and of the precautions which should be taken against them. Then it goes on to high explosives and tells

where is the safest place when H.E. bombs are dropping (see diagram p. 287, Vol. 3). Next it describes shelters of every kind, Morrison and Anderson, refuge rooms and public shelters. During these cold nights it is useful to know that a simple heater can be made by placing a flower-pot on a couple of bricks to raise it from the ground, placing a lighted candle by the drain hole at the bottom of the flower-pot (without, however, blocking up the hole), and then turning a second flower-pot upside down on top of the first flower-pot, edge to edge. After a time the top flower-pot will give off considerable warmth—sufficient for a small shelter. Other chapters in the book deal with war gases, and the respirators which are a complete protection against them ; simple first-aid ; and lighting restrictions—domestic and vehicle. It is good to see that the compilers of the book have not forgotten that animals, too, are entitled to a share of A.R.P.

LONDONERS LUNCH TO MUSIC

" Dame Myra Hess gave her first formal piano recital yesterday (Nov. 2) since she has become a D.B.E. A full house and an overflow covering half the available stage—chairs then giving out—welcomed her . . . And the great pianist proceeded to play late Beethoven as only she among women pianists can."—Peterborough in the " Daily Telegraph "

MOST music-lovers know how, with the outbreak of war and the consequent enforced change of habits of the London public, Miss Myra Hess (as she then was) decided to cancel her American tour in order to sustain as far as she could the cause of music in England ; and launched in cooperation with the Trustees of the National Gallery the " National Gallery Lunch-Time Concerts." She herself opened proceedings by giving a piano recital on October 10, 1939, and since then, up to the end of October this year, 556 concerts have been given. The attendance has averaged 2,000 per week, and 227,000 people paid for admission ; 1,947 different artists have appeared, and the Musicians' Benevolent Fund, to which all profits go, has benefited by £3,350. While it is safe to say that all artists of any repute in this country have appeared at the concerts, Dame Myra has made it her business to encourage the younger and unknown musicians by regularly sandwiching them in between the " stars."

It is interesting to note that a very large proportion of the audiences at these now famous concerts are in uniform. Yet the B.B.C. is still not convinced apparently that the men (and women) of the Army, Navy, and Air Force feel the need for something more than variety, selections from light opera, and febrile crooning.

One of the 27 sergeant-cameramen who are being sent to the Middle East by the new Army Film and Photo Unit. They are equipped with a miniature still camera, cine-film camera and a revolver. *Photo, Planet News*

IT MUST BE A COMBINED JOB

Until superiority is gained in the air none of our other arms can operate to the full limit of its own power. Then, and not till then, will the general defensive turn to the grand and final offensive.—Colonel Moore-Brabazon, M.P., in a broadcast

BRITAIN'S No. 1 airman, now Minister of Aircraft Production, is undoubtedly right. Without a strong and thoroughly flexible air force, capable of universal application, Britain cannot win this machine war. The bitter lessons of Norway and France and Crete, plus those of the rapidly overrun countries of Europe, have driven home the truth of that doctrine. The full use of the air arm with air superiority, in offence and defence, is essential. One of the brightest aspects of the Libyan offensive is the evidence of air and land cooperation ; the aeroplane is helping the tank and the infantry generously, as well as carrying out at greater distances its own operations, both tactical and strategical. " Hurrybombers " and cannon aircraft strafe the Nazi forces while the tanks engage them, army cooperation and reconnaissance machines are continuously active, and Fortresses deal with the enemy's supply bases in Africa. All this indicates that the higher authorities of the R.A.F., as well as the War Cabinet, have now gained a true sense of proportion. But no one weapon in this war can be supreme, none by itself can win. Tank weeks, air weeks, warship weeks all serve important purposes, but only a full and carefully planned use of all weapons, from battleships to bayonets, can force decisions.

HISTORY REPEATS ITSELF

German troops occupying the inner part of Rostov left in accordance with orders of the German Command, in order to undertake reprisal measures against the Russian civilians who struck at our rear in the city. This form of warfare is new to the German soldier.—Military Spokesman in Berlin, Nov. 29, 1941

" THIS form of warfare is new to the German soldier "—but not to the Russians. In " War and Peace," Tolstoy tells us that in 1812 " the so-called partisan warfare had begun with the enemy's entrance into Smolensk. Before the irregular warfare was officially recognized by our government many thousands of the enemy's soldiers—straggling, marauding or foraging parties—had been slain by Cossacks and peasants. By October there were hundreds of these companies, differing widely from one another in numbers and in character. Some were detachments that followed all the usual routine of an army, with infantry, artillery and staff officers. Some consisted only of Cossacks on horseback. Others were small bands of men on foot and also mounted. Some consisted of peasants, or of landowners and their serfs. There was a deacon at the head of such a band, who took several hundred prisoners in a month. There was the village elder's wife, Vassilissa, who killed hundreds of the French . . . The irregulars destroyed the Grande Armée piecemeal. They swept up the fallen leaves that were dropping of themselves from the withered tree, and sometimes they shook the tree itself." *Sometimes they shook the tree itself !*

Recently there have been unveiled in the church of Little Missenden, Bucks, stained-glass windows depicting the Battle of Britain and, right, the " Miracle of Dunkirk." These great events are realistically treated : bombs, planes, ships and guns in action are all represented, probably for the first time in this medium. The work is by Mr. G. E. R. Smith and commemorates the completion of 50 years' ministry of the Bishop, Rt. Rev. Philip Herbert Eliot, in the County of Buckingham. *Photo, P. H. Lovell*

Naval Air Strength of the Pacific Powers

BRITAIN. The drawing shows a typical modern aircraft carrier of 23,000 tons, 753 feet long and carrying a complement of 1,600. Its armament consists of sixteen 4·5-inch dual-purpose guns and a large number of aircraft are carried. In the drawing can be seen (1) the Blackburn Roc, a two-seater fighter fitted with a power-operated gun-turret, with 4 guns ; (2) a Fairey Fulmar, an eight-gunned two-seat fighter with a 1,145 h.p. Rolls-Royce Merlin engine.

Britain has lost three aircraft carriers. She still has, in commission or building, the Implacable, Indefatigable, Illustrious, Victorious, Formidable, Indomitable, Furious, Eagle and Hermes, in addition to the Argus, a "Queen Bee" tender for training purposes, and the seaplane-carrier Albatross.

U.S.A. The drawing is of the Ranger, U.S. aircraft carrier of 14,500 tons. Her complement is 1,788, she is 769 feet in length and can take about 80 aircraft. The Ranger carries eight 5-inch A.A. guns and 40 smaller ones and her speed is about 30 knots. When not in action the six funnels are raised to the vertical position. Other carriers are the Lexington, Saratoga, Enterprise, Yorktown and Wasp. The Hornet was recently commissioned and eleven 25-26,000-ton carriers of the Essex class are provided for in the current programme.

The planes shown are (3) the Grumman Sky-Rocket, a twin-engined single-seat fighter, and (4) the Curtiss 77 (SBC-4) Helldiver, a two-seat scout-bomber.

JAPAN. Shown in the drawing is the Soryu, one of Japan's latest carriers, sister ships being the Hiryu and the Koryu. These carriers are of 10,050 tons displacement, 688 feet in length and are armed with twelve 5-inch A.A. guns and 24 smaller. They are said to carry 30-40 aircraft. Possibly completed are the 14,000-ton carriers Syokaku and Zuikaku. In addition, there are the Ryuzyo, of 7,100 tons, completed in 1933, and the Hosyo, 7,470 tons. Then there are the older Akagi and Kaga, each of 26,900 tons, originally laid down as a battle cruiser and battleship respectively.

Japan has a number of ex-mercantile vessels of about 6,000 tons, converted into seaplane carriers, the converted tankers Kamoi and Notoro of 17,000 and 14,000 tons, and three seaplane carriers of 9,000 tons, the Titose, Tiyoda and Miduho.

Japan keeps her new types of aircraft a closely guarded secret, but it seems likely that the Mitsubishi Karigane (5), largely used by the Japanese Army Air Corps, could be adapted for deck-landing. It is a two-seat monoplane, the Mark II version of which is fitted with a 800 h.p. Mitsubishi A.14 engine. The single-seat Zero (6), one of Japan's latest fighter planes, closely resembles the Brewster Buffalo. The Mitsubishi 92 (7) is a two-seat reconnaissance monoplane fitted with a 420 h.p. Jaguar engine.

Specially drawn by Haworth for THE WAR ILLUSTRATED

War in the Pacific: Japan Takes the Plunge

So long had the clouds of war lowered above the Pacific that when the storm actually broke it came with all the greater shock. On December 7 Japan declared a state of war against America and Britain. Swiftly the challenge was accepted. The war had become a world war indeed.

WHILE M. Kurusu and Admiral Nomura, the Japanese envoys in Washington, were closeted with the United States Secretary of State, Mr. Cordell Hull, in Washington, Japanese war planes were actually bombing American naval bases in the Pacific. Mr. Hull did not know that, but his remarks were caustic enough. He had in his hands the Japanese reply to his note of November 26, in which he had made proposals for a peaceful settlement in the Pacific in return for promises by Japan to make no further aggressive moves southward or against Russia. "In all my fifty years of public service," he said, referring to the Japanese reply, "I have never seen a document that was more crowded with infamous falsehoods and distortions—on a scale so huge that I never imagined until today that any Government on this planet was capable of uttering them." The Japanese listened and then, with unsmiling faces, left the State Department.

Hardly had they gone when on America descended the tremendous, almost unbelievable tidings that Japan had dared to attack her. The first announcement was given to the press by Mr. Stephen Early, President Roosevelt's secretary, early in the afternoon. "The Japanese have attacked Pearl Harbour from the air, and all naval and military activities on the island of Oahu, the principal base in the Hawaiian Islands." A few minutes later the President issued a further statement: "a second air attack has been reported. This has been made on army and navy bases in Manila, capital of the Philippines." Then from near and far came in news of fresh acts of Japanese aggression. Guam had been bombed, Honolulu was being raided. American warships had been severely damaged, and one was said to have been sunk.

At the White House President Roosevelt held conferences with his service chiefs and called a special cabinet; Mr. Stimson, Secretary of War, mobilized the Army, and Mr. Knox, Navy Secretary, ordered the fleets to action stations. At the same time, President Roosevelt released for publication the text of an appeal to the Japanese Emperor, one which he had sent on Saturday afternoon, December 6, as a last-minute appeal to keep war from the Pacific. It fell on deaf ears, however. The Japanese militarists were in full control, and they had resolved on war.

Swift came the news from the Imperial Japanese Headquarters at Tokyo that as from dawn Japan had entered into a state of war with the United States and Great Britain. "We, by the grace of heaven, Emperor of Japan, seated on the throne of a line unbroken for ages eternal, enjoin upon you, our loyal and brave subjects: we hereby declare war on the United States and the British Empire." The war, went on the rescript, was necessary to "ensure the stability of East Asia and to contribute to world peace."

A month before Mr. Churchill in his Mansion House speech had pledged Great Britain's word that should the United States be involved in war with Japan, the British declaration of war would follow "within the hour." As soon as he received the news of the Japanese aggression against the U.S.A., Mr. Churchill (he told the House of Commons on the afternoon of December 8) telephoned President Roosevelt with a view to arranging the time of the respective declarations. The President told him that he was sending a message to Congress (which alone can make a declaration of war on behalf of the U.S.A.).

"I then assured him we would follow immediately. However, it soon appeared that British territory in Malaya had also been the object of a Japanese attack, and later on it was announced from Tokyo that the Japanese High Command—a curious form, not the Imperial Japanese Government, but the Japanese High Command —had declared that a state of war existed with Great Britain and the United States. That being so, there was no need to wait for the declaration by Congress. The Cabinet, therefore, which met at 12.30 today, authorized the immediate declaration of war upon Japan."

Then the Prime Minister proceeded to read the text of the communication which

M. Saburo Kurusu (right), Japan's special envoy to the U.S.A., on his way to the White House accompanied by Mr. Cordell Hull, U.S. Secretary of State. *Photo, Associated Press*

had been dispatched to the Japanese charge d'affaires at one o'clock. Dated from the Foreign Office, December 8, it read:

On the evening of Dec. 7 his Majesty's Government in the United Kingdom learned that Japanese forces, without previous warning either in the form of a declaration of war or of an ultimatum with a conditional declaration of war, had attempted a landing on the coast of Malaya and bombed Singapore and Hong Kong.

In view of this wanton act of unprovoked aggression committed in flagrant violation of international law, and particularly of Article One of the Third Hague Convention relative to the opening of hostilities, to which both Japan and the United Kingdom are parties, his Majesty's Ambassador at Tokyo has been instructed to inform the Imperial Japanese Government, in the name of his Majesty's Government in the United Kingdom, that a state of war exists between the two countries.

The Netherlands Government, went on the Prime Minister, had declared war on Japan at 3 a.m. Then he told how he had sent a warning to Thailand, that she was in imminent danger of Japanese invasion. "If you are attacked defend yourselves. The preservation of the independence and sovereignty of Thailand is a British interest, and we shall regard attack on you as attack upon ourselves." Chiang Kai-shek, Generalissimo of Free China, had also been assured that henceforth we would face the common foe together. Finally, said the Prime Minister, it was "of the highest importance that there should be no underrating of the gravity of the new dangers we have to meet." The enemy had attacked with an audacity which might spring from recklessness, but which might also spring from a conviction of strength.

"We have at least four-fifths of the population of the globe upon our side. We are responsible for their safety and for their future. In the past we had a light which flickered; in the present we have a light which flames; and in the future there will be a light which shines over all the land and sea."

Shortly afterwards, the Congress of the United States met in joint session at Washington. Mr. Roosevelt took eight minutes to make his historic declaration.

Yesterday, Dec. 7, 1941, a date which will live in infamy, the United States of America was suddenly and deliberately attacked by naval and air forces of the Empire of Japan.

The United States was at peace with that nation, and, at the solicitation of Japan, was still in conversation with its Government and its Emperor looking towards the maintenance of peace in the Pacific.

Indeed, one hour after Japanese air squadrons had commenced bombing in the American island of Oahu, the Japanese Ambassador to the United States and his colleague delivered to our Secretary of State a formal reply to a recent American message, and, while this reply stated that it seemed useless to continue the existing diplomatic negotiations, it contained no threat or hint of war or of armed attack.

It will be recorded that the distance of Hawaii from Japan makes it obvious that the attack was deliberately planned many days, or even weeks, ago. During the intervening time the Japanese Government has deliberately sought to deceive the United States by false statements and expressions of hope for continued peace.

The attack yesterday on the Hawaiian Islands has caused severe damage to American naval and military forces. I regret to tell you that very many American lives have been lost. In addition, American ships have been reported torpedoed on the high seas between San Francisco and Honolulu.

Yesterday the Japanese Government also launched an attack against Malaya. Last night Japanese forces attacked Hong Kong; last night Japanese forces attacked Guam; last night Japanese forces attacked the Philippine Islands; last night the Japanese attacked Wake Island; and this morning the Japanese attacked Midway Island. Japan has therefore undertaken a surprise offensive extending throughout the Pacific area.

The facts of yesterday and today speak for themselves. The people of the United States have already formed their opinions and will understand the implications to the very life and safety of our nation.

As Commander-in-Chief of the Army and Navy, I have directed that all measures be taken for our defence, but always will our whole nation remember the character of the onslaught against us. No matter how long it may take us to overcome this premeditated invasion, the American people in their righteous might will win through to absolute victory.

I believe that I interpret the will of the Congress and of the people when I assert that we will not only defend ourselves to the uttermost, but will make it very certain that this form of treachery shall never again endanger us.

Hostilities exist. There is no blinking at the fact that our people, our territory and our interest are in grave danger. With confidence in our armed forces, with the unbounded determination of the people, we will gain the inevitable triumph, so help us God.

I ask that the Congress declare that since the unprovoked and dastardly attack by Japan on Sunday, Dec. 7, 1941, a state of war has existed between the United States and the Japanese empire.

When the President had finished and was leaving the Chamber, there was a scene of tremendous enthusiasm, and it was noticeable that men who up to the day before had been amongst the most prominent of the Isolationists were now cheering and clapping as vigorously as the rest. Then the Congressmen met in their own Houses to consider the declaration of war resolution. Only 20 minutes after President Roosevelt had sat down, the Senate passed the war resolution by 82 votes to none; and the House of Representatives was almost as quick, but in this case there were 388 votes against one, the solitary dissentient being Mrs. Jeanette Rankin, a Republican pacifist who voted against the entry of America into the first world war in 1917. "Whereas," the declaration read, "the Imperial Japanese Government has committed unprovoked acts of war against the Government and people of the United States of America . . . be it resolved by the Senate and House of Representatives of the United States of America in Congress assembled that a state of war between the United States and the Imperial Japanese Government, which has thus been thrust upon the United States, is hereby formally declared . . ." America was in the war.

Japan's Place in the New Theatre of Conflict

NAVAL BASES
AIR BASES

By courtesy of the "News Chronicle"

JAPAN HAS STRUCK and her entrance into the struggle will involve a vast area of sea and land in totalitarian war. To the north she may well have to reckon with the Soviet Red Banner Far Eastern Armies of a million men, now concentrated on the Manchurian and Russian Siberian frontier. To the south Thailand and Malaya have come into the land fighting, for an attack on the Burma Road is an essential part of Japanese strategy. The naval war must of a surety spread far and wide from north to south and from east to west in the open Pacific, and about the remotest islands held by Japan, Britain, and the United States. Japan has some excellent bases in the

Marianas and Carolines equipped by Nature with deep harbourage ; and Palau, with its deep sheltered lagoon and high hills for shore batteries, can anchor fifty warships comfortably. A big sea battle between Japanese and American Fleets began on December 8 off the coast of Hawaii with heavy losses on both sides, and great damage to Pearl Harbour, U.S. naval base. The American naval base at Guam was "virtually destroyed."

Five years of indecisive war in China have taken a heavy toll of Japanese effectives, but Japan is said to have 2,500,000 under arms, and another 6,000,000 potential reserves. Whether the latter can be fully equipped, however, is the great ques-

tion, Nippon being poor in mechanization and the resources which build and keep the military machine going. Although Japan has begun her war with violent air attacks on Hongkong, Singapore, the Philippines and other places, her air power has not kept pace with Japanese ambitions, and the fact that she is dependent for 90 per cent of her oil supplies on America, the Dutch East Indies and Mexico is a weak point in her programme of aggression. None the less, the extremists of Tokyo have long visualized a vast Japanese empire stretching from the Arctic to the Equator, from which all European and American influence would be excluded.

Into Battle Go Cunningham's Tanks and M

A 60-pounder gun of a Home Counties Yeomanry regiment i
Western Desert, taken during a reconnoitring patrol (abov
scrub.   R.A.F. armoured cars advancing in a forward area of
"shellbacks," and are extensively used

British Br
forces cros
North Cou
bayonets f

rst Photographs of the Great New Offensive

g from under its camouflage netting (left). Tank driver's view of the
er armoured vehicles stand out clearly in the vast expanse of sand and
(right). On account of their carapace of armour they are known as
ard aerodromes among other dangerous tasks.

d through a gap in the barbed wire defences as the first British
wn on Nov. 18 (left). Above, the Company Commander of a
a last-minute inspection of a patrol. Right, British troops, with
gh a smoke-screen during the first stage of the new Libyan battle.

Libya, Phase Two: Battle of the Parallelogram

Although it is not yet possible to write a complete account of the great battle of the Western Desert, sufficient information has come to hand to form a picture of the operations which constituted the opening phases. What follows is based upon official statements issued in London and Cairo and the despatches received from Reuter's correspondents with the British Forces in Libya.

THE Third Battle of Libya opened with a strategical surprise. For months past war material had been pouring into the Middle East and piling up in the Western Desert, and it was obvious to everyone that a great battle was looming. Yet when General Auchinleck gave the order to advance, the Germans were taken by surprise. The British and Imperial troops swept across the frontier wire, poured down from the high ground to the escarpment, rushed across the great minefields cleared by the sappers, and were in among the enemy, behind his main defences in the very centre of his armoured troops, almost before he was aware that zero hour had struck again. But "Old Rommel," as the men of the German Afrika Korps almost affectionately call him, was swift in his recovery. Whatever may be said about the Italians, the Germans rallied immediately and fought back hard. So there began a battle which may be compared to a vast and bloody game of chess—one that is being played out in Central Cyrenaica, between the Egyptian frontier and Tobruk, with thousands of tanks as the key pieces, and troop lorries and supply vehicles as the pawns.

The struggle that ensued has been called the Battle of the Parallelogram, since it was mainly fought in a vast parallelogram in the desert, bounded on the north by a road from Tobruk to Bardia and on the south by the Trigh-el-Abd track, or Slave Road, which runs from El Gobi in the west to Sidi Omar, some 40 miles south of Bardia. When the battle opened on November 18, the enemy infantry, German and Italian, occupied a series of strongly fortified posts between Bardia and Sidi Omar. To the west in the parallelogram were General Rommel's two armoured divisions, while just outside it, beyond the Tobruk-El Gobi track, lay an Italian armoured division—the Ariete.

Our attack was launched with a twofold objective. We had to overcome the Bardia-Sidi Omar line, but this would have been a difficult operation so long as the enemy's armoured forces were intact. Accordingly it was essential to compel these to give battle.

The role assigned, therefore, to our armoured forces was to sweep westwards, south of Sidi Omar along the Trigh-el-Abd, and then to bend northwards towards Tobruk, between the two German armoured divisions and the Italian armoured division. The task of our infantry was, in part, to outflank and roll up the Bardia-Sidi Omar line, and in part to follow up our armoured forces.

The result was that the two German armoured divisions, reinforced by the Italian division from the west of the Tobruk-El Gobi track, were compelled, as planned, to give battle south-east of Tobruk.

So began what may be called the first phase of the Libya battle (see page 327). It was a struggle unlike anything that may be conceived on a European battlefield. All the units engaged were completely motorized

and could range in any direction, regardless of natural obstacles—which, however, in any case were practically non-existent. The desert, indeed, affords as much freedom of movement to motor vehicles as does the sea to men-of-war. So fighting may begin in one area, drift into another miles distant, and may be broken off without decisive result. In this vast battlefield, so stark and strange, there was no recognizable front.

"After passing through miles of country thick with British motor transport, we were about to enter an empty patch of desert when a captain held up his hand and shouted 'Don't go on!' He told us the enemy were directly ahead, and laughed heartily at our ingenuousness, calling to his friends: 'Here's a bunch of crazy war correspondents who wanted to walk right into Jerry's parlour!'"

LIBYAN BATTLEFIELD, scene of fierce tank battles. The arrows show where two Nazi panzer divisions, separated in the first phase of the battle, managed to link up by smashing through the narrow British corridor to Tobruk.
Courtesy of the "Daily Sketch"

Very different is this sort of war from any that has been fought in the past. For instance, in this campaign the generals are in the front line. We are told of a brigadier who led his men into battle in a staff car, and when only 800 yards from 15 German tanks, stood up on the roof to observe the enemy through binoculars. Another commander of one of our tank brigades occupied the gunner's position in a tank, and started the action by himself firing upon the enemy. Yet another commander, a famous fire-eating desert veteran, whose armoured force has been in heavy action since the offensive opened, has almost constantly led his tanks in person.

"It is an amazing sight," says one of his junior officers, "to see him dashing about amidst our tanks in his car and waving the forces forward with a flag. The other day I saw him come alongside one tank, rap on its side with the butt of his flag, and bawl 'blue murder' at the erring tank commander who emerged from the turret. He had just previously received a bit of shrapnel in the shoulder, but refused to stop to have it attended to."

Another contrast is the extraordinary difficulty in refuelling tanks and other vehicles scattered far and wide across the desert; indeed, the whole question of supplies in such a campaign as this is makes the quartermaster's job, as the captured Nazi general, von Ravenstein, said, a nightmare. Yet our supply columns have kept in touch, even though they are deemed the special prey of Rommel's tanks, "armoured corsairs" specially detailed for the purpose. Many

losses have been inflicted by the enemy on our swift-moving columns, but the supply organization is now so vast that, so it is claimed, it would take more tanks than the Germans have in Africa to upset it. Between the battlefield and Egypt (we are told) lie mile upon mile of what was recently enemy territory, but is now covered as far as the eye can reach in any direction with British motor transport, thousands of vehicles with ample room for dispersal between each. The scene is said to be like a great trek to the American West, as envisaged by a Hollywood film director. The lorries with their canvas tops look just like covered wagons, and in between them our A.A. gunners are seated comfortably on portable chairs with guns at the ready. While awaiting the order to set out, drivers while away the time by kicking a football about the sand.

While the terrific clash of the armoured forces was taking place, particularly at Sidi Rezegh—described as being littered for three miles with "tangled wrecks of some panzer regiment, blackened and twisted. Ammunition and petrol lorries, now misshapen hulks of iron, shared the fate of the tanks"—the garrison at Tobruk burst south-eastwards through the invading lines, and joined up with the British force which had advanced from the east and south. The junction was not consolidated, however. This was revealed in a communiqué from Cairo, on Dec. 1.

"In the afternoon of yesterday," it read, "German infantry with tank support again attacked our positions about Sidi Rezegh, where they were successful in making a penetration into our defences." And a further communiqué issued on the following day stated that "Yesterday the enemy threw into the battle all his available armour on a comparatively narrow front. Very heavy fighting throughout the day in the area Rezegh-Bir el Hamid-Zaafran resulted in a junction between the German forces which had advanced from the south and south-west with those originally disposed about Zaafran."

This brings us, then, to the beginning of December, when the position was hardly such as to warrant the optimistic accounts which had emanated from the Military Spokesmen at Cairo in the opening days of the offensive. The Germans had suffered heavy losses in tanks and lorries and in man-power, but so, too, had the British, the New Zealanders operating along the coast, and the South Africans who were literally overrun at Sidi Rezegh by Rommel's tanks during November 21-23, with the loss of some twelve hundred men.

Such had been the fury of the struggle, so heavy the casualties, so wearing the pace of the mechanized forces, that the need for a lull was paramount. For 11 days of desperate tank and infantry battles Cunningham's forces had striven with Rommel's in an attempt to bottle them up and destroy their total armoured strength. In that, so far, they had not succeeded: the link with Tobruk was broken, and Rommel's forces in the desert to the west were once again in contact with his main body in the parallelogram itself. So both armies fell apart like two exhausted wrestlers after a long bout. The first and second rounds, the first and second phases, were over.

Now, rather than continue the guerilla fighting which was as exhausting as inconclusive, the British Command decided to establish its forces along an "offensive line" running from El Gobi to the south-east of Sidi Rezegh. To this line the infantry units retired for a badly needed rest, while within and behind it the tanks were refuelled, regrouped, and overhauled.

Knocking the Stuffing Out of 'Sawdust Caesar'

LEADERS IN LIBYA : Air Vice-Marshal A. Coningham, C.B., D.S.O., M.C., D.F.C., A.F.C., Air Officer Commanding the Western Desert, left, with Acting Air Marshal A. W. Tedder, C.B., Air Officer Commanding-in-Chief, R.A.F., Middle East. In Sicily direct hits on a power station at Porto Empedocle, the port for Girgenti, on the southern coast, send up clouds of yellow and black smoke, right. During the month of November over 1,000,000 bombs were dropped on Italian targets by our aeroplanes operating from R.A.F. bases in Malta.

ITALIAN SUPPLY SHIP of about 1,000 tons caught in the Mediterranean by our bombers. Hits were registered amidships, and the vessel eventually sank after a heavy explosion.

AXIS TRANSPORT vehicle in North Africa before an air attack, above. In the photo below the car has been completely obliterated by a bomb from R.A.F. Mediterranean Command.

IN SOUTH ITALY—at Locri in Calabria—a low-flying medium bomber reduces a war factory to smoke and debris. Pilots reported that they saw people wave to them as they flew over the target.

Photos, British Official : Crown Copyright

Our Diary of the War

WEDNESDAY, NOV. 26, 1941   816th day

Air.—Enemy patrol vessels and barges attacked in the Straits of Dover. Night attack on Emden and N.W. Germany as well as the docks at Ostend.

Russian Front.—Germans made small gains on Moscow front at the price of very heavy losses. Russian advance on Ukraine front.

Africa.—After regrouping and reinforcements on both sides, a second great tank battle began in Libya, mainly around Sidi Rezegh. To the south Indian troops captured Jalo. German armoured column crossed Egyptian frontier south of Sidi Omar, but was attacked and split up.

General. — Lebanese independence proclaimed by Free France.

THURSDAY, NOV. 27   817th day

Air.—Enemy supply ship sunk off The Hague by Beauforts. Enemy convoy off coast of Normandy attacked by Fighter Command, also shipping at Boulogne and aircraft at Berck. Night attacks on Düsseldorf, docks at Ostend and enemy aerodromes.

Russian Front.—Germans claimed capture of Klin, north-west of Moscow, and Tula was almost encircled. Russian counter-drive in Southern Ukraine continued.

Mediterranean.—Night raid on Naples by R.A.F. Royal Arsenal hit.

Africa.—Elements of British main forces in Libya linked up with detachments advancing from Tobruk. Sidi Rezegh lost and recaptured. In Abyssinia, Gondar, the last Italian stronghold, surrendered.

Home.—Few raiders over East Anglia and S. Coast by night.

FRIDAY, NOV. 28   818th day

Russian Front.—Further Russian advance in the Southern Ukraine. Soviet troops recaptured several villages to the north-west of Moscow. Slight Russian advance on Leningrad front.

Africa.—Axis forces contained east of a line Tobruk-Sidi Rezegh reorganized for an attempt to break out. Italian Bologna division badly cut up in an action east of Tobruk. British forces captured Bir el Hamid. Heavy night raid on moles, shipping, and stores at Benghazi.

Home.—Slight enemy activity by night over S. Wales and S.W. England.

General.—More reinforcements reached Singapore for the Malaya Command. Two German soldiers killed in a Paris restaurant.

SATURDAY, NOV. 29   819th day

Sea.—Admiralty communiqué announced that H.M. submarine Tigris had sunk 5 enemy ships and seriously damaged a sixth and that H.M. submarine Trident had sunk 3 enemy ships and seriously damaged 4 others in the Arctic. Two were transports packed with troops for the Murmansk front.

Russian Front.—Soviet forces crossed the Don and drove the Germans out of Rostov. Von Kleist's army forced to retreat in disorder towards Taganrog. Russians recaptured several villages south-east of Kalinin.

Africa.—Big new tank battle began. Gen. Von Ravenstein, commander of the 21st German Panzer division, captured. British patrols reached Cyrenaican coast between Jedabia and Benghazi. Night raids by R.A.F. on Derna and Benghazi.

General.—All leave for British troops in Singapore stopped. Two more Germans soldiers killed by an explosion in Paris.

SUNDAY, NOV. 30   820th day

Air.—Over 150 tons of bombs dropped on Hamburg, one of the many targets of Bomber Command's night attacks. Emden, Bremerhaven, Wilhelmshaven, Kiel, and Lübeck also bombed.

Russian Front.—Marshal Timoshenko's armies steadily pursued Von Kleist's forces towards Taganrog and drove back Hun-

garian and Rumanian troops in Donetz Basin. Little change on Moscow front, where the Germans claimed the capture of Volokolamsk. Russians admitted loss of Tikhvin.

Africa.—R.A.F. announced that from start of Libyan battle to midnight on Nov. 30, 176 enemy aircraft had been destroyed for certain. Furious tank battle continued near Sidi Rezegh. Heavy night raid by R.A.F. on Benghazi.

MR. CHURCHILL'S MESSAGE

On the Eve of the Libyan Offensive of Nov. 18, 1941

I HAVE it in command from the King to express to all ranks of the Army and R.A.F. in the Western Desert, and to the Mediterranean Fleet, his Majesty's confidence that they will do their duty with exemplary devotion in the supremely important battle which lies before them.

For the first time British and Empire troops will meet the Germans with an ample equipment in modern weapons.

The battle itself will affect the whole course of the war. Now is the time to strike the hardest blow yet struck for final victory, home and freedom.

The Desert Army may add a page to history which will rank with Blenheim and with Waterloo. The eyes of all nations are upon you. All our hearts are with you. May God uphold the right.

MONDAY, DEC. 1   821st day

Sea.—A surface force under Capt. Agnew in H.M.S. Aurora sank two Italian supply ships and the escorting destroyer Alvise da Mosto in the Mediterranean.

Air.—Hudson aircraft of Coastal Command made night raid on docks at Kristiansund, Norway.

Russian Front.—Russians continued their advance in the Rostov sector. Moscow thrusts held. Germans claimed capture of Balaclava, in Crimea.

Africa.—Hard fighting still going on at Sidi Rezegh. Forces of 15th Panzer division succeeded in getting through to the west before British closed gap between Tobruk and Sidi Rezegh. Italian Ariete division suffered heavy losses.

Home.—Bombs dropped on S.W. Coast town after dark. One enemy raider destroyed. H.M.S. Mendip shot down a Heinkel 111 off East Coast.

General.—State of Emergency proclaimed in Singapore and the Federated Malay States. Pétain and Darlan had a secret

meeting with Goering at St. Florentin-Vergigny, 80 miles S.E. of Paris.

TUESDAY, DEC. 2   822nd day

Sea.—Powerful units of Britain's Eastern Fleet arrived at Singapore. Australian Government announced loss of H.M.A.S. Sydney after she had sunk the German armed merchantman Steiermark.

Russian Front.—Rostov pursuit of Nazis continued. Soviet troops sweeping southwest from Voroshilovgrad drove Italian and Hungarian troops towards Saalino, 100 miles north-west of Rostov.

Africa.—Rommel succeeded in breaking through the Tobruk corridor and linking up his 15th and 21st Panzer Divisions. Germans recaptured Sidi Rezegh and Bir el Hamid. Command H.Q. at Nairobi announced that enemy prisoners taken at Gondar numbered 11,500 Italian and 12,000 native troops. The attacking force numbered less than half the enemy.

Home.—Enemy activity at night over S.W. England. Two enemy raiders destroyed. Mr. Churchill described Government's new man-power policy in the House of Commons.

General.—Italian official Stefani agency reported a " vast conspiracy against the State." Three Axis divisions reported engaged against Serbian forces in Western Moravia.

WEDNESDAY, DEC. 3   823rd day

Russian Front.—Soviet troops, pursuing Von Kleist's army, reached Taganrog. On the Moscow front Soviet troops recaptured several villages in the Kalinin sector.

Africa.—Slackening in tempo of Libyan battle pending new phase of the battle.

General. — Washington revealed that Turkey had for some time been receiving Lease-Lend aid from U.S.A.

THURSDAY, DEC. 4   824th day

Russian Front.—Russians in Taganrog. Russian cavalry occupied Khartsissk, 50 miles north-west of Rostov. In Moscow sector, heavy fighting around Mojaisk. Soviet forces recaptured some positions near Tikhvin, on Leningrad front. New Russian counter-offensive in Arctic Karelia.

Africa.—Lull in the fighting continued. Extremely bad weather conditions hampered operations. Much patrol activity.

General.—In India, Pandit Jawaharlal Nehru, former President of Congress, was released from prison. Fighting between Serbs and Axis forces continued in Moravia.

H.M.A.S. SYDNEY, 6,830-ton cruiser of the Royal Australian Navy, was lost, presumably by an explosion following a hit, after sinking the armed German raider Steiermark of 9,400 tons. On July 19, 1940, she sank the Italian cruiser Bartolomeo Colleoni and damaged another. Inset shows the Sydney's crest. *Badge, copyright by H.M. Stationery Office; Photo, Wright & Logan*

Men and Machines that Rule the Desert Sky

NIGHT FIGHTERS have played an important part in the Libyan battle in which the air cooperation of the R.A.F. has proved of such immense value. Aircraft of a night fighter squadron operating in the Middle East are seen, right, flying in formation above a layer of cloud.

Wing Commander R. G. YAXLEY, M.C., D.F.C., has been awarded the D.S.O. for courageous leadership in connexion with the magnificent achievement of the Beaufighters of the R.A.F., which, up to November 27, had destroyed at least 44 enemy aircraft since the battle of Libya began. Below, close-up of the nose of a Beaufighter, showing the long chord engine cowlings.

Photos, British Official: Crown Copyright

The crew of a Glenn Martin bomber of the S.A.A.F. buckling on their parachutes before taking off on a raid, above. Below, one of the Tomahawks which have wrought havoc among the tanks and transport columns of General Rommel, and shot down many enemy aircraft.

'Hercules' of Today on the Factory Line

A battery of crank-case drilling machines at a factory producing Bristol Hercules engines, such as are fitted to the Bristol Beaufighter and Short Stirling. The Hercules is a 14-cylinder radial sleeve-valve engine.

The Hercules Mark III is one of the most powerful air-cooled motors in the world. Its fourteen cylinders, as shown above, are arranged in two banks. An impressive characteristic of this engine is its cleanness and simplicity.

Below, a mechanic fits up a Hercules engine on the test bench ready for its trials. The Hercules III is rated at about 1,375 h.p., and to give best performance at height and near the ground it has a two-speed supercharger and controllable pitch airscrews are fitted.

This view along the finishing line at a Ministry of Aircraft Production shadow factory shows Hercules engines being completed. The finished product is seen in the foreground and its size may be gauged by the standing figures.

A transport driver (in civilian life a silk weaver) takes a new Hercules engine to the test bench. The efficiency and reliability of aero-engines such as this make possible the fine performance of British aircraft.

Photos, Keystone P.N.A., G.P.U. and " Daily Mirror "

Your Waste Paper Is Wanted—for Shells!

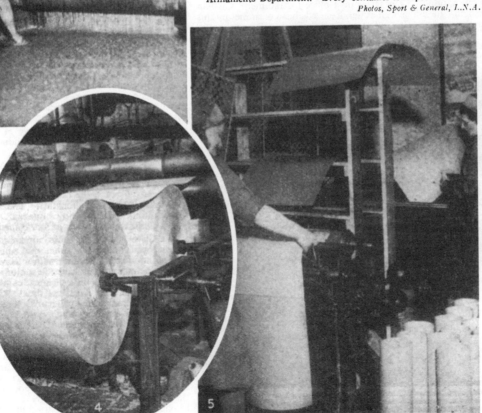

JUST one of the thousand ways in which waste paper can help—and help tremendously—to win the war is illustrated in this page. When the waste paper is collected, either by the Council lorry or by Boy Scouts doing their day's "good turn," (1) it is taken down river—we are speaking of London—to one of the great salvage dumps (2). Then it is passed through a variety of processes, including refining (3), which ensures that there are no lumps left. Eventually the mass of waste paper, made up of torn-up letters, old envelopes, scraps of newspaper, bits of cardboard, and so on— waste of the lowest grade, No. 13—is converted into "board," which has a variety of wartime uses. In the case in point huge rolls are taken to a factory where ammunition containers are being made in vast quantities. There it is cut into sheets by power-driven machines (4), or by machines worked by girls (5). At this stage the sheets are glued together and made into rolls, but before they are fit to receive the shells they have to pass through more processes. Roll is placed in roll, bottoms and lids are attached, and web handles affixed by girls' nimble hands. Some of the work involved is exceedingly dirty, e.g. dipping the containers in wax and painting them, but for the most part it is done by women and girls.

The basic wage is 33s. 6d., plus a production bonus, depending upon the output of the individual "shop" but averaging 18s. Women employed on "dirty work" get £1 per week extra. The finished containers (6) have to be passed by a woman inspector of the Chief Inspectorate of Armaments Department. Every container is inspected and stamped before it is issued to Ordnance

Photos, Sport & General, I.N.A.

'Friendly Places' for Britain's Serving Men

Of the ills that beset the soldier—the sailor and the airman, too, for that matter—boredom is one of the worst. How shall he spend the hours which separate the last parade from Lights out? Here in this article by the Rev. Townley Lord, D.D., the well-known Baptist minister, we are told something of the great work done by the Y.M.C.A. and other voluntary organizations.

IT is an accepted principle of modern warfare that soldiers, sailors and airmen need and repay careful attention to their general well-being. Recently an R.A.F. officer was arranging for some of his men on leave to have accommodation. They were pilots and observers, and the officer was heard to remark : " These boys cost a lot to train and every one of them is very valuable : we ought to look after them in the best possible way."

Today the men and women who compose our fighting and associated services are fortunate in the organizations which minister to their needs. There are, of course, official services maintained as part of the general administration, such as N.A.A.F.I., the concert parties organized by E.N.S.A., and so on.. But a very considerable amount of comfort and good cheer is provided by organizations such as the Church Army, the Salvation Army, and the Y.M.C.A.

In the struggle of 1914-18 these organizations made a fine and widely appreciated contribution to the general welfare of the troops. When the present conflict began their activities were again directed towards serving the national need. How well and valiantly those needs were met is illustrated by the story of canteen service prior to the collapse of France and in the evacuation of Dunkirk ; but since that time, as our national effort had steadily gained strength, these varied ministries have increased their range and effectiveness.

Following the tendency of modern warfare, these various services have become "mobile."

The Y.M.C.A. has at the present time over 800 mobile canteens serving isolated units, gun crews, searchlight companies, balloon barrage groups and men in lonely defence posts. Salvation Army canteens were prominent in Greece, twelve of them, indeed, being lost in that epic campaign. The Church Army has 100 mobile canteens estimated to reach over 100,000 men every week.

FROM A Y.M.C.A. VAN, Commander F. Hallows, R.N. (retd.), serves buns and tea to men of the Forces. He is 65, and is believed to be the oldest voluntary helper driving a Y.M.C.A. tea car.
Photo, L.N.A.

A mobile canteen is a sort of travelling universal provider : it combines the restaurant, the general store and the library ; it can even act as post office for the men. Civilian as well as Service needs have been met by this fleet of motorized helpers. During heavy raids on our towns and cities these canteens have been much in evidence. In one Midland city, for instance, following a raid, a single group of canteens provided over 70,000 meals for the homeless.

Even more imposing than the work of these mobile units is the service rendered by the various centres in camps, billeting areas, railway stations, docks, etc. The Y.M.C.A. alone reports 1,134 of these centres in Great Britain and Northern Ireland. The Church Army has 150, while the Salvation Army has 500, stretching from Iceland to Singapore and serving, it is estimated, between two and three million men and women of the Forces every week. The Y.M.C.A. has centres as far afield as Iceland, the Middle East, Iraq, India, Burma and Malaya.

These organizations, of course, have a strong religious basis, and while it is never obtruded on men and women whose needs at the moment when they make their way to the huts may be primarily physical, there are always well-organized facilities for the culture of the mind and for religious activities. The Y.M.C.A. is especially prominent at the present time through its educational programme. It has a trained staff of organizers, including a large proportion of university men. At least 250 lectures are given every week in Y.M.C.A. centres, and there are discussions, dramatic readings, musical circles and popular concerts. There is a strong demand for classical music as well as jazz, and for lectures on serious literary themes.

Side by side with this goes work of a definitely religious nature, for these organizations cooperate effectively with the chaplains. Sunday services, week night gatherings, community hymn-singing go on in the Church Army, the Salvation Army and the Y.M.C.A. The first-named organization in particular has extended this service to the civilian population. Nightly services in public air-raid shelters are a feature of London life today.

A recent venture is the provision of clubs and hostels both for officers and non-commissioned ranks. The Canadian Y.M.C.A. has made great strides in this direction. Near one of the London railway termini a Salvation Army hostel provides accommodation for officers at the rate of five shillings for private room and breakfast. The same organization has recently opened Red Shield Clubs for the wives of servicemen.

Are these varied activities appreciated ? If you want to know, watch the constant flow of inquirers at the Information Bureaux. Watch the men as they leave the stations and make a bee-line for the nearest canteens. As one of the men described them, " they are friendly places where you can get together, have a meal, enjoy a song, write a letter, and generally feel ' at home.' " It is a great job they are doing in crowded camps, at the ports, in lonely outposts, on desert sands, in bleak Iceland, and in blitzed civilian areas. This is certainly religion in action. When the full story comes to be written we shall learn of tireless service that goes round the clock, of hardships willingly embraced, of courage that can go the extra mile, and of heroism under fire.

SALVATION ARMY workers loading supplies on to a canteen train. This is one of four hundred trains equipped with portable canteens for the troops, details of which were given in Vol. 4, p. 138. The service is run jointly by the Army Welfare authorities, the Salvation Army and Y.M.C.A., with the cooperation of the L.M.S. Railway.
Photo, Fox

'Neath Tropic Palms Toil the Gordons

GORDON HIGHLANDERS, though you would never guess their regiment from this unorthodox kit, are here seen in the Far East making defence obstacles from tree trunks felled in the neighbourhood. British, Imperial, Indian and Malay troops are now established in force at various strategic points in the Far East and have had intensified training in the science of jungle warfare. Japanese forces are now attacking our positions in Malaya, but the Gordons are not likely to be caught napping. Their motto is " Bydand "—" Watchful."

Photo, British Official: Crown Copyright

I Was There! ....Eye Witness Stories of the War

'Your Bren Gun Carrier Shot Up My Car'

First German general to be captured by the British in this war was General von Ravenstein, Commander of the 21st German Panzer Division, who was "put in the bag" in the course of the battle outside Tobruk. Here is his story, as told to the B.U.P. correspondent.

ANY commander who wants to be successful must know the ground over which his troops are fighting. I was out on reconnaissance in my car in the El Duda area where I intended to launch certain operations.

In the course of my scouting I crossed a ridge over which I couldn't see, and had the misfortune to run into a British Bren gun carrier, which shot up my car and wounded my driver. [A later report had it that the carrier was manned by some of General Freyberg's New Zealanders; the general's car had been previously shot up by the R.A.F. and by Indian troops.] I had no choice but to give myself up. It is something which might happen to anyone in this damned desert.

The desert is a perfect battle ground for armoured forces such as are engaged at present. The way I was captured shows the difficulties of this kind

of campaign. Rapid manoeuvres make it a game of surprises, a paradise for a tactician, but a nightmare for a quartermaster.

The scene on the flight deck of H.M.S. Ark Royal as she listed over after being torpedoed. Men can still be seen at their posts in the superstructure while airmen and ratings are clustered around the ship's planes. See also pp. 342-3. *Photo, British Official*

monkeys the men began to slip down to the destroyer's forecastle. I walked forward, found a clear space, and in turn slipped down fifteen feet of rope to the destroyer. From there I saw a scene I shall never forget.

From the flight deck 60 feet above us, from the boat deck and the weather deck, men were swarming down ropes dressed in all kinds of clothes. Many were half naked. Those on the ship were waving and cracking jokes with others who were already safe down the ladder. From the flight deck swung a 17-stone lieutenant-commander, red-faced and jovial. "Come on, landlord," called a voice.

'We Realized the Ark Royal Was Finished'

Torpedoed in the Western Mediterranean on November 13, the famous aircraft-carrier Ark Royal sank on the following day while she was being towed to Gibraltar. Reuter's special correspondent, who was on board the Ark when she was torpedoed, tells this vivid story of her end.

I WAS in my cabin washing before going in to tea when a torpedo hit us amidships on the starboard side. There was a sudden shuddering crash. The lights went out. I was flung against the wall. For fully a minute the ship shuddered like a harp string.

Grabbing a lifebelt I ran out along the passageway. In the dim light I saw the officers and ratings filing up the ladders leading to the upper deck. Often I have heard of the coolness of Navy men in a crisis,

and these men were as calm as though they were going down the gangway at Gibraltar.

I arrived on the quarter-deck to find a score of officers pumping up their lifebelts. The Ark Royal was listing alarmingly to starboard, and the white waves flowing past were ominously stained with dark brown oil. The fuel in the engines was still driving us forward, but every minute the deck slant increased till it was difficult to stand upright.

Suddenly the vibration of the engines beneath our feet died away, restarted for a moment, and then stopped. We glanced at one another, and then through the loudspeaker above us came the words, "Everybody to the port side." Almost before we could move came the voice again : "Prepare to abandon ship."

We reached the boat stations on the weather deck and found that it was impossible, owing to the heavy list, to launch the motor-boats. Crowding the decks were hundreds of the ship's crew, some in overalls and some in underwear. Ropes began to snake down from the flight deck, and cork rafts splashed into the sea.

Then we saw a destroyer pulling in alongside. An officer ordered the men to form up four deep, and although, for aught they knew, the ship might have heeled over and gone down any moment, they obeyed instantly. Soon the destroyer came close under our rails. Ropes leaped up from her and were caught and made fast. "First men over," ordered an officer. Like agile

Towards the bows I could see men in rubber boats and one or two swimming in the water. Whalers launched from the ship were already picking them up. For nearly an hour men slid down ropes till the decks forward were packed with men.

Then we heard a piercing whistle. Gazing upward we saw the captain's head over the edge of the flight deck. Cupping his hands, he shouted to the men to go aft and make room for their comrades. The Ark Royal seemed to have steadied. The captain, certain senior officers and engineer officers with a strong body of men remained.

As we veered away from the side we realized how severely hit she was. She lay at a steep angle to the water which suggested a motor-car on the road with both wheels off. Hissing clouds of steam were pouring from her. Silently we gazed at her.

Destroyers were now circling the stricken

Gen. VON RAVENSTEIN, commander of the German 21st Panzer Division in Libya, the story of whose capture by a British Bren gun carrier is given above. *Photo, E.N.A.*

Capt. L. E. H. MAUND, Captain of H.M.S. Ark Royal, the last moments of which are related in this page by Reuter's special correspondent aboard her. *Photo British Official*

carrier, to prevent any attack on the Ark Royal again. Not until darkness hid their ship did the officers and men of the Ark Royal seek warmth below decks from the biting wind.

Two hours later we heard the joyful thrill of a voice calling all the remaining members of the engine-room staff to return aboard the ship. One of the Navy's small craft drew alongside by the light of torches, and burly stokers scrambled eagerly over the rails from the deck. Smoke from the Ark Royal's funnel was black against the sky, billowing over the ship. Against the faint glow of the lights of Gibraltar, which she was trying to make so desperately, we could see the dark bulk of the carrier.

We returned below, and then the ship increased her speed and we were told we were on the way to Gibraltar. Two tugs were then towing the Ark Royal and destroyers and other small craft were standing by. At Gibraltar the survivors were farmed out to the various ships in the harbour at breakfast-time. We saw the destroyers returning and thought the Ark Royal would be home soon.

There was stunned silence among those of her officers in the ship when they were told gently by another officer that she had sunk 25 miles away.

From one of her engineer officers I heard of the fight to save her. " We found the switchboard smashed," he said, " but managed to get the dynamos working with portable apparatus. We got the pumps started, but the water was rising fast. The captain called for steam in the remaining boilers. We managed to get some steam up, but after a while the gauges fell, the lights dimmed, and we knew we had set ourselves a hopeless task. After receiving our report the captain ordered everybody to abandon ship. A destroyer came alongside and took us off.

Just before she sank she had a list to starboard of 35 degrees. We realized she was finished. She toppled over like a tired child. Her stern reared up for a moment and then gently she slid beneath the waves."

Radio Officer IAN A. PHILLIPS of the Mercantile Marine, who was torpedoed three times in a month, relates some of his thrilling experiences below.

I Was Torpedoed Twice in One Morning

Torpedoed three times within a month—twice in one morning—Ian A. Phillips, a young radio officer in Britain's Mercantile Marine, spent 15 days in an open boat on the Atlantic and travelled something like 1,000 miles before he reached the safety of Ireland's north-west coast. The story of his experiences, exclusive to " The War Illustrated," is told below.

I JOINED my ship, of which I was chief radio officer, in August, and we left England in convoy three days later. We had been at sea some days when German aircraft bombed the convoy in the late afternoon, and in the evening a submarine attacked and sank one of the escort ships.

The next day submarines again attacked the convoy, and just after three o'clock in the morning my ship caught two torpedoes. She sank in fifteen seconds. I was blown through the deck-head of the radio room on to the main deck. I jumped into the sea. It was fortunate I had my life-jacket on as I cannot swim. I floated around for about two and a half hours before being picked up by one of the other ships in the convoy. Two days later the convoy was again attacked by submarines and also bombed by a Focke-Wulf Kondor, but my own ship got through safely to Lisbon.

I signed on with this ship as third mate and we proceeded to Gibraltar to join another convoy. We sailed in September. After being shadowed by a German aeroplane, we were again attacked by submarines when we had been at sea about a week. On the second day of the attack, ten minutes after midnight, my ship was torpedoed and sank within an hour and a half. I jumped overboard before she went down and was in the water four and a half hours before being picked up by a ship's lifeboat. We got aboard at about 5 a.m. At 6.30 a.m. this ship, too, was torpedoed and sunk. Again I had to jump for it, and it was once more my life-jacket that saved me. I was picked up by the ship's lifeboat at eight o'clock.

There were 22 of us in the boat, packed like sardines, and the seas were running high in a north-westerly gale. At 8.30 a.m. we sighted a warship and burnt signal flares, but we were not observed, and the chances of rescue faded out as the ship disappeared. We put out a sea anchor and hove to as the weather was bad. Next day the weather was still bad. We opened a case of 6-lb. tins of corned beef. It had had canvas nailed about it as a protection against the weather, but the nails had entered the tins and the meat was bad and useless. We were still hove to.

The following day we hoisted sail and headed for the Portuguese coast, but the next day we were running before a north-west gale and shipping plenty of water. Four days after the sinking, a Welsh fireman died.

The wind changed to the south, and as it kept in this quarter the following day we decided to make for Ireland. For four days we made good progress. Then an Arab fireman died. We were all getting a bit weary by now. No one had slept and no one had been dry since we got into the lifeboat. We looked a queer lot with our bearded faces and increasing thinness.

Though we made good progress, the weather continued bad. The waves were between 30 and 40 feet high, and the boat took some holding. We shipped plenty of water. Later the waves were shorter and steeper, a sure sign of shallower water, and we began to look for a sight of land. Rain fell during the night, but we welcomed this, for we spread a sail and had a good drink. Our daily ration of food was half a biscuit and an eggcupful of water.

A Filipino sailor died that day. The next day there was still no sign of ship or land. Then, two days later, we saw the light of the Slyne Head lighthouse. It was a cheering sight, but the seas were the worst I have seen for years and the coastline was bad, all rocks. At 9.43 a.m. after being at sea in an open boat for fifteen days, and covering approximately 1,400 nautical miles, we landed on a small patch of sandy beach at Keerenmaur, near Clifden, Galway, Eire, and were lifted from the boat by fishermen, who gave us hot tea, milk and whisky.

I Met 'Captain Cortez' Just Back from Tobruk

Not long ago the special correspondent of the " Daily Mail " in Alexandria interviewed a Spanish captain who had just been congratulated by Adml. Sir Andrew Cunningham on the completion of his 25th voyage to Tobruk as the master of a cargo steamer.

LET us call him Capt. Cortez. I wish I could relate the story of his last trip to Tobruk as he told it to me, in a mixture of Spanish, French and English, with a wealth of gesture and pantomime which made him leap from one side of his battered little bridge to the other.

Attacked three times during daylight on the last day, shelled as she entered the harbour, and bombed and shelled at intervals throughout the night and next day, his ship nevertheless discharged her cargo.

When I offered my congratulations to this sturdy little band on the way they stuck their job, Capt. Cortez said : " Why, it is nothing to us. We have nothing more to lose except our lives."

He was more in his element talking of how they clipped pieces off the wing of one of three attacking Messerschmitt 109s.

" We no can see them," he said, " but I get my big gun straight in sun because I know they are there. I am all time working machine-gun, swinging it in figure of eight to throw cone of bullets where they must be. Then I hear noise them diving, but still no see. I tell my first officer, ' Wait. No fire yet.' He want to fire. I say : ' No. Noise get louder.' First one machine come one side us and drop bombs ; then another come other side. His bombs fall only 20 yards away. Then third machine come straight. I see him. I say ' Fire.' Gun go.

" He almost over funnel when he turn, but pieces from his starboard wing drop off and one fall on our deck. Beautiful ! He go wobbling away, getting lower and lower.

" In the bows my man is working another machine-gun when piece cannon-shell go through his thigh. ' Stick it,' I cry, but poor fellow he presently faint and fall beside his gun. He all right in hospital now. I stop his bleeding with bottle peroxide hydrogen and put him sleep with bottle whisky "

SKIPPER MAX, who commanded a German U-boat in the last war (left), now an anti-Nazi, has, like the " Captain Cortez " mentioned in this page, been running a transport between British bases and Tobruk.
Photo, British Official

Editor's Postscript

THE rich Indo-China possessions of the disintegrating French Colonial Empire are being impudently grabbed by the Japs from the palsied hand of Pétain, while the traitor Darlan is conspiring for Nazi dominion over all French North-West Africa. In our issue of July 5, 1940, my keen personal interest in that region of overseas France led me to write an article expressing my faith in the patriotism of the colonial governors and military leaders of Morocco, Algeria and Tunisia being able to rally their provinces to the eventual rescue of the Motherland—nothing but a willingness to be defeated need have held them down. Alas, eighteen months later the will to lose has prevailed. In that time Britain has gone from strength to strength in withstanding the hammerings of the Hun upon her great cities and countryside, while steadily arming herself for that great day, which is drawing nearer, when our resolve to rid the world of Nazi tyranny will be crowned with abiding victory—a victory in which, to the sorrow and shame of all good Frenchmen, the worse elements of their countrymen will have no part save that of traitors planning for the defeat of Britain and the Free French forces who are so loyally cooperating for her survival and their own vindication.

JUST what sort of Colonial Empire will be saved for a France that cannot save anything for herself—her honour least of all—no one can define with any confidence of prevision. But when I heard today that the Japs were pouring troops into Saigon, with a view to threaten or attack Thailand, the first thing that came to my mind had nothing whatever to do with the War. It was an instance of human heartlessness exceeding any that I have ever known. I read it years ago in "L'Illustration," where the story and pictures filled a large page. Somewhere in the region of Saigon the French had a leper settlement for the natives. The narrator visited this and was astonished to find a young French boy among the afflicted and abandoned natives. His conductor told him the boy's story. A French couple of the commercial class who had lived some years in Saigon discovered one day to their chagrin that their child of four or five had somehow become a leper—an extremely rare occurrence. So they simply sold up everything they possessed and cleared away, leaving no address or clue to their whereabouts, after abandoning the little chap in some jungle land not far from the leper encampment. He had been found, and here he was, now eight or nine years old, with the fell disease slowly eating away his hands and toes! That was all; but I can never quite get that horrific page of "L'Illustration" out of my thought when I read of Saigon

FROM what one reads and the pictures one sees of Murmansk and Archangel it would be natural to imagine that few days of the long and bitter Arctic winter in these regions would be free from snowfalls. Yet a

colleague of mine, who spent a whole year of his military service at Archangel during the last War, surprised me the other day with the information that he never saw a snowfall or snowstorm there. So far as he could determine, the snow, once the short summer had come and gone, simply "arrived" in the coldest hours of night on the low-lying land along the banks of the Dvina—it never thins from the distant hills that rim the river valley and its fertile plain of wheatland. Once it has arrived in this surreptitious way it stays for the eight or nine months of winter. "But I never saw it snowing in the daytime," my friend insists. And life is quite tolerable, as there are no rains to thaw the snow and

Rear-Adml. SIR TOM PHILLIPS, who has been appointed Commander-in-Chief Eastern Fleet, was previously Vice-Chief of Naval Staff. He is 53 and only 5 ft. 4 ins. in height.
Photo, Bassano

turn it into slush or ice, just illimitable dry, powdery whiteness, which can be banked up and cleared for tracks. They have even electric tramcars in Archangel !

WENT into my library today just as the one o'clock news was coming through . . . "and this is Wilfred Pickles reading it." For the moment I was more interested in Wilfred Pickles than in the news. I had read about this new announcer, and I now listened to him for the first time with rising pleasure. Here was a manner of speech that gave pungency to the English phrases which the announcer was transferring from the typed sheet to the sound waves that carried his living, lively, rhythmic utterances through the ether. There may be a certain art in achieving this naturalness, but it is perfectly concealed, as art should be in speaking and acting. But more probably there is nothing of the kind: it is merely the natural, unaffected utterance

of a man who despises frills and affectations and talks to the microphone as he might talk to you or me. And that goes for Bruce Belfrage also. There are announcers so faultlessly correct according to the approved standards of diction that you can't tell one from t'other—at least I can't, for I have often been wrong in anticipating their vocal "signatures." If the B.B.C. will only encourage individuality in its regular announcers—the speech of its occasional broadcasters it cannot control—it will be doing a good service to the public. For due observance of the rules of correct speech need not, indeed, should not, smother the individuality of the speaker.

AND now, as we go to press the news that we are actually at war with Finland, Hungary, Rumania and Japan since our last issue indicates the ever-increasing speed and spread of the Maelstrom of War which now whirls over every continent and sea on this planet. Before the present number reaches the hands of its readers even some of the fast fading neutrals may have been engulfed. The treachery of Japan was only to be expected and has its merits in its reactions on the United States—where are the Isolationists now ?

JAPAN's criminal folly (at the bidding of Hitler) will prove her cardinal error—an error that may affect a peace-loving world as a powerful cathartic. That race of little yellow men—mere apes of Western culture in all their larger activities—have blindly taken the first step towards national hara-kiri.

IN old Japan of the Ronin and the Samurai, before modern science and invention put into their nimble monkey hands the means and methods for effecting good or evil on a vast scale, they had a code of honour and a secluded god incarnated in the unseen person of the Mikado, the act of hara-kari, or self-disembowelling, to assert one's "honour" was a commonplace. But with their whilom god dressed in military uniform and publicly appearing as the leader of a rapacious, ravening, military power, eager to subject the peace-loving races of the east so that the Japs might lord it over all the Orient, how changed the scene! Yet as the Spanish say, "a monkey dressed in silk is still a monkey." And this new Japan, with all the accoutrement of scientific destruction in her greedy paws, which she will use with the atrocity of a wild animal gone mad, will eventually find her only honour in self-destruction.

GENERATIONS of British traders, officials, and sojourners in the East have borne testimony to the deceit and trickery of the Japanese—the only real "yellow peril" that has ever existed, for the Chinese are as noted for their peaceful disposition as their envious enemies of the islands for their aggressive spirit. Never has the innate treachery of these swaggering invaders of China been so completely illustrated as in their method of making war on Britain and America under cover of peaceful talks at Washington. They have gone one step beyond Hitler, and many steps back to the barbarism of the Mongol Khans.

Printed in England and published on the 10th, 20th, and 30th of each month by the Proprietors, The Amalgamated Press, Ltd., the Fleetway House, Farringdon Street, London, E.C.4. Registered for transmission by Canadian Magazine Post. Sole Agents for Australia and New Zealand : Messrs. Gordon & Gotch, Ltd. ; and for South Africa : Central News Agency, Ltd. December 20th, 1941. S.S. *Editorial Address :* JOHN CARPENTER HOUSE, WHITEFRIARS, LONDON E.C.4.

Vol 5 *The War Illustrated* Nº 116

Edited by Sir John Hammerton

FOURPENCE

DEC. 30TH, 1941

AT SINGAPORE Indian troops arrive to take part in the defence of the great fortress-port. An island of many warriors, including English, Scottish, Australian, Sikhs, Gurkhas and Malays, Singapore has been assembling its forces from all parts of the Empire. Many of these men have been in action against the Japanese troops who succeeded in making landings on the beaches in the north of the Peninsula, and heavy fighting has taken place amid Malayan swamps and jungles.

Photo, British Official: Crown Copyright

NO. 117 WILL BE PUBLISHED SATURDAY, JAN. 10, 1942

WE ARE GOING TO WIN THE WAR—AND PEACE

THE first world war began with a shot fired by a Balkan terrorist. The second will be dated from the bombing of Pearl Harbour by Japanese aircraft dispatched by the war lords of Tokyo, those terrorists of the Orient, while the emissaries of their Emperor were still speaking peace in the corridors of Washington. That was the spark that set all the continents aflame. Hitler made Europe a battlefield ; it was left to Tojo and his fellow militarists to fire the Americas and Asia, Australia, the barren wastes of the frozen north and the glamorous islands of the southern sea.

Japan's attacks in the Pacific, against Britain in Hongkong and Malaya, against the United States in Hawaii and the Philippines, provided, as Mr. Roosevelt put it in his fireside talk to his people on December 9, the climax to a decade of international immorality. "Powerful and resourceful gangsters have banded together to make war on the whole human race." For ten years past Japan has paralleled the course of Hitler and Mussolini in Europe and Africa, but now " it has become far more than parallel : it is a collaboration so well calculated that all the continents of the world and all the oceans are now considered by Axis strategists as one gigantic battlefield."

LOOKING back over a decade which the historians of the future will surely regard as one of the most saddening, even the most shameful, of the century, one sees that the career of plundering and blundering began when Japan invaded Manchuria in 1931. It was a most blatant act of aggression, yet she was permitted to "get away with it." There were protests in Congress and Parliament, in London and Washington, and at Geneva. But Japan had powerful friends and even many sympathizers. Britain's Foreign Secretary, Sir John (now Lord) Simon, came out almost as Japan's apologist. But most of us were not yet awakened from our post-war dreams. After all, Japan was a long way away, and Manchuria—well, did it really matter very much if it were rechristened Manchukuo ?

BUT what followed would provide a fit theme for the musings of Hardy's Spirit of the Pities. To quote Mr. Roosevelt again : " In 1931 Japan invaded Manchukuo—without warning. In 1935 Italy invaded Ethiopia—without warning. In 1938 Hitler occupied Austria—without warning. In 1939 Hitler invaded Czechoslovakia — without warning. Later in 1939 Hitler invaded Poland—without warning. In 1940 Hitler invaded Norway, Denmark, Holland, Belgium, and Luxemburg—without warning. In 1940 Italy attacked France and later Greece—without warning. In 1941 Axis Powers attacked Yugoslavia and Greece and they dominated the Balkans—without warning. In 1941 Hitler invaded Russia — without warning. And now Japan has attacked Malaya and Thailand and the United States—without warning. It is all of one pattern. We are now in this war. We are all in it—all the way."

So it is that 1941 goes out in a blaze of horrific war, and 1942 emerges against a curtain of flame. Vast have been the changes brought about by a year of days and nights,

every one of them loaded with death and destruction. Since last New Year's Eve millions have died—not in their peaceful beds but suddenly cut off in their pride and prime, in the " vast and dusty shambles " or in lonely agony, amid the crash of bombs in close-packed cities, in hospital wards, in blazing aircraft, in the stark cold of the desert night and in the unbroken silence of the ocean depths. It has been a year of tremendous happenings, one whose events have been written in blood on the tablets of history. Blood and tears, toil and sweat have been our lot ; grievous have been our losses, deep our disappointments, heavy the blows we have suffered. Not yet has the day of victory dawned for us. Still Hitler strides the Continent like a colossus, and the tide of his triumphs has hardly been stayed.

YET the year that has gone, culminated though it has in the tremendous onslaught by Japan, has not been without comfort for us. Then we stood—we of the British Commonwealth—almost alone in arms against a multitude of foes, better armed, much better prepared and, in some ways, better led and directed. During those twelve months the gap between our production and that of our enemies has been greatly reduced, though it is not yet entirely closed. The men and women in our factories have laboured loyally and long to repair the deficiencies, to make good the losses. Our armies have grown, our Air Force is more powerful by far, and our Navy (though we have to mourn the loss of many a great ship, of all too many brave men) is still second to none in fighting spirit. But even more important is the fact that, as Mr. Churchill said the other day, we have now at least four-fifths of the population of the globe upon our side (although let us not forget that unarmed millions are of little use against panzers and bombing planes).

The millions of the Red Army, the men who for six months have borne the full brunt of the greatest war machine the world has ever seen—the men who, after fighting every inch of the way back to Leningrad and Moscow and the Don, have of these late weeks turned on their pursuers and for the first time given Hitler a taste of the defeat which he has inflicted so often upon others—these men are our comrades. The Soviet partisans, fighting with rifle, torch and explosive charge among blackened timbers and rubble heaps, in what only a short time ago were flourishing towns and cities—they too are with us. The Chinese, battling so bravely in the yellow mud of their river valleys, bombed and blasted yet still tenaciously defending their native soil against the Japanese invader—these warriors of Free China, these soldiers of Chiang Kai-shek, they too we hail as our comrades.

Then there are the Americans. At long last the jealousies and fears, the distrust and differences, which for generations have kept the two great Atlantic democracies apart, have been wiped from the slate. The men of New York and San Francisco, of Minneapolis and New Orleans, of Detroit, Chicago and Oklahoma—of all the 48 states of the great American Union, from Washington to Texas, from Maine to California—they are our comrades, our brothers-in-arms as well as in spirit.

WE are all in the war now—one war, all the way. We must match the enemy with a grand strategy. " We must realize," to quote President Roosevelt again, " that Japanese successes against the United States in the Pacific are helpful to the German operations in Libya ; that any German success against the Caucasus is inevitably an assistance to Japan in her operations against the Dutch East Indies ; that a German attack against Algiers or Morocco opens the way for a German attack on South America. On the other side of the picture we must learn to know that guerilla warfare against the Germans in Serbia helps us ; that a successful Russian offensive against the Germans helps us ; and that British successes on land or sea in any part of the world strengthen our hands." And the President went on to say that Germany and Italy, too, considered themselves at war with the United States, just as much as they consider themselves at war with Britain and Russia. Another two days, and Hitler and Mussolini, nerved by Japanese victories to one desperate throw, flung down the gauntlet of actual war.

IN speaking for his own people the President was speaking of a surety for us too. " We Americans are not destroyers "—we of the British Commonwealth, of China and Soviet Russia and the Netherlands and Poland and the rest—" we are not destroyers, we are builders. We are now in the midst of a war, not for conquest, not for vengeance, but for a world which will be safe for our children . . . In the dark hours of this day and through the dark days that may come, we will know that the vast majority of the members of the human race are on our side. Many of them are fighting for us. All of them are praying for us . . . **We are going to win the war, and we are going to win the peace that follows."** ROYSTON PIKE

'I ASK that Congress declare . . . a state of war' between the United States and the Japanese Empire : President Roosevelt speaking in the United States Congress on November 8. Behind him is Mr. Sam Rayburn, Speaker of the House of Representatives. *Radioed Photo, Associated Press*

America's Pacific Bases Now Engulfed in War

OAHU island, one of the Hawaii group, where hundreds of people were killed at Pearl Harbour by the Japanese; the photo shows American Air Corps planes lined up on Hickam Field.

GUAM, one of the Marianas, in the Pacific. The American base here was reported to have been wrecked by Japanese bombs and shells.

A coast-defence gun, described as a "12-in. disappearing rifle," guarding the entrance of Manila Bay, on the Philippine island of Corregidor.

AT PEARL HARBOUR, Hawaii, heavily attacked in the Japanese surprise offensive—U.S. destroyers and Clipper plane. Right, Wake Island, midway between Honolulu and Guam, in the Pacific; a U.S. refuelling base it was subjected to heavy attacks by the Japanese.

Photos, Planet News, Keystone, Associated Press, Wide World

War Did Not Surprise the Netherlands Indies

Beneath the spreading fronds of a palm tree an army searchlight of the Netherlands Indies defences projects its beam through the tropical night.

DUTCH DESTROYERS of the Netherlands East Indies Navy guarding a harbour entrance in the Far East. Head of the Dutch East Indies Navy, which will cooperate in the defence of the Pacific, is Vice-Adm. C. E. Helfrich.

THE DUTCH QUEEN'S PLEDGE

YOU know how Germany, in the same fashion as Japan now follows in Asia, has assaulted many countries in Europe one after the other. Japan, possessed by the same spirit of aggression and of contempt for law, follows here, also, in the steps of its German Axis ally. We have learned.

Now that the friendly American and British peoples are being attacked, the Kingdom of the Netherlands puts all its military power, and all its resources, at the disposal of the common war effort.

The Netherlands did not hesitate to defend themselves with courage when they were wickedly assaulted in Europe. The Indies will not waver now that such an attack threatens them in Asia.

I count on the navy, the army and the air force, on all civil servants, and on all civil services, whose war duty now begins. I and all my subjects count on all the courage, the determination and the perseverance of all in the Indies.

Queen Wilhelmina's Proclamation broadcast by Prof. P. S. Gerbrandy in the Radio Orange programme on Nov. 3, 1941

CURTISS HAWK fighter aircraft of the Royal Netherlands East Indies Air Force lined up on the airfield at Bandoeng, Java.

ANTI-TANK GUN, drawn by a tractor on which its crew are seated, passes through a village in the Dutch East Indies. Left, an anti-aircraft gun during night exercises in the Far East. The Royal Netherlands Indies Army numbered before the war some 37,000 men, with numerous reserves.

Photos, Sport & General, Michael Lorant, Keytsons and Wide World

Hong Kong: British Outpost Menaced by Japan

THE HARBOUR AT HONG KONG, at the mouth of the Canton River. The Japanese bombed and attempted to invade this British colony on December 8, 1941. Preparations against attack, however, had been proceeding for some time. In the photographs beneath are one of the air-raid shelters which have been bored deep into the hills upon which Hong Kong is built, and torpedo boats on guard in the vicinity of the island.   *Photos, Fox, Associated Press*

BRITISH TANKS IN LIBYA advancing through a mined area in the desert. The heroism of our tank men is one of the glorious chapters of the whole war. Enemy mines, bombs, shell-fire, blinding sand-storms—all these they take as a matter of course. They have created new records in human endurance. Four days in a tank was regarded as the limit, but many of the tank crews fighting in Libya have remained in action for eight or twelve days subsisting on dry pack bully and biscuits. Knocked out of one tank they will crawl sometimes to another to keep up their attack on the enemy.

Photo, British Official : Crown Copyright

'For Good or Ill It Is Auchinleck's Battle'

In the House of Commons on December 11 Mr. Churchill gave "the best account I can of where we stand and how we are." He paid a high tribute to Russia's magnificent stand (see page 376), welcomed China as a worthy ally, described Japan's cold-blooded attack and the tragic loss of the Prince of Wales and the Repulse (see page 371). Most of his speech, however, was devoted to the Libyan battle, and below we reprint the most important passages.

THE Libyan offensive did not take the course which its authors expected, though it will reach the end at which they aimed. Very few set-piece battles that have to be prepared for a long time in advance work out in the way that they are planned and imagined. The unexpected intervenes at every stage. The will-power of the enemy impinges itself upon the prescribed or hoped-for course of events.

Victory is traditionally elusive. Accidents happen and mistakes are made. Sometimes right things turn out wrong and quite often wrong things turn out right. War is very difficult, especially to those who are taking part in it or conducting it.

Still, when all is said and done, on November 18 General Auchinleck set out to destroy the entire armed force of the Germans and Italians in Cyrenaica. Now, on December 11, I am bound to say that it seems very probable that he will do so.

The picture that was made beforehand by the commanders was of a much more rapid battle, and they had the idea which I expressed that the entire German armoured forces would be encountered by our armour forces in a mass at the outset and that the battle would be decided in a few hours.

This might have been the best chance for the enemy. However, the sudden surprise

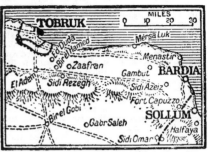

By courtesy of "The Times"

the enemy had gradually accumulated on the coast. For us the foundation of everything was supply and mechanized transport, and this was provided on what had hitherto been regarded as a fantastic scale. Also we had to rely on our superiority in armour and in the air. Most of all in this struggle, everything depended for us on an absolutely unrelenting spirit of the offensive, not only in our generals but in the troops and everyone in action.

That has been forthcoming and is still forthcoming. All the troops have fought all the time in every circumstance of fatigue and hardship with one sincere insatiable desire to engage the enemy and destroy him if possible, tank for tank, man for man, and hand to hand. Behind all this process, working out at so many different points and in so many separate combats, has been the presiding will-power of the C.-in-C., General Auchinleck. Without that will-power we might very well have subsided on to the defensive and lost precious initiative which here in this Libyan battle we have for the first time felt strong enough to maintain. The first main crisis of the battle was reached between November 24 and 26.

On November 24 General Auchinleck proceeded to the battle headquarters, and on November 26 he decided to relieve General Cunningham and appoint Major-General Ritchie, a comparatively junior officer, in command of the 8th Army in his stead.

This was immediately endorsed by the Minister of State and myself. General Cunningham had rendered brilliant service in Abyssinia and was also responsible for the planning and organization of the present offensive in Libya which began with surprise and success and which had now apparently turned the corner.

He has since been reported by the medical authorities to be suffering from serious overstrain and has been granted sick leave. Since November 26 the 8th Army has been commanded

of the Tobruk garrison, including Poles, all played an equally valiant and active part.

At the beginning of the offensive I told the House that we should, for the first time, be fighting the Germans on equal terms in modern weapons. This was quite true. Naturally there have been some unpleasant surprises, and also some awkward things have happened, as might be expected. Those who fight the Germans fight a stubborn and resourceful foe, a foe in every way worthy of the doom prepared for him.

Some of the German tanks carried, as we knew, a six-pounder gun. Although it can carry many fewer shots, it is sometimes more effective than the guns with which our tanks are mainly armed. Our losses in tanks were a good deal heavier than we expected. It may be that at the outset, before it was disorganized, the enemy's recovery process for damaged vehicles worked better than our own. They are very good at that.

Our Air Force was undoubtedly superior throughout in numbers. Although the Germans have drawn, in the most extravagant manner, air reinforcements from many quarters, including the Russian front, that superiority has been more than maintained. Great satisfaction has been expressed by the troops and military authorities about the way in which they have been helped and protected by the action of the R.A.F.

About half and sometimes more than half of everything in men, munitions, and fuel which the enemy send to Africa is sunk before it gets there by our submarines, cruisers, and destroyers and by the activities of our Air Force. In this way, therefore, the prolongation of the battle may not be without its compensations to us.

From the point of view of drawing weight from the vast Russian front, the continuance of the fighting is not to be regarded as evil. The first stage of the battle is now over. The enemy has been driven out of the positions which bar our westward advance. Everything has been swept away except certain pockets at Bardia and Halfaya, which are hopelessly cut off and will be mopped up or starved out in due course. It may definitely be said that Tobruk has been relieved or, as I should prefer to state, has been disengaged. The enemy, still strong, but severely mauled and largely stripped of his armour, is retreating to a defensive line to the west of Tobruk. Some substantial reinforcements of British troops are available close at hand.

I am making a rule never to prophesy or to promise or guarantee future results, but I will go so far on this occasion as to say that all danger of the Army of the Nile not being able to celebrate Christmas and the New Year in Cairo has been decisively removed.

IN THE LIBYA CAMPAIGN the wounded have been speedily transferred from the battlefield to the hospitals in Egypt by De Havilland and Bristol transport planes prominently displaying the Red Cross.
Photo, British Official: Crown Copyright

and success of our advance prevented any such mass trial of strength between the armoured forces, and almost at the first bound we reached right out to Sidi Rezegh, divided the enemy armour, and threw them into confusion.

In consequence of this a very large number of detached actions took place over an immense stretch of desert country.

The battle, though equally intense, became both dispersed and protracted. It became a widespread and confused battle of extremely high-class combatants, mounted on mechanized transport and fighting in barren lands with the utmost vigour and determination.

Although we have a large army standing in the Middle East, we have never been able to apply in our desert advance infantry forces which were numerically equal to those

with great vigour and skill by General Ritchie, but during nearly the whole time General Auchinleck has been at the battle headquarters. Although the battle is not yet finished, I have no hesitation in saying that, for good or ill, it is General Auchinleck's battle.

Watching these affairs, as it is my duty to do, from day to day, and even from hour to hour, and seeing the seamy side of the reports that have come in, I have felt my confidence in General Auchinleck growing continually. Although everything is hazardous in war, I believe we have found in him, as we have in General Wavell, a military figure of the first order. The newspapers have given full and excellent accounts of the strangely interspersed fighting in which the British Armoured Corps, the New Zealand division, the South African division, the Indian division, the British 70th Division, and the rest

Our Searchlight on the War

MEN, MACHINES AND COURAGE

The position they had to storm was a fort flanked by huge minefields, row upon row of barbed wire, and traps of all kinds. Throughout the British attack the Italians kept up a ferocious cross-fire . . . The infantry braved the mines no sappers could tackle beforehand in so deadly a cross-fire—and broke through.—*Description of the fighting in Libya*

WITH each passing century war becomes more and more horrible and destructive. While this is to be deplored, it is a matter for sober rejoicing that the courage of man keeps pace with the diabolical weapons of science. Death-dealing machines become increasingly ingenious, and the tank and aeroplane have speeded up the rate of casualties. In less than six months 8,000,000 men have been killed, wounded, taken prisoner or are missing on the East Front. From this it might be assumed that the war would soon end if only because such losses must neutralize the power of the armies. But Germany and Italy, Russia and ourselves still have immense resources in man-power. Nor must we forget that every year new young recruits are available for service. The lesson of the tank in Libya and elsewhere is that it is still an auxiliary to the infantry. Where opposing sides are more or less equal and the machines are knocked out, the infantry has to get down to hand-to-hand fighting. The hope of the Allies is, of course, in a vast superiority of machines. We must build so large a mechanical armoury that our wastage in tanks and aeroplanes is of no consequence. Not until then is a decision possible. Not until then can we roll up the Nazi octopus that strangles the greater part of Europe and a large area of Russia.

BARBARISM AND CULTURE

A Nazi soldier, taken prisoner, spat in a British officer's face while being interrogated. With commendable restraint and dignity the officer wiped his face and reminded the German that he might have been killed for resisting while a prisoner of war. An Italian pilot, taken prisoner in Cyrenaica, said he looked forward to learning to read the English classics in the original during captivity.

THE tragedy of Italy, once the centre of culture in Europe, in being allied to Germany, is glaringly illustrated in these two incidents. This is not to say that all Italians are longing to read Shakespeare, but the fact remains that the Italian people are fundamentally civilized, with a thin veneer of Fascism, while the Nazis do not know and have never really known the ideals of civilization. The latest generation of louts have been taught to loathe all culture lest any predilection for humanism should interfere with their instincts to destroy. That the Italian people ever allowed themselves to follow their comic-opera Caesar to perdition is somewhat mystifying until we remember that the art of assassinating tyrants is not so simple as it was. Modern armaments and a ruthless bureaucracy have made revolution extremely difficult, and the wishful thinkers who still pin their faith on revolt either in Italy, Germany, or the occupied territories must surely disabuse their minds. Ribbentrop, who has nothing to learn from Hitler or Goebbels in lying, probably

spoke the truth when he told the quislings in Berlin the other day that "the tank and dive-bomber precluded the possibility of revolt in disarmed territory." Revolt in Europe, generally, will come, as it did in 1918, only when the Nazis have been severely thrashed. The dictator who holds all the weapons is unassailable in his own country, or on conquered territory. The Italians are paying the price of their folly in allowing Mussolini to rise and sell Italy to the hereditary enemy.

R.A.F. ATTACKS ON GERMANY & OCCUPIED TERRITORY

Sept. and Oct., 1941   *Based on official statistics*

Date	Main Raids	Other Raids	Date	Main Raids	Other Raids
Aug.			Oct.	Nuremberg**	
31 N	Essen**		12 N	Bremen*	
	Cologne**	1	13 ND		4
Sept.	N	1	14 N	(S. Germany)	
2 D	(Bremen)	1	Oct.	15-20 N D	10
2 N	Frankfurt**		20 N	Bremen**	
	Berlin*	3		Wilhelms-	
Sept. 3-6	D, N	8		haven*	
7 N	Berlin***	3		Emden*	
8 N	Kassel**	2	21 N		5
9 D		1		(N.W. Ger-	
10 N	Turin**			many)	
Sept. 11, 12 N		12	23 N		3
13 N	Brest***		24 N	(Rhine and	
15 D		1		W. Germany)	1
15 N	Hamburg***		26 N	Hamburg	
16 N		2		(N.W. Ger-	
17 D	(N. France)	1		many)	4
Sept. 17-27 N D		22	28 N	(S. and S.W.	
28 N	(Turin			Germany)	2
	Genoa)	2	29 N		4
Sept. 29-Oct. 12 N D		37	30 N	(N.W. Ger-	
				many)	5

Summary : *Heavy raids in Sept. and Oct. 14 ; Other raids : Sept., over 71 ; Oct., over 67.*
Asterisks indicate strength of raids. Names in brackets lighter or more general raids. In some cases raids on aerodromes are listed as single raids, but may represent two or more places raided. N, Night. D, Day.

CAN LONG-TERM BOMBING WIN ?

The R.A.F. must be enlarged until it can bring a decisive influence to bear on events by bombing operations sustained throughout the 24 hours. The time available for building up that bombing fleet is diminishing.—*Major Oliver Stewart in the " Observer "*

MR. CHURCHILL has given the glad and most significant news that the R.A.F. is now "at least equal in size and numbers " to the German, and has thereby put a term to the long years of air failure and disappointment. Are we making the fullest use of that equality ? We can now meet, according to Major Stewart and other authorities, the enemy's attempts to destroy our industrial strength by a 24-hour bombing offensive. We can also acquire local air superiority, as we have done in Northern France in recent months.

At the end of the last war we had 22,600 planes —the biggest air force in the world. That was thrown away, and laboriously, at great expense

Petty Officer A. E. SEPHTON, posthumously awarded the V.C. for great courage and endurance during a Nazi dive-bombing attack on the cruiser Coventry off Crete on May 20. Two cruisers, the Coventry and Phoebe, went to the rescue of a British hospital ship, after she had radioed S O S, while a squadron of German planes were attacking her. P.O. Sephton, in one of the gun director towers, was critically wounded by machine-gun bullets from a low-flying Nazi dive-bomber. Despite great pain Sephton refused medical attention and carried on with his duties. He died later in the day.   *Photo, " Daily Mirror "*

and suffering we have built it up again on an even larger scale. But time, which has so often and so foolishly been said to be against Hitler, races on, and it does not seem that we are even now remotely approaching a 24-hour attack. In two normally favourable months, according to official figures given in the accompanying table, the R.A.F. carried out 14 heavy raids and about 140 lesser raids on German Europe—say 160 in all, in 60 nights and days. Attacks so spread out can hardly be considered a serious offensive, and in November there was an 11-day period without a single raid. Some critics declare that the enemy has proved for us that long-term strategical bombing cannot win without land operations. The bomb can destroy buildings and people, but it cannot occupy territory. The question remains : will it destroy morale with anything less than 24-hour bombing ?

MONSTROSITIES OF THE AIR

The U.S. Navy has just launched at Baltimore a 67-ton Martin flying-boat, named Mars, which is capable of flying to Europe and back non-stop or of carrying 150 soldiers and their equipment several thousand miles.—*" The Times "*

AMERICA has always been the home of " the biggest yet," but even the new monster flying-boat of the air is, it is reported, to be exceeded in weight and size. As the photograph shows, Mars dwarfs the men attending on it until they suggest Lilliputians. How many men and how many thousand hours of their work, amateurs of the air may ask, were engaged in its birth ? Would not those men and those man-hours expended upon the excellent Martin Maryland bombers which come from the same factory and have already given such good service to the R.A.F. in the Middle East, have given us 10, 12, or more machines that would have achieved war results twenty times as effective ? Super bombers carry super bomb loads, but air monsters of this kind surely put too many eggs in one basket. Our big bombers, Manchester and Halifax, are an undoubted success, but even they, an air authority has stated, must be supplemented by smaller, faster, more easily manufactured machines. And all the time, while the factories labour to increase output, the enemy shifts his industries farther from our bombing bases and disperses them widely over the regions he has occupied. It is a race against time . . . and ingenuity. Nature made the same mistake a few million years ago by allowing the reptilian life of the world to grow to such gigantic sizes that the creatures lost their mobility and died out because of the inconvenience of their sheer bulk. Where Nature erred let Martin and Modern Mechanism beware !

THE MARS, the world's largest flying-boat, a 67-tonner built in America by the Glenn Martin Company. She is fitted with four 2,000-h.p. engines and six gun turrets, and is capable of flying across the Atlantic and back without a stop. The Mars was damaged recently when one of her motors caught fire as she was taxi-ing on the water.   *Photo, Sport & General*

Our American Allies Active in the Atlantic

PATROL COMMANDERS of the U.S. Atlantic Air Patrol, which helps to keep the Lease-Lend line open, checking positions of their patrol planes at a secret base. Right, a Catalina flying boat returning to its mother ship after a 12-hour patrol.

ON AIR PATROL over the North Atlantic, an American flying boat helps to protect a large convoy taking war material to Britain. These patrol planes, which operate for the specific purpose of seeing that the Atlantic sea-lanes are kept open for the safe passage of America's "tools" to the Democracies, work from secret bases.

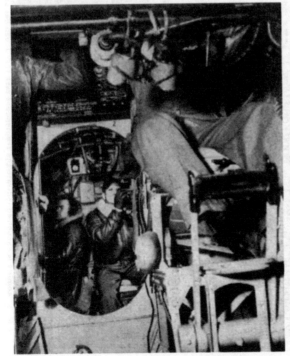

U.S. NAVY PATROL aircraft flying up the rugged east coast of Greenland against a background of snow-covered mountains. Left, the interior of a U.S. Navy Atlantic Patrol flying boat.

Photos, Keystone, Associated Press

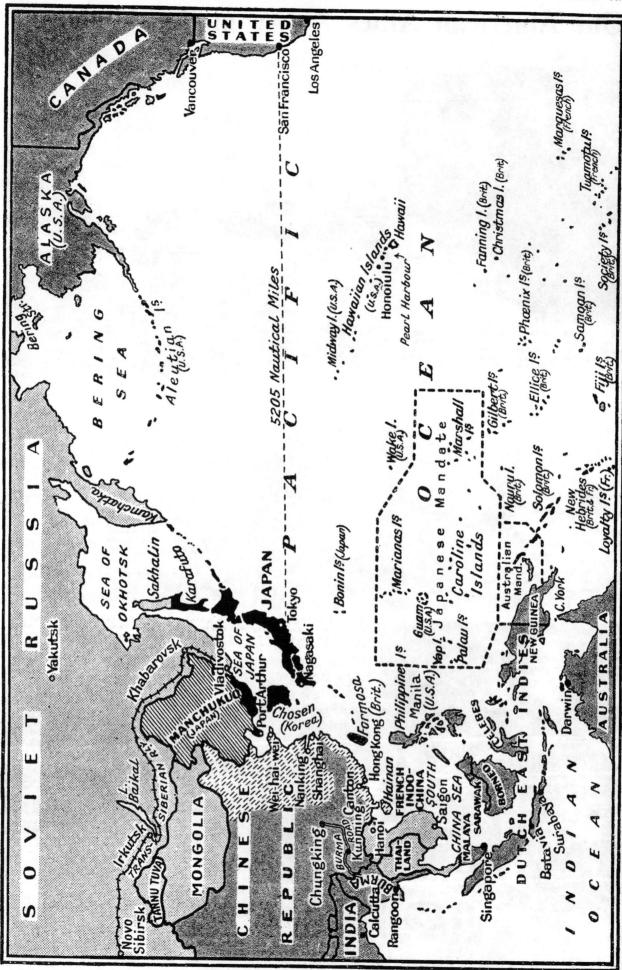

THE FAR EASTERN ARENA, where Japan has staked her whole existence on a war gamble with the Democracies, can be followed in this map. While she was talking peace in the traditional Hitlerian style, Japanese aeroplanes, ships and soldiers were attacking far and wide. Hong Kong, Thailand, Malaya, the American naval bases at Guam, the Philippines and the Hawaiian Islands, were furiously and simultaneously brought under Japanese fire. Long anticipating war with America, Japan was able to make good use of the islands over which she holds a mandate. Even a general survey of this vast scene of conflict is enough to indicate the tremendous task that Japan has undertaken, especially in view of the fact that her war with China continues to absorb so great a part of her military machine.

First Round to Japan in the New World War

" No honest persons today or a thousand years hence," said President Roosevelt in his broadcast
on December 9, "will be able to suppress a sense of indignation and horror at the treachery
committed by the military dictators of Japan under the very shadow of the flag of peace borne
by their special envoys in our midst." Below we tell of what that treachery coupled with
daring and military might, was able to achieve in the war's first few days.

THE second world war opened on Sunday,
December 7, when Japan, without (it
need hardly be said) a declaration of
war, delivered a series of almost simultaneous
attacks against a number of American and
British possessions in the Pacific.

Most important of these was that on Pearl
Harbour in Hawaii, the main base of the
United States Fleet in the Pacific. It had for
its objective the crippling of the American
fleet, so that for the time being, at least, it
should not be able to sail out and join the
British Far Eastern squadron at Singapore.
It must have been prepared for long before,
since Pearl Harbour is nearly 4,000 miles
from Japan, and even 2,000 miles from the
nearest Japanese bases in the Caroline and
Marshall Islands. For a week and more the
Japanese aircraft carriers must have been
negotiating their approach, until on that
Sunday morning they had arrived within
striking distance. Then the planes were
launched, and shortly afterwards the American ships and forts were being deluged with
bombs. It was a bold stroke, if a treacherous,
and it was not without success. Col. Knox,
U.S. Navy Secretary, admitted the loss of
one battleship (the Arizona), three destroyers
and a large number of aircraft, while 2,729
naval men were killed ; altogether what
President Roosevelt described as constituting
a serious set-back.

Attacks on the Bases

Other American bases in the chain which
links San Francisco with Manila were also
attacked almost at the same time. Midway
Island and Wake were heavily bombed ;
and Guam, dangerously situated in the midst
of the Japanese mandated islands, was not
only bombed but invested by Japanese
warships and invaded by Japanese troops.
Imperial H.Q. at Tokyo announced on December 10 that the landing had been successful, and the following day they claimed to
have occupied the capital, Agana, and taken
350 prisoners, including the Governor.

Almost at the same hour as the onslaught
on Pearl Harbour, Japanese planes raided
the Philippines. The first air attacks were
delivered on a number of Army and Navy
bases near Manila, and the capital itself was
attacked on December 9. Then on the next
day these air attacks were followed up by
attempted landings in considerable strength
on Luzon, the northern island of the Philippine group. Japanese troops were got ashore
at Aparri and elsewhere, and parachutists
were also said to be in action. The enemy,
reported General MacArthur, U.S. Commander-in-Chief in the Far East, were in
considerable strength and were using Army,
Navy and Air Force in close conjunction. The
American defending force was small, but it hit
back hard. The position in Luzon was said
to be in hand, and one Japanese battleship,
the Haruna, was set aflame, while another,
the Kongo, was claimed to have been sunk.

Invasion of Malaya

While these blows were being delivered
at America's outposts in the Pacific, the
Japanese also went into action on the Asiatic
mainland. On that same Sunday Hong Kong
was bombed, and the next day Japanese
troops exchanged shots with the British
outposts. At first, however, there was no
attack in force, since Chinese bands struck
at the rear of the Japanese attackers. Then
far to the south, beyond Cape Cambodia, a

**MALAYAN WAR ZONE, showing by arrows
the Japanese attacks on the peninsula. Land-
ings were made round Singora, Patani, and
Kota Bharu, the first two places being in
Thailand, which soon capitulated.**
By Courtesy of the " Daily Mirror"

fleet of Japanese transports, heavily guarded
by warships, set Japanese troops ashore in
Malaya and Thailand.

Thailand's resistance was brief. After
five and a half hours only Bangkok announced on December 8 that resistance had
"ceased temporarily." The Japanese occupied Bangkok, and before the week was out
news came of the conclusion of a Thai-
Japanese agreement, giving the latter the
right to occupy Thai bases and to send
troops across Thailand against Burma and
the Malay States.

In Malaya the first Japanese landings were
effected at 1.30 a.m. (local time) on December
8, at the mouth of the Kelantan River.

' A VERY HEAVY LOSS '

IN my whole experience, I do not remember any
naval blow so heavy or so painful as the sinking
of the Prince of Wales and the Repulse.
These two vast, powerful ships constituted an essential
feature of our plans for meeting the new Japanese
danger as it loomed up against us in the last few months.
These ships had reached the right point at the right
moment, and were fitted in every respect for the tasks
assigned to them.
In moving to attack the Japanese transports which
were disembarking troops at the Krau Isthmus, Admiral
Phillips was undertaking a thoroughly sound, well-
considered offensive operation, not indeed free from
risk, but not different in principle from any similar
operation we have repeatedly carried out in the North
Sea and the Mediterranean. Both ships were sunk
by repeated air attacks by bombers and torpedo aircraft.
These were delivered with energy and determination,
both high-level attacks which secured hits, and three
assaults by torpedo aircraft, by nine aircraft in each
wave which struck our ships with several torpedoes.
There is no reason to suppose that any new weapons
or explosives were employed or any bombs or torpedoes
of exceptional size.
The continued waves of attacks secured their purpose,
and both ships capsized and sank, having destroyed seven
of the attacking aircraft. The escorting destroyers
came immediately to the rescue and have now arrived
at Singapore crowded with survivors.
We have reason to believe that the loss of life has
been less heavy than was at first feared. But I regret
that Admiral Sir Tom Phillips—one of the ablest brains
in the naval service—is among those reported missing.

IT is a very heavy loss that we have suffered . . . It may
well be that we shall have to suffer considerable
punishment, but we shall defend ourselves everywhere
with the utmost vigour in close cooperation with the
U.S. and the Netherlands Navies. The naval power of
Great Britain and the U.S. was very greatly superior,
and is still greatly superior, to the combined powers
of the three Axis Powers.—*Mr. Churchill in the House
of Commons, Dec. 11, 1941*

Apparently their objective was Kota Bharu
aerodrome, which was being defended by
Imperial troops drawn from our forces at
Singapore. Another landing was soon made
at Kemassin, east of Kota Bharu, and after
severe fighting the British and Indians
were compelled to withdraw to a line south
of the aerodrome. Yet another Japanese
landing was attempted at Kuantan, 150 miles
to the north of Singapore. When news of
these landings was flashed to Singapore, the
newly-appointed C.-in-C. of Britain's Far
Eastern Fleet, Admiral Sir Tom Phillips,
took his ships to sea, with a view to intercepting the Japanese invaders. Before he
could engage, however, Japanese air attacks
were anticipated and he about turned.
Then disaster overtook him : the two British
warships, Prince of Wales and Repulse,
were sunk by bombs and aerial torpedoes
(see Mr. Churchill's account on left), the
Repulse at 2.29 and the Prince of Wales at
2.50 p.m. on December 10. Meanwhile,
Singapore was being subjected to a series of
heavy air attacks. Each was beaten off in
turn by the guns of the fortress and the
fighters of the R.A.F. of Far Eastern Command. On December 9 ships of the Netherlands Indies fleet arrived at the port, Queen
Wilhelmina's Government having declared
a state of war with Japan the previous day.

From yet other corners of the vast Pacific
came tidings of war and Japanese thrusts
and counter-thrusts. Japanese planes were
reported over San Francisco ; air-raid warnings were sounded in New York ; Canada and
Australia made ready for invasion. Japanese
landings were reported from South Burma,
while from Thailand the invaders threatened
the Burma Road, the lifeline of Free China.
At Chungking the news of the extension of
the conflict brought from Chiang Kai-shek a
declaration of war against Japan, so that
after four years· of invasion the Japanese
could no longer describe the China war as an
" incident." The A.B.C.D. front (America,
Britain, China, Dutch East Indies) was at
last a fighting entity.

Germany Declares War

Great events, but still the record of that
earth-shaking week was not concluded.
Suddenly the world's attention was switched
away from the Pacific to Berlin, where at
2 p.m. on December 11 Hitler flung down the
challenge of war to the United States and
Mussolini came goose-stepping after. In
Washington the news was received with
surprise but with grim resolution. At·
9.30 a.m. (American time) Hans Thomsen
brought to the State Department the German
Government's formal notification that Germany was at war with the United States.
At noon Congress received a message from
the President :

On the morning of December 11 the Government of
Germany, pursuing its course of world conquest,
declared war against the United States. The long-
known and long-expected has thus taken place. The
forces endeavouring to enslave the entire world now are
moving towards this hemisphere.
Never before has there been a greater challenge
to life, liberty and civilization. Delay invites great
danger. Rapid and united effort by all the peoples of
the world who are determined to remain free will
ensure world victory for the forces of justice and
righteousness over the forces of savagery and barbarism.
Italy, too, has declared war against the United States.
I, therefore, request Congress to recognize a state of
war between the United States and Germany and
between the United States and Italy.

With unanimous voice, the Senate and
House of Representatives both voted for war
against Germany and Italy.

Britain's Bastion at the Crossroads of the Orie[nt]

A general view of Singapore looking across the city. In the background, to the right, is Singapore Strait, looking towards the China Sea, while the hills in the left background are beyond the naval base in Johore Strait. At this base, on the north-east coast of Singapore Island, twenty-two square miles of deep-sea anchorage are available.

SINGAPORE ROADS, abov[e] of native craft. The island only town is Singapore itself

gapore, Chief Objective of the Japanese Invaders

Singapore received its baptism of fire from the air at dawn on Dec. 8, and the A.R.P. services immediately went into action. Above, a Chinese air-raid warden looks out towards the Victoria Memorial Hall (centre) and Fort Canning (background). Oval, left, Government House, Singapore; the present Governor is Sir Thomas Shenton Thomas.

wded with shipping, for Singapore, the " Crossroads of the East," is a free port and handles an enormous volume of trade. Left, Singapore River, with its cluster out 26 miles long by 14 wide, with an area of 220 square miles and a population of some 750,000—Malays for the most part, but with many Chinese, Indians, etc. The tamford Raffles in 1819 following the leasing to him of the island by the Sultan of Johore and the Chief of Singapore.

Photos, G. H. Metcalf, F. Henle, Brandt

Now Finland Is Numbered Among Our Enemies

Two years ago, when Finland was attacked by Soviet Russia, Britain and America watched her gallant stand with intense sympathy. Much material help was accorded her, indeed, by the Democracies, and at one time there was even talk of sending a British expeditionary force to her aid. Yet, such is the whirligig of war, Finland is now amongst our declared foes.

WHEN Hitler made war on Russia last summer, Finnish divisions marched with the Nazi legions. Finland actually declared war on the Soviet Union on June 27, and Field-Marshal Mannerheim, the Finnish C.-in-C., declared in an Order of the Day that Finland had embarked at the side of Germany on a " holy war " against Russia. At first the Finns professed that their war was not part of the trial of strength

had pushed northward along the Leningrad-Murmansk railway, one of the most important Russian links with the outside world. In the lake region of the Salla they attempted to capture the town of Kandalaksha, while in the far north, in the Murmansk sector itself, they rendered invaluable help to their German allies.

In the light of these operations it became increasingly difficult for the Finns to main-

sent a note to the Finnish Government, in which he had warned them that Britain was bound to consider Finland a member of the Axis, since it was impossible to separate the war which Finland was waging against Russia from the general European war. "If, therefore, the Finnish Government persists in invading purely Russian territory, a situation will arise in which Great Britain will be forced to treat Finland as an open enemy, not only while the war lasts but also when peace comes to be made."

At the beginning of October Stalin sent a request to the British Government, asking for a declaration of war on Hitler's three satellites who had invaded Russia—Finland, Hungary and Rumania. Fresh attempts were made to induce Finland to break off the war. A last appeal was made at the end of November, when the Finnish Government were given till December 5 to cease military operations. At the same time the Russians announced their evacuation of the naval base of Hango, ceded to the Soviet in 1940. A reply was received from Helsinki, but it was completely unsatisfactory. So at 1.1 a.m. on December 7 a state of war with Finland—and also with Rumania and Hungary—came into being.

Finland had made her choice. Yet there must have been many in the little country who regretted the course of events. Certainly, their gains to date have been few and barren. The territory they have recovered from Russia is nothing but " scorched earth." Most of the men are at the front. There is a serious food shortage; traffic has been dislocated; stocks of fuel are low; casualties must have been heavy. These things seem a heavy price to pay for Nazi friendship. Nor do they represent the closing of the account.

between the Great Powers. This pretence was kept up for some months, and as late as September 14 we find Mr. V. Tanner, Finnish Minister of Trade and Industry, declaring at Helsinki that " This is for us an entirely defensive war by which we desire to obtain secure frontiers and a lasting peace."

But what constitutes " secure frontiers " ? At first it was claimed that the Finns sought nothing more than the re-occupation of the territories captured by the Red Army in the campaign of the winter of 1939–40. But even in July Marshal Mannerheim declared that his Army's objective was " a great Finland " and " liberation of the Karelian people on both sides of the frontier." This meant, apparently, the extension of the Finnish frontiers up to the old frontier on the Karelian Isthmus, to the river Svir in the gap between the lakes of Ladoga and Onega, and from Lake Onega northwards up to the most southern point of the White Sea. Some Swedish observers declared that the Finns' objectives were even more extensive—that it was intended to claim all the territory up to the west coast of the White Sea, at least as far as Kandalaksha, and possibly even to include the Kola Peninsula and the ice-free port of Murmansk.

From the outset Finnish divisions joined in the attack on Leningrad, attacking the Russians across the Karelian Isthmus, and thus immobilizing a large number—some put it at 30—of Russian divisions. By October the Finns were back on their old frontier; they had cleared the western and part of the eastern shores of Lake Ladoga and penetrated into Russian territory between Ladoga and Onega. After occupying the capital of Soviet Karelia, Petrozavodsk, they

Gen. von Falkenhorst (right), Commander-in-Chief of the German Army in Norway, photographed on a visit to Field-Marshal Mannerheim, C.-in-C. of the Finnish Forces, who is seen left.
Photo, Sport & General

tain their attitude of disinterestedness in the struggle elsewhere. On July 29 Finland broke off diplomatic relations with Britain, yet Britain was still disinclined to recognize Finland's defection from the democratic camp. Finland, it was apparently felt, was still not hopelessly lost; and for months diplomatic efforts were made to persuade her to withdraw from the war once her troops had established themselves on her 1939 frontier.

In August Mr. Cordell Hull, the American Secretary of State, made overtures to Finland, expressing the view that Stalin was prepared to make peace on most reasonable and honourable terms. Then on September 24 it was announced that Mr. Eden had

MURMANSK-LENINGRAD front, showing the important Murmansk-Leningrad and Archangel-Vologda-Leningrad railways. A branch line from Soroka the exact location of which has not been divulged, links the two railways. In the far north there has been little substantial change for three months, while Tikhvin, on the railway to Vologda was recaptured by Soviet troops on December 8.

From Finland to the Ukraine One Great Battle

In the facing page is told how Britain found herself compelled to declare war on Finland, the once highly democratic country which on Nov. 25 joined the Axis. The two photographs above were taken in the Far North sector of the Russian front, and show, left, Finnish troops on the move in Eastern Karelia, where the roads are completely waterlogged, and, right, a flame-thrower being used by a Finnish detachment in an attack upon a Soviet position.

This remarkable photograph from the Russian Front, which comes from German sources, is described as showing the road to Kiev littered with Soviet equipment left behind when the Russian forces were trying to escape encirclement. It is now the turn of the Germans to seek to escape from the pincers of Timoshenko's armies in the southern Ukraine.

Photos, Planet News, Associated Press

Our Diary of the War

FRIDAY, DEC. 5, 1941　　　　*825th day*

Air.—Enemy shipping attacked by R.A.F. off N. Coast of France.

Russian Front.—Several successful Russian counter-attacks on the Moscow front. Russians still advancing in the southern Ukraine. Situation still serious around Tula.

Africa.—Fighting flared up again in Libya with heavy German attacks on El Duda. Indians made successful attack on Bir el Gobi.

Mediterranean.—Night attack on Naples by R.A.F.

General.—German major shot in Paris.

SATURDAY, DEC. 6　　　　*826th day*

Air.—Coastal Command attacked enemy shipping off Norwegian coast.

Russian Front.—Soviet troops advancing towards Mariupol. Successful Russian counter-attacks in the Kalinin sector.

Mediterranean.—Naples again raided by R.A.F.

Africa.—British troops recaptured ground lost near El Duda. Contact renewed with Tobruk.

Home.—Britain declared war on Finland, Rumania and Hungary.

General.—M. Litvinov, new Soviet Ambassador to U.S.A., arrived at San Francisco. President Roosevelt sent personal message to Emperor of Japan.

SUNDAY, DEC. 7　　　　*827th day*

Russian Front.—Timoshenko's armies continued their advance from Rostov. Russian troops forced their way into Kalinin.

Africa. — Intensive fighting throughout Libyan battle area. German armoured divisions moving west. Sidi Rezegh recaptured by British. Italian Bologna division badly cut up.

Far East.—Japan declared war upon Britain and the United States. Japanese air raids launched against U.S. naval bases in the Pacific; Pearl Harbour (Oahu Island), Wake Island and Guam heavily attacked. Raids on army and naval bases in the Philippines.

MONDAY, DEC. 8　　　　*828th day*

Russian Front.—Germans driven from several villages around Kalinin. Russian advance in the Taganrog area continued.

Africa.—Rommel's forces being slowly driven westwards.

Far East.—Constant air attacks on U.S. Pacific bases. Japanese troops landed in Northern Malaya. Singapore and Hong Kong bombed. Thailand capitulated within a few hours of a Japanese invasion of the country.

Home.—Britain declared war upon Japan. Small number of enemy aircraft attacked N.E. England at night.

General.—President Roosevelt asked Congress for declaration of war against Japan. Canada, Costa Rica, Dominica, Haiti, Honduras, Nicaragua and Free France declared war against Japan. China declared war against Japan, Germany and Italy. The Netherlands govt. declared war against Japan.

TUESDAY, DEC. 9　　　　*829th day*

Air.—Coastal Command attacked enemy shipping off Dutch coast. Offensive sweep over N. France by Fighter Command.

Russian Front.—Russians claimed recapture of Tikhvin, in Leningrad sector. Russians continued to advance on S. Front.

Africa.—El Adem captured by British and Tobruk relieved. Enemy retirement westward accelerated. Tripoli attacked by R.A.F. at night. Landing grounds at Derna and Gazala attacked.

Far East.—Bitter fighting for aerodrome of Kota Bharu, in N.E. Malaya.

Home.—Junkers 88 shot down in daylight off N.E. coast.

General.—Remainder of the British Empire

declared war against Japan, as did Cuba and Panama.

WEDNESDAY DEC. 10　　　*830th day*

Sea.—H.M.S. Prince of Wales and H.M.S. Repulse sunk off the coast of Malaya. Japanese battleship Haruna sunk off Philip-

MR. CHURCHILL ON RUSSIA

SIX weeks or a month ago people were wondering whether Moscow would be taken, or Leningrad, or how soon the Germans would overrun the Caucasus and then the oil-fields of Baku. We had to consider what we could do to prepare ourselves on the long front from the Caspian Sea to the Mediterranean. Since then a striking fact has become evident.

The enormous power of the Russian Army and the glorious steadfastness and energy shown in resisting the frightful assault have now been made plain. On the top of this has come the Russian winter, and on top of that the Russian Air Force. Hitler forced his armies into this barren and devastated land. He has everywhere been brought to a standstill. On a large portion of the front he is in retreat. The sufferings of his troops are indescribable. Their losses have been immense.

The cold, snow, and piercing winds blow across the icy spaces and ruined towns and villages, and along the lines of communication assaulted by guerillas. There is a stubborn unyielding resistance by the Russian people who defend every stone, every house and every yard of their soil.

All these have inflicted upon the German Army and the German nation a bloody prop, almost unequalled in the history of the war. This is not the end of the winter. It is the beginning.

The Russians have now regained a definite superiority in the air over large parts of the front. They have the great cities in which to live. Their soldiers are habituated to the severity of their native climate, and they are inspired with the feeling of advance after a long retreat and of vengeance for monstrous injury.

In Hitler's launching of the Nazi campaign on Russia we can now see, after less than six months of fighting, that he has made one of the outstanding blunders of history, and the result so far realized constitutes an event of cardinal importance in the final decision of the war.—*House of Commons, Dec. 11, 1941.*

pines. Japanese cruiser and destroyer reported sunk off Wake Island.

Air.—Daylight raids on objectives in N.W. Germany.

Russian Front.—Moscow announced re-

capture of Yelets, in the Don battle area. More local successes for the Russians in both the Moscow and Leningrad sectors.

Africa.—Mobile forces attacked Rommel's formations moving N.W. and W. from El Adem.

Far East.—Mass attacks against island of Luzon, in Philippines. Landings at Aparri, Vigan and Lingayen. Japanese attempted new landing at Kuantan, in Malaya.

THURSDAY DEC. 11　　　*831st day*

Air.—More daylight raids on objectives in N.W. Germany.

Russian Front.—Soviet troops continued to advance in many sectors. A hundred villages recaptured in the Russian counter-attack around Yelets. Many villages also recaptured in the Tikhvin area. Soviet advance continued on the Southern Front.

Africa.—Mr. Churchill announced that Gen. Sir Alan Cunningham had been replaced as commander of the 8th Army by Maj.-Gen. N. M. Ritchie.

Far East.—Penang heavily bombed. Reports stated that Japanese attacks on the Philippines, Malaya and Hong Kong were being successfully held. Australian bombers based on Dutch East Indies raided Japanese air bases on Pobra Island.

Home.—Very slight air activity over N.E. England by night.

General.—Italy and Germany declared war on U.S.A. U.S.A. declared war against Germany and Italy.

FRIDAY, DEC. 12　　　*832nd day*

Sea.—Admiralty announced that an Italian cruiser was badly damaged and probably sunk by British submarine in the Central Mediterranean.

Russian Front.—Further striking successes reported from Moscow. Germans abandoned much material in their retreat. 400 towns and villages said to have been retaken by Soviet troops in a week's fighting.

Africa.—Swifter progress in Libya where Gazala was surrounded.

Far East.—Japan. battleship badly damaged off the Luzon coast. Japanese gained three footholds on Luzon, but were heavily engaged. Garrisons at Wake and Midway Islands continued to resist invaders. In Malaya, fierce fighting reported in Kedah area on the Thai frontier.

2nd EAGLE SQUADRON Spitfires fly over the Stars and Stripes as they set off on a sweep. This squadron, led by Sq. Ldr. R. Powell, D.F.C., is the second of the three American Eagle Squadrons to be formed in Britain as units of R.A.F. Fighter Command.　　　*Photo, Fox*

London Pools To Drown 'Fire-bomb Fritz'

This huge water tank in the devastated area of Fore Street, London, has been improvized against further Nazi efforts to set fire to the City. For the past few months demolition squads have been working on this heavily blitzed site, and the débris has been cleared, but reconstruction must wait until after victory.

Circle, firemen are filling a tank in the basement of a wrecked house in Bond Street. It holds 350,000 gallons. So deep are some of these reservoirs that lifebelts are placed in handy positions in case of accidents.

Photos, L.N.A. and "The Times"

Like circular swimming pools with diving-boards attached, these nine emergency tanks seen in the photograph on the left have been sunk into the ground on the site of a street which was destroyed by bombs. Here is a side-light on the war which reveals the fantastic shifts to which the cities have been forced by the invention of the aeroplane. No writer of fiction ever imagined that one day our quiet Victorian streets would be so curiously transformed.

Above, this reconstruction of several basements makes a large receptacle for an emergency supply of water. Much of the fire damage in London was due to a shortage of water caused sometimes by the destruction of the mains.

Photos, Sport & General and Planet News

Aircraft Without Airscrews—A New Development

Based upon articles in " Flight " by G. Geoffrey Smith, Managing Editor

Drawn for THE WAR ILLUS-
TRATED *by War Artists Ltd.*

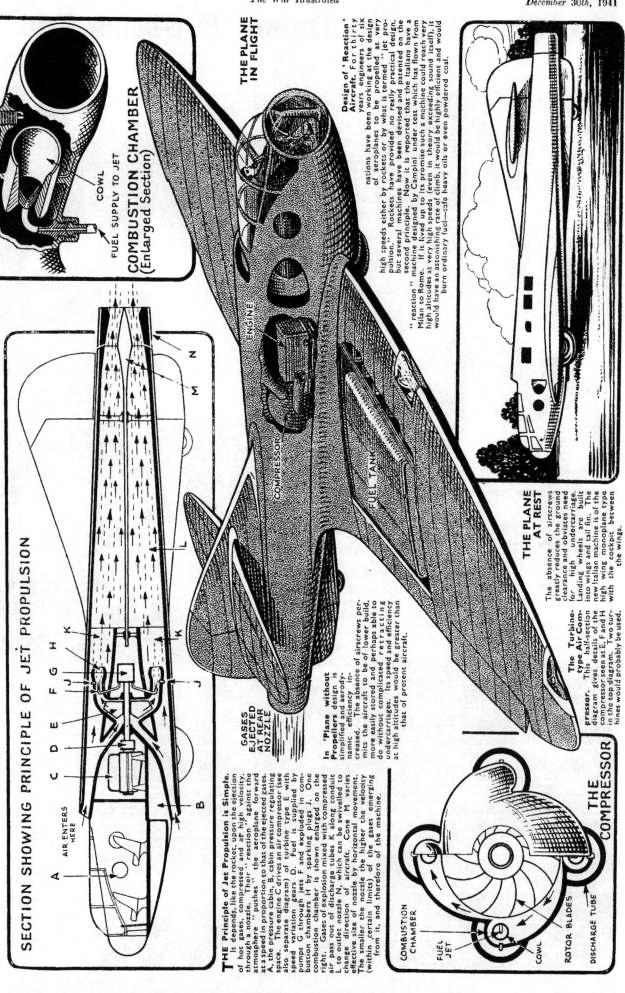

COMBUSTION CHAMBER
(Enlarged Section)

H.T. LEAD

FIRING PLUG

COWL

FUEL SUPPLY TO JET

THE PLANE IN FLIGHT

ENGINE

COMPRESSOR

FUEL TANK

SECTION SHOWING PRINCIPLE OF JET PROPULSION

A B C D E F G H J J K K L M N

AIR ENTERS HERE

THE Principle of Jet Propulsion is Simple. It depends, like the rocket, upon the ejection of hot gases, compressed and at high velocity, through a nozzle. Their " reaction " against the atmosphere " pushes " the aeroplane forward at a speed in proportion to that of the ejected gases. A, the pressure cabin, B, cabin pressure regulating space. The engine C drives an air compressor (see also separate diagram) of turbine type E with speed variation gears D. Fuel is supplied by pumps G through jets F and exploded in combustion chambers H by sparking plugs J. One combustion chamber is shown enlarged on the right. Gases of explosion mixed with compressed air pass out of discharge tubes K along conduit L to outlet nozzle N, which can be swelled to change direction of aircraft. Cone M varies effective size of nozzle the higher the velocity (within certain limits) of the gases emerging from it, and therefore of the machine.

GASES EJECTED AT REAR NOZZLE

In 'Plane without Propellers design is simplified and aerodynamic efficiency increased. The absence of airscrews permits the aircraft to be of lower build, more easily stored and perhaps able to do without complicated retracting undercarriages. Its speed and efficiency at high altitudes would be greater than that of present aircraft.

Design of ' Reaction ' Aircraft. For thirty years engineers of six nations have been working at the design of aeroplanes to be propelled at very high speeds either by rockets or by what is termed " jet propulsion." Rockets have provided no really practical design, but several machines have been devised and patented on the second principle. Now it is reported that the Italians have a " reaction " machine designed by Campini under test which has flown from Milan to Rome. If it lived up to its promise such a machine could reach very high altitudes at very high speeds (even in theory exceeding sound itself), it would have an astonishing rate of climb, it would be highly efficient and would burn ordinary fuel—safe heavy oils or even powdered coal.

THE PLANE AT REST

The absence of airscrews greatly reduces the ground clearance and obviates need for high undercarriage. Landing wheels are built into wings and tail fin. The new Italian machine is of the high wing monoplane type with the cockpit between the wings.

The Turbine-type Air Compressor. This half-section diagram gives details of the compressor seen at F, and H in the top diagram. Two turbines would probably be used.

THE COMPRESSOR

COMBUSTION CHAMBER

FUEL JET

COWL

ROTOR BLADES

DISCHARGE TUBE

Gondar Falls: The End of An Empire

"Not a single leaf remains in the wreath of laurels with which the counterfeit Caesar, the toothless beast of prey, Mussolini, decorated himself," wrote "Pravda," famous Russian newspaper, on the morrow of the fall of Gondar, last of the Italian strongholds in Abyssinia. "The East African Empire of Italy, so proudly proclaimed in Rome, has collapsed like a house built of the sand of the African desert."

FOR months the Italians in Gondar, deep in the mountains to the north of Lake Tana, kept their flag flying—until long after, indeed, every other Italian stronghold in Abyssinia had surrendered. But it fell at last. On the evening of November 27 the Union Jack was run up over the offices of the Bank of Italy in Gondar. Only the town's inaccessibility enabled it to hold out so long, and in order to subdue it British engineers with East African labour had to build a mountain road up which the guns and lorries were able to move. This highway, constructed all unknown to the Italians, was their undoing.

Before dawn on November 27 a heavy artillery barrage was put down by African and Indian batteries, and this, combined with deadly air bombing, enabled the infantry to advance. Up the rocky slopes they clambered, and by midday the attackers had turned the enemy's southern flank and were assailing his rear. The final assault was delivered by East African troops; indeed, more East Africans fought at Gondar than in any other single engagement. Men of the King's African Rifles occupied the enemy's forward positions at Defeccia and Maldiba, east of the town, and at about 2 o'clock in the afternoon clouds of smoke arose as the garrison fired their ammunition dumps and store houses. Step by step enemy resistance was overcome, and only one Italian battery near the strongly fortified position at Diva was still firing when at 3 p.m. white flags were hoisted here and there.

At 3.30 General Nasi, the Italian commander, sent an envoy to ask for an armistice. Major-General C. C. Fowkes, Commander of the Imperial division concerned in the operations, replied that surrender must be unconditional. So two or three hours more passed. Then there was the noise of fighting in the streets, while at the same time a message was received from the enemy in the Ambazzo area, which was still holding out, also asking for terms of surrender. A little later General Nasi agreed to surrender unconditionally, and the "Cease Fire" was sounded. Some 11,500 Italian prisoners were taken and 12,000 native levies. They were permitted to march out with the honours of war.

The next day General Wetherall, G.O.C.-in-C. East African Command, reviewed the conquerors. On the parade were men from the Mother Country —a battalion of the Argyll and Sutherlands was mentioned — East, South, and West Africa, the Sudan, India, Ethiopia, both regulars and irregulars, and a detachment of Free French —the whole presenting a magnificent and stirring picture. Following the parade there was a march

GONDAR and district, which was finally cleared of Italian power and influence by the British forces under Major-Gen. C. C. Fowkes on November 27.
By courtesy of "The Times."

past, General Wetherall taking the salute. Then a personal message from him was read out by individual companies, ten different translations being necessary to ensure that the diverse nations on the parade all understood.

With the capture of Gondar the East African force has accomplished its immediate mission in defeating the last of the Italian forces opposed to us.

To carry this out we have advanced nearly 3,000 miles, defeating in many battles an enemy superior to ourselves in numbers and artillery. We have accomplished our task owing to our superior leadership, the valour of our soldiers and the bravery of our airmen.

Some of the troops which have fought at Gondar are veterans, but the majority have seen little or no previous fighting. In the difficult and stern fight for this peace, you have all displayed the same fighting spirit.

Though in this theatre of war we have defeated our enemy, the time has not come to relax. It is only for us a breathing space in which to perfect ourselves in our own tactics and the mastery of our weapons. We do not know what plans our enemy will make for the future, but that he will fight us to the end is certain.

I have had a wire from the head of the Army in London congratulating you on the fine feat of arms entailed in the capture of Gondar. I, your present C.-in-C., am proud of you, and I am certain that whatever calls may be made on you in the future will be met with the same valour and success as you have recently displayed.

So ended the Italian Empire in East Africa. Of the great army of 300,000 troops with which Mussolini planned to invade the Sudan and possibly Egypt, only a few wanderers in the region behind Assab were left at liberty; the rest were all in the British prison-camps or under the African soil. Only six years have passed since on October 3, 1935, the Italian troops crossed the Mareb from Eritrea into Abyssinia, and so began that discreditable episode which was hailed by the Duce as a revival of the glories of ancient Rome. Following the crushing of the Abyssinian levies by sheer weight of metal, wholesale air-bombing and the shameful use of poison gas, the Negus fled to England, and Mussolini came on to the balcony in Rome and announced that Victor Emmanuel, King of Italy, had assumed the title of Emperor of Abyssinia. "This is the goal towards which for 18 years the eruptive energies of the young generations of Italy have been disciplined," he roared.

Now the tables have been turned. With the exception of the few wanderers just mentioned, there is not an Italian left in arms in the whole of East Africa, and Haile Selassie reigns again in Addis Ababa.

A general view of Gondar, showing the ruins of the old Portuguese town and fort. The last Italian stronghold in Abyssinia, it was surrendered unconditionally by General Nasi, the Italian commander, with 23,500 men, half of them Italians, and fifty guns. It was officially announced that our forces numbered less than half the enemy. The fall of Gondar brought Mussolini's East African Empire to its inglorious conclusion.
Photo, E.N.A.

At Last Every Briton Will Be Mobilized

Early in December the Government produced plans for the complete mobilization of Britain's man- and woman-power. Some account of the new proposals is given below, together with quotations from just a few of the many interesting speeches made by M.P.s in the course of the debate in the House of Commons which opened on December 2.

MOVING a resolution in the House of Commons on December 2, that in the opinion of the House " the obligation for National Service should be extended to include the resources of woman-power and man-power still available," Mr. Churchill said that 1941 had been occupied with the problems of production. The crisis of equipment is now largely over. The year 1942 will be dominated by the crisis of man-power and woman-power. Great new supply plants must be staffed ; powerful armies must be maintained at home, in the East and in India ; the Air Force is to be greatly extended in 1942, and still further in 1943 ; the Navy is growing continuously ; and, apart from our own needs, we must keep our supply engagements to Russia.

A heavy burden will fall upon us in 1942, said the Premier, and it will be necessary to make great demands upon the nation. These demands will intimately affect the lives of many men and women ; they will make further inroads upon our comfort and convenience, the character and aspect of our daily life. There will be a general moving up nearer the front which will affect a large block of the people. In a word we shall have " another instalment of toil and sweat, of inconvenience and self-denial, which I am sure will be accepted with cheerful and proud alacrity by all parties and all classes in the British nation."

Then Mr. Churchill proceeded to detail the Government's proposals. With regard to men, the system of block reservation was to be changed to one of individual deferment of military service ; the age for compulsory military service was to be raised from 41 to 51, while the limit was lowered to 18½. It was also proposed to register boys and girls between 16 and 18. Then as for women, although it was not proposed to compel married women, even those without children, to join the services, married women might volunteer, and in any case they would continue to be directed into industry. Unmarried women were to be required to serve in the uniformed Auxiliary Forces of the Crown or Civil Defence, but at the outset only those between 20 and 30 would be affected. Why is it that we have to make this demand on women for the Army ? the Prime Minister asked. Because the " two vultures " of Invasion and the Air Raider still hang over us. In conclusion, he gave a promise that the new powers would be exercised without any discrimination between person and person and class and class. " There must be no soft jobs for the privileged and hard grind for the poor."

Sweeping powers, indeed, but not too sweeping—so, at least, almost every speaker considered in the debate that followed. But speaker after speaker complained that the powers previously given to the Government had not been used as efficiently and effectively as they should have been. Compulsion, in other words, is not enough. Man- and woman-power must be properly utilized.

There must be no waste. But, so it is alleged, there is plenty of waste at present.

Hitler can produce 4,000 planes and 2,500 tanks a month, averred Mr. Horabin (N. Cornwall, Lib.) ; the enemy is fully organized for total war, but we are using only half of our potential capacity because the Government lack the moral courage to tackle the big problems—the transfer from a money to a production economy, a wages policy, conscription of management, the Civil Service . . .

Sir John Wardlaw-Milne (Kidderminster, Con.) was more explicit. He said that some

GRANDMOTHER MAKES GUNS and sets an example to the young women of the country. Mrs. Mary Connors, 55-year-old widow, who has eight grandchildren, says " our boys must have the guns " as she works at the breech of a 25-pounder.
Photo, Central Press

of the girls in the Fighting Services are doing only four-and-a-half hours' work a day, have the whole of every second week-end off, and their duties are such as girls of a similar age in civil employment are doing for eight or nine hours daily. Sir John also quoted from letters sent to him as Chairman of the Select Committee on National Expenditure. " The majority of the women," wrote one from an ordnance factory, " waste an average of four hours a day, making cups of tea and powdering their noses."

Mrs. Hardie (Springburn, Labour), who is a pacifist, declared that in her opinion war is not a woman's job, but since women are involved in it, she thought it was unfortunate that older women " are very much inclined to sacrifice younger women and get them out of the way so that they can take the places themselves."

Mrs. Mavis Tate (Frome, Con.) believed that very much more might have been done to absorb women into industry and the Forces before compulsion was introduced. She severely criticized the Minister of Health's proposal that grannies and aunts should look after the children of munition workers. Nursery schools ought to be established, yet the number of such schools is woefully small. Then she went on to describe how the other day she paid a visit incognito—she dressed up as the mate of one of the workmen—to a certain aerodrome and aircraft factory where,

she had been told, there was a tremendous waste of time.

" In the factory I saw men sleeping in a shed, men whose work it is to wheel out a few aeroplanes in the morning and wheel them back again at night. In the interval they do absolutely nothing. I saw large luxury motor-coaches which drive the men to work in the morning from about 15 miles away. The men who drive those coaches that tremendous distance of 15 miles in the morning and 15 miles at night are earning £7 a week, and they have no work whatever between the time they drive the men to work in the morning and drive them back at night. In the middle of the day they drive a coach out again—what for ? To take themselves half a mile to the canteen. It is too exhausting for them to walk. I say that while you get that sort of example— and I could give one example after another—you will not get real enthusiasm."

Another distinctly individual contribution to the debate was made by Mr. James Griffiths (Llanelly, Lab.), whose argument paralleled in large measure that put forth some few days before by Sir G. Schuster— that the ideal way of organizing the nation for National Service would be to put all, irrespective of person or class, on a common war footing. Then Mr. Griffiths made an appeal that there should be no quibbling by the Ministry of Pensions with regard to pensions that might have to be paid to the older men, the men between 41 and 51.

" They are the men of my own generation. In the main the men of that generation began work at 12 or 13 years of age. It was a generation which was half decimated in the last war, a generation that has borne 30 odd years of hard industrial toil. Many hundreds of thousands of them went through the experiences of the years from 1914 to 1918. They are now at an age when they are liable to crack. Every time I visit my native village I note with dismay that more of my generation have fallen by the wayside because they have been unable, at their age, to stand the strain of modern industrial life. When these men are called up there will be a larger percentage of breakdowns among them than among the younger generation."

Another Labour member, Mr. A Edwards (Middlesbrough, East), took the line, somewhat unusual in his party, of criticism of the Civil Service machine.

" Some of the best minds and most efficient men in the country are to be found in the Civil Service. They carry a very grave responsibility. But with the machine under which they have to work, they simply cannot do what is required. Everything in this country has speeded up except the Civil Service, which is so constructed that it cannot speed up . . . We have created a veritable Frankenstein which will destroy us if we do not deal with it. You can get the best brains you like from all industries, but as long as they have to go at the speed of the permanent officials, production will not be speeded up. That machine destroys and frustrates every effort."

But for the most part the Labour members were concerned with putting forward the view that there should be a great extension of public control and planning of industry— that conscription of property, no less than conscription of life, is vital for the proper organization of our war effort. They made this demand, not out of any traditional belief in the virtues of nationalization, but rather because in their opinion " by taking over wealth, privilege and economic power "— to quote from Mr. Griffiths again—" we shall give the people of this country an incentive—a sense of a great cooperative effort in our mission. We shall build a dynamic democracy, and not only beat Hitler and all the other forces that make for war, but we shall win the peace as well."

Russia's Factory Front Is Still Unbroken

Director of a clothing factory in Kutais (right) receiving young girl students who have applied for work. All over Russia young boys and girls are replacing men in the factories.

Centre right, Mrs. Petushkova, a Russian war worker, operating a lathe in a Russian factory. She is doing a man's job with skill and efficiency.

Below, a young girl worker operating a drilling machine in a big steel works of Western Russia. She is one of the great army of Soviet women workers.

At the foot of the page Russian munition workers pause a moment while a comrade reads the latest bulletin from the front. They know that the defence of Russia depends upon them no less than the soldiers engaged in the front line.

Photos, Planet News

I Was There!.... Eye Witness Stories of the War

Rommel Asked Me, 'Aren't You Glad?'

During his three days' captivity among the Germans in Libya, a staff sergeant of the R.A.O.C. met General Rommel face to face and was under fire from British guns. Below we give the story Sergeant Weallens told to F. G. H. Salusbury, "Daily Herald" special correspondent in Libya.

Sergeant E. Weallens, R.A.O.C., who was captured by the Nazis in Libya, saw General Rommel, and escaped. He describes his experiences in this page.   Photo, Topical

IT was on November 21, round Bir el Gubi. We had gone out to bring in a damaged vehicle, but my lorry got stuck in the sand and three of us were taken prisoner. The Jerries took us to an interpreter.

Just then a big staff car dashed up and all the Jerries jumped up as if they were on strings and started to " Heil Hitler."

There was a red-faced, strongly built fellow in the car—not too tall when he stood up. He "Heiled Hitler" too, and seemed very pleased with himself, especially when the Jerries crowded round and some of them made signs to ask if they could photograph him. When he spoke to them they were as pleased as Punch.

Then he saw us lads and he beckoned us over. I stood to attention, but I didn't salute him, and he said to me in English, "Well, Englander, aren't you glad you're out of it ? " I said " No." I said I'd like to be back with my own people. I thought he was Rommel then, and I know now because I've seen photos of him. He wore a great-coat with belt and revolver—the full trappings—and bits of ribbon in his buttonhole, German style. He was quite good-humoured, quite a cheerful-looking chap.

As we were taken away they all "Heiled Hitler" again, and Rommel went off.

They bunged us in a troop-carrier with ten Jerries. That night we went straight into action. We were dashed to hell by our own guns. Don't talk to me about our guns ; I've had my whack of them. The second day we were in the fighting round Sidi Rezegh. The third day we went. south and were hammered again. It was a proper fight.

The panzer chaps went out in those caterpillar things, then they decided to turn, and we came back through the barrage, and that was the worst of all. The column stopped and they put us on the ground. We had been there only ten minutes when our tanks came blazing through.

One of the Jerry wagons next to us went up in flames, and, knowing that it contained ammunition, I said to the lads, "Let's edge away like." So we edged away, and by the time that the Jerry rearguard came up we were safe on our bellies in the bushes.

As luck would have it I still had my compass. I'd wrapped it up in a couple of handkerchiefs and they passed it over—so we were able to make our way back in the right direction.

First thing we heard was a wireless set talking in English, so I called out "Are you British ? " and they said "Yes. Who are you ? " I said "Staff sergeant of the Ordnance Corps and a couple of lads. For Heaven's sake take us in ! "

On the day we were captured we had nothing at all to eat. The second day we had some weak tea and brown bread. The Jerries had stew once a day and some hard tack. They treated us all right. One of the lads in our truck was about 20, and he slipped us a cigarette—just human nature I guess. So I showed him a photograph of my wife and kids.

On the third day an order of the day was issued announcing that Moscow had fallen. It was just before we went into the barrage, and I got the idea that the order was read out on purpose to cheer them up.

From Berlin We Flew Homewards in Flames

When the crew of a Wellington bomber which raided Berlin on November 7 were washed up at Ventnor they had spent 57 hours in their rubber dinghy after flying over Germany in flames. Their amazing story is told here by the captain of the aircraft.

ON the outward journey on Friday evening (November 7) we encountered broken cloud as we crossed the sea, and this thickened into impenetrable masses as we got into Germany. About 30 miles from Berlin we came under fire, the German batteries shooting up at us through the cloud with predicted fire. I think it was here that we were first hit. One shell went off right underneath us. We heard a crack and everything in the aircraft shook.

But we went on to drop our high explosives on Berlin. The target was obliterated by cloud before we could drop our incendiaries and we kept these, intending to put them down on the way back.

We were on the course for home, still well inside Germany, when we were hit again by guns which opened up suddenly on us. Shells burst all round the Wellington.

Then, almost simultaneously, the second pilot and the rear-gunner reported that the aircraft was on fire. Opening the door behind me and looking back, I saw that the fuselage was filled with blinding, choking smoke. Flames were coming up through the floor and were beginning to lick up the sides.

The incendiaries had caught fire, and, 12,000 feet up, the bomber was ablaze along the whole length of the bomb racks, a target for every gun within range. While the wireless operator tapped out a message to base : " Hit by flak," the second pilot went back to tackle the fire. He shouted in the observer's ear as he passed him to tell me to jettison the incendiaries. Then, with the fire extinguisher, he tackled the fire. When the extinguisher ran out, he poured coffee from the thermos flasks on to the worst parts of the fire.

NEAR TOBRUK, Nazi armoured vehicles taking part in a night attack. In such a lorry as the one seen above, Sergeant Weallens, and two comrades, with ten Germans, found themselves in action against the British. "Don't talk to me about our guns," he writes, "I've had my whack of them." After being under British fire at Sidi Rezegh and elsewhere, Sergeant Weallens and his fellow-prisoners were put down somewhere in the Western Desert, and made good their escape.
Photo, Keystone

It seemed to have "quite a decent effect," he said. Meanwhile, the wireless operator had left his set and had gone back to try to get through to the rear of the bomber to wind out his trailing aerial, which would give him greater range and also a better chance of getting a "fix" of their position. But the smoke and flames beat him back. For ten minutes he was unable to get through.

Unable to talk to the others over the "intercom." because my mouthpiece was not working, I stuck to the controls. The front-gunner, who had been let out of his turret, stood beside me to carry messages between me and the rest of the crew. The smoke was so thick that at times I was forced to hold my head outside the window to be able to breathe. Back in the middle of the plane, the second pilot was fighting the fire blindly. "You couldn't see an inch in front of you," he said.

Then I threw open my escape hatch and gradually the smoke cleared as the wind rushed through the interior. After struggling for nearly ten minutes, the wireless operator was able to grope his way back to the trailing aerial. Then he went forward again to work on his set. As the bomber flew on he and the observer were checking up on their position. Repeatedly the wireless operator sent out messages. At the end of every message he added an S O S signal.

We tried to jettison the incendiary containers, but they would not drop. The electrical switch system was not working. As the blazing bomber flew on, it was still under fire from the flak batteries on the ground. You could hear the crumps all round us. I can't make out how it was they didn't blow us out of the sky. I was expecting that at any minute after we had got away from the guns enemy fighters might come up "to finish us off."

The rear-gunner remained in his turret—at one time cut off by fire and smoke from the others—to meet a fighter attack. But no fighters appeared. Until he opened his ventilators he was half choked. All the time we were under fire he was reporting the positions of the flak. He said he could hardly hear the others' voices over the "intercom."

Eventually the fire inside the aircraft was put out, but the incendiaries were still burning. I found that I could close the bomb doors—or what was left of them—and the fire died down for a minute, then flared up again. Several times we tried opening and shutting the doors in the hope that we might get it out altogether. Then, we decided to keep them closed to hide as much light as possible from the ground defences.

Looking through the astro hatch, the second pilot saw for the first time that while he had been fighting flames inside the aircraft, fire had burnt away part of the fabric of one of the wings.

Gradually we lost height until—over two hours later—we crossed the enemy coast at a height of only 1,000 feet. The incendiaries were still burning. We knew it was touch-and-go to cross the sea. We thought we'd take a chance on coming down in the water rather than come down in enemy territory, so we flew on. Twenty-five minutes after we had crossed the coast the engines spluttered and failed. All the petrol had gone. We had been flying then nearly three hours after the bomber had caught on fire.

Everything had been made ready for coming down in the sea. When the bomber hit the water, its back was broken. Because of the damage to the aircraft I was unable to get the tail down to make "a decent landing," and the aircraft went into the water nose down. It went underneath for

practically the whole of its length, and then the empty petrol tanks in the wings floated it to the surface again. The flotation gear had been burnt away.

The wireless operator was still working at his set, sending out signals, when the machine hit the water. Within a minute the aircraft sank, but during that time all the crew managed to get out. We were in the water hanging on to the dinghy's ropes. One by one we clambered into the dinghy. One of us was a non-swimmer. I had one leg injured and my face was cut through being badly thrown forward against my instrument panel when we hit the water. The others who had been able to get into positions for a crash landing were unhurt.

We just sat in the dinghy waiting for dawn to break. The next day—Saturday—was really lovely—sunny and warm—and the sea was like a mill-pond. At about ten in the morning we saw some Hurricanes in the distance, but they didn't see us. About half an hour after we'd come down in the sea a plane dropped some Very lights above us. It must have been fairly high because we couldn't hear the engines very loud. We signalled an S O S with a torch. We paddled all Saturday. The crew was marvellous—not a grouse, not a moan. We paddled most of the night, too, taking it in turns, two at a time. It helped to keep us warm. On Sunday the weather was bad the whole time, big seas were

running, but the dinghy was first class. When the water came over, we baled out with tins. We rationed our food and drink for six days. We had biscuits and chocolate, rum and water.

On Sunday night the wind came up stronger still. When the sun came up the next morning we saw a buoy go swishing by. We seemed to be moving at a devil of a speed with the tide. Seeing the buoy sort of bucked things up. Then we saw the coast in the distance. We were afraid we were going to be carried past it so we all paddled like dingbats, but we were being taken in pretty fast. After a time we could see people. Then, as we got nearer, we waved. We could see them waving back. We paddled to within 20 yards of the shore and then a big sea more or less washed us up to the rescuers who had waded out.

Four members of a bomber crew whose aeroplane was hit by German "flak" over Berlin, and later came down in the sea. The crew's amazing experiences are described in this page.
Photo, Keystone

On My Way to Kuibyshev from Moscow

As the Germans drew ever nearer to Moscow, those people of the city who were not required in the fighting line or the factories were evacuated to Kuibyshev, 450 miles away on the Volga. Among them was the well-known Russian writer, Vsevolod Ivanov, whose account is printed below.

I STOOD on the bank of the broad, full-flowing Volga at Kuibyshev. Around me lay a large town, with smoking factory chimneys, motor-cars whirling by blowing their horns, large steamboats plying up and down the river . . .

I came here from Moscow. Many friends have come with me and many more are still arriving by train and by steamboat. The tale of our journey is brief and essentially the same in all cases. There is no room for "civilians"—if one can speak of civilians in this war—near the trenches. I was a non-combatant and needed quiet for my work: I was ordered to leave.

On the way out here there was a great deal of sadness in the faces of my fellow-travellers. But when troop-train after troop-train passed us going towards the west a new expression appeared on those sad faces. One realized that this was the sadness of parting, not the sadness of death and decay.

Our train moved along slowly. Frequently we were shunted aside to allow passage to the numerous trains loaded with troops, guns, motor vehicles. Sometimes our train halted at some tiny wayside station amid snow and oak trees from which the leaves had scarcely fallen.

Then I would go and visit the Red Army men in their cars. The walls of the cars were decorated with posters and hand-

written newspapers produced by the soldiers themselves. Here was a call to smite the German hard "so that he'll never forget our plains and never think of invading them again." There were caricatures of the enemy, drawn if not with skill at least with wrath. Almost every one of these wall-newspapers urged railwaymen to greater speed. One declared outright: "We have been waiting and begging for this moment for four months. Drive us faster, comrades!"

I got into conversation with some of the men. They were artillerymen from Siberia. Thickset, of no great stature, but with evidently inexhaustible strength. They apparently knew what they were in for, and they would probably fight like Siberians who are accustomed both to hard scraps and hard weather.

The most moving sight in our journey was to see the meeting between factories which were being evacuated to the east and the troops moving towards the west. On one track stood cars loaded with guns, on the other track rows of cars loaded with machinery which made the guns. A damp heavy snow fell, covering the tarpaulins with a white shroud. One could imagine the machines saying to the guns, as they met for a moment: "Don't worry—we'll soon be sending you some brothers."—*Soviet War News*

Editor's Postscript

In these distressful days of lightning change from hour to hour, it is beyond man's wit to forecast the state of things even so near as a week ahead. "The shape of things to come" indeed! There is no more shapeliness in them than in the flood from a burst water-main. So, although this issue of THE WAR ILLUSTRATED is dated for the day of publication while I am writing nearly a fortnight in advance of that, what disturbing or heartening events happen meanwhile might make anything written today seem woefully wide of the mark. I shall therefore confine this note to an expression of the hope and belief that all the disasters of the last few days— these being some of the heavy blows which Mr. Churchill has so often warned us to expect—all these notwithstanding, I look to a great redressing in 1942. The treachery of Japan has disclosed a deplorable state of unreadiness in America, for which the Isolationists may be thanked. That our Trans-atlantic allies will soon recover from these staggering blows must not be doubted; that the Anglo-Saxon world, now fused into one mass of furious energy, will go forward to eventual and overwhelming victory is certain. If the shadows that overhang the ending weeks of 1941 are heavy, like all shadows they will pass; and if 1942 cannot take the world through to daylight, we can at least hope it will bring the first streaks of dawn. The Eastern windows have at the moment of writing opened to darkness, but "say not the struggle naught availeth," and so into the New Year of Hope!

My week-end reading has been rather a "mixed grill." Until now I have known of Willa Cather, one of the most distinguished American novelists, only by reputation. One whose judgement in books has never failed me put a copy of "A Lost Lady" in my hand, and having started to read this short novel in the train I read nothing else that evening—not even the newspapers—until I had finished what is one of the finest of the many fine examples of story-telling that have come to us from America. The story runs to no more than 35,000 words, and yet there are no fewer than ten characters in it who stand out "in the round" as living creatures of life's drama whom the reader is not likely to forget.

I am not likely to forget "A Lost Lady" for another reason. One of the dominating figures in the story is that of a horrid American type: the cruel, ruthless small-town young man who tramples his way to material success as mercilessly as any Italian gangster, but contrives to keep within the law, often by qualifying himself as lawyer. We first meet this particular rascal when he is eighteen, trying to impress a group of quite decent youngsters by capturing a woodpecker and, with devilish dexterity and a tiny razor blade, slitting its eyes so that the poor creature amused him by its wild eyeless flight among the tall beeches . . . to the horror of the younger lads. With true insight the novelist does not bring him to a bad end, for it just isn't true that evildoers are always or often punished—except in novels and melodramas. This loathsome young sadist is left flourishing. But I shall link him now with the actual Neapolitan nobleman who used to keep three thousand quails on his lovely estate, all with their eyes made blind by red-hot bodkins: a horror that has often haunted my mind since I first heard of it in Naples more than thirty years ago.

A rare instance of swift punishment for cruelty I find related in Prof. E. M. Butler's bulky life-study of Rainer Maria Rilke, the mystic German poet, to whose work, still little known in England, I have only recently been introduced by the same friend who has put me on to Willa Cather.

Admiral HAROLD R. STARK, known as "Betty" Stark to the American fleet, is U.S. Naval Commander-in-Chief. He has served in the U.S. Navy as Chief of Ordnance and as commander of cruisers of the American Battle Force.   *Photo, Associated Press*

The young Rilke (who had been brought up as a girl until he was five and had twenty-four different nurses before his first birthday!) scored one up on a bully at an Austrian military academy: "One Christmas Eve, when they were all packing for the holidays, a brutal senior, seeing the little boy lost in happy dreams beside his brimming valise, tossed it up to the ceiling and broke into coarse laughter as the contents scattered over the room. Suddenly to his own surprise and even horror, René (as Rainer was then known) heard his own voice saying loudly and emphatically: 'I know that you won't get home for the holidays.' His tormentor began to laugh, slipped, fell and broke his leg. He did *not* get home for the holidays, and this evidence of prophetic or psychic gifts earned their owner a not unenviable reputation in that barbarous community."

And this week-end, too, I may confess my failure in attempting to renew a very slight acquaintance with the work of a popular author—the late John Buchan. (I am not interested in him as Lord Tweedsmuir.) I started out joyfully with Dickson McCunn, retired grocer of bookish tastes in search of romance, and elderly hero of "Huntingtower." Buchan's delightful mastery of the Glesca dialect as exemplified by McCunn at times and always, in its lower depths, by the "Gorbals Die-Hards," could not fail to rejoice one whose youth had been spent in St. Mungo's grey, grimy, but go-ahead city.

All went well until we got to Huntingtower, when began a great stir about stolen jewels, a prisoned maiden, and a bunch of characters who could have walked out of any boys' paper yarn in the last fifty years or so. All told, mind you, in the most vigorous and scholarly manner. I felt that I knew where the Gorbals Die-Hards originated: it was in the Den at Thrums, and somehow under the lead of Tommy and Corp Shiach they were more credible. So having finished the chapter "Of the Princess in the Tower" I skipped the next two hundred pages and read the last two just to make sure that it all came out according to the formula of my old friend Charles Pearce, who, forty years ago, used to keep five or six yarns of a similar kind (not so finely written, be it said) running simultaneously in as many different boys' papers! It seems a pity to find so much good writing and power of characterization, as well as humour, devoted to this sort of story.

One passage in "Huntingtower" reads quaintly in these rationed days: Mrs. Morran "had been baking that morning, so there were white scones and barley scones, and oaten farles and russet pancakes. There were three boiled eggs for each of them . . . there was skim milk cheese" . . . but that's enough! Yet I can make those who like eggs, boiled, fried, or poached, still more jealous of the plenteous past by turning to P. G. Hamerton's "A Painter's Camp in the Highlands." Malcolm was the name of an extraordinary Highlander who used to do the author the honour of visiting him at his camp on the island of Inishail in Loch Awe. "By way of preparing himself for the more serious business of breakfast, it is a custom of his, when eggs are obtainable, to beat a dozen of them together in a basin with whisky and sugar, and eat the whole raw mess with a spoon, like soup." That was just a sort of cocktail, for when breakfast came along with trout, mutton chops and eggs, Malcolm had the nerve to complain because he was given only four boiled eggs! "Go and boil six and twenty," he said to the serving man, "you'll find two dozen in the box in my boat." The author privately instructed his servant just to boil another four for the ravenous Highlander "which, with the four he had eaten, the plates of mutton chops, the plates of trouts, the loaf of bread, and the six cups of a strong coffee, I considered a sufficient breakfast." Twenty eggs for his breakfast! Are we one-egg-a-fortnighters envious?

Printed in England and published on the 10th, 20th, and 30th of each month by the Proprietors, The Amalgamated Press, Ltd., The Fleetway House, Farringdon Street, London, E.C.4. Registered for transmission by Canadian Magazine Post. Sole Agents for Australia and New Zealand : Messrs. Gordon & Gotch, Ltd. ; and for South Africa : Central News Agency, Ltd. December 30th, 1941.   S.S.   *Editorial Address :* JOHN CARPENTER HOUSE WHITEFRIARS, LONDON, E.C.4

Vol 5 The War Illustrated Nº 117

Edited by Sir John Hammerton

FOURPENCE

JAN. 10TH, 1942

TOBRUK RELIEVED. New Zealanders smile as they pass a " Matilda " tank, one of those which sallied out from Tobruk to link up with the New Zealanders at El Duda. General Freyberg, V.C., Commander of the N.Z. Division, stated in his report to the New Zealand Government : " It is fair to claim that the part played by the New Zealand Division, which has destroyed a large portion of the German force, together with a great deal of their equipment and material, will prove a great contribution to the campaign."

Photo, British Official : Crown Copyright

NO. 118 WILL BE PUBLISHED TUESDAY, JAN. 20

FOUR HUNDRED MILLION CHINESE OUR ALLIES

ALTHOUGH the Chinese have been fighting the Japanese invaders since the summer of 1937, there was no formal declaration of war until the other day. The Japanese have always referred to the struggle in which a million-and-a-half of their troops are engaged as the " China incident." They cán employ that half-contemptuous expression no longer. On December 9 Dr. Quo Tai-chi, Foreign Minister in General Chiang Kai-Shek's government in Chungking, announced that China had decided to declare war on Japan, Germany, and Italy. A few days later a Chinese government spokesman declared that China was eager to contribute her share in the fight and '' whatever we can do is being done and will always be done.'' He disclosed that General Chiang Kai-Shek had formally proposed to Britain and the U.S.A. that a military alliance should be formed against the Axis, directed by a unified command and in agreement on the grand strategy of the war.

FOR four years the Chinese have been fighting the Japanese. They have suffered great reverses. Many of the Chinese provinces and the whole of the coastline are in enemy hands, together with nearly all the most important cities. Hundreds of thousands of Chinese have been killed in battle or died of wounds, or from hardship and famine brought about by war's dislocation of the country's economy. But the Chinese people are tough ; they have tremendous staying power and are hardened to suffering and to want. Time after time the Japanese, realizing the impossibility of conquering the huge mass of China—at least within an appreciable time—have offered to come to terms. But the only man capable of speaking for China as a whole is Chiang Kai-Shek, and he at the very beginning of hostilities told his people that '' there is no looking backward : we must fight to the bitter end.'' All the Japanese have been able to do is to persuade some fifth columnists of a most unsavoury type —disreputable politicians, traitors and crooks and bankrupts—to accept office as their puppet underlings in North and Central China. At Nanking there is what purports to be a Chinese government under a certain Wang Ching-wei, and a year ago this was formally recognized by the Japanese, and by Germany and Italy six months later. But Wang has a reputation for inconsistency and disloyalty, and must prove but a slender support for Japanese pretensions. He is a poet as well as a politician ; maybe he would have been safer if he had stuck to poetry.

CHIANG KAI-SHEK is the personification of Free China. He, more than any man, has brought a united China into being. For many years following the deposition of the last of the Manchu emperors in 1911, China was one vast battle-field in which war-lord fought war-lord, the Communists fought the Nationalists, and the people paid the price. But since 1927 Chiang Kai-Shek has been China's national leader. Sometimes he has been (and is again today) the Prime Minister—President of the Executive Yuan, as they put it ; always he has been Generalissimo of the Chinese armed forces. In China today he occupies a position com-

parable with that of Churchill in Britain, Roosevelt in America, and Stalin in Russia.

Not for many centuries has China produced so strong and vigorous a character. Born in 1887 in a seaside village of Chekiang province, he came of moderately well-to-do stock, neither rich nor poor. His mother seems to have been a remarkable woman, and he has expressed his deep indebtedness to her influence. He received his military training in Japan, and even served for a time in the Japanese Army. On his return to China he became an ardent Republican and served Sun Yat-sen in various civil and military capacities ; in particular, he was head of the military academy at Whampoa, where Russian tutors trained the officers of China's Nationalist armies. Then he came into prominence as a leader of the Nationalist forces operating from Canton. Followed years of campaigning against one war-lord or the other and, more particularly, the Communists. In 1928, having defeated every rival, he became virtual dictator. Since then he has been chiefly engaged in captaining his people against the Japanese invaders.

IF Chiang Kai-Shek is China's No. One, then No. Two is his wife, Mayling Soong, whom he married in 1927. '' Madame,'' as she is styled throughout China, is as remarkable a personage as her husband. She is the youngest of the three Soong sisters and, like them, was educated in America. Her eldest sister, Ai-ling, is the wife of H.H. Kung, at present Minister of Finance at Chungking, and generally reputed to be China's most able financier. The second, Ching-ling, is the widow of Dr. Sun Yat-sen. Of the three brothers, T. V., T. L., and T. A., the best known is T. V., who was China's Finance Minister for nine years up to 1933, and has always been one of the most pronounced opponents of the Japanese. All the Soongs are Christians—Soong *père*, after an American education, was converted

to Christianity, returned to China as a missionary and helped to found the first Y.M.C.A. in Shanghai ; Chiang Kai-Shek is a Christian, too, though he was not when Mayling married him. He knows his Bible and quotes scripture on occasion, but his Christianity is of the variety of Cromwell and Chinese Gordon ; at times he has shown in actual campaigning a certain ruthlessness.

BUT while Chiang Kai-Shek dominates the Chinese scene, he has a number of most capable subordinates. Those of his family, or rather, his '' in-laws,'' have been just mentioned. Also included in the innermost circle at Chungking is the Australian journalist, W. H. Donald, who entered the General's service in 1934 as a kind of confidential adviser and friend, and has the reputation of being the only man who dares say '' no '' to him—and says it quite often. Another striking personality is Dr. Quo Tai-chi, who last April was appointed Minister of Foreign Affairs, following a term of office in London as Chinese Ambassador. His place in London was taken by Dr. Wellington Koo, who, after a brilliant career at Columbia University, became Chinese Minister to the U.S.A. at 27, and won renown by his capable handling of Chinese affairs at Geneva. Yet another great Chinese must be mentioned— Dr. Hu Shih, who for some years past has been Chinese Minister at Washington. Dr. Hu, the '' Voltaire of China,'' is the father of the Chinese Renaissance, since he it was that popularized the use of Pai-hua, a colloquial, much simpler form of Chinese than the classical Mandarin. By means of Pai-hua every Chinese may hope to learn to read and write —a revolution indeed.

THESE, then, are the men who are the leaders of Free China. Under their immediate control is about half the Chinese population, and their authority extends far into Japanese-occupied territory. They have built up a great army of about a million

SOLDIERS OF FREE CHINA. Very different from the ill-equipped and hastily organized troops which first met the Japanese invaders four years ago is Chiang Kai-Shek's army of today. The Chinese cadets we see here are now to be counted among our comrades-in-arms.
Photo, Associated Press

men, while the irregulars must number at least two millions more. They have worked an economic revolution in their once backward and backwater provinces—and here let us mention the Chinese Industrial Cooperatives, the movement launched in 1938 through the inspiration of Mr. Rewi Alley, a New Zealander. Nor is their influence bounded by the limits of China : the eight million Chinese who have their homes in Indo-China, Malaya, Burma, the Dutch East Indies and the Philippines have sent to Chungking millions of dollars to pay for war needs.

FOR years Free China has been fighting one of the partners of the Axis. While we were appeasing Hitler and Mussolini, China was fighting Hitler's and Mussolini's ally. Moreover, we have endeavoured to appease Japan. Chungking, as the '' Economist '' pointed out a few weeks ago, '' has been bombed by planes using American petrol ; the cities of China have fallen to soldiers wearing British wool and carrying weapons forged by British machines.'' For four years and more China fought a lonely battle against our enemy, as well as hers. Only now has that fact been at long last recognized. Today China has her place in the world-wide Freedom Front. ROYSTON PIKE

After Four Years of War Free China Fights On

During four years of bitter warfare against the Japanese, the Chinese have worked hard to become self-sufficient in armaments, and, left, Chinese workers are seen packing "potato masher" grenades in a Chinese munitions factory. Above, women of the Chinese Red Cross.

CHINESE TANKS manoeuvring in a typically Chinese terrain with rice-fields in the foreground. Many new brigades of light tanks have been established in General Chiang Kai-Shek's army, these units being especially suited to the type of country in which they have to operate. Inset map shows the direction of the Chinese attempt (black arrows) to create a diversion in the rear of the Japanese forces which attacked Hong Kong.

Photos, Mrs. T. Muir and Associated Press.   Map, Courtesy of the "Daily Mail"

In Libya 'Only One Order—Attack and Pursue!'

THE BRITISH OFFENSIVE in Libya, which after its initial successes had at one time seemed to be developing into a stalemate, resumed its forward momentum in the middle of December. "Give the enemy no rest," ordered Gen. Auchinleck. "There is only one order—attack and pursue!" These photographs from the Libyan front show : top, Indian infantry charging through gaps in enemy wire made by the Bren carriers during the attack on Jalo. Centre, captured Italians waving white handkerchiefs and holding up their hands as a British escort, marching backwards, keeps them covered. Below, a British cruiser tank passing a blazing German tank set on fire during a fight with British units.

Photos, British Official

South Africa 'Ueber Deutschland' in the Desert

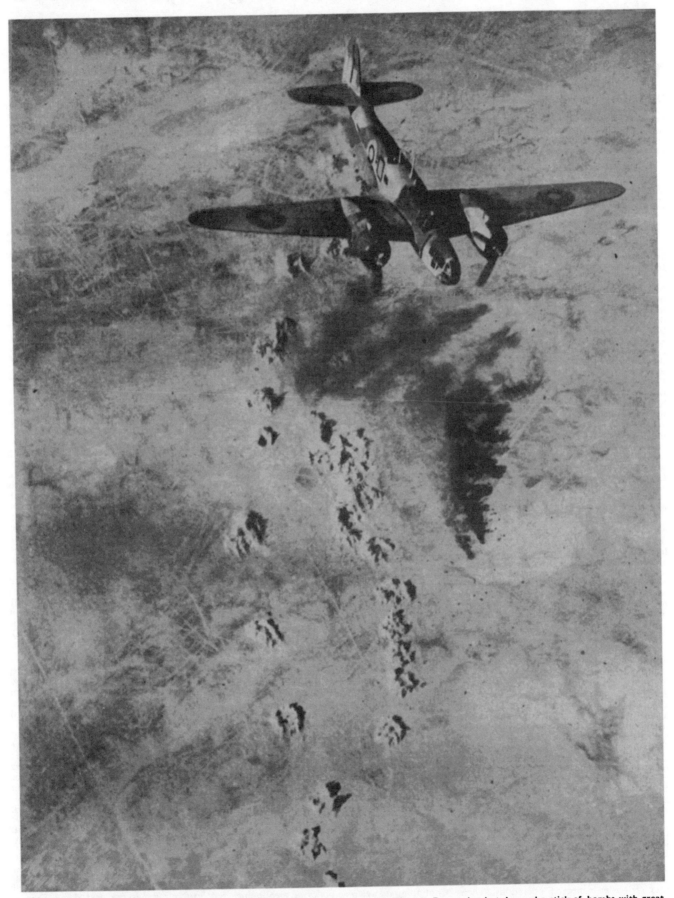

A MARTIN MARYLAND bomber of the South African Air Force, operating in the Western Desert, has just dropped a stick of bombs with great accuracy upon an enemy transport column. Continuous and effective air attack upon enemy supplies and lines of communication has proved of inestimable benefit to the British land offensive in Libya. The Glenn Martin 167-B4, known in the R.A.F. as the Maryland, is a mid-wing monoplane powered by two 1,050 h.p. Pratt and Whitney Twin Wasp or two Wright Cyclone engines.

Photo, British Official : Crown Copyright

Rommel in Retreat Through Cyrenaica

Launched with such high hopes of victory and attended at the outset by some measure of success, the offensive by Britain's 8th Army in the Libyan Desert soon lost its impetus, and after a few days it seemed likely that the struggle would deteriorate into one of attrition. But following General Auchinleck's arrival at advanced H.Q. the offensive was again assumed, and ere long Rommel was " on the run."

WHEN General Auchinleck, Commander-in-Chief Middle East, arrived at the 8th Army's H.Q. in the Libyan Desert on November 24, he was quick to appreciate that the situation was going none too well. One of his first acts was to change the command (see page 367). Then he issued to the new Commander, Lt.-Gen. N. M. Ritchie, an Order of the Day.

There is no doubt whatever that the enemy will be beaten. His position is desperate. He is trying by lashing out in all directions to distract us from our objective, which is to destroy him utterly. We will not be distracted, and he will be destroyed. You have got your teeth into him. Hold on. Bite deeper and deeper, and hang on until he is finished. Give him no rest. There is only one order—attack and pursue. All out, everyone.

Then began what Mr. Churchill described as Auchinleck's battle. At its outset the Imperial troops were grouped along an " offensive line " running from El Gobi to Sidi Rezegh. Another British force was holding Tobruk, but Rommel had succeeded in breaking the corridor which for a short time had joined the garrison and the army attacking from the south. The enemy were also holding Sollum and Bardia, but they were being harassed continually by New Zealanders and British. This was the position at the beginning of December ; what followed we may discover from the communiqués issued from British G.H.Q. Cairo—albeit none too clearly since " in this fluid battle which has ranged on the main front with local fluctuation over an area of some 1,600 square miles since November 20, the centre of gravity has altered almost daily as our or the enemy's main tank concentrations mass for attack or counter-attack."

That was said on December 2 ; the day before the enemy had thrown into the battle all his available armour on a comparatively narrow front, and there had been heavy fighting in the area Rezegh-Bir el Hamed-Zaafran. That same day R.A.F. H.Q. announced that British, South African and Free French aircraft had been in action against enemy tanks and transport in the neighbourhood of Sidi Rezegh, while Bardia and Benghazi had also been raided. The German contribution to the picture was the claim that since the beginning of the fighting more than 9,000 prisoners, including three generals, had been brought in, while 814 British tanks had been captured or destroyed, and 127 British aeroplanes shot down.

For a few days there was a marked lull throughout the desert. Fighting continued, particularly to the south-east of Tobruk, but both sides, exhausted by the terrific battles of the past fortnight, were engaged in re-grouping and reforming their forces. There was air activity on both sides, but heavy rain seriously hampered operations. Then, on December 5, Cairo reported that " the tempo in Eastern Cyrenaica has again quickened." The enemy delivered three

heavy attacks on Ed Duda, south-east of Tobruk, and gained a little ground ; Indian forces were in action against enemy troops near Bir el Gobi, and in the frontier area New Zealand troops engaged an enemy column west of Menastir. The next day came the news that the armoured forces of both sides had joined battle on December 6, and then on December 8 came the news that the British pressure throughout the whole battle area was steadily increasing. A tank action west of Bir el Gobi was reported, and amongst the regiments named as having distinguished themselves were the King's Dragoon Guards, 11th Hussars, and the Border Regiment ; and it was made known that the Rifle Brigade, the King's Royal Rifles, and the Royal Sussex Regiment (at Sidi Omar) had also been doing excellent work. Fighting patrols of the Borderers were clearing the Sidi Rezegh area, and had recovered a New Zealand divisional dressing station which had been overrun by the

COAST OF LIBYA, showing the sites of the principal engagements fought by the British 8th Army during its advance through the province of Cyrenaica.   *Map by courtesy of " The Times "*

enemy during the attack in which he had occupied Sidi Rezegh about December 1.

First news of a most important development was contained in the Cairo announcement of December 9. " In the main area between Tobruk and Bir el Gobi," it read, " there was some westerly movement of the enemy." But neither the scale nor the degree of this movement seemed at first more than local, and it was thought that it was possibly an endeavour by the enemy to gain some temporary respite from the incessant attacks by our mobile columns. But it was more than that. " The westerly movement of the enemy," reported Cairo on December 10, " has now apparently accelerated under the vigorous pressure of our forces, with the fullest and most effective cooperation of our air forces. The remaining enemy armoured forces are endeavouring to cover this westerly movement." . . . It was also announced that British troops from Tobruk had joined hands in El Adem on December 9, with South African and Indian troops from the south-east. " The siege of Tobruk has therefore been raised, and road communication has been opened with the east." Continuing its welcome policy of mentioning particular units engaged in the fighting, Cairo reported that South African armoured cars and mobile columns of the Buffs

Punjabis and Rajputs had been working round the enemy's right arm towards Acroma.

General Ritchie's mobile forces continued to attack the enemy, whose trend of movement was north-west and west from El Adem. British armoured forces went into action against a number of German tanks which were endeavouring to interfere with operations being carried out west of El Adem by Sikhs, Punjabis, and the Royal Sussex Regiment ; farther east the South Africans cleared up the area north of the Trigh-Capuzzo, and New Zealanders and Poles mopped up in the neighbourhood of Tobruk. Still the news continued to be good. Came December 12, and Cairo announced that " in spite of the bad weather and heavy sandstorms which have now continued for two days, our advance is everywhere being pressed with the utmost vigour in a north-westerly direction." Meanwhile, the R.A.F. were, as always, exceedingly active, not only over the Libyan battle area proper, but along the enemy's lines of communications and base ports, right back to Benghazi and beyond.

On December 13, 14, and 15 German lorry-borne infantry, supported by the remaining German tanks, delivered three counter-attacks with the greatest determination. The brunt of the onslaught was borne by the 4th Indian Division in the centre of our line. Ably backed up by battalions of the 4th Sikh Regiment and 1st Punjab Regiment, the Buffs, supported by the 21st Field Regiment, Royal Artillery, played the decisive part in finally defeating the counter-attacks in which about 20 German tanks and a number of Axis aircraft were destroyed. This counter-attack of Rommel's was a gallant effort, but it was of no avail. Ritchie's 8th Army rolled on.

Slowly the centre of the battle in Cyrenaica moved westward. Gazala was surrounded by New Zealand troops, and the road from there to Derna and the aerodrome at Derna were heavily bombed. In spite of bad weather with low clouds and rain, the Imperial forces made steady progress, so that a month after the opening of the offensive Cairo was enabled to claim that the war was going definitely in our favour. On December 16 heavy sandstorms and general bad weather slowed down the rate of advance, but on December 18 British G.H.Q. in Cairo announced that " the Axis forces in Eastern Cyrenaica are now in full retreat. After five days of intensive fighting, in which all remaining German and Italian resources had been thrown into the battle . . . the enemy's front has everywhere been broken."

By nightfall of December 18 Derna aerodrome had been captured and the town itself fell into our hands the next day. Then at 11 a.m. on Christmas Eve British troops entered Benghazi. They had covered 250 miles in 5 days.

British Planes and American Tanks in Libya

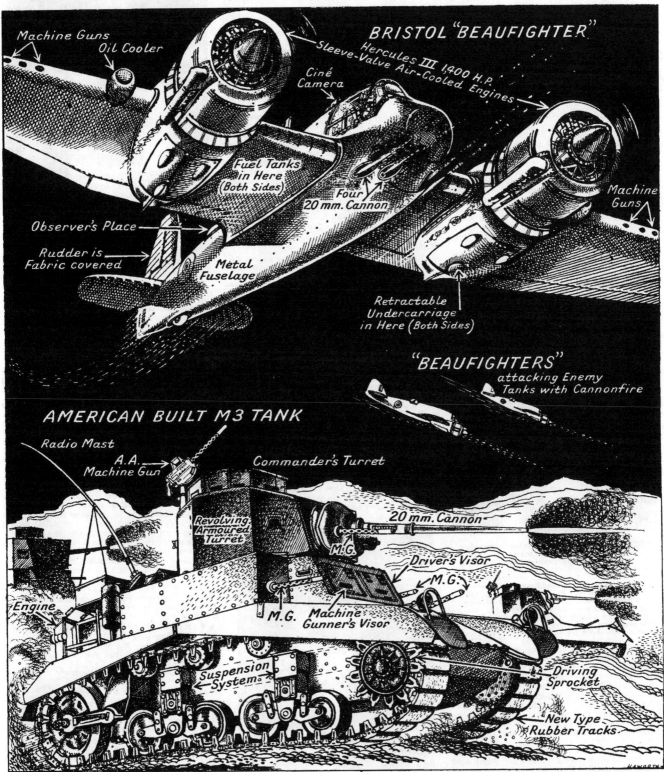

Machine Guns
Oil Cooler

BRISTOL "BEAUFIGHTER"
Hercules III 1,400 H.P.
Sleeve-Valve Air-Cooled Engines

Ciné Camera

Fuel Tanks in Here (Both Sides)

Four 20 mm. Cannon

Machine Guns

Observer's Place

Rudder is Fabric covered

Metal Fuselage

Retractable Undercarriage in Here (Both Sides)

"BEAUFIGHTERS" attacking Enemy Tanks with Cannonfire

AMERICAN BUILT M3 TANK

Radio Mast

A.A. Machine Gun

Commander's Turret

Revolving Armoured Turret

20 mm. Cannon

M.G.

Driver's Visor

M.G.

Engine

M.G. Machine Gunner's Visor

Driving Sprocket

Suspension System

New Type Rubber Tracks

HAWORTH

BATTLING IN LIBYA, the two units shown in this diagram have dealt heavy blows to the German-Italian forces.

The Bristol Beaufighter, latest of a long line of famous Bristol designs, combines tremendous fire-power, long range, high speed and manoeuvrability. An all-metal mid-wing monoplane, fitted with two Bristol Hercules engines, it has a nominal top speed of 330 m.p.h. at 14,000 feet, its service ceiling being just under 30,000 feet. The exceptionally heavy armament includes four 20 mm. cannon in the fuselage and six machine-guns in the wings. The Beaufighter, which has a wing-span of 57 ft. 10 in. and a length of 41 ft. 4 in., incorporates several interesting features, such as a cabin heating system and special escape facilities enabling the crew of two to bale out into a patch of still air. The navigator-observer-wireless operator is responsible for reloading the guns (the cannon are drum-fed), which are all sighted and fired by the pilot. In the first few days of the Libyan campaign one squadron of Beaufighters was reported to have shot down 36 enemy planes without loss to itself.

American M.3 11-ton tank. These fast-moving armoured vehicles, used in the Libyan campaign, incorporate many interesting features, notably the unorthodox construction of the caterpillar treads. These are of rough rubber, so tough that they are said to last better than steel and they do not break so easily. The tank is well armed and armoured for a light tank. The photograph, right, shows one of the many German Stukas brought down from the Libyan skies. *Diagram specially drawn for* The War Illustrated *by Haworth ; Photo, British Official*

Our Searchlight on the War

LOOKING BACKWARD AND FORWARD

Time is at heart neutral, but he can be made to fight on the side that makes best use of him.

TO win the war we must fight, watch and work as if Germany were on our threshold, as indeed she is, and cease to talk about time being on our side ; but we can temper the ordeal with a little optimistic reasoning. Hitler is not so strong as he was in 1939, in spite of the fact that he has enslaved the greater part of Europe. He has lost the flower of his army, and millions of sullen serfs are a doubtful asset. On the other hand, the Allies are immensely stronger than they were when war broke out. While Hitler has been squandering his power to the point of desperation, Britain and the United States have, by the exigencies of strategy and circumstances, conserved theirs. It is now a moot point whether the Channel Ports, the loss of which filled us with dismay, were worth keeping in view of our unpreparedness at the time ; but it needed Mr. Churchill's vision to tell us that the fall of France made no difference. Hard though the task before us may be, Britain is certainly in a better position today than she was in 1916. At that time we were hanging on even

OSCAR THE CAT is looking somewhat nervously at the camera man, for having escaped twice from torpedoes, Oscar is hoping for peace—and the plenty that some cats contrive to get even in wartime. He is technically a German, and was rescued from the Bismarck. Adopted by the Ark Royal, Oscar had to take to a floating plank when the Ark went down, but a destroyer, catching sight of him, signalled his position to a rescue ship. Oscar was picked up and is now on parole at a Sailors' Rest in Northern Ireland. *Photo, Topical-Press*

more grimly than we are today, and Russia was falling to pieces. The Soviets, both unwilling and unready to come in in 1939, are pushing Germany back with a colossal strength and courage which humanity will ever remember with gratitude. And across the Atlantic the United States, with an immense army already in training and all her war factories getting into high gear, is ready for her great part in Freedom's battle. In 1917 a month elapsed after the declaration of war before the order was issued to recruit units of the regular army to war strength, and, except for small arms, American soldiers were dependent on British and French equipment. These are cheering facts. If Hitler could not win in 1940 after Dunkirk he is not likely to win now.

CAN THE BOMB BREAK GERMANY ?

The bomber is a weapon which, if properly handled and used with ruthless efficiency, can ruin Hitler's hopes.—Sir Archibald Sinclair at Newcastle, Dec. 6

THE Minister for Air agreed, as we all do, that this war, unlike the last, must end in Germany with the close cooperation of air, sea and land forces. But he is an unrepentant advocate of the policy of long-term bombing and seems confident that the "huge, ponderous campaign, inexorable in its slow but devastating development, would break the military power and sap the war-will of the German people." Sir Archibald

admits that the damage "we are surely doing" to the German military machine is not yet apparent in any slackening of the military effort, and he appears to ignore the fact that the more concentrated Nazi bombing on this country, so much smaller than the German Reich with its wide-flung industries, produced no slackening in our military effort. Shirer in his "Berlin Diary" said he could see no moral effect of the "night bombing of Western Germany of which the B.B.C. has been boasting." And in the Ruhr centres, "which the Allies were supposed to have bombed so heavily" in May 1940, he could see no considerable result. "The factories were smoking away as usual." Lars Moen, speaking of the bombing of Antwerp in "Under the Iron Heel," said that the September raid damage was "disappointingly small," and that there was not much to be said for night raids. Even now, a year later, we have little evidence that the "beautiful bombs" and the heavier bombers are producing any lasting results. Are we to endure a five years' war to justify Sir Archibald Sinclair's faith in large-scale bombing ? Goering failed miserably. Can Sinclair succeed ?

PACIFIC SHOCKS

The United States Services were not on the alert against a surprise air attack.—Colonel Knox, Secretary of the U.S. Navy

THE Allies' preliminary losses in the Pacific have been appalling. The simple truth is that America in 1941, like France and Britain in 1939, had hoped until the last minute to escape from war. Quite obviously the American fleet and Air Corps were not ready for the Japanese onslaught, and the United States has had to pay a heavy price for being off her guard. Why, also, did the Allies bemuse themselves with the thought that Japan was far too involved with China to take on other enemies ? The lesson to learn is that Japan and Germany have completely abolished the idea of peace, and regard war as the natural and perpetual occupation of mankind. It is difficult for the Democracies to see life in this way, but we may well have to borrow something of this dreadful philosophy from our enemies before we are able to overthrow them. Why be surprised at any kind of barbarism that the Japanese commit, such as the bombing of the open and undefended town of Manila ? The Japanese, in cruelty and efficiency, have proved themselves to be the Prussians of the East. The Allies have the material resources for victory, but these must be girded up with totalitarian vision and ruthlessness.

Lt.-Commander M. D. WANKLYN, D.S.O., of the submarine Upholder, the first submarine commander in this war to be awarded the V.C. He received the honour for relentless attacks on at least 13 enemy ships, including a U-boat, cruiser, destroyers, transports, tankers, and supply ships. On one occasion a Nazi destroyer tried to ram the Upholder. She escaped and dived, then returned to sink a large troopship. Although 37 depth charges were dropped about her Lt.-Commander Wanklyn brought the submarine safely home. *Photo, Keystone*

AIRGRAPH LETTERS, some of the million or so from the Middle East which the Post Office delivered recently in Britain. To economize space and time, soldiers' letters are written on a standardized form, filmed in miniature, and reprinted in England for distribution. *Photo, Wide World*

SENTENCE THEM NOW !

The Vichy Government are informing the German authorities of the "deep uneasiness in all Frenchmen" about the "massive repression" constituted by the latest German reprisals order.—Reuter

THE German mind has been suffering from severe shocks during the past few weeks. It is beginning to realize that the Nazi victories are of little avail. The fall back in Russia, the reverse in Libya, the entry of America into the war, point to the defeat of Hitler. The Germans cannot fail to see that they are opposed by a hostile and resolute world, and fear is creeping upon them. Is not the time opportune to warn those Nazis responsible for the murder of hostages in various occupied countries that the world is watching them personally, and that their names will appear on a list of criminals to be hanged after the war if they do not stop these atrocities ? The Allies should draw up a list of the Nazi butchers—the Heydrichs and Stülpnagels—and make a joint declaration that these men will answer for their crimes with their lives. The V campaign might cite their names at the end of its broadcasts.

PERVERSITIES OF PÉTAIN

All Mr. Churchill's books and articles are to be placed on an Index by the Vichy Government. Pétain is taking a personal interest in this Index.

MARSHAL PÉTAIN will be 86 next April. He has exceeded the commonly accepted span by 16 years. His defence of Verdun was a great patriotic effort, but even at that time he disliked the British and was reputed to be a "defeatist." The Nazis remembered this streak in his nature and have made him their tool. But there are other curious defects in his character. Pétain is a reactionary with an aversion for "progress" and democratic freedom. His befogged mind would like a return to pre-Revolution France, and he suffers from a fatalistic feeling that France, in being tortured by Germany, is expiating her sins. Could defeatism go farther ? He

NEW BADGE issued to about 60,000 workers on the domestic side in hospitals throughout England and Wales. *Photo, British Official : Crown Copyright*

probably clings to office under the delusion that he is of some use to his people, but a vast number of Frenchmen would condemn this *vieillard* for much of the misery prevailing in France. To put the works of the great leader of Democracy upon the Index is not the least cowardly decision of Vichy. To such humiliation has Pétain, aided by a terrified political scum, brought the once proud land of *Liberté*.

At Pearl Harbour Japan Tried for a 'K.O.'

HICKAM FIELD, with planes and hangars burning furiously, is seen above after a Japanese attack on Pearl Harbour, Oahu Island, on Dec. 7. In the foreground is a Flying Fortress. Above right, a Japanese two-man submarine, used in the attack on U.S. ships at Pearl Harbour, captured by U.S. naval forces. Circle, Admiral Kimmel, Chief of the U.S. Pacific Fleet at the time, who was replaced by Rear-Adm. Nimitz.

A gutted hangar and wrecked planes at Hickam Field, on Oahu Island, Hawaii, after the raid by Japanese planes. Casualties among the personnel at America's great air base in the Pacific were very heavy, and the losses in aircraft severe. Hickam Field lies midway between Pearl Harbour and Honolulu.

FIRST details of American losses in the Japanese attack on Pearl Harbour, Hawaii, on Dec. 7, were given by Col. Knox, U.S. Navy Secretary, on his return on Dec. 15 from a visit of investigation. The battleship Arizona was sunk through "a lucky hit"; three destroyers, the Cassin, Downes and Shaw, each of 1,500 tons, were also sunk, together with a minelayer, the Oglala, and an old wireless-controlled target ship, Utah. The battleship Oklahoma capsized, but Col. Knox stated she could be righted and repaired. Casualties among personnel amounted to 2,729 naval officers and men killed and 656 wounded, while Army casualties totalled 168 killed, 223 wounded and 26 missing. Losses in aircraft were severe.

"The U.S. surface ships were not on the alert against a surprise air attack," said Col. Knox, "but the Japanese failed in their purpose—to knock out the United States before the war began."

U.S. WARSHIPS lost in the Japanese attack on Pearl Harbour included the 32,600-ton battleship Arizona (above), sunk through what Col. Knox described as "a lucky hit." The 29,030-ton battleship Oklahoma (left) capsized. Both were completed in 1916.   *Photos, Planet News, Keystone, Wide World, Dorien Leigh*

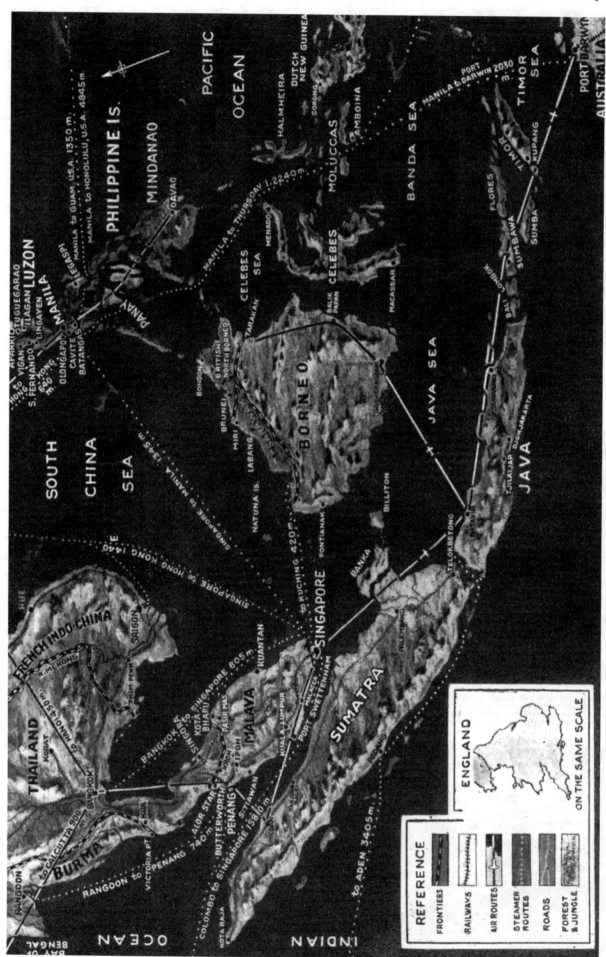

WHERE JAPAN ATTACKED is made clear in this map of the South Pacific, which shows Malaya, the Netherlands East Indies and the Philippine Islands. Owing to the conditions under which the Japanese launched their attack it was almost inevitable that the situation in the Far East should develop adversely for the Allies in the opening stages. After the first three weeks of fighting in the Pacific the Japanese had penetrated in Malaya to the Island of Penang and Ipoh, centre of the tin mining area. Sarawak, too, was invaded, and landings in North Borneo were reported. Medan in Sumatra was bombed. Hong Kong was attacked and, though the defence was fierce, the garrison was forced to surrender on December 25. In the Philippines attacks upon Luzon, where landings were vigorously countered by U.S. forces, were supplemented by an invasion of Mindanao.

Map, Courtesy of "The Crown Colonist."

Battle in Malaya: The Threat to Singapore

" The initial surprise attack, with no declaration of war, and the decision of the Thai Government to offer every facility to the enemy, have made things very difficult for us," said Sir Shenton Thomas, Governor of the Straits Settlements, on Dec. 16. " They have not gone as we hoped. But that is nothing new in the history of the British Empire." Below we set the military developments against a Malayan background.

LAND of perpetual sunshine, of jagged mountains and dense tropical jungle, of tin mines and rubber plantations—that is Malaya where today, for the first time in history, soldiers of the British Empire are struggling with the Japanese for mastery in real war.

Malaya is the southern extremity of the " leg " which reaches out from Burma through Siam to the islands of the East Indies. It is all British, with an area of 52,500 square miles, and a population of over five millions—more than two million Malays and almost as many Chinese, some 700,000 Indians, and only 25,000 or 30,000 Europeans among the rest. Politically, Malaya extends beyond the peninsula to include certain islands. It is divided into the colony of the Straits Settlements (Singapore Island, Penang Island with Province Wellesley, Malacca, Labuan off British North Borneo, and Christmas and Cocos Islands in the Indian Ocean south-west of Sumatra); the Federated Malay States (Perak, Selangor, Negri Sembilan and Pahang); and the Unfederated Malay States of Johore, Kedah, Kelantan, Trengganu and Perlis.

The first Japanese landings were made on December 8 in Thailand, at Singora and Patani, little unprotected ports on the east coast and not far to the north of the Malayan frontier. Then in Malaya itself the Japanese were got ashore at the mouth of the Kelantan River north of Kota Bharu ; and at Kemassin, due east of Kota Bharu. A day or two later another landing was in progress at Kuantan, in Pahang, about 180 miles north of Singapore as the aeroplane flies. The beaches on the east coast of the Malay Peninsula are for the most part long and sandy, sloping up to rows of coconut palms, behind which the native fisherfolk have their huts. During the winter months this coast is exposed to the full blast of the north-east monsoon, and the great rollers of surf pounding on the sandy beaches must have added to the difficulties of the landings, particularly if these were effected in the face of determined machine-gun fire. There is no reliable port on the east coast from Bangkok to Singapore. Very different is the west coast, which is dotted with ports for much of the way from Penang to Malacca and Singapore, and is sheltered from the monsoons by the mountainous backbone and by the island of Sumatra. It is on this side of the peninsula that most of the rubber estates are situated, as well as the most important tin mines.

Evacuation of Penang

Why did the Japanese land where they did ? In the Singora area it was, we may be sure, to secure the narrow isthmus, and thus not only cut the railway from Bangkok to Singapore, but interrupt the British communications between Burma and Malaya. Yet a third reason was to secure a foothold for the attack on Kedah and move down the railway along the west coast of Malaya. By Dec. 10 Kedah had been penetrated by the Japanese invaders, and heavy fighting was reported there on Dec. 12. Then on Dec. 18 it was announced from Singapore that " Our troops in south Kedah and the Province of Wellesley were successfully disengaged and are now reorganizing south of the River Krian." Shortly afterwards the withdrawal had exposed Penang, and on Dec. 19 it was announced in Singapore that, following heavy raids by Japanese bombers, a complete evacuation of Penang had been carried out.

H.E. Sir Thomas SHENTON THOMAS, G.C.M.G., O.B.E., Governor of the Straits Settlements and High Commissioner for the Malay States.   *Photo, Lafayette*

The landings in Kelantan had for their chief objective the aerodrome at Kota Bharu ; not until this was in their hands could the Japanese safely develop their offensive across the isthmus against Penang. Kelantan is, for the most part, a mountainous, roadless jungle which might be expected to present an impenetrable obstacle to the invaders ; roads there are none. Very much the same conditions prevail behind Kuantan, though here

THE MALAY PENINSULA, showing southern Thailand and the battle areas where British and Japanese forces have been heavily engaged.
Map by courtesy of " News Chronicle "

there is a road leading up the valley of the Pahang river into the heart of the province of that name, and to Selangor beyond.

The real Japanese menace continued to develop along the western coast, where Japanese troops appeared in force, operating from Singora. Within a few days the Japanese overran territory of vast economic value, while their columns threatened Taiping, headquarters of the native Malay Regiment, and even the ports far to the south, in particular Port Swettenham and Malacca.

Even more ominously significant was their air superiority, due to their ever-increasing hold on the country's aerodromes. When the campaign opened the Japanese could operate from nearly 90 land and seaplane bases, scattered over Indo-China, and another 20 in Thailand were granted them when that country capitulated after a few hours' resistance. In the whole of Malaya there are 11 Government aerodromes, but within a short time, following the capture by the Japanese of Alor Star and Sungei Patani in Kedah, Bharu in Kelantan and Butterworth in Wellesley Province, these were reduced to six, viz. Batu Pahat (Johore), Ipoh, Sitiawan and Taiping (Perak), Kuala Lumpur (Selangor), and Singapore. Many of these aerodromes were bombed over Christmas, and the invaders were coming dangerously close to Ipoh. On December 26 Japanese bombers raided Kuala Lumpur, capital of the Federated Malay States. Among the buildings hit was the mosque, where three worshippers were killed—an incident which profoundly shocked the Moslem population, since the raid was carried out on a Friday, the Moslem Sunday.

But while the situation in north-west Malaya remained unchanged, for a few days at least, elsewhere the Japanese were exceedingly active. Rangoon, the great port of Burma, was heavily bombed on Christmas Day—the same day on which the survivors of Hong Kong's little garrison capitulated to the Japanese hordes. About the same time enemy landings were taking place in Sarawak : numerous enemy transports anchored off Kuching, the state capital, were bombed by British aircraft on December 24, and Dutch submarines and aircraft were also busy, sinking (it was claimed) three large troop transports and one tanker. Sarawak, it was learned, had been evacuated by the handful of British which the " White Rajah's " Government had at their command, but not before the valuable oil wells and plant had been put out of action. Then on December 28 Medan airport in Sumatra was heavily bombed. Everywhere the Allies were forced to remain on the defensive, although on December 18 it was announced that Portuguese Timor was occupied by the Allies.

So as the year drew to a close the situation in Malaya was black—far blacker, indeed, than had been deemed possible only a few weeks before.

On December 26 the War Office announced that Lt.-Gen. Sir Henry Pownall had arrived in Singapore and assumed the appointment of Commander-in-Chief, Far East, in succession to Air Vice-Marshal Sir Robert Brooke-Popham ; it transpired that General Pownall had been appointed to this command in November when he vacated the post of Vice Chief of the Imperial General Staff. " This is a belated recognition by those in authority of unfittedness and incompetence," commented Mr. W. M. Hughes, former Australian Prime Minister.

'The Defence of Hong Kong Will Live in the Stor

IT was on Dec. 18, 1941, that Japanese troops landed in strength on the island of Hong Kong.

Steadily they infiltrated inland. The artillery personnel of Forts Collinson and D'Aguilar were withdrawn to Stanley after the destruction of their heavy guns. A British counter-attack on the afternoon of Dec. 19 proved unsuccessful. On Dec. 22 the enemy landed more troops on the north-east coast and attacked unceasingly. By then the island had been split into three parts—an isolated British force in Stanley, the enemy to the east of the Gap at the head of Tai Tam Bay, and the British to the west, with small British pockets holding out in isolated positions.

The enemy kept up incessant attacks accompanied by intensive bombardment from the air and by mortars and artillery. The water and food situation became desperate. On Christmas Day the military and naval commanders informed the Governor that no further effective resistance could be made, and the surrender took place at 7.5 p.m.

Lord Moyne, Secretary of State for the Colonies, sent the following message to Sir Mark Young : " It is a good fight you have fought, and I send you and all who have held out so splendidly against overwhelming force the thanks of his Majesty's Government. The defence of Hong Kong will live in the story of the Empire, to which it adds yet another chapter of courage and endurance."

Top left, Major-General O. M. Maltby (left), G.O.C. China Command, Canadian detachment which took part in the defence of Hong Kong Canadian reinforcements, whose arrival was announced by Ottawa on

HONG KONG, the Crown Colony captured by Japan, lies at the m is a general view looking northward from Victoria Peak. The penins street in Hong Kong leading down to the Bund. Above, an Indian gun the invaders before the garrison was overwhelmed.

Photos

he Empire—It Is a Good Fight You Have Fought'

BRAEMAR HILL

NORTH POINT

CAUSEWAY BAY

KELLET I.

EAST POINT

HARBOUR

DOCK

NAVAL YARD

J. K. Lawson (reported killed in action) commanding the
Young, K.C.M.G., Governor of Hong Kong. Bottom left,
marching through the streets of Hong Kong to their camp.

a river and is an island 32 square miles in area. Top right
n the mainland, also forms part of Hong Kong. Right, a
of Hong Kong's defence guns which wrought havoc among
t & Fry, E.N.A., Paul Popper. Map by courtesy of "The Times"

In the Philippines America Stands at Bay

After their heavy blow at the U.S. Fleet at anchor in Pearl Harbour, the Japanese Army went into action against the Americans in the Philippine Islands. By way of background to the story of the fighting, we give below some particulars of the country which is providing a land battlefield for the two great Pacific Powers.

No wonder the Japanese want the Philippines, that great group of islands—they number over 7,000, though only 466 are bigger than a square mile—which lie on the far side of the Pacific from San Francisco, off Asia's south-east coast. Altogether the Philippines have an area rather smaller than that of Japan, but they have a bigger acreage of arable land and support a population only one-fifth of Japan's; they are, indeed — Mindanao especially—some of the least populated areas of the Orient. And if we add to this fact the facts that the Philippines have a highly fertile soil and are rich in minerals—gold, iron, chromium, and manganese in particular—we shall see that there are plenty of reasons for Japan's act of aggression.

Unfortunately for Japan, but fortunately for the Philippines, the attack was launched in 1941 and could not be delayed until five years later. In 1946 the American protectorate over the " Commonwealth of the Philippines " is due to lapse, and the Commonwealth will then automatically assume full sovereignty and become a republic. If the Philippines stood alone, they could hardly be expected to withstand the full might of Japan; as it is, they are backed by the strength of the great American democracy.

President Manuel Quezon

For nearly 400 years the Philippine archipelago was part of the King of Spain's dominions. Then in 1898 war broke out between Spain and the U.S.A. After six months Spain sued for peace, and in 1899 the Philippines were ceded to the United States as part of the spoils of victory. At the time many of the Filipinos were in revolt against the Spanish administration, and it was only with some difficulty that the Americans were able to bring their new possession under control. Among the leaders of the rising was one Manuel Quezon, then in his early twenties. In the years that followed national feeling continued to grow, and in 1934 President Roosevelt signed the Tydings-McDuffie Act, which provides for the establishment of Philippine independence— not at once but, as mentioned above, in 1946; by the same Act there came into being the Commonwealth of the Philippines, and its first President was, and is, Don Manuel Quezon. He is a most colourful personality, excellent at poker and even better at politics; a man with a taste for display, yet not one to stand on ceremony—at least, among friends.

He is a typical Latin, revealing in his appearance as in his attitude and character the touch of Spanish blood in his veins.

Under the Tydings-McDuffie Act the U.S.A. retains certain rights over the Philippines; in particular, all legislation affecting currency, imports and exports and immigration must be approved by the President of the U.S.A.; foreign affairs are under the control of the U.S. State Department; and, even more important, America is responsible for the defence of the islands— until 1946.

MacArthur the C.-in-C.

Here we must make the acquaintance of General Douglas MacArthur, C.-in-C. of the American Forces in the Far East. In the last war MacArthur won a great reputation as a front-line general with the American forces in France. From 1922 to 1934 he served in the Philippine division of the U.S. Army, and in 1935 he went back to the Philippines at the invitation of President Quezon, to act as his military adviser. The story goes that Don Manuel asked him: " Can the islands be defended ? " and when MacArthur replied " Yes " immediately offered him the job. The General is the virtual creator of the Filipino Army, which under American leadership is giving a very good account of itself against the Japanese. MacArthur was also responsible for the islands' defences. In 1936 he had a plan which he submitted to Washington—one which, he declared, would cover every foot of shore line in the islands of the archipelago and make the most ruthless and powerful enemy pause. If this programme were carried out, he said, it would take 500,000 men, 10 billion dollars, tremendous casualties, and three years to invade the Philippines successfully. In 1937 MacArthur retired, and many of his plans were shelved. Not until last July, when President Roosevelt smelt danger again in the Far East, was MacArthur sent back to Manila.

When the war began on that first Sunday in December, 1941, General—or rather, Field-Marshal MacArthur, as he holds that rank in the Philippine Army—had under his command more than 10,000 American troops, 20,000 Filipino regulars, and 130,000 reservists. The first Japanese landings were effected on the great northern island of Luzon —at Aparri on the north coast, at Vigan, Lingayen, and San Fernando on the west, and at Legaspi in the extreme south-east.

Confused fighting continued about the scenes of the landings for some days, while from the outset the Japanese bombers were busy, paying particular attention to the American air base at Clark Field, north of Manila, and their naval base at Cavite. By December 17 General MacArthur reported that the situation was well in hand. But at dawn on December 20 further landings were affected this time in the island of Mindanao.

Still greater landings were reported on December 22, when 80 transports were sighted in the Gulf of Lingayen. It was estimated that some 80,000 to 100,000 Japanese troops, making six or eight divisions, were now taking part in the attack, and seven distinct fronts could now be distinguished in Luzon. Light tanks were reported to be in action south of Agoo, and soon came the news that they were striking inland from the Gulf of Lingayen. Particularly heavy fighting took place in this area north-west of Manila, since from here the approach to the capital was the least difficult of those taken by the invaders. Although heavily outnumbered, the American and Filipino troops kept up a tough resistance, and it was here that General MacArthur himself took the field.

Savage Bombing of Manila

Meanwhile, Japanese bombers were active all over the islands. Manila had been bombed several times when General MacArthur, in an effort to save it from destruction, declared it an open town. The Japanese reply was prompt and characteristic. A Japanese military spokesman declared that the Imperial forces would not " consider their action in any way restricted by such a unilateral announcement," and after a preliminary reconnaissance to make sure that the city was undefended, waves of Japanese bombers attacked Manila on December 27. Considerable damage was done to the harbour and several vessels were sunk, but still more was done in the residential and business districts where there were no military objectives. On the next day the Japanese bombers returned and wreaked even more havoc. " There is little need for black-out here tonight," said Bert Silen, National Broadcasting Company reporter; " a bright moon is shining and its colour is tinged with red." But the people of Manila were not cowed. " London took it and we can," was a widely heard comment; and some murmured some such words as " Just you wait. Our day is coming, and our slogan will be ' Remember Manila.' "

MANILA, capital of the Philippine Islands, showing the River Pasig which divides the city. After Manila had been bombed several times by the Japanese, it was declared an open town and (reported Washington on Dec. 26) all military forces and the civil government were withdrawn. Yet on Dec. 27 and 28 Manila was subjected to a series of terrific air raids. The city's population in 1939 was 623,362.   *Photo, Associated Press*

Invaded Commonwealth of the Western Pacific

PHILIPPINE ISLANDS, scene of numerous Japanese attacks. Relatively small-scale landings were made at Aparri, Vigan and Legaspi to establish beach-heads, and these were followed on December 22 by a major attack around the Gulf of Lingayen. Right, a Japanese bazaar in Manila.

Left, Manuel L. Quezon, President of the Commonwealth of the Philippines. Right, General Douglas MacArthur, commanding the U.S. land and air forces in the Philippines.

The great archipelago of the Philippines stretches from the north of Borneo to within a day's steaming of Formosa, and contains more than 7,000 islands and islets. Above is a highway over the mountainous country near Manila, the capital, which stands on the largest island, Luzon. There is a small Philippine army, men of which are seen, right, manning a heavy machine-gun against air attack. Gen. MacArthur, formerly Chief of Staff of the U.S. Army, was loaned to organize the defences of the Commonwealth; he is a Field-Marshal of the Philippine Army.

Photos, Mrs. T. Muir, Lubinski, Associated Press; Map, G.P.U.

Our Diary of the War

SATURDAY, DEC. 13, 1941   833*rd day*

Sea.—British forces sank two Italian cruisers and an E. Boat during a night engagement in the Mediterranean.

Russian Front.—Red Army continued to make progress in the Moscow sector.

Africa.—British forces closing in on defensive positions covering Gazala.

Far East.—Japanese made further advances in N.W. Malaya and were reported to have occupied U.S. Base at Guam. Fresh landing attempts in Philippines flung back. Dutch submarines sank four laden troopships off Malaya. Chinese launched offensive against Japanese troops investing Hong Kong.

SUNDAY, DEC. 14   834*th day*

Russian Front.—Russian advance in Moscow area continued. Large German forces surrounded at Klin.

Africa.—Battle swinging westwards in Libya. Hundreds of Axis prisoners captured near Bir Hakeim.

Far East.—Heavy Japanese mechanized attack in N.W. Malaya with fighting along the borders of Burma. Hong Kong garrison rejected an ultimatum to surrender.

MONDAY, DEC. 15   835*th day*

Sea.—Admiralty announced that British submarines had sunk six Axis ships in the Mediterranean.

Russian Front.—Russians recaptured Klin and three towns in the Tula area.

Africa.—In Libya enemy counter-attack beaten off. Imperial troops captured over 1,000 prisoners.

Far East.—British withdrew in N.W. Malaya. Garrison evacuated from Victoria Point in face of powerful Japanese attack. Hong Kong heavily attacked.

TUESDAY, DEC. 16   836*th day*

Russian Front.—Kalinin recaptured by Red Army, six enemy divisions being smashed. Russians began new offensive against Finnish forces south of L. Onega.

Africa.—Fierce battle in Libya around Alem Hamza, 15 miles S.W. of Gazala. British armoured forces reached a point 30 miles west of Gazala.

WEDNESDAY, DEC. 17   837*th day*

Sea.—Admiralty announced sinking of Italian submarine Ammiraglio Caracciolo in Mediterranean by the destroyer H.M.S. Farndale.

Air.—R.A.F. made heavy attack on Brest docks at night.

Russian Front.—Aleksin and Shchekino, in the Moscow area, recaptured by Russians.

Africa.—Battle at Alem Hamza continued. Axis forces offered strong resistance at Halegh el Olebam, west of Gazala. By nightfall main British infantry forces had reached the general line of the Tmimi-Mekili road.

Far East.—Japanese reached a point 10 miles from Penang. Three enemy landings made in Sarawak, where British forces withdrew after destroying oil refineries. Japanese demand for surrender of Hong Kong rejected by Sir Mark Young, the Governor.

THURSDAY, DEC. 18   838*th day*

Air.—R.A.F. made daylight and night attacks on the docks at Brest.

Russian Front.—Powerful Russian offensive developing in Karelia against the Finns.

Africa.—British victory in Libya after three-day battle in the Gazala area. British troops advanced thirty miles in a day.

Far East.—Dutch and Australian troops landed in Portugese Timor to forestall an expected Japanese aggression. New Japanese attack on N.E. Malaya driven off with heavy losses. In Kedah British retired to a new line leaving the coast opposite Penang in Japanese hands. Heavy artillery duels at Hong Kong.

FRIDAY, DEC. 19   839*th day*

Russian Front.—Russians recaptured more towns and villages on Moscow front, including Ruza, Terusa and Kanino.

Africa.—Derna airfield in Libya captured by British. Derna and Mekili occupied without opposition. Forward mechanized patrols reach a point 25 miles W. of Giovanni Berta.

Far East.—Penang evacuated by British troops. Further British withdrawal on mainland of Malaya. Japanese claimed to have captured most of Hong Kong. Further land and air activity in the Philippines.

SATURDAY, DEC. 20   840*th day*

Russian Front.—Volokolamsk recaptured by Soviet troops, and at least two German divisions routed near southern shores of L. Ladoga. Three Nazi transports sunk by Soviet submarine.

Africa.—Imperial forces in full pursuit of Rommel's broken columns in Libya.

Far East.—Japanese troops landed in force on island of Mindanao, mainly at Davao. At Hong Kong, Imperial forces still holding out.

Home.—A few bombs were dropped by raiders during the night at scattered points.

General.—Washington announced that Admiral Ernest J. King, commander of the U.S. Atlantic Fleet, had been appointed Commander of the Combined U.S. Fleets.

SUNDAY, DEC. 21   841*st day*

Russian Front.—Moscow announced that Gen. Meretsov's forces had advanced 45 miles beyond Tikhvin.

Africa.—British armoured forces attempting to head off Rommel's forces and force them to give battle west of Benghazi.

Far East.—Japanese invaders of Malaya thrusting towards Ipoh, 300 miles north of Singapore.

General.—Hitler declared himself Commander-in-Chief of the German Armies. Field-Marshal Von Brauchitsch being superseded. Col. Knox announced that 14 enemy submarines had been sunk or damaged in Atlantic by U.S. Navy.

MONDAY, DEC. 22   842*nd day*

Russian Front.—Russians still advancing along the railways leading to Leningrad.

Africa.—Pursuit of Axis forces in Libya

continued. It was announced that British had entered Cirene, forty miles west of Derna.

Far East.—An attack in force launched upon the Philippines by a new Japanese force of some 100,000 men. Fierce fighting in the Lingayen coastal areas.

General.—It was revealed that Mr. Churchill, together with Lord Beaverbrook and chiefs of staff, was in Washington.

TUESDAY, DEC. 23   843*rd day*

Sea.—Admiralty announced that six more enemy ships had been accounted for by submarines in the Mediterranean.

Russian Front.—Russians occupied more localities, including the important railway junction of Gorbachevo and the towns of Cherepov and Odeyev.

Africa.—British tanks reached the coastal plain of the Gulf of Sirte.

Far East.—Imperial forces continued to hold out in the western half of Hong Kong. More Japanese forces landed in the Philippines. Wake Island, in mid-Pacific, invaded by Japanese.

General.—First Anglo-U.S. War Council held at the White House, Washington.

WEDNESDAY, DEC. 24   844*th day*

Russian Front.—Further Russian successes in the operations to relieve Leningrad.

Africa.—Imperial troops entered Benghazi and also took Benina.

Far East.—Japanese pressure on Hong Kong increased. Japanese attack on island of Luzon, in the Philippines, developed with a thrust towards Manila.

General.—President Roosevelt and Mr. Churchill broadcast from Washington.

THURSDAY, DEC. 25   845*th day*

Russian Front.—Moscow announced the recapture of Kaluga.

Africa.—German forces at Jedabia, 100 miles south of Benghazi, attempting to cover Rommel's retreat into Tripolitania.

Far East.—The garrison at Hong Kong was forced to surrender. The Japanese made a landing near Kuching, capital of Sarawak.

General.—It was revealed that Gen. Wavell had visited Chunking for discussions with Gen. Chiang Kai-Shek. St. Pierre and Miquelon, French islands in the Gulf of St. Lawrence, taken over by Free French.

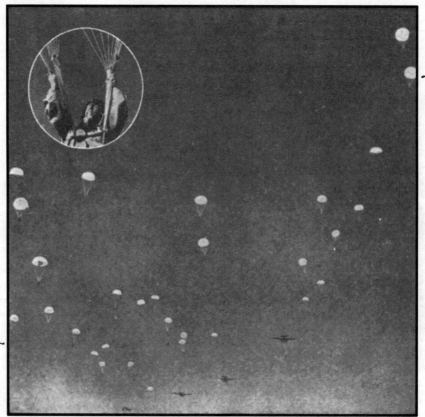

SPECIAL AIR SERVICE is a volunteer branch of the Army cooperating with the R.A.F. in the Middle East. The training is similar to that of parachute troops in this country, and members of the Service are seen here descending from R.A.F. planes. Inset, one of the S.A.S. about to touch ground.

Photos, British Official : Crown Copyright

They Have Won Honours in Freedom's Cause

Free French Cross of Liberation

Capt. Jean Morlaix, Cross of Liberation. This Free French air ace has so far destroyed 16 enemy planes.

Adolphus Gibson, D.S.M., for bravery in H.M. Transport Dorien Rose. He is a coloured fireman in the Merchant Navy.

Capt. Pierre Lusyne, O.B.E. and **Belgian Croix de Guerre,** for heroic work in the evacuation of Dunkirk.

Captain René Lusyne, O.B.E. and Belgian Croix de Guerre. With his brother (left) he brought hundreds of B.E.F. to safety.

Belgian Croix de Guerre

Lt.-Cmdr. (E) Dudley Chandler, D.S.C. and **Bar.** D.S.C. for gallantry in Greek waters. Bar for work in Mediterranean.

A.B. Benjamin Phillips, B.E.M., for gallantry in the performance of his duties. Able Seaman Phillips is a Swansea man.

Ch. Engineer A. Drummond, O.B.E., for preventing serious consequences from a leak in the side of a bombed vessel.

Capt. Francis Pretty, O.B.E., for dealing promptly and efficiently with damage when his ship was bombed on convoy.

Chief Petty Officer R. G. Mackenzie, D.S.M., for gallantry during the evacuation of Namsos in the Norwegian campaign.

Second Officer Richard Ayres, M.B.E., for devotion to duty. He was sole survivor of a boatload of 31 men from a torpedoed ship.

Lt. (Act. Capt.) D. E. Evans, G.M., for gallantry in salvaging a captured German tank from a blazing ship at Suez.

Capt. (Temp. Maj.) Godfrey Rigby, G.M., for his participation in the same exploit. Maj. Rigby comes from St. Annes, Lancs.

Capt. (Temp. Maj.) C. R. Clark, G.M., for gallantry and devotion to duty in company with Capt. Evans and Maj. Rigby.

Lt. (Temp. Capt.) H. J. Hunt, O.B.E., for conspicuous gallantry in carrying out hazardous work in a very brave manner.

Lt. Hugh Morrison, O.B.E., for throwing unexploded bombs into the sea after a Mills bomb had fallen among them.

Lce.-Sergt. David Carrick, B.E.M., for gallantry conduct during an air raid. Lce.-Sgt. Carrick is in the Cameronians.

Flt. Lt. George Barclay, D.F.C., for gallantry and devotion to duty in operational duties against enemy aircraft.

Flg. Off. G. A. Daymond, No. 71 (Eagle) Squadron, R.A.F., **D.F.C.,** for gallantry in flying operations against the enemy.

Actg. Flt. Lt. C. G. Petersen, No. 71 (Eagle) Squadron, R.A.F., **D.F.C.,** for outstanding qualities of leadership in air sorties.

Plt. Off. Carrol Mc-Colpin, No. 71 (Eagle) Squadron, R.A.F., **D.F.C.,** for great courage and resource in action.

Lt. N. E. Goddard, Fleet Air Arm, **D.S.C.,** for gallantry, daring and skill during operations against the battleship Bismarck.

Sqdn. Ldr. A. R. Barton, D.F.C., No. 249 Squadron, R.A.F., **Bar to D.F.C.** for gallantry and devotion to duty in air operations.

Miss Elizabeth Owen, G.M., for bravery while acting as stewardess on the St. Patrick, sunk by enemy action.

Sister Rosamund Ledger, A.R.R.C., for devotion to duty in her hospital work in the face of enemy action.

Mrs. Rowena Jones, B.E.M., for gallantry during a heavy air raid on Merseyside.

Mrs. Dorothy Batt, B.E.M., for continuous bravery during heavy air raids on Bristol.

Miss Patricia Dewing, B.E.M., for working telephones in a blazing fire substation while bombs fell.

Mrs. Elizabeth Plumb, B.E.M., for bravery while a stewardess on the Rangitane, sunk in the S. Pacific.

Lampman Albert Bentley, B.E.M., for gallant conduct during enemy air raids on a railway station.

Mr. Fred Bassett, Stationmaster of Charing Cross Station, **M.B.E.,** for leadership and courage.

Inspector Edward Sinden, B.E.M., for gallant conduct during heavy air raids on the station where he worked.

Capt. J. D. Archer, assistant dockmaster, **G.M.,** for heroism during heavy air raids in the dock areas.

Capt. F. T. Moynihan dockmaster P.L.A., **G.M.,** for gallantry during enemy raids on London docks.

Albert Covell, lock foreman, **G.M.,** for devotion to duty during the heavy air raids on London docks.

Retreat from Moscow: Will 1942 Repeat 1812?

In 1812 Napoleon marched on Moscow, and after a few days' occupation of the capital set out on the retreat which has lived in history as the supreme example of the nemesis that overtakes the conqueror who does not know when to stop. In 1941 Hitler's armies took the road to Moscow. Now they are on the retreat. Will Hitler's armies die like Napoleon's in the Russian snow?

"MY soldiers," said Hitler in an Order of the Day issued to his troops on October 2, "you have prepared the ground for the last vast stroke which will smash our foe before winter sets in. Step by step preparations have been made to bring the enemy into the situation in which we can now give him a mortal blow. Today marks the beginning of the last decisive battle of this year."

Then began the great German drive on Moscow. For weeks it continued, and day by day the German hordes drew ever nearer to the Russian capital. The climax of the great battle was approached on November 16, when von Bock launched the last and greatest wave of the offensive. The German plan was to break through the Russian lines and encircle Moscow with a wide outflanking movement, while pressure was maintained in the centre. Directly engaged in the offensive were 51 divisions—13 tank, 33 infantry, and five motorized infantry divisions. Most of the armoured and mobile strength was massed on the flanks, the attack in the centre being entrusted mainly to infantry. The enemy objectives were Tula, Kashira, Ryazan, and Kolomna to the south of Moscow; and Klin, Solnechnogorsk, Rogachev, Yakhrona, and Dmitrov to the north. When these had been carried, the final assault would be delivered from all three sectors at once and, so it was believed, Moscow must fall.

When the battle began, von Bock concentrated on his left flank, facing the Russian right flank in the Klin sector, the 3rd and 4th

Tank groups commanded by Generals Hoth and Huepner, consisting of the 1st, 2nd, 5th, 6th, 7th, 10th, and 11th tank divisions, the 36th and 14th divisions of motorized infantry, and the 23rd, 106th, and 35th infantry divisions. Then in the Tula sector there were concentrated the 2nd motor mechanized army of General Guderian, consisting of the 3rd, 4th, 17th, and 18th tank divisions, the 10th and 29th motorized infantry divisions, and the 167th infantry division; and against the centre the 7th, 9th, 12th, 13th, 20th, and 43rd army corps, and the 19th and 20th tank divisions. This vast host of 51 divisions was assembled between Kalinin and Tula.

From November 16 to December 5 the Russians under General Zhukov fought a stubborn defensive battle. Many of the German attacks were smashed, others were nipped in the bud by vigorous counter-attacks. The Germans made progress, but nowhere was that progress comparable with that which had been made in the summer and autumn offensives. Yet the invader got very near to Moscow—just how near was not revealed until weeks later when the shadow was lifted from the capital. North of Moscow the advanced German columns reached the village of Ikshaeon on the Dmitrov highway, and Kriukovo on the Leningrad railway; in the centre, the Volokolamsk sector, they appeared to have penetrated to halfway between Istra and Moscow; while on the Mojaisk highway they reached Kubinka. At certain points, then, they were less than 30 miles from Moscow. Yet, as fate would have it, not a German soldier glimpsed the glittering cupolas of the Kremlin—other than as prisoners. But near as was the enemy, the situation in the capital remained completely calm. Many of the people had been evacuated, and those who remained were already inured to life in the front line. A state of siege had been proclaimed; food was severely rationed, and the black-out was very strict. Air raids became a regular feature, as many as seven occurring in one day. But the damage done by Hitler's bombers was quickly repaired, and the citizens' response took the form of devoted toil, building barricades and deepening the fortifications.

Turning of the Tide

Then on December 6 the tide turned. On that day the Russians from the defensive turned to the offensive. On both flanks heavy blows were dealt at the now largely exhausted and severely battered German forces. The Russian success was swift and overwhelming. By December 11 the position was as follows:

(a) General Leliushenko's forces were smashing the 1st tank and 14th and 36th motorized infantry divisions, having captured Rogachev and surrounding the town of Klin.

(b) General Kuznetsov, having captured the town of Yakhrona, was pursuing the retreating 6th and 7th tank and 23rd infantry divisions of the enemy to the south-west of Klin.

(c) General Vlassov was pursuing the 2nd tank and 106th infantry divisions, after having occupied the town of Solnechnogorsk.

(d) General Rokossovsky was pursuing the 5th, 10th, and 11th tank divisions, an S.S. division, and the 35th infantry division, and had occupied the town of Istra.

(e) General Govorov broke through the defences of the 252nd, 87th, 78th, and 267th infantry divisions, and occupied the districts of Kulodiakino and Lokotnya.

(f) General Boldin, having routed to the north-west of Tula the 3rd and 4th tank divisions and an S.S. regiment of the "Germania" division, surrounded the 296th infantry division.

This photograph from the Russian front shows a German soldier on outpost duty in the thick snow, wearing a white camouflage cloak and helmet cover. *Photo, Associated Press*

(g) The First Cavalry Guard Corps of General Belov, having routed the 17th tank, 29th motorized infantry, and 167th infantry divisions of the enemy, was pursuing their remnants and had occupied the towns of Venev and Stalinogorsk.

(h) General Golikov was pushing back to the south-west units of the 18th tank and the 10th motorized infantry divisions, and had occupied the towns of Mikhailov and Epivan.

By then, in five days' offensive, the Russians claimed to have occupied and freed from the Germans over 400 populated centres, and to have captured 386 tanks, 4,317 lorries, 604 motor-cycles, 305 guns, 109 trench-mortars, 715 machine-guns, and 546 automatic rifles. In addition, large numbers of tanks, lorries, guns, etc., had been destroyed. Moreover, the Germans were estimated to have lost on the field of battle more than 30,000 killed.

For a while the Germans did their best to minimize the reverse which their armies had suffered—a reverse which was all the more significant following the smashing defeat of Von Kleist at Rostov. In Berlin the military spokesmen declared that the winter was colder than usual, and had come earlier than had been expected. One report had it that the Germans were retreating according to plan in order that their troops might winter in more comfortable quarters; Moscow should consider itself lucky that it had been saved by the Russian winter—but saved only for a few months, since in the spring the German offensive would be resumed in greater strength than ever before. But in actual fact it was not General Winter who beat von Bock—it was General Zhukov. "The Nazi invaders," declared the Soviet Information Bureau, "are being beaten now not by the terrible frost, but by our glorious Red Army. And the frosts, real Russian frosts, are still ahead."

A few days later "Pravda," the famous Moscow newspaper, wrote that "The Nazi hordes are rolling back. The roads are strewn with the bodies of German soldiers, burnt and damaged vehicles and guns. Such is the inglorious end of the second general offensive against Moscow, proclaimed by Hitler. The promised peace has not materialized for the German people. The promised rest in warm flats in the Soviet capital has not materialized for the German troops. The rout of Hitler's picked divisions with colossal fresh losses has resulted in a complete failure of his plans for the encirclement and capture of Moscow." In a word, the attack on Moscow, which had been launched with such a fanfare of trumpets, with such an outburst of Hitlerian boasts and bombast, was a fiasco.

Moscow sector of the Russian front. On December 15 the Russians recaptured Klin, Kalinin was retaken on the following day, and on December 20 Moscow announced the re-taking of Volokolamsk. On Dec. 26 Kaluga was reoccupied. *Map, courtesy of "The Times"*

Hitler's Greatest Offensive Peters to a Close

Even when the Germans had captured Mariupol, on the Sea of Azov, Russian guerillas left them no respite. On the right is a dramatic photograph of street fighting in the town, while below smoke pours upwards after Partisans have dynamited points near the railway station.

"The German retreat (writes 'Pravda'), has created good conditions for a still wider development of guerilla warfare. Guerillas now have better opportunities to annihilate the invaders, to capture their equipment and to use it against them. The ranks of the German Army have been thinned. A large number of their divisions have ceased to exist as a fighting force. Military discipline is beginning to deteriorate. The fighting spirit has cracked ... Guerillas, a great and responsible mission has fallen to your lot. Be worthy of that mission. Death to the Fascist robbers!"

SOVIET LONG-RANGE GUN, from a well-hidden position in a pine forest, is engaged in counter-battery work, firing at enemy gun-sites miles away. The Russian gunners played a great and gallant part in stemming the gigantic Nazi offensives on the Eastern Front.

Photos. Keystone and British Official

Britain and America Have Invasion Barges Too!

There seem to be only four men in this invasion barge, but you can tell that to the Marines who are hidden away inside. The Royal Marines have had intensive training with these specially constructed craft.

Left, the concealed Marines in readiness for landing. Above, mechanized section of the landing-party losing no time in getting away.

U.S. MARINES of the Atlantic Amphibious Force are seen, left, driving what they call a " K Jeep " tractor, trailing a field-piece, off a landing barge into shallow water on the edge of a beach. Right, British Royal Marines moving off in convoy after landing a gun. Naval assault landing craft were used in the British landings on Vaagso and Maalo Islands off the Norwegian coast on Dec. 27.

Photos, Fox and Keystone

Torpedoed! Just One Episode in the War at Sea

AN AMERICAN FREIGHTER, the S.S. Lehigh, sunk by a submarine when 75 miles off Freetown, Sierra Leone, is seen going to the bottom in the series of photographs, left, taken from a lifeboat in which survivors escaped. Top right, British warships on convoy escort during an air attack in the Mediterranean; a cruiser with guns at extreme elevation is passing astern of the warship from which the photograph was taken. Oval, the Liverpool H.Q. of Sir Percy Noble, C.-in-C. Western Approaches, who is seen (centre) with his staff. Above right, the destroyer Kimberley approaching a rowing boat full of British soldiers who had escaped from Crete, navigating with a sixpenny compass.

Photos, British Official; Keystone, Central Press

I Was There! .... Eye Witness Stories of the War

I Saw 'Repulse' and 'Prince of Wales' Go Down

Only newspaperman on board H.M.S. Repulse when she was torpedoed by the Japanese off Malaya on December 10, 1941, was O. D. Gallagher, famous "Daily Express" war reporter. Here is his story—grimly vivid and unique in the annals of the war at sea.

THIS is the simple story of a naval force which went into north-eastern Malayan waters on Monday, December 8. Prince of Wales and Repulse were the backbone of this force. I was in Repulse. The aim of the force was, in the words of the signal of C.-in-C. Admiral Sir Tom Phillips, sent to all ships:

The enemy has made several landings on the north coast of Malaya and has made local progress. Meanwhile fast transports lie off the coast. This is our opportunity before the enemy can establish himself.

We have made a wide circuit to avoid air reconnaissance and hope to surprise the enemy shortly after sunrise tomorrow (Wednesday). We may have the luck to try our metal against the old Jap battle-cruiser Kongo or against some Jap cruisers or destroyers in the Gulf of Siam.

We are sure to get some useful practice with our high-angle armament, but whatever we meet I want to finish quickly and so get well clear to eastward before the Japanese can mass a too formidable scale of air attack against us. So shoot to sink.

In a message to the men and officers of the Repulse on Tuesday evening her Captain, William Tennant, said:

We are making for the nor'-east coast of Malaya, and shall be off the nor'-east corner at dawn. We shall be to seaward of Singora and Patani, where Japanese landings are taking place.

Though we may, of course, run into Japanese forces anywhere during the day, I think it is most probable that only submarines and aircraft are likely to be sighted. Some time at night and at dawn the fun may begin. We must be on the look-out for destroyer attack tonight.

If we are lucky enough to bump into a Japanese convoy tomorrow, it will be of most invaluable service, and seriously upset their plans. Having stirred up the hornets' nest, we must be expecting plenty of bombing on our return tomorrow.

But at 5.20 that same evening a bugle sounded throughout my ship Repulse over the ship's loudspeakers giving immediate orders to the whole ship's company and filling every space of engine-room and wardroom with its urgent bugle notes, followed by the order: "Action stations! Enemy aircraft."

I rushed on to the flag-deck, which was my action station. It was a single Nakajima Naka 93 twin-floated Jap reconnaissance plane. She kept almost on the horizon, too far for engagement, for a couple of hours. A voice from the bridge came out of the loudspeakers: "We are being shadowed by enemy aircraft. Keep ready for immediate action to repel aircraft."

At Sea With No Air Support

Two more Nakajima Naka 93s appeared. They kept up a long relay watch on us. What an admiral most wishes to avoid had happened. His ships were out at sea, sufficiently distant from shore to prevent him receiving air support before dawn the following morning, when a mass enemy air attack now seemed certain. We had not yet sighted any enemy naval force or received reports of an enemy transport convoy.

At 9.5 p.m. came a voice from the loudspeakers: "Stand by for the Captain to speak to you." Captain: A signal has just been received from the Commander-in-Chief. We were shadowed by three planes. We were spotted after dodging them all day. Their troop convoy will now have dispersed. We will find enemy aircraft waiting for us now. We are now returning to Singapore."

Then followed a babble of voices and groans. A voice said: "This ship will never get into action. It's too lucky." So it was. In the message from the Captain

the previous day he noted that Repulse had travelled 53,000 miles in this war without action, although it trailed the Bismarck and was off northern Norway and had convoyed throughout the war.

I slept in the wardroom fully clothed and awoke to the call "Action stations" at 5 a.m. on Wednesday. It was a thin Oriental dawn, with a cool breeze swept through the fuggy ship, which had been battened down all night as a result of the order to "darken ship."

The sky was luminous as pearl. We saw from the flag-deck a string of black objects on the port bow. They turned out to be a line of landing barges, "like railway trucks," as a young signaller said. At 6.30 a.m. the loudspeaking voice announced: "Just received message saying enemy is making landing north of Singapore. We're going in." We cruised in line-ahead formation, Prince of Wales leading, the Repulse second, and with our destroyer screen out, down the Malayan coast, examining with the help of terrier-like destroyers all coves for enemy landing parties.

Prince of Wales looked magnificent. White-tipped waves rippled over her plunging bows. It shrouded them with watery lace, then they rose high again and once again dipped. She rose and fell so methodically that the effect of staring at her was hypnotic. The fresh breeze blew her White Ensign out stiff as a board.

As we sped down Malaya's changing coastline the wag of the flag-deck said travel-talkwise: "On the starboard beam, dear listeners, you see the beauty spots of Malaya, land of the orang-outang." Again the loudspeaker announces: "Nothing sighted." The Repulse sends off one of her aircraft.

We drift to the wardroom again until 10.20 a.m. We are spotted again by a twin-engined snooper of the same type as attacked Singapore the first night of this new war. We can do nothing about it, as she keeps well beyond range while her crew presumably studies our outlines and compares them with silhouettes in the Jap equivalent of Jane's Fighting Ships. At 11 a.m. a twin-masted single-funnel ship is sighted on the starboard bow. The force goes to investigate her. She carries no flag.

I was looking at her through my telescope when the shock of an explosion made me jump so that I nearly poked my right eye out. It was 11.15 a.m. The explosion came from the Prince of Wales' port side secondary armament. She was firing at a single aircraft. We open fire. There are about six aircraft. A three-quarter-inch screw falls on my tin hat from the bridge deck above from the shock of explosion of the guns. "The old tub's falling to bits" observes the yeoman of signals.

That was the beginning of a superb air attack by the Japanese, whose air force was an unknown quantity. Officers in the Prince of Wales, whom I met in their wardroom when she arrived here last week, said they expected some unorthodox flying from the Japs. "The great danger will be the possibility of them flying their whole aircraft into a ship and committing hara-kiri." It was nothing like that. It was most orthodox. They even came at us in formation, flying low and close. Aboard the

Repulse I found observers as qualified as anyone to estimate Jap flying abilities. They know from first-hand experience what the R.A.F. and the Luftwaffe are like. Their verdict was: "The Germans have never done anything like this in the North Sea, Atlantic or anywhere else we have been."

They concentrated on the two capital ships, taking the Prince of Wales first and the Repulse second. The destroyer screen they left completely alone, except for damaged planes forced to fly low over them when they dropped bombs defensively.

At 11.18 the Prince of Wales opened with a shattering barrage with all her multiple pom-poms, or Chicago Pianos as they call them. Red and blue flames poured from the eight-gun muzzles of each battery. I saw glowing tracer shells describe shallow curves as they went soaring skywards surrounding the enemy planes. Our Chicago Pianos opened fire; also our triple-gun 4-inch high-angle turrets. The uproar was so tremendous I seemed to feel it.

Direct Hits on the Repulse

From the starboard side of the flag-deck I can see two torpedo planes. No, they're bombers. Flying straight at us. All our guns pour high-explosives at them, including shells so delicately fused that they explode if they merely graze cloth fabric. But they swing away, carrying out a high-powered evasive action without dropping anything at all. I realize now what the purpose of the action was. It was a diversion to occupy all our guns and observers on the air defence platform at the summit of the mainmast.

There is a heavy explosion and the Repulse rocks. Great patches of paint fall from the funnel on to the flag-deck. We all gaze above our heads to see planes which during the action against the low fliers were unnoticed. They are high-level bombers. Seventeen thousand feet. The first bomb, the one that rocked us a moment ago, scored a direct hit on the catapult deck through the one hangar on the port side.

I am standing behind a multiple Vickers gun, one which fires 2,000 half-inch bullets per minute. It is at the after-end of the flag-deck. I see a cloud of smoke rising from the place where the first bomb hit. Another comes down bang again from 17,000 feet. It explodes in the sea, making a creamy blue and green patch ten feet across. The Repulse rocks again. It was three fathoms from the port side.

Two planes can be seen coming at us. A spotter sees another at a different angle, but much closer. He leans forward, his face tight with excitement, urgently pounding the back of the gun swiveller in front of him. He hits that back with his right hand and points with the left a stabbing forefinger at a single sneaker plane. Still blazing two-pounders the whole gun platform turns in a hail of death at the single plane. It is some 1,000 yards away.

I saw tracers rip into its fuselage dead in the centre. Its fabric opened up like a rapidly spreading sore with red edges. Fire . . . It swept to the tail, and in a moment stabilizer and rudder became a framework skeleton. Her nose dipped down and she went waterward. We cheered like madmen. I felt my larynx tearing in the effort to make myself heard above the hellish uproar of guns. A plane smacked the sea on its belly and was immediately transformed into a gigantic shapeless mass of fire which shot over the waves fast as a snake's tongue. The Repulse had got the first raider.

For the first time since the action began we can hear a sound from the loudspeakers, which are on every deck at every action station. It is the sound of a bugle. Its first notes are somewhat tortured. The young bugler's lips and throat are obviously dry with excitement. It is that most sinister alarm of all for seamen : " Fire ! "

Smoke from our catapult deck is thick now. Men in overalls, their faces hidden by a coat of soot, man-handle hoses along decks. Water fountains delicately from a rough patch made in one section by binding it with a white shirt. It sprays on the Vickers gunners, who, in a momentary lull, lift faces, open mouths and put out tongues to catch the cool-looking jets. They quickly avert faces to spit—the water is salt and it is warm. It is sea water.

The Chicago Pianos open up again with a suddenness that I am unable to refrain from flinching at, though once they get going with their erratic shell-pumping it is most reassuring. All aboard have said the safest place in any battleship or cruiser or destroyer is behind a Chicago Piano.

There is a short lull. The boys dig inside their overalls and pull out cigarettes. Then the loudspeaker voice : " Enemy aircraft ahead." Lighted ends are nipped off cigarettes. The ship's company goes into action again. " Twelve of them." The flag-deck boys whistle. Someone counts them aloud : " One, two, three, four, five, six, seven, eight, nine—yes, nine." The flag-deck wag, as he levels a signalling lamp at the Prince of Wales : " Any advance on nine ? Anybody ? No ? Well, here they come."

It is 12.10 p.m. They are all concentrating on the Prince of Wales. They are after the big ships all right. A mass of water and smoke rises in a tree-like column from the Prince of Wales' stern. They've got her with a torpedo. A ragged-edged mass of flame from her Chicago Piano does not stop them, nor the heavy instant flashes from her high-angle secondary armament. She is listing to port —a bad list. We are about six cables from her. A snottie, or midshipman, runs past, calls as he goes : " Prince of Wales' steering gear gone." It doesn't seem possible that those slight-looking planes could do that to her.

The planes leave us, having apparently dropped all their bombs and torpedoes. I don't believe it is over, though. " Look, look," shouts someone, " there's a line in the water right under our bows, growing longer on the starboard side! A torpedo that missed us. Wonder where it'll stop." The Prince of Wales signals us again, asking if we've been torpedoed. Our Captain Tennant replies : " Not yet. We've dodged nineteen." Six stokers arrive on the flag-deck. They are black with smoke and oil and in need of first aid. They are ushered down to the armoured citadel at the base of the main-mast. The Prince of Wales' list is increasing. There is a great rattle of empty two-pounder cordite cases as Chicago Piano boys gather up the empties and clear for further action.

' A Mortally Wounded Tiger '

Twelve-twenty p.m. . . . The end is near, although I didn't know it. A new wave of planes appears, flying around us in formation and gradually coming nearer. The Prince of Wales lies about ten cables astern of our port side. She is helpless. They are making for her. I don't know how many. They are splitting up our guns as we realize they are after her, knowing she can't dodge their torpedoes. So we fire at them to defend the Prince of Wales rather than attend to our own safety.

The only analogy I can think of to give an impression of the Prince of Wales in those last moments is of a mortally wounded tiger trying to beat off the coup de grâce. Her outline is hardly distinguishable in smoke and flame from all her guns except the fourteen-inchers. I can see one plane release a torpedo. It drops nose heavy into the sea and churns up a small wake as it drives straight at the Prince of Wales. It explodes against her bows. A couple of seconds later another explodes amidships and another astern.

Gazing at her turning over on the port side with her stern going under and with dots of men leaping from her, I am thrown against the bulkhead by a tremendous shock as the Repulse takes a torpedo on her port side astern. With all others on the flag-deck I am wondering where it came from, when the Repulse shudders gigantically. Another torpedo.

Now men cheering with more abandon than at a Cup Final. What the heck is this ? I wonder. Then see it is another plane down. It hits the sea in flames also. There have been six so far as I know. My notebook, which I have got before me, is stained with oil and is ink-blurred. It says : " Third torp."

The Repulse now listing badly to port. The loudspeakers speak for the last time : " Everybody on main deck."

We all troop down ladders, most orderly except for one lad who climbs the rail and is about to jump when an officer says : " Now then—come back—we are all going your way." The boy came back and joined the line. It seemed slow going. Like all the others, I suppose I was tempted to leap to the lower deck, but the calmness was catching. When we got to the main deck the list was so bad our shoed feet could not grip the steel deck. I kicked off mine, and my damp stockinged feet made for sure movement. Nervously opening my cigarette case I found I hadn't a match. I offered a cigarette to a man beside me. He said : " Ta ! Want a match ? " We both lit up and puffed once or twice. He said : " We'll be seeing you, mate " and I replied : " Hope so. Cheerio."

We were all able to walk down the ship's starboard side, she lay so much over to port. We all formed a line along a big protruding anti-torpedo blister, from where we had to jump some twelve feet into a sea which was black—I discovered it was oil. I remember jamming my cap on my head, drawing a breath and leaping. Oh, I forgot—the last entry in my notebook was : " Sank about 12.20 p.m." I made it before leaving the flag-deck. In the water I glimpsed the Prince of Wales' bows disappearing.

Kicking with all my strength, I with hundreds of others tried to get away from the Repulse before she went under, being afraid of getting drawn under in the whirlpool. I went in the wrong direction, straight into the still spreading oil patch, which felt almost as thick as velvet. A wave hit me and swung me round so that I saw the last of the Repulse. Her underwater plates were painted a bright, light red. Her bows rose high as the air trapped inside tried to escape from underwater forward regions, and there she hung for a second or two and easily slid out of sight.

Swimming in a Sea of Oil

I had a tremendous feeling of loneliness, and could see nothing capable of carrying me. I kicked, lying on my back, and felt my eyes burning as the oil crept over me, in mouth, nostrils and hair. When swamped by the waves I remember seeing the water I spurted from my mouth was black. I came across two men hanging on to a round lifebelt. They were black, and I told them they looked like a couple of Al Jolsons. They said : " Well, we must be a trio, 'cos you're the same." We were joined by another, so we had an Al Jolson quartet on one lifebelt. It was too much for it, and in the struggle to keep it lying flat on the sea we lost it.

We broke up, with the possibility of meeting again, but none of us would know the other, owing to the complete mask of oil. I kicked, I must confess somewhat panicky, to escape from the oil, but all I achieved was a bumping into a floating paravane. Once again there were four black faces with red eyes gathered together in the sea.

Then we saw a small motor-boat with two men in it. The engine was broken. I tried to organize our individual strengths into a concerted drive to reach the idly floating boat. We tried to push or pull ourselves by hanging on the paravane, kicking our legs, but it was too awkward, and it overturned. I lost my grip and went under. My underwater struggles happily took me nearer to the boat.

After about two hours in the water, two hours of oil-fuel poisoning, I reached a thin wire rope which hung from the boat's bows. I called to the men aboard to help me climb the four feet to the deck.

They tried with a boat-hook, but finally said : " You know, we are pretty done in, too. You've got to try to help yourself. We can't do it alone." I said I could not hold anything. They put the boat-hook in my shirt collar, but it tore, and finally they said : " Sorry, pal, we can't lift you. Have you got that wire ? " " Yes," I said. They let me go, and there I hung. Another man arrived and caught the wire. He was smaller than I was. I am 13 st. The men aboard said they would try to get him up. " He's lighter than you," they said. They got him aboard, during which operation I went under again when he put his foot on my shoulder. The mouth of one black face aboard opened and showed black-slimed teeth, red gums and tongue. It said : " To hell with this ! "

He dived through the oil into the sea, popped up beside me with a round lifebelt, which he put over my head, saying : " Okay. Now let go the wire." But I'm sorry to say I couldn't. I couldn't bear to part with it. It had kept me on the surface about 15 minutes. They separated us, however, and the next thing I was being hauled aboard at a rope's end, which they could grip as it was not oily or slimy.

Another oil casualty was dragged aboard, and later 30 of us were lifted aboard a destroyer. We were stripped, bathed and left naked on the fo'c'sle benches and tables to sweat the oil out of the pores in the great heat.

Left, Captain J. C. Leach, R.N., in command of H.M.S. Prince of Wales, was posted missing after the vessel had been sunk off Malaya on December 10. Missing also was Admiral Sir Tom Phillips (centre), C.-in-C. of the Far East Fleet, whose flagship she was. Capt. W. G. Tennant, R.N. (right), commanding the Repulse, was saved.   *Photos, Associated Press, Planet News, Vandyk*

Editor's Postscript

WHAT of 1942? I am no prophet, nor son of a prophet, but I offer the suggestion that it is going to be the Big Year of the War. Not in mere "victories"—for the vanquished have often more victories to their credit than the final victors. And so it is likely to be in this universal smash-up. It is highly improbable that we shall see an end to the struggle this year, but it is most likely that, after having to suffer many new set-backs, still more "sweat and blood and tears," the shape of future events will be shadowed forth in bolder outline. It will be a year of great decisions, with the smoke of battle clearing here and there to reveal the course which the clashing forces of Tyranny and Democracy will have to pursue in 1943. At any rate, for all who can stand up to the pain and pressure of life in wartime it is going to be the peak year of sensational happenings and world-wide devilishness, such as old Earth has never witnessed in its millions of years. A great time in which to be alive, and to remain alive with eager eyes towards the peace that must come. At least, that's my opinion—and my name isn't Nostradamus!

MY regular readers will remember that before the guillotine descended upon our paper supplies and we were able to give a much larger publication, and issue it weekly into the bargain, I occasionally devoted a page to comment upon the letters that came to me from all parts of the world that had not yet been made inaccessible by German occupation. Although the area of the globe across which postal intercourse can still take place has been vastly reduced within the last eighteen months, and the exigencies of the paper situation have forced our publishers into various self-denying ordinances, whereby the original weekly issue of a million copies of THE WAR ILLUSTRATED has had to be restricted to a point considerably below the half-million level, the volume of my correspondence scarcely shows any decline. Had I the space to deal with it, this would offer an excellent illustration of how effectively the sea-ways of the Empire have been, often at great sacrifice, maintained by the energy and resource of the British Navy and our splendid merchant service.

IT has long been impossible, however, to find space for what always proves an attractive feature—talks with my correspondents. But among the letters to hand this week there is one, coming to me over four thousand miles, that simply demands publication:

British Legation, Port-au-Prince.
Dear Sir John,

On the threshold of the third year of war may I congratulate you on the service that your WAR ILLUSTRATED has given to Great Britain. Among the various types of literature which the publicity side of this Legation receives from London and elsewhere, yours is undoubtedly the most popular and copies go to the various outposts and are snatched up avidly by people here.

I hope you will be able to continue the good work.   Yours sincerely,
                            R. A. N. HILLYER, H.M. Minister.

IT is indeed a pleasure to receive such a letter, not only because of the satisfaction it gives me in its recognition of the interest of our publication, but of its appraisal as a contribution to the war effort. Mr. Hillyer's letter has come to my desk via Air Mail, but as I have received many scores of letters from distant parts of Canada, Australia, and New Zealand, as well as from all parts of Africa North and South, carried hither by mail steamers, that is only a further proof that THE WAR ILLUSTRATED does "get about." The dramatic change in the War situation,

Major-Gen. NEIL METHUEN RITCHIE, whose appointment as Commander of the 8th Army in Libya was announced by Mr. Churchill on December 11, 1941, has now been granted the acting rank of Lieut.-General. Gen. Ritchie is 44.   *Photo, Vandyk*

the Japanese attack in the Pacific, and the Axis hostilities menacing the Eastern seaboard of America, and especially these island approaches, may bring experiences of the most exciting kind to Mr. Hillyer, who was appointed H.M. Minister Resident and Consul in Haiti (the "Magic Isle" of Seabrook's fascinating book) at the beginning of 1939.

CAME across by chance on one of my bookshelves today "Life's Questionings" by William Romaine Paterson: a brilliant little book of aphorisms which express in gobbets of gleaming prose much of his somewhat pessimistic philosophy of life expounded at length in "The Nemesis of Nations" and in "Problems of Destiny." On the first page at which I opened the book I read: "It is a sign of the fundamental wickedness of the human race that during the French Revolution small gold and silver guillotines were worn as jewelry by the women." A reminder that there may be lots

of work for the guillotine again before the growing mess in France is cleaned up. But probably firing squads will save time.

PATERSON'S apophthegms are well worth reconsidering today: there is not one of the 116 pp. that does not contain three or four arresting thoughts for these times, all pithily phrased. "Only a man like Caesar could make love to a woman and carry on a war at the same time" lets out the sexless maniac of Berchtesgaden, but the gross-living gangster of the Palazzo Venezia has already proved its truth. Paterson is one of my oldest friends and we last corresponded in Spanish shortly before the War when he was staying at Sitjes near Barcelona perfecting himself in that language—the eighth or ninth on his list! One of the most brilliant alumni of Glasgow University, at the age of twenty-five, he made a great success as a novelist under the name of "Benjamin Swift." Many of my old readers will recall his "Nancy Noon."

WITH hearty approval I note the tightening up of the existing rules that regulate the Home Guards—if, indeed, they hitherto have had anything resembling rules or regulations. A strong body used to gather in our village, where there is great need of an effective unit, but attendance during the last six months had notably thinned, the enthusiasm lowered. "Why didn't you turn up at last meeting, Brown?" "Oh, it was mother's birthday." The same question to Jones brought the answer: "Had some letters to write." What Robinson's response was I don't remember; quite possibly "sore feet." Arrangements to collect the men to attend a group lecture and special instruction four or five miles away were not carried out, and those assembled in uniform awaiting transport spent the evening yarning at the Blue Pig.

NOW this is very bad for discipline, and very much to the disquiet of the serious-minded members of the local group, squad, platoon, or whatever it calls itself. So, not a day too soon has the step been taken to place a reasonable amount of compulsion on the Home Guard, with appropriate penalties for the non-discharge of their not-too-onerous duties. Fortunately our rural scene has not yet been sullied by paratroops or any sort of invader, else I should have trembled for the "show" our locals would have put up. But a recent tightening up of discipline, will, I am sure, produce the desired results. A hard-working non-com. in the H.G. assures me the case I describe is exceptional. I hope he's right.

A GLEAM of humour in the gloom of war is worth a hundred groans. And nothing better have I heard than the statement in a broadcast from America about the first experimental black-out along the Pacific Coast cities. According to this the performance of America's A.R.P. left much to be desired at many places. Los Angeles was a brilliant exception. Its general black-out was effective. But there is a great sky-sign advertising the hospitality of the celluloid metropolis to all arriving by air. Somebody forgot the switch, and this was left blazing with increased brilliancy from the encircling gloom: "Welcome to Los Angeles."

Printed in England and published on the 10th, 20th, and 30th of each month by the Proprietors, The Amalgamated Press, Ltd., The Fleetway House, Farringdon Street, London, E.C.4. Registered for transmission by Canadian Magazine Post. Sole Agents for Australia and New Zealand : Messrs. Gordon & Gotch, Ltd. ; and for South Africa : Central News Agency, Ltd. January 10th, 1942.   S.S.   *Editorial Address :* JOHN CARPENTER HOUSE, WHITEFRIARS, LONDON, E.C.4

Vol 5 · N° 118

The War Illustrated

Edited by Sir John Hammerton

FOURPENCE

JAN. 20TH. 1942

TO CAIRO FROM LIBYA come these Axis troops, not as conquerors but as prisoners. They are some of the thousands of German and Italian prisoners captured by Gen. Ritchie's 8th Army in Cyrenaica. Escorted by Scottish troops and Egyptian mounted police, these men are seen marching through the City of the Caliphs on their way to the citadel, or El-Kala, in the background, which was built by Saladin in 1166. Within the citadel stands the Mosque of Mehemet Ali, flanked by tall minarets.

Photo, British Official : Crown Copyright

NO. 119 WILL BE PUBLISHED FRIDAY, JAN. 30

THE UNITED NATIONS DECLARE, FOR FREEDOM

ON the first day of 1942 the Grand Alliance of the Democracies against the Axis powers was concluded at Washington, when the representatives of 26 nations signed a solemn declaration of mutual support and resolved to fight the war together to a successful finish.

The "Declaration By the United Nations," as it was officially styled in the published text, although historians may prefer to call it the Declaration of Washington, opens with a list of the Governments signatory thereto. Then it goes on, "Having subscribed to a common programme of purposes and principles embodied in the Atlantic Charter ; and being convinced that complete victory over their enemies is essential to defend life, liberty, independence and religious freedom, and to preserve human rights and justice in their own lands as well as in other lands ; and that they are now engaged in a common struggle against savage, brutal forces seeking to subjugate the world, declare :

"1.—Each Government pledges itself to employ its full resources, military or economic, against those members of the Tripartite Pact and its adherents with which such a Government is at war.

"2.—Each Government pledges itself to cooperate with the Governments signatory hereto, and not to make a separate armistice or peace with the enemies."

"The foregoing declaration may be adhered to by other nations which are or which may be rendering material assistance and contributions in the struggle for victory over Hitlerism."

No special ceremony attended the signing of what Mr. Cordell Hull, the U.S. Secretary of State, described as "one of the greatest documents in history." After President Roosevelt had signed for America and Mr. Churchill for Britain, the representatives of the other signatory states proceeded to the White House, and, with their overcoats over their arms, passed into the room of Mr. Berle, Assistant Secretary of State, where the document lay ready for their signature. Mr. Litvinov, the Soviet Ambassador, signed for Russia, and Mr. T. V. Soong, just reappointed Chinese Foreign Minister, for China. Dr. Loudon, Queen Wilhelmina's Minister in the States, signed for the Netherlands, and the British Dominions were represented by Mr. Leighton McCarthy for Canada, Mr. R. G. Casey for Australia, Mr. Frank Langstone for New Zealand, Mr. Bajpai for India, and Mr. Ralph Close for South Africa. Then, one by one, the envoys of the other nations added their signatures—of Belgium, Luxembourg, and Greece, of Norway, Poland, Czechoslovakia, and Yugoslavia, of Costa Rica, Cuba, the Dominican Republic, Salvador, Guatemala, Haiti, Honduras, Nicaragua, and Panama.

SWIFT on the heels of the publication of the Declaration of Washington came the announcement of the first major decision of the new Alliance. On January 3 it was announced in Washington that, as a result of proposals put forward by the United States and British Chiefs of Staffs, and on their recommendations to President Roosevelt and to Prime Minister Churchill, and with the concurrence of the Netherlands Government and the Dominion Governments concerned, the system of a unified command was to be established in the south-west Pacific area. Henceforth, all the forces in this area—the area was not precisely defined, but it was authoritatively stated to include Singapore, Malaya, the Dutch East Indies, and the Philippines—would operate under one Supreme Commander : "At the suggestion of the President, in which all concerned have agreed, General Sir Archibald Wavell has been appointed to this command." Major-General G. H. Brett, Chief of the Air Corps of the U.S. Army, was appointed Deputy Supreme Commander, and General Sir Henry Pownall was appointed General Wavell's Chief of Staff, while Admiral Thomas C. Hart of the U.S. Navy was given command of all the naval forces in the area. At the same time, went on the announcement, His Excellency the Generalissimo, Chiang Kai-Shek, had accepted supreme command over all land and air forces of the united nations, which were now or might in the future be operating in the Chinese theatre.

WITHIN a few hours General Wavell was on his way to take up his new command. "I am fully conscious that it is a great responsibility which rests on me," he said on January 4. "The sudden and treacherous attack by Japan has given her forces an initial advantage. This is the advantage which a murderer, thief or cheat can always gain against an unsuspecting ordinary and decent citizen." The situation might become worse until the tide turned, and in any case it would not be possible to reverse it at one blow. "We must hold on with what we have until we can collect our forces for the return blow," he added. "The combined forces of Britain, the United States, China, the Netherlands East Indies and Australia cannot fail in the long run to throw out the Japanese freebooters from the places they have temporarily seized."

HISTORY has known other Grand Alliances —one of the most famous is that against Louis XIV of France, in which Mr. Churchill's ancestor, the Duke of Marlborough, so distinguished himself—but never has there been any Alliance to be compared with this tremendous "instrument of war, which is just as tremendous a forger and welder of the peace that is to follow after." Compared with the Declaration of Washington, the Axis and the Tripartite Pacts look small enough. On our side there are now ranged four-fifths of the world.

THIS was made outstandingly clear on January 6, when Mr. Roosevelt delivered the most historic of all his vital Messages to Congress : "The consolidation of the united nations' total war effort against our common enemies is being achieved. That is the purpose of the conferences which have been held during the past two weeks in Washington, Moscow, and Chungking . . . We shall not fight isolated wars—each nation going its own way. We of the united nations will so dispose our forces that we can strike at the common enemy wherever the greatest damage can be done. The militarists in Berlin and Tokyo started this war, but the massed angered forces of common humanity will finish it."

IN these circumstances it is almost difficult to realize that this time last year we of the British Commonwealth were alone, with no ally in arms beside us. America was in the working war but not in the fighting war. Russia—amazing thought when we think of the six months of struggle along the road to Moscow and back—was still Hitler's ally. The Chinese were fighting the Japanese, whom we were still trying to appease . . . What, or rather, whom, have we to thank for the tremendous transformation ? First and foremost, Mr. Churchill and President Roosevelt ; but perhaps our thanks are due almost equally to Messrs. Hitler and Tojo. If Hitler had learnt the lesson that Napoleon never learnt—when to stop ; if Tojo had never thought what a wonderfully clever thing it would be to catch the Yanks unprepared—then we might still have been sustaining the struggle alone, or almost alone.

WHAT a vast difference, then, has been brought about in our situation and in our prospects by a brief 12 months ! An even greater difference may be brought about before we have torn the last leaf off 1942's calendar—that is, if we work as we ought to work, and if we fight as we can fight and must. The armies of the Axis will be crushed on the field of battle, their navies will be sent to the bottom or driven to surrender at another Scapa, and their air fleets will be swept from the skies. Germany will at last experience all the woes and wrongs which she has inflicted upon so many innocent peoples. These things shall be. They will proceed inevitably, inexorably, from the Declaration signed in Washington on January 1.

GEN. SIR ARCHIBALD WAVELL, Supreme Commander of the forces of the united nations in the South-West Pacific, being helped into parachute equipment before leaving Malaya after an inspection of Singapore's defences. *Photo British Official*

E. ROYSTON PIKE

Malta Had 60 Raids in Christmas Week

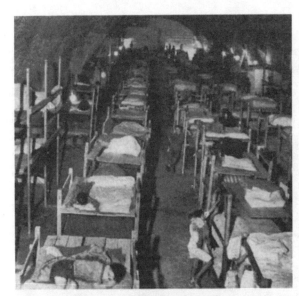

Maltese Shelter dug deep beneath the island rock. Malta has thirty long underground galleries of great antiquity which have been adapted to serve as shelters against air raids.

KING'S CHRISTMAS MESSAGE TO MALTA

Malta the Indomitable sent the following Christmas message to King George VI :

" Please convey to his Majesty the King the loyal and devoted Christmas greetings of the people and garrison of Malta and all parties in the Council of Government. Now, as ever before, Malta stands determined to play its part in the Empire struggle until the day of victory comes."

In his reply to Lt.-Gen. Sir William Dobbie, Governor of Malta, His Majesty said :

" Please convey to the Government, garrison and people of Malta my sincere thanks for their Christmas message. I send them my best wishes, in confidence that the coming year will find them as undaunted and resolute as ever in the defence of the island."

Maltese Families have endured a thousand air attacks—there were 60 air raids on the island during Christmas week. Fortunately the workable island rock has provided safe shelters and civilian casualties have been relatively small. These young Maltese are seated outside a shelter entrance.

VALETTA HARBOUR is, naturally, one of the main objectives of Axis raiders, and this photograph was taken at the height of a raid. But air attack on Malta has proved very costly to the enemy, enormous numbers of enemy planes having been brought down by the island's defences—A.A. guns and the indomitable fighters of the R.A.F. And Malta hits back, for British bombers based on the island have dropped millions of bombs on enemy targets in Sicily and S. Italy.

Photos, British Official : Crown Copyright ; Planet News

Our Troops in Libya Wear the Smile of Victory

Hundreds of cans full of petrol fell into British hands when this fuel dump, between Bardia and Tobruk, was captured. The loss of fuel supplies by capture or bombing has been a great blow to Rommel's panzers.

BARDIA COULD NOT EMULATE TOBRUK

THE New Year began well in Libya with the capture of the fortified seaport of Bardia. During the night of January 1-2 units of the First and Second South African Divisions—the South African Police, Kaffrarian Rifles and Royal Durban Light Infantry—supported by British tanks and medium artillery as well as by the Polish Field Artillery Regiment and by the New Zealand Cavalry Regiment, carried the strong defences of Bardia at the point of the bayonet. The operation was magnificently supported by units of the Mediterranean Fleet.

The Bardia garrison held a position of great natural strength, made even more formidable by the application of military science and engineering. But though the German and Italian garrison had before it the magnificent example of Tobruk to show what a resolute defence could accomplish, they surrendered unconditionally after an attack of less than 48 hours.

Although naval and air bombardment and artillery fire contributed to the capture of the fortress, it was the bayonet attack at night which really sealed its fate. Rather than face a repetition of the attack, the enemy decided to surrender, and on Friday morning, January 2, two Axis emissaries approached the British lines with a flag of truce. They asked Gen. de Villiers, commanding the British forces in the attack, to make a rendezvous with Maj.-Gen. Arthur Schmidt, the Axis commander, with a view to negotiating the surrender. The terms were soon settled and nearly 8,000 prisoners were taken by the Imperial Forces when they entered the town later in the day.

Maj.-Gen. Schmidt, the first German general commanding a large force to surrender to the British in this war, was Chief Administrative Staff Officer of the African Panzer Groups.

THE LIBYAN ADVANCE has brought regiments from home as well as Imperial troops into the limelight. Above, some cheery lads of the Essex Regiment are seen at El Duda, while at the top of the page two no less cheerful machine-gunners of a North County regiment sit in a captured enemy gun pit. Circle, a remarkable shot by the Germans. The shell went right down the muzzle of a British tank gun and split it in two.

Photos, British Official: Crown Copyright

In Pursuit of Rommel Across the Desert

VICTORY IN LIBYA is crowning the efforts of General Ritchie's 8th Army, which, by the end of 1941, had almost cleared the province of Cyrenaica of the enemy. Photographs from the Libyan front in this page show : top, Axis tanks, armoured vehicles and mechanized transport ablaze in the desert after capture by South African troops. Below, British military traffic making its way along the Tobruk-Bardia road. The New Year opened with Gen. Rommel brought to bay at Jedabia, 100 miles south of Benghazi, where he strove desperately to break out of the ring slowly closing round him.

Photos, British Official : Crown Copyright

CHURCHILL SPEAKS FOR BRITAIN IN AMERICA:

MR. CHURCHILL in America ! It was at 1.4 a.m. on December 23, 1941 that the dramatic announcement was made in London that " The British Prime Minister has arrived in the United States to discuss with the President all questions relevant to a concerted war effort. Mr. Churchill is accompanied by Lord Beaverbrook, Minister of Supply, and a technical staff. Mr. Churchill is the guest of the President." This was followed by the news that the Prime Minister had arrived at the White House in Washington and had gone into immediate conference with President Roosevelt.

Followed days of intense activity in which Mr. Churchill and his experts (who included Admiral Sir Dudley Pound, First Sea Lord ; Air Marshal Sir Charles Portal, Chief of the Air Staff ; and Field-Marshal Sir John Dill, lately Chief of the Imperial General Staff) discussed with the President and his colleagues such vitally important matters as the establishment of an Allied War Council to direct and coordinate strategy on every front and on all the seven seas, the combination of the man-power of Russia and China with the illimitable industrial resources of America and Britain, and the pooling of war materials and supplies—indeed, every aspect of what is now a world-wide struggle of the Democracies against the Axis Powers.

High lights of Mr. Churchill's visit were his addresses to the Congress of the United States on December 26 and the Canadian Parliament four days later— utterances which, thanks to radio, had an audience of uncounted millions ; some of the most important passages in one and the other are reprinted below.

Premier's Speech to U.S. Congress

THE fact that my American forbears of so many generations played their part in the life of the United States and that here I am, an Englishman, welcomed in your midst, makes this experience one of the most moving and thrilling in my life, which is already long and has not been entirely uneventful. I wish indeed that my mother, whose memory I cherish across the vale of years, should have been here to see. I cannot help reflecting that if my father had been American and my mother British, instead of the other way round, I might have got here on my own.

In that case this would not have been the first time you would have heard my voice. In that case I would not have needed any invitation, but if I had it is hardly likely it would have been unanimous.

As a " child of the House of Commons," one who was brought up in his father's house to believe in Democracy, Mr. Churchill declared that all his life he has been in harmony with the tides which had flowed on both sides of the Atlantic against privilege and monopoly, and has steered confidently towards the Gettysburg ideal of " the government of the people, by the people, for the people." Then he described how much he had been impressed and encouraged by the breadth of view and sense of proportion which he had found in all quarters in America. The United States had been attacked and set upon by three most powerful armed Dictator States.

The quarrel is opened which can only end in their overthrow or ours. But here in Washington in these memorable days I have found an Olympian fortitude which, far from being based upon complacency, is only the beginning of an inflexible purpose and the proof of a sure, well-grounded confidence in the final outcome. We in Britain had the same feeling in our darkest days. We, too, were sure in the end all would be well.

You do not underrate the severity of the ordeal to which you and we have still to be subjected. The forces ranged against us are enormous. They are bitter, they are ruthless. They have a vast accumulation of war weapons of all kinds. They have highly-trained, disciplined armies, navies and air services. They had plans and designs which had long been tried and matured. They will stop at nothing that violence or treachery can suggest.

It is true that on our side our own resources in man-power and materials are far greater than theirs. But only a portion of our resources are as yet mobilized and developed, and we both of us have much to learn in the cruel art of war. We have therefore without doubt a time of tribulation before us.

During the best part of the last 20 years, the Premier went on, the youth of Britain and America have been taught that war is evil, while during the same 20 years the youth of Japan and Italy have been taught that aggressive war is the noblest duty of the citizen, and that it should be begun as soon as the necessary weapons and organization have been made. We had performed the duties and tasks of peace ; they have plotted and planned for war.

But now at the end of December 1941 our transformation from easy-going peace to total war efficiency has made very great progress . . . Provided that every effort is made, that nothing is kept back, that the whole man-power, brain-power, virility, courage and civic fortitude of the English-speaking world, with all its galaxy of loyal, friendly and associated communities and States—provided that is bent unremittingly to the supreme task—I think it reasonable to hope that the end of 1942 will see us quite definitely in a better position than we are now, and that the year 1943 will enable us to assume the initiative upon an ample scale.

Some people might be momentarily depressed when the Premier and President alike spoke of a long and hard war. But the British and American peoples would rather know the truth, sombre though it may be. Moreover, all the tidings will not be evil. Already mighty strokes of war have been dealt against the enemy by the Russian armies and people. Wounds have been inflicted upon the Nazi tyranny and system which have bitten deep and will fester and inflame not only in the Nazi body but in the Nazi mind.

The boastful Mussolini has crumpled ; he is now but a lackey and serf, the merest utensil of his master's will. He has been stripped of his African Empire and Abyssinia has been liberated. The British armies in the east, which were so weak and ill-equipped at the moment of the French desertion, now control all the regions from Teheran to Benghazi and Aleppo and Cyprus to the shores of the Nile.

There are good tidings also from the blue waters. The lifeline of supplies which joins our two nations across the oceans—that lifeline is flowing steadily and freely in spite of all the enemy can do. It is a fact that the British Empire, which many thought 18 months ago was broken and ruined, is now incomparably stronger and is growing stronger with every month. Lastly, to me the best tidings of all is that the United States, united as never before, has drawn the sword for freedom and cast away the scabbard.

Then the Premier proceeded to discuss what, viewed quite dispassionately, appears an irrational act—Japan's war against the United States and the British Empire.

They have certainly embarked upon a very considerable undertaking. And after the

PRESSMEN AND PREMIER. Mr. Churchill, smoking his inevitable cigar, and seated next to President Roosevelt, takes great delight in answering the questions fired at him by American journalists at a Press conference at the White House on the occasion of his recent visit to Washington.
Photo, Planet News

HISTORIC WORDS IN WASHINGTON AND OTTAWA

ADDRESSING U.S. CONGRESS on Dec. 26, Mr. Churchill is seen before a battery of microphones which enabled his speech to be listened to by millions all over the world. Behind him is Mr. William P. Cole, Acting Speaker of the House, and on the right Vice-President Henry A. Wallace.

outrages they have committed upon us at Pearl Harbour, in the Philippines, in Malaya and in the Dutch East Indies, they must now know that the stakes for which they have decided to play are mortal.

When we compare the resources of the United States and the British Empire with those of Japan, when we remember those of China, which has so valiantly withstood invasion and tyranny, and when also we observe the Russian menace which hangs over

Japan, it becomes still more difficult to reconcile Japan's action with prudence and sanity.

What kind of a people do they think we are ? Is it possible that they do not realize we shall never cease to persevere against them until they have been taught a lesson which they and the world will never forget ?

Next Mr. Churchill turned from the turmoil and convulsions of the present to the broader basis of the future.

Twice in a single generation the catastrophe of world war has fallen upon us. Twice in our lifetime has the long arm of fate reached across the ocean to bring the United States into the forefront of the battle itself. If we had kept together after the last war, if we had taken common measures for our safety, then this renewal of the curse need never have fallen upon us . . .

It is not given to us to peer into the mysteries of the future. Still I avow my hope and faith, sure and inviolate, that in the days to come the British and American people will, for their own safety and for the good of all, walk together in majesty, in justice and in peace.

contrary, we must drive ourselves forward with unrelenting zeal. In this strange, terrible world war there is a place for everyone, man and woman, old and young, the hale and halt —service in a thousand forms is open. There is no room now for the dilettante, for the weakling, for the shirker, for the sluggard . . . The enemies ranged against us have asked for total war. Let us make sure they get it.

Mr. Churchill then looked back on the years of war. He mentioned Hitler's felonious invasion of Poland, "the phoney war," the assaults on Norway, Denmark, Belgium and Holland— absolutely blameless neutrals ; the hideous massacre of Rotterdam, the great French catastrophe. If only the French had decided to continue the fight from North Africa . . .

But their generals misled them. When I warned them that Britain would fight on alone, whatever they did, their generals told their Prime Minister and his divided Cabinet : " In three weeks England will have her neck wrung like a chicken." Some chicken ! Some neck !

Mr. Churchill proceeded to describe how the tide is now turning against the Hun. Britain is growing stronger every day. The Russian Army, under their warrior leader, Joseph Stalin, is fighting furious war with increasing success. General Auchinleck is mopping up the German and Italian forces who have attempted the invasion of Egypt. The mighty republic of the United States has entered the conflict in a manner which shows that with her there can be no withdrawal except by death or victory. After a passage in French, greeted with a roar of appreciation by the bilingual Canadian M.P.s, Mr. Churchill resumed in English.

We may discern three main phases or events in the struggle that lies before us. First there is the period of consolidation, of combination and of final preparation. The second phase may be called the phase of liberation. There is a third phase which must also be contemplated—the assault upon the citadels and the homelands of the guilty parties both in Europe and Asia . . . Let us then address ourselves to our task, not in any way underrating its difficulties and perils, but in good heart and sober confidence, resolved that, whatever the cost, whatever the suffering, we shall stand by one another true and faithful comrades and do our duty, God helping us, to the end.

Address to the Canadian Parliament

IT is with feelings of pride and encouragement that I find myself here in the House of Commons of Canada invited to address the Parliament of the Senior Dominion of the Crown . . .

Then followed many paragraphs devoted to a survey of Canada's magnificent contribution to the Imperial war effort, in troops, in ships, in aircraft, in food, and in finance.

The peoples of the British Empire may love peace, they do not seek the lands or wealth of any country, but they are a tough and hardy lot. We have not journeyed all this way across the centuries, across the oceans, across the mountains, across the prairies, because we are made of sugar candy.

We do not ask that the rules of the game should be modified. We shall never descend to the German and Japanese level. But if anybody likes to play rough we can play rough too. Hitler and his Nazi gang have sown the wind. Let them reap the whirlwind. Neither the length of the struggle nor any form of severity which it may assume will make us weary or will make us quit.

Then came a tribute to " that great man," the President of the United States, with whom Mr. Churchill had spent the last week, concerting the steps which will bring about " the total and final extirpation of the Hitler tyranny, the Japanese frenzy, and the Mussolini flop."

The crisis is upon us. The power of the enemy is immense. If we were in any way to underrate the strength and resources or the ruthless savagery of that enemy we should jeopardize not only our lives, for they will be offered freely, but the cause of human

freedom and progress to which we have vowed ourselves and all we have. We cannot for a moment afford to relax. On the

IN OTTAWA, in the Chamber of the Canadian House of Commons on Dec. 30, the scenes of enthusiasm which had been witnessed a few days before in Washington were repeated when Mr. Churchill addressed the members of the Canadian Legislature. Here he is seen making his speech while members applaud. In the background sits the Speaker of the House of Commons.   *Photos, Keystone*

Our Searchlight on the War

FRANCE'S YEAR OF HOPE

After France fell certain French Generals were unwise and mean enough to say that " in three weeks England will have her neck wrung like a chicken."

THE Russian victories and the entry of America into the war have had a profound effect on the true France. 1942 will be a year of increasing hope and possibly resurgence of the French people. Nothing, of course, but treachery can be expected from the Vichy Government, who are the gaolers of compatriots. France is said to possess two trump cards, North Africa and the French fleet, but even

Indian public of all castes and creeds are now able to see the difference between British imperialism, so called, and Japanese and German aggression, even though the Congress Working Committee has the effrontery to say that the British Government is an arrogant imperialism undistinguishable from Fascism. Subjugation of Asia is the Japanese ambition, and if it came about there would be no room in India for democratic evolution. Sir Firoz Noon advises the potential munition workers of India to plunge into the production of more and more guns and ammunition for defence. Such is

Atlantic success, has received little notice. A year ago we were in the gravest danger of being starved into submission. Our arteries with the United States were being cut right and left by Hitler's bombs and torpedoes, but our seamen and an efficient war direction have turned a near defeat into a near victory. There are no words noble enough to praise the men concerned in this triumph. We can only humbly thank them and be proud of them, for the Battle of the Atlantic is the very foundation of all our victories—and it is still going on. Everything depends and has depended upon Britain's will and power to keep this sea open. Had we failed the Nazis would have won.

MR. EDEN IN MOSCOW. Wearing a black fur coat and an R.A.F. fur cap, Mr. Anthony Eden is seen, left, saluting after detraining at Moscow on his arrival for important discussions with Mr. Stalin. Mr. Molotov is seen, centre, and on the right is Sir Stafford Cripps. Mr. Eden on his return described the talks as " full, frank and sincere." *Photo, British Official: Crown Copyright*

Vichy realizes that nothing is to be gained by handing these over to Germany. The men of Vichy, however, have so compromised themselves that they now depend for their lives, miserable as they are, upon a Nazi victory. As the chance of that victory recedes so will France pass out of her despair into defiance. The question is one of heroic leadership in France itself, inspired by the splendid attitude of Free France. If our late Ally has an evil genius for fostering the worst politicians in the world, she has also a good genius for producing fine patriotic figures. We do not doubt that some great leader who will help to restore the soul of France is lurking somewhere in that tragic land.

MANILA'S MARTYRDOM

According to a British United Press message, United States naval authorities have allowed it to be understood that no major contact with the Japanese Fleet can be expected for months, perhaps a year.

THE tragedy of Manila and the Philippines is one of the supreme lessons of the war. An amiable and peace-loving people is overwhelmed by the yellow locusts from Nippon. Britain cannot afford to criticize the United States for neglecting the defences of the Philippines. We, ourselves, have lost—temporarily—the Channel Islands, Hong Kong and much of Malaya, but the lesson to be learned is that both great Democracies proved unequal to their responsibilities. They were not able to protect the freedom-loving peoples. Let Britain and America revise the idea that freedom in itself has some magic power of self-preservation. To guard it we must be stronger than any combination of powers that might threaten it. The Democracies must also revise their ideas about peacetime armaments, and all malcontents who howl about the cost of navies, armies and air forces must be silenced. America is preparing to spend £37,000,000,000 on a Victory Programme. Britain is already spending £400,000,000 a month. Had the Allies in common spent a fraction of these figures before the war, Hitler and Mussolini could not have risen to challenge the free peoples.

WISDOM FROM INDIA

Some Indian leaders who today even in the face of this extreme danger are behaving in a sulky manner will never be forgiven by future generations for their indifference to the dangers of India.—Sir Firoz Noon

SINCE the Japanese entered the war a few responsible Indian leaders have warned their countrymen of the futilities of political discord and civil disobedience. Perhaps the

the only way to ensure India's eventual freedom, the same freedom for which the Allies are fighting. Victory is essential to all our aspirations, and if it is not achieved the Germans and Japanese will put democracy in the concentration camp; Indian politicians and peoples would then really know what Fascism is. Mr. Gandhi has resigned his leadership of the Congress Party, but continues a symbolical opposition to all wars, whatever that may mean. His departure is a good sign, since Mr. Gandhi's attitude to the world crisis is hopelessly unpractical. At a time when all the seas and lands are full of bombs, torpedoes and tanks, civil disobedience and non-cooperation would appear to be an Indian form of hara-kiri.

GREATEST VICTORY OF ALL

Replying to questions in Ottawa, Mr. Churchill said that in the last five months the net losses of ships were only one-fifth of the preceding five months.

THE traditional way of taking our pleasures, or victories, sadly may account for the fact that Britain's best New Year gift, the Battle of

SALVAGE AND SALVATION

Will the drive for salvage of all kinds change our national habit of extravagance into one of thrift ?

IN the old days of peace and plenty an intelligent Frenchman, asked what had impressed him most about England, replied that he was astonished by the wasteful and extravagant habits of the people of all classes. The opinion seems to have been confirmed by the immense value and utility of salvage of all kinds from food to metals and paper. We now collect these unconsidered trifles to help to save our very lives from the predatory foe. As to whether the world will be immensely poorer or richer after the war there are two schools of thought—those who believe that the cupboard of life will be bare, and those who think that a new system of economics and world cooperation will usher in a time of great prosperity. In either case the idea of national thrift might well continue, for thrift is a basis for success and happiness in life. The extravagant may appear to have a good time, but the careful man is not only the better citizen, but fundamentally the happier. To make thrift possible, however, post-war Governments must set an example. We must get back to a system that does not rob Peter to pay Paul, in other words, to reasonable taxation and better employment and wage conditions which will obviate the dissipation of public money. Surely the best social system is one which makes the individual proud and secure in his own efforts. It is the abuse of wealth and not its accumulation which is bad.

ANGLO-RUSSIAN FRIENDSHIP

What matters in foreign affairs is not the form of internal government of any nation, but its international behaviour —Mr. Anthony Eden.

IN his splendid broadcast on his visit to Russia, Mr. Eden expressed the feelings of all liberal-minded men and women in regard to Anglo-Soviet relations. The war for freedom has brought Russia and Britain together in idealistic amity. The magnificent fight of Russia and Britain on behalf of the human spirit has won the admiration of both peoples. Contrasts in forms of government must be no bar to an increasingly fruitful understanding. Let it be admitted that we have something to learn from the Soviets and that the Soviets have something to learn from us and progress is inevitable. At heart, the Russian and British peoples want the same things, freedom from aggression, freedom to develop their national genius, peace and prosperity. Neither is a war-mongering race ; but, like all peace-loving men, they make the greatest warriors when the call comes to defend themselves against cruelty, injustice and tyranny.

SANDBAGS IN SAN FRANCISCO piled up around the Pacific Telephone and Telegraph Building on the morning following the Japanese attacks on America's Pacific outposts. The threat to American cities on the Pacific coast caused the authorities to order immediate protective measures against the possibility of Japanese bombing attacks from aircraft carriers. *Photo, Planet News*

All These Things Constitute a Naval Base

THOUGH it is not intended to represent any known harbour, this drawing illustrates the characteristic features which may be found in any large naval base, whether situated in the Pacific or elsewhere.

The most important feature, of course, is the harbour (1), which must be capable of providing shelter for a fleet and room for the largest battleship to manoeuvre. The entrance to this harbour is protected by a net and boom (2) against the encroachment of hostile submarines. Minefields (3) guard the distant approaches. At (4) and (4a) are the emplacements of long-range coastal artillery which defend the base against enemy warships, and batteries of searchlights (5) are sited to illuminate the harbour approaches.

Fighter aircraft, as well as reconnaissance and bomber planes are stationed at the airfield (6), which has multi-directional runways. One of several A.A. defence systems, with its gun-sites, predictors, range-

finders, sound locators and searchlights, is seen on the high ground (7). Seaplanes and long-range flying boats have hangars and repair workshops with ramps leading down to the water's edge (8) and a berth for aircraft-carriers is seen at (9).

Not the least important feature of the base of this kind is the oil and fuel storage with a jetty along which fuel is pumped into the storage tanks (10). A submarine depot ship, which houses a foundry, plumbers', copper-smiths' and carpenters' shops, light and heavy machine shops and electrical and torpedo repair shops, is seen berthed at (11) with some of the submarines it services. At (12) are larger workshops, forges, etc., where all heavy repairs to warships can be carried out, and in this connexion the large travelling cranes and gantries (13) are used.

The cruiser (14) is in the refitting berth, being made ready for sea again. A large power-house is seen at (15) and at (16) are storehouses. Alongside rise the aerial

masts of the radio station (17). A large dry dock, in which major repairs and refits are carried out, is at (18), and adjoining it is the pumping plant (19). Dry docks are usually constructed in close proximity to wet docks in order that, after discharging her cargo or stores, a vessel may, when required, be dry berthed without loss of time. If there is no space availabe for a graving dock a floating dock may be used. Barracks, administrative offices and a parade ground for troops or Marines are situated at (20).

The strategical importance of such a base is obvious, and that is why Japan is making such strenuous efforts to deny our own and the U.S.A. Fleets the use of Singapore, Pearl Harbour and other similar bases, and why our Bomber Command makes continuous heavy raids upon the German-controlled bases at Brest, Dunkirk, La Pallice and Lorient.

Diagram specially drawn by Haworth for THE WAR ILLUSTRATED.

The Ordeal in the Philippines and Malaya

The Japanese plan of campaign was to surround Singapore by the conquest of the Philippines and Malaya and the occupation of Borneo. Though their initial efforts, aided by immensely superior forces, and a treacherous surprise attack, met with considerable success, victory will remain with the Democratic powers when their great strength and strategy are fully coordinated.

As the war in the Pacific developed it was obvious that the Japanese were working to a long-prepared plan. Their strategy was to conquer the Philippines, and thus assure their ocean flank. Malaya and Borneo were secondary operations with the intention of surrounding and reducing Singapore. Hence the Japanese initial concentration against Manila, capital of the Philippine group. By December 29, 1941, they had as many as 200,000 men on Luzon, with reinforcements continually arriving.

The invaders struck with fanatical fury regardless of losses. During the night of December 29-30 the Japanese army operating in North Luzon attacked Cabanatuan, about 60 miles inland from the Gulf of Lingayen, along a mile front, meeting with strenuous American and Philippine resistance, while enemy forces, which had landed in overwhelming numbers in the region of Mauban, southeast of Manila, pressed forward in a long battle line. Making rapid advances, the Japanese had fought their way into Luisiana and Dolores by December 30 and were then within 45 air miles of their objective.

A statement from General MacArthur's headquarters on the next day prepared the world for the fall of Manila. It said : " The enemy is driving in great force from both north and south. His dive-bombers practically control the roads from the air. The Japanese are using great quantities of tanks and armoured units. Our lines are being pushed back." General MacArthur, with United States and Philippine troops, continued to inflict heavy losses on the enemy along an arc-like front stretching 200 miles from the Cavite navy yard across six provinces. While Mr. Stimson, U.S. War Secretary, praised the General's heroic stand, he pointed out that America must face the fact that the Japanese were overwhelmingly strong. " I am confident," he said, " that we can and will defeat them in the end, but we cannot do that by looking through rose-coloured spectacles."

Flaming Wreckage of Manila

It was announced on January 3 that the American and Filipino troops had left Manila and that the near-by naval base of Cavite had also fallen. All defence works, industrial and supply facilities, including fuel, were destroyed, and ships and stores were removed by the defenders. The Japanese entered the city amid the flaming wreckage of their own bombs, at 1 a.m. New York time. Meanwhile, the Allied troops were still holding strong positions to the north of the city, and the fortifications in the Manila Bay area, including Corregidor, Fort Hughes on the island of Caballo, Fort Drum on El Fraile Island, and Fort Frank on Carabao Island. The masterly way in which General MacArthur had conducted his defence was justified by the fact that he had extricated his forces from annihilation between the Japanese pincers. On January 4 it was learned that he was entrenched in the mountainous region of the Zambales and Pampanga provinces, two miles across the water from Corregidor. There was no thought of evacuating the U.S. and Filipino soldiers from the island of Luzon. Their courageous stand had at least resulted in diverting and holding more than a quarter of a million Japanese from objectives in Malaya.

While General MacArthur was consolidating his positions in Luzon, a formation of heavy American bombers attacked the

MALAYA, where at the beginning of the New Year Japanese forces were thrusting forward south of Kota Bahru on the east coast and had reached Ipoh on the west.
Courtesy of " The Times"

Japanese naval units at Mindanao, the most southerly of the Philippine islands. An enemy battleship suffered three direct hits, a destroyer was sunk and several other ships were severely damaged. The American planes, which had operated from a secret base, returned without loss. A conspicuously brave incident in this action was the fight put up by the small American seaplane tender, U.S.S. Heron, for seven hours against fifteen Japanese planes. The Heron shot down several of the attackers. She was assailed by a veritable storm of bombs and three torpedoes. One of the latter scored a direct hit, but still the Heron kept afloat and reached port. Her Commander, Lieut. W. L. Cabler, was awarded the Navy Cross and recommended for promotion.

Simultaneously, General MacArthur, operating in Pampanga province, to the

LUZON, chief island of the Philippines. Manila, the capital, was occupied by the Japanese on Jan. 2. The Americans and Filipinos, after withdrawing, held strong points to the north, where a fierce battle went on.
Courtesy of the " Daily Mirror"

north-west of Manila, struck back at the Japanese, inflicting on them one of the worst defeats since their landing on the island. The enemy in this engagement lost at least 700 killed. The defenders of Corregidor, which the Americans still held in Manila Bay, beat off the fourth successive enemy attack.

In Malaya, after a brief respite, following the British retreat from Ipoh, the great tin centre in north-west Malaya, fighting was resumed on a large scale. An announcement from Combined Headquarters, dated December 30, stated that the enemy were attacking in strong force in this area, though further air raids on Kuantan and Kelantan on the east coast of Malaya had caused very little damage. A matter for congratulation was the calm way in which the Malays of the north stood up to Japanese frightfulness. Although the Kelantan Volunteer Force consisted of no more than 100 strong, with a few Europeans, they carried out their duties with a stoical indifference to danger, guarding bridges and other points, and preventing panic generally among the inhabitants. Many stories of individual heroism in the Malay ordeal could be told, but that of Major F. Harvey and his assistant Lieut. Foo Kia Peng, two Salvation Army officers, has received special mention. When the bombs began to fall on Penang, which capitulated to the Japanese, these two devoted men decided to remain to aid the wounded. When Lieut. Foo's car was destroyed by a bomb he commandeered a rickshaw and was continuously on duty removing the injured to the hospital, organizing a refugee camp, finding cooks, and setting an example to the suffering inhabitants by his own resource and courage.

Malayan Jungle Fighting

Strange indeed was some of the hand-to-hand fighting in the Malayan jungle. At an advanced outpost, south of Ipoh, a Highland captain, once a reserve Rugby forward for Scotland, having used up all his ammunition, attacked the Japanese with his hands. His C.S.M. battered the enemy with a Tommy gun. An orderly also entered the fray, and these three men killed at least 12 Japanese, and managed to escape unhurt, save that the C.S.M. blistered his fingers by grasping the hot barrel of the gun.

Enemy pressure on the Perak front continued to force our troops farther south of Ipoh towards new positions near Bidor, about 70 miles north of Kuala Lumpur, which is the second largest city in Malaya after Singapore. Maintaining their attacks from the north with a great number of small tanks, armoured cars and Bren-gun carriers on January 5, the Japanese also threatened the British left flank by further landings on the west coast of Malaya at the mouth of the Perak and Bernam rivers.

In the north-east sector the enemy drove down the coast of Trengganu to positions 30 miles north of Kuantan, a port for rubber and tin transit. Here they later gained possession of the aerodrome, some 190 miles from Singapore.

After four weeks of fighting the Japanese could be said to have had all the advantages and initiative. Our losses, particularly in rubber- and tin-producing areas, were undeniably heavy. We had to fight rearguard actions all the way against a vastly superior number of men and machines.

Manila's Preparations for Attack Came Too Late

BLACK-OUT in Manila was put into practice just before Japan launched her attack. The extinguishing of the lights proved prophetic, for Manila was the main objective of Japanese invasion forces and fell on Jan. 2, 1942.

Above, modern architecture in the capital of the Philippines. Below, the Escolta—the Broadway of Manila, —reported to be in flames when the Japanese entered.

FILIPINOS test their gas masks during a demonstration of civilian defence at Manila, city with a population of over 623,000. Once they had occupied the city the Japanese compelled all white civilians to remain indoors under penalty of being shot if they ventured into the streets.   *Photos, Planet News, Lubinski*

Russians strike back, as Mr. Eden put it, "withou
and transport abandoned by the roadside as the
houses in Kalinin set ablaze by the Germans befo
to endure the cold. Right, Red Army troops un

Armies Strike Hard at the Retreating Germans

ut respite." Top, German guns, armoured vehicles
reated from Klin, north-west of Moscow. Left,
d the town. Oval, German prisoners, ill-equipped
ov advancing from a locality recently recaptured.

Hitler in Command: The Russians Sweep On

The end of 1941 saw the German armies retreating here slowly, there fast, along the whole of the front from Leningrad to the Black Sea. At this crisis of the war the Fuehrer assumed direct responsibility for the future course of the campaign. But the Russians, aided by General Winter, still advanced.

JUST before Christmas 1941 von Brauchitsch, Commander-in-Chief of the German Army, was sacked by his Fuehrer. In an announcement issued from Berlin on December 21 it was recalled that Hitler personally assumed the command over the whole armed forces of the German Reich on February 4, 1938, since " reasons of state imperatively demanded that all powers should be concentrated in one hand." Moreover, " the realization of an inward call and his own will to take upon himself responsibility weighed with the statesman Adolf Hitler when he resolved to be his own Generalissimo. The course of this war has more and more confirmed the recognition of this fact, but it was fully shown only when the campaign in the East assumed proportions exceeding all past notions. The vastness of the theatre of war, the close connexion of the conduct of land operations with the political and economic war aims, and also the numerical size of the army compared with the other part of the armed forces, have induced the Fuehrer to follow his intuitions and to influence in the strongest possible manner the operations and the equipment of the army, and to reserve to himself personally all essential decisions in this sphere. Following up his decision of February 4, 1938, the Fuehrer therefore resolved on December 19, 1941, while fully recognizing the merits of General Field-Marshal von Brauchitsch, to combine in his own hands the leadership of the whole armed forces with the supreme command of the army."

Why Brauchitsch Was Dismissed

According to the most generally accepted view Brauchitsch was superseded because of the failure of the attack on Moscow ; the German Army had suffered its first major disaster and the C.-in-C. had to pay for it. But reliable information has come into the hands of Dr. Benes, President in London of Czechoslovakia, which points to serious differences between Hitler and Brauchitsch. According to these reports the latter is reported to have told his master that 1,075,000 German soldiers had been killed on the Russian front up to November 15 ; that Germany could not win the war, either on the field of battle or in the political arena ; but that she might not lose the peace if she were helped by mistakes both diplomatic and political made by the Allies.

Following his assumption of the supreme command, Hitler addressed a personal appeal to the German Army. " From the new eastern front," ran one passage of his exordium, " nothing else is expected today than what the German soldiers achieved in four Russian winter campaigns 25 years ago. Every German soldier must set an example to our loyal allies . . . Preparations for an immediate resumption of offensive operations in the spring, until the enemy in the east is finally destroyed, must be taken at once . . . I know war from the four years of mighty conflict in the west, from 1914 to 1918. I experienced personally the horrors of almost all the battles as an ordinary soldier. I was wounded twice and was even threatened with blindness. Thus nothing that torments you, weighs upon you, and oppresses you, is unknown to me . . . What I can do for you, my soldiers, by way of care and leadership, will be done . . ."

What of the men to whom this appeal was addressed ? Hundreds of thousands of them were retreating from Moscow, just as Napoleon's legions had retreated 130 years

before and in much the same conditions. They were hungry and tattered, cold and miserable in the extreme. The icy blast pierces the ersatz uniforms—many of the men seem to be without overcoats—so that in order to keep out the cold they swathe themselves in rugs and old eiderdowns tied round their waists with string, wrap their necks in petticoats and Russian children's shawls. How woeful was their plight was confessed by Hitler himself. In a statement read by Goebbels over the German wireless, the Fuehrer claimed that " fighting an enemy vastly superior in number and material, our troops have gained tremendous victories," but in the next breath went on to say that " if the German people want to make a Christmas present to the front they must give their warmest clothing which they can spare in war and be able to replace later in

RUSSIAN FRONT. The shaded area indicates ground recovered by the Russians in their counter-offensive up to the end of 1941.
Courtesy of the " News Chronicle "

peace." Goebbels went into more detail. " We who on the home front enjoy a modest but secure Christmas must deny ourselves. What we miss means simple discomfort compared with the privations of the soldiers at the front." So the " little doctor " appealed for gifts of " felt-lined boots, socks, stockings, vests, pullovers, warm woollen underclothing, chest protectors, head, ear and wrist covers, jack boots, large blankets, ground sheets, thick fur-lined gloves, scarves and wind-proof jackets." So, under the supervision of Nazi collectors, every German home at Christmas was searched for anything and everything that might help to keep the soldiers warm. " Even single gloves are valuable," said an announcer over the German radio, " for if a soldier has one hand warm he already feels better ; failing anything better, he who has no other things to spare can perhaps find some old rag which may be made into warm lining."

Napoleon Did Not Winter in Russia

One German newspaper published an " alphabet," with a phrase for each letter ; e.g. under S, " Stalin is warmly clad, therefore see that our soldiers are still more warmly clad." Another had it that Napoleon's Grande Armée was defeated in Russia by the cold, but this could not happen to the German army of today since their people at home would not leave them in the lurch. But the compiler of the alphabet did not mention that even the last stragglers of Napoleon's army had recrossed the Russian frontier on their way home well before Christmas in that fateful 1812. Moreover, the Germans in 1942 are striving to hold positions far to the east of any they held in the last war. During the Great War, Major Gribble of the " News Chronicle " has pointed out, the Germans never held the line farther east than Riga, Minsk and Czernowicz ; there is not a point on this line which is less than 350 miles west of the positions now held by Hitler's armies in Russia—at some points the difference is 600 miles. The average day temperature in the existing German positions is from 10 to 15 degrees colder than on the old lines held during the Great War.

Compared with the Germans, their Russian foes were far better off. They were now better equipped, fresher, and in many places more numerous ; they were, moreover, inured by long experience to conditions which, to the man from the genial Rhineland or even the plains of Prussia, must seem hellish. Still more, they had now the confidence of victory. All along the line they were pushing back the Germans. The threat to Moscow had been averted, and Kaluga, it was announced on January 1, was recaptured by Gen. Boldin—a reverse which Hitler strove in vain to counter by dispatching a crack German division from Cracow in troop-carrying planes. When they were smashed, he himself flew to Smolensk in the hope of preventing a debacle. In the north, too, the defenders of Leningrad were on the offensive ; while in the south the Russians, by a brilliantly conceived stroke, recrossed the Straits of Kerch and invaded the Crimea.

No wonder Hitler's New Year message to his people struck a sombre note. " Now, on New Year's Eve," it concluded, " we can only pray to our God Almighty that He may grant the German people and her soldiers the strength to support with a brave heart all that is necessary to safeguard liberty and the future."

Hawaii Paid the Grim Penalty of Unreadiness

A.A. machine-gun and crew at Wheeler Field, American airfield in the middle of Oahu Island, Hawaii. They came into action when Hickam Field, farther south was attacked on Dec. 7.

An improvised gun emplacement made from a wrecked plane after the surprise attack by the Japanese on Hickam Field, near Honolulu.

Left, Hangar No. 3 at Wheeler Field, Oahu Island, after military areas in Hawaii had been bombed by the Japanese on Dec. 7, 1941.

AT HONOLULU (above) furniture was moved hurriedly into the street after the Japanese had begun their bombing and fires had broken out. Right, the scene at Pearl Harbour on Dec. 7 as Japanese planes attacked. The pall of smoke on the right comes from the burning U.S. battleship Arizona

Photos, Wide World, Keystone, Associated Press

Our Diary of the War

FRIDAY, DEC. 26, 1941　　846th day

Russian Front.—Moscow announced recapture of Naro Fuminsk, S.W. of Moscow.

Africa.—In Libya, British forces harassed main enemy forces in the Jedabia area.

Far East.—Lt.-Gen. Sir Henry Pownall arrived in Singapore as C.-in-C. Far East. Engagements between patrols in the area of Sungei-Siput, Perak, and north of Kemaman, in Trengganu. Japanese landed heavy forces near Atimonan, 75 miles S.E. of Manila on the Island of Luzon. Heavy fighting in the area of Lingayen Gulf.

General.—Mr. Churchill addressed both Houses of Congress in Washington.

SATURDAY, DEC. 27　　847th day

Air.—Düsseldorf and targets in W. Germany attacked in heavy night raid by R.A.F. Docks at Brest and Boulogne also attacked, and airfield at Sola, Norway.

Russian Front.—Red Army continued to advance, and good headway was made in the direction of Orel.

Africa.—Pressure on enemy continued in the Jedabia area.

Far East.—In Malaya, small activity around Blanja in the Khemor area. Kuala Lumpur raided by Japanese bombers. In the Philippines, Manila suffered a heavy air raid.

General.—Raid by combined force of Royal Navy, Army, and R.A.F. on the Norwegian Islands of Vaagso and Maaloy. It was disclosed that Mr. Eden had been in Moscow for discussions with Soviet leaders.

SUNDAY, DEC. 28　　848th day

Air.—Wilhelmshaven, Emden and Rhineland were main targets of night attack by R.A.F. Docks at Dunkirk also bombed.

Russian Front.—Soviet forces attacked all along the front. Moscow announced recapture of Belev, Likhvin and Novosil. Gen. Meretsov s forces reached River Volchow.

Far East.—Manila again heavily raided by Japanese bombers. Enemy pressure increased from the south-east of Luzon. Dutch airfield near Medan, in Sumatra, attacked by Japanese bombers.

MONDAY, DEC. 29　　849th day

Air.—Night attack by Coastal Command on enemy shipping at La Pallice.

Russian Front.—Red Army advancing on Leningrad, Moscow and Donetz fronts.

Far East.—Evacuation of Ipoh, in Malaya, by British forces announced. Four night raids on Singapore. Great battle between Chinese and Japanese raging in north Hunan. In Philippines, Gen. MacArthur's defence lines shortened north of Manila. Corregidor heavily bombed by Japanese.

Home.—Enemy air activity by night over N.E. coast. 3 enemy bombers destroyed.

General.—Mr. Churchill attended meeting of Canadian War Cabinet at Ottawa.

TUESDAY, DEC. 30　　850th day

Air.—Halifax bombers made a daylight attack on the docks at Brest. 7 enemy fighters were destroyed by escorting Spitfires. Coastal Command made another night attack on docks at La Pallice.

Russian Front.—Moscow announced that Kerch and Feodosia, in the Crimea, had been recaptured by units of the Soviet Caucasian army. Zozelsk and Lugorski-Zavod, south of Moscow, also recaptured.

Africa.—Tank battle developed in the Jedabia area.

Far East.—In the Philippines heavy enemy pressure developed in the north-eastern sector. Malaya put under martial law. Numerous air raids on Port Swettenham.

Home.—Mr. Eden arrived back in London from Moscow.

General.—Mr. Churchill addressed members of the Canadian Legislature in the House of Commons at Ottawa. Mr. Gandhi resigned leadership of the All-India Congress Party.

WEDNESDAY, DEC. 31　　851st day

Sea.—Admiralty announced the sinking of five enemy schooners by British submarines in the Mediterranean and damage to an Italian destroyer.

Russian Front. — Moscow officially announced the recapture of Kaluga and with it news that 16 German divisions under Gen. Guderian had been routed.

Africa.—Rommel striving to keep open his southern flank to maintain supply lines from Tripoli. Bardia defences attacked.

Far East.—Two night raids on Singapore. Violent fighting south of Ipoh. In the Philippines Japanese mechanized forces pressed toward Manila from north and south.

THURSDAY, JAN. 1, 1942　　852nd day

Russian Front.—Russian troops recaptured several towns, including Staritsa, 120 miles N.W. of Moscow.

Africa.—British attacked during night of Jan. 1-2 by units of 1st and 2nd South African Divisions supported by tanks, artillery and naval units.

Far East.—Big battle raging north of Manila. Officially announced that British forces had withdrawn from Sarawak. Sharp fighting at Kuantan in Malaya. Japanese-occupied aerodrome at Gong Kedah raided at night by R.A.F. Communique from Burma reported small Japanese infiltration into Bokpyn in the Mergui district, but enemy withdrew when British columns arrived.

General.—Admiralty announced a raid on the Lofoten Islands. British forces were in control for three days.

FRIDAY, JAN. 2　　853rd day

Sea.—Admiralty announced that British naval units in the Mediterranean had sunk one Italian and two German submarines and taken prisoners the crews.

Air.—Bomber Command made night attack on naval bases at Brest and St. Nazaire.

Russian Front.—Moscow reported recapture of Malo Yaroslavets, north of Kaluga.

Mediterranean.—Night raid on Naples by R.A.F.

Africa.—South African troops and British tanks captured Bardia, 8,000 Axis prisoners.

Far East.—Manila occupied by the Japanese. Fighting going on to the north of the city. In Malaya three attacks were made by enemy on the Perak front. Landing in Lower Perak repulsed. Enemy occupied outskirts of Kuantan. Two air raids on Rangoon, and one on Singapore.

General.—Twenty-six powers signed a joint declaration at Washington, binding themselves not to make a separate armistice or peace with the enemy.

SATURDAY, JAN. 3　　854th day

Sea.—Admiralty reported a five-day attack by U-boats on a British convoy. 2 merchant ships were lost, but over 90 per cent of the convoy arrived safely. An ex-American destroyer, H.M.S. Stanley, and the auxiliary vessel H.M.S. Audacity were sunk. At least three of the attacking U-boats were destroyed and two Focke-Wulf aircraft were shot down, with a third severely damaged. Admiralty also announced the loss by enemy mines in the Mediterranean of the cruiser H.M.S. Neptune and the destroyer H.M.S. Kandahar

Russian Front.—Russian troops pressed forward towards Mojaisk.

Africa.—In the Jedabia area British mobile columns continued to harass the main enemy concentrations.

Far East.—More Japanese attacks on Corregidor. American and Philippine troops consolidating new positions. In Malaya heavy fighting continued in the Perak area. Japanese landed in British North Borneo.

General.—A joint announcement issued by Pres. Roosevelt and Mr. Churchill stated that Gen. Wavell had been appointed Supreme Commander of the Unified Command of the South-West Pacific Area. Maj.-Gen. G. H. Brett was appointed his Deputy, and Gen. Sir Henry Pownall his Chief of Staff. Admiral Hart, commanding U.S. Asiatic Fleet, assumed command of all naval forces in that area under the direction of Gen. Wavell, and Gen. Chiang Kai-Shek was given command of all land and air forces of the united nations operating in the Chinese theatre.

SUNDAY, JAN. 4　　855th day

Air.—Daylight raid on Germany by Bomber Command.

Russian Front.—Fighting reported in the streets of Mojaisk. Moscow announced recapture of Borovsk, 25 miles S.E. of Mojaisk.

Mediterranean.—Enemy submarine base at Salamis, near Athens, raided by R.A.F. during night of Jan. 3-4.

Africa.—Enemy positions at Halfaya heavily attacked from the air.

Far East.—Big battle still raging between Chinese and Japanese in Hunan province. In the Philippines, Corregidor was again attacked from the air. Fighting continued in Pampanga province, north of Manila. In Malaya, the Japanese reached a point 35 miles N.W. of Kuala Lumpur and made fresh landings on the west coast of Malaya.

General. — Pres. Roosevelt and Mr. Churchill attended a conference of the Allied War Council in Washington.

ST. PIERRE-MIQUELON, French island group off the south coast of Newfoundland, was seized by Admiral Muselier, Commander of the Free French naval forces on the evening of Dec. 24, 1941. Free French Marines are here seen marching along the dockside at St. Pierre.

Photo, Associated Press

War Reaches India's Eastern Gate

Lt.-Gen. T. J. HUTTON, C.B., recently appointed G.O.C. Burma in succession to Lt.-Gen. D. K. McLeod. He was formerly Chief of the General Staff in India.

IN THE BURMESE JUNGLE British troops with rifles and tommy-guns advance, suitably camouflaged, during training exercises.　Burma is now threatened by the Japanese occupation of Thailand.

RANGOON, capital and seaport of Burma, has been the target of severe bombing attacks.　In the first of these, on Dec. 23, 1941, there were about 600 civilian casualties. American pilots, originally enlisted to defend the Burma Road, are now being used to help the British airmen defend Rangoon.

Little land fighting has yet taken place in Burma.　Victoria Point, in the extreme south, was evacuated by its small garrison on Dec. 15, since it was considered untenable, and the first engagement with enemy troops was reported in a communique from Army H.Q. on Jan. 1, 1942, which stated that a small party of Japanese who had infiltrated into Bokpyn, in the Mergui district, withdrew in face of our columns.

On Jan. 2 it was confirmed from New Delhi that picked Chinese troops were moving into Burma to help in its defence.

BURMA has been improving her defences in recent months and, above, Shan peasants are clearing and levelling the ground for a new airfield. Burma has a land frontier of about 1,700 miles, bordering on China, Indo-China and Thailand.

Planes of a British bomber squadron are seen in formation over the famous golden pagoda called Shwe Dagon at Rangoon, Burma's capital. The aerodrome there was attacked on Christmas Day 1941, and the city has since suffered many more air raids.

Photos, Ministry of Information, Lafayette, Planet News

'We'll Defend the Indies to the Last Man'

Of all the members of the A.B.C.D. front in the Pacific war zone, the Dutch were the most fully prepared and hence already have a number of successes to their credit, achieved by their bombers and submarines against the Japanese transports and landing-parties. In this article we tell something of the Dutch Empire in the East Indies which, though Holland is in Nazi occupation, is so vigorously continuing the war.

A FORTNIGHT before the Japanese struck in the Pacific, the Dutch colonies in the East Indies were put on a war footing, and hardly had the news arrived of the attack on Hawaii, Manila and Singapore, when the Netherlands Government, here in Britain and in the Orient, declared war against the aggressor. Acting on Queen Wilhelmina's instructions, the Governor-General of the Netherlands East Indies, Jonkheer van Starkenborgh Stachouwer, broadcast the news to the people of the Indies at 6.30 a.m. on December 8. At the same time, the Commander-in-Chief in the Netherlands East Indies, Lt.-Gen. TerPoorten, mobilized the Army, dispatched forces to the outer islands as a protection against attack, and interned some 2,000 Japanese and a number of suspect Chinese. Moreover, they promised and dispatched all possible aid to their new allies, more particularly to the British at Singapore.

'Everything to Fight For'

The determined note of the Dutch resistance was sounded in an address broadcast by Gen. TerPoorten on December 22. The day had come, he said, for the Army to defend the country with all the means at its disposal against a barbaric and dishonoured enemy. "Already various hostilities have taken place in the archipelago, and already we may speak with pride of the blows inflicted on the enemy. We have everything to fight for—our honour, our freedom, our home—in brief, our happiness, without which life is not worth living."

A few days later, when the Japanese had claimed to have made landings in British Borneo, General TerPoorten vowed that the Japanese would not be allowed to get away with the oil they were draining from the damaged wells, "because our Air Force will bomb hell out of them." But, he went on, the Dutch needed immediate material support, particularly bombers, fighters and A.A.

guns. Given these without delay, they could defeat even a large-scale Japanese attempt to land on their islands. In any event, "the Indies form the first line of defence which will be defended to the last man."

Certainly the Netherlands Indies would prove a rich prize for the Japanese robbers. For centuries they have been famed as among the world's richest islands. When the Dutch went there first they sought spices and such-like exotic produce; now the islands' immensely fertile soil produces rubber, sugar, copra, tobacco, tea and coffee, while from their bowels are derived oil and copper, lead and bauxite. Then the hillsides are carpeted with dense forests, filled with valuable timber.

Altogether the islands of the Dutch East Indies cover an area of about 735,000 square miles, inhabited by more than 60,000,000 people. Most important of the far-spreading group is Java, which, with a population of about 40 millions, may claim to be one of the most densely populated areas in the world—784 people to the square mile, compared with England's 703.

In Java are situated the chief interests, the principal arsenals and dockyards. Batavia (pop. about 260,000), the capital of the Dutch Indies, lies near its western end, while near the opposite extremity is situated Surabaya, the great naval base. To the west of Java lies the far larger island of Sumatra, much of which is covered with tropical jungle, although along the coast may be found many a town amongst the finest examples of town planning in the Orient; then to the east stretches a far-flung chain of islands divided by narrow seas—Bali, world-famous for its temple dancing girls, and Lombok, both outposts of Hinduism in a Mahomedan world. Next come Sumbawa, Flores and Timor, while to the north of these are Celebes and the Moluccas, on one of which is the naval base of Amboina. These are just a few of the scattered islands which are amongst the jewels

Jhr. A. W. L. Tjarda van Starkenborgh Stachouwer, Governor-General of the Netherlands E. Indies, who, in a broadcast on Dec. 31, 1941, declared that the Netherlands Indies would fight to the end. *Photo, Associated Press*

of Queen Wilhelmina's crown. They are the scene of a rich and complex civilization, which dates back for many hundreds of years.

As for the people, they are for the most part Indonesians, for the Javanese have mixed with the Chinese, and there is a Hindu element in Sumatra, Bali and parts of Java; there are also Arabs and, of course, a number of Europeans. In Java there are some 50,000 Europeans. Note that whereas in India the half-castes—Eurasians, as they are called—are ostracized by white "society," in the Netherlands Indies a dash of white blood confers the status of European. In years gone by racial intermarriage was encouraged, and, indeed, the Dutch burghers and traders can have needed little inducement to find their wives amongst the local women, since the charms of the girls—of Java and Bali in particular—have long been famous.

To defend their rich territories in the Orient, the Dutch have a considerable local army, navy and air force. The Royal Netherlands Indies Army is a fully equipped and highly trained professional force of some 30,000 men. All the members of the various population groups are represented in its ranks, and while most of the officers are Europeans, quite a number of them are natives. All able-bodied Dutch in the islands were made liable for military service in 1940, and more recently compulsory service has been extended to the native population.

Dutch Power in the East

The Netherlands Far East Fleet is comprised of cruisers, destroyers, submarines, various small ships and auxiliary craft, and a Fleet Air Arm; the naval base at Surabaya is one of the most formidable in the Far East. Coming to the Air Force, it is equipped with American-built machines—Martins, Lockheeds, Curtisses, Brewsters and Ryans. It is on her air arm that the Netherlands most chiefly relies in this new war that has been thrust upon her—on her air arm and on the hosts of small craft, submarines and motor-torpedo boats in particular, which are eminently fitted for service in the island-dotted seas of the Indies. Indeed, in the first weeks of the Japanese invasion of Malaya and the Philippines Dutch submarines and aircraft did invaluable work in destroying 15 enemy aircraft, 2 cruisers, 2 destroyers, 9 transports, 2 tankers and 2 merchant vessels.

DUTCH EAST INDIES, long coveted by Japan, not only for the strategic position occupied by the archipelago which separates the Indian Ocean from the Pacific, but also on account of its vast riches in petroleum, tin, rubber, and crops. Japanese air attacks have been made at various points in the archipelago, while Dutch submarines and aircraft have taken energetic counter-measures.

Where the Dutch Face the Japanese Onslaught

The Dutch Colonial Government has long been alive to the dangers of fifth column activity in the Dutch East Indies. Here members of the Batavia Home Guard are guarding an administrative building during exercises.

THE DUTCH EAST INDIES have met the Japanese onslaught with calm and courage, and the deeds of the Netherlands forces there, by sea and in the air, have been prominent in the news from the Pacific theatre of war. Left, the Post Office at Medan, Sumatra, the airfield of which has been bombed by Japanese planes. Right gun crew of a destroyer of the Netherlands East Indies Navy. Centre right, view over the volcano of Papandayan, Western Java, showing the difficult nature of the country for an invader. *Photos, Planet News, E.N.A., Mrs. T. Muir, Sport & General*

Bomb Bursts

Prinz Eugen

Halifax Aircraft

Gneisenau

Scharnhorst

BREST NAVAL BASE was the objective of heavy daylight raids by the R.A.F. on Dec. 18 and 30. It was during the former raid that the photograph above was taken showing Halifax aircraft attacking the German battleships Scharnhorst and Gneisenau and the battle-cruiser Prinz Eugen at their repair berths. During the month of December the R.A.F. carried out nine night raids on Brest in addition to these two daylight raids. These intensive attacks show that the R A F is determined to keep the German naval units immobilized. Submarine repair shops and depots at Brest as well as at La Pallice have also received the constant attention of our heavy bombers.

Photo, British Official; Crown Copyright

Hong Kong's Fight to the Bitter End

For most of the world Christmas Day 1941 was saddened by the news that Hong Kong, Britain's outpost in China, had been compelled to capitulate to the Japanese besiegers. Below we give a day-to-day account of the colony's gallant stand against truly overwhelming odds.

WHEN Japan struck in the Pacific, Hong Kong stood to arms at once. The garrison, numbering some 8,000 men at most, was of truly Imperial character. It consisted of the 2nd Bn. Royal Scots and 1st Bn. Middlesex Regiment; two Canadian battalions—Winnipeg Grenadiers and the Royal Rifles of Canada—under the command of Brigadier-General J. K. Lawson; the 2/14 Punjabis and 5/7 Rajputs, together with the Hong Kong Volunteer Defence Force and the normal complement of R.A., R.E., and Royal Signal units, etc., the whole force being under the command of Major-General O. M. Maltby. Units of the Royal Navy and of the Hong Kong Naval Volunteer Reserve and detachments of the Royal Marines co-operated with the military force.

On December 8 Japanese forces, estimated at one division with a second division in reserve close behind, crossed the frontier of the Hong Kong leased territories on the mainland. Heavily outnumbered as they were, the garrison withdrew according to the previously arranged plan, blowing up roads and bridges behind them.

Dec. 9. In the afternoon our forward troops on the Taipo Road withdrew into the prepared "Gindrinkers Line," on Castle Peak Road. At about 11 p.m. Sing Mun redoubt, which was held by a platoon of the Royal Scots, was captured by the enemy by surprise.

Dec. 10. Attempts by the enemy to break through towards the Taipo Road failed. However, as reserves had been used in this fighting, a readjustment of the line was carried out at dusk.

Dec. 11. Strong enemy pressure developed in the morning on our left flank, held by the Royal Scots. The two left companies were driven in by heavy and accurate mortar fire, but the situation was stabilized by the use of all available reserves, including a company of the Winnipeg Grenadiers. The Royal Scots, nevertheless, suffered severe casualties.

Dec. 12. The island of Hong Kong was subjected to sporadic bombardment by artillery and from the air, but casualties were few. The civil population was reported to be calm, but their morale was considerably shaken. Monetary problems and rice distribution gave cause for serious anxiety.

First Japanese Ultimatum Rejected

Dec. 13. A difficult day. Shelling increased in intensity and accuracy, and various guns and searchlights were put out of action. The Japanese presented an ultimatum, which expired at 3 p.m. and was rejected out of hand. The Chinese were reported to be mopping up Japanese troops near Tashui, 25 miles north-east of the Hong Kong border, and near Lingehan, some 12 miles nearer.

Dec. 14. There was systematic shelling by the enemy. The morale of the civilian population was still shaky owing to difficulties over the distribution of rice, but otherwise control improved.

Dec. 15. It was reported that more than half of the pill boxes between Lyemun and Bowrington were out of action. Movements of the enemy towards High Junk and Clear Water Bay areas were observed, and further parties were seen to have landed on Lamma Island.

Dec. 16. Aerial bombing and artillery shelling were on an increased scale, with a high standard of accuracy on military objec-tives. One enemy aircraft was brought down into the sea.

Dec. 17. Our counter-battery fire silenced a section of enemy artillery on Devil's Peak, another on Gun Club Hill, and three mortars on the water front.

At 3.5 p.m. the Governor sent to Lord Moyne, the Colonial Secretary, in London a telegram. "After some further bombardment I have today received another letter signed by the Japanese military and naval commanders-in-chief, asking me to confer about surrender on considerations of humanity. The following is the text of my reply: ' The Governor and Commander-in-Chief of Hong Kong declines most absolutely to enter into any negotiations for the surrender of Hong Kong, and he takes this opportunity of notifying Lt.-Gen. Takaishi Sakai and Vice-Admiral Masaichi Niimi that he is not prepared to receive any further communication from them on the subject.' "

Dec. 18. "Another peace offer by the Japanese was flatly rejected this morning," announced Hong Kong, "to their evident surprise. During the night of December 18-19 the enemy succeeded in crossing the bare 500 yards of intervening water and in landing on Hong Kong Island, in the Tai Koo area and Lyemun, whence they steadily infiltrated to Wongnai Chung Gap and Tytam Gap."

Dec. 19. Counter-measures against the Japanese parties which had succeeded in landing in the neighbourhood of North Point and Tai Koo were continued.

Dec. 22. The enemy landed further troops on the north-east coast and attacked continuously. A counter-attack on the 21st from Stanley towards Ty Tam Tak had failed, although a certain number of the enemy were killed at a cost of about 100 Canadian casualties. A counter-attack by a company of Winnipeg Grenadiers to retake Wongnai Chung Gap also failed in the face of concentrated mortar and light machine-gun fire, which inflicted heavy casualties.

Dec. 23. For the 24 hours ending 5 p.m. the enemy had kept up incessant attacks, accompanied by intensive bombardments from the air, mortars and artillery. Some ground on Mount Cameron lost during the night was recaptured by the Royal Marines, but counter-attacks by the force at Stanley towards Stanley Mound failed. However, the Middlesex Regiment successfully repulsed a determined attack at Leighton Hill. But the water and food supply was desperate, for the reservoirs and depots were in enemy hands.

Dec. 24. The enemy continued to subject the garrison to heavy fire from dive bombers and mortars, and by means of incendiary bombs set the countryside all round Mount Cameron on fire.

Dec. 25. "The Governor of Hong Kong," announced the Colonial Office, " reports that he has been advised by the military and naval commanders that no further effective resistance can be made. He is taking action in accordance with that advice." The statement went on: " It will be remembered that the Japanese effected landings in strength at several points on the island on December 18. To many it seemed that the end must be near. Yet for seven days, under relentless observed artillery fire, not only from the mainland, but from heights on the island, the garrison fought on, refusing three demands to surrender.

"The water supply soon gave cause for anxiety. Important reservoirs fell into Japanese hands; water mains were destroyed by bombardment. The Public Works Department struggled bravely to effect a remedy, but the enemy destroyed the pipes again and again. Two days ago there remained but one day's supply. Military and civilian casualties were heavy, but under the inspiring leadership of Sir Mark Young the morale of all was admirable."

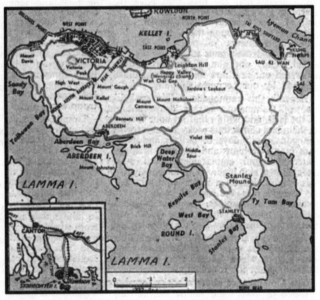

An account of the surrender of the island was forthcoming from the Domei Agency. "Sir Mark Young, the Governor of Hong Kong," it read, " and the Commander of the British garrison there, at 7.5 p.m. yesterday (Dec. 25) unconditionally surrendered with their forces to the Japanese as the result of a parley with the Japanese military and naval authorities which took place at the Peninsular Hotel at Kowloon from 6.50 p.m. until 7.5 p.m. yesterday. Sir Mark stayed at the Peninsular Hotel overnight under the protection of Japanese troops and returned to Hong Kong to prevent the destruction of establishments and materials in the British Crown Colony, with a Japanese staff officer today. During the historic conversation Sir Mark stated: ' I am here to become a prisoner by ordering the entire British forces to cease all resistance.' It is understood that the remaining British troops, estimated at 6,000, have been ordered to disarm by noon."

" So ends a great fight against overwhelming odds," to quote from a Colonial Office statement again. " The courage and determination of the Royal Navy and troops from Great Britain, Canada and India, as well as the local volunteer units, and many Chinese, will long be remembered."

I Was There! .... Eye Witness Stories of the War

We Went to Vaagso with the Commando Men

On December 27, 1941, for the first time British soldiers, sailors and airmen combined in an assault on the Nazi-occupied European coastline. Their raid on the Norwegian island of Vaagso is here described by Reuter's correspondents who accompanied the expedition.

In charge of the Commando troops in the Vaagso raid on December 27, 1941, was Brig. J. C. Haydon, D.S.O. (left). The naval forces which cooperated in the raid were led by Rear-Adm. H. M. Burrough, C.B. (right).

Photos, Universal and Lafayette

WE left our base with Christmas decorations still hanging up in the ward-room, and early on the morning of December 27 were off the entrance to Vaagso Fjord waiting for dawn—the zero hour for the attack to begin.

The ship's crews had been closed up at their action stations for an hour or more and there was not a sound as, in line ahead, we gently slipped round the headland and steamed down the fjord towards the town. Everything was ready for the first step—the bombardment of the two coastal batteries which the warships had to carry out first to enable the soldiers to make a safe landing.

Once inside the fjord assault craft with soldiers veered out of line and the warships went ahead to take up their positions. No attempt was made to interfere with this, and it seems that the first knowledge the German gunners had of our arrival was a hail of high explosive shells which rained relentlessly down upon them, reducing their gun emplacements to piles of shattered masonry and their guns to twisted pieces of metal. Only one gun of the two batteries answered our fire, and this was immediately silenced by our accurate shooting.

Beneath this cannonade a thin snakelike line of Commando barges drove straight to the islet, and within half an hour the men in them had climbed its rocky slopes, stormed the guns as in days of cutlass and pistol, shot many Germans and taken 20 prisoners. Later the gun emplacements and stores were blown sky high. Simultaneously with this assault, led by a major who serenaded his men across the smooth water to the strains of his bagpipes, the main landing—which I made in the leading barge with members of the Army film unit—took place.

As the naval bombardment died down the Hampdens swept over the head of the tiny bay in which Vaagso Port lay nestled thickly against the towering cliffs.

The Commandos chose a rocky foreshore on which to lower their ramps, and as they landed smoke bombs dropped from 50 feet up. This screen, through which a German machine-gun fired a few rounds ineffectually, gave the landing-party complete cover. It was perhaps a little too close, but it could

not have been better timed. The R.A.F. had scored an early bull's eye.

I waded ashore with the rest, knee-deep through rocky pools and acrid fumes, on to ledges of snow. It was a weird and confusing experience, through which the Commando troops, led by dashing young officers and hard-bitten sergeants, emerged to begin a series of assaults through and around the narrow town from west to east.

It was then that the fun—Commando fun 1942 style—really started. The officers of the troops concerned gathered up their forces for the most desperate of all the tasks that short swift day. They had to advance down the main street.

A Troop Without An Officer

One officer had slipped on getting out of the boat and jammed his leg between it and the rocks, but he struggled on, limping badly. Another encountered immediate machine-gun fire, and with his men engaged and killed five of the enemy before setting fire to an ammunition dump. Later, he was killed trying with a corporal to storm a hotel from which a number of German officers were firing. A third officer was sniped in the back soon afterwards. At one time the entire troop was without an officer in command.

Despite casualties, all ranks pursued their task with great gallantry both before and after they were reinforced by a floating reserve. One man I saw fought brilliantly. He was the corporal who went with his captain to storm the hotel. After the officer had been shot he managed to chuck a grenade into the building, which then caught fire.

Many Germans were roasted to death in houses they made into strong points, and from which they doggedly refused to emerge, even when grenades or a fusillade of shots had set the rooms about them on fire. Resistance was particularly stubborn in the centre of the town which, as the morning grew older, began to blaze as more and more houses holding snipers and small parties of the enemy came under heavy fire, including 2-inch and 3-inch mortar shells.

While we were still dodging behind boulders and slinking over the first half-mile, and whilst the first of the Norwegian

men, women and children, anxious to go to England, were running back to our barges—some in tears, some laughing and all rather scared—two warships rode majestically past the town sending a wash ashore for four miles or more of Nazi inland waterway space.

Heavy gunfire reverberated down the fjord to add to the clamour of explosions. Another German coastal battery four miles away over the hills tried to get the range of our warships, but their fire was ineffective.

Deprived of reinforcements, the nearest neighbouring garrison was over the water 25 miles away. The Germans got little help from their air force, although the aerodromes at Trondheim, Stavanger, Lista, Aalborg and Herdla are all within striking distance.

The land operations, carried out in the extreme confusion of close hand-to-hand fighting, smoke and flame, tested the Commandos' communication system to the hilt and as the battle progressed many messages could only be got through by word of mouth.

The lieut.-colonel commanding the battle on shore showed an inspiring disregard of danger in his anxiety to keep it under control. He escaped unscathed, although he had at least one narrow escape. A German opening a door threw a stick grenade in his path, but he jumped clear. Then the Nazi walked out. He was immediately shot.

Demolition work was sometimes unavoidably risky owing to the closeness of the canning and oil factories to the fighting. I and several others had to duck rather hastily

HERDLA AERODROME, about 100 miles down the coast from Vaagso Is., was heavily attacked by Blenheims of Bomber Command during the combined operations of December 27 to prevent enemy aircraft from assisting the German garrison attacked by the British raiding-party. The photograph was taken from one of the attacking Blenheims, and shows bombs bursting on the airfield. The Me 109 on the exrteme left, taxi-ing on the airfield, was destroyed.

Photo, British Official: Crown Copyright

‖‖‖‖‖‖‖‖‖‖‖‖‖‖‖‖‖‖‖‖‖‖ I WAS THERE! ‖‖‖‖‖‖‖‖‖‖‖‖‖‖‖‖‖‖‖‖‖‖‖

The remarkable photographs in this page were taken during the combined raid on the occupied islands of Vaagso and Maaloy on December 27, 1941. Left, four German prisoners, one of whom carries a white flag of surrender, being escorted to a British transport. Right, one of the few British wounded being evacuated on one of the landing craft. At least 120 Germans were killed during the raid.

when the biggest of them was blown up, and a little later, when the only German tank in town, a small light model, was demolished in its garage. Pieces of the burning metal whistled past me up the street and wounded two of our men 200 yards away.

The Germans, though outnumbered, fought to the last and were good physical types. By skilful use of cover and by using almost flashless and smokeless cordite they showed that they have mastered one of the ugliest features of modern war—street-fighting. Some German troops, including a small unit spending Christmas at Vaagso and who were out early on a route march, made for high ground, and one soldier was

still sniping when, all tasks completed, the last of the Commandos were re-embarked.

It was just three in the afternoon as we steamed out of Vaagso Fjord. Almost the entire German garrison of upwards of 200 men had been killed, wounded, or taken prisoner ; all the industrial plant was dynamited, and the coastal guns spiked. The Navy destroyed 16,000 tons of merchant shipping, two armed trawlers and an armed tug. R.A.F. and Naval cooperation was of first-class vigour, and, as one Commando sergeant described it, " so comforting." No soldier, sailor or airman who took part failed to realize their complete interdependence in modern warfare.

I Watched a Practice Alert in India

Formed only 18 months ago, the Indian Observer Corps has thousands of keen-eyed and keen-eared watchers who cover all the areas vulnerable to air attack. Reuter's special correspondent sends this account of the air defence exercises he witnessed in Northern India.

COLUMNS of armoured vehicles, taking part in the week's air defence exercises, passed me roaring their way north as I went to visit the secret headquarters of the India Observer Corps somewhere in Northern India. They were followed by heavy guns.

In the headquarters I found a large table with a map of the surrounding districts so arranged that the path of the approaching aircraft reported by the observation posts by means of direct telephone connexions could be plotted with complete accuracy.

Two mock air raids were taking place when I arrived. With quiet efficiency young Indians received telephone reports and

marked the position of the raiders on the map, while at the desk above them others reported to fighter aircraft command, A.R.P. authorities and anti-parachutist detachments. On the first day, I was told, these keen youngsters dealt successfully with no less than nine simultaneous raids.

The mock air raids took a realistic turn when the sirens sounded and the warplanes, whose path I had been watching plotted, appeared overhead. Detonations in the vicinity indicated that they had succeeded in dropping a few bombs. But a few minutes later one of the outlying observers reported that at least two raiders had been shot down

in his area, and the appropriate indicator was triumphantly placed on the plotting map. These young Indians, many of them evidently scarcely out of school, did their job with superb efficiency which could only be attained by their own keenness coupled with skilful training.

The great air defence exercises entered their second phase with aircraft representing enemy air forces attacking various local targets. Hostile aircraft flew at a great height over the cantonment area of Peshawar. The alarm was sounded and full defence precautions were immediately taken by the civil and military authorities. No bombs were dropped and presumably the enemy's object was merely to spy out the land.

Later in the day a short but sharp attack by enemy dive-bombing was made on a post in the Khyber Pass, but this was repulsed without any serious damage being caused.

Soon after dark some " bombs " fell unexpectedly in the Noshera area, evidently dropped by enemy aircraft operating at a very great height in the sub-stratosphere. The umpires of the directing staff ruled that these bombs, if real, would have caused a certain amount of damage to a main road and railway in the vicinity. Arrangements were at once made to effect the necessary repairs.

All civil and military A.R.P. and P.A.D. (preparation for air defence) services are in a constant state of readiness. Black-out and other defence measures have been strictly enforced and everyone is waiting with keen interest for further developments in these realistic and instructive exercises.

ON VAAGSO ISLAND an oil factory burns fiercely after demolition by the British Commandos. British soldiers are seen guarding against snipers or surprise counter-attacks. Right, British troops after street fighting in the main street of Vaagso, where they attacked and captured the German H.Q. The German military commander was taken prisoner as was the naval officer in charge of the convoy control port.   *Photos, British Official*

Editor's Postscript

How many of the millions who listen to the B.B.C. every day of their lives realize that they are utilizing the greatest of all modern inventions for world-happiness? Not one in ten thousand, I'll bet. They accept this superlative achievement of human skill just as indifferently as the packet of cigarettes for which they had to queue up—nay, the trouble of getting the latter gives it for the moment a superior value to the priceless gift of radio. That nation shall speak peace unto nation through etheric space does not thrill them greatly. No wonder when we consider that through most of the years in which radio has been at the command of men it is War that has been spoken. Without wireless this world war could not have come to pass: certainly not in its manner of coming and continuing. Without (1) the misuse of this marvel of science in spreading lies, hatred, and threats of horror and nation speaking war unto nation, (2) the coordinating of the movements of armies and navies and ships at sea, and (3) guiding the death-dealing bombers to their targets—without these no such universal war as we are witnessing could have developed on this planet.

Few, indeed, ever think of that when listening to exponents of the lowest form of melody, known as "crooning," which my dictionary rightly defines as "a hollow, continued moan." Moaners would be a better description for its exponents. Nor can you be impressed with the wonder of wireless when your receiver sometimes assaults your ears and senses with the crude and crapulous jokes of men indiscriminately dubbed "comedians," some of whose prototypes before Marconi's day collected their fees in their hats by the sad sea waves.

Yet, think of the wonder of wireless when on December 26 last you could listen while all the world listened to the greatest oration since Lincoln's two minutes' masterpiece at Gettysburg in November 1863, heard by a few hundreds only. Churchill's thirty-five minutes of superbly-balanced oratory, in which he had the greatest theme in modern history for exposition—the uniting of all freedom-loving nations under the lead of the entire English-speaking world for the extinction of tyranny, wars, murder, and slavery—this great speech will echo down the ages and untold millions through the world were able to listen to the actual words of flame and fervour as they issued from his own eloquent lips. A tremendous occasion, which thrilled into a renewed fervour of life the countless millions of listeners who shared the orator's sympathies and ideals, while it must also have confirmed their faith in their deliverance for the oppressed and tortured who could hear it in those lands where the Nazi slavery has been imposed.

Just what followed his historic speech on the broadcast that night I don't know. I certainly didn't listen. But as likely as not it might have been: "We are now taking you over to Cock-eyed Caravan in Soho for dance music by Billy Bonehead and His Boys, with Minnie Moaner." That's the pity of it—what a juxtaposition. But, of course, the B.B.C. cannot be expected to cater mainly, or even largely, for high-brows, when one remembers the intellectual standard of its major body of listeners—after seventy years of free education. Nor am I in any degree against amusement and entertainment, with or without music, featuring largely on the programmes. I owe too many good laughs from B.B.C. entertainers—no listener can be more eager than, at any time, I for a good comic turn—to grudge the quantity that is daily dished up. It's the curiously poor quality of much of it to which I take exception.

GEN. Sir H. R. POWNALL, recently appointed Chief of Staff to General Wavell in the new Pacific Command, served in France and Belgium through the last war and in 1938 was Director of Military Operations and Intelligence at the W.O.   *Photo, Walter Stoneman*

So important is the part that radio is playing in the life of all nations today I feel we must do more than tolerate it or take it for granted. Its place in our everyday life is increasingly important and after the War it may revolutionize more than one of our cherished institutions. It can only benefit by criticism. Just now it has attained to titanic stature because of the paper famine. The B.B.C. is clearly usurping many of the time-honoured functions of journalism. With the exceptions of the "Daily Telegraph" and "The Times" among the London dailies I found the others astonishingly empty on the morning after Boxing Day when they had actually three days' news to offer their readers. Except for a few brilliant columns of exclusive writing, they mainly consisted of the news bulletins, to which we have listened several times over, reprinted and slightly garnished with flaring headlines.

I fear that our daily papers (except those named) are in grave danger of losing individuality by over-compression in order to print a maximum of copies from their available quotas. It magnifies the office of the B.B.C., and no greater disaster to our social and intellectual life could happen than the B.B.C. emerging from the War as the prime source of national information, instruction, and amusement. That would be a big step towards totalitarianism. The B.B.C. as a stronghold of Bureaucracy would be a menace to the very freedom for which we are fighting and enduring unimagined privations. It must not be, yet things could easily drift that way—are drifting in my opinion, and only strong, free, individual newspapers will stop the drift.

My thoughts have turned thus after reading an attractive pamphlet "B.B.C. at War," by Antonia White, in which the multifarious activities of the Corporation are described and illustrated in a way that makes one feel "hats off to the B.B.C." But there's the very point of danger. My first impulse was to pen a glowing tribute to the War work of this great national monopolist organization; it is impossible to withhold admiration for the scope, enterprise, and general good sense of its ever-widening activities, only the least worthy of which are best known to a public incurious about the best. Its continuous foreign broadcasts in its European News Service are models of honest statement and judicious comment, as I can personally vouch from being able to follow them in three of the many foreign languages in which they are issued. Especially do I like to listen to the fine, vigorous phrasing of the Spanish announcer, though the Italian and French are equally praiseworthy and the English bulletins in the European service sometimes seem to me more pithy and pointed than those in the Home Service.

The vividness of the news is immensely enhanced by the recordings from B.B.C. observers on all fronts of the War, and the men and women that are often brought to the microphone to relate personal experiences help not only to give immediacy to the news but to enlarge its appeal and its international value. All this is splendid, and I'm backing much of our propaganda of understatement against all the hysterical, over-emphasized, and exaggerated emanations from enemy sources. But, I repeat, it will be a bad day for Britain if the present news monopoly of the B.B.C. should ever become an established and regularized competitor with the free press of a free people.

Not content with having made a great success of the Brains Trust, I see that the B.B.C. is even giving "Any Questions" a book all to itself . . . and private publishers are starving for paper! The publications department of the B.B.C. has always seemed to me a questionable form of activity in a country where we have not yet copied our Russian Allies by nationalizing the book-publishing trade as well as the Press. I am sure that is as foreign to British ideas as the Russian alphabet is to our school children.

Printed in England and published on the 10th, 20th, and 30th of each month by the Proprietors, The Amalgamated Press, Ltd., The Fleetway House, Farringdon Street, London, E.C.4. Registered for transmission by Canadian Magazine Post. Sole Agents for Australia and New Zealand : Messrs. Gordon & Gotch, Ltd. ; and for South Africa : Central News Agency, Ltd. January 20th, 1942.   S.S.   *Editorial Address:* JOHN CARPENTER HOUSE. WHITEFRIARS. LONDON. E.C.4.

Vol 5 *The War Illustrated* Nº 119

Edited by Sir John Hammerton

FOURPENCE

JAN. 30TH, 1942

DUTCH MARINES, forming part of a landing-party from a destroyer on manoeuvres. Sturdy lads like these are now giving a good account of themselves in the Dutch East Indies, invaded by the Japanese. Ever since the outbreak of hostilities in the Far East the armed forces of the Netherlands East Indies have made an impressive showing against the enemy. Their deeds by sea and air were prominent in the news from the Far East from the very first, and now the land forces are at grips with the Japanese on the island of Celebes.

Photo, Sport & General

THE 'LAST PHASE' OR 'THE MOST DANGEROUS'?

BY THE EDITOR

THESE questions arise out of a recent statement by one of the greatest leaders of the British Commonwealth : Field-Marshal Smuts. After Mr. Churchill, there is no spokesman of Empire whose words command greater respect, whose every public utterance deserves closer attention. Yet, on this one occasion I very respectfully ask if he has said the right word. The last phase ? Surely not. The most dangerous ? Almost certainly.

How do we stand at the time of this writing ? In a very critical position with no great clearing of the clouds. They are low, if not lowering ; but while low clouds might have led to an unwise naval action by offering a tenuous substitute for the substantial roof of R.A.F. fighters which was not available (as it should have been), and the consequent disaster might well have raised up a British Jeremiah to echo " Woe ! Woe ! Ansaldo," the low clouds that hang over the War World today must not, and will not, depress those world-wide forces that are making the supreme stand for freedom. They will rather intensify the effort needed for their dispersal. And that effort will certainly mark 1942 as the War's most dangerous year.

The Last Phase is still far off. Various critical phases must, and will, be presented to us before the final one is discernible. What are the facts as distinct from rumours, guesses and wishful thinking ?

Most consolatory is the colossal resurgence of Soviet Russia. But consolation, let us remember, is needed only where grief is. The progress of our Libyan campaign, though lacking the dash and irresistibility which had been hoped for it, is still unmistakable, and its slowing down should not ultimately detract in any degree from the greatness of the victory which already seems assured. It is proving a bitter campaign against a ruthless, resourceful and implacable foe, whose cooperation with the dispirited forces of the despicable Mussolini has imparted a certain stiffening to stuff which of itself would long since have crumbled. The Nazis in North Africa—there thanks to the perfidy and treachery of Vichy France—have supplied the steel reinforcement to the low quality cement of the Italians. So far, there is no mistake about our North African victory, but not until we have driven Nazi and Fascist from Tripoli can it be regarded as one hundred per cent solidified.

We can disregard most, if not all, of the stories about Germany's difficulties in Occupied and Unoccupied France. The plain truth is that all France is " occupied " and is not only destitute of the means to eject its invaders, but is more likely to help

them by further and far-reaching " collaboration." See what will happen to the French Fleet at Dakar, at Oran, at Bizerta when the most dangerous phase develops with the entrance of Spain and the overrunning of Portugal by the Nazi hordes ! Unless we are secure from Egypt to Tripoli and the Tunisian frontier by then the low clouds will surely lower. Possibly the American navy will be able to give such effective cooperation to the British before then as to dispose of the hostile French and their Nazi masters at Dakar and to profit from the Trans-Saharan railway which the enemy is now hurriedly constructing. Possibly. And we will leave it at that.

Still with our eyes on the West, we can derive comfort from the rising success of Anglo-American cooperation in the Battle of the Atlantic, the crucial importance of which is liable to be overlooked as we strain our vision Eastward while America strains hers Westward, and Australia looks with an anxious eye to her near North.

The treachery of Japan—for which both Britain and America ought to have been prepared—has produced a new phase of the War which closely resembles the First. Our American critics who rated Chamberlain and his appeasement policy, when German treachery was finally revealed with the rape of Poland, were in no better case when their own Government was talking at Washington about ways of peace with the rascally repre-

sentatives of their trans-Pacific enemy, who was even then sending armadas of destruction against every U.S. base from the Philippines to Honolulu. Indeed, there should be in America, if our Allies will think back to Chamberlain Britain in Aug. 1939, and their own condition on Dec. 7, 1941, something of that fellow-feeling which in adversity makes us wondrous kind. And I think there is. Britain was more fortunate in having no such mischievous fifth columnist as the foolish flying fellow Lindbergh masquerading as a national hero on his cheaply earned world publicity. (And, incidentally, it would be almost a crime against decency to allow him a hand now in helping the Anglo-American cause in view of his avowed hatred of all things British.)

But vast and catastrophic as the successes of Japan in her panther-like attack on Western civilization may appear, these should be related mainly to elements of surprise and treachery and are not to be regarded as mortal blows. They carry in them the seeds of their own undoing. The far-reaching nature of those blows, the immense dispersal of Japan's effort, is the best guarantee of their eventually being rendered nugatory Japan is over-reaching herself. She is causing imponderable financial loss to the British and the Dutch and in a smaller measure to the Americans—for which again the traitors of Vichy can be thanked in their shameful surrender of Indo-China—but she has cemented the A.B.C.D. union. And when the forces which Japan has so wantonly attacked have rallied from these initial blows, as they assuredly will even if it takes another year and greater blows are still to fall upon us, Japan will be driven from the mainland of Asia and from the Malay archipelago back to her own islands, where—and that day shall come—her present friendly enemy Russia will be constrained to join with the amalgamated forces of America, the British Commonwealth, China and the splendid Dutch in the " erasure " of the rookery cities of that aggressive race of a bastard civilization which unites the worst elements of the western whites with the worst of the yellow men.

For ourselves we can be of good cheer. Our blunders made good, our firm and effective handling of Syria, of Iraq, of Persia, of North Africa and our defence of Egypt and the Suez Canal, our reconquest of Abyssinia and East Africa, and the amazing defence of gallant little Malta (which Mussolini was to capture in two days !), and—but really if we " think on these things " and many others to Britain's credit we can still keep high hearts even when the clouds are low.

I repeat : we find ourselves in the War's most dangerous year, but the Last Phase is still beyond mortal vision.

J. A. HAMMERTON

Field-Marshal SMUTS, here seen on a British warship in Durban Harbour, said on Jan. 10 that the war had " now entered its last and most dangerous phase."

Photo, Wide World

Britain's Premier Speaks in Canada's Parliament

PREMIER IN OTTAWA, where he met with an enthusiastic reception during his recent visit to Canada. Left, Mr. Churchill stands bareheaded on the steps of the Canadian House of Commons acknowledging the greeting of the vast crowd which gathered to see him. On the right he is seen inspecting a guard of honour provided by the Canadian Army, outside Parliament Buildings, Ottawa.

In the Canadian House of Commons, at Ottawa, Mr. Churchill delivers his address to the assembled members of the Canadian Legislature on Dec. 30, 1941. The salient points of his speech are given in page 415. Mr. Mackenzie King, the Canadian Prime Minister, in introducing Mr. Churchill, referred to him as " the personification of Britain's greatness."

Photos, British Official : Crown Copyright

They Know the 'Green Hell' of Jungle Warfare

The Dogras are among the Indian regiments which have been carrying on highly successful guerilla warfare behind the enemy lines in Malaya. Men of the Dogra Regiment are here seen crossing a lake in rubber boats.

A tommy-gunner of the Manchester Regiment in the Far East decks his helmet with some ferns as camouflage.

Men of the Argyll and Sutherland Highlanders in Malaya under cover on a jungle roadside. One of their regimental mottoes is " Sans Peur "— Fearless.

AUSTRALIAN TROOPS in Malaya now have an opportunity of putting into practice the intensive training they have had in jungle warfare. Right, an A.I.F. sentry on duty in a mosquito net.

Photos, British Official: Crown Copyright; Wide World

In Malaya the Indians Prove Their Worth Again

GURKHAS in Malaya training amid the dense tropical undergrowth. These sturdy troops, men of the 9th Gurkhas, have now had an opportunity of putting their training into practice and the heavy losses sustained by the Japanese during their advance in Malaya are in no small part due to the fine fighting qualities of the Indian troops taking part in the defence of the peninsula.
Photo, British Official : Crown Copyright

Modern War in an Ancient Roman Province

FOLLOWING the fall of Bardia, an account of which was given in page 412 of this Vol., the British 8th Army continued its successes in the Western Desert by the occupation of Jedabia, and the storming of Sollum at the bayonet point.

Sollum, near the Egyptian frontier, was held by the Axis as an outlying post of the Halfaya position. The village was stormed by the Transvaal Scottish on Jan. 12, and on Jan. 17 the Halfaya garrison, numbering 5,500, surrendered.

Jedabia, where Gen. Rommel had left a strong holding force on his retreat towards Tripolitania, was by-passed by Gen. Ritchie in his pursuit of the main Axis forces and was dealt with later.

Above, left, many Nazi bombers destroyed in Libya lie in what is known as the " Graveyard of the Stukas." Circle, left, men of the Free French " Lorraine " bombing squadron, co-operating with the R.A.F. in the Western Desert. Above, a Sikh soldier picks off enemy snipers from the balcony of a ruined house in Derna.

ANCIENT CYRENE, with its ruined temples, is here seen from the modern macadamized road above the town on which armoured cars of the South African Field Force are moving. Cyrene, originally a Greek colony, lies between Derna and Barce and was captured by the British during the advance of the 8th Army to Benghazi at the end of Dec. 1941.

Photos, British Official : Crown Copyright

Strengthening the Defence of Britain's Airfields

R.A.F. REGIMENT, specially formed for airfield defence, will include mobile and static units and will be trained on Commando lines. Here a detachment going on duty passes the crew of a Bristol Beaufort.

Behind a barrier of barbed wire two machine-gun crews in a concrete pill-box help to guard this R.A.F. Bomber station. The experiences in Crete and Malaya have proved the need for a better system of airfield defence.

AIRFIELD DEFENCE in this country is now being put on a sounder basis. Men of the newly formed R.A.F. regiment are erecting barbed wire entanglements around a British aerodrome.

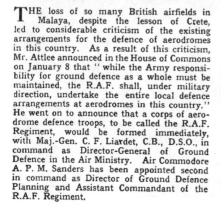

Maj.-Gen.
C. F. LIARDET

Air Cdre.
A. P. M. SANDERS

THE loss of so many British airfields in Malaya, despite the lesson of Crete, led to considerable criticism of the existing arrangements for the defence of aerodromes in this country. As a result of this criticism, Mr. Attlee announced in the House of Commons on January 8 that " while the Army responsibility for ground defence as a whole must be maintained, the R.A.F. shall, under military direction, undertake the entire local defence arrangements at aerodromes in this country." He went on to announce that a corps of aerodrome defence troops, to be called the R.A.F. Regiment, would be formed immediately, with Maj.-Gen. C. F. Liardet, C.B., D.S.O., in command as Director-General of Ground Defence in the Air Ministry. Air Commodore A. P. M. Sanders has been appointed second in command as Director of Ground Defence Planning and Assistant Commandant of the R.A.F. Regiment.

Stopping all cars, a member of the R.A.F. Regiment covers the occupants with his tommy-gun until the corporal of the R.A.F. Service Police on duty has examined their passes.

Photos, British Official : Crown Copyright ; Fox

Our Searchlight on the War

PUNISH THE GUILTY!

The Allies "determine in a spirit of international solidarity that (a) those guilty and responsible, whatever their nationality, are sought for, handed over to justice and judged, (b) that the sentences pronounced are carried out." *Inter-Allied Conference at St. James's Palace declaration.*

STALIN has made it perfectly clear that Germany will be punished for her crimes. Although he talks about Hitlerite Germany he has no doubt now that the whole nation are responsible for plunging the world into a sea of blood. Whether we call it revenge or retribution (and the dictionary indicates that these are one and the same thing), the conscience of humanity will not allow the enemy to escape judgement. But we can be sure that, as soon as Hitler is beaten, a moan of self-pity will go up, even as the Germans repudiate the leader they once deified. Retribution must take the form of making it absolutely impossible for the Germans to smash the world again, and that

NEW RIFLE AND BAYONET issued to British troops. The new rifle, the No. 4, has a slightly longer barrel than the old Lee-Enfield. The bayonet is only 6 ins. long, with a sharp point and four fluted sides. *Photo, G.P.U.*

can be done by internationalizing flying in Germany, and prohibiting German control of any aeroplanes whatsoever. As for the ringleaders in crime, from Hitler to quislings of all nations, they must be put on trial and punished. The inter-Allied Conference at St. James's Palace have made this a principal war-aim. Let no man try to frustrate the necessary procedure when the time comes.

THE FATHER OF THE FEAST

Lord Woolton has received about 13,000 letters addressed to him personally by housewives and others during the last year. The Minister treats these letters seriously, and to each of the 13,000 correspondents a reply was sent.

THE task of feeding the nation in wartime was never likely to be a sinecure, but, of all the Ministries, that pertaining to Food seems to be the most popular. Lord Woolton has been both competent and lucky. His work might have been far more harassing if the Battle of the Atlantic had gone against us. As it is, we have all had quite enough to eat, and submit with good humour to necessary reductions, and are grateful for occasional increases. Intelligent and economical housewives, who know all about the complexities and perplexities of feeding a family even in peacetime, can appreciate the difficulties of feeding a nation in wartime, and we doubt if the most critical would say that they could do it better than Lord Woolton, in the circumstances. The Minister is in the position of being as generous a host as possible on a limited and hazardous larder. Nor will we begrudge him his fan mail, including the letter from "Chuffy," the black cat that begged not to be deprived of his little drop of milk because he catches mice for the Government. It was a wise move to cancel the winter bonus of extra quantities of rationed foods, although we might have drawn on our reserves. The entry of Japan into the war

and new demands on shipping in consequence compel us to husband our stocks. If we are not laughing and growing fat, we are doing nicely, thank you, and it is at least an aesthetic joy to see so few "corporations" among the middle-aged. No lady need worry now about slimming, and no gentleman can hope to throw his weight about.

ENSA'S FULL HOUSE

The Entertainments National Service Association is known to British troops everywhere, from the Arctic north to tropical Africa.

IF war has become increasingly cruel and dangerous it has also become, paradoxically, more humane. Everything possible is done to mitigate suffering and boredom, and "all talents" are harnessed in totalitarian effort. The artist, writer, and actor now have a definite part to play in keeping up the morale of the people, whether they are on the fighting fronts or working in munition factories. Before the fall of France the total number of entertainments given in France by E.N.S.A. amounted to over 5,500. They were attended by 2,242,559 persons. Mr. Basil Dean tells us that, since July, 1940, E.N.S.A. has played to audiences totalling 50,000,000. The tremendous amount of good- that the organization does is incalculable. Modern war is far more boring than exciting. In trying to abolish this boredom E.N.S.A. is helping to keep us all on the alert for the means of achieving victory. The men and women on the entertainments front bring good cheer and set us all an example. To keep cheerful is a national service in itself. Make a resolve to be an unofficial member of E.N.S.A. and ridicule all rumourists and malcontents.

HALF-AND-HALF MEASURES

We do not like Government control, but the day has now come when we must consider, not our preferences, but what must be done if the war is to be won. One thing is clear. We "cannot serve God and Mammon"—Government control and private enterprise. *From a letter to "The Times"*

WHEN we recall the state of affairs immediately after Dunkirk Britain has done wonders on the production front, but results are still not good enough. Competent judges of industry, including workers and managers alike, believe that production could be increased by 40 per cent. There are delays, bottlenecks, discontent about wage anomalies. Some workers get too much, others too little. Old grievances between Capital and Labour crop up here and there. Employers worry about E.P.D. Workers complain about income-tax. Some think that industries engaged in munitions should come under Government control, and that only in this way can Britain ensure a totalitarian effort. Such control is contrary to the democratic scheme of things, but if it would produce that extra 40 per cent none but the selfish and unpatriotic would oppose it. Russia completely understands the significance of

MAJ.-GEN. G. H. BRETT, newly appointed Deputy-Commander of the forces of the United Nations in the S.W. Pacific, has been tabled for promotion by Pres. Roosevelt. *Photo, Planet News*

totalitarian war. The practical unity and efficiency among the Soviet people of all kinds are illustrated by an incident related in the "Soviet War News." A Russian invented a new weapon called the P.P.S. gun. Though Hitler's armies were at the gates of Moscow a factory was ordered to begin mass-production of this sub-machine-gun within thirty days. In peacetime six months would have been necessary. Workers of all grades went to it with a will, and the gun was on the assembly lines within eleven days.

WORLD NAVAL WAR

The tragedy of Malaya is due to overwhelming Japanese sea and air power. Japan's navy is now a dominant factor in the war, redressing the German lack in this respect.

IN no spirit of carping criticism it can be said that had America been as prepared to hold the Pacific as Britain was ready to hold the Atlantic, she would not have lost her bases, and the Japanese could not have swamped the Malayan Archipelago. Nippon's temporary victory, far more than a local one, may mean a vast extension of the naval war if the yellow Prussians can get into the Indian Ocean and the Atlantic. Hitler has found his match on land in Russia, but if he can stabilize the East Front he will concentrate on Egypt and North Africa. Constant Axis raids on Malta may be the prelude to an effort to capture this fortress and Gibraltar, as part of the enemy's effort to command the seas. Britain must hold Malta and Gibraltar at all costs.

EN ROUTE FOR RUSSIA, part of the vast quantities of medical supplies being sent to the Soviet Union by various organizations, including the British and American Red Cross and the L.C.C., are here seen being dispatched from London Headquarters. *Photo, L.N.A.*

Japan's Formidable Power in the Pacific

CRUISER
Tone Class

BATTLESHIP
Nagato Class

2 MAN
SUBMARINE

← Approx. 300 ft →

42 ft

Battleships.

The most powerful of all are the Nissin and the Takamatu, both due for completion during 1941. They are over 40,000 tons, carry nine 16-in. guns, and have a speed of 30 knots. The Haruna was reported sunk off Luzon on Dec. 11, 1941, leaving nine others, and of these the Nagato and Mutu are the most recent. Two of these remaining battleships are said to have been badly damaged. The Nagato and Mutu are approximately 700 feet long and have a displacement of 32,720 tons. Completed in 1920-1921, they were reconstructed during 1934-1936, when A.A. and anti-submarine protection were increased, and the speed raised.

The main armament is eight 16-in. guns (A) with twenty 5·5-in. (B), eight 5-in. A.A. (C). There are also four submerged torpedo-tubes, and three aircraft are carried—the catapult is seen at (D).

The main belt of armour is said to be twelve inches or thirteen inches thick, with 14-in. armoured gun-turrets. Searchlights are shown at (E). Complement is 1,332.

Japan is thought to have at least four " pocket battleships " building or completing.

Cruisers.

Japan is known to have twelve 8-in.-gun, six and possibly more 6-in.-gun, and seventeen 5·5-in.-gun cruisers, and most of them appear to have a speed of about 33 knots.

The Tone class (Tone and Tikuma) shown here displace 8,500 tons and are 614½ feet long. They were completed in 1938-39.

The twelve 6·1-in. guns are all mounted forward of the control tower (F) and there are also eight 5-in. A.A. guns (G) and other smaller guns. Four banks of triple torpedo-tubes (H) are mounted. Four aircraft are carried and there are two catapults (J). The aircraft-incline at the stern is an unusual feature (K).

The aircraft shown is a Navy type 96; a type normally carried on Japanese warships.

Submarines.

The Japanese Navy has many submarines, some of which are reported capable of crossing the Pacific and back without refuelling. Perhaps the most interesting, however, are the tiny 2-man vessels used in the attack on Pearl Harbour (see p. 393). These submarines are taken on board a merchant vessel or warship to within a hundred miles of their objective and are then slung overboard (1).

The diagrammatic drawing (2) illustrates the following features:—(A) Two 18-in.-torpedo tubes, (B) ballast tank, (C) Officer at the periscope controls, (D) batteries, (E) Engineer seen tending the electric motor, (F) compressed-air bottles, (G) fore and aft trimming tanks, (H) hydroplanes. A 300-lb. explosive charge is said to be carried in these vessels, for what purpose is not clear. (3) Comparison between a standard Japanese submarine and a 2-man vessel. Whereas a standard submarine costs approximately £500,000, the midget vessel would probably cost about £5,000.

Specially drawn by Haworth for THE WAR ILLUSTRATED

The Yellow Tidal Wave in the Far East

The capture of Kuala Lumpur and Tarakan, the Dutch island off the coast of Borneo, mark the second phase in the Japanese encirclement of Singapore. After five weeks of fighting the enemy held four-fifths of Malaya and approached the back door of the great naval base.

WITH the exception of the fine courage of our troops, fighting against heavy odds, there was little to relieve the lengthening story of Japanese Malayan successes during the second week of the new year.

There was a continuous onslaught of fresh enemy soldiers against tired men deplorably handicapped by a lack of aerial reconnaissance. The Japanese had augmented their forces by new landings at the mouth of the Bernam River on the west coast, further threatening our flank guarding the northern approaches to Kuala Lumpur. Emerging from the forests where they had employed ingenious guerilla tactics, the enemy were now able to make use of the good roads and communications of the rubber estates, and their advance with heavy and light tanks became less difficult.

Kuala Lumpur, a city of 100,000 inhabitants in the centre of the plantations, was now within their grasp from the north-west, but the enemy were also attacking in the north-east corner of Malaya, where our men were forced back on Kuala Lipis, and at Kuantan, half-way down the east coast.

Increasing their tank-power with twelve-ton vehicles, the Japanese crashed through our defences north-west of Kuala Lumpur, releasing hordes of infantry from the lorries following behind. The city's position became more and more critical, and it was decided to abandon it, after the scorched earth policy had been strictly applied. Stocks of food were therefore distributed to the public, and the native population enjoyed a great share-out of free gifts. Food, drink, clothing and many other portable goods were piled on bicycles, rickshaws, ox-carts, and motor-cars, and hurriedly removed. Immovable things, likely to be of use to the invaders, such as reserves of oil and machinery, were destroyed. Carrying out a skilfully organized withdrawal, our forces took up new positions at Seremban, fifty miles south of Kuala Lumpur, and though the road was a continuous mass of soldiers and transports, an orderly retreat was maintained throughout.

The Gurkhas, who had particularly distinguished themselves in the defence of the city, standing up to tank attacks and dive-bombing with almost superhuman courage, were in no wise dispirited by the grim fortune of war, but marched back to continue the fighting in due course, singing cheerfully as they went. The fall of Kuala Lumpur was confirmed on Jan. 12.

In this map of Malaya successive stages of the Japanese advance towards Singapore are shown by white lines with dates in the panel on the right.

Map, courtesy of the " Daily Express "

How was it that the Japanese had so quickly been able to overrun so difficult a country as the Malayan Peninsula ? The fact is that their successes throughout were due, in the first place, to immense superiority in men and machines, but credit must be given to their cunning methods of infiltration. Where the terrain did not admit of attack by tanks, innumerable small parties of the enemy "trickled" through the jungle. Clad in light garments, and armed with small-calibre weapons, these free-lance infantry were ordered to advance independently and make their way against our forces as best they could. Hiding here, there, and everywhere in the forest, the ubiquitous gunmen in vast numbers crept forward to their objective. The jungle, which was thought to be impenetrable, was no obstacle to these agile fanatics, who had obviously been rehearsed for fighting amid the intoler-

able tropical heat and tangled vegetation. As the enemy approached nearer Singapore air raids became more frequent, and a formation of 70 aircraft attacked on Jan. 12, causing fifty-five casualties.

Elsewhere in the far-flung area of Asian conflict, the Allies scored a minor success by raiding aerodromes at Bangkok twice within 24 hours, after a flight of 300 miles over jungle and mountains from bases in Burma. The R.A.F. were supported by five aircraft of the American Volunteer Group. At least seven enemy planes were destroyed.

Working to a prepared plan of possessing themselves of the Dutch East Indies, the Japanese on the night of Jan. 10-11 attacked the island of Tarakan (north-east of Borneo), where they met with fierce opposition from the garrison. In this engagement bombers of the Netherlands East Indies Air Force scored two direct hits on enemy transports, and shot down three Japanese planes. An offensive was carried out simultaneously against Minahasa (North Celebes), where men of the Netherlands garrison struck back at seaborne troops and parachutists.

Tarakan soon fell into enemy hands, but the Dutch garrison had time to destroy the oil wells, some of the most valuable in the East Indies. The oil from these wells is so pure that it needs no refining, and can be pumped, as fuel, direct into tankers. Part of the Tarakan Dutch garrison escaped to the mainland.

Meanwhile, Gen. MacArthur on the American front in the Philippines had had time to reform his hard-pressed legions. They were now occupying strong positions in the mountains of Luzon, north-west of Manila. The Japanese, however, were daily moving troops into the line and landing fresh reinforcements with the intention of attacking on a large scale.

On Jan. 11 the enemy struck against Gen. MacArthur's right flank in tremendous force, but American and Filipino troops held firm. The Japanese suffered heavy casualties, but made no progress. This battle in the mountains was accompanied by fierce attacks on the fortified island of Corregidor and the Bataan Peninsula.

Later news from the Philippine theatre of the war indicated that Gen. MacArthur's army had proved definitely superior in artillery to the Japanese, and columns of mechanized units as well as infantry concentrations had been shattered.

IN THE PHILIPPINES Gen. MacArthur's troops have been putting up a magnificent resistance in face of heavy Japanese attacks. Left, a 12-in. long-range gun on the island fortress of Corregidor which guards Manila Bay. Right, Fort Drum, at the entrance to the bay. Gen. MacArthur has kept relatively large Japanese forces employed against him which might have been used elsewhere and has denied the invaders the use of Manila Bay.

Photos, E.N.A.

First Cities of Malaya that Fell to the Enemy

IPOH, the post office and town hall of which are housed in the building seen above, is a centre of the tin mining industry in Malaya, a country which is one of the world's largest producers of tin. The town, which lies in Perak on the railway from Singapore to Bangkok, was occupied by the Japanese after British troops had been withdrawn towards the end of December 1941.

KUALA LUMPUR, a centre of both tin and rubber industries, fell into Japanese hands, according to Tokyo reports, on Jan. 11, 1942. The Mosque, above, is the religious centre of the native population, as is that at Kuala Kangsar, north of Ipoh, seen centre right. Centre left is the impressive railway station in Moorish style at Kuala Lumpur, capital of the Federated Malay States. All the buildings in this page were designed by Brig.-Gen. A. B. Hubback (retd.), C.M.G., D.S.O., F.R.I.B.A., former Government architect to the Federated Malay States.

From the Leningrad
padded suits to prote
German mechanized
the Moscow front.

Photos, British Official; Planet News

nts come these photographs, severa o them from a new Soviet war film, showing : 1, a Soviet anti-tank gun in action on the Leningrad front. The crew wear e cold. 2, guns of a Soviet armoured train opening up on German positions during the fighting at Tula, south of Moscow. 3, Soviet bombers setting out to attack ont of Moscow. 4, Cossack cavalry detachment, leaving their horses in a wood, charge a German position in the Moscow sector. 5. Red Army artillery in action on winter equipment, Red Army men are lined up to receive decorations. 7, volunteers from Leningrad on reconnaissance.

New Year Begins Well for the Red Armies

Despite Hitler's assumption of the High Command the beginning of 1942 saw the Russians
sweeping inexorably forward over the whole of the vast Eastern Front. Soon the German
propaganda claim that their troops were withdrawing merely to rectify the line became untenable, and reports of a wholesale sacking of generals began to come out of Germany.

THE capture of Kaluga on Dec. 30, 1941, was one of the most important operations by the Red Army since the beginning of their counter-offensive, for it placed the whole German army in that sector in an extremely precarious position.

Preparations for this operation began in the middle of December, a few days after the launching of the great Russian counter-offensive, when Gen. Boldin's forces routed the 3rd and 4th German tank divisions and an S.S. regiment of the Germania division to the north-west of Tula. This attack was rapidly followed up and Gen. Guderian's 2nd Panzer Army was forced to make a hasty withdrawal southwards. The Germans then made a stand at Kosaya Gora, ten miles from Tula, a strongly fortified point of resistance; but this place was outflanked, and the Russians, by a pincer movement, recaptured Shchenkino, inflicting heavy losses

moved secretly towards Kaluga, and, the Nazis having weakened this sector, the Russians drove a deep salient into the Nazi lines, forming a triangle based on Alexin and Krapivna with its point near Kaluga, which at that time was about 40 miles in the rear of the German front line.

On Dec. 21, without pausing in their march, the Red Army men attacked Kaluga. Capturing the only bridge over the Oka river, they broke into the southern suburbs. Fierce fighting ensued in which streets changed hands several times, and the enemy, receiving hastily dispatched reinforcements from other sectors, resisted stubbornly. But the Red troops, too, were now receiving reinforce-ments in considerable numbers, and a ding-dong battle ensued which went on for a week. The German command hurled all its available planes into the battle, and those sections of the city recaptured by the Russians were

In the Leningrad sector Gen. Fedyuninsky's troops continued to advance, and by the beginning of 1942 the German troops in that area, having lost all the positions which they had captured during September, October and November 1941, took shelter behind the defensive line which they had built in August of last year. But though the German High Command wished to rest its sorely-tried troops, Gen. Fedyuninsky gave them no respite. To make matters worse for the German armies before Leningrad a new thrust by the Russians below Lake Ilmen threatened to trap them.

Nor was the Russian advance confined to the Moscow and Leningrad fronts. The close of 1941 saw the towns of Kerch and Feodosia, in the Crimea, once again in Russian hands.

The landing on the Kerch peninsula was a brilliant operation carried out by troops of the Caucasian Front commanded by Lt.-Gen. Dmitri Kozlov, in cooperation with the Russian Black Sea Fleet under Vice-Adm. Oktyabrsky. The first step was a frontal attack launched against Kerch on Dec. 26, when troops under Lt.-Gen. Vladimir Lvov crossed the Kerch Strait with the intention of drawing upon themselves and immobilizing all the available German forces. Then, three days later, a flank attack was launched against Feodosia by troops under Maj.-Gen. Pervushin.

Despite falling snow and pouring rain and a heavy storm which delayed the landing of some of the troops, the operations, which are said to have been personally planned by Stalin, were carried to a successful conclusion. Gen. Lvov's troops met with fierce resistance, but they managed to land and hold their ground until reinforcements came up and the German resistance was broken.

'The Crimea Must Be Liberated'

When reports reached the German armies that Feodosia had been quickly captured by Gen. Pervushin, the Nazis, fearing to be cut off, rushed westwards along the roads leading to the interior of the Crimea.

To Lt.-Gen. Kozlov, Commander of the Caucasian Front, and Vice-Adm. Oktya-brsky, Commander of the Black Sea Fleet, Stalin sent his congratulations, ending with these words: " The Crimea must be liberated from the German invaders and their Rumanian and Italian lackeys." These words were taken to heart and further Crimea landings took place within the next few days, notably at Eupatoria, on the west coast, menacing the German armies besieging Sebastopol.

These Russian columns landing on the west coast of the Crimea struck right across the peninsula in the direction of Djankoi, a railway junction at the base of the Perekop Isthmus, in an endeavour to cut off the German forces in the Crimea from the mainland.

In the sector of the Donetz basin, too, Timoshenko's shock troops pressed forward, and by Jan. 14 hundreds of Russian tanks had rolled across the solidly frozen Donetz river and reached a point only eight miles from the great city of Kharkov. Following in the wake of the tanks, Russian cavalry and ski-troops armed with sub-machine-guns helped to break up the German defence line east of the city.

And so the year 1942 opened auspiciously for the Soviet Union, with the invader in retreat from Leningrad to the Crimea.

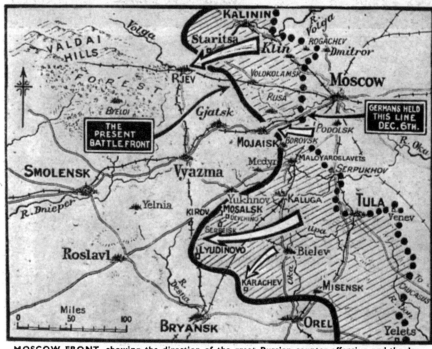

MOSCOW FRONT, showing the direction of the great Russian counter-offensive and the deep wedge which, by Jan. 13, had been thrust into the German line south-west of the Russian capital. German forces in the area between Mojaisk and Vyazma were threatened by an encircling pincer movement from Rjev and Mosalsk. *Map, Courtesy of the " Daily Telegraph "*

on the Germans, driving Guderian's forces from the main highway and cutting them off from repair bases and the main roads. They retreated once more.

Meanwhile, Gen. Zhukov had con-centrated a group of mobile shock troops in the Tula area, consisting of infantry, cavalry, tanks and artillery. The route of march of this shock group was deliberately made through a district with poor roads which must have appeared to the Germans impassable. The flanks of this body were protected by Soviet forces north and south, and the northern party launched a feint attack on the Makarovo-Kaluga highway. The Nazis fell into the trap and transferred their 137th Infantry Division to this point.

Meanwhile, from the south a mobile unit of automatic riflemen, travelling all through the night, broke into Dubno, some miles in the enemy's rear, and created great confusion.

The enemy's attention being thus diverted north and south, the main mobile group

subjected to frequent and heavy raids; but the Red Army continued to press the enemy farther west, and on the morning of Dec. 30 the Red Flag of the Soviets again waved over Kaluga.

To celebrate the New Year the Red Army captured yet another position of great importance, Malo Yaroslavets being reoccupied by the Red Army on Jan. 1, 1942, after a week of steady progress, by concerted blows from the north, west and east. Violent street fighting in the town lasted a whole day and night. Vast quantities of material were abandoned by the Germans. " We found tanks, armoured cars and guns in good order literally at every step," said Maj.-Gen. Golubev. " Large fuel and am-munition dumps were intact. We captured about 50 enemy tanks and armoured cars, about 100 lorries, over 60 guns, over 150 machine-guns, 500 bicycles, and whole depots of shells, explosives, cartridges, grenades and fuel. The enemy is fleeing and losing his picked cadres of men and officers."

The Two R.A.F.s 'Mid the Snow of Northern Russia

SYMBOL OF COOPERATION between the British Royal Air Force and their Soviet comrades, this photograph shows an R.A.F. officer of the British detachment in Russia with Captain Andruskin of the Red Air Force at an observation point on an airfield in the northern sector of the Russian Front. Behind, men of the R.A.F. stand on guard. The Russian airmen were very impressed by the British Hurricanes sent to Russia, and many of their pilots are now handling these aircraft with great success.

Photo. Planet News

Our Diary of the War

MONDAY, JAN. 5, 1942   856*th day*

Air.—R.A.F. heavily attacked docks at Brest and Cherbourg during the night.

Russian Front.—Russians claimed an advance of 45 miles in two days in the Crimea. Almost the whole of the Kerch peninsula cleared. New Russian offensive launched against Kharkov.

Africa.—British mobile columns active in the Jedabia area.

Far East.—U.S. bombers hit a Japanese battleship and sank at least one enemy destroyer off Davao. West of Manila a Japanese attack repulsed with heavy losses. In Malaya, British troops made further withdrawal south of Ipoh. Chinese claimed a big victory near Changsha, in Hunan.

TUESDAY, JAN. 6   857*th day*

Air.—Night attack on Brest by R.A.F.

Russian Front. — Soviet communiqué announced sinking of three enemy transports in the Barents Sea. Berlin admitted Russian landing at Eupatoria, in the Crimea.

Africa.—British troops of the Brigade of Guards in action near Jedabia.

Far East.—In Malaya, British forces withdrew from the Kuantan area.

General.—President Roosevelt, addressing Congress, announced his armaments programme. New Navy-R.A.F. raid on Norway carried out at night. Helle Fiord, between Bergen and Trondheim, entered. Three enemy vessels sunk and a factory shelled.

WEDNESDAY, JAN. 7   858*th day*

Air.—Night attack on Brest by R.A.F.

Russian Front.—Soviet landing in the Crimea continued. Red Army reoccupied Meshchovsk, 40 miles S.W. of Kaluga.

Africa.—Axis forces at Jedabia retreated westward under cover of a heavy sandstorm.

Far East.—Heavy fighting in the Philippines to the N.W. of Manila. Corregidor heavily bombed. In Malaya, Japanese claimed to have captured the whole of the Kampar area, 90 miles N. of Kuala Lumpur.

General.—President Roosevelt presented to Congress the greatest Budget in history, calling for an expenditure of over £13,000,000,000.

THURSDAY, JAN. 8   859*th day*

Air.—Night attacks by R.A.F. on Brest and Cherbourg.

Russian Front.—Soviet pressure continued all along the front. Offensive against Kharkov making steady progress.

Africa.—British pursuit in Libya slowed down by bad weather. Rommel withdrawing towards El Agheila.

Far East.—Heavy fighting in Malaya between the Slim River and Kuala Lumpur. R.A.F. twice raided Bangkok. An American submarine sank four Japanese ships in the Pacific. In the Philippines, Japanese bringing up reinforcements.

FRIDAY, JAN. 9   860*th day*

Sea.—Admiralty announced that the cruiser H.M.S. Galatea had been sunk by enemy action in the Mediterranean.

Russian Front.—Russians advancing from Kaluga captured three more towns and entered the province of Smolensk.

Mediterranean.—Malta had its 200th raid in five weeks. Maj.-Gen. Beak, V.C., appointed G.O.C troops in Malta in succession to Maj.-Gen. Scobell.

Far East.—In Malaya an all-day battle north of Kuala Lumpur resulted in heavy casualties on both sides. Lull in the fighting in the Philippines. R.A.F. attacked Japanese air base at Raheng, in Thailand.

SATURDAY, JAN. 10   861*st day*

Russian Front.—Russian forces continued to advance in the Donetz Basin, crossing the Donetz River at many points.

Far East.—Japanese at the outskirts of

Kuala Lumpur. Intensive patrolling and artillery duels in the Philippines. Japanese landed at night at four points in the Dutch East Indies.

Home.—Enemy night raiders over N.W. England and Midlands. A few bombs on Liverpool.

General.—Mr. Duff Cooper recalled from Singapore.

SUNDAY, JAN. 11   862*nd day*

Sea.—Admiralty announced sinking of a large enemy transport laden with troops in the Ionian Sea. A medium-sized supply ship was also torpedoed and severely damaged.

Air.—R.A.F. made yet another night raid on Brest.

Russian Front.—Moscow announced the recapture of Lyudinovo, 40 miles north of Briansk, and of the important railway junction of Tikhonova Pustyn, a few miles north of Kaluga.

Far East.—In Malaya the Japanese forces entered Kuala Lumpur. In the Philippines a Japanese attack north-west of Manila was repulsed with heavy losses. U.S. Navy Department announced an enemy attack on naval station at Tutuila, American island in Somoan group. Chinese claimed successes against Japanese in Hunan, north of the Yangtse, in South Annui and in Suiyan. Allied planes scored hits on two enemy cruisers off Dutch Borneo.

MONDAY, JAN. 12   863*rd day*

Russian Front. — Soviet forces closing around Orel. Further Russian progress in the Crimea.

Africa.—Pressure on Halfaya increased. Sollum captured by the Transvaal Scottish regiment.

Far East.—In Malaya, British troops withdrew to positions north of Seremban. In Dutch East Indies, Tarakan surrendered to Japanese. In the Philippines another Japanese assault on Gen. MacArthur's position was beaten off.

TUESDAY, JAN. 13   864*th day*

Sea.—Admiralty announced that an Italian supply ship of 5,000 tons was torpedoed and seriously damaged in the Mediterranean.

Russian Front.—Russian troops occupied Kirov, in the province of Smolensk, and Dorokhove, near Mojaisk. In the Leningrad area, Starayo Rusa, 10 miles south of L. Ilmen, was reoccupied by the Red Army.

Africa.—Occupation of Jedabia by British forces announced from Cairo.

Far East.—Further British withdrawals in Malaya.

General.—Inter-Allied conference at St. James's Palace. They signed a declaration placing among their chief war aims the juridical punishment of those guilty of barbarities against civilians.

WEDNESDAY, JAN. 14   865*th day*

Air.—R.A.F. made heavy night attack on Hamburg and N.W. Germany.

Russian Front.—Russians within eight miles of Kharkov. On the Moscow front Red Army recaptured Medyn, 25 miles west of Malo Yaroslavets. In the Crimea, Soviet detachments reached Kolash, a few miles from Djankoi.

Mediterranean.—Malta had 14 air raids in a single day.

Far East.—Heavy raid on the Rangoon area. Japanese invasion fleet which captured Tarakan reported moving south. In the Philippines General MacArthur's troops beat off two more heavy attacks. Gen. Wavell established his H.Q. in Dutch East Indies.

General.—U.S. set up a unified War Production Board under Mr. Donald Nelson.

THURSDAY, JAN. 15   866*th day*

Air.—R.A.F. made heavy night raid on Hamburg and Emden.

Russian Front.—Soviet troops pushed forward to cut Kharkov-Kursk railway.

Far East.—Japanese claimed to have crossed the frontier of Johore. U.S. submarine sank 17,000-ton Japanese liner. In Luzon, Gen. MacArthur's troops still held their ground.

General.—W.O. announced that command of British and Indian land forces in Iran and Iraq is to pass from C.-in-C. India to Gen. Auchinleck, C.-in-C. Middle East.

FRIDAY, JAN. 16   867*th day*

Russian Front.—Red Army began direct attack on Mojaisk. Soviet forces pressed forward towards Perekop Isthmus, in Crimea.

Africa.—Rommel's forces in Libya took up defensive position south of El Agheila.

Far East.—Australian reinforcements in action in Malaya. U.S. naval forces sank three Japanese transports and two cargo vessels. Dutch announced sinking of two Jap destroyers during attack on Tarakan.

General.—Gen. Sir Alan Hartley appointed C.-in-C. India.

SATURDAY, JAN. 17   868*th day*

Air.—Enemy shipping at St. Peter's Port, Guernsey, attacked by Beaufort aircraft.

Russian Front.—Russians pressed forward in all sectors of the Moscow front.

Africa.—Axis garrison at Halfaya surrendered unconditionally. 5,500 prisoners taken.

Far East.—Japs heavily attacking right flank of Gen. MacArthur's position in Batan peninsula. Japanese reported to have made new landing on Subig Bay, Luzon.

Japanese aircraft raided Moulmein district in Burma. In Malaya, Japs made new landing near Muar.

Home.—Mr. Churchill arrived at Plymouth by flying-boat from Bermuda.

General.—Germany officially - announced death of F.-M. Von Reichenau.

TRAINING MERCHANT GUNNERS in a London bus. A large number of London buses have been transformed into mobile gunnery schools. They are sent to docks to give lessons in A.A. gunnery to captains and crews of the Merchant Navy.   *Photo, Central Press*

Dutch East Indies Caught in the Tide of War

Menado Bay, Celebes, viewed from the mountains fringing the coast, is seen right. Menado Bay is a fine natural harbour in the Minahassa region of the Island of Celebes, where the Japanese landed at three points on Jan. 10.

Below, a scene in the harbour of Macassar, Celebes. Macassar, with a population of 53,700, is the most important city in the Celebes. It lies at the opposite end of the island from Menado Bay.

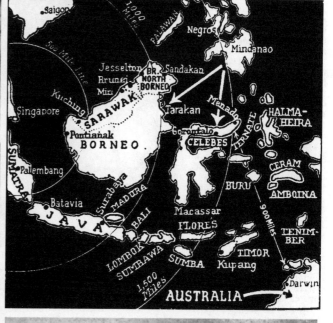

Above, Kuching, capital of the State of Sarawak. Three Japanese landings were made in Sarawak, an independent State under British protection, c. Dec. 17, 1941. British forces withdrew after destroying oil refineries.

Tarakan, the Dutch oil-port off the N.E. coast of Borneo, surrendered to the Japanese on Jan. 13 after the small garrison had fought for two days against heavy odds. The map shows where Japanese forces landed in the Dutch East Indies.

Photos, E.N.A.
Map, the " Daily Mirror "

'ONLY ALL-OUT WAR WILL HASTEN VICTORY'

In his Message to Congress on the " state of the Union " on Jan. 6, 1942, President Roosevelt
gave striking evidence of the unity and determination of the American people, and of the immense
plans for war production to be put immediately into effect. Below we print some of the most
important passages from this momentous speech.

EXACTLY one year ago today I said to
this Congress : " When the dictators
are ready to make war upon us they
will not wait for an act of war on our part.
They—not we—will choose the time and
place and method of their attack." We
now know their choice of the time : a peaceful Sunday morning—Dec. 7, 1941. We
know their choice of place—an American
outpost in the Pacific. We know their choice
of method : the method of Hitler himself.

After reviewing the long-prepared schemes of
conquest of Japan, Mussolini and Hitler, Mr.
Roosevelt stated that Japan's sudden entry into
the conflict had failed in its purpose of terrifying
and confusing the United States.

This reassembling of the
seventy-seventh Congress is proof
of that ; for the mood of quiet,
grim resolution which here prevails bodes ill for those who
conspired and collaborated to
murder world peace. That mood
is stronger than any mere desire
for revenge: it expresses the will
of the American people to make
very certain that the world will
never so suffer again . . .

Powerful and offensive action
must and will be taken in proper
time. The consolidation of the
united nations' total war effort
against our common enemies is
being achieved. That is the purpose of the conferences which
have been held during the past
two weeks in Washington, Moscow, and Chungking. That is the
primary objective of the declaration of solidarity signed at Washington on Jan. 1, 1942, by the
26 nations united against the Axis
Powers . . . These 26 nations
are united, not in spirit and
determination alone, but in the
broad conduct of the war in all
its phases.

For the first time since the
Japanese and Fascists and Nazis
started along their bloodstained
course of conquest, they now face
the fact that superior forces are
assembling against them. The
militarists in Berlin and Tokyo
started this war, but the massed,
angered forces of common humanity will
finish it.

The destruction of the material and spiritual
centres of civilization was the purpose of Hitler
and his Italian and Japanese chessmen, who
would wreck the power of the British Commonwealth, Russia, China and the Netherlands, and
then combine all their forces to achieve their
ultimate goal, the conquest of the United States,
knowing that victory for America meant victory
for freedom and the institutions of democracy.

Our own objectives are clear : the objective
of smashing the militarism imposed by the
war lords upon their enslaved peoples ; the
objective of liberating the subjugated nations;
the objective of establishing and securing
freedom of speech, freedom of religion,
freedom from want and freedom from fear
everywhere in the world.

Victory required that the superiority of the
United States in munitions and ships must be
overwhelming—so overwhelming that the Axis
nations could never hope to catch up with it—and
they must not only produce arms for their own
and the allied forces, but be prepared to put weapons
into the hands of those men in the conquered
countries who stand ready to revolt against their
oppressors.

I have just sent a letter of direction to the
appropriate Departments and Agencies of our
Government ordering that immediate steps
shall be taken :

1. To increase our production rate of
aeroplanes so rapidly that in this year of
1942 we shall produce 60,000 planes, 10,000
more than the goal set a year and a half ago.
This includes 45,000 combat planes—bombers,
dive-bombers and pursuit planes. The rate
of increase will be continued so that next
year, 1943, we shall produce 125,000 aeroplanes, including 100,000 combat planes.

2. To increase our production rate of tanks
so rapidly that in this year of 1942 we shall

U.S.A. DECLARES WAR. President Roosevelt signing America's
declaration of war against Japan on Dec. 8, 1941, after Congress had
given its approval with only one dissentient voice.
Photo, Associated Press

produce 45,000 tanks ; and to continue that
increase so that next year, 1943, we shall
produce 75,000 tanks.

3. To increase our production rate of anti-aircraft guns so rapidly that in this year,
1942, we shall produce 20,000 of them ; and
to continue that increase so that next year,
1943, we shall produce 35,000 anti-aircraft
guns.

4. To increase our production rate of
merchant ships so rapidly that in this year,
1942, we shall build 8,000,000 deadweight
tons, as compared with the 1941 production
of 1,100,000. We shall continue that increase
so that next year, 1943, we shall build
10,000,000 tons.

I rather hope these figures will become
common knowledge in Germany and Japan.

Production for war (went on the President)
depends on the speed and efficiency of the workers,
on the diversion of basic materials from civilian
use, and on the cutting of luxuries and other non-essentials—in' a word, only an " all-out " war
by individual effort and family effort in a united
country would hasten the ultimate all-out victory.
Whereas the U.S.A. had hitherto devoted only 15

per cent of the national income to defence, the
programme for the coming year would cost more
than one-half of the annual national income.

Then Mr. Roosevelt gave a warning against
defeatism, always one of the chief weapons of
Hitler's propaganda machine, and against suspicion and mistrust between one individual and
another, one group and another, one race and
another, one Government and another.

We cannot wage this war in a defensive
spirit. As our power and our resources are
fully mobilized, we shall carry the attack
against the enemy—we shall hit him and hit
him again wherever and whenever we can
reach him. We must keep him far from our
shores, for we intend to bring this battle to
him on his own home grounds.

The American armed forces
must be used at any place in all
the world where it seems advisable to engage the forces of the
enemy . . . American armed
forces will operate at many points
in the Far East. American armed
forces will, on all the oceans, be
helping to guard essential communications which are vital to the
united nations. American land,
air, and sea forces will take stations
in the British Isles, which constitute an essential fortress in this
world struggle.

We know (continued the President)
that we may have to pay a heavy
price for freedom, and we are prepared to pay it. To the question,
" When will the war end ? " there
was only one answer : it will end
just as soon as we make it end by
our combined efforts, strength, and
determination to fight through, and
work through until the end—the end
of militarism in Germany and Italy
and Japan.

That is the spirit in which the
discussions have been conducted
during the visit of the British
Prime Minister to Washington.
Mr. Churchill and I understand
each other, our motives, and our
purposes. Together, during the
past two weeks, we have faced
squarely the major military and
economic problems of this greatest
world war. All in our nation
have been cheered by Mr.
Churchill's visit. We have been deeply
stirred by his great message to us.

After paying tribute to the British people, the
Russian people, the Chinese, the Dutch, and all
the governments in exile, Mr. Roosevelt concluded :

But we of the united nations are not making
all this sacrifice of human effort and human
lives to return to the kind of world we had
after the last world war. We are fighting
today for security and progress and for peace,
not only for ourselves but for all men, not
only for one generation but for all generations
. . . We are fighting, as our fathers have
fought, to uphold the doctrine that all men are
equal in the sight of God. Those on the
other side are striving to destroy this deep
belief and to create a world in their own
image—a world of tyranny, cruelty, and
serfdom.

That is the conflict that day and night now
pervades our lives. No compromise can end
that conflict. There never has been, there
never can be, a successful compromise
between good and evil. Only total victory
can reward the champions of tolerance,
decency, freedom, and faith.

The American Machine Speeds Up for War

Multiple drill, which combines a score of operations in one, in use in the workshops of General Motors at Rochester, New York, now turned over entirely to the production of tanks, lorries, and other war material.

AIR RAID SIREN being installed at San Francisco. The Pacific seaboard of the United States is now shown to be definitely vulnerable to hostile attack.

Hawaiian sentries on guard outside a power sub-station in Honolulu. Hawaii has passed from a Pacific playground to a battle area.

LOS ANGELES DEFENCES include many anti-aircraft guns, and above a gun crew are digging an emplacement for the gun standing in the camouflaged background. Right, a U.S. bomber being loaded with a cargo of 600-lb. bombs. *Photos, Sport & General, Planet News, Keystone, Fox*

The Soldier Who is Winning the War for Russia

Mr. Hamilton Fyfe, famous as a Special Correspondent of world-wide experience and War
Correspondent of the " Daily Mail " with the Russians during the Great War until the collapse of
Tsarist Russia, contributes this study of the Soviet soldier, whose new national spirit and patriotism
inspire him to achievements which were far beyond the reach of the spiritless armies of the Tsar.

MAKING allowance for the help given
the armies of the Soviet Union by
the weather—and it must be a large
allowance—the rapidity of their advance
since they took the initiative from the enemy
and began to push the Nazis back proves
that there is in them a very different spirit
from that of the armies, commanded first
by a Grand Duke, then by a weak-minded
characterless Tsar, with which I served as
correspondent for two years during the last
war.

The trouble then was that the men had no
belief in their officers. It would be hardly
too much to say that most of the regimental
officers were hated. As for staff officers,
they were so completely out of touch with

they had grown up with. Nothing of that
sort of fraternization between men and
officers was known in other units of the
Tsar's forces.

Today the whole attitude of both has been
changed. I felt the change as soon as I
renewed my acquaintance with the Russian
soldier a few years ago. He had always
been a likeable fellow. Too fond of vodka
perhaps, when he could get it, poor devil !
The way it was taken was very often like
this : a bottle containing rather more than
half a pint would be bought for ninepence.
The neck would be knocked off against a
wall, then the spirit was swigged off at one
go. In a few minutes it took effect. The
drinker fell down, wriggled or was rolled

ardour that used to blaze among Arab tribes
in the Sudan on the proclamation of a Holy
War. Every man of them is aware that he
fights to rid the soil of his country of a
pestilent, treacherous, deliberately inhuman
foe.

Not that they refuse to look on the German
soldier as a fellow-man. They have been
told how Hitler and his gang befoozled
the German mind. On the Nazi leaders,
on the S.S. detachments, on anyone who
bellows " Heil Hitler " or " Sieg Heil ! "
they have no mercy. They do not torture
them, they just kill them as poisonous
reptiles are killed. But for the deluded
rank-and-file they feel pity. They are
friendly with them, and the Germans,
thawing under kindness, make the remarks
and give vent to the feelings which are at
once radioed to Germany to break down
the civilian dependence on Hitler.

That is one among the many results of
instructing the soldier in numerous directions
as well as the purely military. He is taught
to understand his enemy. He knows that,
while troops cozened and conscripted will
show energy and even courage when things
go well, they quickly lose heart when they
are on the run. Therefore he makes every
possible effort to keep them moving and to
make them move still faster.

The quantity of material they lose shows
how well the Russians are succeeding in
this. In a few weeks they have captured
3,500 tanks, 2,000 guns, and 30,000 motor
trucks or troop-carriers. They lost heavily
in their retreat and the Nazis were able to
use many of their tanks against them, for
they had mobile repair shops not far in the
rear. Now it is the turn of our allies to
patch up tanks they find abandoned and put
them into action against their former owners.

That the Germans had to abandon their
Panzer equipment on so large a scale shows
how hard driven they were. For this much
credit, of course, must be given the High
Command of the U.S.S.R. forces. The
direction of tactics has been very clever.
This was always a strong point in the Russian
Army. Alexieff in the last war was a superb
worker-out of retreats. The Soviet generals
have had a more welcome task. They
have worked out the method of a victorious
advance.

They are not content to push forward
a few tanks and a few lorryloads of infantry
and to make a chance dent in the enemy line,
sending more troops and tanks if the way
is kept open, or else leaving the detachment
to its fate, if need be. They open up a
wide gap and take care to keep it open.
Many German punches into the Russian
front were countered ; the attackers were
cut off and annihilated. That does not
happen to the Russian thrusts. For they
are not only planned with skill and attention
to the smallest detail ; they are carried out
with intelligence as well as dash.

Nothing is left to chance. No lives are
deliberately sacrificed. The Russian soldier
knows this, and he responds with the best
he can give. To him must go the thanks
of the civilized world for turning the tide
of battle against the enemy, who had had it so
long in his favour. He has begun the
process which will engulf the Nazi system,
extirpate its armed forces, and teach the
German people that sheep-like devotion to
an aggressive dictator is as disastrous as was
their worship of a foolish, bumptious emperor.

SOVIET GUNNERS chatting with Major Laptev, the commander of their artillery unit, after a
successful shoot in which they silenced six batteries of German guns which had been harassing
the Red Army lines.   *Photo, Planet News*

the various fronts that the fighting men
scarcely knew of their existence. When
staff work was particularly bad, the whole
of the blame was put on the generals commanding, which was often unfair. But a
widespread impression prevailed that anyone above the rank of major must be grafting
and getting rich at the expense of all below
them. And the brutal way most officers
used to treat their men—if not brutal, it
was as a rule contemptuously harsh—created
the feeling that there was nothing in common
between them.

There were exceptions to this. I was
once the guest of a Cossack regiment. One
day I was given an exhibition of rhythmic
movement and agility by the " regimental
dancers." As we sat watching them the
colonel told a couple of young subalterns
to join in and show what they could do.
Then a captain took his place in the ring.
Finally the colonel himself, carried away
by the music and the stamping, and no doubt
by the recollections they brought back to
him, dashed in and danced as well as any
of them. But all those Cossacks probably
came from the same district, the same group
of villages. They could be compared with
the British soldiers of the middle of last
century who followed " the young squire "

into a corner, and slept heavily for hours.

The army is not teetotal now, far from it,
though quite a number of abstainers can be
found in all ranks. Many of them abstain
in order to set a good example, so that the
Cause may not be smirched by drunkenness
among its defenders. There is truth in
very little. It is frowned on by the moderate
drinkers. No Party member would take
too much liquor in public. Self-respect
and the fear of being degraded prevent that.

There has been intensive teaching, too, not
only about the harm done to the Cause by
the lack of self-control, but about the danger
of intoxication when the mercury in the
thermometer drops to twenty or thirty below
—even fifty at times. Pictures of drunkards
frozen stiff have more effect maybe than
exhortations to be " good Communists."

Yet it would be a mistake, and a big one,
to assume that such exhortations are wasted.
The stubborn resistance offered to the Nazi
invaders, the determination to destroy
everything that could be useful to them,
the gallantry with which key points were
held, and now the vigour of the advance
that is driving the hated Germans back
where they came from, prove that these
Russians are filled with something like the

The Battle that Never Ceases—the War at Sea

Clinging to the keel of an upturned ship's lifeboat, too exhausted to move, are four survivors from a torpedoed merchant ship. Only one had sufficient strength to reach for the line thrown by a rescuing warship. Right, British destroyers, the German U-boats' nightmare.

TANKER ABLAZE as she sinks into the Atlantic as a result of enemy action. Left, aircraft guarding a convoy on its way to the Middle East. The war at sea is still the most vital of all the battles in the world-wide war.

Photos, British Official; Central Press, Planet News

I Was There!.... *Eye Witness Stories of the War*

I Got Right in the Middle of Eleven Messerschmitts

Separated from his squadron during a sweep over France, a Polish Spitfire pilot spent an exciting hour before landing at a South Coast aerodrome with one gallon of petrol in his tank. He here relates his adventures in his own words.

JUST after leaving the English coast on a fighter-bomber operation, I lost touch with the rest of my squadron, so I flew across to France on my own.

Near Hazebrouck I was just catching up with one of the Polish Squadrons when an Me. 109 got between me and another Spitfire in the rear section of this squadron. The German could not have been more than twenty yards in front of me, and he was creeping up on the Spitfire, which was about the same distance in front of him. I dared not open fire for fear of hitting the leading Spitfire. But suddenly the other Spitfire changed direction, and in that split second I opened fire with my machine-guns from dead astern. The enemy dived, and I followed, firing all the time. Black smoke appeared from the cockpit and then flames. I did not care to follow him down too far in case of attack from behind. So I broke off and looked for the squadron again—but they had disappeared.

Then, about 5,000 feet below me, I saw 12 aircraft flying towards the coast. I was sure they were friendly, so I flew down to join up with the last section of them. But on getting to within 20 yards I saw the black crosses on their wings. They were Messerschmitts.

I attacked the leader of the rearmost section on the starboard side, opening fire at point-blank range. He simply fell away in an uncontrollable spin, with black smoke pouring out. I attacked another, but in the middle of my burst I knew that I myself was being attacked. Then my guns stopped firing, and I had to take evasive action.

Somehow I got right into the middle of 11 Me.s, who must have thought they were being attacked by several aircraft. They all started flying in different directions, head on, sideways, zooming and diving. On several occasions collisions were averted only by inches. Owing to my guns having stopped, I had made up my mind to ram anything which came near, but every time I tried the enemy managed to get out of the way.

By this time we were almost over the sea near Calais, and suddenly—possibly as a result of anti-aircraft fire—my aircraft turned on its back and shot upwards. I was unable to right it, as the aileron control seemed to have failed, but I managed to get into a dive and pulled out almost at sea level.

M. RACZKIEWICZ, President of Poland, at a march past of a Polish Wing of the R.A.F. He presented decorations to Polish air aces.
Photo, L.N.A.

There were no Huns in sight, so I endeavoured to find my way home, and landed with one gallon of petrol. My radio and all the pneumatic system had ceased to function, but my only injuries were a few small splinters in my left leg.

One French Family Kept Me for Seven Months

Captured at St. Valery in June 1940, Pte. John Morris, of Kingston-on-Thames, reached home after 16 months in France. The story of how he was befriended by the French people, reprinted from the "Surrey Comet," is told below by Pte. Morris himself.

AT the beginning of June 1940 I was attached to a group of East Surreys. We had a roving commission and our job was to hold up the enemy's advance for as long as possible in order to give other units of the B.E.F. a better chance to embark.

After several days of hard fighting we were forced to surrender at St. Valery. From there we were marched for 12 days towards the interior. We had hardly any food and had to rely upon the generosity of the French, who would line the roadside and give us anything they had. The Germans even objected to this and on one occasion a guard struck me with his rifle butt when I was about to take a piece of bread offered me by a kindly French peasant.

At night we were turned into a field, like a flock of sheep, and left to find whatever shelter we could. If we wanted any breakfast we had to get up at four o'clock, improvize mugs from any rusty tin cans we were lucky enough to find in the ditches, and then were issued with some coffee and black bread.

At the end of 12 days of this wretched existence I decided to make a break for it. I chose a good moment and made a dash for a swamp. I was there four hours before two small French boys found me. They were really grand. They took off their own clothes so as to rig up some sort of change of garment for me, and they even brought me a slice of their valuable bread spread with sugar. Then they showed me the way to the village and took me to one of their countrymen.

I could speak French and between us we planned out the best route for me to take. He fixed me up with a good suit of clothes, gave me some money and told me where to go for aid when I reached my destination. I had an uneventful trip and I reached the town in question after five days of walking.

In this town I found willing help. The place was full of German soldiers and I had to watch my step all the time. I got hold of an identity card. I was introduced to my "mother" and "father," two "brothers" and a "cousin." We were a very happy family. I stayed with these grand people for the best part of seven months. During part of that time we had five German officers billeted with us.

POLISH FIGHTER SQUADRON with the R.A.F. flying past in formation during a review by the Polish President and Mr. Anthony Biddle, American Ambassador to Poland. Polish fighter pilots are doing good work with the R.A.F., and in this page one of them relates some of his adventures.
Photo, British Official: Crown Copyright

I WAS THERE!

Here are British cadets in the U.S.A. lined up to receive preliminary instruction at Riddle Airfield, Florida. It was in June 1941 that the first batch of 550 cadets set sail for America. They receive the same training as U.S. pilots under the supervision of American Air Corps officers.
Photo, British Official : Crown Copyright

I was accepted as a member of the family who had " just got back from Portugal " (I had been having French and Portuguese lessons from a French professor each day and by now was quite proficient in both languages). When my " mother " told them I was also able to speak English this intrigued the Germans greatly, because they too " had a smattering of English," and so we conversed in the old mother tongue !

By now it was time for me to get moving again, and I went to the commandant to apply for an " ausweiss," or permit, to cross the demarcation line. My identity card stood up to close scrutiny, and with my two " brothers," who were trying to get across to join General de Gaulle, I got on a German troop train going south.

We settled down in a carriage which was already occupied by two German soldiers,

and resigned ourselves to the two days' journey. At lunchtime we got out our meal, which consisted of white bread and jam, and the Germans duly produced their inevitable ration of black bread and sausage. By a little bit of bartering here and swopping there we had a two-course lunch—black bread and sausage, first course, and, for sweet, white bread and jam.

Eventually we arrived in Paris, where my " brothers " and I parted. (I have since heard that they managed to reach England and are now serving with the Free French Army.)

I waited in Paris for a few weeks until everything was prepared for the next stage of my journey. I was given fresh supplies of money and clothing and was instructed how to reach Marseilles, from where I managed to reach England.

A friend and myself decided we couldn't miss the opportunity of seeing Niagara Falls, and we managed to get a lift in a car which was making the double journey. We went there in uniform, and were attacked every five minutes by Americans wishing to photograph us.

A day or two later we entrained for Pensacola, Florida, in air-conditioned coaches which were clean because the windows were kept shut. We changed at Cincinnatti, Ohio, and breakfasted at the station, which was a grand modern affair with a large domed ornamental roof, a marble floor and corridors leading down to the platforms below, from which electric " horses " pulled long trains of baggage trucks.

On arrival at Pensacola we were taken to the naval air station, which is really a marvellous place. The buildings are of brick with white, 20-foot-high stone pillars supporting the porches. Each building is larger than the old school. They are two-storey buildings with marble floors, balconies, showers, classrooms and central heating. Flight students, as we are called, have officers' messing facilities with coloured waiters. We have more than we can eat, and the food is beautifully prepared.

Owing to the fact that our passes ashore are not available yet, we spend our spare time on the beach, which consists of silvery sand. There is plenty of shade from the sun and the temperature of the sea is so high that one can stay in for hours on end. The " ship " is provided with a cool, air-conditioned cinema, where a different programme is shown every night.

At the " ship's " store anything can be purchased very cheaply, from milk shakes, toilet preparations and clothes to cameras and cigarettes, etc. The latter cost 25 cents (1s. 3d.) for 40, with a box of matches thrown in !

We Are Learning to Fly in the U.S.A.

Among the R.A.F. cadets who went to America for their training was Michael Rowe, of Kingston-on-Thames. Some of his first impressions of Canada and the United States in the days before war had reached their shores are here reprinted from the " Surrey Comet."

A**FTER** an uneventful voyage across the Atlantic it was evening when we finally docked in Canada. For the first time in nearly two years we saw the undimmed lights of a city without black-out. The quay itself was floodlit.

Our quarters were semi-permanent bungalows with every convenience. Our first taste of unrationed Canadian food was quite a shock ; there was plenty of everything. For a few days, I must admit, we did nothing but eat.

When we reached the shopping centre by street car, we found shops which remained open nearly all night and milk bars on every corner. There were no " pubs," as all alcohol is controlled ; if one required any beer one had to get a permit at a liquor store, but the beer wasn't worth the trouble of getting.

On arrival at Toronto we found that we were billeted right inside Toronto Exhibition. We were liberally surrounded by livestock—bulls, cows, horses, sheep, etc. We went there in order that the necessary papers for each of us could be made out and signed by the U.S. Consul before we changed our uniform for civilian togs and our Canadian dollars into American dollars and crossed into the States.

The " Ex." includes a livestock exhibition, a large fair, and exhibits of a hundred and one articles of various manufacturers, while there was a 24-hour typing marathon between teams from U.S.A. and Canada which continued throughout the exhibition. In addition there were numerous bandstands, dance pavilions, Ford car races, and demonstra-

tions and firework displays. Last, but not least, crowds of people, all of whom were very friendly towards us, especially the girls ! in !

AN AMERICAN INSTRUCTOR is here seen making notes on the performance of an R.A.F. pupil : his left wing and tail are a little too low. The U.S. Army Air Corps is training 8,000 British pilots a year, and in this page a young British R.A.F. cadet tells of some of his experiences in Canada and America.
Photo, Fox

Editor's Postscript

THE torpedoing of the French passenger steamer Lamoricière by a submarine of a " foreign power " in the Mediterranean with heavy loss of life, is the usual crude Nazi effort to make increase of bad blood between Vichy France and the Allies (idea : might have been a British, Dutch, Polish, or Free French submarine!), but it is not likely to be any more successful in that respect than the torpedoing of the U.S. ship Athenia at the beginning of the War when Goebbels made the infamous suggestion that Churchill was the instigator of that atrocity.

ONE of my various Mediterranean crossings was in the Lamoricière, and it proved the next worst thing to a dreadful journey years before from Alicante to Algiers in the Jebel Zarzar, one of those speedy little vessels built originally for carrying the mails to Port Said. The Lamoricière left Tunis in an evening of African loveliness and everything seemed set for a delightful trip ; the appointments of the ship perfection (it had been built in a British yard only a year or two before) ; service in the dining-room better than on most French liners. I got talking to a man from Marseilles who had just completed a course of study in Spanish but could not speak it with any fluency. He made a bargain with me that I'd talk Spanish to him and let him reply in French, just to get his ear in, and we yarned so until one in the morning, arranging to meet at breakfast and have a great day. The fates intervened. The ship was almost empty of cargo, the wind freshened, in the morning not one passenger could scramble to the dining-room!

WE had an airy deck cabin, but it was an effort to stand erect even for a minute. Fortunately the stewards could stagger from kitchen to cabins, and during the whole of that day they had to serve the passengers in their beds! My wife and I enjoyed all our meals ; there wasn't the slightest tendency to *mal de mer* ; we just could not get up and dress. All the other passengers spent the day similarly, and not until the vessel docked at Marseilles next morning did anybody sit down again in that charming dining-room. The rueful countenance of the jolly fellow from Marseilles when I met him at breakfast showed how sincere was his regret at what we had missed. The sinking of the Lamoricière must bring the total number of vessels I have sailed in that have since been sunk in the Great and the Greater Wars up to ten or more. I can name just now the old Oronsa, the Lusitania, the Empress of Britain, the Lapland, and the Rajputana. But there were several others whose names elude me. What a foul thing that old dual-whiskered beast Tirpitz invented when he started the policy of sinking at sight!

OUR American friends have amused me all my life, since the distant days of Max Adeler and Artemus Ward, and the unique Mark Twain. How much we of the older generation owe of high spirits and entertainment to those old American humorists ! Rather outmoded today. But in one particular America has not changed in half-a-century : its readiness to foretell the wonders its men of science are going to perform—some day. A goodly number of the many marvels its scientists have promised have undoubtedly been brought to perfection, or approximately so ; the talking picture, the cheap motor-car, are examples. But others are still very remote from realization. Nearly fifty years ago American papers were full of an epoch-making invention whereby no more coal would be wasted by the greater part of its heating value being dissipated up the chimney. An American had perfected a process for extracting the heat-giving element from the coal without having to burn it in a furnace ; a few buckets of coal would do the work of tons! I have never yet had the experience of travelling in an American train utilizing this marvellous process, nor in any steamboat so equipped. Like many of their sensational discoveries it's death trod upon the heels of its birth.

AND now comes the president of the U.S. Association of Science Writers (N.B.— " writers," not experimenters) with the yarn that—again some day—a ten-pound bomb will be manufactured which will blast a hole 25 miles in diameter and wreck every structure within 100 miles. And this will be accomplished by the simple process of releasing the terrific energy contained within the atoms of uranium. One of these beautiful little bombs would destroy all Berlin. Two, I suppose, would turn London and its eight millions into the dust whence they came. I

GEN. CHIANG KAI-SHEK, placed in supreme command of all land and sea forces of the United Nations operating in the Chinese theatre of war. 55 years old, he is acknowledged to be one of the world's greatest generals.   *Photo, Associated Press*

hope that Lord Beaverbrook will indent for the first of those handy little ten-pounders. Good thing America is now in the War, as Hitler might have got in first with his reservation. I wish I could believe this American " science writer " (Jules Verne had nothing on any of them), for an assortment of these ten-pound uranium bombs would solve the problem of how to get rid of Germany from this planet.

IN a comparison between the Russian soldier of 1812 and 1941 a correspondent in " The Times " remarks that the Russians' " fighting qualities have remained the same : great tenacity, courage and endurance ; supreme skill in guerilla fighting, fanaticism and *psychic resistance to defeat*." Quite a few Germans who should know their countrymen have written to the effect that Germany expects to be defeated. " Let us die like the Goths," is a line by a Nazi poet. Death is a favourite theme among German artists and writers, and the Dance of Death has inspired many a Teuton painter. Their most popular modern poet, Rainer Maria Rilke, whose life by Prof. Butler I am reading this week-end, infuses many elements of genuine beauty into his melancholic philosophy of despair. A psychologist might diagnose the whole Hitler effort as a monstrous gesture of despair. Beneath a veneer of glory a profound tendency to melancholy and defeatism is ready to express itself at the destined moment.

COMPLETELY amoral, Hitlerism has no spiritual support when things go wrong, and the retreat of the Nazis on the east front may even be the beginning of the rot. Germany expected Britain to fall to pieces after Dunkirk, precisely because she herself would have collapsed in similar circumstances. She also expected Russia to disintegrate under the Nazi sledgehammer in the summer and autumn of 1941. But both Britain and Russia were able to draw on that reserve of inner power which is common to all righteous causes assailed by the forces of evil. This quality is a kind of immortal genius greater than courage itself. No one can deny that the Germans are brave, but they are lacking in that superlative stamina which is ultimately more powerful than armaments. The most hopeful sign as the war proceeds is that more and more men and women in Occupied Europe and beyond are increasing their " psychic resistance to defeat."

WE must all take an occasional holiday from the War, and I can always find surcease in books that have no bearing on the conflict. Such a book is Mr. Grant Richards' record of his friendship with A. E. Housman. No poet could have been happier with his publisher than the author of " A Shropshire Lad ": from 1897 till Housman's death in 1936 their friendship was unimpaired. This mutual understanding and respect seem to have been one long holiday, for publisher and poet seldom met but to travel in pleasant places, either in England or France, and collect a memorable vintage or some culinary *chef d'oeuvre* at a favourite restaurant or inn. A. E. Housman emerges from Richards' memories not as a dry scholar or Olympian recluse but as a genial and fastidious host.

Printed in England and published on the 10th, 20th, and 30th of each month by the Proprietors, The Amalgamated Press, Ltd., The Fleetway House, Farringdon Street, London, E.C.4. Registered for transmission by Canadian Magazine Post. Sole Agents for Australia and New Zealand : Messrs. Gordon & Gotch, Ltd. ; and for South Africa : Central News Agency, Ltd. January 30th, 1942.   S.S.   *Editorial Address* : JOHN CARPENTER HOUSE, WHITEFRIARS, LONDON, E.C.4

Vol 5   # The War Illustrated   Nº 120

Edited by Sir John Hammerton

FOURPENCE

FEB. 10TH. 1942

AMERICA'S VANGUARD COMES TO BRITAIN. This radioed photograph shows United States infantrymen, of what is officially styled
" The United States Army Forces in the British Isles," marching through the streets of a port in Northern Ireland after their disembarka-
tion on Jan. 26. To the music of the " Star-Spangled Banner " they came down the gangways, and they reciprocated their welcome with
" There'll Always Be An England." Officially welcomed by the Duke of Abercorn, Governor-General of Northern Ireland, Major-General
Hartle, the American G.O.C., smilingly replied, " We are very glad to be here. I assure you."   *Photo, Keystone*

WHAT THE WAR HAS TAUGHT US ABOUT JAPAN

THE old joke about the British War Office " always preparing for the last war " was a wisecrack, with a core of reality to it. But it would not be fair to blame only the War Office for our unreadiness to keep our military methods up to date. It is a failing which affects large numbers of Britons, many of them holding important responsible posts—but not showing very much sense of responsibility.

How often we have to learn vital facts about enemies after they have begun war against us ! We are not, it is true, alone in this. It would be impossible to imagine a ruder and more unpleasant awakening than the American people had when the Japanese, whom they had despised, ridiculed, spoken of with contempt as monkeys, sank two of their battleships the moment war started, and within a few weeks made America's position in the Philippines almost untenable.

WHENCE this refusal to face realities ? The plain truth is that both the Americans and we ourselves were misled by those who ought to have studied the realities and to have kept us better informed —that is to say, the diplomats and also some of the Press correspondents in Japan. For example, I see in the " Daily Mail '' an article telling us how dearly we must pay for not knowing what harm the Japanese could do us as one of the Axis Powers. That article is by Mr. Ward Price, who, for years, was engaged in cracking up Hitler and Mussolini and the Japanese !

But while many have failed us in recent years, it is not at all fantastic to ask how much two gentlemen named W. S. Gilbert and Arthur Sullivan contributed half a century ago to make us, and a good many Americans, too, think lightly and condescendingly of the Japanese. Very large numbers of people must have got their ideas of Japan from " The Mikado," must have found it difficult to take seriously a country they had seen represented in a comic light. Silly ? Yes, but the great majority are unfortunately prone to be silly in just that way.

DID we not underrate the Boers when the South African War began in 1899, because we had seen them pictured in cartoons as peasants with bushy beards and long, curly pipes, in clothes looking the very reverse of military smartness ? Did not the French fancy they could safely take on the Germans in 1870 for the reason very largely that they had been taught to think of them as dreamy, scholarly, unpractical folk ? And were not the Germans equally disillusioned in 1914 when they imagined our men to be the " flannelled fools at the wicket and muddied oafs at the goal," of whom Kipling wrote in a bad temper, never having been any good at games himself and disliking everybody who was ?

Public opinion is such a curious mixture, made up of very few facts, a great deal of ignorance and prejudice, lies deliberately invented, jokes tossed about. We did not feel contempt for the Japs, as Americans did. They had been our allies for a long time. We had sympathized

with them in their war against the Tsardom and fought with them against Imperial Germany. But we did not, when the alliance came to an end, learn to look on them as possible, even probable, enemies in the Far East, where our interests clashed with theirs at so many points.

WE were told up to the time of their sudden, treacherous attack (treacherous, because their envoys were actually engaged in negotiations at Washington when their air force began bombing) that there was not much likelihood of their making war —at any rate not just then ! We were assured that they lacked necessary war materials. We were given to understand that their aircraft were flimsily built and their pilots unreliable. What a lot we have had to learn painfully since then !

The first lesson, and the most valuable if we take it in the right spirit, is that they had decided long before on the kind of warfare they meant to go in for, and had prepared for it with meticulous care. Let us select a few examples of this.

They got Germans to instruct them in dive-bombing, and they practised on the Chinese.

They realized the importance of what Napoleon called " having one man more than the enemy has," and resolved to throw in their strength without considering losses. Our reports continually say : " We were heavily outnumbered." They have copied in Malaya the methods of China's guerilla bands which try to get behind the force they are attacking and never make frontal assaults.

Another saying of Napoleon's (or was this one Wellington's ?) they have acted upon with thoroughness and cunning—about " the importance of knowing what is going on behind the hill over there."

THEY were practising Fifth Column tactics long before Hitler, long before the Spanish Civil War which gave rise to the

expression (one of the generals on Franco's side said he had four columns converging on Madrid and a fifth inside the city, meaning, of course, sympathizers with the rebellion). Now we know why the Japanese who settled in such large numbers in the countries their Government coveted were mostly photographers, barbers, dentists, gardeners and indoor servants.

No surprise or alarm was felt when a professional cameraman was seen taking pictures. No thought of hostile ears being open damped down gossip in barbers' shops. Dentists could mix on friendly terms with prominent persons in a community. Valets and cooks could pick up odds and ends of information. Over the cultivation of flowers or vegetables employers often become confidential with their outdoor employees. As long as thirty-five years ago British Columbians wondered why Japanese came over to Vancouver in such regular streams and seemed most of them to have plenty of money. Californians asked the same question. Now they know the answer.

THAT same genius for working underground was displayed in the secrecy which shrouded their preparations for war. A former British Ambassador in Tokyo has made the naive confession that " while we know Japan has been building hard for the last five years in her naval dockyards, that is all we do know, and she may now be in possession of two or three forty-thousand-ton battleships." The same lack of information was admitted about Japanese building of aircraft. They were said to aim at 30,000 a year and to be able to produce no more than 10,000; but no one really knew. It may well be asked, What do our Embassies do with the Secret Service funds with which they are liberally provided at the expense of British taxpayers ?

We might inquire also why the correspondent of " The Times " at Singapore should say : " The Japanese are employing novel tactics in fighting quite unlike any that has taken place during the last five years in Europe, Asia or Africa." In this sounds the familiar note of astonishment that anyone should do anything new ! The Japanese are superior to us in jungle warfare. They have developed the German method of infiltration. To make a way through the thick bush in any sort of formation is out of the question. Therefore they tell off small groups, even single men, to aim at reaching a point some miles ahead. They climb trees for concealment, and for sniping. They lie in water-logged paddy fields, where they may be submerged for hours at a time.

SO, to sum up, the chief lessons we have to learn from the war with Japan up to the present are (1) never to underestimate those who may become our enemies ; (2) always to look ahead and prepare for the warfare that is coming rather than that which is past ; (3) to insist that our diplomats, secret service agents, and colonial officials shall be men of quick mind and close observation, who will give us warning of dangers before and not after they occur.

H. HAMILTON FYFE

JAPANESE TANK passing over an emergency bridge during army manoeuvres. The Japanese invading armies have managed to land tanks in considerable numbers both in Malaya and Luzon. *Photo, Associated Press*

Today It Is Bombs on Singapore : Tomorrow ?

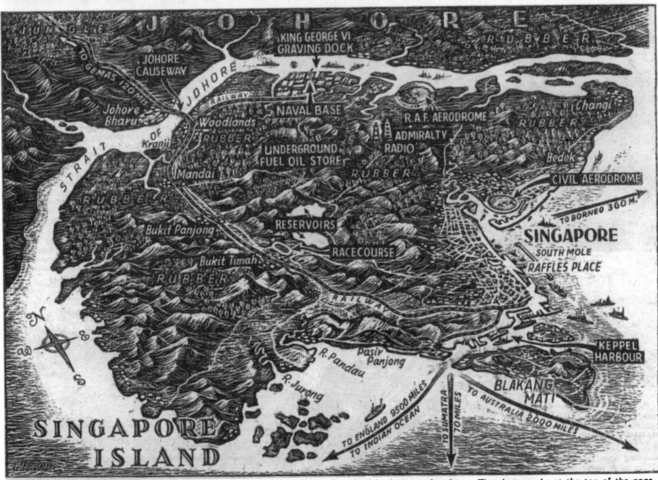

SINGAPORE ISLAND, a relief map of which is seen above, has been heavily raided by Japanese bombers. The photographs at the top of the page show Tamil workmen clearing up raid debris after bombs had fallen in the residential and business quarter of the town of Singapore.

Photo, British Newsreel. Diagram specially drawn for THE WAR ILLUSTRATED *by Harrop*

The Gun that Knocks Out the German Tanks

THE Royal Regiment of Artillery is equipped with one of the best guns in the world—the 25-pounder "gunhow," which combines the functions of a howitzer and a high-velocity field gun. Its pedigree is derived from its predecessors, the 4·5 howitzer and the 18-pounder field gun, which were the standard field pieces prior to the last World War.

The range of the British 25-pounder is said to be far greater than that of its German equivalent, and whereas the latter has a traverse of only 60 degrees, the British gun, by means of the traverse wheel which constitutes its ground platform, can sweep through a complete circle.

It has proved its great value in the Libyan campaign, where again and again it has turned the tide. Used as a high-velocity gun it created havoc among the German tanks, achieving the same results as the Russian anti-tank planes (see page 474). In some cases a single shell passed through two German tanks and even then did further damage beyond. 25-pounder field regiments are now completely mechanized, and as our forces expand and production increases this British "gunhow" is likely to have considerable influence on the course of future campaigns.

Bottom left is the badge of the Royal Regiment of Artillery, with its mottoes meaning "Everywhere" and "Where Duty and Glory Lead."

The British 25-pounder gun is featured in this page. Top, a close-up; centre, an action photograph taken near Tobruk; right, diagram indicating the gun's salient features.

Photos, British Official

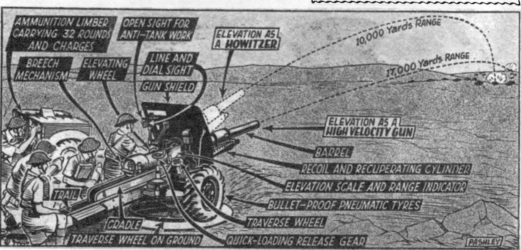

AMMUNITION LIMBER CARRYING 32 ROUNDS AND CHARGES — OPEN SIGHT FOR ANTI-TANK WORK — ELEVATION AS A HOWITZER — 10,000 Yards RANGE — 17,000 Yards RANGE — BREECH MECHANISM — ELEVATING WHEEL — LINE AND DIAL SIGHT — GUN SHIELD — ELEVATION AS A HIGH VELOCITY GUN — BARREL — RECOIL AND RECUPERATING CYLINDER — ELEVATION SCALE AND RANGE INDICATOR — BULLET-PROOF PNEUMATIC TYRES — TRAVERSE WHEEL — TRAIL — CRADLE — TRAVERSE WHEEL ON GROUND — QUICK-LOADING RELEASE GEAR — PASHLEY

Australia's Record Score in the Libyan 'Test'

Men of an Australian Fighter Squadron in Libya sorting out mail from home (above). Right, Tomahawks of the R.A.A.F. in the Western Desert.

A member of the R.A.A.F. gets his breakfast in the desert, circle. An American-built Tomahawk of the R.A.A.F. in flight over Cyrenaica, centre right.

Members of the R.A.A.F. now flying Blenheim bombers in the Libyan battle are perched on top of one of their aircraft which bears as its emblem a kangaroo speeding forward with a bomb. The R.A.A.F. in the Middle East has a record of having brought down 18 enemy planes for every one of its own that has been lost.

Photos, British and Australian Official

Australia Meets the Threat of Invasion

Until the entry of Japan into the struggle, Australia seemed to be far removed from the war's main battlefields. Now, however, following Japan's attacks on the islands lying off the continent's northern coast, she finds herself in the front line indeed.

"FOR the first time in history Australian territory has been attacked; for the first time in history a foreign invader is trying to get a footing on Australian territorial soil. The enemy's next stroke may well be an attempt on the mainland itself." So declared Mr. J. M. Forde—Army Minister in the Commonwealth Government and Acting Premier in the temporary absence at Perth of Mr. Curtin, the Labour Prime Minister—in a broadcast to the Australian people on Jan. 23, following the news that Japanese troops had effected landings in New Guinea and the Bismarck Archipelago, territories mandated to Australia by the League of Nations after the last war.

The invaders first made their appearance early in the morning of Jan. 21, when strong forces of Japanese aircraft appeared over the Bismarck Archipelago and northern New Guinea. Shortly afterwards several towns in New Ireland and New Guinea were bombed. On the next day a Japanese armada approached Rabaul in New Britain. Rabaul and other places in the archipelago were raided by Japanese planes, launched from several aircraft carriers; and on Jan. 24 numerous Japanese landings were reported

could be settled or would almost settle itself as soon as Hitler and his Nazis had been routed in Europe, the Middle East, and the Atlantic. Naturally enough, such a view found small countenance in the Antipodes. For the Australians and New Zealanders the struggle in Malaya—the gateway to Australia—is no side-show, but a most vital battle. Small wonder, then, that the criticisms of the conduct of the Malayan campaign were caustic in the extreme. Bitter, too, were the denunciations of the civil and military administrations at Singapore; ineptness and inefficiency were only two of the ingredients constituting what was scathingly referred to as the "Singapore mentality."

"It is a pity so much will have to be suffered by gallant soldiers and innocent people," said Mr. Herbert Evatt, Commonwealth Minister for External Affairs, on Jan. 23, "to prove that Malaya is not a side-show but a primary and vital struggle between the Democracies and the three Axis powers. We can weaken Hitler and his power to invade Britain and attack the United States by an all-in fight against Japan now, not later. Later may be too late . . . If Japan is allowed to control or accumulate

ment, he went on, regarded the Pacific struggle as primarily one in which the United States and Australia must have the fullest say in the direction of the Democracies' fighting plan. "Australia looks to America, free from any pangs as to traditional links or kinship with the United Kingdom. We know the problem that the United Kingdom faces, but we know that Australia can go and Britain still hold on. We are determined that Australia shall not go . . ." Australian policy would be shaped towards obtaining Russian aid and working out, with the United States as the major factor, a plan of Pacific strategy, with the British, Chinese and Dutch forces.

This statement by the Labour Premier aroused much criticism in Australia, and Mr. Curtin soon found it advisable to declare that he was not suggesting for a moment any weakening of the ties between the United Kingdom and Australia. Australia looked towards the United States, he said, as England looked to France when the *entente cordiale* was concluded; the new relationship to the United States was a military alliance, necessitated by geographical considerations. His article meant that Australia as part of the British Commonwealth must face the strategic problems of our own defenders with realism, and it was because Australians wished to remain part of the Commonwealth that they insisted that their voice should be heard. And that voice (so it was urged "down under") was not being heard, or heard sufficiently. Cabling from England to his newspapers in Australia, Sir Keith Murdoch argued that Britain was taking a tremendous responsibility, "unwise in any event, but shattering in effect if things go wrong, in deciding for all British people everywhere, including the nine million whites in the South-Western Pacific, 12,000 miles away, all matters relating to strategy and the direction of the war."

So Sir Keith Murdoch urged the entry of a "stout Dominion element" into the War Cabinet, and the plea was immensely reinforced on Jan. 24, when it was announced that Mr. Curtin had asked Mr. Churchill to accord Australia a seat in an Imperial War Cabinet and also in a Pacific War Council, both yet to be formed.

Meanwhile, Australia was making ready to meet the invader. The cream of her young men, 200,000 volunteers, were operating in the Australian Imperial Force, fighting in the jungles of Malaya or in the Middle East, but all men capable of bearing arms were mobilized by Mr. Forde on Jan. 24.

Some there were who visualized the almost immediate descent by the Japanese on the Australian mainland; others were of the opinion that if war came to Australia it would take the shape of air raids on Darwin, and on Cairns, Townsville, and other places on the east coast of Queensland. The Japanese might attempt a drive across the continent from Darwin to Adelaide, or along the Queensland coastal belt to Brisbane and perhaps to Sydney. But Australia is a country of vast distances and of indifferent communications. Thus it seemed on balance more probable that the Japanese would attempt to consolidate their hold on both sides of the Torres Strait, for the strait is an Allied life-line, and through it (we may presume) planes and ships are being rushed from America to the support of the Netherlands East Indies, Malaya and Singapore. If that life-line be cut, then the tide of succour must be diverted some thousands of miles round the south of the Australian continent.

NEW GUINEA and the islands of the Bismarck Archipelago. Rabaul, within 800 miles of the Australian mainland, was attacked by the Japanese on Jan. 22, and very heavy air attacks were made over the entire archipelago. The arrows show direction of Japanese threats to Australia. The Torres Strait is only 100 miles wide. *Courtesy of the "Daily Mirror"*

to be taking place in New Guinea, the Bismarck Archipelago and the Solomon Islands. Following the issue of the communiqué giving this news, Mr. Forde declared that: "Australian militia forces are probably in action against Japanese troops trying to gain a foothold on our shores. There can be no doubt that we will hear the roar of cannon along the coast of this country, and that the Japanese plan to attack Australian towns." A similar warning was uttered by Mr. Curtin, the Prime Minister, in a nation-wide broadcast. The country must be prepared, he said, for the shelling and raiding from the air of her cities. Japan had "mountains of supplies and equipment" and so was able to take the offensive everywhere. Nor could he hold out any hope that the Allies had reached the end of their reverses. Australia must just stick it until the Allies had won the Battle of Production.

In this hour of supreme and altogether unexpected crisis many voices were raised in Australia in criticism of the policy of the Allies. On every hand the view was expressed that the war leaders in London and Washington regarded the struggle in the south-west Pacific as a side-show—something which

vast stores of raw material in the Pacific, the economic blockade to some extent can be turned against the Empire. If Japan is allowed to bring more and more strategic bases under her sway, her powerful navy and air force will then turn and help Hitler to subjugate Britain and the United States." Then Mr. J. Beasley, Minister for Supply and Development, after declaring that "the rising sun is nearly overhead," urged that ships, guns, planes, and troops must be got to Malaya *now*. "The Battle of the Pacific won, we can beat the Japanese navy here; the Battle of the Pacific lost, the Japanese navy is ready for service in the Atlantic. So the Battle of the Pacific is the Battle of the Atlantic."

This point of view was not new; indeed, it had been expressed by Australian politicians and Australian newspapers since the opening of the Japanese war, even earlier. Shortly after Christmas Mr. Curtin himself had "spilt the beans" in an article in the "Melbourne Herald," in which he had declared that Australians refused to accept the dictum that the Pacific struggle should be treated as a "subordinate segment of the general conflict." The Australian Govern-

Now India Triumphs Where Rome Held Sway

INDIAN TROOPS IN LIBYA include the Rajput Rifles. Men of this regiment are here seen clearing the ruins of ancient Cyrene after its capture. The Indian regiments in Libya have fully maintained their great traditions, and the 4th Indian Division was mentioned in dispatches from Cairo for the gallant manner in which it beat off three strong German counter-attacks, delivered with superior forces, on Dec. 13, 14 and 15, 1941. The Indian Army has now grown to nearly 1,000,000—more than four times its pre-war size.

Photo. British Official: Crown Copyright

Our Searchlight on the War

SALUTE TO GREECE

Neither famine nor threats have persuaded the Greeks to surrender any of the British and Anzac officers and soldiers who remain in hiding among them. The Greek death rate each day from starvation and exposure in Athens and Piraeus alone exceeds 2,000.

THE tragedy of Greece is the supreme sorrow and irony of the war. To recall that this beautiful land and valiant people thrashed the contemptible Fascist bully only to be ground down by the German homicides is to make one despair at the terrible, if temporary, power of evil over good. It is the bitterest news to know that such heroism as the Greeks displayed is rewarded only by cruelty and starvation, and that men and women fall down and die in the streets of Athens, the fount of Liberty and the shrine of Demosthenes. Under the auspices of the International Red Cross we are trying to get food through to Greece, and we hope that Turkey and Egypt will be able to do something. The German, Italian and Bulgarian scum now in occupation take pleasure in making Greece suffer for her courage. We can only console ourselves with the knowledge that the eclipse of Hellas is no more than a miserable phenomenon that will pass. There will come a time when Greece will rise again greater in power and even more profound in spirit for her sublime defiance and grief. While the Allies fight and toil with that

H.R.H. the DUKE OF CONNAUGHT, who died on Jan. 16, 1942, at the age of 91. He was a great-uncle of the King and senior Field-Marshal of the British Army. *Photo, Wide World*

object, the whole civilized world salutes her. The future of Greece is bound inextricably with ours. She will be unleashed from the tyranny of the mechanized savages who now pollute her soil.

REICHENAU THE RUTHLESS

He was "the standard-bearer of the thoughts of a new age," one who imparted lustre to the "eternal verities" of the German soldier, and whose name would live for ever in the history of the German people and its armed forces.—Hitler's Order of the Day on the death of Marshal von Reichenau

NAZI butcher number one on the east front, Marshal von Reichenau died mysteriously, but his crimes will live after him. It is interesting to compare Hitler's eulogium with the Reichenau Document, a secret order signed by the commander of the 6th German Army, and discovered by the Red Army among other Gestapo papers at Klin after the Germans' precipitate retreat. No plainer incitement to torture and murder emanated from the councils of the sadistic Gestapo. Lest any German soldier should misunderstand his duty he is frankly told that his task "goes beyond the scope of the normal functions of the military." Some Nazis are acting "frivolously" in allowing any food to the Russians. Such an act is "unnecessary humanitarianism." Unless the Russians behind the German lines collaborate with the Nazis they are to be exterminated. All buildings which are not of use as quarters for German army units, as well as all "symbols of the domination of the Bolsheviks, must be destroyed. No treasures of history and art in the east are of the slightest consequence." There is authentic evidence in a

further document appended to this order that Hitler inspired this policy. "The standard-bearer of the thoughts of a new age" carried out his master's ideas to the letter. All Nazi thoughts have one beginning and one end. They begin with envy and hatred and end with pillage, murder and destruction. In that sense the "eternal verities" of the German soldier have a meaning. They are true to the nature of the blond beast.

GANGSTERS AND MYTHS

Japanese propaganda has been endeavouring to prove that parts of South America were once conquered and civilized by Japan.

LIKE the German tribes who excite their barbarous mentality with dreams of Aryanism and supermen, the Japanese are trying to prove that they are the only civilized Asiatics. The truth is that, in spite of their arts, which, in any case, do not approach in grandeur and antiquity those of the Chinese, the Japanese are an essentially primitive people. While they have quickly assimilated the industrial ideas of the west they have never acquired any of our superior ethical standards. It is no mere accident that the two most backward nations, spiritually, are now fighting side by side under a similar oligarchy of murder for the enslavement of mankind. Not only do the Japanese hope to spread their tyranny over Asia, but they have cast covetous eyes on South America, and the complete break of the 21 South American states with the Axis is a logical policy. The two Americas must unite against Japanese and German aggression. As part of their imperialistic programme the yellow men long ago started a propaganda drive in Peru, and many books were published by the Japanese in Spanish to the effect that they were the founders of the Inca empire. Needless to say, this surprising and ingenious idea is repugnant to Indo-Americans who believe in an original kinship with the civilized Chinese.

IF THE NAZIS INVADE US

Quite a few Englishmen are wondering how best they could serve their country in the event of a German invasion in force.

WE must never forget that Britain is still the chief obstacle to German world domination. She stopped the enemy in 1940, and she stopped him alone. The Nazis may come at us some day in full fury. With our characteristic optimism there is a tendency to think that the Home Front has seen the worst. Civil Defence rose splendidly to the occasion under bombing and will do so again when the time comes, but forced inactivity must naturally affect discipline and enthusiasm. All male civil defenders should include in their training a compulsory course of arms instruction, so that, in an emergency, they can take their place in the Home Guard. When the Germans were first nearing Moscow there was a Soviet *levée en masse*, and total mobilization for *service with the army* of every able-bodied man and woman between 16 and 50. The men were sandwiched among the regulars, the women were ordered to dig trenches and set tank traps. They stopped the Germans, but they were able to do this only because they had been training for some months previously.

PACT OF BLOOD

From the prairies and the teeming cities of Iowa and the North-West, these American soldiers had come thousands of miles, not to sojourn among strangers, but among grateful friends and among comrades of the British fighting services.—Sir Archibald Sinclair, in welcoming American troops landed in Northern Ireland

THE arrival of United States soldiers in Northern Ireland is a historic and heartening event. As in 1917 so in 1942, the New World comes to help save Europe from the old Germanic curse. It was the presence of American troops in ever-increasing numbers on the battlefields of France that finally convinced the Kaiser that Germany could not win. The sons of their fathers again take up the challenge thrown down by tyranny. They, like us, will look upon this war as part of the old unfinished war of 1914-18. But this time the nations will not slip back into isolationism, indifference and cynicism, for the progressive peoples in Britain, America and Russia are determined on collaboration in the ideals of freedom, justice and peace. In welcoming the American troops, how truly thankful we are that Ulster remains part of the Empire! The vision and patriotism of Northern Ireland recalls the splendid work of Earl Craigavon. Meanwhile Mr. de Valera's Eire clings to an out-moded and increasingly dangerous neutrality—a not too happy status for any nation professing liberty at this supreme crisis in human fate.

Railings being removed from Parliament Square, Westminster, to provide war scrap. Inset, Mr. G. M. Carter, appointed Director of Demolition and Recovery. *Photos, Keystone, Associated Press*

WISE FINANCIAL POLICY

"No war, least of all this present one, so stupendous in its expenditure, can be waged without a measure of inflation."—Sir Noton Barclay

OUR financial and monetary policy in this war is far more effective than it was during 1914-18. A measure of inflation is inevitable at a time when the earning power of the nation is universally increased, but high taxation, E.P.D., and the curtailment of spending power due to rationing and the general limitation of purchasable articles have reduced consumption. Whereas in the last war certain luxury trades appeared to flourish, and the new rich of all classes were able to squander their money, if they felt so inclined, there is little to buy in the present circumstances. The policy of restricting the supply of goods is the simplest way of preventing over-consumption, for real inflation begins when many people buy more than they need. Inflation, like a high temperature, generally results in a collapse, or financial slump. This happened after the last war as a result of an orgy of over-spending, speculation and capital expansion. Any excess of purchasing power over production should therefore be watched, and wartime control of finance should not be suddenly abandoned. We must get back to freedom in this respect, but restrictions should be gradually modified to avoid unhealthy financial conditions.

An operational barge, where small balloons of London's river balloon barrage units are kept. One of the balloons is going to be transferred by R.A.F. speed boat to a destroyer whose balloon needs repair. *Photo, Fox*

In Russia the Poles Are Forming an Army

Men of the Polish divisions now being raised on Russian soil are seen above, marching along a country road in Russia. They are being equipped by Britain and the United States.

Gen. Sikorski, Polish Premier and C.-in-C., inspects the Polish Women's Auxiliary Service formed in Russia. Circle, Gen. Anders, commander of the Polish forces raised in Russia.

POLISH ARMY IN RUSSIA, now nearly ready to take the field, symbolizes the new policy for cooperation between Free Poland and the Soviet Union. The original agreement between Russia and Poland, reached shortly after the Nazi invasion of Russia, gave the Poles the right to form an autonomous army to fight under Soviet High Command. Two divisions were originally envisaged, but at a conference between Mr. Stalin and Gen. Sikorski in Dec. 1941 the number was brought up to 100,000 men. Mr. Stalin agreed that 25,000 Polish soldiers should be sent to the Middle East. Centre, Polish infantry training in Russia. Below, Polish artillery.

Photos, Polish Ministry of Information

Fighting Amid the Snow

The Red Army in Action

Specially Drawn for
THE WAR ILLUSTRATED
By Haworth

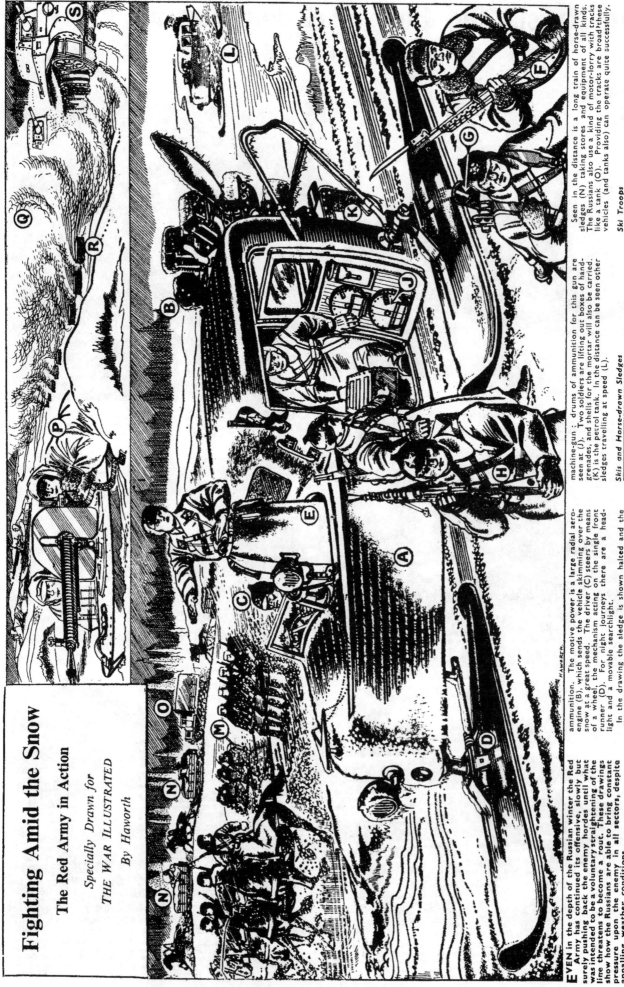

EVEN in the depth of the Russian winter the Red Army has continued its offensive, slowly but surely pushing back the enemy hordes until what was intended to be a voluntary straightening of the line threatens to become a rout. These drawings show how the Russians are able to bring constant pressure upon the enemy in all sectors, despite appalling weather conditions.

Air Sledges

In the main drawing is shown a powerful air sledge (A); it carries six men and an officer as well as arms and ammunition. The motive power is a large radial aero-engine (B), which sends the vehicle skimming over the snow at a great speed. The driver (C) steers by means of a wheel, the mechanism acting on the single front runner (D). For night journeys there are a head-light and a movable searchlight.

In the drawing the sledge is shown halted and the officer (E), watching the enemy through his field-glasses, directs the operations of the sledge crew. The arms these men carry illustrate the types of light weapons used by the Russians: (F) an automatic rifle with a short knife-like bayonet, (G) a small mortar, (H) a light machine-gun; drums of ammunition for this gun are seen at (J). Two soldiers are lifting out boxes of hand-grenades, and shells for the mortar will also be carried (K) is the petrol tank. In the distance can be seen other vehicles travelling at speed (L).

Skis and Horse-drawn Sledges

Another method by which the Russians move large numbers of men quickly is shown at (M). By means of a special harness and a pole each cavalryman pulls two infantrymen on skis along with him. Sometimes two horses are harnessed together to take six men.

Seen in the distance is a long train of horse-drawn sledges (N) taking stores and equipment of all kinds. The Russians also use a kind of motor-lorry with tracks like a tank (O). Providing the tracks are broad these vehicles (and tanks also) can operate quite successfully.

Ski Troops

The inset drawing shows (P) Russian ski-troops with machine-guns mounted on sledges. The two men pull the sledge by means o a harness. A white smoke-screen (Q), made by smoke pots (R), is often used to cover the movements of tanks (S), which are painted white.

Mojaisk Falls: the Great Retreat Goes On

When Russian troops entered Mojaisk on the morning of Jan. 19, the final stage of the offensive operations in this sector of the Moscow front was completed, and the last direct threat to the Russian capital, whose imminent fall Hitler has so often proclaimed, was removed.

MOJAISK, captured by the Germans on Oct. 14, 1941, was certainly intended to remain in German hands for the winter. Of great strategical importance, barring a main road and a railway, it was converted into a bastion by the Nazis, with three general lines of defence which included several strongly fortified villages, concrete blockhouses, earthworks, and barbed wire.

General Zhukov probably decided, when the Russian counter-offensive was launched on Dec. 6, that nothing could be gained by a frontal attack on so strong a position. He set out, first of all, to outflank it north and south, and the map in page 446 shows how, by Jan. 13, 1942, the Soviet armies on the Moscow front had thrust deep wedges into the German lines reaching nearly to Rjev in the north and Lyudinovo in the south, thus threatening the Nazi forces at Mojaisk with encirclement. By a series of operations which began in Dec. the Germans were driven back from their advance positions at Svenigorod and Golitsino, almost at the gates of Moscow, to the defences of Mojaisk, where they were held while the outflanking movements were made with great success.

Mojaisk being the key to the Russian capital, it was here that the Germans had probably concentrated more war material than at any other point of the front, which would explain why they defended the place with such ferocity when strategically, with the two arms of a pincers closing around it, the position was indefensible. Moreover, between it and Smolensk, 200 miles in the rear, there were no natural obstacles which could be turned into a line of defence.

Having seriously defeated the enemy at Dorokhovo, south-east of Mojaisk, on Jan. 13, the Soviet forces hurled the Germans back on to the Mojaisk defences. The outskirts of the town were encircled by a powerful line of fortifications, but the Russians, by marching over trackless land, by-passed many strong points and infiltrated through the German defences with great skill, appearing suddenly before Mojaisk itself.

The battle for Mojaisk proper began on Sunday, Jan. 11. Lieut-Gen. Govorov, whose forces captured the town, told a war correspondent of "Pravda" how the place was stormed. "In the northern, eastern, and southern outskirts of the town," he said, "the Germans had constructed rows of

GEN. VON REICHENAU, who commanded a German Group on the Ukraine Front, has died, according to a Berlin statement issued on Jan. 17, "as the result of a stroke."
Photo, International Graphic Press

blockhouses. In the centre brick houses were transformed into strong points. It was possible to overcome this formidable system of defence only by means of concentrated artillery and trench-mortar attacks. In the eastern sector the firing points and enemy blockhouses were subjected to terrific direct fire by our artillery. Dive-bombers attacked the retreating enemy columns day and night."

While this reduction of the fortifications was proceeding the pincers movement north and south of the town was making such headway that, under the threat of being surrounded, the Germans were compelled to evacuate the town, leaving only a rearguard to cover their retreat. Then Soviet infantry broke through into the south-west suburbs of Mojaisk and occupied the railway station. At the same time other units, entering the northern suburb, wiped out the defending bodies of Germans. Street by street the German rearguard was mopped up, Soviet troops finally

penetrated into the western part of the town, and on Jan. 19 Comrade Koltunov raised the Red Flag once more over the building of the City Soviet. So ended what, in effect, was the siege of Moscow.

Four days after the recapture of Mojaisk a large meeting of the working population of the town was held, and the secretary of the Mojaisk committee of the Bolshevik Party, who, while the Germans were in occupation, had been directing guerilla operations in the district, announced that the restoration of the town would begin immediately, special repair brigades having been formed.

An interesting sidelight on the campaign is given by the "Daily Telegraph" Special Correspondent in Russia, who states that the Germans got away most of their heavy equipment from Mojaisk by rail, having reduced the Russian broad gauge to their standard European one. Now the Russian Labour Corps are working like ants to change it back again.

Following the fall of Mojaisk the Russian troops pressed on, and the next major operation was the deepening of the wedge that had been driven into the German lines on a seventy-mile front from Kholm to Toropets, midway between Moscow and Leningrad. The main objective on this front was the freeing of the Leningrad-Ukraine railway, fifty miles west of Kholm, one of the German army's lifelines. By Jan. 24 the Russians were reported to be within forty miles of the important railway centre of Veliki Luki, and Russian forces advancing south from Staraya Toropa and Zapadnaya Dvina directly threatened Smolensk, where Hitler had established his winter H.Q., with envelopment. A flanking movement from the south in the direction of Yelnia accentuated this menace.

Moreover, the greater part of the German armies lying between Novgorod and Lake Peipus receive rations and supplies by the Leningrad-Ukraine line and its seizure by the Russians would be a heavy blow to the besiegers of Leningrad. Apart, too, from the importance of the railway itself, the development of the Russian advance westwards towards Pskov represents a growing menace to the German troops freezing in front of Leningrad. Should the Soviet troops continue to advance at the same rate of speed, the assailants of Leningrad may be forced to beat a hasty retreat towards the Baltic States to avoid being cut off.

YASNAYA POLYANA, near Tula, was the home of Leo Tolstoy, the great Russian writer, who was born and was buried there. Russian officers are standing by Tolstoy's grave after the recapture of the town. On the left is part of the burial ground of German soldiers. Tolstoy's house, which had been for many years a Tolstoy museum, was sacked and defiled by the Nazis when they captured the town. Relics, manuscripts, books and pictures were either stolen or destroyed and the furniture was used for making fires for heating German troops. *Photo, Planet News*

'Victory or Not, An Episode of War Most Glo

Left, Sikh troops entering
Above, a Blenheim bomber

IN Cyrenaica a new battle
forces began to push eas
occupied Jedabia, and swiftly
midway between Jedabia and
the convoys attacked in the
achieved a tactical surprise f
which comprised our advance
Afrika Korps These light fo
panzers came up against the
major scale developed.

All the same, when Mr.
speech in the House of Com
Libya battle, " whether you
highly profitable transaction,'
61,000, and to everyone engag

Top right, tired and dejected It
armoured car column having

Left, German heavy calibre bombs abandoned on Derna aerodrome being examined by a
rechristened. A British tank crew affixes the new name—Democracy Lane—over the
in Cyrenaica.

ing the battles in Cyrenaica.
rfield in the Western Desert.

, 1942, when Gen. Rommel's
neila. Two days later they re-
north and north-east of Msus,
ay, strongly reinforced, despite
our naval units and aircraft,
hing the British light forces
ong armoured columns of the
ckwards, and when Rommel's
ed strength a tank battle on a

describe the campaign in his
e was able to claim that the
not, must be at the moment a
re 18,000 against the enemy's
rious episode

w right, men of a South African
nner in recaptured Benghazi.

boye, the Axis Highway being
an notice-board somewhere

Bitter Battles for Malaya and Burma

Having borne the brunt of the fighting in Malaya for five weeks, British and Indian troops were reinforced by the Australian Imperial Force on Jan. 16. Some valiant delaying actions were fought, the Australians quickly adapting themselves to the ingenious military "jiu jitsu" of the Japanese hordes.

AFTER seven weeks of war the Japanese had "saturated" the Malayan Peninsula. Their filtering tactics covered nearly the whole terrain, innumerable troops seeping down the east and west coasts and spreading far and wide throughout the forests and plantations.

It was a war of ambush and trap on both sides, and the enemy, having the advantage of superior numbers in men and machines, exploited a system of guerilla war specially adapted to forest land. It was obvious that the Japanese were avoiding a pitched battle on a large scale until within striking distance of Singapore.

After the fall of Kuala Lumpur and Port Swettenham British forces consolidated at various points in the Negri Sembilan area. Here, though fatigued by five weeks' continuous campaigning, they were able to delay the Japanese until relieved by the Australians. The news that these splendid soldiers were in action in Malaya for the first time was a source of renewed hope and encouragement not only to the defenders of Singapore but to the whole of the British Empire.

We can imagine with what heartfelt relief the tired British and Indian soldiers watched the "Aussies" take up their positions in the line about 150 miles from Singapore. Mr. Forde, deputy Prime Minister and Minister for Defence Coordination, announced on Jan. 16 that the Australian Imperial Force had had its first encounter with the Japanese and had inflicted heavy casualties on them. He had earlier received a message from Major-Gen. Gordon Bennett, G.O.C. A.I.F. in Malaya, which said:

"I am alive and fit, and commanding the forces covering the western sector with British, Indian and Australian troops. They are now in action contacting the enemy. Our troops are eager to fight. I trust the enemy will soon realize that I am alive."

The last sentence is in contradiction of the Japanese lie, deliberately put out to gain information about the A.I.F. positions, as to the capture and death of Gen. Gordon Bennett.

The change-over was a skilful military manoeuvre, the whole of the A.I.F. reaching the front without a casualty under cover of a heavy storm. Had the weather been fine the Japanese might have discovered the Australian positions and dive-bombed the advancing columns. It was not long before news of a heartening success relieved the monotonous chronicle of British retreats and evacuations in Malaya. On Jan. 18 the world learned that the Australians had killed about a thousand of the enemy, using those very methods of ambush which the Japanese themselves had found so effective.

For instance, in the region of Muar on Jan. 18 the Japanese launched an attack with ten medium tanks. A party of Australians with two concealed anti-tank guns allowed the tanks to pass down the road. When the enemy machines were thirty yards away the rear gun came into action. With loud shouts of

"Whacko!" the Australians fired at point-blank range. The close-up tanks made a perfect target, and five were put out of action and caught fire, their ammunition exploding at the same time. As the sixth tank was shielded behind the others an Australian raced down the road and destroyed it with hand-grenades. The remaining four tanks were picked off by the Australians' second gun. Japanese infantry, for whom the tanks were the spearhead, deployed among the rubber plantations, where the Australians engaged them for a whole day with

bayonet and Tommy gun. Our men, greatly outnumbered, were in danger of being surrounded, but were relieved by reinforcements with Bren guns and armoured cars.

It is not surprising that man for man the Australians, with their splendid physique and freer intelligence, are greatly superior to the Japanese. The story of an Australian corporal, stripped to the waist, moving through the jungle and engaging six Japanese, is by no means exceptional. Finding his bayonet useless on this occasion, he threw it away and, using a sharp chopper called a *purang*, he dispatched the entire Japanese party.

As the enemy drew nearer Singapore our fighter and bomber aircraft, though limited in numbers, had greater opportunities of bombing Japanese concentrations and several valuable offensive sweeps were made in the Muar-Batu Pahat area. Here a number of barges which were bringing fresh Japanese forces into Johore were successfully attacked.

The important town of Batu Pahat fell into enemy hands. The R.A.F., however, accounted for about 100 Japanese planes during the week ending Jan. 24. Singapore

GEN. WAVELL, Supreme Commander of the forces of the United Nations in the S.W. Pacific, left, talking to his deputy, Maj-Gen. G. H. Brett. In the middle is Rear-Adm. Thomas Hart, commanding the naval forces of the United Nations in the same area. This radioed photograph was taken at their first meeting " somewhere in the Dutch East Indies."

Photo; Associated Press

suffered heavily in a big raid on Jan. 21, 383 persons being killed, 625 admitted to hospital and 100 detained at first-aid posts. In this raid the Japanese lost 13 planes.

By Jan. 28 the battle was raging 50 miles from Singapore itself; and on that day the Straits Settlements Government ordered the evacuation of a coastal strip one mile wide on the northern shore of Singapore Island.

Yet another move in the Japanese dream of Asia for the Asiatics was opened up by the enemy on Jan. 17. Spreading from Thailand across the mountains, the yellow plague advanced and took Myitta and then the coast town of Tavoy, centre of the tin industry in Burma. In the face of superior forces our troops were withdrawn some thirty miles from the Thai frontier. Myawadi and Moulmein were bombed by enemy aircraft on Jan. 20, and army headquarters reported that a fierce battle was raging between British and Siamese troops on the new Burma front in the Kawkareik area. It was learned on Jan. 26 that heavy Chinese reinforcements were proceeding to Burma.

MALAY PENINSULA, showing the battle areas in Burma and Johore. In the Burma area Siamese troops were the first to cross the frontier, some 45 miles east of Moulmein in the region of Palu. They were followed by strong Japanese attacks on Sukli and Tiwakale.

Map, Courtesy of the "News Chronicle"

Ashore in Triumph Goes the Rising Sun

JAPANESE INVASION TROOPS are seen in action in these first photographs of Japanese landings "somewhere in the Pacific." Top, hauling equipment ashore from invasion barges. Centre, a smoke screen being laid, according to the German caption, to cover the landing of Japanese troops. Below, Japanese invasion troops advancing after landing preceded by the banner of the Rising Sun. Circle, General Sugiyama, Commander-in-Chief of the Japanese Army. General Sugiyama was made Chief of the General Staff in 1940 and directed the first Japanese assault on French Indo-China.

Photos, Keystone, Wide World

Our Diary of the War

SUNDAY, JAN. 18, 1942 869th day

Russian Front.—Red Army pressed forward on three main fronts. Fierce street fighting in Mojaisk.

Mediterranean.—Comiso aerodrome, Sicily, attacked by Hurrybombers. Night attack on aerodrome at Catania, Sicily.

Far East.—In Malaya, heavy fighting in Northern Johore, in the region of Batu Anam. Japs claimed capture of Batu Pahat. In the Philippines, Gen. MacArthur's forces beat off heavy Japanese attack in Batan peninsula. Bangkok raided by R.A.F. on night of Jan. 18-19.

Home.—German aircraft dropped bombs on a Shetland island. Admiralty announced destruction of a Dornier bomber by destroyer Walpole.

General.—U Saw, Prime Minister of Burma, arrested for alleged complicity with Japanese.

MONDAY, JAN. 19 870th day

Sea.—Admiralty announced sinking of destroyer Vimiera.

Russian Front. — Russians recaptured Mojaisk, removing the last direct threat to Moscow. Germans claimed to have re-occupied Feodosia in the Crimea.

Far East.—In Malaya further landings were made on the west coast by Japanese troops. It was reported from Rangoon that the enemy had occupied Tavoy in Lower Burma.

TUESDAY, JAN. 20 871st day

Air.—R.A.F. attacked Emden at night.

Russian Front.—German armies in Mojaisk sector retreating towards Vyazma. Soviet announced recapture of Ostashevo, 100 miles north of Rjev.

Far East.—In Malaya heavy fighting between mouth of Muar river and Batu Pahat. In the Philippines new attacks on Gen. MacArthur's positions in the Batan peninsula held. U.S. War Dept. announced that a Japanese cruiser was sunk by American bombers off Mindanao. Heavy Jap air raid on Sabang, off N. Sumatra. Communiqué from Rangoon reported crossing of Burmese frontier east of Myawaddi by Thai troops. Melbourne announced a heavy Japanese air attack on Rabaul, in New Guinea.

Home.—Few enemy raiders dropped bombs on E. Coast after dusk. N.E. coast town bombed and machine-gunned by single raider during daylight.

WEDNESDAY, JAN. 21 872nd day

Air.—R.A.F. made heavy night attack on Bremen and Emden. R.A.F. daylight sweep over N. France.

Russian Front.—Germans falling back towards Smolensk. Fierce fighting outside Borodino, 12 miles west of Mojaisk.

Far East.—Heavy air raid on Singapore in which 13 enemy aircraft were destroyed. Heavy fighting continued between Muar and Batu Pahat. In Philippines, Gen. MacArthur's troops made a successful counter-attack. One of his guerilla bands gained a local success in a surprise raid against an enemy aerodrome at Tuguegarao. More large-scale air attacks on New Guinea.

Home.—A few bombs at night in E. Anglia. A daylight raider dropped bombs on one of the Shetland Islands.

THURSDAY, JAN. 22 873rd day

Russian Front.—Red Army units 25 miles west of Mojaisk. Uvarovo recaptured. Fierce fighting in the Valdai Hills and around Rjev.

Africa.—Gen. Rommel's forces made a surprise sortie in Libya.

Far East.—Heavy fighting in Western Johore. In Luzon, Philippines, Japs reported to be throwing in an entire army of 200,000 men. Japanese invasion armada off Rabaul, New Guinea. Moulmein, in Southern Burma, bombed by Japanese.

Home.—Dover area shelled for 3½ hours by German coastal batteries. A few bombs dropped by night in E. Anglia.

FRIDAY, JAN. 23 874th day

Russian Front.—Moscow reported a Soviet advance of 65 miles on a seventy-mile front between Moscow and Lake Ilmen.

Far East.—Japanese forces landed on Kieta, one of the Solomon Islands. Imperial troops made a further withdrawal in Malaya. In air battles over Rangoon at least 21 Japanese planes were shot down. Attacks on American and Filipino forces in Luzon repulsed. Dutch announced that their bombers made twelve direct hits on four enemy warships and four transports in Macassar Strait.

Africa.—General Rommel's forces re-occupied Jedabia.

SATURDAY, JAN. 24 875th day

Russian Front.—New Russian advance continued on a wide front. Soviet troops advancing upon the Leningrad-Ukraine railway in the direction of Veliki Luki.

Africa.—British and German forces engaged north-east of Jedabia.

Far East.—At least 16 more Japanese planes destroyed at Rangoon. In Malaya, Japanese claimed to have captured Yong Peng, 65 miles N.W. of Singapore. Enemy gained some ground in Luzon. U.S. Navy Dept. announced that American destroyers had attacked a Japanese convoy in Macassar Strait, sinking two ships and damaging others. Dutch bombers scored direct hits on transport and a destroyer and capsized a big passenger liner. A British ship destroyed a Japanese submarine. Japanese thought to have landed at Rabaul. Chinese planes destroyed two enemy transports off Indo-China. Night attack by British bombers on Bangkok.

General.—Official report on U.S. Navy losses at Pearl Harbour published.

SUNDAY, JAN. 25 876th day

Russian Front.—Moscow announced the recapture of Netidovo, on the railway line from Rjev to Veliki Luki. German defences around Rjev breached.

Mediterranean.—Air Ministry announced that R.A.F. and Navy aircraft had carried out a 24-hour attack on an enemy convoy in which a 20,000-ton liner was hit and believed sunk, a cruiser, destroyer and two merchant ships were damaged and a battleship probably hit.

Africa.—Tank battle still raging in the neighbourhood of Antelat, 50 miles N.E. of Jedabia.

Far East.—First communiqué issued from Gen. Wavell's Pacific H.Q. announced that during a 48-hour attack on the enemy convoy in Macassar Strait three ships were destroyed, four others probably sunk and 12 damaged out of the Japanese armada engaged in landing forces at the oil port of Balik Papan, in Dutch Borneo. In the Philippines, Gen. MacArthur launched a heavy counter-attack on Japanese troops in a Batan peninsula, scoring a "smashing success." A British communiqué from Burma announced that large Chinese reinforcements were pouring into Burma. In Malaya, British troops maintained their positions.

Home.—Bombs were dropped by enemy raiders on S.W. coast at night. One enemy bomber destroyed.

MONDAY, JAN. 26 877th day

Air.—R.A.F. fighter sweep over N. France. Hanover and Emden heavily attacked at night as well as the docks at Brest.

Russian Front. — Red Army advance towards Vyazma on central front continued, as did the advance towards Veliki Luki.

Africa.—Axis forces in Libya reached points beyond Msus, between Jedabia and Mekili.

Mediterranean.—Admiralty announced that five Axis ships had been torpedoed in Mediterranean. Three considered sunk.

Far East.—U.S. Navy Dept. announced that a U.S. submarine had torpedoed and possibly sunk a Japanese aircraft carrier in the Macassar Strait. Dutch and American planes continued to attack the Japanese convoy lying there. 10,000 Japanese reported to have landed at Rabaul, in New Guinea. In Malaya, Singapore announced capture of Batu Pahat, on the west coast, by Japanese.

Home.—Troops of the United States Army landed in Northern Ireland.

TUESDAY, JAN. 27 878th day

Sea.—Admiralty announced loss of H.M.S. Barham on Nov. 25, 1941, torpedoed in the Mediterranean.

Russian Front.—Moscow announced that Red Army troops on the Kalinin front were vigorously advancing.

Africa.—Tremendous attack by Allied air forces played havoc with Rommel's columns.

Far East.—More Japanese landings in Malaya. In Burma R.A.F. blew up the Kawkareik-Myawaddi road east of Moulmein. British garrison at Mergui evacuated. Batavia reported Japanese air raids on Macassar, Pontianak, Belawan, Padang, Parepare, Tanjong Pinang, Riouw Archipelago, and Amboyna. R.A.A.F. bombers sank three Japanese ships in Rabaul harbour. Chinese forces reported nearing Kowloon. Japanese ships hit in Macassar Strait now reported to include 11 warships and 17 transports sunk or badly damaged. U.S. Navy Dept. announced that Midway Island was still holding out.

Home.—Prime Minister reviewed the war situation in the House of Commons.

General.—Canada announced that she would send Britain as an outright gift £225,000,000 worth of munitions and food.

TWO KINGS MEET at luncheon at the Dorchester Hotel, London, following the signing of the Yugoslav-Greek agreement on Jan. 15. King Peter of Yugoslavia (left) emphasizes a point as he discusses the new Balkan Union with King George of the Hellenes.

Photo, Associated Press

Muller the Nazi Pilot Won't Fly Again

Left, as a German plane approaches, Red Army soldiers man their A.A. gun, while another estimates the height with a range-finder. Above, the German plane turns to escape the fire.

The plane is hit and hurtles to the ground, above. Right, beside the wreckage of the machine lies the body of the pilot.

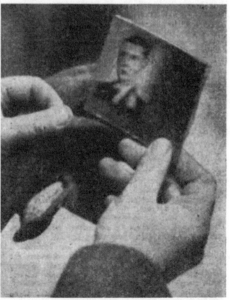

The concluding stages of this dramatic incident, photographed during the opening of the great Russian counter-offensive, are seen above. Left, the gun and instruments of the wrecked aircraft are dismantled by the Red Army men. Right, a Soviet soldier examines the dead pilot's identity card—his name was Muller. There have been many Mullers lying in the snows of Russia since the Russians took the initiative on the Eastern front and the arrogant Luftwaffe has been severely mauled.

Photos, British Official: Crown Copyright

Russia Has Tank-Busters—Where Are Ours?

Rifle Bullet 7·7 mm. = ·303 in.
Cannon Shell 20 mm. = ·78 in.   37 mm. = 1·45 in.   50 mm. = 1·96 in.

German Mark IV Tank

75 mm. Cannon

Stormovik Type Armoured Plane 37 mm. Cannon in Nose

The Russians quickly realized that the most effective weapon against the tank was not the bomber, or even another tank, but a special anti-tank plane. It had to be armoured to fly low over its target and provided with cannon firing armour-piercing shell. As the Nazi Mark IV tank was almost immune against the normal 20-mm. cannon, heavier calibres were needed. The Stormovik was first adapted with 37-mm. (nearly 1½ in.) cannon, as seen in the diagram, and then special Stalin anti-tank planes were produced. The comparative sizes of cannon shell are indicated top left. *Specially drawn for* THE WAR ILLUSTRATED *by War Artists Ltd.*

IT was recently stated in "The Times" that : "Tanks in the open have proved that they cannot at present be dominated by the opposing air arm. No doubt the tacticians of the air have not shot their bolt ; possibly armoured aircraft carrying quick-firing cannon may reassert the authority of air fleets over land fleets."

Most of our air correspondents seem to agree that the German heavy tank is not yet being effectively dealt with from the air. Experience has shown that the fast moving tank is a small and very difficult target for the bombing aeroplane, and there is a complete lack of evidence that panzer units in Libya have been seriously damaged by high or low flying bombers. Many motor vehicles have been destroyed from the air but not many tanks. The "tank-buster" is clearly a very urgent need, but it has taken more than two years of mechanized fighting to disclose it. It is an unhappy comment upon the supposed close cooperation between our air and mechanized forces that, at this stage of the war, it has to be admitted, as more than one commentator does, "that we still need an efficient anti-tank aeroplane." The Beaufighter is the one machine reported in the N. African campaign to be armed with cannon, but it carries only 20 mm., and at least 37-mm. cannon are needed to deal with the heavily armoured German Mark IV tanks seen in this diagram. Their cannon fire a shell nearly equal to 4-in. calibre.

THE army authorities decided some time ago that the only weapon to deal with the tank was the tank, and we were told at the opening of the offensive that for the first time our men were meeting the Hun on equal terms with equal equipment. All the news from Libya has shown, however, that this method is not quickly decisive and results in heavy casualties in men and machines. We have our air superiority, and the R.A.F. has done excellent work both in cooperating with our troops and in destroying the enemy's supplies and communications. Without this domination of the skies the desert offensive would never have had hope of success.

Tanks with air support are a chief weapon of the German offensive and specialized weapons are needed to deal with them from the air. This is particularly important in view of Rommel's proved capacity in repairing damaged tanks on the field and putting them into service again. Well-armoured planes able to fly low and attack with heavy cannon in power turrets are required, and it is understood that such machines were designed many months ago.

Our Russian allies saw the need for an effective air weapon against the heavy tank early in their fighting, and with the quickness of decision

Photo, British Official : Crown Copyright

which they have so frequently shown, put anti-tank planes into production at once. They first made a new Stormovik, well armoured and provided with 37-mm. cannon, as shown in action in the diagram. Their newest anti-tank plane, the "Stalin" type, of which no details have been released, is armed with large bore cannon and is claimed to possess unprecedented armour-piercing strength. Early in Dec. 1941 one detachment of a Red Air Force unit flying the new

plane had destroyed 80 tanks in a short period. A squadron similarly equipped destroyed 608 tanks in three months.

German tanks in Libya, such as those in the photograph above, have mostly been knocked out by artillery fire, especially by the 25-pdr. the "gunhow" illustrated in page 460. Anti-tank guns and artillery have a valuable and well-recognized part in the destruction of tanks, but no gun can have the mobility of the plane.

Martel of the Tanks Meets 'Sheila'

Lt.-Gen. G. LE QUESNE MARTEL, D.S.O., M.C., first Commander of the Royal Armoured Corps, is here seen chatting to a tank driver during recent Infantry versus Tanks exercises. General Martel has been associated with tanks since they were first employed, having served on the Staff of the Tank Corps in France for eighteen months in 1917-18. He was Assistant Director of Mechanization at the War Office from Oct. 1936 to Dec. 1937, and Deputy Director until Feb. 1939. He commanded the 50th Division during the Battle of France and led the counter-attack at Arras on May 23, 1940, when a handful of British tanks fought a great battle against superior numbers of enemy tanks.   *Photo, Keystone*   Page 475

Now It's Scrap Rubber that's Wanted

Old tires are now of great value to the war effort. Here is a dump in the Old Kent Road, London, awaiting removal.

These women are removing worn treads from tires too old to be suitable for re-treading. They will later be processed.

RECLAIMING RUBBER is an essential part of the war effort now that the rubber plantations in Malaya have been overrun by the enemy. Scrap rubber of all kinds is required to augment the supplies of crude rubber. Oval, part of a seven-acre pile of discarded rubber at the Akron plant of the Goodyear Co., in America. This will be regenerated. Above left, old treads of tires stored to await processing. Right, a girl weighs out chemical ingredients to be mixed with "reclaimed" rubber to make it suitable for various trade requirements.

Photos. Associated Press, Sport & General

The Farmer Works Though Winter Grips the Land

"The nation wants all you can produce, and will pay for it," Mr. R. S. Hudson, Minister of Agriculture, told farmers at Newcastle on Jan. 16. He went on to speak about new food problems added to those which already confronted the country by reason of recent events in the Pacific. There could, he said, " be no relaxation, no respite. It was to them that over 40,000,000 of our people were looking for a very great deal of the wherewithal to sustain them in this fight for their—and farmers'—existence." Even in the winter work goes steadily forward on the farms, and in this page are shown, top, a tractor levelling ground in Gloucestershire, and, below, a team of horses hauling timber at Bramham, Yorks. *Photos, Fox*

I Was Amazed that Our Beaufort Ever Got Home

The quality of our aircraft and the courage of the men who fly them are both exemplified in the following story of a Beaufort's adventures off Norway, which was broadcast by the sergeant-pilot in command.

THE other day we were ordered to attack a convoy of large enemy ships off the coast of Norway. Three aircraft were to go, led by the squadron commander. Unfortunately, my aircraft was delayed a little in getting off the ground and as such operations are worked to the split second, the other two Beauforts went on ahead. We had about three hundred miles to go before reaching Norway, and before getting there I did everything to catch up with the other two aircraft, but I couldn't though I ran into evidence of their work. There was a big black pall of smoke on the horizon, just where we knew the convoy to be, and I soon saw it to be a large ship on fire and listing over.

I picked another ship of about 7,000 tons,

went in and released my torpedo. Then, Charlie, the rear gunner, yelled through the inter-com.: "Look out, skipper—Messerschmitts!" At the same moment I heard the rattle of a German's guns and the pouf of his cannon shell. The Messerschmitt hit us first time, and I saw tracers going past my head, then the gunner yelled again, "Another one coming in, skipper." They hit us again. I heard our guns going all the time. Charlie, very calmly, said: "I think I got him," then a second later: "Here comes another from the beam." There was a terrific explosion at the back, and the rear guns stopped. The observer crawled back, and a few seconds later came to tell me: "Charlie's been hit pretty badly."

All this time I was throwing the aircraft

BEAUFORT in flight, with its bomb doors open, showing a torpedo ready to be launched against enemy shipping. The Beaufort is used for bombing, torpedo-bombing and reconnaissance. *Photo, Central Press*

about, but we were then only about 20 feet above the water. All the time the two Messerschmitts were coming in and letting us have everything they'd got from 20 yards. Every time they hit us my Beaufort shuddered, and I had to fight the controls to keep her out of the sea.

Later I found that the rear gunner, who had been unconscious, had come to, and had opened up again. We were certain he got one of the Messerschmitts. He filled its belly with lead at less than 20 yards, and didn't see anything more of the Jerry. Then the rear guns stopped again, and I was chased all over the place. There was some inviting cloud, but I couldn't get the aircraft high enough, we were so badly hit. I thought a thousand times that we must go into the ditch. But I had to laugh when the observer calmly pulled out his watch and announced that the scrap had lasted for nearly twenty minutes.

Only Just Above the Sea

Our guns began again, and I thought, "By Jove, those boys are all right." They had dragged themselves up to the guns and were still fighting. Then the one remaining Messerschmitt came round the front of us. He must have thought we were finished, but after one more squirt from our guns he turned away in a hurry, and we didn't see him again.

We had to go home then, and we found that we were heading south instead of west, with about three hundred miles to go in a damaged aircraft. We were just skimming the waves. It was raining hard, blowing a gale, and all the perspex—that's the glass—had been shot away. We were wet and miserable, and there were two men badly hurt. I said, "We'll have to go down in the water," but then we found that the rear gunner and the wireless operator had collapsed and couldn't move.

We were still only just above the sea. So we decided to try to get home, and we took off our Mae Wests to make a bed for Charlie, as he was really hurt. It took three hours before we made a land-fall, and then we were about two hundred miles south of where we should have been. That's how we had been chased.

When I tried to turn the aircraft right, I found that she wouldn't turn, although I managed to coax her to eighty feet. So we turned out to sea again in a wide circle to the left, and lost sight of land. Anyhow, we got home at last. But on getting ready to land I saw the undercarriage swimming about in the breeze. So I just prayed and crash-landed. I was amazed that the Beaufort ever got home after all she'd been through.

This enemy ship was destroyed by a Beaufort torpedo-carrying bomber. Top, the vessel being attacked off the Norwegian coast. The aircraft has just cleared the ship's mast and a bomb has struck the poop. Above, a second later, the bomb has exploded, smoke and flame leaping up by the mainmast. A pilot's story of how his Beaufort attacked an enemy convoy is given above.

Photos, British Official

We Dived Into Oil to Save Our Ship

How the valuable whale factory ship Svend Foyn—a British vessel manned by Norwegians—was saved after she had been torpedoed in a gale is described here by a young Norwegian who worked amid swirling oil, sea water, and crashing machinery.

OUR ship the Svend Foyn was homeward bound with 20,000 tons of oil in her tanks when we ran into bad weather. Then we were torpedoed. The Svend Foyn opened fire on the U-boat and drove it off, but a hole had been blown in her side and the sea came washing in. In order to trim the ship it became necessary to pump some of the fuel oil from two of the tanks, but the valves lay ten feet below swirling black oil and water.

The captain told me and three other pump men that the only chance of saving the ship was to go down and turn on the valves of the fuel tanks. So we put on diving equipment, and as soon as the sea calmed down a bit, the chief engineer gave the word and we dived down. It was useless to attempt to use an underwater torch—the most powerful torch would not penetrate six inches through the black viscous oil—and everything had to be done by touch. We spent four nightmare days in this way.

Each time I went down I swallowed pints of oil and water. In between dives my feet slipped on the wet, oily deck as the ship lurched this way and that. But I managed to turn the valves.

The second day was, I think, the worst of the four. The weather was certainly no better. Now some of the 60-ton boilers, used for rendering down the blubber, had broken completely loose. I was scared once or twice as they charged about the ship. Then they crashed right past me and floated out to sea. Other steel parts of the ship had also broken adrift in the gale. The deck still tilted at all angles.

By the third day we had lightened the ship a bit, and it was mostly a question of releasing oil. Things still looked so bad that for most of the day the captain had us standing by the lifeboats. On this day the pump-room door was forced open by the heavy seas. One of my mates and I were sent down to close it. We had to fix a stanchion against it. Time and time again we tried, but always, when we had nearly succeeded, the seas burst the door away from our grasp. Then suddenly my mate lost his foothold and vanished. Then the seas washed him towards me, and as he was being whisked by, I managed to grab him.

On the fourth day we finished the job of trimming the ship. The seas moderated a bit, and we came safely into port with the bulk of our valuable cargo intact.—"*Daily Mail*"

Chinese Guerillas Helped Us Escape from Shanghai

From Shanghai, seized by the Japanese in the first days of their Pacific onslaught, several British and Americans escaped with the help of Chinese guerillas. One of the Americans, Francis Lee, told the following story to a "Daily Mail" correspondent.

BRITISH and Americans met behind closed doors all over Shanghai when the Japs took over. On everyone's lips there was only one word—"Escape." But all roads were blocked and many foreigners were arrested while trying to get away.

I did not want to be a prisoner for the rest of the war, so I took a chance, and after several secret rendezvous in parks, alleyways, kitchens, and cafés I contacted a trusted friend. He is a Chinese guerilla commander in Kiangsu province, and he rushed an emissary to guerilla headquarters to see what could be done.

At 2 a.m. on Christmas Day a shivering farmer knocked at the door and whispered, "Sampan waiting in creek two miles from Shanghai. Come tonight." On Christmas night, while most of Shanghai's foreigners were dismally celebrating, I rounded up two friends. We stuffed our pockets with medicines, tooth-paste and soap. Then, feigning to be holiday drunks and smiling and waving to the Jap sentries, we passed the barricades and reached the appointed village.

There, almost in sight of the Japs, boatmen beckoned us to where a sampan, covered with matting, was waiting. We put off down stream at once. The first problem was to pass a strongly garrisoned town. But the boatmen, whistling merrily, briefly replied to the Jap officer's hail, "No passengers."

Eventually we disembarked and reached an abandoned house, from which a Chinese boy burst brandishing a Mauser and shouting, "I am a Chinese soldier." He led us to a barn where the colonel of a guerilla unit, known as the "National Salvation Army," wrote down our destination and then burnt the paper in the candle. He also wrote out a safe conduct pass which his adjutant folded double, indicating that it was a Chinese guerilla dispatch.

It was moonlight, with snow falling intermittently, when we sailed off again into the maze of canals and waterways of Central Kiangsu. Often our boatmen hailed from a distance Japanese soldiers who dared not emerge from their positions at night owing to a complete guerilla control over the countryside.

Penetrating deeper into guerilla regions, we met Major-General Mayungkan, director of political propaganda in Kiangsu. Here I saw peasants undergoing guerilla training. They do not stay long in one place, and their headquarters is constantly being moved to avoid detection. But they are fully supplied with radios and telephones to contact the numerous units, including those operating in Shanghai.

The guerilla commander had the most surprising knowledge of world affairs. He is in constant contact with spies in the Nanking puppet government. He revealed that the Japs have been so harassed by guerillas who blow up the Shanghai - Nanking and Shanghai-Hangchow railways that they lined the tracks with electrically charged wires and employed hounds to smell out the explosives. But guerilla technicians cut the wires and laid false trails for the hounds. The Chinese manage to confine the Jap troops to their few garrisons and retain full control of the countryside.

The commander presented us with loaves, clean underwear captured from Soochow, one of the strongest Jap-garrisoned towns, and sent us to the house of a farmer named Fang, whose wife prepared supper, while her 8-year-old daughter played with the guerillas' Mausers and listened entranced to stories of desperate nocturnal raids.

From here lay the last and most dangerous lap of our escape. Ahead of us was the heavily guarded Sashing-Soochow railway and Hangchow-Nanking highway, both of which we had to cross to reach Free China. Crossing the railway meant taking a sampan past the inspection point under a bridge.

Resourceful guerillas make use of the Nanking puppets, who live in mortal fear of their lives. Thus it was that a high official was made to act as our accomplice. By a trick that I cannot describe, we got through. A few hours later Chinese farmers welcomed us, shouting, "Long live the A B C D front." They asked when America and British planes were going to bomb Japan, and showed us the ruins caused by Jap bombings.

A Toast in Boiling Water

On the shore of Tai Lake we met two British Army officers, Major Sidney Hunt and Captain Raymond Dewar-Durie, and Mr. Watts, a Kailan mining engineer, who had also escaped from Shanghai. With guerilla sailors we crossed the lake in a junk and arrived at 2 a.m. at a secret rendezvous.

In single file the three Britons and we three Americans, guarded by guerillas, marched along a path, and suddenly emerged on a Jap-controlled highway down which we walked for half a mile, listening to the rumble of artillery off to the right, indicating a skirmish which the guerillas had started to distract attention from our escape. Thus we walked the whole night. Dawn found us filing into a ghostly ruined town of Free China, where a few bedraggled survivors of the terrific bombardment exist in poverty-stricken despair.

In a burned teahouse, with a rickety table and broken cups, Britons, American, and Chinese drank a toast in boiling water to the united front. A day later guerillas, proudly shooting off their Mausers, escorted us to the first inhabited town of Free China, where the flag-waving population gave us a community tea-party and anxiously questioned us when the United States and British bombers would begin to arrive.

Similar to those whose activities are described in this page, these Chinese guerillas—farmer-fighters from the southern provinces—are ready to harass the Japanese invaders. *Photo, G.P.U.*

Editor's Postscript

WHILE it can be argued that war brings forth some of the finest qualities in humanity—self-sacrifice, heroism, love of country, comradeship, and so forth—no argument is needed that it more readily brings forth the worst. Lying, deceit, selfishness, inhumanity: all these, and more, flourish abundantly in wartime. And I am inclined to the view that society in the post-war world will go through a period of lowered morals before we get back the old decencies of life. Here, I agree, it can be argued that much of the sanity we all so anxiously wish to recover was lost before the present War broke loose. For the moment, however, I am concerned with only one thing that has deteriorated alarmingly: accepted honesty in social dealings. The alacrity to blame the War for every instance of slackness and lack of the accepted courtesies of civilized life is universal.

MANY of our great public services have carried on, and are carrying on, splendidly despite endless difficulties; especially the railways. On the whole the Post Office has stood up well to the strain, for though we can all give instances of irritating delays we can also give many more examples of efficiency. "Lost in the post" is a favourite excuse; "You didn't get my letter?" a common explanation of someone's neglect. Very few of these complaints are justified. Since September 3, 1939, I have written many, many hundreds of letters and I have no record of a single one of these failing to reach its addressee. But the number of letters that I haven't received because of alleged postal inefficiency is considerable. And I just don't believe they were ever written. It's so easy to shirk an obligation by the simple process of telling a whopper. Having always had about as low an opinion of mankind in this respect as that of the Preacher, I just ignore this now popular excuse and write down those who proffer it as liars—unless good evidence to the contrary is forthcoming. Cadging letters, requests for help, financial or otherwise, never by any chance fail to reach me. Perhaps the writers make the address unusually clear in such cases.

TALKING about lies, we have become so familiar with the apocryphal biographies of film stars, invented by a class apart known as "press agents," that even the least informed reader now accepts them as pleasing fiction. But a good deal of fiction used to be circulated about famous authors before the rise of these mayflies of the film world. I happened to turn to the late Lord Birkenhead's "Last Essays" tonight to read again his brilliant and outspoken "Reflections in a Library." My eye fell on this: "It is claimed for Balzac that he could write a novel almost at a sitting, sustained by draughts of black coffee." Whoever was the first to claim this for Balzac was certainly no true man, as it is notorious that Balzac was a most painstaking author. Turning to Mary F. Sandars's life of him I read: "writing did not at any time come easily to

him, and 'Stella' and 'Coqsigrue,' his first novels, were never finished; while a comedy, 'Les Deux Philosophes,' was also abandoned in despair."

I WISH that Lord Birkenhead had applied to the statement he quoted that searching scrutiny for which he was famous as a lawyer, for if he had taken the pains to look over half-a-dozen volumes of Balzac (which I have just done) he would have found that the shortest of them, "The Quest of the Absolute," runs to ninety thousand words, while "The Chouans," in common with most of his full-length novels, contains about 150,000 words. Written "almost at a sitting"! Anything from three to six months would have been a fair estimate of the time required by a fairly fast practitioner in creative composition—apart from the desideratum of genius. Had the matter in hand raised a legal question, Birkenhead would assuredly have considered the possibility of any human being writing at the express speed of a thousand words an hour (even full of black coffee) getting away with a novel of only ninety thousand words "almost at a sitting." Edgar Wallace might have spun one of his yarns at two thousand words an hour, for he used to dictate at top speed to a shorthand writer while walking about his study, and, even so, his average time for one of his novels would have been about fifty hours. In this way Edgar could certainly turn out a good readable yarn inside a week—but Balzac was no Wallace, or rather, the other way round!

IN glancing through "The Chouans" (which is concerned with the guerilla royalists of the French Revolution) the

following passage seems to me worth quoting for its application to the present distressful times in which the French are living once again:

"'Do you notice, mademoiselle,' he said, 'how little our feelings flow in their accustomed channels in these times of terror in which we live? Is there not a striking and unexplainable spontaneity about everything that takes place around us? We love nowadays, or we hate, on the strength of a single glance. We are bound together for life, or we are severed with the same speed that brings us to the scaffold. We do everything in haste, like the nation in its ferment. We cling to each other more closely amid these perils than in the common course of life. Lately in Paris we have come to know, as men learn on the battlefield, all that is meant by the grasp of a hand.'

"'The thirst for a full life in a little space,' she said, 'was felt then because men had so short a time to live.'"

Today in Paris that thirst for a full life can only be allayed by the reflection that it will be unattainable until the Nazi has been compelled to evacuate the once proud *ville lumière* where his polluting presence has only temporarily put out the light. Parisians must just go on thirsting and hoping that the short time to live may prove long enough to carry them through to the day when a draught of full life may again be theirs.

A Word to our Readers who have not preserved their Serial Numbers for Binding

The heightened interest of the War has coincided with the severest stage of the paper famine. When we ought to have been increasing the size of each number, printing more and more copies, we have had drastically to reduce both size and circulation. This has led to some unavoidable disappointment. Those who had not begun two years ago getting their numbers bound up now find it difficult to complete the four volumes now completed. Arrangements latterly made for the convenience of those who have regularly bound their volumes, however, are working as satisfactorily as prevailing restrictions will allow.

But among my very large circle of readers there are many thousands who must feel the need to possess an adequate permanent history of the War, and the opportunity to secure the best available is now open to them. The first three volumes of my other highly successful publication, written as a continuous narrative of events and superbly illustrated, "The Second Great War: A Standard History," are now obtainable in the splendid edition expressly printed for the Waverley Book Co., who offer the work on easy instalment terms.

It is naturally a more costly production than "The War Illustrated," but the subscription terms bring it well within the means of a large body of my readers, and as nothing comparable with "The Second Great War," in regard to literary contents and documentation, and particularly illustration, is ever likely to be produced, I would advise those readers who may be interested to send a postcard at once to THE WAVERLEY BOOK CO., 96, Farringdon Street, London, E.C.4, asking for full particulars of their present exceptional offer which enables you to examine the volumes now ready in your own home free of all charge or obligation.

Here again delay in writing might lead to disappointment, for the edition now available cannot be indefinitely extended owing to the limitation of stocks, and the fourth volume will soon be on sale. In "The Second Great War," I may add, I have had the expert cooperation of Sir Charles Gwynn, K.C.B., D.S.O. as Military Editor, whose name and experience give the work a cachet of authority.

Maj.-Gen. H. GORDON BENNETT, C.B., C.M.G., D.S.O., V.D., G.O.C. Australian Imperial Forces in Malaya, served in the last World War from 1915 to 1918.
Photo, British Official

Printed in England and published on the 10th, 20th, and 30th of each month by the Proprietors, The Amalgamated Press, Ltd., The Fleetway House, Farringdon Street, London, E.C.4. Registered for transmission by Canadian Magazine Post. Sole Agents for Australia and New Zealand: Messrs. Gordon & Gotch, Ltd.: and for South Africa: Central News Agency, Ltd. February 10th, 1942. S.S. *Editorial Address*: JOHN CARPENTER HOUSE, WHITEFRIARS, LONDON, E.C.4.

Vol 5 # The War Illustrated Nº 121

Edited by Sir John Hammerton

FOURPENCE

FEB. 20TH. 1942

CORREGIDOR ROARS DEFIANCE. One of General MacArthur's big guns in action against the Japanese invaders of the Philippines. Corregidor is the rocky island fortress which stands at the entrance to Manila Bay, denying its use to the Japanese invaders. Though heavily attacked from the air, it continued to hold out, affording valuable assistance to the American-Filipino troops on the Batan Peninsula. On Feb. 1 a Japanese force assembling at Ternate to attack Corregidor was blasted by the heavy artillery of the fortress.

Radioed photo, Keystone

THE RUSSIANS EXPECT TO WIN BY THE WINTER

FROM all the fronts the news is bad, and we are told on high authority that before we can expect it to get better it will almost certainly get worse. From all the fronts save one. From Russia, and from Russia alone, for weeks past the news has been good, is still good, and may well get better.

Really the Russians are amazing fellows. Last year from June to November they were in retreat. They put up a tremendous fight, it is true ; they proved themselves in battle to be far stouter and more determined than had been expected even by those who counted themselves among the Soviet's friends, even admirers. Then at the beginning of December the communiqués began to tell a different story. The Russians, who had been retreating, began to advance ... And the reversal of fortune which began at Rostov has not yet been checked. Still Stalin's men are recapturing, yard by yard and mile by mile, field by field and village by village, the territory which they scorched and abandoned in the great withdrawal of last year. How long this counter-offensive will be maintained none can say. But it is significant that the Russians themselves believe that Hitler's armies have still plenty of punch left, and that when the snows melt and the ground thaws the line of battle may once again draw nearer to Moscow.

THIS was one of many interesting points contained in the talk given by Sir Stafford Cripps at the Ministry of Information a few days ago. "The general conception in Russia is that the Germans will be driven back a long way (he said). A new German offensive is anticipated in the spring, which may make some headway into Russia. Then I think the Russians will give the *coup de grâce* to the Germans in the autumn or winter. I do not think the Russians will stop at the German borders, but are out to defeat the Germans conclusively."

Here are some more things Cripps told us ; we ought to take careful note of them since they come from a man who really knows Stalin, who really knows his Russia and the Russians, and who (O rarity amongst our diplomatists !) has a diplomatic triumph to his credit.

MANY people, he reminds us, thought that Russia would not be able to cope with the German blitz attack because of her inability to organize behind the fighting line. But the Russians have not only kept their 2,000-mile-long front in being during a fighting retreat over hundreds of miles, but they have carried out a scorched earth policy, moved their key industries into safe zones, and, to crown all, maintained supplies for an army of 9,000,000 men. "I don't suppose that all the 9,000,000 are fully equipped for front-line fighting in the winter, but the equipment of the troops in the front line and reserve is very adequate." By June the Russians will have an army twice as big as before the war, and it will be fully equipped.

How are we to account for this extraordinary achievement ? The answer lies in the loyalty and determination of every individual Russian. Even before the war Russian feeling against the Germans was very strong, but when Hitler launched his attack every single Russian individual, man, woman and child, made up his or her mind that at all costs they would defend their country against the German invaders. Of course, the cost has been enormous in terms of suffering and domestic tragedy. Food has been short, since transport has had to be concentrated on supplying the army. People have gone cold, "and unless you have lived in Russia it is difficult to realize what it means when the temperature is 30 degrees or 40 degrees below zero. If all their windows are broken it is impossible to maintain any warmth, and the trouble is that so many windows were broken." Yet, in spite of all, "when I returned to Moscow last month, I had never seen the population with their tails higher up. They were magnificent . . ."

ANOTHER encouraging feature is that the Russians have discovered and use a number of very young generals. Particularly in the fighting on the Moscow front a great many young officers in the thirties have shown their brilliance and have been promoted to commands. They have done magnificently, but all the same, the plan for the defence of Moscow and the counter-attack was conceived by Premier Stalin. Although in the veteran Marshal Shaposhnikov he has a most competent Chief of Staff, Stalin himself (Sir Stafford Cripps makes plain) is the brain of the Russian resistance, the real military genius of the war on the Eastern Front.

Then in the matter of war production the Russians have worked wonders. Many of their industries in the areas overrun or threatened by the Nazis were moved to the east in good time, and some of these are already functioning afresh. Industrial development in the Urals and beyond is very great indeed—at least double or treble their

capacity at the beginning of the war. But, none-the-less, the Russians need our help ; and so far they have been very satisfied with the assistance we have given them in the way of planes and tanks. Altogether, then, concludes the Man from the Kremlin, we have every reason to be optimistic about the issue of the coming campaign.

YES, they are amazing people, the Russians. But those of us who know our history should not be so very surprised. Under Stalin and the Bolsheviks the Russians have done well ; but when all things are considered they—the rank and file of the army, the junior officers, the great mass of the people —did well even under "the purblind, corrupt, incompetent tyranny" that was the Tsarist regime. Mr. Churchill once protested against that forthright description, but Mr. Lloyd George, out of greater knowledge and broader sympathy, has maintained that Tsarism fell "because every fibre of its power, influence and authority had rotted through and through." Yet under that rotten system the Russians fought for nearly three years—three years of almost continuous, one might say altogether senseless, slaughter. In his "War Memoirs" Mr. Lloyd George quotes message after message sent by the Russian C.-in-C.'s Chief of Staff to the War Minister in Petrograd. As early as April 1915 he was complaining that "the question of cartridges and rifles is a bloody one." A month later, "from all armies the cry goes up 'Give cartridges.'" Another week : "Yesterday the Germans dropped on to a section of one of the regiments 3,000 heavy shells. They demolished everything. And we fired barely 100." In their metal-battered trenches the unarmed living among the Russians snatched the rifles of the fallen ; and when rifles failed, as they so often did, they fought with knives and bare fists. The casualties were horrible ; but when someone in the Duma complained, a Russian general is reported to have said, "Don't worry yourself. Thank God, of men, at all events, we have enough." That sort of thing went on for nearly three years.

THAT is what the Russians were like a generation ago ; their grandfathers were the same, the men we fought in the Crimea, and their great-grandfathers who put Napoleon "on the spot." Do you remember that famous chapter in Tolstoy's "War and Peace," in which he describes the battle of Borodino in 1812—the battle which was not a battle but a prolonged massacre ? Napoleon had used all the old manoeuvres that had been invariably crowned with success, yet so far from victory being secured, "from all sides the same tidings kept pouring in, of killed or wounded generals, of reinforcements needed, of the troops being in disorder, and the Russians impossible to move." They ought to have fled, according to all the rules of Napoleonic experience. But they stood— and died rather than give way. Afterwards they put up an obelisk at Borodino—it is only 10 miles from Mozhaisk, where Hitler's men are dying today—with the inscription "End of offensive. Beginning of flight and ruin of the enemy." Perhaps it is there still.

SIR STAFFORD CRIPPS, M.P., photographed on his return to London from Moscow after relinquishing his post as Ambassador to the U.S.S.R.
Photo, Central Press

E. ROYSTON PIKE

From Across the Atlantic New Comrades Come

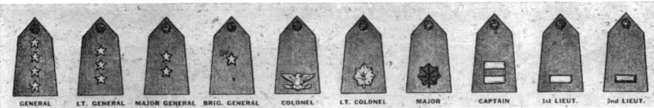

GENERAL   LT. GENERAL   MAJOR GENERAL   BRIG. GENERAL   COLONEL   LT. COLONEL   MAJOR   CAPTAIN   1st LIEUT.   2nd LIEUT.

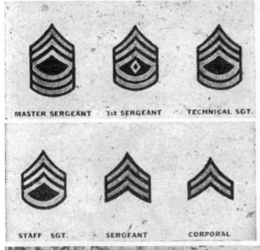

MASTER SERGEANT   1st SERGEANT   TECHNICAL SGT.

STAFF SGT.   SERGEANT   CORPORAL

INSIGNIA worn by commissioned and non-commissioned officers in the United States Army are seen above and left. When the insignia are the same (viz. 2nd Lt. and 1st Lt. : Major and Lt.-Col.) the higher rank is in gold and the lower rank in silver. Among N.C.O.s the rank of Master Sergeant corresponds to our R.S.M. A single stripe (not shown left) denotes a 1st class Private. A 1st Sergeant is also known as a top sergeant. The ordinary infantry sergeant is known as a line sergeant. The men's olive green cap is piped with a colour denoting the arm of the service, but the officer's piping of black and gold is invariable.

' OLD GLORY ' FLIES IN IRELAND as a detachment of American troops, some of the first contingent to come to the United Kingdom since the last war, marches from the quayside after disembarking at a Northern Ireland port on Jan. 26. The contingent was under the command of Maj.-Gen. Russell P. Hartle, and its safe arrival was described by Sir Archibald Sinclair, in his speech of welcome, as " a gloomy portent for Mr. Hitler." Symbolic of the understanding between the two great democracies is the handshake with which a British sergeant greets a newly arrived American colleague, centre right.

Photos, P.N.A. and The Daily Mirror

VANCOUVER (above), which celebrated its jubilee in 1936, is the great Canadian terminal point on the Pacific. It lies at the wooded western edge of British Columbia and, standing on the south side of Burrard Inlet, it has one of the finest natural harbours in the world.

SYDNEY (below), in New South Wales, at the other end of the Pacific, is the most important port in Australia, and the harbour, thirteen miles in depth, is cut up into bays and headlands which provide some 200 miles of sea frontage. The photograph shows Harbour Bridge, opened in 1932.

Great Cities Now Hear the Winds of War

SAN FRANCISCO (above), chief port of America's Pacific coast, has a magnificent land-locked bay providing a vast natural harbour approached through a gap in the coastal mountains called the Golden Gate. This view of the city shows the San Francisco-Oakland Bay Bridge.

YOKOHAMA (below), the seaport of Tokyo, lies on a wide, unsheltered bay, and the harbour is mainly protected by breakwaters built in 1896. A mere fishing village in 1859, it now has over 700,000 inhabitants. It has been largely rebuilt since its devastation by earthquake in 1923.

If Only There Were More Australians!

Never in Australia's history has she found herself in so dangerous a position as now, when the Japanese invaders are already establishing their hold on the islands lying just to the north. What is said below of the Commonwealth may help towards an understanding of the strategic problem.

SEVEN million Australians—and a hundred million Japanese! There in a nutshell is the nightmare which for many years has oppressed the Australian imagination; and today, when the yellow flood is actually lapping Australia's northern coasts, the nightmare has become a reality.

So few are the Australians, and so vast is the territory which is theirs to hold—if they can. England has just over 700 people per square mile, but Australia has only a fraction over two per square mile; and Australia is fifty times the size of England and Wales. There are fewer Australians than there are "Londoners." Australia is as big as the United States, but there are 43 people for every square mile of the American Union. To add to the contrast, most of Australia's three million square miles have no people at all; nearly half the Commonwealth's population is concentrated in the capital cities, in Sydney and Melbourne, Brisbane, Adelaide and Perth. New South Wales is the most populated of the States comprising the Australian Commonwealth, and some half its people live in Sydney. This great metropolis on the Pacific ranks indeed as the third largest city in the British Empire, surpassed only by London and Calcutta. And in Australia, as in Britain, there is a drift to the towns; Australia's cities, like ours, eat men.

But it is only fair to point out that less than two hundred years ago Australia was inhabited only by wandering tribes of aborigines, men in the lowest scale of human life. There are 60,000 of them left, and some 20,000 half-castes; but for the rest the Australians are almost entirely of our own stock. Eighty-six in every hundred were born in Australia, and eleven in the British Isles; Australia, it has been said, is more British than Britain—only a little less British than New Zealand.

Those seven millions include some of the most vigorous, mentally and physically, of the world's folk; for the most part a sophisticated people, and exceedingly urbanized. They have a high standard of living, one of the highest in the world; and a high standard of living does not go well with a high birth-rate. Contraception is cheaper than babies—and far less trouble. Australia's birth-rate is higher than England's—17·4 per thousand compared with our 14·9—and its death-rate is lower, 9·4 compared with England's 12·4; but compare this with Japan's birth-rate of 31 per thousand and death-rate of 17·6. Only three millions have been added to Australia's population in the last 40 years, and it is estimated that only a million more will be added in the next forty. But Japan's population in 1935 increased by over a million, and in several years recently that figure has been approached. Moreover, since the death-rate is falling as well as the birth-rate, Australia's young people are dwindling as compared with the middle-aged and old—just as they are in England.

Of course, a very large part of Australia is unfitted for human habitation—or perhaps we should say for white habitation. Forty per cent of the continent is returned as "unoccupied or occupied by the Crown"; of its 1,900 million acres only 22 million are under crops. Moreover, man is not making much headway against nature. Erosion by wind and rain is terrific. Australia's deserts are encroaching steadily on the fringe of cultivated land; and in their blindness the pastoralists and settlers are aiding their march by cutting down the trees and burning the bush wholesale. Irrigation and a vigorous policy of land colonization on a huge scale are the paramount needs, but they both require labour; and where is the labour to come from? Particularly in the tropical north and in Queensland there are vast tracts seemingly suited for the settlement of oriental peoples, who might indeed manage to get a living where the white man would find it impossible. The Japanese say that, given a chance, they could make good. But to a man the Australians are grimly resolved that they will never be given that chance . . .

A vast unpeopled heart—the dead heart, it is often called—with here and there on the circumference, on the coast or near it, a cluster of population or an area given up to agriculture or to industry: that is Australia. In between the settlements, the congeries of civilized life, stretch for hundreds, even thousands, of miles almost entirely unpopulated wastes. The chief, almost the only, means of communication are the railways, mostly government-owned. (Unfortunately there is no universal railway gauge in Australia, the gauges varying from 3 ft. 6 in. to 5 ft. 3 in.) Each State has its own local system, converging on its capital, but nearly 2,000 miles of the 28,000 miles open belong to the Commonwealth. Chief among these Federal lines is the Trans-Australian, 1,108 miles in length, which links Kalgoorlie in Western Australia with Port Augusta in South Australia. By way of this line the west coast has railway connexion with the east coast, more than 3,000 miles away.

There is still no railway directly linking the north of Australia with the south. But there is now direct communication across the "inland" between Darwin and Port Augusta. From Darwin the North Australia Railway, a Commonwealth line, runs for 316 miles to Birdum; and from Alice Springs in the very heart of Australia—the Centre, as Australians call it—another Federal railway, the Central Australia, runs to Adelaide. From where the line from Darwin peters out into nothingness at Birdum to where its fellow begins at "the Alice" is some 600 miles of wild, hardly explored bush country —at least, that was its state up to two years ago. Now, however, from Larrimah, a new railway siding just north of Birdum, to Alice runs Australia's strategic highway, a fine all-weather road along which thunder the military convoys from the south to Darwin. The road was built under military supervision by some 400 navvies who worked day and night with the assistance of every mechanical aid. The job—621 miles of first-class road— was completed in record time, the road-makers' greatest triumph being the stretch of 300 miles from Tennant Creek to Birdum, which was built in ninety days.

Other new roads have been built of late years, or are in process of construction. One of the most important links the Queensland coast with the North-South road at Tennant Creek; this road too, though it had to be cut through country even more difficult than the Centre, was built at the rate of 3 miles a day. A third is the 1,000-mile Overland Road between Port Augusta in South Australia and Norseman in Western Australia.

These roads not only afford greatly needed means of communication, but are opening up vast new areas, which, when peace returns, will be calling out for the pioneers. But will the call be answered?   E. R. P.

AUSTRALIA, showing the main road and rail communications. The North Australia Railway, from Darwin to Birdum, is now linked to the Central Australia Railway, which runs from Adelaide to Alice Springs, by a new strategical highway.

Specially drawn for THE WAR ILLUSTRATED *by Harrop*

Australia's Heart Is No Longer 'Dead'

DARWIN, with its fuel-oil installation and airport, is a focal point of Australia's defence. Two years ago it was famed for its "Wild West" atmosphere, but now it is essentially a "Services" town.

ALICE SPRINGS, top, in the "Centre" is the railhead where the motor-lorries forming the military convoys of the Central Australian road pick up their loads en route for Birdum and Darwin.

Australia has conscription for her home defence forces; above, men of the Darwin battalion in that town's tropical setting.

For years there was a gap of 1,000 miles between the railway systems of Australia's east and west. Then in 1917 the Commonwealth built the Trans-Australian Railway. Left, a train crossing a typical stretch in the Nullarbor Plain.

Photos, Courtesy of the Australian Government, Keystone

Page 487

Our Searchlight on the War

THE INFERNO OF SINGAPORE

It is learned authoritatively that the defenders of Singapore are well supplied with food and water and are prepared to hold out to the last.

A CHAPTER unique in the history of sieges is being written by the defenders of Singapore. Destiny has brought the great naval base into an unforeseen predicament. Designed as a naval base, it is now threatened by hordes of Japanese soldiers and aeroplanes. That the island and its inhabitants will suffer from enemy bombardment is inevitable, but it is to be hoped that everything possible is being done to increase the number of fighter aircraft to frustrate the Japanese. The people of Britain, who, to some extent, were similarly placed after the fall of

ROYAL OBSERVER CORPS member wearing the new battle dress of blue-grey serge. A woven circular badge, as shown above, is worn on the left breast. The blue beret bears the R.O.C. metal badge. *Photo, Associated Press*

hand, since we are all hoping earnestly that victory will come sooner than later, is there any evidence that the enemy is feeling pressure on the home front? It is reported that Hitler has withdrawn the bulk of the Luftwaffe from the Eastern front. If this is so, there are two conclusions: (1) that the Nazis are anxious about the defence of the Reich, and (2) that Hitler is about to attack elsewhere. To abandon air support on the East front in the heat of hostilities suggests the former. During the last few weeks Germany has lost either through "heart trouble" or forced resignation several old Army generals. Conflict between the Army and the Nazi Party is no secret. As the Army clique weakens in influence so Hitler's personal friend, General Dietrich, commander of

TANK TRANSPORTER used to save wear of tank tracks on hard roads. This transporter, which has a 130-h.p. engine, is carrying a Mark IVa cruiser tank. At the back is a folding "runway" to facilitate loading and unloading. *Photo, British Official*

France, when the thin line of the R.A.F. stood between them and disaster, will understand the feelings of the defenders of Singapore. While their position is one of supreme peril it is also one of great honour. Singapore will ultimately remain British. To have taken part in the present ordeal will ever remain an enviable one. A plucky English girl, who decided to stay on "to be of use," cabling from Singapore to her anxious mother, says, "Everything O.K. Nothing to worry about." Such is the spirit that "wins these 'ere wars," as the Cockney says, with a grim smile.

AUSTRALIAN INCIDENT

Mr. Curtin, the Prime Minister, on his return from Western Australia, replied to the allegations casting doubt on the unity of Australia and Great Britain, saying that they had amazed and shocked him.

WE hope that the recent statements by Australian leaders have cleared the air, and that we shall hear no more of disloyalty and disunion. Mr. Hughes and Mr. Menzies, in their frank attitude towards the situation, have done Britain and Australia a great service. There is no discord between the Mother Country and the Commonwealth, but only admiration and gratitude for mutual courage and determination in the joint struggle for survival. If, however, there is any Fifth Columnism in Australia, and Mr. Hughes has definitely stated that there is, it was wise to denounce it outright, so that it can be watched and restrained. There are two kinds of Fifth Columnists : rank traitors, of whom Quisling is the prototype, and unconscious defeatists, men who are temperamentally afraid, who when things go wrong begin to jitter and express their funk in unreasonable criticism. We notice that such critics in this country seldom have a word of praise for Mr. Churchill and the Government when things go right.

INVASION—OF GERMANY?

Commenting on Hitler's last speech, the Turkish paper Yeni Sabah says that "the speech shows that the German nation is beginning to shake. The German leader appears more afraid of the people's morale than the enemy."

RUSSIA has told us that the *coup de grace* will be inflicted on Germany this year. In the light of Soviet military achievements it is not for us to be sceptical. The Allies, however, must prepare for a long war. Better remember the old song which runs, "It may be for years . . . ," and be on the safe side. On the other

the S.S., increases his power. The S.S. may be likened to some of the later Roman Praetorian guards who were used to bolster up the reigning tyrant. Meanwhile, that obsequious lieutenant of death, Himmler, is adding to the number of his police troops whose real purpose is to thwart revolution in Germany, although they have been used in the Russian campaign. Goering and Heydrich also command armies semi-independent of the German military machine. Are these to be used against the German people should they revolt when the Russians reach the Reich frontier?

A VOICE FROM RIOM

"It is a man already condemned whom you invite to reply to the summons of your courtroom. What is this but a mockery? What effect can my reply have? Has not the issue been already settled before you?"—From the defence of M. Léon Blum, French Socialist ex-Premier

THE curtain has been lifted from the secret trial of Frenchmen arrested on a charge of war guilt by the publication of M. Blum's defence, smuggled out of France, and published in England. We hope that the French people will get to know of M. Blum's brave attack on his accusers. The men who are responsible for the betrayal and ruin of France are not at Riom ; they are at large and working in close collaboration with the Germans. The Riom trials are on a par with the Reichstag fire conspiracy whereby the innocent were tried by the guilty. The grim farce of Riom was staged by the Nazis, with the connivance of certain Frenchmen who, rather than lose their money and power, preferred to hand their country over to the enemy. The Riom idea was an effort to delude the French

people stunned by the sudden collapse of France. Since that evil day our late ally, in the popular sense, has had time to know who are the real culprits. Hence the delay in arriving at any verdict. France is aware that as long as the enemy is in control justice and mercy are dead.

NORWAY IN BONDAGE

Speaking in German, surrounded by Nazi emblems and Nazi bayonets, Quisling, on being appointed Prime Minister of occupied Norway, thanked Hitler and the German Commissar, Terboven.

THE Nazification of Norway makes little progress. According to "Judas" Lie, quisling chief of the police, the "state of emergency demanded most ruthless action against the people, including the use of firearms . . ." While every form of brutality and repression is in operation, Quisling himself has the effrontery to talk about the beginning of a new era in Norway as a free and independent country. Reading such ludicrous statements, one wonders whether words, in Nazi parlance, have entirely reversed their meaning. Quisling's own paper is even called Fritt Folk, meaning free folk. The people of Norway have been assaulted, robbed and frequently murdered. Yet Quisling tells them they are free ! There is something to be said for the theory that Hitlerism is a disease, and those who catch it are quite incapable of forming a sane judgement.

TIN MINERS working on the rock face of a Cornish tin mine with a huge drill. With the loss of tin mines in the Far East, production in the Cornish mines is being increased. In late years tin mining almost ceased in Britain. *Photo, G.P.U.*

So This Is the Way the Japanese Land

SOMEWHERE IN THE PACIFIC a party of Japanese troops forces its way ashore on Allied territory. The drawing does not profess to show any particular landing, but it gives a rough guide to the methods adopted.

Landing Troops

Standing offshore (A) is a transport seen in the act of hoisting wooden sampan-like barges each containing a hundred soldiers plus equipment. They row to shore and unload stores and equipment (B). Some troops, carrying light arms, will make their way through the thick jungle (C). Others are seen scaling the heights in the foreground by means of a rope ladder (D), which has bamboo rungs and round wooden attachments which keep the ladder away from the cliff.

Hauling and Erecting Guns

At (E) a party are hauling a small field-gun up the cliff ; one man is stationed upon a ledge part way up, and assists in keeping the wheel which is being hoisted from dragging against projecting rock. The gun barrel is being carried away slung from a

bamboo pole (F). The erection of a similar small gun is seen in detail in the immediate foreground. The barrel is being lowered on to the recuperator mechanism (G); the breech mechanism and sighting apparatus are fixed on afterwards. The shield (H) is being brought up. (J) is a stereo-telescope used in range-finding. Near by is a Japanese officer; his sword is of the ancient Samurai type (K).

Arms and Equipment

These include: (L) light machine-gun, (M) heavier type of M.G. carried in two parts, (N) small grenade-thrower, (O) grenades in pouches, (P) rubber shoes for running, (Q) small digging spade, (R) water-bottle.

INSET is a Japanese two-man tank ; the machine-gunner is seen in the revolving turret (1), and the driver at (2). A large type of tank, probably 15–18 tons, is seen at (3). Three methods of transport are seen : (4) is a peculiar two-wheeled rickshaw affair which is dragged by man-power. Pack ponies and modern lorries are also used.

Specially drawn by Haworth for THE WAR ILLUSTRATED

The Battle of Singapore Has Started

After eight weeks of bitter war on the beaches and in the jungles of Malaya, the Japanese had succeeded in overrunning the Malay Peninsula and looked across the Johore Strait at the Island of Singapore, where the British forces now stood at bay.

"THE Battle of Malaya has come to an end," said Lt.-Gen. A. E. Percival, G.O.C. Malaya, in a statement issued on Jan. 31, " and the Battle of Singapore has started . . . Today we stand beleaguered in our island fortress. Our task is to hold this fortress until help can come, as assuredly it will come. This we are determined to do."

For a week it had been only too certain that the whole of the Malay Peninsula would have to be evacuated by the Imperial troops, and all during that week the Australians, British and Indians fought a series of fierce rearguard actions. The enemy enjoyed almost complete control of the air, and dive-bombing and machine-gun attacks were almost incessant. By day the men who for weeks had been battling in the jungle strove to hold up the Japanese advance; and night brought them no rest since some had to dig new gun-pits and slit trenches, while the rest withdrew yet another stage towards Singapore. As they went back they blew up roads and bridges, burnt villages and plantations, so that their way was marked by a heavy pall of black smoke.

The last points of contact between the Imperial forces and the enemy were near Pontian Besar on the west, somewhere near Kotatinggi on the east, and at Kulai in the centre. Two battalions of the Australians, with the Gordon Highlanders and Argyll and Sutherlands, kept the enemy at bay while their comrades completed the last lap of 20 miles and marched across the Johore Causeway into the island of Singapore. The withdrawal was completed on the night of Friday, Jan. 30, without the loss of a single man.

The crowded causeway was as clear as Piccadilly Circus at noon, since the moon was brilliant, the most brilliant of the month. Hour after hour the troops poured over the causeway and, once across, pulled off the main roads to their pre-determined positions. Then, tired and filthy, they tumbled from their transports to snatch a few hours' sleep under the rubber trees before going to their new battle stations. A complete change of clothing was given to every man, and there were lashings of hot food available. When the time came for the rearguard to withdraw, the Gordons went first, then the Australians, and finally the Argylls.

"The sight as these tired men—Australians, Indians, Englishmen, Scotsmen—withdrew into the fortress was one I shall never forget," writes W. T. Knox, News Chronicle Special Correspondent. "Two pipers of the Argyll and Sutherland Highlanders—that regiment which first engaged the Japanese on Dec. 8 and has since fought 11 heroic battles against them—were the last to cross the causeway. They piped over the Australians and the Indians, the East Surreys, the Leicesters, the Manchesters and the Loyals; they piped over the Gordons and the Australian sister regiment to the regimental march, 'The Cock of the North.' Then the air changed to 'Blue Bonnets' and 'Jenny's Black E'e' as the Argylls crossed the causeway. Tired Indian and Australian transport drivers woke and grinned as they saw these gallant men go by."

After the last man had crossed there was a pause. It was nearly morning and the quiet waters of the Johore Strait gleamed in the growing light. The day drew on, and then

WAVELL TO SINGAPORE

The Japanese are straining every nerve to keep the advantage gained by their initial treacherous surprise and to gain a quick success. Once their impetus is thwarted they will soon lose courage. Our task is to check them and to gain time for the great reinforcements, which we and our American Allies are sending to the Eastern Theatres.

We are in a similar position to the original British Expeditionary Force which stopped the Germans and saved Europe in the first battle of Ypres. We must be ourselves worthy successors of them and save Asia by fighting these Japanese. We have now reached an area where we cannot be constantly outflanked and where the enemy cannot exploit his superior mobility.

You must yield no strip of ground without fighting hard and leave nothing behind undestroyed that could be of the least service to the enemy. Our friends and Allies, the Dutch, are carrying out this policy in every part of the Netherlands East Indies with sacrifice and resolution.

I look to you all to fight this battle without further thought of retreat and make the defence of Singapore as memorable and successful an exploit as the defence of Tobruk, which British, Australian and Indian troops held so long and gallantly.—Feb. 4, 1942

the order was given to blow up the causeway. There were two explosions; one wrecked the steelwork lock system for passing ships through at the northern end, while the second, which rocked the earth and could be heard all over the island, blew a great gap in the causeway itself. Rails and railway sleepers were flung high into the air and a great cloud of smoke went up.

"A gentle breeze was blowing up the Straits from the east, causing the water to lap gently against the length of the causeway that remained," wrote The Times Special Correspondent in Singapore. "There was no sign of movement on the farther bank. Coils of barbed wire could be seen covering the causeway on the hither side of the breach. On the south side of the Straits of Johore, for 15 miles on each side of the causeway, the Imperial forces—British, Australian, Indian, and Malay—were concealed in jungle, scrub, and swamp. Roads were given up almost entirely to military traffic. Because of the frequent air-raid alerts there were few civilians, Asiatic or European, moving about. . . .

Except for the murmuration of aeroplanes high up in the sky, the occasional fire of A.A. guns, and the distant explosions of bombs, it would have been a perfect morning in the tropics."

So on that Sunday morning the siege of Singapore began. What its cosmopolitan population had regarded as being almost outside the bounds of possibility was now a fact; the enemy were at the gates, separated by only a three-quarter-of-a-mile-wide strip of placid water. But after the first shock they were quick to accustom themselves to the changed conditions; and under the stress and strain of war, in face of the ever-present possibility of wounds or death, a new fellow-ship began to show itself between the hitherto so superior whites and the Asiatics, brown and yellow.

Garrisoned by a truly Imperial force—one made up of Australians, Highlanders, men from Lancashire and the English shires, Indians (Punjabis, Gurkhas, Jats, Baluchis, and Garhwalis), the Malay Regiment and the Sarawak Rangers—Singapore made ready to fight to the last. The situation was grim. Japanese bombers seemed to be everywhere, and the two aerodromes on the island could hardly be used by the British fliers. From every corner came news of fresh Japanese successes: from the Indies to the east, and from Burma to the north, where the Japanese had occupied Moulmein and were threatening to cross the Salween River, thus threatening Rangoon.

But none-the-less Singapore refused to be downhearted. " Substantial reinforcements have been received," announced the Governor of the Straits Settlements, Sir T. Shenton Thomas, in a midnight broadcast on Jan. 31. "Here we are and here we stay . . . each of us to do our bit. This is total war . . . It will be grim, no doubt, but no more grim than in Britain, Russia and China; and if the people of these countries can stand up to total war, so also can we . . . all we have to do is to hang on grimly and inexorably, and for not very long; and the reward will be freedom, happiness, and peace for every one of us."

MOULMEIN, a town of Tenasserim, in Southern Burma, at the estuary of the Salween River, was evacuated by the British about Jan. 31. It is one of the most picturesque of Burmese towns, and above is Temple Hill with its ornate pagodas. The map shows the Salween River and the railway from Rangoon to the Burma Road, main artery of China's war supplies. *Photo, Paul Popper*

'We Stand Beleaguered in Our Island Fortress'

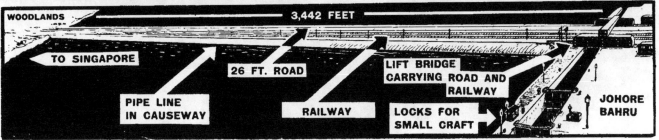

WOODLANDS — 3,442 FEET — TO SINGAPORE — PIPE LINE IN CAUSEWAY — 26 FT. ROAD — RAILWAY — LIFT BRIDGE CARRYING ROAD AND RAILWAY — LOCKS FOR SMALL CRAFT — JOHORE BAHRU

JOHORE CAUSEWAY, linking Singapore Island to the mainland of Malaya, was blown up after the last British troops had been withdrawn from Johore. Top, a view of the Causeway with the Penang express passing. Above, the Causeway in diagram form.

SINGAPORE ISLAND, showing its position in relation to the mainland of Southern Malaya. About midnight on Feb. 8, Japanese detachments crossed the strait at its narrowest point and landed north of Choa Chu Kang.

DEFENCES OF SINGAPORE being further strengthened as the Japanese menace grew. Left, a machine-gun post on a road leading out of the city. Above, Singapore's inhabitants digging trenches to help in the defence of the city.

Photos, Associated Press, E.N.A. Map, The Evening News. Diagram, The Daily Mail

Over a Countryside Held Fast in Winter's [

Red Army men wearing warm fur caps are seen sighting a trench mortar in wintry surroundings (left). Over the frozen fields Soviet infantry are charging an enemy position with fixed bayonets (above).

This is the PE-2, new twin-engined bomber of the Soviet Air Force, details of which are still a closely-guarded secret. One of the most significant factors of the air war in Russia is the way in which, despite tremendous difficulties, Russian maintenance has stood the strain. Col. Stefanovsky, of the Red Air Force, considers that Soviet air weapons are definitely superior to the German.

ALMOST beyond a do
Moscow and Lening
began. Failing in that t
that they could maintai
worst of the winter unti
powerful spring offensiv
realized this; and realize
upsetting the Nazi plans
the rigours of a Russian
acclimatized. The Red /
anything up to 50 degrees
for days and nights in su
During the summer fig
experience in ski-ing we
and set aside for winter
decision has borne fruit.
were trained to make lon
for that physical endura
considers one of the mo
training, long-distance gr
5,000-verst (4,170 miles
Moscow, w

Photos, British Offici

A Red Army machine-gun crew in action (right). Machine-guns are often mounted on sledges (see diagram p. 466). Circle below, German prisoners taken by Red Army men in a recaptured village on the Moscow front.

ded to capture
Russian winter
ably considered
t through the
be ripe for a
High Command
best chance of
full extent by
eir troops were
ained to stand
tay in the open

th considerable
ecially trained
ps. This wise
sands of troops
, and as a test
al Timoshenko
es of military
as the famous
Khabarovsk to

; G.P.U.

A reconnoitring party of Soviet ski troops wearing white camouflage cloaks, hoods and gloves. The Russians have thoroughly reorganized their military ski-ing in the light of experience gained during the Finnish war. Ski-ing has been introduced into all branches of the services, and a platoon in full equipment recently covered 6½ miles in 52 minutes.

Hard Knocks for the Japanese Aggressors

Japan's initial victories have given the enemy temporary command of the south-west Pacific, but though it must take the Allies time to recover and assemble their full striking power, American, Dutch and British ships and planes have by no means lost the means and skill to inflict great losses on their opponents.

ELATED and, perhaps, too confident, and underestimating the strength of the Allied forces in Borneo and Java, the Japanese assembled a huge convoy off the Philippines. It consisted of at least forty ships, protected by about fifteen warships. In coming through the Macassar Strait, which is only eighty miles wide, this large convoy was obviously taking a grave risk. As the Dutch reconnaissance planes gave information of the approach of the enemy ships intense preparations were made to attack them, not in the open sea but in the confined area between Borneo and the Celebes.

On Jan. 23 Dutch Army aeroplanes swooped out of the sky on the straggling target, taking the Japanese commanders completely by surprise. Raining their bombs amid transports and battleships, the bombers scored a direct hit on a large warship and sank a cruiser of the heaviest type. Two other cruisers, a destroyer and four large transports also were seen to be burning furiously. So ended the first day of this brilliant counter-stroke against the Japanese hastening to land forces at Balik Papan, and probably on the island of Java.

On the following day the Dutch planes went into action again and wrought further havoc among the confused lines of the convoy. At least two heavily laden transports were sent to the bottom. But this time the enemy endeavoured to defend the convoy by the use of fighter aircraft operating from a carrier in the vicinity, but the Dutch, in addition to bombing their objectives on the sea, scored a victory in the air.

Continuing the battle on the third day, aircraft completely destroyed a heavy cruiser, set fire to a second cruiser and transport, and shot down four intercepting Japanese Navy "O.O." aeroplanes.

After these fierce daylight attacks the Dutch planes, assisted by American naval units which had hurriedly come into battle from the southern end of the Macassar Strait, attacked the enemy at night. Using bomb and torpedo with deadly effect, seven transports were destroyed and two severely damaged. The Japanese aircraft-carrier was also sunk by an American submarine, and a Dutch submarine accounted for another enemy cruiser and destroyer.

Caught in the Strait the convoy anchored off Balik Papan, a port on the west coast of Borneo. It was joined by a second convoy consisting of a great number of ships and invasion barges, and though the Allies continued to attack by plane, scoring many direct hits among the disembarking

ADML. CHESTER NIMITZ, Commander of the American Pacific Fleet, stated that his fleet would " bring the war to the enemy's front door."
Photo, Associated Press

soldiers, the Japanese succeeded in landing and keeping a foothold on this part of the island.

Total enemy losses in the battle of the Macassar Strait amounted to one battleship or heavy cruiser, 6 cruisers, 18 transports, 3 destroyers, 1 aircraft-carrier and 16 aircraft. These figures indicate the magnitude and success of this engagement, but its effect on the enemy's plans was incalculable. Such large convoys were no doubt intended to bring a quick and decisive action in Java and the Celebes. The Allied command, by rapid and efficient coordination frustrated, for the time being at least, the conquest of Java, a key point in our defence of the south-west Pacific, as well as inflicting on the enemy one of the heaviest defeats in the history of the Japanese Navy.

Destroyers in Action

An incident in the naval war which will take its place in the chronicle of courage was the engagement on Jan. 26 between two British destroyers, the Vampire of the Royal Australian Navy and the Thanet

on the one side, and a Japanese cruiser and three destroyers on the other. The conflict began after dark in the region of Endau, on the east coast of the Malayan Peninsula, when our naval forces attacked a Japanese transport about to land troops. Our destroyers raced into action against heavy odds. After a running fight one Japanese destroyer was sunk, the second was damaged, the third retired. It is regrettable that the Thanet, after a valiant fight, was sunk. These destroyers were veterans of the last war and mounted guns of only 4-in. calibre as compared with the Japanese 4·7 weapons.

America's Fleet Hits Back

Heartening news of American naval successes in the Pacific was received on Feb. 2. This time the U.S. Fleet, so completely destroyed by Japanese propaganda, struck a surprise blow at Japanese naval and air bases in the Marshall and Gilbert Islands. The importance of these bases in the scheme of Japanese aggression is this constant use as centres from which to attack the Philippines and Dutch East Indies. Though few details were published in the Navy communiqué the attack was made in considerable strength, and aimed at several bases.

Admiral Chester Nimitz, Commander-in-Chief, Pacific Fleet, reported that many enemy auxiliaries were sunk or damaged, and Japanese military installations on shore were hit by naval aviation units and shell fire. The enemy also lost a number of planes, some being shot down and others being destroyed on the ground. Eleven American aircraft failed to return.

We can imagine that this hard punch from Uncle Sam must have greatly cheered American and Filipino soldiers in Luzon, where General MacArthur is the hero of the hour. His splendid stand amid the hills of the Bataan Peninsula is one of the finest military feats of the war. When Pearl Harbour was smashed the islands were cut off from their supply. The General, who had made a long and careful study of the terrain, held a meeting with his officers. He is reported to have said, " Any machine-gun nest can be captured if the attacker is willing to pay the price. So can the Philippines be captured if the enemy is willing to write off his losses."

A brave statement, which meant that MacArthur was going to defend his positions to the last man. The Japanese swarm like ants over Luzon and Mindanao. Their ships and planes surround the island, but MacArthur, in his much shortened front, north-west of Manila, in rugged mountainous country, the sea on both sides, and Corregidor forts behind him, is putting the price of Japanese victory higher every day.

On Feb. 2 two enemy attempts to land troops on the west coast were obliterated, although the Japanese invaders were composed of the famous Tatori shock troops. Another attempt at midnight was also foiled with very heavy losses. In this action an American patrol vessel did valiant work in dispersing Japanese barges full of troops, and even fought off an enemy warship and destroyer. Not a single Japanese soldier reached the shore alive. In the eastern sector, round about Pilar, the Japanese, with the 65th division, attempted a frontal attack which was part of an enveloping movement in conjunction with the 141st and 122nd regiment of infantry. These manoeuvres were completely frustrated.

H.M.S. THANET, an " S " class destroyer of 905 tons, completed 1918-19, was lost when she and H.M.A.S. Vampire attacked a Japanese cruiser and three destroyers off Malaya on Jan. 26.

Page 494
Photo, Wright and Logan

Half the Globe Is the Pacific Battlefield

SEEN FROM THE MOON the Pacific Ocean must seem to cover half the terrestrial planet. It embraces about three-eighths of the total sea area of the world, and this map gives some idea of the vast distances involved in traversing this new arena of war. From Panama to Singapore is a matter of 11,800 miles.

Drawn by Felix Gardon, and based on material from Life Magazine, New York

FOLLOWING the sudden Japanese attack on Pearl Harbour on Dec. 8, 1941, little was heard of the United States Pacific Fleet until the announcement from Washington on Feb. 1, 1942, of the surprise attack on the Marshall and Gilbert Islands. (See p. 494.)

"Events have emphasized the importance of our Pacific forces in the broad strategy of the Allied war effort," said Admiral Chester Nimitz, Commander-in-Chief of the U.S. Pacific Fleet, after this action. "This war will keep us busy every moment of every day and night across the vast reaches of the Pacific—specifically those areas where we can most effectively harass the enemy and contribute to our foreign security . . . Every ship and every man of the United States Pacific Fleet is now being used to the fullest extent to bring the war to the enemy's front door."

Admiral Nimitz had hoped to encounter large enemy combatant vessels, but his report indicated that none were to be found, and some idea of the difficulty experienced in making contact with the main battle fleets of the enemy in the Pacific may

be gained from the map above, showing the vast distances which separate the continents.

The Japanese have a great advantage in operating much closer to home than either the British or American forces. Japan is only 1,250 miles from Manila, and with Indo-China and Thailand in her grasp she found herself within easy striking distance of Burma and Singapore. Moreover, her naval movements are protected on one flank by her vassal states bordering the South China Sea.

MODERN fighting ships have not an unlimited radius of action; their fuel capacity is relatively small. Though individual ships may roam the seas for weeks or months at a time, refuelling as opportunity presents itself, a battle fleet, with its attendant ancillary units, cannot remain at sea under war conditions for more than a few days at a time. So, in the vast expanse of the Pacific, naval strategy must hinge on the number of bases available. Even with the recent increase in the number of potential bases in the Pacific, it still remains true that in the main the

great battle fleets are dependent on shore communications, and therefore the fleet which can work closest to its home bases has an advantage.

But as an element in naval strategy the islands of the Pacific are of the utmost importance. Since 1919 Japan, under the Treaty of Versailles, has had mandatory powers over several of these island groups, though, under the Mandate of the League of Nations, the use of these islands for warlike purposes and their fortification were forbidden, and under the Washington Treaty of 1922 the British Empire, the U.S.A. and Japan agreed to maintain the status quo in many of the most important strategic positions in the Pacific.

BUT in 1934 Japan decided to terminate the Washington Naval Treaty, in 1935 she withdrew from the London Naval Conference, and the limitations in the size of the battle fleets of the three Powers imposed by agreements of 1922 and 1931 lapsed, as did the provision against fortifying the island bases. So Japan forged ahead with plans for naval domination in this vast ocean.

WEDNESDAY, JAN. 28, 1942   879th day

Air.—Night attack by R.A.F. on Boulogne area, the docks at Rotterdam and objectives in Munster.

Russian Front.—Russian troops advancing in direction of Smolensk from Staraya Toropa and Zapadnaya Dvina. Further Russian progress towards Yelnia.

Far East.—In Malaya heavy fighting around Rengit, 50 miles from Singapore. Government of Straits Settlements issued orders for the evacuation of all persons and livestock from a coastal strip one mile wide on the northern shore of Singapore Island. Eight enemy raiders shot down in a daylight attack on Rangoon. In the Dutch Indies stiff resistance offered to Jap landings at Kendari and Sempara in the Celebes. Nine enemy air raids on Emmahaven, in Sumatra.

THURSDAY, JAN. 29   880th day

Sea.—Admiralty announced sinking of a U-boat by Free French corvette Roselys.

Air.—R.A.F. offensive sweep over N. France.

Russian Front.—Moscow announced recapture of Barvenkova and Lozovaya, on the Ukraine front. Myatlevo, 45 miles S.E. of Vyazma, and Sukhinichi, 140 miles S.W. of Moscow, also retaken by Red Army.

Africa.—Benghazi again in Axis hands, Rommel's forces reached Regima, five miles beyond Benina aerodrome.

Far East.—In Malaya, Japanese reached Ulu Sedili, 38 miles from Johore Bahru. Batavia announced landing by Japanese at Pamangkat, on west coast of Borneo. At least 12 enemy planes destroyed by British and American pilots in the Rangoon area.

FRIDAY, JAN. 30   881st day

Russian Front.—Moscow announced the recapture of several more inhabited points.

Far East.—In Malaya, Japanese reached Kulai, 18 miles from Singapore Island. Fighting in Burma developed east of Moulmein. Japanese in Luzon reinforced. Fighting continued in and around Balik Papan, in Borneo. Dutch guerillas active in the Minahassa peninsula of Celebes. Japanese transports sighted off Amboyna.

Home.—Boys of 17 registered for national service.

General.—Hitler, in a speech made in Berlin, warned Germany that the road ahead was likely to be hard and difficult.

SATURDAY, JAN. 31   882nd day

Russian Front.—Kuibishev announced that Russian troops in the Southern Ukraine had broken through the German lines and were pressing forward. Red Army troops reported within 37 miles of Dnepropetrovsk.

Far East.—An Army communiqué from Rangoon announced that our forces had evacuated Moulmein. In Malaya, British forces were withdrawn from the mainland on to Singapore Island and the causeway over the Johore Strait was breached. Tokyo announced that their forces had captured Sambas, in Dutch Borneo, after a successful landing. Amboyna heavily shelled and bombed.

SUNDAY, FEB. 1   883rd day

Sea.—U.S. Navy Dept. announced that an attack had been made by surface and air units of the U.S. Pacific Fleet on Japanese bases in the Marshall and Gilbert Islands.

Russian Front.—Red Army units made further considerable advances on the Ukraine front.

Africa.—Gen. Rommel's spearhead reached a point 27 miles east of Barce.

Far East.—From Singapore Island British batteries shelled Japanese positions and supply roads on the mainland unceasingly. In the Philippines, a Japanese force at Ternate, assembling for an attack on Corregidor, was wiped out by the heavy guns

of the fortress. In Burma, British took up new positions along the western bank of the Salween River. Japanese parties which landed at Amboyna on Jan. 31 reached the vicinity of the aerodrome.

General.—Vidkun Quisling made puppet Prime Minister of Norway by the Nazis.

MONDAY, FEB. 2   884th day

Russian Front.—Russian drive into the Ukraine continues. On the Leningrad front units of Gen. Meretskov had a local success on the west bank of the Volkhov River. Russians admitted recapture by Germans of Theodosia, in the Crimea.

Africa.—Rommel's Libyan advance continued, the spearhead of the attack reaching a point only 60 miles from Derna.

Far East.—Japanese massing for assault on Singapore. In Burma, stiff fighting along the line of the Salween River. In the Philippines another heavy attack on Gen. MacArthur's position was beaten off with heavy losses to the enemy. Further Japanese reinforcements landed on the island of Amboyna. American aircraft sunk two enemy transports off Balik Papan.

General.—The Egyptian cabinet resigned. Berlin announced that Goering had been in Italy over a week. He visited many units of the Luftwaffe and conferred with Mussolini and the King of Italy.

TUESDAY, FEB. 3   885th day

Russian Front.—Red Army advanced in most sectors. Fierce fighting around Rjev and near Kharkov.

Africa.—Rommel's advance slowed down. British mobile columns continued to harass the enemy.

Far East.—Two Japanese attempts to land troops on the west coast of Luzon were foiled and heavy losses inflicted on the enemy. Surabaya, main Dutch naval base on island of Java, had its first air raid. Heavy Japanese air attacks on Singapore.

General.—Mr. Eden announced in the House of Commons that an agreement had been signed in Addis Ababa recognising Abyssinia as once more a free and independent country.

WEDNESDAY, FEB. 4   886th day

Russian Front.—Moscow reported that many towns and villages in the Smolensk area had been recaptured. Kuibishev radio stated that Timoshenko's armies had pierced the German defences on the Kharkov front.

Africa.—Gen. Rommel's troops reached Derna.

Far East.—Dutch and Japanese forces still battling for Amboyna. Chinese troops captured Cheng Mook-Tou, 30 miles from Hong Kong. Another Jap attack in the Philippines

broken up. More air raids on Singapore. Koepang, capital of Dutch Timor, bombed and machine-gunned. British and Indian troops continued to hold the Salween line in Burma.

Home.—Lord Beaverbrook appointed Minister of War Production. Sir Andrew Duncan became Minister of Supply.

THURSDAY, FEB. 5   887th day

Sea.—Admiralty announced the loss of H.M. submarine Triumph.

Russian Front.—Timoshenko's armies launched big pincers movement on Kharkov. Fierce fighting in the sector between Leningrad and the Valdai Hills.

Africa.—Little change in the general position.

Far East.—Heavy artillery duels across the Johore Strait. Surabaya again raided. Japanese aircraft raided Port Moresby, in New Guinea.

General.—New government formed in Cairo with Nahas Pasha as Premier.

FRIDAY, FEB. 6   888th day

Air.—Night attack by R.A.F. on docks at Brest.

Russian Front.—Fierce fighting on an 80-mile front from Bieigorod to Kursk.

Mediterranean.—Two enemy supply ships torpedoed by naval aircraft.

Africa.—Axis forces claimed capture of Tmimi, S.W. of Bomba.

Far East.—Samarinda, oil port on the E. coast of Borneo, occupied by Japs. In the Philippines fresh Japanese landings at Luzon reported. At Singapore the gun duel across the Johore Strait continued. 10 Japanese raiders shot down over Rangoon.

General.—Anglo-U.S. combined Chiefs of Staff Group established. Munitions Assignment Board set up in U.S. under Mr. Harry Hopkins.

SATURDAY, FEB. 7   889th day

Air.—Offensive patrols by Bomber Command over North Sea. N.E. coast of Germany raided.

Russian Front.—Red Army continued to advance in the four main sectors of the Eastern Front.

Africa.—Little change in the land situation.

Far East.—Japanese air raids on Surabaya. Northern areas of Singapore Island heavily shelled. Batavia announced occupation of Pontianak by Japanese. Japanese cruiser sunk by Dutch aircraft near Amboyna.

General.—U.S. Navy Dept. announced that all naval units in Australia and New Zealand area had been combined under Vice-Admiral H. F. Leary, designated Commander of the Anzac Forces.

H.M.S. TIGRIS, which recently inflicted severe losses on German transports and supply vessels in Arctic waters, is a " patrol type " submarine of the Triton class. Her captain, Commander H. F. Bone, D.S.O., D.S.C., R.N., is seen in the conning tower of the Tigris.

Bardia, 'Bastion of Fascism,' Captured Again

OUTSIDE BARDIA large batches of Axis prisoners are congregated near the desert highway after the recapture of that " Fascist bastion " on Jan. 2. Bardia was recaptured by units of the 1st and 2nd South African Divisions under the leadership of Maj.-Gen. I. P. de Villiers, M.C., and the prisoners taken amounted to 7,500, including the German commander of the garrison, Maj.-Gen. Schmidt. In addition, over 1,000 British prisoners of war there were released.

Photo British Official: Crown Copyright

464-1: MR. CHURCHILL AND THE CRITICS

WHEN on his return from Washington Mr. Churchill discovered that his Government was being attacked so widely and so severely, he decided that he must ask the House of Commons for a vote of confidence, '' because things have gone badly and worse is to come.'' So on Jan. 27 the Prime Minister opened a three-days' debate.

After some account of the Battle of Libya the Premier went on to discuss the fighting in the Far East. For nearly two years Japan had threatened an attack, and in anticipation of the blow '' every scrap of shipping we could draw away from our vital supply routes, every U-boat escort we could divert from the Battle of the Atlantic, has been busy to the utmost capacity in carrying troops, tanks and munitions from this island to the East.'' But we had also to help Russia, try to beat Rommel and form a stronger front from the Levant to the Caspian. Some 60,000 men were concentrated at Singapore, and the Prince of Wales and the Repulse had been sent out east : but priority in modern aircraft, in tanks and in anti-aircraft and anti-tank artillery had been accorded to the Nile Valley. Then came some account of what had been decided in Washington. The vanguard of an American army has already arrived in the United Kingdom ; the league of 26 United Nations had been formed ; measures had been devised to defend our possessions against Japan ; and a vast common pool of weapons and munitions, raw materials and shipping had been established. '' So (concluded the Premier) it is because I see the light gleaming behind the clouds and broadening on our path, that I make so bold now as to demand a declaration of confidence of the House of Commons as an additional weapon in the armoury of the United Nations.''

★ Tragedy of the Repulse and the Prince of Wales

FIRST to follow the Premier was Mr. Peth-ick-Lawrence (Lab., Edinburgh, E.). After a caustic reference to those who pay lip service to Mr. Churchill's leadership while in fact they are seeking to undermine it, he referred to the anxiety felt about many things, particularly about what has been happening in the Far East.

Why were the Prince of Wales and the Repulse sent to eastern waters without being assured of adequate aircraft protection ? It is no answer for the Prime Minister to say that greater aircraft protection than was actually sent was not available ; if these important ships could not be properly protected by aircraft, why were they sent at all ?

Cmdr. Sir A. Southby (Con., Epsom) declared that it was a fatal blunder to dispatch the capital ships to the Far East. By themselves they could not hope to engage the Japanese fleet. They lacked not only adequate fighter protection but destroyer protection. '' I cannot believe that expert naval officers at the Admiralty failed to advise that in the circumstances those ships should be accompanied by an aircraft carrier.''

★ 'No Zeal, but—Plenty of Overtime!'

Sir Herbert Williams (Con., Croydon, S.) expressed himself in highly critical fashion. He declared that it was wrong that the Prime Minister should also be Minister of Defence : '' You have one man dominating the chiefs of staff who are, after all, only employees whom he can sack at any moment.''

This view was strongly rebutted a little later by Mr. Attlee. But, went on Sir Herbert, '' I don't want to change the Prime Minister. I want a changed Prime Minister . . .'' Then he proceeded to belabour the Civil Service machine.

Whitehall swarms with committees, and they are all reasons for not coming to a decision about something or other. The way in which correspondence is handled in Government departments is quite stupid. I have been a Minister and seen the rotten system at work. But it is tolerated—tolerated by Ministers, nine-tenths of whom have never in their lives earned £500 a year in ordinary industry. No one in the commercial world would ever take the job of a Parliamentary secretary. There is no zeal in our Government departments, but there is plenty of overtime.

★ Russia Has Done It : Why Not We ?

Dr. Haden Guest (Lab., Islington, N.) made a pertinent comparison between Britain's position and Russia's.

Does the House not realize that during 20 years or little more Russia has built up out of colonial people, who were in some cases much more primitive than colonial peoples in our own Empire, a vast, powerful, and enthusiastic army which is now repelling the Germans in Russia ? Why have we not built up something of the kind in the East ? We have had two years to prepare. Why have not these two years been used ? How is it that our people in Malaya were so lacking in foresight and knowledge, perhaps so preoccupied with the prices of tin and rubber and so little preoccupied with the defence of Empire interests, that they did not raise the formidable defence force which they might have raised ? Why have we not organized the man-power in India and Burma, with their 400,000,000 people ?

★ Let Us Cooperate with India's Millions

Mr. S. O. Davies (Lab., Merthyr) also pleaded for the full utilization of '' the vast potential arsenal of human and material power that lies undeveloped, unused, and largely treated with contempt, in India.''

When the Secretary of State for India tells the public that India is today the main arsenal of war of both the Middle East and Far East, he is not only talking nonsense, but comes pretty near to being charged with deliberately misleading the people of this country. There is one aircraft works in a country that can boast a labour power amounting to 150,000,000 men and women. There may be 1,000,000 men in the Indian Army, but the population of India is 400,000,000. What is the Government fighting for ? Is it to make the world safe for free peoples ? Are they fighting for the principles that are laid down in the Atlantic Charter ? If so, India has the first call on them, not merely humanly speaking, but strategically.

★ 'Don't the Germans Have Dust-Storms ?'

Opening the second day's debate, Sir J. Wardlaw-Milne (Con., Kidderminster) protested against the '' flights of fancy '' indulged in by the authorities at Singapore. '' If the Commander-in-Chief knew that we were not ready he should have kept his mouth shut.'' Then he turned to an interesting side-issue.

Nothing has disgusted me more in the last few weeks than some of the communiqués which we have read. I realize that in Libya the weather has been bad. It is right that we should be told that it has been bad. But you would think, to listen to the statements that we get from the B.B.C., that the dust-storms fall only on the British troops and that the Germans never had a dust-storm ; and again that it is '' not cricket,'' that it is '' hitting below the belt,'' for the Japanese to land in sampans and proceed up creeks. Really these things are very childish . . .

For the rest, Sir John's speech was devoted to a criticism of our industrial effort.

Our production has gone up tremendously, '' but when the Prime Minister says it is four or ten times, or whatever it was, more than it was in 1917 he might as well tell us that it is 100 times more than it was in the Boer War, or a thousand times what it was at Agincourt . . .

★ Did Malaya Go Short for Russia's Sake ?

As so often in recent months, Mr. Shinwell (Lab., Seaham) was highly critical. Why not two votes of confidence ? he asked, one in the Prime Minister and another in the remaining members of the Government. Probably 90 per cent of the House would vote for the Prime Minister ; probably 95 per cent of Hon. Members would vote against the second —and they might include the Prime Minister, who, presumably, knows his Government . . . Mr. Shinwell was particularly contemptuous of the suggestion that the Far East had been deprived of supplies because of our Russian commitments.

This is surely fantastic. Apart from some raw material, it was only in September that we began to assist Russia with aircraft and tanks, and then obviously only in small quantities. In the time available it is doubtful whether we have sent to Russia much more than 1,000 aircraft, 1,000 tanks, and probably the same number of guns. This is only about a couple of weeks' production, that is, if the Government's declarations about our rapidly extending output are accurate. It is only chicken feed in relation to the vast needs of our ally in her epic-making resistance.

★ We Have 18,000,000 Men, the Axis Has 15,000,000

Mr. Noel Baker (Lab., Derby) declared that the salient factor of the present situation was the predominance of the Allies.

On the most conservative computation, the United Nations have 18,000,000 men in arms, mobilized, trained, equipped. The Axis cannot have more than 15,000,000 ; and 3,000,000 of them are the reluctant serfs of the senile criminal in Rome. Our production of arms has great defects ; but with the production of Russia it must now equal or very nearly equal the output which Hitler can achieve ; and on top of that we have the 45,000 tanks and the 60,000 aircraft which President Roosevelt has promised for this year. We have still vast unmobilized resources ; the Axis Powers have none.

So the great debate drew to a close. There were many more speeches, filled with criticism for the most part, but criticism professing to be of the most helpful kind. Then on Jan. 29 the Prime Minister made his reply. No one could say that it had not been a necessary debate, he said. Many would think it had been a valuable one. He had heard or read every word, and declared himself ready to profit to the full from the many constructive and helpful lines of thought that had been advanced. '' I shall not be like the saint, to whom I have before referred in this House but whose name I have unhappily forgotten, who refused to do right because the devil prompted him. Neither shall I be deterred from doing what I am convinced is right by the fact that I have thought differently about it in some distant, or even in some recent, past.'' Already he had one change to announce—the appointment of a Minister of Production [Lord Beaverbrook].

Then he came to the question of the sinking of the Prince of Wales and the Repulse. If Admiral Tom Phillips's action had been successful, the invasion of Malaya would have been paralysed at its birth. '' In the opinion of the Board of Admiralty the risks which Admiral Phillips took were fair and reasonable, in the light of the knowledge which he had of the enemy, when compared with the very urgent and vital issues at stake on which the whole safety of Malaya might have depended . . . I could not bring myself to pronounce condemnation of his audacious, daring action.''

The Prime Minister concluded with an avowal of confidence that we shall bring this conflict to an end in a manner agreeable to the interests of our country and the future of the world. '' I have finished. Let every man now act in accordance with what he thinks is his duty in harmony with his heart and conscience.'' On the House being divided, 464 voted for the motion of confidence and one, Mr. J. Maxton, against.

Women are Making Britain's Giant Bomber

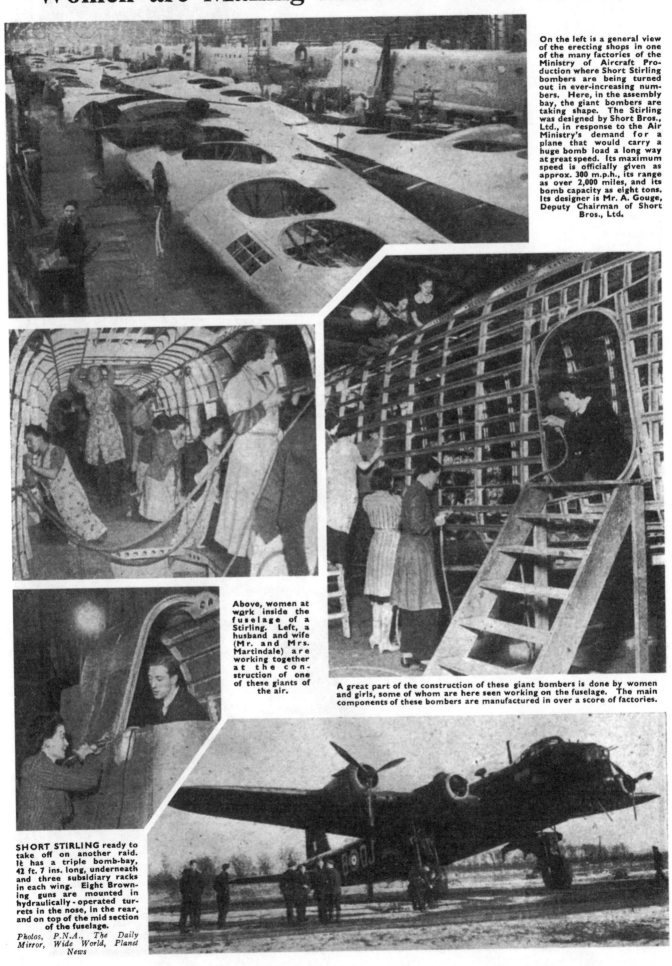

On the left is a general view of the erecting shops in one of the many factories of the Ministry of Aircraft Production where Short Stirling bombers are being turned out in ever-increasing numbers. Here, in the assembly bay, the giant bombers are taking shape. The Stirling was designed by Short Bros., Ltd., in response to the Air Ministry's demand for a plane that would carry a huge bomb load a long way at great speed. Its maximum speed is officially given as approx. 300 m.p.h., its range as over 2,000 miles, and its bomb capacity as eight tons. Its designer is Mr. A. Gouge, Deputy Chairman of Short Bros., Ltd.

Above, women at work inside the fuselage of a Stirling. Left, a husband and wife (Mr. and Mrs. Martindale) are working together at the construction of one of these giants of the air.

A great part of the construction of these giant bombers is done by women and girls, some of whom are here seen working on the fuselage. The main components of these bombers are manufactured in over a score of factories.

SHORT STIRLING ready to take off on another raid. It has a triple bomb-bay, 42 ft. 7 ins. long, underneath and three subsidiary racks in each wing. Eight Browning guns are mounted in hydraulically-operated turrets in the nose, in the rear, and on top of the mid section of the fuselage.

Photos, P.N.A., The Daily Mirror, Wide World, Planet News

H.M.S. DUKE OF YORK, the latest addition to Britain's sea power, is now in commission, and it was recently revealed that Mr. Churchill travelled in her across the Atlantic on the occasion of his visit to America. Laid down in May 1937 the Duke of York is a sister ship of the King George V and the ill-fated Prince of Wales. This new battleship has a displacement of 35,000 tons and her armament includes ten 14-in. and sixteen 5·25-in. guns. She carries four aircraft launched by catapult. Her normal complement is 1,500. This photograph of the Duke of York was taken looking towards her forward gun turrets. Her commander is Capt. Cecil Harcourt, R.N., who was appointed Director of the Operations Division at the Admiralty soon after war broke out.

Photo, British Official: Crown Copyright

Meet the Men of Queen Wilhelmina's Navy

NETHERLANDS ARMS, with the proud device "I will uphold," on the bridge of the Dutch ship Van Meerlant, serving with the Royal Navy.

DUTCH MECHANICS at a Royal Dutch Naval Air Service operational base in Scotland have a lift on the bomb tractor. Dutch and Dutch Colonial airmen are working in close cooperation with the R.A.F.

Lieut.-Commander J. F. van Dulm, captain of a Dutch submarine cooperating with the Royal Navy in the Mediterranean which on the night of Nov. 28 1941, sank the German submarine U.95.

THE DUTCH SUBMARINE which torpedoed and sank the German submarine U.95 in the Mediterranean is seen, left, arriving at a British port. On the right, Kapitanleutnant Gert Schreiber, captain of the U.95, steps ashore to go into captivity, followed by the survivors of his crew. The torpedo fired by the Dutch vessel sank the U.95 in six seconds.

Photos, British Official ; Crown Copyright ; Planet News

I Was There! .... Eye Witness Stories of the War

With Unbelievable Suddenness the Barham Sank

Told by Capt. C. E. Morgan of the Valiant to Massy Anderson, Reuter's special correspondent, this dramatic story of H.M.S. Barham's sinking off Sollum on Nov. 25, 1941, has a tragic interest in that Mr. Anderson himself went down in the Galatea a few weeks later.

Malayan native soldier of the British forces shows his approval on finding the wreckage of a Japanese plane shot down in Malaya.
Photo, British Official

IT was like something one sees on the films [Captain Morgan of the Valiant said to Reuter's correspondent, Massy Anderson]. The 35,000-ton ship disappeared with unbelievable suddenness; it was only 4 minutes 35 seconds exactly from the moment the torpedoes struck until she had completely disappeared.

Our battleships were proceeding westwards line ahead, with the Valiant immediately astern the Barham and with, a destroyer screen ahead out, ahead of the battle fleet. At 4.23 p.m., carrying out a normal zigzag, we turned to port together, thus bringing the ships into echelon formation.

Suddenly, at 4.25, I heard a loud explosion, followed by two further explosions a couple of seconds later. Fountains of water and two enormous columns of smoke shot skywards. The smoke formed an enormous mushroom, gradually enveloping the whole of the Barham, except the after part, which was subsequently also blotted out as the ship slid into a vast pall of smoke.

As the explosions occurred the officer on watch gave the command "Hard to port," to keep clear of the Barham.

Fifteen seconds later I saw a submarine break the surface, possibly forced there by the explosion. Passing from left to right, the submarine was apparently making to cross the Valiant's bows between us and the Barham. He was only about seven degrees off my starboard bow and 150 yards away, though he must have fired his torpedoes from about 700 yards.

As the periscope and then the conning-tower appeared I ordered "Full speed ahead, hard starboard." But, with the helm already hard to port, I was unable to turn quickly enough to ram him before he crash-dived only 40 yards away on our starboard side. The submarine was visible for about 45 seconds, and, simultaneously with our ramming efforts, we opened fire with our starboard pom-poms. He was so close, however, that we were unable to depress the guns sufficiently and the shells passed over the conning-tower.

I then gave the order "Amidships," again to avoid turning into the Barham, which was still under way with her engines running but listing heavily to port. As we came up on her beam she heeled further about 20 or 30 degrees, and through the smoke I could see all her quarter-deck and forecastle. Men were jumping into the water and running up on the forecastle.

The Barham was rolling on a perfectly even keel with neither bows nor stern sticking into the air. For one minute she seemed to hang in this position; then, at 4.28, she suddenly rolled violently, her mainmast striking the surface of the sea sharply a few seconds later.

I saw water pouring into her funnels. There followed a big explosion amidships, from which belched black and brown smoke intermingled with flames. Pieces of wreckage, flung high into the air, were scattered far and wide, the largest piece being about the size of my writing-desk. I immediately ordered "Take cover" as the wreckage started flying, and that was the last we saw of the Barham, which had run almost a mile since the moment she was hit.

When the smoke cleared the only signs left were a mass of floating wreckage.

The screening destroyers, which were some distance ahead of the battleships, sped back and dropped depth charges, while the others picked up survivors. The destroyer flotilla leader, Jervis, came racing down my starboard side asking for the submarine's position, but by this time we had drifted a long way past the spot where he dived, and it was impossible to give the exact location.

I think the torpedoes struck between the mainmast and the funnel, and the final explosion was probably the six-inch magazine going up, as the explosion was not loud enough for 15-inchers. Had it been the latter I should probably not be here myself, as we were only three cables (600 yards) distant.

The speed with which the Barham sank led to a heavy toll of lives, some 700 being lost. Many of the 600 survivors had remarkable escapes. Some were blown high into the air from inside the ship. Vice-Admiral Sir Henry Pridham-Wippell, whose flag the Barham was flying, was picked up after being an hour in the water. He had escaped by climbing into the water down the starboard glacis. The Barham's captain, Capt. G. C. Cooke, and most of the senior officers were all killed.

How We Fought on the Beach at Kota Bharu

The story of the Japanese landing at Kota Bharu in Malaya and of the gallant fight our men put up against overwhelming odds is told below by the Brigadier in charge of the British forces.

WE were up against the possibility of landings anywhere on 35 miles of coastal beaches, all eminently suitable for landings.

I saw the biggest threat as being most likely to come from the beaches south of Kota Bharu. Our railhead was at Kualakrai, 42 miles distant, where we had considerable stores. That railway was most vulnerable to attack because it was only a single track and had several bridges.

We were just about to be reinforced when the Royal Australian Air Force located Japanese transports off Cambodia Point. Four ships were seen 100 miles north of Kota Bharu moving southward, and about an hour before midnight on Dec. 7 the beach look-out posts reported ships offshore.

Next morning one 18-pounder on the beach opened fire against the ships. I informed the commanding officer at the R.A.F. station and the Australian Air Force. Hudsons went off to attack. The first sortie failed, but just before dawn they hit a 15,000-tonner, which burned all day long.

Meanwhile, fighting had begun on the beaches. One Indian officer said the Japanese landed 60 barges drawn by motor-boats. Each motor-boat carried an anti-aircraft gun, and each barge held 60 men, making a total landing force of 3,600. I am inclined to think that may have been an exaggeration.

Previously we had blacked-out the whole district, but on the night of the landing the Company Commander saw two lights shining above a house in a high position, providing a guide to the enemy.

The Japanese also entered Kuala Paamat, a small bay south of the entrance to the Kelantan River, thus escaping our land-mines. We attacked with artillery, mortars and machine-gun fire from pill-boxes.

My men in the pill-boxes fought with the utmost bravery either until they were killed or until their ammunition ran out. I sent

H.M.S. BARHAM was sunk by torpedoes off Sollum on Nov. 25, 1941. In this page Capt. Morgan of the Valiant, which was steaming immediately ahead of the Barham when she was hit, tells the dramatic story of her sinking. H.M.S. Barham was a battleship of the Queen Elizabeth class, completed in 1915 and later reconstructed. *Photo Wright and Logan*

IN MALAYA the British forces, though heavily outnumbered, and without sufficient air support, gave an excellent account of themselves, as is evident from the story of the fighting at Kota Bharu given in these pages. Heavy floods added to their difficulties, and on the left a convoy of 25-pounders is seen on a flooded road, while the nature of the terrain in which the British were fighting is shown, right, where a gun crew are manoeuvring their piece into position among dense tropical growth.
Photos, British Official; Associated Press

reinforcements to restore the pill-boxes at the river mouth, where the Japs also landed, but could not do so effectively. We did pin the enemy that day, but it was impossible to throw him out.

Four squadrons of planes came up to help us, while six Wildebeeste torpedo-bombers took off, but were unable to do any damage. Meanwhile, the three aerodromes were being heavily bombed. There were 27 casualties from one bomb alone.

During the morning there came reports of 20 more ships seen just off land.

By the evening we had lost half our air strength either on the ground or in air combat. By 8 p.m. on Dec. 8 our air arm had ceased to function, but the Japanese bombers were still coming over, I believe from land bases.

The next day the R.A.F. and the Australian Air Force were ordered to fly off all serviceable aircraft because of the air superiority of the enemy. This was most serious from my point of view. I had reports that hundreds of Japanese were now detraining across the Thai border, while the smoke of ships, including Japanese warships, had been sighted behind the small islands lying off the coast.

We withdrew to our second line running south-east from Kota Bharu to the coast. The Japanese attacked heavily with fresh troops, and some of my men on the right flank were cut off. We were forced to drop back to the Kochong line, which we held for 96 hours. We then had to drop back to Machang because the Japanese were filtering round our flanks to the rear. At Machang we held on for two more days.

Our next withdrawal was to the Nal River, five miles north of Kualakrai. On the following day one of our patrols, consisting of four Bren-carriers, was wiped out by the Japanese with hand grenades. The crews were killed by tommy guns. The Japanese climbed trees and ambushed the patrol, dropping grenades on each machine.

They started to bomb Kualakrai then. We launched a counter-attack, which was unsuccessful. Next day we began to leave Kualakrai and spent the night at Manikurai. We blew up the railway bridge, but also bombed the railway at three points behind us and hit two trains.

The Japanese always had local numerical superiority. Our posts at Kota Bharu fought with the greatest bravery until overrun by the enemy.—*The Daily Mail*

Ivan Is an A.R.P. Warden in Moscow

Of all Moscow's A.R.P. wardens, none is better known than Ivan Semyonovich. So well known is he that the Soviet journalist Yozovsky decided to make his acquaintance. This is his account of the interview reprinted from the Soviet War News.

THERE was no trouble in finding him. You only had to mention his name and everyone said : " Oh, yes—you want Ivan Semyonovich—certainly, right this way."

I arrived at an A.R.P. post. A bunch of fine strapping lads were there, strong and capable-looking. Their leader must be a hero of a chap, I thought.

Imagine my surprise when I met Ivan Semyonovich—a puny little grey-haired old man. He was quick to notice my embarrassment and read my thoughts. "Yes," he said, a little defiantly. "I am sixty-four years old and retired on a pension. I used to be a house-painter."

It appears that when war was declared he went to his house committee and presented the following document which he had composed himself :—

" In view of the scoundrelly attack of Hitler's gangs on our Socialist fatherland of working people, I declare myself mobilized until the final annihilation of the Fascist abomination. I undertake to fulfil all obligations in the defence of houses from air attack.
(Signed) IVAN SEMYONOVICH FEDOSEYEV. June 22, 1941."

Then he got busy. He collected fire equipment. He collected people to use it. He showed the people how to work the equipment. I asked him how he did it all.

" It's a question of the right approach," he said, twirling his grey moustache. "That's what you need in dealing with people. For instance, we had one chap in our house, a very respectable citizen—yes, you should see his grand whiskers—but full of the wrong ideas.

" As soon as it got dark he used to make a bee-line for the air-raid shelter. Never mind, I thought to myself, I'll cure him. I tipped off the women in the shelter—and they knew what to do. They gave it to him good and proper. Pretty soon he came slinking along. 'Ivan Semyonovich,' he says, ' for goodness' sake give me something to do. Those women will be the death of

me.' Well, now he's manning a hose at the top of the house, as brave as they make them. That's the right approach for you."

So we went up on the roof. I realized then that the roof was to Ivan Semyonovich like a ship's bridge is to a captain. Everything was in ship-shape order : spades, axes, hooks, fire-tongs, piles of sand, fire-hoses and stirrup-pumps.

His eye landed on an empty bucket. " Hey, Sasha—what's this ? " " Plenty of time to refill it before nightfall," said Sasha. " That's what you say. And supposing the siren goes this minute . . . what then ? Go on, jump to it, lad ! "

Advising, prompting, scolding—he kept everyone busy and happy. Talkative, full of jokes and good cheer—that's the captain of this A.R.P. group. He walked about the roof as he talked to me, twirling his moustache, waving his arms and paying no attention to me whatever. I might have fallen over the parapet and the captain would still go on talking.

When I sat down he took this for a sign of weakness. " Feeling a little tired," he said. " Poor chap. It's on account of your youth. When you reach my age you'll have more strength and experience. Who knows—you might even be appointed an A.R.P. chief ! "

'Always a Cheery Word'

I heard afterwards how during a raid he had worked all night, going from point to point, helping wherever the danger was greatest. Always a cheery word of encouragement. No wonder the people in his team are so fond of him. When one of his men was burned on the face he helped to tend him. " There'll be a red mark there," the man said. " Where . . . " cried Ivan Semyonovich. " I can't see any red mark. Nonsense, man—you're handsomer than ever."

When I left this unheroic-looking, sixty-four-year-old hero, I mentioned that I intended to write something about him in the papers. He beamed with pleasure.

" Now that's fine," he said. " That's what I call the right approach." Coming closer to me, he added in a confidential whisper. " You can't imagine how nice it is to read about yourself in the papers. Gives you a real thrill."

So here is a little testimonial to one of the many Muscovites, old or young, man or woman, who have sprung out of obscurity into the front line of battle—the battle against the fire-bomb and the high-explosive. In Moscow, as in London, the Ordinary Man is doing his bit. **Page 503**

HAPPENED to be reading the most illuminative thing I've ever read about Rudyard Kipling, T. S. Eliot's essay with which he prefaces A Choice of Kipling's Verse, when the six o'clock news was turned on " and this is Wilfred Pickling it " . . . or words to that effect. " In Burma we have withdrawn from Moulmein . . . ." I'd heard enough for the moment. Turned to page 187 and read, for possibly the 187th time, Mandalay:

> By the old Moulmein Pagoda, lookin' lazy at the sea,
> There's a Burma girl a-sittin', and I know she thinks o' me ;
> For the wind is in the palm-trees, and the temple bells they say :
> "Come you back, you British soldier ; come you back to Mandalay !"

WHAT memories these words awaken ! First read and re-read in the 'nineties . . . Franklin Clive, in that rich bass of his, now so long mute, singing the song time and again at the old Savage Club to a noble tune composed by a Brother Savage . . . somebody later setting it anew (as somebody always will) to a tune that seemed to destroy its rhythm and could not be listened to by those of us who were caught by the first setting . . . One is tempted to ask how Kipling would have reacted to the events now happening in the East. A vain thought, perhaps, for it would not have been the Kipling of Barrack Room Ballads who would have made " great verse " of them. That ichor of enthusiasm, which inspired our prophet of empire in his early spontaneous poetry, is a stuff that does not endure. Perhaps the events of our strange new times are too great even for great poetry. They seem to have overwhelmed the imagination of our best living poets.

MORE than once I have expressed my disappointment at the extent to which the horse is still being used in war. The thoroughness with which British cavalry and the R.H.A. had been mechanized was, no doubt, the reason for my hoping that horses, these innocent victims of Man's inhumanity, would be less involved in this last great killing time. But the use being made of them in the German, Polish, Russian, Italian, Yugoslavian and other armies has shown how unfounded was my hope. While I can rejoice wholeheartedly in the killing of Germans and am glad that their Fuehrer holds them as low in his esteem as the Kaiser who dubbed them cannon fodder, I hate to think of the horses they are sacrificing, for whom I feel equal sympathy with the Russian horses that are doomed to slaughter in the defence of our Soviet allies. The swift death of any creature, man or beast, by bullet or bomb, matters little : what horrifies the mind is the prolonged agony that has to be borne by the mangled bodies on the battlefields before merciful death arrives. The Russian loves his horse just as the British trooper makes a chum of his mount, whereas to the dehumanized Hitler-bred soldier the horse is merely a means to an end, while the Italian and the Spaniard are traditionally and instinctively cruel to their animals.

ONLY recently I realized that a considerable proportion of the horses used by the Nazis are Irish-bred. Thanks to a young Irish girl, who is a keen lover of horses and writes me most surprising letters from time to time, have I been put wise in this regard. She tells me, for instance, that four members of the German Jumping Team who attended the Dublin Horse Show in August 1939 arrived some months earlier in Eire and were frank enough to admit to a reporter of The Cork Examiner that they were buying up horses for the Nazi army. Rittmeister Brickmann, one of the team, told a relative of hers at the show that they had to round up their purchases and get them shipped to Germany before the end of the following week, which, as she points out, would just allow these Irish horses to get to Germany one week before Hitler decided to " put a stop to this lunacy " in Poland. " Anyway," she goes on, " I saw in an Irish paper, about a week after war was declared, that the last of the 10,000 horses bought by these Germans in this country had arrived at Hamburg. The last one disembarked was a fine grey mare, bought at Clonmel Fair, and the Germans had painted ' Clonmel ' on her side in green letters."

MY young correspondent gives practical evidence of her interest in horse lore by sending me an article, published in the magazine, Riding, for April 1939, entitled " Horses in the Next War." From this it is clear that the Nazis would have an eye to the rich booty awaiting them in the shape of horses as soon as they got hold of Yugoslavia with its more than one million horses, Poland and Rumania also having immense herds of horses to be seized for war transport and cavalry remounts. The concluding paragraph of the article in Riding (it was written by Mr. Eric Hardy, F.Z.S.) is worth reprinting in this connexion :

> For the last few years the Germans have been buying horses and have added a troop of mounted infantry to each regiment of foot, and stocky Norwegian-bred pack-horses are being imported for mountain warfare. Many of these were used in the march into Austria. She is also relying upon them in the event of a long war and shortage of motor fuel. The British Army has kept but two regiments of regular cavalry, besides those of the Household, as sufficient ! The Swiss, like the French, are using cavalry in conjunction with their mechanized troops, but the British Army's almost complete discarding of the horse has caused amazement abroad. Are we so sure we shall never be called upon to fight in hill country ?

I HOPE that I am not lacking in humour, but I often wonder why some of the Government appeals to common sense and common decency are so designed and worded as to suggest that the mass of the public are nitwits or cretins. If it is necessary to spend large sums and valuable time of artists and technicians in producing posters warning people not to sneeze in one another's faces, not to tear off the protective netting on buses and trains, not to walk off fast travelling transport in the black-out, not, in fact, to behave like lunatics or worse, one is forced to wonder whether education is of the slightest use. That some people do destroy the netting applied to glass for their protection is obvious to any traveller, but I am inclined to think that a heavy fine or term of imprisonment would be far more effective and economic than a poster widely circulated at a time when there is supposed to be a paper famine. I am not amused by these general reflections on the intelligence of the herd, and they are certainly not true of the majority of Britons. If they were, our plight would indeed be hopeless. Humour and wit are aids to the strain and fatigue of life at all times, but they are worthy of better subjects than criminal idiocy or foul manners which need a drastic cure or correction and not a semi-sympathetic guffaw.

"BORROWING " grows apace. One of the later developments is the pinching of hotel reading-room periodicals by guests. I mentioned to a floor waiter at a West End hotel yesterday that, although I had often seen the weekly illustrateds lying on the hall porter's counter, boldly stamped with the hotel name, and ready for placing in the reading-room, it was months since I had found any one of them on the table, where the chief reading matter consisted of copies of The Plumbers' Record, Chamber of Commerce Journal, Undertakers' Gazette, Gas World, and such like. " Quite right, sir," said he, " these are never, never taken away, but The Tatler, Sketch, Illustrated London News, Sphere, and Punch usually disappear the same day as they are placed on the reading-room table. Sometimes we are lucky enough to find one or other of them in a bedroom." Thus scarcity makes " borrowers " of us all. I am apprehensive that a day may come when it will be risky to leave one's shoes at the bedroom door. Fortunately that day is not yet. Meanwhile, keep an eye on your overcoat in any restaurant now unless you have committed it to the care of the cloak-room attendant.

GEN. DOUGLAS MacARTHUR, intrepid leader of the American and Filipino forces in the Philippines, commanded the famous Rainbow Division on the Western Front in the last war.
Photo, Central Press

Printed in England and published on the 10th, 20th, and 30th of each month by the Proprietors, The Amalgamated Press, Ltd., The Fleetway House, Farringdon Street, London, E.C.4. Registered for transmission by Canadian Magazine Post. Sole Agents for Australia and New Zealand : Messrs. Gordon & Gotch, Ltd. ; and for South Africa : Central News Agency, Ltd. February 20th, 1942. S.S. *Editorial Address:* JOHN CARPENTER HOUSE, WHITEFRIARS, LONDON, E.C.4.

Vol 5 **The War Illustrated** N° 122

FOURPENCE

Edited by Sir John Hammerton

FEB. 28TH, 1942

THROUGH ARCTIC SEAS pass our convoys and their escorting warships delivering war material to Russia. The decks and super-structure, like those of the warship above, become thickly encrusted with ice as the spray freezes. But, weather and foe notwithstanding, the convoys get through laden with weapons and supplies for use against the Axis on the Russian Front.

Photo, Associated Press

NO. 123 WILL BE PUBLISHED TUESDAY, MAR. 10

ARE WE WINNING THE WAR?

BY THE EDITOR

IN the first week of the War the writer was asked by a young journalist, who has since done admirable work for British propaganda, if he thought the Allies would win. So indignant did I feel that any Briton should ask such a question at such a moment that I fear my answer was a rude one. The shock of doubt implied by the question made it sound little short of treasonable. Had there been many like that young man in Sept. 1939 going about asking the same question we might have lost the War by now. To enter upon a life-and-death struggle with a doubt as to its issue is to weaken the incalculable advantage of the will to win. An aged and death-awaiting philosopher might be pardoned if he expressed some such doubt. Philosophic doubt is one thing (and a commendable thing), but a doubting spirit in youth, with its physical powers to lend a hand in the opening of a fight for its own freedom, is another and a damnable thing.

THAT we shall win the war must be the faith and belief of every Briton. And though the same sirens that startled me with a false alarm on the morning of Sept. 3, 1939, after listening to Chamberlain's declaration of War, have moaned their warnings a thousand times since (the third today had just sounded as I began writing) my faith in Victory has not diminished. But in the two years and a half that have passed there have been many moments when that faith has been sorely tried—none more trying than the fall of Singapore, while three of the major vessels of the Nazi fleet, so long sheltering in the harbour at Brest, had brazenly sailed through the Straits of Dover and joined the rest of Hitler's navy in their home waters behind the fortress of Heligoland.

NONE-THE-LESS, there is but one answer to the larger question, "Shall we Win?" Today, with more confidence than ever, the affirmation of ultimate triumph can be made. Our very survival after the bursting of the French bubble—"the greatest Army in Europe" now some miserable millions of ragged starvelings rotting in prison camps or labouring as helots for the enemy, the vaunted Maginot Line so much junk !—is the chief guarantee of our final victory. These foolish things of France in which we were induced to put our trust are almost forgotten ; in their place a mightier army than France ever possessed, one of which we had been kept as completely in ignorance as we had been stupidly led to lean upon the other, is fighting gloriously for a Russia of newly revealed strength and vision. In cooperation with a Britain that survived the defection of a once-powerful ally, Soviet Russia is proving a worthy partner in the war against Nazi aggression. And if it required the intrusion of Japan to bring America wholeheartedly into the conflict, all the initial and easily achieved successes of that treacherous and still semi-barbaric power will yet prove worth our suffering for the sake of America's eventual and decisive contribution to Victory.

HITLER'S cardinal mistake, has been his attack on Russia, and his urging Japan into the conflict may yet prove less wise than it appears. His pressure on Spain and Vichy will probably bring these two crippled but trouble-making powers into the conflict as our open enemies. That may be his final error. Both of them are already fighting Britain covertly in the Mediterranean and North Africa, restrained only from full and open "collaboration" by fear of civil war at home, and civil war in Vichy France and Franco Spain will tend rather to shorten than to lengthen the War should the anti-democratic leaders of those countries take the final step.

ONE thing stands out beyond all doubting : this year of 1942 is going to see the climax of the War ; everything is piling up for that. The brilliantly conceived and boldly executed move of the Scharnhorst, the Gneisenau and the Prinz Eugen (whose value to the Nazi fleet is more than doubled by the loss of the Prince of Wales and the Repulse) portends a sea affair of the major sort at an early date. Worse trials than any since the Fall of France await the Democratic Powers. But hourly the potential might of America is developing. Her initial disasters, unexpected though they were, are acting as a spur to supreme endeavour and cannot for long exert a paralysing effect on American activities in the Pacific.

THE audacious approach of the Japs to Australia's northern shores has had an electrical effect upon our kinsmen of the southern continent, who are wisely bestirring themselves to increased effort and are agreed that they would rather defend themselves by uniting with the Americans, Dutch, and British in taking the offensive against the Japs at such points on the invaded islands to the north and north-west as the strategy of General Wavell may determine, than wait to repel any attack in force on the Australian mainland. New Zealand, whose North Island is even more

SIR EARLE PAGE, P.C., G.C.M.G., Australian special Envoy to Britain, whose function is to establish Cabinet liaison with the British Government. *Photo, Lafayette*

inviting to Japanese landings, is also at the peak of alertness. But, despite the immense resources of a war-hungry nation of nearly one hundred millions, it is difficult to see how the threat to the British Dominions of the South Pacific can be translated into a menacing reality. Years of preparation and a treacherous stroke account for their speedy, spectacular victories, but treachery has done its worst and the forces now being brought to life by America, whose main theatre of the War must be the Pacific, will, with the aid of British and Australian forces and generalship, and the help of China's fighting millions, redress the ravages of the yellow wing of Nazi gangsterism, not in a month or two but possibly before the year has run its course. Next year assuredly.

MANY a time in the War of 1914-18 there were periods when the question " are we winning the War ? " might have been asked with even less obvious reasons for an affirmative answer. And not the least anxious of these periods started with the great German offensive on March 21, 1918, when the Huns broke through with forty divisions along the fifty-five-mile front between Scarpe and Oise and swept the Allies back to the west, recapturing all the ground gained by us at such sacrifice in 1916-17, and pressed on, with only brief local set-backs, until it looked as though they would regain Amiens, the extreme point of their first penetration in 1914.

When Foch had assumed the supreme command on the Western Front in April and Haig had issued his famous " backs to the wall " order, who that remembers those days can forget their anxiety ? Did we look like winning the War then ? Yet by July 18 the tide was already on the turn, by August 8 the invaders were suffering blow upon blow from British, French and American counterattacks until, with Austria cracking under Italo-British pressure, by Oct. 11 the beaten legions of the Kaiser were in widespread retreat. Seventeen days later Austria had capitulated ; on the last day of that month Turkey surrendered ; five days later the Huns were in full retreat everywhere on the Western Front, the red flag of revolt hoisted at Kiel and Hamburg by the sailors of a fleet which had so long rotted there afraid to face the British in open water.

No more than five months had sufficed for all the decisive events that changed the fortunes of the Kaiser and his Hunnish legions from the appearance of victory to the certainty of débâcle.

Now that is worth recalling at such a time as we are passing through at present, albeit there is hardly any comparision between the opposing forces of the War today and those of 1918. Its literally world-wide diffusion, its bewildering complexities of direction, its dark intriguing, its impact on every land and people and on every inhabitant of the countries involved, its ferocity by sea and air undreamt of in 1918 ; its ever-shifting areas of explosion . . . in a word we are caught up in Total War which makes the geography of any earlier war more like topography : local rather than universal. Still there is this to remember : local victory or defeat can have a repercussion which will affect even the

SOME REFLECTIONS IN A DARK HOUR

Vice-Adm. C. E. L. Helfrich (below), C.-in-C. of the Netherlands East Indies Navy, who now succeeds Admiral T. C. Hart as Commander of the Combined Naval Forces in the A.B.D.A. area (S.W. Pacific).

Vice-Adm. Herbert F. Leary, U.S. Navy (below), appointed to command the combined Australian - New Zealand naval forces. His title is Commander of the Anzac Forces.

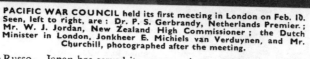

PACIFIC WAR COUNCIL held its first meeting in London on Feb. 10. Seen, left to right, are : Dr. P. S. Gerbrandy, Netherlands Premier.; Mr. W. J. Jordan, New Zealand High Commissioner ; the Dutch Minister in London, Jonkheer E. Michiels van Verduynen, and Mr. Churchill, photographed after the meeting.

remotest reaches of a Total War. The Russo-German struggle, for instance, is affecting Britain's home defence far more than most of us realize, and should our Soviet Allies extend or retain their winter gains when the Nazis return to the attack this Spring the effect will be magical. It might easily daunt a Darlan and frighten a Franco, not to say how it might react on Mussolini's sorely tried Italians.

ALMOST more disturbing to the British cause than events in the Pacific is our second retreat in Libya, for which we have the vermin of Vichy to thank even more than that formidable and ingenious Nazi General Rommel. For essential to our grip on the Mediterranean is the capture of the North African coast as far west as Tripoli, and essential to our ultimate victory is the command of the Mediterranean. Our second advance to Benghazi, though indecisive, may still rank as a victory in view of its discomfiture to Rommel ; what has twice been done may well be done a third time with more enduring result: The Egypt that may have to be defended now is at least a pro-British Egypt, and a Nazi failure in attacking it might prove to be the beginning of our third and final capture of Libya with a strong, swift move into Tripolitania, bringing us up against the Tunisian frontiers of Vichy and the final show-down in that part of the world. But it took Britain five months to re-shape another Army of the Nile for the second advance to Benghazi, so that a speedy pursuit of even a beaten Rommel from the Egyptian frontier, with any assurance of a permanent lodgement at the end, is not to be looked as an early event. Meanwhile Gen. Smuts has told us that " South Africa is in dire peril," while a knowledgeable critic has said that if we are still holding Burma and Egypt at the end of 1942 the year will not have been ill-spent !

THE really decisive blow is most likely to come, however, when the present pact of non-aggression between Soviet Russia and

Japan has served its purpose, just as Hitler's pact with Stalin served its ends—at both ends. This depends, of course, on the outcome of the Nazi-Soviet Spring campaigns in which so much of our fortune of war is bound up. If Russia holds fast on the west, then with her help, China's cooperation, and that unquestionable aerial supremacy which is surely shaping to reality in Britain and America, the destruction of Japan's cities and war centres will kill the yellow octopus at its head ; its tentacles will loosen wherever they are now clinging on Pacific isles and Asiatic mainland.

Not till then is the consciousness of impending defeat likely to awaken in the mind of Nazidom.

OBVIOUSLY, we have far to travel on a rocky road beset with difficulties and dangers, but it happens often, when the spirit is most depressed and the end still seems distant, that a backward glance will show how far we have travelled, and taking heart thereat we move on. Our surprise when we do arrive is to realize how near the end we had come when it still seemed far off. *J. A. HAMMERTON*

NEW ZEALAND GUNNERS serving in the Middle East are firing their 25-pounder at long range against enemy tank concentrations. A description of this gun, one of the world's best, is given in page 460.

Photos, British Official, Wide World, Sport & General, Associated Press

In Rangoon: Gateway to the Burma Road

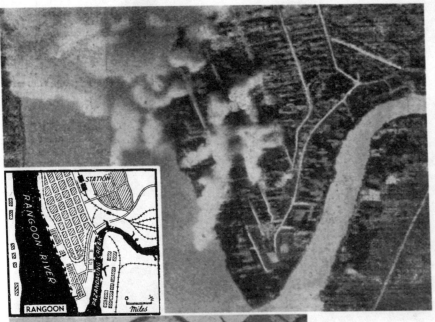

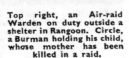

Top right, an Air-raid Warden on duty outside a shelter in Rangoon. Circle, a Burman holding his child, whose mother has been killed in a raid.

Top left, photograph radioed from Tokyo to Berlin showing Japanese air bombardment of Rangoon. A map of this quarter of Burma's capital is inset. Above, a bomb-wrecked street in Rangoon, a city of over 400,000 inhabitants.

BURMA'S CAPITAL and seaport, Rangoon, has been heavily attacked from the air by the Japanese, though at great cost to themselves. Above, left, is one of the surface shelters in a main street of the town. Right, relief map of Burma. The Japanese crossed the Salween in considerable force and occupied Martaban on February 10, and on Feb. 16 occupied Thaton, only 50 miles from the Rangoon—Mandalay railway.

Photos. Keystone, British Newsreels. Maps, The Daily Mail and The Daily Express.

In Java They Prepared for Imminent Attack

Leaving one of the bomb-proof command centres at Surabaya, Java, are Jhr. Tjarda van Starkenborgh Stachouwer, Governor of the Dutch East Indies (left), and Vice-Adm. C. E. Helfrich, Commander of the Allied Naval Forces in the S.W. Pacific.

BATAVIA, capital of the Netherlands East Indies, is a great emporium of the East. Javanese women are here seen doing their washing by the canal bank.

JAVANESE SHELTER of novel design. The air-raid shelters in Java are built in this strange shape to deflect what might otherwise be a direct hit. Many places in Java have been the targets of Japanese raiders, including Surabaya and Batavia, the capital.

SURABAYA, strongly fortified naval base in Java, is a fine city with a quarter of a million inhabitants, and on the right is one of its wide modern streets. The base has been heavily attacked by Japanese aircraft. On the left is one of the special highway barricades erected alongside roads around Surabaya. In case of invasion they can be tilted across the road.

Photos, Paul Popper, Associated Press, Pictorial Press, E.N.A.

Their Tomahawks 'Scalped' the Japs Over Burma

Air Vice-Marshal D. F. Stevenson, D.S.O., O.B.E., who has taken over the Burma Air Command. He was formerly A.O.C. No. 2 Group, Bomber Command, R.A.F.

Photo, Lafayette

A pilot of the American Volunteer Group wearing the national Chinese emblem on his flying jacket.

Maj.-Gen. Claire Chennault, in charge of the American volunteer pilots who have done such good work at Rangoon. He was an American infantry lieutenant in the last war.

Photo, Wide World

Airmen of the American Volunteer Group playing a ball game in front of one of their Tomahawks, as they await a call to take the air.

Photos, British Newsreel

IN a special Order of the Day, Air Vice-Marshal D. F. Stevenson, commanding the R.A.F. in Burma, paid high tribute to the airmen of the American Volunteer Group, who up to the end of January had shot down over 100, probably 130, Japanese aircraft in fourteen fights at the cost of five of their own pilots killed in action and one taken prisoner. This Order expressed the deep admiration of the R.A.F. and praised the Americans in these words : "The high courage, skilful fighting and offensive spirit displayed mark the A.V.G. as a first-class fighting force."

These airmen, who have been doing such fine work at Rangoon, are Americans who resigned U.S. commissions to join the China Air Force and protect the American lease-lend convoys passing along the Burma Road. Under the terms of their contract with the Chinese Government they are paid 500 dollars for every Japanese plane destroyed.

Because they fly Tomahawks the pilots of the A.V.G. are known as Scalper Squadrons, and since they enlisted in the China Air Force as civilians all Scalper officers are addressed as "Mr." These men, by their victories above the paddy fields of Burma, are helping to avenge Pearl Harbour.

Above, a Tomahawk being loaded up with ammunition by men of the A.V.G. Below, some of them are refuelling a Tomahawk. Their planes are painted to resemble the head of a shark.

The Strange Case of Mr. De Valera's Ireland

Speaking on Feb. 3, Mr. De Valera warned the Irish people that, in a war situation that might last for four years more, Ireland might become a cockpit. Attacked by one or both belligerents, she would defend her liberty : hence, "we should not be satisfied until we have 250,000 men trained as soldiers." But (it may be asked) would they suffice against panzers and dive-bombers ?

BECAUSE he was an American citizen—he was born in New York in 1882 of a Spanish father and an Irish mother—Mr. De Valera was not shot in 1916 for his part in the Easter rising in Dublin. Other commandants of the insurgent Republicans were given short shrift, and he was sentenced to death by the British military tribunal. But in 1916 America had not yet entered the war, and it was thought that it would not look too good for an American citizen to be put up against the wall. So Eamon De Valera was reprieved . . . lived to protest 25 years later against the coming of American troops to Northern Ireland without previous consultation with the Eireann Government of which he is the head.

Years ago " Dev " was cordially hated on this side of the Irish Sea. Nor was this surprising, since he was one of the most prominent of those who took up arms against the British in Ireland. Nothing could curb his intransigent spirit. He fought us; he fought his old revolutionary colleagues when they made peace with Lloyd George and established the Free State. Even when he made his peace with the Treatyites he still maintained his fierce hostility to the British and to those who, in his opinion, were too friendly to British men and ways.

All that is long ago, however. Since 1932 he has been the Premier of Southern Ireland ; and today De Valera and Eire are almost synonymous, so extraordinarily tenacious is his hold over his people's imagination. He is still as fanatical as of yore, still an extremist of extremists ; but Ireland's Roosevelt, as he might well be styled, has other qualities that endear him not only to his friends but to former foes. He is a man of deep religious conviction, a strictly practising Catholic, and no bigot : he is a man of simple life who neither smokes nor drinks, but in his leisure moments plays chess, listens to the wireless and dabbles in mathematics. He has a wife and family, and they live in quite a small house in a Dublin suburb. His salary as Taoiseach (Prime Minister) is £2,500 per annum, but he takes less.

Following the establishment of the Irish Free State in 1921, the Irish question, so far as Britain was concerned, seemed to be settled. Two questions only kept the two countries apart : the partition of Ireland into the 26 counties of Eire and the six of Northern Ireland, and the continued occupation by the Royal Navy of the three ports of Cobh (Queenstown), Lough Swilly and Bere Haven. But war has brought new differences, created fresh difficulties. Eire alone amongst the nations composing the British Commonwealth is neutral. The German Embassy still functions in Dublin, and Herr Hempel has, no doubt, proved himself exceedingly useful to his masters in Berlin. British airmen who are forced down in Eire are interned. Irishmen who have enlisted into the British Army have to change into " civvies " before they are allowed into Eire to visit their relations. Yet across a not very well guarded frontier a large British army, now reinforced by a strong contingent of Americans, keeps watch and ward in Ulster. So strange is the situation that it has given rise to much unfavourable comment on this side of the water.

Why should British and American ships bring foodstuffs and fodder to Eire, when Mr. De Valera " walks by on the other side " of the war ? How long could Eire remain neutral if it were not for the British Navy who guard the seas around her shores, and the British Army in the north ? Why won't Mr. De Valera come in on the same side with Mackenzie King, Smuts, and Curtin ? *Why won't the Irish people let us use those ports?*

That question of the ports takes us back to 1937, when Mr. Chamberlain handed them

EAMON DE VALERA, Taoiseach or Prime Minister of Eire, at work seated beneath a plaque of the late Arthur Griffith, one of the founders of the Sinn Fein movement and of the Irish Free State, now Eire.
Photo, Topical

back to Eire. Today we wish he had not done so ; but at the time the move found plenty of defenders, and Lord Chatfield, who was First Sea Lord at the time, has recently restated the case for their return. Opposition in Eire to the occupation of the ports by the United Kingdom was increasing, and it was obvious that unless we were willing and able to hold them by military force they would be useless for naval purposes. To have made them secure against land attack in time of war by a hostile Eire would have required considerable military forces, and these we did not possess over and above those needed to fulfil our Continental obligations. Even if we had retained them, there was little chance that the Royal Navy would be able to make use of them in time of war. On the other hand, there was a hope that an improved atmosphere would be created that might enable the Navy to use the ports in wartime by consent, and in any case there was a greater chance that the ports would be denied by Eire herself to the enemy for hostile action against us. Of course, no one thought at that time that France would collapse, and that the strategic naval position would become what it has been. But at least it may be urged that,

while we have been able to control the submarine menace without the use of the Eire ports, those same ports have been up to now effectively denied to the Germans.

Eire, then, is not in the war ; all the same, she has not been able to escape its effects. Apart from the German bombs which fell on Dublin by mistake, the war has brought many changes to Irish life. Since the island is by no means self-supporting, there is severe rationing of foodstuffs, fodder, petrol, and all kinds of fuel. Wheat is short, and oats and barley have to be used in the loaf. Sugar is getting scarce, and the tea ration is half an ounce per week. Many Sunday trains have been cut, and the private motorist has almost left the roads. Very little coal is imported from England, and the people have been told to use turf in their grates as their fathers did. The imports of building materials, too, have been largely reduced, so that the much needed rehousing of the people has been stopped. Something not far from famine, Mr. Sean Lemass, Minister for Supplies, has said, may arise in Eire unless the people exert themselves strenuously to avoid it.

Such deprivations are only to be expected in a country at war, but the Irishman, and still more the Irishman's wife, find it difficult to understand why they should be necessary in Ireland since Ireland is neutral. We find that lack of understanding surprising ; but then we do not realize to what an extent the Irish are a censored people. There are three censorships in present-day Eire : the religious and moral censorship exercised by the Catholic Church ; the political censorship of controversial and " sex " books directed by the Government ; and, thirdly, the wartime censorship carried out in pursuit of the neutrality policy. So complete is this that the Irish people are shockingly ignorant of the war and of the issues at stake. Letters to Eire have to run the gauntlet of two censorships. Newspapers are strictly censored, and also the wireless and films. Recently, we are told, an Irish news reel was banned from the cinemas because it showed children at the London Zoo feeding the elephants ; the children were carrying gas-masks, and it was considered that the gas-masks might evoke sympathy for Britain — which would be inconsistent with Eire's neutrality ! No photograph of Mr. Churchill, nor of Hitler or Mussolini, is permitted on the screen. No battle incidents may be depicted. Such words as Fifth Column, sabotage, and refugees are cut out of any film sequence.

In spite of this official blanketing of the war, there are some Irishmen who do realize the issues at stake, e.g. Mr. J. M. Dillon, a leader of the opposition Fine Gael party, who has repeatedly urged that an approach should be made to the U.S.A. as well as to Britain lest Ireland should be turned into a " German Gibraltar in the Atlantic." For the most part, however, Irishmen follow Mr. De Valera's lead, and trust him to see the thing through. And he, though he prophesies no smooth things, still puts his trust in that neutrality which betrayed Holland and Belgium, Denmark and Norway.

E. ROYSTON PIKE

Our Searchlight on the War

ARE BIG SHIPS OBSOLETE?

It has been assumed that the 83,000-ton French liner Normandie, which was destroyed by fire in New York harbour, was being converted into an aircraft carrier.

THE big ship in this war has proved the biggest failure. The small ships—our little corvettes, for instance—have been a great success. The 27,000-ton Ark Royal, launched in 1937 and costing £3,215,639, did valiant service, but she was too large a target to escape the ubiquitous torpedo, and was sunk in the Mediterranean on Nov. 13 last. We need not recapitulate the melancholy record of big naval craft losses and their crews during the present conflict. But to ignore the lesson of these casualties would be extremely foolish. The floating leviathan by itself has become obsolete. Since an aircraft carrier with a large number of its own planes cannot protect itself, is it unreasonable to assume that huge battleships, even if accompanied by fighter escorts, are far too vulnerable? If the Normandie was being fitted up as an aircraft carrier her loss by fire may be a blessing in disguise, for her chances of going to the bottom with 75 aeroplanes and her crew would have been even greater than those of the Ark Royal. The question to ask is how long an aircraft carrier must be to carry a few aeroplanes? The need is for a large number of small, fast and easily manoeuvrable floating aerodromes, not for colossal targets such as the Normandie would have proved to be.

Dr. FRITZ TODT, Hitler's chief engineer, was killed in a plane crash on the Russian front on Feb. 8. *Photo, Universal*

COMMERCIAL QUISLINGS

The daily list of convictions for black market traffic increases in length. This criminal commerce is the most appalling disgrace of the war.

WHILE the Ministry of Food has done splendid work in trying to give everybody a square food-deal, a minority of unscrupulous sellers and buyers defy the law and make immense profits by so doing. Nor do the heavy fines inflicted upon them have any effect. The fact that our seamen are sacrificing their lives to keep Britain supplied with essentials is nothing to these heartless profiteers. They take their blood money and prosper. They are worse than highwaymen, who did, at least, run the risk of being shot or hanged. The traffic, of course, could be stopped at once if the British public solemnly resolved, as a whole, to have nothing to do with the black marketeers. The man or woman who obtains something extra in this contemptible way is a nauseating specimen, and we do not doubt that there are some who boast about their "triumphs." They should be reported to the police. While there are far too many official warnings in the form of posters to the citizen not to behave like a congenital idiot, we have not yet noticed any appeal to the public to denounce the black marketeers, and to avoid them on the grounds of common patriotism. Furthermore, is it sufficient to fine companies guilty of this crime? The people responsible should be imprisoned without the option, and their names should be given the widest publicity.

SERVICE COOPERATION

The training of a large proportion of the Luftwaffe was based on co-operation with the land forces of the Reich, whereas that aspect of cooperation was largely overlooked in our case.—*A correspondent in The Times*

THE R.A.F. in itself will not bring us victory. The Navy alone cannot win the war, and the Army would be helpless without the support of the other two arms. Recent controversy has suggested that a tradition of independence rather than co-operation still lingers. It is of paramount importance that the three Services should know how to combine to the full when the opportunity arrives to destroy the German armies. The enemy's initial victories were due to his new idea of using the Luftwaffe, in conjunction with heavy tanks, as mobile artillery, while the Allies, thinking in terms of the last war, were employing the few aeroplanes they possessed for reconnaissance, isolated bombing and individual combat. The Battle of Britain was, of course, a unique occasion, and it is hardly likely that the circumstances that made the R.A.F. sole arbiters in this action will occur again. We are preparing to smash Germany on land, so completely, in fact, that Allied armies can march through her territory and occupy it throughout. To ensure such a victory the R.A.F. and the Army will have to work in the closest cooperation. Let us by all means continue to bomb military objectives in Germany, let us be ready for the eventuality of great sky battles, but let us also remember that the Army must have overwhelming fighter support, working in the closest possible conjunction with the military.

REBIRTH OF A NATION

When peace came one of the gravest problems facing the nation would be that of unemployment. It was to be hoped that priority would be given to rebuilding the homes of the people.—*Lord Sankey*

COMPREHENSIVE plans for reconstruction after the war are by no means premature, for there is a vast amount of work to be done, and we must be ready to do it. This time a land fit for heroes must be no rhetorical joke. Change

Brig. J. C. CAMPBELL, who won the M.C. in 1919, has been awarded the V.C., the D.S.O. and a bar to the D.S.O. for gallantry during operations in Libya. The V.C. was awarded for most conspicuous gallantry at Sidi Rezegh in Nov. 1941 while in command of a small force which was repeatedly attacked by large enemy formations. Throughout the action, in which he was wounded, "his magnificent example and his utter disregard of personal danger were an inspiration to all who saw him." *Photo, The Times*

and progress are long overdue. The programme will probably be a happy mean between those who would apply the "scorched earth" policy equally to all that is good or bad in our traditional system, and those hard-faced cynics who hope that the more things change the more they will remain the same. One reform is imperative above all others. Whether it means a modification of the capitalistic system or not, the British people are not going to suffer the degradation of mass unemployment. Another important reform will be the final abolition of the slums; but the authorities must make sure that speculative jerry-builders do not disfigure the countryside with new slums. The health and prosperity of the nation will depend to a large extent on rural economy, and that means an agricultural system which makes farming and farm labour a living industry. In spite of the cranks who hint at revolution, the British public, always strongly individualistic and dubious about political extremism, will prefer to express the national genius for evolution. It would appear that the nation-planners will have to work outside the baleful influence of party politics or their efforts will be frustrated. It is difficult to visualize the kind of world that will evolve from the present chaos, but of this we can be certain. Reconstruction will demand immense natural resources and unlimited labour. True wealth is inherent in these factors if they are allowed to exercise a reasonably free play, and are not hindered by gold standards and suchlike financial strait jackets which tend to restrict trade and consumption of goods.

FIREMEN ICEBREAKERS dealing with the thick ice formed on emergency water tanks in a London street during a recent cold spell. *Photo, Planet News*

THE NORMANDIE, fire-ravaged and waterlogged, lying on her side in the mud and ice of Hudson River, following the disastrous fire which broke out aboard her on Feb. 9. It was said to have been caused by a welder's torch igniting bedding. *Photo, Planet News*

More Men for Gallant Malta's Defence

GOING ASHORE AT MALTA are these troops who formed part of a large convoy which recently arrived safely at the Grand Harbour. The intensification of the air raids on Malta, the massing of Luftwaffe units in Sicily and the recent visit there of Goering are portents that an attempt may soon be made to wrest this vital base from British hands. Inset, Vice-Admiral Sir Ralph Leatham, K.C.B., Flag Officer in Charge, Malta. Commanding the troops in Malta is Maj.-Gen. D. M. W. Beak, V.C.

Photos, British Official : Crown Copyright

The Tragic Story of Singapore's Fall

The fall of Singapore with the loss of many brave lives and some 50,000 prisoners was a major defeat for the Empire. Once again it was a case of inadequate mechanical support. Our troops put up a magnificent defence to the last and covered themselves with glory, but they were overwhelmed.

ON Feb. 12 the Empire was confronted with the blackest day since Dunkirk. The public was shocked by the news of the imminent fall of Singapore, the lynch-pin of Britain's power in the Far East. We had been prepared for bad tidings, but that the city's defence should collapse within 52 hours of the Japanese invasion of the island was beyond belief. There was still some doubt as to the finality of this disaster, for the news came from Japanese sources, echoed by Berlin.

But as the day wore on we learned that the situation was not entirely hopeless, that our troops had refused to surrender and were counter-attacking. Let us recapitulate the great story of the defence of Singapore.

For a day or two at the beginning of February there was an ominous lull along the south coast of Johore facing Singapore Island, broken by occasional gunfire across the narrow strait. The Japanese were preparing for their great assault, assembling troops, tanks, heavy guns, barges, fighter and bomber aircraft. The British did their best to break up these concentrations. Meanwhile, the enemy increased their vicious raids on Singapore city.

On Feb. 6 there was still no sign of any Japanese mass attack. Our artillery continued to bombard enemy movements in the Johore Bahru area. British and Imperial troops, assisted by Chinese volunteers, manned every yard of the coast, the whole beach bristling with machine-gun nests and observation posts. Mortars and other weapons were placed where they could do most damage to the enemy immediately he struck across the water. The intermittent artillery duel gathered in intensity, and the enemy attacked with low-level bombing and machine-gun fire.

On the eighth day of the siege Singapore city realized its close proximity to the invader. Residential areas were bombarded with medium artillery fire at the extreme range of twelve miles, our heavy guns answering in loud cannonade. Doors and windows rattled everywhere, ceilings cracked, houses collapsed under the vibrant shock of this terrific gun duel. As each dawn rose, blood-red over the beleaguered and smoking island, the battle of shell and counter-shell increased throughout the long and brilliant tropic day. At regular intervals Japanese bombers came over and dropped their loads of death among the inhabitants. Europeans, Malays, and Chinese went about their work of defence and succour.

Landings on the Island

The first news of a Japanese landing nearing Singapore was published on Feb. 9, when it was learned that enemy patrols had succeeded in occupying Ubin Island in the north-east part of the strait on the previous morning. Next day the Japanese landed in force on the western shore of Singapore between Sungei Kranji and Pasa Laba under a heavy barrage and fighter and bomber support. Our troops attacked with supreme vigour and courage, inflicting heavy losses, and our tragically outnumbered aeroplanes did their best to stem the yellow tide. The R.A.F. destroyed and damaged 19 enemy aircraft.

On landing the Japanese followed the same tactics as in Malaya, splitting up into individual groups and filtering through the mangrove swamps, jungle, and rubber plantations. On the same day they claimed to have smashed British gun-emplacements and pill-boxes at the end of the causeway two and a half miles east of the Kranji river, and that their troops had reached a point ten miles from Singapore.

The British Navy under continuous fire had been playing a vital part in Malayan coastal waters, harassing the enemy, and small vessels were being used to evacuate scattered units of British soldiers who had been cut off in the retreat from the Peninsula. As many as a thousand were rescued by the same methods as used at Dunkirk. Similarly, small craft of the Royal Navy and Netherlands Navy also rushed in and out of Singapore harbour in the south of the island to take off women and children.

What had happened to the great naval base? The fortification, which had been twenty years building and cost perhaps £60,000,000, had to be submitted to the "scorched earth" policy. The splendid floating dock for a 45,000-ton battleship, the smaller docks, the barracks for thousands of workers—all the accumulated engineering and scientific skill of a generation was ruined as far as its original purpose as a great naval depot was concerned. But in spite of fanatical Japanese efforts to capture the position with tanks, dive-bombers, and fighters, the British forces, according to information received from Bombay early on Feb. 13, were still in possession, and had made the naval base the pivot in a defensive line running south through the centre of the island to Tanglin, the racecourse suburb, north-west of Singapore, down to the coast in the region of Pasir Pajang. The strategic significance of this line was to defend the reservoirs, north-west of the racecourse, on which the city's water supply depended.

The Japanese penetrated this south-west corner of the city, and immediately boasted that it had fallen and that their flag was flying over the centre. But the boast was premature. Singapore was doggedly fighting on, General Yamashita's demand for its surrender having been rejected.

Our troops continued fighting all round the Singapore defence perimeter, and to the north and west of the island. Such was the position on the morning of Feb. 13. But, as has been proved so often, courage is not enough. Without mechanical support it is wasted. As the hours passed in that tragic week it was only too clear that Singapore would fall. General Percival was compelled to surrender unconditionally, and he and General Yamashita met at 2.30 (local time) on Feb. 15 and signed the necessary documents.

PACIFIC BARRIER of island masses which, stretched across the seas between the continents of Asia and Australia, separates the Pacific Ocean from the Indian Ocean. Japan's object is to capture the whole of this vast archipelago and then secure control of the Indian Ocean. While the tragedy of Singapore, described in this page, was being played out, the Japanese were also attacking Borneo and the Celebes, where they had landed substantial forces, while many military and naval objectives, such as Surabaya, Rembang, Madiean, Malang and Port Moresby were subjected to violent air raids.

Map by Courtesy of News Chronicle.

So They *Did* Scorch the Earth in Malaya

RUBBER PLANTATION in Malaya razed to the ground by the British before the Japanese invaders arrived. Hundreds of acres of rubber plantations were destroyed in this manner.

JAPANESE TANKS were destroyed in large numbers during the fighting in Malaya. A tree has fallen across the tank in the foreground and a member of its crew lies dead beside it. In the background another burns.

MINING A BRIDGE near Kuala Lumpur, these Indian sappers are making sure that the Japanese advance shall be delayed as long as possible.

A thick pall of pungent smoke hangs in the air as a rubber factory is destroyed by British forces during their withdrawal through the Malay Peninsula. Thousands of bales of rubber were burnt, factories set on fire and machinery smashed.

Photos, British Official; Associated Press and Keystone

FOR a year and a half, said Mr. Churchill in his Sunday evening broadcast on February 15, a ceaseless stream of ships, men and materials has flowed from this country to build up our armies in the Middle East. Most of the convoys now have to go round the Cape, each ship making only three voyages in the year, but sometimes they take the far shorter if far more dangerous passage through the Mediterranean.

The dramatic photographs in this page were taken at the height of an Axis attack upon a British convoy. More than a hundred German and Italian aircraft, torpedo-carriers and bombers, made a fierce and prolonged attack upon an important British convoy passing through the dangerous waters of the Mediterranean. The attacking aircraft were met by a terrific barrage from the guns of the warships escorting the convoy, and although the attack was pressed hard and lasted for five hours, the enemy planes were eventually driven off without any damage having been inflicted either on the convoy or its escort.

In the upper photograph an Italian Savoia torpedo-bomber is seen crashing into the sea in flames, while on the right is a cruiser of the convoy's escort with her guns raked to extreme elevation. In the lower photograph a bomb is seen exploding very close to an escorting cruiser during the attack, and the sky is filled with the puffs of smoke from the exploding A.A. shells. One of the supply ships which formed part of the convoy is visible in the centre.

Photos, British Official: Crown Copyright

What the Russians Have Done This Winter

WHAT the Red Army had accomplished in the first two months of its great counter-offensive has been clearly summed up by Mikhail Kalinin, Chairman of the Presidium of the Supreme Soviet.

" For nearly two months now," he said, "the Red Army has been successfully developing its offensive. During this time some units have advanced at least 250 miles. The fact that our troops have passed to the offensive is by no means accidental. It is a consequence of the tactics employed by them during their retreat. The Red Army's defence was an active defence. In all their operations our troops followed the principal rule of the Soviet Command—exhaust the enemy's strength to the limit and inflict on him the heaviest possible losses. During the retreat our army coped with this task more brilliantly than in any past war.

" The Germans measure their successes by the number of towns they seize and the area of territory they occupy. Our commanders, on the other hand, measure our successes by the losses which the enemy has suffered and by the extent of his exhaustion. Hitler, undeterred by heavy losses, sacrificed everything to his delirious plan for capturing Moscow. He has already paid dearly for it and will pay still more dearly. With staunch troops and a skilful Command, Moscow was the perfect place for resisting and defeating the enemy. And on Nov. 6 and 7, at a time when it seemed that the German army had achieved its greatest success at the approaches to the capital, Stalin confidently called upon our army and the whole Soviet people to inflict utter defeat on the invaders.

" My words are inadequate to describe the effect of Stalin's speech on our population and the army. I can only say that our strength seemed to redouble. It was one of the most remarkable events in the history of the war. During the retreat our army fought heroically and the enemy paid a heavy toll for every inch of our territory The Red Army's efforts were not futile. They created the conditions for our offensive. The initiative passed to our troops. Town after town, district after district. are being liberated from the yoke of the Nazi invaders. The hour is not far distant when all our Republics now occupied by the Germans will return to their family."

SOME idea of what the Red Army has done since it began its counter-offensive at the beginning of December may be gained from the map in this page, which shows the line of the farthest German advance into Russia and the approximate line reached by the Red Army at the end of January. At first sight it seems little. A vast area has still to be recaptured before the Germans are pushed back to the line from which they started. But, considering the vast strength of the German Army and their paramount desire of creating a static front for the winter, the relentless drive of the Red Armies in conditions which were formerly supposed to preclude offensive action is a good omen.

A few weeks ago the enemy was at the gates of Moscow, Leningrad seemed hopelessly beleaguered, Rostov was in the hands of the Germans, and Axis forces had overrun the whole of the Crimea. Today Smolensk, 230 miles from Moscow, is threatened by pincers movements from north and south ; the operations for freeing Leningrad have made substantial progress : Timoshenko's forces stand at the gates of Kharkov ; the Germans have been thrown out of Rostov, and a portion of the Crimea, including Kerch, is once again in Russian hands, thus removing an immediate threat to the Caucasus.

It must be remembered that the Germans are making every effort to stem the Soviet offensive until the spring, in order that after mustering their forces they can once again launch a mighty offensive. The main object of the Russian High Command therefore is to give the Germans no respite, to make them use their reserves and to prevent their main forces from eluding pursuit. Not to delay for an instant, to continue the relentless drive westward, such is the avowed aim of the Red Army and its leaders.

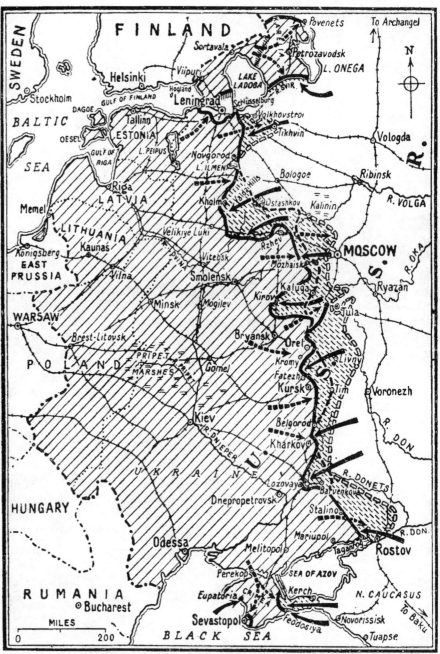

Courtesy of The Manchester Guardian

DURING January the most pressing need of the Germans on the central sector of the front was to try to save the few main railway lines of communication westward. But one of them, from Moscow to Riga, passing through Rzhev, was cut for a hundred miles or more when the Red Army, developing a strong offensive from the region of the Valdai Hills, drove a deep wedge into the German line between Lake Ilmen and Rzhev. Leaving Rzhev in a deep pocket from which the only way of escape was southwards to Vyazma, the Russians cut this railway from Olenino to a point not far from Velikiye Luki. There remained the railway and highway to Smolensk, but these, too, were threatened by the Russian advance from Kaluga to Kirov.

Then, while the Germans were endeavouring to parry the thrust from the Valdai Hills, a powerful offensive was launched by Timoshenko's armies in the region of the Donets basin, and though Kharkov, strongly fortified by the Germans, remained in Nazi hands, the Red Army captured the junction of Krasnograd and made good progress towards the Dnieper, Lozovaya and Barvenkova, between Donets and Dnieper, both being recaptured. Moreover, the German High Command, it was reported, were obliged to put into the south-western and southern fronts against Timoshenko's drives large numbers of reserves which it had been intended to withhold for a possible spring offensive.

Meanwhile the operations for the relief of Leningrad continued and the Russians drove several wedges into the zone near Schlüsselburg, while the beleaguered garrison co-operated by making frequent sorties.

But no one more than the Russians themselves realizes that there is yet a long way to go before the invader is driven from their homeland. They do not underestimate the enemy s potential and realize that the whole winter production of an enslaved Europe may be hurled against them in the spring. But they have complete confidence both in the Red Army and its Command, and in Mr. Stalin's wise and efficient leadership. Russia does not wait on Hitler's will but presses forward with inexorable strength.

They Fight and Die for Mother Russia

NAZI BARBARITY is exemplified in the photographs above found on a dead German officer in Russia. On the left Nazis test the ropes on which five Soviet villagers, seen right a moment before the table was knocked from under their feet, were hanged.

Left, a Russian guerilla band, with rifles and a sub-machine-gun, thread their way through high grass to find the enemy. Below, an American-built Tomahawk in service with the Red Army and its Soviet crew.

Page 519

WELCOMING GUERILLAS who have safely returned to their native village after activities in the German rear. President Kalinin recently stated that Stalin's call for guerilla warfare was an exceptionally important factor which helped to inflict heavy losses on the enemy and caused demoralization among his troops. *Photos, British Official*

Our Diary of the War

SUNDAY, FEB. 8, 1942   *890th day*

Sea.—Admiralty announced loss of the destroyer Matabele.

Air.—Enemy bomber shot down off Belgian coast.

Russian Front.—Heavy fighting near Schlusselburg in the Leningrad sector.

Africa.—Little change in the land situation. British holding defence lines in Gazala area. Night raid by Axis aircraft on Alexandria.

Far East.—Japanese reported to have landed on Ubin Island in Johore Strait. In the Philippines, heavy aerial bombardment of MacArthur's positions.

General.—Dr. Fritz Todt, Hitler's chief engineer, killed in a plane crash in Russia.

MONDAY, FEB. 9   *891st day*

Russian Front.—Red Army units made a further advance in the Donetz area.

Mediterranean.—Admiralty announced the torpedoing of two enemy supply vessels by naval torpedo-bombers on the night of Feb. 6.

Africa.—British forces made contact with enemy 12 miles west of Gazala.

Far East.—Strong Japanese forces landed on the N.W. corner of Singapore Island. Batavia raided by Japanese aircraft. Japanese claimed to have crossed the Salween River, in Burma.

General.—The French liner Normandie, now U.S. auxiliary ship Lafayette, caught fire and capsized in New York harbour.

TUESDAY, FEB. 10   *892nd day*

Russian Front.—Russians claimed to have driven deep wedges into German zone around Leningrad.

Mediterranean.—Admiralty announced two more enemy supply ships sunk.

Africa.—Active patrol work in the area south of Derna.

Far East.—Japanese landed reinforcements on Singapore Island. Imperial forces compelled to yield ground. Japanese claimed to have occupied Martaban, in S. Burma. Jap landing at Gasmata, in New Britain, and at Macassar, in South Celebes. Heavy fighting in the Batan Peninsula.

Home.—Enemy night raider dropped bombs on a N.E. coastal town.

WEDNESDAY, FEB. 11   *893rd day*

Russian Front.—Continued fierce fighting in the Leningrad sector.

Africa.—No change in the land situation.

Far East.—British forces made a further withdrawal on Singapore Island. Japanese bombed Samarai, off S.E. coast of New Guinea. Further Japanese landings in South Celebes.

THURSDAY, FEB. 12   *894th day*

Sea.—German battle cruisers Scharnhorst and Gniesenau and cruiser Prinz Eugen from Brest made a dash from there to a German port via the Straits of Dover. A sea and air encounter developed. German ships, heavily escorted and screened by fighter aircraft, escaped towards Heligoland Bight, but several torpedo hits believed to have been scored on them. British lost 42 planes in the battle.

Air.—Big offensive sweep over N. France.

Russian Front.—Fighting around Leningrad continued. Big battle still raging around Kharkov.

Mediterranean.—British bombers attacked targets at Salamis, in Greece, and Heraklion, in Crete.

Africa.—Patrol activity in front of Gazala. Heavy night raid by R.A.F. on Tripoli.

Far East.—British forces resisted fiercely on outskirts of Singapore town. Japanese flung in more troops and tanks. In Burma, a big Japanese attack in the Pa-an area repulsed. Japanese claimed capture of Macassar.

Home.—Daylight raid on S.W. coastal area. One Dornier destroyed.

FRIDAY, FEB. 13   *895th day*

Air.—R.A.F. made night raids on Cologne, Aachen, and the docks at Le Havre.

Russian Front.—Red Army troops reported to have entered White Russia. Krasnograd, 70 miles S.W. of Kharkov, claimed to be recaptured. Big battle around Zhisdra, on the central front.

Far East.—Japanese pressure on Singapore increased hourly. In Burma more heavy fighting in the Pa-an area.

General.—U.S. Navy Dept. announced that in the combined air and sea attack on the Japanese bases in the Marshall and Gilbert Islands on Feb. 1, the enemy ships sunk included: one modern cruiser, two

CZECH SABOTAGE

SINCE March 1939 more accidents have taken place on Czechoslovak railways than during the whole preceding twenty years of the Republic's administration. The greatest number of accidents occurred when the German Army was marching east for new conquests, or during troop movements from east to west. Bridges were damaged, rails torn up, and military trains had to stand for hours in sidings or on the open lines outside the stations. Telephones ceased to function whenever military orders had to be sent, and food supplies for the Army were held up all over Bohemia and Moravia for "unaccountable reasons." In some cases railway warehouses containing Army food supplies were actually blown up.

Sometimes a rail broke just before a military train passed over it. Sometimes a point or traffic signal was blocked. At other times the cause of the accident was more complicated, as in the case of the breakdown near the station of Josefova Hut on the Pilsen-Cheb line. Above the track here was a steep cliff, but all the time the railway was under Czech administration the linesmen guarded against landslides by continually making tests. One day, however, the cliff crashed down on to the line a few minutes before a military transport passed through. Scores of German soldiers were killed on the spot, while others were so severely wounded that they had to be taken to hospital where many of them died later. A large quantity of military material was destroyed at the same time.—*From Volcano Under Hitler, by Jiri Hronek.*

ocean-going submarines, one 17,000-ton liner, three 10,000-ton tankers, five 5,000-ton cargo boats, two auxiliaries, two minesweepers, and a number of tugs and small craft.

SATURDAY, FEB. 14   *896th day*

Air.—R.A.F. made night attack on Mannheim and N.W. Germany.

Russian Front.—Further advances on the Kalinin front. Leningrad fighting continued.

Mediterranean.—Many aerodromes and military targets in Sicily bombed by R.A.F. Particularly effective raid on Gherbini.

Africa.—In Libya 18 Kittyhawks, attacking formation of 30 Axis planes, shot down 20 and damaged the rest for no loss.

Far East.—Imperial forces still resisting in Singapore, where Japanese pressure increased. Japanese made an attack on Palembang, Sumatra, with parachutists. Heavy artillery duelling in the Philippines. Enemy attack in Burma slackened.

SUNDAY, FEB. 15   *897th day*

Air.—R.A.F. carried out an offensive sweep over N. France. Bomber aircraft made night attack on docks at St. Nazaire.

Russian Front.—Moscow reported severe fighting in the Kerch Peninsula.

Mediterranean.—Naval aircraft attacked units of Italian fleet and certain hits were obtained by torpedoes on two cruisers and a destroyer. A second destroyer probably hit.

Far East.—Singapore fell. In Sumatra, Japanese launched a full-scale attack on Palembang. In Luzon, the Japanese regrouped their forces for a new offensive. In Burma, Japanese reported to be attacking Thaton.

Home.—A few bombs dropped by night in N.E. England and S.W. Scotland. An enemy bomber was destroyed.

General.—Oil refinery on Aruba Island, in Caribbean, shelled by U-boat.

MONDAY, FEB. 16   *898th day*

Russian Front.—Soviet forces continued their attacks in the Leningrad sector. Moscow announced appointment of Boris Bannikov as People's Commissar for War Supplies.

Africa.—Patrol activity continued.

Far East.—MacArthur's positions in Batan peninsula shelled for 24 hours. Japanese forces occupied Thaton, in Burma. Heavy fighting around Palembang, captured by the Japanese.

Home.—Enemy bomber destroyed off S.W. coast.

General.—35,000-ton U.S. battleship Alabama launched 9 months ahead of schedule.

TUESDAY, FEB. 17   *899th day*

Air.—Enemy shipping off Dutch and Norwegian coasts attacked by R.A.F.

Russian Front.—Moscow radio broadcast to people of White Russia on their coming liberation as advanced Soviet forces entered the province.

Africa.—British patrols attacked Rommel's advanced positions.

Far East.—Japanese reinforcing their Burma front. Fighting continued around Palembang, in Sumatra.

General.—Total mobilization of men, women and materials ordered in Australia.

OCEAN VANGUARD, first of a fleet of merchant ships to be built in America for Britain. She is an all-welded ship. Here in the engine-room are Engineers T. Dorman and E. Hughes   *Photo, Keystone*

Strange Adventure of a Sunderland's Crew

WRECKED BRITISH AIRMEN, whose Sunderland flying-boat crashed off the Libyan coast, are seen, left, sitting on a wing of the aircraft as it drifted towards shore. Soon after they landed the crew were taken prisoner by Italians (above).

FOUR miles off the coast of Cyrenaica a Sunderland flying-boat crashed into the sea after an engagement with two Messerschmitts, one of which was shot down. The crew were blown to the shore on a wing torn from the plane, and Italian soldiers captured them as they landed. The next morning, after the party had trekked along the coast all night, the leader of the Italians decided to make for Benghazi with his men, and left the British in an Arab village. There they found an Arab guide, who led them towards the British lines. On the way they overtook a dozen of their former captors, who threw away their rifles and joined the party. This strange occurrence was repeated four times in the course of the journey, and by the time the New Zealand Flt.-Lieut. in charge of the wrecked airmen arrived within the British lines he was able to hand over a hundred or more Italian prisoners.

The flying-boat, which drifted towards the Libyan coast at the mercy of waves and wind, soon became a total wreck. The strange adventure which befel! the crew, who from being captives became captors, is told on the left.

Two officers of the party are seen above drinking from a rain pool. The dog went through the whole adventure. Right, the captors captured. Some of the Italians who threw away their rifles and joined the R.A.F. party are seen heading for the British lines. *Photos, British Official: Crown Copyright*

Repairing Rommel's Tanks

How the Nazi Maintenance Units 'Go to It'

Specially drawn for
THE WAR ILLUSTRATED
By Haworth

RECENT reports from Libya have shown that the Germans have perfected methods by which they can very quickly repair damaged tanks and get them back into battle again. This drawing illustrates a German repair and replenishment camp somewhere in the Libyan desert.

Tank Transporters and Trucks

In the background (A) a Mark I light tank (6 tons) is being unloaded from a big tank transporter. These transporters are used to haul derelict tanks vehicles are fitted with winches to haul derelict tanks

aboard. (B) A Mark II tank (9 tons) which has lost its track is being towed in—a tank in this condition can still manoeuvre its turret and fire its guns but would be motionless.

(C) Tanker trucks carry petrol, oil, and water ; a great many of these are needed to keep an armoured division supplied. (D) Repair and workshop lorries. (E) Camouflaged tents for tank crews. (F) Small tracked vehicle used to carry petrol and oil to tanks ; the cans of petrol are being brought up to refuel a Mark III 18-ton tank carrying 50-mm. gun seen on the extreme right.

Making the Mark IV Ready

The tank in the foreground is a Mark PZ IV being re-stocked with ammunition and having minor adjustments made. This tank, which has been such a tough proposition in Libya, weighs 22 tons, has a crew of 5 and a speed of about 25 m.p.h. (maximum). The large 75-mm. gun and an M.G. are seen at (G) ; the turret is, of course, pointing towards the rear of the tank. The commander (H) is handing shells for the large gun into the turret ; the shells are being unloaded from a small wheeled ammunition carrier which is seen at (J). A second M.G. is seen in a

ball-mounting at (K). The gunner is being assisted in reloading with fresh cartridge belts. The next trap-door gives access to the driving position which has a heavily armoured vizor (L).

On the left some adjustments to the engine are being made ; note the large air filter (M), the winch wheels (N), which utilize the tank's own power to haul itself on to a transporter if required. (O) Testing and adjusting the track ; if any weak links are found the spare track links at (P) can be unlocked and fitted in. German tank corps men, like the British, wear berets.

Above 'Hell-fire Pass' Rose the White Flag

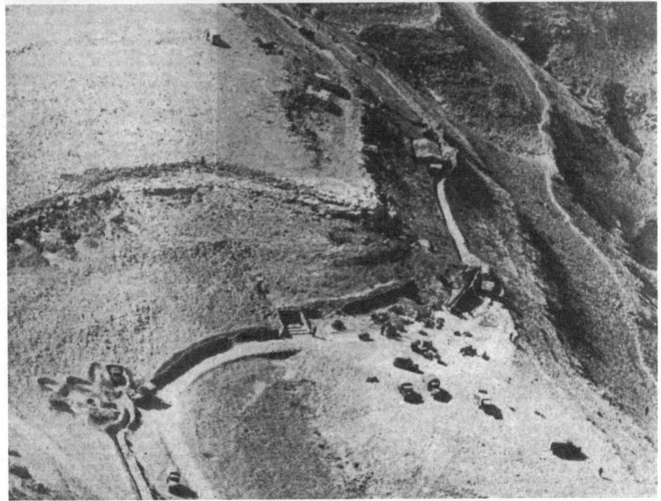

THE SURRENDER OF 'HALFAYA to Gen. Ritchie's troops took place on Jan. 17, 1942, and about 5,500 Axis prisoners were taken. Top left, a flag of surrender hoisted on one of the enemy's gun positions. Top right, the scene at the enemy H.Q. at Halfaya after Maj.-Gen. de Villiers, seen right, had received the surrender of the Axis garrison. Below, an aerial photograph showing Axis transport abandoned at the side of the famous Halfaya Pass. The Halfaya position had served the Germans well, pinning down a large British force and compelling British supply columns to make a long detour.

Photos, British Official: Crown Copyright

Are We Pulling Our Weight in Production?

" Can you do more than you are doing now to help the common cause ? Are you making a hundred per cent effort ? " These were questions put by Sir Stafford Cripps to the millions who heard his B.B.C. postscript on Feb. 8. Below we discuss the frequently-made allegation that ours is not an all-out effort in production.

RECENTLY a number of Soviet Trade Union delegates visited some 60 factories, works, mines, and shipyards in this country, held a number of meetings, and talked with several hundreds of working men and women ; their findings make interesting reading. " British industry is working well," said Mr. Shvernik, the delegation's leader, " and possesses all that is required to increase the output of all forms of armaments. Organization of production is good and equipment is excellent." What impressed the delegation even more was the splendid morale of the British workers.

But there is another side to the picture. According to Mr. Shvernik, in a number of factories there is insufficient utilization of

workers and some the employers ; nearly everybody blames the Government. To blame is easy, but sometimes the accusations are based on all too little knowledge.

No doubt amongst the workers there are many absentees, but we should not jump to the conclusion that such absenteeism as exists is just the result of that Monday morning feeling. Numbers of the workers in the factories are in the Home Guard or Civil Defence, and only those who have had to work seven days a week for weeks and months on end, with many a spell of night-work, are in a position to criticize those who take an occasional day off. Maybe there are some who earn such good money that they refuse to put in a few hours' overtime, or who

for Barnard Castle, " there are girls getting up at three o'clock on these dark winter mornings and travelling 30 miles in order to be ready to start work at seven. The next week they are on a different shift, and reach near home about midnight. After the bus drops them, they have to walk a mile or two miles in the black-out to reach their homes. Talk about courage ! It requires some courage to walk two miles or so in the black-out at midnight in some of those lonely districts, yet the girls are doing it. Of course they are complaining ; it is their right to complain, and it is the duty of the Government to try to ameliorate the conditions."

" Go to it," says a much displayed Government poster. Those girls plodding through the Durham streets must feel just a trifle resentful when they read the exhortation. No doubt the man on night shift who comes home with the milk thinks much the same— though he probably expresses himself more forcibly. Or that may be beyond him.

Then what about the factories ? We have all read of the one where things as a rule were pretty slack, but it was swept and nicely tidied up so that everything was in apple-pie order when the King paid it a visit. In how many factories is there delay owing to the shortage of materials or a break-down in transport, because the orders are not continuous, or there is a too frequent change-over from producing one item to turning out another ? How many mushroom firms are there which have been started by people with no real knowledge of the business, but who are anxious to get their hands on a Government contract ? How many contracts have gone to the monster firms who have a pull with the Government departments—who have grabbed orders right and left (although there is no possibility of their executing them at once) so as to cut out the small men ?

Then if there are workers who refuse to work overtime because of income tax, are there no firms who declare that the excess profit tax of twenty shillings in the pound takes all the incentive out of industry ? There are still many firms working on the cost-plus system, so that it is a distinct advantage to them to push their costs to the highest level. There are whole industries engaged on war work whose costs are never revealed to the Government auditors. The trade associations fix a price for a certain job, and this or that Ministry is forced to accept it. This they do all the more readily since in many cases the controls which have been established in Whitehall are staffed by officials of the employers' federations, by whom they are paid.

In his postscript Sir Stafford Cripps said that one thing is plain—that the total supply is insufficient to fill all the needs, and that " had our efforts in production been greater, we should not now be retreating in North Africa." We may not agree with the last statement ; we may, perhaps, prefer the opinion of those who assert that we are not short of arms in Libya but of the right sort of arms, " and for that blunder (to quote from a recent editorial in The Evening News) the blame must rest not on the little man in the workshop, but on the brass hats in the War Office, who still seem to derive too little mental nourishment from their prolonged lunches." But no one will cavil at Sir Stafford Cripps when he states that " Each hour of work that you lose, each day that you do less than you might by way of productive labour, whether as worker or as manager . . . makes our total effort less effective and lets down someone, somewhere, who is offering his life to save for you all the things that you value in life." E. R. P.

SOVIET DELEGATES in a British factory. Delegates of the Soviet Trades Unions, who have been visiting British factories, are chatting to a workman at a northern tank factory. Centre, Mr. Shvernik, Secretary of the All-Union Central Council of Trades Unions. *Photo, Keystone*

the equipment, machines, tools, lathes, etc., on hand ; the number of women introduced into industry is inadequate ; and some factories adopt an incorrect attitude towards the initiative of the workers, paying no heed to their rationalizing proposals—there is an unwillingness to listen to the voice of the working man and woman and the shop stewards ; and there is even in some factories a limitation of output. " On our territory," concluded Mr. Shvernik, " there is a life and death struggle with Hitlerism ; on your territory there is not."

Really we should not need a Russian to tell us of these things. The correspondence columns of the newspapers and their editorials, the speeches of back-bench M.P.s, and, indeed, the conversations of every day, have rubbed home the same lesson. Months ago Sir John Wardlaw-Milne alleged in the House of Commons that our productive effort was only 70 per cent of what it might be, and Mr. Bevin has asked that it may be increased by 40 per cent. Then we have Sir Stafford Cripps confessing that since his return from Russia he has felt in this country " a lack of urgency," a feeling that we are not all-out in our effort and determination.

Many and varied are the reasons advanced for this state of affairs. Some blame the

object to working overtime altogether since they will have to pay income tax on their extra earnings ; but these are few. Many a skilled engineer engaged in the vital work of setting up machines for the novices to work finds in his pay packet less than £4 at the end of the week.

Why should not more married women go out to work ? is a question frequently asked, often by those who think that so far as their own wives are concerned a woman's place is the home. But how can a married woman with small children go out to work unless there is a day nursery at hand which will look after her youngsters ? There are only about 300 day nurseries in the whole of the country, providing accommodation for some 15,000 children. And is it to be expected that a woman worker should have to cook her own meal when she returns home after a hard day's work ? There are numerous factories still without canteens, and in the whole of Britain there are only some 1,200 British Restaurants. Even when the children go to school the arrangements for feeding them are shockingly inadequate, and reflect most strongly on the foresight and capacity of the local educational authorities.

Then there is the matter of travelling to and from work. " In my division," says Mr. Sexton, M.P.

Some At Least Are Working 'All Out'

British Valentine tanks lined up on the quay of a British port ready for shipment to Russia (right). Lord Beaverbrook calls this "one of the finest of all tanks."
Photo, J. D. Forbes

A corner of a British shipyard in wartime (below). Amid a forest of steel the outline of a new vessel takes shape.
Photo, Central Press

Mrs. Grace Swain (above), once an upholstress, whose husband is in the Army, now screws jackets for guns. Below, an impressive scene in a gun factory where gun production is in full swing.
Photos, Central Press, Fox

I Was There! .... Eye Witness Stories of the War

We Fought Our Way Through the Malayan Jungle

Cut off in the Malayan fighting, units of Australians and Indians made their way through swamp and jungle in small parties, carrying their wounded with them. Here are some of the stories they told when they finally reached the British lines.

PRIVATES Frank Johnson, Bob Drouin and Trevor Davis, of the A.I.F., described their adventures in diary form as follows:

Saturday, Jan. 17.—At dusk a Victorian unit was 11 miles south of Muar. The Japanese attacked. We beat them off and settled down for the night, with patrols thrown out and outposts guarding our camp.

Sunday—At 6.30 a.m. the enemy again launched an infantry attack, followed by tanks. Bayonet fighting lasted about a quarter of an hour, and then in the next half-hour our anti-tank guns got ten tanks. It was quiet for the remainder of the Sunday, and we prepared to push on to Muar to try to contact the Indians.

Our colonel, who had been down a road to the rear to contact a New South Wales unit, was picked off by a Japanese machine-gunner while returning to us. There were snipers up the trees on all sides, shooting at us all the time.

On Sunday night there was a short bayonet attack against one of our companies in which the enemy came off second best. We gained the impression that the Japanese were in-filtrating in large numbers all round us. There were snipers around, mortars were lobbing shells in the middle of us all the time, and there were large numbers of enemy infantry along the road in both directions.

Monday.—Quiet except for snipers and mortar shelling until the afternoon, when the enemy artillery barrage began, with shells first dropping behind us, then lowering gradually until they got the range perfectly, dropping them all over our camp.

We were now outnumbered, and after repulsing them our infantry commander decided to withdraw. Our infantry, withdrawing down the road ahead of the transport, was heavily engaged by five machine-gun posts and mortar fire. Our transport was then cut off, and our unit decided to break up into small parties and go through the jungle.

Thirty-six of us set out in one party, travelling through the jungle swamps up to our waists, through vines, creepers, with thorns cutting us to pieces.

Tuesday.—We rejoined other members of our unit who had joined up with a New South Wales unit. The New South Wales men had been engaged all Monday fighting back 11 miles, to where we found them four miles north of Parit Sulong Bridge.

Wednesday.—We attacked Parit Sulong Bridge. The enemy also attacked us from behind, using at least one tank, artillery, and an air bombardment. We could not take the bridge, which had been held earlier in the week by British forces. Those forces, we later learned, were seven miles farther south—just seven miles between us and safety and reinforcements.

Our commander made the final decision to let us break up into small parties to try to escape. We three made our way through the jungle with the help of friendly Chinese, and reached a British unit after a 15-mile journey.

The story of their escape was told by Corporal G. Bingham and Signalman Max Bendit in the following words:

After the commander told us on Wednesday that we could split up, most of us decided to hang on as long as possible, though we were foodless and almost without ammunition.

The wounded were our biggest worry. Most of us had some souvenir to bring home, like bullet grazes and shrapnel wounds, but we were worrying more about other chaps—we couldn't leave them.

When the question was getting desperate on Wednesday the commander sent five trucks of wounded over the bridge. They were clearly marked with the Red Cross, and the Japanese allowed them to reach a road-block. An officer driver tried to get the Japanese to allow the wounded out, but the Japanese demanded unconditional surrender, though they let the wounded return to our camp.

Then the commander asked us what we would like to do. We decided to fight it out. They were still sniping, shelling, machine-gunning, and mortaring from all sides.

On Thursday three of our planes dropped food and medical supplies, but some of us would have preferred ammunition.

Volunteers stayed with the badly wounded. Those of us able to get along, including the walking wounded, set out in small parties—ours had 11 fit men and 20 wounded.

We had the same jungle journey as others before us, crossed various rivers, sometimes wading, sometimes swimming, helping the wounded all the time. Chinese living in the jungle fed us, and a Malay guided us for five miles along a river.—*Daily Herald.*

Australians making their way through the jungle in Malaya. How some rejoined their units after being cut off by the Japanese is told in this page. *Photo, Associated Press*

Chased by a U-boat, We Gave Her the Slip

The Battle of the Atlantic still goes on unremittingly, and here is the story of a typical wartime Atlantic crossing, told exclusively to THE WAR ILLUSTRATED by J. C. R. Birney, who not long ago was a passenger on a homeward-bound freighter.

WE felt very nautical and noble getting up at 3.0 a.m. in the chilly dawn, piling on sweaters, heavy coats, scarves and finally life-saving jackets, to take our turn at the eternal watch for U-boats. But the early morning watch passed uneventfully enough, and then I retired to my diminutive cabin to snatch some sleep. Lying down on the bunk, with my coat and shoes by my side, sleep soon came; but not for long. A continuous sounding of bells, penetrated by pleasant dreams of firm, dry land. Listening for a moment, I got up swearing, "Another of those damn' boat drills, just as I'd got to sleep, too!" and poked my head out of the porthole. Nothing. So, without bothering to put on my shoes, and still half-asleep, I tottered out on to the deck to see what was afoot.

As I turned left out of the door to look over the side, I realized what was happening; almost before I knew where I was I was back in my cabin scrambling into shoes, coat and life-saving jacket. For there, large as life, and quite close to our starboard beam, was a U-boat. By the time I was back again on the deck the U-boat was pretty well dead astern. It must have surfaced somewhere on our starboard bow, and as soon as we had sighted it we had swung round as hard as we could go to put it astern. The regulations laid down that when the alarm sounded all the passengers should find their way to the forward saloon, a tiny room on the level of the lower deckwork and reasonably well-protected from flying shell or other splinters. Since there were only a few men on board, and excitement ran high, we could not resist the temptation to get on as high a deck as possible and watch the fun. We kept well out of the way, but I suspect that the skipper and his crew were too busy to attend to us. By this time everyone was, of course, at action stations ; we lost no time in bringing the field glasses to bear on our pursuer. There she was : the vicious bow wave cascading over her bulging prow gave an impression of speed which sent a chilly shiver down my spine.

The pursuit had been going on for some time ; our ship, flogged to her limit, was pounding along at a pace she had never dreamed she could do. Suddenly the ship's bells rang again, in a different rhythm. We thought for a moment that everything was over bar the shouting, when—Baang ! The diminishing rush of a shell departing on its way reminded us that most certainly it was not. We stood open-mouthed and rooted to the spot, while the brown puff of cordite drifted silently to port. The gunners worked hard to reload, and we waited to see the result of our shot.

It seemed an age before we saw the great waterspout of our shell a little to port and some way short of our target. But before long another bang, and another diminishing whoosh marked our second shot on its way. I had my eyes glued to the U-boat, when I noticed a small brown puff of smoke drifting away from her. Just for a second, realization of what this meant escaped me ; then, " She's firing back at us," I shouted.

This time it really did seem a long time. In a ship you are the only target. It would be ten seconds, perhaps, before that shell arrived ; meantime, there was just nothing you could do about it. So we just kept looking over the side of the ship.

All the Shots Went Wide

Crack ! It had arrived. Dead in our wake. We were thankful to see it was a long way short, although we knew that the first would only be a ranging shot. Meanwhile our second shot had arrived. Somewhat to starboard but still in front of its target. Then, " Puff ! "—our adversary's second shot was on its way. Craaa-ck ! There it was ; a little way to one side, but certainly a good way short. Hope was born that we, at least, were out of range, and we noticed too that the conning tower and bow wave of our pursuer were a good deal less pronounced than they had been some time ago. We felt we could breathe more freely, though the U-boat was still between us and home.

In an hour's time the U-boat was hull down ; the weather fortunately was worsening, and light rain squalls showed on the horizon. This offered an opportunity, we altered course and gained, after some time, the shower ; under cover of its protective curtain we altered course again. Half an hour later, emerging from the squall, we found that the U-boat was lost to view. Easing down the engines, we began cautiously to edge round to the north to bring us back on our homeward track.

But evidently our pursuer had calculated aright, for he showed up again, low down on the starboard quarter, still hot on the chase. Again the engine telegraph clanged, and every ounce of speed was ordered as we changed course to the eastward once more.

Our skipper had the measure of his opponent, however. By the judicious use of rain squalls, and by so altering his directions to give our pursuer a false idea of our intentions, he managed to draw well away. Night covered us with its welcome darkness and we were able to work our way round in a huge circle until, by dawn the following day, we were heading for home again. All the same, during the night, there were few of us who did not obey strictly the regulations ; we even went to bed with our shoes on.

Evidently our skipper's tactics had completely confounded the enemy, for the next day we saw no sign of him. It was only when we had to slow down to half-speed to give opportunity for some first-aid repairs to our over-strained engines, that we realized how near disaster we had been.

I Saw the Poles Go Over the Top at Gazala

Poles were among the troops from Tobruk that took part in the British advance in Libya in Dec. 1941. The Daily Mail correspondent, Alexander Clifford, who watched them make an assault at Gazala, wrote this vivid account of the scene.

THE artillery barrage was starting up as I reached Gen. Kopanski's headquarters, just a couple of miles from the enemy lines. All our batteries were behind us, firing over our heads.

Gen. Kopanski's headquarters was a motley collection of Australian, British, German and Italian vehicles with the red and white Polish flag flying above it. I found the general standing at the foremost edge casting a searching eye over the battlefield.

Before us his troops were strung out in parallel lines across the landscape waiting to move and lounging among tussocks and camel scrub until zero hour struck. Gen. Kopanski tapped his watch and held it to his ear to make sure it was still going.

Suddenly the quick pop-popping of automatic weapons began to rattle all along the line until the air around us was singing with bullets. A low-flying enemy plane was dodging in and out among the scudding clouds, and everyone was firing at it as it came along. Almost at the same moment Gen. Kopanski looked up from his watch and said " Thirty seconds to go."

All across the plain ahead of us men were getting to their feet. They stretched themselves as men always seem to do before going into battle. For a moment they hunched their shoulders against the wind, and their greatcoats blew out stiffly behind them. They turned up their collars and tilted their tin hats to windward. Then they hoisted machine-guns on to their shoulders or picked up rifles and held them across their bodies.

Dead on time they started to move. They had to walk across a little dip, then over a shallow ridge, then through another hollow, and on to the skyline. Then they would be in action. They went slowly but very steadily. They were so close there was no need to use field glasses to watch them.

There came a moment when the entire horizon ahead of us was covered with an almost unbroken hedge of men silhouetted blackly against the billowing, wind-driven clouds. The Italian barrage grew more excited and erratic. Gen. Kopanski muttered : " They aren't getting much opposition or they wouldn't be standing up."

Almost as he said it an enemy shell cracked down at the right-hand end of the line, and when the ginger-coloured smoke cleared away about 50 yards of the line was gone. But a couple of seconds later they popped up again from the ground where they had thrown themselves, and continued their steady march.

Now the whole first line with its patrols sprayed out before it went down over the skyline. Gen. Kopanski began to use his field glasses. " It makes a nice change for the boys," he said, " after being cooped up in Tobruk." I looked sharply at him, but he had spoken with utter seriousness. The Poles are like that.

From over the ridge machine-guns began to fire in quick, stuttering bursts. Then came the sharp, whip-lash crack of rifles. Each sound came detached and clear on the driving wind. The front line was at close quarters with the enemy now, but the rear units were still breasting the rise on to the skyline. Imperceptibly the whole tempo of the battle quickened.

Inside the canvas lean-to attached to the truck beside me an artillery major was rapping orders down a telephone in rich consonantal Polish. The 25-pounders behind us paused in their steady firing to increase the range. Then they started again, and their shells went whimpering over our heads almost non-stop. Sometimes the wind would drop for a second and the noise of the guns would reach us with startlingly redoubled loudness.

By now all the men had topped the ridge and gone down to the battle. On the left a battery of anti-tank guns bounced forward among the tussocks and disappeared.

A dispatch rider came bumping out of the smoke ahead and gave Gen. Kopanski a message. The Polish guns suddenly began firing right over the front line on to the enemy batteries. Machine-gunning had extended right and left on the Polish flanks. The New Zealanders and Indians were in action and the engagement was general all along the front.

Later, as the sun went down garishly among the heavy rainclouds and darkness closed in, a chill wind set us shivering.

We turned aside to make camp for the night, leaving the Poles and Indians and Maoris thrusting ahead into the gathering dusk.—*The Daily Mail.*

POLISH SOLDIERS firing from behind the scanty shelter of a desert boulder. How Polish troops from the Tobruk garrison made an assault upon the enemy at Gazala is told above by a correspondent of The Daily Mail who saw the attack.

Photo. British Official ; Crown Copyright

Editor's Postscript

I AM glad to see that the President of the Library Association has written to the Press warning enthusiasts in the present drive for paper salvage against the danger of sacrificing something that might be of much greater value preserved as a book than by its addition to the mountain of pulp that we are all so anxious to augment. Several cases within my own experience, and indeed in my own home, where every bit of scrap has been most reverently contributed to the national collection, have made me acutely aware of the need for Mr. Esdaile's warning. I know of several valuable books that have been unwisely sacrificed to produce no more than a handful of pulp, and in my own case a large collection of letters descriptive of my travels in South America, carefully preserved by me for nearly thirty years, as they contained a great mass of information likely to be of value for a book that I have long projected, have gone to the local salvage dump !

In this particular case I had no occasion in all those years to refer to those letters, until the other night when I wished to verify the name of a vessel in which I had made a longish Pacific journey and which was torpedoed in the last War. It was on looking for the collection that I discovered it was well on its way to making perhaps 5 ounces or 6 ounces of pulp, and I think this was an instance in which its previous condition was more valuable than its present. But, with this reservation, I do seriously appeal to my readers to relax no effort which they are able to make towards increasing the supply of paper for pulping. There are uncountable tons of waste paper in British homes—old florists' catalogues, some of which are bulky enough to make a volume of THE WAR ILLUSTRATED, costumiers' luxurious spring and winter folios of new designs, and local ironmongers' illustrated offerings of "everything for the home," not to say thousands of nostalgic catalogues from the motor makers, which in the happy past seemed to breed with the rapidity of rabbits—send all of these at once to your local paper salvage director and so help in this great national effort to save shipping space for the urgencies of war.

ANOTHER danger of the moment in the undiscriminating bureaucratic manner of carrying out departmental orders is that many pieces of charming old wrought iron work will be sacrificed without materially helping towards the total of scrap needed by our iron foundries and steel works, while possibilities of huge contributions will be passed by. There is probably enough steel work in the Blackpool Tower to provide a new destroyer, but I have not seen it suggested anywhere that it should be pulled down and so utilized as Blackpool's contribution ! Personally I should hate to see it go, as many of my memories are associated with it, for there was a time when I was myself a Blackpudlian, away back in 1894, when I edited The Blackpool Herald, and the Tower was only two or three months old. But even in those early days it was realized that it could not stand for ever, and how could it die better than by furnishing a really enormous quantity of raw material for armaments in the hour of Britain's greatest need ? Nor is it the only steel apparatus of amusement to be found at our holiday resorts that could furnish forth really substantial contributions of the precious metal without destroying in the process objects of beauty and cultural value.

THERE is also, I am told, the probability that the Eiffel Tower will soon be dismantled by the Nazis for a similar purpose, and as the Blackpool Tower is by way of being one of its progeny, though not aspiring to the magnitude of the parent, why should not the son be made to do his job for freedom before the father is forced to provide war weapons for tyranny ?

WE are so used to the lying propaganda of Goebbels that one can hardly believe one's eyes when the erudite doctor writes the truth. He tells us in a recent number of Das Reich that the Germans are politically immature, are not sure of themselves, and are lacking in the necessary instinct to take the right path for successful historical development. We could not put it better ourselves. The political ineptitude of the enemy, allied to a tragic and atavistic hatred of civilization, has long been Europe's curse. The Germans have never wanted political experience because the idea of freedom is a complete mystery to them. It is this blind spot in Teuton psychology which, in the last analysis, will bring them down, for the vast majority of mankind, nurtured upon incontrovertible political truths, will in no circumstances submit to a race that is morally in the Stone Age.

FOR the Germans to rule the world they would have to kill off the rest of humanity. Hitler's policy of extermination in this respect is entirely logical but not entirely practical. But when Goebbels says that the Allies did not beat Germany in the last war he is repeating the old lie. The Kaiser's armies were utterly routed in the autumn of 1918, as Hitler's will be when the Allies are strong enough to do it. We refrained from carrying the war into Germany on purely humanitarian grounds, and though Foch's decision was applauded at the time it has proved to be one of the greatest blunders. On the lie that Germany was not defeated in the field Hitler was able to lay the foundations for a new war of aggression. In electing and following this monster, who could repeat the historic disaster of the Kaiser, the Nazis have proved, as the war-minded Germans before them, that they are without political experience or moral conscience.

ISN'T there some member of the Brains Trust whose teeth are set on edge every time he hears one of the numerous B.B.C. announcers talking about Corregidor with a hard g ? It sounds horrible to the ear attuned to Latin languages. A corregidor (literally a corrector) is the Spanish for chief magistrate (he figures prominently in Sabatini's latest romance "Columbus"), and any one of them would have a fit if he heard himself called a cor-eggy-dor. The name must be pronounced cor-rej-ee-dor. Most English dictionaries (they surely have one somewhere at the B.B.C.) gives the word, which has been long adopted into the acquisitive English language, with its proper pronunciation. You will often see the Latin word "corrigenda" ("corrections") at the end of an English book, but if you pronounced it corigg-enda you would be lowering yourself to the level of the B.B.C. Possibly it has eggs even on its Brains Trust, just as most of us are now apt to think in terms of eggs, but there must be at least one brain there that might have been trusted to rise above eggs. Perhaps the announcers are in much the same case as the M.P.s in Iolanthe—you remember the lines :

When in that House M.P.s divide,
    If they've a brain and cerebellum, too,
They've got to leave that brain outside,
    And vote just as their leaders tell 'em to.

BUT I cannot imagine the Spanish announcer accepting the "eggy" version of the word. It may be an American solecism (Americans are very loose linguists), and as the U.S.A. have been holding the island of Corregidor for 43 years perhaps they may have got even the natives to mispronounce the word. I am entirely ignorant of the island's history—never heard of it until a few weeks ago—but I refuse to believe that whoever christened it gave its name a hard g. All words in languages derived from Latin where a g is followed by an i or an e demand the soft g, which is pronounced like our j. That is elementary, my dear Watson. As Cor-rej-ee-dor one can imagine this island with some sort of penal establishment or "house of correction," as Cor-eggy-dor it doesn't mean a thing to me. But you know how editors can be wrong at times . . .

SIR R. DORMAN-SMITH, who succeeded Sir Archibald Cochrane as Governor of Burma on the expiration of the latter's term of office in May 1941. *Photo, Press Portrait Bureau*

Printed in England and published on the 10th, 20th, and 30th of each month by the Proprietors, The Amalgamated Press, Ltd., The Fleetway House, Farringdon Street, London, E.C.4. Registered for transmission by Canadian Magazine Post. Sole Agents for Australia and New Zealand : Messrs. Gordon & Gotch, Ltd. ; and for South Africa : Central News Agency, Ltd. February 28th, 1942. S.S. *Editorial Address:* JOHN CARPENTER HOUSE, WHITEFRIARS, LONDON, E.C.4.

Vol 5   # The War Illustrated   N° 123

FOURPENCE

Edited by Sir John Hammerton

MAR. 10TH, 1942

DARWIN PREPARES. Already bombs have fallen on Australian soil, and the landing of Japanese forces in New Guinea and Timor presents a direct threat to the continent of Australia.   The little town of Darwin in the north of Australia, less than 400 miles from Timor has now become one of the most important strategic bases in the Empire. Here are stationed thousands of A.I.F. troops as well as large air and naval establishments and a strong garrison of home defence forces. The photograph above shows a gun crew of the Australian Artillery at Darwin laying an 18-pounder.

Photo, Sport & General

NO. 124 WILL BE PUBLISHED FRIDAY, MAR. 20

SINGAPORE: THE WAY TO LOSE AN EMPIRE

NOT since 1781, when General Cornwallis with 7,000 British regulars surrendered to Washington at Yorktown, has the British Empire suffered such a blow as the fall of Singapore. Yorktown lost us the American colonies; it marked the end of one British Empire. Will the historians of a hundred years hence write that Singapore marked the beginning of the end of another?

As yet the magnitude of the disaster is not completely realized. Our spirits are depressed, it is true, but our minds are too numbed to appreciate the full force of the blow we have suffered at the hands of a race which for years we have regarded half contemptuously as mere Orientals. When I was a boy I remember studying the pictures in The Illustrated London News of the Russo-Japanese War: "Fancy, that great big Russian soldier being taken prisoner by that little Jap!" It is not pleasant to think of those thousands of British, Australian, and Indian troops being counted on the quays of Singapore by these same Japs and shipped off to captivity in Formosa or some other far distant island of the Pacific.

WHY has this thing come upon us? Did we deserve it? Could we have avoided it? Can we learn from it so as to avoid a similar —perhaps even greater—blow in the future? Why did Singapore fall? To begin with, it was never a fortress in the military sense at all; it was a naval base from which it had been intended that the ships and planes of the Allies should sally forth to keep the Japanese hundreds of miles away. All its guns pointed out to sea, and the possibility of an attack from the land, down the Malayan peninsula, had hardly been considered. Unlike Malta and Corregidor, it was not built on a rock, but on a swamp. Unlike Tobruk, it had a vast civilian population, most of whom, unlike the people of Moscow, were just so many spectators of a conflict which they seem to have concluded was no concern of theirs.

EVEN so, how were the Japanese able to batter their way over 600 miles in eight weeks, and by the end of the tenth week to have marched in triumph into Singapore? The first reason was our shockingly weak air force. At the very outset we lost half our fighter strength, mostly on the ground, and the planes which our pilots had to take up were Brewster Buffalos, Hudsons, and Wirraways—old types which were no match for the Japanese fast-climbing fighters. We had a few bombers, but the Japanese had more, and dive-bombers in plenty. "The day after the Japanese landed on the island," reports a Special Correspondent of The Times and The Manchester Guardian in a dispatch— truly a dreadful document— published on Feb. 18, "when Japanese dive-bombers, accompanied by hundreds of fighters, were bombing and machine-gunning our men unmercifully, there were six Hurricanes, and six only —a seventh was having its wheels repaired—giving our men 'air support.'" Hardly less important was the crippling loss inflicted on the Royal Navy, when at the very beginning of the battle two of our finest ships were sacrificed in what must seem to be, despite

all the official excuses, an act of sublime folly. "All our troubles flowed from Japanese sea and air superiority," says Sir Keith Murdoch; "we never really had a chance on land."

WITH 60,000 men—Mr. Churchill's figure —we tried to hold a country larger than England, against an army far more numerous than ours, and far better equipped. The enemy were, moreover, toughened and acclimatized, whereas our troops were not only far fewer than the enemy but many of them, to quote The Times Special Correspondent again, "never seemed to be physically up to the mark. Some had been too long in this tropical climate and had gone soft. Others had only just arrived, and were not accustomed either to the terrain or to the climate. One brigade was plunged straight into jungle fighting in Johore three days after it arrived in Singapore after eleven weeks at sea." We made a bad start when the troops in Kedah left their strong positions and crossed the isthmus to meet the Japanese at Singora, and were caught half-way. More heavy casualties were suffered in the long retreat through the jungle. "The British lost heavily in great stands as they retired," Sir Keith Murdoch has declared, "and when the Australians came in north of Johore the Indians were tired and almost finished. The Argyll and Sutherland Highlanders suffered heavily in men." If only we had had planes, tanks, guns, and sufficient men, he concludes, there is no reason why we should not have held the Japanese in the north. If only . . .

"ONE British soldier is equal to ten Japanese," said a wounded Tommy to Cecil Brown, correspondent of Columbia Broadcasting, "but unfortunately there are eleven Japs." Then the American went on to make those accusations against the Singapore authorities for which the military banned him from the microphone. This is what he cabled on Jan. 14, a month before Singapore fell. Already it was a touch-and-go affair, such was the incredible and unbelievable unpreparedness. He spoke caustically of the Singapore mentality, of

civilians who were apathetic towards everything, except making tin and rubber money, having *stenghas* (whiskies) between 5 and 8 o'clock in the evening, keeping fit, being known as a 'good chap,' and getting thoroughly 'plawstered' on Saturday night." To the suggestion of any and every change, however slight, they rejoined "with a snort through the nose overhanging a whisky glass—' can't be done.'"

NOT only Cecil Brown, but every observer has commented on the failure to use the vast resources of Asiatic labour which should have been available. With the exception of the more progressive and politically conscious of the Chinese community, the bulk of the Asiatic population remained spectators from start to finish. When Penang was bombed in December, says Mr. F. D. Bisseker, a member of the Legislative Council, "the civilian population evaporated in the most amazing manner," so that the essential services were disrupted and there ensued "looting, pollution, dirt, stink, debris, rats, blood—innumerable horrors which cannot be mentioned." So it was at Singapore. The Times Special Correspondent, after alleging that "the Government had no roots in the life of the people of the country," states that the people hastened to get as far as possible from the scene of hostilities, so that bomb-craters on airfields were not filled up because no Asiatics, and not enough Europeans, were available for the work; there was no native labour at the docks, so that soldiers had to be taken away from military duties to load and unload ships; thousands of people could have been brought away from Singapore but for the fact that there were not enough Europeans to man and stoke the numbers of small ships and launches that were lying in the harbour; while early on in the war, of the 12,000 Asiatics normally employed at the naval base, only 800 were reporting for duty.

HERE is a point we should do well to dwell on and to ponder. Malaya is the first instance of a British colonial possession which has been directly attacked. The enormous preponderance of its people are not of British nationality, still less of British descent, although they have been under British rule for many years. Under that rule the material progress has been striking, but the people themselves have been regarded as coolies—as so much yellow and brown labour whose muscles may be conveniently used in the tin mines and on the rubber plantations. We—or rather the "Singapore wallahs"—have treated the people as coolies. Is it surprising that in the hour of testing they acted as coolies, "did a bunk" into the jungle? Is the same thing happening now in Burma? *Will it happen in India?*

"A GREAT Empire and little minds," said Burke, "go ill together." We have them both, the Empire and the little minds —the yes-men, the Party hacks, the Colonel Blimps, the nincompoops and lickspittles, the blatherers of Army spokesmen in Cairo and far nearer home. But if we want to keep the one we must get rid of the others—and quick.

E. ROYSTON PIKE

JAPAN PRESSES ON! Although taken in China, this photograph well suggests the dash and high efficiency which have sent the Japanese surging over Malaya into the "fortress" of Singapore.

America's Air Watch Over the Atlantic

U.S. 'BLIMP' on patrol duty along the sea lanes of the Atlantic takes a close look at a freighter. The American Navy uses a number of these small airships for reconnaissance work.

At Wheeler Field on Jan. 9 these two American airmen —Lieuts. George M. Welch and Kenneth M. Taylor—were awarded the Distinguished Service Cross for bringing down four and two Japanese planes respectively. Wheeler Field lies north of Pearl Harbour on Oahu Island, scene of the first Japanese attack on the U.S.A. on Dec. 7, 1941.

BARRAGE BALLOONS are now being mass-produced in America. Here is the new balloon room at the Firestone Tire and Rubber Company plant at Akron, Ohio. The room is large enough to accommodate twelve inflated balloons at a time.

Left, pilots of a pursuit squadron of the U.S. Army Air Corps standing by ready to beat off any enemy attempt to raid America's Eastern seaboard.

Photos, Wide World, Keystone, Central Press

What the Cameraman Saw at Sarawak

SARAWAK, where the Japanese made their first landings on Dec. 17, 1941, lies on the N.W. coast of Borneo. The photograph at the top of the page shows the port of Miri, which is the centre of an important oilfield. Centre, one of the first photographs received of the invasion of Sarawak, showing Japanese infantry with a light field-gun after landing. Above, Japanese troops climbing over an obstruction are lit by the glare from a blazing petroleum field set alight by the defenders before it could fall into enemy hands. *Photos, L. T. Lucas, Keystone*

Oilfields Now 'Scorched' by Our Dutch Ally

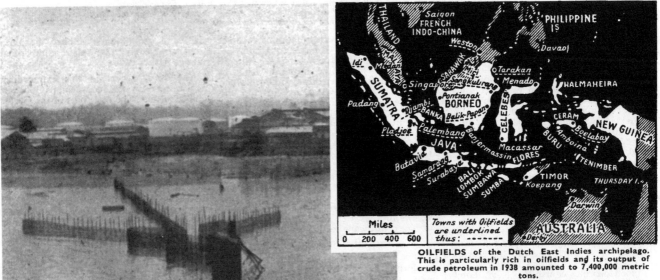

OILFIELDS of the Dutch East Indies archipelago. This is particularly rich in oilfields and its output of crude petroleum in 1938 amounted to 7,400,000 metric tons.

An oil well in the centre of the island of Sumatra belonging to the Nederlandsche Koloniale Petroleum Maatschaapij.

BALIK PAPAN, on the east coast of Borneo, is one of the most important oil ports of the Netherlands East Indies. It has extensive oil-product manufactories as well as refineries. Some of the storage tanks and plant are seen above, with the edge of the jungle in the background.

SUMATRA is an island, rich like Borneo, in petroleum deposits. Above are seen the oil tanks at Palembang, attacked by the Japanese on Feb. 14. The output of the Palembang oilfield is 4,250,000 tons a year. Below, part of the oil installations of the Royal Dutch Oil Company at Pladjoe, Sumatra.

TARAKAN, rich oil island off Dutch Borneo, captured by the Japanese in January. It is stated to be, for its size, the richest oil land in the world. *Photos. L. T. Lucas, G.P.U., E.N.A.* **Page 533**

From Brest Hitler's Ships Got Safe Home

" The most daring and successful (within limits) action of any that I think we have faced since The Dutch sailed up the Medway nearly 300 years ago "—so Mr. Amery, Secretary of State for India, described the action which we review below.

A T 1.35 on the morning of Feb. 13 the Admiralty and Air Ministry issued a communiqué to the effect that the German warships, Scharnhorst and Gneisenau (26,000 tons each), and the 10,000-ton cruiser, Prinz Eugen, accompanied by torpedo-boats, E-boats and minesweepers, had been in action in the Channel with our aircraft and destroyers. The significant paragraph in the communiqué read as follows : " When last sighted, the enemy, which had become separated, were making for the ports in the Heligoland Bight."

It is hardly surprising that the public were startled by this sensational, if brief, information. They had long been under the impression that the English Channel was inviolate, at least to German battleships. Further, as a result of 110 night and day bombing attacks on these ships, immured for nearly a year at Brest—Mr. Churchill disclosed on Feb. 17 that 4,000 tons of bombs had been dropped in the course of 3,299 bomber sorties, at a cost of 43 aircraft and 247 Air Force personnel—they had reason to think that the familiar S & G and the Prinz were hardly fit enough to take so long and hazardous a trip.

The mystery deepened still more when it was learned that Bomber Command had visited Brest only a few hours before the departure of the German vessels, and that it was not until about 11 a.m. on Feb. 12 that R.A.F. aircraft reported that an enemy squadron was approaching the Dover Straits from westward heavily escorted by fighter aircraft. Thus more than three hours of daylight in which an attack on these German ships might have been fatally effective was apparently lost. This delay in getting to grips with the enemy, and the possibility of lack of cohesion between Coastal Command and the Admiralty, and between the other R.A.F. Commands and the Admiralty, became the subject of an official inquiry, appointed by Mr. Churchill in accordance with his peech on Feb. 17.

Let us try to follow the course of this engagement. Having reached a point of 400 miles from Brest, and being already near the Narrows on their way to the open North

Sea by 11 a.m. on Thursday morning, it can be assumed that the German squadron had started some time before midnight. Admiral Ciliax had chosen the moment well ; he lacked nothing for meteorological intelligence and the weather was excellent for this purpose. The ships hugged the French coast and were protected by relays of fighter aircraft from aerodromes all the way. They formed a vast umbrella of steel over the whole convoy. This weather, so favourable to the enemy, was a great handicap to our air reconnaissance ; as it happened the battleships were " spotted " between Berck and Le Touquet by two Spitfires flying low beneath the clouds on a shipping reconnaissance. These were furiously attacked by 12 Me.109s as well as A.A. fire, but they managed to escape to their base.

Swordfish into the Inferno

Our first aircraft to get into action were six Swordfish from the Fleet Air Arm, which were ordered to take off when the enemy ships were reported at 11.35 a.m. to be at the western entrance to the Straits of Dover. Led by Lieut.-Commander E. Esmonde, D.S.O., R.N., they attacked heedless of the overwhelming odds against them. They well knew how vulnerable were their machines to the enemy's fighters, and that the German ships would put up a veritable flaming wall of " flak." But each pilot, like a modern Icarus, flew into the inferno, pressed his attack home as best he could, and disappeared. Not one Swordfish returned to its base, and of the 18 men composing their crews only five were saved by our light craft.

Next, a formation of British torpedo-bombers with an escort of fifty fighters, followed at short intervals by fresh waves of fighters and Hurricane bombers, rushed to the assault. The sea and air battle unique in the history of warfare increased in violence. The sky was literally alive with conflicting planes darting all over the place, diving, ascending, stalling, and crashing. Bomb,

shell and cannon-burst stabbed the almost impenetrable grey atmosphere with brilliant orange flashes of fire.

The Navy's part in this extraordinary action was no less conspicuous for verve and heroism. The first ships of the German convoy were sighted at about 12.30 p.m., when a number of M.T.B.s struck in against heavy fire and enemy aircraft which dived on them continuously. The M.T.B.s hung on grimly, releasing their torpedoes, but owing to a heavy smoke screen it was impossible to say whether any of these had taken effect.

A magnificent effort was made by our destroyers. Called from the North Sea, they could only join issue with the swift-moving enemy ships if they risked the mine-fields. There was no time to make a detour through the swept channels. Straight across these fields of death our destroyers, under Captain C. T. M. Pizey, stormed into battle, defying a whole arsenal of naval guns. Eighteen 11-inch guns, twenty-four 5·9s and twenty-eight 4·1s belonging to the Scharnhorst and Gneisenau. In addition, there were eight 8-inch and twelve 4·1 guns on the Prinz Eugen and innumerable other weapons, not to mention the aerial armament and hurtling bombs. Everything was done by German aircraft to divert our fire from its main objective, the huge German battleships.

The British destroyers put their helms over at about one mile and three-quarters from the enemy and let go their torpedoes. Lieut.-Commander E. C. Coats, R.N., of H.M.S. Worcester went even closer in and engaged the battleships from no more than across a mile and a quarter of turbulent sea. The Worcester was hit and set on fire forward. She was stopped, her crew got the fire under, started her engines again and were able to bring her back to port under her own steam.

Another destroyer attack was made on the Prinz Eugen led by H.M.S. Mackay (Captain J. P. Wright, R.N.). The German

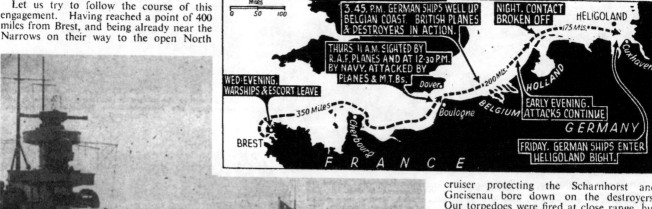

WED. EVENING. WARSHIPS & ESCORT LEAVE

3.45 P.M. GERMAN SHIPS WELL UP BELGIAN COAST. BRITISH PLANES & DESTROYERS IN ACTION.

THURS 11 A.M. SIGHTED BY R.A.F. PLANES AND AT 12:30 P.M. BY NAVY, ATTACKED BY PLANES & M.T.Bs.

NIGHT. CONTACT BROKEN OFF

HELIGOLAND

EARLY EVENING. ATTACKS CONTINUE

FRIDAY. GERMAN SHIPS ENTER HELIGOLAND BIGHT.

cruiser protecting the Scharnhorst and Gneisenau bore down on the destroyers. Our torpedoes were fired at close range, but owing to bad visibility it was not certain whether she had been hit. Notwithstanding all these valiant efforts, the enemy ships escaped about nightfall on Feb. 12, and entered a German port in Heligoland Bight.

Our losses in aircraft amounted to 20 bombers (including 5 machines of the Coastal Command), 6 Swordfish, and 16 fighters. As far as is known, the enemy lost about 20 fighters and some escort ships. There is no doubt that some damage was done to the enemy's big ships.

Naturally enough, the Nazis were cock-a-hoop. In a broadcast on Feb. 14 Rear-Admiral Lützow boasted that " for the first time for 250 years a fleet of an enemy of Britain has dared to enter the Channel . . .

The German battleships Scharnhorst (left) and Gneisenau photographed when they were at Kiel. The story of their escape from Brest to a German port via the Dover Straits is told in this page and the map traces their route and shows where they were attacked.

Photo, E.N.A. · Map by Courtesy of News Chronicle

Salute to the Men Who Gave Them Chase

Sub.-Lieut. E. Lee (below) was the only one who escaped un-injured of the 18 men who flew their six Swordfish into action against the German battleships. Only five men, four of them wounded, returned from the engagement.

Lieut. Commander E. Esmonde, D.S.O. (below), who led the Swordfish attack on the German warships in the Dover Straits, was killed, together with his crew, after having sent a torpedo straight at the leading battleship.

The Wing Commander of a Blenheim Squadron which took part in the attack (third from left) chats with his men on returning to their station. At least one hit on a German battle-cruiser was scored by this squadron.

Captain C. T. M. Pizey, R.N. (centre), who led the destroyer attack in H.M.S. Campbell, photographed after the action with Gunnery Officers Lieut. M. B. Collings (left) and Lieut. A. E. Fanning.

RACING INTO ACTION against the Scharnhorst, Gneisenau and Prinz Eugen off the Dutch coast are H.M.S. Worcester and other destroyers. The Worcester, braving the Germans' heavy guns, went into within a mile and a quarter of the enemy before firing her torpedoes. She was hit and set on fire, but returned safely to harbour. Centre right, H.M.S. Campbell, flotilla leader, a destroyer of 1,530 tons, carrying six 21-inch torpedo tubes in triple mountings and armed with five 4·7-inch guns.

Photos, Planet News, Associated Press, Wide World, Wright & Logan, The Daily Mirror

Our Searchlight on the War

MILLIONS OF WASTED HOURS

Lord Gainford pointed out in the House of Lords on Feb. 10 that pottery work is not an industry vital to the war effort. In any case, it is an extraordinary muddle that growing children should be allowed to work fifty-three hours a week at a trade which is dangerous to their health, when there is other labour available.

IT would be interesting to know how much potential labour in Britain is being wasted by ridiculous restrictions. Take the A.R.P. personnel, for instance. There are 250,000 full-time Civil Defence workers. Apart from " clocking in and out " on their shifts they have been able to do very little work of national importance for months. Many patriotic wardens and firemen admit a sense of frustration and would be glad to amalgamate their duties with work more directly concerned at the moment with the war effort. It is true that arrangements are now being made for this reservoir of labour to be more effectively used, but this concession from Trade Union interests is so hedged with restrictions as to

H.M. THE QUEEN watching parcels being packed for Indian prisoners of war during a visit to India House on Feb. 17. Her Majesty was keenly interested in the work of the Indian Comforts Fund, which also sends food and clothing to Indian soldiers and seamen. *Photo, P.N.A.*

produce an almost negative result. Skilled Civil Defence volunteers can be employed only on " constructional work of national importance connected with civil defence," and they receive the modest sum of 5s. a week for up to 24 hours' work, or 7s. 6d. if over 30 hours' work. In such capacity they can exercise their peacetime trades for not more than six hours a day. Nor must they be employed alongside men engaged under ordinary industrial conditions. Under no circumstances may, for example, the painter or carpenter in Civil Defence uniform work on the same ladder or at the same bench as his fellow-craftsmen. Where is the comprehensive plan that will make practical use of idle hands in the place where they are most wanted—the war factories ?

BELGIAN ' COOLIES '

In 1941 the Belgian national expenditure totalled 36,640,000,000 francs, while the revenue was only 15,530,000,000 francs. The official costs of German occupation, which were 15,150,000,000 (as against 4,500,000,000 in 1940), practically equalled the total revenue.—I.T.F. ; *Facts and Figures about the Dictatorships.*

THESE figures are eloquent of the working of the New Order in Belgium. The Nazi Herrenvolk, or overlords, have appropriated the whole of the Belgian people. They either work for the tyrant, starve, or go to the concentration camp. In addition to this crippling penalty Belgium had to deliver in 1941, 7,850,000,000 francs' worth of goods and labour for which she had nothing but a credit balance in Berlin. Of this amount 6,500,000,000 francs represent a compulsory loan of goods, and over 1,000,000,000 francs remittances from Belgians working in Germany to their families which the German authorities did not pay out, but caused the Belgian bank to issue in advance. This is what the German Brusseler Zeitung describes as Belgium's contribution towards financing the war against Bolshevism and its allies. The cynicism of this remark is typical. Russian communism, or Bolshevism, as

the Germans and their lickspittles in Spain and Italy persist in calling it, is a genuine effort to improve the lot of the workers. Nazism is a system whereby all the workers are turned into coolies to enrich a minority of German overlords. Hitler hopes that the workers of the world will be united some day, not in freedom and prosperity, but in a chain-gang for the benefit of the German peoples as a whole.

COLLECTIVE SECURITY

It is not necessary that an international organization aiming at security and collaboration should include from the start all the European nations. But it is essential that Great Britain and Russia should take their stand by the side of the lesser States.—*Dr. Nintchitch, Yugoslav Minister for Foreign Affairs*

THE League of Nations failed because certain nations were neither ready for nor wanted the democratic principles inherent in its structure. The United States, whence it originated, in President Wilson's mind, deserted the League, but Britain "joined up," and, true to the disarmament policy upon which it was founded, disbanded her armies and " scuttled " her ships. History repeats itself, but it is to be hoped most fervently that no such folly will inspire our post-war politicians. Do we not owe our present troubles to the futility of pacifism, which is incompatible with a Great Power ? It was an invitation to the political pirates in Germany, Italy and Japan to hoist their Jolly Rogers and set forth for the loot in the form of riches that Britain left about like "unconsidered trifles." We have temporarily lost our possessions in the Far East, but the question might be asked whether we deserved to hold them. Britain will get them back at great cost, but whether we can keep them will depend on our will and strength to defend them. Make no mistake, Hitler, Mussolini, and the Japanese aggressors are not phenomenal freaks. Such men are only super-cracksmen and they recur in history. The progressive nations, Britain, Russia and the United States will take charge of the future, but as armed guardians of the peace, and not pacifist visionaries.

BACK TO THE MUD

The Ostdeutscher Beobachter reports that among the ruins of Wolkowysk a large quantity of stone axes, tinders and flints, iron weapons and bone spindles have been discovered. With the aid of these it will be possible to establish the national-political features of this area in ancient times.

SOMEBODY once brilliantly diagnosed the whole Nazi movement as a *nostalgia for the mud.* It may well be that the Germans are the missing link between the ape and the human being, and have managed to outwit evolution and remain like their original parents. Here is something for the scientists to get their teeth into, but is it not strange, to say the least, that the Germans are always delving into the remote past for facts or legends applicable to, if not explanatory of, their aboriginal pedigree? Surely their historic and interminably boring desire to be supermen is an acknowledgment of their conscious inferiority. Whether the stone axes, iron weapons and bone spindles found at Wolkowysk fit in perfectly with the national-

political features of Nazism or not, there is no doubt that they symbolize the time-lag in Nazi psychology. When Hitler's swastika fades as the national emblem, the Neanderthal skull (which was found near Düsseldorf) and two stone axes might be adopted.

COLONEL BLIMP'S PROGRESS

Mr. David Low, the cartoonist, first drew his engaging character, Colonel Blimp, eight years ago. Are there as many Blimps in the Empire today as then ? We hope not.

IF ridicule could kill, Mr. David Low's Colonel Blimp, that fatuous type of military expert, who is always preparing for the last war and pompously wrong about everything in this, would long ago have been interred without military honours. The famous cartoonist has recently told us over the wireless that the idea of Blimp occurred to him about ten years past when in a Turkish bath he was listening to a couple of fat asses in their birthday suits telling one another that what Japan did was no business of Britain. "Someone ought to draw something about all this," said Low to himself, *sotto voce,* under the steam. Whether there are fewer Blimps in this country than there were in 1931 who can say ? But it has been suggested that the Blimp mentality has not decreased in numbers east of Suez. A well-known Blimp is the one who is always painfully surprised when the enemy does something rather unusual, unexpected and successful, as if the whole art of war was not to surprise your opponent and take him off his guard. Does Blimp then still use the expression, " It isn't cricket," or has he awakened to the crass idiocy of such a remark ? Let us preserve a Blimp or two. We could ill afford to spare the laughter he gives us in these grim days.

HOME GUARD PIKE, described by Lord Croft, Under-Secretary for War, as "a most effective and silent weapon," is considered a " last hope " by at least one Company Commander. This Home Guard certainly seems to prefer his tommy-gun. *Photo, G.P.U.*

Britain's War Cabinet: Old Faces and New

SIR STAFFORD CRIPPS, Lord Privy Seal and Leader of the House of Commons.

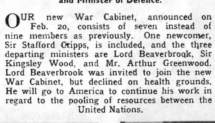

MR. WINSTON CHURCHILL, Prime Minister and Minister of Defence.

MR. OLIVER LYTTELTON, Minister of State, with general supervision over production.

OUR new War Cabinet, announced on Feb. 20, consists of seven instead of nine members as previously. One newcomer, Sir Stafford Cripps, is included, and the three departing ministers are Lord Beaverbrook, Sir Kingsley Wood, and Mr. Arthur Greenwood. Lord Beaverbrook was invited to join the new War Cabinet, but declined on health grounds. He will go to America to continue his work in regard to the pooling of resources between the United Nations.

MR. ANTHONY EDEN, who remains Foreign Secretary.

MR. C. R. ATTLEE, Deputy Prime Minister and Dominions Secretary.

MR. ERNEST BEVIN, Minister of Labour and National Service.

SIR JOHN ANDERSON, Lord President of the Council.

Photos, Central Press, Topical Press, Associated Press, Wide World, Fox

From Rangoon to Darwin One Long Battle

Confused indeed was the position in the south-west Pacific following upon the disastrous surrender of Singapore. Fighting went on continuously in a score of places, and here it is possible to reflect only the high lights of the vast struggle. See map in page 514.

SINCE the Burma Road is the Chinese life line, and since the continued resistance of China is one of the principal hopes and mainstays of the Allies, there was ever-deepening anxiety as the Japanese pushed relentlessly towards Rangoon, ocean terminus of the great highway.

Moulmein was evacuated by the British on Jan. 31, and fresh positions were taken up on the western bank of the Salween. Here a determined effort was made to halt the invader, but the Japanese were in overwhelming strength, and by the capture of Martaban on Feb. 11 and Thaton on Feb. 16 they outflanked the Salween defenders. Once again General Hutton's men were compelled to fall back, this time to positions which had been hastily prepared along the line of the Bilin river. Action was swiftly joined, and the Japanese preponderance in arms and men was soon made apparent. There was a gallant diversion on the part of Chiang Kai-shek's Chinese operating from the Shan states, who delivered a big thrust at Chiengmai, northern terminus of the railway to Bangkok. But soon it was apparent that the Bilin line could not be held much longer, and the week-end brought news of fighting on its western side, between the Bilin and the Sittang. This brought the Japanese within some 75 miles of Rangoon; and the significance of their advance was apparent from an official statement issued on Feb. 20 from Chungking, concerning the results to date of General Chiang Kai-shek's visit to India. It was revealed that concrete measures had been decided upon for the transportation of supplies direct from India to China, by a new route whose capacity would exceed that of the Burma Road. "The use of Rangoon," it went on, "as the port of entry has therefore been abandoned, and its approaches have been mined."

No details of the new road were issued, but it was generally assumed that the reference was to the partly completed Assam Road which has been under construction since the summer of 1939. As the map in this page shows, it runs from Chungking to Sadiya in Assam, which is the railhead of the Bengal-Assam railway, giving it connexion with Calcutta and Chittagong on the Bay of Bengal. Its total length is given as about 2,200 miles, of which (so far as is known) only 500 miles have been constructed as yet. The difficulties involved are enormous, greater even than those which confronted the builders of the Burma Road. Its "roof" is 9,000 feet, several thousand feet higher than that of the Burma Road. Between Chungking and Batang the road, running in a generally westward direction, must cross great rivers and several mountain ranges before, at Batang, it arrives in the Lower Himalayas. Here it proceeds south-west through some of the most mountainous country in Asia, a jumble of great ranges and precipitous defiles. Then just before entering Assam it drops from the clouds to the Brahmaputra valley. From Chittagong to Sadiya is about 600 miles; from Calcutta it is about 300 miles farther.

But the building of the Assam Road is part of a long-term policy; for the present the Burma Road is of much greater importance, and the Burma Road, following the threat to Rangoon, is now as good as closed. Moreover, consequent upon the Japanese triumph at Singapore, it may be expected that the Japanese fleet will make an incursion into the Indian Ocean with a view to cutting the far-stretched lines of Allied communications—those which lead to and from India by way of the Persian Gulf, round the Cape, and from Australia.

While the threats to Burma and India,

THE ASSAM ROAD, the presumed course of which is shown by the dotted line in the map above, is understood to be the new route by which supplies will be sent to China. The use of Rangoon as the port of entry for Burma Road supplies was abandoned before the end of February. *Courtesy of The Daily Telegraph*

and ultimately China, were developing, the Japanese conquests in the Dutch East Indies continued. Two days before Singapore's fall the Japanese launched a large-scale attack by sea and air against Palembang in south-east Sumatra, a great oil centre and one of the chief Dutch settlements in the Indies. The next day, Feb. 14, Japanese shock troops to the number of 700, armed with tommy-guns, light mortars and other weapons, were dropped by parachute in an attempt to capture the oil refineries, and clear the way for the landing of troops from the flotilla of transports which nosed their way through the narrow strait between Sumatra and the island of Banka. The parachutists were practically all wiped out by the Dutch defenders without much trouble; but under cover of a heavy bombardment the Japanese put thousands of men into small craft of every kind, sloops and motor-boats, rowing boats and rafts, in which they pushed up the Mosei river in the direction of Palembang. "Murderous havoc was played among the thousands of invaders," said an official account, "by the R.A.F. Hurricanes and Blenheims," but such was the weight of the enemy onslaught that it soon became apparent that the fall of Palembang could not be delayed more than a few hours. So the Dutch once again adopted their "scorched earth" tactics. Oil wells, installations, refineries and equipment—all went up in flames. It was described as the greatest voluntary destruction the world has ever seen, greater even than the blowing up of the Dnieper Dam in Russia. Said a spokesman over Batavia radio on Feb. 17, "We have lost the oil, but this loss is small compared with the fact that the Japanese too have lost it. We still have other sources of oil. They have not."

While the Japanese were battering their way into Palembang, other detachments of the apparently inexhaustible enemy were drawing a net round the great and vital island of Java. To the north of Borneo they seized Banjermassin, advancing along the coast from Balik Papan; in Celebes, Macassar was theirs. On Feb. 19 Darwin in Northern Australia was raided for the first time by Japanese aeroplanes; and on the next day Japanese landings were effected in Timor and Bali.

In Bali, which is separated from Java by only two miles of water the Dutch fought a determined delaying action. The Japanese were in considerable strength, and fierce fighting developed in the neighbourhood of Den Pasar, where is the island's one aerodrome and only good port, which they had no sooner secured than they were heavily bombed by Flying Fortresses, flown by American pilots. Their position, indeed, was not altogether a happy one, since not only were they bombed from the air, but they were cut off on the seaward side.

On the night of Feb. 19 an Allied squadron, consisting of Dutch cruisers and Dutch and American destroyers, attacked the strong concentration of enemy warships and transports off the east coast of Bali. One of the Allied destroyers was torpedoed and sunk, but the enemy had by far the worst of it. The battle continued for some days, and a statement issued by the Dutch East Indian Government on Feb. 23 declared that it could be assumed that the greater part of the fleet—nineteen was the figure mentioned—in which the Japanese set out for the conquest of Bali had been destroyed or badly damaged. The single ship which succeeded in escaping destruction had fled.

Said an Indies Government spokesman in Batavia the same day: The magnificent successes of the Allied sea and air forces justify the belief that the conquest of Bali means to the Japanese as pyrrhic a victory as the conquest of the burning homes at Tarakan, Balik Papan and Palembang."

Foes and Friends on the Pacific War Fronts

Radioed from Tokyo to Berlin, this photograph shows the opening phase of the Battle of Singapore from the Japanese side. Japanese troops are in position on the mainland facing the island, awaiting zero hour for the assault.
Photo, G.P.U.

Taken aboard a Japanese invasion barge, this photograph shows Japanese troops about to make a landing on the shores of Luzon, in the Philippines —where General MacArthur still puts up a great resistance.
Photo, Keystone

Below, transporting light artillery by pack horses over the difficult terrain of the island of Java. Java contains the headquarters of General Wavell's Command.
Photo, Sport & General

This radioed picture from Melbourne shows Pacific Naval chiefs in conference in Australia. Left to right are : Vice-Admiral H. J Leary, U.S. Navy, Commanding the Combined Naval Forces in the Anzac area ; Vice-Admiral Sir Guy Royle, R.N., First Naval Member of the Commonwealth Naval Board, and Commodore W. E. Parry, Chief of N.Z. Naval Staff. *Photo, Planet News*

Below, the Government House and War Memorial at Darwin, seaport of Northern Australia, only separated from the Japanese forces which invaded Timor by the 300 miles of the Timor Sea.
Courtesy of Australian Govt

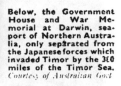

In Burma 'We Intend With the Men and Material

RANGOON, capital and seaport of Burma, at the mouth of Rangoon River, was the objective of strong Japanese thrusts. The photographs show, top left, shrines at the base of the great Shwe Dagon pagoda ; top centre, British soldiers in Rangoon, with the Shwe Dagon pagoda in the background ; above, shipping in Rangoon harbour.

Photos, Paul Popper, British Official: Crown Copyright; Fox, G.P.U.

hich Continue to Flow to Us to Attack the Enemy'

BURMA'S DEFENCES are now being tested in the struggle with the Japanese invaders. Top right, an Indian trench mortar detachment at Mandalay. Left, Burman personnel of Burma's R.N.V.R. training with heavy artillery at a Naval depot. Above, a convoy of hundreds of laden lorries passes along the famous Burma Road. The quotation at the head of the page is taken from a message to the Burmese people from the Governor, Sir R. Dorman-Smith, on Feb. 8.

In Russia the Cossacks Ride Again

Are the days of cavalry over ? The Soviet High Command does not think so, and the daring
and successful exploits of the Cossacks on the Eastern front have shown that the horse can
negotiate ground over which tanks and motor-lorries cannot advance ; mounted men armed
with automatic weapons can gallop over rough ground that would slow up any motor-cyclist ;
and cavalry bands, well handled, can be a terror to the enemy's unprotected flanks.

ON the vast Russian front, from the Ukraine to Leningrad, the Don, Kuban and Terek Cossacks are fighting the Nazis with all their traditional skill. Of course, it would be folly to throw cavalry, unsupported, into a modern battle, and the Soviet cavalry units are supplied with machine-guns, artillery and even tanks. The cavalrymen themselves are taught not only horse-riding but also bayonet-fighting, bomb-throwing, trench-digging and ski-ing.

The horse is the means of locomotion which enables a blow to be struck quickly and unexpectedly. For instance, recently the Germans made a break-through near a very important point. For twenty-four hours Cossack troops raced from one flank to another, through forests and across rivers covered with thin ice, where no tank could venture, went into action and checked the enemy until the breach could be repaired.

On one occasion the 2nd Guards Cavalry Corps, with their famous leader Major-General Dovator (since reported killed in action) at their head, broke through the German front line, penetrated deep into the enemy's rear and for many days, behind the backs of the German generals, smashed headquarters, dispersed transports and disrupted communications. Into such a panic were the Germans thrown that an Order had to be issued announcing to the Nazi troops that, contrary to rumours, not 100,000 but only 18,000 Cossacks had penetrated their rear. In fact, there were only 3,000, but they twice scattered the headquarters of the 6th German Army.

This is how one of Dovator's successful raids was carried out. The Cossacks took no baggage train with them, but carried everything they needed on their horses. After smashing an advanced battalion of the 66th "Hitler" Infantry Regt. and routing the Rumanian Royal Guard, they penetrated about 60 miles into the enemy positions. There they became complete masters of the situation, damaging roads and communications, burning stores and destroying motor columns and fuel lorries. For twelve days

they harried the enemy without respite. On the second day of the raid they ran into the 9th battalion of the 430th Infantry Regt. and after a pitched battle destroyed it.

When informed by partisans that the Germans were forming special detachments to exterminate his Cossacks, Gen. Dovator broke up his formation into small groups which began acting independently in all directions. Making their base in a dense forest, the Cossacks appeared in the night or at dawn where they were least expected. From the surrounding woods stranded Red Army men and officers rallied to the Cossacks and Dovator furnished them with rifles and machine-guns captured from the enemy. In twelve days he had thus armed a detachment of 1,000 men. Destruction during the raid included 2,500 German soldiers, 10 guns, 87 machine-guns, 115 lorries, six tanks, two ammunition dumps and three wireless stations. When it was time for them to return to their lines, local inhabitants led them through dense woods to the rear of the German front line. On a misty morning they charged their way through the Germans from the rear, broke through and returned safely to their own units, leaving behind them over 1,000 armed men as guerillas.

Hero of the Soviet Union

Major-General Lev Dovator commanded the Red Cossack Corps which was recently renamed the 2nd Guards Cavalry Corps. For his daring and heroism in battle he was awarded the title of Hero of the Soviet Union. Another famous Russian cavalry commander is Major-General Byelov, commander of the 1st Guards Cavalry Corps, whose troops fought splendidly in the Ukraine later and in the defence of Moscow, routing the Germans after they had broken through in the Tula sector.

A woman war-correspondent, Eugenie Krueger, went to interview Dovator when he was fighting on the Moscow front. It was no easy matter to find his headquarters. The only accurate direction that could be given her was—" Look for Dovator where

the fighting is hottest." When she did reach his H.Q. she summed up her impressions of the man in this manner :

" The day was drawing to a close when the General returned from the main line. Without pausing to remove his coat he walked over to the table and, unfolding a map, proceeded to explain the situation and the plan of subsequent operations. His speech was quick, laconic. Giving little time to minor detail, he tried to make everybody understand his main idea. His enthusiasm is contagious, his speech picturesque and expressive. This is how he speaks of his Guardsmen :

" ' Our weapons ? Rifle ! Sabre ! Hand-grenade ! Fire bottles ! There is one of my commanders, believe it or not, he once got on a horse and attacked a tank. Queer chap. But what can you do with him if he actually did destroy the tank ? And he is by no means young. I scolded him, but inwardly I thought : This old boy is made of real stuff, he is a real Guardsman.' "

Yes, they are all made of the real stuff, these Cossacks—and the Nazis fear them. In the letter of a German N.C.O., one Kurt Gerch, we read : " The most terrible thing I have ever experienced is a Cossack attack. We were blinded by the glitter of their sabres and deafened by their savage shouts."

And here, to end with, is the tale of the five messengers. A squadron of Cossacks was trying to fight its way out of a deep valley, where they were being hemmed in by German tank detachments. Their commander had to send for reinforcements and chose five dispatch riders for the job, hoping that one, at least, would get through. All were given sealed envelopes with an identical message, and they made for the only gap in the German ring which was covered by cross-fire from German machine-guns. In full view of the Germans they climbed the hillside. In a moment not less than ten machine-guns were trained upon the horsemen. The five Cossacks fell from the saddle, seeming to trail lifeless from the stirrup as their horses dragged the men along the snow-covered ground. As soon as the horses disappeared over the brow of the hill the seemingly helpless riders sprang into the saddle again. All five reached headquarters.

SOVIET CAVALRY are seen galloping into action on the Eastern Front in this photograph radioed direct from Moscow to London. Colonel-General Gorodovikov, a Soviet cavalry commander, stated recently : " Formidable Cossack groups are gathering on the Don, in Kuban and Terek. The peoples of the North Caucasus and Daghestan, the Turkmenians and Tajiks, the Kazakhs, Kalmucks, Bashkirians, Tartars and other descendants of Jenghiz Khan's troops are forming new cavalry units."

Photo, Planet News

Red Horsemen Eager for the Fight

SOVIET CAVALRY, emerging from their hiding-place, gallop forward to attack the enemy. The Cossacks have a reputation as horsemen second to none, and their furious attacks have time and again demoralized the German infantry.

A group of Cossacks, members of the Soviet Popular Volunteer Force, are seen on the right receiving instruction from their leader. They have raided German communications with great effect.

COSSACKS played a great part in the defence of Moscow, and here some of them are seen trotting along a forest ride near the outskirts of the city. Stalin himself praised them for their splendid work.

The old mother of Marshal Budenny stands at the roadside of her native village, waving to Cossacks of her son's old regiment who have formed themselves into a People's Guard.

Photos, British Official: Crown Copyright; Keystone

Our Diary of the War

WEDNESDAY, FEB. 18, 1942 900th day

Sea.—Admiralty announced the successful passage of important British convoys through Mediterranean. Five enemy planes shot down, four more probably destroyed. One enemy heavy cruiser torpedoed by submarine; two cruisers and destroyer torpedoed by naval planes.

Russian Front.—Russians claimed capture of Zakhorova, west of Bryansk. Heavy fighting in the Crimea.

Africa.—Widespread patrol activity in Libya.

Far East.—Japs launched heavy attack against British line on Bilin River, Burma. Off Sumatra, where Jap forces pushed towards Sunda Straits, many invasion barges were sunk by Allied bombers. More Jap reinforcements landed in Luzon.

Home.—A Dornier 217 shot down off East Coast. Single raider bombed E. Anglian coast.

General.—Gen. Chiang Kai-shek had a long conversation with Mr. Gandhi in Calcutta.

THURSDAY, FEB. 19 901st day

Sea.—Two E-boats destroyed during night attack on a British convoy. One enemy bomber destroyed and four others damaged.

Russian Front.—Capture of Kresty, 80 miles N.W. of Smolensk, announced by Russians.

Far East.—Japanese who had crossed the Bilin River driven back. Chunking announced new overland route in use to replace Burma Road. Rangoon stated to be closed as a port of entry and its approaches mined. Allied reinforcements reported to have reached Java. U.S. fighters shot down 6 Jap planes over Surabaya. Fierce fighting in Palembang area, Sumatra.

Home.—Important changes in the War Cabinet announced (see page 537). Air Marshal Harris appointed A.O.C.-in-C. Bomber Command. Night bomber raided E. Anglian town.

Australia.—72 Japanese bombers raided Port Darwin, on northern coast of Australia, at 10 a.m. Second raid, by 21 bombers, about noon. At least six enemy aircraft destroyed.

General.—Riom trial opened.

FRIDAY, FEB. 20 902nd day

Air.—Fighter Command set an E-boat on fire during offensive patrols over Channel and N. France.

Russian Front.—Fighting in all sectors reached great intensity.

Far East.—Islands of Bali and Timor attacked by Japs. Invasion fleet off Bali heavily attacked by Allied bombers. Burma battle continued along Bilin River.

SATURDAY, FEB. 21 903rd day

Russian Front.—Heaviest fighting was around Leningrad, Rjev, Orel, Kursk, Kharkov, and the Crimea.

Africa.—In Libya a patrol of the Royals penetrated as far as Msus, raiding Rommel's base. Enemy vehicles were destroyed and prisoners captured.

Far East.—Allied H.Q. announced that losses inflicted on Jap invasion fleet on Feb. 19-20 off Bali were at least 1 cruiser sunk and five damaged; 2 destroyers sunk; 1 transport sunk and six damaged. In Burma, Japs advanced towards Pegu.

SUNDAY, FEB. 22 904th day

Air.—Bomber Command made night attack on ports and other targets in N.W. Germany. Docks at Ostend also bombed.

Russian Front.—Fifteen inhabited localities in a southern front sector reported to be occupied as the result of one day's fighting.

Africa.—Nazi forces moving up in Libya.

Far East.—In Burma fighting continued between the Sittang and Bilin Rivers. Enemy drive from Palembang towards the Sunda Strait, in Sumatra, being held up by Dutch forces.

Home.—Changes in six Ministries were announced from Downing St.

MONDAY, FEB. 23 905th day

Russian Front.—Moscow communiqué reported recapture by Red Army of Dorogobuzh, 45 miles east of Smolensk.

Far East.—Little change in Burma. Japanese invasion fleet off Bali driven off with heavy loss. Japanese force on Bali fighting to hold part of the island.

Australia.—Part of the Northern Territory placed under military control.

General.—President Roosevelt broadcast from Washington.

One Crime Only Can Rob Us of Victory

HOW do matters stand now? Taking it all in all, are our chances of survival better or are they worse than in Aug. 1941? How is it with the British Empire or Commonwealth of Nations? Are we up or down?

The first and greatest of events is that the United States is now unitedly and wholeheartedly in the war with us . . . When I survey and compute the power of the United States and its vast resources and feel that they are now in it with us, with the British Commonwealth of Nations all together, however long it lasts, till death or victory, I cannot believe there is any other fact in the whole world which can compare with that. That is what I have dreamed of, aimed at and worked for, and now it has come to pass.

BUT there is another fact, in some ways more immediately effective. The Russian armies have not been defeated, they have not been torn to pieces. The Russian people have not been conquered or destroyed. Leningrad and Moscow have not been taken. The Russian armies are in the field. They are not holding the line of the Urals or the line of the Volga. They are advancing victoriously, driving the foul invader from that native soil they have guarded so bravely and love so well. More than that : for the first time they have broken the Hitler legend. Instead of the easy victories and abundant booty which he and his hordes had gathered in the West, he has found in Russia so far only disaster, failure, the shame of unspeakable crimes, the slaughter or loss of vast numbers of German soldiers, and the icy wind that blows across the Russian snow.

HERE, then, are two tremendous fundamental facts which will in the end dominate the world situation and make victory possible in a form never possible before. But there is another heavy and terrible side to the account, and this must be set in the balance against these inestimable gains. Japan has plunged into the war and is ravaging the beautiful, fertile, prosperous, and densely populated lands of the Far East . . . Tonight the Japanese are triumphant. They shout their exultation round the world. We suffer. We are taken aback. We are hard pressed. But I am sure even in this dark hour that " criminal madness " will be the verdict which history will pronounce upon the authors of Japanese aggression, after the events of 1942 and 1943 have been inscribed upon its sombre pages.

No one must underrate any more the gravity and efficiency of the Japanese war machine. Whether in the air or upon the sea or man to man on land they have already proved themselves to be formidable, deadly, and, I am sorry to say, barbarous antagonists. This proves a hundred times over that there never was the slightest chance, even though we had been much better prepared in many ways than we were, of our standing up to them alone while we had Nazi Germany at our throat and Fascist Italy at our belly. It proves something else. And this should be a comfort and reassurance. We can now measure the wonderful strength of the Chinese people who under Generalissimo Chiang Kai-shek have single-handed fought this hideous Japanese aggressor for four and a half years and left him baffled and dismayed . . .

YOU know I have never prophesied to you or promised smooth and easy things, and now all I have to offer is hard adverse war for many months ahead. I must warn you, as I warned the House of Commons before they gave me their generous vote of confidence a fortnight ago, that many misfortunes, severe torturing losses, remorseless and gnawing anxieties lie before us. To our British folk these may seem even harder to bear when they are at a great distance than when the savage Hun was shattering our cities and we all felt in the midst of the battle ourselves. But the same qualities which brought us through the awful jeopardy of the summer of 1940 and its long autumn and winter bombardment from the air, will bring us through this other new ordeal, though it may be more costly and will certainly be longer. One fault, one crime, and one crime only, can rob the united nations and the British people, upon whose constancy this grand alliance came into being, of the victory upon which their lives and honour depend. A weakening in our purpose and therefore in our unity—that is the mortal crime. Whoever is guilty of that crime or of bringing it about in others, of him let it be said that it were better for him that a millstone were hanged about his neck and he were cast into the sea.

Mr. CHURCHILL in his " Singapore has fallen " broadcast, Sunday, Feb. 15, 1942.

FLYING FORTRESSES under construction in one of the Boeing Aircraft Company Plants at Seattle, Washington, New models of this famous four-engine bomber incorporate several advancements over previous types.
Photo, Central Press

Hitler's Guns Fire Across the Straits

Hitler confers with Prof. Albert Speer, the German architect. Herr Speer succeeded Dr. Todt, after the latter's death, as Hitler's Chief Engineer.

GERMAN COASTAL GUNS on the French shores still bombard the Dover area and Channel convoys from time to time. Above, one of these heavy German guns has just fired and the shell is hurtling across the Dover Straits. Top left, men of the Todt Organization, formed by the late Dr. Fritz Todt, are seen indulging in a little recreation after working on a battery emplacement on the French coast. These German guns are the object of constant attention by the R.A.F. during their offensive sweeps over the Channel.

Photos, Sport & General, Keystone

Sansom's Rough-Riders Have Powerful Mounts

The 5th Canadian (Armoured) Division, known as Sansom's Rough-Riders after their Divisional Commander, Maj.-Gen. E. W Sansom, arrived in Britain on Nov. 22, 1941. Canadian tank men are seen above during exercises in England using American "General Lee" tanks. It has been disclosed that some of Canada's own new heavy tanks, a type known as the "Ram," have already reached Britain.

The former Fort Garry Horse, crack Canadian cavalry regiment, is now a unit of the Canadian Armoured Division, and is training with American "General Lee" 30-ton cruiser tanks like that on the left. Note the American-type crash helmets.

Photos, Central Press

Vital Links in the War of Machines

TREADS FOR TANKS being assembled in a U.S. factory. These treads are put on to the rollers of the tank in two sections. First of all, the tank is hoisted by crane and lowered into the bottom section; then the upper part is lowered from a crane and pulled over the rollers as shown in the photograph. Finally the two parts are bolted together by hand. *Photo, Central Press*

Above Singapore Floated the Flag of Japan

" Never has Britain lost so much face in the Orient. A fortress deemed impregnable has been reduced in nine weeks." So read the New York Times on the morrow of Singapore's fall. " Not since the collapse of France has the anti-aggressor cause suffered so catastrophic a blow."

SHORT of food, water, petrol and ammunition, his troops surrounded in Singapore city and the centre of the island, General Percival realized that it was impossible to carry on the defence any longer. This he indicated in a message to General Wavell. The last British communiqué was issued on Saturday, Feb. 14.

Today (it read) the enemy has maintained his pressure, supporting his attacks with a number of high-level bombing raids by large formations of aircraft, continual shelling by his artillery, and low dive-bombing attacks. His artillery have also shelled the town intermittently throughout the night and this morning. Our troops, British, Australian, Indian and Malay, are disputing every attempt to advance further towards the heart of Singapore town. In the town itself the civil defence services are making every effort to deal with the damage and civil casualties caused by hostile shelling and bombing.

On the afternoon of the next day, Feb. 15, a peace mission, headed by Major C. H. D. Wild, attached to the British General Staff, with four British officers, was dispatched to the Japanese Army headquarters with a white flag of truce. They were handed the Japanese peace terms and left the headquarters at 4.15 p.m., after arranging for a meeting between the leaders of the two armies.

Later on Sunday evening the meeting was held in the Ford motor plant at the foot of Bukit Timah hill, in the centre of the island. Accompanying Lt.-Gen. Percival were Brig.-Gen. K. S. Torrance, Major Wild, and Brig.-Gen. T. A. Newbiggin. They were met by Lt.-Gen. Tomoyuki Yamashita, Commander-in-Chief of the Japanese Expeditionary Force in Malaya. The meeting lasted 49 minutes. General Yamashita demanded unconditional surrender. According to the Japanese News Agency the following conversation ensued :

Lt.-Gen. Yamashita. I want your replies to be brief and to the point. I will only accept an unconditional surrender.

Lt.-Gen. Percival. Yes.

Have any Japanese soldiers been captured ?—No, not a single one.

What about the Japanese residents ?—All the Japanese residents interned by the British authorities have been sent to India. Their lives are fully protected by the Indian Government.

I want to hear whether you want to surrender or not. If you want to surrender I insist on its being unconditional. What is your answer, yes or no ?—Will you give me until tomorrow morning ?

Tomorrow ? I cannot wait, and the Japanese forces will have to attack tonight.—How about waiting until 11.30 p.m. Tokyo time ?

If that is to be the case, the Japanese forces will have to resume attacks until then. Will you say yes or no ? (Lt.-Gen. Percival made no reply.)

I want to hear a decisive answer, and I insist on an unconditional surrender. What do you say ?—Yes.

All right, then, the order to cease fire must be issued at exactly 10.00 p.m. I will immediately send 1,000 Japanese troops into the city area to maintain peace and order. You agree to that ?—Yes.

If you violate these terms the Japanese troops will lose no time in launching a general and final offensive against Singapore city.

THEY WERE IN MALAYA

British and Imperial forces which took part in the Malayan campaign and the defence of Singapore.

(i) 18th British Division, comprising 53, 54, and 55 Inf. Bdes., including battalions of

R. Northumberland Fusiliers	Suffolk Regt.
R. Norfolk Regt.	Beds & Herts Regt.
Cambridgeshire Regt.	Sherwood Foresters

(ii) 8th Australian Division : 22nd and 27th A.I.F. Bdes.

(iii) 9th and 11th Indian Divisions, including battalions of :

East Surrey Regt.	Dogra Regt.
Leicestershire Regt.	Baluch Regt.
Argyll and Sutherland Highlanders	Hyderabad Regt.
Punjab Regt.	Sikh Regt.
Jat Regt.	Frontier Force Regt.
Rajputana Rifles	Frontier Force Rifles
Royal Garhwal Rifles	Gurkha Rifles
	Indian State Forces

(iv) 1st and 2nd Malay Inf. Bdes., containing battalions of :

Loyal Regt.	Manchester Regt.
Gordon Highlanders	Indian and Malayan Bns.

Besides the artillery regiments included in the above Field formations, a number of Coast Artillery Units, A.A. Regts., A/Tk. Regts. and Searchlight Units ; while in addition to the Engineer Units included in the above there were a number of Fortress Companies, R.E. and Army Troops Companies. Also R.A.M.C., R.A.S.C., R.A.O.C., etc., Indian Medical Services, Army Nurses and local volunteer battalions.

Lt.-Gen. Tomoyuki Yamashita, C.-in-C. of the Japanese expeditionary force in Malaya, who dictated the terms for the surrender of Singapore *Photo, Wide World*

General Yamashita also accepted full responsibility for the lives of the British and Australian troops, as well as the British women and children remaining in Singapore. " Rely upon Japanese *Bushido*," he declared. (Bushido is the ancient Japanese code of chivalry.)

The unconditional surrender dated from 7 p.m. Singapore time (12.30 p.m. British time), and three hours later fighting ceased along the entire Singapore front. Following the capitulation the civilian population was reported to be quiet but bewildered. The civil defence and fire services were carrying on, and the telephone girls were still at their posts. " Ragged Tommies and Anzacs," cabled the Japanese Domei Agency war correspondent in Singapore, " stumbling with fatigue after being driven before the relentless Japanese juggernaut, are enjoying their first real rest in a month and a half."

At 8 a.m. on Monday, Feb. 16 (1.30 a.m. B.S.T.), the Japanese army, tanks in the van marched into Singapore. The flag of the Rising Sun was hoisted over the Government buildings, and guards were stationed in the suburbs, " and are completing the work of cleaning up seditious elements." Meanwhile the Japanese naval forces completed the occupation of all the defence positions, including those of the Seletar naval base, the Keppel harbour, and Fort Changi. " At a joint conference a British officer gave a detailed explanation regarding the port facilities, after which a decision was reached regarding the disposal of British warships remaining in Singapore ports."

How many men actually surrendered was not clear, but the number was very large, since no evacuation of the fighting services had been contemplated. The first Japanese claim comprised 60,000 men—" campaigning forces, fortress guards, and volunteers, made up of 15,000 of the British metropolitan forces, 13,000 Australians, and the remainder Indians." It was also stated that there were still a million inhabitants left in Singapore.

Then on Feb. 21 Berlin radio, quoting Tokyo reports, stated that the number of prisoners at Singapore was now given as 73,000. Among them were 8,000 wounded, under medical care. It was also claimed that 300 guns, 2,000 machine-guns, 200 tanks and armoured cars, one steamer of 10,000 tons and three 5,000-ton tankers were also captured.

SINGAPORE raid damage in Raffles Square, named after Sir Stamford Raffles, founder of Singapore. A Japanese bomb hit the building in the corner strewing wreckage all over the square, and these Malayan workers have been cleaning up. A concrete pill-box is marked with an arrow on the left.

Photo, Associated Press

In Corregidor MacArthur Still Held Out

Top, rows of shells in their racks in the underground ammunition depots ready to feed the big guns of Corregidor Island.

Above, American soldiers running to their action stations along a naturally camouflaged pathway on the fortress island of Corregidor.

Circle, a gunnery officer receiving firing data from the observation posts at a gun site on Corregidor Island.

Photos, Associated Press from Paramount News

Above, American gunners on Corregidor working the range-finder. The heavy guns of the island fortress guard the entrance to Manila Bay.

Left, a giant howitzer forming part of the powerful Corregidor defences. The island has proved a valuable flanking bastion for MacArthur's gallant forces.

Singapore Was Burning as I Packed My Bag

This dramatic picture of Singapore in the last days before its fall was written on the eve of his departure on Feb. 11 by C. Yates McDaniel of the Associated Press, the last foreign correspondent to leave the island.

THE sky over Singapore is black with the smoke of a dozen huge fires today, as I write my last message from this once beautiful, prosperous and peaceful city.

The roar and crash of cannonade and bursting bombs which is shaking my typewriter, and my hands which are wet with the perspiration of fright, tell me without need of an official communiqué that the war which started nine weeks ago, 400 miles away, is today in the outskirts of this shaken bastion of Empire. I am sure there is a

JAPANESE SNIPERS

Equipped for fighting independently behind the enemy lines for two weeks to a month, a Japanese sniper carries :
Gas mask.
Green combination mosquito net camouflage hood covering helmet, head and shoulders.
Green corded net to camouflage rest of body.
Black wire eyescreen against sun glare.
Coil of rope for climbing trees and tying himself to trunks and branches to prevent the recoil of the rifle from dislodging him.
Five-inch-long sack of rice.
Small bag of hard tack.
Half a pound of hard candy.
Package of concentrated food.
Tin of field rations. Small tin of coffee.
Vitamin pills.
Tin of chlorine to purify water.
Mess-kit. Canteen.
Antidote for mustard gas.
Quinine, stomach pills, gauze, pads, bandages (packed in a nest of wicker baskets and in the gas mask).
Spare socks, gloves, toothbrush.
Torch with rotating vari-coloured lenses, one colour apparently intended as a sign of recognition, a visual password.—*Clark Lee, Associated Press War Correspondent*

bright tropic sun shining somewhere overhead. But in my many-windowed room it is too dark to work without electric lights.

Over the low rise where the battle is raging I can see relay after relay of Japanese aeroplanes circling, then going into murderous dives on our soldiers who are fighting back in the hell over which there is no protective screen of our own fighter planes. But the Japanese are not completely alone in the skies this morning, for I just saw two "Vildebeestes"—obsolete biplanes with an operating speed of about 100 m.p.h.—fly low

over Japanese positions and unload their bomb burden with a resounding crash.

It makes me ashamed of myself sitting here with my heart beating faster than their old motors when I think what chance those lads have of getting back in their antiquated machines. If ever brave men earned undying glory those R.A.F. pilots have this tragic morning.

There are many other brave men in Singapore today. Not far away are A.A. batteries in open spaces—they must be to have a clear field of fire. Please overlook the break in continuity, but a packet of bombs just landed so close I had to duck behind a wall which I hoped would, and did, screen the blast. But those gun crews are keeping on fighting, their guns peppering the smoke-limited ceiling every time Jap aeroplanes come near, and that is almost constantly

The "All Clear" has just sounded—what a joke, for from my window I can see three Japanese aeroplanes hedge-hopping not a mile away.

A few minutes ago I heard a tragic two-way telephone conversation. Eric Davis, director of the Malayan Broadcasting Corporation, urged the Governor, Sir Shenton Thomas, to give permission to destroy an outlying broadcasting station. The Governor demurred, saying the situation was not too bad. Davis instructed the station to keep on the air but to stand by for urgent orders.

We tuned in to the wavelength of the

Punjabi Sepoys, in tropical kit, manning a Bofors A.A. gun forming part of the Singapore defences. A tribute is paid to the bravery of the A.A. gun crews at Singapore in the eye-witness account in this page.
Photo, Associated Press

station in question. In the middle of a broadcast in Malay urging the people of Singapore to stand firm the station went dead.

My colleagues left last night, and the military spokesman gave his daily talk on the situation to an audience of three—the representatives of two local newspapers and myself. Henry Steel (of Richmond, Surrey), an Army Relations Officer who has seen us through the bad situation from the Thai border to Singapore, has just told me I have 10 minutes to pack up and leave, so I am embarking with about a 50-50 chance of getting clear.

Grim Was Our Flight From the Doomed City

The majority of the British women and children were evacuated from Singapore before the final Japanese assault. From The Daily Mail correspondent, Cedric Salter, came this impression of the scene on one of the liners engaged in the work of rescue.

WOMEN and children are sleeping on the decks, in hammocks slung from all conceivable supports, and on the floors of packed cabins and saloons aboard this great North Atlantic liner, now a rescue ship. The liner landed Indian reinforcements at Singapore before picking up

900 British women and 500 children to carry them to safety.

Twice we have been attacked. Once a bomb fell only 30 yards away, blotting out one of the tugs helping to nose us out of harbour. All four of the tug's crew were killed, and a dozen small holes were drilled in our own side. But after three days we were out of range of enemy bombers.

There is still need for unceasing vigilance, however, against submarines or surface raiders. In my two-hour turns on watch, shared with the mere handful of men on board, I have seen nothing but the endless waste of blue water. Fierce line squalls occasionally scud across our path, lashing us at our look-out posts with warm rain, which a minute later rises in steam from our clothes as the scorching sun reappears.

The drama of life goes on aboard ship. There have already been four births. Most of the women have left homes and husbands behind in besieged Singapore, but even so the ship has something of the holiday air it used to have on its peacetime fashionable summer cruises.

Only for the hushed quarter of an hour when the news is broadcast from London is there any tension. Gaiety then dies out of faces as the grim story is told of those left behind.

Beach pyjamas or shorts are the mode. But the wearers must wait on themselves, carrying heavy trays from the kitchens to release the skeleton staff of overworked stewards for the actual cooking. Long lines

A Vickers Vildebeeste torpedo-bomber flying over H.M.S. Coventry in the Solent. How brave pilots of the R.A.F. were sent up against the Japanese over Malaya in these slow and obsolete biplanes is told in the dramatic story above.
Photo, Central Press

of drying laundry continually flutter in the hot tropical wind.

The greatest hardship is the black-out. It means that every porthole and door must be sealed at night against showing a light. In the airless temperatures of the hundreds the heat becomes intolerable. The result is that now, after nearly a week, some of the

children are pale and fretful. Their mothers even are showing signs of strain.

I am writing this in my " quarters "—a mattress under the long muzzle of a gun mounted aft—as Lights Out is being sounded. The faintly phosphorescent wake is stretching away towards the east as the ship bears its cargo from danger towards friendlier land.

books of reference. Two dartboards and some billiard tables and the remains of a hastily eaten meal were all that remained in one of the petty officers' messes. One of the oil tanks was on fire. Flames were leaping up and gusty clouds of black smoke were blowing over the Straits of Johore. Two or three Japanese reconnaissance aeroplanes were wheeling round in clouds like kites. The purr of their engines, now swelling, now dying away, went on all the afternoon.

My Farewell Visit to the Great Naval Base

The special correspondent of The Times, who paid a visit to the great Singapore base shortly after it had been evacuated by the Navy, described this " most moving experience " in the following dispatch.

HERE was one of the great naval bases of the world. It was more than a base; it was a self-contained city, covering several square miles. It had been nearly 20 years a-building, millions of tons of earth had been moved, one whole river had been diverted. It had cost perhaps £60,000,000.

Here were a floating dock, towed 8,000 miles from England, that could accommodate a 45,000-ton battleship; a smaller floating dock for the repair of destroyers and submarines; a graving dock able to accommodate with a few feet to spare the Queen Mary or the Queen Elizabeth. Here was a giant 500-ton crane able to lift an entire gun-turret out of a battleship. Here were workshops for the repair and maintenance of machinery and guns; an Admiralty transmitting station, one of the most powerful in the world; wharves for revictualling and refuelling ships; huge underground oil and armament depots; shore accommodation for the crews of ships; whole residential areas of small villas, such as might be found in any London suburb; and 17 football fields.

Brain Centre of the Far East

Here was a large concrete administration building which had been the brain centre and the nerve centre of British Far Eastern strategy. Here were barracks that housed a labour force of 12,000 Asiatics. Just off the shore of the base were 22 square miles of deep sea anchorage which could accommodate with ease a combined British and American naval force. Next door were the great airfield and the R.A.F. establishment of Seletar, an air base complementary to the naval base, huge hangars, repair shops, administrative buildings, houses for personnel, runways from the sea for seaplanes, and great oil tanks.

But the Japanese advance down the mainland had obliged the Navy to evacuate. A few Indian sentries were on duty at the gate. Hardly anyone was to be seen where formerly

there had been scenes of such tremendous activity. The Japanese were lobbing mortar shells into the base from across the Strait in a desultory fashion. An occasional lorry, going down to bring away supplies, sped to the warehouses. On the waterfront British troops were in position, seeking what protection they could from the mortar shells.

We crept along, keeping behind buildings as far as possible. Even so the Japanese must have spotted us as we crossed one rather exposed stretch, for one mortar shell landed with a resounding crack only 50 yards in our rear.

The great floating dock had been sunk just off the shore. Its upper works rose above the still water of the Strait. The great crane still stood, one of its girders scarred by a shell. Shells had also fallen through the roofs of the boiler shop, the light machine shop, and the foundry. One or two had struck the administration building, from which everything had been removed.

The room of the Commander-in-Chief, the scene of so many vital conferences in the past—indeed, it was here, perhaps, that was taken the fateful decision to send the Prince of Wales and the Repulse on their last voyage—was empty save for a large Admiralty chart of the world on the wall and some odd

Such were the last days of the great Singapore naval base. Like the Maginot Line it never came fully into action at all. That was its supreme tragedy. Two months before it had been the greatest Allied naval base in one half of the globe. It was now one military sector out of many such sectors in the defence of an island. It had been tucked away at the back of the island as if an attack on the base

A view of the foundry at Singapore Naval Base. The base was officially inaugurated on Feb. 14, 1938, when Sir Shenton Thomas opened the new graving dock. Scores of millions were spent upon it, but the great base was hardly used except for the week when the Prince of Wales and the Repulse put in there just before their disastrous sally.

from the mainland was a possibility that had never occurred to its designers. Indeed it had been built on the premise that our Navy and Air Force would never permit an enemy to come within 100 miles of Singapore. But Singapore's back door had become its front door. One machine-gun firing across the Strait was worth all the 500-ton cranes in the world.

SINGAPORE NAVAL BASE, the graving dock of which could accommodate the largest warship afloat, is now in Japanese hands. In this page a correspondent of The Times describes his farewell visit to the base shortly after it had been evacuated by the Navy. On the left of the photograph is the great floating dock, built at Wallsend and towed out to Singapore in 1928. It now lies sunk just off the shore. *Photos, British Official*

Editor's Postscript

THERE's usually more than one way to any one place, and I have derived amusement lately from watching how certain religious leaders (chiefly bishops) and certain able non-religious publicists (chiefly socialists) by different paths of reasoning have arrived at the same happy meeting place, where the banner under which both sides join hands bears the words : " Spare the German people ! " I can understand the bishops better than the super-humanitarians of the extreme left. But both are elements of some danger to the future of the world in that now farther-off event to which I sincerely believe we are moving : the final overthrow of Pan-German expansionism—not merely Nazism. For Nazism in the ultimate examination is merely a German disease, which can be cured only by a major surgical operation. The Free German movement in Britain which has been lifting its head within the last few weeks should be carefully watched, although we know that many worthy individuals are prominently identified with it. Hitler was not the only German survivor of the last war who swore to be revenged upon the victors. Even among the socialist republicans the smouldering hatred of the French and British, which was to be expected after so humiliating a defeat, was beginning to glow into redness long before Hitler came to fan it into flame. And among the anti-Nazi Germans are many whose chief difference from Hitler is political. Their aims were the same, their methods different.

HAD Hitler never arisen another German-made war would have had to be fought, not perhaps for another generation, which would have suited many of us much better, but in the long run would not have been much better for humanity at large. I assert that no atrocity of this War is a new thing to German (not just Nazi) mentality. Every expression of hate is the same as in the last war—only more so. The difference is not in kind, but in degree. Just reflect on that and see if you don't agree with me. I haven't the space to illustrate my contention in detail just now, but you can take it that had the Kaiser possessed the means of frightfulness which Hitler commands it would have been used in equal measure. Kaiserism was milder simply because it had not the means to do ill deeds which makes ill deeds done. The leopard's spots remain even if you whitewash him. A shower of rain will reveal them. There is no change of skin or heart in the German of today, and once more I am glad that I have never approved the early injunction of our Ministry of Information which urged British editors to distinguish between the German people and the Nazis. The " good Germans " are at present in a hopeless, negligible minority.

HAVING occasion to refer to one of Kipling's books last night I was interested to notice that the set to which it belonged (published round about 1900) bears on a fly-leaf the sign of the swastika with Kipling's autograph enclosed within a circle. On the front of the binding the swastika is also used in association with an elephant's head. And, as though to be right either way, the hooked cross in one of the devices is given in reverse to the other. It occurred to me that a day may come in a very distant future when any of Kipling's books bearing the swastika that may still survive may suggest that they were the work of a Nazi author ! For I am sure that this ancient good luck symbol which has been used for thousands of years in every part of the world by peoples in all stages of culture will become peculiarly Germanic : the symbol of Germany's great bid for world-domination, losing entirely its old Sanskrit significance of " Well-being, or good luck."

MUCH nonsense has been written about its evil meaning when the arms of the cross are turned upwards or downwards (I don't know which), but to Kipling it was evidently acceptable either way. And I venture the opinion that it has always been used indiscriminately in this respect, just as the Nazis use it either as filling a conventional square or tilted diamond-wise. I am afraid I was one of the many who ten or twelve years ago contemned the swastika as a childishly primitive badge for a great national European movement to adopt, or I would not have chosen it as a feature of the design for the binding cases of my Manners and Customs of Mankind, its ancient symbolism being the only reason for doing so. There seems to be little doubt about its Aryan origin, which first commended it to Hitler, but the world knows the sort of " well-being " it now stands for, and when the Nazis have shot their last bolt its evil meaning will have been made

Lt.-Gen. HEIN TER POORTEN, Commander-in-Chief of the Royal Netherlands East Indies Army, now heavily engaged with the Japanese invaders. *Photo, Associated Press*

clear to all the world : the swastika as a bringer of good luck will no longer influence even the most primitive of savages.

ONE of my readers, at present on military service, is good enough to question my reference to the Athenia as an American ship, for which many thanks. He reminds me that it was a Clyde-built vessel of the Donaldson-Atlantic Line, and I must attribute my lapse of memory to the fact that the Athenia was carrying a complement of passengers who were all U.S. citizens returning to America, the vessel having been chartered for that purpose ; a fact well known to the Nazi U-boat Commander who sank it. On that particular voyage it should have had the immunity from sea attack to which any American vessel at that time was entitled. Readers will remember that Goebbels broadcast that it had been " sunk by instructions of Winston Churchill " in order to create a situation which might have induced the U.S. Government to demand reparation, and so produce an " incident " between Britain and U.S.A. There actually were many evil-minded persons in America at that time, and later, ready to use the Goebbels lie to foster ill feeling. The crime attracted world-wide attention because it was the very first instance in this War of German frightfulness at sea, and all the facts and illustrations were fully given in the first two numbers of WAR ILLUSTRATED.

AT no time more than today do we stand in need of an occasional laugh. I am as eager as anyone to be taken out of my gloomy self and always ready for a laughmaking wisecrack. You will not believe me when I say that I was found by my wife in a state of helpless hilarity on my study floor tonight. But the cause thereof could be traced by any alienist to a paragraph in an evening paper I was clutching, wherein it was stated that a comedian, whom I know only by name, is starring in a London show while he is sending out a show of his own entitled "You Lucky People." The paper goes on to say : " Writing the material for his star, Vic Wise, Tommy has worked out a stunt, whereby Trinder, the boss, will talk on a radio set to Vic. ' Don't you realize that I can sack you ? ' he will ask Vic. ' Yes, and I can turn you off,' returns Vic – doing so." Now ain' that jus' too funny ? We ought to be very grateful for those highly-paid stars who can think out such side-splitting quips . . . we lucky people !

BEFORE any of my readers spend tuppence-ha'penny to correct me I must amplify what I wrote about Corregidor, as I observe, re-reading the paragraph, that in seeking after brevity I have not made a good job of it. While it is correct to state that, in languages derived from the Latin, the sound of g, when followed by e or i, is soft like j, in Spanish the pronunciation cannot be so easily represented by our j sound as it can in French or Italian. The true sound is something like a combination of the guttural ch (as in Scots "loch") and "hay." Thus the soft g in Corregidor is better represented for the strictly Spanish pronunciation as Cor-*ech-ee*-dor, the *ech* being made noticeably guttural. But the "eggy" sound has no sort of warranty.

Printed in England and published on the 10th, 20th, and 30th of each month by the Proprietors, The Amalgamated Press, Ltd., The Fleetway House, Farringdon Street, London, E.C.4. Registered for transmission by Canadian Magazine Post. Sole Agents for Australia and New Zealand : Messrs. Gordon & Gotch. Ltd. ; and for South Africa : Central News Agency, Ltd. March 10th, 1942. S.S. *Editorial Address :* JOHN CARPENTER HOUSE. WHITEFRIARS LONDON. E.C.4.

Vol 5 *The War Illustrated* Nº 124

Edited by Sir John Hammerton

FOURPENCE

MARCH 20TH, 1942

STIRLINGS IN FLIGHT. Here are some of our 30-ton heavy bombers in the air. Despite its great size the Short Stirling is said to be very easy to manoeuvre, and these bombers, together with Halifax, Manchester and Lancaster bombers, are coming into service in increasing numbers, ready, in the words of Sir Archibald Sinclair, " to strike hard at the vital centres of German war industry and transport."
Photo, P.N.A.

NO. 125, NEW 6d. FORTNIGHTLY ISSUE, ON SALE THURSDAY, APRIL 2

INDIA & CHINA: A TURNING-POINT IN THE WAR

THEY'RE serving drinks to the conquering Japanese in the bars of Singapore. Japanese officers are trying to make themselves comfortable in the armchairs of Hong Kong's most exclusive clubs. Japanese armies have chased us out of Malaya, and threaten to repeat the performance in Burma. Any day now their warships are expected in the Bay of Bengal. Soon Colombo may be shelled ; soon bombs may be falling on the crowded bazaars of Calcutta. And then what ? What will be the reaction of the Indian masses to the strokes of war ? Will they stand fast and fight back ? Will they panic ? Or will the truth of Matthew Arnold's famous lines be manifested once again :

> The East bow'd low before the blast,
> In patient, deep disdain.
> She let the legions thunder past,
> And plunged in thought again.

THAT was the reaction of the masses of Malaya. From beginning to end of the campaign which brought the Japanese in triumph to the gates of Singapore, the bulk of the native population of the Malayan states remained as passive spectators of a fight that was none of their business. A change of masters, yellow Japanese instead of white British—perhaps to most of them it did not matter very much (though it *ought* to matter). Of Burma, is there reason to believe the same may not be said ?

We talk easily enough of India, as easily as we talk of Germany or America, Australia or Japan ; we see its great red shape on the map, we can visualize something of its appearance and its people. To the educated Indian, to such men as Nehru and Gandhi, to the Indian intelligentsia, "India" means something. But 90 per cent of the peninsula's 400 millions live in villages—there are 700,000 of them—and to the villager India is just a name ; perhaps not even that, since only 12 per cent of the people are counted as literate. To the peasant the village is his all. The horizon marks the end of his world. Empires come and empires go, but he still toils in his pocket-handkerchief of a field, just as his ancestors did ages ago when *our* ancestors were dressed in woad and modesty.

IGNORANT as most Indians are, they are also the victims of a grinding poverty. Most of the agriculturists are in debt ; many, indeed, are in the grip of the moneylender from the cradle to the grave. Wages, judged by Western standards, are a mere pittance ; the average income is only about £4 or £5 *a year*. In India the most gloomy theories of Malthus, Ricardo and Marx seem to be borne out by the facts, since always and everywhere the population is pressing upon the means of subsistence. The fact that since the beginning of this century the population of India has increased by 115 millions constitutes a most striking tribute to the Anglo-Indian health administration ; but while British rule has enabled millions more to be born and to survive the perils of an Indian infancy, it may well be argued that the lot of the individual peasant has not been commensurately ameliorated. And the townsman is in no better position. The slums of the Indian cities are reputed to be the worst in the world ; Calcutta can show fouler dens

than can Warsaw or Naples, Glasgow or Shanghai.

AN Indian coal miner gets about 7d. a day ; a worker in a textile factory receives a daily wage of 8d. or 9d., though some get as much as 2s. Very long hours are worked, and child labour is still widespread. To be fair to the oft-maligned British capitalist, it should be remarked that the mills and mines, where the evils of our own Industrial Revolution of a century ago are paralleled and perhaps surpassed, are to a large extent owned and worked by Indians.

What can these poor and lowly folk know of the world outside, of the world war ? Little news percolates to the remote village or to the hovels in which men, women, and little children live and die in an environment of disease, squalor, and ancient dirt. What can they know, when only a tiny fraction of the population has ever sat at a school desk ? Still, after a century and a half of immense effort, the mass of the people is dull and spiritless. Theoretically they are free, but, as Macaulay once declared, "Electors meet in vain where want makes them the slaves of the landlord, or where superstition makes them the slaves of the priest."

Yet in China, just across the frontier, men and things are very different. Like India, China has a people counted in hundreds of millions ; but, unlike the Indians, the Chinese show themselves to be possessed of a national spirit, think of themselves as one people, have pride in their great past, confidence in the present, and hope in the future—all things unknown to most Indians. Great and strange is the contrast, and it is not easy

GEN. CHIANG AND 'MADAME.' "A great man and a great lady"—so the Viceroy of India described the Chinese Generalissimo and his consort when they visited Delhi last month.
Photo, Associated Press

to discover its why and wherefore. Something is due to race, and more to history ; something to religion, or rather ethics, and as much to social organization. But perhaps the most important factor is political. The Chinese have embraced with ardour the gospel that was preached by Sun Yat-sen 30 years ago, whose fundamental principles are Nationalism, Democracy and Social Justice. This gospel has captured the Chinese imagination and evoked a response such as not even Gandhi has been able to evoke in India.

CHIANG KAI-SHEK has shown the world that oriental masses *can* be stirred out of their apathy. Confronted by immense difficulties, by age-old traditions, by fettering systems of class and convention—quite as hampering in their way as the Hindu caste system—the Chinese Generalissimo and the other inheritors of the Sun Yat-sen tradition have worked a revolution fit to be compared with that of the Jacobins or the Bolsheviks. The Chinese are fighting to defend their liberty, their own liberty, their own way of life. They are fighting for the decencies of human existence against an enemy for whom these decencies seem to have no meaning. China knows what she is fighting for. India does not. She cannot defend her freedom since she is not yet free (so the Congress spokesmen declare).

Obviously Chiang Kai-shek has much to teach us, and it is not surprising that his visit to India a few weeks ago was hailed as a possible turning-point in history. During his fortnight's stay he met not only the Viceroy and members of the Indian Government, but Mr. Gandhi, Pandit Jawaharlal Nehru, Mr. Jinnah, President of the Moslem League, and many another leader of the Moslem and Hindu factions. The visit set the seal upon the comradeship in arms of two great nations, as the Viceroy happily declared in his speech of welcome to the General and Madame Chiang, who "concentrate and symbolize the glorious resistance of Free China to the onslaught of Japanese aggression."

THEN on Feb. 21 was published the text of a long message from Chiang Kai-shek to the people of India, in which he appealed to them for the sake of civilization and human freedom, to give their united support to the principles of the Atlantic Charter . . . to wholeheartedly join the Allies—China, Great Britain, America, and the Soviet Union—and participate shoulder to shoulder in the struggle for survival of the free world until complete victory has been achieved. He appealed also to Britain : "I confidently believe that our ally Great Britain, without waiting for any demands on the part of the people of India, will as speedily as possible give them real political power, so that they may be in a position further to develop their spiritual and material strength and thus realize that their participation in the war is not merely an aid to the anti-aggression nations for the securing of victory, but also a turning-point in their struggle for India's freedom."

Chiang Kai-shek had spoken. The whole world heard him, and nearly the whole world approved. India waited.   E. ROYSTON PIKE

Changsha Was a Great Victory for Our Allies

Types of Japanese prisoners captured by the Chinese armies during the Changsha battles at the beginning of January 1942, when the Japs lost 21,000 men.

Top right, two camouflaged Chinese soldiers using trench mortars captured from the enemy. Above, Chinese soldiers who fought in the Changsha battles, with hand grenades slung over their shoulders.

Above, a pile of Japanese war material collected after the brilliant Chinese victory at Changsha.

Right, Chinese soldiers collecting rifles abandoned by Japanese infantry in their flight. By many successful actions against the invaders of their country the Chinese have shown that the Japanese army is not invincible.

Photos, British Official: Crown Copyright

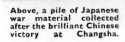

There's No Pause for the R.A.F. in Libya

THE LIBYAN CAMPAIGN was not marked by any major land operations during the month of February, but the R.A.F. were incessantly active, raiding Axis supply lines, stores, troop concentrations and ports. The top photograph shows a formation of Blenheim bombers setting out on a raid over Cyrenaica with their escorting fighters. Below, bombs from aircraft of the South African Air Force exploding with good effect on Barce aerodrome.

Photos, British Official: Crown Copyright

Planes and Destroyers Keep the Convoys Safe

A recent night attack by E-boats and Dorniers on a British convoy in the North Sea was smashed by British destroyers and Defiant aircraft. Men of the Defiant squadron are here seen in front of one of their planes.

A gunner looking along the sights of his Oerlikon A.A. gun, ready for any raiding Dornier which may try to attack the convoy.

A destroyer keeps a watchful eye on a merchant convoy while a plane of Coastal Command circles overhead (centre right). Above, as dusk falls, another convoy reaches harbour after having crossed the Atlantic in the teeth of the Axis submarines and aircraft. Nevertheless, as Mr. Churchill recently warned us, our anti-U-boat flotillas and naval light forces of all kinds have been, and are strained to the utmost limit by the need for bringing in the food by which we live and the materials for the munitions with which we fight.

Photos, P.N.A., Fox

R.A.F. Hurricanes Within the Arctic Circle

One department of this " hard and adverse " war on which Britain has a right to congratulate herself is the great assistance that she has been able to give to Russia in planes, pilots and technicians. This cooperation has played an important part in the great Russian counter-attack.

NOT until after the war can we expect to know the full facts as to Britain's aid in machines and technicians on the Russian front, but the story of the R.A.F. Wing which arrived home recently after its successful mission to far-northern Russia is typical of the excellent working arrangement that we have had with our Soviet friends during the past few months.

It begins in September last when the German " steamroller " was moving, apparently with irresistible force, across the vast territories of our Ally. The Russians carrying out their masterly retreat found themselves in need of emergency munitions.

Leaving the warm English sunshine the R.A.F. Wing, which was composed of two squadrons of the latest type of 12-gun Hurricane fighters, under command of Wing-Commander H. G. N. Ramsbottom-Isherwood, A.F.C., found their way to that mysterious No-man's-land at the extreme north-west of Russia. The previous winter's snows had not entirely melted in this bleak and twilit world well within the Arctic Circle. The Wing's objective was to help to resist the German armies driving in the direction of Murmansk, through Norway and Finland, and also to demonstrate Hurricane fighters to Russian pilots and crews.

Russian hospitality made up for the cold atmosphere and sinister scene, and at first the British airmen had almost too much to eat and drink. There was a superabundance of fresh meat, ham, smoked salmon, butter, milk, but few fresh vegetables. If there was no beer, champagne, vodka and even brandy were always available.

" We worked at first," said the Wing-Commander, " as an independent unit and made our own plans, but the Russians soon adopted our ideas. We escorted the Russian bombers ourselves, and never lost one."

The Russians learned with amazing rapidity and thoroughly. Strange aircraft, new engines, unusual gadgets offered no serious problems to the Soviet pilots and technicians. Day after day, in icy cold weather, with rolled snow above the soil of the aerodrome, our pilots did " readiness " duty as they did in this country during the Battle of Britain. The Wing accounted for at least fifteen German aircraft definitely destroyed and many others damaged.

Attacks on the Aerodrome

On one occasion the enemy tried to raid the Anglo-Russian aerodrome in force. They sent over twelve bombers in formation to try to wreck the place. The Russian warning system, however, was so efficient that our pilots had ample notice of the attack and were able to destroy three raiders and damage nearly all the others. They gave the Germans such a rough handling that they never tried to attack the aerodrome with more than one or two aircraft at a time, and then only when clouds offered plenty of protection.

Describing the first demonstration of the Hurricanes, one of our pilots said :

Russian generals, admirals, Air Ministry experts and engineers were all present. We had been told something was expected of the machines, so we gave all they had got. We dived on the group of officials, roared round hangars, flew straight at them at practically ground level, and did some acrobatics which seemed to delight them all.

The General in charge of the Russian Fleet Air Arm in the north was the first to take a Hurricane up. He had everything explained to him as he sat in the cockpit. A woman interpreter —a schoolmistress—translated our words into

Russian and, like everyone else, she was most thorough. To make quite sure that the General understood everything thoroughly, she made him repeat each phrase. With the tail of the aircraft jacked up, he sat in the cockpit familiarizing himself with the controls. Next morning he took-off, and after a circuit he made a perfect landing. Once we had taught a few of the Russian pilots to fly, they in turn became instructors to their countrymen, and in a surprisingly short time they were most efficient. Meanwhile, our ground experts were teaching their opposite numbers about engine maintenance, radio equipment and so on. One of the Russian engineers obtained 98 out of 100 marks at an examination on the maintenance of the type of Merlin engine fitted to these Hurricanes. You have to hand it to these people. They certainly do learn fast. Almost the very day the Wing became operational in Russia our pilots destroyed three Huns and probably destroyed another. A few days later— the next day of good flying weather—we had more victories, and when the Russians saw we were there to kill Germans, as well as to pass on our knowledge of the Hurricane, nothing was too much for them to do for us.

I am afraid that when we were approaching our Russian aerodrome some of us expected to see a few mud huts in the midst of a swamp. Instead, we lived in brick-built, properly furnished and heated buildings. The Russian ideas on aerodrome dispersal are at least as advanced as ours, and their camouflage systems are superb. The command post, in which Wing-Commander Isherwood, our C.O., had to spend a good deal of his time, contained a bombproof operations room to which warnings of approaching enemy aircraft came with surprising speed. The Russian Observer Corps is most efficient, and so are the anti-aircraft defences.

Our boys sometimes did four bomber escorts in a day. Sept. 26 was a typical day. Two flights of one of our squadrons took off with fast Soviet dive-bombers and a flight of heavy bombers. The sky above the vast aerodrome seemed full of aeroplanes. They were all back in an hour without loss. One flight of our squadron was jumped on by six ME 109s. The Hurricanes turned on the Huns and, picking out their targets, sent three Messerschmitts into the ground.

Our aircraft had not even a single bullet-hole in them, and the Soviet bombers were able to do their job unmolested. The Russian General telephoned a message of thanks. On another bomber escort next morning our boys shot down two more German aircraft before lunchtime.

Later on, by the way, the sun could just be detected below the horizon as we went to lunch. There was scarcely any real daylight, but the coldest temperature we recorded was five degrees above zero.

On the whole, the food was extremely good. My first breakfast at our aerodrome was of steak, champagne and brandy. Afterwards we had more normal meals, and there was always plenty of good butter, ham, smoked salmon and splendid soups.

While we are naturally happy to return home (he concluded), many of us were sorry to leave Russia, and I, for one, have returned home feeling very confident of the part Russia is playing in this war.

The following tribute was paid to Wing-Commander Ramsbottom-Isherwood by Divisional Commissar A. Nikolaiev, dated Nov. 29, 1941: " Under your command," it read, " the airmen of the Wing of the Royal Air Force have bravely fought against our common enemy—Hitler's Germany. Your personal manliness. daring and able handling have been greatly valued by the Soviet Government. I am glad to congratulate you with the award of the High Order of the Union of Socialist Republics, 'The Order of Lenin.' I am convinced that the friendly military co-operation between the English and Soviet airmen will be further strengthened in future."

Soon after their return to England, Wing-Commander Ramsbottom-Isherwood, Squad. Leader A. H. Rook and Squad. Leader A. G. Miller were awarded the D.F.C.

'SHOT' WITH A SMILE, these British pilots of the R.A.F. Wing which went to Russia leave with their Soviet comrades a film record of a highy successful visit. Top, R.A.F. pilots at the entrance to the Russian dug-out seen in the opposite page.
Photos, British Official

When Our No. 151 Wing Was in Russia

No. 151 WING, R.A.F., having successfully completed its mission in Russia, is now back in Britain. Here are pilots of one of the squadrons in their dug-out dispersal hut in Russia. The furniture they made themselves.

MID RUSSIAN SNOWS sentries of the R. A. F. Wing in Russia patrol an aerodrome on the edge of a frozen lake.

This sturdy Hurricane (right) is parked out in the open in Russia with only a camouflage net as covering against the weather.

An R.A.F. flying field in Russia before the advent of the winter weather (below). The aircraft originally sent to Russia have now been supplemented by large deliveries of Hurricanes, which are piloted by members of the Red Air Force.

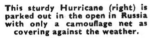

A Russian officer watching an R.A.F. pilot don his parachute. Having demonstrated Hurricane fighters to the pilots and ground crews of the Soviet Union, the R.A.F. Wing has returned, leaving their aircraft and equipment in capable hands.

Photos, British Official: Crown Copyright   **Page 559**

Our Searchlight on the War

PROBLEM OF MORALE

> The errors, the defects of temperament that caused the defeat of France, are not peculiarly and essentially French; they are human, and we are all in our different ways liable to them.—*Mr. W. Somerset Maugham*

A GRAPH of public morale since the war began would show that the highest point was reached in the summer and autumn of 1940. Those perilous months, from the Battle of Britain to the burning of London, were wonderfully inspiring. Although our position after Dunkirk looked nearly hopeless the national morale was such that our defeat was unthinkable and our victory a fact. History would not be wrong in recording that the spirit of the British people at

MILITARY POLICE of the Polish (left) and Free French Forces are now on duty in London assisting and examining the passes of their soldiers now in training in this country.　*Photos, Keystone*

that time saved the world from German domination. Our naval defence, our successes in the air and in Libya, and the work of Civil Defence at home brought 1940 to a close on a note of triumph. Though our position is now incomparably stronger materially than it was then, there is a feeling that the national morale is not so high. Is this not due to the fact that a large number of people are not doing enough, and some, through no fault of their own, are idling away their time? The collapse of France gave Britain her "finest hour," but it also placed us on the defensive where we have been, with the exception of Libya, ever since. The news of our paratroop raid near Havre came as a great tonic. May we hope that the time is near when we shall see the enemy harassed by simultaneous attacks in various parts of his straggling coast line? To pass from the defensive to the offensive is the business of 1942. We must beware of the Maginot complex.

BRITAIN'S PATH

> Our goal might be the same as that of Soviet youth, but the path by which we should reach it must be defined by our own environment and not by that of Russia or any country.—*Sir Stafford Cripps, M.P.*

WE have in Britain the political experience, the technical efficiency, and the traditional fortitude to build a great and prosperous future. It only suffices for us to be true to ourselves and to exploit our native genius at its best to make post-war Britain a happy land. While the ideals of freedom approximate in all nations fighting against the tyrants, each of the Allies has its own problems to solve in its own particular way. A small island, which depends for its life upon sea-power and which is loosely tied by sentiment to far-flung Dominions, is not the environment for experiments in totalitarian communism. Our democratic ideals are not the fruit of a generation

of toil. They are deep-rooted in the past, and have matured throughout the centuries, adapting themselves resourcefully to new circumstances and modern conditions. The march of socialism in Britain has proceeded step by step as a matter of evolution. The British people will work out their own destiny. They are too wise to discard a constitutional system which, in spite of its faults, and they can be remedied, has kept them in the forefront of the world for so long.

THE MISSING BLITZ

> Germany gave up the attempt to "coventrate" England a long time ago, since it appeared that the bombing of towns does not produce decisive results.—*Berlin Correspondent of the Stockholm Tidningen*

CERTAINLY, the bombing of Britain did the enemy no good. It aroused the national spirit to a mood of defiance and resolution which proved to the world that we were invincible. That, combined with our aerial victories in the autumn of 1940, was the first sign that German aggression could and would be stopped. But the Berlin correspondent forgets to state that, when Germany had overwhelming air superiority, she was able to conquer Europe with comparative ease. With his thousands of planes, Hitler blackmailed various European capitals into surrender. Rotterdam he "coventrated." The threat to Paris played a great part in the collapse of France. Had the Allies now the same numerical superiority in planes as Hitler had in 1939, we could win the war immediately by attacking Germany in such force that resistance would be hopeless. This is a point to remember. Nor must we forget that it would suit the Nazis perfectly to call off the bombing of military objectives now that the Allies have reached parity and probably gone beyond it. The real reason for the blitz holiday is because Germany has lost so many planes and skilled pilots on the East Front.

FRENCH REVOLUTION, PART II

> In spite of the zones into which the country is divided, France is secretly engaged in bringing about the greatest revolution.—*General de Gaulle*

IN regard to France the British public have shown a commendable restraint and sympathy, but some impatience is inevitable. Our late Ally

THE OWEN GUN, invented by 27-year-old Evelyn Owen of the A.I.F., fires 30 rounds in 3 seconds, is considered far more deadly than any other sub-machine gun, and costs only a fraction of the price of the Thompson sub-machine gun. It is being mass-produced in Australia.　*Photo, Australian Official*

under *force majeure* is working for the enemy, but the French people cannot help themselves. They are subjected to a kind of penal servitude by the Germans. Armed with all the machinery of repression, the Nazi jailors stand over a prostrate nation. But the spirit of France is not dead, and it is for the United States, Britain, and Russia to help to sustain that spirit. General de Gaulle tells us that France is secretly engaged in bringing about the greatest revolution in her history. Such an event is, of course, a historic necessity, not only for the resurrection of France, but for the benefit of the world as a whole. The Vichy quislings must be well aware that their days are numbered. They are like men under sentence of death, but the date of their execution has not been fixed except in the inscrutable calendar of fate. They are between the devil of Hitler and the rising storm of French popular hatred. The storm will break as soon as France regains confidence in herself. The Allies, in remembering all that France has done for civilization, must help her regain that confidence, and convince her that her future will be no less great than her past.

A QUADRUPLE ALLIANCE

> I want to see England in real alliance with Russia and the United States—and if China were a strong and regular power (as it might be some day), I say the alliance should be quadruple. *Charles Villiers to Mme. Olga Novikoff* (1866)

CHARLES VILLIERS, the great humanist and reformer, in writing to Mme. Novikoff, an advocate of Anglo-Russian friendship, uttered a wish that may well become a true prophecy. The world is now clearly divided between criminal tyrannies and constructive reformers—the Axis on the one hand trying to destroy civilization, and the Allies on the other trying to preserve and increase it. The New Order must revolve round Britain, the United States, Russia and China, and if these Powers can consolidate eventual victory in a progressive alliance there should be great hope for the future of mankind, and the end of all political and military gangsters who try to dominate the world, not for the benefit of their peoples, but for their own personal vanity. The rise of such murderous megalomaniacs must become impossible, and healthy democracies can prevent it. The dictators were able to impose their systems upon their hysterical peoples and destroy the happiness of millions only because the Allies fell apart after the last war and refused to agree upon a common policy of peace, security and progress.

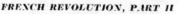

DOUBLE LAUNCHING in the United States. Down the slipways at the Philadelphia Navy Yard goes the newly launched U.S. destroyer Butler, while on the left the destroyer Gherardi awaits its turn.　*Photo, Wide World*

War's Flames Light Up the African Sky

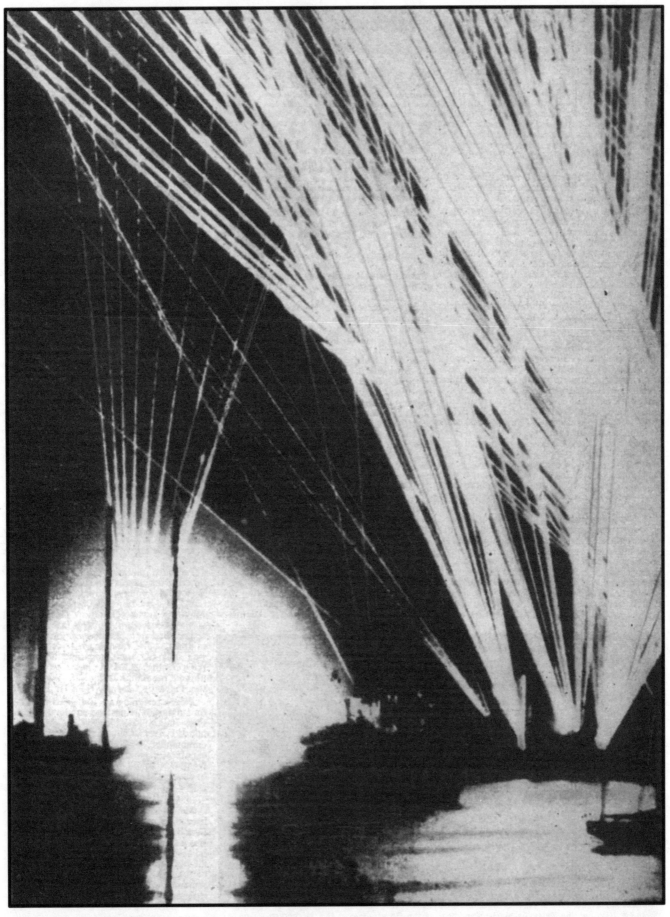

FLAK OVER TRIPOLI during a night visit by bombers of the R.A.F. This photograph, received from enemy sources, shows the tremendous barrage which British aircraft encounter during their frequent visits to the Libyan harbour to which come supplies and reinforcements for General Rommel. The flash on the left was made by the explosion of a heavy British bomb. *Photo, Keystone*

They Fought Like Wild Cats in Java

Fresh from their great triumph at Singapore, the Japanese turned their attention to Java, the last outpost of the Allies between the great continental masses of India and Australia. Below we describe the opening phase of the conflict.

ON the eve of the Battle of Java, Lt.-Gen. Hein ter Poorten, C.-in-C. of the Dutch forces in the Netherlands East Indies, broadcast an inspiring call to his men. "Fight like wildcats, and fight like hell," he urged them. The situation was serious, but if there was no reason for light-hearted optimism, there was also none for pessimism. The enemy was at the end of long lines of communication ; they were seeking desperately for food and oil. The Dutch were fighting for their existence and their families ; and, moreover, they had the assistance of thousands of British, Australian and American troops who had now arrived in Java.

The battle opened with a sea engagement. An enemy fleet of 40 transports, closely guarded by some 20 warships, including several heavy cruisers, and watched over by a host of seaplanes, was reported to be making for Surabaya, the great Allied naval base in the east of Java. At once orders were given for the Allied squadron operating in the eastern portion of the Java Sea to go into action. Contact was established west of the island of Bawean late in the afternoon of Feb. 27, when the opposing fleets—the enemy being greatly superior in number of ships and fire-power—were still separated by 12 miles or so. A fierce engagement developed and destroyer attacks were launched on both sides. At this phase of the battle one Allied cruiser was damaged and had to leave the fighting line, and a Dutch destroyer was hit by an enemy salvo and sank. But the enemy did not go scatheless. Many hits were obtained on their ships. A large Japanese cruiser of the Mogami class was set on fire ; another eight-inch-gun cruiser apparently received considerable damage, and yet a third heavy cruiser was sunk. At least three Japanese destroyers were left behind, burning or sinking ; nevertheless the enemy fleet continued to steam on at high speed.

The action continued during the night and at a long distance, and now it was that the Netherlands Navy received a crippling blow. Two fine cruisers which had received strict orders from the Navy C.-in-C. to attack by all means and regardless of risks were torpedoed. "Probably," said an official report, "in the course of their very gallant and daring action against a superior enemy force they advanced into the Japanese line

of submarines." Their sacrifice was the subject of a fine tribute by Batavia Radio.

"We realize fully what the heavy loss of cruisers means, and we are not downhearted. Instead, we are filled with deep pride for those heroic men who sacrificed themselves. We bow to those brave Dutchmen and Indonesians who were filled with the spirit of devotion, and who went out to attack, not thinking of the outcome of the battle, but having only one aim. They did not die in vain. They leave a memory which will live as a brilliant example to the men of our army and air force who have now themselves taken up arms against the invaders. By this unbelievably courageous act at sea, a new and glorious chapter has been added to the history of the Dutch fleet."

During the next night (Saturday, Feb. 28) the Japanese, undeterred by the Allied sea and air defences, which inflicted some damage on the transports and the escorting warships, succeeded in landing at three main points on the northern coast of Java—at Bantam and Indramayu, 50 miles west and 100 miles east of Batavia respectively, and over a wide front east of Rembang. Fierce fighting continued throughout the Sunday. The enemy endeavoured to carry out strong infiltration, mainly by light armoured cars and lightly armed cyclists. They suffered heavy losses at several points, but before nightfall the Dutch admitted in an announcement from Bandoeng that the Japanese had overrun a large part of the plains of Krawang in the Indramayu section. Only a few thousand struggled ashore at first, through a hail of bombs and machine-gun bullets, but the stream of men continued without a break so that soon they were pressing on to the interior. Fighting doggedly all the way the Allied forces went back, blowing up railway and road bridges as they went, so as to prevent, if possible, the junction of the invading forces. The Dutch also adopted the most intense " scorched earth " tactics, but there was no wholesale evacuation of the civilian population. In general the people met the invaders with admirable calm. Only a few high Dutch officials were ordered to leave their posts in the threatened regions and repair to Batavia or (when this was abandoned as the capital) to Bandoeng—and even they were told to leave their wives and children behind. The police were reinforced and ordered to stay behind, whatever happened, so as to help the civil adminis-

MAJ.-GEN. H. D. W. SITWELL, G.O.C. the British troops in Java. *Photo, Lafayette*

trators to maintain public order and confidence.

That British were playing their part in the battle was revealed in an Order of the Day.

"British troops in Java," it read. "We have the honour to be about to fight with our Dutch and American allies in defence of the last stronghold of democracy in the South-West Pacific. The Japanese are skilful and well-armed opponents, and likely to be in superior numbers. They fight better in attack than in defence, and therefore our best chance is to attack whenever we can. 'Attack' and not 'defence,' must be our watchword. The British in the past have always displayed their finest qualities in the darkest hour. An historian describing a battle fought in Spain about 130 years ago, where victory was snatched from defeat in the face of an overwhelming superiority of numbers and equipment, wrote : ' And now the whole world was to see with what glory and majesty the British soldier can fight.' The eyes of the world are on them now. Let them see it again."

From the quotation from Napier's description of the Battle of Albuera in the Peninsular War careful commentators surmised that the Order was penned by General Wavell himself. Maybe it was so, but now General Wavell was recalled from the A.B.D.A. front and re-established in his old position of C.-in-C. in India. The reason given for the change was that the swift Japanese advance had reduced the A.B.D.A. area to practically nothing more than Java itself. Wavell's place was taken by Lt.-Gen. Hein ter Poorten.

Before returning to India General Wavell sent a farewell message to the Netherlands East Indies, in which he declared that he handed over his command to the Dutch commanders with confidence, knowing their capabilities and skill, their unswerving resolution to do everything for the defence of Java. " I have found them men of deeds rather than of words, and have learned to appreciate the worth of what they do."

Meanwhile, the situation in the island was becoming ever more difficult ; indeed, the Dutch authorities admitted that the struggle was a desperate one. The East Indies Army, however, would endure to the bitter end, and all commanders were given orders to fight to the last. In their great ordeal the people remained resolute and calm, and in a broadcast message Queen Wilhelmina, after declaring that " the Dutch Navy will rise again, stronger than ever before," promised that " to help the East Indies in the great struggle we shall do the impossible . . ."

JAVA, island of the Malay Archipelago and seat of the Government of the Netherlands East Indies, was invaded by Japan on the night of Saturday, February 28. Landings were made at three points—east and west of Batavia—the capital, and west of Surabaya, and by March 9 the Japanese claimed complete victory. *Map by courtesy of News Chronicle*

Over Java Has Swept the Japanese Tornado

FLYING DUTCHMEN of the Royal Netherlands East Indies Air Force, some of whom are seen above, have fought magnificently in the defence of Holland's territories in the Far East.

IN JAVA there are extensive forests through which roads, like that above, have had to be cut. The total mileage of highways in Java is about 17,000.

MINES AND SHELLS for the protection of the great naval base of Surabaya being towed to an ammunition depot. One of the Japanese landings in Java on Feb. 28 was made to the west of this important base, in the vicinity of Rembang.

BATAVIA, capital of Java, seen from the air. The city was declared an open town by the Dutch Indies authorities, and at 8.30 p.m. on March 5, "without firing a shot," the Japanese marched in.

Photos, British Official; E.N.A., Sport & General

Galloping forward into battle across the frozen plains go men of Maj.-Gen. Byelov's 1st Guards Cavalry Corps. How the Cossacks ride again in Russia is the page is from an article by Col. Gen. Gorodovikov in Soviet War News. Below, Red Army ski troops are on their way to the front line, clad in white c Centre, right, a derelict German tank lies abandoned in the snow after the Nazis have retreated.

Left, a typical young Soviet warrior with his machine-gun. Right, a group of Germans captured by the Re are suffering from their inadequate protection against the rigours of a Russian winter.

Photos, P.N.A., British Official; Keystone

542 ; the sentence at the top of
and riding on tanks and sledges.

STALIN GREETS THE GLORIOUS RED ARMY

THE Red Army is 24 years old. It was on Feb. 23, 1918, that it went into action for the first time—at Pskov and Narva, when it defeated the Germans who were advancing on Leningrad. This year the anniversary was celebrated with more than usual enthusiasm, since once again the Russian soil feels the German invaders' tread ; and the occasion was seized by Stalin, as People's Commissar for Defence, to issue a special Order of the Day.

After reviewing the great achievements of the Red Army in its 24 years of life, Stalin proceeded to tell of the treacherous attack made on Russia by Fascist Germany last summer. "The enemy expected that the Red Army would be routed after the very first blow and would lose its ability to resist. But the enemy miscalculated badly. He did not realize the Red Army's power, nor the strength of the Soviet rear and the determination of our people to win ; he did not realize the unreliability of the European fear of Fascist Germany. Finally, he did not realize the internal weakness of Fascist Germany and her army." True, in the first months of the war the Red Army was forced to retreat and evacuate part of the Russian territory ; but none in the Red Army or in Russia doubted that this retreat was but temporary. Having accumulated fresh strength, having been reinforced with men and equipment, the time came when the Red Army was able to pass to the offensive. Within a short time the Germans suffered one blow after another, at Rostov and Tikhvin, in the Crimea and before Moscow. In a succession of violent battles the Red Army drove the Germans back from Moscow, and still keeps pressing them westwards. Hundreds of towns and villages have been liberated.

STALIN speaking in Moscow during the 24th anniversary celebrations of the Bolshevik Revolution in Nov. 1941, while the hitherto victorious German army was only some thirty miles away. *Photo, British Official*

★ Nazis on the Verge of Catastrophe

THE German Fascists (continued Stalin) thought their army invincible, more particularly since it had the support of troops drawn from Italy, Rumania and Finland, whereas the Red Army has no such support. Yet now they are on the verge of catastrophe.

Now the Germans no longer possess the military advantage which they had in the first months of the war as a result of their treacherous and sudden attack. The momentum of this unexpectedness and suddenness, which constituted a reserve force for the German Fascist armies, has been fully spent. Now the fate of the war will be decided not by such a factor of surprise, but by permanent factors—stability of the rear, morale of the Army, quantity and quality of divisions and Army equipment, organizational ability of the Army Command.

Under the mighty blows of the Red Army the German troops, rolling southwards, are sustaining huge losses in man-power and equipment. They are clinging to each line in the attempt to postpone their destruction. But the enemy's attempts are in vain. The initiative is now in our hands, and the painful efforts of Hitler's weakened, rusty machinery are unable to withstand the drive of the Red Army.

The day is not far off when the Red Army, by its powerful blows, will throw the bestial enemy back from Leningrad, and will clear them out of the towns and villages of White Russia and the Ukraine, Lithuania, Latvia, Estonia, and Karelia, will free the Soviet Crimea, and the Red banners will again fly victoriously over the whole Soviet land.

However, it would be unpardonable shortsightedness if we were to rest content with the success already achieved, and to believe that we had already done away with the German troops. This would be empty boasting and conceit unworthy of Soviet people. One must not forget that there are still many difficulties ahead. The enemy is suffering defeat, but he has not yet been routed, still less has he been finished off.

But the enemy is still strong, and the more often he is defeated the more furious will he become. Therefore it is necessary that the training of reserves for assistance to the front should not be relaxed in our country for a single moment. It is necessary that fresh Army units should go to the front one after another, to forge victory over the bestial enemy. It is necessary that our industry, especially our war industry, should work with redoubled vigour. It is necessary that the front should receive every day increasing quantities of tanks, planes, guns, mine-throwers, machine-guns, rifles, automatic rifles, and ammunition.

★ The Red Army's Supreme Task

Then Stalin proceeded to compare the war aims of the Red Army with those of Hitler's Fascists.

The Red Army's strength rests above all in the fact that it does not wage a predatory imperialist war, but a patriotic war, a war of liberation, a just war. The Red Army's task is to liberate our Soviet territory from the German invaders, to liberate from the yoke of the German invaders the residents of our towns and villages who, before the war, were free and lived like human beings and who are now oppressed and suffer pillage, subjection, and famine ; and, lastly, to liberate our women from the disgrace and outrages to which they have been subjected by the German Fascist fiends.

What could be nobler and loftier than this task ? No single German soldier can say that he is waging a just war, because he cannot fail to see that he is forced to fight for the plundering and oppression of other peoples. The German soldier lacks any lofty, noble aim in the war which could inspire him and in which he could take pride. Any Red Army man, on the other hand, can proudly say that he is waging a just war, a war for liberation, a war for the freedom and independence of his Motherland. The Red Army pursues its noble and lofty war aim, which inspires it to heroic feats.

This, properly speaking, explains why the patriotic war brings forward thousands of heroes and heroines in our country who are ready to face death for the freedom of their Motherland. This is the source of the strength of the Red Army. This is also the source of the weakness of the German Fascist Army.

★ Hitlers Come and Go : Germany Remains

Then came a denial of the view sometimes expressed in the foreign press, that the Red Army's aim is to exterminate the German people and destroy the German state.

This, of course, is a stupid lie, and a senseless slander against the Red Army. The Red Army has not and cannot have any such idiotic aims.

The aim of the Red Army is to oust the German occupationists from our country and liberate Soviet soil from the German Fascist invaders. It is very likely that the war for the liberation of our Soviet land will result in the ousting or destruction of Hitler's clique. We would welcome such an outcome. But it would be ridiculous to identify Hitler's clique with the German people and the German State. The experience of history shows that Hitlers come and go, whereas the German people and the German state remain.

Lastly, the strength of the Red Army lies in the fact that it does not and cannot entertain racial hatred for other peoples, including the German people, that it has been brought up in the spirit of the equality of all peoples and races, in the spirit of respect for the rights of other peoples.

The Germans' racial theory and their practice of racial hatred have brought about a situation in which all freedom-loving peoples have become the enemies of Fascist Germany. The theory of race equality in the U.S.S.R. and the practice of respect for the rights of other peoples has brought about a situation where all freedom-loving peoples have become the friends of the Soviet Union. This is another source of the strength of the Red Army, and this is also a source of the weakness of the German Fascist Army.

★ No Racial Hatred in the Red Army

Next Stalin protested against the view that the Red Army is inspired by feelings of racial hatred. In Russia, he pointed out, any manifestation of such hatred is punished by law, and the Red Army is quite free from it.

Sometimes the foreign press engages in prattle that the Soviet people hate the Germans just because they are Germans, and that the Red Army exterminates the German soldiers just because they are Germans, because it hates everything German ; and that therefore the Red Army does not take German soldiers prisoner. This, of course, is a similar stupid lie, and senseless slander of the Red Army.

Certainly the Red Army has to annihilate the German Fascist occupationists since they wish to enslave our Motherland, or when they, being surrounded by our troops, refuse to lay down their arms and surrender. The Red Army annihilates them not because of their German origin but because they wish to enslave our Motherland. The Red Army, like the army of any other people, is entitled to annihilate and bound to annihilate the enslavers of its Motherland, irrespective of their national origin.

★ If the Enemy Does Not Surrender

Recently, continued Stalin, German garrisons at Kalinin, Klin, Sukhinichi, Andreapol and Toropets had been surrounded by Red Army troops who promised to spare their lives if they surrendered, but as the Germans refused to lay down their arms they had to be driven out by force, and many of them were killed.

War is war. The Red Army takes German soldiers and officers prisoner if they surrender and spares their lives. The Red Army annihilates German soldiers and officers if they refuse to lay down their arms and attempt, arms in hand, to enslave our Motherland. Remember the words of our great Russian writer, Maxim Gorky : "If the enemy does not surrender he must be annihilated."

"Comrades, Red Army men and Red Navy men, commanders and political workers, men and women guerillas," concluded Stalin, "I congratulate you on the twenty-fourth anniversary of the Red Army ! I wish you complete victory over the German Fascist invaders. Long Live the Red Army and Red Navy ! Long live the men and women guerillas ! Long live our glorious Motherland and its freedom and independence ! Under Lenin's banner onward to the defeat of the German Fascist invaders ! "

Eighteen Young Airmen—And Every One a Hero

Already we have told of the action on Feb. 12, when, despite gallant efforts on the part of our airmen and destroyers, the Nazi ships from Brest made a successful passage to a home port (see page 534). Now we give some further details of the heroic part played by the Swordfish planes.

Lieut.-Commander EUGENE ESMONDE, D.S.O., R.N., awarded a posthumous V.C.

ON the morning of Thursday, Feb. 12, 1942, Lieut.-Commander Esmonde, in command of a squadron of the Fleet Air Arm, was told that the German battle-cruisers Scharnhorst and Gneisenau, and the cruiser Prinz Eugen, strongly escorted by some 30 surface craft, were entering the Straits of Dover, and that his squadron must attack before they reached the sand banks north-east of Calais.

Lieut.-Commander Esmonde knew well that his enterprise was desperate. Soon after noon he and his squadron of six Swordfish set course for the enemy, and after ten minutes flight were attacked by a strong force of enemy fighters. Touch was lost with his fighter escort, and in the action which followed all his aircraft were damaged. He flew on, cool and resolute, serenely challenging hopeless odds, to encounter the deadly fire of the battle-cruisers and their escort, which shattered the port wing of his aircraft.

Undismayed, he led his squadron on, straight through this inferno of fire, in steady flight towards their target. Almost at once he was shot down, but his squadron went on to launch a gallant attack in which at least one torpedo is believed to have struck the German battle-cruisers, and from which not one of the six aircraft returned.

His high courage and splendid resolution will live in the traditions of the Royal Navy and remain for many generations a fine and stirring memory.

Col. THOMAS ESMONDE, his great-uncle, won the V.C. in the Crimean War.

IT will live in history—the story of the eighteen men who flew their six obsolescent Swordfish biplanes, laden with torpedoes, straight into the Scharnhorst, Gneisenau, and Prinz Eugen through a terrific curtain of fire. But the story, though one of supreme individual courage and steadfast devotion to duty, is not one which reflects much credit on those primarily responsible. The speed of these Swordfish biplanes, when fully loaded, is about 100 m.p.h., and they were therefore extremely vulnerable to the large escorting force of enemy fighters. Not one Swordfish returned to its base, and of the crews only five men, three of whom were seriously wounded, survived the action.

The supreme courage displayed by their leader, Lieut.-Commander E. Esmonde, is made clear from the official citation which accompanied the announcement of the posthumous award of a V.C. (see panel above). Decorated by the King for a previous exploit only the day before this action, Esmonde sent a torpedo straight at the leading battleship before he crashed. With him died his observer, Lieut. Williams, and his air-gunner, Petty-Officer Clinton.

The C.O. of the airfield from which the doomed machines took off told a News Chronicle reporter that for nearly half-an-hour these Swordfish were our only planes striking at the enemy battleships protected by a great force of aircraft estimated at nearly 400 planes. He said : " I wished all my men good luck—they knew what they were after

—and I heard nothing until many hours later when five survivors were brought ashore by the Navy. Every plane had taken terrific punishment before they had got over the enemy's destroyer screen."

Following Esmonde were Sub.-Lieut. C. M. Kingsmill and Sub.-Lieut. R. M. Samples, pilot and observer respectively of a Swordfish that was badly hit early in the action by cannon shells from an enemy fighter. Both were wounded, but with part of the aircraft shot away and the engine and upper wings in flames, they flew on undaunted until they had taken aim and fired their torpedo. Then they turned and tried to come down near some ships, but these opened fire, so they flew on until their engine stopped and the plane came down in the sea, where they were picked up. Both officers were awarded the D.S.O. and the Conspicuous Gallantry Medal was given to their air-gunner, 1st Class Naval Airman D. A. Bunce, who stayed at his gun engaging the enemy fighters, one of whom he probably shot down.

In the wake of Kingsmill, Sub.-Lieut. B. W. Rose pressed home his attack. His aircraft, too, had been hit early in the action, but, though in great pain from a wound in his back, he held on his course. Another hit burst his petrol tank, but steadily he flew on, getting within 2,000 yards of the enemy before releasing his torpedo. Then he flew back across the fire of the enemy escort and, his aircraft ablaze, came down in the sea. He has been awarded the D.S.O., together with his observer, Sub.-Lieut E. F.

Lee. Their air-gunner, Leading Airman A. L. Johnson, D.S.M. (mentioned posthumously in dispatches), had been killed before they reached the enemy escort vessels, and Sub.-Lieut. Lee stood up in the cockpit directing the pilot so that he could evade the enemy fighters until at last the aircraft came down in flames. Then, although under fire, he got his wounded pilot into a dinghy, where he stayed, tending him, while a terrific battle raged overhead, until both were rescued. To the News Chronicle reporter, Sub.-Lieut. Lee, a fair-haired boy of 20, said : " It was pretty frightful. We went straight in with the Germans giving us everything they had. There was a terrific moving mass of aircraft all around us, but as we wheeled away and went rushing into the sea I caught a glimpse of the second flight coming in. That flight was never heard of again."

The men who comprised this flight were Lieut. J. C. Thompson, R.N., Sub.-Lieut. R. L. Parkinson, R.N., Sub.-Lieut. C, R. Wood, R.N.,Sub.-Lieut.W. Beynon, R.N.V.R., Sub.-Lieut. E. H. Fuller-Wright, R.N.V.R., Act. Sub.-Lieut. Peter Bligh, R.N.V.R., Ldg. Airman E. Tapping, Ldg. Airman W. G. Smith, and Ldg. Airman H. T. Wheeler, all of whom were mentioned posthumously in dispatches.

The last that was seen of them was as they flew steadily onward towards the battle-cruisers under the leadership of Lieut. Thompson. Their aircraft shattered, they carried on through the inferno of fire to carry out their orders and attack the target. Not one of them came back.

FLEET AIR ARM HEROES of the action against the Scharnhorst and Gneisenau in the Channel—the 18 men, pilots and crews of the six Swordfish planes who showed " courage beyond praise "—were honoured in a mass award announced in the London Gazette on Feb. 27. Above left, Sub.-Lieut. E. Lee, reporting to the C.O. of the airport from which the Swordfish took off. Right, a Fairey Swordfish, the now obsolete type of torpedo-carrying plane in which the " suicide squadron " attacked the German warships. *Photos, Planet News, Associated Press, Central Press, The Daily Mirror*

Our Diary of the War

TUESDAY FEB. 24, 1942   906th day

Air.—Spitfires made an offensive sweep over N. France. Mines laid at night in enemy waters.

Russian Front.—Moscow reported important victory over 16th German Army near Staraya Russa.

Far East.—In Burma, Imperial Forces fell back to the west bank of the Sittang River. An enemy submarine shelled oil refineries on Californian coast. Japs raided Java airfields. News received of fresh landing by Japs near Koepang, capital of Dutch Timor. Japanese planes raided Port Blair on the Andaman Islands in the Bay of Bengal.

Home.—Night raid on East Anglian coast town.

WEDNESDAY, FEB. 25   907th day

Russian Front.—Fierce battles continued on the Smolensk front. Lichninskaya, on the Kharkov front reported recaptured by Russians.

Far East.—Batavia announced sinking of five large Jap transports in the Macassar Strait. R.A.F. and A.V.G. in Burma destroyed at least 30 enemy bombers and sunk two enemy river boats.

THURSDAY, FEB. 26   908th day

Air.—Night attack by R.A.F. on Kiel and Wilhelmshaven.

Russian Front.—Big Russian blow north of Lake Ilmen.

Far East.—21 enemy aircraft shot down in the Rangoon area. In the Pacific, American submarines torpedoed four Japanese ships, including two transports. In the Philippines, Gen. MacArthur counter-attacked with considerable success. Jap planes again raided the Andaman Islands. Australian planes made night attack on Rabaul.

FRIDAY, FEB. 27   909th day

Air.—Night attack by R.A.F. on Kiel and Wilhelmshaven.

Russian Front.—Moscow announced that Red Army had begun liberation of the Kursk province. Heavy fighting continued around Staraya Russa.

Far East.—Japanese supply lines on the Burma front heavily attacked by R.A.F. and A.V.G. MacArthur's forces made gains of from one to five miles along the entire Bataan front. Japanese heavy cruiser Mogami and three destroyers put out of action off Java.

SATURDAY, FEB. 28   910th day

Air.—Blenheims made daylight attack on docks at Ostend. Night attack on Kiel and Wilhelmshaven. Fighter Command attacked airfields in occupied territory.

Russian Front.—Heavy Russian attacks in the area S.E. of Lake Ilmen, on the Donetz front and in the Crimea.

Far East.—Sea battle continued against Japanese expeditionary force making for Java. Jap aircraft attacked Port Moresby.

Home.—German bomber destroyed off E. Anglia.

General.—British parachute troops, infantry, and naval forces made a successful combined raid on the night of Feb. 27-28 on the German radiolocation post at Bruneval, near Le Havre.

SUNDAY, MAR. 1   911th day

Sea.—British M.T.B.s torpedoed Nazi tanker near French coast.

Russian Front.—Red Army continued a methodical progress on all fronts.

Far East.—Japs made night landings on Java at three points: in N.W. Bantam, in the Bay of Indramayu and east of Rembang. In Burma, Rangoon-Mandalay railway reported cut by Japanese.

Home.—Bombs dropped by night on a district in S.W. England.

MONDAY, MAR. 2   912th day

Russian Front.—Russian southern armies launched new offensive. Heavy fighting continued in Smolensk, Staraya Russa, and Leningrad areas.

Far East.—Jap invaders of Java advanced to Soebang and Blora. Japanese claimed to have bombed wireless station and naval base at Christmas Island.

Atlantic.—U-boat shelled island of Mona, in the Caribbean Sea.

General.—Downing Street announced that Gen. Wavell would resume his command as C.-in-C. India.

TUESDAY, MAR. 3   913th day

Air.—Night attack by R.A.F. on armament factories in Paris. Another force attacked French Channel coast.

Russian Front.—Timoshenko's forces made considerable advance towards Dnepropetrovsk. In the Smolensk area the Russians reported recapture of Korobetz. Karijevja, south of Staraya Russa, also recaptured.

Far East.—Fierce fighting in Java. U.S. Navy Dept. reported that an American naval squadron had destroyed 16 out of 18 Jap bombers which attacked it, for the loss of two fighters. Action took place west of the Gilbert Is.

General.—Arrival of Gen. Wavell in India announced.

WEDNESDAY, MAR. 4   914th day

Russian Front.—Gen. Boldin demanded surrender of Orel, encircled by Red Army. Red Army pushing forward towards Yelna.

Far East.—Japanese continued to advance in Java. Bandoeng, new seat of Government, bombed four times. In Burma, Japs crossed River Sittang and reached Waw, 15 miles west. In the Philippines, U.S. bombers sunk more than 30,000 tons of enemy shipping in Subic Bay. Jap fighters machine-gunned intallations at Darwin, N. Australia. Australian planes raided Jap airfields and shipping at Gasmata, New Britain.

General.—Disclosure of safe arrival of a further large contingent of American troops in N. Ireland.

THURSDAY, MAR. 5   915th day

Russian Front.—Moscow announced recapture of Yukhnov, in the Smolensk area.

Far East.—Battle raging for Pegu, 40 miles above Rangoon. In Java, Japanese advanced half-way across the island, and captured Batavia, the capital.

Home.—Operation of the National Service Acts extended to include men from 18 to 46 and women from 20 to 31. Bombs dropped in daylight on South Coast.

General.—20 Frenchmen executed in Paris by the Nazis as a reprisal for the shooting of a German sentry. Announced that 100 Poles had been shot as a reprisal for an attack on two German policemen in Warsaw.

FRIDAY, MAR. 6   916th day

Russian Front.— Battles raging around Theodosia and Sevastopol. Further Red Army advance in the Donetz area.

Africa.—Free French motorized units captured three Italian posts in Fezzan.

Far East.—Batavia—claimed by Japanese —officially reported to have been evacuated. British tanks in action in Burma, north of Pegu.

Home.—New Defence Regulation made civilians liable to labour service in event of invasion.

SATURDAY, MAR. 7   917th day

Air.—Night attack by R.A.F. on naval base at St. Nazaire.

Russian Front.—Heavy Russian attack launched along the Moscow-Smolensk railway in the Gzhatsk sector.

Far East.—Japs attacked Bandoeng, H.Q. of Allied forces in Java. Port Moresby, New Guinea, raided by Japanese aircraft.

Home.—Enemy aircraft destroyed during slight night activity.

SUNDAY, MAR. 8   918th day

Air.—R.A.F. made daylight attack on Matford lorry works at Poissy, near Paris. Other bombers attacked power station at Comines, near Lille, and railway yards at Abbeville. Night raids on Essen and the Ruhr.

Russian Front.—Russians reported to have recaptured Sichevka, 45 miles north of Vyazma.

Far East.—Japs claimed occupation of Rangoon. New Jap landing on island off New Guinea coast. In Philippines, MacArthur's guns smashed Japanese reinforcements. Suicide of Japanese C.-in-C. in Philippines reported. Communication with Java cut.

Home.—Bombs on three towns on N.E. coast of England at night. Admiralty announced destruction of a Heinkel 111 by trawler Cornelian.

MONDAY, MAR. 9   919th day

Russian Front.—Red Army launched new attack between Taganrog and Stalino.

Far East.—U.S. Navy Dept. announced that U.S. submarines had torpedoed a Jap aircraft-carrier, three cruisers, a destroyer and a naval tanker. Official announcement of fall of Rangoon. Lt.-Gen. Sir H. R. Alexander appointed G.O.C. Burma.

ROLLS-ROYCE MERLIN XX aero-engines in production. Women war-workers have quickly adapted themselves to precision engineering, and these girls are seen at work in a corner of the assembly shop.

Australia Must Work Now as Never Before

BREN CARRIERS on the assembly line in an Australian railway workshop which now turns out machines of this kind as well as the locomotives seen on the left. With the fall of Singapore and the rapid advance of the Japanese forces in the Dutch East Indies, Australia realized her danger. Bombs have fallen on the Commonwealth, at Darwin, Broome and Wyndham. "Our honeymoon is finished," said Mr. Curtin, the Prime Minister. "Now we must fight or work as never before."

Photo, Sport & General

Today It's 'The Horror That Is Greece'

Honour and interest alike demand that everything should be done to help the Greeks, who, as is told below, are now in the most desperate plight. The British Government has agreed to waive its rules of blockade in their favour, but so far the amount of foodstuffs which have reached our sorely-stricken allies is very small.

THE Greeks are starving. They are dying in their thousands of famine and the diseases caused by malnutrition. Between Oct. 1, 1941, and Jan. 26 last, some 40,000 Greeks died from these causes. The mortality is particularly heavy in Athens and its port, the Piraeus, but the situation is just as tragic in other cities and the country districts. In the Greek islands, too—in Chios and Syra in particular—the situation is frightful. Recently the inhabitants of Syra telegraphed to Athens, "Send wheat or coffins." A very large proportion of the deaths are among the younger generation. Whooping cough and diphtheria are taking a terrible toll of child life, and there is a great need of serums, quinine, and cod-liver oil for the children who are wasting away. Those who survive are hardly better off. Starvation is causing young girls of 13 to take up prostitution, and Axis agents are engaged in a flourishing white slave traffic between Greece and Vienna and Budapest.

Last January the News Chronicle published a letter from a man in Athens. "The food situation is getting worse. Now I dare not walk in the streets. I keep to the house and the garden, for it is impossible to walk through Athens without seeing, every three or four hundred metres, some poor person fainting or dying in the street from hunger. Hungry children are everywhere searching the garbage for scraps to eat. This is what you see in the street. It is impossible to contemplate what goes on behind the walls of the homes in the poor parts of Athens." The lack of food extended to all classes, he went on; there were no black markets any more because there was no food for them to deal in. "So many people have died here that there is no longer any wood for coffins. At night, hearses, boarded up against outside gaze, leave the city for mass burials in the country outside." Yet, in spite of all, "the spirit of the people is wonderful. No one here will falter. Now, as never before, you can be proud that you are a Greek."

Even in peacetime Greece was not a self-supporting country, and before the war she imported at least a third—sometimes very much more—of her wheat requirements. With the cessation of imports the Greeks would have had to tighten their belts, but they would not have starved. The present famine is enemy-made; it is directly due to the plundering in which the Nazis and their Italian allies have engaged from the very moment they crossed the frontier into Greece last spring.

"As the German armies swooped southwards in the wake of their armoured divisions," M. Tsouderos, Prime Minister of the Greek Government in Exile, has declared, "they plundered and pillaged everything in their path. Cattle, crops of every nature, clothing, and movables were taken from the inhabitants of towns and villages. Shops were stripped of their commodities, and all stocks were commandeered. The way was thus paved for the general famine which is now sapping the roots of the Greek nation."

Hundreds Die Daily

In the same document—a White Paper on German, Italian, and Bulgarian atrocities in Greece and Crete, recently published by the Greek Government—M. Tsouderos declares that the "food conditions under Axis rule are appalling beyond words. In the Athens-Piraeus area, 450 people are perishing daily of hunger; 500,000 inhabitants in this area have to rely on public assistance for the very barest meal. The Italians view this situation with satisfaction, as the resistance of a starving population is greatly reduced. Whenever an Axis ship happens to be sunk in the proximity of Greek waters, the occupation authorities deliberately suspend the distribution of the bread ration for three days, falsely alleging that the ship sunk was bringing food to Greece from the Axis Powers."

All through the White Paper runs a note of horror. "At no time in history has organized crime on so large a scale been instituted as part of the technique of invasion and conquest." From the beginning the invaders conducted themselves in the most savage fashion. Mention is made of the orgy of destructive bombing indulged in by the Italian Air Force at Corfu—a zone which had been demilitarized since 1864 and did not possess a single anti-aircraft gun, yet it was attacked on over 30 occasions. When the Nazis entered Greece, they conducted themselves in the same brutal fashion. "These Teuton masters of a new philosophy did not respect one single principle of international law or human decency . . . Towns and villages were reduced to ruins; old men, women, and children were deliberately massacred by machine-gun fire." Whole towns were wiped out; Red Cross hospitals, clearly marked, were completely destroyed; and five Greek hospital ships, again bearing unmistakable Red Cross markings, were sunk by German aircraft, and their survivors machine-gunned as they tried to keep afloat.

Even worse than the treatment of Greece was the invasion of Crete. The three principal towns, Canea, Heraklion, and Retimo, were bombed time and again until not a wall was left standing. "The wretched inhabitants, as they struggled to escape from their primitive shelters, were mercilessly butchered by the machine-guns of aircraft flying at low level, and the agony of mutilated women and helpless little children left these raging beasts unmoved."

Perhaps the most horrible story is that which tells how on the eve of the Battle of the Kalamas River nine Italian tanks deliberately moved backwards and forwards over the bodies of Greek wounded soldiers, although no fighting was in progress. Would it were not true; but the Greek Government declares that the incident is authenticated by trustworthy eye-witnesses.

Looting the Conquered

Not even the cessation of armed resistance on the mainland and in Crete has brought an end to the terror. Hundreds of hostages have been, and are being, shot; and often the pretexts for this butchery are alleged assistance to British prisoners in their attempts to escape, alleged concealment of arms, sabotage, and trespassing on petrol dumps. "On June 29 last a young woman and a boy of 13 were shot in University Avenue in Athens by German guards, because they appeared to show some sympathy for British prisoners who were being led past." Housebreaking, theft, and assaults upon women by the Italian and German soldiery are common practices, and go unchecked; looting in every possible form is carried on in the most systematic manner. It is that looting which, as we have seen, is one of the chief reasons why today the Greeks are starving.

To quote from another Greek Government memorandum issued a week or two ago, "The enemy's efforts are deliberate. Together with the body he wishes to destroy the soul of the Greeks. The civilized world, those who remember that they owe some debt to the Greece of the past and the Greece of the present, must oppose these efforts with every means available." Food is the first essential, and already certain stores—beans, split peas, potatoes, onions, fish, and eggs—have reached the half-starved people by way of Turkey under the auspices of the Greek Government. Now comes the news that in Egypt a cargo of 8,000 tons of cereals is waiting shipment to Greece, providing the Axis permission may be obtained, and Dingle Foot has stated in the House of Commons that the Italian safe-conduct has been received, and that, moreover, the British Government has financed the chartering by the Swedish Red Cross of a vessel to carry relief to Greece.

But what are 8,000 tons when even in a good year Greece imported 400,000 tons at least?

GREECE STILL FIGHTS on the side of the Allies, for several units of the Greek Navy are taking part in the common struggle. Here the crew of a Greek destroyer, the Coundouriotis, are seen at gun practice.   *Photo, British Official: Crown Copyright*

Glimpses of Europe Under the Nazi Boot

Land under cultivation in the region of the Zuider Zee, Holland, for the production of more food (above). How much the Dutch themselves will get is problematical.

Polish Jews, with their shovels, arriving by lorry to work as demolition squads under the watchful eyes of the Nazis. The persecution of the Jews continues unabated in Poland.

Some of the thousands of French people who left the occupied towns of France for the unoccupied zone when the Germans came, travelling (top right) in the cattle trucks so familiar to British soldiers in the last war. Above, a railway bridge across the Rhône, near Lyons, said to have been destroyed by saboteurs.

Grave of a British airman in a Norwegian cemetery, tended and adorned with flowers by Norwegian sympathizers (left). Norwegians turn their backs as a Nazi band parades through the streets of Drobak, near Oslo (above). This photograph was smuggled out of Norway.

Photos, Sport & General, Keystone, Planet News

Far Below Ground They're Making Planes

FLUORESCENT LIGHTING installed in a machine shop hewn out of oolite, a kind of limestone, in what was recently a disused underground works, now being converted into a factory.

Section of a drilling shop already in operation in what was once a chalk mine. Air conditioning plant is installed, and all vital departments of underground factories are immune from enemy action.

UNDERGROUND FACTORIES for aircraft production are being made by the conversion of disused underground works such as chalk mines and quarries. What is being done in this way is shown in the remarkable series of photographs in this page. Lower left, a store room hollowed out of solid chalk. Oval masked painters spraying the hewn-out walls of an underground factory with distemper. Right, workers at an underground factory leaving for lunch. The nearby canteens are situated above ground.

Photos, P.N.A., Fox.

Our Parachutists Led the Way at Bruneval

A COMBINED raid, in which the Royal Navy, Army and R.A.F. cooperated, was carried out on the night of Feb. 27 against an important German radiolocation post at Bruneval, 12 miles north of Le Havre.

The carrying force of bombers was led by Wing-Commander P. C. Pickard, D.S.O., D.F.C.

The parachute descent force, led by Major J. D. Frost, was dropped, in bright moonlight and slight mist, within easy reach of the objective, despite enemy flak concentration upon the low-flying aircraft during the run-up.

Diversionary operations were carried out by fighter aircraft. The ground operations were carried out according to plan in the face of strong enemy opposition. In spite of all efforts by German defence troops the apparatus was completely destroyed and heavy casualties were inflicted by our parachutists.

Men of the supporting infantry return home after the successful raid on a German radio-location post at Bruneval.

German prisoners, captured during the raid on Bruneval, being searched aboard one of the returning vessels.

Above, troops engaged in the Bruneval raid opening up machine-gun fire upon beaches from their landing craft during a rehearsal of the raid. During the actual raid the German beach defences, taken in the rear by the parachutists, were covered from seaward by the landing craft military escort (found by the Royal Fusiliers and the South Wales Borderers, Home Forces), and overcome.

Having completed their tasks, our troops made their way to Bruneval beach under cover of fire from our light naval forces, commanded by Commander F. N. Cook, Royal Australian Navy. Here are some of the parachute troops after the raid.

Wing-Com. Pickard, D.S.O., D.F.C., the leader of the R.A.F. carrying force of bombers which took part in the raid, examines a captured German steel helmet.

I Was There!....*Eye Witness Stories of the War*

'Inside Ten Minutes the Beach Was in Our Hands'

The following account of the British parachute raid on the German radio-location station at Bruneval, near Havre, was given by Reuter's Special Correspondent, who accompanied the expedition in a " combined operations " ship.

For some days all those who took part had waited. Training and rehearsals had been completed. Everything was satisfactory, and all that was needed were the right conditions. Since the Navy, the Army and the R.A.F. each had vital parts to play, weather conditions to suit all services were necessary—little or no wind for the parachutists, good visibility for the R.A.F. and the right tide for the Navy. In winter few days can fulfil all those conditions.

As each day passed, so spirits sank in the wardroom of the ship in which I had lived during the final training and rehearsal for the parachute troops and the light landing craft. Then glumness and depression were rapidly transformed into jubilation when word came round late on Friday afternoon (Feb. 27): "The job's on tonight."

The sun shone brilliantly from a clear sky when the naval flotilla sailed to the cheers of other craft. As the pastel shades of the sky darkened into night the escorting craft faded into vague shapes distinguishable only by their wake—a silver streak in the light of the moon.

While the flotilla steamed steadily to the French coast, those who were to man the landing craft blacked their faces with burnt cork and paraded the wardroom in sheer high spirits, giving imitations of well-known black-faced comedians.

We were well within "enemy waters" when the light landing craft left the mother ship and went on with the escort. Just before leaving, echoing through the ships, came the stirring melody "Land of My Fathers," sung by the Welshmen who formed a large part of the soldiers' protection crews. Small, undefenceless though the landing craft seemed, yet stowed away within them were guns and ammunition sufficient to deal hardly with either air or E-boat attack.

With all guns shelling, the craft could bristle arms like a porcupine quill. Also on board were duffle coats for the parachute troops on the way back, bully-beef, biscuits, and condensed milk, large reserves of petrol and a jar of jam.

I stood in the bow of the ship and watched the craft slowly merging into the silver greyness of the far distance. Beside me stood a member of the gun crew whom I recognized as one of the wardroom stewards —an unfailingly cheery man who had a slang description for nearly every dish. Up to then I had only seen him as a dexterous waiting steward. Yet there he stood, looking with envious eye at the departing flotilla. His attitude was typical of those who had to stay behind. "I'd give a quid to be going with you," said one lad, while persuasive attempts to stowaway were also made. For us, it was anti-climax. We had to wait now till it was all over. But at that very moment all was activity on the aerodromes, where the parachute troops were climbing into the Whitley bombers which were to drop them.

The R.A.F. timing was excellent. They found their spot at exactly the right moment, and from only a few hundred feet the parties of paratroops were landed in a few minutes. The Air Force was also in at the end of the operation. As dawn took away the protective cover of darkness from the returning craft, the R.A.F. threw over them a powerful "umbrella" of fighters. " It was lovely to see half the British Air Force swooping round us," said one parachutist officer when we got back.

All the crews of the aircraft which dropped the parachutists came to the ship to await the return of the parachute troops. The commander of the squadron was pointed out to me. He stood in the wardroom in a manner known to millions, with his fair hair smoothly brushed, with his head held slightly back and rather to one side—the pilot of "F" for Freddie in "Target for Tonight." The Air Force men had a strong Empire flavour. There were seven Canadians, some New Zealanders and one Australian in the dark blue of the R.A.F.

Later, Reuter's Special Correspondent received first-hand reports of the operation itself. This is what he wrote :

A charge led by a Seaforth Highlander sergeant proved the turning-point in the raid by British paratroops on the French coast at Bruneval, 12 miles north of Havre, in the early hours of the morning of Feb. 28. The purpose of the raid—the destruction of a valuable German radio location post— had been achieved, the Navy waited off shore, yet still the Germans held the approach to the beach. The party attacking the beach had been pinned down for some time by accurate machine-gun fire from the beach fort, the minimum time expected for the raid had already expired, danger to the paratroops themselves grew as each minute passed, danger equally increased for the light Naval craft.

Then above the noise of firing could be heard the shouts of the Seaforths, "Cabar Feidh," indicating that one party of paratroops, which had been dropped a little off the mark, had joined up with the main force and was now coming into action. ("Cabar Feidh" is one of the Seaforth Highlanders' mottoes and is Gaelic for "Antlers of the Deer.")

"Inside ten minutes," said Captain John Ross, the second in command, "the beach was in our hands." The Germans holding the fort had all either been killed or captured, or had fled to a near-by wood.

Captain Ross, who emphasized what a complete surprise the raid was to the Germans, said he was sure that right up to the end they did not really know what was happening. At no time did they hold the least initiative, and though they fought well so long as they held the attackers off, "when it came to fighting at close quarters they gave in."

This remark was echoed by most of the paratroop officers. The Germans were stubborn when behind cover and in a good position, but if suddenly confronted at a distance of only a few yards—and much of the fighting was done at no greater range— they generally turned and ran.

The commanding officer, Major J. D. Frost, told me that his men "did excellently." He went on : "On the way across in the planes, you would never have thought

THE BRUNEVAL RAID, an account of which is given in this page, was a highly successful essay in Services cooperation. Seen here returning after the attack, these landing craft held a military escort which covered the operations of the parachutists from seaward. More photos are in page 573.
Photo, British Official: Crown Copyright

Major J. D. FROST, who commanded the parachute descent force in the Bruneval raid described below. *Photo, British Official*

it was an operational flight. It was more like a joy ride. Every machine, I think, had its own concert party. It was by no means so frightening as everybody had expected. You sat at the hole, looked down and saw a few tracer bullets go past below—and jumped."

The Germans, while still holding the beach fort, called out in excellent English "The boats are here," in the hope of misleading the paratroops into believing a Naval officer had shouted and getting them to chance a run for the beach under machine-gun fire.

Both Major Frost and Captain Ross had nothing but praise for the R.A.F. "They put us down ten yards from where we wanted to be," said Ross, " and within two minutes of leaving the plane the troops were armed, organized and ready to fight."

"The real hero," said the Major, " was the officer commanding the section which was dropped away from the bulk of the troops." Only 20, the youngest officer of the party, and therefore known as "Junior," he had to find his way, frequently under fire, in an area quite unknown to him. When "Junior" took his first look round and failed to recognize any familiar landmark he knew he was lost.

"I don't think there's any feeling quite so unpleasant as suddenly finding yourself in enemy territory and not knowing where you are," he said. "Then I saw another plane going along low down and I knew in which direction to go, and after a while I saw the lighthouse. Then everything was all right.

"For the whole two hours or more of the operation there was never a moment when some firing was not going on. Yet nowhere did I see any sign of life in the houses. Two of my men went through a village, but there were no lights, no furtive peering by the edges of curtains."

It was a former Fleet Street man, 22-year-old Lieutenant Peter Young, who was assigned the task of dealing with the radio-location post, and so complete was the surprise of the attack that he had almost reached his objective before encountering any opposition. The German sentry challenged the approaching troops twice and then fired. The paratroops, who had held their fire as long as possible, "rubbed him out," said Lieutenant Young. "After that we hunted them out of cellars, trenches and rooms with hand grenades, automatic weapons, revolvers and knives.

"Most were killed, but some ran away, and one tried to hide over the edge of the cliff. Having got there, he wanted to surrender, and I looked over to see him with his hands up. At the time I thought I had seen nothing funnier than a German trying

to scramble up the lip of a cliff with his hands up."

The post being captured, it was the turn of the sappers. Their task was to destroy the apparatus ; and destruction could scarcely have been more complete. To the sappers also fell the duty of searching the beach for mines and laying anti-tank mines.

One of the parachutists told me they got

away just in time. "The Germans had an armoured division about 50 miles away, and as we left the beach I saw a column of headlights coming towards us, though still some distance off," he said.

When the Verey signal flashed, the Naval craft came in "like a swarm;" took the men on board and were steaming back to England in a surprisingly short time.

In Spite of All I Got Safe From Singapore

The Associated Press correspondent, C. Yates McDaniel, one of the last to leave Singapore (see page 550), arrived in Batavia on Feb. 20 after the adventurous seven-and-a-half-day journey which he describes below.

THE ship in which we got away from Singapore was passing a group of peaceful little islands when two Japanese light bombers circled and glided over us. The old ship shuddered when bombs exploded just astern. A few minutes later two more planes were over, not more than 500 feet up. This time they did not miss. The decks seemed to bounce up to meet us as we flopped on our faces. We found a gaping hole through the forward hold. Ten minutes later there was another ear-splitting crash, followed by the hiss of escaping steam. The ship listed and began settling.

After surveying the damage the captain ordered the remaining two lifeboats over the side. After an hour of baling, rowing, and sailing we grounded on a coral reef and waded ashore on the little island of Banku. A hundred men and a girl settled down for a miserable night on the narrow beach. Japanese planes knew exactly where we were, and we knew there was little hope of rescue by our own people.

On the early morning of Feb. 14 we were breakfasting on a cigarette tin of muddy water, which neither tasted nor smelled like tea, and one small biscuit, when the look-out reported that small launches were approaching our ship, which was still barely afloat.

An hour later our lifeboat returned, reporting that the launches belonged to a rubber planter on a neighbouring island who would try to take us off at nightfall.

Our hopes were dimmed soon after by the drone of the Japanese planes. Up and down they flew, and then we heard bombs exploding. They circled over us again and there were more bombs. Towards noon a formation of seven bombers circled over our stricken ship. I saw two bursts forward. The ship reared up by the stern. Our captain turned away and took off his cap.

The first and only muster of the ship's company and passengers showed 131 men and one woman unharmed, one Australian soldier and one Chinese stoker killed by bombs, and one sailor badly burned and three slightly injured.

After sunset the first officer, who had been out in a launch, reported that he had taken off six badly wounded women from other ships in which casualties were heavy. All hands were ordered to muster on the beach. We waited an hour in the darkness, knee-deep in water, while the officers decided how to get us out to the launches. Even our lifeboats could only approach within half a mile. We were finally ordered to make our way the best we could.

The next 45 minutes were the worst I have ever experienced as I clambered over coral rocks and slipped into holes. I kept my cameras and my films of burning Singapore and the bombing of our ship high over my head until within twenty yards of the nearest boat, when I plunged off a rock into a ten-foot hole. I could have cried, but had to carry on swimming until I was hoisted into the lifeboat. Somehow, with one workable oar and everybody shouting different orders, we managed to push against the wind and the tide to the launch.

Fifty-one men and one girl, exhausted and soaked, with their legs bleeding, piled into a launch licensed to carry fifteen. Waves rolled over the deck where we sprawled, wet and shivering, but still hoping we would make Sumatra before dawn brought Japanese bombers.

Daybreak found us approaching the mouth of a river, up which we worked our way until late afternoon. Then we rounded a bend and saw the White Ensign over warships anchored by a wharf. Ashore we found members of the Malayan Command staff from Singapore.

Early the next morning, Feb. 16, we resumed the slow journey up-river. At noon we reached a motor roadhead, hungry and cramped, but were soon cheered by the warm hospitality of the Dutch military and civilians, who fed us sumptuously and provided a lorry for the 400-mile drive across Sumatra. On the next afternoon we reached north-west Sumatra. Hotels were full of refugees from Malaya and Southern Sumatra, but a good Dutch lady took us in and fed us. The next morning we were told there was a chance of getting away by warship if we pushed on.

We hired pony carts and drove to the railway station during the beating of tom-toms which gave an air-raid alarm. Half an hour later we left the train at a port. The effects of earlier bombing were everywhere. Twice during the day the Alert sounded, but no planes appeared. Late in the afternoon I saw a British destroyer on the horizon steaming at full speed towards harbour. Half an hour later the destroyer was alongside.

The officers quickly and efficiently shepherded us aboard and allotted places for 176 men, women, and children—British soldiers and sailors, Americans and Dutchmen from the Sumatra oilfields and rubber estates, and six weary members of the last party from Singapore.

Lt. EVAN CHARTERIS led the parachutists which dropped away from the main body. He is referred to as " Junior " in the story. *Photo, Lafayette* **Page 575**

Editor's Postscript

ADAPTABILITY is the main factor in survival. The weird and futile prehistoric monsters on which Nature tried her 'prentice hand so unsuccessfully for a few million years in the Primary and Secondary periods, disappeared because they were unable to adapt themselves to the changing conditions of the Earth's temperature and the altered areas of land and water in their feeding grounds. The few species that survived and still hold their own in the struggle for existence are only pocket editions of their progenitors of the Cretaceous period. Adaptability is possibly the most vital quality in all forms of material success. In the politician it becomes opportunism ; but in the explorer, the inventor, the man of action, it is essentially what it is termed. It has no place, however, in the poet or the inspired artist. Mr. Epstein (quite rightly) resolutely refuses to adapt himself to popular taste, and as resolutely refuses to become extinct, even though many of his later works of art might look better against a background of the Late Pliocene Age, when Java man was raising his ape-like howls in the very jungles where our Dutch allies are now at death grapple with a modern ape-like creature who has become formidable just because, unlike prehistoric Java man, he has proved highly adaptable.

Well, dear readers, this is a little excursus before I have to tell you about our own need for adaptability. This paper problem ! Once again the blow has fallen upon us, but this time, I am told, more hopefully than before, that it may be the last. Our quota of printing paper is again reduced : not so drastically as in the earlier and more cruel cuts, but heavily enough to cause some heart-burning.

I NEED not recapitulate the long story of how the Fury with the abhorred shears has been hovering over the printing presses of THE WAR ILLUSTRATED for a year or more, longing to snip short the reels of paper that are fed into them. She has got away with many a cut : one actually approximate to 100,000 copies weekly, in itself an enviable circulation. Since the last very big cut was forced upon us, however, it was determined that not again would we disappoint a large section of our loyal subscribers by reducing our printing order to the point at which the amount of paper to be saved had been obtained—at the loss of another 40,000 subscribers or so. Never again, it was resolved, would we just cut off a large percentage of our readers by limiting our printing order to the amount dictated by our paper quota.

YOU will remember that we made various alterations to the number of pages in each issue, and to the published price, and finally (as it was hoped) to the incidence of publishing. Instead of appearing weekly we have been issuing every ten days since No. 104, and in this way supplying every one of our subscribers instead of regretfully sending many more thousands of them away empty-handed, week after week, by direct cuts in circulation equivalent to the reduction in our own paper supply.

ALTHOUGH this once-every-ten-days publishing has proved successful and has prevented widespread disappointment to readers (for remember THE WAR ILLUSTRATED is the *only* popular picture-record of the War whose circulation is still calculated in hundreds of thousands), I have never liked it, and if there are readers who have found it as irritating at times as the editorial staff have found it, I fancy they would be equally glad to hear of a simpler alternative which will meet every objection.

A FORTNIGHTLY publishing date solves all our difficulties and will enable me to carry out some noteworthy improvements

SIR JAMES GRIGG, K.C.B., K.C.S.I., Britain's new War Minister, was for several years Finance Member of the Viceroy's Council in India. He is 51.
Photo, Associated Press

in the presentation of the publication. A fortnightly of the exact size of the present issue would be inadequate as an up-to-date current War record. So, starting with No. 125 each issue will be *increased in size* by eight pages. Four of these will carry beautiful *gravure printing* in different colours on tinted paper. The slower printing possible with a fortnightly issue will improve all our pages, quite apart from this gravure supplement, and it will also be possible to trim the edges of the pages, which up till now has not been practicable. Each of our fortnightly issues, I feel sure, most of my readers will think worth any two of the weekly or tenth-day issues. But the increase in price will be no more than twopence, so that the two fortnightly numbers at sixpence a copy will involve no extra expenditure per month compared with the present three fourpennies. Following the present issue, the first of the new series, No. 125, will appear on Thursday, April 2 (the day before Good Friday). Thereafter we shall publish every alternate Friday.

THE only way to meet the distressing paucity of paper is to put the paper available to better use, and that's what my scheme for THE WAR ILLUSTRATED succeeds in doing. I know each number will be so great an improvement on any previously published that I am looking forward quite excitedly to seeing the first copy !

And here are all the things attained by the fortnightly publication of THE WAR ILLUSTRATED at sixpence :

(1) A greatly improved, enlarged, and pictorially enriched current record of the War.
(2) Every existing subscriber able to secure a copy.
(3) No confusion about publishing dates, as it will be on sale each alternate Friday (some places on the Thursday).
(4) More than ever worth binding in volume form, by reason of the lovely coloured gravure supplements in every fortnightly number.
(5) The difficulty of the paper quota overcome.
(6) No increased expenditure on the part of subscribers.

WELL, if we of THE WAR ILLUSTRATED had n o t been more adaptable to the conditions in which we are living (Spencer's theory of "life," by the way) than those prehistoric monsters (or Mr. Epstein) I can't guess what would have become of this unique and continuous current picture-record of the War. And, actually, instead of being defeated by the horrid (but essential) restrictions of the Paper Controller (publishers' wives personify him in their lullabies as the ogre from which their mother love protects their little ones) we are about to blossom out into a new and fuller life !

FOR the benefit of the many thousands who bind their serial numbers into volume form, let me add that Volume 5 of THE WAR ILLUSTRATED will be complete with No. 130 appearing on June 12. This is also by way of a warning, for I urge all who have bound the first four volumes to note the date at which Volume 5 concludes and lose not a moment then in getting the loose numbers to the binders. For a day may come—alas, almost certainly will come—when no more binding cases can be manufactured and the remaining loose numbers thereafter may have to be kept until the end of the War before facilities for binding them can be available.

BY way of P.P.S., this will interest my readers. In 1934 I issued one of my most successful serials, WORLD WAR : 1914-18, which consisted of twenty-four pages of black and white, four pages of gravure printing and four pages of wrapper, price sevenpence. Although the printing and paper we were then able to provide were greatly superior in WORLD WAR, compared with the cheaper rotary printing of THE WAR ILLUSTRATED, the comparison of material value, considering present difficulties, justifies my claiming that our new fortnightly will be a triumph in economic production. The new fortnightly issue of THE WAR ILLUSTRATED will consist of twenty-eight pages in black and white, plus four pages of the finest gravure printing, price sixpence ! If any reader were to complain of this as value for money I should not like to have him as a friend.

Printed in England and published fortnightly by the Proprietors, The Amalgamated Press, Ltd., The Fleetway House, Farringdon Street, London, E.C.4. Registered for transmission by Canadian Magazine Post. Sole Agents for Australia and New Zealand : Messrs. Gordon & Gotch, Ltd. ; and for South Africa : Central News Agency, Ltd. March 20th, 1942. S.S. *Editorial Address:* JOHN CARPENTER HOUSE, WHITEFRIARS, LONDON, E.C.4.

Vol 5 *The War Illustrated* N° 125

Edited by Sir John Hammerton

6ᵈ. FORTNIGHTLY   APRIL 2. 1942

SIR STAFFORD CRIPPS, Lord Privy Seal, who has gone to India as a member of the War Cabinet to consult with representatives of all parties on the acceptability of a new Government plan " to aid India in the realization of self-government," to use Mr. Churchill's own words. Sir Stafford Cripps will also, during his visit, consult with the Viceroy and General Wavell upon the military situation. India is the subject of a special article and of the photogravure section in this number.   *Photo, Topical Press*

NO. 126 WILL BE PUBLISHED FRIDAY, APRIL 17

HONGKONG & NANKING: A TALE OF HORROR

HARDLY had Hongkong fallen, when horrible tales began to be told of the things that were done by the Japanese in their hour of victory. Refugees who managed to reach Kwantung in Chinese territory reported that in Kowloon, the mainland portion of the colony, " after dark nothing but screams and cries and police whistles were heard from Dec. 12 to Dec. 25." Homes and shops were looted, and gangsters went about demanding money as the price of their " protection." British women had been raped both in Kowloon and Hongkong, and some had been rounded up and handed over to Japanese officers.

AT first there was hope that these stories contained (as most atrocity stories do) an element of excited exaggeration. But day by day evidence has accumulated, and we are now assured that the testimony of eye-witnesses has established the fact that, following the capitulation, Japanese troops were let loose to indulge their savage hates and brutal lusts—that they embarked upon an orgy of licence in which were involved the military prisoners, now disarmed and helpless, and the civilian population, without distinction of race or colour, sex or age. Some account of the terrible happenings that are alleged to have occurred was given by Mr. Eden, Secretary of State for Foreign Affairs, in a statement made in the House of Commons on March 10.

" It is known (he said) that 50 officers and men of the British Army were bound hand and foot and then bayoneted to death. It is known that 10 days after the capitulation wounded were still being collected from the hills and the Japanese were refusing permission to bury the dead. It is known that women, both Asiatic and European, were raped and murdered, and that one entire Chinese district was declared a brothel, regardless of the status of the inhabitants. All the survivors of the garrison, including Indians, Chinese, and Portuguese, have been herded into a camp consisting of wrecked huts without doors, windows, light, or sanitation. By the end of Jan 150 cases of dysentery had occurred in the camp, but no drugs or medical facilities were supplied. The dead had to be buried in a corner of the camp.... Most of the European residents, including some who are seriously ill, have been interned, and, like the military prisoners, are being given only a little rice and water and occasional scraps of other food."

THE Japanese guards, Mr. Eden continued, were utterly callous, and repeated requests made by General Maltby, the General Officer Commanding, for an interview with the Japanese commander had been curtly refused, which presumably means that the Japanese High Command have connived at the conduct of their forces. Fortunately, there is some reason to believe that conditions have slightly improved recently, but still the Japanese Government have refused their consent to the visit to Hongkong of a representative of the Protecting Power (the Argentine Republic), and no permission has yet been granted for such a visit by the representative of the International Red Cross Committee. Moreover, since the Japanese have required all the foreign consuls to withdraw from territories they have invaded since the outbreak of war, it is clear that their treatment of prisoners and civilians will not bear independent investigation.

In opening his statement Mr. Eden declared that the barbarities indulged in by the Japanese at Hongkong were of the same kind that aroused the horror of the civilized world at the time of the Nanking massacre in 1937. But memories are short, and it may be doubted whether what happened at Nanking four years ago made any deep and lasting impression on the public conscience. After all, in those days China seemed a very long way away, and what happened to the Chinese could *never* happen to us or ours . . .

THE story of Nanking's sack is full of horrors, and this is no place to dilate upon them; details will be found in, e.g., Edgar Snow's " Scorched Earth," where it is stated that some 50,000 Japanese troops were let loose in the city for over a month in an orgy of rape, murder, looting, and general debauchery, which has nowhere been equalled in modern times. The number of slaughtered has been put at no less than 42,000, a large percentage of whom were women and children, and not a female between the ages of 10 and 70 escaped violation. Thousands of stores and houses were systematically stripped of all their stocks and furnishings by gangs of soldiers working under their officers' supervision, and then set ablaze. The homes of foreign diplomats were entered and their servants murdered. Privates did as they pleased ; officers either participated themselves, or excused the conduct of their men by explaining that as a conquered people the Chinese could expect nothing else. Japanese Embassy officials were aghast at the excesses, but were powerless to do anything to stop it.

Nanking was no isolated instance of Japanese frightfulness. The fate of the Koreans and the Formosans makes a grim chapter in the chronicles of Japanese militarism. Shocking things were done in Manchuria before it became the puppet state of Manchukuo. Shanghai had its scenes of terror in 1932, and one appalling incident in particular is remembered, when at the Kiangwan racecourse some Japanese officers (to quote Edgar Snow again) " lined up a number of captured Chinese civilians, including women and children, and ordered their newly-arrived troops to use them for bayonet practice. When a soldier made a clumsy thrust he had to repeat the performance until he had perfected his technique, or overcome his timidity."

Then for the last five years, as General Chiang Kai-shek told the Indians in his special message the other day :
" the civilian population of Free China has been subjected to almost daily bombings from the air and bombardments by heavy artillery. In every place invaded by the Japanese troops men, women and children have been assaulted or killed. Young men, educated people, and men with ideas and intelligence have been singled out for torture and specially severe treatment. Institutions of culture, objects of historical interest and value, even articles necessary for the people's livelihood, such as cooking utensils, ploughs, and tools have been destroyed. In places under Japanese military occupation robbery, rapine, incendiarism and murder are frequent occurrences. Moreover, the Japanese soldiers have, with official connivance, opened opium dens, gambling dens, and houses of ill-fame everywhere in order to sap the vitality of the Chinese people, and destroy their spirit. Such is the disgraceful conduct of the Japanese . . ."

WHY do Japanese soldiers commit these crimes against humanity ? It is because they are *trained* to do it; because, from the day he first puts on his uniform, all the training of the Japanese soldier makes for endurance, hardness, contempt for pain suffered—which inevitably leads to indifference to pain inflicted. From his mother's knee he is taught that no career is so honourable as that of the soldier. He sees himself as a humble instrument of the Emperor's will, destined to contribute his mite to the conquest of East Asia, perhaps of all Asia, perhaps the whole world. If he is a private he boasts that he belongs to an army which has never been defeated ; if he is an officer, then he needs no reminder that a Japanese officer should never be captured alive. He is taught the code of *Bushido* (his profession of which was denounced by Mr. Eden as " a nauseating hypocrisy ") which embodies the seven military virtues— loyalty, valour, patriotism, obedience, humility, morality, and honour. He is taught that no privilege is so great as to die for the Emperor ; if he is killed in battle he will go to no wishy-washy heaven, or join the houris in the Moslem paradise, but his name will be enshrined in the family temple. He will be remembered and revered by his children's children, and although not quite a god like his Emperor, he will be something of a " godlet."

THESE are the men we are up against ; these are the things they believe and the things they do. We may exhaust all the adjectives of condemnation, but, as Mr. Eden said in concluding his statement, " we can best express our sympathy with the victims of these appalling outrages by redoubling our efforts to ensure Japan's utter and overwhelming defeat."

E. ROYSTON PIKE

WOE TO THE CONQUERED ! Reports of Japanese atrocities at Hongkong have deeply moved public opinion, but such happenings have long been everyday occurrences in China. This picture of human misery, a woman weeping over her husband's corpse, dates from the sack of Nanking in 1937. *Photo, Associated Press*

Where the First Bombs Dropped on Australia's Soil

AFTER A JAP RAID on Darwin in which considerable damage was done to property. The huge crater in front of the demolished post office is shown in this photograph radioed from Melbourne.

DAMAGE AT DARWIN. A building in the Main Street in this important North Australian town, after a Japanese bomb had fallen (top left). Darwin was raided for the first time on the morning of Feb. 19 and a second raid followed an hour or two later.

Circle, men of the A.I.F. manning the Darwin Defences entering a sand-bagged observation post.

Right, the smashed jetty at Port Darwin after the first raids on Australia. In the two attacks made on that day, six enemy aircraft are known to have been destroyed.

Photos, Keystone, Planet News, Sport & General

Where the Invader Is Next Door to India

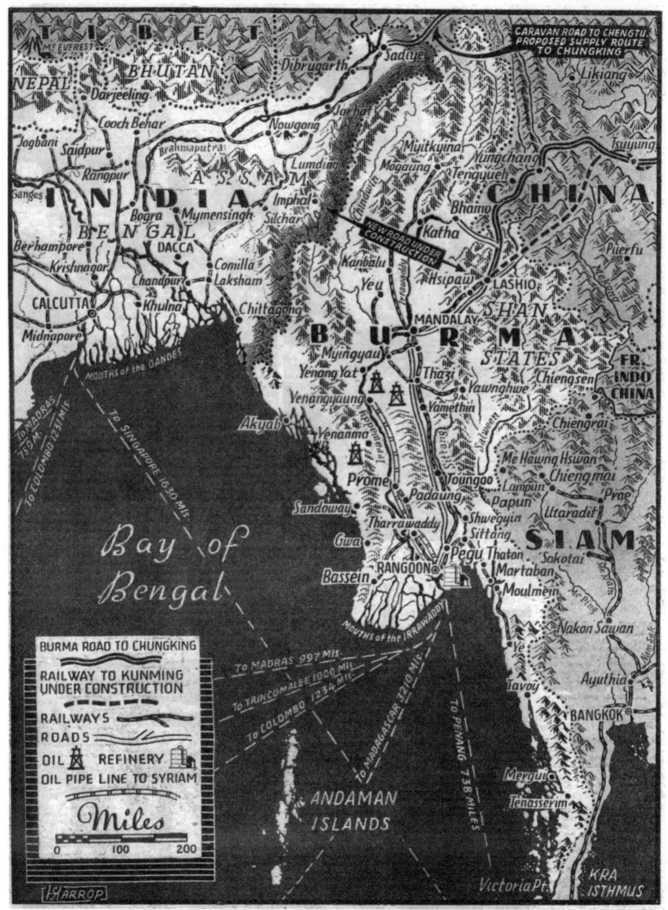

BURMA, separated from peninsular India by the Bay of Bengal, and from Bengal and Assam by parallel mountain chains covered with thick jungle, is the bastion which covers India's eastern land flank. It is, too, the connecting link between India and China, and as such its conquest would be of inestimable value to Japan. With Malaya, Thailand and Indo-China in the grip of Japan, the threat to Burma is a grave one, made even more serious by the fall of its capital, the seaport of Rangoon, which was evacuated on March 8.

Specially drawn for THE WAR ILLUSTRATED *by Harrop*

'Too Few, Too Late': The Tragedy of Rangoon

Less than a month after the Japanese marched into Singapore they added Rangoon to their list of conquests. Below we give an account of the last hours of the great city—one of the chief centres of British political and commerical greatness in the Far East—and of the supremely gallant efforts made to save it by General Hutton's all too small and weak force.

"THE loss of Rangoon," General Wavell told L. Marsland Gander, The Daily Telegraph special correspondent, who interviewed him at New Delhi on March 13, " is in some respects even more serious a blow than the loss of Singapore. It brings the war much closer to India, and threatens our communication with China. As in Malaya, reinforcements were insufficient, they arrived too late, and were insufficiently trained." To which must be added the fact that once again the Japanese were greatly superior in the air.

But there is consolation—although of a very sorry kind—in the fact that it was a dead and ruined city that was abandoned to the Japanese. Weeks before the last British troops marched out, a thorough-going " scorched earth " scheme had been elaborated to the smallest detail, and when the moment came it was carried out in the most ruthless fashion. Great warehouses, docks, quays and jetties were blown up or set on fire. The smoke from burning petrol dumps billowed to heaven. Hundreds of trucks and cars which had arrived by boat were destroyed in their cases without being unpacked. Other stocks and stores were dumped into the harbour. Finally, the important Syriam oil refineries, 20 miles down the river, were completely demolished beyond repair, and the pipe-line bringing oil from the fields 300 miles to the north was cut.

While this organized destruction was going on, there was an outbreak of hooliganism and looting by the city's criminal elements. One night the largest department store in the city was ransacked ; the looters smashed what they could not take away and dumped quantities of abandoned goods in the streets. " Asiatic quislings," wrote O. D. Gallagher of The Daily Express, " whose emotions against the whites have been worked up by the Japanese radio, sneak around the city at night as fire-bugs. Buildings burned all day. Debris littered the streets with the bodies of dead dogs and dead looters, shot during the night by military patrols."

No City So Well Defended

Another eye-witness of the drama was Philip Jordan of the News Chronicle. He cabled on March 1 that it was not safe to go into the centre of the town without some kind of weapon, and often as not the only way to deal with the looters was to shoot them without mercy. He drew a picture of a dead and tragic city, filled with relics of family life left behind. As yet there was an abundance of food and drink, and if you turned looter and cared to get drunk several times a day you could do so without so much as by your leave. " Such is Rangoon today," he concluded, " slices of great and unnatural peace, and great and unnatural horror ; a lily festering in sunlight. But the abiding memory will always be of great bravery against great odds."

None described that battle with a more powerful pen than Philip Jordan himself. In a dispatch telegraphed on March 3 he declared that Rangoon had been defended with a gallantry which, even if it had been equalled, had never been surpassed in the military history of the British Empire. " Without respite, without relief, without adequate sleep, short of equipment and sometimes without food for as long as six days at a time, a force formed from among British regiments as well as Indian and local troops has been fighting a regularly reinforced and freshened Japanese force, at least three times as large, for the past 44 days." Lt.-Gen. Hutton's troops had done more, suffered

more, and endured more than any troops who have yet fought in this war. " No city in the world has yet been defended as Rangoon has been defended by Britain's forgotten men. But if they are forgotten now, if they seem remote now, the time will come when their names will head the roll of military glory."

Then Mr. Jordan proceeded to tell of the great stand which had been made by Hutton's men on the banks of the Sittang River.

THEY FOUGHT IN BURMA

British.—Duke of Wellington's Regiment, King's Own Yorkshire Light Infantry, Cameronians, West Yorkshire Regt., Gloucestershire Regt., Royal Tank Corps.

Burmese.—Burma Sappers and Miners, Burma Rifles, Burma Army Service Corps.

Indian.—Indian Artillery, Indian Signal Corps, Jat Regiment, Baluchi Regiment, Dogra Regiment, Frontier Force Regiment, Gurkha Rifles, Indian Army Service Corps, Indian Hospital Corps.

If they are forgotten now, the time will come when their names will head the roll of military glory.—Philip Jordan, in the News Chronicle.

In the early hours of the morning of Feb. 23 (he wrote), it was found to be impossible any longer to hold the bridgehead on the east side of the Sittang River. Although many of our troops —men of the K.O.Y.L.I. and the Duke of Wellington's Regiment—were on the wrong side of the river fighting the enemy, our sappers, at 5.30 a.m., blew up the bridge "efficiently and gallantly." There then began what one man who took part in it described as " a party that made Dunkirk look like a picnic." And it is impossible to disbelieve him. Bombed, shelled, machine-gunned from the air, mortared, hundreds of doomed men began to swim the river, at this point some 800 yards wide.

For the next three days and the next three nights hundreds of heads bobbed in torn waters, struggling to reach the far shore. How many men were drowned, how many died beneath the cruel punishment from the air, is not yet known Abandoning all but their arms and the clothes they stood up in, men plunged into the swift current and struck out for " home." Those who could not swim snatched logs, clusters of bamboos, anything that would float, and kicked their way across—not to safety but to positions from which, without any rest, they would be forced to fight again, even though they had already fought since Jan. 16.

A brigadier who himself swam the river and whose red tabs are today sadly but honourably faded as a result, says that he saw gallantry there that he never saw even in the last war ; that he saw and experienced a situation there more desperate than any he had ever known. He says that perhaps the most wonderful thing of all was the way in which the wounded were cared for and ferried across beneath the blaze of the Burman sun and the hail of Japanese steel. Doors, rafts, anything in fact on which a man could be laid were launched, and men acting as outboard motors slowly yet painfully ferried them across.

But this is not all. Then when there was no ferry of any kind to be found, men lowered the wounded gently into the water and, treating them as life-savers treat drowning men, swam them to the far bank. Thus the remnants of one of the most gallant forces of history came back to reform, to re-equip, and to fight again.

On March 4 it was officially announced in Rangoon that the Japanese had crossed the Sittang, and that the British patrols were in contact with the enemy at Waw and northeast of Pegu. Two days later the decision was taken by the military authorities—who had been left in charge of the city by Sir Reginald Dorman-Smith when he removed the seat of Government to Mandalay on March 3—to withdraw the last British forces. So the final essential demolitions were put in hand, and the next day Rangoon was even more than it had been before a dead city, lying under a pall of smoke rising from the fires caused by the demolition parties and the bands of saboteurs and looters.

According to the Japanese, a general attack on Rangoon began at nine o'clock on the evening of Saturday, March 7. The British encampment in the neighbourhood of Mingaladon, they claimed, was surprised by the Japanese right wing, while their left attacked it from the rear. Finally at dawn the next day they entered the city and hoisted the flag of the Rising Sun above the railway station. High columns of smoke were still rising to the sun from the burning wharves as the Japanese marched in ; warehouses and docks were still smouldering. In almost plaintive tone the Japanese complained of the ruthless plundering of Japanese establishments and destruction worked by the British troops before they made their retreat.

RANGOON—a study of Burmese types at an open-air market-place. When Rangoon fell on March 8 fires were raging all over the city, many of them caused by looters and saboteurs. *Photo, Paul Popper*

Still the Story Is One of Retreat in Burma

INDIAN TROOPS use sturdy Texas mules to carry the guns of a mounted battery over the rough terrain of Burma (left).

HOMELESS BURMESE, victims of the Japanese air raids on Rangoon, line up at a food distribution centre. Circle right, Burmese labourers building surface shelters in Rangoon, which was heavily raided in the days prior to its evacuation.

RANGOON RIVER

DOCKS AND WAREHOUSES

DALHOUSIE STREET

FRASER STREET

SULE PAGODA ROAD

FIRE STATION

British troops crossing a river in Burma. Burma's rivers, Salween, Bilin, and Sittang, have been the scene of fierce fighting to hold up the Japanese advance.

RANGOON, the fall of which was officially announced on March 9. When the Japanese occupied the town only a shell remained. The "scorched earth" policy left nothing of use for the invaders.

JAP INGENUITY overcame the difficulty of this destroyed bridge in Burma. One girder was left on which the Japs placed railway lines. By transferring railway wheels to the lorries they got wagons across.

Photos, Planet News, G.P.U., Keystone, British Official: Crown Copyright

The Inevitable Tragedy of Java's Fall

Shortly after midday on Saturday, March 7, there came a final message from the Dutch in Bandoeng, and below we quote its most important passages. The last words from the cable station were, "Now we shut down. Long live our Queen! Good-bye till better times."

JUST a week after the Japanese landings in force, organized resistance in Java came to an end. From Tokyo came a report that shortly before midnight on Saturday, March 7, a Dutch general, carrying a white flag, approached the Japanese lines and offered to open negotiations for surrender. The next afternoon at three o'clock the commander of the Japanese forces met the Dutch Governor-General, Jonkheer A. W. L. Tjarda van Starkenborgh Stachouwer, at Kalidjati. It appears that the Governor-General consented at first to the surrender only of the troops in the Bandoeng sector, but on the Japanese commander insisting on the unconditional surrender of all the Dutch forces in the island, Jkr. Stachouwer promised to order the cessation of hostilities at 10 o'clock on the following morning. The number of troops affected, claimed the Japanese, was 93,000 Dutch and 5,000 British, Australians and Americans.

Tragic as the surrender was, it was none the less inevitable. Dutch officers who escaped to Australia asserted that the Japanese had landed another 50,000 men in Java on March 7, and that they had some 60,000 in the neighbourhood of the Dutch naval base of Surabaya. Resistance in Eastern Java was dwindling to a close, and the Japanese claimed to have entered Surabaya, itself, which they admitted was burning "because of the incendiarism carried out by the retreating Dutch troops." Most of Western Java had been overrun, too, and the defence lines around Bandoeng pierced.

'Whatever Made You Fight?'

An account of the "unconditional surrender" of the Dutch forces was issued by the Japanese News Agency. "Cars displaying the white flag draw up before the buildings on Kalidjati aerodrome (it read). The men who descend from them are General ter Poorten (the Dutch C.-in-C.), his Chief of Staff, Lt.-Gen Buckels, a staff officer and two interpreters. They stride into the building behind the guides, and take the seats to which they are motioned.

"The conference begins. The Japanese commander permits ter Poorten and other officers, to be named by ter Poorten, to keep their swords. Ter Poorten smiles faintly in thanks. Then he brings out a list of armaments and weapons in Java, and places it on the blue and white striped table-cloth. He explains the items in a tired voice. Our commander bends over the list, and glances up in amazement. 'The number of guns you have is very small,' he says; 'it does not amount to the artillery brought here by us. Whatever made you fight in the circumstances?' Ter Poorten smiles in his embarrassment: 'That's true. It is certainly true,' he says."

Batavia, the capital of Java, had been evacuated by the Dutch some days before. The story of its fall was told by the war correspondent of a Tokyo newspaper.

On the afternoon of Thursday, March 5, the Japanese arrived at a narrow river, some four miles to the north of the city, where they were met by a group of Dutch and Indonesians carrying white flags, who stated that they represented the Government in Batavia and were waiting to convey a message of surrender. Learning that Batavia had been declared an open city and that the Allied troops had been withdrawn, the Japanese commander gave the order to enter, and at 8.30 p.m. his troops marched in. Following a meeting with the Mayor and the provincial Governor, the Japanese commander issued a proclamation, in which he declared that he had taken over the duties of the Governor-General; that local laws would remain valid where they did not interfere with the military administration, and that the Japanese authorities would respect the lives, religion and rightful property of the people, who in turn must respect the orders of the Japanese Army and officials. Wilful violation of Japanese orders, communication with the "enemy," destruction of property, etc., would

be severely dealt with. "The military administration," the proclamation concluded, "aims at the rapid restoration of peace and order and normal conditions in the Netherlands East Indies, on the principles of co-existence and co-prosperity for all."

On Saturday, March 7, the Netherlands News Agency in Bandoeng sent a last message to the outside world, reviewing the course of the fighting and not hesitating to point the moral.

Jap Supremacy in the Air

The situation in Java, at least in the west part of the island (it began), had become critical, as the result of a Japanese break-through of the defences of the north side of the volcano of Tangkuban Prahu—a success achieved the previous day in the face of desperate resistance by the Netherlands East Indies troops. The Dutch were not only far inferior in numbers, but they were continuously harassed by the Japanese Air Force, against which the Allies could no longer put up effective resistance. "The tragedy now unfolding itself in the previously peaceful valleys north of the Tangkuban Prahu crater—known to thousands of tourists for its beauty—is the more heart-rending for Dutch people when they recall that a great part of the Dutch Air Force was lost in the unavailing defence of Malaya." In the Netherlands East Indies, the message went on, there had been some criticism of the way in which the Allies had conducted the campaign in Malaya and Singapore, but now that Dutchmen were having to fight in the same circumstances judgement might be less severe. However, the conditions in Java were even more unfavourable than in Malaya, since the Japanese were probably in the proportion of at least five to one—to say nothing of their superiority in the air, where they had absolute mastery.

When Japan, on Dec. 8, declared war the Netherlands East Indies immediately threw into the struggle all their forces in the air and on the sea, "in an aggressive spirit, which has been much praised by public opinion in all the countries

fighting against tyranny." This policy carried with it the risk of quick exhaustion of the Dutch forces, but the risk was taken in the expectation that reinforcements would soon arrive in the Far East. During January the Outer Provinces (i.e. the Dutch islands other than Java) were lost one by one, but it was still expected that in February reinforcements would arrive to enable Java to be held and later the initiative to be taken. But these reinforcements never came.

True, the Allied Fleet and Air Force in offensive actions scored great successes, and aeroplanes came in, particularly United States bombers, which proved a formidable weapon. But their value decreased since there was insufficient fighter protection and protection for the airfields, while the fighters available were not of the quality to meet the Japanese on equal terms.

By the end of February Java was practically surrounded. Then the enemy launched his attack. In a heroic attempt to prevent the enemy landings, the Allied fleets did the utmost they could do (see pp. 562, 595). Again they were faced with enemy superiority, and the kernel of the Dutch Fleet was lost. Following the battle, Surabaya could no longer be used as a base for cruisers and destroyers, and the necessary protection from heavy bombers could no longer be given. Heavy losses were inflicted on the enemy during the landings which began on Saturday, Feb. 28, but these successes were dearly paid for. After they had overcome Dutch resistance at sea and in the air, the Japanese had practically free play. Nothing could prevent them from landing just as many men and as much material as they wanted.

Without sufficient protection in the air the troops were practically powerless. So Batavia had to be abandoned, and the Dutch forces were concentrated on the plains around Bandoeng, since this was easier to defend than the flat country of the north coast. This was the position when the message ended.

Bandoeng fell, as we have seen, on March 9. At the last moment Dr. van Mook, Lt. Governor-General of the East Indies, and members of the Government and high officers of the fighting services—15 in all—escaped by air to Australia. Their plane took off from "the last strip of runway available." Arrived in Adelaide, Dr. van Mook declared in an interview, "I hope Australia gets support in time. Java's lesson is more aeroplanes, more ships."

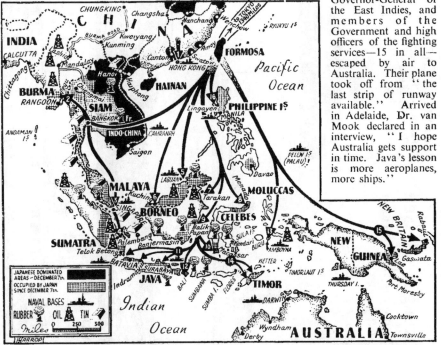

JAPAN'S LIGHTNING CAMPAIGN is illustrated in detail in this map. The arrowheads show: 1, Hongkong, captured on Dec. 25, after a short siege. 2, Burma; Rangoon the capital was evacuated by the British on March 8. 3, Malaya; on Dec. 8 the Japs landed at Kota Bharu. Singapore fell on Feb. 16. 4, Sumatra, attacked on Feb. 14. Southern Sumatra now in Japanese possession. 5, N. Borneo, invaded Dec. 17. 6, Sarawak, invaded at same time. 7, Tarakan, invaded Jan. 10. 8, Celebes, where first Jap landing was made on Jan. 12. 9, Balik Papan, scene of Jap landing on Jan. 23. 10, Macassar, where Japs landed on Feb. 10. 11, Java, three landings made on Feb. 28. Batavia fell on March 6. 12, Bali, where a Jap landing was made on Feb. 20. 13, Amboyna, large naval base, where Japs landed on Jan. 31. 14, Timor. On Feb. 20 Japanese troops landed in both Dutch and Portuguese Timor, only 450 miles from the mainland of Australia. 15, New Britain. Enemy landings made at Rabaul on Jan. 23 and Lae on Jan. 25. 16, Philippines, where the Japanese made their first landings on Dec. 10. American and Filipino forces are still holding out in the Bataan Peninsula. *Map by courtesy of News Chronicle*

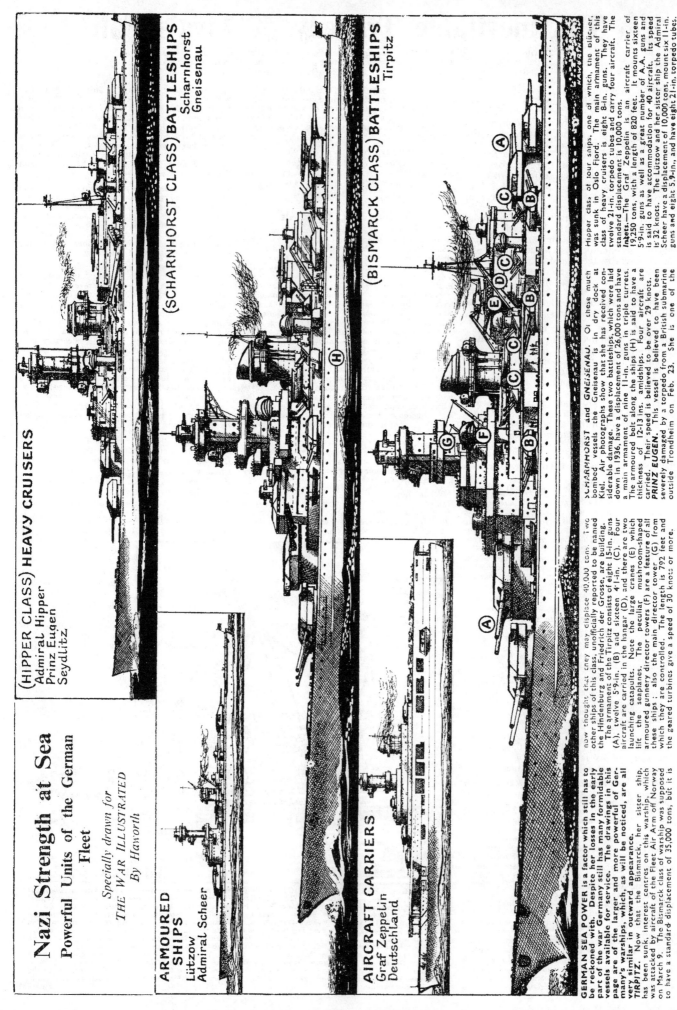

Nazi Strength at Sea

Powerful Units of the German Fleet

Specially drawn for THE WAR ILLUSTRATED By Haworth

(HIPPER CLASS) HEAVY CRUISERS
Admiral Hipper
Prinz Eugen
Seydlitz

ARMOURED SHIPS
Lützow
Admiral Scheer

(SCHARNHORST CLASS) BATTLESHIPS
Scharnhorst
Gneisenau

AIRCRAFT CARRIERS
Graf Zeppelin
Deutschland

(BISMARCK CLASS) BATTLESHIPS
Tirpitz

GERMAN SEA POWER is a factor which still has to be reckoned with. Despite her losses in the early part of the war Germany still has many formidable vessels available for service. The drawings in this page are of the larger and more powerful of Germany's warships, which, as will be noticed, are all very similar in outward appearance. Now that the *Bismarck*, her sister ship, has been sunk, interest centres on this warship, which was attacked by aircraft of the Fleet Air Arm off Norway on March 9. The Bismarck class of warship was supposed to have a standard displacement of 35,000 tons, but it is now thought that they may displace 40,000 tons. Two other ships of this class, unofficially reported to be named the Hindenburg and Friedrich der Grosse, are building.

The armament of the *Tirpitz* consists of eight 15-in. guns (A), twelve 5·9-in. (B) and sixteen 4·1-in. (C). Four aircraft are carried in the hangar (D), and there are two launching catapults. Note the large cranes (E) which lift the seaplanes. The peculiar mushroom-shaped armoured gunnery director towers (F) are a feature of all these ships ; also the main director tower (G) from which they are controlled. The length is 792 feet and the geared turbines give a speed of 30 knots or more.

SCHARNHORST and GNEISENAU. Of these much bombed vessels the Gneisenau is in dry dock at Kiel. Air photographs show she has received considerable damage. These two battleships, which were laid down in 1936, have a displacement of 26,000 tons and have a main armament of nine 11-in. guns in triple turrets. The armoured belt along the ships (H) is said to have a thickness of 12-13 ins. amidships. Four aircraft are carried. Their speed is believed to be over 29 knots.

PRINZ EUGEN. This vessel is believed to have been severely damaged by a torpedo from a British submarine outside Trondheim on Feb. 23. She is one of the Hipper class of four ships, one of which, the Blücher, was sunk in Oslo Fiord. The main armament of this class of heavy cruisers is eight 8-in. guns. They have twelve 21-in. torpedo tubes and carry four aircraft. The standard displacement is 10,000 tons.

Injets.—The Graf Zeppelin is an aircraft carrier of 19,250 tons, with a length of 820 feet. It mounts sixteen 5·9-in. guns as well as a great number of A.A. guns and is said to have accommodation for 40 aircraft. Its speed is 32 knots. The Lützow and her sister ship the Admiral Scheer have a displacement of 10,000 tons, mount six 11-in. guns and eight 5.9-in., and have eight 21-in. torpedo tubes.

Inside the Nazi Fortress of Heligoland

Looking west, elderly German sailors on guard in Heligoland, the strongly fortified Nazi base in the North Sea, not far from the Kiel Canal.

'Against England,' such is the meaning of the inscription on the crude caricature of Mr. Churchill in a Heligoland gun emplacement.

HIGH STREET, HELIGOLAND on a quiet day. Right, entrance to the underground fortifications. Circle, German soldier entering the secret, camouflaged fortress. Though bristling with every kind of defence, Heligoland has frequently been visited by the R.A.F., and many valuable photographs, one of which appeared in Vol. 11, page 47, of The War Illustrated, showing the positions of the new harbour and mole, gun emplacements and entrances to the underground barracks, have been taken.

Photos, Keystone

Our Searchlight on the War

EMPIRE AND DEMOCRACY

The loss of Britain's Far Eastern possessions and the threat to India have raised the question of our future imperial policy and responsibility. It has even been asked whether the idea of empire is compatible with true democracy.

BRITISH dominion over a large part of the globe was the result of no preconceived plan. Unlike Germany, we were never obsessed with that inferiority complex which found expression in the word *Weltmacht*. One fact is paramount above all criticism. If we are not loved as rulers we are not universally loathed as the Germans are. In the nature of things no empire can hope to be popular with the governed, for the simple reason that no race likes to be controlled or influenced by another. Britain has admittedly made mistakes, but surely far fewer than might have been expected, considering the difficulties of holding a balance between innumerable castes, creeds and prejudices of the races that make up our imperial population. It is something that we have, on the whole, kept order in India, and much that we have brought many benefits of civilization to the Indian peoples. Looking back on our long administration we are

Irreplaceable relics of English history have been removed from Westminster Hall to a safer place. Workmen are dismounting the statue of William Rufus. *Photo, Planet News*

entitled to ask, and not apologetically, whether the Empire would have been better off under any other system, or if such a system would have worked at all. It is to our credit that we have gradually modified the old idea of imperial domination, and prepared the way for a genuine co-partnership with India. The British people devoutly hope that India, with the help of the Allied nations, will weather the storm that threatens to destroy the whole idea of racial freedom, dignity and progress. In the face of this peril Britain and India must be linked as never before.

HOW TO GROW MORE FOOD

During the spring and summer months every acre of available land should be brought under cultivation, and a seven-day week should become obligatory on all agricultural workers.

THE whole burden of the Allied war effort depends on ships. We can do nothing without them. While waiting for American and British shipyards to increase our tonnage to a point commensurate with the enormous demands of the war how can we best economise our prevailing shipping space? By decreasing our food

imports we would have more space for the transport of soldiers and munitions. We have by no means reached the limit in Britain's food production, and this will not happen until every available square yard of our soil is under cultivation. Everybody must know of some field, derelict land or parkland which is not " doing its bit " for victory. It is also a question of time as well as space. Much more food could be produced if the whole agricultural industry were geared to a seven-day week. Saturday afternoons and Sundays should be regarded as normal working hours. Once the principle of week-end work is accepted, arrangements could be made for workers to have a half-day's holiday in rotation. Payment for Sunday work should be at the same rate as the normal weekday hours. At this supreme crisis in our fate the industrial worker, in this respect, should not be in a privileged position as compared with the fighting services. The general application of a seven-day week would enormously increase the working hours over the period of the coming year.

WATCH MADAGASCAR!

In the past year more than 400 French vessels sailed from Mediterranean ports to Madagascar. If this island falls into Axis hands it will be one of the greatest strategic disasters of the war.

HAS Britain learned the real lesson of Japanese aggression ? Are we sufficiently aware that the Japanese onslaught in the southern Pacific is not a local war, but a deep-laid plan, with Hitler, to gain command of the oceans? The fatal weakness of Germany, in her mania for world-power, has always been lack of sea-power. She lost the 1914-18 war because of this. Until Japan struck so successfully against the Allies in the Far East, we could confidently count upon our naval arm as a decisive weapon in ultimate victory. Hitler's main problem has been and still is to cut our sea communications. Without Japan's aid he could not hope to do this, but with his Axis partner " mopping up " ocean bases everywhere Nazi strategy is simplified. The Japanese territorial conquests are immense, but could the Axis gain control of the seas they might realize the dream of dividing the world between them. The American West Pacific bases, with Singapore, Java and Rangoon, have gone. We must make sure that Ceylon and Madagascar do not fall into enemy hands. If the Japs could control Madagascar and its 135 airfields the Allies' lifeline with the Mediterranean and South Russia would be in the gravest jeopardy.

IF INVASION COMES

The new Defence Regulations provide for the conscripting of the services of civilians in threatened areas.

THE Home Guard and A.R.P. services know what to do in the case of invasion, but what about the rest of the public? The original instructions told them to " stay put." Under the new Defence Regulations they can be conscripted, and quite rightly. But the machinery for doing this would appear to be too cumbersome for the rapid mobilization necessary in such an emergency. First, the competent military authority must contact the Regional Commissioner. He, in turn,

Flg. Off. KENNETH CAMPBELL, R.A.F.V.R., awarded the V.C. for most conspicuous bravery. Pilot of a Beaufort aircraft, he made a daring torpedo attack on an enemy battle cruiser in Brest harbour at dawn on April 6, 1941. Despite the formidable defences, he skimmed over the Mole and launched his torpedo at point-blank range. The aircraft did not return.
Photo, British Official: Crown Copyright

contacts the Ministry of Labour, and eventually the local National Service Officer collects and assembles and instructs the workers required. They must be employed only on non-combatant duties, and will be paid at stipulated rates. It might well be asked whether there will be time under the stress of H.E. and probably gas bombs, tanks, machine-guns, flame-throwers for such leisurely bureaucratic niceties. Will the conscripted have to fill up forms and render an account for overtime ? We should all be trained now either as fighters or workers or both, so that we know what to do immediately the detestable foe sets foot upon our sacred shores.

KILLING RUSSIA WITH WORDS

The Bolsheviks who could not defeat the German troops and their allies in one winter, will be annihilatingly defeated by us in the coming summer.
—Hitler, on March 15, 1942

THE British nation has been accused of foolish optimism, and in some respects there has been much wishful thinking and complacency. There is nothing complacent about Mr. Churchill's speeches. He has not hesitated to warn us of the magnitude of our task, nor offered false hopes of easy victory. The supreme and most fatuous optimist in the world is Adolf Hitler, and his super-confidence is not the least of his many serious blunders. He led the German people to think that the war would be over almost before it had begun. They expected it to end with the Polish campaign. Then, 1940 was to be victory year. Something went wrong again. Well, certainly 1941. Having annihilated the Soviet armies in the autumn of 1941, the end was near. But the Russian soldiers mysteriously came to life again and hit back. Moscow, Leningrad, and the Caucasus which, according to Hitler, should be part of the German Reich now, are still in possession of the so-called Bolsheviks. The German armies are being battered, broken and destroyed, though Hitler is gaining many great " defensive victories." When Stalin's soldiers reach the German frontier will the Fuehrer, still regarded by some people as a marvel of genius, talk about defensive victories ? Maybe, by then the hysteria of victory will have changed to hysteria of defeat, for the German mind swings between two extremes.

Admiral HAROLD STARK, who is assuming a new post as Commander of the United States Naval Forces operating in European waters. *Photo, Topical Press*

Australia 'Stripped for War' and 'Fighting Mad'

AUSTRALIAN MANHOOD is well exemplified in these sturdy fellows. Engaged on road-making in the vicinity of Darwin they are "diggers" in both senses of the word, and are verily "stripped for war."

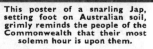

HE'S COMING SOUTH

It's fight work or perish

This poster of a snarling Jap, setting foot on Australian soil, grimly reminds the people of the Commonwealth that their most solemn hour is upon them.

IN a broadcast message to America on March 13, Mr. Curtin, Prime Minister of Australia, urged the necessity for the closest cooperation between his country and the United States. Then, in resolute terms, he restated the Commonwealth's determination to wage war to the uttermost.

Britain has fought and won in the air the tremendous battle of Britain. Britain has fought and with your help has won the equally vital battle of the Atlantic. She has a paramount obligation to supply all possible help to Russia. She cannot at the same time go all out in the Pacific. We are her sons and on us the responsibility falls.

We are as firmly determined to hold and hit back at the enemy as courageously as those people from whose loins we spring, those people who withstood the disaster of Dunkirk, the fury of Goering's blitz, the shattering blows of the battle of the Atlantic. We are fighting mad. Our people have a Government that is governing with orders and not with weak-kneed suggestions. We Australians are a people who, while somewhat inexperienced and uncertain as to what war on their soil may mean, are nevertheless ready for anything, and will trade punches, giving odds if needs be, until we rock the enemy back on his heels.

Out of every 10 men in Australia, four are now wholly engaged in war, as members of the fighting forces or making the munitions and equipment to fight with. The other six, besides feeding and clothing the whole 10 and their families, have to produce the food and wool and metals which Britain needs for her very existence. We are not, of course, stopping at four out of 10. We had over three when Japan challenged our life and liberty ; the proportion is growing every day. We are mobilizing womanpower to the utmost. From four out of 10 devoted to war, we shall pass to five and six. We have no limits.

We have no qualms here. There is no fifth column in this country. We are all the one race, the English-speaking race. We will not yield easily a yard of our soil. We have great space here, and tree by tree, village by village, and town by town we will fall back if we must . . .

MR. J. CURTIN, Australian Prime Minister, speaking at Melbourne. On the left is Mr. N. J. O. Makin, Navy Minister.

Photos, Sport & General

(Continued)

FOR remember, we are the Anzac breed. Our men stormed Gallipoli. They swept through the Libyan Desert. They were the men of Tobruk. They were the men who fought under bitter, sarcastic, pugnacious Gordon Bennett in Malaya and were still fighting when the surrender of Singapore came. These men gave of their best in Greece and Crete. They will give more than their best on their own soil, where their hearths and homes lie under enemy threat.

Our Air Force are in the Kingsford Smith tradition. Our naval forces silently do their share on the Seven Seas. Our fighting forces are born attackers. We will hit the enemy wherever we can, as often as we can, and the extent of it will be measured only by the weapons to our hands.

Australia is a nation stripped for war. Our minds are set on attack rather than defence. We believe, in fact, that attack is the best defence. Here in the Pacific it is the only defence we know. It means risks, but safety first is the devil's catchword to day. Business interests in Australia are submitting with a good grace to iron control and drastic elimination of profits. Our great labour unions are accepting the suspension of rights and privileges which have been sacred for two generations, and are submitting to an equally iron control of the activities of their members. It is now work or fight for every one in Australia.

This war may seem the end of much that we have painfully and slowly built in our 150 years of existence, but even though all of it go, there will still be Australians fighting on Australian soil until the turning-point be reached, and we will advance over blackened ruins through blasted and fireswept cities, across scorched plains, until we drive the enemy into the sea.

Once Again New Guinea Has Scenes of Savagery

SALAMAUA, the airfield of which was seized by the Japanese about March 8, became the seat of administration of the mandated territory of New Guinea in 1938 after the former capital, Rabaul, had been destroyed by volcanic eruption in June 1937. Right, a general view of the new capital.

IT was on Jan. 20 that the first heavy Japanese air attack was made on Rabaul, seaport and chief town of New Britain, largest island of the Bismarck Archipelago in the mandated territory of New Guinea. Two days later a Japanese invasion armada was sighted off the island and landings were effected shortly afterwards. Following this, Japanese landings were made on the neighbouring island of New Guinea and airfields were seized at Lae and Salamaua. The danger to Australia was grave, since New Guinea is separated from Queensland only by the 90-mile-wide Torres Strait. But bombers of the R.A.A.F. and the United States have made daily and continuous attacks upon the Japanese bases, blasting the airfields they occupy and inflicting much damage upon their convoys in the Huon Gulf, betwen New Guinea and New Britain. Australian troops and militia in the Huon Gulf country of N.E. New Guinea waged a steady guerilla warfare against the invaders, retiring into the hills to swoop down upon the Japanese by night. The Japanese occupied Lae and Salamaua about March 8. No infantry infiltration had been made towards Port Moresby a week later.

The main street of Salamaua. Tropical fruits, especially coconuts, grow abundantly, and coffee, cocoa and kapok are also grown.

PORT MORESBY, the harbour. Port Moresby, which lies on the Gulf of Papua, in the Commonwealth Territory of Papua, which is the S.E. part of New Guinea, has been heavily bombed by the Japanese and would provide them with a valuable base for any contemplated invasion of Australia.

MADANG, seaport of New Guinea, on Astrolabe Bay, was the commercial capital of the former German protectorate, Kaiser Wilhelm's Land. It was then known as Friedrich-Wilhelmshafen. On the right, a native Papuan from the Upper Purari river in his war dress.

Photos, Sport & General, E.N.A., Paul Popper

Outstanding Personalities of the Indian Scene

Sir STAFFORD CRIPPS and Mr. M. A. JINNAH, President of the Moslem League, in conversation during Sir Stafford's visit to India in 1939.

Marquess of LINLITHGOW, Viceroy and Governor-General of India since 1936. He is the 33rd to hold an office first filled by Warren Hastings in 1774.

Mr. Jawaharlal NEHRU is leader of the Congress Party, the most powerful organization of the Indian Nationalists.

Gen. Sir A. WAVELL, G.C.B., who was re-appointed C.-in-C. of the army in India in March 1942. He held the position from July 1941 to last January, when he took up the A.B.D.A. Command.

Pandit M. M. MALAVIYA is the 80-year-old leader of the Mahasabha, the anti-Congress party of Orthodox Hindus.

Mrs. Vijayalakshmi PANDIT, elder sister of Mr. Nehru, was the first Congress woman minister.

Rt. Hon. V. S. Srinivasa SASTRI, a Liberal leader and former Indian High Commissioner to S. Africa.

Sir Tej Bahadur SAPRU is perhaps the most famous Indian Liberal. He is an Allahabad lawyer.

Mrs. Sarojini NAIDU, poet and orator, ardent opponent of purdah and child marriage.

Moulana Abul Kalam AZAD (left), the 50-year-old Moslem theologian and philosopher who is the present president of Congress, although this is a predominantly Hindu party. Dr. R. B. AMBEDKAR is the champion of the Untouchables in their revolt against the Indian caste system. Sardar Vallabhbhai PATEL is a Congress leader in Bombay, Madras, Sind and the Central Provinces. Subhas Chandra BOSE (right) is India's most extreme left-wing politician. He has been president of Congress, but for some time past he has found a haven of refuge in Berlin under Nazi patronage.

Photos, Sport & General, Bassano, Fox, Wide World, Associated Press, Topical Press, Planet News, Lafayette

They Speak for the Indians in a Fateful Hour

In the House of Commons on March 11 Mr. Churchill announced that Sir Stafford Cripps was about to go to India, "to satisfy himself upon the spot by personal consultation that the conclusions upon which we are agreed, and which we believe represent a just and final solution [of the Indian question], will achieve their purpose." Some of the persons whom the Lord Privy Seal may be expected to meet are the subject of this article.

AT 4.30 this morning India's most famous personality rose from his bed, said his prayers (devout Hindu that he is), and went for a brisk walk through the dusty and fly-blown little village where he has his home. Arrived back in his cottage—it has been called a hovel—he drank a mug of goat's milk and made a meal of fruit and a handful of dates. Then he sat down at his spinning-wheel, where he does what he would have every Indian peasant do—makes his own *khaddar* (home-spun cloth), or, cross-legged on the mud floor, listened to what a visitor had to say, and in return spoke off his own gospel of India for the Indians—an India from which not only British rule but slums and pestiferous villages have been banished, and the man of high caste goes into the temple side by side with the man of low caste, even the untouchable.

Mr. Gandhi is in his early seventies. He was born in 1869 of a well-to-do family, and at 19 went to England, where he was a student at University College and was called to the Bar by the Inner Temple. Then in 1893 he went to South Africa, where he won fame not only as a lawyer but as a champion of the rights of the Indian settlers. During the Boer War he organized and led a Red Cross unit in the field. Then in 1914 he returned to India, and soon won by common consent the leadership of the Nationalist movement. He it was who, rejecting any thought of an armed revolt, instituted the campaign of non-violent disobedience (*satyagraha*) to the laws imposed by British rule, and in 1922, and again in 1930 and 1933, he was sentenced to imprisonment for his anti-Government activities. In 1924 he was President of the Indian National Congress, and throughout the twenties he was at the height of his power. More than once he has expressed a will to retire from politics and has withdrawn into what he hoped would be obscurity, only to be drawn back into the political vortex. At present he holds no official position in the Nationalist movement, but still he is the apostle of passive resistance to the British Raj. Yet although he hates British Imperialism he has no hate for the British themselves. Deeply religious—not for nothing has he been given the title of Mahatma (Great Soul)—he is yet completely opposed to caste, that basic principle of Hinduism. By all save a handful of India's 400 millions—by Moslems as well as by Hindus, by the men of high caste and of none, and no less by the British community—he is held in the highest reverence. Not since Buddha died, it has been said, has an Indian been so loved.

Nehru's Vision of a New India

If Mr. Gandhi is the most famous of present-day Indians, it may be claimed that the most powerful personality is Mr. Jawaharlal Nehru: certainly he is the most interesting, since in him East and West are fascinatingly intermingled. He comes of an old and very wealthy family of one of the highest castes, the Kashmiri Brahmins, so that the blood which runs in his veins is some of India's bluest. From childhood he had an English tutor, and in 1905, when he was 16—he was born in 1889, the same year as Hitler—he was sent to England and followed the road which leads through Harrow to Trinity College, Cambridge, and the English Bar. He learnt to appreciate England, and in particular English literature; it has been said that hardly a dozen men alive write English as well as he. Returning to India in 1912 he flung himself with all the

ardent enthusiasm of youth into the Nationalist movement, and soon came to be regarded as an extremist; altogether he has spent seven years in gaol because of his part in the civil disobedience campaign.

But Nehru is more than a Nationalist; this leader of the peoples who are literally saturated with religion is an agnostic, while in political matters he is a socialist—and there are not many socialists in India. "I see no way of ending the poverty, the vast

MR. GANDHI has been for many years the uncrowned king of India's many millions. Above we see him on a visit to Simla in 1939.
Photo, Fox

unemployment, the degradation and the subjection of the Indian people, except through Socialism," he has written in his autobiography. He advocates disarmament, but he is no pacifist; like Mr. H. G. Wells he believes that national armies should be abolished, and that an international air force should police the world. There is no Indian more anti-Nazi, more anti-Fascist, more anti-totalitarian than Nehru, yet by an unhappy paradox he ranks amongst Britain's most bitter opponents. In this war all his sympathies are with Britain and her allies, yet only recently was he released from the prison to which he had been sentenced for urging Indians to take no part in the war effort. The goal of India, he has said, is a "united, free, democratic country, closely associated in a world federation with other free nations. We want independence, but not the old type of narrow, exclusive independence. We believe that the day of separate warring national states is over."

More than any man in India, Nehru represents Congress, the largest of the Indian political parties and ever since its

foundation in 1885 by a retired Anglo-Indian Civil Servant, the main instrument and expression of Indian Nationalism. Its membership runs into three or four millions, less than 1 per cent of the total population, although (such is the poverty of the Indian masses) quite a considerable proportion of these are not able to afford the annual subscription of 4 annas (say 5d.). At the base of the Congress structure are the individual members in the towns and villages; these choose delegates to Congress committees in the provincial capitals, which in turn choose the All-India Congress Committee. This committee appoints the President—Nehru has held the position four times, a quite exceptional honour—who with 14 associates forms the Congress Working Committee. The present President of Congress is M. Abul Azad. He is a Moslem, which is a reminder of the fact that though the great majority of Congress members are Hindus, its membership also includes many Moslems. Other outstanding Congress personalities include Sardar Vallabhbhai Patel, a leading right winger; Babu Rajendra Prasad, a past President; Khan Abdul Gaffar Khan, a leader of the Moslem element; Bhulabhai J. Desai; Chakravarti Rajagopalacharia, former Premier of Madras; and the poetess-social reformer, Mrs. Sarojini Naidu.

Spokesmen of the Moslems

Next in size and importance to Congress is the Moslem League, which is as strong in its demand for Indian independence as Congress, yet declares its strongest opposition to any scheme for an All-India parliament, since this (it maintains) would involve the domination of the Moslems by the Hindu majority; hence it advocates the establishment of a Moslem-controlled state, comprising the provinces of Sind, the Punjab, and the North-West Frontier, with the Indian state of Kashmir and possibly Afghanistan. This demand for Pakistan, as it is called, is most closely associated with the name of Mr. Mohammed Ali Jinnah, the League's President. But of India's 90 million Moslems, less than one per cent are members of the Moslem League; and the Premiers of Sind, Bengal and Punjab (Mr. Allah Bakhsh, Mr. Fazlul Huq, and Sir Sikander Hyat Khan) have declared themselves opposed to Pakistan, although in each of these provinces there is a Moslem government.

Although Congress and the Moslem League are by far the most powerful of India's political parties, there are several others. The Mahasabha is the orthodox Hindu party; it is much more conservative than Congress and strongly opposed to it, chiefly because Congress leaders are apt to be somewhat lax in the matter of caste distinctions. Its most prominent figure is Pandit Malaviya, who has been twice President of Congress and is famous as a scholar. Then there is the National Liberal Federation, among whose most prominent members are Sir Tej Bahadur Sapru, Mr. M. J. Jayaker, and Rt. Hon. Srinivasa Sastri. As a rule, the Liberals are prepared to work in close cooperation with the British and favour Dominion Status as the immediate goal rather than complete independence. There is also an Indian Socialist group which strives to influence Congress in a socialistic direction from within. Finally, there are the Untouchables, although these are a class rather than a party. Their spokesman is the prominent lawyer, Dr. B. R. Ambedkar, who, the son of a poor "Untouchable," has waged relentless war on caste.　E. R. P

Photo, W. Bosshard

India Dreams of—Dominion

Since 1911, Delhi, the old Mogul capital of India, has again become the Imperial capital of India, and outside the old city, in what is known as New Delhi, stand the legislative buildings seen above, in architectural style a blending of East and West, expressive of a cooperation between Briton and Indian which should be the keynote of Indian administration.

Photos, Courtesy of High Commissioner
for India, Paul Popper, Fox

From Cities of 'Richest Ind'

1, Assembly Building, formerly the Senate House, of Madras, capital of the Madras Presidency.   2, Modern office block in Chowringhee Road, the main thoroughfare of Calcutta; very different are the shops and houses in the purely Indian quarter.   3, The Babu Ghat on the Hooghli River, where the natives of Calcutta seek relief from the torrid heat.

Great Centres of Imperial Rule

Photos, Dorien Leigh, Lubinski

4, The Char Minar, focal point of the life of Hyderabad, capital of the state of that name and the residence of the wealthy Nizam. 5, The natural harbour of Trincomalee, on the north-east side of the island of Ceylon. 6, New Delhi, the circular Council House, comprising buildings erected for the Legislative Assembly, and the Chamber of Princes.

India—Old and New

Photos, Dorien Leigh, Fox

The smoking chimneys of the Tatanagar iron and steel works at Jamshedpur, Calcutta, largest industrial plant in India, which symbolize India's great arms-production effort, are in striking contrast to the peaceful, age-old scene of an Indian ricefield.   But while India's potential economic resources are enormous, they are still largely undeveloped.

Fierce and Bloody Battle in the Java Sea

The Battle of the Java Sea was a heavy defeat for the United Nations, since all but one of the thirteen warships of the Allied squadron that went into action against the Japanese were sent to the bottom. Here is the story, reminiscent in its grimness of Jutland 26 years ago, as told in an Admiralty communiqué issued on March 14.

Although full information is not yet available, it is now possible to give some account, so far as particulars are at present to hand, of the events in the Java Sea on Feb. 27 and subsequent days, during the Japanese invasion of Java.

On the afternoon of Friday, Feb. 27, an Allied force, consisting of H.M.A.S. Perth (Captain H. M. L. Waller, D.S.O., R.A.N.), H.M.S. Exeter (Captain O. L. Gordon, M.V.O., R.N.), the United States cruiser Houston, and the Dutch cruisers De Ruyter and Java, was at sea north of Surabaya. The Allied cruisers were accompanied by the destroyers H.M.S. Electra (Commander C. W. May, R.N.), H.M.S. Jupiter (Lt.-Com. J. V. J. T. Thew, R.N.), and H.M.S. Encounter (Lt.-Com. E. V. St. J. Morgan, R.N.), and the Dutch destroyer Kortenaer. This force was under the sea command of Admiral Doorman, whose flag was flying in the De Ruyter. The whole naval force in the area was under the strategical control of Admiral Helfrich, of the Royal Netherlands Navy.

At 4.14 p.m. on Feb. 27 this Allied force made contact with a Japanese force about half-way between Bawean Island and Surabaya. The Japanese force consisted of at least two Nati class cruisers of 10,000 tons armed with ten 8-in. guns, and a number of other cruisers. The Japanese cruisers had with them thirteen destroyers organized in two flotillas.

Action was joined at extreme range. Almost at once one of the Japanese destroyer flotillas launched an attack, but this was driven off by the fire of the Allied cruisers, and one of the enemy destroyers was seen to be hit by shells from H.M.A.S. Perth. Soon afterwards the other Japanese destroyer flotilla delivered a torpedo attack. While action was being taken to avoid these torpedoes, H.M.S. Exeter was hit by an 8-inch shell in a boiler-room. This reduced her speed and forced her to drop out of the line. Only one of the torpedoes launched in this attack took effect. This hit the Dutch destroyer Kortenaer, and she sank.

The three British destroyers were ordered to counter-attack the Japanese destroyers, who were retiring under cover of a smoke-screen. Very little information is available about the result of this counter-attack. H.M.S. Jupiter reported seeing only two enemy destroyers, both of which she engaged with gunfire. H.M.S. Electra was not seen after she had disappeared into the smoke screen, and it is presumed that she was sunk.

As soon as the Allied cruisers, except H.M.S. Exeter, who was unable to keep up, drew clear of the smoke, they again engaged the enemy, this time at shorter range. Less than half-an-hour later the enemy cruisers turned away under cover of a smoke screen. It was seen that one of the enemy heavy 8-in. gun cruisers had been hit, and was burning fiercely. Admiral Doorman led his force round, and chased the enemy to the north-eastward, but he failed to regain touch with them in the fading light.

THE JAPS HAD 105 WARSHIPS

From the outset we sought the offensive and struck the aggressor blow upon blow during the period in which the Outer Provinces, where less strong defences were disposed, were lost one after the other as had been foreseen.

Java, the barrier, remained. It remained until Friday and Saturday, Feb. 27 and 28, 1942, when Helfrich, then in command of the joint naval forces, was forced to battle with a Japanese armada convoying 60 troop carriers on their way to the north coast of Java. At that moment the Japanese had 14 cruisers, 55 destroyers, 25 submarines, 5 aircraft-carriers and 6 seacraft-carriers, i.e. more than 100 warships, in our East Indian waters.

The battle against the Japanese fleet had success, but the attempt against the troop-carriers, which were shielded by a front of submarines, failed. A large part of the Allied fleet, the strength of which was less than one-third of the enemy's naval forces, was lost.

Dr. P. S. Gerbrandy, Netherlands Prime Minister, in a broadcast to the Dutch people, March 11, 1942.

After nightfall the Allied cruisers sighted four enemy ships to the westward, and engaged them, with what results is not known. Admiral Doorman attempted to work round these enemy ships in order to locate the convoy, which was expected to be to the northward. This was found to be impracticable owing to the high speed of the enemy, and Admiral Doorman then turned his force to the southward to close the coast of Java, intending to sweep to the westward along the coast in an attempt to intercept the Japanese invasion convoys.

Half-an-hour after the Allied force had turned to the westward along the coast of Java H.M.S. Jupiter was disabled by an under-water explosion. She sank four hours later. H.M.S. Jupiter was not far from the mainland of Java, and a number of survivors have already reached Australia.

At 11.30 p.m., when the Allied cruisers were about twelve miles north of Rembang, two enemy cruisers were sighted between our ships and the coast. They were at once engaged, and a number of hits were secured on the enemy. The De Ruyter was hit by one shell. Immediately afterwards the De Ruyter made a large alteration of course, presumably to avoid torpedoes fired by the enemy. The other Allied cruisers were conforming when underwater explosions occurred simultaneously in the De Ruyter and Java. Both these Dutch cruisers blew up and sank at once.

It is impossible to assess with accuracy the damage inflicted upon the enemy during the actions on Feb. 27. Observers in H.M.A.S. Perth considered that one Japanese 8-in. gun cruiser had been sunk, a second 8-in. gun cruiser damaged, and a destroyer sunk. It has also been reported that a cruiser of the Mogami class (8,500 tons, fifteen 6·1-in. guns) was set on fire, and three destroyers seriously damaged and left on fire or sinking. H.M.A.S. Perth, who had received some damage, reached Tanjong Priok at seven o'clock in the morning of Saturday, Feb. 28. With the enemy in command of the sea and air north of Java in overwhelming force, the Allied Command was faced with the problem of extricating the remaining Allied ships from a very dangerous situation. The way to Australia was barred by the 600 miles long island of Java, with the straits at either end of it under enemy control.

After dark on Feb. 28 H.M.A.S. Perth left Tanjong Priok with the intention of passing through the Sunda Strait during the dark hours. During the night a report was received from H.M.A.S. Perth which indicated that she had come into contact with a force of Japanese ships off St. Nicholas Point at about 1 p.m. Nothing, however, has been heard of H.M.A.S. Perth or the U.S. cruiser Houston since that time.

The same night H.M.S. Exeter, who was unable to exceed half speed, left Surabaya accompanied by H.M.S. Encounter and the U.S. destroyer Pope. At forenoon on Sunday, March 1, H.M.S. Exeter reported that she had sighted three enemy cruisers steering towards her. No further signals were received from H.M.S. Exeter, H.M.S. Encounter, or the U.S. destroyer Pope. The Dutch destroyer Evertsen encountered two Japanese cruisers in the Sunda Strait. She was damaged and was beached. The destroyer H.M.A.S. Stronghold (Lt.-Com. G. R. Pretor-Pinney, R.N.) and the sloop H.M.S. Yarra (Lt.-Com. R. W. Rankin, R.A.N.), are also missing and must be considered lost. It has not been possible to form any estimate of the damage inflicted on the enemy by these ships during their last actions.

LOST WARSHIPS of the Allies, sunk during the action in the Java Seas. Top, the Dutch cruiser De Ruyter, 6,450 tons, flagship of Admiral Doorman. Left, H.M.A.S. Perth, 6,980 tons. Right, H.M.S. Exeter, 8,390 tons. Admiral Sir W. James, C.-in-Chief, Portsmouth, described the battles in the Java Sea as " among the fiercest and bloodiest battles ever known .... the Dutch, British and American sailors fought to the last gun against impossible odds."

Photos, Wright & Logan, Sport & General

'Smite the Enemy Day and Night' Said Stalin

RED ARMY SKIERS before Moscow. As related in pages 492-493, Russia's specially-trained ski troops have played a great part in the Soviet's counter-offensive. Thousands of them have been training in Siberia.

MACHINE-GUNNERS of the Red Army in their emplacements near the village P. Though Hitler has "annihilated" the Red Army five times in his communiqués, it continues to advance westwards !

SOVIET ARMOURED CARS advancing over the snow through a forest on the Eastern Front, proceded by motor-cyclists. Soon they will help to liberate another Russian town or village.

WRECKED SUPPLY TRAIN of the Nazis, caught by Russian fire. Above, right, German trenches in a wood on the Russian Front. Stalin's instructions to his bombers are : "Smite the enemy incessantly day and night, without giving him time to recover, destroying his fortified bases and depriving him of the possibility of bringing up reserves."

Photos, British Official : Crown Copyright ; Planet News, Sport & General

'We Shall Forget or Forgive Nothing'

THIS RUSSIAN PEASANT, her home in flames, stands in the snow, pathetic witness of the destructive fury of the invaders of her country. Of the "universal robbery, devastation, abominable violence, outrages and massacres perpetrated by the German Fascist invaders against the peaceful population" Mr. Molotov gave a lengthy account in the Note he sent to all Governments with which the U.S.S.R. has diplomatic relations. And as *Pravda* stated on Jan. 5, "We shall forget nothing, we shall forgive nothing. Not one single atrocity will remain unavenged." *Photo. Keystone*

Our Diary of the War

TUESDAY, MAR. 10, 1942   920th day

Air.—R.A.F. bombers raided targets in the Ruhr at night.

Russian Front.—More localities on the Leningrad front captured by the Red Army.

Mediterranean.—Cairo announced that a cruiser, a merchant vessel, and a destroyer were torpedoed and set on fire by British aircraft.

Far East.—R.A.A.F. bombers heavily attacked Japanese invasion forces in New Guinea. Port Moresby raided by Japs for tenth time. Japs made a further landing on New Guinea at Finschhafen.

Home.—Mr. Eden told the House of atrocities committed by the Japanese on the garrison at Hongkong.

WEDNESDAY, MAR. 11   921st day

Russian Front.—Red Army breached a strongly fortified line on the Kalinin front.

Africa.—Free French announced capture of Axis outpost at Temessa.

Far East.—Army communiqué stated that fresh Japanese landings had been made in the Irrawaddy delta. Australian and American bombers carried out dawn to dusk attack on Japanese forces in New Guinea.

Home.—Mr. Churchill announced that Sir Stafford Cripps would go to India to negotiate on Government plan to end the long constitutional deadlock. Greek Maritime Court opened in London.

THURSDAY, MAR. 12   922nd day

Air.—R.A.F. made night raid on Kiel and other targets in N.W. Germany.

Russian Front.—Local successes by Soviet troops in several areas.

Far East.—Relentless air attack on Japanese in New Guinea continued. Thirteen enemy ships reported sunk or put out of action. Washington reported that a U.S. submarine had sunk three enemy freighters, and one passenger and cargo ship in Japanese waters.

Home.—Enemy aircraft shot down off Welsh coast.

FRIDAY, MAR. 13   923rd day

Air.—R.A.F. bombers attacked marshalling yards at Hazebrouck. Night raid on Cologne.

Russian Front.—Gigantic battles raging along the whole front. Several important points recaptured on the Donetz front.

Far East.—Operations proceeding in Burma in the Nyaungebin–Shwegyin area. U.S. Flying Fortresses blasted Jap airfields at Lae and Salamaua in New Guinea. Tokyo claimed occupation of Medan, capital of Sumatra.

SATURDAY, MAR. 14   924th day

Sea.—Admiralty communiqué on the three-day battle of the Java Sea gave Allied losses as twelve ships. British: Cruiser Exeter; Destroyers Electra, Jupiter, Encounter and Stronghold. Australian: Cruiser Perth and Sloop Yarra. U.S.: Cruiser Houston and Destroyer Pope Dutch: Cruisers Java and De Ruyter; Destroyer Kortenaer. Japanese losses not known. In English Channel, two E-boats sunk by surface patrols.

Air.—R.A.F. fighters destroyed 10 enemy aircraft without loss to themselves during offensive sweep over Channel.

Russian Front.—New Russian attack in Crimea.

Far East.—Officially disclosed that large contingents of U.S. troops were in Australia. In Burma, Jap patrols moving in direction of Taikkyi.

Home.—Enemy raiders over S.W. England at night.

SUNDAY, MAR. 15   925th day

Sea.—Five German E-boats sunk and five damaged by Navy and R.A.F. in night to dawn fight in the Channel. Destroyer Vortigern lost.

Russian Front.—Big Crimea battle continued. On central sector Red Army attacked Olshanks and Chotinetz, S.W. and N.W. of Orel. Railway to Kursk reported cut.

Africa.—R.A.F. carried out big daylight air raid on Martuba aerodrome in Libya.

Far East.—Gasmata and Rabaul heavily bombed by Australian and American bombers. In Burma, R.A.F. continued to hammer Jap concentrations and supplies.

General.—Hitler made excuses for Russian failure in speech at Berlin.

MONDAY, MAR. 16   926th day

Russian Front.—Soviet troops captured a number of villages in various sectors. Capture of a Black Sea port announced by Moscow radio.

Mediterranean.—Island of Rhodes attacked by British bombers and naval units before dawn.

Far East.—Jap fleet movements reported off W. Australia. Rabaul and Gasmata again bombed by R.A.A.F.

TUESDAY, MAR. 17   927th day

Russian Front.—Soviet communiqué stated that Russian forces had broken through enemy defensive positions on the S.W. sector of the front. Big-scale battle for Kharkov developed.

Africa.—Cairo communiqué reported repulse of strong enemy column in the Cherima area, 20 miles south of Tmimi.

Far East.—U.S. announced that Gen. MacArthur had been appointed Supreme Commander of all the United Nations Forces in the S.W. Pacific. Maj.-Gen. John Wainwright to command in the Philippines.

WEDNESDAY, MAR. 18   928th day

Russian Front.—Stalin's armies closed in still further on the Rjev-Vyazma pocket. Gzhatsk reported encircled by Red troops.

Far East.—Communiqué from Sydney announced that 23 Jap ships had been destroyed in Allied air raids on Salamaua and Lae, in New Guinea. In Burma, Japs advancing up Irrawaddy river. Allied troops in action south of Kanyutkwin.

Home.—Bombs dropped at night near S.W. coast of England.

THURSDAY, MAR. 19   929th day

Russian Front.—Big battle in progress around the Smolensk road. Battle for Kharkov continued.

Far East.—American general, Lt.-Gen. Joseph Stillwell, appointed Commander of the Fifth and Sixth Chinese Armies in Burma.

Home.—A few bombs dropped at night in rural areas of S.W. England.

General.—Mr. R. G. Casey, Australia's Minister in Washington, appointed Minister of State and representative of the British War Cabinet in the Middle East.

ANY OLD CLOTHES ?—FOR NAZIS

FOUR days before Christmas, 1941, Dr. Goebbels announced a collection of winter clothing and skis for the troops fighting on the Russian front. The newspapers spent a day or so explaining why it should be necessary to take such a step on behalf of an army so well-equipped as the German army was supposed to be, and why it had not been done earlier. Then the Nazi Party apparatus set itself in motion.

A considerable degree of pressure was employed, and it was made clear that counter-propaganda and sabotage, and theft of the articles collected, would be punished with death. Some of the provincial newspapers printed the names and addresses of families who gave little or nothing, and in some cases the refractory were arrested as saboteurs. In Silesia workers who were able to prove that they had no articles of clothing they could spare were forced to hand over 10 marks and a number of clothing coupons. But the wireless was careful to announce that expensive furs need not be given up, as they were too valuable a part of the national wealth.

The general public showed little trust in the collectors. Some persons insisted on having receipts for the articles handed over, while others sewed labels with their names and addresses into the garments, though this was forbidden. Skis and furs belonging to Poles and Jews, both in Germany and Poland, were simply confiscated. Industrial undertakings and wholesalers had to give up a part of their stocks—two per cent in the clothing industry. After the collection had been extended for a further week it was announced that 56,000,000 warm garments had been collected, among them 2,900,000 fur garments, 1,800,000 pairs of underpants, 2,400,000 ear protectors, etc. It appears that each sock and glove was counted as a separate garment.

The Nazi Party naturally made as much propaganda about the affair as possible. New trainloads of troops off for the front were publicly equipped at the railway stations. The broadcasting stations gushed. " You should have seen the joy of the soldiers, it was simply unbelievable," said a speaker over the Frankfurt radio on January 9. But for the most part the army had the job of sorting out the garments and distributing them, and a considerable part of the woollen articles found their way into the shoddy mills.

COLLECTIONS were made in twelve different countries. In Norway the police had already confiscated blankets as far back as October. In November the Rumanian Government had insisted on all Jews giving up a part of their clothing for the army ; Jews who were so poor as not to be liable for income tax were required to give up at least a shirt, a pair of underpants, a pair of socks, two handkerchiefs and a towel ; those who had none to spare had to buy them. During the new collection all Rumanians had to give up a blanket, two pairs of socks and two pairs of woollen gloves. The garments were collected by committees which were always accompanied by policemen. In Bulgaria money was collected to buy sheepskins. Belgian and Spanish Fascists organized collections for their own legionaries, and Slovaks and Croats for soldiers of their own nationality in Hitler's army in Russia. In Holland, Sweden and Switzerland collections were organized by Germans, but the Swedish Government forbade the export of the articles collected. In the Bohemian Protectorate the puppet President Hacha also organized a collection for the German soldiers.—I.T.F.

'A Foreign Field that Is for Ever England'

WAR GRAVES OF TOBRUK where lie, far from England's shores, those men of the British and Imperial Forces who fell in a siege which formed one of the most glorious pages in Britain's military history. To quote the famous lines of Laurence Binyon—" They shall not grow old as we that are left grow old : Age shall not weary them, nor the years condemn."

Photo, British Official : Crown Copyright

French Papers Published at the Risk of Death

There is no liberty of the press in present-day France. The recognized newspapers which still appear in that unhappy country are Nazi-inspired and Nazi-controlled. Nevertheless, throughout the land, in both occupied and unoccupied zones, Frenchmen, at great risk, print and distribute clandestine broadsheets which tell the truth about what is going on in their own country and the outside world.

IT is said in St. John : " the truth shall make you free," and today all Frenchmen who hope for freedom are risking imprisonment, if not their lives, to print, distribute or secure a copy of the secret newssheets which alone have dared to print the truth. Despite the dire penalties which threaten all those people found to be in possession of these clandestine publications, they are distributed in thousands under the very eyes of the Nazis and of the police.

There are scores of these illegal news-sheets and pamphlets. Some of them are cyclostyled ; some are hand printed from toy printing sets ; others are printed on presses assembled from parts got together at great risk, and with great difficulty. Here are the titles of some of them : *L'Humanité, Pantagruel, Valmy, Résistance, L'Ordre Nouveau, Liberté, Peuple de France, Libération, Le Feu, La Voix de Paris, La Guerre Continue, La France Continue, Les Petites Ailes de France.* Many bear a motto or device which illustrates their tendency. Thus *Liberté* prints at the top of the page Foch's dictum : " A nation is never conquered until it accepts to be."

To avoid discovery by the police these underground publications must be continually on the move. Thus it is no uncommon thing to find on some of them, like *La Voix de Paris*, the mention, after the date : *Après le 32me déménagement* (After the 32nd move). Passed on from hand to hand, these newssheets keep their countrymen informed of what is really going on in their own land, of the double-dealings of the traitors of Vichy, of the mass executions of which no details are officially made public, and of the need of continued resistance, even though passive, against the invaders.

How one of these papers—*Valmy* —was produced has been related in the newspaper France, published in London, by the man who risked his life for months to issue it, M. Paul Simon, a Frenchman who won the *Médaille Militaire* in the last war. Here is part of his story :

" The first two numbers were made with the help of one of those toy printing sets the rubber type of which is placed in a tiny four-line composing stick. The first number, of which fifty copies were printed and hand-corrected, was a month's work. The title was stencilled. The second issue took just about as long but this time we printed a hundred copies. The work was done in my dining-room. There were four or five of us busy on it, including one woman. For the second number we ran out of printing ink. This was a serious matter, since to obtain any more we should have had to ask for a buyer's permit from the police, a step which, as you will understand, we hardly felt inclined to take. The third and fourth numbers were typewritten, 150 and 300 copies respectively being printed. But there was a far greater number than this in circulation. In large private businesses the employees copied them either on the typewriter or duplicating machine so that often the copies were far better than the original. Typists would pass a whole day tapping them out, often with the tacit approval of their employers."

Now arose the question of distribution. M. Simon and his assistants applied the principle of the pentagon. Each of the five members of the original group was given a certain number of copies. He would then start other groups, the members of which would, in turn, start others, so that they themselves didn't know who the distributors were, and many times M. Simon was himself offered a copy of *Valmy*. What the total circulation of the paper and its copies was he has no idea, but one single organization managed to print 10,000 copies of each number.

" We ourselves (to continue our quotation) printed 500 and 2,000 copies respectively of numbers 5 and 6 with a stencil and a roller squeegee. Then we ran out of ink again, but managed to procure some from German offices. On July 14 (French national fête) *Valmy* appeared on blue paper with red and white lines and this time was

CLANDESTINE PAPERS which Frenchmen risk their lives to print and distribute. These and the voice of the B.B.C. are the only means by which Frenchman can get to know the truth.
By courtesy of La France Libre

printed in a real printing works. But from August onwards repression became very stringent. One never knew, on leaving in the morning, whether one would not be arrested before night. Our October number we had to burn as a result of a sudden alert. In November we found ourselves without a printer as ours went out of business. We found another, but one fine day the printer's daughter, frightened, threatened to denounce us. So we decided to go back to our old methods. The next issue was due to appear on a Saturday afternoon before Christmas. On the Friday I got wind of the news that I was to be arrested, so I immediately disappeared. I had learned a week previously that the editor of another clandestine newspaper had been shot.

" We received much anonymous help. Our paper was given away, not sold. The cost was at first met from our own pockets, but soon we received many gifts and our expenses were largely covered by the voluntary participation of the public. If such a thing were necessary, this in itself would be a proof of how the people of France are resisting the invader."

Another of these underground newspapers, *Libération*, gave the first eye-witness account of the execution of French hostages at Nantes, telling how the men were led to a quarry and there massed against the walls while a machine-gun opened fire upon them : " An hour later," goes on the story, " lorries arrived and young and old were carted away, leaving behind a trail of blood and against the wall of the quarry dark pools of blood and crimson patches on the quarry walls.

" Next day thousands of people came with flowers and covered the bloodstained stones. These flowers are a pledge of revenge, a pledge that will be kept before long. A few days later the Nantes Kommandatur published a list of 48 names. Two names were missing and will not be revealed. The Germans are ashamed to admit that the two names were those of women."

Valmy was the second clandestine paper to be printed in occupied France. The first was *Pantagruel*. This paper, in one of its first numbers, commented thus on the bombing of French ports by the R.A.F. : " If we admit that the English are fighting for us at the same time as for themselves, and that is the true case, they are no more to be blamed than our own soldiers who blew up our bridges and destroyed our fortresses. That is one of the unhappy necessities inherent in war, and one can only judge them with fairness in recalling the reasons which dictate the acts." That is good sense and sound patriotism. " It is our ardent hope," states *Pantagruel*, " that an English victory will save France from the loss of several of her provinces, her colonies, from economic slavery and from forced inflation."

Here are some typical comments from other clandestine papers : *La Guerre Continue*: " Marshal Bugeaud, who conquered that North Africa which we are now handing over to Germany, liked to say—' An army of sheep led by a lion is more to be feared than an army of lions led by an ass.' The English have Churchill ; we have Darlan."

L'Ordre Nouveau : " When the Germans and their agents talk of a New Order—an order under which apparently nothing works and one dies of hunger—when they talk of ' collaboration,' it is well to remember the declarations these same Germans have themselves made and which are being repeated in Germany today. Here are some samples :

' We must show that we are in this world to be masters of it, and that we dominate Europe.'
Deutsche Allgemeine Zeitung. Oct. 1940.

' After the war Germany must digest all the conquered territories.'
Voelkischer Beobachter. July 20, 1940.

' After the war, when we need labour, it is clear that the German workers must have the lion's part and that foreigners will only be employed as unskilled labourers.'
Das Schwarze Korps. Nov. 21, 1940."

Despite all the efforts of the German and Vichy authorities to stamp them out, the forbidden pamphlets still pass from hand to hand, ill-printed proofs that " great is Truth, and mighty above all things."

Who Were the Real Criminals at Riom?

GUARDED COURT HOUSE at Riom at the opening of the "Supreme Court," when MM. Daladier, Blum, Guy la Chambre, Jacomet and Gen. Gamelin were arraigned on charges of war guilt. Right, Admiral Herr (in uniform), one of the judges, entering the Court House.

AT Riom, little town in the department of Cantal, in unoccupied France, began on Feb. 19 the much publicized and long deferred trial of MM. Daladier and Blum, former French premiers, M. Guy la Chambre, former Air Minister, General Gamelin, generalissimo of the French armies at the beginning of the Battle of France, and M. Jacomet, former War Minister. They are arraigned on charges of war guilt. M. Pierre Cot, also accused, is at present in America. Two members of the French Government which was in power shortly before the capitulation, M. Reynaud, former French premier, and M. Mandel, Minister of the Interior, are confined in the fortress of Portalet on charges which have not yet been fully defined. The Riom trial was instituted at the instigation of the Germans, who wished France, by a solemn verdict, to admit her responsibility for the war. The Vichy government, faced with a growing spirit of resistance in France, dared not openly lead the debates into this channel. Instead, it pursued the course of seeking to place upon the accused the responsibilities for France's defeat and took the opportunity thus afforded it of wreaking vengeance upon its political adversaries.

THE RIOM TRIALS opened on Feb. 19. In this photograph, the only one allowed to be taken in the Court Room, are seen eight of the nine judges, including the president of the Court, M. Caous, who are trying former members of the French government. On the left is the Prosecuting Attorney, M. Cassagneau.

Photos, Associated Press

AFTER THE PARIS RAID on the night of March 3, when bombers of the R.A.F. destroyed the Renault factory at Billancourt which was turning out tanks for Germany. This photograph, taken from an R.A.F. reconnaissance plane which flew over the works on the following day, shows the still smouldering ruins and the complete destruction caused to the factory buildings after the R.A.F. crews had, to use their own words, "pranged it." A marks the gaping hole in the top of the gasometer, and the letters B indicate wrecked tanks in an assembly shop which was entirely destroyed by fire. This shop was producing 27 tanks a week for Germany. A chaos of wreckage remains of what were once engine shops, rolling mills, stores departments, modelling departments, assembly shops, repair shops and foundries.

Photo, British Official

These French Factories Worked for Hitler!

BOMBS ON POISSY, near Paris, where Boston bombers of the R.A.F. attacked the Matford factory on the afternoon of March 8. This factory was engaged on the production of army lorries and transport vehicles for the Nazis.

DAMAGE AT BILLANCOURT after the R.A.F. had bombed the Renault works (see also photograph in page 602). These are the gutted foundries and rolling mills.

RAIDED RENAULT WORKS are shown again in the lower photographs. Circle left, the tank assembly shops, with many of the tanks clearly visible amid the wreckage. Above, I denotes the still smouldering ruins of workshops; 2, wreckage of the modelling department. *Photos, British Official: Crown Copyright* **Page 603**

Short Shrift for 'Black Market' Traitors!

There's a battle being waged in Britain—a battle, to use the vivid phraseology of Admiral Sir William James, quoted below, of the People against the Parasites. Here we give an account of a few of the shameful activities of the "black marketeers."

OF late weeks the British public has woken to the fact that a dangerous form of Fifth Columnism has developed in our very midst. The "Black Market" traitors have so increased in numbers and entrenched themselves that, though thousands of convictions have already taken place, very many more cases are still awaiting settlement before the Courts of Justice.

An underground organization has been gnawing into the vitals of the people's morale like an ever-growing colony of rodents. So widespread and mysterious have been its ramifications that in the existing state of the law it was very difficult to abolish it. Not a day has passed but somebody has been prosecuted or imprisoned. The "small fry" have paid their fines or gone to gaol, but the "big bosses" behind the scenes have not infrequently managed to escape.

Black-market trade has become a form of profiteering far more vicious than ever occurred in the last war. In the first place, it is definitely illegal. In the second, it causes unrest by interfering with the excellent system of rationing and inducing people to break the law. Hardly surprising, then, that normal, decent, patriotic citizens have been nauseated by the unending list of prosecutions and the trivial punishments awarded, and have expressed their indignation that such treachery and corruption could flourish, especially at a time when Britain was threatened as never before in her history.

To what end, they ask, are our seamen facing death by night and day to bring in the food necessary to our salvation if such vermin as the black-market dealers are allowed to wax fat upon this scandalous business? Said the Chairman of the South Shields Food Committee recently, "We've shed more blood and tears than any other seafaring town, just so that this country can get its food. We are not going to be kind to the traders who exploit it. We can't rely on magistrates any more. They just inflict paltry fines."

Food, clothes, petrol, whisky—everything controlled or uncontrolled—apparently they can, or could, be had in large quantities if people were prepared to pay the price demanded. Shoppers have been encouraged to defeat the law by dishonest shopkeepers, and in some places regular days when these offences could be committed with impunity have become part of a commercial routine.

How have the black markets, which range over the length and breadth of Britain to a lesser or greater extent, been kept supplied? There is little doubt that the basis of this traffic was in an organized system of wholesale theft. Here are some figures: A Great Western Railway official has said that £200,000 worth of merchandize had been stolen during the year 1941, and over 1,000 arrests had been made. The Southern Railway has lost £160,000 worth of goods, and the value of pilfering on the L.N.E.R. has amounted to £300,000. The corresponding figure for the L.M.S. is more than £500,000.

It must be remembered that the railways have been largely denuded of their permanent, fully responsible staff, and have had to employ a number of temporary hands.

The docks provide an obvious and fruitful source for goods for the racketeers. From five ships which had arrived in Liverpool 2,153 carcases disappeared, their eventual destination being dealers on the black market. Profits to be made on the black market have been enormous. Sugar worth £50 was sold for £162. 45,000 eggs were sold at 4s. 6d. a dozen. Chocolates were retailed at 2s. 4d. a pound above the legal price. These are typical instances of hundreds revealed in various Court cases. A restaurant run by enemy aliens, with a meat ration equivalent to the value of £1 per week, had been in the habit of supplying 300 steaks a day.

There has been no consistency in punishing the culprits. The public, however, long ago came to the conclusion that, generally speaking, the penalty was quite inadequate to the crime. One of the largest firms in South Shields was fined £1 and £1. 1. 0 costs for trading in illicit stocks. A cinema was fined £1,500 for obtaining excess rations. Some criminals went to prison, and some did not.

In the debate in the Commons on March 3, Major Lloyd George quite rightly reminded the public that "there could be no black market unless there was someone prepared to buy . . . It was the people who wanted something more than their neighbours who were responsible for the profits being made in this business. It was about time people realized that they had a duty to the State."

As a result of the growing storm of indignation, much heavier penalties for black-market crimes were announced on March 11. It was agreed that the existing Defence Regulations were inadequate, and instead of three months' imprisonment on summary conviction and two years on indictment, it was decided to raise the term of imprisonment to 12 months on summary conviction and 14 years' penal servitude on indictment. In regard to fines, it was decreed that the criminal must pay a sum at least equal to the benefit which, in the opinion of the Court, he had derived from the offence. In some cases the fine could be three times the price at which the offender had offered to sell or buy the goods in question.

Meanwhile, Scotland Yard have been concentrating their attention on the "big bosses" behind the racket, and it is hoped with the very much heavier penalties and a skilful and relentless offensive against all and sundry connected with the traffic, to stamp it out. Under the new Regulations a provision to cope with persons who receive commissions or other valuable considerations in respect of illegal transactions has been inserted. Since stocks for the black market depend to a large extent on theft, the new Regulations are designed to apply to cases of stealing or receiving controlled articles. But it is for the public also to assist in every way by treating this sinister business as a form of treachery, and where possible to report any racketeers that come to their notice. Let it be a patriotic point of honour with us to frustrate these criminals and bring them to justice. If there are no customers, the market would soon die a natural death . . .

THE BILL. *From the cartoon by Illingworth in The Daily Mail*

'PEOPLE v. PARASITE'

WE are now fighting the greatest and fiercest war of all time, and the stakes for us are the continuance of our existence as a nation. We are fighting on several fronts, in the Far East, in the Middle East, in all the seven oceans, and we are fighting in our own country the battle of the People against the Parasites.

Hardly a day passes without decent men and women being exasperated and infuriated by reports of police-court cases which are evidence that, though we have entered the most fateful year in our history, and though our sailors, soldiers and airmen are daily giving their lives for their country, we are nourishing in our midst individuals who were so aptly described recently as vermin, who are not only doing nothing whatsoever to help the war effort, but are thriving in sleek comfort on the proceeds of illicit dealings in commodities necessary to the well-being of our people. I do not know why these able-bodied men enjoy immunity from serving the country in the armed forces or the workshops nor do I know where they get their petrol, but I do know that this battle of the People against Parasites must be won by the people, and can be won if the people close up their ranks and take the offensive.

We can win the battle in this part of England, and win it quickly, if every member of the Naval personnel in the Command and every man and woman in the Royal Dockyard will from now on consider it his or her bounden duty to the country and to the men in the battle areas, to report to his or her commanding officer, or other suitable authority, when they have evidence that the parasites are at their filthy work.

I know that there are many people whose natural instinct is to avoid becoming involved in any cases where the law is put in motion, but the times are so serious that I feel it is my duty to call on every one to fight with vigour and determination in the battle of the People against the Parasite.—*General Order issued by the Commander-in-Chief, Admiral Sir William James, Portsmouth*

Rommel's Tanks Charged At Us Full Tilt

Written by Reuter's Special Correspondent with the British troops in Libya, this dispatch gives a vivid picture of the conditions prevailing in that strange battleground. It was sent off from near Sidi Omar on Nov. 25, 1941.

I WAS standing outside H.Q. here near Sidi Omar when light tanks rushed up, reporting that they had engaged a force of between 30 and 40 German tanks which were now coming at full speed in our direction, endeavouring to take us in the rear.

An officer came out of his office, and looking through his glasses said: "They are about two miles off and coming in fast. Tell the artillery to smarten them up a bit." He was quite unconcerned, and found time to shake my hand and indulge in a few moments of social pleasantry, more as though welcoming a guest to a tennis party than directing a battle at its most trying moment.

Indeed, after watching the tanks for a few moments more, he turned back into his office and went on with his work.

This confidence in our defence proved well founded. The Germans had chased our light tanks, who with their superior speed had drawn them on into an area which was heavily mined by us, and where anti-tank guns and 25-pounders — ingeniously camouflaged — were ready to open up from close range.

The Germans came on at full tilt, as though not suspecting a trap. At the H.Q. officers stood on the roof of cars, the better to see the approaching clash. The Germans opened fire at our first defence line, but their guns could not make the range. Then the tanks turned broadside on and shot among our front, firing wildly as they went. The din was tremendous, for no sooner had the Germans exposed their flanks than our guns opened up on them. Columns of smoke shot up into the air as our shells burst, some of them oily black in colour, signifying that a tank had been hit. One tank—quite close to us by this time—burst into flames at once. The others slowed down and turned away, plainly damaged.

For about 15 minutes the fight continued, the Germans turning this way and then that in an effort to get within range of us. Then, seeing that they were out-gunned, they turned away and made off to the west. Some made the error of drawing away in single file along a ridge. They stood out on the horizon like toys and gave us beautiful targets. Our shells crashed in among them and did further damage. When the smoke had cleared, our men went out and found 13 German tanks knocked out, some of them completely destroyed by fire. Those which were merely holed were set on fire and destroyed, to prevent the Germans recovering them at any future time. Later, 15 German tanks were reported moving away to the west: these are believed to be the only survivors of this fight.

Changing the Wheel Under Fire

Before this happy culmination, however, there had been many anxious moments. We knew that fresh British tanks were on the way, but at the moment of the attack we had only light ones not intended to engage the German heavies. Furthermore, a great mass of transport had crowded back into this area for safety after Axis tank columns had raced down our left flank from El Gobi almost into Egypt.

A small party of war correspondents took part in this temporary withdrawal, travelling with a huge convoy carrying the staff of one of our army corps which made a forced march throughout the night and drove through minefields in order to take up a new position. As we drove to this point we passed lorry-loads of German prisoners being rushed to the rear. We wondered what they were thinking as German tank shells burst on the right of us, not more than two miles off, but with blank faces they hung on to the lorries like tired passengers on a crowded bus. At one point one of our cars had a puncture and we had to change the wheel.

We found ourselves left behind our column. As we worked we looked every now and then over our shoulders to note the German shell bursts creeping up on us, denoting that the tanks were getting nearer and nearer. One could not help recalling the exaggerated suspense scenes in early film dramas, when the villain giving chase seemed to be catching up with the hero and heroine all the time. It was difficult to imagine that we, too, were not players in an unreal drama.

On arriving at last in this area we were heavily shelled by German and Italian batteries holding out along the frontier to the north and apparently determined to sell themselves dearly. For most of the morning we were obliged to lie in shallow, hastily-dug trenches. Our cars were hit by fragments as the shells burst all around. As the German tanks were withdrawing after the battle described above, British bombers appeared in force and dived upon them. Indian troops near us stood up on their lorries, waving and cheering as our planes roared down to do their deadly work.

The Nazis withdrew some miles to reform, evidently with the intention of attacking the next day. But they are not being left undisturbed. British night bombers are over them now. Flares are falling on their encampment, and bombs are following them down. The night sky is also lit up by flames from a

ENEMY TANKS, armoured vehicles and mechanized transport ablaze and smoking after their capture by South African troops in Libya. An eye-witness account of the destruction of many of Rommel's tanks during a desert engagement is told in this page by Reuter's special correspondent, who mentions how the flames from burning Nazi tanks lit up the night sky. *Photo, British Official: Crown Copyright*

Nazi tank still burning after four hours.

Three Italian prisoners brought in to our lines by the Indians were very fearful and pleaded that they should not be killed as they all had *bambini* at home. One of them, a corporal. said he had found the other two dying of thirst in the desert, and all of them had agreed to surrender as soon as they could find the British. "I tried to surrender months ago," the corporal told me, "but my officer had me handcuffed and I lost a stripe. I never wanted this war, and there are many more at home like me." All three seemed afraid that they might be sent to

India, and asked in chorus: "Please, can't you arrange to send us to London?"

Other Italian prisoners I saw complained that they had had only a cupful of water apiece in the last three days. Of two wretched men just brought in, one was half-crazy with thirst and the other so hungry that he was trying to suck some nourishment out of an old discarded food tin that he had picked up. The few German officers among the prisoners seemed docile enough, as did the Germans of other rank. The rigours of this campaign seem to have taken the harshness and stiffness out of many a Nazi.

fields themselves are a military secret, but I believed the enemy could drill three brand-new wells in less time than it would take them to open one of the old shafts.

The destruction of the wells, because of the large area to be covered, required all Monday and most of Tuesday. During this time a small force of Dutch soldiers fought a desperate fight against a much larger enemy unit, holding the Japanese at bay until the work had been completed.

The Japanese air troops actually did succeed in capturing one refinery on the banks of the Musei river, and hoisting the Rising Sun flag. The capture was effected when enemy troops, obviously operating with complete knowledge of the defence arrangements, landed in the refinery grounds inside the military guard and drove civilian employees out at the point of guns.

How We Scorched the Oil Wells at Palembang

This remarkable story of the destruction of the great oil plant at Palembang in Sumatra after the Japanese parachute attack was told to William Dunn, the Columbia Broadcasting System's correspondent, by Mr. L. W. Elliott, an official of the Standard Oil Company.

THE first Japanese parachutists landed at Palembang near the Standard refinery and inside the Shell refinery, only a short distance away, shortly after 9.50 on Saturday morning (Feb. 14). The paratroops in the latter refinery were eventually blown up with the plant.

By noon the Standard plant began to evacuate all non-essential employees. The refinery staff included 70 Americans, 300 Europeans and 3,300 native employees, all of whom have been accounted for. An operation crew kept on duty, together with Dutch army units, who were in constant contact with the enemy, and army experts waiting to blast the entire plant.

By two on Sunday morning the army experts went to work and in one hour destroyed all vital instruments, machinery and loose equipment. Time was then allowed for Dutch and native troops which had been holding off the enemy at four major points to retire to safety.

When this allotted time had elapsed fire bombs released simultaneously by an electrical system set the entire refinery stock ablaze with a deafening roar. Millions of barrels of petrol and crude oil petroleum products and priceless aviation petrol burst into immediate and inextinguishable flames.

This was only the beginning, however, for there still remained 81 miles of subterreanean pipe-line and the great oilfields themselves

to be destroyed. Native crews, working by hand, ignited fuses which set off dynamite blasts spaced every few hundred feet for the entire 81 miles of the pipe-line, and did so in record time. The pipe-line passed under three large rivers. Dynamite charges had long ago been placed within the pipe itself as near the centre of the rivers as possible and explosions occurred at those points.

The methods used to cut off the flow of oil permanently from hundreds of wells in the

The hoisting of the Japanese flag was the first definite signal to the outside world that the enemy was in possession, but it was also the signal for a small military force to launch an heroic drive on the refinery to enable the planned destructions to take place.

The drive was successful so much so that the refinery joined all others in the district in a blinding blast of flames. Inside were the invading force and their Japanese flag.— *The Daily Telegraph.*

Through Snow and Ice Our Ships Struggled to Russia

This account of how supplies from Britain reached the Russian northern ports in spite of severe wintry conditions was given by Reuter's Special Correspondent, who travelled in a warship escorting one convoy.

As we steamed farther and farther north, the hours of daylight grew shorter until it was light for barely four hours. The cold was intense and the wind, which always seemed to blow at gale force, brought snow-storms whirling round the ships, making navigation almost impossible, and the task of keeping stations in the lines of ships a nightmare.

Spray froze directly it touched the ships. Gun mountings had constantly to be de-iced and the breeches kept covered so that they could be fired, while the ice was as much as six inches thick on the barrels and armoured plating. Inside the ship, electric radiators were kept going day and night, but the cold

was so great that ice formed on the cabin walls from condensation.

Sheepskin coats, fur caps, balaclava helmets, fleece-lined gloves, and special thick underwear were issued from the ship's stores and it was virtually impossible to recognize shipmates in the muffled figures to be seen on deck which showed only the end of a nose and two eyes.

The task of anchoring the ship on arrival was made more difficult by the fact that on the forecastle everything was frozen fast. Special steam jets had to be fitted before the anchors could be let go, and it was only after half an hour's hard work with these jets, and axes and hammers wielded by the anchor

PALEMBANG, a street in the market. The Japanese made a parachute attack on Palembang, great oil-producing centre in Sumatra, on Feb. 14. How the oil plant and the wells were destroyed while a Dutch covering force held the enemy at bay until the destruction had been completed is related above by an official of the Standard Oil Company

Photo, E.N.A.

AID FOR RUSSIA is being fully maintained despite the difficulties which beset our convoys. Here are ships of one such convoy carrying valuable supplies steaming through the ice-covered waters of the Arctic. How British supplies have been reaching Russia's northern ports is described in an eye-witness article in this and the preceding page. *Photo, Fox*

party, that the capstan could be freed from its coating of ice and the cable prised loose from the deck.

Once we were at anchor a Russian naval captain and two lieutenants came on board. After completing their business with the captain, they were brought to the wardroom to be introduced to the ship's officers and have a drink. When everyone had a glass, a toast was called, " To the damnation of Hitler," which the Russian captain heartily

reciprocated, and responded with a toast to three great men, " Churchill, Stalin, and Roosevelt."

In the meanwhile, the merchant ships had gone ahead and were berthing, while preparations were immediately put in hand for the task of unloading their stores of aeroplanes, tanks, guns, munitions and medical supplies. Thus another cargo of arms reached our allies fighting on the northern front without loss or damage to a single ship.

for St. Thomas, in Portuguese West Africa, with cargo of wine and potatoes.

We had an absolutely grand time on board. From the captain down to the deck-hands they could not do enough for us. They treated us right royally—the captain even insisted that we should have our meals before he or any of his officers sat down. The first mate taught us to navigate in Portuguese, and we ended up by taking a watch for them. It helped to repay their kindness.

On the fourth day after we had been picked up, I was taking a sun-sight on the bridge when I saw two destroyers approaching. At that distance we couldn't tell whether they were friendly or not, so we kept out of sight until they got closer and we saw the Union Jack. Then we started shouting and waving our arms to attract their attention. But they stopped 200 yards away and hoisted flag signals, asking the Congo for her identity. The Congo replied, and our hearts sank into our borrowed boots as the destroyers turned away, satisfied that she was a neutral, and made off at twenty knots.

The Portuguese Treated Us Right Royally

Coming down in the Atlantic with engine trouble, the crew of a Lockheed Hudson were picked up by a Portuguese cargo ship and "treated right royally" before being taken off by a British destroyer. The following story was broadcast by the pilot.

WHEN our engine conked out over the Atlantic I looked for a Portuguese steamship I'd seen earlier. When I found her I gave the order " ditching stations," and put down on the sea about half a mile from the ship. The jolt threw me forward, my head hit the windscreen, and I was knocked out. When I came to I found that the water was over the top of me. I made one mad scramble and got through the emergency exit in the cockpit roof.

The boys had got the dinghy out. Even in this moment we got a laugh. The two air gunners had taken off their flying boots, and they started to get into the dinghy from opposite sides. Suddenly one of them yelled : " Sharks " ! His feet had floated up underneath the dinghy and had touched the other gunner's feet.

Then we found another snag. The dinghy was still attached to the Hudson's door by the tube through which it is inflated with compressed air. Clippers are stowed in the dinghy specially for cutting this tube, but they were so securely packed up that we couldn't undo them. We all tried hard, but our hands were too cold. The Hudson was still floating, but she might go down at any moment—and take the dinghy with her. Finally my second pilot took the door right off the Hudson. We brought it into the

dinghy, and cut the tube later, at our leisure.

The Portuguese ship had put about by now, and was making for us. All we had to do was sit there until she arrived. Suddenly we heard aeroplane engines. It was another Hudson from our patrol, flown by a pilot we call " Tich," who has the D.F.C. and D.F.M. He had come to make sure we were all O.K., and he flew round us with a wingtip just clear of the water, until the Portuguese ship picked us up. Then he waggled his wings and pushed off.

I was feeling pretty dicky by this time. I'd lost a lot of blood from the gash in my head, and they took me straight off to the ship's sick bay. The attendant there gave me a glass of port to pull me round. He looked at my head, dressed it, and said, " Alla right—very good." I found by experience that this was all the English he knew. But he made a beautiful job of my head, and, what's more, he lent me his pyjamas.

The others were quite all right after a hot bath. They dressed themselves in civilian clothes lent them by the Portuguese, and then sat down to a slap-up feed—six-course dinner, with wine and liqueurs, and a fresh-killed chicken as the big dish. I got up for lunch the next day, and found that the Congo —that was the ship's name—was bound

'Comings here—peoples aboard'

Suddenly the destroyers circled. They came back, and this time closed right in. An armed party put off. In a few moments they had boarded us, and we were saying good-bye to the Portuguese. They were very sorry to see us go—the captain had tears in his eyes.

On board the destroyer I found that just as the destroyers were leaving the Congo that first time, one of the wireless operators had picked up a strange message. It read : " Comings here—peoples aboard ! " and it had been sent out from somewhere very near. Those were almost the only words of English that the Congo's wireless operator knew, and he had done his best to get a message through for us.

That was why we'd had an armed party boarding us—the destroyers expected to find Germans or Italians, but, instead, they found four Englishmen.   **Page 607**

Editor's Postscript

HISTORIANS will agree that the two greatest surprises of the War were (1) the collapse of the French Army, and (2) the courage, fortitude and efficiency of the Russian Army. For years preceding the War, Europe, and especially Britain, had been deluded by the idea that France, whatever the vagaries of her politics, was an impregnable bulwark against German aggression. At the moment of peril her patriotism and military genius could not fail her. As soon as the alarm sounded all political corruption would disappear and the true France would emerge defiant and invincible. I remember my friend Henry D. Davray, most sincerely Anglophile of all French journalists, illustrating this to me in pencilled diagrams on the tablecloth of the restaurant where we were dining one night before the calamity had come upon us. It all looked dead easy and most reassuring in the pencilled diagrams; but what a world of fantasy we lived in then! All his theories proved no more indelible than the pencillings on the tablecloths. France fell because internal discord had so undermined the national spirit that unity, even in the face of aggression, was impossible. Sincerity and idealism had given way to cynicism and despair, and a kind of *sauve qui peut* for place, power and possessions was the result.

THE reverse is the story of modern Russia. After her defeat in 1918 Russia had to rebuild her world anew. The Soviets achieved in a generation what had taken the other great nations of Europe a hundred years to do, and a collective national idealism permeated the whole social fabric. Unlike the French people the Russians had been given something to believe in. If the rest of the world was unaware of this, it is because it was never allowed to know what was really happening in Russia. Here again political prejudice obscured the view. In no department more than in the Red Army, which celebrated its 24th birthday on Feb. 23, is the progress of modern Russia so conspicuous. Cradled in the revolution, its military spirit and technical efficiency increased year by year in readiness for the ordeal which Stalin knew would come upon it.

BUT while there was reason enough for you and me to be kept in ignorance of what a splendid military machine the Soviet generals were building up, it is absurd to think that the man who made the greatest mistake about Russia was the one who had most opportunities for knowing all that was happening there: Adolf the Omniscient! In marching east Hitler made the defeat of Germany inevitable, as I have pointed out in a recent number. Yet, how could Hitler have refrained from attacking Russia? In "Mein Kampf" he explicitly states that parts of Russia were to be German colonies; and in any case Nazism cannot exist in Europe unless it destroys all other systems of government.

MR. GEORGE ORWELL writes an excellent article on Kipling in that excellent monthly Horizon, which I usually read from title page to imprint every month with great spiritual profit . . . But Mr. Orwell must not be allowed to get away with the assertion that " it is possible that it was Kipling who first let loose the use of the word ' Huns ' for Germans." Which reminds me that an old lady, writing to me on behalf of self and partner, when I started publishing World War in 1934, said that she would cancel her order if I allowed the Germans to be called Huns, as she had protested against my doing so in THE WAR ILLUSTRATED of 1914-18. I replied that not all the old ladies in England, Scotland, Tunbridge Wells, or the Empire would pre-

Lt.-Gen. SIR H. R. L. G. ALEXANDER, who succeeded Lt.-Gen. Hutton as G.O.C. Burma, was the last man to leave the beaches at Dunkirk. He was recently G.O.C. Southern Command.
Photo, Topical Press

vent my doing so. It is one of the few things about the late unlamented Kaiser that I admired : his honesty about the Huns. For he was " the onlie begetter " of " Hun " as a title for the German (of all classes, let me add, even including the liberal-minded Professor Haeckel, who approved the War of 1914).

ONE of few encyclopedias in which you will find this point elucidated is my own Universal Encyclopedia—I saw to that. " Gain a reputation like the Huns under Attila," said William of the withered arm when sending his troops out to China for the relief of the Peking legations in 1900, he, poor posturing fool, personating Attila! Hence Hun and all that the word implies has stuck to the German ever since, and I shall be glad if Mr. Orwell will make a note of this. Mr. Orwell, by the way, is a writer of taste as becomes every contributor to Horizon. Perhaps he would tell me what he means by the phrase " sooner or later " which he uses while criticizing other phrases. Sooner than

what ? Later than when ? I'm always open to learn. Myself I write " soon or later," which in a sense answers both of my questions by rendering them unnecessary.

A NEW book on Thomas Hardy reminds one of a great writer and an essentially kind spirit. One wonders what the Sage of Wessex would have made of this most terrible of all wars. When he wrote The Dynasts he was concerned with what was regarded in Victorian times as the culminating drama of conflict. Hardy lived to see the Napoleonic wars surpassed by the Kaiser's war of 1914-18. But once more Britain's genius triumphed. Yet within a generation the struggle began again with increased violence, and a totalitarian significance involving nearly every human being in cruelty and suffering. Such a repetition of history might well justify Hardy's so-called pessimism.

BUT the author's fatalism was never of the cynical kind. It derived from the deepest sympathy with human beings thrust against the inscrutable forces of destiny. He was too profound a poet, and had too great a sense of beauty, including the beauty of tragedy, to forget the courage and dignity of men and women in the appalling predicaments of this life. The courage and dignity of the free peoples, opposed to the tyrants and their hordes of slaves, provide the strongest grounds for our hope. They are a spiritual barrier against which Hitlerism cannot in the end prevail. We survived Dunkirk and we shall survive Singapore and Rangoon, and any other incidental defeats because faith in our cause is invincible. Britain has been going through a dark period of the war, but to be depressed about it is to loosen the sinews of that faith and resolution. Thomas Hardy, who wrote some fine patriotic poems, would never have despaired of our victory in the Second World War, and he would surely have given us some memorable poem to console and hearten us, pessimist though he was.

I AM glad to be reminded by one of my readers who shares my anxiety about the fate of the horse in the present war, that the R.S.P.C.A. is actively engaged in a big drive to raise £100,000 for the purchasing of veterinary requirements which would, as far as humanly possible, alleviate the inevitable sufferings of the horses which are so essential to the war effort of our Russian Allies. As I pointed out in my last reference to this subject, the Russian is as sympathetic to his horse as the Arab is traditionally supposed to be (thanks in large measure to Caroline Norton's once famous poem), but I cannot recall any similar trait in the German being celebrated in verse or prose, and I am certain that nothing but the commercial value of their animals and their usefulness in the war is likely to appeal to the Nazis. All lovers of animals will be only too delighted to help even in the smallest way to minimize the suffering of the horses, be they used by enemy or Ally (I note that a great many of the Nazi cavalry have happily fallen into the hands of the Russians) and if that £100,000 can be raised by the R.S.P.C.A., it is obviously going to be quickly turned to merciful use. Sir Robert Gower, R.S.P.C.A., 105, Jermyn Street, London, S.W.1, will receive and acknowledge contributions.

Printed in England and published every alternate Friday by the Proprietors, The Amalgamated Press Ltd., The Fleetway House, Farringdon Street, London, E.C.4. Registered for transmission by Canadian Magazine Post. Sole Agents for Australia and New Zealand : Messrs. Gordon & Gotch, Ltd. ; and for South Africa : Central News Agency, Ltd. April 2, 1942. S.S. *Editorial Address* : JOHN CARPENTER HOUSE WHITEFRIARS, LONDON, E.C.4.

Vol 5 # The War Illustrated N° 126

Edited by Sir John Hammerton

6ᵈ FORTNIGHTLY   APRIL 17, 1942

FAMOUS AMERICAN GENERALS, MacArthur (right) and Wainwright, photographed together in the Philippines, where the heroic resistance of American and Filipino troops has been a source of inspiration to the United Nations. On Feb. 22 President Roosevelt asked Gen. MacArthur to transfer his H.Q. from the Philippines to Australia. When the General arrived there on March 17, after an adventurous journey, he was appointed Supreme Commander of all the United Nations Forces in the South-West Pacific. Gen. Wainwrght was left to carry on MacArthur's great fight in the Philippines.

Photo, Keystone

NO. 127 WILL BE PUBLISHED FRIDAY, **MAY 1**

THE THIRD SPRING OFFENSIVE

BY THE EDITOR

WHEN our thoughts should be joyously turning with those of the poet to the hounds of spring " on winter's traces " clearing the way for " a summer-to-be," they must turn rather to the Hounds of Hell which now, for the third springtide of the War, are being unleashed upon us. Herein lies the most horrid of the transformations which Hitlerism has produced. The spring offensive has become a regular feature of the War, whose makers had planned that it would need no second spring.

Not with equanimity can we recall the spring of 1940 when, with the Scandinavian campaign, came " the first real crunch of the War " (as Mr. Churchill phrased it). The British Navy did great work then, up to its best traditions, inflicting on the Nazi sea-power losses which, proportionate to its pre-war strength, equalled, if they did not exceed, any that the British Navy has sustained, even in the recent dire disasters of the Pacific. But the Allies lost the fight for a hold on the Scandinavian main. And in that abortive campaign were sown the first seeds that blossomed into a veritable *fleur de mal* when France fell from us in the tragic days of June.

NOT with greater pride, but with less mortification, can we recall Hitler's next spring offensive. The signal fact that Britain, despite the criminal treachery of Nazi-ruled France (which in Indo-China was already preparing the way for Japan's cunning attack of the following winter), despite the loss of our self-sacrificing Allies of Greece and Yugoslavia, the supreme fact that Britain was still battling almost alone in shining disproof of the melancholy axiom that " the broken heart it kens nae second spring," provided the greatest cause for courageous hope. And had not we the historic battle of Cape Matapan to the credit of our Navy, were we not wiping out the Italians in North-East Africa, re-conquering Abyssinia, advancing through Libya and making prisoners of an immense proportion of the Duce's army, albeit unable to save the territories of our gallant Balkan allies ? Furthermore, we had but recently won the greatest of all our battles—the Battle of Britain—by virtue of which we survive and fight today. And though our head was bloody in the Battle of London which raged into this second spring, most assuredly it was unbowed.

Let's think on these things as the third spring offensive is upon us, and especially let us remember that the Nazi plans for the second of the series were frustrated, thanks to our timely occupation of Syria, our firmness in Iraq and Persia, and in some measure to the delaying action of our friends of Yugoslavia. Thus, although Hitler's fancy turns in springtime to thoughts of hate and war, hate has its disappointments no less profound than love.

IN the third spring we are actually better placed than before, even allowing for the dreadful things that have happened in the Pacific. In closest cooperation with Soviet Russia, America and China, the greatest potential of fighting strength and armaments production in the history of the world has come into being. As Mr. Churchill has said : " It now seems that we and our Allies cannot lose this war except through failure to use our combined overwhelming strength and multiplying opportunities."

General Smuts, whose voice carries imperial authority, has said that the pressure of this third spring offensive will be felt at its strongest in the Middle East, on India, and in the Indian Ocean. Certainly all the indications point in these directions, and it is hardly possible that Turkey will be able to ride the coming storm without being drawn in. But along her eastern flank Germany has vast Soviet forces opposing her, armies whose fighting power has been the grand surprise of the War, while the Japanese, with all their cheap and showy victories to consolidate, have the swiftly-growing might of the world's most powerful republic soon and relentlessly to press upon them in recapturing from them the fruits of their felony.

And if, as a gambler's last throw, Hitler decrees the invasion of Britain, there is every reason for believing we are ready. M. Maisky has adjured us to think in terms of 1942, not 1943. Events are compelling us so to think, but long views have sometimes more merit than short. At all events it will not be long before we all know vastly more than any man alive knows today.

* * *

TO all of us who endured the four years of the last war the hateful calamity of the present World War is bearable only by contemplating our experiences in 1914-18. The perils that confront us may be more fearsome than those we survived four and twenty years ago, but in the mere fact of that survival abide encouragement and hope. It is this, I think, that lends a certain serenity to those of the older generation in facing up to the trials and tribulations of the present hour ; this, that in some measure, sustains our Prime Minister in his tremendous task. And it is a crowning mercy that in this dire time of spiritual trial the leadership of the British race has fallen to one whose unquestioned genius, whose unrivalled qualities of mind and heart were nurtured to their finest issues in high responsibility of statesmanship and in courageous public criticism throughout the forty-two years of this eventful century. This should always be our first thought in discussing the problems and perplexities, foreseen and unforeseen, with which each new day now presents us.

THE recent parliamentary pother about a newspaper incident, which need not be more definitely specified, reflected no great credit on either side, but a careful and impartial examination of the evidence forces one to a verdict for Mr. Morrison. The role of Smart Alec, which so many journalists of the lusty younger breed find easy to discharge, has really less to do with the freedom of the press than with the vapourings of the irresponsible. Nothing could be more mischievous in moments of national peril than to allow the accumulated wisdom of the nation to be brushed aside by presumptuous and exhibitionist youth, splendidly daring in its inexperience, because, forsooth, things unforeseen have brought disaster upon the best-laid plans of the most experienced.

HAD one the space which the paper famine forbids it would be a simple matter to show how hopelessly wrong some of our most trusty military experts have been, not only in this war, but in every war that has been fought in the modern era. Advice on high politics, military strategy, and tactics is so plentiful just now that if one went across to the " local " tonight one would be certain to find three or four of the " regulars," with as many pints in them, ready and willing to put their counsel at the service of the War Cabinet. This is at once the weakness and the strength of Democracy. Yet, with all its absurdities, I prefer it to any New Order in Europe or Asia.

HARDLY any detail of criticism that is being advanced against the British High Command today is new. It has all been stated in similar language whenever arms have been in action throughout the eventful story of the upbuilding of the British Empire. And in its partial eclipse it is worth remembering that the worn-out cliché that Britain loses every battle except the last one seems nowise short of truth. It is merely another way of saying that, although the British are not a warlike or aggressive race, they have unique powers of endurance, fortitude, recovery, which show best only when their assailants have stirred them to righteous anger. Well, there's cause enough for that anger now, and it is rising rapidly, but its best expression should take the form of furious energy in war production rather than in carping criticism of the Government, or the hunting for scapegoats when things go wrong, as they are apt to do at times.

Lt.-Gen. SIR W. DOBBIE, indomitable Governor of the indomitable little island of Malta. "We have been sorely tried," he said in a recent broadcast, " but are not crushed . . . We shall persevere until, by God's help, we shall win through."   *Photo, G.P.U.*

J. A. HAMMERTON

Soon 'Attack' Will Be the Anzacs' Watchword

Above, gun examiner (with pencil) and draughtsman examining plans of a 3·7-in. anti-aircraft gun in an Australian army inspection depot where the guns are checked before and after proof. Circle, general view of the machine-shop in an Australian factory producing anti-tank guns.

Many new shipyards have been opened in Australia as part of an extensive shipbuilding programme, and below are some of the new wharves and stages being laid down at an Australian port, while in the background a cargo ship is being converted for war purposes.

Photos, Australian Official, Sport & General

Above, Bren guns made in Australia are being examined by (left to right) Brigadier Milford, Mr. J. K. J. Jensen, Controller - General of Munitions Administration, Maj.-Gen. Northcott and Maj.-Gen. Stantke. Australia's production of war material is rapidly increasing.

The Australian soldiers of today have already proved that they are of the same "Anzac breed" as their fathers who fought in the last war. They believe in the offensive spirit, and below recruits are being instructed in guerilla tactics for disarming an opponent. The man on the ground originally had the rifle.

Photos, Australian Official, Wide World

Page 611

Free China's Young Womanhood Goes to War

WOMEN OF CHINA receiving musketry training at barracks in the Hunan Province, where some 20,000 girls are being trained for service with the Chinese Army (left).

Members of the Chinese Students' Corps starting for the front (below). Chinese youth is whole-heartedly in the war effort, and women as well as men are playing their full part in the struggle of the democracies.

AT THE RANGES Chinese women, training for service with the Army, are taught how to handle a rifle with efficiency. Above, two of them are seen practising correct aiming.

Thousands of Chinese women are serving, too, with the army medical units. On the right some of them are practising stretcher-bearing in the first-aid section of their training.

Photos, British Official: Crown Copyright; Keystone

They're Building Roads from India into China

SUPPLY ROUTE TO CHINA. The fall of Rangoon having closed the sea outlet of the Burma Road, new highways between India and Chunking are being completed with all possible speed. One of these is the Assam Road, the presumed course of which is given in the map in page 538. The road seen under construction in these photographs is said to lie between Loshan (Kiatingfu) and Sichang (Ningyuanfu) and is presumably a link between the Burma Road and the Assam Road. Right, the highway winding through the mountains. Below, a temporary bridge in use while a permanent span is being built.

The construction of these new lifelines between India and China is an immense task, for the roads have to be driven through wild country, swift rivers and streams have to be bridged, and landslides frequently delay work. Above, coolies carrying engineers across one of the streams that had to be bridged. Left, cars about to proceed after a landslide had been cleared away.

Photos, Associated Press

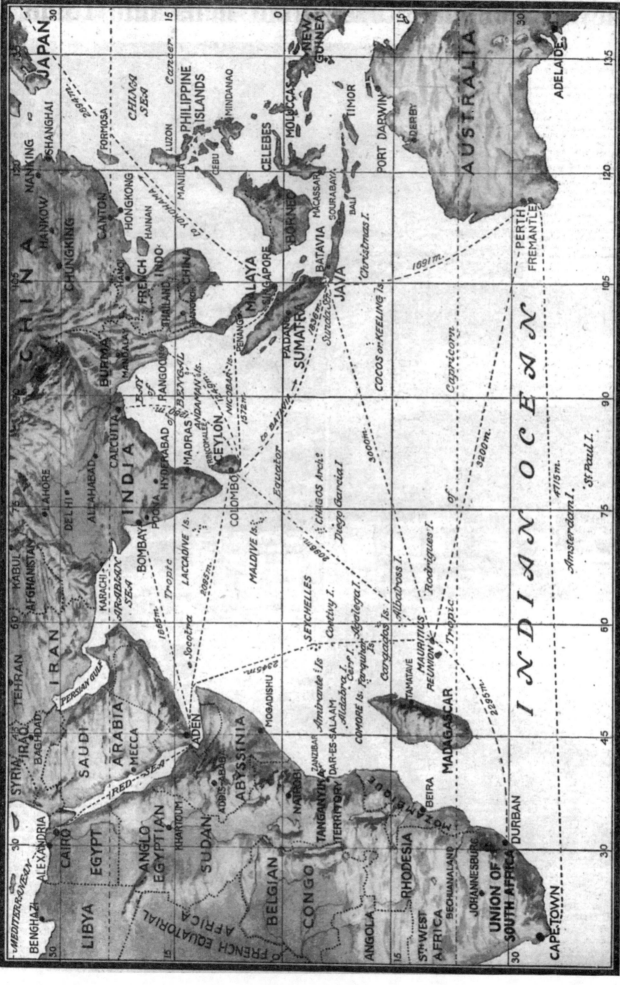

THE INDIAN OCEAN. Washing the shores of Africa, Asia, and Australia and, in the far frozen south, Antarctica, stretches the vast expanse of the Indian Ocean. Since Singapore's fall it, like the Pacific, has become a battlefield, and any and every day brings tidings of fresh warlike incidents in one of its innumerable corners. Japanese submarines are reported to be operating in Indian waters, and as early as Jan. 29 an American freighter was torpedoed and sunk only ten miles off Madras. Of the ocean's many islands—the most important are shown in the map—the Andamans in the Bay of Bengal were evacuated on March 12 by the British, and seized ten days later by the Japanese.

Specially drawn for THE WAR ILLUSTRATED *by Felix Gardon*

War's Monsoons Threaten the Indian Ocean

Already dominant over a vast expanse of the Pacific, the Japanese are now extending their tentacles of aggression to the Indian Ocean. Here we tell of this new area which has been suddenly brought into the war zone, and in particular of those islands which have a strategical significance of the first order.

FOR many years Singapore has been called the Gateway to the East. Now, following the Japanese triumph, it is rather the Gateway to the West. Already the Andaman Islands in the Bay of Bengal have been occupied by the Japanese, and the Nicobars are threatened. Japanese warships may even now be preying on the shipping whose routes lie between Africa and Australia.

Hardly less important than the Mediterranean, the Indian Ocean is criss-crossed by British supply lines. Since the Mediterranean is largely barred to our convoys by Axis planes and submarines, the greater part of the British and Australian supplies and reinforcements for the Middle East, as well as for North Africa, must make the long voyage round the Cape of Good Hope, after which they have to traverse some 3,000 miles of the Indian Ocean before they reach the less exposed waters of the Red Sea. The Imperial route between Britain and Australia also goes round the Cape, and includes more than 4,700 miles of the Indian Ocean between Freemantle and Cape Town. To reach Aden and Bombay, Colombo and Calcutta, our ships after leaving Durban are in the open waters of the Indian Ocean; and so, too, are the ships which take Allied supplies to Russia through the Persian Gulf, and those which bring back Persian oil for our war machine. And now this so recently British ocean is threatened by enemy fleets and raiders; Ceylon may be blockaded, Calcutta may be shelled from the sea, and soon reports may come of Japanese landings on "India's coral strand."

Rather less than half the size of the Pacific —its area is given by geographers as some twenty-eight million square miles—the Indian Ocean is flanked on the west and north by huge land masses, from which have been detached in immeasurably remote ages a number of island fragments. These islands are not so numerous or so widespread as those of the Pacific, but their strategical importance is just as great.

All Eyes on Madagascar

Perhaps the most important is Madagascar, which ranks as the world's fourth largest island. It is nearly a thousand miles long by 360 miles wide, and it provides a home for nearly four million people, belonging to one or the other of the Malagasy tribes. Until 1895 the island was independent under its own sovereign, but in that year the French deported Queen Rànàvalona III to Algiers, and henceforth ruled the island as a French colony. The people accepted the change—they could hardly do otherwise; but to this day they have shown themselves a trifle resentful of the Westernizing process, and particularly in the country districts their Christian profession is but a veneer on the deep-seated belief in the ancient gods.

Like most tropical islands Madagascar is exceedingly fertile; in the uplands large numbers of cattle are bred, and the valley plains bear rich crops of rice and sugar, coffee and tobacco. The woods are full of valuable timber, and there are also considerable mineral workings. But in the present state of world history Madagascar's importance is strategical rather than commercial; and it may be noted that there are a number of good harbours in the island, in particular Majunga, Diégo Suarez, and Tamatave.

This being so, it is easy to understand the concern with which the news was received in Allied circles, that a Japanese mission was about to be dispatched to Madagascar, if it had not actually arrived. The island's Governor-General, M. Annet, is an ardent supporter of Vichy, and it was feared that France was about to abandon Madagascar to the Japanese just as she abandoned Indo-China in 1940—with disastrous consequences to the Allied cause. In Washington M. Henry-Haye protested that Marshal Pétain's Government had not the slightest intention of doing any such thing; but it has to be remembered that behind Pétain stands Admiral Darlan. No wonder, then, that the United Nations decided to keep Madagascar under close observation; so close, indeed, that Nazi-occupied France declared that

General Smuts was preparing to seize the island from South Africa.

To the north-east of Madagascar lie the Seychelles, a scattered group of some ninety islands and islets, with a total area of only 156 square miles. The chief island of the Seychelles proper is Mahé; its outer dependencies include Aldabra, Amirantes and Farquhar, Coetivy and Agalega, and we may be sure that the Japanese strategists have their eyes on them as possible bases for their surface and underwater raiders. The Seychelles have been a British colony since their capture from the French in 1794; the population is estimated at thirty-two thousand, and the chief product is coconuts.

Lying 500 miles to the east of Madagascar is the British island of Mauritius; though its area is only 720 sq. miles, it is densely populated, such is the tropical exuberance of its soil. Its population of some four hundred thousand is a medley of Negroes, Malays, Chinese, Ceylonese and Indians; Indian coolies are largely employed on the sugar plantations. The governing officials are of course English, but for the rest, the upper class are descendants of the original French colonists. Under the same government are the Oil Islands or Chagos Archipelago (the most important is Diégo Garcia) lying almost in the middle of the Indian Ocean, and Rodrigues, some 350 miles to the north-east. Lying to the south-west on the direct line of communication with Durban is Réunion, a French island still professing allegiance to Vichy.

From Mauritius to Colombo, the chief port and capital of the British island of Ceylon, is a matter of some two thousand miles. Much has been written of this "pearl of the Indian Ocean," of its natural loveliness and its charming and colourful people; but today the emphasis is on sterner things. At Trincomalee there is an important naval base, the most important left to us in these waters now that Singapore has gone; but for the rest the island is largely indefensible. Until only a year or two ago there was only one small aerodrome, a few miles outside Colombo, but it is reported that aerodromes have since been built for the use of the R.A.F.

ANDAMAN ISLANDS, in the Bay of Bengal, 800 miles from both Calcutta and Trincomalee, were occupied by Japanese troops on March 23. Withdrawal of the British and Indian forces there was completed on March 12. The photograph shows Aberdeen Island viewed from Ross Island, across Port Blair harbour. *Photo, E.N.A.*

and Naval air arm. Trincomalee is declared to be impregnable—from the sea; but the Japanese, if they come, may be expected to attack it from the land, just as they did Singapore; and Ceylon has a great expanse of low-lying coastlands fringed with palms which might make excellent cover for enemy landings. Fortunately for the Cingalese, the island is close to India, and could thus be readily reinforced and supplied.

Lying well out from the Indian peninsula are several groups of islands: the Laccadives, 200 miles west of the Malabar coast of Madras province, to which they are politically attached: the coral islets of the Maldives, 400 miles south-west of Ceylon, of which they are a dependency; and in the Bay of Bengal, the Andamans and Nicobars. The Andamans are particularly interesting from the sociological point of view, since the original inhabitants are represented by half-savage aborigines, while the bulk of the population are convicts or ticket-of-leave men.

To complete the list we may mention the Cocos or Keeling Islands—some twenty coral islets with a population of about a thousand, chiefly engaged in growing coconuts—and Christmas Island, which lies some 500 miles to the east of Cocos and 200 miles south of Java. Its importance is derived from the large natural deposit of phosphate of lime, which constitutes its sole export; before the war most of it used to go to Japan. Maybe the Japs have already returned to the island, not as peaceful traders, but as warriors in the cause of "co-prosperity."

Hawaii Ready to Avenge the Felon Blow

Top, giant Flying Fortresses of the Hawaiian Air Force Bomber Command flying in formation over the island. Above, two sergeants check over the ammunition belt of a machine-gun in the fuselage before taking off. Aircraft of this type have been used with great success in bombing Japanese positions in New Guinea.

Centre right, crew of a Flying Fortress of the Hawaiian Air Force Bomber Command going aboard their aircraft. Right, one of the Flying Fortresses being loaded up with 300-lb. bombs by an ordnance crew. Hawaii, fast recovering from the shock of Japan's surprise assault on Dec. 7, 1941, has been rapidly reinforcing its already powerful defences.

Photos, Wide World, Planet News

Japanese Islands Blasted by America's Fleet

On Feb. 1 the U.S. Navy Department announced that an attack had been made by surface and air units of the U.S. Pacific Fleet on Japanese bases in the Marshall and Gilbert Islands. Here are some of the first photographs to be received of this action. Top, an ammunition dump and two fuel dumps ablaze after an attack by U.S. planes. Above, mechanics refuelling and rearming a U.S. Navy plane on its return from the very successful raid.

Centre left, a carrier-based Navy plane taking off during the attack on the Marshall and Gilbert Islands. Left, guns in action aboard one of the U.S. cruisers which took part in the attack. The enemy ships sunk included one modern cruiser, two ocean-going submarines, a large liner, three tankers, five cargo boats, two auxiliaries, two minesweepers and numerous small craft.

Photos, Keystone, Planet News, Associated Press

Our Searchlight on the War

SELF-DENIAL WEEKS

The need is for ships and shipping space. Such is the indispensable foundation of all our war efforts. As a nation Britain is still consuming far too much. A series of self-denial weeks would greatly help to economise tonnage.

ALL over the European mainland where the blond Nazi beast has left his mark, people are suffering from starvation or semi-starvation. What is the position in Britain? Taking the

WARSHIP WEEK in London. Mr. A. V. Alexander, First Lord of the Admiralty, addressing the crowd from the deck of H.M.S. Trafalgar, constructed for the occasion in Trafalgar Square. *Photo, Sport & General*

nation as a whole we are living almost as well as in pre-war days. There is enough and more than enough to eat, drink, and smoke. We have been told to tighten our belts, and that will be no hardship. Thanks to our valiant seamen the supply of commodities has been such that, as compared with other nations, we hardly know that there's a war on. Our immunity is purchased at the expense of brave men ready to face every peril in order that Britain shall survive. There is not the slightest doubt that the average person could save on the consumption of food, drink, tobacco and other so-called necessities, at least for a limited period. If everybody agreed to eat one slice of bread less per day for a week shipping space available for purely military purposes would be substantially increased. Why not reserve certain weeks in the year as self-denial weeks, especially during the warmer, lighter months from May till the end of October? We have had our War Weapons Week and our Warships Week. Self-denial weeks, with the object of saving on consumption in every possible way, would be an inspiring gesture of a truly religious character. Let the Spartan spirit of our Merchant Navy find expression also on the home front. The Church might give a lead with self-denial sermons, the Press, the Wireless, and the prestige advertisers could help to popularize the idea. The first week in June, August and October might be devoted to this national service in patriotic thrift.

H.M.S. RAILINGS

Gates and railings during the week ending March 21 yielded a record total of 12,000 tons—more than sufficient in dead weight of metal to replace a heavy cruiser. London's share was 5,591 tons.

THE salvage of railings has proved one of the most practical and valuable emergency orders of the war. There is no little symbolism in the fact that these bits of old iron that once more or less protected the Englishman's home in the private sense are now being used nationally

to stop the German gate-crasher. We have said farewell to our railings without any particular regret. On the whole, they were anything but beautiful and not very useful. The fashion for cheap iron work in domestic architecture and round open spaces was already passing before the War, and it is hardly likely to revive again. Somehow or other, such cast-iron reserve does not fit into the larger scheme of freedom for which civilization is fighting. There are many other kinds of railings that will have to go before the new world can be built, but they are in the nature of mental barricades to reforms long overdue.

EUROPE'S DARKEST AGE

It is inevitable that Fascism should curse the intellectuals. Historians will call the years of Hitler's easy victories the " black-out of Europe." The Fascists dread men who think—men on whose features shines the light, whether it emanates from the birth of new ideas, or as a reflection from the past.—Ilya Ehrenburg

TO say as some people do that Hitler has brought Europe back to the Middle Ages is an insult to the men who built the cathedrals and instituted the ideal of chivalry. In the whole history of the world there is no epoch foul enough to be compared to Hitlerite Germany, for Nazism is a deliberate and diabolical plan to destroy the human mind. All that is fine in past experience, whether in religion, art, poetry and philosophy, must necessarily be obliterated before Hitler can realize his mad dream of chaining mankind to the chariot of the Herrenvolk. The link that binds truly civilized men together is a belief in humanity as the chosen vehicle for the expression of truth and justice, though great minds differ as to these ideals, and the method of their attainment. It has remained to the Nazis to exalt lying, plunder and murder into cardinal virtues. Hitler's hatred of all culture, even German, is due to the fear that the system he has created is doomed whatever victories he may achieve, for it is impossible to deny the spiritual force behind man's instinct and longing for perfection. This power is proof against all the machinery of death, as the Nazis will ultimately learn.

PLEA FOR OPTIMISTIC RESOLUTION

Could Hitler have seen into the future would he have set his military machine in motion? He hoped to destroy the nations piecemeal. He has temporarily subjugated some, but the greatest Powers in the world are now ranged against him in overwhelming strength and resolution.

WITH the warmer and more cheerful weather may we hope that Britain will forget her long winter of discontent, and in a spirit of renewed optimism and unity get on with the war? This is no time for pessimism. We must look at the war as a whole, and not concentrate on reverses which, in regard to our initial weakness, were inevitable. The electorate as well as the leaders they chose to guide them during the abysmal period between the two wars must take their fair share of blame. They demanded disarmament and sought peace almost at any price. History can record no more tragic example of political

RECCE CORPS dispatch rider keeping various units in touch during exercises. The Army Reconnaissance Corps is called " the armed eyes of the Army." *Photo, British Official: Crown Copyright*

myopia than occurred during the twenty years between 1919 and 1939. While we were all talking and acting peace the dictators were preparing to destroy us. Even with the Hun at our gates we refused to have conscription. The wonder is that Britain has not only survived but that she can visualize victory on the horizon. Let us remember our deliverance with gratitude to all the men who have helped to save us. Our defeats are deplorable, but do we realize how great, how providential perhaps, have been our victories? They brought us through the darkest days when we stood alone, and they are the foundation upon which the Allies will triumph. Pessimism in the face of our grand record of courage and endurance is an unworthy and dangerous attitude of mind.

THE WREN CHURCHES

It is an important and interesting fact that only one of the blitzed Wren churches is a total wreck.

WREN was undoubtedly one of Britain's greatest architects, and though his work in London has suffered cruelly as a result of German raids the essential structure of many of his churches survives. This fact must be remembered in any plans for general reconstruction of the town. Wholesale demolition of such aesthetically valuable buildings, though damaged, would be a great loss to our architectural heritage. The Wren churches that can be restored must have their place in the new survey of London. Just as we cherish Old Masters in painting, so must we preserve the classics of architecture. It is to be hoped that Wren churches will be given more space, and thus seen to better advantage.

ITALIAN PRISONERS, mostly captured in the Tobruk area, at work in a London Park. All the prisoners have large, circular patches on the back for identification purposes. *Photo, Keystone*

We Must Have Ships, Ever More Ships

ANOTHER MERCHANT SHIP is nearing completion on the stocks and will soon be launched from one of Britain's yards. Speaking at Liverpool on March 22, Mr. Attlee stated that the naval tonnage we completed in the last quarter of 1941 was four times as much as in the last quarter before the war and merchant shipping twice as much. Current production is greater than at any time in the last war, when there were more yards, more men and no "blitz" and black-out to contend with.

Photo, Keystone

More Than 1,600 Air Raids On Malta!

Scenes from the raids on Malta. Circle left, a policeman on duty at the Royal Naval Dockyard watches the battle imperturbably. Centre, a workman descending by rope from a building on which he was working. Right, dockyard workers entering a rock shelter following an "imminent danger" signal.

Above, the charred wreckage of a Ju 88 dive-bomber shot down over Malta by Hurricane fighters. Circle right, an R.A.F. Wing Commander in charge of a Blenheim squadron based on Malta. The small bombs painted on "Old Joe's" fuselage denote the number of raids this aircraft has carried out on enemy territory and shipping.

MALTA UNDAUNTED by more than 1,600 air raids still goes about its business with calm and dignity. This is Kingsway, main street of Valletta, with many of its shops, churches and houses destroyed by bombing. But Malta is magnificently defended : even the Germans admit as much. "In Malta," said a speaker on the German radio on March 15, "the British possess air defences which are unequalled." They should know. Hundreds of Axis planes have been brought down there by British Spitfires, Hurricanes, and A.A. guns.

Photos, British Official

They 'Ride in Whirlwinds and Direct the Storm'

WHIRLWINDS, in mass formation, are seen above, their four 20-mm. cannon, mounted in the nose, being clearly visible against the clouds. These cannon, whose great fire power makes the Whirlwind a dangerous opponent for the Luftwaffe pilot, are seen close up on the right. A mechanic is about to take off the covers. Below, members of a Whirlwind squadron in front of one of their planes. The Whirlwind single-seat monoplane fighter is powered with two Rolls-Royce Peregrine engines, each of 850 h.p. An unusual feature which distinguishes this aircraft is the tail unit, the tail planes being set far above the line of the fuselage and towards the upper extremity of the high fin.

Photos, Fox, Associated Press

MacArthur and His Yanks Arrive 'Down Under'

While American airmen were plastering the Japanese troops and transports in the New Guinea area, a great host of their fellow-countrymen were quietly arriving at Australian ports. Below we describe their coming, and something is told also of the dramatic advent of their commander, gallant MacArthur of Philippine fame.

IN the Prime Minister's office in Canberra the telephone rang. Mr. Curtin picked up the receiver. It was the American General Brett at the other end—Brett, Deputy C.-in-C. of the A B D A front. "MacArthur has arrived," came the brief statement; "I am sending you a fuller message by plane." Already two airmen—by happy augury, an Australian and an American—were flying to Canberra; and soon the Prime Minister had General Brett's message in his hand.

"The President of the United States," it read, "directs me to present his compliments, and to inform you that General Douglas MacArthur, of the United States Army, has arrived in Australia from the Philippines. In accordance with his directions, General MacArthur has assumed command of all the United States Army forces here. Should it accord with your wishes and those of the Australian people, the President suggests that it would be highly acceptable to him and pleasing to the American people for the Australian Government to nominate General MacArthur supreme commander of all the Allied forces in the south-west Pacific. Such nomination should be submitted simultaneously to London and Washington. The President is in general agreement with the proposals regarding the organization and command of the Australian area, and regrets that he has been unable to inform you of General MacArthur's pending arrival, but feels certain that you will appreciate that his safety during the voyage from the Philippines required the highest order of secrecy."

Forthwith, Mr. Curtin sent an enthusiastic cable to President Roosevelt.

"General MacArthur's heroic defence of the Philippines has evoked the admiration of the world and has been an example of the stubborn resistance with which the advance of the enemy ought to be opposed. The Australian Government feels that his leadership of the Allied forces in this theatre will be an inspiration to the Australian people and to all the forces which will be privileged to serve under his command."

On the same day (March 17) the American War Department in New York announced that General Douglas MacArthur, accompanied by Mrs. MacArthur and their four-year-old son, by his Chief of Staff, Brig.-Gen.

Richard K. Sutherland, Brig.-Gen. Harold H. George of the Air Corps, and several other staff officers, had arrived that day in Australia by aeroplane. It was stated that General MacArthur was to be Supreme Commander in that region, including the Philippine Islands, in accordance with the request of the Australian Government; and it

Gen. MacARTHUR (left) shaking hands with one of Australia's military leaders on arrival for his first conference in Melbourne. Photograph radioed from Australia.

was revealed that as early as Feb. 22 General MacArthur had been ordered by President Roosevelt to transfer his headquarters from the Philippines to Australia as soon as the necessary arrangements could be made. General MacArthur had requested that he might be permitted to perfect arrangements within his command in the Philippines, and the consequent delay had been authorized by the President.

Escape from the Philippines

How did MacArthur get to Australia? The story of his escape from the enemy-infested Philippines makes dramatic reading. By a fortunate chance a squadron of six American motor torpedo-boats arrived in the Philippines shortly before the outbreak of war, and it was in these M.T.B.s that he decided to make his escape, although some of his senior officers urged that he should make the attempt by submarine. But General MacArthur put his trust in Capt. Bulkely's little ships.

Soon after sunset on March 12 the little party started off in four motor torpedo-boats. In the early hours of the next morning the boats were separated, and most were late in arriving at the appointed rendezvous. At nightfall the boats put out to sea again, but now they were only three, as one had developed engine trouble and the passengers had to be transferred. All three ships sighted enemy destroyers, but they managed to get by undetected, and by noon they reached their second rendezvous.

Here they went ashore and pushed inland to where it had been arranged for three Flying Fortresses to pick them up. But the planes were late. After three days and nights the little party began to fear that the planes had been shot down.

But on the fourth night they heard the welcome drone of the bomber's engines and

soon two Fortresses—but only two—came to land. MacArthur squeezed the whole party into the two planes, leaving perforce a quantity of baggage and arms behind. They took off at midnight on March 16 and, after flying over an area under Japanese control, managed to reach Darwin safely between 8 and 9 o'clock in the morning. Making a quick transfer to another plane, they resumed the southward journey via Alice Springs.

But MacArthur was by no means the first American to arrive "down under." For weeks past, indeed, thousands of American troops and airmen had been arriving at Australian ports. The first clue to their arrival was when it was announced on Jan. 6 that "American visitors might make payments in Australian currency." Convoy after convoy of great luxury liners, cargo boats, and warships, crossed 12,000 miles of the South Pacific, dodging the submarines which tried in vain to penetrate the American Navy's protective curtain.

Hardly had the troopships docked when the men in Yankee uniform streamed down the gangways, followed by an endless chain of vehicles, transport trucks and guns of every calibre. As they passed through the city streets on the way to camp they were stared at, then delightedly mobbed, by the Australians, who could not do too much for the American visitors. But still their presence was not officially announced, and the Australian girls greet their new-found "dough-boy" friends with "Hullo, Official Secret, how do you like it here?"

Early in January a U.S. Army headquarters was set up in Australia, and very shortly in several of the provincial capitals American soldiers far outnumbered their Australian comrades. American airmen were there, too, in great numbers and the sight of American planes, including Kitty-hawks and Flying Fortresses, became a familiar spectacle in the Australian sky. But it was not until March 17 that Mr. Stimson, the U.S. Secretary of War, announced in Washington that "units of the United States Army, including both air and ground troops in considerable numbers, are now in Australia."

It was on March 21 that General MacArthur reached Melbourne, and from his hotel he issued a statement to the press.

"I am glad" [he said], "to be in immediate cooperation with the Australian soldier. I know him well from World War days, and admire him greatly. I have every confidence of the ultimate success of our joint cause, but success in modern war requires something more than courage and willingness to die; it requires careful preparation. This means the furnishing of sufficient troops and material to meet the known strength of a potential enemy. No general can make something out of nothing. My success or failure depends primarily on the resources that the respective Governments place at my disposal."

"My faith in them," he concluded, "is complete. In any event I will do my best. I will keep the soldier's faith."

U.S. AIRMEN now operating from Australia examine the wing of their bomber riddled with bullets from Jap fighters while raiding enemy-occupied territory. *Photo, Planet News*

Australia Remembers—and Prepares

In the Great War the Australians played a great and noble part. The memory of those who served lives as an inspiration in the present hour of trial; it is symbolized in this impressive stone temple, the War Memorial in Melbourne. Within is a " Rock of Rememrance," so placed that a shaft of light from an aperture in the roof strikes it at **11** a.m. on November **11**.

Twixt Palm-fringed Shore and Desert

Darwin, little town in Northern Territory with a peacetime population of about 1,000, is now a vital strategic base with thousands of troops stationed in and around it. 1, Engineers of the A.I.F. laying a bridge over a swamp near Darwin. The country hereabouts is of a tropical nature and the rainfall heavy. 2, Australian Light Horsemen galloping over the sand dunes of the interior.

PM

Darwin's Defenders Make Ready for War

3, Men of the A.I.F. making a clearance through the jungle for a new road. Many such roads are now being made. 4, Soldiers of the Darwin battalion marching beneath pandanus palms and gum trees in the Darwin sector. 5, Axemen of the A.I.F. Engineers, stationed near Darwin, felling trees for bridge building. Australia works as she will fight—with all the vigour of a young people.

Most Australians Live in Cities!

Photos, Wide World, Fox

Third largest city in the British Empire is Sydney, capital of the state of New South Wales; one of its finest residential districts is seen in the top photograph. In the centre is the old Government House, now dwarfed by modern skyscrapers. Left, Unity Building and Town Hall, Melbourne, capital of Victoria. Right, the City Hall of Brisbane, capital of Queensland.

St. Nazaire : Most Daring Raid Since Zeebrugge

Just four weeks after the raid on Bruneval, another combined operation was delivered on March 27–28, this time against the Nazi U-boat base at St. Nazaire. What follows is based on the official communiqués ; accounts by Gordon Holman, Reuter's and Exchange correspondent, and other eye-witnesses, will be given in our next number.

ALL was quiet in St. Nazaire that Friday night. The tide was running high, and low clouds obscured the moon, now nearing the full. In the harbour basin German U-boats lay at anchor, where a quarter of a century ago a great host of Americans landed to help win the first Great War. Most of the town's population and the garrison were abed and asleep, but the German sentries were awake, and every now and then the searchlights swept the waters of the estuary. From north to south they wheeled and then back again, and for hours there was nothing to report. But at length—it must have been round about midnight—the probing finger of light picked out a number of darkened ships swiftly making their way through the narrow channel which lies between the shore and a line of sandbanks. At once the alarm was given, and the curtain went up on a drama such as has not been played since the Zeebrugge raid of St. George's Day in 1918.

ST. NAZAIRE, the large dock. This photograph was taken when the Normandie was there and gives an idea of the size of the dock, which is large enough to hold the German battleship Tirpitz. The picture of H.M.S. Campbeltown was superimposed to show how she rammed the dock gate. *Photo, Courtesy of The Daily Mail*

What followed has been tersely related in a series of official communiqués. The first, issued on the morning of Saturday, March 28, merely stated that " a combined operation was carried out in the early hours of this morning by units of all three Services in a small raid on St. Nazaire." The second, issued late the same evening, gave the news that a signal had been received from the raiding force which was now returning safely. Twenty-four hours later the third communiqué was much more detailed.

Carried out in the early hours of March 28 by light forces of the Royal Navy (under the command of Cmdr. R. E. D. Ryder, R.N.), Special Service Troops (led by Lt.-Col. A. C. Newman, of the Essex Regiment), and R.A.F. aircraft, the raid was primarily directed against the large dry docks and the harbour installations at St. Nazaire.

H.M.S Campbeltown (ex-American destroyer U.S.S. Buchanan), with bows specially stiffened and filled with five tons of delayed action high explosive, forced her way through the doubled torpedo baffle protecting the entrance to the lock and rammed the centre of the main lock gate. The force of the impact was such that the destroyer came to a standstill only when her bridge was abreast the gate itself. As soon as the bows of the Campbeltown were firmly wedged, Special Service Troops landed as arranged and set about the work of demolition. The pumping station and dock-operating gear were destroyed, and other demolition work was carried out according to plan.

Meanwhile a motor torpedo boat had fired two delayed action torpedoes at the entrance to the U-boat basin and a motor launch had taken off the crew of

Commander R. E. D. Ryder, 34-year-old polar explorer, who commanded the naval forces in the raid on St. Nazaire. *Photo, News Chronicle*

The docks at St. Nazaire, showing the lock gates rammed by H.M.S. Campbeltown and the entrance to the U-boat base at which delayed action torpedoes were fired. Lt.-Cmdr. Beattie, commanding the Campbeltown, was reported missing. *Photo, Associated Press*

the Campbeltown. A large explosion, followed by a smaller one, was seen and heard by our returning forces at 4 a.m., which was the time the delayed action fuses were due to go off.

The raid caused panic among the enemy, who fired indiscriminately at friend and foe. The enemy's 6-in. guns sank one of their own flak ships at the time she was engaging our returning forces.

Only a small proportion of the diversionary bombing could be carried out on account of low cloud for fear of inflicting casualties on the French civilian population.

Their task accomplished, our troops commenced to withdraw in motor launches detailed for the purpose to rejoin the covering force of destroyers. Enemy machine-guns appear to have prevented the full withdrawal of some of our forces.

Five German torpedo boats came into sight and opened fire on our motor launches. The escorting destroyers drove them off and forced them to retire. (Although classed by the Germans as torpedo boats, these vessels are similar to our "S" class destroyers.) Beaufighters, Hudsons and Blenheims of Coastal Command provided air protection to our returning forces.

As was only to be expected, the German High Command claimed that the raid had been a complete failure. But German war correspondents who were there paid high tribute to the British forces who had taken part in the operations. " Even after being isolated from the main force," wrote one correspondent, ". certain British units continued bitter resistance. They established themselves in houses, and kept up fire from the windows, fighting with terrific fury."

Another wrote of Scottish troops who, wearing rubber-soled shoes, landed swiftly and silently on the shore without being seen by the German defenders ; " they advanced on the town and established themselves in the houses, resisting every attack most stubbornly." Yet another, quoted by the official German news agency, revealed that it was not until 8 a.m. that the harbour and town were once again completely in German hands.

This last fact is eloquent of the magnificent stand made by those of the raiders who had been unable to regain the boats ; it was proof that for four hours after the raid's end they maintained a fierce resistance. The Germans claimed about a hundred prisoners, and there were many casualties not only in the landing force but in the accompanying ships. When the expedition arrived back in port on Sunday, March 29, the White Ensign was flown at half-mast, and naval ratings were kept busy carrying wounded men on stretchers to the waiting ambulances. But, as Gordon Holman wrote : " The men who paid the bill were the last who counted the cost."

SOLDIERS OF THE RED BANNER. In the Far East, as is told in the article in the facing page, Soviet Russia has a powerful, numerous and well-equipped army; this photograph shows a Russian patrol somewhere on the frontier between Siberia and Japanese-controlled Manchukuo. Just how strong these Red Banner armies are is a matter of conjecture, but it may be confidently assumed that they are well capable of meeting any thrust of the Japanese if the aggressive instinct of the war lords at Tokyo should embolden them to go north after their all-too-easy successes in the south.

Photo, Planet News

Page 628

Stalin Has Another Army in the Far East

"If they dare poke their pig's snout into our Soviet garden," Stalin is reported to have said once when the Japanese were adopting a particularly truculent attitude, "it will get a rap which they will never forget." This article tells of the men who may be expected to give that rap if and when it is required.

FIVE thousand miles beyond Moscow, right on the other side of Asia in the provinces that fringe the Pacific, Russia's Army of the Far East stands ready for war. Really it is three armies : the Army of the Transbaikal Military District on the Mongolian border, and the First and Second Red Banner Armies with their headquarters at Vladivostok and on the Amur river.

As long ago as 1935 the Red Army in the Far East (says Max Werner) was in a position to put about 300,000 men into the field against Japan. That was but a beginning, however, and there can be no doubt that every year that has passed has seen a considerable increase in its strength. By the autumn of 1938 it was reliably reported to have numbered over half a million. Today its field strength is reported to be a million, and some military writers are of the opinion that the Russians could put three million men into the field against the Japanese. Certain it is that in addition to the first-line troops there is a very large number of reservists—men who, after they have completed their period of service, have settled as colonists in the vast and still sparsely peopled areas which constitute the Far Eastern command. For some years past young Russians have been encouraged to enlist in the Red Banner armies. The encouragement consists not only in appeals to patriotism, to the desire for change and adventure and " see the world at the army's expense," but of pay somewhat higher than that of the ordinary Red Army man. Thus the Red Banner armies have claim to be regarded as a " corps d'élite," since they contain a very large element of the most vigorous and enterprising of Russia's young manhood. Moreover, they are reported to be particularly well supplied with all the machinery of modern war—with heavy guns in plenty, masses of light artillery, mechanized cavalry and several thousand tanks. To what extent the Red Banner armies have had to contribute in men and equipment to the war against Hitler can hardly be determined, but it seems safe to assume that their strength has not been seriously diminished.

All authorities lay stress on the fact that the Far Eastern army is entirely separate from that which is fighting so valiantly in the west ; it has been the definite policy of Stalin and the Russian military authorities to create and maintain it in a state of both military and economic independence. To an almost complete extent its supplies are derived from local sources ; and here we must remember that the Far Eastern provinces of the Soviet are vast in extent (some 3,000,000 square miles), of huge productive capacity, and possessed of still vaster potentialities. During the last ten or a dozen years the whole face of the Soviet Far East has been transformed. Extensive schemes of hydro-

electric development have been carried out. Great towns—Khabarovsk, capital of the Far Eastern Territory, and Komsomolsk, a centre of the machine-tool industry, Cheremkhovo on the Baikal coal-field—have arisen on the sites of obscure villages or in the heart of the unpeopled *taiga*. Steel plants and coal mines provide some of the most important of war's raw materials ; while oil, that other prime essential, comes by pipeline from the Russian (northern) half of the island of Sakhalin. Save perhaps for wheat the Far East Regions provide all the foodstuffs required for their population and the Army, while in Vladivostok huge canneries have been established to deal with tremendous quantities of fish—today as in the past one of the most important of the elements in the Russian soldier's diet. Then the Far Eastern Command has its own shipyards, its own plane factories, and its own plant for the production and repair of tanks and other war vehicles.

Doubling the Trans-Siberian

None of this development would have been possible unless it had gone hand in hand with an immense extension of the transport system. At the time of the Russo-Japanese war of 1904-5 the Trans-Siberian Railway to Vladivostok was a single track, so that only a one-way traffic was possible ; the goods trucks as they arrived at the Far Eastern terminus were flung off the line and dumped. Lack of supplies was one of the main reasons for Russia's defeat in that war of a generation ago, but such a situation should never arise again. By 1938 the Trans-Siberian railway's tremendous length had been double-tracked, and work is now proceeding on the treble-tracking of considerable lengths. Moreover, a new Siberian railway is being, or has been, constructed, running to the north of the old line, from Taishet in Central Siberia through Bodaibo and Komsomolsk to Sovietskaya, on the Pacific facing Sakhalin. Connecting links between the two railways have been built, in particular one between Komsomolsk and Khabarovsk. The road

Marshal V. BLUECHER, mystery man of the Soviet Army, whose name has been associated, rightly or not no one yet knows, with the Red Armies in the Far East. *Photo, G.P.U.*

system, too, has been developed in the most revolutionary fashion, since there is now a network of motor-roads linking all the centres of industry and of strategy in the Far East, from Outer Mongolia to the shores of the Sea of Okhotsk. Werner describes this road building as probably the biggest strategical transport feat of our generation.

Guarding the vital Trans-Siberian and North Baikal railways is a vast and powerful defence system running from Vladivostok to Lake Baikal and hugging the Amur and Ussuri rivers where they form the border with Japanese-controlled Manchukuo. Built between 1932 and 1937, this Far Eastern Maginot Line is reported to be three miles deep and to include 5,000 concrete pill-boxes armed with cannon and machine-guns and numerous gas-proof and bomb-proof subterranean chambers. Behind this fortified zone are sited a number of aerodromes (see map).

Vladivostok is the main base of Russia's Far Eastern fleet, since it is the only Russian port in the Pacific which is ice-free, or can be kept free by ice-breakers, throughout the year. Of late years its repair yards have been extended and a floating-dock installed. At the same time a new town and port has been brought into being at Sovietskaya, while a new naval base has been constructed at Nikolayevsk at the mouth of the Amur river. Yet another new naval base is at Petropavlovsk in Kamchatka.

To end on a personal note, who are the Soviet commanders in the Far East ? That is an official secret, but two men have been associated for years past with that vital region : Marshal Vassili Bluecher and General Grigori Stern. Bluecher is a man in his early forties who was largely responsible for the establishment of the Soviet Mongolian Republic, after which he commanded the Communist armies in China which were cooperating with General Chiang Kai-shek. Stern is not yet forty, but, according to report, he fought for the Government in the Spanish Civil War, and in 1938 was recalled to Russia to become Bluecher's chief-of-staff. In 1938 he was in command of the Soviet forces which defeated the Japanese in the battle of Changkufeng on the Manchukuo border, and again in the next year in Outer Mongolia. At the beginning of last year he was reported to be bringing the Russian defences in the Far East into a still higher state of efficiency, ready for the day when (so the Russians have long anticipated) the Japanese war lords go north as well as south.

RUSSIA'S PACIFIC FRONT faces the islands of Japan, while on land it runs for many hundreds of miles with that of Japanese-controlled Manchukuo. Of particular interest, then, are the Russian air and naval bases shown in this map. From Vladivostok to Tokyo is some 700 miles.

Our Diary of the War

FRIDAY, MAR. 20, 1942   930th day

Russian Front.—Fighting fiercest around Leningrad and west of Staraya Russa.

Mediterranean.—Heavy air attacks on shipping in the Grand Harbour at Malta.

Far East.—Jap forces advanced along the Markham valley of New Guinea from Lae. Port Moresby raided by Jap bombers. In Burma, Chinese cavalry inflicted considerable casualties on a mixed enemy force.

Home.—Bombs dropped after dark by enemy bombers in S.W. England.

SATURDAY, MAR. 21   931st day

Russian Front.—Heavy fighting in the Donetz sector. Russians reported nearing Orel.

Mediterranean.—Admiralty announced sinking of two large enemy supply ships in Central Mediterranean by British submarine. Malta defences destroyed 17 enemy aircraft in heaviest raids of the year.

Africa.—Free French H.Q. announced that Gen. Leclerc's columns had raided new Italian outposts in Zuila-Temessa district, N.E. of Murzuk.

Far East.—In Burma, heavy fighting around railway junction of Letpadan. Japs advancing towards Toungoo. Derby and Broome, in W. Australia, attacked by enemy aircraft. Allied bombers raided Rabaul; hits scored on two enemy cruisers.

SUNDAY, MAR. 22.   932nd day

Sea.—Naval forces under Rear-Adm. Vian, covering passage of a convoy through Mediterranean, made contact with an Italian force. Italian battleship torpedoed and set on fire; two cruisers damaged. British losses, one merchant ship sunk; one destroyer hit.

Russian Front.—Moscow announced 12,000 Germans killed in ten-day battle on the Kalinin front.

Africa.—Cairo announced that mobile columns of the 8th Army had carried out a successful two-day raid behind Rommel's lines in Libya.

Far East.—Japs made daylight raid on Darwin and Katherine. Allied planes heavily bombed Lae in New Guinea.

General.—Sir Stafford Cripps arrived in India.

MONDAY, MAR. 23   933rd day

Russian Front.—Russian forces reported to have surrounded Novgorod.

Mediterranean.—Admiralty announced two U-boats, two supply ships, six schooners and a motor transport vessel sunk by British submarines.

Far East.—At least 12 enemy planes destroyed in attack on Mingaladon aerodrome. U.S. Navy Dept. announced that a U.S submarine had sunk three Jap ships and damaged two others in Japanese waters. Port Moresby raided by Jap planes.

Japanese occupied the Andaman Islands in the Bay of Bengal.

Home.—Night raids over S.E. Coast. Two enemy aircraft destroyed.

TUESDAY, MAR. 24   934th day

Air.—R.A.F. made daylight attack on power station at Comines, near Lille, and other objectives in N. France.

Russian Front.—No material change. Heavy fighting in Donetz sector and on the Kerch peninsula.

Far East.—Heavy raid on Port Moresby. In Philippines, Corregidor raided by 54 Japanese heavy bombers. Three shot down. A.V.G. bombers attacked enemy airfields at Chiengmai and Lamphun, in Siam. Chinese forces in Burma resisting Jap drive to Toungoo.

Home.—Night raids over S. Coast. Formation of a General Staff for War Production announced.

WEDNESDAY, MAR. 25   935th day

Air.—R.A.F. sweep over N. France. Heavy night raid on Essen and targets in the Ruhr. Daylight attack on shipyards at Le Trait, west of Rouen. Night attacks on docks at St. Nazaire.

Mediterranean.—Heavy air raids on harbour at Malta. Three enemy aircraft destroyed, 3 probably destroyed and 8 seriously damaged. Many others hit.

Far East.—U.S. Navy Dept. announced successful naval raids on Wake Island and Marcus Island by Vice-Adm. Halsey's Pacific Fleet "Task Force." Chinese forces threatened with being cut off on Toungoo front in Burma. Port Moresby again raided.

THURSDAY, MAR. 26   936th day

Air.—R.A.F. attacked shipping and docks at Le Havre in daylight. Eight German fighters destroyed. Night raids on Ruhr. Daylight attacks on oil refinery near Ghent and airfields in Holland.

Russian Front.—Germans lost at least 11 aircraft in heavy raid over Murmansk. Soviet troops made further progress in Leningrad sector.

Mediterranean.—Violent air raid on Malta. Four enemy bombers shot down, another probably destroyed and four damaged.

Far East. — Chinese troops defending Toungoo against heavy Japanese attacks. Chinese troops advancing towards Jap bases at Tangaw and Heighong, in Siam. In Philippines, Corregidor raided seven times in twenty-four hours. Allied bombers raided Jap shipping at Kupang, Timor.

Home.—Night bombs on N.E. Coast.

FRIDAY, MAR. 27   937th day

Air.—R.A.F. bombers with fighter escort attacked objectives at Ostend. Night attack on aerodromes in Low Countries.

Russian Front.—Russians made combined land, sea and air attack behind German lines at Murmansk, where Nazis were preparing an offensive.

Far East.—Twentieth raid on Port Moresby. In Burma, Jap forces continued their pressure against Chinese and British units around Toungoo.

Home.—Daylight "hit-and-run" raids on S.W. Coast. Night bombs on N.E. Coast and E. Anglia.

General.—General Sir Thomas Blamey appointed Commander-in-Chief of the allied land forces in Australia. President of the Philippines' arrival in Australia officially announced. Another attempt made on the life of Marcel Déat, leader of pro-Nazi National Popular Party in France.

SATURDAY, MAR. 28   938th day

Air.—Fierce air battle over Channel. At least 13 German aircraft destroyed for the loss of 5 British planes. Heavy night raid on Lubeck. R.A.F. dropped leaflets on Paris.

Far East.—Japanese making great effort to capture Toungoo.

General.—Attack by British Navy, Army and Air units on the German naval base at St. Nazaire. Main dock gate blown up by ramming it with an ex-American destroyer (H.M.S. Campbeltown) filled with tons of high explosive. Special Service troops carried out prearranged demolitions in the dockyards. Bulgaria declared war on Russia. H.M. the King broadcast to the nation.

SUNDAY, MAR. 29   939th day

Air.—Coastal Command made night attack on enemy shipping off Norwegian coast. Fighters made offensive sweep over N. France.

Russian Front.—Big German counter-attack in Kalinin sector smashed after five-day battle. Heavy Soviet attacks in Donetz area.

Far East.—Toungoo, in Burma, partly evacuated by Chinese forces. Japanese force striking west of the Irrawaddy threatened Prome.

Home.—Single raider dropped bombs at night in E. Anglia.

General.—British proposals for India announced in New Delhi.

MONDAY, MAR. 30   940th day

Sea.—Admiralty announced loss of H.M.S. Naiad, 5,450 ton cruiser.

Russian Front.—Russians recaptured an extensive district in the Smolensk area. Heavy Soviet attacks north-east of Taganrog.

Far East.—Jap forces driven back on Irrawaddy front by British tanks. Chinese still holding part of Toungoo. In the Philippines a new Japanese attack repulsed with heavy losses. Darwin raided by Japanese aircraft.

General.—Sir Stafford Cripps broadcast to India's peoples from New Delhi. Anti-war riots reported at Sofia.

TUESDAY, MAR. 31   941st day

Sea.—Admiralty announced safe arrival at Murmansk of important convoy for Russia despite four German attempts to annihilate it. Three U-boats were severely damaged, if not sunk. The enemy lost one, possibly two, destroyers.

Russian Front.—34 inhabited places on the Kalinin front recaptured by Soviet troops in two days' fighting. On Donetz front, Kharkov reported encircled by Russian troops. Moscow communiqué announced sinking of a U-boat and an enemy transport in Barents Sea.

Far East.—Heavy fighting at Shwedaung, 10 miles south of Prome, in Burma. Battle for Toungoo, on the Mandalay road, still raging. In Australia, Japanese planes raided Darwin. R.A.A.F. bombers blasted airfield at Koepang, Dutch Timor.

General.—Australian Army reorganized in two commands.

H.M. Submarine TALISMAN comes home. Her successes in the Mediterranean are denoted by her own "Jolly Roger." The bars represent enemy supply ships sunk, the transfixed U the sinking of an enemy submarine, the crossed guns and star denotes a gun action with an Italian destroyer and the dagger another successful exploit. *Photo, British Official*

Is Sweden Next on Hitler's Programme?

New Swedish aircraft. Most of Sweden's aeroplanes are of foreign type built under licence, though the aircraft department of the Götaverken builds training planes of its own design.

SWEDISH TROOPS on Gottland, big island in the Baltic. These soldiers are at musketry practice before the old town wall of Visby, seaport of Gottland. Left, men of Sweden's "Home Guard," who would augment her standing army in case of invasion.

SWEDISH WARSHIPS lying off Stockholm. With the approach of spring, rumours were circulating that Sweden might prove to be the next victim of a Nazi attack. Sweden has a small but useful fleet—it is stated to include two cruisers, three coast defence ships which may be classed as battleships, and a number of smaller vessels—which Germany would no doubt like to gain control of, but Sweden has had time to put her defences in order, and it is unlikely that a German attack would go unchallenged.

Photos, L.N.A., Black Star, Keystone

Those Magnificent Men of the 'Red Duster'

Raising in the House of Commons on March 19 the question of the Mercantile Marine, Mr. A. P. Herbert urged that a message of good will, hope, admiration, and gratitude should be sent to the gallant officers and men who are facing such great dangers. Several spoke in support, but an appeal for a Royal Commission to inquire into seamen's conditions was rejected.

PERHAPS the greatest story of the war is that which tells of the part that is being played by the Merchant Navy. But for this mysterious flotilla of all sizes and conditions, pitching, tossing, fighting—and alas, sometimes sinking—in the Seven Seas ; but for a devoted band of sailors who have made up their minds to " deliver the goods " or die, Britain herself would have been sunk.

When the average longshoreman talks glibly about the Battle of the Atlantic, which has been variously won, lost and won again, has he the faintest conception what it means ? The veil is occasionally lifted. So many tons of shipping have been destroyed in so many months. Another chapter in the chronicle of sublime courage appears in the newspapers. Something almost incredibly brave and grand, like the epic fight of the Jervis Bay, echoes across the vicious Atlantic. We read of men on rafts under a pitiless sun in a sea infested with sharks, men singing and joking as if they were enjoying a Bank Holiday on Hampstead Heath. In Arctic latitudes sailors in open boats laugh and try to cheer each other as the food and water fail and the cold paralyses their limbs. And all this because Britons are so brave and kind and patriotic that they are willing, happily willing, to face every conceivable horror so that their country shall live.

Even in peacetime it is a hard life to be a merchant sailor. Ten to one the elements are against you. Food is none too good, ships are old, and working conditions are sometimes as foul as the weather. But in time of war it is one long gamble with ubiquitous death.

Then there are books which tell of the endless struggle against odds, Nature's and the enemy's. One such is Warren Armstrong's The Red Duster at War (Gollancz). Mr. Armstrong tells us that " *effective* tonnage for carrying foodstuffs and raw materials and troops at the outbreak of this war was barely 14,000,000 gross tons, as compared with 17,500,000 tons in 1914." To confront and shoulder responsibilities immensely greater than in 1914 we possessed 2,000 fewer vessels in 1937-8— 28 per cent of the world's tonnage instead of 44 per cent !

We had lost after nineteen months of war 5,500,000 tons of shipping, more than three times as much as was sunk in a similar period of the last war.

These figures speak volumes both as to the suicidal policy which allowed our merchant shipping to rot in peacetime, and of the heroism and resource of the Merchant Navy since the Germans resumed their traditional plan of murder on the high seas by sinking the Athenia on the very first day of the war. A merchant seaman quoted by Mr. Armstrong puts the position regarding the decline and fall of tonnage into forcible language :

" When there was stink of war in the air wherever you went, and when every damned country was building battleships, aeroplanes, guns and tanks, and raising new and bigger armies, navies and air forces—and when Britain had forgotten to think in terms of merchant ships ! Show me the battleship that can fight, the bomber that can fly, or the tank that can go into action—the armies, navies or air forces that can be moved, clothed, munitioned, fed and maintained—*or the munition factories that can work without the existence of an adequate Merchant fleet !* and you'd be showing me something worth looking at ! *Wasn't* that the real position in 1938, less than a year before we were at war again ? And what was happening ? Economic experts seriously planned a more or less wholesale lay-up of U.K. merchant shipping ! "

While the public was being regaled with picturesque stories of the launching of the new luxury liners, the Mauretania and the Queen Elizabeth, the shipbuilding industry as a whole was coming to a standstill and thousands of skilled men had drifted and were drifting away into other industries. What was wanted was a large number of small vessels between 1,500 and 5,000 gross tons, "which includes the general utility tramp - steamers *on which we must rely for supplies both of food and raw materials,*" and it was precisely in this category that the 2,000 reduction between 1914 and 1939 was made.

Only a few men seemed to realize that when the new war began Britain would be dangerously handicapped unless she greatly increased the number of merchant ships. In a Parliamentary debate at the end of 1938 Lt.-Cdr. Fletcher (now Lord Winster) uttered a reminder of our lack in this respect. How were we to bring in three-quarters of our food, the raw materials, essential for munitions, to transport our troops, and to feed 4,000,000 more mouths in this country than during the last war ? In 1914 we imported 646,000,000 gallons of petroleum. In 1935 those imports had gone up to 2,808,000,000 gallons.

While Britain was laying up ships our foreign competitors were building and subsidizing. Our shipping trade was sinking to zero. The Japanese took 61 per cent of the Calcutta–Japan business, which was *wholly* British in 1911. Between 75 and 92 per cent of our coal exports was carried in foreign ships. It is almost beyond belief that at the end of 1938 Britain, within a year of a fight for her very life, was last on the list in regard to shipping construction. The United States was top with 420,931 tons, Germany came second with 381,304. Then came Japan, the Netherlands, Italy, Denmark and Sweden, with poor little Britain "knocking up " the grand total of 71,156 tons.

Since then things have, of course, changed for the better. But it obviously needed a great war to redeem our birthright—the command of the sea ; and that we have done this is a great tribute to all concerned in the tradition of the Red Duster. As soon as their country was in danger the merchant sailors came flocking back to the flag.

As Mr. Armstrong poignantly says : " The spirit of the Merchant Navy has never failed. Because it has not failed, let there not be built a companion memorial to that which was erected on Tower Hill after the world war of 1914, to commemorate the bravery of our Merchant seamen. *Rather let Britain give her Merchant Navy a better, a far more practical memorial. Let us, at long last, give our Merchant Seamen a square deal !* "

THEY ' DELIVER THE GOODS,' these men of the Merchant Service, whether it is food for Britain's larder or supplies for our fighting men. Above, gun drill under the Red Ensign. Top, all hands to the boats during practice drill on a merchant ship. *Photos, British Official*

On Such Ships As This Britain's Cause Depends

TYPES OF ANTI-AIRCRAFT GUNS

High-Angle Type · Pom-Pom Type · 20 mm. Cannon · Machine Gun

LIFE RAFT

Drinking Water 3 Qts. per Person · 2 lb. Tin of Biscuits · Tin of Chocolate (160 Tablets) · 6 oz. Tin of Pemmican · 1 lb. Malted Milk Tablets

STANDARD 24 ft. SHIP'S LIFEBOAT 32 Persons

OUR DEPENDENCE UPON SHIPPING, not only to bring supplies and food across the Atlantic, but also to carry war material and soldiers to the many battle fronts, is well known. To offset the losses incurred at sea, ships are being launched at an ever-increasing rate, which has been made possible by standardization and simplification of design and construction of the tramp steamers which form our vast carrying fleet.

Britain has always excelled in the building of tramp steamers, and this drawing shows a typical product of our shipyards unloading cargo at a busy port.

Interesting features of this type of ship are : (1) Comparatively small and compact main engines of approx. 2,000 b.h.p. Fuel oil and fresh water are in tanks below engine-room. (2) Exhaust-heated steam boiler which supplies power to all auxiliary machinery. (3) Two of the four large cargo holds which have a capacity of over 500,000 cubic feet. (4) Steam winches. (5) Cargo-hauling derricks, each capable of hauling 2 tons. All holds, hatches and derricks are standard pattern, thus making for rapid assembly. (6) Wheel-house (protected against M.G. fire). (7) Wireless

room. (8) Captain's cabin. (9) Engineers' and officers' cabin. (10) Galley. (11) Crew space in the 'tween decks. (12) Anti-U-boat gun. Various types of anti-aircraft guns used for defending merchant ships are shown in the inset drawing. (13) Two life rafts are slung ready for speedy launching in an emergency. A similar raft is seen in the small inset—this type can support at least 20 persons : X, one of two buoyancy drums ; Y, wooden framework ; Z, lifelines.

The standard 24 ft. lifeboat is provisioned as follows: 14 tins of biscuits, 14 tins of chocolate, 75 tins of pemmican, 28 tins of malted milk tablets, with 3 quarts of water per person. This works out at 14 oz. of food per person.

Regulation Equipment : A, portable wireless transmitter ; B, stays for canvas boat cover ; C, cover ; D, oars and mats ; E and F, provision lockers and water tanks (other similar ones elsewhere on the boat) ; G, manual pump ; H, kapok-filled buoyancy chambers. Much other relevant equipment is carried, including boat-repairing equipment, blankets and massage oil. At least one lifeboat is motor-driven.

David Fights Goliath in the Mediterranean

"That one of the most powerful modern battleships afloat, attended by 2 heavy and 4 light cruisers and a flotilla, should have been routed and put to flight with severe torpedo and gunfire injury, in broad daylight, by a force of 5 British light cruisers and destroyers, constitutes a naval episode of the highest distinction, and entitles all ranks and ratings concerned and, above all, their commander, to the compliments of the British nation."—Mr. Churchill

FOR the days and nights of many weeks Malta had been bombed. Now supplies were running short. The arsenals had to be replenished, the storehouses refilled, the tanks refuelled. So from Alexandria convoys were dispatched.

One convoy left " Alex " on March 20, accompanied by a squadron of the Mediterranean Fleet commanded by Rear-Adm. P. L. Vian. Throughout that day and most of the next it ploughed on its way through heavy seas and foul weather. But at dusk on March 21 five German transport planes, escorted by an Me.110, on the way to Crete from Libya, spotted the mass of ships. Swiftly the enemy sped on to their destination, but as they went they sent back a message of what they had seen. In the convoy they knew then what to expect ; the next day, they realized, would bring against them the Nazi dive-bombers and, perchance, the Italian fleet. Their anticipations were fully justified, but until Sunday afternoon the convoy kept on its course until it had arrived 150 miles S.E. of Malta. Here the naval battle was joined.

Early on Sunday afternoon (said an Admiralty communiqué issued on March 25) an enemy force consisting of four cruisers was sighted to the northward. The enemy was at once attacked by our light cruisers and destroyers under the command of Rear-Adm. P. L. Vian, D.S.O. The enemy was driven off without having inflicted any damage to our convoy, its escorts, or its covering force.

Soon after 4.30 p.m. Admiral Vian again sighted the enemy. This time the enemy consisted of one battleship of the Littorio class, two heavy 8-inch-gun cruisers, and four other cruisers, accompanied by destroyers. Despite the great disparity of force, Admiral Vian at once led his light cruisers and destroyers to the attack, in order to drive them away from the convoy. During the brilliant action which followed our destroyers delivered a torpedo attack on the enemy, closing the powerful enemy squadron to a range of three miles before firing their torpedoes. In pressing home this attack the destroyers received valuable support from our light cruisers.

This determined attack against a greatly superior force not only inflicted serious damage on the enemy but threw him into confusion and forced him to retire without having made contact with our convoy. The Littorio class battleship was seen to be hit amidships by a torpedo. She was also hit by gunfire from our cruisers and set on fire aft. Severe damage was also inflicted upon one enemy cruiser, and a second enemy cruiser was hit.

By the skilful use of smoke screens our force avoided serious damage. Some damage was, however, suffered by one of our cruisers and three of our destroyers. Casualties were not heavy.

of sandwiches and tangerines. This was quickly followed by more Junkers 88s and Italian aircraft, but all the bombs and torpedoes missed.

Suddenly, shortly before 2.30 p.m., the look-out spotted several suspicious vessels on the horizon. Admiral Vian left part of his force to guard the convoy, and sheered off with the remainder to engage the enemy. Battle ensigns were run up at the mastheads and all ships increased speed. Ploughing through heavy seas in battle formation, with their flags streaming in sunshine and the high wind, our ships were an inspiring sight as they raced into action.

A few minutes later the enemy ships, now fifteen miles away, were identified as three cruisers, and the British force immediately laid a smoke screen to hide the convoy and our own positions. The enemy also began to lay a smoke screen. He opened fire at 2.35 p.m. at twelve miles away, the first salvo falling over a mile from us. The second salvo was nearer, and the third 600 yards away. By now we had increased speed to 30 knots, and the sound of the wind tearing through our rigging almost drowned the thump of the enemy guns.

Having closed range sufficiently, we opened fire at the enemy cruisers. For several minutes the world became just a turmoil of stifling black and yellow smoke. Ear-splitting gunfire, whistling shells, and shouted orders, and through all this I could hear the hiss of our shells as they left the guns. Several more aircraft attacked us, and

Above, the British Anti-Aircraft ship Curacoa (4,290 tons). Ex-cruisers, converted into anti-aircraft ships, were amongst the British squadron which drove off a superior Italian force when it tried to smash a Malta-bound convoy on March 22. The British force was under Rear-Adm. Philip Vian, seen below on the bridge of his old ship, the Cossack. He was made K.B.E. for this action. *Photos, British Official*

Among the eye-witnesses of what he aptly described as a " David-and-Goliath battle " was Reuter's Special Correspondent ; he watched it from the bridge of Rear-Adm. Vian's flagship.

Our first encounter (he wrote) came at 9.30 in the morning, when four Italian Savoia torpedo-bombers, flying close to the water, launched a fruitless attack against our destroyer screen. Small groups of torpedo planes made five or six more attacks, during the morning, but all their " fish " were easily avoided. The one excuse they can offer is the fearsome barrage put up by our ships. The first German plane to appear was a Junkers 88, which dropped four red flares ahead of us at 1 p.m., soon after we had finished our action station lunch

through a break in the smoke I saw a Junkers 88 waltzing away to avoid our fire. Now numerous bombers attacking the convoy were faintly visible in the distance . . .

At 4.22 p.m. I heard the most reassuring sound of the day, a voice ordering the cooks to the galley to make tea. But the lull was short, for at 4.40 we sighted the enemy again. This time they included a battleship. Immediately afterwards we were hit. A swirl of smoke and bits of burning cloth enveloped me . . . Above the din I heard the Gunnery Officer urging on his men with exhortations like " Beat it up," " Let's show 'em what we can do."

Reward came when one of our shells hit the battleship, apparently holing her quarter-deck, through which flames shot up close to the after turret, preventing it from firing. All the time the Admiral and the Captain, their faces blackened by smoke, were directing operations with uncanny calm. Towards the end of the action the destroyers went in and launched torpedoes. We also made a torpedo attack within range. At 6.45 p.m. came news that the enemy was turning away, but fire was exchanged until nightfall, when we had a final visit from the torpedo bombers.

"Then in the darkness we rejoined the convoy," concluded the correspondent, "which was safe and sound in spite of the air attacks to which it had been subjected while we were grappling with the fleet."

U-boats Take War to the Dutch West Indies

ARUBA, island of the Dutch West Indies off the coast of Venezuela, the oil refineries of which have been shelled by German U-boats. Below right, a German submarine returning to base after cruising in American waters.

A Dutch marine stands guard near an unexploded torpedo on the beach at Aruba. In the background a British tanker, struck by another torpedo during a U-boat raid on shipping in the area, is being taken in tow.

BLAZING OIL lights up the night sky over Aruba as a tanker burns after being hit by a German torpedo during a submarine raid on the island on Feb. 15. Left, the tanker photographed from a bombing plane which was sent out on a search for the U-boat.

Photos, Sport & General, Associated Press, Keystone

Fortunate Few Who Escaped From Hongkong

A Petty Officer of the Royal Navy who escaped from Hongkong with Admiral Chan Chak's party. He wears a Chinese identification note.

ON Christmas Day 1941, 83 Britons and Chinese from Hongkong made a bold bid for safety and ran the gauntlet of the Japanese in five motor torpedo-boats, one of which was sunk, with the loss of 16 on board.

The original party comprised 26 British officers, 35 other ranks, one civilian (Mr. MacDougall), and 21 Chinese. Their escape was largely due to the courage and resourcefulness of the one-legged Chinese Admiral Chan Chak, liaison officer between Chinese and British authorities. The 67 survivors landed on the coast of Kwangtung.

Members of the party which escaped from Hongkong photographed with Chinese officers and the lorry which bore them to Shaokwan.

Left, Admiral Chan Chak with Commander Hugh Montague, R.N., who escaped with him. Above, Mr. MacDougall, of the Ministry of Information, who received a bullet in his left shoulder.

Photos, Pictorial Press, Associated Press

I Was There! .... Eye Witness Stories of the War

I Saw Terrible Things Happen in Hongkong

Among the few people who escaped from Hongkong following its capture by the Japanese was Miss Phyllis Harrop, an assistant in the Secretariat of Chinese Affairs, and well known for her work against the dope and vice gangs in the Colony. Here is what she said in interviews given in Chungking.

THREE things aided my escape from the Colony at the end of January (Miss Harrop told a Special Correspondent of The Daily Mail in Chungking, capital of Free China, on March 13): (1) Previous experience—I had escaped from the Japanese in various parts of China three times before; (2) I have many Chinese friends; (3) I have an extensive knowledge of the Cantonese dialects. My Chinese friends were only too willing to help. With their help I was able to penetrate the Japanese Army and Navy cordon surrounding Hongkong and to escape to the mainland.

For six weeks I wandered alone through large areas of South China, daily evading Jap sentries, and always in fear of my life. In the end—though I cannot tell you how—I contacted guerillas and marched through South Kwangtung, sharing the life of these Chinese soldiers who brought me through to safety at Kweillin. From there I flew to Chungking today.

When I got away the Colony was still in a state of chaos. Japanese gendarmerie were supposed to be in control, but looting was rampant. In the streets no woman was safe from Japanese soldiers, no matter what her colour or race.

Condition of the Internees

All foreign civilians have been interned under appalling conditions—men, women, and children alike. British, American, and Dutch, including children, are interned on the Stanley Peninsula of the island itself. Prisoners of war have been imprisoned in Samshuipo and a camp in Argyle Street, Kowloon. So far as I know the civilian prisoners are made up as follows: British, 3,000; American, 600; Dutch, 70.

Their rations consist of two bowls of rice daily. No foreign food is available, because the Japs collected all foreign food stocks in the island and shipped them to Japan. Dysentery is rife among these civilians. Many have died for lack of medical attention. The Japs let them die. Those who are left bury their dead where they can in corners of the camps. Medical supplies are non-existent. All were seized by the Japanese almost as soon as they arrived and were wantonly destroyed. The Japanese simply said, contemptuously: "We have our own remedies: we don't want foreign medicines."

Industry on the island has come to a complete standstill. Unemployment among the Chinese population is on a wholesale scale. There is a tremendous shortage of food and the sufferings of the crowded Chinese population are beyond description. This is a situation created by the Japanese themselves. They are trying to ease things now by evacuating as many Chinese and neutral foreigners—mostly Portuguese—as they can. For the rest, they continue their policy of stripping the island bare. Iron railings and metal of every description have been collected for shipment to Japan. Even the ornamental bronze lions at the entrance to the Hongkong and Shanghai Bank have been taken away.

The atrocities are not exaggerated. Some I saw with my own eyes—in my own house. My Chinese houseboy was bayoneted in the stomach and killed for no apparent reason. Thirteen other Chinese were murdered in the same house. My amah [woman servant] was raped by three or four Japanese and was in a serious condition when I last heard of her.

Foreign women who were raped included an Englishwoman of my acquaintance who was first slashed in the face with a soldier's belt. Her husband afterwards found her body with bayonet wounds in the stomach. The Japanese shot none of their victims; they bayoneted them all to death.

More details of these atrocious happenings were given by Miss Harrop to the Chungking correspondent of The Daily Telegraph.

Most of the raping of British and other European women concerned volunteer and professional nurses. None was killed. In one district, apart from many Chinese cases, seven European women were killed with bayonets after being raped.

A British merchant whose wife was my friend told me himself: "I was a wounded A.F.S. volunteer. I was taken to hospital, where my wife was a volunteer nurse. I heard her voice next door on Christmas Day at 3 p.m., the hour when the colony surrendered. Shooting, Japanese came into the hospital. I heard shouts. After a while I managed to get out to search for my wife. I found her dead—outraged, her face slashed, and bayonet wounds in her stomach. Others were also raped and killed. I hid under a bed, pressing against the wall beside my wife's body, trying to escape the Japanese, who stormed all over the place. Coming into the room, the Japanese, without looking under the beds, systematically bayoneted through all the mattresses, again stabbing my wife's body and almost killing me. I myself buried my wife near-by."

There were many other similar cases among the foreign community, especially among the Chinese. In my own block of flats, where I was the only foreigner among 40 Chinese, practically all the women were raped and all the men bayoneted.

(How did I escape assault myself? I don't know. I suppose it was my lucky star.)

While the atrocities against foreigners ceased with their internment, those against the Chinese went on. I myself saw on the waterfront at the end of January a long queue of Chinese standing waiting, when the Japanese, without reason, beat up at least a dozen men and women with bamboo poles and threw them into the harbour to drown. I walked along the harbour past the bodies

MISS P. HARROP, first foreign woman to escape from Hongkong since the Japanese occupation, tells in this page of the terrible things she says happened there.

of Chinese who had been killed. A Chinese woman of about 22 was stopped at the corner of Wyndham Street and stripped by Japanese soldiers. They cursed her and made her stand naked in the middle of the road. She was still standing there when I passed by an hour later.

The Colonial Secretary, Mr. Gimson, who arrived in Hongkong only the day before the outbreak of war, protested in a letter to the Japanese against the atrocities after the surrender. The next day he was arrested and gaoled in the central prison, where he was kept two days without any charge or even questioning. He was then released and is now interned in the Stanley Camp, where he is the acting head of the British community. The Governor, Sir Mark Young, is completely isolated, apparently in the Peninsular Hotel in Kowloon, where he went on Christmas Day to surrender. The Medical Director, Dr. Selwyn Clark, his wife and others received special orders from the Colonial Secretary and are acting as liaison officers with the Japanese, doing urgent work in the colony.

The Japanese took off the golden Royal Crown badges from the caps and sleeves of all Hongkong's constables, who continued policing the streets before their internment. Invariably the Japanese trampled on the badges. I met a constable I knew walking about the centre of the city wearing his badges. I asked him, "How did you keep the crowns?" He pulled out of his pocket a handful of the badges, saying, "As fast as they are pulled off I put on fresh ones."

This is characteristic of Hongkong's spirit.

We Bombarded Rhodes from Sea and Air

In the sea and air attack on the Island of Rhodes in the early hours of March 16 there was a split-second cooperation between the Navy and the R.A.F., as described in the following eye-witness account.

WE sailed early, and it was not until late in the afternoon, when the captain made an announcement over the ship's loudspeakers, that we knew why we had put to sea. To reach our objectives we had to sail well into the narrow enemy waters of Rhodes—between Rhodes and Turkey. The captain explained that our aircraft would drop flares and would spot for the naval bombardment.

All the first day and most of the night we bowled along at high speed, but as we came abreast of Rhodes we slowed down to reduce the bow wave and wake, lest these gave us away. We had also to negotiate minefields.

Standing on the bridge I could see the Turkish mainland looming through the dark starry night on our right across the flat, calm water. Suddenly an eerie glow to my left

told me that our aircraft were dropping flares before bombing the Rhodes airfields. Tracer shells and bullets rocketed skywards from the ground defences, while searchlight beams fumbled uncertainly among the clouds.

This began soon after midnight and continued for a considerable time until we turned to approach Rhodes town. Punctually we established communication with our aircraft, and the atmosphere became tense as we crept towards the shore. Around me on the bridge figures—ghostlike in white anti-flash helmets and long white gauntlets—made final adjustments to the instruments or spoke quiet orders down the voicepipes. The dim purple and green glowing dials of the instruments were the only pinpoints of light anywhere.

Then the flares dropped by our aircraft

ISLAND OF RHODES, in the Aegean Sea. The devastating blow which British bombers and units of the Royal Navy dealt this Italian island before dawn on March 16 is described in an eye-witness account below.
Photo, Topical

began floating down on Rhodes town. Red, white and green tracer bullets shot up to meet them, but failed to hit the flares or planes. In the midst of a burst a string of bullets would twist and waver, indicating uncertainty on the part of the gunners. Nearer and nearer we crept and I wondered how long it would be before we were sighted and fired at.

When we were only four miles from the town one of the ships began firing starshells which floated down over the target. In the glare I could easily make it out. I could also see the streets and houses in Rhodes and felt uneasily certain that we must be obvious to the shore batteries. But if we were the defenders were so surprised that we were able to hurl the greater part of our quota of shells into the target area before they replied. Still the anti-aircraft gunners were sending up tracers in desperate, unsuccessful attempts

to put out the flares which floated to the ground, where they continued burning brightly for a considerable time, lighting the surrounding area with a fierce glare. I could also see anti-aircraft shells bursting among the clouds.

Minutes passed, then between the shattering crashes of our broadsides, we heard the air torn by shells from the shore batteries intended for us, but splashes in the water where they fell showed that they had not got our range.

Twenty minutes after the action began the fleet was steaming away, having delivered several hundred shells, weighing 40,000 pounds, at the targets. With ack-ack guns still firing, and through the pall of smoke which we laid to cover our retreat, it was difficult to see the full effects of our bombardment, but fires were burning, and it is believed that considerable damage was done.—*Reuter*

English considerably. High light of our visit was the concert given on board our ship by Russian sailors from a neighbouring naval base. It was an extraordinarily good show, lasting for two hours, and consisting mostly of folk songs and peasant and gipsy dances.

The choir comprised some 30 to 40 sailors, and they sang so well that the concert had to be given in two " houses " to enable as many of our ship's company as possible to attend. Both houses were packed. The applause after every song and dance was tremendous, but when a Russian naval officer came on to the stage and sang a song of which he had written both the words and music called " Okay, Great Britanny," the sailors cheered to the echo. The words of the song were, unfortunately, all Russian until at the end of the chorus came the phrase " Okay, Great Britanny, and Russki Soviet land, hurrah ! "

After the concert the Russian officers came to the Wardroom while the sailors were entertained forward by our sailors. In the Wardroom a buffet supper had been arranged and the party was soon in full swing, with a lot more singing, this time from Allied choirs. When the Russians had to leave the captain thanked them for the concert, and spoke for everyone when he told them that he hoped they had enjoyed

The Russians Sang to Us, 'Okay, Great Britanny'

The friendly hospitality shown by the Red Navy to the crews of H.M. warships escorting the convoys to the Russian Arctic ports is described here by Reuter's correspondent with the Home Fleet.

I RECENTLY sailed in a British escort vessel and spent some time along the North Russian coast. Parties and entertainments were given on both sides and the main difficulty, that of language, was overcome by

a genuine desire on each side to get on with the other. A knowledge of French proved a great help, but by the end of an evening we had increased our Russian vocabularies while the Russians had augmented their

SOVIET SAILORS aboard a Russian submarine, typical of the men who lavished their hospitality on the crews of British warships convoying supplies to Russia. The "extraordinarily good show" provided by such a party of sailors is described in this page.
Photo, Planet News

their visit as much as we had enjoyed having them on board.

On shore the Russians could not do enough for us, and when one of our officers tentatively asked whether it was possible to go ski-ing in the neighbourhood an unlimited supply of skis was put at our disposal. Ski-ing parties were immediately organized and some much-needed exercise was thoroughly enjoyed.

How We Dug the Japs Out of Their Foxholes

The following graphic account of what he described as a "battle of the foxholes," was given to Reuter's special correspondent with the American and Filipino forces by a young staff-sergeant, after a mopping-up action on the west coast of the Bataan Peninsula sometime in February.

FOR ten days we had not seen a Japanese, then the order came to close a gap between two companies of the 45th infantry. I went forward with the platoon and we took up positions. We soon found that we had got into a "battle of foxholes." It was our job to dig them out.

The Japanese have their own method of constructing the hide-outs we call "foxholes." First they make a small round hole in the earth just large enough to take one man. Then, from the hole, they hollow out a kind of dug-out chamber big enough to shelter four or five men. These foxholes were well camouflaged with leaves and tree branches and we had great difficulty in detecting them. We were working with tanks, and as they advanced they sounded their sirens. This was the signal for us to advance and deploy in a covering action.

Once we found we had advanced beyond one Japanese foxhole without seeing it, and then we came across another in front of us. We took to earth pretty quickly then, as we found ourselves between two fires, but we got to work with rifles and grenades and cleaned out the hole behind us and then crept up to the one in front.

I saw a Japanese soldier cautiously poking his head out of his hiding-place. I fired my rifle, which jammed, then I snatched a pistol from one of my men and let the Jap have a clipful.

At times we were only twenty to thirty feet away from the Japanese, both Americans and the invaders being concealed in holes in the ground. When using grenades at such short range there is nothing to worry about as long as you are well down in your hole when your grenade goes off.

We were not particularly impressed with the efficiency of the .26 calibre Japanese rifle—those captured were obviously inferior to the American Garand—but the Japanese .38 calibre quick-firing machine-gun, mounted on a low tripod, was a well-made weapon. The Jap hand grenades were smaller than ours, and in some cases were thrown from sticks fitted on to the casing. The Japanese also used a small portable landmine which detonated as soon as the button on top was stepped on.

During these operations my company captured 11 out of 12 parachute supply containers dropped by Japanese planes. In addition to ammunition, they contained compressed meat, oatmeal and sacks of rice, and they came in very useful.

The ice on the deck of this British warship gives some idea of the hardships experienced by the men who convoy supplies to Russia.
Photo, Associated Press

JAPANESE SOLDIERS in action with a light machine-gun. This may be one of the .38 calibre quick-firing machine-guns mentioned in this article by a staff-sergeant of Gen. MacArthur's forces as being used by the Japanese in their attack on the Philippines. The Japanese rifle, which one of these men is carrying, did not impress him as being as good as the American Garand.
Photo, Black Star

Editor's Postscript

ALTHOUGH personally I'm far more concerned about winning the war—*and* the peace to follow—than worrying about our plans for a brave new world, at times I'm tempted to speculate on the kind of world that may follow the second German effort to destroy our civilization. I am not among those who take a sour and hopeless view of the future, who prophesy lean years and leaner purses. Paradoxically enough the forces of destruction-construction work hand in hand, and though we shall have squandered a great deal of money, so-called, in preserving our liberties, the potential of real wealth in labour and natural resources is so unlimited that properly planned recovery could be effected within one generation. It would appear to be a matter of switching over intelligently from the destructive to the constructive impulse. In the modern scientific world, poverty, where it is not the result of individual folly or crime, should have no place.

ONE of the lessons of the last great slump was that there need be no dearth of commodities. The problem was one of bridging the gulf between producer and consumer. Any system that permits the sabotage of tons of coffee, fish, vegetables, fruit, wheat, and many other necessities in order to keep up prices which a large number of people cannot afford to pay is surely a kind of economic barbarism which ought to disappear with the political barbarisms against which we are fighting. Economists have been well aware for a long time that the trouble is one of over-production and under-consumption. The goods are there, or can be there, but the money token by which they can be transferred from the producer to the consumer is all too limited.

THAT is not to advocate the light-hearted grand share-out that world-reformers used to insist upon (do these simple-minded agitators still survive in Hyde Park ?). Such an idea is both unpractical and against nature, and no bureacracy could ever make it work. The new system, whatever it be, must still give free play to individual enterprise, brains and ambition, but it must also recognize the fact that there is enough for all if the machinery of distribution can be properly adjusted. The need is for purchasing power in the form of wages based on a high rather than a low standard of living. The war will have increased the productive capacity of vast territories like Canada, Australia, India, Russia and China, as well as our own and the United States, and the industrial potential everywhere will be immense beyond the imagination of any Victorian economist. It is a complex subject, but the salient fact is that the world is a rich one now and not a poor one, and need not alternate between artificial booms and slumps. It should not be beyond the wit of man to keep it on an even keel of reasonable prosperity. But that is listening to the voice of optimism, which can justify itself only with intensified concentration upon the great business of winning the war.

"ESTO es muy Churchill" is a phrase, I'm told, now used in Barcelona, meaning it's a real good thing ! Away back in the eighteen-eighties we schoolboys had a similar catchword, "It's all sirgarnet," signifying an nth degree of all rightness, derived no doubt from our satisfaction at Sir Garnet Wolseley's Tel-el-kebir victory in the Arabi Pasha rebellion, but I guess the phrase was going out of use by 1885, when, as Lord Wolseley, he arrived within sight of Khartoum with his flotilla too late to save Gordon and his garrison. I hope "this is the real Churchill" will have a longer vogue in Barcelona no matter what happens in Madrid.

MR. R. G. CASEY, formerly Australian Minister in Washington, who has been appointed Minister of State and representative of the War Cabinet in the Middle East. *Photo, Lafayette*

IT is worth mentioning, I think, that I am frequently being surprised by the efficiency of our Overseas Communications. This very week, for instance, I have had letters from readers in Gibraltar and Malta, which have taken only two or three weeks to arrive at my desk. Both are from correspondents who have been subscribing to THE WAR ILLUSTRATED since its first number, and during the 32 months that have elapsed each of them is missing only one of our numbers to complete his volume up to date. From a reader in Toronto, whose letter is just to hand, I am very pleased to quote the following:

"You began the issue of this publication Sept. 16, 1939. An examination of our file this morning disclosed a very remarkable fact. Through all these intervening months from Sept. 16, 1939 to Dec. 30, 1941, THE WAR ILLUSTRATED has made the journey over the ocean to this office in absolute safety with one exception, copy No. 79 issued under date of March 7, 1941, is missing."

I think that my readers will agree with this correspondent's added comment:

"If that is not a tribute to the Navy and the convoy system, I do not know where you would find a better illustration. Britannia rules the waves ! Britain delivers the goods!"

ALTHOUGH there is mighty little that I can find to admire in the national life of Eire, apart from its poets and playwrights (I am now revelling in Sean O'Casey's latest book, Pictures in the Hallway) I doubt if Dublin Opinion, the self-styled "National Humorous Journal of Ireland," has many more appreciative readers than I. (We have nothing quite so characteristic over here). I have just been enjoying its twentieth anniversary number. But what interested me most in it was a prophecy: the one incontrovertible, accurate, unassailable, cast-iron prophecy of the war ! As one to whom the drama of life is streaked with comedy, I am glad to find this astounding prophecy in a comic journal. Be it known then that, in its issue of January 1929, Dublin Opinion published a cartoon, now before me, in which a typical Irishman is being blown to blazes by A.A. guns, Zeppelin and strange air bombers, while the caption reads (in English which these comedians of Eire still use in preference to their native lingo): "Progress. Victim of New, Bloody, and Dramatic Invention in World War 1939." Can you beat that for prophecy ? Remember it was disclosed to an indifferent world of Irishmen ten years before the event ! Many a true word spoken in jest. Meanwhile, all the best to Dublin Opinion.

IF you are a hard-working, hard-hit civilian and should light your fire in your humble grate one morning with a bit of the morning paper, which has brought you neither increase of hope nor comfort of mind, you're no patriot. But if you're a care-free soldier lad you can do what you like with your wastepaper. For there would seem to be no effective brake on waste so far as the military are concerned. Near where I'm writing is a house in which nine sergeants are billeted. One of them frankly told the owner, a lady who has removed to a small cottage, that they didn't know what to do with their wastepaper. They were cluttered up with it and could only think of burning it ! Horrified at the thought, the good lady herself arranged to get this precious "waste" transported to the village salvage centre. It is quite in keeping with our haphazard organization that the Army should have had no clear instruction in this vital salvage drive. In my opinion the greatest factor of waste in respect to paper, food, petrol and rubber is the Army. I have seen country lanes littered with empty pasteboard packets that have brought a plethora of cigarettes from Canada while we are starving for Canadian pulp and paper.

"ALL I know about the wireless," I overheard my wife tell a friend last night, "is the switch you press for turning it off." In the present state of that great institution the B.B.C. a more intimate acquaintance with the uses of the wireless set is hardly called for. My nightly ambition is to hear the nine o'clock news without the tail end of the stuff preceding it . . . and that goes for Big Ben, too.

Printed in England and published every alternate Friday by the Proprietors, The Amalgamated Press, Ltd., The Fleetway House, Farringdon Street, London, E.C.4. Registered for transmission by Canadian Magazine Post. Sole Agents for Australia and New Zealand: Messrs. Gordon & Gotch, Ltd.; and for South Africa: Central News Agency, Ltd. April 17, 1942. S.S. Editorial Address: JOHN CARPENTER HOUSE, WHITEFRIARS, LONDON, E.C.4.

Vol 5 *The War Illustrated* N° 127

Edited by Sir John Hammerton

6d. FORTNIGHTLY

MAY 1, 1942

INDOMITABLE MALTA thrills to the sound of the pipes and drums as British troops, followed by an enthusiastic crowd, march down a badly bombed street. Enduring the heaviest blitz ever concentrated on one small area, the people of Malta, inspired by the resolute bearing and courage of the Governor, Sir William Dobbie, have given to the world an unequalled example of calm fortitude and smiling bravery. Malta has deserved well of the Empire. (See article in page 659)

Photo, Sport & General

NO. 128 WILL BE PUBLISHED FRIDAY, MAY 15

INDIA: SIR STAFFORD OPENS THE DOOR

WITH the Japanese armies moving steadily up the Burmese valleys to the gates of India, with the Bay of Bengal laid open to the Japanese fleets by the fall of Singapore—the British Government in London decided to send an emissary to India to enlist the support of its people, and, perhaps still more important, of its politicians, in the war effort of the United Nations. The man choosen for this difficult and invidious task was Sir Stafford Cripps, the eminent lawyer who, after being expelled from the Labour Party because of his too advanced views, proved an exceedingly capable ambassador to Moscow and is now Lord Privy Seal and a member of the War Cabinet.

SIR STAFFORD CRIPPS' appointment was announced by the Prime Minister in the House of Commons on March 11. "He carries with him the full confidence of the Government," said Mr. Churchill, "and he has in their name to procure the necessary measure of assent, not only from the Hindu majority but also from those great minorities, amongst which the Moslems are the most numerous and on many grounds preeminent." Travelling by air, Sir Stafford arrived in Delhi on March 23, and forthwith issued a statement to the Press:

"I have come here because I am, as I have always been, a great friend and admirer of India," he said, "and because I want to play my part as a member of the British War Cabinet in reaching a final settlement of these political difficulties which have long vexed our relations. Once these questions are resolved, and I hope they may be quickly and satisfactorily resolved, the Indian people will be able to associate themselves fully and freely not only with Great Britain and the other Dominions, but with our great allies, Russia, China, and the United States of America, and together we can assert our determination to preserve the liberty of the people of the world. There is no time to lose . . ."

ENSUED a period of intense discussion, of ardent and sustained deliberation. Never had New Delhi seen such a coming and going, hardly affected even by the heat of the tropical day. Within 24 hours of his arrival, and while he was still a guest in Viceroy's House, Sir Stafford Cripps had met General Wavell, India's C.-in-C., members of the Viceroy's Council, and a galaxy of provincial governors. Swift on their heels came those who claimed to speak for India's 400 millions, for prince and peasant, for Brahmin and pariah, for the leagues in which the politically conscious Indians—so few compared with the great illiterate mass—are bound by ties of sentiment and interest. Day after day went by. Hopes were raised, died away, raised again into new life. Formulas were framed, proposals propounded; rumour ran wild through the teeming bazaars, and even the corridors of official Delhi echoed to the whispers of controversy.

THEN on March 29 the text was published of the "Draft Declaration of Discussion with Indian Leaders." For the first time the terms of the proposals which Sir Stafford Cripps had taken to India were revealed. After stating that his Majesty's Government had as their object "the creation of a new Indian Union, which shall constitute a Dominion associated with the United Kingdom and the other Dominions by a common allegiance to the Crown, but equal to them in every respect, in no ways subordinate, in any aspect of its domestic or external affairs, the document proceeded to promise that immediately on the cessation of hostilities steps would be taken to set up an elected body, charged with the task of framing a new constitution for India. H.M. Government would undertake to accept and implement forthwith the constitution so framed, subject only to the right of any province to retain its present constitutional position or to receive the same full status as the Indian Union. A treaty would be negotiated between H.M. Government and the constitution-making body, covering all necessary matters arising out of the complete transfer of responsibility from British to Indian hands; it would make provision for the protection of racial and religious minorities, but would not impose any restriction on the power of the Indian Union to decide in the future its relationship to the other member states of the British Commonwealth.

FINALLY it was stated that during the critical period which now faces India, and until the new constitution could be framed, his Majesty's Government must inevitably bear the responsibility for and retain the control and direction of the defence of India as part of their world war effort. The task of organizing to the full the military, moral and material resources of India must be the responsibility of the Government of India, with the cooperation of the peoples of India, and so the immediate and effective participation of the leaders of the principal sections of the Indian people was invited, in the counsels of their country, of the Commonwealth, and of the United Nations.

Those leaders rejoined with no certain or united voice. None save the Liberals showed any willingness to accept the proposals as they stood. The Hindu Mahasabha and the Sikhs of the Punjab hastened to give a point-blank refusal. The Moslem League was gratified at the virtual acknowledgement of the principle of Pakistan—self-determination for the Moslem provinces—but waited to see how the Congress cat would jump. The Indian Princes were lukewarm for the most part in their attitude, and the Scheduled Classes were similarly unenthusiastic. But the main challenge to the scheme came from the Congress party.

BEHIND closed doors the Congress leaders wrestled and wrangled, and only now and again did there emerge a murmur of the wordy strife. It was generally believed that Pandit Nehru was in favour of acceptance of the Government's proposals, and also maybe Dr. Azad, the President of Congress; but against them was ranged a solid block of opposition, of men who refused to believe that any good thing could come out of British promises. At last they came to an agreement. They gave their answer, and it was "No."

In a resolution, published on April 11, the Congress Working Committee expressed regret that, though self-determination for the people of India was accepted in principle in the British Government's proposals, it was fettered and circumscribed and its execution was to be deferred to the future, until after cessation of hostilities. They objected to the "complete ignoring" of 90 millions of people in the Indian states, and to the power given to a province to remain outside the Union. Then the question of defence was another stumbling block: the Committee (they declared) had no desire to upset in the middle of the war the present military organization and they accepted that the higher strategy of the war should be controlled by the War Cabinet in London, which would have an Indian member. But they strongly objected to the continuation of the India Office, and asked for definite assurances that the new government of India would function as a free Government, the members of which would act as members of a Cabinet.

IN his reply, Sir Stafford Cripps referred to these suggestions:

The first, that the constitution might be changed now, had been made for the first time the night before, and it was generally believed that it was practically impossible in the middle of the war. As for the second, the establishment of a truly national government: this would involve constitutional changes of the most complicated character and on a very large scale. Were such a system to be introduced under the existing circumstances the Cabinet (nominated presumably by the major political organizations) would be responsible to nobody but itself, could not be removed, and could in fact constitute an absolute dictatorship by the majority. This suggestion would be rejected by all the minorities in India, nor would it be consistent with the pledges given by H.M. Government to protect the rights of these minorities.

MAULANA AZAD in a further message, declared that the Working Committee "was not interested in Congress as such gaining power, but was interested in the Indian people as a whole having freedom and power." (An interesting comment on this is Sir Stafford Cripps' remark at Karachi on April 13: "Congress wanted all or nothing—they could not get all, so they got nothing"). So the negotiations broke down. But the door to future success had been opened.

E. ROYSTON PIKE

SIR STAFFORD CRIPPS on the way to India. "You have done everything in human power," said Mr. Churchill when the Cripps mission had ended in disappointment. *British Official: Crown Copyright*

Colombo Where the Air Defences Were Ready

Lt.-Gen. Sir H. R. POWNALL, who assumed the military command of the island of Ceylon on March 14, went as Chief of Staff with the B.E.F. in France when war broke out.
Photo, British Official

Air Vice-Marshal J. H. D'ALBIAC, Air Officer commanding the R.A.F. in Ceylon, was in charge of the British air forces in Greece during the campaign there.
Photo British Official

Above, the new town hall, Colombo; and below, a view of the quayside. Colombo has one of the largest artificial harbours in the world, with an area of over six hundred acres. The present population of the city is about 300,000.

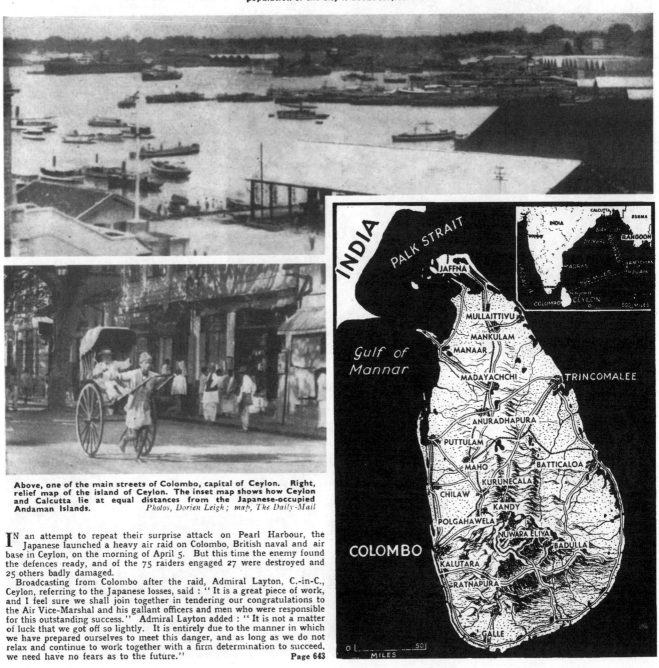

Above, one of the main streets of Colombo, capital of Ceylon. Right, relief map of the island of Ceylon. The inset map shows how Ceylon and Calcutta lie at equal distances from the Japanese-occupied Andaman Islands.
Photos, Dorien Leigh; map, The Daily-Mail

IN an attempt to repeat their surprise attack on Pearl Harbour, the Japanese launched a heavy air raid on Colombo, British naval and air base in Ceylon, on the morning of April 5. But this time the enemy found the defences ready, and of the 75 raiders engaged 27 were destroyed and 25 others badly damaged.

Broadcasting from Colombo after the raid, Admiral Layton, C.-in-C., Ceylon, referring to the Japanese losses, said : " It is a great piece of work, and I feel sure we shall join together in tendering our congratulations to the Air Vice-Marshal and his gallant officers and men who were responsible for this outstanding success." Admiral Layton added : " It is not a matter of luck that we got off so lightly. It is entirely due to the manner in which we have prepared ourselves to meet this danger, and as long as we do not relax and continue to work together with a firm determination to succeed, we need have no fears as to the future."

America's Soldiers Arrive Safely in Australia

U.S. CONVOY is seen above heading for its destination somewhere in the Pacific Ocean. Left, war material being loaded on to a vessel about to leave for the S.W. Pacific with a convoy from an American port.

THOUSANDS of American soldiers, airmen and ground crews have crossed and are crossing from America to theatres of war in the S.W. Pacific, escorted by units of the American and Imperial navies. Large numbers of these men, who will fight many thousands of miles from their homes, had never been on a sea voyage before, for many of them come from States in the Middle West.

William Courtenay, "Sunday Times" Correspondent with the American Forces in Australia, describing his ocean crossing in an American troopship, said that his voyage was uneventful save for a storm on the last two days "with visibility at zero and a gale blowing at seventy miles an hour on the surface for 48 hours. The troops were thrilled at the experience of the long voyage and safe arrival at the journey's end. All looked forward to quick action, most agreeing that they would be out of America for well over two years."

With the troops travelled Negro stevedore battalions, to unload the great stores of war material and equipment which accompanied the fighting men, who are seasoned soldiers, ready to go into action anywhere at a moment's notice.

Below, anti-aircraft gunners aboard one of the transports included in an important American convoy which safely reached Australia.

Photos, Keystone, Planet News

Crowded Decks for the Pacific Crossing

EN ROUTE FOR AUSTRALIA, these American soldiers on a transport forming part of an important convoy are enjoying the brilliant sunshine of the Pacific crossing. All are wearing lifebelts because of danger from Japanese sea and air raiders, and rubber rafts are stacked ready for any emergency. Some of the men have obviously been washing their " smalls " to judge from the lines of washing hung out to dry.

Photo. Planet News

Russia's Murmansk Door Must Be Kept Open

Vitally imperative is it that the sea route to North Russia should be kept open, since it is the main route by which British and American war supplies are being sent to Stalin—and Stalin's army is the main obstacle to Hitler's victory on the continent of Europe. Because of this, Nazi attempts to close Russia's Arctic Gateway are being intensified.

WELL beyond the Arctic Circle a great convoy of Allied ships, carrying American and British planes, tanks and munitions to Murmansk, and strongly escorted by British cruisers and destroyers—one report had it, by an aircraft carrier as well—was spotted by Nazi reconnaissance planes north-west of Tromsoe on March 27. The news was radioed to the Nazi authorities in Norway, and squadrons of Junkers 88 dive-bombers at once took off to attack the convoy. But as they dived through the snow-clouds they were met by Fleet Air Arm fighters and a terrific anti-aircraft barrage. Within a few minutes the attackers had had enough and they—or what was left of them—winged away to their base.

But the Nazi reconnaissance planes continued to shadow the convoy, and it was plain to the Commodore that another attack might be expected at any moment, whether from the air or by some of the German warships which were known to be in Norwegian waters. At Trondheim was based a heavy German naval squadron comprising (so it was reported) the Tirpitz, Admiral Scheer, Admiral Hipper, Prinz Eugen, and auxiliary units. Moreover, the German destroyer squadrons based on Tromsoe and Trondheim had both been reinforced during the past ten days.

On the morning of Sunday, March 29, the naval attack started, when a German destroyer flotilla began to shell the convoy. But for once the weather was in our favour, since high seas and heavy snowstorms every now and again hid the ships of the convoy from the destroyers, and the British escort ships at once hit back vigorously in defence of their charges. Despite very bad visibility, salvos from the Trinidad (Capt. L. S. Saunders, R.N.), one of our latest cruisers, crashed on to the leading Nazi destroyer and in a few minutes left it a crippled and blazing hulk. Then the Trinidad set out to chase the other enemy destroyers, which at once sought safety in flight. They escaped in the snowstorm.

A few hours later there came another attack by Nazi destroyers. Again they were unsuccessful, and one of them was hit by gunfire from H.M.S. Eclipse (Lt.-Cmdr. E. Mack, R.N.), lost speed and eventually stopped. Two more enemy destroyers arrived on the scene, however, before the *coup de grâce* could be given, and the Eclipse had to break off the action and return to the convoy.

The convoy sailed on, but it was attacked yet again, for the fourth time, just as it was entering Kola Bay, the inlet in which lies the harbour of Murmansk. This time destroyers from Tromsoe made the attack, supported by dive-bombers from Kirkenes and Petsamo and a

H.M.S. TRINIDAD, Fiji Class cruiser of 8,000 tons, crippled one of the German destroyers which recently attacked a large Allied Russia-bound convoy and gave chase to two others which escaped.
Photo, British Official

pack of U-boats. Things were looking pretty bad when, in response to a message from the Commodore to the Soviet Naval H.Q., a number of Russian fighters took off from Murmansk and sped to engage in the battle. Soon a full-scale air-sea-battle ranged over a wide area, but once again the attackers were foiled and the long convoy steamed triumphantly into Murmansk. Berlin admitted the sinking of a Nazi warship, but claimed with ridiculous exaggeration that heavy loss had been inflicted on the convoy and their naval escort. For their part, the British Admiralty admitted that the Trinidad and Eclipse had both suffered some damage, but both had returned safely to harbour and there were very few casualties.

So one more convoy had got through—one more, for, judging from the Nazis' reports of the activities of their U-boats in Arctic waters, the Barents Sea in particular, it was but one of many. For months past, aided by the twenty hours of winter darkness in every twenty-four, guns, tanks, planes and munitions of every kind have been pouring into Murmansk ; and now that the ice has melted they will be pouring into Archangel too. It has been generally assumed that they have been destined for the main battle-front

between the Baltic and the Black Sea, but it is interesting to note that some Nazi writers have expressed the view that the war material has been piling up in Murmansk ready to be used in a great Scandinavian offensive to be launched by the British and Russians together in the spring—an offensive aimed at occupying the northern coast of Norway, pinching off the narrow strip of Finland, and so effecting a land junction of the British and Russian forces. Maybe this is but a Nazi dream, but it might have the makings of a very bad dream indeed for the Nazis, since they would be faced with the necessity of sending reinforcements and supplies to a front in the Far North, while at the same time they were mounting their last, most desperate and most determined offensive against the Russians in the Ukraine and the Caucasus. Thus they would have to maintain a north-south supply line cutting right across the main east-west line—a delicate and potentially dangerous operation.

But there is the possibility that the Germans will do the attacking at Murmansk. From Stockholm recently came a report of a conference held at the H.Q. of Gen. Dietl, commander of the German-Finnish forces at Petsamo, at which Field-Marshal Mannerheim, Finland's C.-in-C., was reported to have agreed to a request—or a demand—that the Finns should bear the brunt of an offensive to be launched shortly against Murmansk and Soroka on the White Sea—in other words, a renewal of the offensive which has been halted since last July, when the Finns and their Austrian allies reached the river Litsa, a mere 15 miles inside Soviet territory from the Finnish frontier.

Whatever form the offensive takes, whether the Nazi-Finns initiate the offensive or whether it is snatched from their hands by the Russians, Murmansk remains in the front line of importance. Even in the last war it was important because of the railway to Petrograd, and here it was that in 1918 British, French and American troops carried on an ill-fated expedition against the Bolshevists and "White" Finns. Today it is much more important, when its population has grown from a mere 2,500 or 3,000 to some 120,000, and it is Russia's most important fishing and shipping centre in the Arctic, and a principal base of the Red Navy, well-equipped with modern docks and shipyards. Particularly rapid has been its growth since the double-tracking of the Leningrad railway and the completion of the White Sea Canal. Although it is 600 miles north of Leningrad, which is ice-bound in winter, Murmansk's harbour is open all the year round, thanks entirely to a stray current from the comparatively warm Gulf Stream.

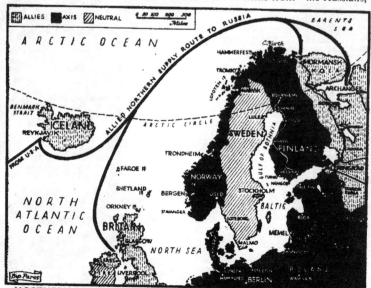

NORTHERN SUPPLY ROUTE to Russia from Britain and America through the Arctic Ocean. The unsuccessful attack by the Germans at the end of March on a large Murmansk-bound convoy led to the first official intimation that America was sending supplies to Russia over this route. Note the railway from Murmansk to Leningrad.
Map, Courtesy of The Daily Express

What Our Airmen Saw of the Tirpitz

TIRPITZ, Germany's giant battleship, photographed by an R.A.F. reconnaissance plane in Aas Fjord, Norway. From amidships on the starboard side she is protected by an anti-torpedo boom, while floating camouflage lies on both sides of her bow and stern. Heavy white camouflage material covers the barrels of the 15-in. guns.

A DARING CLOSE-UP, to take which the airman dived to only 100 feet above the battleship, shows a section of the Tirpitz as she lay in Aas Fjord. Taken from the port side, the photograph shows the central portion aft of the bridge. Left, an R.A.F. photograph of the Tirpitz steaming at speed in Trondheim Fjord. *Photos, British Official* Page 647

What Free French Africa Means To Us

Gen. Mangin, who led the victorious offensive of the French 10th Army in the Compiegne sector in June 1918, once said : "He who holds the Chad holds Africa." Some idea of the strategical (and also the economic) importance to the Allies of Free French Africa is given below.

LOOK at the map of Africa. In the centre of the continent lies a huge block of French territory bounded on the north and south by Libya and the Belgian Congo, on east and west by the Anglo-Egyptian Sudan and Nigeria. This great territory, made up of the French Cameroons, Ubangi-Shari, the Chad Territory, Middle Congo and Gabon, has, fortunately for the Allies, rallied to the cause of Free France.

This African group of colonies is of great strategical interest. Its coast line on the South Atlantic, stretching for some 600 miles, has a number of modern ports like Libreville, Port Gentil, Pointe Noire and Douala, the two latter perfectly equipped with jetties and quays in deep water. Moreover, this group of colonies binds together British West Africa and British East Africa, forming a solid block right across the continent from the Atlantic to the Red Sea.

ing in modern warfare. Here, too, are men who escaped from Dunkirk and Norway, as well as magnificent native troops from the African hinterland. And more Frenchmen are constantly arriving from Great Britain after completing their training in this country. From Brazzaville went the Free French troops who distinguished themselves in Libya, in Eritrea, and in Syria. At Yaundé, in the Cameroons, a new depot has been created for the Foreign Legion.

But of all the Free French territory in Africa, probably none is more important than the Chad, the cross-roads of the continent of Africa. Here roads radiate in all directions, while northwards lie important oases in the heart of the Libyan desert. During the past year much work has been done in constructing new roads and perfecting existing ones in this area. Thousands of natives have been employed on this work ; and today the

From it radiate roads to the lake, to Kano, terminus of the railway from Lagos, to Abeche, to Fort Archambault, to Carnot, to Yaundé. Maybe there are more, of which nothing has yet been said. With Fort Lamy in Axis hands the main route across Africa from Atlantic to Red Sea would be lost to the Allies. The importance of this supply route jumps to the eye when one looks at the map of Africa. Stores and supplies of many kinds can be unloaded at Lagos or Douala for dispatch to the Middle East ; supplies which otherwise would have to make the long journey around the Cape with all its attendant hazards of mine and submarine. That the Axis is alive to the importance of Fort Lamy is shown by the fact that it has already been attacked from the air. The nearest Axis air base for use against French Equatorial Africa is at Ghadames, 1,500 miles away.

The economic resources of Free French Africa, too, are by no means negligible. The Cameroons are rich in cocoa, coffee, timber, palm-oil and palm kernels ; then come minerals, such as tin ore, plumbago, wolfram, mica, iron ore and gold, which is extracted in ever-increasing quantities. Some geologists hold that French Equatorial Africa has gold deposits as rich as those of the Transvaal. From the north come cattle and hides ; farther south the cultivation of cotton has started, while Gabon is particularly rich in timber, exporting in normal times some 400,000 tons per annum, almost all of which, before the war, was sent to Germany. The economic development of Free French Africa is now under the direction of M. Adolphe Eboué, Governor-General of Free Equatorial Africa, and former Governor of the Chad. M. Eboué was the first Colonial governor to rally to General de Gaulle. A native of Cayenne, in French Guiana, he held various administrative posts in the Colonial Service and when, in 1936, he was made a Colonial Governor, his was the unique distinction of being the first native functionary to rise to that rank. The present Governor of the Chad is Captain Pierre Olivier Lapie, who distinguished himself in the fighting at Narvik with the Foreign Legion.

The important role already played by the Free French African ports and the even more important part they may play in the future cannot be overstressed. As sea bases for patrolling both the sea routes across the South Atlantic and the Cape route to the Indian Ocean their value can immediately be assessed on glancing at a map.

Finally, it is important to remember that Free French Africa is six times as large as metropolitan France and, with a population of six millions and considerable economic resources, constitutes a valuable asset on the side of the United Nations.

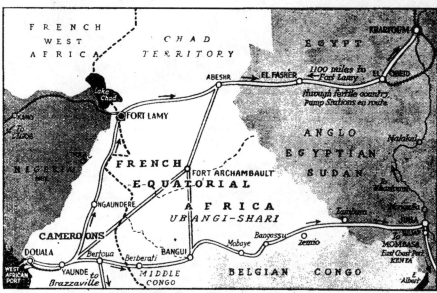

Allied communications through Free French Africa are shown in this map. Two great motor roads now cross Central Africa, one from Lagos or Douala through Fort Lamy to the Sudan, and the other from Douala to Juba and on to the Indian Ocean.   *Map, Courtesy of The Sphere*

Through this territory runs an important life-line from Britain and the United States to the Middle East, the vital supply route which goes from Lagos, the British port in Nigeria, across the heart of Africa, to Khartoum, Port Sudan and Massawa. Another important link is the road running from the Free French port of Douala through Bangui to Juba, whence supplies can be diverted through Kenya to Mombasa on the Indian Ocean, or up the Nile to Khartoum.

Situated in the territory are many air bases and modern aerodromes which enable Britain to maintain regular air communication between her colonies of Gambia, Sierra Leone, the Gold Coast and Nigeria on the one side and Egypt, Kenya and the Sudan on the other. Had French Africa been entirely controlled by Vichy, Nigeria would have been isolated and surrounded by hostile or German-controlled neutral territories.

At the time of the Armistice between Pétain and the Axis, military preparedness in the French Cameroons and French Equatorial Africa was almost non-existent. But since then much leeway has been made up. Brazzaville, capital of the Free French Middle Congo, has become the receiving station for vast supplies of material and men for the Free French Empire. Here, in Brazzaville, at the Camp Colonna d'Ornano—the Free French Saint-Cyr—officer cadets receive their train-

interior of French Equatorial Africa, for long impenetrable, can be reached from the coast by car and lorry in four or five days.

Defending the Chad territory is a Free French column under the command of General Leclerc. That this young general is by no means a partisan of static defence is shown by the recent series of remarkable raids he has carried out against the Axis outposts in the south of Tripolitania. At the beginning of March his forces captured an enemy advanced post at Fezzan, in the southern Libyan desert, hundreds of miles from the Chad. A few days later the posts of El Uigh, El Chebir, El Gatrun, Tegerhi, Temessa and Tassawa were likewise captured with insignificant losses. Tassawa lies in the heart of Italian Tripolitania, and the capture of this place constituted a grave threat to the right flank of the Italian forces in this area.

These raids were analogous to those carried out the year before by Free French Forces under the late Lt.-Col. Colonna d'Ornano, when the Méharistes, or Camel Corps, made successful attacks on Murzuk and Gatrun. These raids have their significance, for one of the benefits which accrued from the adhesion of the Chad to the Free French cause was that any Italian push into the heart of Africa could be forestalled.

Fort Lamy, which lies just south of Lake Chad, is the strong point of the territory.

'Recognition' by U.S.A.

To the United States no less than to Britain the maintenance of the vital highways across central Africa is of supreme importance, especially as America is now building up big supply bases in Eritrea. This importance was given official recognition by the State Department at Washington on April 4, when it was announced that a decision had been taken to establish an American Consulate-General at Brazzaville. By so doing the United States has recognized that the French Territories of Equatorial Africa and the Cameroons are under the effective control of the French National Committee in London, with which the American Government is cooperating. The first American Consul-General to Brazzaville will be Mr. Maynard Barnes, formerly First Secretary to the American Embassy in Paris and afterwards in Vichy.

Where Flies the Flag of the Fighting French

Left, men of France's possessions in the Pacific who have rallied to Gen. de Gaulle. They now form part of the Bataillon du Pacifique operating with the Free French Forces in Libya. The U.S.A. has recognized the French National Committee's authority over French possessions in the Pacific as well as in French Equatorial Africa.

Below, war material being transported over the Congo-Ocean railway which links Pointe Noire with Brazzaville. Pointe Noire, like Douala, is a well-equipped port on the Atlantic coast.

Above, stores being unloaded at Douala, the Atlantic seaport of the French Cameroons. From here a road runs through French Africa to the Nile and the Indian Ocean. Douala lies just near the frontier of British Nigeria.

Aircraft on the airfield at Fort Lamy in the Chad territory. They are planes which have taken part in raids on Kufra and the Fezzan region. The enemy has paid tribute to the importance of Fort Lamy by bombing it twice, although it lies a great way from the nearest Axis air base.

Photos, Forces Françaises Libres

Our Searchlight on the War

WOMEN AS FIGHTERS

There are strong men and weak men, and there are strong women and weak women. There is no differentiation between the sexes in the Soviet Union.—Valentina Grizodubova, Soviet ace woman pilot and squadron leader

ONCE having admitted the principle of totalitarian war, the recruitment of women for the fighting services is perfectly logical. In Russia there are hundreds of girl fighter pilots, and they are as efficient and brave as the men. Sex-equality has reached the limit in Russia, and presumably those women who want to fight

UTILITY WEAR. Left, a Brenner Sports model in brown and natural diagonal weave tweed. Right, one of the men's Utility tweed suits.

Photo, Wide World

Our tradition of freedom implies more than mass-production, high wages and secular pleasures. Communism has become the fashionable panacea, but there can be little doubt that any kind of State despotism is alien to a people whose genius for freedom has developed in progressive continuity for centuries. The need is to restore what is best in our tradition, and surely one of the first things is that yeoman's independence which has nearly been submerged in competitive industrialism. Rationalization of farming which would sweep away the small holdings and merge them in large collective units under state control would tend to destroy the character of the nation. The freedom for which we are fighting also means the freedom of rural communities to preserve certain features of our country life which are wholly and happily English. As Mr. Massingham points out in an excellent article in The Fortnightly Review on the future of farming, "The function of the State is to encourage its nationals to do as far as is humanly possible without it, so that a vigorous and regional self-government is its true purpose, not a bureaucracy using revolutionary powers to paralyse it."

THE CLOSED SHOP

The Ministry of Food and the Board of Trade plan the "telescoping" of businesses which will result in reducing the nation's 750,000 shops to between one-half and a third of this number.

NAPOLEON contemptuously called us a nation of shopkeepers. He learned that we could also win wars. What Hitler calls us doesn't matter. Britain's war with the Nazis, however, is forcing us to close a large number of retail businesses. Time and energy necessary to run these must be diverted to the national business of the war. The man in the street who has often marvelled at the innumerable shops in London and other large cities will also wonder if this emergency measure will have a permanent effect on our highly individualistic trading methods. The "small man" is naturally concerned as to whether this forced closure of his shop will make it difficult for him to resume his trade in peacetime. Shopkeeping, after all, is only one means of livelihood, and the multiplication of marts does imply a waste of time and money in the support of a vast army of middlemen. It remains to be seen whether all this energy in purveying goods from the producer to the consumer could be applied in a more creative sense to the benefit of the nation as a whole. The question ultimately is one of employment and the opportunity to make a living. Could some system be devised whereby the redundant "clerks of commerce" could find an outlet for their talents in more constructive and equally lucrative channels they might be happier in such work. The future of shops, like the future of other things, is still obscure.

POOL VAN being loaded for general delivery in the St. Pancras area. London now has a new pool delivery scheme and people living more than a mile from the stores where they shop will receive deliveries only once a week.
Photo, Topical

alongside their menfolk have no difficulty in doing so. As a choice between fighting against the Nazis and living under their bestial system we do not doubt that there are many women in this country who would be quite prepared to shoulder arms and defend their homes and children if the need arose. Certain crises in human fate justify the most drastic attitudes. But as a general principle civilization is quite rightly opposed to the idea of the woman soldier. It is not a question of weakness or strength, courage or cowardice. Nature has decreed that woman's responsibility is a creative one. Her function is to give and not to take life, and this, in itself, is her heroic contribution to the scheme of things. Christian chivalry, right down the ages, has regarded woman as the gentler sex, and gentleness also is a virtue. It would be no sign of progress if this tradition were discarded. If there must be wars, it is better that men should do the fighting. A world in which all women were trained to the use of lethal weapons could not claim to be civilized, sex-equality notwithstanding.

THE ENGLISH HERITAGE

Though nobody says it and everybody talks in the air about Democracy, what we are really fighting for is the English tradition based upon an extremely ancient rural Democracy . . .—Mr. H. J. Massingham in The Fortnightly Review

LISTENING to some of our well-meaning reformers, one might imagine that up to 1939 Britain was a land of untutored savages exploited by a few plutocrats and ex-public school boys. Admitting that disgraceful poverty existed, we still had a standard of living much higher than any European country ; and the immense bill for social services was proof of a considerable effort, at least, in humanism. Whatever the shape of things to be, we should not lose sight of the fact that we are fighting, firstly, for spiritual values, for unless these survive no amount of scientific materialism will make Britain happy.

HITLER AND FRANCE

The Nazis, after nearly two years of alternate cajolery and brutality, have completely failed to impose their New Order on France.

HITLER has found it impossible to "digest" France. Having "destroyed" her, as he promised to do in Mein Kampf, he expected her to collaborate in his plans for enslaving Europe. German psychology is so stupid that it is quite mystified because Hitler's victims will not shake hands with their oppressors. The Riom trials, which were staged to prove that France and not Germany was responsible for the war, have been a great disappointment to the Nazi hierarchy. To occupy the whole of France with Gauleiters and troops at a time when, thanks to Russia, Hitler's manpower is waning, and British and American strength is increasing, will tend to weaken the Nazi war effort. Germany is well aware that the spirit of France must rise in proportion to the Allied victories when the tide turns against the Nazi tyranny. The appointment of Laval or any other French traitor to be Statthalter of France must only further consolidate French patriotism. There is but one solution for the horrible mess that the Germans have made of Europe, and that is to retreat within their own frontiers. Though they cannot be expected to do this of their own free will the time is coming when they will be forced to do it.

UNDER NEW MANAGEMENT, this captured Junkers 88, now bearing British markings, is serving as an R.A.F. instructional aircraft. Several enemy aircraft, captured and reserviced, are now being used for instructional purposes.
Photo, British Official : Crown Copyright

Soviet War Workers Beat Every Record

Russians of all classes are generous donors of blood for the wounded. Left, packing blood for transport to the front at a blood transfusion institute. Above, Russian munition workers riveting anti-tank grenades.

Above, sub-machine-guns in the making at a Soviet factory. In the background are war slogans. Below, workers in a Soviet railway depot finishing the armoured train they built and presented to the Red Army on its 24th anniversary.

In the shell-making shop of one of Leningrad's many plants where Soviet workers are striving to maintain an ever-increasing output.

RUSSIAN WAR TROPHIES, including these aircraft of the Luftwaffe brought down in Russia, are being shown to the Soviet people at an exhibition in the Gorky Central Park of Culture and Rest, Moscow. This tangible evidence of the success of their armies against Hitler's mighty, but not invincible, military machine, has had a heartening effect upon the inhabitants of Russia's capital, who not so long ago could hear the thunder of the enemy's guns at their very gates.

Photo, Planet News

Russia Will Smash Hitler's War Machine

RED ARMY men in action (right). Centre, photograph radioed from Moscow to London, showing Russian sappers, in snow camouflage, cutting a passage through enemy barbed wire. Shells from a German battery are bursting in the rear. Bottom, a heavy Russian tank ramming a German tank during a Red Army advance.

Photos, Planet News, Keystone

GERMANY ON THE DOWN GRADE

PRESIDENT KALININ of the U.S.S.R. has summed up, in an article in the Russian newspaper Izvestia, the last nine months of the war between Germany and the U.S.S.R. Here are some of his remarks :

At present German aviation does not dominate the air. The Germans are still able to hurl considerable numbers of planes against one sector or another. They are compelled to do this to protect their units from our attacks. This is forced on them by our command, and results in enormous losses. Our tank forces are also gradually approaching the Germans' in quantity, in two ways—we are destroying German tanks in large numbers, and our own tanks are increasing in numbers. In quality they are greatly superior to those of the Fascists.

The German Command has made innumerable failures. It is sufficient to recall that it failed to prepare in time enough winter clothing for its army. Another of the weaknesses of Germany, weaknesses which predetermined its inevitable defeat, is the inability to organize productive work in the conquered countries and those which are " in alliance."

The spring brings new difficulties for the German Army. Before the occupation troops could feed themselves on plunder ; now there is nothing left.

All these things provide ground for the conclusion that the fighting capacity of the German troops has declined. The Fascist Army has passed its zenith and is now on the down grade. It depends on our strength and the valour of the Red Army how much time elapses before the final collapse of Hitler's war machine.

We have sufficient strength for this task, and even more than we sometimes believe.

At Bataan They Fought to the Last Cartridge

"A long and gallant defence has been worn down and overthrown. We have nothing but praise and admiration for the commanders and men who have conducted this epic chapter in American history." So spake Mr. Stimson, U.S. Secretary for War, when giving out the news on April 9 of the fall of Bataan, where for four months a gallant little force of Americans and Filipinos had held a great Japanese army at bay.

AT 10.30 on the morning of April 9 the American War Department issued this announcement: "A message from General Wainwright at Fort Mills (on Corregidor Island in Manila Bay), just received by the War Department, states that the Japanese attack on the Bataan Peninsula succeeded in enveloping the east flank of our lines in the position held by the II Corps. An attack by the I Corps, ordered to relieve the situation, failed, due to the complete physical exhaustion of the troops. Full details are not available, but this situation indicated the probability that the defences on Bataan have been overcome."

At a press conference later in the day Mr. Stimson revealed that, the day before, President Roosevelt had sent a message to General Wainwright expressing full appreciation of the enormous difficulties confronting him, and telling him he had nothing but praise for his method of conducting the defence and for his soldierly conduct throughout. Furthermore, any decision that the General reached now would be in the interests of the country and his splendid troops.

The U.S. War Minister went on to say that the day before, General Wainwright had reported that he had 36,853 effectives at his command on the Bataan Peninsula, not including the wounded, some 20,000 civilians, and 6,000 Filipino labourers. The greater part of the armed forces were Filipinos. The Americans were made up largely of the 31st Infantry Regiment, the crews of two tank battalions and units of self-propelled artillery, together with Air Force ground crews, and sailors and marines from the abandoned Cavite naval base. Air Force personnel numbered about 5,000 men at the start of the invasion, and of these some 2,000 fought as infantrymen in the later stages, after their aircraft had been put out of action or transferred, as had been a number of long-range bombers, to the Netherlands East Indies and Australia. (American air losses were very heavy on the first day of the invasion, revealed Mr. Stimson; and Robert Waithman, News Chronicle correspondent in New York, gave the unofficial estimate that on December 8 most of the between 500 and 600 planes which the Americans had on Luzon island were destroyed by Japanese bombs.)

Igorots Ride the Tanks

As mentioned above, the greater part of the defenders of Bataan were natives of the Philippines, who proved themselves to be of the finest fighting quality. As an instance, take General MacArthur's story of an action in February.

A company of Igorot tribesmen had "died to a man in their foxholes without flinching or thought of retreat." Their comrades sought to avenge them; and when the General ordered a counter-attack, the Igorots climbed on top of the American tanks and guided them through the dense bamboo jungle. The little force closed in on the enemy. "Bataan," reported General MacArthur in his dispatch, "has seen many wild mornings, but nothing to equal this. Always above the din of battle rose the fierce shouts of the Igorots as they rode the tanks and fired their pistols. No guns, no thicket, only death itself could stop that mad rush. Of all the bloody spots on the peninsula, that proved to be the bloodiest. When the attack was over the remnants of the tanks and of

BATAAN Peninsula, showing the line between Subic Bay and Manila Bay held by the American and Filipino troops for four months against superior forces. The island fortress of Corregidor, which still held out, lies five miles off the southern tip of Bataan.
Courtesy of The Daily Telegraph

the Igorots were still there, but the 20th Japanese Infantry Regiment was completely annihilated. Many desperate acts of heroism have fallen under my observation in many fields of battle in many parts of the world. But for sheer breath-taking and heart-stopping desperation I have never known the equal of those Igorots riding the tanks."

The American and Filipino troops in Luzon had had their food rationed since January 11, the day after General MacArthur took up his position in Bataan. Immediately following, attempts were made under the direction of Brig.-General Hurley to send supplies into the Philippines from an American base in Australia. General Hurley did manage to get several shiploads of supplies into the Philippines and part reached Corregidor and Bataan.

For every ship that arrived he lost nearly two ships, however. All the same, said Mr. Stimson, the defenders were never short of ammunition. "Our troops," he said, "outnumbered and worn down by successive attacks by fresh troops, exhausted by insufficient rations and disease prevalent in that peninsula, finally had their lines broken and enveloped by the enemy."

From the Japanese news agency came an account of the last phase of the battle for Bataan. The final assault was launched on April 3, and for nearly a week General Yamashita strove to drive the defenders from their positions. After taking Limay on the east coast of the peninsula, the Japanese vanguard drove into Lamao, forcing the American and Filipino troops to fall back in the direction of Mariveles on the peninsula's southern tip. After heavy Japanese dive-bombing several thousands of the defenders surrendered in the Limay and Lamao region (so it was claimed), among them being the Commanders of the 21st Division and the 22nd Infantry Regiment.

Last Hours on the Peninsula

The ferocity of the attack may be gauged from a statement by a Japanese staff officer, who is quoted as saying that several hundred guns were trained on each square mile of the front, which was 12½ miles wide and 19 miles deep. On the first day of the operations—on April 3, that is—there was a six-hour barrage; this ceased at 3 in the afternoon when the Japanese infantry occupied the American advanced lines. Then artillery and infantry attacked alternately in the following days until American and Filipino resistance was exhausted. Throughout, the Japanese, thanks to their complete air superiority, were using fresh troops; altogether, it was estimated they had available some 100,000 men.

By April 8 the end was in sight, and from Corregidor came a message telling how throughout the night nurses dazed with fatigue and war-weary troops and civilians had been making the passage across the narrow channel separating the Bataan peninsula from Corregidor.

"They have braved Japanese bombers and the shark-infested seas in a bid for refuge from the clutches of the Japanese, who have overrun the peninsula. Some have come in rowing-boats, but most of them swam and were picked up in mid-channel by other small craft. And as they made the perilous trip the Japanese bombed and viciously machine-gunned them. Some of the soldiers had gone many nights without sleep, or had had little to eat during the final days of the battle against overwhelming odds. The only thing they wanted was sleep. Some of the nurses, who came in small boats, stumbled as they set foot ashore from weariness after long days of work under constant fire. Meanwhile, from this island fortress we could hear tremendous explosions, and see fires as the scorched earth policy was being carried out. Soldiers, veterans of many bombing attacks, wept openly as they heard the San Francisco short-wave station broadcast the news, 'Bataan has fallen'."

Fighting on the peninsula ceased on April 9. In a message from Corregidor, which was now once again furiously bombed and shelled, to President Roosevelt, General Wainwright said that everything possible had been done to hold Bataan with the limited number of troops under his command. But "the overwhelming air and artillery superiority of the Japanese finally overcame the dogged resistance of the hungry and exhausted defenders." A few days later he sent a "no surrender" message. "Bataan has fallen, but Corregidor will carry on. On this mighty fortress the spirit of Bataan will continue to live."

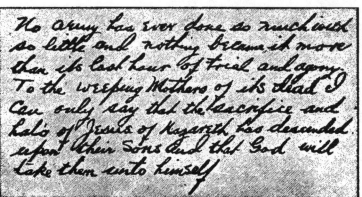

No army has ever done so much with so little and nothing became it more than its last hours of trial and agony. To the weeping Mothers of its dead I can only say that the sacrifice and halo of Jesus of Nazareth has descended upon their Sons and that God will take them unto himself

This photograph, radioed from Australia, is of General MacArthur's personal tribute to his old comrades, the gallant defenders of Bataan, who, after a resistance of four months which made history were overwhelmed by the vastly superior weight of enemy forces.
Photo. Planet News

Photo, Wide World

America Thunders Defiance

In the workshops, the factories and the steel mills of the United States of America the weapons of war are being forged, not only for the great republic herself, but for all those who stand beside her in defence of Democracy.   An enormous 16-in. gun, similar to those defending Corregidor, is here being tested at Fort Tilden, military camp on Long Island, N.Y.

'Action Stations' Has Sounded

1. Motor-cycle troops of the 66th Regt., U.S. 2nd Armoured Division, going into action during manoeuvres, led by a machine-gun armed "jeep," or scout car. 2. 12-in. mortar guns at Fort Corregidor, Manila Harbour, manned by U.S. Coast Artillery gunners. 3. An American 37-mm. anti-aircraft gun in action during exercises at La Guardia Field, N.Y.

Pho
Spe

Guns and Men on the Alert

4. A 37-mm. anti-tank gun being hoisted on to a dummy transport plane; photograph taken through the side window of a scout car. 5. A 155 howitzer manned by a gun crew of the 113th Field Artillery, U.S. 30th Division, practising in gas masks. 6. American tanks on exercise advancing through a smoke screen. The crew wear crash helmets.

Photos, Planet News, Wide World

Soldiers of Uncle Sam

The U.S.A. is raising, and equipping, great armies to fight in any corner of the globe. The U.S. Army uniforms shown top, are, left to right : snowshoe trooper; summer or tropical field ; winter field ; armoured forces ; ski trooper ; paratrooper ; summer mounted. Above, training with light assault boats. Ten of these boats nest inside each other on a single truck.

Malta: So Small in Size, So Great in Spirit

In assuming the Colonelcy-in-Chief of the Royal Malta Artillery, which most ably supports the R.A.F. in the active defence of the island, the King, in a special message to Lt.-Gen. Dobbie, said: "I have been watching with admiration the stout-hearted resistance of all in Malta—service personnel and civilians alike—to the fierce and constant air attacks of the enemy in recent weeks."

JUST a red dot on the blue expanse of the Mediterranean—that is the map's picture of Malta. But in history Malta, although it is smaller than the Isle of Wight, has a place surpassing in greatness and grandeur that of many a state larger far in territory but not to be compared with it in the heroism of its people, the valour of its defenders, its importance in the strategy of a world-wide conflict.

Since that summer day in 1940 when the mouthing megalomaniac, Mussolini, appeared on the balcony of the Palazzo Venezia and bellowed forth to the crowd of frenzied Fascists massed in the square below him the news that Italy had gone to war—since

'WHY WE HAVE NOT TAKEN MALTA'

MANY people in Germany ask : "How can Malta still carry on after all these attacks ? It should be knocked to pieces by now." These people look at the map and see a tiny island, like a pin's point. They overlook that, after two years of war, Malta is one great fortress. It is armed to the teeth. The A.A. guns are tremendously strong. The other defences are standing up to the heaviest test. Ammunition dumps and fuel stores are hidden in deep caverns of the rock—invulnerable from the air for all practical purposes. *From the sea Malta is practically invulnerable.* You will remember that Italian M.T.B.s tried to penetrate the Malta defences and to enter the harbour of Valetta. Not one of these courageous naval units returned. To fight Malta we have to attack from the air and cut off her sea communications. But you cannot expect the Luftwaffe to sink the island with bombs.—*Gen. Quaade, Luftwaffe spokesman, April, 3 1942.*

that day, not yet two years ago, Malta has borne the full brunt of an almost continuous air assault. More than 1,500 air-raid alarms have been sounded in the island, sometimes as many as eight in one day. In these circumstances life on the little island is eventful enough ; it is both tough and dangerous. As the morning sun comes up from the eastern sea the sirens may churn out their first warning of the day. There is no panic, since the Maltese have seen more aerial combats than any other people in the British Empire. Rarely do they miss a dogfight, and they cheer themselves hoarse as a plume of black and white smoke streaking across the azure sky speaks of the doom of yet another German or Italian pilot.

For the most part the men continue with their work until the shell splinters become too numerous or the bombs fall too close to be comfortable. Then, for a brief space, they join their womenfolk—the mothers who have gathered their children like chickens under the maternal wing—and make quietly and unhurriedly for the safety of the rock shelters.

Fortunate indeed is it for the islanders that Nature has provided them with so solid a foundation. Beneath their feet some 6,000 air-raid shelters have been tunnelled out of the solid rock, and another 1,500 are in course of construction. Most of them are over 100 feet down, and in some there is accommodation for as many as 1,500 people, with a bunk provided for each. Nearly every shelter is equipped with electric light and wireless, with washing and cooking facilities ; and some of them have small altars erected in a quiet corner, where regular evening services are held and where solitary prayers may be, and are, offered to our Lady of Victories.

Although the Axis spokesmen claim that Malta must soon be starved into submission, the food situation is, in fact, remarkably good, considering the dangers and difficulties

that attend the island's provisioning. There are two meatless days a week ; but fish is always available, and there is plenty to eat for all. Soup kitchens have been organized, and there those islanders who have lost their homes through enemy action are able to obtain a substantial meal for a few pence. The Government provides warm clothing for those who have lost their all, and makes grants of money in necessitous cases. The local milk-marketing board makes a point of seeing that every child has its supply of fresh milk daily.

The inspiration of the island's magnificent defence—and not only of its defence but of the offensive spirit which actuates its defenders on land, sea and in the air—is the sixty-year-old General Dobbie. "England doesn't seem to realize the magnificent job he is doing," a man just back from Malta told The Star the other day, "holding that tiny fortress on the enemy's doorstep. Think of it ! Only 70 miles from Sicily, where the Luftwaffe are concentrated ; as open to attack as are our South Coast towns from the Nazi bases on the Continent, yet worse off

MALTA'S DEFENDERS. Left, Maj.-Gen. D. M. W. Beak, V.C., D.S.O., M.C., commanding the troops in Malta. Centre, Air Vice-Marshal H. P. Lloyd, Air Officer Commanding R. A. F., Malta. Right, Sir E. St. John Jackson, Lieut.-Governor of Malta. Photos of the Governor, Lt.-Gen. Sir W. Dobbie, and Vice-Adm. Sir R. Leatham, Flag Officer in Charge, are in pages 513 and 610.
Photos, British Official: Crown Copyright, Vandyk, Keystone

than we are because there can be no retreat to other aerodromes far inland."

Gen. Dobbie is in very truth a Christian warrior, a soldier in the evangelical tradition of Cromwell and his Ironsides, of Capt. Hedley Vickars, who "walked with God before Sebastopol" in the Crimea, of "Chinese" Gordon who found in his Bible the inspiration which nerved him to meet with sublime contempt the Mahdi's spearmen. To quote from The Star again, "Dobbie still lives 'with a Bible in one hand and a sword in the other.' He still holds his Bible classes in his home just as he did at Chatham and later in Malaya. He is still a teetotaler. Even in the hottest attack —and believe me, the Luftwaffe know how to drop bombs on Malta—Dobbie will go out imperturbable, regardless of self, thoughtful of others. I have seen him helping to rescue people from their wrecked homes and urging on the civil as well as the military defence. And it is largely because of his personality that the Maltese have come to respect and like the British."

Foremost in the defence of the island is the Royal Air Force, and well do Air Vice-Marshal Lloyd and his squadrons deserve the congratulations which were sent them by Sir Archibald Sinclair last autumn. "The brilliant defence of the island by the Hurricanes (wired the Air Minister), the audacious attacks of the Beaufighters on enemy air bases, the steady and deadly slogging of the

Wellingtons at the enemy airports, the daring and the dextrous reconnaissances of the Marylands, culminating in the tremendous onslaughts of the Blenheims and Fleet Air Arm Swordfish on Axis shipping in the Mediterranean, are watched with immense admiration by your comrades in the R.A.F. and by your fellow-men at home."

But the Royal Navy, too, is playing a magnificent part in Malta's defence—and offence ; and when we remember the much more than century-old association of the island with his Majesty's ships it is not surprising that the Navy holds a unique place in the affections of the islanders. Not so many ships put in at Valetta as in the days of peace ; but ships still call, and, large or small, they are sure of a tremendous reception. One such occasion was on December 13 last, when three British destroyers, followed by another of the Dutch Navy, entered the harbour after a triumphant clash in which they had sent to the bottom two of Mussolini's cruisers with one of his destroyers and an E-boat. Then the age-old bastions overlooking the harbour, the cobbled wharves

and the long waterfronts are crowded with a cheering population, ships are manned, and military bands on the quayside play "Rule, Britannia," and "Roll out the Barrel."

Recently Air Vice-Marshal Lloyd spoke of the difficulties which have to be faced in the island's offensive-defence. Looking for the enemy is very difficult, he said, since the area of sea is enormous. "We patrol the seas to the east and to the west every day and all day. To the east it is over 350 miles to Greece. When we arrive there we have to cover something like 500 miles of Greek coast and open sea from Italy to Africa. To the west we have 200 miles to the Tunisian coast, and in the south 200 to Tripolitania." Well might he describe it as a tremendous undertaking, one which imposes a terrific strain on the young and courageous pilots. All the same, "We in Malta dominate this part of the Mediterranean. We strike the enemy wherever it hurts him most. And it hurts him grievously."

Then, in conclusion, Air Vice-Marshal Lloyd said that Malta was on the eve of great events, in which she would play a part greater even than heretofore in the enemy's defeat. "Malta has every reason to be proud of the past ; she has every reason to be proud of her part in this war, and the full story of that has yet to be told. When it is told, it will amaze many people. The best, however, is yet to come. God speed that day ! "

Ever Nearer to India Stride the Japanese

Day by day the Japanese are getting nearer to India, now revealed as their principal objective in the Far Eastern war zone. Below we describe a number of clashes on land, sea and in the air, in which the enemy still on balance had the advantage.

TOWARDS the end of March, or early in April, the Japanese High Command sent a numerous and powerful fleet into the Indian Ocean. On April 4 it was observed steering towards Ceylon, and (said Mr. Churchill in the House of Commons on April 13) it comprised at least three battleships, including one modernized 16-in.-gun Nagato type, and five aircraft-carriers, together with a number of heavy and light cruisers and destroyer flotillas.

Very soon this great force made its presence felt. First, from the aircraft-carriers sped a host of bombing planes to raid ports in Ceylon and on the Madras coast. Colombo was the first target. Maybe the Japanese were hoping to repeat their success at Pearl Harbour in the opening hours of the war; if so, they were disappointed. The defences were ready, and out of 75 raiders, 25 were shot down by our fighters and two, engaged in a low-flying attack, by anti-aircraft fire; five more were probably shot down and another 25 damaged. Although the harbour and the suburb of Ratmalana were dive-bombed and machine-gunned, the damage caused was reported to be slight and the casualties few. Over half the people killed were patients in a medical establishment.

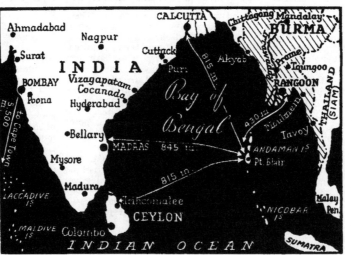

INDIAN OCEAN where Japanese submarines and aircraft are operating against Allied shipping and men-of-war. From aircraft-carriers, probably based on the Andamans, they have launched air attacks on Colombo and Trincomalee.
Courtesy of The Daily Mirror

and a near miss on one aircraft-carrier was claimed. "But whether any damage was done I have no knowledge," said Mr. Churchill on April 13; "I know this, however, that practically all our aircraft taking part in the attack were shot down or seriously injured or became unserviceable."

Then on Easter Monday, April 6, a British convoy was intercepted off the coast of Orissa by two Japanese heavy cruisers and a destroyer. Forming a triangle, the enemy ships opened a barrage of gunfire, which lasted about half an hour. Several merchant ships were sunk, but between

H.M.S. DORSETSHIRE, 9,975-ton cruiser, sunk in the Indian Ocean by Jap air attack.

This attack on Colombo was made on Easter Sunday, April 5. The next day the first bombs fell on the Indian mainland, when the harbour at Vizagapatam and the town of Cocanada were raided by a small number of Japanese aircraft. Then on April 9 a large force of enemy bombers and fighters carried out an attack on Trincomalee, the British naval base in Ceylon. Some damage was caused to the harbour and aerodrome buildings, and there were a few casualties amongst the dockyards naval and civil personnel. But 21 of the raiders were destroyed for certain, 12 were probably destroyed, and two more damaged.

Following these attacks British torpedo aircraft sallied out to attack the carriers from which the Japanese planes had been launched. On the day of the Colombo attack there were thunderstorms and low cloud, so that they were unable to make contact with the enemy. After the Trincomalee raid, however, it was reported that contact had been established,

H.M. aircraft-carrier HERMES, sunk off Ceylon by Japanese bombs. She was completed in 1924.

four hundred and five hundred survivors reached the Orissa coast in their lifeboats. Three days later the Japanese claimed to have sunk 20 merchantmen and damaged 23 others

in the Indian Ocean up to April 7. Moreover, in the same communiqué they declared that they had sunk two British cruisers, and the next day they added to their list of victims an aircraft-carrier.

These naval losses inflicted by enemy aircraft were admitted by the Admiralty within a few hours: the cruisers H.M.S. Dorsetshire (Capt. A. W. S. Agar, V.C., D.S.O., R.N.) and H.M.S. Cornwall (Capt. P. C. W. Manwaring, R.N.) and the old aircraft-carrier H.M.S. Hermes (Capt. R. F. J. Onslow, M.V.O., D.S.O., R.N.). More than eleven hundred survivors, including the two commanding officers, were rescued from the cruisers; and a large proportion of the ship's company of H.M.S. Hermes reached land, since at the time she was sunk she was only about ten miles off the eastern coast of Ceylon.

Mr. Churchill had little to add to the communiqués when he made a statement on the sinkings; he did disclose, however, that the British fleet in the Bay of Bengal was under the command of Admiral Sir James Somerville, "an officer who for the last two years has been commanding in the western Mediterranean and has almost unrivalled experience of the conditions of modern war."

While the Japanese were scoring these successes at sea, their armies were pushing steadily ahead through the valleys and jungles of Burma. General Alexander's little army and the Chinese army under the American General Stilwell fought valiantly, but they were compelled to fall back up the valleys of the Irrawaddy and the Sittang. The Japanese overcame the desperate Chinese resistance in Toungoo on April 1, and to the west the British were compelled to evacuate Prome on April 3. The same day Mandalay was savagely bombed. Two days later the heavy bombers of the American Volunteer Group struck back at the Japanese in Rangoon, but their effort was small and weak compared with the enemy's punch. For still it was the old, old story. In the sky of Burma, as in the skies of so many other places where the United Nations have warred against the Axis, air superiority was the enemy's strongest card.

H.M.S. CORNWALL, 10,000-ton cruiser of the Kent class, sunk by Japanese air attack in the Indian Ocean.
Photos, Central Press, Associated Press

With Uncle Sam's Men on the Emerald Isle

'YANKS' IN IRELAND are rapidly settling down in their new environment, and training exercises and manoeuvres are now in full swing. These photographs show : top, a "jeep," or "blitz buggy," as the Americans term their small scout cars, towing an anti-tank gun during exercises along the coast of Northern Ireland. Centre, American snipers busy among the rocks. Above, the first shooting practice of American gun teams using British artillery in Northern Ireland.

Photos, Fox, Associated Press

Our Diary of the War

APRIL 1, 1942, Wednesday   942nd day

Air.—R.A.F. made night attack on Matford motor-works at Poissy, near Paris, as well as on other targets in N. France, Belgium and Germany. Boulogne docks bombed by day.

Mediterranean.—In more mass raids on Malta 17 enemy aircraft destroyed and many damaged.

Burma.—Chinese withdrew N.E. of Toungoo. Battle for Prome developing.

Australasia.—R.A.A.F. made another heavy raid on Koepang, in Dutch Timor.

General.—Washington announced 28 Axis submarines destroyed to date by U.S. Forces. First meeting of Pacific War Council held at White House, Washington. Call-up of all Australian single men between 18 and 45 and married men between 18 and 35.

APRIL 2, Thursday   943rd day

Air.—R.A.F. attacked Matford works at Poissy by night, also docks at Le Havre.

Russian Front.—Soviet forces made considerable advance S.E. of Kharkov.

Home.—Night raids on South coast.

APRIL 3, Friday   944th day

Sea.—Admiralty announced loss of H.M. destroyer Heythrop.

Mediterranean.—Heavy raids on Malta. During March 59 enemy aircraft were destroyed over Malta, 23 probably destroyed and 94 damaged.

Burma.—British forces withdrew from Prome to positions north of the town. Mandalay heavily bombed.

India.—Flying Fortresses of U.S. Air Forces in India attacked Japanese shipping in the Andaman Islands.

Australasia.—R.A.A.F. made another heavy raid on Koepang. Port Darwin raided : five of the raiders destroyed.

APRIL 4, Saturday   945th day

Air.—Sweep by R.A.F. over N. France. Railways near St. Omer attacked.

Russian Front.—Moscow announced more successes on the Leningrad front and the sinking of two enemy transports in the Barents Sea.

Burma.—Japanese thrusting towards Burma oilfields at Yenangyaung.

Australasia.—R.A.A.F. attacked enemy aerodromes at Lae in New Guinea and Koepang in Dutch Timor. Many Japanese aircraft destroyed over Port Darwin.

General.—U.S. State Dept. announced that the U.S.A. recognized the authority of the Free French throughout French Equatorial Africa and the Cameroons. Repatriation of some sick and wounded British and Italian prisoners began following an Anglo-Italian agreement for the exchange. U.S. Navy Dept. announced that U.S. submarines had sunk at least one and probably two Japanese light cruisers near Christmas Island. Jap ships sunk or damaged by U.S. Navy to date totalled 132—56 warships and 76 non-combatant vessels.

APRIL 5, Sunday   946th day

Air.—Gnome-Rhone aero-engine works at Gennevilliers raided at night by Whitley bombers. Other aircraft of Bomber Command raided objectives in Germany, including Cologne, and the docks at Le Havre.

Mediterranean.—Day and night air battles over Malta.

India.—Japanese aircraft raided Colombo, British naval base in Ceylon. Of 75 raiders, 27 were shot down. Five more were probably destroyed and 25 others damaged.

Burma.—American heavy bombers attacked docks at Rangoon.

Philippines.—Heavy Japanese attack on the Bataan Peninsula repulsed.

Home.—Enemy bomber destroyed off E. Coast.

APRIL 6, Monday   947th day

Air.—Night attack by R.A.F. on Ruhr and Rhineland.

Mediterranean.—More mass raids on Malta.

India.—Harbours at Vizagapatam and Cocanada, in the province of Madras, bombed by Japanese aircraft.

Philippines.—Japanese made some gains on Bataan Peninsula at a heavy cost.

Australasia.—R.A.A.F. attacked Rabaul and Gasmata, in New Britain, and Koepang in Dutch Timor.

Home.—Bombs dropped on S. Coast. H.Q. of the first Canadian Army, under command of Lt.-Gen. A. G. L. McNaughton, established in the U. Kingdom.

General.—U.S. Navy Dept. announced sinking of three more Japanese ships by U.S. submarines.

APRIL 7, Tuesday   948th day

Sea.—Admiralty announced loss of H.M. destroyer Havock off the Tunisian coast, and submarine Tempest.

Mediterranean.—Another fierce raid on Malta. At least nine raiders destroyed.

Burma.—British destroyed oil and cement installations in retirement north of Prome.

Philippines.—Heavy casualties on both sides in the Bataan Peninsula.

Australasia.—R.A.A.F. attack on Lae, in New Guinea.

General.—Reported from Norway that all Norwegian clergymen had resigned en masse.

APRIL 8, Wednesday   949th day

Air.—R.A.F. made big offensive sweep over N. France. Night attack on N.W. Germany and docks at Le Havre.

Russian Front.—Rumanian 18th Division reported shattered in big battle on the Ukraine front.

Mediterranean.—Air blitz on Malta continued. Nine enemy aircraft destroyed and many damaged.

Africa.—Cairo communiqué reported increased activity in the forward area by Rommel's troops.

Burma.—Imperial forces reported holding positions north of Thayetmyo, Irrawaddy river port.

Philippines.—Huge Japanese forces attacking American-Filipino troops on Bataan Peninsula.

Australasia.—Japanese seizure of Lorengau, in the Admiralty Islands, reported.

General.—Gen. Marshall, Chief of Staff of the U.S. Army, arrived in London. Ali Pasha Maher, former prime minister, arrested by Egyptian Government.

APRIL 9, Thursday   950th day

Sea.—Admiralty announced sinking of British cruisers Dorsetshire and Cornwall by Japanese aircraft in Indian Ocean, and that an Italian 10,000-ton cruiser had been sunk by British submarine in the Mediterranean.

Air.—R.A.F. made night raids on a number of localities in N. Germany.

Russian Front.—Berlin radio admitted that Soviet forces had by-passed German defence lines on Kharkov-Byelgorod road.

Africa.—In Libya a British column reported engaged with the enemy S.W. of Gazala. Alexandria had its third air raid in three days.

Indian Ocean.—Trincomalee, Ceylon, raided. 21 Jap planes certainly destroyed, 12 probably destroyed and two more damaged.

Burma.—American Volunteer Group pilots shot down 10 Jap aircraft and damaged 2 without loss.

Philippines.—Washington communiqué indicated that American resistance in Bataan had ended.

Australasia.—Allied bombers carried out heavy raid on Rabaul, New Britain.

APRIL 10, Friday   951st day

Sea.—Admiralty announced sinking of aircraft-carrier Hermes by Japanese air attack off Ceylon. British submarine sunk two enemy supply ships in Mediterranean.

Air.—R.A.F. made night raid on Ruhr, and also attacked docks at Le Havre.

Mediterranean.—Two more heavy air raids on Malta.

Africa.—Clashes between advanced units in Cyrenaica.

Burma.—Japs launched three-pronged drive from Toungoo.

Philippines.—Washington announced sinking of a Jap cruiser off Cebu by U.S. torpedo boat. U.S. submarine sunk armed Japanese ship near the Celebes.

Australasia.—Japs claimed occupation of Christmas Island. R.A.A.F. raided Koepang, Dutch Timor. Japs raided Port Moresby.

General.—Delhi reported that Congress had rejected British proposals for settlement of Indian problem.

APRIL 11, Saturday   952nd day

Air.—R.A.F. sweep over N. France.

Russian Front.—Soviet troops reported to be within sight of Bryansk.

Mediterranean.—Two more heavy raids on Malta. R.A.F. made night attack on Crete.

Burma.—Japs launched heavy attack on British positions S.W. of Taungdwingyi.

Philippines.—U.S. War Dept. announced that 12,000 Japanese had landed on the island of Cebu. Intensive air attacks on Corregidor and Fort Hughes.

APRIL 12, Sunday   953rd day

Air.—Large R.A.F. sweep over N. France. Night attack on Channel ports, the Ruhr, Le Havre, aerodromes in Low Countries and France, and N. Italy.

Mediterranean.—Two more heavy raids on Malta.

Philippines.—Corregidor raided 12 times in 24 hours.

Australasia.—Allied bombers attacked Rabaul in New Britain, Lae in New Guinea and Faisi in the Solomons. Koepang, in Dutch Timor, raided by R.A.A.F.

APRIL 13, Monday   954th day

Air.—Large-scale sweep over N. France.

Mediterranean.—Malta blitz continued.

Philippines.—10 Japanese air raids on Corregidor. The fort's guns sunk enemy boats in harbour at Mariveles.

General.—Appointments announced of Adm. Sir James Somerville as C.-in-C. Eastern Fleet and of Lord Louis Mountbatten as Chief of Combined Operations.

APRIL 14, Tuesday   955th day

Air.—R.A.F. daylight sweep over N. France lasted from 10 a.m. to 7.30 p.m. Night raid on industrial targets in the Ruhr and docks at Le Havre.

Russian Front.—Red Army reported making good progress N.E. of Byelgorod.

Mediterranean.—More air raids on Malta. Nine enemy planes brought down.

Burma.—On the Sittang front Chinese withdrew to north of Yedashe.

Indian Ocean.—R.A.F. destroyed or damaged 13 Japanese flying-boats in a raid on Fort Blair in the Andaman Islands.

Philippines.—Corregidor bombed and shelled by Japs for 5th day in succession.

Australasia.—Australian bombers attacked Lae in New Guinea and Koepang in Timor.

Home.—Sir Kingsley Wood introduced the new Budget.

General.—Laval appointed Chief of the Vichy Government. In Australia, Mr. Curtin, the Prime Minister, was sworn in as Minister of Defence. Persian Government broke with Japan.

VICE-ADML. LORD LOUIS MOUNTBATTEN, Chief of Combined Operations, in conference with Combined Operations chiefs at their headquarters. Left to right : Gp. Capt. A. H. Willetts, Rear-Adml. H. E. Horan, Maj.-Gen. J. C. Haydon (who commanded the troops in the Vaagso raid on Dec. 27, 1941), Lord Louis Mountbatten, Air Vice-Mshl. J. M. Robb, Brig. G. E. Wildman Lushington (Royal Marines), Cdre. R. M. Ellis.

Photo, Planet News

Death from the Air in the Bowels of the Earth

A STREET OF BOMBS in a depot of R.A.F. Maintenance Command driven into the heart of a mountain. The bombs the men are trundling down a ramp are 500-lb. high-explosive blast bombs, and stacked on the left are 500-lb. semi-armour-piercing bombs. For everything except pay and rations—for spare motors or aircraft, for petrol and oil, for uniforms, oxygen, compasses, dope and bombs, or any other of the 750,000 separate items which keep an air force in the air, the R.A.F. must go to Maintenance Command.

Photo, Topical Press

Yugoslavia's Airmen in the Middle East

The youngest member of the Yugoslav Seaplane Squadron, a fourteen-year-old apprentice, stands proudly beneath the emblem of his country.

Yugoslav airmen are still carrying on the fight. Above, an aircraft of the Royal Yugoslav Seaplane Squadron on service in the Middle East takes off on patrol.

Left, Yugoslav pilots checking their course before setting out on one of their daily patrols over the Mediterranean. Above, armourers bombing up an aircraft of the Royal Yugoslav Seaplane Squadron.

Photos, British Official: Crown Copyright

Bombs on Germany—The R.A.F. Strikes Again

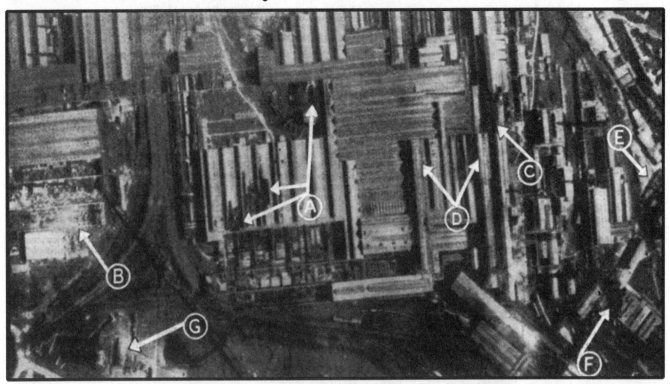

BOMBER Command has been taking the war on to Germany's doorstep in no uncertain manner. Among the very heavy raids on Reich territory recently carried out by aircraft of Bomber Command were those on the important Baltic seaport of Lübeck and the Thyssen steelworks at Hamborn, in the Rhineland. The photograph above, taken in daylight by an R.A.F. reconnaissance plane, shows damage done to the Thyssen steelworks by the raid on the night of March 9. (A) Two direct hits on a large shed—probably plate or stock shed. One gap in the roof is 65 yards across and the other 50 yards across. (B) Direct hits on storage yards—damage by fire. (C) Large shed, probably part of the steel rolling works, burned out. (D) Blast effect—roofs damaged over a wide area. (E) Long workshop burned out. (F) Large shed partly destroyed. (G) Large shed badly damaged by blast. The Thyssen steelworks are a great plant with power station and coking plant, eight blast furnaces, 21 basic steel furnaces and four electric steel furnaces. In addition to producing steel for war weapons the factory makes finished railway lines. *Photos, British Official*

DESCRIBING the raid on Lübeck, the C.O. of a Wellington Bomber Squadron said it was the most amazing blitz he had ever seen since he started bombing eighteen months ago. "We found a great area round the docks completely enveloped in flame. It wasn't a question of counting the number of fires ; the whole area was one gigantic fire." So great were the fires started by the R.A.F. that fire brigades from Schwerin, Stettin and Stralsund were sent to Lübeck to cope with them ; Stralsund is 120 miles from Lübeck and Stettin is 150. The photograph of Lübeck below was taken at the beginning of the raid and shows incendiaries burning and fires starting. The thin white lines are the incendiaries and the thicker ones the fires ; they appear as lines on account of the speed of the aeroplane. The target was an important one, for Lübeck has important shipbuilding yards where submarines as well as surface vessels are constructed. As a seaport where many railways and inland waterways join, Lübeck handles a great volume of traffic between Germany and Scandinavia and is used also for sending supplies to Norway, Finland and the North Russian Front.

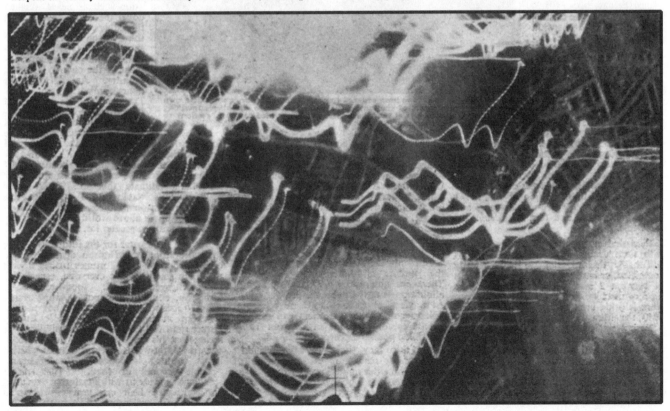

Critical Indeed Will Be 1942's Harvest

Not often in wartime does Parliament find time or opportunity to discuss the state of British agriculture, but on March 18 there was an interesting and informative debate on the subject in the House of Commons. It was opened by Mr. R. S. Hudson, Minister of Agriculture, on whose speech the present article is largely based.

WE may have to tighten our belts a good deal more this year, said Mr. Hudson ; but we can do it, and will do it, cheerfully. All the same, no effort is being spared to see that everything that *can* be produced in this country to lessen the belt-tightening, is being produced. Moreover, every ounce of foodstuffs that we produce here lightens the task imposed on our shipping—on that shipping so sorely needed for so many other purposes vital to our final victory. It is only sober truth that the harvest of 1942 may well be a critical factor in the future history, not only of this country, but of the world.

What the Minister of Agriculture had to say concerning British farming was highly encouraging. When this year's ploughing season is completed there will be something like six million more acres under the plough in the United Kingdom than before the war. Our average wheat acreage for the ten years before the war was just over 1,600,000 ; last year that had been increased by more than a third, and, moreover, whereas before the war a great deal of the produce from that acreage went to the feeding of livestock, practically the whole of it now goes for human consumption. A potato acreage of rather more than 700,000 in 1938 has been raised to well over a million acres—an increase of nearly sixty per cent. In 1938 some 2,500,000 tons of vegetables were produced, and in 1941 this was increased to nearly 4,000,000 tons. The oat acreage is up from 2½ million to nearly 4 million, and this year we are aiming at a record sugar-beet acreage of 405,000 —the maximum the existing factories can deal with.

Another interesting fact revealed by the Minister is that we are today probably the most highly mechanized farming country in Europe, and over 7,000 tractors under State ownership are being hired to farmers. Power farming is far less well developed in Germany ; though the Nazis have increased their arable acreage, the increased ploughing is dependent on prisoner-of-war labour. In other respects, too, our farming position shows to advantage ; thus the cereal harvest in Continental Europe both in 1940 and 1941 yielded less than the pre-war average, and Germany's potato and root crops tell the same tale.

Remarkable progress has been made with farm drainage work. Much land is still badly drained, but we have already completed, or have in hand, the improvement of between 2 and 3 million acres. Every kind of machine that will speed up drainage work is being brought into service. In July 1940 the Ministry of Agriculture did not possess a single excavator ; now it has 250, and before the end of the year it hopes to have 400. But there are still thousands of miles of ditches which are not doing their job, and in consequence tens of thousands of acres which are waterlogged and not producing maximum crops. So farmers, landowners and County Agricultural Com-

mittees must make it their watchword, " To fight to the last ditch."

But although much has been done to increase the productivity of Britain's soil, much more could be done if the labour were available. Because of the town-dominated politics of our age there has been for many years past a steady drift of the more young and vigorous from the country to the towns ; and although in wartime this drift is no longer noticeable, tens of thousands of skilled agricultural workers have been taken into the Army. Thus it is that there is now a distinct shortage of labour in the fields, and this shortage will have to be made good by unskilled labour and by the Women's Land Army. The latter has now passed the

Many R.A.F. stations have been ordered to grow a large proportion of their own crops, and these pilots of the famous Eagle Squadron are learning something about agriculture on one of the " home farms " now joined to R.A.F. stations to grow food for the airmen. *Photo, Wide World*

25,000 mark—an increase of more than 15,000 on the total of a year ago ; but Mr. Hudson is emphatic that there is still room for many more women on the land, to do work which is second-to-none in national value. Over 90 per cent of the Land Girls are turning out splendidly, and there is no longer any difficulty in getting farmers to take them. More use is to be made, too of school-children, Italian prisoners, and voluntary land clubs.

Not only the farmers are responsible for the product of the nation's foodstuffs. There are now nearly 1,750,000 holders of allotments—nearly double the pre-war figure. At a very conservative estimate allotment holders and private gardeners can produce vegetables to the value of between 10 to 15 million pounds a year.

Are there any limits to what Britain's soil can be made to produce—apart, of course, from the limitations of size ? Some part of the land would not repay the costs of cultivation even at wartime prices, but the uncultivable area is much smaller than

has often been supposed, since under the stress of war many thousands of acres of swamps, heath and rugged mountainsides have been made to bear bountiful crops, or at least to carry stock. Another limitation is that of labour, to which we have already referred ; given more men, given more Land Girls, then the land will provide yet more bountiful harvests.

But there are many who are of the opinion that one of the most important limiting factors is the system of land-holding and land-ownership. Some are urging that large-scale mechanized farming should be favoured, and this has been tried, indeed, in some districts, with striking success, e.g. on the Dagenham estates of the Ford Motor Company. Others take the contrary view, maintaining that the prairie system of farming is quite unsuited to England and the English character, and that it is intensive farming that should be encouraged, i.e. the production of milk and dairy produce, vegetables and fruit— relying for our bread supply still very largely or almost entirely on the import of grain from overseas. But intensive farming demands a degree of cooperation between farmers in the way of marketing, use of tractors, mechanical plant, and so on, and the English farmer up to now has shown himself to be far less cooperatively inclined than the farmers of, say, New Zealand or Denmark. Then, as always, there is the question of expense. Where is the money to come from, asks the farmer—asks, too, the landowner, now staggering under a burden of taxation such as never weighed down the shoulders of his forefathers ? So we come to the demand that the State should make itself responsible for the proper development of the country's basic industry. As the eminent agricultural expert, Sir Daniel Hall, has expressed it in a recent book, " Agriculture can only be placed on a sound and progressive footing if the State obtains the control of the land that ownership confers." How far the State has gone already in the matter of financing agriculture may be seen from Sir D. Hall's estimate that in 1938-9 over £100 millions was paid in subsidies to farmers, remission of taxes, and the maintenance of prices above world level. Today the figure must be greater far.

But that is a matter for the future. Today, to quote from Mr. Hudson again, " The crisis of our national fortunes makes it all the more essential that everyone, especially those engaged in the food-production campaign, should think not of what he is going to receive, but of how much he personally can manage to contribute." Every farmer must feel a personal responsibility for seeing that his fields are properly cultivated, and every farm-worker that the farm on which he is working is producing the greatest possible amount of food. " That spirit alone will provide us with maximum production, without which our past efforts and sacrifices may well prove to be in vain."

Spring's Drive on the Land in Full Swing

Twenty-year-old George Stennett (centre) runs an 800-acre farm of his own, of which 700 acres is under the plough. Here a drill is being filled with oats for sowing. Mr. Stennett also has 250 ewes and 300 lambs.

The National Federation of Young Farmers' Clubs gives the youth of Britain a chance to serve their country. Boys of Holbrook School are selecting potatoes from the clamp for use in the school canteen.

Joan Hill, working with the Women's Land Army on a Northants farm, scatters "the good seed on the land" in a manner which has not varied since the days of the Bible (circle).

Photos, Fox, The Daily Mirror, Central News

Below left, Hertfordshire Land Girls are seen "lining" a ditch in readiness for the motor excavator which another girl is handling. Below right, Peggy Ayres, once in the printing trade, now drives a two-furrow plough.

Page 667

Into Action On Land Goes the Royal Navy

The Navy, too, is training to strike at enemy-occupied territory. Above, sailors prepare for demolition work. One section establishes telephone communications while others guard them with revolvers and grenades.

A naval demolition party, led by officers, laying charges on a vital bridge-head ready to blow it up.

Above, ratings of a naval raiding party dressed in their special raiding gear assemble on the deck of a warship before transport to shore.

Some of the naval raiding party, carrying lengths of cable and equipment, trudge through a mountain stream on their way to the rendezvous (right).

Photos, British Official

We Went With the Raiders to St. Nazaire

Supplementing the official story of the raid on St. Nazaire (*see* page 627), here are eye-witness accounts by Gordon Holman, Reuter's and Exchange Telegraph correspondent, and men who participated in the operations.

OUR journey to St. Nazaire was undertaken with an escort of destroyers (wrote Gordon Holman). There were alarms but absence of air attack. A dramatic moment came when at nightfall we changed direction and began our run into the enemy stronghold. The whole force moved silently and without the slightest glimmer of light. I was in a motor gunboat with Commander "Red" Ryder, and Lieutenant-Colonel A. C. Newman, commanding the naval and military forces respectively.

The German flak rose into the sky in staccato bursts of fire. As we entered the estuary tracer shells went up on either side forming a strange Gothic archway of fire.

GORDON HOLMAN, who covered the raid for the Press.

Suddenly, as we pushed up the estuary towards our objective, two powerful searchlights swept the water, picking up the leading ships as if it had been daylight, and the Germans fired a burst of flak. There was a brief and tense interval and then there came another and more continuous burst of fire, which was answered by the Campbeltown.

The match had been set to the conflagration. In a second the whole river was covered with a fantastic criss-cross pattern of fire, marked by the varied coloured tracer shells and bullets. The roar and rattle of gunfire so filled the night that it was impossible to hear orders shouted only a yard or so from the bridges of the motor launches to the gunners on the deck below. Dozens of searchlights lit the scene, but accurate fire from the ships soon reduced the number.

The British force, which had been moving slowly, cracked on all the speed they had, and continued up river towards St. Nazaire and the docks. They went in face of fire from many shore positions which gave the raiders all they had got. The Campbeltown attracted the defenders' attention and she continued on her way under constant heavy fire from both sides of the river.

Our motor gunboat blazed her way past the last barrier before the entrance to the dry dock. She then swung round in comparatively wide water, and, while shells screamed over the top of us, we watched the Campbeltown finish her last journey by magnificently shooting up a German flak ship, which she left in flames before speeding up for the charge into the dock gates. She piled herself up on them with the sureness of a ferret diving into a hole.

Soon a new and even grimmer note was added to the constant cannonade by the roar of big explosions. "There go the first demolitions," said Colonel Newman. "I told you they would get in." He almost

begged to be landed at once, so that he could get to his men on shore.

Then our M.G.B. nosed her way round the stern of the Campbeltown, which was stuck up by the bows as if climbing a steep hill, and got alongside the jetty of a small inner harbour. Colonel Newman, giving a final tightening pull to his equipment, jumped ashore followed by his adjutant and small headquarters staff. "Good luck," we shouted, and he disappeared round some blazing buildings, towards the dry dock.

Heavy fire was coming from the direction of the main basin and also across the harbour. Screened from the former by some buildings, we lay alongside the jetty for a few minutes while survivors of the Campbeltown scrambled on board. We then headed out into the main channel again, and immediately came under the fire of German shore positions. "Round the corner" they swept the M.G.B. with rapid fire at a range of less than 50 yards. Although a number of the crew were wounded we replied with machine-gun and pom-pom fire. On the exposed forecastle gun a gunner took careful aim at a German pill-box and scored a direct hit, which caused the captain to shout from the bridge: "Well shot, do it again." But the gunner had fired his last shot—he was killed immediately.

There was no sign of the pace slackening out in the harbour. The glare of fires from both burning German and British vessels made a light nearly as strong as the searchlights. Inshore great fires were raging in many places, and the battle was intensified from time to time by a shattering explosion. A big burst of fire went straight down the inner basin, indicating that the Commandos had secured yet another position and were

Lt.-Cmdr. BEATTIE, in charge of the Campbeltown when she rammed the basin lock gates at St. Nazaire. He was reported missing after the raid. *Photo, G.P.U.*

raking the U-boat moorings with mortars and Brens.

Commander Ryder twice attempted to get alongside the mole, which was still held by the Germans, but the fire power was intense, and we were driven off. The crew of the exposed decks—the Germans were able to fire down on them from concrete emplacements—fought with magnificent courage. Our M.G.B. was the last of the small White Ensign armada left in the harbour. Although there was the possibility that we had been holed, and that damage had been done to vital controls, we made a full-speed dash down the river.

As it was the run was a nightmare experience in which one small M.G.B. became the target for literally hundreds of enemy guns at comparatively short range. Picked out by searchlights we made our best possible speed as gun after gun took up the attack. Only a hard turn to port prevented us running into a German flak ship lying in the middle of the river. She opened fire on the M.G.B. at 20 yards range, but with our last shells we silenced her, and then, as we escaped, saw her destroyed by the concentrated fire of her own shore batteries, who believed, apparently, that it was the M.G.B. lying disabled in mid-stream. Aided by this muddle, which was only one of many such incidents for the Germans, who frequently shot up each other in their anxiety, we raced down the estuary under the fire of the heavier batteries at the entrance. Turning and twisting to avoid the powerful searchlights, we reached the open sea. The deck was littered with wounded men. A young lieutenant crawled about administering first aid as best he could in the dark on the slippery metal decks.

Behind us was a scene of blazing destruction which reminded one of the worst London blitz nights. Fires raged everywhere, and the Germans were still shooting away madly in all directions. The Commandos, continuing their systematic destruction under the cover of assault parties, had clearly persuaded the enemy that large forces were still in occupation. The one tragic moment from our point of view came with the realization that some of the fighting Commando troops on shore could not be evacuated. Colonel Newman had probably realized the likelihood of this contingency arising while

Lieut. Col. A. C. NEWMAN, who led the Special Service troops in the St. Nazaire raid, was reported missing afterwards. He was attached to the Essex Regt. *Photo, British Official*

These two photographs afford proof of the success of the St. Nazaire raid described in this page. Above, photograph taken by a reconnaissance plane before the raid :- 1, the lock gate in position. Below, the same area after the raid. The damaged outer lock gate to the Penhouet Basin is seen at (A), lying against the western side of the dock, blown off its sill and badly buckled. The damage to the machine-house (C) that operated the gate can also be seen. The concrete dam is shown at (B).

Photos, British Official : Crown Copyright

he watched the initial stages of the attack. He raised no question on the matter and not for one minute did he hesitate to go ashore and take his headquarters staff with him. The Commandos themselves in the heat of the battle were probably the least worried of all with regard to their own withdrawal.

The explosions round about the docks which the Commandos engineered covered the survivors from the Campbeltown with debris. The Commandos were fighting with great gusto on shore at this period. They had overcome all difficulties about landing and the speed of their penetration into the strongly held enemy forward position was a great achievement. Sweeping aside all opposition they went straight to their pre-assigned post, the covering parties getting their guns and mortars into position to hold

off any enemy attempt to interfere with the destruction of the dock installation.

The highly trained key-men of this part of the operation were the demolition bodies. Working with a speed that must have amazed the Germans, they fixed heavy charges of explosives to bridges, dock gates, and important buildings and blew them sky high in a matter of minutes. One of the biggest bangs in the early stages was the explosion that accounted for the power-house of the dock. Another explosion almost certainly destroyed the gates of the main basin. Thunderous explosions were still going on when the last of the naval forces had to withdraw.

Chief Engineroom-Artificer Harry Howard was on the Campbeltown when she rammed the dock gate.

The ship was definitely well jammed into the block (he said)—a good 10 to 15 feet. The captain did his job wonderfully. The ship was doing about 15 knots at the time. We put on everything we had. Then the crash came and all of us in the engine-room were thrown to the plates.

When we recovered we had to wait for the order " abandon ship." I went to find out what was happening. I learned from the first lieutenant that all steam was finished, so I brought all the men up.

I went on all-fours along the upper deck to where most of the men were still stationed in shelter. The fo'c'sle was blazing. There were showers of bullets of all kinds. As we climbed down the ladder on to the dock some of the men were hit. Others carried the wounded as we ran round the buildings, still under fire, to the point where the motor gun-boat was waiting. This was the boat that had put the military commander and others ashore.

Before we left I found out that most of the men of my department were on board. There was a fusillade of bullets seeming to come from everywhere. For 50 to 70 yards after we pulled out it was terrible.

A naval officer who played a leading part in the attack gave another graphic description of the scene.

How completely the raid took the Germans by surprise (he said) is shown by the fact that it was several minutes between the time their searchlights picked up the British ships as they made their way up the Channel and the time the firing started. It takes a lot of decision to start firing at a strange ship in your waters.

We saw a German guardship of about 600 tons and thought he was going to shoot us up, but before he could fire we got a direct hit on his gun.

As soon as the Germans on shore heard the firing they opened up on to this wretched flak ship of theirs, firing absolutely indiscriminately. They did not seem to mind where their own men were, but just blazed away. They were shooting at their own friends across the dock from the house-tops. Most of the opposition came from the house-tops—some of the high houses gave us a lot of trouble.

Campbeltown's Terrific End

I got the impression that they were ready for the air raid, but I am pretty sure they did not expect us from the sea, otherwise they would not have let us get so near to their dock wall before opening fire.

It was only after we had fired upon this flak ship that they began. Then they sent up fire the like of which I have never dreamed of. Our light craft replied with all the guns they had, but some of our ships were knocked out.

The Campbeltown actually got within a hundred yards of the lock gate before she came under fire. Then a terrific fire was opened on her from all sides, but she soon rammed the lock gate with a tremendous, splintering crash. As she struck I saw a large flash, but what caused it I do not know. Half the Commandos were crowded in the Campbeltown and as soon as she came to rest they leapt ashore.

Lieutenant-Commander Beattie went below with other officers to see that the fuses were all right for the main explosive charge, as the impact of the collision might have disarranged them.

Coming behind the Campbeltown I landed Colonel Newman on the south side of the old entrance to the submarine basin. He went up to join his men in that area.

After that I went across to see the scuttling charges of the Campbeltown go off. We then ordered in another of our light craft, which fired two delayed-action torpedoes at the little lock gate.

A house was burning fiercely not far away, throwing a lurid light over the quay. It had evidently been fired by the Commandos. There was rifle and machine-gun fire all over the place. I saw some men come round a building not far away. They wore blue dungarees, and I thought they were British—until they opened fire on me.

I was ashore about a quarter of an hour waiting for Commander Beattie. I saw about 20 or more of the crew pass me on their way to be re-embarked. I expected the officers would be behind them, but I did not meet any. Commander Beattie was the principal performer in this raid. His name must be mentioned. He was seen ashore by his crew. Whether he lost his way behind some of the buildings I don't know. He may have joined up to fight with the Commandos.

We were unable to bring off Lt.-Col. Newman and some of his men, but I think myself he was expecting that and was perfectly prepared to go on fighting until it got daylight.

Here are some of the Special Service troops who took part in the St. Nazaire raid, photographed on their return. In the centre is the officer who led them. *Photo, Planet News*

We Weathered a Wild Night in the Atlantic

Besides U-boats and aircraft, our ships have to face another enemy in the North Atlantic—the weather—as is vividly described below by an R.N.V.R. Lieutenant in the ex-American destroyer Richmond.

A HARSH yellow sunset and a steeply falling glass gave warning that it was going to blow. By 8.30 p.m., when I took over the watch from the Gunner, the storm was approaching its full fury. The Richmond's motion was wild and fantastic: she was shipping it green and bumping cruelly. The ship was practically hove to. With wheel hard a-starboard, and the starboard engine going dead slow and the port half ahead, it was just possible to keep the ship under control.

A tremendous sea struck the Richmond, rolling her over to a frightening angle and shattering the glass in the wheelhouse window and hurling everybody on the bridge in a sprawling heap to leeward. The roar of the gale drowned the noise of splintering glass, but not the language of the Gunner, who had hit a tender portion of his anatomy on the engine-room telegraph.

The Quartermaster, a young Devon man with just over a year's service, was thrown clear of the wheel, but fought his way up the steep slope of the slippery bridge and again grabbed the spokes of the wheel. "Is she steering all right, Quartermaster?" bellowed the Captain, in a voice which could be just heard faintly above the scream of the gale. "Yes, zur," yelled the Quartermaster. "Everything in the garden's lovely." An odd remark, but one which showed the right spirit.

A still bigger sea struck the Richmond. The ship was not so much rolled over as pressed down by hundreds of tons of water. The roll recorder registered 58 degrees. The destroyer righted herself to an angle of 30 degrees, and there she lay while the sea rained blow after blow after blow. The fuse-box was broken and there was a firework display as the fuses blew. Below decks everything was in darkness since the blowing of the fuses, and the electricians were hard at it running extra leads and rigging emergency lighting. A heavy sea beat in the wardroom scuttles and bent the ship's side, buckling several main frames and the deck. A torrent of water poured down the hatch into the fore messdeck.

At once men jumped to the burst-in scuttles and held them down to stop the inrush of seawater, while seamen, stokers, cooks and stewards set about shoring them up under the directions of the Engineer. Nearly all the proper shores had been washed overboard, but with mess tables, stools, a gun rammer and other odds and ends they made a workmanlike job of it.

Havoc of the Storm

A tour of inspection showed that most of what was movable on deck had been swept overboard. The motor-boat was gone. The searchlight tower was buckled and twisted and presented a ridiculously drunken lopsided appearance. The engine-room escape hatch, a strong steel cylinder riveted to the deck, had been torn off and lay in the lee scuppers.

The ship's cat, Minnie, was missing for a time and there was great anxiety until a leading seaman discovered her crouching terrified in the seamen's bathroom. In some mysterious way she had made her way aft along the upper deck without being swept overboard. The seaman put her down his oilskin trouser leg and carried her back to her terrified kittens. The cat family were then made comfortable in the Engineer's bunk.

With the coming of daylight the storm blew itself out and all hands busied themselves clearing away the wreckage. Shortly after noon the Richmond sighted the coast. One more Atlantic crossing was safely over.

Shipping green seas, a British destroyer ploughs through the waves on her task of searching for enemy submarines. What it means to be on a destroyer in the full fury of an Atlantic storm is vividly recounted in this page by an R.N.V.R. Lieutenant. *Photo, Keystone*

WHEN it was published in December of last year I was not attracted to a book by M. Henry Torrès on Pierre Laval. I think it must have been the dust-cover that put me off : " Life Story of a Cynic, Crook, Traitor." That sounds a little cheap and sensational. But I came upon the book last week in the house of a friend who advised me to read it. He presented me with his review copy, and having once begun to read I was kept engrossed to the final word. In importance I do not hesitate to describe it as one of the major books of the War. Brilliantly translated by Mr. Norbert Guterman, whose name is unknown to me, the literary style is so admirable that I should like to read it all over again in the original French if I can come by a copy. It is something far more than a mere biography of one of the greatest gangsters who have ever exploited the national affairs of a great nation with the same sort of ruthlessness as Al Capone and his gang exploited the vice and dirt of Chicago : it is a lucid and convincing account of French high politics from the Great War of 1914 to the Total War of today, and from its pages the reader, unfamiliar with the low cunning and foul intrigue which characterized the profession of politician in Paris, will gain a neon-clear vision of the evil forces that were long at work for the destruction of the Third Republic.

READ especially in association with the evidence which M. Daladier and M. Léon Blum have so fearlessly given at Riom to the discomfiture of the Fascist French, it will convince even the most fervid Francophile (such as myself for many a year) that there was something rotten in the state of our ally, and had all these facts been known to our own political leaders their whole attitude should have been modified in the face of the Nazi menace. At least it can be said that had all the facts as revealed in this authoritative history of Laval's machinations, plus the Riom evidence, been at the disposal of our own political leaders and their implications made available to the British public through Parliament, it is hardly conceivable that we could have joined forces with France to destroy Hitlerism with the slightest expectation of accomplishing that mighty task together. But that, of course, is only being wise after the event. What every Briton has good cause to be thankful for, with the knowledge now at his command, is that British political life has at no time, and least of all in the present century, bred such self-seeking, such deliberate defeatism, such anti-social knavery as has characterized French politics for many years past.

LAVAL is no lone wolf, M. Torrès names and describes a whole pack of them. He sees in General de Gaulle the one focal point of renascence, and there are many genuine patriots still on French territory who, when the great hour strikes, will assuredly assert themselves and those principles of liberty which France gave more than a hundred years of intellectual and physical energy to establish —and the Pétain-Laval defeatists lost to her

in a fortnight. Let me add that, regarded only as the authentic life-story of a master crook, this record of how the ill-favoured spawn of a low-class provincial café-keeper rose to fabulous wealth and international power, and now quisling "dictator" of France, while still remaining a semi-literate boor, makes a fascinating romance of crime which outstrips any invention of the novelist.

AFTER finishing with the Laval book I picked up the latest arrival on my table : Strictly Personal by W. Somerset Maugham, a small but valuable addition to the literature of this war. The only thing about it that I do not like is its title. Mr.

Maugham, whose prose style is to me a constant delight, has a very instructive story to tell, and tells it in his own masterly way. His adventurous escape from the Riviera in a coaling boat ; his various literary missions for the Ministry of Information, in France, in England, and in America ; the amusing and significant contacts he made with many odd personalities in his wide travel, are all narrated with that penetrating eye for character which has won his place among the half dozen foremost English novelists of his time.

STRICTLY PERSONAL is much more important than a brief record of things that happened to a famous writer in the first two years of the War, for it contains the mature and dispassionate reflections of a serious student of modern life whose many years of residence in France, and his intimate knowledge of French character, endow with authority his acute observations on the state of the French people with whom it was Britain's unhappy lot to join hands against Nazism. In all that he tells us of the common

people he is objective and therein more acceptable as a contributor to the proper understanding of the immeasurable tragedy of France than if his point of view were " strictly personal."

EVEN his frank and good-humoured account of things as he found them on returning to England has an air of detachment which carries the conviction of " things seen " with an impartial eye. Anyone who reads Strictly Personal will not only be charmed with the personal element of its narrative, but will obtain an authentic picture of a France that went unwillingly to war, ill-prepared, incompetently marshalled and with the will to lose ; the reasons for this deplorable attitude of mind being made manifest with greater detail in the description of the miasmatic sludge of French politics which, as I have indicated above, makes the life of the Traitor Laval by M. Torrès so revealing.

HOW's this for stellar pre-science ? I find it in one of the various rival editions of Old Moore's under the month of May : " Disturbed conditions crop up in Fleet Street after the disappearance of a well-known journal. Almost at the same time a new one arises on unusual lines with a policy designed rather to put the brake on the fast-moving reforms which are now canvassed so eagerly in many quarters." A well-known journal did almost disappear in March, but what is outside all probability is that a new one could arise. Old Moore was reckoning here without the Paper Controller.

HERE is another astrologer glibly interpreting the stars for May : " The passing of the two of the major planets from Taurus into Gemini in May will entirely alter the course of the war. The conjunction of Saturn and Uranus will destroy the conditions that began in 1935 and reached a climax in 1939. This spring and summer will witness the destruction of the Nazi regime, and the removal of Germany and Italy from the ranks of our enemies. Moreover, an even more welcome change will follow the passing of Saturn and Uranus out of Taurus, for we shall finally free ourselves from the hampering and restricting influences that have held us in check since the beginning of the war, and shall be in a position to follow a policy of vigorous offence." I will only comment on this excerpt which I've taken from an article on the Astrological Outlook by Vivian B. Robson, B.Sc., in The Queen of March 25, by expressing the hope that these most desirable things may happen, while stating my conviction that Saturn and Uranus will have no more to do with the course of events than Flanagan and Allen.

A CORRESPONDENT writes, apropos an article which appeared in the 123rd number of THE WAR ILLUSTRATED, that the terminus of the Assam-Bengal Railway is at Saikhooa Ghat on the southern bank of the Sobit River, Assam, and not at Sadiya on the north bank, as stated in the article. My correspondent, Mr. E. Clear Hill, A.M.I.E.(Ind.), informs me that he constructed the first portion of the road from Sadiya to Sonpura when he was in charge of the newly created P.W.D. subdivision of Sadiya in 1913-14, so that I must regard this correction as authoritative.

Vice-Adm. SIR GEOFFREY LAYTON, appointed Commander-in-Chief, Ceylon, in March 1942, with acting rank of Admiral for the duration of the appointment. *Photo, Lafayette*

Vol 5 *The War Illustrated* N° 128

Edited by Sir John Hammerton

6d FORTNIGHTLY

MAY 15, 1942

THE PACK HORSE still has a place in modern warfare. Recently Northern Command's Pack Transport Company has taken part in some important exercises when this photograph was taken. This Company's work is to carry supplies and ammunition for the Infantry over country where wheeled transport is impossible. Each horse carries 320 lb., and a Company can carry twenty-seven tons of supplies. Many of the horses belonging to the unit were well-known hunters before the war, and some of them are International Show jumpers.   *Photo, Planet News*

NO. 129 WILL BE PUBLISHED FRIDAY. MAY 29

LAVAL: THE TRIUMPH OF TREASON

BY THE EDITOR

THE full horror of the French debacle is only now emerging. In the stunned amaze of her second Sedan the Allies of France had not envisaged the ultimate abomination which faces them today: a France at the mercy of the lowest created thing her changeful history has ever brought to prominence and power. Such bloodthirsty revolutionaries as Fouquier-Tinville and Marat had at least the redeeming virtues of enthusiasm for the republic and genuine antagonism to the oppressors of the people : qualities that not so long ago were recognized and are now applauded in the pioneers of the Soviet Republics of Russia. But this sewer rat who, by a cruel twist of fate and by long connivance with the ruthless enemies of his country, has come to exercise under Hitler tyrannical power for evil over his hapless fellow countrymen, is utterly devoid of all those ideals of public good that have ever made men do evil that good may come : his whole career has been marked by a callous indifference to every prompting of patriotism ; he has been completely devoted to his own personal interests and ambitions.

TIME was when the name of Laval had honour in France. The seigneurs and counts of Laval were great figures in feudal times, an André de Laval was Marshal of France in the heroic day of Joan of Arc. Quebec has its Laval University as a memorial of the devoted bishop who fathered so well the early colonists when the Count de Frontenac held the town against the English attacks. But for generations to come this name will connote to France and to all the world besides everything vile, perverse, abominable. Even the historic, castled town of Laval in Brittany may be tempted yet to re-christen itself when the infamy that is about to be brought upon France by the scoundrel who bears its name will have obscured for ever what of honour its tradition retained.

For, make no mistake about it, France under this vile quisling is going to plumb the deepest depths of shame. His elevation to power at the hands of Hitler is the first desperate success of the Third Spring Offensive.

To know something of the villain of the piece makes possible a shrewd guess at the dénouement of the drama, and Laval's life of political and social crime has been mercilessly laid bare by one who has known him intimately through his whole tortuous career, M. Henry Torrès, whose life-story of Laval I reviewed in page 672 of THE WAR ILLUSTRATED, and to which I shall here return for some forceful phrases.

Whatever we may think of Hitler and Mussolini, with whom Laval will now play third fiddle in their devil's orchestra, both of them are immeasurably his superiors, not merely in organized power but in personal character. They at least, however wildly mistaken in their ideals of national progress and in their political ideologies, however bloodthirsty in their methods, started with the notion of devoting their personal talents to the aggrandisement of their respective nations.

NEVER for one moment of Laval's life has he been influenced by such grandiose notions. Because his country had attained

to imperial grandeur while he was still a dirty little boy listening to the vinous vapourings of his father's customers in the miserable *bistro* attached to the paternal butcher's shop at Châteldon in Auvergne (only a little way from Vichy and but little farther from Riom where his later career was to find its landmarks), because France was imperially great and politically rotting the mind of this repulsive Auvergnat peasant had no flicker of patriotic impulse such as undoubtedly imbued both Mussolini and Hitler, but only the impulse to enrich himself at his country's expense.

PIERRE LAVAL was Prime Minister of France 1931-1932; Foreign Minister after the assassination of Barthou in 1934, and Prime Minister again in 1935-1936. *Photo, Wide World*

To this one end he applied his high endowment of low cunning, first to local politics in Aubervilliers, that industrial outer suburb of Paris, where a pretence of sympathy with the trade-unionists, the socialists, and the poor, won him the support of the toilers and established him for years as mayor or political boss, whence progress to the Chamber of Deputies and thence to the Senate was effected by intrigue and a beguiling tongue. Almost devoid of education, his capacity for humbug was phenomenal. With a knowledge of law such as could have been acquired from an elementary textbook he worked up an extensive practice as a " poor man's lawyer," his tricky and ingenious mind and his complete lack of scruple being of much greater value to him than years of legal studies.

HE was socialist deputy for the Seine at the beginning of the War of 1914, and there is no record that he ever contributed one day's energy towards the victory. There is, on the contrary, overwhelming evidence of his defeatism. As a deputy he was immune

from service in the trenches (his age was thirty-one), although many patriotic deputies refused to take advantage of this provision and died fighting the invader. Laval pleaded his varicose veins ! There is an historic utterance of his in the Chamber on Jan. 21, 1917. " Without Russia we would not have been at war. Russia betrayed France. Long live France ! Down with Russia ! " By the same process of reasoning and with far more justification some British M.P. might stand up today and exclaim : " Without France we would not have been at war. France betrayed Britain. Long live Britain ! Down with France ! "

But during, and immediately after, the war Laval the defeatist was busy making useful contacts with crafty collaborators and intended victims, making big money from shady transactions with rogues in high finance, and slyly edging away from his pretended sympathies with the poor and oppressed, so that ten years later he was a self-styled Independent and as such became Senator for the Seine in 1926. The dirty little peasant from the mean little pub at Châteldon was planting his feet on what M. Torrès calls " the foothills of power," for he had been Minister of Public Works in 1925 and was now Minister of Justice, shamelessly misusing his power in both offices.

IN the incessant shuffling and re-shuffling of the French political groups his genius for intrigue had brought him by 1931 to the position of Premier and Foreign Minister, and now with vast financial resources, darkly secured (he had been deep in the great Stavisky swindle of 1929 but wriggled free with his gangster cunning), and a venal press at his command, his course for further profitable adventure in politics and finance was full set. He was not only Prime Minister but he was head of a gang : it was as though Boss Croker of tainted Tammany memory, having attained to the mayoralty of New York had become U.S. Secretary of State.

Foreign Minister again in 1934, he was Premier as well as Foreign Minister in 1935-36, when he and the Duce became thick as thieves and the abortive Laval-Hoare pact was a by-product of their friendship, while the Franco-Soviet pact (which he had signed with no intention of observing it) proved one of the factors in ending his premiership in the next year, as Germany found in it no obstacle, but rather a pretence, for denouncing Locarno on March 7, 1936, and reoccupying the Rhineland.

With the fall of his Ministry in 1936 he and his fellow defeatist Brinon, mainly through their control of important newspapers, carried on their insidious campaign for an " understanding " with the Nazis. " With Italian assistance," says M. Torrès, " he continued to work for a policy of Franco-German collaboration in which France was to play the part of a vassal state." And today, just six years later, he finds himself the active head of this vassal state. What a dark romance of history is here !

PERHAPS its most dramatic moment came in the confusion of June 1940, when he reappeared in the flight to Bordeaux as the tried and trusted friend of Germany and Italy, as one who had given hostages to the enemy in years of covert and overt collaboration and was to be associated with Pétain at the burial of the Third Republic. M. Lebrun, President of France, no genius, no heroic figure, but a man not devoid of courage, was prepared to leave for Morocco at the head of a Parliamentary delegation which he, by virtue of his office, had named. The ship was ready to convey them, but Laval went to Lebrun and warned him: "If you leave this French soil you will never set foot on it again." And the cowardly defeatist prevailed: the one great chance of a regenerated France was lost: the traitor had triumphed.

Pétain's hatred of the man, due less to natural repulsion from a loathsome personality than to his own senile self-conceit, soon relieved the subsequent Vichy government of its most sinister personality, whose ultimate triumph over the vain old man is now complete, and will be merciless. Writing in the spring of last year M. Torrès concluded his scathing exposure of Laval's evil life with these words:

"Today the traitor is in Paris, surrounded by his old gang — Déat, Doriot, Eugène Deloncle (chief of the Hooded Men), Jean Goy, Jean Luchaire, Jean Fontenoy, all of them vultures who were able to spread their wings only over the charnel-house of defeat. He is also surrounded by the curses of the people of Paris, unanimous in their hatred for him and in their faith in the liberation of France by a victory of the Allies. His sinister figure still stands out against the background of all the events which mark

the gradual sinking of his country into abjection; directly or indirectly, by his emissaries, he is still playing a part in the enslavement of France."

Precisely one year later events have justified M. Torrès. On April 19 Laval's new Vichy Government was announced, and there is not a name included therein that does not denote an enemy of the old republic, a jackal eager to hunt in Laval's pack for the picking up of a living such as Hitler will throw to them. Pétain, a defeatist in the last War despite his success at Verdun, whose mission to Franco Spain had marked him in 1939 as the possible leader of a complacent France which would leave Germany a free hand in Central and Eastern Europe—"the flag of Verdun held in decrepit hands was to screen the surrender of France," says Torrès—Pétain passes into the dim realm of the impotent as a mere figurehead for the Laval gangsters; he has no more power in his hands today than ex-President Lebrun in his Gestapo-guarded country home. In

Food pours into Marseilles from North Africa, but most of it goes to Germany. Above, a German (left), Italian (right) and two Frenchmen inspecting shipments. Top right, fresh vegetables are loaded on a train bound for Germany. Bottom, potatoes for Germany being unloaded at Marseilles. *Associated Press*

his 90 seconds' broadcast to the Vassal French on April 19 he had the dishonesty to assert that Laval had been his coadjutor in founding "the new Order which was to assure the rebirth of France" (an honour from which he took the earliest opportunity of dissociating him) and that now "at a moment as decisive as June 1940" he "finds himself" (note these words) "associated with him once more to continue the task of national recovery."

The raw truth is that this old man is militarily and politically dead, but he just won't lie down. He is content to be used by Hitler via Laval as a symbol of a France that for the time being is voiceless at home and whose spirit finds release only in the words and deeds of De Gaulle and the Fighting French.

From every point of view the situation is tragic: one of history's ghastliest tragedies. We have now to face a France reorganizing for Anti-Allied effort, a France that is being forced to work for the Nazis and is almost certainly going to be made to

fight against her former and still faithful allies. Almost more menacing than Laval at the helm of a storm-tossed ship of state is Darlan in command of the Armed Forces of the so-called French Empire. He is no less anti-British than the new head of the Government. A small-minded man, like Pétain a prey to personal jealousies, and anxious only to stand in with the side which he hopes will win the War, Darlan is as much our enemy as Goering or Raeder and will not scruple to use the French fleet against the Allies when his Nazi masters command him. The hope of France in that event lies in the sturdy Breton sailors who may have a word to say when the order is given.

Meanwhile, the only change in the situation is: that Vichy France now comes into the open as an enemy country, which it has been *de facto* since its Syrian forces fought the British in the middle of 1941; since it opened the way for Japanese aggression by the surrender of Indo-China the year before, since it began deliberate cooperation with the Nazis in North and West Africa, and aided in every way short of actual fighting the preparation and progress of General Rommel's attack on Egypt, which was based not only on Italian Tripoli but also upon French Tunisia with its ports of Bizerta, Sfax, and Gabes and its coastal roads and railway to Tripoli. Whatever the feeble Pétain dictatorship may have been, the Laval Vichy Government is now an avowedly hostile Government. Laval, in his new capacity of German gauleiter, has categorically named Britain as the enemy and accused this country of having dragged France unwillingly into the War. Britain and her Allies must now face all the implications of that fact; and hostility by air, by land and sea as part and parcel of Hitler's new Western offensive.   J. A. Hammerton

Retreat Through Burma: Fighting All the Way

"The stubborn resistance," said General Wavell in his broadcast from Delhi on April 21, "that the tired and heroic defenders of Burma are putting up after four months of fighting, almost without rest or relief and in most difficult conditions, against superior numbers, is proof of the quality of our men."

WHEN Rangoon's fall was imminent the garrison marched out to fight their way northward along the road and railway to Prome and Mandalay. Their withdrawal was hampered at every step by rapidly increasing enemy forces, and the march tested the men's courage and endurance to the utmost. The situation was grave in the extreme; the danger of a complete collapse of British resistance within Burma had drawn very near, since both at Rangoon and at Pegu, fifty miles to the north-east, the Japanese were making great efforts. But on March 7 the situation was retrieved, if only for the time being—retrieved by a mere handful of British troops. At Pegu the Hussars (light tanks) smashed the ring which the Japanese had drawn about them, while the Rangoon garrison, with the Gloucesters in the front, fiercely attacked a road block which the enemy had contrived at Taukkyan.

Taukkyan had been converted into an improvized fortress: but the Gloucesters, despite their inadequate artillery support and the enemy superiority in the air, pushed relentlessly up the road, pursuing the Japanese from cover to cover. That night the survivors of a sadly thinned battalion slept in the heart of the enemy's defences. Next day the attack was renewed at dawn, and the garrison broke through. This battle of Taukkyan-Pegu was on a small scale, but it was fought for a great prize; had the Japanese won, Burma would have been lost to Britain straightaway. Moreover, it was the first defeat inflicted on the Japanese army. The Gloucesters, on whom fell the heaviest losses, shared the honours of the day with the Hussars, a squadron of the Royal Armoured Corps, the Frontier Force Rifles from the Punjab, two anti-tank batteries and some field artillery.

The retreat continued northward. On March 19 the Gloucesters were in action again at Letpadan, half-way from Rangoon to Prome; in a spirited little engagement they killed and wounded nearly a hundred of the enemy, and rescued seventeen men of the Gurkha Rifles who had been taken prisoner. Ten days later, when the British force had almost completed its withdrawal to Prome, the Gloucesters turned at bay once again, and surprised and mowed down the Japanese advance guard which had rushed headlong into the village of Paungde.

Now it was decided to deliver a counter-stroke and Paungde was selected as the target. A few hours after they had occupied it in triumph, the Japanese were driven out of the town by the Hussars, supported by the Gloucesters, the West Yorks, the Duke of Wellingtons and the Cameronians. One enemy battalion took refuge in the jungle, only to be ringed round by the British and wiped out with relentless precision by tommy-guns, bombs and bayonets. This brilliant little affair disrupted the Japanese plans for the swift encirclement of Prome. But the British force at Paungde was in no enviable position, since the Japanese vanguard had succeeded in by-passing the town and had reached Shwedaung, where the road to Prome touches the River Irrawaddy, and had there established a succession of road blocks, which effectively separated the British spearhead at Paungde from the main body at Prome. The Japanese engineers, in spite of the little time at their disposal, had made the most of the possibilities of the ground; moreover, they were being effectively aided by a considerable

PROME, in Lower Burma, on the left bank of the Irrawaddy, 160 miles north of Rangoon, was captured by the Japanese early in April. This photograph shows the celebrated pagoda, visited by hosts of pilgrims, and the gigantic modern statue of Buddha.
Photo, E.N.A.

number of Burmese, so numerous—the figure of four thousand was mentioned—as to constitute a Burma army.

These Burmans, reported William Munday, of the News Chronicle, the only war correspondent in that front line, fought with fanatical fury, being imbued with the belief that the charms they wore, and the "oath water" they had drunk in swearing allegiance, made them immune to bullets. Spurred on by Japanese officers who remained in the background, the Burmans in their uniforms of blue trousers and white shirts were mowed down in hundreds as they threw themselves on to the British bayonets and into the path of rifle and tommy-gun fire. Few of them could have retained their belief in their oaths and potions when the Indians of the Frontier Force hurled themselves upon them at a river crossing near Shwedaung. In this one brush alone three hundred Burmese disloyalists were killed, and another seventy captured.

When the British at Prome realized the plight of the little force cut off at Paungde a counter-attack by way of rescue was planned. But before it could be mounted the troops at Paungde—Hussars, West Yorks, Duke of Wellingtons, Gloucesters, Cameronians and Frontier Force Rifles—decided to make their own extrication. Hard fighting went on for many hours; when a number of strong points had fallen into their hands and several lines of stubbornly held defences had been pierced, the British paused for a breather and to re-organize. Then they went forward again, and by the evening of March 30 the Japanese barrier had been overrun and the reunited British forces stood ready in Prome to resume the struggle.

But their stay in Prome was short. Japanese strength grew from day to day, from hour to hour even. On the evening of Wednesday, April 1, the British covering force in Prome was attacked by the enemy in considerable strength, and their defences in the jungle country east of the main road and the high ground south of Prome were overrun. After much hard fighting the British moved back to fresh covering positions north of Prome early on April 2. As they withdrew to their new positions they were heavily bombed by Jap dive-bombers and harassed continually by the enemy, who had followed hard on their heels. At the same time, the menace of the Burmese fifth columnists increased with every British reverse; many of the tribesmen in the Prome region had been in revolt against the British as recently as 1931, and they now hastened to take up arms again against us. But the withdrawal continued, and the Japanese pressure was successfully withstood.

Fighting was wellnigh continuous, and every now and again it developed into local battles. Thus on April 11 there was a fierce struggle south-west of Taungdwingyi, and other enemy columns were engaged as they advanced up the main road from Sinbaungwe; the same communiqué gave news of successful actions fought by a detachment of Royal Marines, operating on the Irrawaddy during the withdrawal of our forces from Prome. Two days later it was announced that the British had established positions near Minhla, covered by the King's Own Yorkshire Light Infantry, "who for days have fought a magnificent action at Myingun." The communiqué went on to refer to the British forces in the Taungdwingyi area who were still holding their positions covering the right flank of the Chinese operating north of Toungoo.

By April 13 the Japanese advance elements were reported to be south of Magwe, over one hundred miles north of Prome, and uncomfortably close to the great Burmese oilfields at Yenangyaung, even Mandalay itself.

Friend & Foe On India's Doorstep

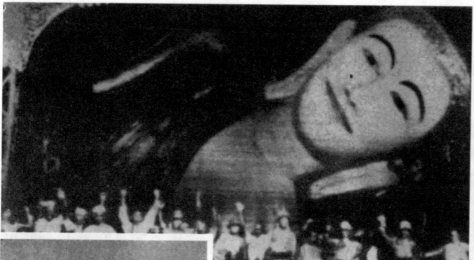

Japanese soldiers and Burmese before the reclining statue of Buddha at Pegu, Burma, after the Japanese had occupied the town (above left). Lieut.-Gen. Joseph W. Stilwell, of the U.S. Army (right), commanding the Chinese Forces in Burma (see text panel below).

UNITED STATES military representative in China and Commander of the Chinese in Burma, Lieut.-Gen. Joseph W. Stilwell, is particularly qualified for his post. He has seen fifteen years' military service in the Far East and is a fluent speaker of several Chinese dialects.

Gen. Stilwell, born in 1883, passed out of West Point Military Academy when he was 21 and joined the 12th Infantry in the Philippines. During his military career Gen. Stilwell has had two periods of service in the Philippines and three later and longer periods in Peking and Tientsin, where he studied Chinese, commanded troops and learned to understand the Chinese mind as few Westerners have done, winning the confidence and affection of the Chinese leaders, who hold him in high regard.

During the last war Gen. Stilwell served with the British 58th Division, the French 17th Corps, the American 2nd and 4th Corps, and at United States General Headquarters. For his part in the chief attacks made by the American army, against the St. Mihiel salient and in the Woevre, he was awarded the United States Distinguished Service Medal. The chief characteristics of his work are said to be ingenuity, exactitude and persistence.

Chinese General Officer commanding a formation in Burma, with a British officer (above left). The forest of derricks in the great Burmese oilfield at Yenangyaung (right). Installations were destroyed before the British withdrawal.

Above, women and children seeking shade under the wing of an R.A.F. aircraft on a Burmese aerodrome while waiting to be evacuated by air. Map, the Burmese battlefront showing the Japanese thrusts (black arrows) against the British-Chinese positions in Upper Burma.

Photos, British Official, Wide World, Sport & General. Map by Courtesy of The Daily Express **Page 677**

Behind the American Lines in Bataan

BATAAN finally fell because sickness struck down the brave defenders whom the Japanese had been unable to conquer. Lt.-Col. William Kennard, a doctor attached to the American Air Forces in the Philippines, has told the story of how, night after night during the month before Bataan fell, four ancient aeroplanes known as "the bamboo fleet" braved Japanese fighters to carry badly needed medical supplies to the troops on the peninsula.

Ten days before the collapse a very high percentage of the troops in the front line were down with malaria. "Sometimes," said Kennard, "30 or 40 per cent of the front-line men were lying on their backs. They were treated as well as possible and returned immediately to fight at a point where other men had fallen out ill. Actual war casualties were kept at a minimum during the last two or three months, but the number of disease victims climbed. Hospitals and field medical units did excellent work, but were handicapped by the lack of drugs." That is the real answer to the question, "Why did Bataan fall?"

Above, an American soldier in a slit trench on the Bataan Peninsula gets a Molotov cocktail ready for action against a Japanese tank. Right, Japanese prisoners captured in the Philippines.

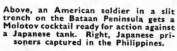

Maj.-Gen. JONATHAN M. WAINWRIGHT, who commanded the U.S. troops in Bataan Peninsula, is seen seated in conference with his staffs officers. Gen. Wainwright withdrew to Corregidor after the collapse of the Bataan defences on April 9.

Above, soldiers and civilians at an early morning service at the Catholic Chapel at Hospital No. 1, in Bataan. Right, American officers take cover from Japanese fire in a "fox hole" on the Bataan Peninsula.

Photos, Associated Press, Topical Press, Planet News

From Australia to the Philippines and Back

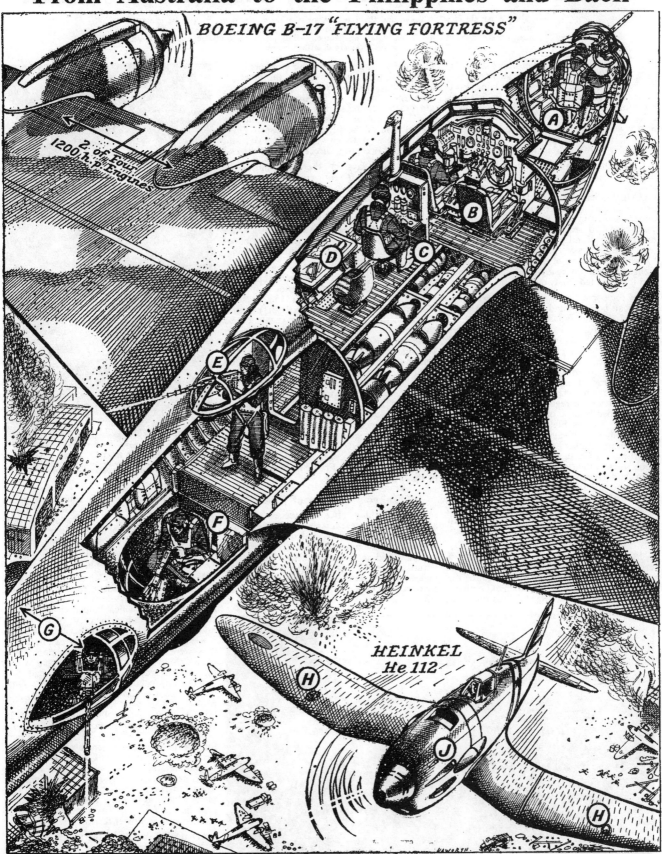

BOEING B-17 "FLYING FORTRESS"

2 of four 1200 h.p. Engines

HEINKEL He 112

HAWORTH.

FLYING FORTRESS is the name given to the gigantic Boeing B-17 four-engined bombers, some of which took part in the recent remarkable raid from Australia to the Philippines (see page 680). These aircraft have also inflicted great damage on Japanese shipping and airfields in New Guinea.

The Flying Fortress is an all-metal mid-wing monoplane, with a wing span of 103 feet 9 ins. and a length of 67 feet 10 ins. Its range is from 2,000 to 3,000 miles according to load and it has a speed of 300 m.p.h. at 14,000 feet. It has a very high service ceiling. Driven by four Wright Cyclone engines of about 1,200 h.p. each, it can carry a very heavy bomb load.

Operating the Boeing. (A) Front gunner and bomb-aimer. (B) Pilot and second pilot's place. (C) Wireless operator. (D) Navigator's table. An engineer also has a place, but this is not shown. (E) Rear upper gun position. (F) Rear lower gun

position. (G) Port and starboard gun positions in "blisters" on the side of the fuselage. The bombs can be seen in the hatches, ready to be released. The Norden sight used by the Americans for bomb-aiming is extremely accurate.

Japanese Machines. Seen attacking from below is the Japanese version of the Heinkel 112 single-seat fighter. It is armed with two cannon (H) and two machine-guns (J) synchronized to fire through the propeller disk. The 910 h.p. Mercedes-Benz engine gives a maximum speed of 350 m.p.h. at 12,300 ft.

Damaged on the ground can be seen several Japanese long-range bombers of the Mitsubishi T 97 type. These aircraft are driven by two Kinsei 14-cylinder radials of 870 h.p., have a speed of 220 m.p.h., and a defensive armament which usually consists of seven 7.7 mm. machine-guns.

Specially drawn for THE WAR ILLUSTRATED *by Haworth*

Bombs on the Japanese : America Hits Back

"Just a sample of what Tokyo and the Japs everywhere are going to get," said the leader of one of the flights of American bombers which went to the Philippines in mid-April. The very next week-end bombs did actually fall on Tokyo. Both of these dramatic and heartening occurrences are described below.

AT 10.30 that Saturday morning (April 11) thirteen heavy American bombers—three were four-engine Flying Fortresses and ten were twin-engine B.25s—took off from an Australian aerodrome on a 2,000-mile flight to the Philippines. Their leader was Brig.-Gen. Ralph Royce, Chief of Staff of General Brett, Commander of the Allied Air Forces in Australia.

Flying throughout the day across enemy-infested seas and islands, the squadrons reached the Philippines before dark, but night had fallen when they landed at an aerodrome hidden in the bush in territory still under American control. Here comrades were ready to receive them with stocks of bombs, spares and petrol. Here, too—or at least within easy reach—were American fighter planes ; one of these on several occasions was sent up against the Jap bombers, and it accounted for two of them.

But for some hours after their arrival the American bombers had the air to themselves, so hard did the Japanese find it to believe that a powerful air striking force was within reach of their bases in the Philippines. But on Sunday morning they learnt of that fact to their cost. First, the heavy bombers took off and flew towards Manila ; they sank one enemy transport near Batangas, but were unsuccessful in their search for Japanese warships near Corregidor. So they flew on and dropped a stick of bombs on the aerodrome of Nichols Field, destroying hangars and damaging runways. The same morning the medium bombers attacked transports and escorting vessels at Cebu, and in the afternoon their attention was divided between Cebu and Davao. The next morning transports and installations at these two places were bombed again ; enemy planes were shot down and ships sunk, and the bombers also smashed up Japanese troop reserves which were just about to deliver a counter-attack against the American infantry at Davao.

"Our raids threw the Japanese into a terrific panic," said General Royce on his return. "Imagine their bewilderment at the sudden appearance of a big bunch of bombers, which let loose everything they had on them.

They did not know where the bombers came from, and their radio used up the ether all day Sunday, trying to find from where we came and a means of stopping us." At last a Japanese reconnaissance plane—"Photo Joe," the Americans nicknamed him—spotted one of the Flying Fortresses. Dive-bombers began to come over in twos and threes, and one got a direct hit on a Fortress.

After two days in the Philippines the American aircraft took off on Tuesday and returned without mishap to their base in Australia. They took back with them 45 passengers—34 Army men and key civilians from Bataan, Corregidor and other districts, who managed to escape under the very noses of the Japanese, and eleven of the personnel of one of the Fortresses, which was the only casualty of the operation.

Ten minutes ahead of schedule time General Royce's bomber landed on the blacked-out airfield on April 15. As the General emerged, Maj.-Gen. Rush Lincoln, Chief of the U.S. Air Corps, hastened to congratulate him and to hand him, on President Roosevelt's instructions, the Distinguished Flying Cross. "He has demonstrated to the highest degree the spirit of offensive action," said General Brett, in an announcement concerning the raid ; "he took the fight into enemy territory, and created dismay and destruction at a time most important to our forces, and he has returned." The same decoration, "for heroism and extraordinary achievement in an aerial flight against an armed enemy," was also conferred on Lt.-Col. J. H. Davies and Capt. Frank P. Bostrom, two of the flight commanders.

Tokyo's Baptism of Fire

Only a few days after this successful foray against the Japanese in the Philippines, the Americans struck again—but this time at the seat of Japanese power. "Shortly after noon today," said a broadcast from Tokyo on Saturday, April 18, "enemy bombers appeared over Tokyo, inflicting damage on schools and hospitals." Later statements added that Yokohama had been attacked at

Brig.-Gen. RALPH ROYCE, Chief of Staff to Gen. G. H. Brett, who led the spectacular bombing raid from Australia to the Philippines.
Photo, Topical

the same time as Tokyo, while two hours later Nagoya and Kobe were also raided, and alerts were sounded in Osaka and Kyoto. These would seem to be all the ascertained facts ; for the rest the story is one of confused enemy reports to which the Americans were careful to add nothing.

First, the Japanese claimed to have shot down three of the raiders, then it was nine ; a little later the number was reduced to one—a solitary plane which landed in the mountains of central Japan, its crew of five being taken prisoners. Nor was it clear whence the planes had come. Tokyo asserted that they were flown from aircraft-carriers, three of which (it was stated) had appeared off the eastern coast of Japan, but had fled without approaching Japanese shores. One, it was reported without confirmation, was sunk. But it was further stated that the hostile planes were North American B.25 bombers—and these planes are not generally used by the U.S. Navy. But some support for the theory that carrier-based planes were used came from Chungking, where it was stated that the planes had arrived safely at their destination, wherever that might be. Then Moscow announced that an American plane which, so its crew asserted, had taken part in the raid on Tokyo, had landed at Khabarovsk in Soviet territory.

What of the results of the raid ? Here, too, the reports were confusing. At first Tokyo tried to minimize the matter, but this did not go well with a statement attributed to Mr. Shigemitsu : "The British," said the former Japanese Ambassador in London, "have endured deluges of bombs for more than two full years. If we lose our composure, the Americans and British will clap their hands and laugh at us. Compared with the German raids on London, today's raid would not even be worth mentioning as an air raid."

U.S. FLYING FORTRESS which took part in the 3,600-mile bombing raid against the Japanese in the Philippines on April 13 and 14. Pilots who were engaged in the raid are seen consulting a map beside their giant aircraft.
Photo, Associated Press

Where the First Bombs Dropped on Japan

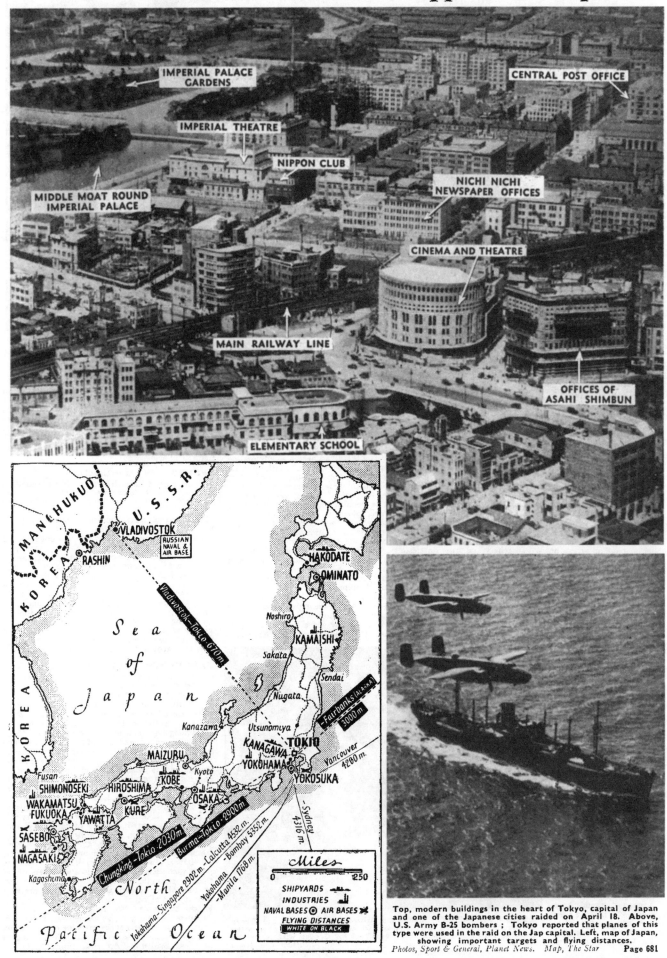

IMPERIAL PALACE GARDENS

CENTRAL POST OFFICE

IMPERIAL THEATRE

NIPPON CLUB

NICHI NICHI NEWSPAPER OFFICES

MIDDLE MOAT ROUND IMPERIAL PALACE

CINEMA AND THEATRE

MAIN RAILWAY LINE

OFFICES OF ASAHI SHIMBUN

ELEMENTARY SCHOOL

MANCHUKUO

U.S.S.R.

VLADIVOSTOK

RUSSIAN NAVAL & AIR BASE

HAKODATE

OMINATO

RASHIN

Noshiro

KOREA

Sea of Japan

KAMAISHI

Sakata

Vladivostok—Tokio 670 m.

Sendai

Nugata

Fairbanks (ALASKA) 3000 m.

Kanazawa

Utsunomiya

MAIZURU

KANAGAWA

TOKIO

Vancouver 4280 m.

Kyoto

YOKOHAMA

Fusan

KOBE

YOKOSUKA

SHIMONOSEKI

HIROSHIMA

OSAKA

Sydney 4316 m.

WAKAMATSU

KURE

FUKUOKA

YAWATTA

Chungking—Tokio 2030 m.

Burma—Tokio 2900 m.

SASEBO

NAGASAKI

Calcutta 4532 m.

Bombay 5352 m.

Kagoshima

Yokohama—Singapore 2902 m.

Yokohama—Manila 1768 m.

North

Pacific Ocean

Miles
0   250

SHIPYARDS
INDUSTRIES
NAVAL BASES   AIR BASES
FLYING DISTANCES
WHITE ON BLACK

Top, modern buildings in the heart of Tokyo, capital of Japan and one of the Japanese cities raided on April 18. Above, U.S. Army B-25 bombers; Tokyo reported that planes of this type were used in the raid on the Jap capital. Left, map of Japan, showing important targets and flying distances.

Photos, Sport & General, Planet News.   Map, The Star   Page 681

Our Searchlight on the War

HITLER'S ERSATZ ARMY

"You'll think I'm prejudiced, perhaps—just being sentimental about the 'good old days,' as we're inclined to be at 50. But I do honestly think the fathers were better soldiers. Hitler has ruined the German army."—*Lieut.-General Rokossovsky, in an interview with the Soviet War News*

LIEUT.-GENERAL ROKOSSOVSKY is one of Russia's greatest generals, and the defender of Moscow. He fought against the Germans in the last war, and is therefore in a position to compare the Kaiser's soldiers with Hitler's. The latter is not a real but an ersatz army, he says. There is no

HOME GUARD F.A. Home Guards, including many who were gunners in the last war, are now taking over field artillery for local defence. These men are firing an 18-pounder during exercises in the West Country.
Photo, British Official: Crown Copyright

true military virtue in it, and this he explains is due to the character, or rather lack of character, of their leaders. Here is an important but little realized fact. Hitler's continual boasts about his soldierly qualities and war service in 1914-18 are nauseating, for he was never a soldier by nature. He was and still is the political gangster, and whatever talents he possesses are founded on vicious instincts. His genius is not for military strategy but for treachery, and this is the weapon which has placed him where he is. Treachery and true courage can never blend, and those who employ treachery corrupt all men who follow them. The German army, no doubt, is physically and mechanically strong, but it is devoid of those moral qualities upon which victory depends.

TIME'S REVENGES

A bust of Lenin has recently been placed in Holford Square, London, opposite the house where the founder of the Russian revolution lived during 1902-3.

FORTY years ago an anonymous and mild-mannered Russian political refugee might be seen going and coming to his modest room in Clerkenwell. Nobody at that time imagined that this middle-class intellectual with the Mongolian face was to revolutionize the vast continent of Russia, and influence the human mind to a universal degree. Lenin was an opportunist of genius as well as a master organizer. In permitting him to travel through Germany in 1917 to lead the revolt which brought Tsarist Russia out of the war, Germany unwittingly laid the foundations of Sovietism. For Germany's war of revenge it would have been better had she tried to bolster up the effete and corrupt system of Tsardom. Hitler's in-

tuitions about what he affects to call Bolshevism have been right. His hatred of the new Russia is founded on fear, a fear fully justified by the fact that Germany is grinding herself to pieces on the idealism which is at the root of Lenin's creed. Lenin was as great in the political as Napoleon in the military sense, and it is fortunate for Russia and for ourselves that his power was assumed by Stalin, who never had any delusions that the revolution of 1917 would not have to be ultimately defended against the German people, the most reactionary and servile race in the world. The British people, who do not like revolutions and have no need for them, will none the less welcome this belated honour to Lenin. Time has brought Britain and Russia together in the fraternity of blood. Who is there among us who does not now salute the man who passed in and out of the door of the house in Holford Square, one of the greatest exiles happy, at least, in that freedom which Britain has never failed to accord to persecuted nationals of other lands?

POPULATION PROBLEM

Children under fourteen now constitute about 22 per cent of Britain's population. At the present rate of decline they will sink to 10·2 per cent in thirty years and 4 per cent by the end of the century.

FROM 1821 to 1921 the population of England and Wales trebled itself. During the past twenty years there has been a steady decline. This fall is one of the big questions lurking in the background of social reconstruction. For what kind of a population is the new Britain intended? It is useless to plan for youth if, in forty years' time, the country will be peopled mostly by aged persons. The statisticians inform us that by 1981 the proportion of young people will be reduced by another third if retrogression continues at the present rate. Speculation as to the decline offers some interesting theories. Nobody will pretend that the teeming millions who inhabited Britain in late Victorian times were well fed, well housed and generally prosperous. The poverty of the cities was an abomination. On the other hand, a certain religious and social discipline among all classes, combined with a feeling of optimism that life was worth while, kept the registrars busy. The last war, the uneasy peace that followed, and the present war, the decline in religion, the increase

RAILWAY POLICEWOMAN, Miss Phyllis Piper, the first to be appointed in England, in her new uniform on her first day of duty. She was formerly in the L.N.E.R. offices.
Photo, The Daily Mirror

of secular pleasures, the motor-car, high taxation —all these in varying degrees are responsible for the empty pram. As between the birth controllers and the high population fanatics we must strike a happy medium. Britain is a small country, and 40,000,000 is probably too high. A lower population, if it could be kept healthily static, might be a good thing.

FREEDOM IS IMMORTAL

In their efforts to enslave Europe the Germans are trying to do the impossible. Intimidation and death only strengthen the courage and resolve of those who are determined to be free.

SOME of the greatest heroes of the war are those anonymous journalists who, under the shadow of torture and death, are producing the underground press of Europe. A collection of these secret papers should be made and housed in a special library, and kept for all time as a symbol of the unconquerable human will. Poland has suffered more than any other nation under the Nazi heel, but the secret anti-Nazi press in that country is read by 3,000,000 people. The system of circulation is ingenious, and known as the "rule of three." According to the Soviet War News the distributor knows no more than two other people connected with the movement—the person from whom he gets the paper and the one to whom he passes it.

JAP PILOTS MUST 'DO OR DIE'

It is a formidable fact that Japanese pilots will not suffer themselves to be taken prisoner. If they are shot down they endeavour to commit suicide.

A CABLE published in The Daily Mail from a special correspondent at Colombo is a remarkable revelation of the Oriental fatalism prevailing among aviators fighting for the Mikado. About to be captured in the cockpit of his crashed machine a Japanese airman had to be pinioned by British soldiers to save him from committing suicide. Explaining his conduct through an interpreter he said that to be taken prisoner was an insupportable shame, but since this humiliation had befallen him his life was, in any case, finished. As a prisoner he had lost his status, and there was nothing further to live for. If the ideal of bushido or chivalry to a beaten foe is a myth, the law of hara-kiri is very much a fact. Should this principle apply to the Japanese forces generally, the Allies are confronted, it would appear, with an alarming obstacle to victory. Careful analysis, however, tends to prove that such a mentality is a weakness rather than a strength. Suicide is the ultimate expression of masochism, and a nation that practises it as a kind of ritual must be one of low psychological standards. We may conclude that the Japanese fighting man, as an individual, does not exist. He is but part of the machine of aggression, and man against man is no match for the higher developed British and American mind.

FOOD FOR GREECE. Archbishop Athenagdras, head of the Greek Orthodox Churches in the U.S.A. and Canada, blessing food aboard the Swedish ship Sicilia bound from New York for Greece with its mercy cargo.
Photo, Wide World

When Our Raiders Swooped on Rommel

DESERT RAID on Rommel's lines in the Western Desert. Above, the raiding party, with vehicles kept well apart to prevent less of a target, moves off at dawn. Circle right, men take cover as an enemy plane spots and tries to bomb them.

Left, one of the British 2-pounder guns accompanying the raiding party firing at enemy motor transport. Concusssion causes the dust to rise in clouds. Above, a German wireless truck, one of the many enemy vehicles set on fire by British guns.

Above, British officers evolve a plan to reduce an enemy strong point. Right, the plan has succeeded and prisoners are shepherded back.

GERMAN TANK, captured during the raid, taken away for examination. Right, a trio of prisoners, exhausted after their experiences at the hands of the British raiders, fall asleep on reaching British lines.

Photos, British Official: Crown Copyright

BREITSTRASSE, LÜBECK, showing the devastation caused by the R.A.F. raid on the German Baltic port on the night of March 28. This photograph was published in the Hamburger Fremdenblatt, which fulminated against the "savagery" of the British, having conveniently forgotten the manner in which the Germans had formerly gloated over the "Coventration" of British cities. An aerial photograph of the raid on Lübeck, taken from an R.A.F. plane, is given in page 665.

Photo, British Official: Crown Copyright

Augsburg— 'This Memorable Feat of Arms'

On April 17 R.A.F. Bomber Command delivered a daylight attack on a vital war factory at Augsburg in the heart of Germany. Here we tell of this most daring enterprise, and also of the R.A.F.'s rapidly increasing offensive in Western Europe.

AUGSBURG, the famous old Bavarian city thirty-five miles to the north-west of Munich, is also one of the most important industrial centres of Hitler's Reich. Among its many factories is one where half the Diesel engines used by the German submarine fleet are made ; and it was this factory—the M.A.N. (Maschinenfabrik Augsburg Nürnberg)—in the outskirts which was made the target of the R.A.F. on April 17.

Round about 3 in the afternoon a force of twelve Lancaster bombers, consisting of four sections led by Sqn.-Ldr. J. S. Sherwood, D.F.C. (No. 97 Squadron), Sqn.-Ldr. J. D. Nettleton (No. 44 " Rhodesia " Squadron), Flt.-Lt. D. J. Penman, D.F.C., and Flt.-Lt. R. R. Sandford, took off for their eleven hundred miles' flight there and back. Hardly had they got across the Channel when Nettleton's formation was fiercely engaged by enemy fighters, and four of his six bombers were shot down south of Paris. After this, however, there was no fighter opposition, and the force pressed on through a cloudless sky.

For most of the way they flew low, hedge-hopping for hundreds of miles through enemy territory. They did so because going low is very much safer for the bomber, since ack-ack gunners are hard put to it to shoot at a target so near the ground, while the belly of the machine, the most vulnerable part of a bomber, is not exposed to fighter fire.

At about 6.20 p.m. they were flying along the shores of Lake Constance. " First came two," said an astounded eye-witness on the German-Swiss frontier, " right down the middle of the Rhine ; a few hundred yards

there were still bombs from ours and two other aircraft to come. I saw the bombs explode as we flew away."

The factory was very strongly defended by A.A. guns. There were gun posts on the roof, and one crew saw more than one of these posts wiped out by the bursting bombs. But so intense was the anti-aircraft fire that three of the Lancasters were brought down after making their attack. The five remaining aircraft, although all damaged by A.A. fire, landed safely at their bases by midnight.

On his return, Sqn.-Ldr. Nettleton, who led the first formation—of the six his was the only plane to return—gave his account of the raid.

" As soon as the French coast came into sight," he said, " I took my formation down to a height of 25-30 feet, and we flew the whole of the rest of the way to Augsburg at that height. Soon after we crossed the coast about 25 to 30 enemy fighters appeared. A fierce running fight developed. It was our job to pierce straight through to our target, so we kept in the tightest possible formation, wing tip to wing tip so as to support each other by combined fire.

We went roaring on over the countryside, lifting over the hills and skimming down the valleys. Fighter after fighter attacked us from astern. Their cannon shells were bursting ahead of us. We were continually firing at them from our power-operated turrets. We rushed over the roofs of a village, and I saw the cannon shells which had missed us crashing into the houses, blowing holes in the walls and smashing the gables of the roofs.

" The fight lasted fifteen minutes or so, and aircraft were lost both by ourselves and the Germans. One by one our planes were shot up

AUGSBURG, Bavarian city where big Diesel engine factories were raided in daylight by the R.A.F. on April 17, lies about 35 miles N.W. of Munich and about 550 miles from London.
Map, Courtesy of The Evening News

Our bombs, of course, had delay action fuses or they would have blown us all up. We roared on past the town. Then I had the painful experience of seeing my last surviving companion catch fire. Hit all over by flak, it turned out of the formation, and I was thankful to see it make a perfect forced landing. I feel sure that the crew should be all right. At that moment all our bombs went up. I had turned and so could see the target well. Debris and dust were flying up.

" Then I set course for home. The light was beginning to fail. I was not attacked again. Until it was dark we again flew a few feet above the ground. Then we rose to a normal height and got home without further incident."

The Germans described the raid—the deepest penetration into German territory yet achieved in daylight in this war—as " senseless propaganda," but they made the significant admission that " the damage done in this attack to our war economy caused an interruption of production in one factory for a few days . . .

Hardly had the raiders returned when official recognition of their bravery was announced. Sqn.-Ldr. Nettleton received the V.C., Flt.-Lt. Penman the D.S.O., and 18 others D.F.C.s or D.F.M.s.

Out-bombing the Nazis

Dramatically effective as was the Augsburg raid, it finds its place in a picture of a rapidly-rising offensive by the R.A.F. In 33 nights—March 20 to April 20—German aircraft dropped fewer than 300 tons of bombs on Britain ; on each of six of those same nights the weight of the R.A.F. bombs on Germany was more than 300 tons. During one week it was 1,000 tons.

Another interesting comparison : no fewer than 200 Nazi planes flew inland into Britain during that same period. But on one night recently the R.A.F sent out a force of more

HEROES OF THE AUGSBURG RAID. Left, Flt.-Lt. R. R. Sandford, one of the section leaders of the force of Lancaster bombers, reported missing after the operation. Centre, Sqn.-Ldr. J. D. Nettleton, who was given the V.C. on his return. Right, Sqn.-Ldr. J. S. Sherwood, D.F.C. and bar, another section leader reported missing.
Photos, British Official, News Chronicle, Fox

behind them were the six others. I could hardly believe my eyes. In Constance the sirens began to scream only after the first two bombers were over the town. Not one shot was fired. It took everyone completely by surprise that the British should dare to come in broad daylight."

Shortly after 8 o'clock the eight Lancasters came in sight of their target. Augsburg is a notoriously easy place to pick out from the air ; and, said the rear-gunner of the aircraft piloted by Flt.-Lt. Penman, who was leading the last section, " You could not mistake the Diesel engine sheds, they were as big as hangars on an aerodrome." All the aircraft bombed from a low level, two diving to two hundred feet, and heavy bombs were seen to burst on the target. " Before we dropped our bombs I could see large bomb holes in the sheds," said the rear-gunner just quoted, " and

and sent down. My own rear gunners found their guns had jammed ; they had been working them, probably, so fast that they had become white-hot. When the Germans had given us all they had we found only two of us were left. By then we were almost defenceless, but their fighters gave up—probably they were running out of ammunition. After that we had no more trouble until we reached the target. We swept on across France and skirted the border of Switzerland into Germany. I pulled the nose of my aircraft up a trifle to clear a hill, pushed it down the other side, and saw the town of Augsburg.

" We charged straight at it. Our target was not simply the works, but certain vital shops in the works. We had studied their exact appearance from photographs, and we saw them just where they should be. Low-angle flak began to come up at us thick and fast. We were so low that the Germans were even shooting into their own buildings. They had quantities of quick-firing guns. All our aircraft had holes made in them.

" The big sheds which were our target rose up exactly ahead of me. My bomb aimer let go.

' NO LIFE WAS LOST IN VAIN '

We must plainly regard the attack of the Lancasters on the U-boat engine factory at Augsburg as an outstanding achievement of the Royal Air Force. Undeterred by heavy losses at the outset, the bombers pierced in broad daylight into the heart of Germany, and struck a vital point with deadly precision. Pray convey the thanks of his Majesty's Government to the officers and men who accomplished this memorable feat of arms in which no life was lost in vain.—*Mr. Churchill, to Air Marshal A. T. Harris, C.-in-C. Bomber Command.*

than 300 planes. As to losses, the Axis lost more aircraft—140 was the figure—in their attacks on Malta than the R.A.F. lost (112) in all its day and night attacks on Germany. Thus the R.A.F. is developing an offensive whose aims are to cripple Germany's industrial production and, perhaps as important, to keep the German aircraft occupied, preventing them from being employed in Malta, Libya, or in Russia.

War on Wheels: Making the Army Mobile

It is a far cry from the chariots of the ancient world to the armoured fighting vehicles of today, but the idea at the back of each is the same—to outflank the enemy by superior speed or to break through the enemy's lines by a combination of mass and momentum. Napoleon himself said : "The strength of an army is estimated by multiplying the mass by the velocity."

FOR centuries the horse was the only motive power superior to the marching capabilities of the infantry, but following the development of the internal combustion engine the armies of the Great Powers have undergone a process of increasing mechanization, and today the whole Army travels on wheels.

It is probably the infantry which has gained most in strength and mobility following this mechanization. Not only can men be carried over long distances in vehicles designed for the purpose, and with them the loads formerly carried in the pack, but wheeled transport enables the men to carry many more auxiliary weapons such as mortars, Tommy guns, light machine-guns and anti-tank rifles.

journey which, a few years ago, could only have been covered as the result of a severe forced march. Such movements of troops are carried out by the R.A.S.C. Troop-carrying Companies.

A vehicle which has had a great effect on infantry tactics is the small tracked armoured vehicle known as the Bren "carrier." Its main purpose is to carry fire power from one part of the battlefield to another and to support and cooperate with the infantry and infantry tanks. Carrier platoons also have, as an integral part of their composition, motor-cycles and motor-cycle combinations, for reconnaissance and inter-communication. Infantry machine-gun battalions are now entirely motorized, the guns, crews and

In the Royal Artillery pneumatic tires and petrol engines have worked wonders in the speed of transportation of heavy guns. Until recent years field artillery was horse-drawn except for very heavy guns. Today, except for mule-borne mountain and pack artillery used in difficult country and the super-heavy guns, like those that fire across the Channel, which are on railway mountings, the artillery, on large pneumatic tires, is drawn by "Scammell" lorries or trucks.

Lorries, light and heavy, are the backbone of the R.A.S.C. today. Since this corps is the supply and transport branch of the Army, providing and delivering supplies, medical stores, fuel and lubricants for every branch of the Service, its transport duties call for a vast number of vehicles. The corps, too, has troop-carrying units, bridge companies (carrying pontoons, girders and bridging stores for the Royal Engineers), runs the Army's petrol depots, supplies it with rations, maintains large mechanical repair shops and vehicle depots, and even provides and operates motor-boat companies for operations on inland waterways. For repair and recovery the R.A.S.C. has one workshop lorry and one breakdown lorry for every 56 vehicles on its strength.

Even the R.A.M.C. is mechanized today. In addition to motor ambulances it has its own mobile neuro-surgical units, X-ray units, bacteriological and malarial laboratory units and blood transfusion units. The vehicles of the R.A.M.C. are, incidentally, driven, not by the personnel of the R.A.M.C. but by drivers of the R.A.S.C.

But when one speaks of a modern mechanized army it is of tanks that one thinks first of all, those weapons of war which, since first they slipped out of a misty French dawn on the Somme on Sept. 15, 1916, have revolutionized military tactics and during the last two years have altered the map of Europe. The main types of tank upon which British production is now concentrating are illustrated in photogravure in pages 687 to 690. In hundreds of factories the Crusaders, Covenanters, Matildas and Valentines are coming off the assembly lines in ever-growing numbers.

The **Valentine** is a sixteen-ton fighting tank, formerly known officially as the Mark III infantry tank. Carrying a crew of three—commander, gunner and driver—these tanks are very manoeuvrable and have a speed of about 17 m.p.h. They are armed with a 2-pounder gun and a Besa machine-gun in a movable turret. The **Crusader** (Mark VI cruiser tank) is an 18-ton tank for fighting and reconnaissance. Its powerful engines give it a speed of over 30 m.p.h. and it carries a crew of five—commander, two gunners, gun loader and driver. The Crusader is heavily armoured and has a 2-pounder gun and two machine-guns. Very fast is the **Covenanter** (Mark V light cruiser tank). It weighs about 16 tons and is said to have a speed of 40 m.p.h. The Covenanter, used mainly for reconnaissance and patrol work, is armed with a 2-pounder gun and a Besa machine-gun and carries a crew of four. Perhaps the tank best-known to the general public is the **Waltzing Matilda** (Mark IIa infantry tank), a 28-ton heavy fighting and assault tank. She has an armour-piercing 2-pounder gun with 70 rounds and a medium machine-gun with 3,000 rounds as well as two smoke projectors. In spite of her heavy armour-plating and tremendous weight the Matilda can reach a speed of 16 m.p.h. She has a crew of four.

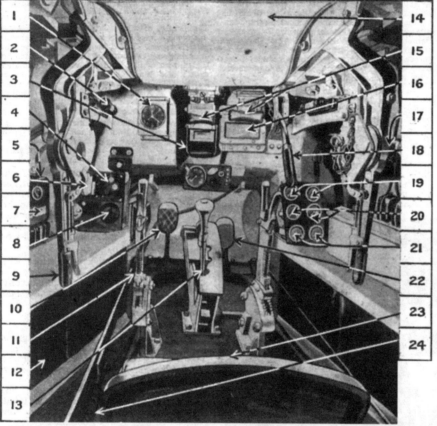

DRIVER'S COCKPIT of a Matilda tank. 1. Stop and trip time clock ; 2. Festoon lamp ; 3. Periscope ; 4. Engine starter switch ; 5. Ammeter ; 6. Engine cut-out ; 7. Electrical switch-box ; 8. Side and tail lamp switch ; 9. Driver's hood operating lever ; 10. Gear change operating pedal ; 11. Steering lever ; 12. Accumulators ; 13. Gear selector ; 14. Driver's hood ; 15. Brow pads ; 16. Bullet-proof glass panel ; 17. Series-parallel switch ; 18. Lever operating visor ; 19. Water temperature gauges ; 20. & 21. Oil and air pressure gauges ; 22. Throttle control ; 23. Driver's seat ; 24. Gear change operating rod. *British Official*

The tremendous variety of vehicles which contribute to the velocity of a modern army ranges from the motor-cycle to the heavy tank, and includes scout cars, light and heavy armoured cars, lorries, supply trucks, troop-carrying coaches, "dragon" troop carriers, baby wireless cars, wireless generating vans, truck-drawn guns, signal trucks, mobile artillery observation posts, mobile pill-boxes, fuel tankers, tank conveyors, ammunition carriers, Bren gun carriers, mobile pigeon-lofts, engineering workshops, break-down lorries and even mobile headquarters.

Infantry are not, as a rule, "embussed" when making very short journeys, as the time and road space needed for embussing, debussing and deploying would not result in any great saving of time ; but for long distances "bussing" is essential, and the troops arrive "fighting fit" at the end of a

ammunition being carried in small trucks. Reconnaissance battalions, in addition to motor-cycles and combinations, are provided with light reconnaissance cars, often mounted with a revolving turret and carrying a smoke-projector and wireless sets.

Motor-cycles are, of course, extensively used by the dispatch riders of the Royal Corps of Signals, another branch of the Service which has been extensively mechanized. The old cable wagon with its six-horse team has now been replaced by the mechanical cable-layer, sometimes known as a "spewer," which throws out the cable while travelling at speed. The wireless equipment used by Signals varies from small portable sets in baby cars to large long-range stations operated from big vans. The Signal Corps is also equipped with armoured cars, tanks and mobile carrier-pigeon lofts.

Photo, British Official: "Crown Copyright"

'Matildas' Waltzing on the Desert Floor

Matilda tanks in the Tobruk area carrying out an offensive patrol in enemy territory. The Matilda, an assault tank designed primarily for attack on prepared enemy positions, has been used with success not only by our forces in Libya but also by the Russians on the Eastern front. Designed for dispersal production, this tank is being made in many parts of the country.

687

'Mechanized' Means Mobility

1, A Bren gun carrier does a vertical dive over a bank, but the crew is unperturbed. 2, Large convoy of heavy army lorries on the road somewhere in England. They are driven by members of the A.T.S. 3, An armed and armoured reconnaissance car of the Reconnaissance Corps on patrol. This is a fast vehicle with a good cross-country performance.

Photos, British
Keystone, Spo

Our New Army on Wheels

4, A Quad, towing a 25-pounder through water, demonstrates the new army methods of water-proofing vehicles. 5, Modern rough-riders have motor-cycles and sidecars as their steeds. This is how the machine-gunner fires while on the move. 6, Bren carriers, escorted by motor-cyclists, speed across a sandy tract in Northern Ireland.

Britain's Cavalry of 1942

Photos, British Official; Sport & General

Top, Covenanter light cruiser tanks on exercise in the South of England. Left, a Crusader 18-ton medium cruiser tank, for fighting and reconnaissance, coming up a slope. Right, a Valentine 16-ton fighting tank of great manoeuvrability photographed in action during an exercise. All three tanks are armed with 2-pounder guns as well as machine-guns.

It's a New China that Fights Beside Us

Side by side with the British in Burma is fighting an army of Chinese, and below we tell something of these allies of ours, allies as hardy as they are gallant. Something is said, too, of the outstanding features of the New China, of which these Chinese soldiers are a product and a part.

DRESSED in their grass-green summer uniform, with their straw sandals and straw hats hanging behind their backs, veteran soldiers of Chiang Kai-shek's army poured into Burma a few weeks ago to play their part in the defence of this dangerously-threatened province of the British Empire. They were lightly-armed and lightly-equipped; such stores as they had were carried in lorries, painted green, with small Chinese flags flying from them, and covered with red-painted slogans. Many of them were drawn from Free China's 5th and 6th Armies, and have had several years of experience of war against the Japanese; thus they know the enemy's methods inside out. Their discipline is superb, and their bravery, their capacity for long-sustained endurance, is hardly to be rivalled.

Not long ago Chinese soldiers were a music-hall joke. The Chinese, being exceedingly civilized and rationally-minded folk, have been wont to look down on the profession of arms; and as a general rule only the riff-raff of society, the ne'er-do-wells, and the urban rabble have become soldiers, whether in the national army or in the private armies of the war lords, or *tuchuns*, who until only the other day periodically wasted the Chinese countryside with their rivalries and raids. But Nationalism has changed all that—nationalism emerging out of the threat to China's very existence that is represented by the Japanese invasion. Not for generations has China been so united, and accordingly so strong, as she is today under the leadership of Chiang Kai-shek. True, the equipment of the Chinese armies is still poor and insufficient compared with that of the Japanese, who have been able to draw on British, American and Dutch arsenals and oil-wells for so much of the war material which they are now using against us. But China's position is steadily getting better. Large quantities of military supplies of every kind have reached her along the Burma Road and through Mongolia from Soviet Russia; and the Chinese industrial cooperatives—the Indusco, as they are called—are turning out ever-increasing quantities of small arms, ammunition, uniforms, and light equipment.

Toughened and hardened by compulsory service in the army, China's manhood is acquiring an altogether new virility—although in China there is still no glorification of war, which continues to be regarded as an unpleasant, indeed disgusting, occupation for intelligent men, one forced upon them by the aggression of lesser breeds from across the sea.

But a change greater and even more fundamental is being worked in the attitude towards life, and in life itself, of China's womanhood—not of *all* the women, of course, but of the more mentally alert, the younger and more vigorous elements in a sex which for thousands of years has been doomed to an existence of passive acquiescence in a state of affairs laid down and ordered by father and husband and son. To quote from a broadcast by Mme. Kung, eldest of the three Soong sisters and Chiang Kai-shek's sister-in-law:

" We have never seen anything like it. Women have escaped from their cloistered lives and are working everywhere: at the front with the fighting men and the wounded; behind the lines with the war-shocked country people; far in the rear, in rural work, in hospitals, in war orphanages, in industrial and community services. And so we are digging in to resist to the bitter end."

There are many Chinese women soldiers in the army that is fighting beside our men in Burma. Though they carry no arms and do no actual fighting, they are right in the front line; they share to the full the hardships of the men and face the same dangers, ever ready to comfort and succour the wounded. " For them there is no lipstick, no powder, no silk stockings or soft beds," reports William Munday, News Chronicle correspondent with the Chinese Army in Burma; " even privacy is denied them:" To quote from one of his vivid cables:

" I visited a Burman bungalow where some of them are billeted in bare rooms with Chinese soldiers. Here at night they spread their blankets on the hard teak floor just as others unroll it in a camp, in the paddyfields, or wherever they happen to be when the fierce sun drops below the horizon. There was no mirror on the walls, none in their packs—just one change of clothing, one blanket. They ate squatting around the communal rice basket, into which they dipped with their fingers. Their only feminine vanity was the delight with which they thrust borrowed revolvers into their belts, or borrowed steel helmets on to their heads, to swagger up and down for a minute until the guns and helmets had to be returned to their smiling owners. I noticed, too, their thick, black hair, always carefully combed; and their cotton khaki uniforms, in which they sleep as well, miraculously uncrushed."

But while recognizing China's valiant struggle against a powerful and much better equipped adversary, we must remember, too, the tremendous progress in the building of a modern state in place of one founded on immemorial custom and age-old tradition. Some details of this New China were given in a recent broadcast by Dr. Wellington Koo.

Following the Japanese invasion of 1937 Chiang Kai-shek established Chungking as the wartime capital of China, and embarked on a vast programme of development in a region which hitherto had been considered as the backwoods of the Chinese Republic.

Within two years over 6,000 new post offices were opened, and 30,000 miles of telegraph lines put up. Over 700 miles of new railways have been opened to traffic; over 3,000 miles of motor roads have been completed, and another 3,000 are under construction. New routes have been opened up for steamboats, and air transport has been developed for both passengers and goods. The production of electrical power has increased

DR. WELLINGTON KOO, Chinese Ambassador in London. He has held many posts in former Chinese governments and was for many years China's representative on the Council of the League of Nations.   *Photo, L.N.A.*

by 25 per cent. The industrial cooperatives (as we have seen) have transformed industry. Very noteworthy, too, is the fact that the lamp of learning has been kept burning. Thousands of students and scores of colleges and universities have migrated from the regions devastated by the Japanese along the coast to the interior provinces of China. But the biggest stride has been made in the field of mass education; in March 1940 a five-year plan was launched to eliminate illiteracy, and already of the 165 millions who were illiterate over 46 millions have been taught to read. And this in a China which is fighting for its very life.

" None of the old-time apathy and stagnation is left," says Dr. Koo; " everywhere one feels an ever quickening tempo of the national pulse, and sees signs of a dynamic new life." And because of China's tremendous manpower and vast potential resources, all this augurs well not only for her own future but for the general cause of the United Nations.   E. Royston Pike

Chinese soldiers on the Ichang front making the most of a period of relaxation. In Burma, Chinese troops have given powerful aid to the British forces around the oil town of Yenangyaung, where they recently covered the withdrawal of hard-pressed British troops across the Pinchaung River.   *Photo, Pictorial Press*   **Page 691**

Chiefs of the United Nations in Chungking

CHUNGKING CONFERENCE of Allied chiefs. This photograph was taken on the occasion of the recent visit of Gen. Wavell and Gen. Brett to Chungking to confer with Generalissimo Chiang Kai-shek. Left to right seated are: Sir Archibald Clark Kerr, British Ambassador to China until Jan., 1942, and now Ambassador to U.S.S.R.; Madame and Generalissimo Chiang Kai-shek; Lt.-Gen. George Brett; Gen. Sir Archibald Wavell. Behind Sir Archibald Kerr is Maj.-Gen. Lancelot Dennys, head of the British Military Mission to China (since killed in an air crash). Between Sir Archibald and Madame Chiang is Mr. Owen Lattimore, personal political adviser to the Generalissimo, behind whom stands Gen. Ho Ying-chin, with, next to him, Brig.-Gen. John Magruder, head of the American Military Mission to China.

Photo, Pictorial Press

GEN. WAVELL SPEAKS TO INDIA

OUR ultimate victory against the brutality and aggression of the Axis Powers is beyond doubt. You have on your side four of the toughest and most enduring races of the world—the British, Chinese, Russians and Americans.

The British may be idle and easy-going in times of peace, but their core is as hard and as unyielding as ever. Adversity picks up the tough heart and reveals that core. They will never give in. The Chinese, though half armed, have stubbornly defended their civilization for nearly five years against the upstart Japanese, and will continue to do so to the end. The Russians have endured an armoured onslaught by the Germans on a scale never equalled, and have thrown it back as they have thrown back so many other invaders. Their endurance is everlasting. And the Americans —of whose determination to assist India to the utmost of their inexhaustible resources Indians have already seen so much evidence—do they strike you as a people who will let go when once they have taken a hold? So our victory is only a question of work and time.

The immediate danger to India is air attack, but I want to get the danger into its proper proportion. The savage ruthlessness shown by Germans against Rotterdam and against some towns and cities in Great Britain has instilled fear, as it was meant to do, in the minds of other people. But it did not break the resistance or terrorize the minds, be it noted, of the Dutch and British peoples who suffered under them . . .

I WAS in Singapore only a few days before its surrender, when it had been experiencing continuous raiding at the maximum scale which the Japanese Air Force could bring to bear. Yet Singapore had few scars and there were few casualties, military or civilian, despite the inadequate defences. . . . I can assure you that if people keep their heads and take precautions laid down by the A.R.P. Service, casualties will not be heavy. Air raids produce more noise and dirt than loss of life or injuries. . . . Already in their attacks on Colombo and Trincomalee, the Japanese had as high a proportion of loss, despite great numerical superiority, as they did in their attacks on Rangoon last winter. Our defence is growing in strength almost daily, and expanding over India.

There is the prospect of invasion by sea and land. That the shores of India are threatened is obvious, and that the enemy might even attempt a landing in force is equally obvious . . . It is impossible to erect defences along the whole immense coastline of India or place soldiers to guard all points.

Our danger is clear to us and seems great. But consider the distance the Japanese are from their bases, the enormous area over which their war effort is already dispersed, the vulnerability to sea and air attack of their line of communications to India, the immensity of the country they would be seeking to conquer. They may raid India. They may even seek to occupy a portion of it temporarily, but as long as India remains true to herself she can never be conquered.

NOTHING can stop us from winning the war; but defeatism and unreasoning panic may hinder and delay the victory. Some of India's most prominent leaders have lately given a stirring call towards resistance against aggression. If all in India, of every class and creed, British and Indian, official and non-official, calmly stay at their posts in office, factory and village, and will work wholeheartedly for India at this crisis, we have nothing to fear.—*From broadcast, April 21*

Out of Italian Prisons into Egypt's Sunshine

FREE AGAIN, wounded British prisoners enjoy the sun on the deck of the Union Castle liner Llandovery Castle, which is seen in the top photograph arriving at Alexandria with repatriated prisoners aboard. Under an Anglo-Italian agreement 129 British prisoners of war and 917 Italians were exchanged for repatriation. The British prisoners travelled to Smyrna in the Italian hospital ship Gradisca, and there were transferred to the Llandovery Castle, which took them to Alexandria. Circle, some of the freed British prisoners at Alexandria. *Photos, Wide World* Page 693

Our Diary of the War

Air.—R.A.F. sweeps over N. France. Docks at Cherbourg attacked. Night attack on the Ruhr, aerodromes in the Low Countries and the docks at St. Nazaire and Le Havre.

Russian Front.—Moscow announced U-boat sunk and enemy destroyer damaged by Soviet warship in Arctic. Red Army troops in Bryansk sector pierced Germans' second defence line.

Burma.—Chungking communiqué announced opening of a major Japanese offensive in Southern Shan States against Chinese eastern flank.

Philippines.—Australian communiqué reported that American heavy bombers had made surprise raids on Jap bases in Philippines on April 13-14, making a 3,600-mile trip.

Australasia.—Allied aircraft made heavy raid on Rabaul.

General.—American residents in unoccupied France urged to sail for home.

APRIL 16, Thursday 957th day

Air.—Over 400 Spitfires made sweeps over N. France. Night raids on Lorient and Le Havre.

Burma.—British took up positions near Yeuchaung.

General.—The King awarded the George Cross to Malta.

APRIL 17, Friday 958th day

Air.—R.A.F. made daylight raid on Augsburg, near Munich. More sweeps over N. France. Night raids on Hamburg, St. Nazaire and Le Havre.

Burma.—British destroyed oilfields at Yenangyaung.

APRIL 18, Saturday 959th day

Air.—R.A.F. sweep over N. France. Attack on Frisian Islands by British planes.

Burma.—British tanks smashed Jap attempt to prevent destruction of oilfields.

Japan.—First air raids by U.S. planes on Tokyo, Yokohama, Kobe and Nagoya.

General.—Laval announced new Vichy cabinet.

APRIL 19, Sunday 960th day

Air.—R.A.F. sweeps over N. France continued.

Russian Front.—Fighting became heavier on the Finnish front.

Burma.—Fierce fighting in the area of the Pichaung.

Indian Ocean.—British planes raided Andamans.

Australasia.—Heavy raids renewed by Allies against Rabaul.

APRIL 20, Monday 961st day

Mediterranean.—Heavy air attack on Malta. 11 raiders destroyed.

Burma.—Chinese troops recaptured oil town of Yenangyaung.

Philippines.—Corregidor and other fortresses in Manila bay heavily attacked.

General.—Vichy announced execution at Rouen by Germans of 30 hostages.

APRIL 21, Tuesday 962nd day

Sea.—Mr. Curtin announced loss of H.M.A.S. Vampire.

Mediterranean. — Malta blitz continued.

Burma.—Battles at Pyinmana and Bawlake.

Philippines.—Japs made new landings on Panay Island.

Australasia.—Allied bombers attacked Rabaul. Port Moresby raided by Japs.

APRIL 22, Wednesday 963rd day

Air.—Daylight raids on Cherbourg peninsula. Night attack on Rhineland and Le Havre.

Russian Front.—Red Army pushed forward six miles in Karelia.

Mediterranean.—Three heavy air attacks on Malta. 30 enemy planes destroyed or damaged. Sicily bombed by R.A.F.

Burma.—Japs launched strong attacks on Loikaw.

Philippines. — Defenders forced to withdraw from Lambunao, Panay.

General.—Commandos raided French coast near Boulogne.

APRIL 23, Thursday 964th day

Air.—Heavy night attack by R.A.F. on Baltic port of Rostock.

Mediterranean.—More Axis planes destroyed over Malta.

Burma.—Japs launched big attacks on three fronts.

Australasia.—Allied air attacks on Rabaul. Three Jap raids on Port Moresby.

General.—S. Africa severed diplomatic relations with Vichy.

APRIL 24, Friday 965th day

Air.—Offensive sweep by R.A.F. over N. France. Docks at Flushing bombed. Rostock again raided.

Mediterranean.—Several more air raids on Malta.

Burma.—Jap mechanised units pushing on towards Mandalay.

Philippines.—Further Jap landings at three points.

Home.—Night raid on Exeter.

APRIL 25, Saturday 966th day

Air.—Rostock again raided at night. Other night targets of R.A.F. were Skoda works at Pilsen, objectives in S. Germany and docks at Dunkirk. Gigantic daylight sweep including submarine targets at Cherbourg and Le Havre, Calais factory and Abbeville railway.

Burma.—Japanese on Salween front pushing N.E. from Hopong.

Australasia.—Darwin bombed. 8 Jap bombers and 3 fighters destroyed.

Home.—Heavy German night raid on Bath.

General.—Washington announced landing of American troops on French island of New Caledonia.

APRIL 26, Sunday 967th day

Air.—R.A.F. sweep over N. France. Rly. yards at St. Omer and Hazebrouck bombed. Rostock bombed at night.

Russian Front.—Red Army strikes in Lapland.

Mediterranean. — Incessant air raids on Malta.

Burma.—Chinese recaptured Taunggyi. Japs nearing Pyawbwe.

Home.—Bath again raided at night.

APRIL 27, Monday 968th day

Air.—R.A.F. sweeps over N. France. Night raids on Cologne and Trondhjem.

Russian Front.—Russians announced capture of Borok, west of Lake Ilmen.

Mediterranean.—Two air raids on Malta.

Burma.—Japs advancing on Lashio.

Australasia.—Darwin bombed by Japs.

Home.—Night raid on Norwich.

General.—U.S. Navy Dept. announced loss of destroyer Sturtevant.

APRIL 28, Tuesday 969th day

Air.—Day sweep over N. France. Night raids on Trondhjem and Kiel.

Russian Front.—German attack on Smolensk front repelled.

Mediterranean.—Three daylight raids on Malta.

Africa.—Many killed and injured in night raid on Alexandria.

Burma.—Lashio heavily bombed by Jap raiders.

Australasia.—More Jap raids on Port Moresby. Allied bombers raided Lae. Mr. Curtin revealed arrival of more U.S. reinforcements in Australia.

Home.—Germans made night raid on York.

General.—President Roosevelt broadcast to U.S. Disclosed that U.S. warships were operating in Mediterranean.

V.C. HEROES OF SIDI REZEGH. Left, 2nd Lt. G. W. Gunn, M.C., R.H.A., who, in an unarmoured car under the heavy fire of 60 tanks, directed the fire of his four anti-tank guns. Finally only one remained. All the crew were casualties except the sergeant. Lt. Gunn, with the sergeant as loader, continued firing until killed. **Right, Rifleman John Beeley, K.R.R.C.,** who carried a Bren gun towards a German post and killed or wounded the entire crew of an anti-tank gun. The post was silenced and Beeley's platoon was enabled to advance. Both men gave their lives for their country. *Photos, News Chronicle and Planet News*

Planning the Course Ahead: Mr. Lyttelton's 'Postscript'

WE have been told often that we are fighting this war to think our own thoughts and live our own lives, and I only want to let our imagination play for a moment on what thoughts we are going to think, and what lives we wish to live. For, make no mistake, we are going to win by our present sacrifices and by our present toil, our right to think them in our own way and our right to live them in our own way. What is that way going to be?

If I can, I want to dispel some of the natural fears which we harbour. One of those fears is that immediately after the war there will be a great wave of unemployment. But there is no reason why that should be inevitable. On the contrary: immediately after the war there will be, an overwhelming demand for those goods which we consume currently for clothes and food and so forth. On top of this demand will be piled the need for re-establishing our stocks. In the clothing industry and in the food industry, there will be an immense need for labour, and our problem for four or five years after the war will not be a problem of unemployment, but a problem of transfer of labour—the problem of getting the peacetime industries going again quickly enough to meet the enormous and impatient demand that there will be for their products.

But these days of immense demand for goods which we consume, like clothes and food and tobacco, cannot be the permanent basis for a national economy. They are like a honeymoon, and when it is over we shall have to find a permanent balance in our economic, and indeed in our whole national, life. Let us agree about the common foundations upon which we wish to build that life, and we *shall* build it. There is nothing that we are more likely to get than the things which we wish for.

I believe there are three things which we all want, and which we must see that we get. The first is to make this a truly cheerful country, a country in which we can laugh when we want and put our tongue out at the people we don't like; a spacious, active, enterprising, gay country. The second is to see that we are never again faced with the horror of mass unemployment. The third is to modernise the capital equipment, by which I mean the transport, the roads, ports, towns, houses and amenities of our country. And the curious thing is that in reaching for the third of these objectives, we shall be going a long way towards attaining the first two.

HOW should we do it? What part should the State play in helping us to do it? I believe it is when what I have called the honeymoon is over that the State will have to take the initiative and the responsibility on whatever scale is necessary in improving the capital assets, the common services and the amenities of our country, all things on which we shall earn a national dividend. Remember, too, that this country's economy, its business life, depend very largely on the import of raw materials and on working those raw materials up into finished products for our own use or for sending abroad. To do this, we want the most efficient transport possible, the most efficient machinery and factories and management. Above all we want the most efficient labour. And surely, for that, what matters most is that we should provide good housing, fine cities and open spaces and all those amenities that go to give us material happiness and contentment and security.

BY all means let us disagree upon matters of detail and how best to achieve what we want, but let us remain united on the main objectives. I believe we can attain that unity, in peace as in war. For example, I am a business man, or rather, I *was* a business man, and I suppose by definition I am a capitalist. But if anybody asked me whether there should be more socialism or more capitalism, more Government planning or more free enterprise, my answer is that there ought to be a great deal more of both. The essence of democracy should be a balance between the organising power of the State and the driving force of the free individual.

So I ask you to exercise the greatest of all human privileges, the right to hope, to foresee, and to plan the course ahead, for by this means the world advances. And if you are inclined to be gloomy, I beg of you at least once a week to indulge in a little wishful thinking. And one day, you know, we shall switch on the news and find that there is no enemy, and we shall pull aside the black-out curtains for the last time. [*April 26, 1942*

'Any More for the Trip to Boulogne?'

COMMANDO RAIDERS who pierced the Channel defences at Boulogne during the early hours of April 22 forming up before crossing the Channel. The attack was made by a force commanded by Major Lord Lovat, and penetrated enemy defences over a frontage of 800 yards. Though the point of attack was one of the most strongly-fortified stretches of the French coast, the attackers spent two hours on enemy-occupied territory and left with all their equipment. Our casualties were very slight. For the actual story, see page 701. *Photo. British Official: Crown Copyright.*

Bloody Was the Battle of New Britain

Rabaul, capital of the Australian island of New Britain, fell to the Japanese on Jan. 23, but several months elapsed before the first full account of the fighting which decided its fate could be pieced together. Here we give the story, based on the cables of G. H. Johnston, The Daily Telegraph's Special Correspondent at Port Moresby.

UNSHAVEN and bedraggled, with cheeks sunken and faces lined, wearing only the tattered rags of their uniforms, the survivors of the Australian garrison at Rabaul returned weeks later to their bases in New Guinea and on the Australian mainland. Altogether some six hundred made their way back through the tropical jungle and across enemy-infested waters—600 out of 1,399. They were defeated ; but what a fight they had put up ! With practically no air support they fought a Japanese invasion force of twenty thousand, supported by at least 150 bombers, fighters, and dive-bombers, and a formidable naval force. Over half their number became casualties ; but the Australians—they included men of the 22nd Battalion of the Australian Imperial Force, originally forming part of the 8th Division which had won distinction in the fighting in Malaya—did not give in until they had made the enemy pay most heavily for his success.

Japanese attempt to land planes on the Rabaul aerodrome came to grief, since, as they roared over the runways, demolition charges were exploded, crashing two of the planes. When darkness fell the Australians took up fresh positions on the slopes of the volcano, Mt. Vulcan. At midnight enemy aircraft came over and dropped parachute flares. At 2.30 a.m. on Jan. 23 the invasion began.

"Over the black waters," said Mr. Johnston, "before Vulcan, the Australians heard the chattering of the Japanese. They saw an occasional flash from their torches and heard their boat-keels grating on the shingle. Then came the sudden flaring of a green light as the troops signalled to the ships that the landing had been made. The invaders wore black singlets and shorts, and their faces were blackened. Little attempt was made at stealth, the enemy apparently supposing that the aerial attacks had wiped out the defenders. A Japanese bugler on the beach played only three or four notes. Then the Australians opened fire, and caused panic among the

guns. Firing from concealed positions the defenders continually swept the wire. The water was red with blood and thick with the bodies of the dead. For an hour the bloodiest battle of the New Guinea campaign went on. Despite the slaughter, the Japanese continued to bring in barge after barge, which bumped over the bodies. It was not long before the Japanese realized the value of the dead. They gathered up scores of bodies, threw them across the wire and clambered over them. Along the beach dead were 6 ft. high for about 200 yards. During the beach fighting, and in hand-to-hand struggles later in the coastal gullies, it is estimated there were at least 1,500 Japanese killed, with fewer than 20 Australians slightly wounded."

Advancing in parties of twelve, armed only with grenades, the Japanese attacked in waves, and by noon were swarming everywhere so that further resistance was useless.

"As the Japanese made a final charge up the beach the Australians coolly outwitted them. Waiting until the enemy were on top of them they ran into the scrub. The invaders, unable to distinguish Australians from their own troops, were momentarily nonplussed. This enabled the Australians to turn off through the bush to a pre-arranged point where trucks were waiting to take them away in one of the most extraordinary withdrawal actions of the war."

Glancing back ere they disappeared into the bush, the Australians saw enemy ships moving up the harbour in line abreast.

Then followed days and weeks during which the Australians struggled through some of the worst jungle country in the world, country which has hardly ever seen a white man—through tropical downpours and slimy morasses, across rivers thick with crocodiles ; they scaled precipices with ropes made from creepers, and bridged chasms by swinging on vines hanging from trees. Their daily diet was one army biscuit and a twelfth share of a tin of bully beef per man. As the days passed some began to drop with fever ; they were carried along on the shoulders of their comrades, who were almost dropping themselves, or borne on hastily-contrived stretchers.

These at last reached safety. But some, alas, fell into the enemy's hands. One party of ten officers and fifty men were trapped at Gasmata by a landing-party from a Jap destroyer. Each Australian officer was handed a revolver and one bullet, and ordered to commit suicide. After the massacre the Japanese steamed away in their warships, thinking that none survived to tell the tale. But three Aussies lived, and, with their hands still tied behind their backs, wandered in the bush for several days before being rescued. Here is what one of them said : he escaped by shamming death after being shot three times :

"The Japanese tied our hands behind our backs and formed us into parties of ten, all tied together. Each party was taken into the jungle. My party was stopped after going a short distance. A Japanese officer drew his sword and ordered his men to fix bayonets. One Australian after another was detached from the party and sent into the bush with a soldier armed with a bayonet. Soon after we heard screams. One of our men asked to be shot, and this was done by the officer. Another of our fellows got loose and dashed into the bush. The officer caught up with him, ran his sword through his back and then shot him. Afterwards several men were bayoneted only a few yards from me without being taken into the undergrowth."

Another atrocity story, almost as horrible, tells of three wounded men in a hut on New Britain. They were discovered by the enemy. One managed to escape, but the others were unable to move. The Japanese set fire to the hut, and both men were burnt to death.

Report has it that there are still small groups of Australians in the hills and jungles of New Britain, waiting for a chance to escape. They and their comrades have much to avenge.

NEW GUINEA, the possession of which is being hotly contested by Japanese and Australian troops. To the north-east is the Bismarck Archipelago, with the island of New Britain where, as is told in this page, there has been most desperate fighting. Here, too, the Japanese have committed atrocities which will befoul their name for all time.
Map, Courtesy of News Chronicle

It was on Jan. 19 that reconnaissance machines of the Royal Australian Air Force sighted heavy concentrations of enemy shipping in the lee of Watom Island, north of Rabaul. Next day the Japanese raided Rabaul with 60 bombers and 20 fighters ; against these the Australians could oppose only five Wirraways, Australian-built machines generally used only for training purposes. All five were promptly shot down, but not before they had destroyed two of the Japanese ; and five more of the enemy planes were brought down by ack-ack fire. On Jan. 21 Japanese reconnaissance planes flew over Rabaul, and the same night Japanese marines from destroyers effected a landing at Kavieng, in New Ireland, in the face of strong opposition by an Australian Commando force. Another enemy detachment landed on the Duke of York Islands, which lie between Rabaul and New Ireland.

Then on Jan. 22 a ferocious attack on shipping and the Australian gun positions about Rabaul was delivered by 110 enemy machines. After hours of almost continuous bombing the Australians—they had no air support—were blasted out of their six-inch gun fort at Point Praed ; but a

landing force. The fire was not returned, the Japanese making off in the darkness."

But the enemy managed to land at other places in the island, and by dawn they had scrambled up precipitous goat tracks near the lip of the volcano. A Japanese soldier was spotted near the peak, signalling seawards ; a sniper got him immediately, and the signaller who took his place promptly shared his fate. Then, as it grew light, the Australians counted off Rabaul a convoy of 25 warships, transports and minesweepers, while beyond them near Watom Island were still more destroyers and three aircraft-carriers.

Under the protection of this powerful force, supplemented by 100 dive-bombers, the Japanese began to land in strength. Their barges, carrying 50 to 100 men apiece, were raked by fire from the Australian mortars, but by sheer weight of numbers the Australians were compelled to withdraw from position after position. They took heavy toll of the invaders, however, as they went back. To quote from Mr. Johnston again :

"Heavy casualties were caused on Raluana beach by 150 members of the A.I.F. Thousands landed at this point. Many becoming entangled in the barbed wire made easy targets for machine-

Getting Ready and the Real Thing 'Down Under'

IN AUSTRALIA coast defences, like those in Britain, have been hurriedly constructed around the coast now that the danger of invasion threatens the island continent. These Australians are erecting barbed-wire entanglements on a sandy cove.

Schoolchildren of Redfern, suburb of Sydney, practising air-raid drill, are told to hold their ears and keep their mouths open. The photograph was taken in a school corridor, for shelters had not yet been built.

BRISBANE, Queensland's capital, sees surface shelters such as are a familiar sight in Britain springing up along her main thoroughfares as the threat of Japanese air attack hangs over the continent. Right, clouds of smoke pouring from a Guinea Airways hangar at Salamaua, New Guinea, after it had been set ablaze during a Japanese air raid on the island.

Photos, News Chronicle, Keystone, Associated Press

Sowing Deadly Mines in the Enemy's Path

MINELAYING to safeguard Britain's coastal sea lanes. Left, a mine being lowered on to a truck which will run it into the ship's hold. Later it will be "sown" against enemy shipping. Top, a "horn" being fixed to a mine. If one of these horns is touched by a vessel the mine will explode. Circle, duffle-coated sailors pushing mines to the stern of the minelayer ready for laying. Above, the mine hits the water after leaving the trap.

Photos, British Official: Crown Copyright; The Daily Mirror, Planet News

Once More 'Illustrious' Sails Out to Battle

H.M.S. ILLUSTRIOUS, 23,000-ton aircraft carrier, which was badly damaged during a dive-bombing attack in the Mediterranean, is again in service after refitting in American and British dockyards. Her present commander is Captain A. G. Talbot, D.S.O., R.N. This photograph shows a Swordfish aircraft which has just landed on the flying deck of the Illustrious and is being taken to the forward lift. H.M.S. Illustrious, which normally carries a complement of 1,600, was laid down in 1937. Accompanying her above is an attendant destroyer. *Photo, Central Press*

What Odds They Faced in Burma's Sky!

Air Vice-Marshal D. F. STEVENSON, C.B.E., D.S.O., M.C., Air Officer Commanding R.A.F. in Burma.

These American-built Brewster Buffalo single-seat fighter monoplanes have been in action on the Burmese front. The two pilots in the foreground, just returned from an operational flight, are both New Zealanders: Sgt.-Pilot T. Beable, of Hangatiki (left) and Sgt.-Pilot W. Christenson, of Christchurch.

Colonel Claire Chennault, until recently commanding the American Volunteer Group in Burma, gives instructions to a pilot, on whose back is seen the A.V.G. flag and instructions in Chinese to safeguard the pilot in case of forced landing. (See also page 510.)

ON A BURMESE AIRFIELD, where coolies are busily working, Kittyhawk fighters of the American Volunteer Group are ready to take off. Cooperating with the R.A.F. in Burma, the pilots of the A.V.G. have scored many successes against the vastly more numerous Japanese. Circle, an Indian pilot with the R.A.F. in Burma whose cockpit is adorned with a painting of the Tiger of Konkan.

Photos, British Official, Pictorial Press, G.P.U., Central Press

I Was There! .... Eye Witness Stories of the War

We Raided Boulogne Beach in Gym Shoes

The daring "small reconnaissance raid" on the French coast near Boulogne which our Commandos carried out in the early hours of April 22, is graphically described below by Reuter's war correspondent, Alan Humphreys.

"**H**ALTEN!" This was the only word spoken by a torch-swinging German forming the one-man patrol that was the first to challenge our Commandos during their two-hour reconnaissance excursion near Boulogne. Tommy-guns spat. A torch went out. We heard no more.

Veiled in night mist our craft crept silently inshore. The Commandos plopped into the shallows and waded to the beach. They were wearing action make-up—jet-black faces. All wore gym shoes, with the exception of one of the officers. He is a former police station inspector in the East End of London. His footwear was a pair of carpet slippers kept in place with elastic. As he clambered over the side he muttered, "I intend to invade France in comfort." His home-made heavy armament was a "cosh."

While we were off the beach searchlights flickered nervously. The Nazis were showing signs of disquiet. As we advanced we could hear whistling, but instead of being met by withering machine-gun fire the Commandos covered the several hundred yards to the safety of the sand dunes at the top of the beach without incident.

Then there was action. But the Commandos were not involved. It was the Naval forces of light craft which had brought the Commandos on this job. While the "little ships" were lying off waiting to bring the Commandos back, they were engaged by a German "flak" ship and smaller craft. The Commandos were getting on with their assignment very quietly. To their surprise all the fireworks came from the sea. These fireworks also caught the attention of the German beach defenders. Their suspicions had been aroused by the presence of our Naval force. They were so engrossed that the Commandos had swept across the sand and were at the beach before they met machine-gun fire.

We had the initiative until the moment when we withdrew—the Germans were always fighting where they were compelled to. We penetrated enemy defences over a frontage of 800 yards. Much of the machine-gun fire was enfilading the beach over the heads of our men. As it dawned on them

that a raid was being made, the Germans fired a shower of Very lights. They went up right and left.

British patrols went out and contacted enemy strong points, cutting communications and thereby preventing reinforcements being sent for. "The pill boxes had not the foggiest idea where we were and what we were doing," said one patrol leader. Remarkable from the military point of view was that, after spending two hours on enemy-occupied territory, every man was withdrawn with arms. Our casualties were negligible.

Major Lord Lovat, wearing the bonnet of his own Lovat Scouts, told me : " We were lucky. During our advance to the sand dunes we might have had to face machine-gun fire." A 21-year-old captain from Glasgow, who came through Dunkirk, said : " We ought to have been cleaned up, but we were not. My sergeant had a very near miss when some of their stuff fell about six inches from him. It was the withdrawal, like all withdrawals, which was the most difficult part of the operation."

A private from Walthamstow told me his experience. " I was clawing my way through the beach wire when I felt my pants catch on it. Just then a Very light went up. It spotlighted everything. I thought I was a goner. Somehow I was not hit."

A Commando, back from the Boulogne raid, hands back unused ammunition. He will probably need it again very soon.

After the Navy's short engagement with enemy warships, which ended in the "flak" ship slinking off, apparently on fire, the eerie silence and darkness of a "Commando night" descended. Then came the rendezvous with the returning Commandos. Slowly sweeping in the direction from which they should appear, the ships scoured the sea. At last, against the pearly grey sea and sky of early morning, came the black shapes of the landing craft. We saw them at last clearly, still black-faced, waving and smiling, their teeth gleaming against the dusky hue. Yes, Britain's task troops had come back from another task—more singeing of Hitler's moustache !

Our Trek Southwards from Bombed Darwin

In the vastness of Australia the evacuation of civilians from enemy-threatened regions presented a very different picture from that seen in England. Here is an account of the first impact of war on Australia, by Mrs. Hilda Abbott, wife of the Administrator of the Northern Territory.

I SHALL never forget the first Jap air raid on Darwin—the cheque I was writing when the sirens went ; the scream of bombs and the cries of the injured ; the crash of concrete that killed our poor little laundry maid ; the roar of planes and guns ; the bullets that sprayed round as we lay in a bed of zinnias ; the scramble to shelter down a cliff face . . .

But it is not of raids on Darwin that I want to tell you—but of the evacuation "trek" across the vast spaces of Australia that followed.

After the first bad raids on Darwin both the Commandant and my husband, the Administrator, said the women must go south. They put the Judge in charge at the railway station, and the A.R.P. men gathered there all the women, the wounded, and the old men. Thirty little children and six nuns, who had been brought in the day before from a lonely mission station, were taken by lorry 70 miles down the line, where they had to wait till we picked them up.

The wet season was not yet over. We were travelling in cattle trucks, and as we

OFF TO BOULOGNE are these Naval ratings, about to embark for the raid on the French coast. The Naval force was under the command of Lt.-Com. Thomas Cartwright, R.N.V.R. Right, Major Lord Lovat, who led the landing-party, giving orders to the officers before setting out for Boulogne ; 53 regiments were represented in the raid. *Photos, British Official : Crown Copyright* **Page 701**

Evacuees from Darwin, on Australia's threatened northern coast, making their way southward in open trucks. An account of the evacuation of civilians from Northern Territory and the difficulties involved is given in this and the preceding page. *Photo, Keystone*

had all been told not to take much baggage, the comforts of cushions and blankets had been left behind. The night was warm, but the truck floor a little hard.

We went on through the forest country. It was a long, hot day. A group of Dutch people were in a goods truck just ahead of ours, and a woman sat with a Turkish towel over her head. They had had terrible adventures getting away from islands in the north. I had met many of them, and had welcomed them to Darwin with a cup of tea. Now I invited the woman to the shelter of our cattle-truck. Her husband was a doctor, and he cared for us all on that journey and attended to all our air-raid injuries.

After our hot day travelling through the forest country we came to Katherine. The constable in charge, the hotel-keeper, the school-teacher—they were all on the little platform to offer us baths and meals and beds. I begged that the train go on as soon as possible ; we were all feeling a slight reaction and as long as we were travelling on into the limitless interior it seemed better. We had refreshing shower-baths in an out-

house at the back of the earthern-floored, funny little hotel, and we carried dishes of water and sponges and food up to the wounded in the train.

Then we were off again. This time we rumbled along through a starry night, and bumps and jolts and bangings could not rob us of a feeling of peace as we lay on the floor, leaning on the children's rolled-up ground-sheets. I think everyone on that train fell quickly into an exhausted sleep.

Next morning we transferred from the train to motor trucks. For hundreds of miles our motor convoy pounded on. It was heavenly, after the train journey, to be out in the open like this, threading through woods, across rolling plains. At given places the convoy stopped for tea, and gradually that welcome break came to be a grim necessity. For tired bodies now ached, every hurt was becoming more painful. In the trucks the temperature went up and the wounded became restless and hysterical.

For three days we pelted on—on where the dust blew and hard hills frowned down, but where women always waited to tend the travellers. Now the outposts of the Macdonnell Range rose before us—grassy hills with flat-topped, rocky ridges. Taller and bigger they grew until the blue ranges came in sight, and grass and sheep and cattle told us that we were nearing a settlement.

After snaking our way through the hills we came to the neat little town of Alice Springs, with its clean bungalows, tidy streets, shade-giving cedars and gum trees, and hoses busy spraying green lawns.

Stiff and cramped, bruised and battered, we climbed down from the trucks, to be welcomed at the schoolhouse with cups of tea and to be shown rows of beds made up for us on the floor. The women of Alice Springs were all ready for us. Good hot dinners were provided at local cafés, and they saw us all made comfortable. The hospitals took in the wounded.—*The Daily Mail.*

PTE. NORA CAVENEY, of Walsden, near Rochdale, Lancashire—the first of Britain's A.A. girls to be killed in action. Private Caveney was working a predictor on a gun-site during an enemy air raid on the South Coast in the early hours of April 17. She was following an enemy plane and was "on target" when she was hit by a splinter of a bomb which fell not far from the emplacement. Another A.T.S., Private Gladys Keel, at once took Pte. Caveney's place. A battery officer said that the girls' discipline under fire was splendid.
Photo, The Daily Mirror

What I Discovered About the 'Doughboys'

The following amusing but informative account of the dress and habits of the "doughboys" was broadcast by Denis Johnston after visiting an American army camp somewhere in the British Isles.

THE first thing you notice is the variety of costume about the place. You picture these "doughboys" in khaki tunics and forage caps very like the British, but with canvas spats extending up the leg nearly to the knee. But very few of them seemed to be dressed like this in private ; they wear light waterproof jackets lined with wool, with zip fasteners up the front—useful little coats. And blue or khaki overalls, called denim suits, when they're working about the place, and gumboots, and, those things you never see on a British soldier— goloshes. They call them rubbers.

On their heads they wear about five different varieties of hats : two types of steel helmet, a sort of deer-stalker's cap, a fur-lined thing with ear-flaps for cold weather, and one or two of them even had the old Boy Scout's hat we used to see them wearing in the pictures, although I believe these are officially withdrawn now. Their gasmasks are in great flat triangular haversacks slung under the left arm, very much bigger than ours but no heavier.

It's sometimes quite hard to tell the officers from the men, if you don't know what to look for. I was puzzled quite a bit over this—what really was at the back of it— because the badges are there all right, and

all the discipline and respect for officers that you find in any other army—the " sirring " and the saluting. (I've never seen so much saluting, with or without hats.) Maybe it's because they usually salute with that grin of recognition they give, because they're run on a more personal basis, or because many of them have been at school together. Anyhow, there you are ; it's a difference that I can't explain, but which you can't help noticing all the time.

Yet at heart they're really very like all other soldiers. They've got the same sort of jokes, and the same sort of complaints, although usually about different things, due mainly, of course, to the different background. For instance, the weather over here is very hard on Americans, because according to their standards of warmth and comfort we don't take the winter seriously. We don't have to in the way they do at home, and consequently they often find it unbearably chilly.

Then they're used to a different kind of food. You can tell that at once by their dixies, their billycans. The British soldier has a deep one because the basis of his cooking seems always to be stew ; the Americans have flat oval dixies because they do not stew, they fry. They're used, of course, to a balanced diet in camp : their bit of green salad, their cereals, their orange juice, and, above all, their milk. They're great milk drinkers, which is hardly true of the British soldier. It's just a matter of habit, and habits have to be taken into account even on active service.

Otherwise their interests are very much the same, and one of the most likable things about them is the fact that they're so young and hard. The doughboy likes to show off his equipment and talk about his home and civil life. The British soldier very often has a photo of his girl in his pocket-book ; but some of these Americans have a pocket-book that opens out into a sort of concertina affair with a regular battery of photographs.

'DOUGHBOY' FROM DAKOTA, Sgt. Lyle Marshal, takes some refreshment after landing in Northern Ireland. *Photo, G.P.U.*

We Ran the Gauntlet Through the Skagerrak

At the end of March 1942 eleven Norwegian ships laid up at Gothenburg, Sweden, attempted to run the blockade through the Skagerrak. Though attacked by German planes and warships, some of the ships reached England, as members of their crews tell below.

IT was late one afternoon that we learned we were to sail at last (said one of the seamen who escaped). After months of exile, dashed hopes and disappointments, our secret preparations were complete. We were off to England !

But we dared not even raise a cheer as we slipped our moorings in the gathering dusk. The only noise came from the ice-floes crunching at our bows. We showed no lights, and as the sky darkened we crept out of Gothenburg harbour. We did not all go out together.

We knew we were taking tremendous risks, but we did not expect things to happen as quickly as they did. The Germans had been tipped off. They were waiting just off the Swedish coast, and they opened up on us immediately. We could do nothing in reply.

Soon shells were screaming all around us. German bombers droned overhead, and it seemed as if nothing could save us. Some of our ships were being fired at from point-blank range. Somehow or other they managed to survive, but it seemed clear that complete destruction awaited us if we carried on, and most of the ships turned back.

Then, quite suddenly, a heavy fog came down. Visibility was reduced to nil and the bombardment stopped. We were in company with a larger ship. With the fog to hide us, we decided to try again. Most of the other ships did the same. With a little luck we felt we would get through.

We crept out again, making for the narrow neck out of the Kattegat. I saw a vivid flash. I think it was the ship which had turned with us on the second attempt. She must have been hit by a torpedo.

We raced on at full speed. Above us we could still hear the roar of the German bombers, and every now and then there was the thud of exploding bombs. In spite of the fog, German warships and U-boats resumed their attack. Torpedoes seemed to fill the sea. But all missed. We were chased for hours, and attacked with every form of weapon—bombs, shells, torpedoes. The fog was our salvation.

At last we were out of the Kattegat. Our chances of escape increased every hour, and we still went on towards Britain.

Then in daylight we saw two planes approaching. A cheer went up from the crew—the planes were British. They came low and everyone jumped about, giving the V sign and waving. It made us very happy to see the R.A.F. pilots waving back

A German Heinkel bomber getting ready to attack one of the ships that, as is told on this page, made the dash from Gothenburg.

[Now the story is taken up by a nineteen-year-old nurse, one of the few women passengers to make the perilous journey.]

Until last November I was looking after sick Norwegian prisoners sent to our hospital from German prison camps. The staff never had any trouble with the Germans, but the Gestapo were always in and out, asking our patients many questions. All doors were guarded day and night.

One night last November I decided I had worked long enough for the Germans. I cannot tell you how I got away, except that I crossed the frontier into Sweden. There I worked again as a nurse, but all the time I was waiting to escape to Britain.

A chance came when I managed to get aboard one of the ships leaving Gothenburg.

We sailed from Gothenburg soon after dark on Tuesday, March 31. Early the next morning we spotted German ships. We turned back. Thick fog came down a little later, and at midday on Wednesday we made once more for the open sea.

An hour later waves of German bombers and fighters began their attack. For seven hours we were bombed and machine-gunned. Not one bomb hit us. Machine-gun bullets ricocheted about the deck.

I think I was more angry than frightened. I stood in the stern, just watching, fascinated that they could attack us so furiously for all that time without hitting us.

The next day armed trawlers shelled us. But they, too, failed.

NORWEGIANS REACH SAFETY. Some of the men who, as described in this page, ran the blockade through the Skagerrak to try to reach England. The men's faces have been purposely blurred so that they may not be identified by the enemy and their relatives made to suffer. *Photos, Planet News*

Editor's Postscript

THOSE lucky American correspondents who were able to see at first hand so much of what has happened since the start of the War before their own country became involved, have had the bulge of their British confrères. What stories they have had to tell; how well most of them have done the telling! Their books are indeed "the abstracts and brief chronicles of the time." I have read most of them. From the Land of Silent People is the latest. This is written by Robert St. John, who "covered" the Balkans for the Associated Press of America through all the shifting scenes of the Axis intrigue and action in Rumania, Greece, and Yugoslavia's heroic tragedy. His book is written with great verve and directness, though destitute of literary grace. But it appears at a time when the paper famine will be its only enemy, for I cannot see its publishers being able to print as many copies as will be called for. At the fateful hour of the Simovich *coup d'état* Mr. St. John shuddered to contemplate the impending slaughter when the mechanized Hun would fall upon the peasant army of the Serbs.

"I THOUGHT back a few months (he writes) when I was living in Bucharest and saw division after division of those grim, grey-uniformed Nazis parading past my window. I remembered watching their twenty-ton, fifty-ton, hundred-ton monsters of steel snorting along Calei Victoriei. I remembered how they amazed Bucharest by never inquiring the way. Most of them, tens of thousands of them, had memorized the map of Bucharest, with its maze of winding streets, before they ever left Germany. And whenever there was any necessity for conversation they talked Rumanian. Maybe not perfectly, but a whole lot better than any of us who had lived in the country for a year or two." He was also impressed with the great travelling repair shops that accompanied the columns. "No matter how much we may have disliked the Nazis, we were impressed by their army. No matter how much we sympathized with the Serbs, we knew theirs was a peasant-cart army." Later on he had a talk with a Serb soldier from a remote mountain district who had never heard of a tank. The poor chap said if there were men in these tanks they must come out, and, as he patted his rifle, "when they come out we shoot them." No wonder he thought then "God help Serbia!" But there will be another and a more epic story to write some day; it will tell how these valiant peasant folk are helping themselves under the dauntless Mihailovich. Pity there will be no lively American reporter there to "write it up" even in the American argot.

RARELY do I pick up any book without finding something in it to which the twisting course of events has not given some new and immediate interest. Reading this week-end the delightful account of her richly coloured life in Paris at the opening of the century by that brilliant Russian lady, Marie Scheikevich, who married a son of the celebrated artist Carolus-Duran, and became the friend of such literary lions as Anatole France, Jules Lemaître, Proust, Cocteau, and many more, I came across this: "To celebrate the return of Brazza to France, Mme. de Loynes gave a dinner followed by a reception. The explorer had that very day broken his arm on leaving the Chamber of Deputies. Having been hastily attended to by a surgeon, he did not fail his hostess, though he was in pain and his arm in a sling. At dessert three servants were needed to bring on the table a ship made of sugar-icing and named Brazzaville."

Brazza has been dead for nearly 40 years, and now the Congo town which he founded

GEN. GEORGE R. MARSHALL, Chief of Staff of the United States Army, who arrived in London on April 8 for important talks with Mr. Churchill and Service Chiefs. *Photo, G.P.U.*

and which that sugar ship celebrated, is in the news again. Very much so, for it is the capital of French Equatorial Africa and the centre of immense activity at this moment as a rallying point of the Free French. It is surprising that Mussolini has not yet laid claim to that territory on the ground that the man who developed it for France was an Italian by birth. Brazzaville lies on the river opposite Leopoldville, the capital of the Belgian Congo, which Stanley was mainly instrumental in bringing under the Belgian crown at the very time that Brazza was mapping out the French Congo, and it is fortunate that these vast friendly lands are neighbours and will yet play an important part in frustrating Axis designs on Africa.

I HAVE just read an article in a London paper which develops the theme "Laval believes the Nazis are beaten." The most expressive comment on this would be Harry Tate's "I don't think, papa." Indeed, I have a feeling that several similar pieces of unexpected information from persons "recently in France" should be received with caution even though the informants are themselves above suspicion. For Laval is too practised in trickery not to encourage confusion of thought about his plans, policies, and personal opinions. It goes against reason to suppose that he has been plotting every hour of his life since the fall of France, to which his earlier machinations had so largely contributed, to snatch supreme power in the vassal state under his chosen masters believing that a day was coming when these same masters would be finally defeated by the Allies he had flouted and denounced. His pose of desiring to placate America, while vilifying Britain, has been assumed only in the hope of setting a little devil doubt to work between the united nations, which might eventually lead to a negotiated peace. He knows what's waiting for him when the Nazis are defeated, if before then the French protelariat fails to produce an avenger such as the old Girondists produced in Charlotte Corday.

THERE are also signs that underhand efforts are being made at present to excuse the anti-British pronouncements of Pétain. That is part of the same game, and possibly originated with the same "sources" that have suggested Laval deliberately excluded from his cabinet such notorious defeatists as his comrades in crime, Déat and Doriot, as a gesture of moderation. These rogues will have greater power outside than inside that gang of dishonest yesmen whom he has imposed upon his unhappy countrymen as a "government," and if Berlin had required their presence in his cabinet Laval would have them there. But we must not let any sympathy for an obtuse and dithering old man whose ineptitude for statesmanship has prepared the way for Laval, blind us to the fact that he has put his signature to many hostile acts against his former allies while promising to follow the path of honour in dealing with those whom the weakness of his own country had betrayed. Fortunately the anti-British nature of Darlan is black enough to resist any whitewashing. But as these triumvirs of vassal France have already by word and deed, jointly and severally, as the lawyers say, shown themselves enemies of Britain and of the Fighting French, it would be folly to think of them in any other guise.

I HAVE just received a postcard from a British prisoner of war in Germany, which has taken barely a fortnight to be delivered from his particular place of internment. His object in writing was to ensure that, although he is doomed to linger in a prison camp for the duration, his collection of THE WAR ILLUSTRATED should go on growing, for which purpose he supplies the name and address of his newsagent at Bromley, who is to gather the serial numbers and binding cases against the happy day of his returning home and adding them to his large collection of popular works originally issued in serial form under the same editorship. I certainly hope it may be possible to carry out his suggestion, as nothing is more pleasant than to return home from a period of even voluntary absence and find the old friends and familiar things you were interested in awaiting you: how much more so the gratification when returning to them after the anguish of imprisonment!

Printed in England and published every alternate Friday by the Proprietors, The Amalgamated Press, Ltd., The Fleetway House, Farringdon Street, London, E.C.4. Registered for transmission by Canadian Magazine Post. Sole Agents for Australia and New Zealand : Messrs. Gordon & Gotch, Ltd. ; and for South Africa : Central News Agency, Ltd. May 15th, 1942. S.S. *Editorial Address :* JOHN CARPENTER HOUSE. WHITEFRIARS. LONDON. E.C.4.

Vol 5 **The War Illustrated** *N° 129*

Edited by Sir John Hammerton

6ᴅ FORTNIGHTLY — MAY 29, 1942

YORK'S GUILDHALL as it appeared on the night of April 28 after it had been struck by incendiaries in one of Hitler's " Baedeker raids " on Britain's cultural heritage. After the legitimate R.A.F. raids on Rostock, where the Heinkel factory and other munition works were destroyed, German officials frankly stated that the Luftwaffe would go out for every building in Britain which is marked with three stars in Baedeker's guide-books. *Photo, Keystone*

NO. 130 WILL BE PUBLISHED FRIDAY, **JUNE 12**

MR. CHURCHILL LOOKS BACK—AND FORWARD

Two years ago Mr. Churchill had just succeeded Mr. Neville Chamberlain in the highest office under the British Crown. It was a difficult hour, dark and dangerous, too. Norway had fallen a few weeks before, and Parliament, voicing the concern of people and Press, was highly critical of the conduct of the war. But the Norwegian débâcle was soon dwarfed. On the very day that Mr. Churchill kissed hands on his appointment as Prime Minister the war on the Western Front really began, when the Germans swept with overwhelming strength into Holland and Belgium ; when he met the House for the first time as head of the Government he declared in words that history will remember that he had nothing to offer but blood, toil, tears and sweat.

Days and weeks passed, and not one but was loaded with disaster. The enemy's blows, so ruthless and unrelenting, were intensified. Paris threw open her gates to the invader. Hitler's panzers roared and rumbled across the plains of Northern France. Calais fell. Boulogne fell. Dunkirk fell. From beaches which only the previous summer had swarmed with happy holiday-makers a host of men in khaki embarked in a fleet of salvage ships, but without their guns, their supplies, their equipment. And Britain stood up alone, almost unarmed, against a host of foes.

Just two years to the day after his accession to office Mr. Churchill gave another of his inimitable broadcasts. Let us look back a little on what we have come through, he invited his audience of many millions ; let us consider how we stand now, and let us peer cautiously but resolutely into the future.

Briefly he reviewed the tremendous period covered by the two years which had passed since he became the King's First Minister. He spoke of France's defeat and fatal surrender, of Mussolini's stroke in the back of a dying France, of Dunkirk, of the imminent threat of invasion, of that solemn majestic hour in which we prepared to conquer or to perish. Time passed. We conquered the Italian Empire. We liberated Abyssinia. We protected the countries of the Middle East. We suffered grievous reverses in going to the aid of the heroic Greeks. Abroad and in our cities we bore unflinching many a heavy blow. Though cheered and helped by President Roosevelt and the United States, we stood alone, neither faltering nor flagging.

Where are we now? continued the Premier. No longer are we unarmed. We are not alone any longer, but in the ranks of the United Nations have mighty allies. By remaining steadfast and unyielding against a Continental tyrant, what has happened before in our island history has happened again : the tyrant has made a fatal blunder. Dictators—even Hitler—as well as democracies and parliamentary governments make mistakes sometimes. One such was made in June last, when, without the slightest provocation and in breach of a pact of non-aggression, Hitler invaded the lands of the Russian people. And this grand blunder was followed by a second. "He forgot about the winter ; there is a winter, you know, in Russia. There is snow there—frost and all that. Hitler forgot about this Russian winter. He must have been

very loosely educated. We all heard about it at school, but he forgot it. I have never made such a bad mistake as that . . ." Because of that mistake more Germans have already perished in Russia than were killed in the whole four and a quarter years of the last war (2,036,893).

What is there in front of Hitler now ? Russian armies, stronger than they were last year, well-equipped with an unquenched constancy and courage. What is there behind him ? A Europe starving and in chains, a Europe burning for revolt. Nor is this all. We are on his track, we and the great Republic of the United States. Already the R.A.F. have set about him so that we now find the Fuehrer mingling terrible threats with his whinings. If we go on smashing up the German cities, his war factories and his bases, he will retaliate against our cathedrals and historic monuments . . . He has even called into question the humanity of these grim developments. What a pity this conversion did not take place in his heart before he bombed Warsaw or Rotterdam ! We have heard his threats before. In September, 1940, reminded Mr. Churchill, Hitler declared he would *rub out* our towns and cities, and he certainly had a good try. Now the boot is on the other leg.

"'Though the mills of God grind slowly, yet they grind exceeding small,' and for my part I hail it as an example of sublime and poetic justice that those who have loosed these horrors upon mankind shall now in their own homes and persons feel the shattering strokes of retributive justice. We have a long list of German cities in which the vital industries of the German war machine are established. All these it will be our stern duty to deal with as we have already dealt with Lübeck, with Rostock . . ."

Then the Premier revealed that the Soviet Government had expressed the view that the Germans in their desperation might make use of poison gas against the armies and people of Russia.

DIÉGO SUAREZ, a general view of Madagascar's principal harbour. Diégo Suarez and Antsirana, site of the naval base itself, which faces Diégo Suarez across a mile-wide stretch of water, fell to the British within 48 hours of their landing on May 5.   *Photo, E.N.A.*

"We are ourselves firmly resolved not to use this odious weapon unless it is used first by the Germans. Knowing the Hun, however, we have not neglected to make preparations on a formidable scale. We shall treat the unprovoked use of poison gas against our Russian ally exactly as if it were used against ourselves, and if we are satisfied that this new outrage has been committed by Hitler, we will use our great and growing air superiority in the West to carry gas warfare on the largest possible scale, far and wide, against military objectives in Germany."

This brought the Premier to a reaffirmation of the British people's "full comradeship of war" with our Russian ally. Our deliveries of tanks, aircraft and munitions are continuing on the full scale ; thanks to the steadfast and faithful courage of our sailors and merchant seamen every convoy to Russia has fought its way through. Is there anything else we can do to take the weight off Russia ? Then the Premier made a reference to that demand for the opening of a second front— a demand which has been voiced most loudly and most often by those who are most critical of his strategical genius. Now, however, he was in no super-sensitive mood.

He welcomed the "militant aggressive spirit" of the British nation. Is it not far better that in the thirty-second month of this war we should find this general desire to come to the closest grips with the enemy than that there should be any signs of war weariness ? Is it not far better that thousands of people gathered in Trafalgar Square should demand the most vehement and audacious attacks than that there should be the weeping and wailing and peace agitations which in other lands and other wars have often hampered the action and vigour of Governments ?

That week, he went on, two islands had been in our minds : Malta, which had just beaten off yet another terrific air attack, and Madagascar.

So as to prevent Madagascar falling into enemy hands by some dishonourable and feeble drifting or connivance by Vichy, it had been found necessary to take certain precautions. More than two months had elapsed since the expedition had left these shores, and "while the troops were on the sea I must tell you I felt a shiver every time I saw the word 'Madagascar' in the newspapers. . . It was with considerable relief that I learned that the difficulties of our soldiers and their losses had not been aggravated, and that the operation had been swiftly and effectually carried out."

Drawing to his conclusion, the Premier remarked that the course of the war seemed to divide itself into four chapters. The first ended with the fall of France ; the second, Britain alone, with Hitler's attack on Russia ; the third he would call "The Russian Glory—may it long continue" ; the fourth opened at Pearl Harbour. In this latest chapter, "Universal War," we are confronted with many difficulties. But, asked Mr. Churchill, is there any thoughtful, sensible person who cannot see how vastly and decisively the awful balances have turned to advantage the cause of freedom ?

"Therefore tonight I give you a message of good cheer. You deserve it, and the facts endorse it. But be it good cheer or be it bad cheer will make no difference to us. We shall drive on to the end and do our duty, win or die. God helping us, we can do no other."   E. ROYSTON PIKE

In Madagascar We Forestalled the Japanese

Maj.-Gen. R. G. STURGES, Royal Marines, commanded troops which landed on Madagascar on May 5.

Rear-Adm. E. N. SYFRET, who was in charge of the Naval forces covering the landing on Madagascar.

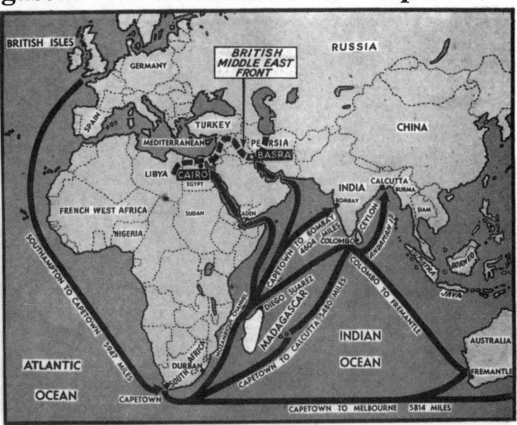

The vital strategic importance of the island of Madagascar is indicated in this map. Had a Japanese force gained possession of the island our lines of supply to Egypt, the Middle East, India, Ceylon and Australia, and the Allied forces holding the line from Tobruk to the Caspian, would have been gravely imperilled.

MADAGASCAR, the road to the south, beyond Fianarantsoa, main highway between the north and south of the island. Right, map of the northern end of Madagascar showing where the British forces landed on May 5. The naval base of Diégo Suarez surrendered 48 hours after the landing. Antsirana had already fallen.

Photos, Walter Stoneman, G.P.U., Paul Popper. Maps by courtesy of The Daily Mail

They 'Sweep' the Nazi Skies and Seaboards

DAYLIGHT SWEEPS in large numbers over Northern France have been an outstanding feature of R.A.F. activity with the coming of brighter days. Top, squadrons of Spitfires take the air for an offensive sweep. Circle, an American-built Boston III bomber, of the type which attacked the Matford works at Poissy in daylight. Right, a Spitfire of a fighter escort accompanying R.A.F. bombers begins to "peel off."

Photos, British Official ; P.N.A.

At Rostock the Nazis *Used* to Make Heinkels

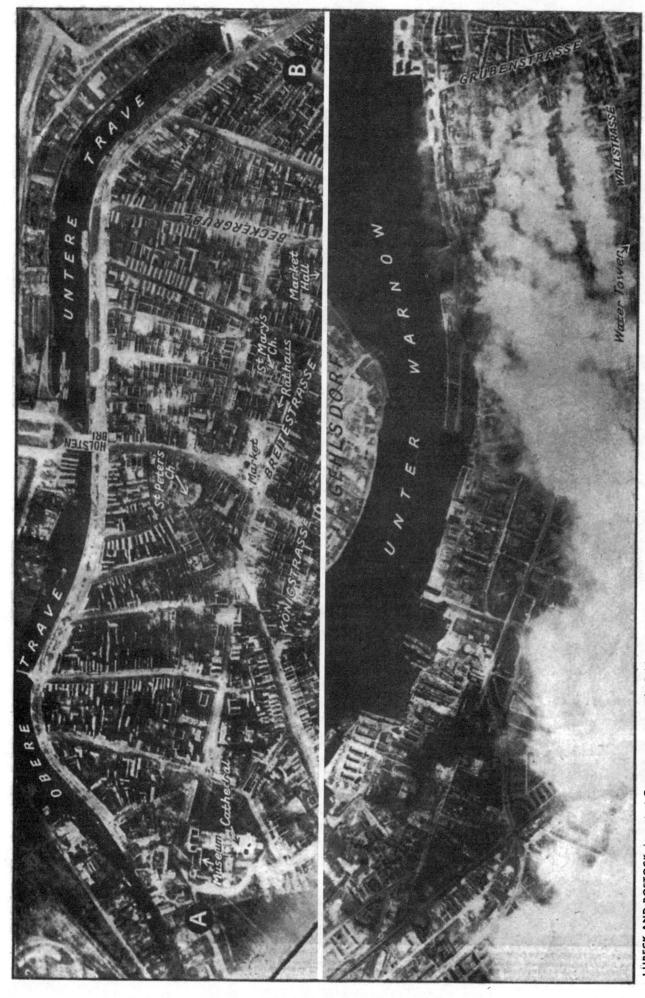

LÜBECK AND ROSTOCK, important German seaports on the Baltic, suffered extensive damage from recent raids by the R.A.F., as the photographs in this page testify. Top, Lübeck: a section of the centre of the city, showing an area of destroyed or damaged buildings stretching over 1,500 yards. Above, Rostock, the city centre and waterfront. A heavy pall of smoke still drifted across the city when this photograph was taken on April 26. An account of the bombing is given in the opposite page.

Photos, British Official

'Baedeker Raids' Are No Reply To Rostock!

The winter lull in aerial warfare was broken at the end of April when the R.A.F. gutted the port of Rostock on the Baltic, and in effect opened a second front on Germany. By way of answer the enemy threatened to destroy the cultural heritage of Britain, and assaulted cathedral cities of no military value, hoping by this species of blackmail to stop night bombing. But the R.A.F.'s hammer-blows at Hitler's war machine continued, and grew in number and weight.

THAT night—the night of April 23—Hitler received a terrific shock. The port of Rostock on the Baltic, a vital link in Germany's communications with Norway, Finland, and North Russia, was the target of the most furious air attack so far delivered in this war. The onslaught was repeated on the three following nights, the R.A.F. giving the enemy no respite until Rostock in a military sense ceased to exist. The Nazi A.R.P. services were taken completely by surprise, our bombs starting to fall before the sirens sounded.

The chief objective was the famous Heinkel aircraft factory. At least three heavy bombs fell on the largest assembly shed. The experimental assembly shop and technical school were also hit, and the railway supplying the works and drawing office were damaged. The big marshalling yards and electricity works suffered extensive damage, and soon became a heap of flaming ruins among which violent explosions occurred as ammunition vans destined for the war fronts caught fire.

The Neptune works were gutted and many ships under construction as well as vessels in the harbour were obliterated. Many of the principal streets of the city, the Luetzow Strasse, Alexander Strasse, St. George Platz are now unidentifiable heaps of debris. An infantry barracks is said to have received a direct hit and about 600 German soldiers were killed. The military damage to Rostock was proved by a remarkable series of detailed photographic records (see pages 709 and 710).

Rostock's Nights of Horror

A Swedish observer spoke of "nights of indescribable horror," when people, awakened by the falling bombs, rushed into the streets in their night clothing. Some 4,000 were killed, he said, and many hundreds more were missing. Rostock became a closed town. Nobody was allowed to visit the place, and nearly all the inhabitants were evacuated, the first "army" of refugees numbering 100,000, were taken to Berlin.

The next effort in these full scale raids was on Cologne. On the night April 27-28 whole sections engaged in war production were wiped out. On the same night, as well as on April 28-29, Trondheim experienced as never before the fury of the R.A.F.

Having blazed a trail round about the fjord the R.A.F. returned to their deadly work. According to eye-witnesses who watched this attack from the Strinda hills, about 100 machines came in from the North Sea at 11.30 p.m. on the second night, and, splitting into four groups, attacked German battleships in Aafjord, 24 miles north-east of Trondheim town, the Nyhavns U-boat base, which had occupied 5,000 Danish labourers about two years in its construction, coastal batteries and fortifications at Agdenaes defending the mouth of Trondheim fjord, and hangars and repair shops at Vearnes airfield, 18 miles north of Trondheim. Our men displayed great skill and courage, defying the heaviest flak and coming down to 500 feet to make sure of their aim. The pilot of one bomber which was hit and was fully ablaze is reported to have tried to crash his aircraft, bombs and all, on to the deck of the German cruiser Hipper. The sound of exploding bombs could be heard fifty miles away on the Swedish frontier. There was panic in Trondheim itself, and thousands rushed for safety into the woods.

On the same night an even larger force of R.A.F. bombers was hammering Kiel where the elusive Scharnhorst was reported to be undergoing repairs, and great fires testified to the efficacy of our missiles among shipyards and factories. A similar attack on Hamburg was also part of this great spring aerial offensive.

Rostock, Cologne, Trondheim, Kiel, Hamburg—there is no disguising the fact that all these places are integral parts of the mighty arsenal which is Nazi Germany. Their power to contribute to Hitler's war effort has been considerably reduced by those night raids at the end of April. This concentrated effort will bulk large in the history of Britain's fight for freedom. On those nights the world, including Germany, was at last convinced that we had won the mastery of the skies.

Needless to say the Nazis sent up a howl of rage. Conveniently ignoring what they had done to British cities when they had a superiority of weapons, our raids were "intolerable" and "inhuman." Their spokesmen tried to console the public by threats of reprisals with the object of destroying every symbol of culture in Great Britain. Castles, Tudor mansions, country houses, sanatoria—all these were listed for vengeance. Said one irate official : " Now the Luftwaffe will go out for every building marked with three stars in Baedeker," such marking indicating some beautiful and time-honoured relic of architectural value. (But in fact Baedeker hardly ever used three stars !). And so it happened that a limited number of Nazi airmen, became chosen " tourists " of insane destruction and death.

On the nights of April 23 five and of April 24 twenty raiders began their work on Exeter. The ancient cathedral city suffered much damage from high explosives and incendiaries on both occasions. On the two

Air Marshal A. T. HARRIS, C.B., O.B.E., A.F.C., Commander-in-Chief Bomber Command, is the man behind the smashing R.A.F. raids on Germany.   *Photo, Charles E. Brown*

following nights (April 25 and 26) Bath, famed for its grand old abbey and perfect 18th-century architecture, was attacked. Great damage was done to residential property, a large number of men, women, and children were killed and injured ; but the city, under the lead of the A.R.P., rose to the occasion. In the Pump Room, 3,000 hot meals were served to the homeless. Many inhabitants who had been sent to Bath as a comparatively safe centre were evacuated. There was, at least, one touch of humour in all this deliberate horror when 25 rheumatism patients went as usual through the flaming debris for their cure to the Royal Baths on Sunday morning.

Exeter was again the Nazis' target on the night of Sunday, May 3, and the next morning one of the pilots who was said to have taken part in the bombing, made a gloating broadcast to the German people.

The fiendish battle against beauty then switched to Norwich, city of unique memories in art and architecture. The place was dive-bombed and machine-gunned for over an hour on the night of April 27 ; many working-class streets were however, smashed and the casualties were heavy. The old Norfolk capital was again raided on April 29.

The fourth place in the Nazi bombers' Baedeker list was York. On April 28, profiting by the brilliance of the moon, the German raiders flew over the north-east coast and descending low released their bombs. They hit a building scheduled under the Ancient Monuments Act, and a large number of shops.

Striking a balance between our raids on German military centres and the enemy's onslaughts on Baedeker points, from April 23 to 29 inclusive the R.A.F. dropped on Germany alone over 1,300 tons of bombs, that is to say, as great a tonnage per night as the whole tonnage dropped by the enemy on the four British cities mentioned above. The Luftwaffe lost 17 bombers, and probably many more, out of about 150 sent over. The R.A.F. lost 40 during the same period.

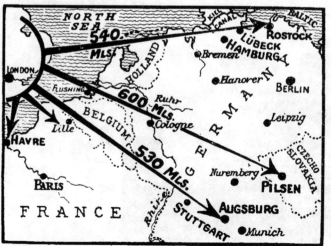

Map showing how deeply the growing British air offensive is penetrating into Germany and German-occupied Europe. Recent important objectives of the R.A.F. are shown.
Courtesy of The Daily Telegraph

They Were 'Starred' by Baedeker, So—

Flames arise from historic York as Nazi bombs fall on the city during the raid on the night of April 28. Five of the 20 raiders were destroyed.

Bath was another historic city recently raided by the Germans. Above, damage done to the Royal Theatre, the first to be built in Bath. Inset above right, the King and Queen talking to residents of the bombed city.

Norwich was the victim of other recent " Baedeker " raids by the Germans, and above is a photograph of damage in St. Stephen's Street. Right, a Union Jack still flutters over the ruins of working-class homes in bombed Exeter. In six nights of raids against England's historic cities, Germany lost at least 17 of a total of 150 raiding planes.

Photos, Associated Press, Keystone, Topical

Links of Steel Across the Libyan Desert

IN LIBYA feverish efforts are being made to speed up communications and augment the existing facilities. New Zealanders and the Indian Corps are beating all records in laying miles of track across the desert. Below, rails being placed on sleepers for a new track under construction. Above, tanks being taken to the base for refitting on one of the new desert railways.

Photos, British Official: Crown Copyright

Our Searchlight on the War

DROWNED IN RUSSIA

Spring floods, with rivers swollen many times their normal size, have held back the German offensive against Russia.

WE are nearing the first anniversary of Hitler's attack on Russia, and it is interesting to view the situation on the East front from a historical standpoint. Though the German onslaught on the Soviets was Hitler's greatest blunder, the truth is that the Fuehrer could not escape, nor did he wish to escape, the destiny which the whole Nazi philosophy created. He began war on Russia with words long ago. In "Mein Kampf" he remarks that "this colossal Empire in the East is ripe for dissolution. And the end of the Jewish domination in Russia will also be the end of Russia as a State. We are chosen by destiny to be the witnesses of a catastrophe which will afford the strongest confirmation of the nationalist theory of race."

The flower of the German army has already perished amid the vast Soviet prairies and round about the great cities of modern Russia. We may or may not see Stalin's hope—the overthrow of the Nazi military machine—this year, but when this does happen the warning words of Bismarck will come true. They are profoundly significant. "Germany, in the interests of her people, must always in every way injure Russia, but never enter into open conflict with her, as the most brilliant and decisive victories of the German armies in the East are bound to be 'drowned' in the endless expanses of Russia, and would, therefore, in the final result, afford no benefit to the German people."

HISTORY REPEATING ITSELF

Four weeks earlier than was expected all our offensive operations ended. Therefore a backward movement was necessary in a general line stretching from Taganrog to Ladoga.—*Hitler, April 26, 1942*

RUSSIA in this war has repeated her historic policy of withdrawal as in Napoleon's time, in 1915 and 1918, but today, thanks to a highly efficient industrial organization and a great popular enthusiasm for the war, she has been able to strike back at the Germans with ever-increasing strength.

In going contrary to Bismarck's cautious policy Hitler has literally dug the grave of the Third Reich, though the Nazis will put up a tremendous fight which will demand all the Allies' strength. We cannot expect the greatest butcher of all time to admit that he made a mistake in underestimating the power of the Russian people. In any case, the salient fact remains that Hitler was determined to wage war on the Soviets, for his intuitions lead him only to one conclusion—violence and yet more violence. Nor is it possible for such a creature to be appalled by the universal suffering and destruction he has caused. He may even yet think that he can win the war. · But the German people, after a year of indeterminate carnage on the East front, must be getting somewhat sceptical. They were completely misled by Hitler into the belief that the Nazi armies could do to the Soviets what they had done all too easily to France.

WHAT OF THE FUTURE?

It is the idealists, the faddists, the progressists, or whatever one may call them, who are reconstructing the world at the present time, and all intelligent people are doing their best to win the war.—*Dr. Headlam, Bishop of Gloucester.*

SOME people's contribution to the war effort is to talk about revolution, as if revolution in itself were the sovereign cure for everything. These worthies apparently fail to see that the war has changed and must continue to change the old-fashioned scheme of things. The kind of world that the extremists hope to create, however, would appear to have no connexion with the past. While improvements must be made, a completely new system of life, however foolproof it may appear in a blue-print, is not com-

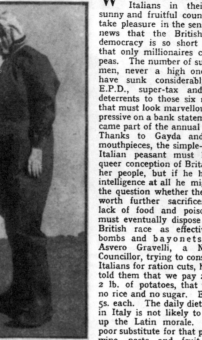
LIFE-SAVING SUIT issued to all sailors serving in the ships of Free Norway.
Photo, Royal Norwegian Government

patible with human nature or experience. The wise men among our reformers are well aware of this, and their objective is not to destroy the good inherent in our past, but to conserve and increase it for the benefit of the future.

THE DIET OF LIES

Only millionaires [in England] can afford peas, beer is poison, and butter is made entirely of lactic acid and mutton fat.—*Asvero Gravelli, on the Rome Radio.*

WE doubt if the benighted Italians in their once sunny and fruitful country can take pleasure in the sensational news that the British plutodemocracy is so short of food that only millionaires can buy peas. The number of such rich men, never a high one, must have sunk considerably since E.P.D., super-tax and other deterrents to those six noughts that must look marvellously impressive on a bank statement became part of the annual budget. Thanks to Gayda and other mouthpieces, the simple-minded Italian peasant must have a queer conception of Britain and her people, but if he has any intelligence at all he might ask the question whether the war is worth further sacrifices since lack of food and poison beer must eventually dispose of the British race as effectively as bombs and bayonets could. Asvero Gravelli, a National Councillor, trying to console the Italians for ration cuts, has also told them that we pay 20s. for 2 lb. of potatoes, that there is no rice and no sugar. Eggs are 5s. each. The daily diet of lies in Italy is not likely to bolster up the Latin morale. It is a poor substitute for that plentiful wine, pasta and fruit which made life so attractive in Italy before Mussolini hitched his wagon to Hitler's swastika with such disastrous results.

A CITIZEN ARMY

I am more convinced of the necessity of maintaining a citizen army in the future than ever I have been, as part of payment for the maintenance of good social service and conditions.—*Mr. Ernest Bevin, M.P.*

HISTORIANS will be puzzled by the fact that the greatest empire in the world managed to exist without some permanent form of conscription. During 1914-18 compulsory service was deferred until January 1916, and then it was applied at first only to single men between 18 and 41. There were subsequent amendments which made all men liable to serve up to 50. Compulsory service was ended on April 1, 1920. We were quicker off the mark in 1939. Even so, the idea of conscription seemed to be abhorrent to our Government until the Nazis struck. This, we feel certain, was not due to public opinion, but only to fear on the part of our legislators that compulsory service would be unpopular with the electors. The ideal of freedom also implies patriotic service in defence of that freedom, and a citizen army such as Lord Roberts advocated before 1914 and on the lines of the Home Guard should become a permanent factor in our national life. The voluntary system is too haphazard, and places us at a great disadvantage as opposed to an enemy or potential enemy with a conscript military organization.

A.A. GIRLS who helped to shoot down one of the German raiders destroyed in an attack on Bath. They are members of a "mixed" battery. *Photo, Keystone*

WARFARE—ANCIENT AND MODERN

The Battle of France will become the classic example of mechanical warfare. It was an event in military art no less significant than the introduction of gunpowder.

THE machine has completely revolutionized the art of war, but in a way not visualized before Hitler attacked the world. Far from turning men into unintelligent robots it has emphasized their individuality to a degree hitherto unknown in military science. The Nazis that overran France were comparatively small in number, but they knew how to use their machines to break down the resistance of their enemy still thinking in terms of trench (albeit concrete) warfare and slow-moving battalions. The Battle of Britain was won by a handful of men who conquered the daylight air singly or in small groups. The ardour and skill of the Soviet guerillas have proved an important factor in the campaign on the East front. The lightly armed and casually dressed Japanese, with their infiltration tactics, were successful in the capture of Malaya. The whole art of modern warfare may be summed up in swift mechanical mobility and agile minds, and the traditional barrack-square methods of training are as out of date as Waterloo and Balaclava. To be a good soldier today demands a high standard of intelligence, a comprehensive education, and an expert's knowledge of machinery and engineering.

SURFACE COAL is now being excavated to augment the country's fuel supplies. It has been estimated that upwards of 50 million tons of surface coal are available for tapping in this country. The photograph was taken at a Warwickshire seam. *Photo, Fox*

America's Dive-Bombers Scored in the Coral Sea

U.S. DIVE-BOMBERS, with one breaking away from the formation to attack. Early reports from the Pacific inferred that the great naval battle in the Coral Sea, fought from May 3 to May 9, was primarily one between the air forces of both sides. Telegraphing from an advanced Allied base, a correspondent described how one Japanese warship was destroyed by "waves of American dive-bombers." Thus the U.S.A. has quickly got into her stride in the naval-air war which will decide the fate of the Pacific.

Photo, Sport & General

No Oil for the Japanese at Yenangyaung!

WHEN, on April 16, it was found impossible to hold the Yenangyaung oilfields south of Mandalay the "scorched earth" policy was put into operation. "An awesome scene of tragic grandeur met the eye as the demolition reached its final stage," reported Reuter's Special Correspondent; "a huge pall of smoke blotted out the sun. The steel sides of the burning fuel tanks buckled and burst with the heat as their contents soared to the sky in a mass of flaming smoke, while hundreds of oil drums burst into flames with a curious hissing noise. Demolition parties, about thirty picked men, worked with a smooth efficiency. Tommies with sledge-hammers smashed material worth thousands of pounds. Gaunt derricks burning furiously stood silhouetted against the horizon, like some strange forest of another world."

Right, a British soldier smashing machinery at Yenangyaung; and, beneath, a night impression of the blazing oilfields.
British Official: Crown Copyright

In Burma the Chinese Fought Beside Us

A squadron leader of the Chinese Air Force giving last-minute instructions to Chinese aviators preparatory to an attack on advancing Japanese columns. On the left, Chinese infantry in a Burmese village purchasing supplies.

SOMEWHERE IN BURMA, Chinese soldiers resting under the concealing branches of a banyan tree. In the foreground is a Red Cross unit with its stretchers stacked. Our Oriental ally, collaborating with British forces in the neighbourhood of Mandalay, has inflicted heavy losses on the enemy, but so superior have been the Japanese in numbers and fire-power, the Chinese and British armies have been separated, and the Burma Road invaded.

Photos, Picture Press, British Newsreels

Not Bravery Alone Could Save Burma

Owing to the impossibility of any civil administration continuing to function in Burma, the Governor, Sir Reginald Dorman-Smith, was ordered by the British Government (it was announced on May 10) to move into India. Resistance in Burma still continued, but the campaign was virtually concluded : Burma had to be temporarily "written off."

FROM the beginning one of the chief objectives—perhaps the chief objective—of the Japanese in Burma was to cut the Burma Road and so sever Free China's principal life-line. And in this at the end of April they were successful. Strongly reinforced Japanese columns swept across the difficult country which lies between the Irrawaddy and the Salween. The Chinese forces put up a strong resistance, but they were heavily outnumbered, and their mechanized equipment was as nothing compared with the tanks, armoured cars and planes with which the Japanese were so well supplied. On April 29 a Japanese mechanized column, numbering (so it was reported) 400 armoured fighting and motor transport vehicles, stormed into Lashio—the Burmese terminus of the Burma Road into China—which had been already converted into a blazing ruin by Japanese bombs and gunfire.

Following their capture of Lashio, the Japanese pushed rapidly ahead along the Yunnan road. Some pursued the Chinese lying in the Irrawaddy valley to the south, more particularly around Yenangyaung. Such an act of destruction must be unexampled in the history of the British Empire ; for months past experts had been perfecting the plans which resulted in the wells being "spiked" for an indefinite period, so that they could be reopened only by fresh boring, requiring elaborate machinery and skilled technicians (see page 716).

By the middle of May, then, the campaign in Burma was practically finished. Fighting continued here and there in the long and jagged front carved out of the tropical jungle, but the word front is hardly admissible, since the Chinese forces under the American General Stilwell were cut off from General Alexander's British and Indians. The Japanese, too, were operating in widely-separated columns : a course which had its dangers, as was seen when the Chinese delivered a sudden counter-stroke at Mandalay, taking in the rear those Japanese who were plunging ahead through Lashio.

Meanwhile, a considerable number of refugees, including a big proportion of British, were being evacuated by air from Myitkyina and from secret bases in the jungle. The planes employed, reported the Daily Mail special correspondent, were seven ancient bullet-holed air-liners, flown by weary American and Chinese pilots. But they carried more than 10,000 refugees from Burma to the comparative safety of India—including several scores of babies, many women, Government officials, and nearly 2,000 wounded soldiers who had been collected at a hospital in Myitkyina. Though often attacked, the planes never missed a day ; each carried 56 passengers and several trips were made in a day.

Burma was as good as lost. The Chinese and the British armies were separated. Worse still, Free China's supply-line was cut. Why did these things happen ?

According to Philip Jordan, the campaign was lost not in Burma but thousands of miles away in London and Canberra.

"What first General Hutton and his men, and later General Alexander, achieved in Burma has been miraculous, and if only London had not let them down, they would have been sitting in Rangoon at this moment. More than once extra divisions were promised and then diverted ; on one occasion when almost in sight of Rangoon, on another without anyone informing Burma that a change of destination had been made. Practically unsupported from the air, British troops fought against huge numbers without rest ; and even if their tails are not right up at this moment, they are fighting the battle with bravery that must for ever rank the K.O.Y.L.I. among the greatest regiments in our history. But the battle has been too uneven . . ."

Victor Thompson, the Daily Herald's correspondent, was more explicit still.

"All parts of our war machine in Burma," he said, "have not equalled the valour of our fighting men," and he proceeded to give eight other reasons than weight of

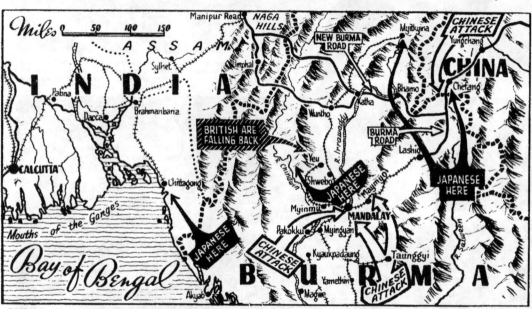

BURMA, showing the principal points of the confused fighting, the Chinese attacking the Japanese from the north and south, the British withdrawing up the valley of the Chindwin. There is no actual front in this amazing campaign among mountainous jungles hardly trodden by the foot of man. *By courtesy of the News Chronicle*

along the Burma Road and were soon on the Chinese frontier, even beyond it ; another column moved rapidly against Bhamo and Myitkyina, terminus of the railway from Mandalay, which was entered by the Japanese on May 8, while yet another force of Japanese troops seized Hsipaw, on the railway which links Lashio with Mandalay. Farther west, a column had moved up the Irrawaddy valley, and so strong was it that the evacuation of the Burmese capital was soon imperative.

On April 28 the British began to fall back from their covering positions 50 miles south of Mandalay ; crossing the Irrawaddy, they took up fresh positions on the River Chindwin, 50 miles to the west, where they were soon once again heavily in action. On the morning of May 1 the last of the Chinese troops in Mandalay withdrew to the north, and the Japanese entered the city. It had been burnt to the ground, said a correspondent of the Japanese Domei agency, and smouldering ruins appeared to spread for miles and miles. "No one—not even a dog —could be seen in the streets."

Before Mandalay fell the Imperial forces in Burma had "scorched" the oil-fields

Of the Allies, the Chinese were perhaps in the better case, since in their retreat every step brought them nearer to the fastnesses of their own country. The British, on the other hand, were struggling through some of the most difficult country in the world, the mountainous jungle which lies between Central Burma and the Indian province of Assam. Writing from somewhere on the Indian border, Philip Jordan, special correspondent of the News Chronicle, described this jungle—a region of great hills and valleys, through which no man has walked before, a region where live "Naga head-hunters, leeches, fever, cholera, great snakes and scores of millions of mosquitoes that carry malaria. And here at the moment live hundreds of men, European, Indian, Anglo-Indian, all struggling northwards towards this little village." Thousands of refugees were streaming along what was described as a road—although much of it is not road at all, but a track cut across the mountains. At one place it is only four yards wide, with a sheer drop of 700 feet on each side ; and at other places, now that the rains of the monsoon have come, "men must wade and fight through sucking mud if they would pass."

opposition for our lack of success, viz., our inability to establish air supremacy and later to provide any air support whatever ; the jungle of Red Tape, which is still slowing down civil government ; lack of co-ordination between all branches of the war effort ; the mystifying faith we seemed to have placed on the loyalty to Britain of the inhabitants of South Burma ; the breakdown, after the war started, frankly admitted by our military leaders, of the British intelligence system ; the difficulty of reinforcement and supply in the absence of good ports and roads into Burma ; the fact that our troops are untrained for jungle warfare ; and, finally, the refugee problem. With more than one million people on the move there have had to be diversions of supplies, dislocation of communications, and shortage of workers in essential jobs.

So Burma has a message, concludes Mr. Thompson. "To you at home, and to all the peoples of all the United Nations. It is : work till you drop to supply modern arms, sort out inefficiency and peacetime procrastination, insist on ruthless and crafty leadership, see that never again are we faced with battles for which we are ill-prepared. We owe that and more to the men who have died in the torrid jungle, and the men I have seen maimed but still of firm spirit in hospital wards behind the line."

New Life Among the Ruins

Amid the fire-gutted ruins of the much-bombed church of St. Giles, Cripplegate, burial place
of the poet Milton, the Rev. H. B. Brewer christens Janice King, granddaughter of Mr. Albert
King, who for 43 years has been verger of the church. The baby is the fourth generation
of the family to be christened in St. Giles. Her father (in uniform) is a R.A. sergeant.

Hitler's Bombers Have Done Their Worst

Photo

1. Washing must be done, bombs or no bombs. The London housewife hangs out her linen close by a scene of havoc wrought by the Luftwaffe. 2. Boys of a London suburb find a water-filled crater makes an attractive boating pool for youthful adventurers. 3. The Lord Mayor's show, martial in character, passes down a blitzed street in the City

Times,
Mirror

But London Is Still Gay and Gallant

4. War or no war, London elects its Queen of the May, whose finery contrasts oddly with the war-scarred background. 5. Among the ruins of the church of St. Andrew-by-the-Wardrobe, the induction of a new rector, the Rev. V. G. Morton, takes place. 6. Amid the ugly ruins of demolished houses these London boys have rigged up an improvized swing.

The Fire Bombs Are Answered

Photos, Planet News, Keystone

Top, Emergency Water Supplies in tanks formed in the basements of wrecked buildings at the corner of Farringdon Street and Charterhouse Street in the City of London. Above, one of Coventry's main streets showing the newly-erected one-storey shops which have enabled the city's life and trade to continue in spite of all that Hitler could do.

Britain's High Command: How the War Is Planned

Following much discussion in Parliament and Press concerning the strategy of the war, crystallized in the suggestion that a Combined General Staff should be set up, the Prime Minister presented to Parliament a White Paper (Cmd. 6351, H.M.S.O., 1d.) whose contents are summarized below, together with some account of alternative proposals put forward by the critics.

NORWAY, Flanders, Greece, Crete, Malaya, Singapore, Bay of Bengal, Burma—together they constitute a chain of disasters such as we have never suffered in our long history as a Great Power. Why did they happen? Are they to be attributed, at least in some measure, to defects in our strategical direction? Is our High Command all that it should be—or could be? In particular, is it true that there has been, and is, lack of co-ordination between the three fighting services?

There are many who think so, and among them are men who have had long and wide experience of the direction of great affairs. To mention but one, here is Sir Edward Grigg, M.P., a former Under-Secretary to the War Office, writing in The Times (April 11) complaining that " once again at Singapore the action of the three services was clearly not combined in a single defensive plan." The two older services, he went on, were once again ordered into action without the indispensable cooperation of the third. For this the fault lay, neither with the Naval, nor the General, nor the Air Staff, but " in the system under which their respective lines of action are combined (or not combined) in a common plan." How does that system work at present? We find the Staff organization outlined in a White Paper, " The Organization for Joint Planning " which was published on April 22.

The ultimate responsibility for the conduct of the war (says the White Paper) rests with the War Cabinet, the Chiefs of Staff being their professional advisers. The Prime Minister and Minister of Defence superintends, on behalf of the War Cabinet, the work of the Chiefs of Staff Committee. In this matter he is assisted by the Defence Committee, which comprises, besides Mr. Churchill as chairman, Mr. Attlee, Mr. Eden, Mr. Lyttelton, the three Service Ministers (Sir James Grigg, Mr. A. V. Alexander, and Sir A. Sinclair), the Chiefs of Staff, and the Chief of Combined Operations.

The position of the three Chiefs of Staff, working together as a Combined, or Joint General Staff, is no new conception, the White Paper goes on. In fact, the Joint Staff advocated from time to time in Parliament and the Press has existed for many years. It has been progressively reorganized and expanded in the light of war experience. It consists of specially selected officers of the three services, who live and work together in the same offices. Thus they learn to think and act in terms, not of three separate units assisting one another for a common end, but of a single fighting unit animated by the same spirit and the same conception of a single task. At their service for information and advice are the three Departmental Staffs of the Navy, Army and Air Force. The organization of this staff is shown in the diagram on the right.

The Joint Planning Staff is, it will be seen, under the direction of three Directors of Plans. These officers divide their time between their own Ministries (Admiralty, War Office and Air Ministry) and the Joint Planning Centre. Each of the planning sections shown in the diagram consists of specially selected officers who work as a team in every sense of the word. They share not only the same tasks but the same office. They not only mess together, but sleep in the same building. They are available for consultation at any hour of the day or night.

As regards the duties of the various sections: broadly stated, the Strategical Planning Section keeps the general situation under constant review, and prepares appreciations of the situation from time to time with recommendations as to the action that we should adopt; the Executive Planning Section is charged with concerting ways and means of putting into effect plans which have been approved; while the Future Operational Planning Section concentrates on the preparation of future plans, even though these may not be immediately within the range of practical politics.

The officers forming the Joint Intelligence Sub-Committee similarly work together, part-time in their own Ministries and part-time as a team; it is their responsibility to collate and assess all information about the enemy, and, in particular, to prepare appreciations of the most likely course of enemy action from time to time.

In addition to the organization shown in the diagram there is the Secretariat of the War Cabinet and its Committees, Military and Civil; its military members constitute the Staff of the Office of the Minister of Defence (Mr. Churchill), and it is their duty to arrange the business, draft the reports, and maintain the records of the military committees of the War Cabinet from the Defence Committee downwards.

This, then, is the directing brain of Britain's military effort, using the word " military " in the widest sense. The organization at the lower levels is hardly criticized; what most of the critics concentrate upon is the lack at the top of a real Combined General Staff with a Chief of its own. To return to Sir Edward Grigg's argument, there should be a Chief of the Combined General Staff responsible for presenting its plans to the Chiefs of Staff Committee, sifting them with that Committee, and thereafter submitting them to the War Cabinet; for seeing that our strategic plans took full account of what the production staff and transport authorities might be expected to achieve; and, above all, that the proper balance between the Services was maintained. As to the C.C.G.S. himself, he should be " a professional or non-Ministerial middle-man."

These suggestions and the White Paper itself provided the House of Lords with a congenial subject for a debate on May 5. Lord Denman and Viscount Swinton, Viscount Trenchard and Lord Milne, Lord Chatfield and Admiral the Earl of Cork joined in supporting the broad principle of a Combined General Staff with its own head; but perhaps the speech which carried most weight was that by Lord Hankey, who for so many years was Secretary of the Cabinet and the Committee of the Imperial Defence. In some ways, he declared, the machinery was a great advance on anything in the last war, but that could not be said of the higher (Ministerial) stage. The increase in the size of the Joint Planning Staff provided a strong additional argument in favour of a Chief of a Joint General Staff to preside over the Chiefs of Staff Committee, to take charge of the whole organization, drive it along, and see that it was functioning properly. Our national habit of self-depreciation, he went on, had led some people to think that the Germans were ahead of us in this matter of the Supreme Control. But he did not believe that was the case, the Germans had made " most frightful mistakes."

Replying to the debate the Lord Chancellor (Lord Simon) expressed the view that to reproduce the Great General Staff of Germany in this country would involve fundamental changes altogether out of the question. But on the subject of the appointment of a Chairman of the Chiefs of Staff Committee he did not actually bang the door.

COMPOSITION OF THE JOINT STAFF

CHIEFS OF STAFF COMMITTEE (1)
and
VICE-CHIEFS OF STAFF COMMITTEE (2)

Joint Planning Staff
(Three Directors of Plans—
Captain, R.N.
Brigadier
Air Commodore)

Strategical Planning Section
R.N.—
1 Captain
2 Commanders

Army—
1 Lt.-Colonel
2 Majors

R.A.F.—
1 Group Captain
2 Wing Commanders

Foreign Office—
1 Counsellor

Executive Planning Section
R.N.—
1 Captain
3 Commanders

Army—
1 Lt.-Colonel
3 Majors
1 Captain

R.A.F.—
1 Wing Commander
1 Sqdr. Leader

Future Operational Planning Section
Director—Colonel
R.N.—
1 Captain
2 Commanders

Army—
1 Lt.-Colonel
1 Major

R.A.F.—
1 Group Captain
1 Wing Commander

Liaison Officers from :—
Ministry of War Transport
Ministry of Economic Warfare
Political Welfare Executive
Ministry of Home Security
and from
other Government Departments when necessary.

Joint Intelligence Sub-Committee
Foreign Office—Counsellor (Chairman)
Three Directors of Intelligence—
Rear-Admiral
Major-General
Air Vice-Marshal
Ministry of Economic Warfare—
Deputy Director-General

Joint Intelligence Staff
(Enemy intentions)
R.N.—
1 Captain
2 Commanders

Army—
1 Lt.-Colonel
1 Major

R.A.F.—
1 Wing Commander
1 Sqdr. Leader
Foreign Office—
1 First Secretary
Ministry of Economic Warfare—
1 Assist. Secretary
1 Principal

Inter-Services Security Board
1 Representative of grade of Lt.-Colonel from each Service

Intelligence Section (Operations)
(Provision of Intelligence to Commanders and Planners about areas which may become the scene of operations)

1 Representative of grade of Major from each Service and Ministry of Economic Warfare

NOTES

(1) COMPOSITION OF CHIEFS OF STAFF COMMITTEE
Chairman :—General Sir Alan Brooke (Chief of the Imperial General Staff).
Members :—Admiral of the Fleet Sir Dudley Pound (First Sea Lord and Chief of Naval Staff).
Air Chief Marshal Sir Charles Portal (Chief of the Air Staff).
Major-General Sir Hastings Ismay (representing the Minister of Defence and directing the Defence Secretariat).
Vice-Admiral Lord Louis Mountbatten (Chief of Combined Operations)—present when major strategical issues or specific combined operations are under discussion.

(2) THE VICE-CHIEFS OF STAFF.
In order to ease the burden of the dual task which devolves on the Chiefs of Staffs of advising H.M. Government on defence policy as a whole, and at the same time directing the work of their own individual Services, each Chief of Staff has a Vice-Chief of Staff as his *alter ego*. The Vice-Chiefs of Staff hold regular meetings at which they deal, in the name of the Chiefs of Staff Committee, with such matters as are delegated to them.
Members :—
Vice-Admiral H. R. Moore (Vice-Chief of the Naval Staff).
Lieut.-General A. E. Nye (Vice-Chief of the Imperial General Staff).
Air Chief Marshal Sir Wilfrid Freeman (Vice-Chief of the Air Staff).
The chairmanship varies according to the nature of the business.

Russia: The Winter War in Retrospect

For the first time since 1918 May Day this year was for the Russians not a public holiday,
a joyous celebration of the achievements of the Revolution, but a day of work, devoted to the
production of yet more weapons to defeat the next German onslaught.

MAY is here. Outside Leningrad the ice is melting fast. From the White Sea to the Black the snows are disappearing before the first genial winds of spring. The rivers are overflowing their banks. Everywhere in the war-blasted countryside trees are in leaf, the flowers are springing in colourful plenty from the so recently frozen earth. There is yet another significant sign of spring's coming to Russia : the Red Army men are changing their felt footgear for leather boots. As yet the snow is turning into slush, the roads are seas of mud ; but soon the ground will become dry and hard, and across it millions of men and all the monstrous machinery of modern war will pass and re-pass in a struggle that may well decide the fate of the world for centuries to come.

What has been happening on the Russian front since the Nazis' furious drive against Moscow was brought to a standstill last December ? It is difficult to form a clear picture, but certain it is that there has been no real lull in the fighting. Hitler and his generals may well have hoped, even expected, that the winter would immobilize the armies and so their troops might be given time and opportunity to recuperate after their terrific exertions of the past few months. But although the winter was inconceivably severe —according to Hitler it was worse even than that which broke Napoleon in 1812— the Russians saw to it that the war went on. Instead of being able to retire to comparatively comfortable winter quarters far behind the line, a great host of Nazis had perforce to remain in the fighting zone. Tanks which should have been withdrawn for overhaul have had to be kept in service ; huge quantities of hoarded war supplies have had to be expended ; lines of communication have had to be kept open. And all the time there has been a steady drain on German man-power.

All the same, it must be admitted that the Germans have done extraordinarily well in an immensely difficult situation. There have been stories of desertions, but for the most part the Nazis have responded to every call that has been made upon them.

The Germans have given much ground, perhaps as much voluntarily as involuntarily, but always they have maintained a continuous front. They are quite a long way now from Moscow, which was once almost within range of their big guns ; winter made them relax their hold on Leningrad, so that across the ice of Lake Ilmen the Russians

have been able to bring reinforcements and supplies and to evacuate two million civilians ; at Rostov in December they suffered what was their first real defeat. But Schlüsselburg and Taganrog at the two extremities of the 1,000-mile front have remained in German hands ; and so, too, have Smolensk, Kharkov and Kiev, most of the Ukraine and the Crimea. At Staraya Russa, south of Lake Ilmen, a large German force has been surrounded, or almost surrounded, for many weeks ; and here and there on the immensely long front there are '' hedgehogs '' in which little German garrisons are set in a sea of Russians ; but, on the other hand, the "sack" at Vyazma on the road from Smolensk to Moscow has not yet been drawn tight. Many of the '' hedgehogs '' or fortified positions have been reduced by the Russians, many thousands of villages have been liberated by the Red Army ; but some of the most fertile, the most thickly peopled and the most industrially developed regions of the Soviet Union remain under the Nazi heel. Hundreds of Russian factories are producing supplies for Hitler's armies ; hundreds of thousands of Russian workers have been compulsorily enlisted in Hitler's droves of slaves. German bridge-heads are firmly placed at all the vital junctions on the far-flung front, and the Nazi armies are dangerously near the Caucasus.

Soviet's Immense Achievement

Yes, the Germans have done well ; but is it too much to claim that the Russians have done better ? Judged by any standard, having regard to any particular, the Soviet's achievement is immense.

As recently as a year ago most of the '' experts '' seemed to be of the opinion that Stalin's army was no match for Hitler's. They professed to find in the opening phase of the Finnish campaign confirmation of their worst suspicions. Red Russia, they urged, was finding great difficulty in worsting little Finland ; how then could she stand against the might of Nazi Germany, a country and people whose every thought and action had long been of war ? Apparently Hitler and his experts thought the same as ours : otherwise they would surely have preferred to keep the Soviets as friends, even half-hearted friends. Russian equipment (it was alleged) was of poor quality and deficient in quantity ; Russian leadership was uninspired, and the Russian soldier was but a dumb brute, unenthusiastic about a war which he did not, and could not, understand ; the peasants were disaffected, the industrial workers were so much factory-fodder, and there were many suppressed nationalities waiting their chance to revolt.

Came June 22, 1941, and a few days, even a few hours, were sufficient to sweep this conglomeration of ignorance, prejudice and misunderstanding on to the scrap heap. The Russian giant, it was revealed, had no feet of clay. On the battlefield a new Russian

manifested itself, one which was at once hailed by Mr. Churchill as a comrade in arms.

Since that June day the Red Army and the Red workers behind the front have made mincemeat of the gloomy prognostications of those who thought that the Finnish campaign was a fair test of capacity in the making of modern war. True, the Russians have been forced to cede vast territories, have suffered enormous losses both in men and material ; but it is just because they have suffered and survived such tremendous hammer-blows that men retain their confidence that Stalin's Russia will weather any fresh storm that may sweep towards Moscow or Baku from the plains of Germany.

Not that Germany is beaten—yet ; far from it. In readiness for the spring offensive Hitler has assembled an enormous host and all his vassal states have been forced to contribute their quota. All through the winter the factories and workshops of the continent have been working at the highest pressure to produce guns, tanks, planes, shells, bombs, equipment of every kind. At any moment now that vast host may plunge forward in a last desperate bid for victory. But not quite a year ago another German army made that venture—and it was a better army, one better equipped and of a higher morale. The cream of Hitler's best divisions are no longer there ; their bodies are peacefully dissolving into the Russian soil, or they lie in the hospital wards, or, maimed and mutilated in body or mind, they have been relegated to the ranks of the Fuehrer's industrial serfs. Of that great host standing to arms at this very moment on the Eastern Front, there is not a man for whom the future is not clouded over by the memory of a winter filled with horrors such as only dreams should be made of.

Stalin's army has been changed, too. Its losses have been enormous, its sufferings cruel. But—he himself declared on May 1— '' the Red Army has become stronger and better organized, its officer corps have been steeled in battle, its generals have gained in experience and are more far-sighted. As for the rank and file, they have become more bitter and more ruthless.''

Even more important, they have come to realize that the invincibility of the German Army is just a myth, a myth and nothing more. The Red Army has taken the measure of the Nazis ; it believes that it can beat them, and, believing that, it probably will. E. R. P.

LIBERATED FROM THE NAZIS! Aragashi, a Russian village from which the former German occupants have been driven out by the Red Army, greets its liberators. Many moving scenes like that depicted above have been enacted in the hundreds of inhabited localities freed by the Soviet forces during their winter advance. But in many of the villages few of the inhabitants are left to witness the return of their victorious soldiers.

Photo. Planet News

Into Action Go Men of the Black Sea Fleet

IN THE CRIMEA Russian Marines are being landed from submarines of the Soviet Black Sea Fleet to attack the enemy in the rear. On May 8 the Nazis launched a fierce attack against the Russians in the Kerch Peninsula.

Left, a column of water rises as a Soviet submarine-chaser drops a depth charge at a lurking enemy submarine. Above, men of the Red Navy cleaning their gun after an engagement. *Photos, Ministry of Information, Planet News* **Page 743**

Our Diary of the War

APRIL 29, 1942, Wednesday 970th day

Air.—Night raids by R.A.F. on Gnome-Rhone aero-engine factory and Goodrich rubber works at Gennevilliers, near Paris.

Mediterranean.—Two enemy aircraft shot down in small daylight attack on Malta.

Burma.—Chungking announced that Japanese have occupied Lashio.

Philippines.—Japanese announce new landings in Mindanao.

Australasia.—Port Moresby raided by Japanese ; Lae and Kupang bombed by Allies.

Home.—Second " reprisal " raid on Norwich.

General.—Hitler and Mussolini meet at Salzburg.

APRIL 30, Thursday 971st day

Sea.—Germans began four-day attack on convoys in Arctic ; cruiser Edinburgh damaged by torpedo.

Air.—Large-scale fighter sweeps over N. France. Le Havre, Flushing, Abbeville, and shipping off Brittany attacked.

Russian Front.—Germans announced Russian attacks on Kerch Peninsula and on central front.

Africa.—Announced from Cairo that Suez Canal and Damietta areas were raided.

Mediterranean.—Five enemy aircraft shot down during daylight raids on Malta.

Philippines.—Heavy bombing of fort and harbour area of Corregidor.

Australasia.—Heavy Allied raid on Lae aerodrome, New Guinea.

Home.—Admiral H. R. Stark, Commander of U.S. naval forces in European waters, arrived in England.

In scattered raids on N.E. coast 11 enemy aircraft destroyed out of 50.

General.—Hitler and Mussolini continued talks at Salzburg.

MAY 1, Friday 972nd day

Air.—R.A.F. fighter sweeps over N. France ; St. Omer and Calais bombed.

Mediterranean.—R.A.F. raided Menidi (north of Athens), Maritza in Rhodes and submarine base at Leros.

Burma.—Japanese entered Mandalay. British withdrew to north of Irrawaddy.

Philippines.—Continued artillery attacks on Corregidor.

Australasia.—Port Moresby raided by Japanese fighters ; allied air activity over Rabaul.

Home.—Minor air raids over S.W. England.

MAY 2, Saturday 973rd day

Sea.—Arctic convoy attacks continue ; cruiser Edinburgh again torpedoed, sunk by our own forces ; one enemy destroyer sunk, another damaged.

Air.—R.A.F. attacked shipping off Norwegian coast on night May 1-2.

Africa.—American service troops officially announced in Middle East.

Burma.—Japanese advance N. of Lashio.

Australasia.—Allies attacked shipping at Rabaul. Four out of 15 Japanese fighters destroyed over Port Moresby.

Home.—Dr. H. Evatt, Australian Minister for External Affairs, arrived in England.

MAY 3, Sunday 974th day

Sea.—Admiralty and Air Ministry announced that damaged Gneisenau sighted at Gdynia.

Air.—In daylight sweeps over N. France Dunkirk and Abbeville attacked. Night raids on Hamburg, St. Nazaire, Kristiansand and shipping off Norway.

Africa.—R.A.F. raided Benghazi harbour ; enemy planes over Alexandria.

Burma.—A.V.G. and Chinese bombed Lashio. U.S. Air Corps bombed Rangoon at night. Japs claimed to have occupied Bhamo.

Philippines.—Heavier artillery and bombing attacks on Corregidor.

Australasia.—Four Jap aircraft shot down over Port Moresby.

Home.—Heavy night raid on Exeter ; seven enemy aircraft shot down.

MAY 4, Monday 975th day

Air.—R.A.F. bombers attacked Le Havre and enemy convoys off Dutch Coast. Night raids on Stuttgart, Skoda works at Pilsen, and Nantes docks.

Russian Front.—Russians report offensive battles in some sectors ; Germans report large-scale air battles on Kerch Peninsula.

Burma.—Japs attack Paoshan on Burma Road. U.S. bombers attacked Mingaladon aerodrome, Rangoon.

Philippines.—Heavy air and artillery attacks on Corregidor ; further Jap landings in Mindanao.

Australasia.—Naval engagement between U.S. and Japs, resulting in sinking of 8 Jap warships and damage to others.

General.—R.A.A.F. airmen stated to be operating in Iceland. Germans announce shooting of 72 Dutchmen for pro-British activities.

Home.—Sharp raid on two S.E. coast towns.

MAY 5, Tuesday 976th day

Air.—Zeebrugge bombed. Stuttgart and Nantes raided for second night in succession.

Indian Ocean.—British troops land in Madagascar and advance on Diégo Suarez naval base.

Burma.—Japs advancing across Chinese frontier up Burma Road.

Philippines.—Japanese made landing on Corregidor at midnight.

Home.—S.E. coastal district raided.

General.—Forty French hostages shot for blowing-up of munitions train near Cherbourg.

MAY 6, Wednesday 977th day

Sea.—Admiralty announced loss of H.M.S. Jaguar (destroyer).

Air.—In sweeps over N. France, Calais, Boulogne and power-station at Caen were attacked. Stuttgart and Nantes raided for third night in succession.

ADMIRAL H. R. STARK, who is in command of the United States naval forces in European waters, being greeted on his arrival in this country by the First Sea Lord, Admiral of the Fleet Sir Dudley Pound (right). On the left is Mr. Winant, the U.S. Ambassador to Britain. *Photo, Keystone*

Africa.—R.A.F. raid Benghazi harbour.

Indian Ocean.—Antsirana, chief town in harbour of Diégo Suarez, Madagascar, captured on night of May 6-7.

Burma.—U.S. bombers attacked Rangoon aerodrome. Chinese occupied Maymyo.

Philippines.—Corregidor falls to Japs after five months' siege.

Australasia.—Allied air attacks on Lae and Rabaul.

Home.—S.E. and S.W. coastal towns attacked by few enemy aircraft.

MAY 7, Thursday 978th day

Air.—R.A.F. bomb Ostend and Zeebrugge. Night attack on enemy convoy off Dutch coast.

Mediterranean.—Seven enemy aircraft shot down over Malta.

MAY 8, Friday 979th day

Air.—Heavy raid by R.A.F. on Warnemünde, near Rostock, in face of intense opposition. Airfields in the Low Countries and N. France and shipping off Norway also attacked.

Russian Front.—Germans open offensive on the Kerch Peninsula.

Africa.—Benghazi raided by R.A.F.

Mediterranean.—Sixteen enemy aircraft destroyed or damaged over Malta.

Indian Ocean.—Japanese bombed and machine-gunned Chittagong area of Bay of Bengal.

Burma.—Japs enter Myitkyina. Announced from Delhi that Japs have occupied Akyab.

Australasia.—Washington and Australia stated that in Coral Sea battle, in progress since May 3, Jap losses believed to be one aircraft-carrier, one heavy cruiser, one light cruiser, two destroyers, four gunboats and two transports or cargo vessels sunk, and damage to another aircraft-carrier, one heavy cruiser, one light cruiser, one seaplane tender and two transports or cargo vessels.

Home.—Night raid on Norwich.

General.—German naval commandant orders night closing of Bergen waters as from May 15.

MAY 9, Saturday 980th day

Sea.—Admiralty announce loss of H.M. trawler Solomon. Stated from Washington that Axis submarines have sunk two merchant ships in Gulf of Mexico.

Air.—In offensive sweeps over N.

France, Hazebrouck and Bruges were attacked.

Africa.—R.A.F. made day and night attacks on Benghazi harbour.

Mediterranean.—Raids on Malta resulted in 30 enemy aircraft being destroyed or damaged.

Indian Ocean.—Japs again raided Chittagong.

Burma.—Further withdrawal of British forces in central Burma. R.A.F. raid occupied aerodrome of Magwe.

Philippines.—Japs report their fleet in Manila Bay.

Australasia.—Of 16 Jap aircraft attacking Port Moresby, three were destroyed.

MAY 10, Sunday 981st day

Sea.—Two cargo ships torpedoed in St. Lawrence River, Canada.

Africa.—Enemy raid on Alexandria resulted in some casualties. R.A.F. fighters in action over Cyrenaica.

Mediterranean.—Sixty-three enemy aircraft damaged or destroyed over Malta.

Indian Ocean.—Japs raided town in Assam, causing some damage and casualties.

Burma.—Announced that Sir R. Dorman-Smith, Governor of Burma, has moved to India.

Australasia.—Allied H.Q. in Australia announce that naval and air battle in Coral Sea has temporarily ceased.

Home.—S.E. coastal town bombed. Sir William Dobbie arrived in London from Malta.

General.—Admiral John Hoover sent by President Roosevelt to negotiate agreement with French commander at Martinique.

Washington confirmed that U.S. bombers raided Tokyo on April 18.

MAY 11, Monday 982nd day

Air.—R.A.F. attacked aerodrome at St. Valery-en-Caux and fired gasholder at Cayeaux ; Coastal Command attacked shipping off Frisian Is.

Russian Front.—Russians report stubborn fighting on Kerch Peninsula.

Mediterranean.—Seventeen enemy aircraft destroyed or damaged over Malta.

Australasia.—U.S. stated that their submarines in the Far East had sunk a Jap destroyer and two cargo ships. Allied bombers attacked seaplane base in Louisiade Archipelago and shipping off Solomon Is. Japs raided Port Moresby.

General.—Pylons of Radio Paris long-wave wireless station reported dynamited.

MAY 12, Tuesday 983rd day

Sea.—Admiralty announced loss of destroyers Lively, Jackal and Kipling in Eastern Mediterranean.

Russian Front.—Stubborn fighting continued on Kerch Peninsula.

Africa.—R.A.F. fighters shot down 13 Junkers 52s off N. African coast.

Mediterranean.—Fourteen enemy aircraft destroyed or damaged over Malta.

Burma.—Heavy fighting still in progress on Burma-Yunnan frontier. U.S. bombers raided Myitkyina aerodrome.

Home.—Single enemy aircraft bombed S. coast.

General.—Germans announced shooting of 24 more Dutchmen for pro-British activities. Bomb attacks on German-occupied hotels in Paris.

At Gibraltar It's Always 'Stand To'

Guarding ammunition in the galleries of Gibraltar's underground defences. Top left, a Bren gun inside a pill-box on the outer defences of the Rock overlooking the surrounding country.

AN ANTI-PARATROOP PATROL moving along a road round the Rock. Circle, a patrol passing through a tunnel to take up position. One of the key-points in the Allies' long line of communications, Gibraltar's fortifications have been completely modernized since the war began. There are miles of tunnels where gun crews stand ready day and night, and all lines of approach from the land are covered by powerful forts and blockhouses. Living quarters within the Rock itself have been brought up to date with electric light, fresh water, etc. *Photos, British Official*

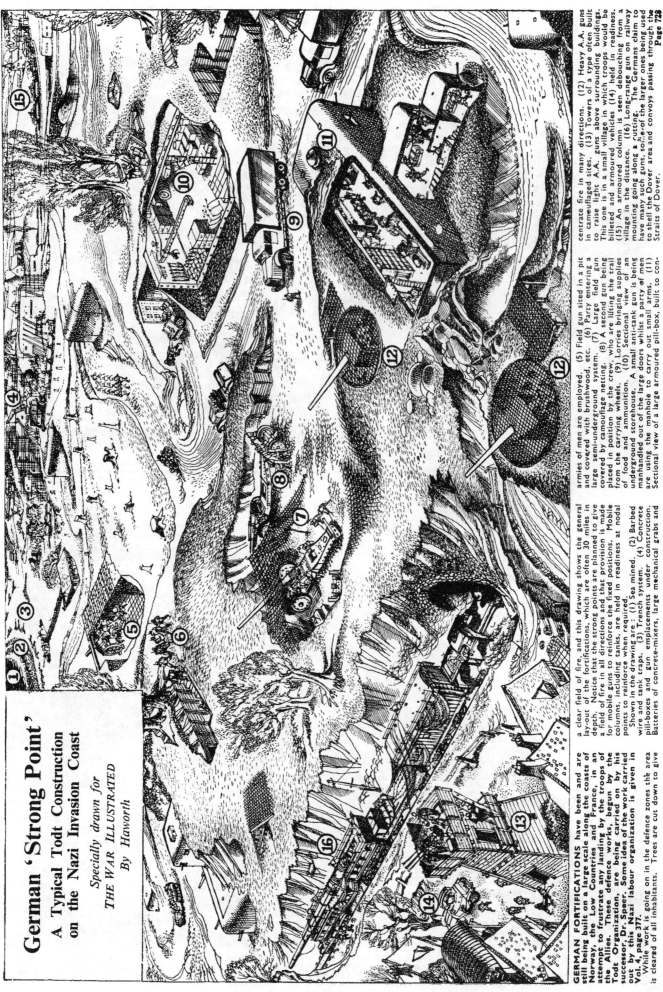

German 'Strong Point'

A Typical Todt Construction on the Nazi Invasion Coast

Specially drawn for
THE WAR ILLUSTRATED
By Haworth

GERMAN FORTIFICATIONS have been and are still being built on a large scale along the coasts of Norway, the Low Countries and France, in an attempt to frustrate any landing by the troops of the Allies. These defence works, begun by the Todt Organization, are being carried on by his successor, Dr. Speer. Some idea of the work carried out by this Nazi labour organization is given in Vol. 4, page 377.

While work is going on in the defence zones the area is cleared of all inhabitants. Trees are cut down to give a clear field of fire, and this drawing shows the general lay-out of the fortifications, which are often 30 miles in depth. Notice that the strong points are planned to give a field of fire in all directions and that provision is made for mobile guns to reinforce the fixed positions. Mobile columns, including tanks, are held in readiness at nodal points to reinforce when required.

Shown in the drawing are: (1) Sea mined. (2) Barbed wire and tank traps. (3) Trench system. (4) Concrete pill-boxes and gun emplacements under construction. Batteries of concrete-mixers, large mechanical grabs and armies of men are employed. (5) Field gun sited in a pit and covered with brushwood, etc. (6) Party entering a large semi-underground system. (7) Large field gun placed in position by the crew, who are lifting the trail from the carrying wheels. (9) Lorries bringing supplies of food and ammunition. (10) Sectional view of an underground storehouse. A small anti-tank gun is being manhandled out of the large doors whilst a party of men are using the manhole to carry out small arms. (11) Sectional view of a large armoured pill-box, built to con-

centrate fire in many directions. (12) Heavy A.A. guns in camouflaged sites. (13) Towers of a type often built to raise light A.A. guns above surrounding buildings. This one is in a small village in which troops would be billeted and armoured vehicles (14) held in readiness. (15) An armoured column is seen debouching from a village in the distance. (16) Long-range gun on railway mounting going along a cutting. The Germans claim to have many such guns, some of the larger ones being used to shell the Dover area and convoys passing through the Straits of Dover.

Now It Is the Nazis Who Fear Invasion

Since Dunkirk we in the British Isles have been living under the threat of invasion. The threat is still there ; it is still possible that Hitler will make a supreme gambler's throw. But of late weeks signs have been accumulating that the Nazis are fearing that the situation may be reversed—that it is we who will do the invading.

OPEN a Second Front ! Relieve the pressure on the Red Army ! Strike now, while the Nazis are sunk deep in the Russian swamps ! This is the demand which is being voiced by men who know, and by men who cannot know, the difficulties involved, the issues at stake—by statesmen of world-wide repute and by humble Service men, grumbling over their half-pints in the canteen at their state of unexpected and unwelcome inactivity.

Here, for instance, is General McNaughton. G.O.C. of the Canadians in Britain, declaring that his force is a dagger pointed at the heart of Berlin ; there is no better-located spot than England, he declares, for offensive action against the coast of Europe from Gibraltar to Spitzbergen (although he agrees that possibly the British offensive may not come until Germany attempts an invasion of England). Here is Mr. Litvinov, the Soviet Union's Ambassador at Washington, asserting that if the German forces could be split or weakened on the Eastern Front by a diversion elsewhere, it would be possible to push the Nazis right back to the German frontier, to Berlin and beyond. And here is Lord Beaverbrook declaring, " I believe in the Russian system, which holds to the faith that the best form of defence is attack. And I believe that Britain should adopt it by setting up somewhere along the 2,000 miles of coastline now held by the Germans a Second Front in Western Europe . . ."

Hitler doesn't like speeches of this kind, on this particular theme. Maybe he suspects that in the summer and autumn of 1940 he missed an opportunity to invade Britain which is hardly likely to recur. Maybe he is not too sure about the morale of his own people, and we may be sure that he knows that there are millions in Europe living (and many of them working) for the day when he and his Nazis will have been wiped from the face of the earth. The possibility of an invasion of Europe by the British and their American allies is realized in Nazi circles, and the Germany authorities in the occupied territories facing the Atlantic, the Channel, and the North Sea have been warned to prepare for blows which may come at any time. Here are just a few indications of Nazi nervousness—and preparedness.

At the beginning of April Gen. Rundstedt, one of Hitler's most successful and experienced commanders, was withdrawn from the Russian front and put in charge of the German defences in France ; and to his new command have been added many fresh troops and a number of aircraft, mostly bombers, under Gen. Coler.

Hundreds of concrete gun-emplacements have been erected at vital points along the coast ; scores of new airfields have been constructed ; minefields have been laid ; and from many districts near the coast, and even in districts far from the coast, the civilian population has been evacuated.

There is significance, too, in the intensification of the Nazis' savage treatment of the dissentient population. Every act or attempted act of sabotage is savagely punished. For every German officer or man shot in the streets of one of the occupied towns the Nazis demand and take the lives of ten or twenty Frenchmen, Belgians or Dutch.

One particular act of terrorism was announced on May 4 by Gen. Christiansen, German Commander in Holland : a German court-martial, it was stated, had taken action against a group of leaders of a secret organization which in its activities and aims was directed against the German occupying power and, moreover, had attempted to gain contact with Germany's opponents. In these proceedings already 79 Dutch people have been found guilty of favouring the enemy, espionage, being in the possession of arms and explosives, and in some cases of breaking their word of honour as officers, and have been condemned to death accordingly. Seventy-two of these sentences have been carried out by shooting. In only seven cases have sentences been commuted to life imprisonment. Within a week 24 more were shot.

Recently further news came to hand of the British Commando raid on St. Nazaire when (it transpires) the French population rose en bloc and for three and a half days fought side by side with the Commando men who had been left behind when the ships withdrew ; in the fighting between 300 and 400 Germans were killed, and after the resistance had been overcome the Nazis shot 500 civilians.

FIELD-MARSHAL VON RUNDSTEDT, recently appointed to command the German armies in Occupied France, is here seen with his Fuehrer.

When peace had been restored the German authorities in the Brest area issued a proclamation threatening to establish a state of siege if " irresponsible elements in Britain's pay and sympathizing with Russia " should " think it opportune to take part in demonstrations or acts which might have disastrous consequences for the whole population." It was ordered that, on the siren being sounded three times at intervals of 30 seconds, all civilians must immediately clear the streets, take shelter in the nearest house and close the windows. Civilians who disobeyed by remaining in the streets or porches, by showing themselves behind closed windows, or by carrying arms may be shot on the spot by patrols. All traffic must stop ; shops, hotels, cafés and schools must close at once . . .

The Germans, it is clear, are getting nervous.

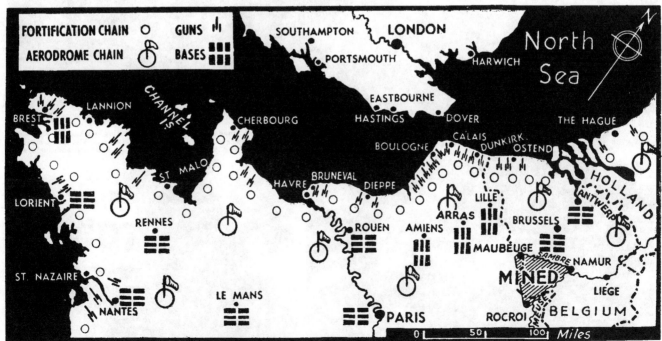

Commando raids upon the French coast and the fear of an invasion in force have caused the German High Command to strengthen considerably the anti-invasion defences set up along the western seaboard of Europe. This map shows the great chain of fortifications stretching from Holland to St. Nazaire. An idea of how the German defences are constructed is shown in the diagram in the opposite page.

Photo, Sport & General.   Map by courtesy of The Daily Mail

America's New Route to Alaska—and Beyond

A great new highway is being constructed across Canada to link the U.S.A. with its new war bases in Alaska over the route shown in the map, left. Above, a plank highway being placed across the frozen Peace River pending the construction of a ferry after the thaw.

Trucks and road-making machinery being rushed to Dawson Creek for work on the new Alaskan highway. The narrow pilot road now being completed will later be widened and surfaced.

Above, a bulldozer carving out a portion of the new Alaskan road. U.S. Army Engineers are blazing a trail through 1,200 miles of Canadian wilderness to build this highway, which Pte. Neff, of Detroit (right), hopes will lead to Tokyo.

Photos, Sport & General. Map by Courtesy of News Chronicle

Corregidor: Epic of 'Grim, Gaunt & Ghastly Men'

AFTER five months of heroic struggle against overwhelmingly superior numbers, Lieut.-Gen. J. M. Wainwright, commander of the American forces on Corregidor Island, was forced to surrender to the Japanese. The news was issued from Gen. MacArthur's headquarters in Australia early in the morning of May 6.

Paying a fine tribute to the men with whom he had lately served, the General said : " Corregidor needs no comment from me. It has sounded its own story at the mouth of its guns. It has enscrolled its own epitaph on the enemy tablets. But through the bloody haze of its last reverberating shot I shall always seem to see the vision of grim, gaunt, ghastly men—still unafraid."

So fell, for the time being, the Allies' last stronghold in the Western Pacific, together with three other forts in Manila Bay, Hughes, Drum and Frank, and the finest harbour in the Pacific.

Towards the end of this epic fight Corregidor was subjected to 13 separate air attacks each day for four days, and was bombarded by many 240-millimetre guns firing from new positions captured by the Japanese. In the final assault the enemy made use of a large number of steel barges in the two-mile trip from the tip of Bataan Peninsula to the island fortress.

A Domei Agency dispatch from a Japanese base in the Philippines gave a description of the last hours before the fort capitulated. " Under cover of darkness and an intensive rolling artillery barrage, Japanese expeditionary forces, which had been biding their time since the complete occupation of the Bataan Peninsula, swarmed across the narrow channel separating Corregidor from the mainland at 8.30 on Tuesday, May 5, in an all-out offensive to crush Gen. Jonathan Wainwright's beleaguered Filipino and American forces. The invasion of the American stronghold was carried out by boats heavily laden with

FORT DRUM, an unsinkable "battleship" of concrete built on top of El Fraile Island in the mouth of Manila Bay (see map, p. 654). Here heavily-armoured turrets mounted 16-inch guns which wrought great havoc on the Japanese troops trying to enter the bay. *Photos, Keystone*

Japanese shock troops, which passed through the mine-studded waters round Corregidor Island. The initial landing was effected at 11 p.m., when a three-column Japanese invasion party crossed over to Corregidor in the face of terrific American fire, with a second and a third landing party following in their wake in rapid succession."

Then followed a vivid account of terrible hand-to-hand fighting with bayonets and sabres, with bombers pulverizing the American fortifications to open points for the Japanese advance. In the same way the other American forts in Manila

Bay were captured, the Japanese announcing that all positions were in their hands by May 6.

Immediately before the fall of Corregidor Lieut.-Gen. Wainwright issued the following message :

" I've been with my men from the start, and if captured I will share their lot. We've been through so much together that my conscience would not let me leave before the final curtain. Americans shaken by the loss of Bataan should not feel the fall of the Manila Bay forts is a double tragedy, but rather an exemplification of the grimness of our spirit when we stay to the end with the job to be done."

Far from disheartening the American public, the loss of the Philippines fight, of which Corregidor was the final episode, came as a new inspiration. In view of the fact that it took the Japanese five months to accomplish what they had hoped to do in twice as many days, America might well claim a moral victory.

ON reports received up till April 15, the U.S. War Department estimated that, including naval personnel, marines, soldiers, Philippine scouts, soldiers of the Philippine Commonwealth Army and various civilians, there were 11,574 persons in the Manila Bay area. With the exception of casualties since that date, these may be presumed to have been taken prisoner.

In the name of the President, the War Department published general orders citing, not individuals, but 30 separate units of the American and Philippine soldiers for their heroism.

In an Australian tribute Mr. Curtin, the Prime Minister, said : " Corregidor takes its place in world history. We had our Tobruk, America has its Corregidor. Standing to that spirit of dauntless gallantry we cannot lose."

ON CORREGIDOR ISLAND, the operating-room in the U.S. hospital after having been hit by a Japanese bomb on Dec. 29, 1941. On the right, General MacArthur's bungalow which was wrecked in the same raid. The General, who was at his post, had a narrow escape, while his wife and small son, having taken cover in a bombproof shelter, were also uninjured. Above, left, a 12-inch gun in the Corregidor fortress. Page 731

Meet the 'Maritimes,' Soldiers on Shipboard

Wearing an anchor badge with the letters A.A., a Maritime soldier practises sighting an Oerlikon gun under the tuition of an officer at a naval gunnery school. Left, life-saving exercises by men of a Maritime regiment.

THE MARITIME REGIMENTS of the Royal Artillery were formed in the summer of 1940, when there were more guns for ships than there were men to man them. There are now four regiments, numbering some 12,000 men, drawn from various branches of the Army. Their specific job is the manning of guns on merchantmen. In the lower photo Maritime gunners, having shot down a balloon during machine-gun practice, wait while a naval officer signals for another to be sent up.

Photos, Associated Press, G.P.U.

I Worked Alongside the Russians for Six Months

Life amid the ceaseless activity of the northern ports of the U.S.S.R., whence convoys of British and American war material are dispatched to the front, was described in the following broadcast by the Hon. J. P. Maclay, M.P., who recently spent six months in northern Russia.

THERE is a strange thrill of satisfaction in watching the ships of a convoy arriving safely at their destination. I used to be down on the quay with the Russian port authorities and their staff watching for the first ship to come slowly round the bend. The Russians had always every detail of the discharging operation fully planned : stevedoring gangs waiting ; the motor-lorries, the girls who were going to tally the cargo, the tugs which were going to work the ships into their berths and the long lines of railway trucks—all standing by ready to commence work, not tomorrow morning but immediately the ship was tied up.

As the ships approached the quay we could begin to realize what this northern passage meant. Ship after ship encased from stem to stern and up to the truck of the masts in hard white ice, their winches slowly turning to keep them from freezing, and on the bridge the captain and a Russian pilot shouting through megaphones to the crew on the fo'c'sle head who are struggling with mooring ropes and wires, difficult and dangerous to handle in the low temperatures. Some of the ships had dents in their sides, and some had chips off their propellers which told a story of a battle with the ice.

Unloading Tanks from Britain

In a few hours' time the ships are safely alongside and the first tanks, aircraft and military vehicles are coming over the side on to the quay and on to the trucks. Everything gives way for tanks and aircraft, and practically always within twenty-four hours after the arrival of a convoy the first railway train, made up of these vital units, is on its way to the interior for immediate use against the enemy. Many of the Russian stevedores are not used to handling this type of cargo, but the British crews were always standing by ready to give a hand or to give advice when required, and ready to drive the winches and handle the gear themselves if the lift was a specially difficult one. The language difficulty was always a problem

and I was often appealed to, both by the Russians and by the ships' crews, to decide some argument which, when I came along with a good interpreter, I found to be no argument at all, as both sides were saying the same thing in a different language.

One only required to be on the spot to know how anxiously the supplies were waited for and how greatly they were appreciated when they arrived. I would like some of our factory workers and engineers to have seen the care and interest with which the Soviet technical experts examined our materials. Every part was looked over with a critical eye and it gave me a good feeling to know that our workmanship could stand up to any inspection or comparisons.

One of the first things which the Russian authorities arranged when the ships came alongside was to issue passes to all members of the crew, but, of course, the language problem was a great barrier. Very few Russians could speak English, and the British found even the Russian alphabet difficult. Our sailors were usually anxious to get to a cinema or find a shop where they could buy something to take home as a memento to their families. In most foreign countries you can have a good guess at the shop signs, but not so in Russia. You may think you have found a restaurant or shop of kinds by seeing people go out and in, but when you get inside you find yourself in the local dispensary or post office. The Russians are naturally a hospitable people and once or twice a week a number of men from each ship were given an invitation to the local concert-hall where there was a dance or concert or cinema and an interpreter was appointed to make sure they were looked after.

I think the British sailors sometimes thought that they would have to teach the Russian girls how to dance the latest dances, but it was very often the other way round. I can remember well the surprise of some Scottish firemen when a Russian girl danced the Highland Fling for them in real Highland Games fashion. The highest compliment

R.A.F. and Russian air mechanics unloading a crate containing a Hurricane, complete with spare parts, from a rail wagon, at a Soviet port. *Photo, British Official*

was paid to her by one of the firemen remarking : " Very weel done, lassie. Even Dunoon wud be proud o' ye."

When convoys were in the port, work continued twenty-four hours a day, but at Christmastime we had parties just the same as at home. I shall never forget one party when I was suddenly called on to make a speech and could not think of anything very weighty to say at such short notice, so I read out a letter I had just received from my four-year-old daughter exhorting me to be most careful not to fall through the ice and finishing up with a request that, when I came home, would I please ask the Russians to send her a reindeer, a wolf and a polar-bear. The speech received the usual polite applause and I thought no more about it until a few days before leaving for home I received an irate signal from the captain of a British warship saying : " Have just received on board a baby reindeer addressed to Miss Maclay, Scotland. Presume you understand this is a man-of-war and not a floating Whipsnade." This was upsetting enough in itself, but my mind at once flew back to my speech and visions of what the next signal might contain if the wolf and the polar-bear also arrived. Luckily, however, the reindeer was the only passenger. But the gift gave me a pleasant warm feeling that the Russian —whom we sometimes think of as only a hard fierce person—could take the trouble to hunt up a baby reindeer to send to a small girl in Scotland.

Short Shrift for Slackers

The stern side of Russia, however, is very stern. Nothing is allowed to interfere with the prosecution of the war. Discipline is severe and mistakes, either by workers or management, are dealt with immediately and ruthlessly. Crimes such as pilfering are regarded as acts against the State and dealt with accordingly. If facilities for doing a job are not available they are improvized, and time and again I used to hear the phrase : " What must be done shall be done." And it usually was done. The Russians knew that all the cargo brought by the ships was urgently required for fighting the war, that men had risked their lives and ships bringing it, and no obstacle was allowed to stand in the way of that cargo getting to its destination either at the front or at the factory.—*The Listener*

BRITISH CONVOY CRUISER in a Russian port after having brought the convoy safely across the Arctic. The voyage was made in almost complete darkness in a temperature sometimes registering 52 degrees of frost. During the hardest weather ships arrived encased in ice. *Photo, British Official*

I Saw Burma's Pagodas Bombed Into Ruins

Japanese bombing raids on the smaller towns of Burma were largely aimed at terrorizing the civil population. A typical raid is described in this dispatch from the Daily Herald's correspondent, Victor Thompson.

THERE are nine planes up there glinting in the sunshine. As we count them we hear the familiar whoosh of falling bombs. We scramble into a slit trench so small that it seems made to measure. The earth sways, and we say : " That must be the other side of the town," and wait for the next series of whooshes.

When the bombing is done we go out to investigate, driving in the direction of a pillar of smoke. Just as the all-clear siren sounds, two cuckoos start calling as if they too were just emerging from shelter. (Yes, there are cuckoos in the wooded hills of Burma.)

The centre of the town has been accurately plastered from at least ten thousand feet. These Japanese are good marksmen whether with bombs or mortars or machine-guns. Fires are already spreading, adding to the heat of Burmese noon.

A fat Burman in his blue and white skirt smeared with red dirt is busy stamping out a little pile of smouldering rubbish in the middle of the road, while his shop burns fiercely apparently unheeded five yards away. Another in a doorway sits asleep with arms folded. Even the crackling of the flames does not wake him. When we go close we see that nothing will wake him any more.

A Yorkshire soldier comes up swearing. He tries to lift a man apparently dazed by blast. " He was cut in two," the soldier keeps repeating. There is little we can do except watch the sketchy A.R.P. services trying doggedly to cope with a situation beyond them.

We pick our way round dead bullocks, which are characteristic of every Burma bombing I have seen, and find several big craters. So the Japanese are now using big stuff as well as the little anti-personnel bombs they usually employ.

There is no evidence that any target of military importance was selected. But then this is the second phase of the Japanese bombing campaign. At first they concentrated single-mindedly on military objectives. Then they turned their attention to the civil population, trying to increase the thousands of refugees on the roads.

While the town burns around us, scorching eyebrows and making breathing an ordeal, we watch the guards posted in the bazaars to prevent looting. We wash off some of the grime by standing under a jet leaking from a fire hose. Firemen are withdrawing to carefully prepared positions. Their enemy is advancing fast.

Well, that is another town written off another once picturesque pagoda-studded town transformed in an hour into ruin and rubbish. Visit such a place as this at night, under the lovely Burmese moon, and the feeling of being in the presence of death is even stronger, the desire to go on tiptoe even more pressing. You begin to feel that all the world is dead except you and the croaking bullfrog somewhere down the river.

Well, that is the war behind the war, a sad story, making Mandalay kin to Coventry and Thazi to Liverpool. These towns are not big. The damage is not huge. The casualties have not been very heavy. But more than a million people are now homeless and on the move, complicating the supply problem of the United Nations. Each whoosh has added to that multitude—which is what it was intended to do.

Life's Not Too Bad in a Workers' Hostel

Thousands of men and women have left their homes to work in arms factories set deep in the countryside. How some of them are housed, fed and cared for is told here by Inez Holden, who lived for some months in a workers' hostel in a Welsh valley.

THIS workers' hostel, built to house about a thousand people, where I have been living for six months, is made up of a main building and several smaller, single-storey buildings, grey in colour, symmetrical in design and functional in purpose. If it had not been set down in a country of great beauty it would look rather like a factory in a futuristic film.

In the centre of the main building there is a reception desk for incoming letters, telegrams, parcels and so on, a post box, two telephone kiosks, a small shop, opened at fixed hours to sell cigarettes and cosmetics, a newspaper and book stall, some armchairs and a sofa. At one end of this building there is the big assembly hall with its stage for dramatic entertainment and screen for cinema shows, and at the other end the large dining hall and kitchens. Along the passage on either side are the various recreation rooms, the library, lounge, reading and writing rooms and the general and accountant's offices.

On the white walls of the writing room I saw reproductions of some of the best French Impressionist paintings. In the passage various notices are pinned up, announcements of concerts, cinema shows, Civil Defence lectures, and information about allotments which can be booked by workers.

Meals are in this order : Breakfast, 5.30 to 9 a.m. ; midday meal, 12.30 to 1.30 ; tea, 4.30 to 5.30 ; supper, 7.30 to 8.30 ; and a light meal from 10.30 to 11 p.m. for the afternoon shift coming off duty. It is usual to have breakfast, a main meal, tea and a light extra meal in the hostel. Most people eat at least one meal a day or night in one of the factory canteens. I found the hostel food good, well cooked, and there was plenty of it.

I slept in a building about two minutes' walk from the reception hall, my room being one of about 15 in a long passage ; there was also a drying room for clothes, three bathrooms and a house steward's room with a telephone for sending messages through to the reception hall. My room was fixed up with a sleeping bunk, a large wardrobe with two shelves, two chairs, a chest of drawers, locker, electric light, a wash basin and running hot and cold water and two windows. I was called by one of the house staff each morning in time for me to bath, dress and get over to the main building for breakfast before going on to the factory. My room was swept and my bed made each day by the house stewardess.

The charge for my complete board and lodging was 22s. 6d. a week ; this is the normal charge for women ; the men pay 27s. 6d. a week. I do not know if this is because they earn more or because they eat more. Probably both.

The sick bay has a sister and two nurses ; it is well equipped and able to deal with all emergency cases.

It is clear, then, that most of the irksome mechanical problems of living are solved here. But there is also the need for warmth and cordiality, possibly something like the fierce intellectual life of the Continental cafés. I do not know how the hostels will cater for this, but I have seen too many people on these dry, pub-closed, cinema-shut Sundays staring in a melancholy way out of the window at the misted Welsh mountains.

There is a certain degree of non-adaptability in some of the people. Several of them have never left home before, and so " Mum and Dad's " design for living is still stamped indelibly on their minds. In spite of national

THE ROYAL ENCLOSURE, MANDALAY, and a general view beyond of the beautiful pagoda-studded city of Upper Burma, which Japanese bombers reduced to smouldering ruins. An air raid on a Burmese town is described in this page. *Photo, E.N.A.*

THE SPIRIT OF MALTA is cheerfully symbolized in this photograph of soldiers clearing away yet another heap of rubble caused by enemy bombs. It was announced on May 8 that General Lord Gort had been appointed Governor of Malta in succession to Lieut.-Gen. Sir William Dobbie. Commander Anthony Kimmins, R.N., describes in this page a recent visit to the Mediterranean fortress.
Photo, Sport & General

upheaval they remain home-bound. I have heard some of them speak of their rooms, critically, as "cells," but it would be impossible to billet a thousand people each in some individual parlour, with an open fireplace, kettle simmering on the hob and "our cat" purring on the hearth.

Others have known so much poverty and unemployment that it must have seemed as if the whole of humanity was conspiring against them; the past despair lives in and with them, and in this mood of maladjustment even the best cannot appear acceptable.

Many of the people, however, contribute a great deal to the communal life. They give free lessons to their colleagues on subjects which they themselves happen to have studied. There are entertainments most evenings, but I remember a night when nothing had been prearranged some of the factory workers volunteered to entertain their comrades; they gave up their free time between two shifts, had only one hour's rehearsal, and in their everyday clothes and without stage effects gave a concert which was both delightful and dignified.—*News Chronicle*

I Went Back to Malta in Wartime

Among the many tributes paid to Malta, the following was broadcast on April 5, 1942, by Commander Anthony Kimmins, R.N., who, like most Naval men, has known the island in peace and in war.

EVERYONE in the Navy knows Malta and everyone in Malta knows the Navy. In the middle of Valetta, the capital, there is a vantage point called the Barracca, which overlooks the Grand Harbour. Many's the time I have stood there before the war and looked down on the scene many hundreds of feet below: the narrow creek of the Grand Harbour and the yellow sandstone rising almost sheer from the water's edge, with hundreds of houses perched precariously on every spare inch of rock. The harbour was usually packed with shipping, warships painted light Mediterranean grey and with white awnings covering their quarterdecks and fo'c'sles. The bells from the many churches seemed to ring continuously: all very gay and picturesque.

The other day I again leant over the rails of the Barracca. There were still the houses rising from either shore, but far too often there were ugly gaps. There were still warships in the harbour, but there was no longer any spotless grey enamel. They were camouflaged, dazzle painted, and dirty with all the marks of countless hours at sea. There were no awnings, because all guns pointed upwards. There were no bells, and it was all much quieter.

As I looked down, I couldn't help remembering the hundreds of hours I had spent flying above Malta in peacetime, and of how on a clear day one could look across from up top and see quite distinctly the coast of Sicily. It was just such a day now, and over there at this moment several hundred enemy

aircraft were grouped ready to take off for the few minutes' flight which separated us. I imagined Field-Marshal Kesselring urging his crews to remove the "Malta menace."

Ansaldo—the Italian spokesman—summed up the meaning of Malta in one sentence: "Malta," he said, "has become a colossal and unsinkable aircraft-carrier, almost within sight of the Italian coast."

Then another thought struck me—what a perfect bombing target! One of the essential measures against bombing attacks is dispersal. But here, round the Grand Harbour and Dockyard, the narrow creeks and absence of flat land had made dispersal impossible.

Then I caught sight of an anti-aircraft position to my left. It was manned by Maltese, men of the famous Royal Malta Artillery. Not far away there was another gun position, manned by English gunners. We'd already had two air raids that morning, and there was a pile of empties beside each gun. But by now the breeches were reloaded with new shells, and there was plenty of ammunition in reserve.

The men of both crews were ready and searching the sky. Each seemed determined to get into action before the other. And that, to my mind, was symbolic of the whole population of Malta. Military, naval, air force or civilian, they never stand at ease. They are constantly on the alert.

Somewhere inside Military Headquarters Major-Gen. Beak, the G.O.C., was making his plans for his various units: his A.A. gunners, his coastal batteries, his infantrymen and his tanks. Gen. Beak is a fighting soldier to his finger tips. He's imbued the whole garrison with the offensive spirit.

Somewhere in Malta are the R.A.F. headquarters, from which Air Marshal Lloyd operates his bombers and fighters. He's another great fighter—he's been fighting on and off since he was 19. He knows all his pilots personally, and they all know and worship him.

It's an amazing sight on one of Malta's aerodromes. On one side you'll find a group of fighter pilots being dished out with cups of tea from a canteen van. They are in full flying kit with their yellow "Mae Wests" round their necks and never more than a few yards away are their Hurricanes and Spitfires. In between whiles there is a constant stream of aircraft landing and taking off from the runways. Wellingtons and Blenheims on their way to bomb the airways in Sicily or off on the longer run to Tripoli; Marylands to reconnoitre Taranto and other Italian ports. When those reports come in more Blenheims take off to intercept and bomb, while Swordfish and Albacores of the Fleet Air Arm disappear out to sea to dive down low and launch their torpedoes.

Now the third of the Service Chiefs, Vice-Admiral Leatham, commanding the dockyard, and the naval units. For many years Malta has harboured and sheltered British warships and merchantmen. Now, in her hour of trial, the Navy and Merchant Navy are determined to stand by her.

There are no Service distinctions or labour troubles in Malta. When a supply ship has to be unloaded, sailors, soldiers, airmen and civilians get down to it as one, no matter how fierce the bombing. For two years now they've held out against enemy attacks, and during the last three months they have withstood heavier and more constant bombing than any other place in the world has ever survived. In this three months they have endured nearly 700 air raids, some of them of several hours' duration.

Never before in history have human beings endured or survived such an attack. Yet life goes on—schools are open, bands play amid the rubble and people listen in the sun: makeshift shops appear from the ruins.

Editor's Postscript

ONLY the thoughtless would expect that the local authorities who take care of the industrial townships, residential and holiday resorts that stud the coasts of Great Britain from Wick in the north-east of Scotland round the shores of England and Wales and as far up the West of Scotland as Oban—more than two thousand miles, I suppose—could guarantee to their fellow citizens any effective measure of protection from Nazi air attacks of the tip-and-run variety. No form of defence has been or can be devized to secure immunity from these nuisance raids ; but it ought to be possible in the more exposed areas, such as the East and South coasts, where this type of attack can be most cheaply carried out, to organize some system of warning to the unfortunate communities who are liable to such disturbing visits. The recent resumption of these raids along the South coast, after ten or eleven months of immunity, would appear to have found the local authorities (whoever *they* may be) no better prepared in this respect than they were two years ago.

THE newspapers of some of these towns are full of complaints from readers and are editorially clamorous that something must be done forthwith to protect the townsfolk. For it is indeed a farce that in printing photographs of the damage in " a South-coast town " where the main street has been bombed and machine-gunned twice in one week, they have to report that " the alarm was given some minutes *after* the first bombs had dropped." In that same town more than a year ago the local journal asserted that the safest time to walk abroad in its streets was *after* an alarm had been sounded or *before* an all-clear ! The marvels of radio-location leave the inhabitants of these South-coast towns quite chilly after being all het-up over the ineptitude of the local siren service. And it seems absurd to me that newspapers which print excellent photos of raid damage may not specify the name of the town. Why are these newspapers allowed to retain the place name in their own titles ? Why should The Sandyshore Gazette be permitted to print that name at all, since it has been obliterated from the gasworks, waterworks, railway station and tramcars ? But to ask these questions is to get no better answer than that recorded ages ago in the comic song " And the Ostrich walked away ! "

FUNNY things still go on in the way of export and import. Paper appears to be the one essential commodity whose import must be rigorously restricted. A vast tonnage of Canadian cigarettes (which are mainly paper if we reckon their superabundant packings) is being imported for the Canadian forces in Great Britain, though many hundreds of them must have been traded off by the recipients in order to get other things more desired. Not long ago I heard of someone in London getting from America a present of two pots of marmalade which had been exported from Dundee in the ordinary way of business ! And in a New York journal recently to hand I was amused and bewildered to read :

" Four Cheeses—Danish blue, royal Danish, English Stilton and American cream—make a pungent, pleasantly tart spread which is to be used for canapés or very special sandwiches. The precious imported varieties are put through a grinder. Then, after the cream cheese has been added, the mixture is beaten until soft and creamy. The final step is the addition of brandy. Two-and-a-half-ounce jars cost 35 cents."

IS it possible that English Stilton, which has always been my favourite cheese and none of which have I been able to touch, taste or handle in any club, hotel, restaurant, hostelry or home for well-nigh two years, has actually been exported to America during that period to enable lucky epicures there to enjoy those " very special sandwiches " ? One might ask : " *How* do they get these Danish cheeses, and *why* should English Stilton be buyable in New York when not a scraping of it can be got in London ? " But I'm sure that Alice would have regarded this as curiouser still : Canadian troops in England are receiving parcels from home containing various choice British brands of tinned meats which had been originally carried overseas to the senders who are now re-exporting them to their country of origin ! The fact that Americans can get good supplies of Scotch Whisky at less than we have to pay for it at home is easier to explain, as its export has been from the beginning of the War an important factor in helping British credits in America. And every time you call for a dubious " double " at your hotel or club you can at least console yourself by knowing that in paying an absurd price for it you are helping the War effort both at home and in America. The lemonade swiller is

MAJ.-GEN. CHARLES H. BONESTEEL, U.S. Army, who now commands the Anglo-American occupation force in Iceland.
Photo, Topical Press

denied that consolation . . . and does he worry ?

TALKING about paper—passing along the Embankment one day this week my eye was caught by an unusual sight : two steam tugs each towing two very large barges filled so high with closely stocked waste-paper that they could just scrape under the wide arches of the new Waterloo Bridge—soon to be opened to traffic it would seem—on their way downstream to some paper mills near the estuary—quite possibly some of these cargoes were destined for certain mills which are controlled by our own publishers, where the paper for THE WAR ILLUSTRATED is made. But perhaps most of these bales of waste were consigned to other pulp and paper works, where the cartridge paper so vital to our armaments supply is manufactured, the roughest, toughest and dirtiest being quite suitable for pulping to make brown paper for all packing purposes. Here was very obvious evidence of the success which had attended the local salvage drives up Westminster way. I was sorry no photographer was at hand to make a picture of the cheering scene. But for all I know the barges may have left a Westminster quay with the official blessing of the Mayor and a fanfare of municipal trumpets as the concluding scene in a most worthy civic effort, and ubiquitous camera-men may have been there to provide graphic record of the occasion. So I may yet find a photograph of the scene to print here on paper to the making of which the heaped cargoes of these barges have contributed ! And by the way, let me remind my readers that there is no let up in this paper-saving campaign. It must go on so long as the War lasts. Many thousands of barge-loads such as I have mentioned will be needed to keep the printing presses going.

JUST a reminder to my readers that with our next number THE WAR ILLUSTRATED will have completed its fifth Volume. Volume V will thus contain the separate numbers from 101 to 130. Further particulars of the publishers' binding scheme will appear in the back pages of the next three issues. For the moment I wish only to repeat the warning already given that all readers who make a point of getting their loose numbers bound into volume form should lose no time after the next one appears in sending these either to the publishers' Binding Department or to their local binder so that the work may be done without delay, while stocks of binding material are still available. I will not stress that when Volume V started I expressed the hope that the " V " might also prove to be the V of Victory. Our hopes ran high then, although really not higher than they ought to run today, when there is even more evidence of the progress of our War effort despite the disasters which have so sorely tried the patience and temper of our people. The most encouraging feature of the War reflected in Volume V is the record of America's entry into the conflict, which more than offsets the flying start that Japan achieved by her treacherous plunge into war. As our sixth volume will cover the next twelve months we must just hope that within that period the victory for which we are striving will either have been attained or be well in sight before its close.

Printed in England and published every alternate Friday by the Proprietors, The Amalgamated Press, Ltd., The Fleetway House, Farringdon Street, London, E.C.4. Registered for transmission by Canadian Magazine Post. Sole Agents for Australia and New Zealand : Messrs. Gordon & Gotch, Ltd. ; and for South Africa : Central News Agency, Ltd. May 29, 1942. S.S. *Editorial Address :* JOHN CARPENTER HOUSE, WHITEFRIARS, LONDON, E.C.4.

Vol 5 | *The War Illustrated* | Nº 130

6d FORTNIGHTLY

Edited by Sir John Hammerton

JUNE 12. 1942

ROSES FOR THE 'OLD AND BOLD.' With colours rose-bedecked, the Royal Northumberland Fusiliers celebrated their regimental day on April 23 in Cairo. A battalion, wearing roses in their caps, marched to All Saints Cathedral. The colours were handed to Bishop Gwynne, who placed them on the altar. After the ceremony the battalion marched past the G.O.C.-in-C., Lieut.-General R. G. Stone. The colour bearers are (left) Lt. W. Sanderson and 2nd Lt. F. Ward, M.C.

Photo, British Official; Crown Copyright

NO. 131 WILL BE PUBLISHED FRIDAY. JUNE 26

BUT JAPAN'S FEET MAY STILL BE OF CLAY . . .

In less than five months, as Dr. H. V. Evatt, Australia's representative to this country, recently reminded us in a Sunday night " postscript," Japan has acquired a new empire. Starting from that grim day in last December, when the United States Navy suffered at Pearl Harbour the heaviest losses in its history, the Japanese have marched along a road of almost uninterrupted conquest. Guam and Wake were captured, and soon after Hongkong ; then the Philippines were engulfed by the Japanese tide, which swept on over Singapore, Britain's principal base in the Far East, and the immensely rich islands of the Dutch Empire in the East Indies. Soon it had swamped the wharves of Rangoon and was foaming furiously up the valleys of Burma. India was directly threatened, and British sea power in the Pacific and the Bay of Bengal was dealt staggering blows. Nothing, it seemed, could stop the mighty avalanche : from Chittagong to New Guinea, from Shanghai to Darwin, the hordes of the yellow men swept on in triumph.

All this must be very surprising to those who hold the belief that the white races are the divinely-appointed masters of the world's destinies. Never, indeed, has the white man's prestige in the Orient sunk so low as in the last few months and weeks. Forty years ago the Japanese showed that they were as good as the Russians ; now they have defeated British and Dutch, Australians and Americans, too.

Obviously amongst us, too, a revaluation of Japan's power and position is an urgent necessity. Unfortunately, such is the darkening and mystifying influence of race, culture, religion and geographical distance, that it is difficult in the extreme for us to think objectively of Japan and the Japanese. Few of us have ever known a Japanese ; fewer still have ever set foot in Japan, while the number of those who, though they may have passed years in the country, have penetrated into the medieval fastnesses of the Japanese home, is infinitesimal. Even when the Japanese were our allies, as they were from 1902 until 1922, they were separated from us by immense barriers of which distance was by no means the principal component. Of course, we knew them in those days to be vigorous, efficient and desperately brave ; but what *could* you make of a people whose statesman or military commanders, when they made a mistake or fell out of the Emperor's favour, saved their honour by committing ceremonial suicide ? Now the Japanese are our enemies ; and difficult as it was to understand them when they were our friends, it is far more difficult when the machinations of the war lords of Tokyo have made them our foes.

But in the matter of Japanese war aims there ought to be little room for misunderstanding. Years ago we were warned of what was coming if the militarists got control and were able to secure the Emperor's semi-religious authority for their designs. It was in 1927 that Baron Giichi Tanaka, at that time Premier of Japan and Minister of War, drew up a " memorial " after a conference at Mukden in what was still Manchuria with other Japanese leaders. This was formally pre-

sented to Emperor Hirohito, who had just succeeded to the throne on his father's death, and though Tanaka fell from power in 1929, the Memorial rapidly assumed among the Japanese the same fame and force as Hitler's *Mein Kampf* had secured in Germany. Often Japanese spokesmen, anxious to conciliate the West for the time being, have denied its authenticity—even its existence—but the best evidence of both may be said to lie in the course of events, which have shown that it contained some pretty accurate prophecy.

For what was the Memorial ? Nothing less than the blueprints of Japanese conquest. Step by step Tanaka plans the absorption of Manchuria, the economic penetration and political domination of China. " Having China's entire resources at our disposal we shall proceed to conquer India, the Archipelago of the Dutch East Indies, Asia Minor, Central Asia and even Europe." In another passage Tanaka says, " In order to conquer the world, we must first conquer China. If we succeed in conquering China, the rest of the Asiatic countries and the South Sea countries will fear us and surrender to us. Then the world will realize that Eastern Asia is ours, and will not dare to violate our rights. This was the plan left to us by Emperor Meiji, the success of which is essential to our national existence."

That was in 1927. But only the other day another clue to Japan's aggressive intentions fell into the hands of our Chinese allies—a Japanese map of what is euphemistically called " the Co-prosperity Sphere," though the only prosperous ones within it are likely to be the Japanese. According to this map the Co-prosperity Sphere embraces the whole continent of Asia with the exception of Arabia, a huge area in the Pacific, and the northern coasts of Australia. " Although it seems the dream of a lunatic," said a Chinese Government spokesman at Chungking, " the map deserves our attention because it represents the settled national policy of Japan in the same way as the notorious Tanaka Memorial which served as a blueprint of Japanese expansion."

Looking at the changes which the last few months have brought to the map of the Pacific area, we cannot but admit that Japan has taken many a big step towards the realization of her colossal dreams. But once again we must remind ourselves to think objectively. In years gone by we have belittled the Japanese ; our experts told us that their planes were no good, their tanks were old-fashioned and their warships top-heavy, while their financial system was most shockingly unsound. " Made in Japan," which we saw so often on the gimcracks which crowded the counters of the chain stores, became a by-word amongst us : where we went wrong was in thinking that everything that was " made in Japan," and more particularly those things which have definitely military value, was just shoddy. Yes, we belittled Japan ; we seriously underestimated the Japanese. But in the hour of their triumph we must be on our guard lest we allow the balance to swing to the other extreme. The Japs are no supermen.

Up to now the advantages have been all theirs. In the first place they are fighting on interior lines. Japan is a Far Eastern power, and to the battlefields in the Far East she can get most easily the most men, the most ships, the most guns, the most planes—and get there first. Then, for more than a thousand years Japan has been a military state, and whatever the fine-seeming facade of modern liberalism, the war lords are the real masters of the state. For years Japan has been stripped for war ; her people, never accustomed to a high standard of living, have become inured to privation. They believe what they are taught—that they must win this war if Japan is to have and to keep a place in the sun. Even more than Nazi Germany, Japan has prepared for war, for this war.

Then there is the question of morale. We have often been defeated in the past, but we console ourselves with the reflection that we always win the last battle. The Japanese require no such consolation. They expect to win not only the last battle but *all* the battles ; and it is a fact worth remembering that the Japanese army—and the Japanese navy, too—has never admitted defeat. Even in China, where the " incident " has become a four-years' war, it is becoming increasingly probable that Japan has never gone " all out." Finally, there is the question of surprise. We do not know what havoc was caused at Pearl Harbour last December 7, but this at least is known, that the Americans were caught napping. Surprise is a great and powerful weapon—but it cannot be used indefinitely.

So that is the position today. Japan is at the top f her form. She is on the crest of a mighty wave of victories. But even the biggest wave must subside, every wave has its trough. It is no wishful thinking to declare that every day that passes must add to Japan's difficulties and dangers. As the American commentator, Nathaniel Peffer, says : " Despite all present appearances Japan is too big for her boots and she will stumble before she has gone much further."

E. ROYSTON PIKE

JAPAN'S DREAM OF EMPIRE as shown in a map which has reached the Chinese Government. Within its boundary are found most of the U.S.S.R., all China, India, Iran and Northern Australia. Areas marked in black are Nippon's empire—at present. *By courtesy of the Daily Herald*

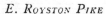

Japanese Tanks at the Front in China

PEACE AND WAR are curiously symbolized by the juxtaposition of these light Japanese tanks with the old Chinese gate. The "yellow Nazis" have been forcing the gates of China for over five years now, but in spite of their superior military strength victory eludes them.

IN NORTH CHINA Japanese army tanks in a victory parade (above). Tanks line up for inspection (right), and, beneath, mechanics servicing tanks while the crews stand on guard. At the end of May the Japanese were concentrating for yet another major offensive against China, in the province of Chekiang, south of Shanghai.

Photos, Pictorial Press

Green Flash: Off Goes the Heavy Bomber

In the nocturnal gloom of the aerodrome, the control officer stands with his Aldis lamp. When the pilot sees the green flash, he takes off for his night excursion over enemy territory.

INSIDE A HALIFAX aircraft of Bomber Command the bomb-aimer is at his post. Beneath, an engineer at the dials which record the pulses of the four engines.

With one blade of her propeller shot away, the rear turret badly damaged, all the instruments gone except the altimeter and rate-of-climb indicator, no brake-pressure, no flaps, no air speed indicator, and two wheels hanging down with flat tires, this Wellington was brought back from a raid on Kiel by a Canadian R.A.F. Squadron Commander. The aircraft skimmed the water at twenty feet, being unable to rise higher, and was crash landed without anyone being hurt. In this photograph the commander is seen, with his observer, examining the damaged propeller.

Photos, British Official

Has Prinz Eugen Lived to Fight Another Day?

PRINZ EUGEN, attacked by torpedo- and bomb-carrying aircraft on May 17, is here seen on that occasion steaming southwards along the Norwegian coast with a protecting destroyer emitting heavy smoke.

PRINZ EUGEN, the German light cruiser, would appear, like Hitler, to have the most diabolical luck. After the R.A.F. torpedo and bomb attack on May 17 near Trondheim, she escaped to Kiel, but, judging by her reduced speed and the fact that she has gone into dock for repairs, some of our missiles took effect.

Reconnaissance discovered the Nazi cruiser running southwards off Lister, on the south-west coast of Norway, escorted by four destroyers. Beauforts with torpedoes and Hudsons with bombs struck against terrific opposition from enemy fighters and heavy flak. Squadron-Leader Dinsdale went in low, let go his torpedo and saw a column of smoke leap up from the stern of the Nazi cruiser. There was an explosion fifteen seconds later, and a sergeant pilot saw a sheet of flame envelop the ship. The escorting destroyers were raked from stem to stern with cannon and machine-gun fire at the closest possible range. Five Me.109s were destroyed and a number of others were damaged

F. Lt. PETT, who took part in the attack. He was awarded the D.F.C. for a similar exploit when the Prinz Eugen forced her way through the Channel on Feb. 12.

Sqdn.-Ldr. J. DINSDALE, who reported that he saw smoke coming out of the German cruiser after he had dropped his torpedo.

BEAUFORT CREW preparing to take off (centre). Above, a Beaufort pilot describing how his torpedo was seen to run towards the Nazi cruiser.

Photos, British Official: Crown Copyright

Another Beaufort pilot making a report to the Intelligence Officer on his return from the attack. Left, the scene of the engagement.

Map by courtesy of The Daily Telegraph

Madagascar: The Taking of Diego Suarez

Lying athwart the lines of communication of the United Nations from the Cape to India, from the Persian Gulf to Australia, the great Vichy-French island of Madagascar must have suggested itself as a most tempting objective to the Japanese. But early in May Britain took steps to see that Madagascar should not be another Indo-China.

TOWARDS the end of February, or may be at the beginning of March, a British Expeditionary Force set sail from these shores, charged with the task of occupying Madagascar—that great island lying off the east coast of Africa which it was feared the government of Vichy-France might be persuaded, or compelled, to relinquish to the Japanese, just as Indo-China was relinquished a year before with results so disastrous to the United Nations in the Far East.

For more than two months the expedition, under the command of Rear-Admiral Syfret, with Maj.-Gen. R. G. Sturges as commander of the troops, was on its way ; but at dawn on May 5 it arrived at the appointed time and without any loss at the appointed place— Courier Bay, just to the west of the northernmost tip of Madagascar. At seven a.m. a note was sent to the French authorities containing certain proposals made with a view to secure their cooperation and to avoid bloodshed. The territory of Madagascar, it was declared, would remain French, and would be restored to French sovereignty after the war. Those members of the civil and military organizations who were prepared to cooperate with the United Nations would be guaranteed their salaries and pensions ; while those who did not wish to cooperate might claim to be repatriated to France when ships were available.

Moreover, the British commanders announced that it was the intention of the United Nations to extend to Madagascar every economic benefit accorded to French territories which had already decided to join the Allies. Reasonable though these terms were, M. Annet, the Governor-General, found it possible to describe them as a demand for unconditional surrender ; and as such, his reply was, " We will defend ourselves to the end."

Already the attack had been ordered. But before the fleet—stated by the French to comprise at first two cruisers, four destroyers, two transports, and an aircraft carrier ; later the figure of ships grew to twenty-three—could enter Courier Bay the approaches had to be swept, since they had been heavily mined. The minesweeping operations were carried out with efficiency and expedition, but while they were in progress the corvette H.M.S. Auricula (Lt.-Cdr. S. L. B. Maybury, R.N.) struck a mine and subsequently sank. Once the way was clear the task of putting ashore the troops, their vehicles and stores was carried out with utmost dispatch, in spite of a marked deterioration in the weather. According to the French authorities the British force numbered about 20,000 men ; the latest information concerning the French garrison made it number 1,500 Europeans and 3,000 Senegalese troops and Madagascar native levies.

Meanwhile, to create a diversion, a British light cruiser took up position off the entrance to Diego Suarez Bay, and at 5 a.m. she lit tar-barrels, raised smoke and fired star-shells. Then as soon as it was light, naval carrier-borne aircraft opened the attack. Their targets, according to a Vichy announcement, were the aerodrome, the port of Diego Suarez, and some French naval units which were lying in the harbour. Four French warships—the auxiliary cruiser Bougainville, two submarines, and the sloop D'Entre-

casteaux—were sunk or driven ashore during the attack.

Meanwhile, Sturges was proceeding with the disembarkation of his troops and armoured units in Courier Bay. Zero-hour for the Commandos was 5.30 a.m., and their first objective was a coastal battery overlooking the Bay ; this was captured very soon by the special service troops and a company of the East Lancashire Regiment. The garrison of the battery was taken by surprise, since all were asleep with the exception of one man engaged in preparing morning tea ; apparently the French were of the view that no large ship could succeed in navigating the dangerous channels and reefs during the hours of darkness. Once they had landed, the troops pressed on from Courier Bay east-

Though not taken in Madagascar, this photo well exemplifies the dash shown by the little party of Royal Marines who, as is told in this page, played so gallant and daring a part in the taking of Diego Suarez. *Photo, Topical Press*

wards across the isthmus along a road, or rather track, which leads from the mangrove swamps of the beach, through thick jungle and tall grass, to Diego Suarez. By four in the afternoon the town was in their hands.

Meanwhile, another force, including the Royal Welch Fusiliers, Royal Scots Fusiliers, East Lancashire Regiment and South Lancashire Regiment, had landed at Ambararata Bay, and they too pressed eastwards, supported by tanks. They reached the tiny village of Mangoky, some six miles inland, without opposition ; but at about eleven a.m. the advance troops were held up by the defence on high ground some five miles south-west of Antsirana. Shortly afterwards an attack was launched, but the position was not finally cleared until evening. By six p.m. the British were in contact with a strongly defended position across the isthmus of Andrakaka which links the naval base on the peninsula opposite the town of Diego Suarez with the mainland. At 5.30 next morning (May 6) the defences lying about two miles south of Antsirana were attacked ; but the attack failed, owing to heavy cross-fire from well-sighted 75s and machine-guns. Snipers, too, concealed in the thick, knee-high grass and in the banks of deep ravines, took heavy toll. The advance

was checked until later in the day when reinforcements were brought up. Darkness had fallen when at about eight p.m. the final assault on Antsirana was launched.

At about the same time a British destroyer took on board a little force of fifty Royal Marines from another warship, and made a spectacularly daring dash for Antsirana. Going at full speed, her 4·7 in. guns, pom-poms, Oerlikons and machine-guns blazing at the French batteries which guarded the half-mile-wide entrance to the harbour at Orangea, she successfully entered the harbour, negotiated the minefields with which it was strewn, and came up alongside the quay of Antsirana in the darkness of the tropical night. And this was done without a single casualty and without any damage to the destroyer.

Armed with tommy-guns and grenades, the Marines leapt on to the quay covered by the fire of a destroyer's pom-poms and machine-guns. " Their numbers were so small," wrote a Special Correspondent of The Daily Telegraph who accompanied the expedition, " that in cold print their orders read like those of a suicide squad." Actually, however, there was only one casualty ; one of the Marines was accidentally shot in the leg by a comrade. Rushing across the quay the attackers came to the high wall of the naval barracks and began tossing their grenades over. Such was the noise and alarm they created that the French officer appeared immediately with the white flag of surrender. In the darkness the Marines' commanding officer ordered the whole barracks to muster on the parade ground, where, in the hurry and darkness, it was impossible to make a thorough search for arms. Only seven Marines could be spared to guard their prisoners, whose numbers proved to be no fewer than 400.

While the Marines were creating this diversion, dashing into the town from the quay, the British troops were attacking strongly from the land side. They met with strong initial opposition, but this they eventually overcame. In the early stages of their assault our troops relieved several pockets of British resistance which had been formed inside the enemy's lines by the rapid infiltration of our advance troops during the attack that morning. As a result it was found that our casualties were far lighter than had at first been feared. The combined assault from land and sea secured the prompt surrender of Antsirana during the night. At two a.m. on May 7 the French naval and military commanders, with the civil administration, surrendered to the British brigadier in charge of the assaulting troops.

Later in the day the coast defence batteries and defensive positions on the Orangea peninsula surrendered, being granted the usual honours of war. That afternoon (May 7) ships of Admiral Syfret's force, preceded by minesweepers, entered Diego Suarez harbour. An armistice was promptly concluded, by the terms of which the French military governor surrendered the Diego Suarez area to Admiral Syfret, all the batteries and forts were occupied by British troops, and the French forces were rounded up and disarmed.

The British casualties were stated to be much smaller than had been anticipated at first : it was believed that about 350 wounded and perhaps under a hundred had been killed.

France's Great Island Saved for Freedom

DIEGO SUAREZ, French naval base in Madagascar, showing how the fortress was attacked. Immediately below is a view near Diego Suarez showing the Caserne des Disciplinaires Coloniaux and, on the right, the military hospital. The bottom photograph is of one of the principal streets in Antananarivo, capital of Madagascar. *Photos, E.N.A., Keystone. Map by courtesy of The Sphere*

Will They Always Lie Becalmed at Martinique?

Adm. Georges ROBERT, supreme authority on the French colonial island of Martinique, West Indies.

The French aircraft-carrier BEARN, which took refuge at Martinique after France collapsed. The U.S. has now demanded her demobilization.

Some of the American planes which were bought by France and carried in the Béarn, and which have lain more or less derelict on the island of Martinique, in the Lesser Antilles, since the summer of 1940.

WHEN Laval was placed at the head of Vichy France, all French colonies excepting those under Free France might be said to be hostile or potentially hostile to the United Nations. Months before Britain had felt compelled to set in train the occupation of Madagascar, and now likewise the United States felt the necessity of securing Martinique in the West Indies. United States' anxiety about this island prompted discussions between Admiral Georges Robert, the High Commissioner, and Rear-Admiral John Hoover, the United States Commandant at Puerto Rico, with a view to immobilizing the power of the island as a base and controlling naval units at anchor there in case they might make an effort to escape to Dakar. Various French naval craft have been at Martinique since the collapse of France, principal among which are the 22,146-ton aircraft-carrier Béarn, and the cruisers Emile Bertin and Jeanne D'Arc. It will be remembered that the Emile Bertin took refuge there with £62,000,000 worth of gold. There are also about 140,000 tons of French merchant shipping at Martinique.

Pathetic relics of French impotence, silent, tarpaulin-covered guns on Martinique (left). Will they speak again in the Allied cause ? Many weapons have been left to rot on the beach. Right, French sailors belonging to the Vichy aircraft-carrier Béarn and the cruisers Emile Bertin and Jeanne D'Arc, finding themselves unable to take part in the war against Hitler do some allotment work.

Photos, British Paramount News

Death Stands Sentinel in the Russian Snow

ON THE EAST FRONT this grim war photograph was taken after Soviet troops had dislodged the Germans from a railway siding. One of the main objectives in the Ukraine is to capture rail junctions and cut communications. This is more important than the taking of towns. Thus the Soviet drive between Bylegorod and Volchansk was planned to cut the Kursk-Kharkov line, and an advance to the Dnieper would threaten von Manstein's communications in the Crimea.

Photo, Planet News

Our Searchlight on the War

ON THE CREDIT SIDE

No other country had ever mobilized its man-power to such an extent as we had had to do.—Mr. Bevin.

THOSE who can remember the political dissensions during the first two years of the last war, the shells scandal, the confusion about man-power, the Mesopotamia miseries, the profiteering and other hindrances to victory, must admit, however captious they are, that things are better this time. The Government is not perfect (no Government ever is), but our organizational methods, in regard to food, labour power, munitions, and the gradual accumulation of striking power are a credit to all concerned. Nor is it fair to blame leaders for disasters whose genesis is to be found in pre-war pacifism. When Mr. Bevin tells us that of 33,000,000 persons in this country between the ages of 14 and 64, 22,000,000 are now in the armed forces, in civil defence and in industry, the nation has every reason to congratulate itself on rising, as it were, to a totalitarian occasion. And it is a tremendous fact that Britain has preserved most of her military power intact awaiting the essential moment when in opening the second front she will be able to strike the Germans down quickly and finally.

SECRET SERVICE SUCCESSES

The case for German world domination was hopeless from the start. At this stage in human development only an atavistic race such as the Germans are could ever expect aggression to succeed.

THE admirable work in connexion with the V campaign, however secret it was, necessarily, revealed, at least, the fact that our close liaisons with patriots in occupied territory were as universal as they were effective. On hearing his name and address mentioned on our wireless many a quisling must have trembled in his shoes when Colonel Britton announced that we were "coming for him." When the complete story can be told there will be some thrilling revelations of the courage and ingenuity of men and women, threatened by death, working for the Allied cause. It was announced the other day that there was a courier service, organized in London by the International Federation of Trades Unionists, operating in half the countries of Europe. Mr. Walter Schevenels, general Secretary of the Federation, said, " Our people are willing to take risks, and from them we get reliable information of what is happening on the Continent. When we want somebody we let the necessary service know, and he is picked up and brought to this country." Part of the Nazi plan was, of course, to destroy the liberty of the workers by disbanding the trades unions, but the workers have secretly reorganized themselves. It is a known fact that 90 per cent of the members of the " conquered peoples " are resisting Nazi domination.

NELSON'S ARMCHAIR

There is no little poetic pleasure in thinking that something from Nelson's famous flagship is helping to win this war.

MANY beautiful and sometimes historic things have changed hands to help the war effort. An armchair with canework seat and rounded back, one of two chairs said to have been in Nelson's state room on board the Victory, was sold recently in aid of London's Warship Week for a hundred guineas. Here is a way in which the " not so rich," harassed by reduced incomes and heavier taxes, can contribute a little extra to the war effort. It is not easy to part with our personal treasures, but a precious antique or picture, or any kind of trinket, is not lost when we dispossess ourselves of it. We may be sure that the purchaser will enjoy it as we once did and still do in retrospect. The collector, in any case, can have only a lease of the things he loves. Ultimately they must go to somebody else. Could there be a better moment than now to pass them on that they might raise money for some cause connected with the war and help to bring that victory without which all enjoyment of artistic or any kind of beauty will become impossible?

OUR CIVILIAN WAR DEAD

With the raids on Baedeker-starred cities there has been a sudden addition to our large number of casualties on the home front.

THE Imperial War Graves Commission, who have so reverently and efficiently looked after the graves of our friends and relatives killed in the last war, have extended their duties to comprise the 42,000 men, women and children killed in the raids on the United Kingdom from the beginning of this war until the end of September 1941, and they have been in contact with the relations of 67 per cent of these casualties. It is hoped to make a complete record of all those who fell on the home front, that their names might ever be linked with " our finest hour." Relatives and friends are asked to communicate with the London offices, 32, Grosvenor Gardens, S.W.1, if they have not already done so. Some poignant facts are often the result of inquiries. A man living in the East End who called concerning his daughter's death was able to supply details of more than 20 members of his family who had been killed, and the ages of war dead range from 11 hours to 100 years. *Dulce et decorum est pro patria mori.*

R.A.F. ON THE MARK

According to a recent statement in Washington an overwhelming air offensive against Germany is being planned by the Joint British and American forces.

THERE are still a few people who are not convinced that Britain's plan of more, bigger and better bombs for German military objectives is an excellent policy. Their argument sometimes follows the line that, whereas the Germans were unable to dislocate our armaments industries, we are unable to destroy theirs. The truth is that Britain is now in a far better position to wage this offensive than ever the Germans were. We have the planes and we have the experience founded upon a consistent study of the whole field of enemy production. If our post-raid photographs of Rostock are not sufficient to convince the doubters, reliable information filters through from neutral sources. A civilian engineer, inspecting the damage to the M.A.N. (Maschinen Fabrik Augsburg Nürnberg A.G.) factory after our raid in April, stated that the R.A.F. success was complete. The damage done affected the three chief departments—armoured vehicles, U-boat engines, and tanks, and at least five months must elapse before normal output could be resumed.

KING HAAKON addressing an audience of Norwegians at the London Coliseum on the 128th anniversary of Norway's Independence Day. *Photo, G.P.U.*

TIME AND TOJO

Within little more than six months the Japanese General Tojo has spread his forces victoriously from Shanghai to the Coral Sea, and the Bay of Bengal.

THERE is a certain parallel between Hitler's and Tojo's methods and their results. Both Axis leaders struck treacherously and both have achieved the temporary conquest of vast territories. Time and the big battalions were on their side. The results of their blitzkrieg must at times even surprise them. There can be little doubt that Hitler and Tojo hoped, by the capture of Madagascar, to link hands in the Indian ocean, and could they have done that the Allies' position would indeed have been precarious. Our well-timed and brilliantly organized descent on the French colonial island has changed the Japanese plan of campaign. But Tojo has every reason to be satisfied with the success of Japanese arms to date. His occupation of Malaya and the Dutch East Indies has placed in his hands centres of inexhaustible supply, for we must not forget that " scorched earth " cannot be a permanent condition of mines and wells. From the Japanese point of view, also, the stopping of supplies to China through Burma is a strategic victory of considerable magnitude, since our Chinese allies are, for the time being at least, isolated from Anglo-American help. Japan is now in a position to attack China from the west along the road to Chungking and from the eastern seaboard through ports that have fallen into her hands.

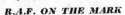

Cordite charges aboard H.M.S. Renown being put into cardboard cases to be sent ashore and stored while the ship is being refitted in dry dock. This is one use for your waste paper. Every vessel of the Royal Navy is thus "de-ammunitioned" preparatory to an overhaul. *Photo, British News Reel*

F/L Kuttelwascher, a Czech fighter-pilot ace. Playing a lone hand at what the R.A.F. call " night intruding," he seeks the Germans in their own " lairs," and has destroyed eight Nazi planes. *Photo, Planet News*

We've Built the 'Persia Road' Into Russia

L.M.S. rolling stock shipped to Persia from England, and called " Churchill's Reply." Trains loaded with supplies for Russia about to move off from the marshalling yards at Ahwaz, about seventy miles from the head of the Persian Gulf. Right, map showing Persian supply route to the Caucasus.

WITHIN the last few months Iran has become a great clearing-house for British and American supplies to the Russian front. Road and rail communications have been vastly improved and increased, and day and night, by iron way and dusty road, trucks and lorries hum with unceasing movement through the romantic land of Omar Khayyám.

What were recently little wayside stations are now great marshalling yards, and immemorial caravan tracks have been widened to take fast modern traffic. The opening of a railway from Khorranshah on the Shatt-al-Arab, some fifty miles west of Bandar Shahpur, to Ahwaz, about seventy miles inland, has greatly speeded up supplies. British soldiers are reminded of home and holidays when they see powerful locomotives, with L.M.S. markings, puffing into Teheran, drawing behind them truck after truck of machinery crates.

THEN begins a thrilling journey across Persia's northern plateau. The dirt road runs between snowcapped mountains, up and down like a gigantic switchback, with views of magnificent scenery on either side. Hour after hour the convoy of lorries eats up the mileage, the Russian drivers, all of whom are skilled mechanics, keeping their places in the line with only one thought—the determination to bring

the munitions of war as quickly as possible to their brothers fighting the Fascist foe.

The last stage of the journey is reached when the convoy descends the road to the Caspian Sea with the port of Pahlevi in sight. An important addition to Soviet armament, having travelled thousands of miles, having defied U-boats and Nazi aeroplanes, is now being unloaded by willing hands. Within a few hours the empty camions—they belong for the most part to the United Kingdom Commercial Corporation, which handles the transit of British supplies for Russia—have turned round and are racing back to refill. The " lease-lend " way in ancient Iran has become one of the main highways to victory.

Russian drivers, under the orders of a Soviet commander, taking over American lorries assembled at Andimishk. Left, the unending stream of vehicles, carrying munitions of war, on their eight-day journey north to Russia. Since the beginning of the year the trickle of supplies to Russia through Iran has become a mighty flood, thanks to the reorganization and development of communications and the enormous increase in the output of the factories of the U.S.A. and Britain.

Photos, British Official: Crown Copyright. Map by courtesy of The Evening News

Kerch and Kharkov: A Two-Way Offensive

The attack on Kerch and the defence of Kharkov are the essentials of the Nazi campaign for 1942.
Two factors dominate all the Germans' calculations: one is oil; the other, food. To continue the
war they want the Caucasus oil. They had hoped to replenish their granaries from the vast
wheat-producing lands of south Russia.

Two pronouncements of great significance were made before the Germans opened their spring campaign in the Kerch Peninsula. The first was by Major Otto Mossdorf, who, in an article in the German press, said that the core of the Red Army is still intact. The second statement was Mr. Churchill's sensational news that Germany had already lost more men in the war against Soviet Russia than during the whole of the last war.

The German people have at last realized that final victory has eluded them, and their appetite for more campaigns in Russia is at a low ebb. An immediate victory was essential, so the German High Command has staged in the Crimea what is described as "an experimental heavy offensive." Rumours of new machines, new explosives, and a paralysing gas were circulated to hearten the home front. It was hoped to smash the Russians into the sea within a day or two, and thus to revive the idea of Nazi invincibility. The attack on Kerch was begun on May 8 by General von Manstein's 11th Army.

With many hundreds of dive-bombers and a new mortar which was used for the first time, and every other destructive device, a collective battering ram hurled itself at the Russian strong points. The Soviet army was beaten back, though not, as the Germans alleged, in panic, but in an orderly retreat, taking up new positions the while inflicting enormous losses on the enemy. Berlin, using the loud pedal of propaganda, endeavoured at first to convey that the Russians had been annihilated. As the days passed, however, insistence was placed on the stubborn defence put up by the Soviet forces, and a certain disappointment could be read into Nazi reports. The communiqués began to tone down. While, on May 18, the Red Army had been obliterated, on May 20 it was still fighting in the neighbourhood of Kerch. Even though the Peninsula, with the exception of isolated segments, had fallen into German hands, this was only a detail in the vast line stretching from the far south to the far north. The Russians announced the evacuation of Kerch on May 24.

While Manstein's forces moved south to the Crimea, Timoshenko's legions were striking west into the Ukraine. Launching the Kharkov offensive, the great Russian Marshal published this Order of the Day: "I hereby order the troops to begin the decisive offensive against our vilest enemy, the German Fascist Army, to exterminate its manpower and war materials, and to hoist our glorious Soviet banner over the liberated cities and villages."

On the eve of battles which may decide the fate of the world the moods of Germany and Russia were in interesting contrast, especially during the opening days of the Kharkov offensive. A note of fear crept into most of the Nazi statements. Goebbels,

Goering and the military experts were obviously on the defensive. There was no confidence either in the German leaders or among the people.

In Russia, on the other hand, there was a feeling of exhilaration and hope. A war correspondent on the Kharkov front wrote:

"Spring has set in and our armies are rolling ahead across fields already covered with young grass. The rumble of tanks fills the air and above,

heading westward, drone the fleets of our bombers. Men with flags stand at our bridges, at river crossings, directing the vehicles towards the front. At one point soldiers have found time to write out in mighty letters of stone, placed across the hillside, the words 'Forward to the West.'

"Back through the recaptured village are pouring columns of German prisoners, men with glassy faces, who do not yet understand what has happened. Many of them are youngsters of 18; they were Hitler's reserves."

Timoshenko's hammer blow between Volchansk and Chuguyev, beginning on May 13 on a fifty-mile front, came as a surprise to von Bock. It anticipated the Nazi spring offensive, and completely wrested the initiative from the Germans. Preceded by heavy artillery fire, described by the Germans as "a dancing volcano," Russian forces made a wide breach in the Kharkov defences, and a large army swept through in a veritable flood of tanks, supported by dive bombers, and motorized infantry under cover of an artificial fog. Nazi strong points were pulverized, and hundreds of villages

were suddenly released from the enemy's grip. Meanwhile, powerful Red bombers struck continuously at Nazi aerodromes, forcing the Germans to withdraw their air power deeper into the rear. By May 14 it was clear that a major operation on the part of the Soviet armies had become a major success, the Russians having penetrated on a wide front to a depth of ten miles beyond the point where they had crossed the River Donetz.

Timoshenko's attack was broadening without losing its drive. Regiments from Moscow, Georgia, the Volga, Uzbekistan and the Donetz Basin went singing into the fray, with the object of liberating the Ukraine. The farthest point penetrated was towards Krasnograd. Here is the vital railway line between Poltava and Lozovaya. Once in possession of Krasnograd the Russians could break von Bock's line of communications with Dnepropetrovsk, and seriously interfere with Nazi reinforcements for the Crimea.

The German High Command, in addition to throwing in heavy reinforcements in a vain effort to halt Timoshenko in the Kharkov sector, tried to embarrass the Soviet Command by a new offensive along the Donetz on a front between Isyum and Barvenkovo, south east of Kharkov, with the intention of striking up against the Soviet armies sweeping west. Whether this was merely a diversionary effort or part of the original Nazi plan of campaign, it constituted a grave threat to Timoshenko's position. could the Nazis break through behind the rear of the Kharkov attack. The speed of modern warfare has made battle lines extremely flexible, resulting in sudden pockets. Without the most careful planning and huge reserves too impetuous an advance is full of dangers. But it would appear that Marshal Timoshenko was well prepared for this Nazi counter-stroke, having placed strong defensive shock-absorbers in positions where they could deal with von Bock's attacks.

The German attempt failed to smash through to the north, hundreds of tanks falling into prepared camouflaged pits, where they were destroyed. The Russians then launched their own tanks against von Bock's forces, causing great carnage among the supporting infantry. On May 21 the Russian High Command put out the reassuring statement that the German counter-thrust north had been held.

Two important facts emerge from the confusion of war on the East front. The first is that the great battles there are not the much heralded German spring offensive. They are definitely a Russian offensive, which has thrust deep into occupied territory. The second fact is that the Russians so far have had command of the air. Their Stormovik dive-bombers, Hurricanes, Tomahawks and Airocobras have shown marked superiority over the Nazi air force

TIMOSHENKO v. VON BOCK. Marshal Timoshenko launched a three-pronged offensive on May 13: 1, north and south of Kharkov; 2, towards railway junction Krasnograd; 3, at Povrosk, against Taganrog. Shortly afterwards an effort to outflank the Soviet armies was made by von Bock between Barvenkovo and Isyum (4). The fifth arrow in the map indicates Kerch, which, the Russians announced on May 24, had been evacuated.

Map by courtesy of News Chronicle

As the Snows Retreat Fierce War Boils Over

GERMAN TANKS, moving along what may well be one of the roads built by the Todt Organization in Russia, have been overtaken by planes of the Red Air Force. On three of them Russian "tank-busters" have secured direct hits.

IN THE CRIMEA, probably in the Kerch Peninsula, where severe fighting between Nazis and Reds flared up on May 8, Cossack sappers are effectively destroying a blockhouse established by the enemy.

ON THE KHARKOV BATTLEFIELD nurses of the Russian Red Cross have won fresh renown for their devoted bravery. In this photograph—like the other two above, radioed from the Russian front — Medical Nurse Olga Usupova, who is reported to have carried 43 wounded Red Army men out of action, is seen tending a casualty during an attack in the Kharkov region.

German army spokesmen, radio reporters, war correspondents, Dr. Goebbels, Goering, and the Fuehrer himself have dilated upon the appalling conditions under which during last winter's campaign in Russia the German soldiers had to live, to fight, and perchance to die. This photograph of German reinforcements struggling along a "road" just affected by the thaw makes eloquent commentary.

British Official; Planet News

All Australia Is Mobilized for War

Since last December Australia has been in the very front of one of the most important of the war zones into which the world is now divided. Some of her towns have been bombed, some of her ships have been sunk in her own waters ; above her hangs the cloud of invasion. How has the Commonwealth reacted to the ever-deepening menace ?

WHEN the war began two and a half years ago the Australians—it is Dr. H. V. Evatt, Australian Attorney-General and special representative to this country, speaking—"without question, without thought of the cost involved, without dwelling upon the fact that The First Great War cost us 60,000 lives and suffering and sacrifice beyond telling, again rushed to the assistance of the Mother Country."

" It was just as simple as that," Dr. Evatt added. And what happened ? Australia sent considerable land, sea and air forces into the thick of the fighting everywhere. As before, the cost was heavy ; as before, the cost was never counted. Many thousands of Australian sailors and airmen have helped in the defence of Britain. They have protected British shipping and have fought the enemy on many fronts, side by side with the sons of Britain and the other Dominions.

Minister, when on the war's first day he made it clear that in 1939 as in 1914 " Australia would be there." True, the Labour Party refused to enter the Government when it was proposed it should be reorganized on a national basis, but its leader, Mr. Curtin, was at pains to demonstrate that their refusal had no anti-war foundation. The Australian Labour Party, he declared, stood inflexibly behind Great Britain, although it maintained its hostility to conscription and the dispatch of Australian forces overseas.

This opposition was carried into the division lobby in Nov. 1939, but it was short-lived, since in June 1940 a special conference of the Commonwealth Labour Party passed a resolution advocating participation in the Empire Aid Scheme, reinforcement of A.I.F. divisions abroad, and compulsory military training.

For a year Mr. Menzies carried on with a Parliament, elected in 1937, in which his

ago, John Curtin graduated from the secretaryship of the Timber Workers' Union of Victoria to the editorial chair of the West Australia Worker, a Labour paper published in Perth. In 1928 he was elected to the Federal Parliament as M.P. for Fremantle ; defeated in 1931, he regained the seat in 1934, and was elected to the Labour leadership in the House of Representatives, i.e. Leader of the Opposition. At the General Election of 1937 he revealed himself as a strong opponent of " foreign entanglements " and conscription, but it is noteworthy that his programme called for the provision of thousands of planes as being more necessary for Australia's defence than warships.

Now this journalist-politician, this man of unconventional ways, but of obvious political foresight, was Australia's Prime Minister, and even his bitterest opponents found little to complain about in his vigorous direction of the nation's war effort, particularly when Japan's entry into the war brought the conflict to Australia's own shores and skies. On Feb. 17, 1942, Mr. Curtin announced that the Commonwealth Cabinet had ordered the total mobilization of all the human and material resources of the country. " Every human being in Australia," he said, " is now at the service of the Government to work for the defence of Australia ; and every material thing—money, machinery, buildings —which can be diverted to war purposes, must be diverted, when directed."

Already—indeed, a week earlier—the War Cabinet had announced a Nine-Point programme of far-reaching measures designed to marshal to the full the nation's resources :

(1) Sale of shares or investment of capital was prohibited save by Government permission, thus eliminating speculation on the Stock Exchanges. (2) Prices of all goods and services were pegged at those ruling on Feb. 10. (3) Profits of all businesses were limited to 4 per cent. (4) Interest rates were put under the control of the Commonwealth Bank. (5) Wages were pegged at the prevailing level, subject to a " margin of tolerance " to allow for changes in the cost of living. (6) All labour transfers were placed under Government control. (7) Drastic penalties were enacted for illegal absenteeism in industry. (8) The Government was given powers to place any area under military control ; and (9) speculation in commodities, e.g. forward dealing in foodstuffs, was prohibited.

Drastic as these measures were, they were only slightly modified before passing into law.

From the beginning of the war with Japan Mr. Curtin made it clear that in his view the Pacific struggle could not, and must not, be treated as a subordinate field. His method of approach was a distinctly realist one, and, knowing Britain's difficulties, he had no hesitation in making a direct appeal to Mr. Roosevelt for American aid. Some of his remarks were perhaps not too happily expressed, and his critics professed to find therein some loosening of the traditional ties with the Mother Country. Any such suggestion, however, was strongly rebutted by Mr. Curtin himself.

As for Australia's policy today, Mr. Curtin summed it up in the same speech under three heads. " First," he said, " the Allies must stand together ; there must be no sacrifice of one allegedly for the common good. Secondly, there must be no half-heartedness or faint-heartedness ; we must not sit sacrosant in a place we have made safe. Thirdly, all the time we are waging the struggle we must keep in mind the cause to which we are pledged—to defeat the enemy. We must not only beat the things for which he stands, but win victory for the things for which we stand."

MR. CHURCHILL WITH DR. H. V. EVATT, Australian Minister for External Affairs and Attorney-General, outside Number 10, Downing Street. After his mission to the United States Dr. Evatt arrived in London, where, as accredited representative, he attended meetings of the War Cabinet and Pacific War Council.
Photo, Planet News

Now it is Australia's turn to need assistance —now, when the danger of Japanese invasion is real, when the Japanese are in possession of vital strategic points in and near New Guinea, which are as much the gateway to Australia as Calais and Dunkirk and Boulogne were to Britain. The defence of the Australian base is of crucial importance, urged Dr. Evatt, since only from Australia can the Japs be attacked ; but, quite apart from this, Britain will see to it that the evil thing of a Japanese invasion shall not come to pass in a British Dominion " owing the same allegiance to the King as you, blood of your blood, flesh of your flesh."

What has been done in Australia to meet the threatened blow ? In a word, the Australians have organized their resources to the utmost. Every Government in turn has devoted itself to that task. When war broke out the United Australian Party was in office at Canberra in coalition with the United Country Party, while the Labour Party was in opposition. Like one man, all three parties, every group and section, stood behind Mr. R. G. Menzies, the Prime

coalition had a majority of fourteen, but his position was one of increasing difficulty. Nor was it improved by the General Election held in Sept. 1940, since this resulted in the return of 37 United Australia-Country members, 36 Labour members and one Independent, who in effect held the balance of power. In the spring of 1941 Mr. Menzies paid a visit to England, where his impressive personality won for him wide popularity and general esteem, but on his return to Australia he sensed a growing dissatisfaction with his Government. Once again he urged the formation of a National Government, and offered to stand down from the premiership in favour of one to be elected by the three parties. His offer was refused, however, and on Aug. 28 he resigned. The following day Mr. A. W. Fadden, Leader of the Country Party and Commonwealth Treasurer, took office, but on Oct. 3 he was defeated on a motion by Mr. Curtin censuring the new Budget provisions as being contrary to true equality of sacrifice. Thereupon Mr. Curtin formed a Labour Government—the first since 1931.

Born in a small town in Victoria 57 years

Hitler's 'Tourists' Came to York

The Gothic Guildhall, York, which was fired on April 28 by Nazi incendiaries in one of Hitler's desperate and infamous " Baedeker " raids. Thus in one dreadful night was destroyed, in obedience to the whim of the modern Hun, a relic of culture which had been cherished by mankind for centuries. Another photograph of the fiery scene is in page 705.

Links With the Glorious Past

In a spirit of vindictive hostility for our legitimate attacks on Nazi war-centres, the Germans bombed and machine-gunned selected English cities from April 23 to 28. Here are some of the scenes of devastation following those raids. 1, A church at York. 2, All that was left of the Market Hall, Exeter. 3, The Boar's Head Inn, Norwich, which was built in 1495.

Photos, *&Gen*

Broken by the Nazi Iconoclasts

Sacred buildings, colleges and fine old houses were like so much kindling to a diabolical holocaust. In spite of the heroic efforts of the fire brigades, many treasures were destroyed, though many more were saved. 4, Ruins of St. Luke's Diocesan Teachers' Training College, Exeter. 5, Firemen at work at Bath. 6, Damage close to Bath's famous Circus.

Nazi Vandalism at Exeter

Bombed on the nights of April 23, 24, and May 3, Exeter was left with many a grievous scar and gaping wound. In the foreground of this photograph a number of dwelling-houses have been shattered by H.E.s or consumed by incendiaries, but rising in serene beauty above the cloud of dust and smoke are the massive Norman towers of the magnificent cathedral.

Alexander's Fighting Retreat Through Burma

" Youngest and certainly one of the ablest generals in the British Army, General Alexander,"
said Mr. Hore-Belisha in the House of Commons on May 20, " was called upon to lead a retreat
which in its circumstances did not differ much from the glory of Xenophon's retreat from Persia
to Asia Minor." As what follows will make clear, it was indeed, a great feat of arms, carried
out against impossible odds

THE final battle in Burma was fought on May 10 at Shwegyin, on the Chindwin opposite Kalewa. Here the headquarters of the 17th division, two infantry brigades, several field mountain batteries and field companies were waiting to be ferried across the river to Kalewa, when a shock party of about 200 Japanese, who had moved up river in motor-boats, with characteristic audacity attempted to bottle them up in the village. The story of the action that ensued may be given in the words of an Indian army officer.

" We heard the sound of machine-gun and mortar fire from the direction of the jetty, from which flat-bottomed paddle-steamers had been taking off from Kalewa carrying our troops, transport, and guns. . . . Our infantry, mostly Gurkhas, shouldered their arms and moved into the forests that cover the hills overlooking the road to the jetty—the hills on which the enemy ensconced themselves. Soon our guns began shelling the enemy positions, and one by one the Japanese guns were either silenced or withdrew beyond range. But the jetty at Shwegyin had been destroyed in earlier mortar shelling by the enemy, so the 17th Division packed their necessities on mules and struck north along the river bank in order to cross the Chindwin at Kalewa.

" It was a difficult march, undertaken at dusk through dense forest that shut out the starlight. The track was smooth and slippery and in parts strewn with jagged boulders. With delight we reached the jungle-fringed Chindwin in the early morning. At the sight of the paddle-steamers chug-chugging over the silky blue surface of the waters, some of us began to croon ' Old Man River.' The Royal Marines were there : these bearded, thick-set men were running the evacuation steamers backwards and forwards across the Chindwin, ferrying men, mules, guns and equipment.

" The monsoon was about to break, and the Chindwin during the past week had risen by three feet, making the old jetty at Kalewa unusable. A new one had to be built by Indian sappers and miners. We crossed the Chindwin with that holiday feeling, marched through Kalewa, and drew from stores our much-needed rations of tea, meat, and butter. Later we made camp in the jungle. The 17th Division was intact, in order and in high spirits, though a certain amount of their transport (including guns and stores) had to be destroyed on the sands near Shwegyin."

After this little affray the British continued their withdrawal up the Chindwin. From the map it would seem that they were heading for the Tamu Pass, which leads from Burma into Assam, to Imphal and Manipur Road ; but by a fortunate piece of prevision a new road into Assam had been under construction for some time past, and it seems to have been so far completed as to have played a very useful part in the evacuation.

Although the time for large-scale operations had passed, Alexander's retreating legion was constantly in action, if not against the Japanese always, then against a Nature which was almost as fiercely hostile. From the Associated Press war correspondent came a vivid picture :

" Across cactus plains and through steamy jungle swamps . . . harassed by enemy fighters and bombers and stabbed at from ambush by bands of native traitors, the haggard, weary riflemen of half-a-dozen one-time crack battalions of the British Isles, Armoured Force crews, and wiry Sepoys from Indian units, are approaching within a few miles of the mountainous Assam frontier." It was a military tragedy for the United Nations, but " for the pitifully small handful of Imperial soldiers who lost Lower Burma and for the few understrength Chinese divisions there can be nothing but praise. They were ordered to do the impossible. Their casualties were appalling in their severity. The majority of stocky, singing Britons I saw hiking into the Salween line in January, and the smiling Chinese legions deploying around Toungoo in March, have been killed."

But out of the death-pockets some retreated; always a new line was established farther back, though always it was weaker than those held before. Every man knew that Burma was doomed when Rangoon fell on March 8, but " for hundreds of miles it was a case of fight and withdraw and fight again. Surrender is not in their vocabulary."

So they drew near the Indian frontier. The first to arrive were the wounded. Victor Thompson of the Daily Herald, who watched them helping each other out of the drab-painted lorries, described the bandaged soldiers as being true sons of the Mons men. " Their faces have grim lines, etched by five months of hard retreating battle," said Thompson, " but they can still laugh, and they can still sing an unprintable song which is to this war what ' Mademoiselle from Armentières ' was to the last." Their first

Allied Generals outside the Chinese advanced headquarters in Burma. Left to right, they are General H. Alexander, G.O.C. Burma, General Sir Archibald Wavell, and General Tu Lee Ming, O.C. Chinese troops in the Toungoo section.
Photo, British News Reel

thoughts were for their comrades, who were still struggling through the almost trackless jungle along the way they had come ; next they asked what was the news from home. Only when they were in hospital and rest camps—in real beds with sheets, with revolving fans in the ceiling, and beer and cigarettes at hand—could they be prevailed upon to talk of their own experiences. Said one Cameronian, " Coolies carried men in litters for three days. It's not a bad way of travelling when you get the knack. My pals call me Dr. Livingstone now." A man of the Gloucesters said that his party had " fed like lords " since the major was a wizard at shooting jungle-fowl with his revolver.

Along the forest tracks, across the mountain paths, they streamed—in lorries and in litters, on foot and sometimes on elephants. Men of many regiments, British and Indian, all tired, all dirty, but all in good heart still. And throughout the retreat *the* tower of strength, the supreme centre of inspiration was General Alexander—" fighting Alex " as the troops called him—who had been the last man to leave Dunkirk beach two years before. In the dusty compound of a Burmese " house-on-stilts " he was interviewed by

Marsland Gander, The Daily Telegraph special correspondent ; he had just crossed the Chindwin in a show-boat-like Burmese stern-wheeler with a thousand troops on board. He had been bombed on the passage and bombed again on the road a few minutes before, but he was as imperturbable as ever. Quiet, friendly and unflurried were the adjectives that sprang to Gander's pen.

" For months we have been living and fighting on supplies that existed here," said the General. " We were really fighting on an island with no communication from the outside world except by air, and we had no air support. The Japanese had two excellent roads ; we also had two roads, but they led nowhere. Now roads have at last been driven through to us. We had almost reached the end of our supplies." One of the greatest difficulties had been the effect of bombing on public utility services. Immediately the Japanese started bombing, railways, powerhouses, waterway communications and even hospitals virtually shut down. Posts and telegraphs were maintained and a skeleton railway staff stuck it, but practically speaking the whole social structure of the country collapsed. You can imagine the problem when hospital menials pack up and run into the bush when the first bomb falls . . .

At last the retreat was over ; General Alexander was fighting no longer in an island with neither bases nor lines of communication ; his little army was now buttressed by the strength of India—which, by his heroic stand, had been given five months to make ready. In a dispatch sent by courier on May 20, Marsland Gander said that General Alexander's Burma army was virtually relieved, although the bulk of the fighting troops were still in Burma. Invested not by the enemy but by great jungle-covered mountains, his relief was not effected in the traditional way of forced marches, skirling pipes, cavalry, or even modern tank charges. Nor this time had the Navy been called upon to play its part. Rather it was accomplished by months of hard work, by sappers, tea-planters and native coolies whose slogan had been " The road must go through."

Slaughter of the Innocents in Burma's Villages

BOMBED BY THE JAPS! A few hours, even a few minutes ago, the village where this photograph was taken was as peaceful perhaps as any of the thousands which pepper the Burmese map. But now it has been raided by Japanese bombers; destruction and death are on every hand; and those of the population who have survived have fled to the jungle.

NEAR TOUNGOO, a patrol of Chinese troops, part of the army commanded by the American General Stilwell, sets out to reconnoitre the enemy's positions. In front marches the standard-bearer carrying the flag—a white sun on a ground of dark blue.

BURMESE REFUGEES set out from their home town which has just been raided by Japanese planes—and they fear may soon be raided again. With their pathetically few belongings piled on light push-carts they wander off, maybe into the jungle or maybe they have chosen the road which after many weeks will lead them into the comparative safety of India. Such terror raids were devised to create havoc, panic and disruption behind the British lines.

This photograph, too, was taken in a Burmese village after the Japanese bombers had come and gone. One of the victims of these savage attacks was a little child, and now the simple funeral procession of family mourners moves along the earthen track to the burial ground on the outskirts of the village.

Photos, British Newsreel

Today in Paris, City of Dreadful Doom

BLINDFOLDING A VICTIM for Nazi butchery, and, on the right, after the executioners have done their work. Beneath, Parisians reading the names of compatriots who preferred to die rather than submit to the German barbarians. Let the Allies remember these crimes against civilization, even humanity.

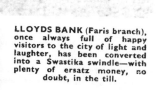

LLOYDS BANK (Paris branch), once always full of happy visitors to the city of light and laughter, has been converted into a Swastika swindle—with plenty of ersatz money, no doubt, in the till.

Butter, eggs and cheese, says the notice over the shop-front, not to mention whipped cream on the window. These are names only, and Parisian housewives stand in queues for hours and frequently go away empty-handed. If there is any milk in the cans it is reserved for the big hotels where Nazi officers have their quarters.

Photos, Associated Press, Keystone

Page 757

BRITISH CASUALTIES

Casualties in the armed forces of the British Empire from the outbreak of war until Sept. 2, 1941:

Officers:
Killed	..	6,295
Wounded	..	4,064
Prisoners of war	..	3,374
Missing	..	953
		14,687

Other ranks
Killed	..	42,677
Wounded	..	42,299
Prisoners of war	..	55,084
Missing	..	28,803
		168,863

Total
Killed	..	48,973
Wounded	..	46,363
Prisoners of war	..	58,458
Missing	..	29,756
		183,550

MAY 13, 1942, Wednesday   984th day

Sea.—Light naval forces attacked enemy convoy off French coast.

Air.—Coastal Command bombers made night attacks on ships off Aalesund and Vaagso.

Russian Front.—Russians on Kerch Peninsula retired to new positions. In Kharkov sector they passed to the offensive and made advance.

Africa.—Small-scale tank and artillery engagements in Libya.

Burma.—British troops made further withdrawal from Chindwin. R.A.F. bombed Akyab aerodrome.

Australasia.—Allied bombers raided ships at Amboina and aerodrome at Rabaul.

General.—Heydrich in Occupied France to organize measures against French patriots.

MAY 14, Thursday   985th day

Sea.—Two enemy armed trawlers left sinking after engagement off French coast.

Russian Front.—On Kerch Peninsula Russians made further withdrawal. In Kharkov sector they continued to advance.

Africa.—R.A.F. bombers made night attacks on objectives in Libya.

Mediterranean.—Eleven enemy aircraft destroyed and ten damaged over Malta.

Burma.—U.S. bombers made daylight raid on Myitkyina.

Australasia.—Enemy aircraft twice raided Port Moresby. Allied bombers attacked Jap shipping at Rabaul and seaplane base on Deboyne Island. Emergency regulations applied to certain districts of Queensland.

Home.—Small enemy attack on S.W. coast.

MAY 15, Friday   986th day

Sea.—Washington announce sinking on May 12 of cargo-boat near mouth of Mississippi.

Air.—R.A.F. attacked three German minesweepers off Cherbourg. Coastal Command made low-level night attacks on two German convoys off Frisian Is.

Russian Front.—Stubborn fighting continued across Kerch Peninsula ; further Russian advance in Kharkov sector.

Burma.—Aerodrome at Akyab bombed by R.A.F.

China.—Japs entered Tengueh in Yunnan.

Home.—Slight enemy activity off E. and S.W. coasts ; two bombers shot down.

MAY 16, Saturday   987th day

Air.—Daylight fighter sweeps over N. France.

Russian Front.—Germans claim to have occupied Kerch town and harbour.

Africa.—Benghazi and Berka raided by R.A.F.

Mediterranean.—Five enemy aircraft shot down over Malta.

Burma.—U.S. bombers raided aerodrome at Myitkyina.

India.—Japs bombed town in E. Assam.

Australasia.—Surprise attack by Allied bombers on aerodrome at Lae.

General.—Announced that more than 2,000 regular officers and cadets of Dutch Army have been sent to prison camps.

MAY 17, Sunday   988th day

Air.—Coastal Command aircraft attacked Prinz Eugen off Norwegian coast by night.

Russian Front.—Russians continue to advance round Kharkov ; stubborn fighting reported on Kerch Peninsula.

Africa.—Raids by R.A.F. bombers on Benghazi and camps in Mekila and Tengeder areas.

Malta.—Nine enemy aircraft destroyed over Malta.

Burma.—Intense fighting continued on Burma Road.

Australasia.—Jap fighters attacking Port Moresby were intercepted.

MAY 18, Monday   989th day

Sea.—Admiralty announced loss of H.M.S. Hollyhock (corvette).

Russian Front.—Russians still advancing in Kharkov area ; intense fighting in area of Kerch.

Africa.—Enemy camps and transport attacked by R.A.F. fighters.

Mediterranean.—Ten enemy aircraft destroyed and five damaged over Malta.

Burma.—Japs land troops on both sides of Chindwin, near Kalewa.

China.—Japs engaged in new drive in Chekiang.

Home.—Small-scale air attacks on coastal districts of S. England.

General. — Rear-Adm. Sir Henry Harwood succeeds Sir Andrew Cunningham as C.-in-C. Mediterranean.

Large contingent of American troops arrive in N. Ireland.

MAY 19, Tuesday   990th day

Air.—Powerful force of R.A.F. bombers attacked Mannheim by night ; submarine base at St. Nazaire also raided.

Russian Front.—Further Russian advance on Kharkov front. Germans started offensive operations in Izyum-Barvenkovo direction, S.E. of Kharkov.

Burma.—R.A.F. kept up raids on Myitkyina and Akyab aerodromes.

Home.—Sharp night attack on N.E. coast town.

General.—Five Jewish hostages shot in Paris for attacks on German soldiers.

MAY 20, Wednesday   991st day

Russian Front.—Russian offensive continued in Kharkov region ; German attacks repulsed in Barvenkovo sector ; fighting still going on in east of Kerch Peninsula.

Mediterranean.—Fleet Air Arm attacked enemy convoy off Malta.

Burma.—R.A.F. attacked enemy troops at Kalewa and Akyab.

China.—Severe fighting continued in Chekiang. Japs made new landings at mouth of Min river, below Foochow.

Australasia.—Allied bombers attacked harbour of Dilli in Portuguese Timor. Jap fighters intercepted over Port Moresby.

MAY 21, Thursday   992nd day

Sea.—Second Mexican tanker torpedoed off Brazilian coast.

Air.—In offensive patrols over N. France, Spitfires attacked shipping.

Russian Front.—Russian offensive continued round Kharkov ; German attacks in Izyum-Barvenkovo region beaten off ; fighting still going on in east of Kerch Peninsula.

Burma.—R.A.F. bombers raided Akyab aerodrome.

MAY 22, Friday   993rd day

Russian Front.—Russians fought offensive battles and consolidated positions round Kharkov ; German attacks repulsed at Barvenkovo.

Africa.—Martuba and Derna aerodromes attacked by R.A.F. bombers.

Burma.—Akyab aerodrome attacked by Blenheim aircraft.

Australasia.—Allied aircraft bombed aerodromes at Lae and Rabaul. Announced that Allied submarines have sunk Jap cruiser and two cargo vessels.

MAY 23, Saturday   994th day

Sea.—Washington Navy Dept. announce submarine attacks on three more U.S. ships in Gulf of Mexico.

Russian Front.—Russians announce evacuation of Kerch Peninsula. On Kharkov front Russians dug in ; German attacks in Barvenkovo area beaten off.

Africa.—Bomber and fighter activity increased over Cyrenaica. Derna landing ground bombed by R.A.F. and enemy transport at Martuba attacked by night.

Mediterranean.—Eleven enemy aircraft destroyed or damaged over Malta.

Australasia.—Allied aircraft bombed Lae aerodrome and attacked shipping at Amboina.

General.—Ten more hostages shot in Paris for attacks on German soldiers.

MAY 24, Sunday   995th day

Russian Front.—Russians still fighting offensive engagements round Kharkov. German attacks at Barvenkovo repelled.

Africa.—Martuba, Tmimi and Benghazi bombed by R.A.F. during night.

China.—Heavy fighting in Chekiang.

Australasia.—Allied bombers raided Vunakanan aerodrome, S.E. of Rabaul.

General.—Broadcast from Germany announced execution of 14 German " Communists " in Mannheim.

MAY 25, Monday   996th day

Russian Front.—Fierce attacks by enemy tanks and infantry in Isyum-Barvenkovo sector.

Africa.—Night attacks by R.A.F. on enemy landing grounds at Martuba and transport between Derna and Bomba.

Mediterranean.—R.A.F. raided targets at Messina by night.

Burma.—U.S. bombers attacked Mingaladon and Rangoon.

China.—Heavy fighting round Kinhwa, capital of Chekiang.

Australasia.—Allied aircraft raided airfields at Rabaul and Lae. Jap flying boats raided Port Moresby by night.

MAY 26, Tuesday   997th day

Sea.—Washington Navy Dept. announce destroyer Blakeley damaged by torpedo in Caribbean Sea.

Russian Front.—German tank and infantry attacks beaten off in Barvenkovo sector.

Mediterrahean.—R.A.F. again raided Messina by night.

Africa.—Enemy columns including tanks began advance eastward, but did not reach our main positions. R.A.F. attacked Tmimi, Martuba and Benghazi.

Burma.—Night raids on Mingaladon by U.S. bombers.

Australasia.—Jap flying boats again raided Port Moresby by night.

General.—Lieut.-Gen. H. H. Arnold, Chief of U.S. Army Air Force, and Rear-Adm. J. H. Towers, Chief of Navy Bureau of Aeronautics, arrived in England.

MAY 27, Wednesday   998th day

Russian Front.—In Kharkov direction Russians consolidated positions ; in Izyum-Barvenkovo area fierce enemy attacks were repelled.

Africa.—Large enemy armoured force heavily engaged by our armoured forces N.E. of Bir Hakeim.

Australasia.—Jap fighters engaged over Port Moresby. Allied bombers raid Rabaul.

General.—Attempt on life of Heydrich at Prague leads to drastic reprisals in Czech Protectorate. As reprisal for murder of two Germans in Lithuania, 400 persons, mostly Poles, executed in Kovno.

Lieut.-Gen. B. B. Somervell, Chief of U.S. Army Supply Services, arrived here.

AIR-RAID VICTIMS

In Britain from the outbreak of war up to the end of April 1942.

Sept. 3, 1939–July 31, 1940	
Killed	310
Severely injured ..	410
	720
Aug.–Dec. 1940	
Killed	22,837
Severely injured ..	28,535
	51,372
Jan.–Dec. 1941	
Killed	20,520
Severely injured ..	21,451
	41,971
Jan.–April 30, 1942	
Killed	1,093
Severely injured ..	1,093
	2,186
Totals	
Killed	44,760
Severely injured ..	51,489
	96,249

Maj.-Gen. E. L. SPEARS, Britain's Minister-Plenipotentiary to Lebanon, arriving at the Petit Serail, Beirut, to hand his credentials to President Naccache. Lebanon was proclaimed a Republic on Nov. 26, 1941, after being occupied by British and Free French Forces. *Photo, Keystone*

The Last Shot Has Not Been Fired in Crete

Although a year has passed since hostilities in Crete officially ended, many British soldiers whose retreat was cut off took to the mountains and, aided by native patriots, have continued the fight against the German invaders. News of some of our men "missing" on the island was confirmed by the publication in a German paper of certain photographs now reproduced in this page. They show, left, German Alpine troops advancing against British and Cretan patriots. Oval, Nazi troops interrogating two British soldiers captured with their Cretan comrades. Right, a ravine typical of the regions where fighting continues.

Beneath, three splendid types of Cretan patriots who fought on against the Nazi oppressor until they were taken prisoner, and, right, German soldiers warning local inhabitants of dire penalties should they give assistance to the British and Cretan guerillas. *Photos, Keystone*

The Home Guard Is Two Years Old

On May 14, 1942, the Home Guard celebrated its second birthday. Some account of the lively progress made by Britain's vigorous citizen army during the past year is here given by our Picture Editor, J. R. Fawcett Thompson, who has been a member of the force since its inception.

"Yours is a great responsibility, having in mind the vital part you have to take in the security of the United Kingdom. The test has yet to come, and when it does the strain on our endurance and on our faith will be great. It will call for the best that is in us of courage and self-confidence." In these solemn words did Lt.-Gen. Sir Bernard Paget, C.-in-C. Home Forces, pay tribute to the Home Guard on the occasion of its second anniversary.

Looking back at the work done and the improvements effected during the past twelve months, it is indeed abundantly clear that the progress made by the force in its second year has been as remarkable—if not, perhaps, as spectacular—as that which characterized 1940-1941. Under its able Director-General, Lord Bridgeman (who succeeded Maj.-Gen. T. R. Eastwood in May 1941), the Home Guard has gone ahead to such purpose that it is now an essential part of Britain's defences against invasion.

If and when the Home Guard goes into action, it will be against the picked troops of the enemy and the training its members are now receiving, based on a full realization of this harsh fact, is being directed to practising units in their battle role. The only advantage the Home Guard can claim over the fully-trained soldier is that he can fight on his own ground, and it is this great asset that must be exploited to the full.

While the force's main operational role has changed little since 1941, the scope of its activities has been enlarged to include the manning of certain anti-aircraft sites and coastal defence guns, thus freeing units of the regular army for service overseas. The former duties were first taken over on a restricted scale early in 1942, but so successfully were they carried out that the scheme was subsequently considerably extended. Recruiting for coastal defence work is about to begin, and there is little doubt that it will meet with an equally enthusiastic reception. A number of transport companies have been formed which will take over vehicles commandeered for military use in the event of invasion, while dispatch riders are now being specially trained under Army supervision. Particular attention has been paid to Intelligence, and all units now have specialist officers skilled in this vital work with contacts in their individual Companies. Close cooperation is preserved with the Police and Civil Defence authorities.

Early in 1942 an important change in organization was made that affected every Home Guard. This was the introduction of compulsion, which meant in effect that after February 16 no member could resign unless in exceptional circumstances, and that a maximum training period of 48 hours per month was obligatory. In addition, power was given in the event of enemy attack for units to be moved outside their own areas should the military situation so dictate. Though at first sight drastic and far-reaching, this alteration proved in practice to be advantageous as far as existing Home Guards were concerned. In point of fact, many thousands of them had for long been putting in more hours of duty than the required maximum, while what small degree of absenteeism there may have been almost disappeared under the new regulations. As regards the conscription of civilians into the Home Guard, the compulsory order has now been applied in all civil defence regions, and in many districts calling-up papers have already been sent out.

New Methods in Training

Since the summer of 1941 notable alterations and improvements have also been made in training, which now comes directly under the C.-in-C. Home Forces. Though the long, dark evenings of the past winter necessitated much time being spent indoors, the instruction and practice then given (e.g. weapons training, sand-table exercises, map-reading) were planned with the object of their being translated into action in the field at the first suitable opportunity. The most significant feature of the field operations themselves was the change over from purely defensive tactics to those of vigorous attack, in which the principle of "Fire and Movement" played a decisive part.

Of definite advantage to training was the recent decision to abolish the always unsatisfactory combined post of Quartermaster and Adjutant, and appoint separate officers for each function. So much good work was done through the year by the two War Office Schools—one in England and the other in Scotland—for battalion, company and platoon commanders, that a third is to be formed shortly in the Midlands which will be capable of handling 70 students at a time for a week's course. For the vast majority of Home Guards, however, it is impossible to get away for a week at a time, and to a proportion of these five Travelling Wings, operating mainly in country districts, have brought instruction on the spot : this arrangement has so well proved its worth that the number of Wings is to be increased to 27. Also planned for the near future is the long-needed establishment of Street-Fighting Schools, an innovation that will receive a ready welcome, especially from city units. Great assistance has been given, too, by the intensive week-end courses energetically provided at the Command Weapon Training Schools, and no praise can be too high for the enthusiastic and hard-working instructors at these camps who have made special study of the Home Guard's peculiar problems and given of their best accordingly.

Cooperation with the Field Army has developed steadily during the year, and combined exercises have become a valuable and increasingly popular part of operational training. In certain areas, moreover, it has been found practical and mutually beneficial to affiliate the Home Guard to regular units.

The position as regards equipment—that ever-present anxiety of the Home Guard—has undoubtedly improved in many directions, and the great majority of units are now fully supplied with clothing, steel helmets and anti-gas equipment. Webbing pouches, now being issued, meet a want of long standing. Most important of all, the supply of personal automatic weapons has certainly been accelerated in recent months—for which, considering the vast demands on the armament industry, the Home Guard should be doubly thankful. Furthermore, a new weapon—the machine-carbine—is being produced in quantity, and will replace to some extent the popular tommy-gun, the latter arm being concentrated in certain Commands only so as to facilitate repairs and replacements.

Four types of grenade are being provided in large numbers, while the Home Guard's two main anti-tank weapons, the Blacker Bombard and the Northover Projector, have by now been issued to many units.

Taking a comprehensive view, therefore, the past year must be recognized as one of steady increase in the fighting power and efficiency of Britain's citizen army, with every prospect of this notable progress being maintained through the months that lie ahead. Mr. Churchill's words to the Palace of Westminster unit when he inspected them on May 12, 1942, fittingly sums up the Home Guard today. "If in 1940," he said, "the enemy had descended suddenly in large numbers from the sky in different parts of the country, he would have found only little clusters of men, mostly armed with shotguns, gathered round our searchlight positions. But now, whenever he comes—if ever he comes—he will find, wherever he should place his foot, that he will immediately be attacked by resolute, determined men who have a perfectly clear intention and resolve, namely to put him to death or compel his immediate surrender."

PALACE OF WESTMINSTER Home Guard were inspected by the Prime Minister on the occasion of the Force's 2nd anniversary. "To invade this island by air," said Mr. Churchill, "is to descend in a hornets' nest . . . There is no part of that nest where the stings are more ready and their effective power to injure more remarkable than here in the ancient Palace of Westminster." *Photo, Topical*

Determined Men Resolved to Kill the Enemy

Smart, purposeful and efficient, the Home Guard have on occasion been justifiably mistaken for regulars. Here is a North-West London unit on the march. The Port of London Authority has its own unit (right, below) specially trained to protect the docks from assault by river.

Week-end camps form a most important part of Home Guard training, since the time available to members during the week itself is very limited. Under the watchful eye of an Army Sergeant-Instructor a class is here learning the mechanism of the tommy gun.

Dispatch Riders are now being trained for work at military H.Q. and in traffic control duties ; above, a Signals Officer is giving instruction in map reading. Circle, West Country Home Guards are taking over field artillery for local defence.

Photos. British Official: Crown Copyright; Fredk. A. Cole, Fox, Topical

THE CONVOY LEAVES AT DAWN. Under protection of escorts, an R.A.F. umbrella and kite balloons, the ships outside a British port are about to take up their stations for their adventurous wartime voyage. The men of the "Red Duster" are at their posts, conscious that upon their patriotism and knowledge of the sea and ships the fate of Britain depends. Our Merchant Navy is a front spread over the Seven Seas. Let us never forget that behind these indomitable men and their motley collection of vessels the cause of freedom has survived, and that without their strength and courage all fronts might have fallen before the Nazi pestilence.

Photo, Central Press

Here's to the Heroes in Britain's 'Subs'!

VICTORY SMILES of Petty Officer H. Fright (left) and Able Seaman James Shanahan, two submarine heroes decorated recently at Buckingham Palace for service in the Tuna and Utmost respectively.

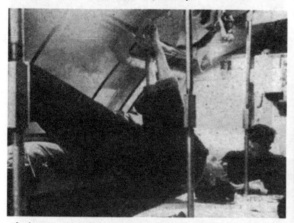

And so to bed, but inside the cramped quarters of a submarine it requires not a little acrobatic skill. A member of a submarine crew hoisting himself into the top bunk.

TRUE TO HER NAME, submarine Thunderbolt (originally the Thetis) has sunk two U-boats, five supply ships, scored six successful gun actions and other operations as marked on her Jolly Roger flag. Lieut. B. J. Andrew (centre), with the Thunderbolt's crew.

Lieut. J. S. WRAITH, D.S.O., D.S.C. (above, left) aboard the submarine Upright, back from a year's "nice work" in the Mediterranean, in the course of which she sank a floating dock, and shot down an enemy aircraft. Left, engine-room aboard a sub. seen through a watertight door.

'Knowing Our Hun' We Must Be Ready for Gas

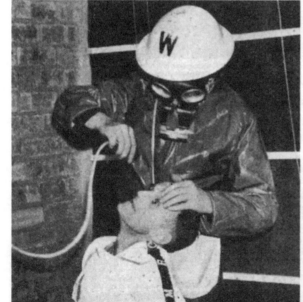

TO THE RESCUE of a gas casualty in a wrecked basement. A realistic rehearsal during a demonstration by the members of the Lambeth A.R.P.

A public gas-cleansing station, now being provided by many local authorities in the event of Hitler's deciding to wage chemical warfare. Find out where your station is !

EYE DOUCHE attention as demonstrated recently by the Lambeth A.R.P. On the right, stripping and identifying clothing by the new pin method. It is essential that gas-contaminated clothing or boots should be put out of harm's way as soon as possible. The public are advised to assist the A.R.P. by studying the handbooks on gas. To be forewarned is to be forearmed. To be gas-conscious is part of the patriotic duty of the citizen.

Photos, Fox

I Went Down to Dover, England's Malta

If there is any town in England which could rival Malta it is surely Dover, which for two years has suffered almost continuous bombardment from the air or from the Nazi long-range guns little more than twenty miles away across the Channel. Here is what David Raymond of Reynolds News saw when he visited the ancient town a short time ago.

YESTERDAY I walked through deserted streets in this town of glaring whiteness. White cliffs, white barrage balloons, white seagulls, white surf, white gashes in the green downs, and a stark stillness in sun-bleached streets—one thought uncomfortably of Elroy Flecker's " long white Sunday that goes on and on."

Through a cottage doorway, over which a sign still said " Bed and Breakfast for Cyclists," I could see the blue sea and an ascending balloon. The balloon was the only thing that moved in this picture of frozen fantasy.

A lot of Dover is like that, but by no means all of it. By contrast, the main thoroughfares presented an almost normal appearance. (One has got used, of course, to the gaps where buildings used to be.) Buses shuttled busily back and fore, women in summery garments went about their shopping, greeting friends, chatting outside well-stocked windows. In a restaurant, nearly full, I was served with the best two-course hot luncheon I have had for a long time. Service was good and quick.

Dover's population is only a fraction of what it used to be. Those who have stayed are mostly engaged on war-necessary work. They have miraculously adapted themselves to living under the daily, nightly threat of bombing, shelling, dive-bombing.

At A.R.P. Headquarters Mr. Scutt, unpaid sub-controller (and a working man), told me:

" Nobody shouts about Dover although we've had a severe hammering here. But the people—and Dover is now a town of working people, the others have gone—have become bomb- and shell-conscious. They have learned to look after themselves. Most people here can now tell you which is a bomb and which a shell, when they hear a bang. They can distinguish enemy from our own aircraft. We have had bombardments lasting five hours at times, but our casualties have been relatively small because the population has cooperated with the authorities."

He added proudly : " We have never had homeless people in Dover—and you can see for yourself (he waved a hand towards the derelict district I had visited earlier) how many homes have been destroyed. We have never even had to put our Rest Centres into full use. The people have become communally minded. They help each other. They take one another in without waiting for the authorities to ask. The working people of Dover have been grand."

Like Malta, Dover is well equipped with underground shelters —deep shelters burrowed into the white chalk cliffs. They could, in a push, accommodate nearly 10,000 persons. One of them has been dug by Civil Defence workers, headed by four miners ; and it runs into the cliff for nearly half a mile. The one I saw was dug during the last war. It was excavated as an experiment to gauge the time it would take sappers to drive a hole through Hill 60. . . . I was taken through it by young Councillor Bushell, a Labour man who is in charge of its maintenance. It can accommodate 1,600 persons safely. There are bunks for 500. One of the tunnels is used as an operating theatre and hospital, with up-to-date equipment on the spot, and electrically heated water.

The shelter has its own auxiliary power plant for use if the main supply is cut off. A canteen is open every night for light, hot refreshment. A kitchen is kept going capable of cooking more substantial meals if necessary. Mobile vans, too, served from British Restaurants make a nightly round of the shelters during blitzes.

During raids most of Dover's population use these shelters. At night, the whole town goes underground. As I came away, women were bringing their bundles of bedding, ready for the night, laying them out to air in the sun. Also underground, I saw what was described to me as one of the most up-to-date of gas decontamination centres.

Incidentally, more people were carrying their gas masks in Dover than I have seen elsewhere. Dover takes no chances. The Nazis are only three minutes away by air. Many miners live in Dover, working in the adjacent coalfield. During blitzes, so I was told, some of them would come home, wash, and go straight down the shelter to join their families, spending the day and

Air-raid damage in Dover, whose population have "taken it" almost continuously for two years. They have, in fact, become used to living under daily and nightly bombing, shelling and dive-bombing. *Photo, Keystone*

night underground. In a black pit by day, in a white pit by night !

Many shops are equipped with shelters for their staffs and customers. If a shell comes over without warning, people in the streets wait for no siren. They go flat down on their tummies just where they are. But they carry on unless things are actually dropping. In fact, their growing indifference to danger is a cause of new concern to the authorities. Thus, too many people are bringing back their evacuated children.

From Hongkong I Marched With Chinese Guerillas

Among the fortunate few who escaped from Hongkong in Admiral Chan Chak's party on Christmas Day 1941 (see p. 636) was Mr. E. M. MacDougall, of the staff of the Ministry of Information. Here is his own story, reproduced through the courtesy of China at War and the North American Newspaper Alliance.

OUR escape from Hongkong meant breaking through three Japanese circles: the ring of troops thrown around the island itself, the sea blockade, and the ring formed by the Japanese army in South China.

It was in surmounting the last of these obstacles that we came to know and to honour the Chinese irregulars who glory in the name of guerillas. For days we marched with them, sometimes almost within speaking distance of Japanese troops, and none of us had any fear. We knew we were in safe hands. The guerillas guided us and cared for us and brought us safely to our destination with the assuredness of homing pigeons.

What do the guerillas of Kwangtung look like ? The average guerilla is a well-set-up youth, lithe and lean, dressed in black clothes, a felt hat of dark colour, and light rubber shoes. Over his shoulder he slings his blanket, and around his waist is strapped a Mauser pistol, his most prized possession. He seems to carry food and to live off the country. Wherever he goes, it is obvious even to the stranger that he has the full confidence of the countryfolk who welcome and feed him. We were told that villagers will often themselves go short in order that the guerillas may eat and be well taken care of. We noticed, too, that all youngsters in villages through which we passed clustered in voluble admiration around our protectors. Ammunition belts were fingered and examined and then reverently handed back to the esteemed guerillas.

Mostly the guerillas were village lads, and their families were securely hidden in the

VETERANS WITH A V, such are the inhabitants of Dover, Britain's own Malta. Here is a typical group of women waiting for a bus. At any moment they might be under fire, for the town is right in Britain's front line. How Dover carries on is described in this page. *Photo, Associated Press*

neighbourhood. Their prime aim in life was to spot a Japanese detachment far from its base at nightfall. "We march until it is almost dark," one of them told me, "and then we make a detour in the hills and get ahead of the enemy, who doesn't know we are within 50 miles. We choose a suitable spot and wait ; and then, as the Japanese walk into our trap——" Here he lifted his Mauser at his imaginary victims. I asked him what happened if there were a great many Japanese. His face broke into a sly smile. "We wait," he said, "and watch and we pick one here and one there." Again the Mauser flashed in youthful hands in a gesture of death. "Are there any Fifth Columnists in this area ? Does anyone ever tell the enemy where you are ? " I asked. He looked at me in some surprise. "Why, no ! " he said. "In this country everyone owes allegiance to the Generalissimo's Government at Chungking. If we find any traitors, we would naturally execute them. No one tells the Japanese anything. When they come, our families shoot them."

The country through which we marched had been the scene of much guerilla fighting. Our party knew it like the backs of their hands. In this gully, they told us, they had a year ago trapped ten Japanese. On that hill they had lost three men, but near the springs they had shot seven. The guerilla at whose side I mostly marched was a lad of 16 from Kwangchowwan, who had left school when he was 13 because he thought it dull, and because there were Japanese to fight. He had been with the Kwangtung guerillas for nearly a year, and claimed nine Japanese victims. "Do you know what the Japanese fear more than anything in the world ? " he asked me, patting his Mauser pistol affectionately. "They fear the voice of this by night."

I asked him about prisoners, and he told me that few prisoners were taken on either side. "When the Japanese catch one of our men, do you know what they do ? They put lighted cigarettes all over his face and kill him slowly. When we take one of them, we cut off his head immediately."

Japanese Trail of Destruction

Guerilla fighting is not pretty, and the village patriots who bear the brunt of it in the lonely hills know the risks they run. You do not have to be told these days where the Japanese have been in China. The mark of their march lies over the countryside like a blight. Untilled fields and ruined villages are their signatures. "But never mind," exclaimed my young guerilla, "one day soon we'll clear them all out and have peace again, maybe a year from now."

Another said to me as we walked : "Do you know we are all brothers now ? Your country and mine both fight against the Japanese, and that makes you and your friends and me and my friends brothers."

The science of guerilla fighting as developed and practised by these soldiers of China seems to depend largely on speed of movement and complete knowledge of the enemy's strength and route. By long habit they can walk all day and all night without rest. They travel light and they travel silently. Their scouts are everywhere, and their assault depends always on surprise. All their tales of encounters with the enemy end on a gleeful, laughing note : "And the Japanese never knew we were there until the bullets began to fly."

One night it was necessary for us to march for 30 miles. The British members of the party, being mostly sailors and unaccustomed to marching, suffered greatly from fatigue, and at the end could scarcely drag one foot past the other. To the guerillas, who were as fresh as paint and ready to march, if necessary, another 30 miles, this was an amazing state of affairs. I heard one whisper to another : "The Europeans walk very slowly and they stumble very often. Are they tired ? "

"Perhaps, but these have marched little more than 30 miles. If they are tired, it is because they wear those great heavy leather boots. No man could walk in those affairs."

The beliefs and hopes of these gallant fighters are very simple : "We know our Generalissimo has the measure of these Japanese, and he will strike when the time is ripe. Meanwhile, we bust their communications, kill their stragglers, and make everything as dangerous and difficult for them as we can. But best of all we love to see an enemy detachment caught far from its base with night coming on." And they patted their Mausers and grinned, and nodded to one another in brotherly understanding.

My Visit to Stalin's Young Soldiers

The visit to the new Russian armies in training behind the southern front which The Daily Express correspondent, Alaric Jacob, describes below left him in no doubt as to the troops' fine quality and high morale.

THE Red Army did me a great honour. During a tour of 1,000 miles, visiting units who have either fought on the southern front already or else are training hard before doing so, a parade was arranged in my honour. I was asked to take the salute. With the Soviet officer I marched on to the parade ground. The senior officer called in a loud voice : "To you, comrades," to which the parading troops responded in a voice which shook the heavens : "May you live long ! "

This ceremonial over, the march past began. There was no band, but the men's voices provided marching music. The leading officer began with a solo, and then the whole company burst into vigorous marching song. They marched with arms swinging wide across the body—two companies of them. They marched and counter-marched, singing as though to burst their lungs. Their artistry was such that their two themes never clashed, but blended into a diapason which suggested illimitable confidence and power.

RED ARMY RESERVES armed with automatic rifles on parade during a review. The enthusiasm of the newly trained soldiers coming into the line on the East Front, singing as they march, is not the least inspiring fact about Russia's war for freedom. A ceremonial review is described in this page.
Page 766
Photo, Ministry of Information

Confidence in their own power. That is the keynote of the Red Army. These men are splendidly equipped. Their transport has seen hard wear. But mark this : all the trucks have new tires. Just before the parade I saw one convoy of big new American trucks go through, driven fully loaded from the disembarkation point hundreds of miles away by Soviet troops.

Consistent in their policy of utter secrecy, which has certainly paid high dividends so far, I have not been permitted to enter the Caucasus proper, but today I am nearer to this vital area than any other foreign correspondent before me. And what do I see ? That the troops the Russians have in reserve are not only great in numbers, but fine in quality.

They are by no means a corps d'élite, but ordinary infantry, tank and cavalry units, recruited in all parts of the Union—Georgia, Armenia, Turkestan, as well as Russia proper. Yet individually and collectively they make a finer impression than picked troops of the German Afrika Korps, whom I saw by the hundred just after being made prisoners in Libya, with all the swagger and jauntiness still in them.

We must throw out the absurd notion that Soviet troops, though very efficient, are somehow rougher and readier than Western armies. Far from it. They do not spit and polish, but a sturdier and more vital body of men no army can boast. In manner they are affable but dignified, quick to smile, disciplined, but without the servility so repulsive among the Germans.

To become an officer you have got to be intelligent, so only high-school graduates can qualify. However, since high-school education is growing, and ten years' tuition is open to all and entirely free, everyone has an equal chance.

Many women are in uniform. The one watching the parade wears a captain's pip, with a revolver slung on her hip. She is an engineer. The widespread belief that Soviet women are actually fighting in the front line is untrue. Most are doctors and medical orderlies, and do all the work of the R.A.S.C. It is not true that girls are flying fighters or bombers.

After the parade we inspected the barracks. Each dormitory is spotlessly clean, beds have plenty of blankets and white pillow-cases, and each runs its own wall newspaper. Pictures of the national leaders decorate the walls. These are adorned with red-painted slogans, e.g. " Greetings to all peoples fighting with us against Fascism," " Fight to the death for the Soviet Fatherland."

The Colonel Calls for Music

When you see films of the Red Army marching to battle singing like an operatic chorus, don't imagine there is anything stage-managed about it. I even saw a squad marching off on fatigue duty carolling like a Cossack choir. The proportion of musical instruments among the troops is as high as the proportion of tommy-guns—and that is plenty. When I commented on the profusion of guitars and balalaikas hanging on the walls, the colonel, an old soldier with a humorous eye, and wearing the Order of the Red Banner, won in the civil war, slapped his thigh and exclaimed : " Right. Let's have some music."

He ordered an officer to call for volunteers among the men. Everyone wanted to be on this parade. Moving into the barrack yard we found the troops already forming a circle, in the midst of which two or three were tuning up accordions and guitars.

Then, with complete lack of self-consciousness, one after another they played and danced Ukrainian, Georgian and Russian dances. One captain from Leningrad called out, dissatisfied : " Come, lads, we can

SOUTH AFRICAN TROOPS, bayonets and grenades ready, searching the ruins of Sollum, Libya, for any enemy that may be in hiding. Writing of British Tommies, an officer on General Rommel's staff described them as " incredibly brave." Extracts from letters discovered on his body-are printed in this page.
Photo, British Official

improve on that," and jumped into the ring. In spite of the heavy top boots he was wearing, he got up on his points like a ballerina, then down on his haunches, doing the famous kick-step.

When the colonel called, " Enough of dancing. Let's have some songs out of you," an impromptu choir formed and began a song with a rousing chorus, called " Three Tank Men went to the War to Fight Against the Hun." Then they went on to the older

Red Army favourites, concluding with the " Hymn of the Bolshevik."

I thanked the colonel for the honour he had done me, and said how much I had enjoyed the Red Army's music, and that I would have much to tell when I returned to the Western desert. The colonel replied : " Give the Red Army's greeting to the Allies in the desert, and tell them we will beat finer and louder music yet out of Fascist hides ! ''

What I Dislike Most Are Those Tommy Patrols!

Not long ago some letters, written by a German officer shortly before his death in action, were picked up on the Libyan battlefield. They came into the hands of Mr. Leonard Mosley, Sunday Times War Correspondent in the Middle East, who translated some of the most interesting passages.

I WAS allowed to read and translate these letters of "Capt. Blank," whom I knew in Germany before the war. Thirty years old and a professional soldier, he was attached to the Foreign Ministry in Berlin right up to the outbreak of war. In Germany he was regarded as among the best type of officer in the new Reichswehr, and when he died from a British machine-gun bullet he was a member of General Rommel's personal staff. Here are some of his comments since he arrived in North Africa.

On the Libyan Battlefront.—It is a bitter thought that I should be here this day, August 1941, sweating like a pig, with bad food, uneatable because of the pestilential flies, when I thought by this time I would be triumphant in Britain.

Why we should have chosen to bring the English to their heels in this horrible desert rather than by way of the Dover cliffs is beyond me. I long to be back in Germany again.

On General Rommel.—It was one of his mornings today, and he was changeable and short-tempered. He is a curious man, sometimes with all the attributes of a great soldier, sometimes childishly petty and indecisive. I hope his plans will carry through, but the Tommies are masters of this desert. They seem to like its heat and dust. I hope we'll trap the wily fellows soon.

On Italians.—How we all, from the General down, despise these pompous, incompetent cockerels. Three days ago one of our patrols returning to our lines was shot up from the rear and six were killed. Italian troops near the place said it was a Tommy desert group, but I don't believe it. That's all they are fit for—stabs in the back. I hate and loathe these café waiters in their gorgeous uniforms.

Yesterday a bold Tommy submarine rose

outside Benghazi and shelled two Italian transports. Our Allies had their revenge today and shot down a plane over the town —a Junkers 88.

And later.—British prisoners were being taken back to our lines yesterday when they were held up among a group of Italian troops. Two Tommies tried to escape and raced up the road. A German officer chased them and fired over their heads, and what did these cockerels do ? A whole Italian gun crew leaped out of their trench and surrendered with their hands up—to two Tommy prisoners.

On the Last Libyan Campaign.—Things are not going well. These fellows are amazing. They never know when they are beaten. The General says everything is all right. If so, why are only half our forces here, and why are we retreating ?

What I dislike are those Tommy patrols. Yesterday one actually had the impudence to raid our G.H.Q. Luckily, I was away with the General at Derna, but they killed Werner and destroyed my files. They left a terrible mess. When will they strike again and how ?

On the R.A.F.—I have just sent out a notice on the orders of the General telling the troops in the south that they will soon have air superiority again and that our planes are concentrating on the Indians in the north. I don't know what the Italians in the north are being told.

They are hitting hard and well, these Tommy planes. Yesterday it was a dump at Barce. Today it was our stores—all our Christmas coffee and 30,000 litres of wine, beer, and spirits smashed into the sand by those infernal bombs.

On British Tommies.—They are incredibly brave. I spoke to some today. They refused to answer my questions and no amount of tricks or persuasion would change their minds. I hope our troops do the same.

Editor's Postscript

IN all the competing plans for rebuilding our devastated towns and villages, in which I take a very tepid interest while the War is still raging, I sincerely hope that Ruskin's harmful advice to Victorian builders will be completely ignored. "Build your house as though it were to last for ever." No greater hindrance to the domestic comfort of the majority of the inhabitants in our built-up areas, if these were built in Victorian times, could be imagined. The destruction of thousands of these old structures will yet prove a blessing in disguise. Their builders kept too close to Ruskin's pernicious advice. Why should our houses last for ever ? We don't ! Few houses, apart from the mansions of the great and noble, that have stood for a hundred years, are good today for anything but pulling down. There are lots of council houses better adapted to notions of modern comfort than thousands of badly designed, inconvenient but solidly built Victorian dwellings that have degenerated into slums just because the horrid things *were* strong enough to last for ever—but for Hitler.

I WAS glad to read some while back that at least one experienced architect had had the courage to oppose this Ruskinian nonsense (though he did not associate Ruskin's name with what he opposed) and take his stand for building lightly constructed but entirely up-to-date dwellings that need not last for much more than thirty years, when they could give way to new buildings that would embody later scientific improvements not yet devised. It was Mr. Donald Gibson, Coventry's City Architect, who advanced this revolutionary idea for housing the populace, and his own skill in quick construction can already be seen in the efficient temporary rebuilding of his "coventrated" city. The number of people in these islands who have tenanted the same house for thirty years is extremely small, but I apprehend an economic difficulty arising, as an estimated duration of thirty years for the homes fit for British heroes to live in is rather near the opposite extreme from the "for ever" ideal. New houses, however, like new clothes, have an exhilarating effect on most people.

ONE of the simplest ways to waste paper is provided by those gold mining companies who from time to time console their shareholders (whose certificates all too often are apt to rank as waste paper) with elaborate reports and plans of the mining operations for the past twelve months. I have just been favoured with such a report and plan from a sound and prospering concern which absorbed a less fortunate company in which I was an original holder and granted me a number of its own shares in exchange for my original holding. The report, which not one shareholder in a hundred will find time to read, or having read would fully understand, contains 16 pages measuring 7 ins. by 10 ins. The plan is printed in four colours on expensive map paper 3 ft. 4 ins. wide by 2 ft. 3 ins. high ! Surely this is quite needless

waste. Most of those who received this elaborate literary and cartographic contribution would bung it unread into the waste basket. The blank back of the map yielded me 16 pages royal octavo, which I shall use for writing some of my articles. For this small favour I return thanks, but I feel that here is a wasteful use of good white paper that ought not to be sanctioned by the Controller.

THAT venerable saw " the nearer the kirk the farther from grace " has a new application today. The nearer your house to a church (especially a cathedral) the nearer you are to bomb danger. I have seen within the last few days some bomb damage on the South Coast, and it was quite evident that (lacking every sort of military object) the beastly young Huns sent over on tip-and-turn raids had deliberately aimed at three churches in widely different parts of the town. One of these, a fine modern edifice, they got plumb in the centre and turned it into a picturesque ruin within five or ten minutes. The other two were very " near misses," but residences standing close by were destroyed, in one case three good houses going down to the one bomb. Long ago I saw a clumsy Nazi try for a railway station and hit a church about a furlong beyond it. He probably got a " highly commended " for that. In coastal towns or country villages the churches are clearly regarded by these cowards of the clouds as attractive targets.

"EQUALITY of Sacrifice." One reads often about this, sometimes with a little misgiving. Although it is amusing to hear a man whose total financial assets might be covered by a tenner tell another whose income tax may

have jumped up to twelve or fifteen shillings in the pound : " Well, we're all in the same boat, ole man," I suppose there is equality of a sort ; each is losing according to his means, and the cheery chappie who is hard-up and happy is losing as much as he has got to lose, which is nil. A correspondent signing himself " Working Proprietor," in a letter to Truth, mentions that his income is " a little less than three times " the amount he has to pay his warehouse foreman. But his income tax is " sixty-six and a half times " that paid by the foreman. I rather gather that when the foreman says to him " we're all in the same boat, guv'nor " a colour floods his vision that is redder than a rose in June. We may be all in the same boat, but some of us have to pull a heavier oar than others. But, of course, some of us possess financial muscles that are stronger than those of other oarsmen.

READING the other night The Scene is Changed, that delightful account of his happy adventures in the world of the theatre at home and abroad, by Mr. Ashley Dukes, author of The Man With a Load of Mischief, I was amused at his reactions to the German inflationary period twenty years ago. He was in Berlin in the summer of 1922 and though living luxuriously " found it hard to spend two pounds a week " on account of the debasement of the mark, but could not feel it to be pleasing or satisfying in any way ! " The sense of robbing a nation by some economic process is ever present," he writes. What misdirected sympathy ! The robbers were the Germans, who were then engaged in paying off millions of foreign debts in debased marks. Admittedly the German investor in national securities suffered equally by having his so-called securities repaid at a time when an investment of £500 had suddenly become worth a pound or so . . . And it was not Hitler nor the Nazis who thought out that dirty trick. This is a thing to bear in mind when your sympathy with the anti-Nazi is canvassed. There are anti-Nazis who are no more our friends than any Hitlerite. I commend to Mr. Ashley Dukes' attention The Greatest Swindle in the World by G. Borsky, and especially Lord Vansittart's brilliant preface to that exposure of the swindling Germans who paved Hitler's way.

NOT long ago I spent some days in the company of a very successful man of business. The most remarkable thing I learned from him was that although he was turned sixty he had never carried a watch ! Surely there are not many like him in this respect. I cannot imagine how he has been able to get along all these years without this prime necessity of organized life. To acquire a watch was one of the first ambitions of my boyhood and I have possessed all sorts in my time from a five shilling Ingersoll to a £25 " hunter " ; but for a number of years—certainly forty—since the once famous cartoonist F. C. G. showed me the merits of the wrist watch " I have used no other." The journalist's life is largely a race against time, and I am plunged in misery if I have ever to get through a day watchless. Perhaps that's why there's a shade of envy in discovering a man who is successfully wandering through life regardless of the flying hours.

Printed in England and published every alternate Friday by the Proprietors, The Amalgamated Press, Ltd., The Fleetway House, Farringdon Street, London, E.C.4. Registered for transmission by Canadian Magazine Post. Sole Agents for Australia and New Zealand : Messrs. Gordon & Gotch, Ltd. ; and for South Africa : Central News Agency, Ltd. June 12, 1942. S.S. *Editorial Address* : JOHN CARPENTER HOUSE, WHITEFRIARS, LONDON, E.C.4